PICTORIAL ATLAS OF THE WORLD

a Salamander book
Published by Salamander Books Limited
LONDON • NEW YORK

PICTORIAL ATLAS OF THE WORLD

A Philip/ Salamander Book

ISBN 0 86101 226 7

Credits

Editor: John Woodward
Editorial consultant: Philip Steele
Captions: Joanna Chapman
Cartographic editor: Ray Smith
Designer: Carol Warren
Picture research: Zena Research
Filmset by SX Composing Ltd
Colour reproductions: Rodney Howe Ltd
Printed in Belgium by Proost International Book Production, Turnhout

The Geographical Consultant

Dr John Salt has been a lecturer in geography at University College London for 15 years. A graduate of the University of Liverpool in 1963, he gained a PhD. four years later. He teaches human geography, with particular reference to population studies. His research interests are in problems of employment and migration, and he has a number of publications in this field to his credit.

The Authors

Jack Tresidder, who wrote the sections on Asia, Australia, Oceania and the polar regions, was born in Whangarei, New Zealand, in 1931, and is a graduate of Otago University. He was formerly a newspaper foreign correspondent and leader writer and has travelled widely on reporting tours of South-East Asia. Now living in London, he is an author and editor with an international publishing firm.

Norman Barrett, who has an honours degree in Physics from Oxford University, is an experienced editor and writer on diverse subjects. He has worked on several international encyclopedias and particularly on publications connected with the sporting world.

Arthur Butterfield, who has lived and worked extensively in South America, has been a freelance journalist and author for many years. He has contributed a large number of articles on varied subjects to countless different publications and was a senior editor on *World Book Encyclopedia* in Britain and in the United States. His special subjects are Latin America, geography, natural history and sport.

Keith Lye has an honours degree in geography and is a Fellow of the Royal Geographical Society. Having lived and worked in Africa for several years, he then returned to London to become a writer, editor, lecturer and broadcaster on African affairs. He has also worked as an editor on *World Book Encyclopedia* both in Britain and in the United States and later as Publishing Manager in the Encyclopedic division of a major London company. He now concentrates on freelance writing and editing.

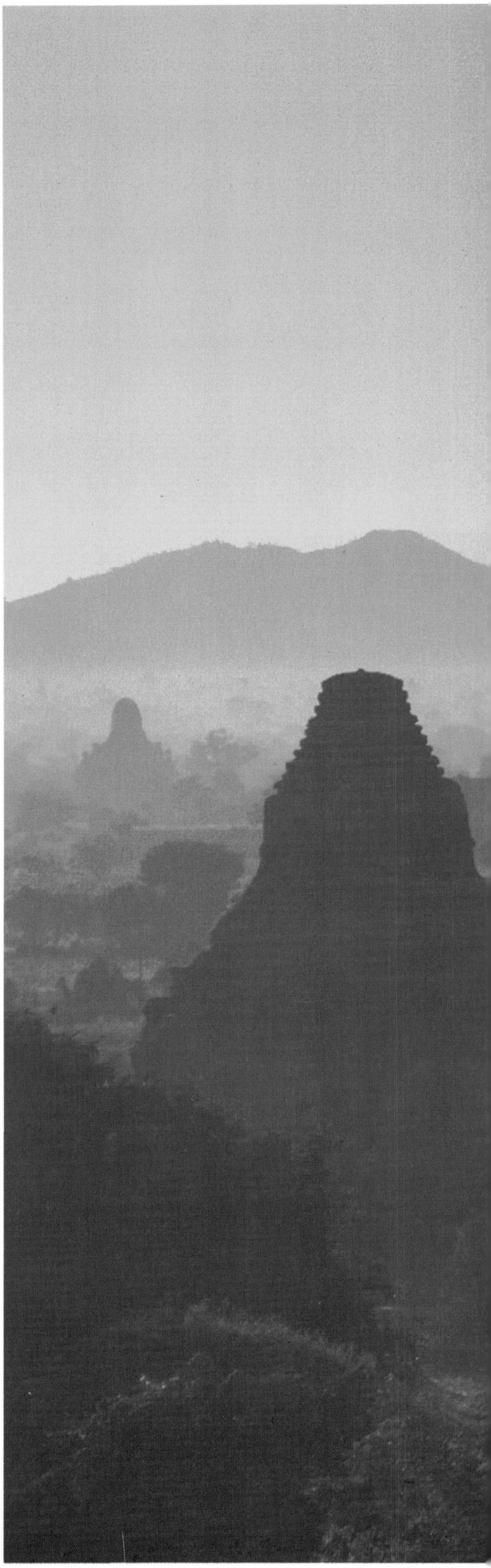

Right: *Ruined temples of the ancient Burmese city of Pagan.*

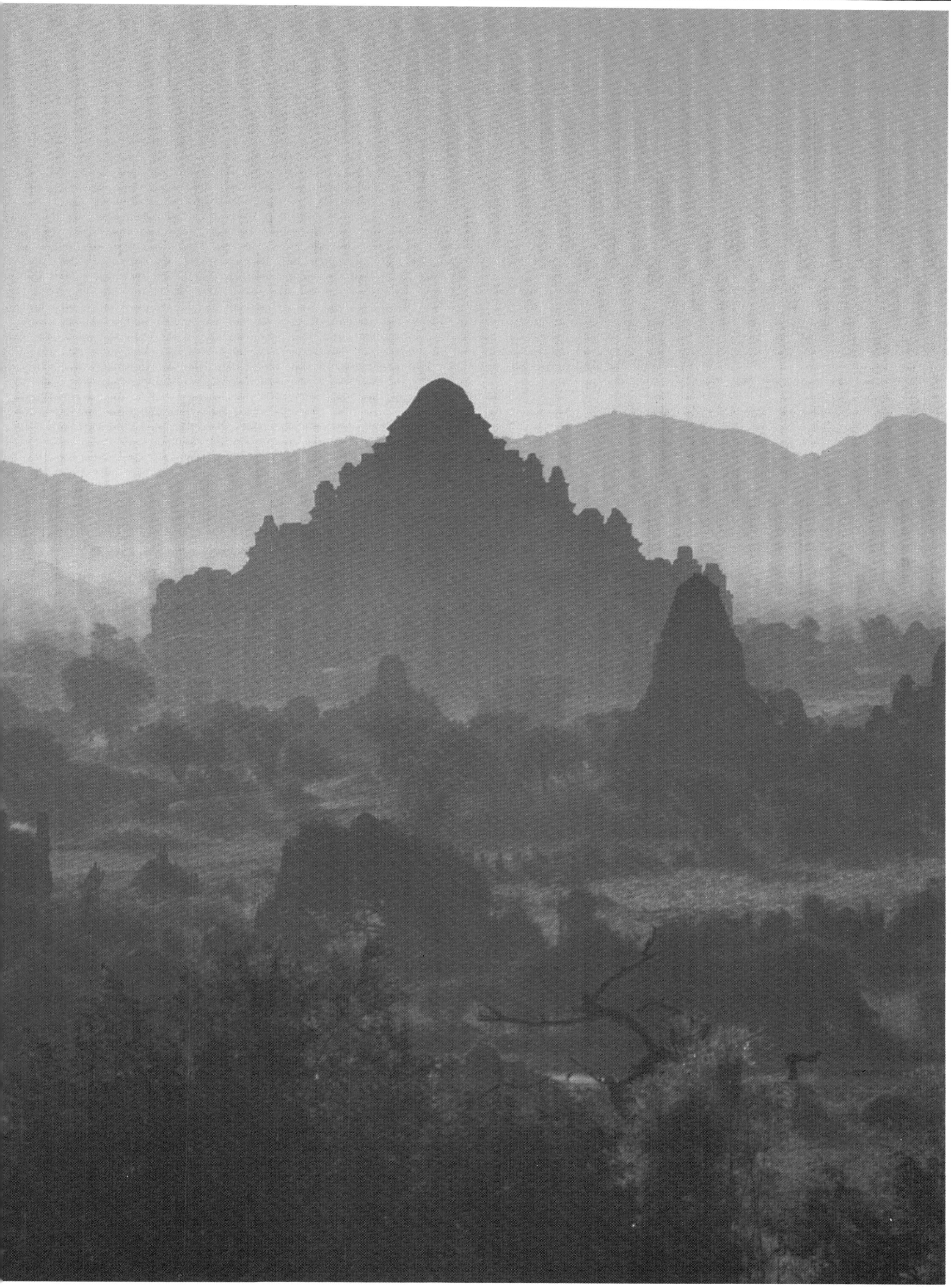

Contents

The World MAP 1-2 12

The Arctic MAP 3 14

Europe MAP 4 16

England and Wales MAP 5 19

Scotland MAP 6 21

Ireland MAP 7 23

Northern France MAP 8-9 24

Southern France MAP 10-11 28

The Netherlands, Belgium and Luxembourg MAP 12 30

Germany and Switzerland MAP 13 32

Austria, Czechoslovakia and Hungary MAP 14-15 36

Romania MAP 16 39

Poland MAP 17 14

Western Spain and Portugal MAP 18 42

Eastern Spain MAP 19 44

Northern Italy and Western Yugoslavia MAP 20-21 46

Southern Italy MAP 22-23 50

Yugoslavia and Bulgaria MAP 24-25 52

Greece and Albania MAP 26 55

Scandinavia and the Baltic Lands MAP 27 58

Denmark and Southern Sweden MAP 28 63

Asia and European Russia MAP 29 64

The Union of Soviet Socialist Republics MAP 30-31 66

European Russia (Central) MAP 32-33 68

European Russia (South) MAP 34-35 70

The Indo-Gangetic Plain MAP 36-37 72

Right: *Machu Picchu, built by the Incas in the high Andes of Peru.*

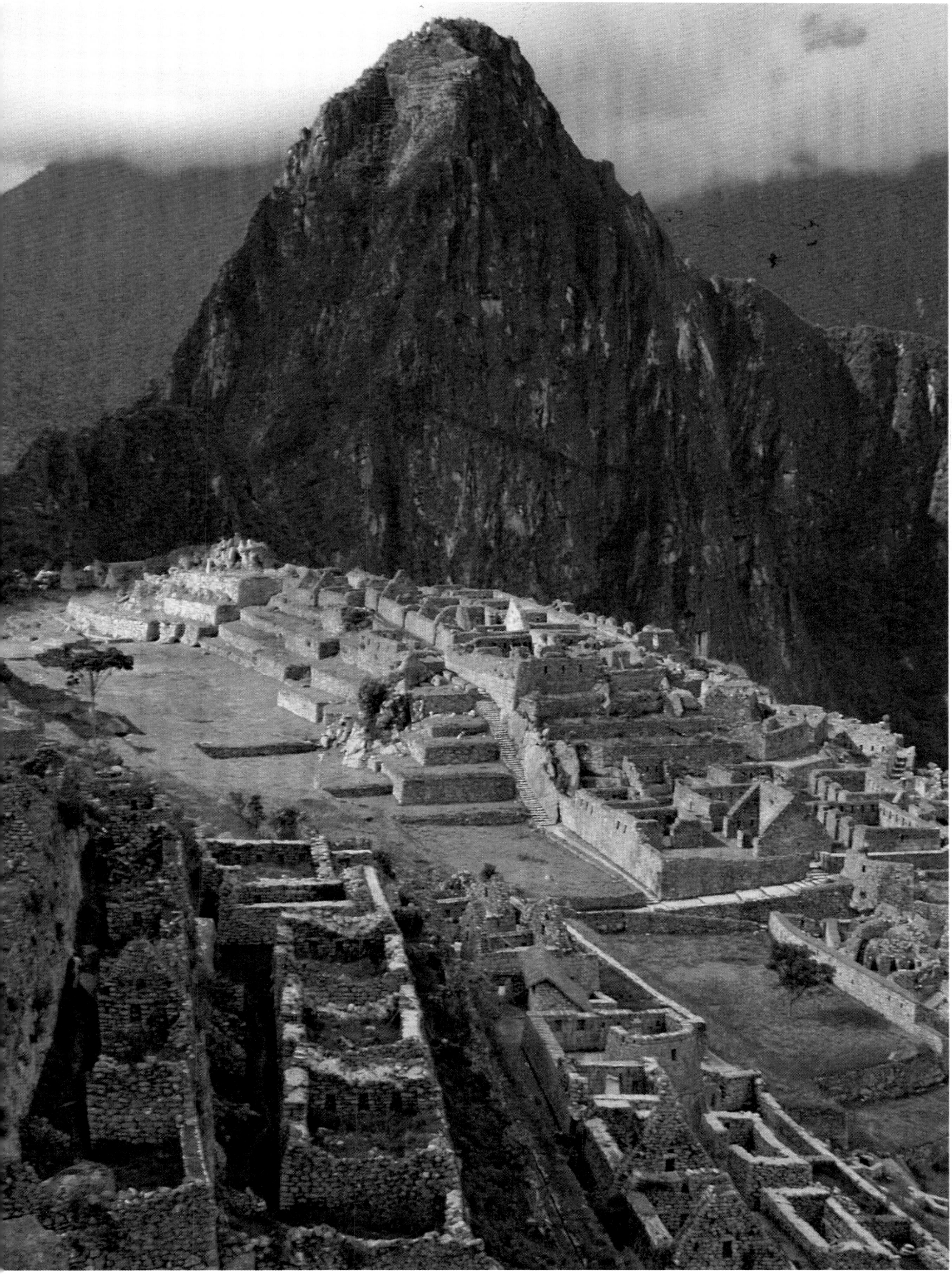

Southern India and Sri Lanka MAP 38 74
The East Indies MAP 39-40 76
Mainland South-east Asia MAP 41 78
China MAP 42 81
Eastern China and Korea MAP 43 84
Japan MAP 44 87
The Near and Middle East MAP 45-46 88
Arabia and the Horn of Africa MAP 47 92
Africa MAP 48 94
Northern Africa MAP 49-50 98
Central and South Africa MAP 51 103
Southern Africa MAP 52-53 106
Australia MAP 54-55 108
Eastern Australia MAP 56 113
The Pacific Ocean MAP 57-58 114
New Zealand MAP 59 116
Antarctica MAP 60 119
North America MAP 61 120
Eastern Canada MAP 62-63 122
Western Canada MAP 64-65 124
The Eastern United States MAP 66 127
The Middle United States MAP 67 128
The Western United States MAP 68 131
Mexico and Central America MAP 69 133
The West Indies MAP 70 135
South America MAP 71 136
South America (North) MAP 72-73 138
South America (South) MAP 74 138
Index to text 144
Index to maps 146

Right: *Dense undergrowth in the New Zealand bush.*

Foreword

The present map of the world is a patchwork of countries with varying shapes and sizes and has evolved over a long period of time. Some parts of the pattern are old, many nations having long and honourable histories. The last four decades, however, have witnessed major change, with the number of independent states more than doubling in the wake of the process of decolonization. Independence has not always severed old ties and many of the new nations still retain social, economic, political and cultural links with a former 'mother' country.

One of the salient features of the twentieth century has been the emergence of three blocs of countries, grouped according to the political and social ideas they espouse and to their different standards of living. The western bloc, which includes North America, Western Europe, Australasia and Japan, is usually regarded as the First of these three 'worlds'. The eastern bloc, the 'Second World', comprises the USSR and Eastern Europe. The 'Third World' includes a wide range of countries, especially in tropical areas, which often have diverse characteristics but whose peoples generally have lower incomes than those of the other two worlds.

The emergence of so many newly independent countries marks a new phase in man's colonization of the world, the principal underlying feature of which is the uneven distribution of population over the earth's surface. For many millennia man has known of and lived in virtually all parts of the land area of the globe. Certain areas with favourable living conditions, such as the fertile, irrigated soils of the Nile valley and the deltas of southeast Asia, have long been foci of settlement. In contrast, three-fifths of the earth's surface has proved too rugged, too high, too cold or too dry to provide the means of livelihood. For over two million years man's numbers increased only slowly. Average length of life in Cromwell's England, 35-40 years, was little better than that of Neanderthal man. But in the last two centuries, and especially in the last thirty years, man's numbers have shot up dramatically to the present 4900 million. What has happened is that the combined advances of hygiene and medicine have precipitated the retreat of death, while in much of the world a fall in birth rates has lagged behind. There are now no empty lands of opportunity to which people can migrate and the burden of massive population increment is becoming intolerable in many countries, particularly the poorer ones where the biggest increases are concentrated. At present rates, for example, Bangladesh's population will double in 23 years, Kenya's in 18. At the same time, a massive redistribution of the world's people is in train. Man is becoming an urban rather than a rural animal and nowhere is this process currently more in evidence than in the Third World where towns and cities resemble teeming ant-hills. In most of the more developed countries the bulk of the population has for decades been town-based and here the principal tendency is now for large city populations to fall as people prefer to move out to surrounding villages.

The availability of food has increasingly given cause for concern. Estimates vary, but it is commonly thought that at least one-tenth of the world's people are undernourished. In fact the food problem is less one of production, more one of distribution to those in need.

Mineral and energy sources have long been prized and today their discovery and exploitation are major tasks of international concern. Larger amounts of raw materials needed, and the demands of new technologies, have meant a continual widening of the scope and intensity of man's search for natural resources. Parallel with the hunger for raw materials has been a thirst for energy, particularly fossil fuels such as oil, and in recent years the strong bargaining position of countries possessing these resources has been apparent.

One of the side effects of growing population and industrialization has been disturbance of the ecological balance in many areas. The ever increasing amounts of waste generated by man's activities have created serious problems of pollution. Rivers and even the sea have in parts been deprived of life and made dangerous to human health. The air in some places has become unpleasant, even dangerous to breathe; it has killed vegetation and poisoned soils as a result of emissions from some industrial processes. A consequence of increasing pollution has been a growing awareness of the need to conserve the environment.

Each of the countries depicted and described in this atlas exists within two separate but related realms. The first is essentially national: each country has its own individual, often unique, problems which arise from the management of its national territory and resources. The second realm is an international one. In a shrinking world no country can act for long in isolation. In the management of the earth's resources for the wellbeing of all its people each country owes some responsibility to the larger community of nations.

Dr John Salt

Right: *The Pont du Gard, a Roman aquaduct near Nîmes in southern France.*

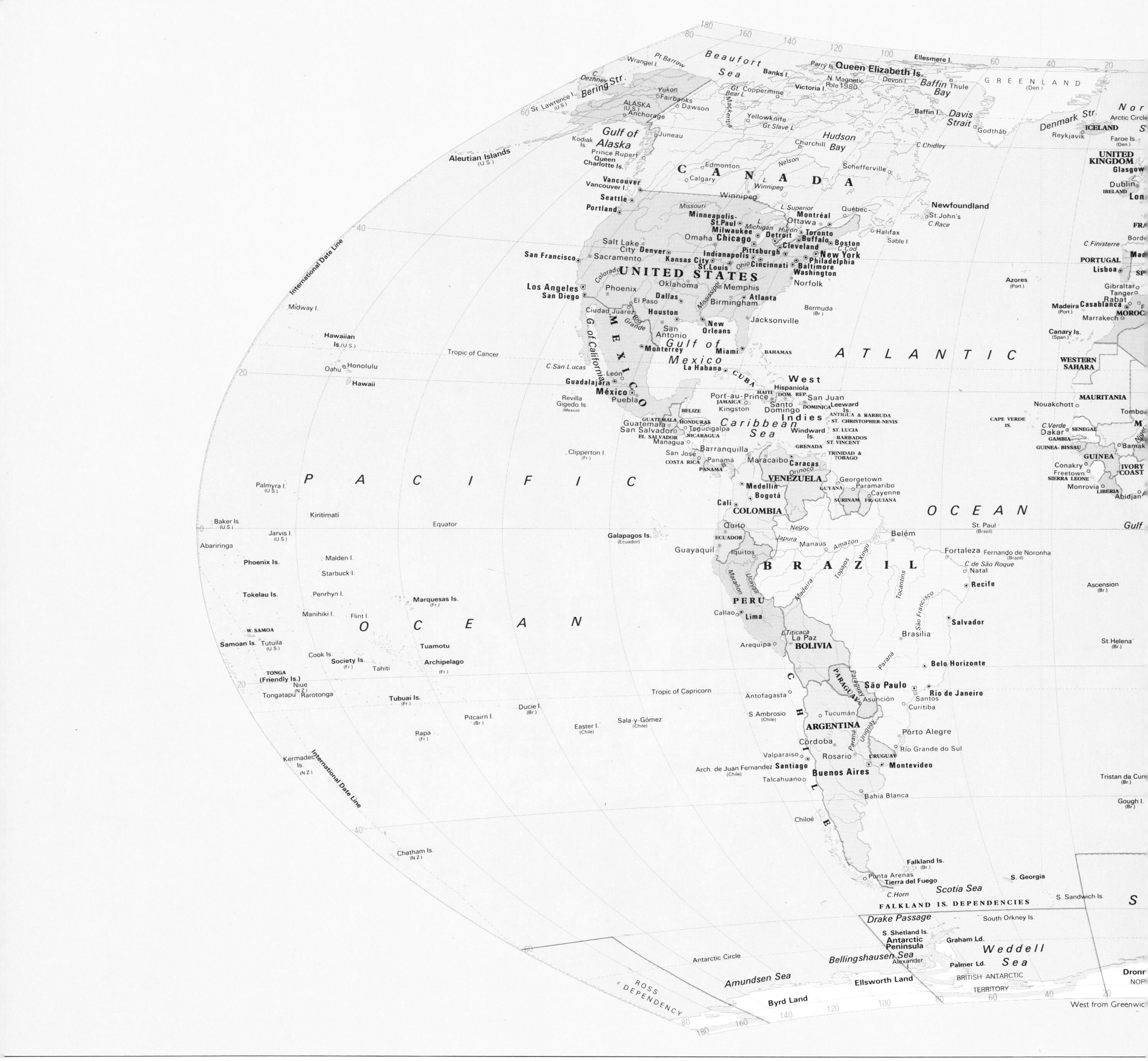

Introduction

A modern and comprehensive atlas has become indispensable both to students of geography and to general readers who want to understand the new economic and political shape of the world. This atlas is unique in that a concise, fascinating and authoritative text, illustrated with striking photographs, supports the fully detailed maps and graphs. The text and maps are indexed separately, so the reader should consult the Index to the Text for information about a particular country or town and the Index to the Maps for its geographical location.

Spellings of place names are in the forms given in the latest official lists and generally agree with the rules of the Permanent Committee on Geographical Names and the United States Board on Geographic Names.

The style of colouring chosen for the maps takes advantage of new developments in cartographic design and production. The inclusion of a hill-shading to complement the political colouring brings out clearly the character of the land and relief features without impairing the detail of names, settlement and communication. The opportunity of new reproduction was also taken to revise coastlines and rivers, boundaries and administrative divisions, railways, roads and airports.

Attention is drawn to the policy adopted where there are rival claims to territory; international boundaries are drawn to show the de facto situation. This does not denote international recognition of these boundaries but shows the states which are administering the areas on either side of the line. The maps are not drawn to the same scale, but each one has its own scale clearly marked where appropriate.

The majority of the maps are accompanied by a small selection of climate graphs. Where possible, towns have been chosen to reflect climatic differences within the area shown on the map, and principal towns are usually included. Complete temperature, pressure and rainfall statistics have been obtained for all except a few stations where pressure statistics were not available. Wherever possible the graphs show average observations based upon long period means, and in all other cases over as long a period as possible. The latest available statistics have been consulted throughout. The figure after the name of the station gives the height in metres of the station above sea-level, so that comparisons between stations can be made after allowing for elevation. For temperature, measurements are given in degrees centigrade; for pressure, millibars; while for precipitation (rainfall and snowfall), the measurements are given in millimetres.

The temperature graphs show the monthly means of daily maximum and minimum actual temperatures; from these the mean monthly actual temperatures can easily be determined by taking the mid point of the bar. The mean annual range of temperature is given above the temperature graphs. The pressure graphs show the mean monthly pressure at sea-level, except in cases of high-level stations, where the height to which the pressure has been reduced is noted. For both temperature and pressure graphs a uniform scale has been employed throughout.

The rainfall graphs show the average monthly rainfall, and above them is given the average total annual rainfall. These graphs have been drawn to show the rainfall on the same scale for all stations to facilitate true comparisons between them. Where the rainfall graph extends over to the temperature graph it has been continued at the side of the graph.

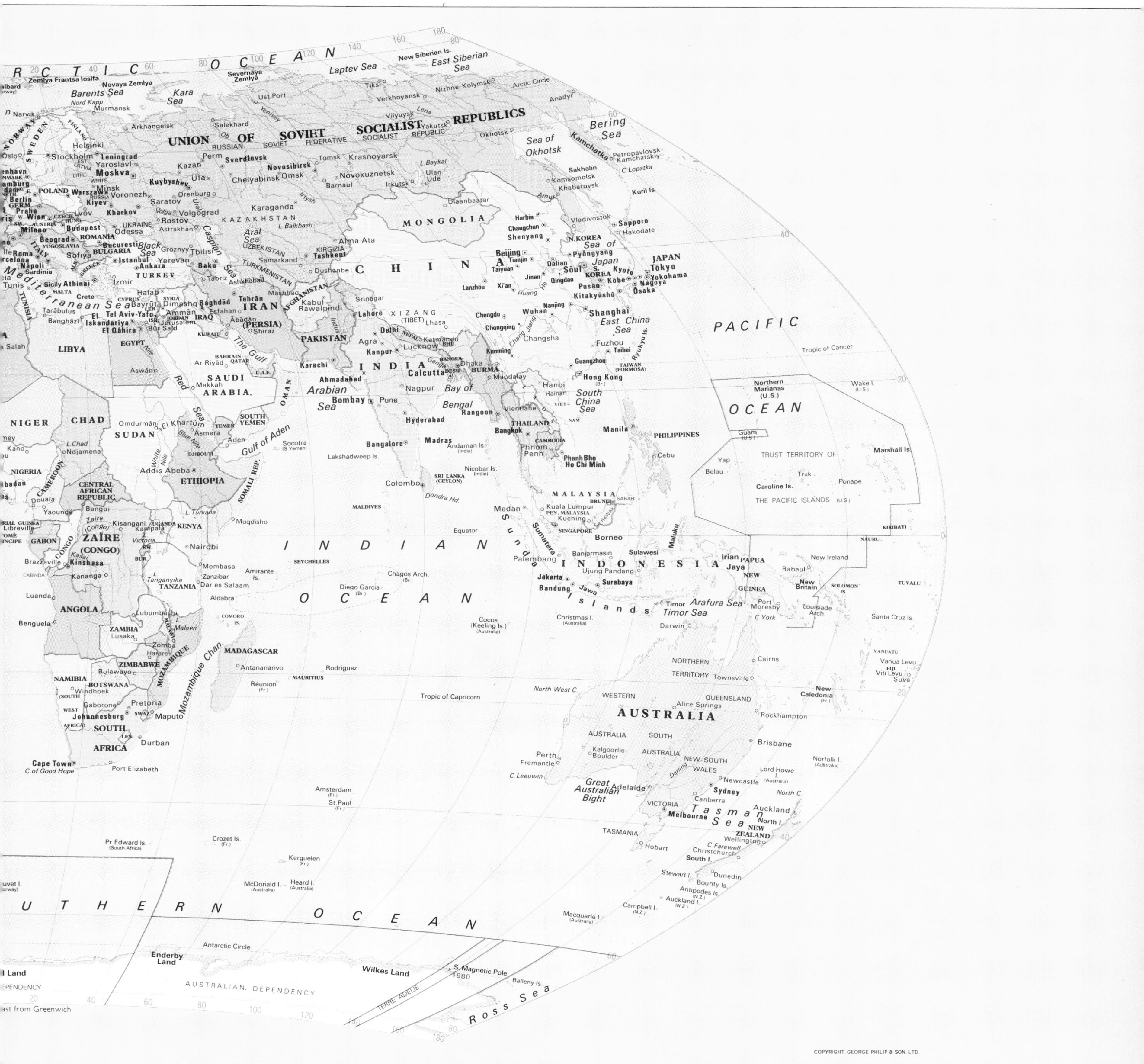

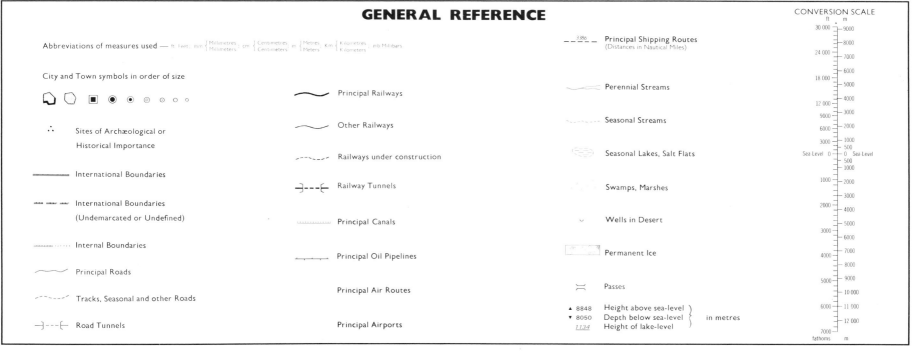

GENERAL REFERENCE

Abbreviations of measures used — ft. Feet, mm {Millimetres / Millimeters}, cm {Centimetres / Centimeters}, m {Metres / Meters}, Km {Kilometres / Kilometers}, mb Millibars

City and Town symbols in order of size

Sites of Archæological or Historical Importance

International Boundaries

International Boundaries (Undemarcated or Undefined)

Internal Boundaries

Principal Roads

Tracks, Seasonal and other Roads

Road Tunnels

Principal Railways

Other Railways

Railways under construction

Railway Tunnels

Principal Canals

Principal Oil Pipelines

Principal Air Routes

Principal Airports

3386 Principal Shipping Routes (Distances in Nautical Miles)

Perennial Streams

Seasonal Streams

Seasonal Lakes, Salt Flats

Swamps, Marshes

Wells in Desert

Permanent Ice

Passes

▲ 8848 Height above sea-level
▼ 8050 Depth below sea-level } in metres
1134 Height of lake-level

CONVERSION SCALE

ft	m
30 000	9000
	8000
24 000	7000
	6000
18 000	5000
	4000
12 000	3000
9000	
6000	2000
3000	1000
	500
Sea Level 0	0 Sea Level
	500
	1000
1000	2000
	3000
2000	4000
	5000
3000	6000
	7000
4000	8000
	9000
5000	10 000
6000	11 000
	12 000
7000 fathoms	m

THE ARCTIC

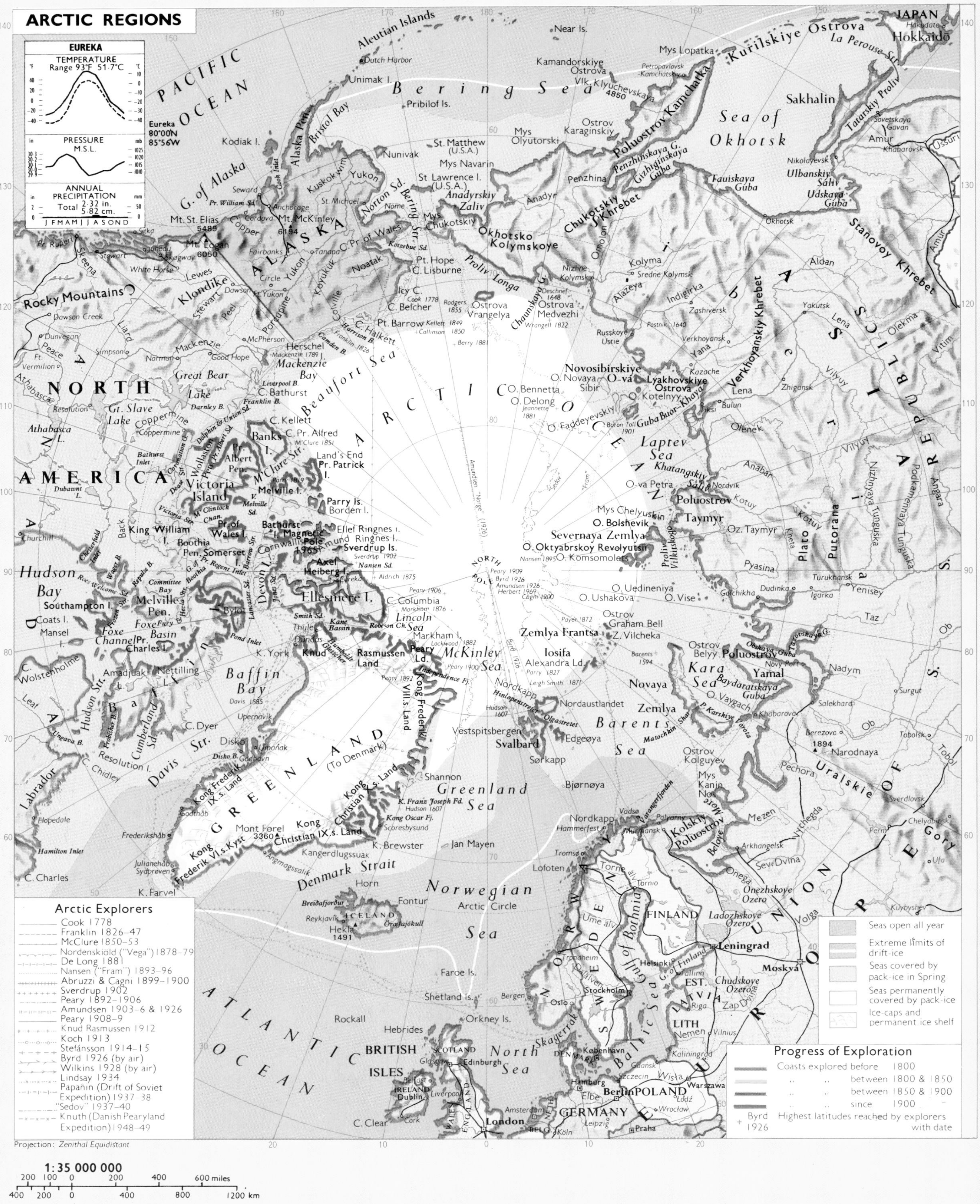

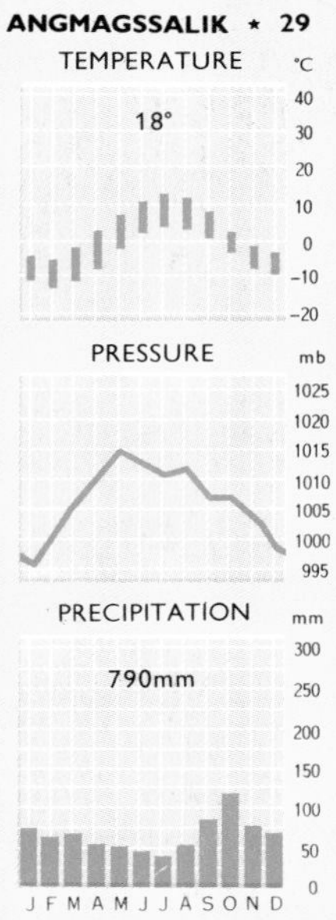

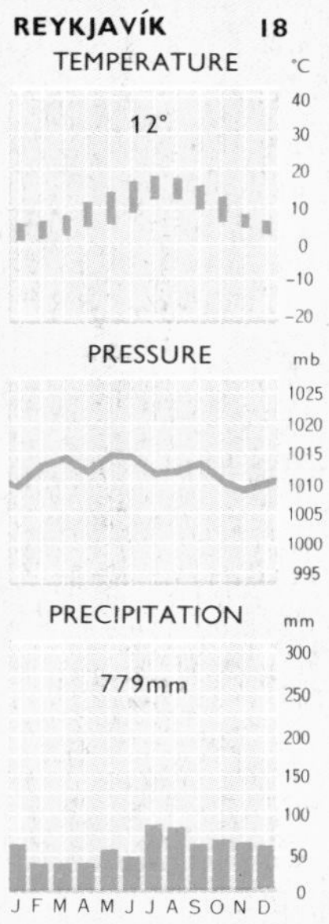

The Arctic Ocean, with its vast area of pack ice, and the Arctic lands in northern America, Europe and Asia make up a total area of 14.2 million km2 (5.5 million sq.m.). This bleak region of continuous cold today plays a vital role in meteorology and aviation and is increasingly being exploited for its minerals and fish.

Although the Arctic Circle itself lies along latitude 66° 30″N, geographers usually define the Arctic limit as the northern tree line and this corresponds generally with a line where average July temperatures do not rise above 10°C (50°F). North of this line lie the island of Greenland, part of Iceland, belts of land in Alaska, Canada, Norway, Sweden, Finland and the USSR and the many islands of the Arctic Ocean. Within this region, winter temperatures average −34°C (−30°F) and the sun rises only between March and September.

Rainfall is low, averaging 15-25cm (6-10in) but slow evaporation leaves the ground damp. Apart from Greenland, the land is generally free of ice but a thick layer of permafrost (mainly gravel) lies beneath the surface. Nevertheless, the topsoil thaws in summer and the plains (tundra) are covered with many species of plants, including moss, lichens, grasses, low shrubs and flowers. Apart from birds, wildlife includes polar bears, foxes, squirrels, hares, voles, lemmings and, during summer, large herds of reindeer and caribou. Some of the world's richest fishing grounds lie near Greenland and Iceland and the Arctic peoples also hunt whales and seals.

Mineral resources are widespread. Coal is found in Alaska, Canada, Greenland, Siberia and the Norwegian Svalbard Islands (Spitzbergen). There is iron, lead, nickel and petroleum in Canada and the USSR, petroleum in Alaska, uranium and thorium in Canada, iron in the Scandinavian Arctic and some gold, copper and tin.

In the USSR, several cities lie within the Arctic, including the ice-free port of Murmansk and the mining centre of Norilsk. The largest group of Arctic peoples are the Yakuts of Siberia (300,000) and the Zyrians (300,000) who are a Finnish race, as are the Lapps (30,000). The Inuit, or Eskimos (100,000) are the most widespread group, living mainly in Greenland, Alaska and Canada. They have probably lived in the Arctic for at least 12,000 years. Although Nordic seamen established settlements from the 10th century, European exploration began in earnest only in about 1500 and was directed mainly towards finding a short sea route to the Pacific. Robert E. Peary

Above: *Dog-drawn sledges are still vital for transport in the wilder areas of north-west and east Greenland.*

Right: *Icebergs broken off the polar icecap can drift well beyond the Arctic Circle.*

reached the North Pole in 1909. In 1958, the US submarine Nautilus travelled under the polar icecap, a distance of 2,945km (1,830 miles).

Today, world airline routes cross the Arctic as the shortest route from Europe to the Pacific. Strategic defence bases are maintained in the region by several nations, chiefly the US and USSR. Weather stations provide invaluable advance information on developments affecting America and Europe, especially the movement of low pressure areas lying between Siberia and Alaska (the Aleutian low) and Canada and northern Europe (the Icelandic low) which often send storms raging southward.

Greenland

Greenland, a province of Denmark with an area of 2,175,600km^2 (840,000sq.m.) is the world's largest island. It has a population of 52,000 and a capital at Godthaab (10,000). Most of the people are a mixture of Eskimo and Danish and the Greenlandic language is closely related to Eskimo. The island was settled by Eskimos from North America by the ninth century and was named Greenland by Norsemen who tried to attract settlers there after the tenth century. A possession of Denmark since 1380, Greenland is now a self-governing province.

Existing crayolite and coal mines are now exhausted, but further exploitation of mineral resources is planned. The population lives mainly by fishing, with some farming in the south-western coastal area. There is a US air base at Thule.

Geologically part of Canada, which is only 16km (10 miles) away at the nearest point, Greenland has mountains rising to 3,660m (12,000ft) in the north, west and east but is mainly a low plateau under a permanent icecap more than 1.6km (one mile) thick. It is deeply indented with fjords. Along the coasts, immense ice floes break off a series of glaciers, the widest of them the Humboldt Glacier, 97km (60 miles) across at the coast. Inland temperatures average −47°C (−53°F) in winter and −11°C (12°F) in summer.

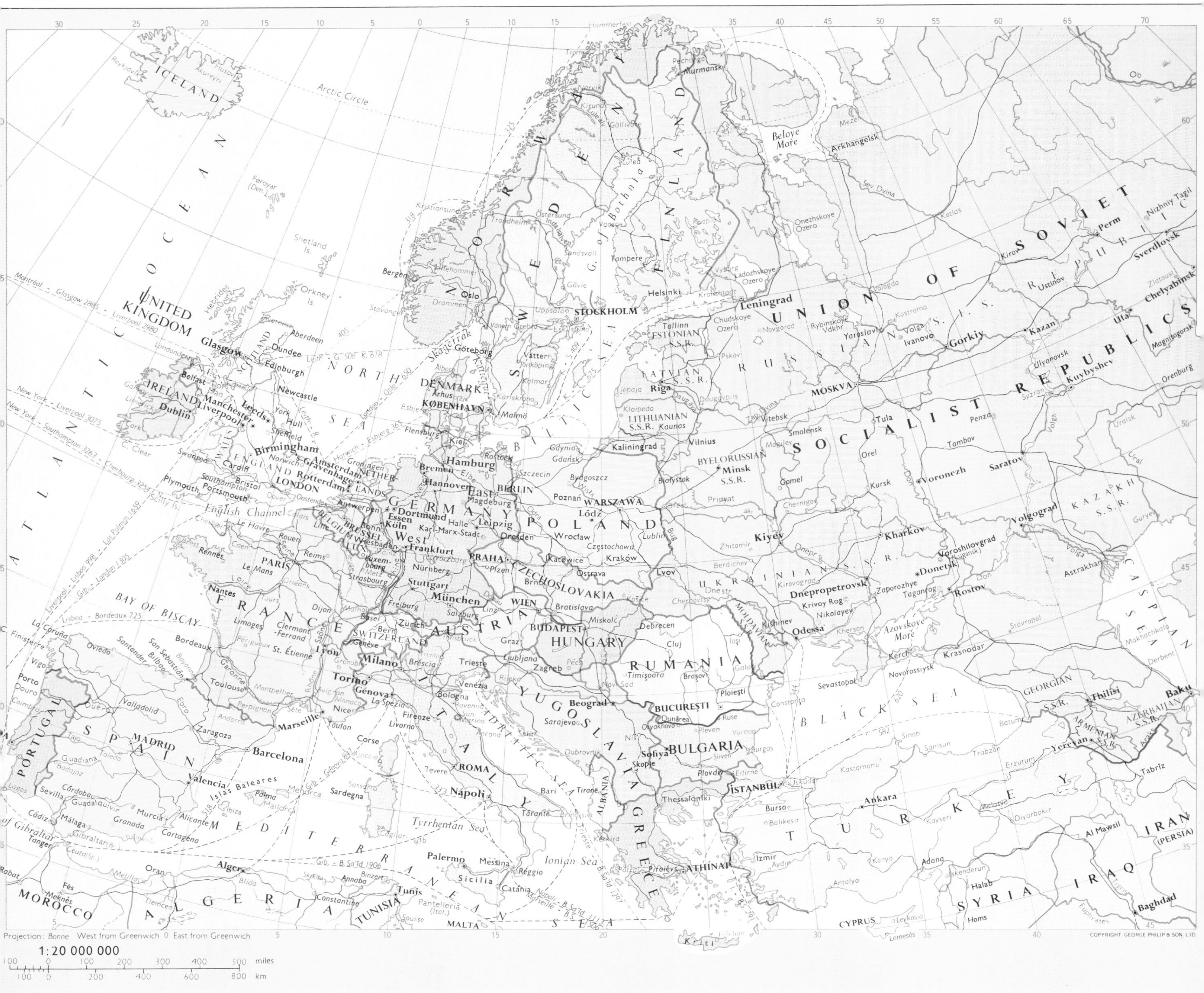

Map 4   EUROPE

Projection: Bonne   West from Greenwich 0 East from Greenwich

1:20 000 000

COPYRIGHT GEORGE PHILIP & SON, LTD

Density of population: Europe

DENSITY OF
POPULATION

B

■ Towns with over
500 000 inhabitants

Inhabitants	per mile²	per km²
	under 2	under 1
	2 – 16	1 – 6
	16 – 32	6 – 12
	32 – 64	12 – 25
	64 – 128	25 – 50
	128 – 256	50 – 100
	256 – 512	100 – 200
	over 512	over 200

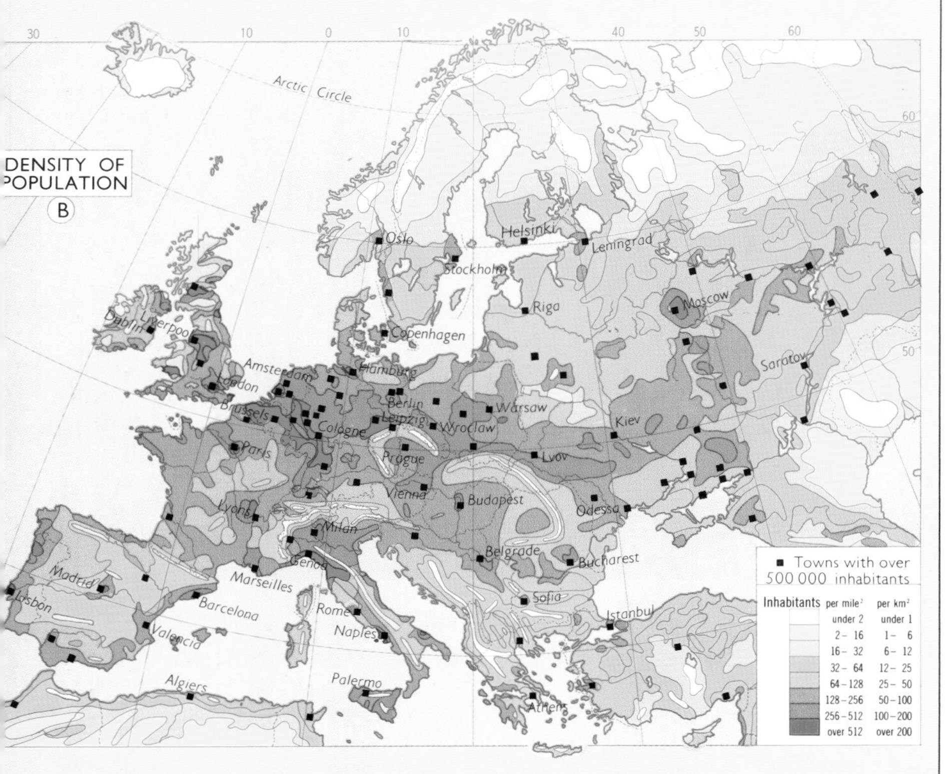

The continent of Europe has been a decisive influence on the economic, social and cultural history of much of the world for more than two thousand years. Since the peak of European power in the 19th century, two shattering wars, the dismantling of colonial empires and the rise of major world powers in America and the East have reduced the relative importance of Europe's political and technological leadership. But the continent includes many of the world's most prosperous economies, has an unmatched heritage of art, architecture, music, literature and science, and comprises a fascinating variety of peoples, languages and landscapes. It owes its position as the cradle of western civilization both to the energy and imagination of its people and to a fortunate combination of natural resources, both mineral and agricultural.

Europe is defined geographically as that part of the Eurasian land mass lying between the Atlantic Ocean in the west and the Ural mountains of the USSR in the east and from the Mediterranean in the south to the Arctic Circle in the north. This huge peninsula has an area of 10,523,000km² (4,063,000sq.m.) and a population of about 770 million,

grouped in 34 nations. Its highest peak is Mt Elbrus in the Caucasus, 5,633m (18,481ft), its longest river the Volga, 3,690km (2,293 miles) and its largest lake the Caspian Sea, 371,800km² (143,550sq.m.). The climate of its western regions is moderated by a warm air stream from the Atlantic. The Mediterranean region is warm and mild, whilst the rest of Europe has a continental climate, with bitter winters in the east. The four main land forms are the ancient, eroded Northwest Mountains, the fertile rolling country of the Great European Plain, the Central Uplands stretching south of this through Central Europe to Portugal, and the Alpine Mountain System of Spain, Switzerland, Italy and the Balkans. More than half the land is farmed, but agriculture employs under a quarter of the workforce. The Industrial Revolution, which started in Britain in the 18th century, soon spread through the continent, thanks to widespread deposits of coal and iron. The heavy industrial capacity of nations such as the USSR, Poland, East and West Germany, Belgium, France and the United Kingdom is today being supplanted by light industries such as electronics.

Although the Cold War tensions that lined up western nations under NATO and eastern Europe under the Warsaw Pact have been reduced, the continent remains divided into two distinct political and economic blocs. Economically the socialist countries are grouped in the Council for Mutual Economic Aid (Comecon) while economic leadership of the west is taken by the European Economic Community (EEC). The EEC includes France, West Germany, Italy, the Benelux countries, the UK, Denmark, Eire and Greece. Spain and Portugal joined in 1986.

The British Isles

The British Isles consist of two main islands and a number of smaller islands off the northwest coast of Europe. They are separated from the continent by the English Channel which is 32km (20m.) across at its narrowest point. The larger of the two islands is made up of three countries–England, Scotland and Wales – known collectively as Great Britain. Together with Northern Ireland, which takes up the northeastern part of the second main island, these countries constitute the United Kingdom of Great Britain and Northern Ireland, and are united under one government. The United Kingdom is often referred to as Great Britain, or simply Britain.

The Republic of Ireland, or Eire in the Irish language, is an independent nation occupying most of the smaller main island with the exception of the northeastern portion.

The United Kingdom

Area: 244,044km^2 (94,226sq.m.).
Population: 55.78 million.
Capital and largest city: London (6.75m).
Languages: English, Welsh and Gaelic.
Ethnic groups: British (descended from Celts, Romans, Angles, Saxons, Danes, Normans), and people of Commonwealth origin, mainly Asian and West Indian.
Main exports: engines, electrical machinery, cars, aircraft, and other engineering products, textiles and clothing, electronics, oil and financial services.
Average temperatures: 4°C (39°F) Jan, 16°C (61°F) July.
Highest point: Ben Nevis 1,343m (4,406ft).

Above: *A view from Little Langdale over the mountains of the Lake District, a beautiful English landscape, with the country's largest lakes and highest peaks.*

The British Isles form a relatively small archipelago and its peoples make up less than two percent of the world's population. But for nearly 500 years they have exercised a profound influence on world affairs. At the end of the 19th century the British ruled the seas and controlled the largest empire the world had ever seen. They started the Industrial Revolution; their legal system and democratic institutions became models for many other nations to copy; and the English language and culture have spread to the remotest parts of the globe.

The characteristics of the English, Scots, Welsh and Irish have sometimes clashed, but at other times have combined to make up a blend of individualism and adventurousness that has produced some of the world's greatest explorers, soldiers, scientists, statesmen, and writers.

The British Isles have been settled since the Stone Age, and today's Britons have many different ethnic origins. Some are descended from invaders: Celts, Romans, Angles, Saxons, Jutes, Vikings, Danes and Normans. Others came to work, such as the Flemings, or to escape persecution, such as French Huguenots and Jews. More recent settlers include immigrants from the Commonwealth: from Africa, from the Caribbean, from India, Pakistan and Bangladesh. Immigrants have often faced racial and economic discrimination, despite their contribution to the cultural variety of the British Isles.

Britain is a densely populated country with nearly 230 people to the square kilometre. More than four-fifths of the people live in England; nearly four-fifths of them live in or near towns, and about a quarter of them are found within 80km (50m) of London.

English is the official language of the United Kingdom. Over half a million people can speak Welsh, which is officially recognized within Wales. Other Celtic languages which may still be heard include Irish, Scottish and Manx Gaelic.

Britain's social welfare system is designed to look after its citizens 'from the cradle to the grave'. It includes free medical treatment, sickness and unemployment benefits, and retirement pensions. Education is free, and is compulsory to the age of 16.

There are two established (official) churches – the Church of England (episcopal) in England and the Presbyterian Church of Scotland in Scotland.

Most Britons are keen on sport. Football (soccer) is the national winter game, and cricket takes over in summer. Rugby, tennis, golf, bowls, and water sports also have large followings.

History and constitution

The Norman Conquest in 1066 marks the last time that the British Isles were successfully invaded. At that time the Channel Islands, which were part of Normandy, came under the English monarch and are today self-governing dependencies of the British Crown. This is also the present status of the Isle of Man, which was taken from Norway in 1266.

In the century or so after the Norman Conquest a bitter conflict developed between the English monarch and the barons, each jealously guarding their own rights. In 1215 the barons forced King John to accept the Magna Carta, a document that guaranteed many of the barons' rights. Wales remained independent until the death of Llywelyn ap Gruffydd in 1282.

In 1266 Norway gave up the Hebrides to Scotland, and in 1468 likewise surrendered the Shetland Islands and Orkney. In 1603 King James VI of Scotland succeeded England's Queen Elizabeth I as James I of England. Thus the two countries were finally united under one monarch. But political union had to await the Act of Union of 1707, which provided them with a common parliament as well as a single ruler. Together with Wales, the two countries from that time became known jointly as Great Britain. In 1801 came a full union of Ireland with England, Wales and Scotland.

Abroad, by the 18th century, Britain had become an imperial power, gaining Canada and India but eventually losing its American colonies. At home, new machines were invented, steam was harnessed as a source of power, and coke was used in the manufacture of iron. Agri-

Above: *A view from the National Westminster Tower, London's tallest building, over the river Thames and St Paul's cathedral.*

cultural workers flocked to the towns to take up better paid jobs in factories. The Industrial Revolution was on its way, and Britain became the workshop of the world, attaining a peak of power and wealth in the second half of the 19th century.

From 1914 to 1918 Britain played a leading role in World War I against Germany and her allies but was left exhausted and impoverished after victory. After the war, southern Ireland became a self-governing dominion, and in 1949 broke away completely as an independent republic.

From 1939 to 1945 Britain was once again on the winning side in World War II, against Hitler's Nazi Germany and Japan. After this even more debilitating conflict Britain tried slowly to adapt to a declining role as a world power and to modernize its industrial plant and outdated labour relations. Many of the old class distinctions began to disappear and a wide programme of socialization was initiated. The once-great empire quickly dissolved as one colony after another claimed and was granted its independence, with India leading the way. Most of them softened the blow by joining the British Commonwealth of Nations (later to be known simply as the Commonwealth), which is a free association of equal and independent states, together with a number of dependent territories, whose head is the British sovereign.

From 1969 onwards, violence in Northern Ireland, which had been simmering for many years, erupted in a series of shootings and bombings. A demand by the Roman Catholic minority there for power-sharing with the Protestant majority in this partly self-governing territory was backed by a terrorist campaign

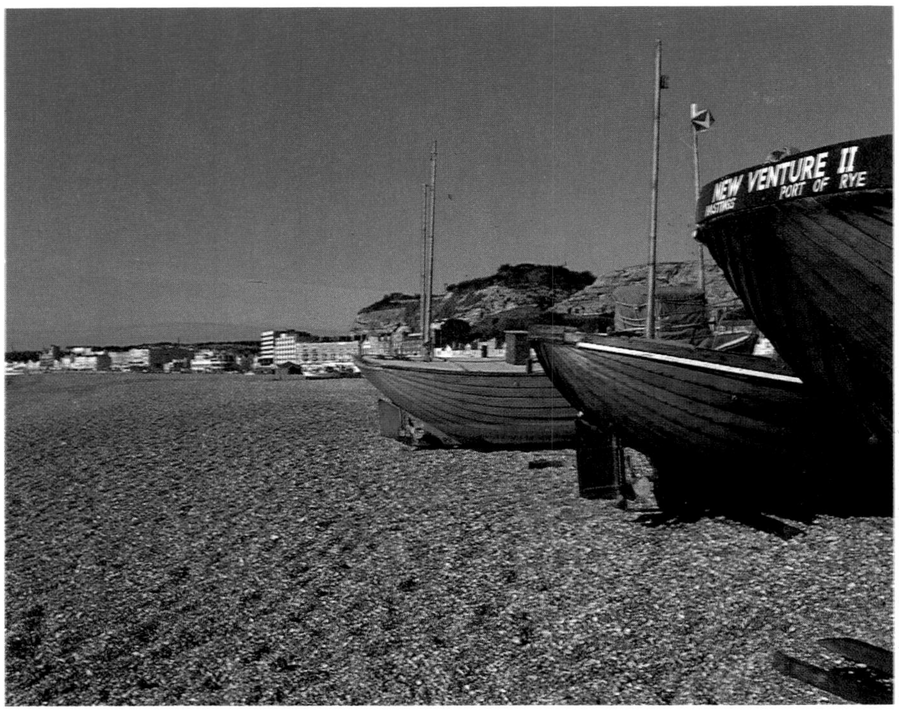

Left: *The ruins of a medieval castle overlooking the old fishing settlement and port of Hastings, now a seaside resort.*

run by proscribed groups such as the Provisional IRA (Irish Republican Army) which sought unification with the largely Roman Catholic republic across the loosely-patrolled border. The Protestants, who strongly support the union with Britain, retaliated with bullets and bombs of their own. Britain established direct rule over Northern Ireland and sent large numbers of troops to the strife-torn area, but by the mid-1980s a solution seemed as remote as ever.

In 1973 Britain was formally admitted to the European Common Market after previous unsuccessful attempts to join. Oil and gas from the North Sea provided a much needed boost for the British economy in the 1980s. Inflation was reduced, but unemployment soared dramatically.

Britain is a constitutional monarchy, with a largely unwritten parliamentary constitution based on well-tried ideas and practices. The House of Commons, with 635 elected members, is the governing body. The House of Lords, which may delay but not defeat bills, has about 1,000 members, most of whom are hereditary peers and peeresses. The monarch is Head of State but the nation is governed by a Cabinet picked by the Prime Minister, usually the leader of the majority party in the Commons.

London is the capital of England, as well as of the United Kingdom. The capitals of Wales, Scotland and Northern Ireland are Cardiff, Edinburgh, and Belfast, respectively. Pressure in the 1970s for devolution of powers in Scotland and Wales has now subsided.

Land and climate

Great Britain is a little under 960km (600 miles) long from north to south, and a little more than 480km (300 miles) wide at its maximum. The scenery is extremely varied for such a comparatively compact area. The Highlands rise in the north of Scotland. The Grampian Mountains form the chief range and include Ben Nevis, Britain's highest point. The land is craggy, desolate, and windswept, with deep fjords (sea lochs) cutting far inland from both the Atlantic and the North Sea.

The Central Lowlands lie to the south of the Highlands, and are made up of the valleys of the rivers Tay, Clyde, and Forth. Rich coalfields and fertile farmland made this region a centre of population and industry. Farther south, the Southern Uplands rise in gently rounded hills. This is sheep-grazing country, and the valley of the Tweed is famous for its woollen mills. The Cheviot Hills, which mark the border between Scotland and England, rise to the south of this region.

England's Pennine mountain chain runs southwards from the Scottish border to Derbyshire. It is often called 'the backbone of England' and its flanks

1:2 400 000
miles
km
KEW 5
TEMPERATURE
°C
13°
PRESSURE
mb
PRECIPITATION
mm
593 mm
J F M A M J J A S O N D
ABERPORTH 133
TEMPERATURE
11°
PRESSURE
PRECIPITATION
990 mm
J F M A M J J A S O N D
SCILLY ISLES
On same Scale
Isles of Scilly
St. Mary's
Penzance
Land's End
St.Ives
NORTH SEA
IRISH SEA
ENGLISH CHANNEL
Bristol Channel
Cardigan Bay
SCOTLAND
Southern Uplands
Pennines
WALES
Cambrian Mts.
Cotswolds
Chiltern Hills
North Downs
FRANCE
Channel Islands
ISLE OF MAN
ISLE OF WIGHT
LONDON
Birmingham
Manchester
Liverpool
Leeds
Sheffield
Bristol
Cardiff
Newcastle
Edinburgh
Glasgow
Projection: Conical with two standard parallels.
West from Greenwich
East from Greenwich
COPYRIGHT, GEORGE PHILIP & SON, LTD.

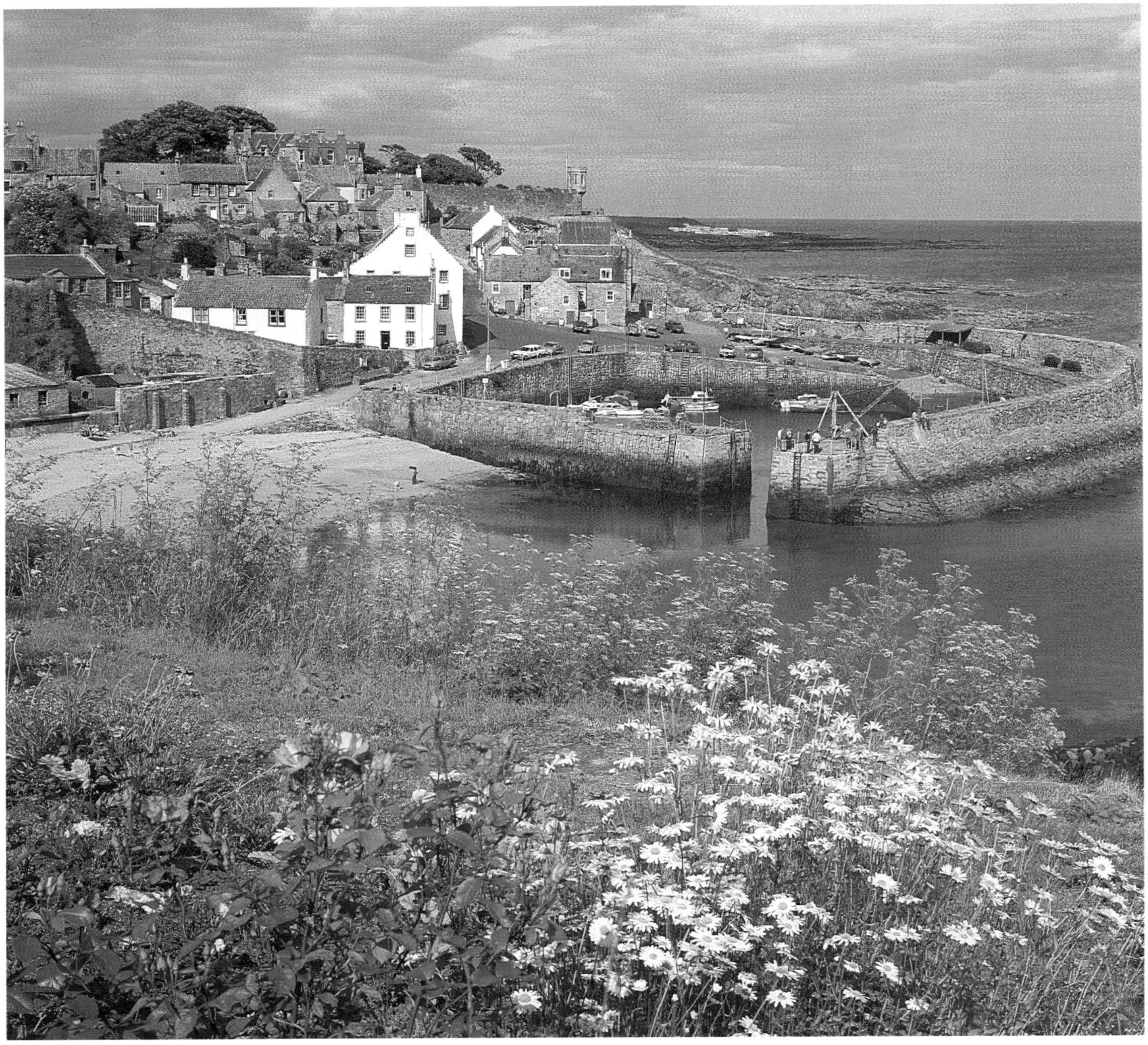

Left: *Crail harbour, Fife, in the Scottish Lowlands where sea-fishing still thrives.*

Below: *British Camp, the Iron Age hill fort on Hereford Beacon in the Malvern Hills, overlooks the lush border country between England and Wales.*

are rich in coal. To the west of the Pennines, England's largest and most beautiful lakes are grouped together in the Lake District, a celebrated tourist attraction.

To the southwest of the Pennines a narrow lowland strip separates them from the magnificent Cambrian Mountains of North Wales. South Wales has extensive coalfields, and much of Welsh industry is centred there.

To the south of Wales, across the Bristol Channel, lies the southwest peninsula. This is made up of Somerset, Devon and Cornwall and is noted for its mild climate and holiday resorts. The region is a huge granite plateau that in many places breaks off in spectacular cliffs where it meets the sea.

The remainder of England is known as the English Lowlands. They include the mainly treeless rolling downs of parts of the south and southeast; the low, flat landscape of East Anglia; and the mineral-rich Midlands plain, which makes up Britain's industrial heart. A third of the people live and work in the southeast, many in London.

Northern Ireland is a land of low hills and fertile lowlands. It is shaped almost like a saucer, with the hills round the coastal rim.

Britain's longest river is the Severn, which rises in Central Wales and flows about 354km (220 miles) into the Bristol Channel. The Thames drains southeastern England, and with London astride it, is the most important of Britain's rivers. The Clyde, Mersey, and Humber also have important estuaries with the ports of Glasgow, Liverpool, and Hull, respectively, located on their banks. The largest lake in the British Isles is Lough Neagh in Northern Ireland, with an area of 398sq.km (153sq.m.).

In spite of its northerly latitude, which is the same as that of icy Labrador, Britain has a temperate climate. In winter the temperature rarely drops as low as −12°C (10°F) or reaches as high as 32°C (90°F) in summer. Its mildness is due to the North Atlantic Drift, which warms the prevailing westerly winds. Rain falls during every month of the year, most of it in the northwest of the country. February and August are the wettest months.

Natural resources

Coal has been Britain's most important natural resource since the early 1600s and reserves are expected to last for at least another 200 years. But the best and easiest seams have already been worked out and new and deeper seams are constantly being explored while older pits are closed. Although annual coal production has been declining, it is still the basis of most electrical power. The main coalfields are located in the East Midlands, South Wales, in the Central Lowlands of Scotland, and along the edges of the Pennines in the north of England.

Britain's iron ore is abundant but of poor quality. As a result, higher grades are imported in large quantities. Fine china clay for making pottery is found in the southwest of England, and chalk and limestone, for making cement, are plentiful in the southeast.

1:2 000 000

WICK   36
TEMPERATURE   °C
10°
PRESSURE   mb
PRECIPITATION   mm
771 mm
J F M A M J J A S O N D

EDINBURGH   134
TEMPERATURE   °C
11°
PRESSURE   mb
PRECIPITATION   mm
676 mm
J F M A M J J A S O N D

SHETLAND IS.
On same scale

Projection : Conical with two standard parallels.   West from Greenwich   COPYRIGHT. GEORGE PHILIP & SON. LTD.

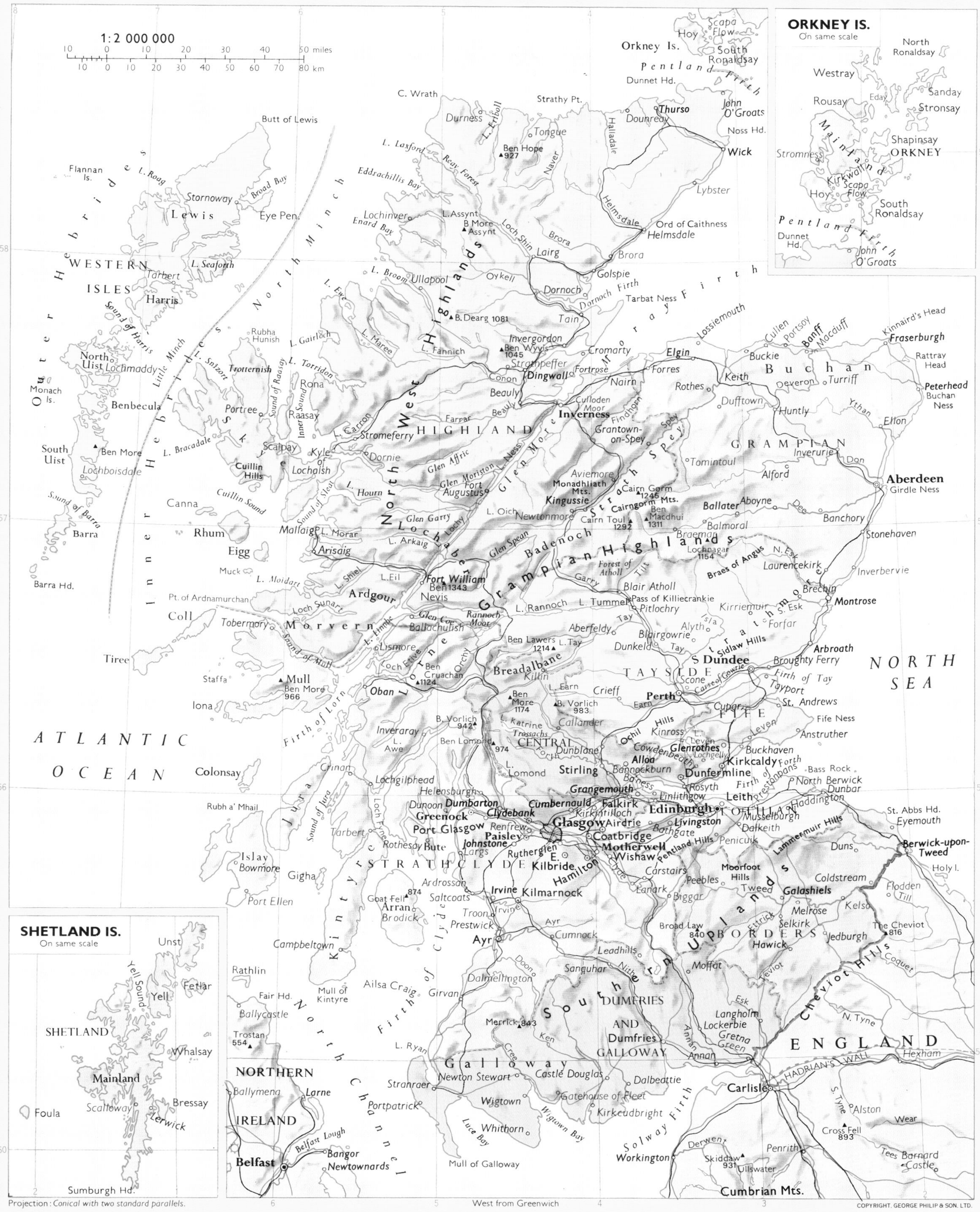

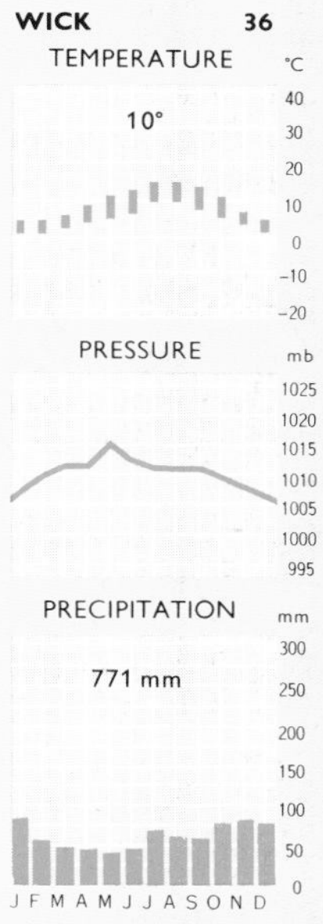

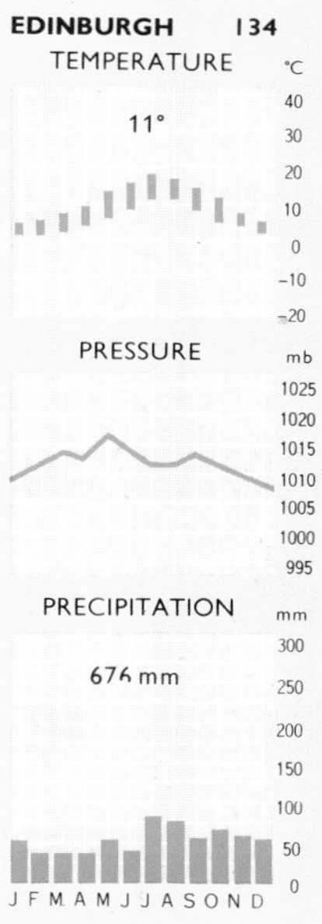

There are large natural gas fields in the North Sea. Supplies were already widely in use by the early 1970s. Huge oil deposits were discovered in the bed of the North Sea in the late 1960s. Britain became an oil-exporting country and by the early 1980s was producing over 70 million tonnes of refined oil annually.

Farming, fishing and forestry

British farmers are unable wholly to feed the country because there is not enough fertile land available. In spite of efficient farming methods and much recent modernization, nearly half Britain's food is imported. The main arable area is in the eastern part of the country, while in general the west is given over to livestock rearing. The principal agricultural products are barley, wheat, oilseed rape, potatoes, and sugar beet. Britain's beef, especially Scottish beef, is world famous. Sheep are reared more for their meat than for their wool. British breeding cattle and sheep are in demand all over the world to improve local stock.

The more sheltered parts of the south favour fruit, flower, and vegetable growing, much of it for the London market. Kent, in the southeast corner of England, has been called 'the garden of England'.

Northern Ireland's specialized and highly mechanized farms produce milk, butter, cheese, beef, bacon, eggs, and poultry.

Fishing has been a traditional industry for centuries. British fishing fleets regularly sail from ports such as Fleetwood, Hull, Grimsby, and Aberdeen to grounds in the North Sea and as far away as the Grand Banks off Newfoundland. Catches include cod, plaice, sole, haddock, hake, herring and skate. In 1982 Britain had a fishing fleet of some 6,500 vessels, which caught nearly 690,000 tonnes of wetfish and 60,000 tonnes of shellfish. The British fishing industry faces increasing competition. In the 1970s Britain became involved in a bitter clash with Iceland over fishing rights.

About 7 percent of Britain is forested, The Forestry Commission is the main timber producer, but much afforested land is privately owned. The country imports most of its timber.

Manufacturing industries

Manufacturing accounts for about 35 percent of Britain's gross national product, and in spite of the loss of captive markets and valuable sources of raw materials with the dissolution of the empire, the country is still one of the leading exporters of engineering products and other manufactured goods. Steel production is decreasing, but Britain remains within the world's top ten producers.

In addition to being the centre of politics, administration, law, insurance, banking, the arts, and fashion, London is also at the heart of the nation's network of transport and communications. Among its major industries are chemicals, clothing, printing, food processing,

Right: *Highlands surround the broad, undulating, central limestone plain near Graignenamanaugh, County Kilkenny.*

Below: *The Protestant cathedral of St Finn Barr in Cork, seaport and county town of County Cork on the river Lee in Ireland.*

paper, furniture, plastics, electronics, and mechanical engineering.

The Midlands, stretching outwards from the sprawling conurbations of Birmingham (2,240,000) [Britain's second city], Wolverhampton (255,000), and Coventry (316,000), has traditionally been the heartland of British industry. The major industries are motor vehicle manufacture, metal products, tractors, and bicycles, and a wide range of other engineering products, as well as pottery. Lancashire has a declining textile industry (formerly cotton but now mainly man-made fibres), and oil refining, shipbuilding, food processing, chemicals, glassmaking, elecronics, paper, and printing are also important. The largest cities in that region are Greater Manchester (2.6m) and Greater Liverpool (1.5m).

The Yorkshire textile industry is better known for its woollen goods and carpets. Sheffield (546,000) is celebrated for its steel and cutlery. Coal, iron and steel, chemicals, and shipbuilding are the major industries of northeastern England. The Central Lowlands of Scotland, with the centre of Glasgow (1.7m) at its hub, produces ships, iron and steel, electronics and woollen goods. Northern Ireland has the largest shipbuilding yards in Britain at its capital, Belfast (360,000). High-quality Irish linen manufacture and tobacco processing are other important industries.

Many British industries are nationalized (government-owned); they include the railways, coal, electricity and parts of the steel industry. They also include the nuclear power stations that have recently become the subject of heated debate.

Trade and external affairs

Britain is one of the world's leading trading nations. Its chief partners are the EEC member states, the United States, Canada, Japan, Australia and New Zealand. Although it imports more than it exports, it is a key financial centre, providing banking, shipping, insurance and other commercial services whose 'invisible' earnings make a significant contribution to its balance of payments.

Although Britain has lost much of its former power and prestige, its experience in statesmanship and its diplomatic finesse is valued abroad in delicate international situations and it has often been called on in the role of 'honest broker'. In addition to the influence it exercises through its world-wide Commonwealth, it retains numerous protectorates, colonies or associated territories. Most of the British territories in Oceania or the Caribbean region are described elsewhere in this book. Britain's only European possession is Gibraltar, a strategically powerful settlement at the entrance to the Mediterranean Sea. The crown colony of Hong Kong is to be returned to the People's Republic of China in 1997. The Falkland Islands (Islas Malvinas) are claimed by Argentina. Following an Argentinian invasion of the islands in 1982 war broke out between the two countries, with much loss of life. Their recovery by Britain has been followed by an uneasy peace.

The Republic of Ireland (Eire)

Area: 70,282km^2 (27,136sq.m.).
Population: 3.6 million.
Capital and largest city: Dublin (526,000).
Languages: Irish (Gaelic) and English.
Ethnic groups: Irish, with Anglo-Irish minority.
Main exports: meat, livestock, textiles, machinery, transport equipment, dairy products.
Average temperatures: 5.6°C (42°F) Jan, 15°C (59°F) July.
Highest point: Carrauntuohill, 1,040m (3,414ft).

The Irish people are descended from a branch of the ancient Celts who spoke a Goidelic language. They are a deeply patriotic and religious people, loquacious, artistic and musical. More than 90 percent of the people are Roman Catholics. The name of the country in Gaelic is *Eire*. Although small in size, Ireland's influence on the outside world has been remarkable, especially through the work of writers such as Joyce, Yeats, Wilde, Shaw and O'Casey.

Most of Ireland's recent history is taken up with the bitter struggle against British rule. From 1845 to 1849 a disease wiped out the Irish potato crop, and as a result more than a million people died of disease and starvation. Many of the survivors emigrated to the United States.

Rebellion against the British erupted sporadically from 1916 to 1921, after which Britain granted the country the status of a dominion. In 1949 Ireland severed its last ties with the British Commonwealth and declared itself an independent republic.

Since that time the Irish Republican Army (IRA), an illegal organization opposed to the partition of Ireland, has been a thorn in the side of the Irish government. Its offshoot, the Provisional IRA, has orchestrated a campaign of violence in Northern Ireland in the 1970s and 1980s.

Right: *Four Courts, by the river Liffey, was rebuilt after the civil war in 1922 and is one of Dublin's finest buildings.*

Projection : Conical with two standard parallels.

1 : 2 000 000

DUBLIN 68
TEMPERATURE °C
10°

PRESSURE mb

PRECIPITATION mm
769 mm

J F M A M J J A S O N D

ARMAGH 62
TEMPERATURE °C
11°

PRESSURE mb

PRECIPITATION mm
849 mm

J F M A M J J A S O N D

Towns underlined in Northern Ireland give their
names to the Districts in which they stand
The remaining Districts are:—

1	Fermanagh	5	Castlereagh
2	Moyle	6	Ards
3	Newtownabbey	7	Down
4	North Down	8	Newry & Mourne

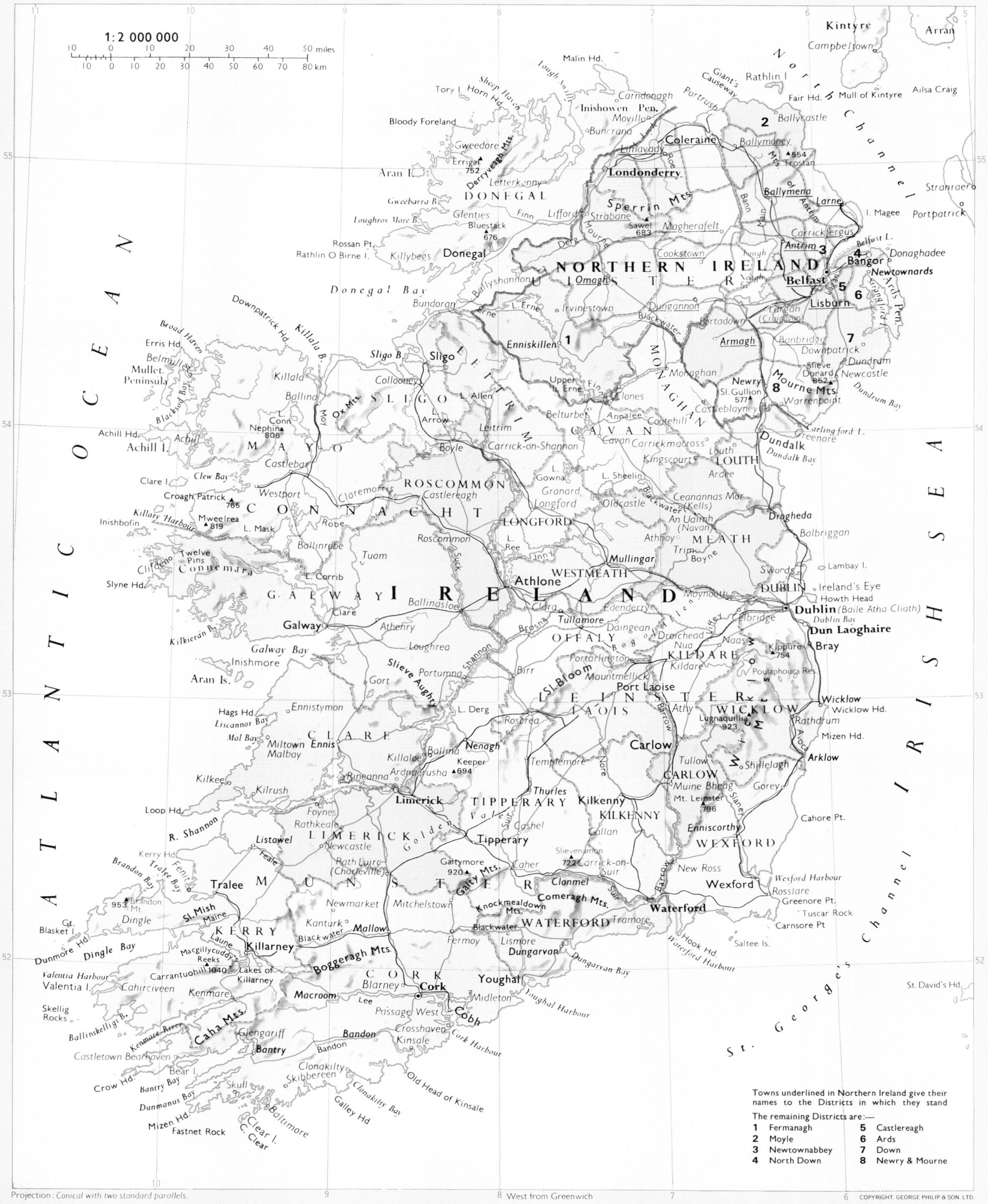

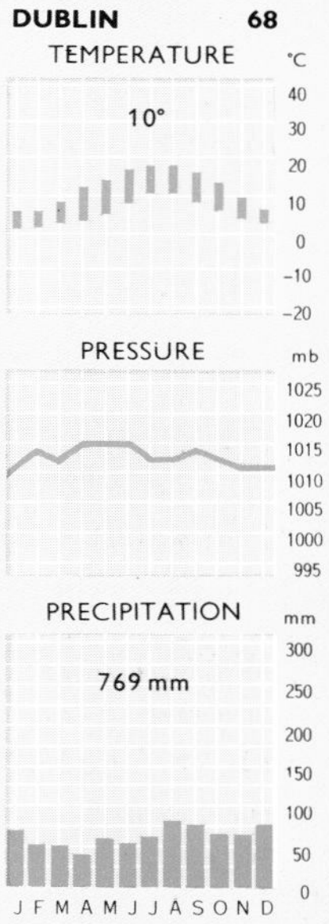

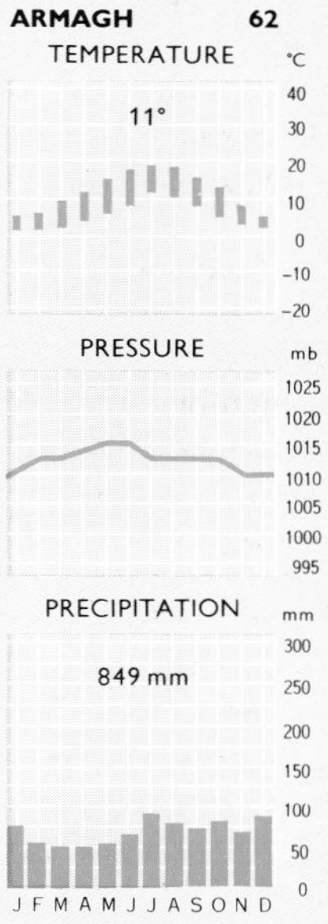

Land, climate and economy

Ireland's plentiful rainfall has made the land so green that it is often called the 'Emerald Isle'. The North Atlantic Drift comes close to the west coast and keeps the climate mild. Physically, Ireland consists of a large central lowland surrounded by a rim of plateaux and hills. Most of the low-lying land is used for cultivation or pasture, although some of it is peat bog. The Shannon, which flows for 386 km (240 miles) is the longest river in the British Isles.

Politically, the land consists of four provinces – Connaught, with five counties; Leinster, 12 counties; Munster, six counties; and Ulster, nine counties. Twenty-six of these 32 counties are in the Irish Republic and the others form the Six Counties of Northern Ireland.

Ireland's greatest resource is its fertile soil. The most important crops are barley, wheat, oats, potatoes, turnips, and beet. Cattle, sheep, pigs, and horses are reared. In the 1960s and 1970s there was considerably increased investment of foreign capital in a number of industrial undertakings such as oil-refining, shipbuilding, fertilizer manufacture, and electronics. Among traditional industries, glass-making at Waterford, and weaving and hand-knitting are well known. Tourism and travel are also major sources of income.

Ireland's major trading partners are the United Kingdom, the United States, West Germany and the Netherlands. Ireland joined the EEC in 1973.

Map 8 NORTHERN FRANCE

BREST   98
TEMPERATURE   °C
10°

PRESSURE   mb

PRECIPITATION mm
1129 mm

J F M A M J J A S O N D

NANTES   41
TEMPERATURE   °C
14°

PRESSURE'   mb

PRECIPITATION mm
741 mm

J F M A M J J A S O N D

DÉPARTEMENTS IN THE PARIS AREA
1 Ville de Paris   3 Val-de-Marne
2 Seine-St. Denis   4 Hauts-de-Seine

Projection: Conical with two standard parallels

1:2 500 000

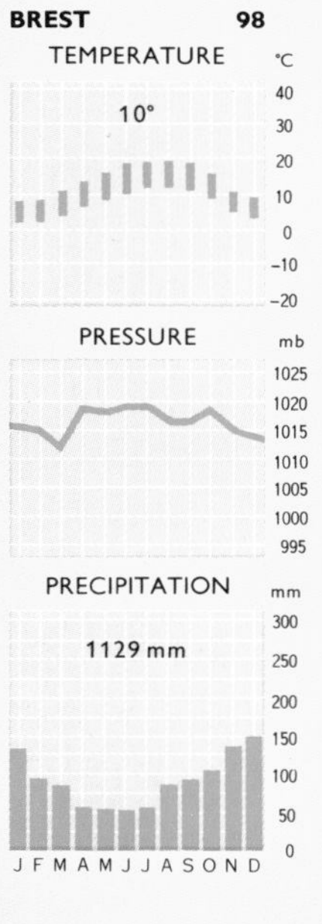

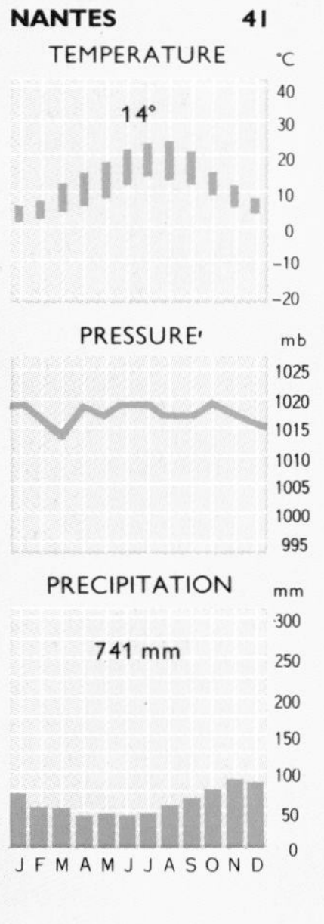

France

Area: 547,026km² (211,207sq.m.).
Population: 54.54 million.
Capital: Paris (metropolitan area, 8.5m).
Languages: French, Basque, Breton, Catalan, German, Provençal.
Ethnic groups: French, Basques, Bretons, Catalans, Flemings.
Main exports: electronics, chemicals, iron and steel goods, aerospace goods, cars, textiles, wines and spirits, luxury goods, beef.
Average temperatures: Paris, 3°C (37°F) Jan. 18°C (65°F) July; Marseille, 6°C (43°F) Jan. 22°C (72°F) July.
Highest point: Mont Blanc, 4,810m (15,781ft).

France is one of the most beautiful and varied of western European nations. It contains temperate fertile plans and rugged, scenic coastlines in the north, plateaux and high mountain scenery, and sunny Mediterranean beaches.

Each region has its own special character, culture and cuisine. France's elegant, cosmopolitan capital, Paris, is one of the world's leading cultural centres and the country has pioneered many artistic developments in architecture, literature, music and painting. French cuisine, cheeses, fashions, perfumes and wines are world-renowned.

After France was liberated from German occupation in 1944, it suffered crippling colonial wars and, as a consequence, political instability. But it has recovered quickly and has made a major contribution to the development of the European Economic Community, of which it was a founder member.

People

The French people are a mixture of various ethnic groups, based upon the original Celtic stock of the Gauls. At different times in its history, France has been subjected to Roman, Moorish and Italian influences from the south. From the north came Norse, and from the east, Frankish and other Germanic influences.

French is a Romance language. A Celtic language, Breton, survives in Brittany and forms the basis of separatist aspirations. Breton nationalism, however, also owes much to geographical remoteness and the relative poverty of its farming and fishing people.

In the southwest, the Basques form a distinctive group, quite different from Frenchmen or Spaniards. The Basque language is of very ancient origin. At the western end of France's border with Spain live the Catalans, whose Romance language resembles that of Provençal. German is spoken in Alsace, which was returned to France from Germany after World War I, and

Map 9

PARIS 75
TEMPERATURE °C
16°
PRESSURE mb
PRECIPITATION mm
619 mm
J F M A M J J A S O N D

DIJON 220
TEMPERATURE °C
18°
PRESSURE mb
PRECIPITATION mm
739 mm
J F M A M J J A S O N D

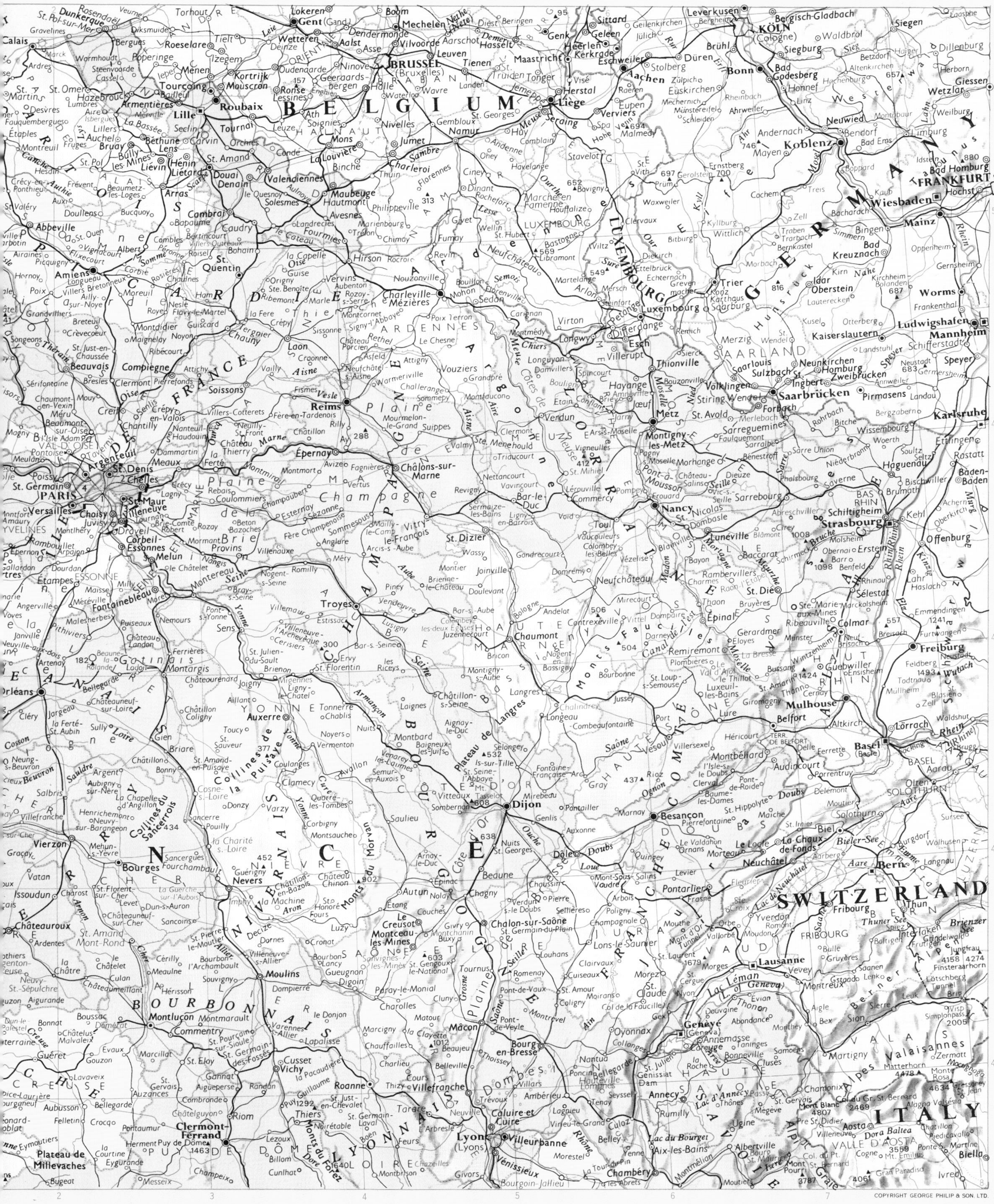

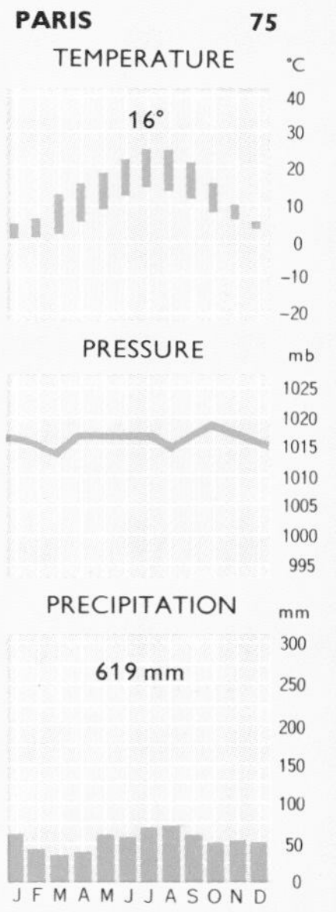

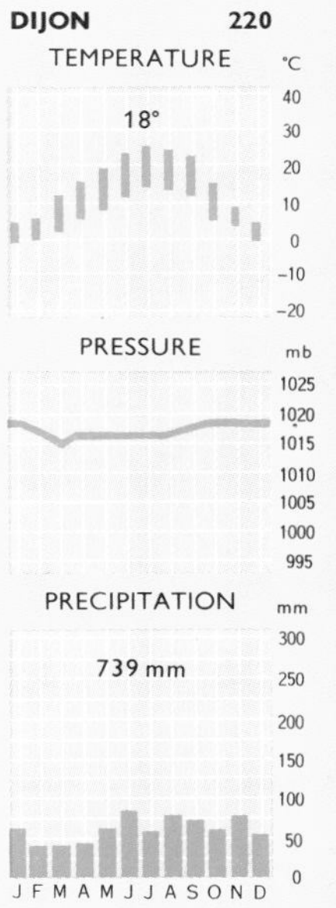

some French-speaking Flemings live in the region bordering Belgium.

In about 1800, France had a population of 27 million – the largest in Europe except for Russia. By 1900 it had increased to 39 million but, in the early 1900s, the birth rate fell. The two World Wars caused the deaths of many of France's active, working male population and this created a serious shortage of workers.

Partly in consequence, after 1945, proportions of children and elderly people had increased relative to those of working age. By 1960, only 56 percent of the people were between 20 and 64 years of age, compared with about 60 percent

in that age range from 1920 to 1940. Immigrant workers filled the gap in the labour force and today there are 1.5 million foreign workers in France – especially Algerians, Spaniards, Portuguese and Italians. The annual rate of population increase is about average for western Europe – about 0.4 percent, or an increase of about 20,000 people per year.

In recent times, France's urban population has increased rapidly. The nation has five conurbations with more than 500,000 people: Paris, Lyon (1.17m.),

Right: *The striking transparent façade of the George Pompidou Centre in Paris.*

Marseille (1,07m.), Lille (0.94m.) and Bordeaux (0.61m.). However, France remains a major farming country. Although the proportion of people engaged in farming has been steadily decreasing, about 10 percent of the labour force still works in farming, forestry and fishing, as opposed to 7 percent in West Germany.

There is no state religion in France, but most people are Roman Catholics.

History and constitution.

Between 58 and 51 BC, Julius Caesar conquered the region that is now France, which the Romans called Gaul. The Celtic population was Romanized and Gaul became a prosperous province. The decline of Roman rule was heralded by border fighting with Germanic tribes.

Finally, a Frankish king, Clovis, overthrew the Roman governor and became the Christian king of the so-called Frankish realm in AD 486. (The name France is derived from the term Frankish.) This realm at first included Aquitaine, northern Gaul and some areas east of the Rhine. Later, the Merovingian dynasty, established by Clovis, added Bavaria, Burgundy, Provence and Thuringia.

The Merovingian dynasty gradually declined in the 600s and, in 751, it was replaced by the Frankish Carolingian dynasty. The second Carolingian ruler, Charlemagne, became extremely powerful and was made Emperor of the Romans by the Pope. Charlemagne died in 814 and, in 843, his empire was divided into three kingdoms. The area containing much of modern France came under Charles the Bald, one of his grandsons.

In 987, the Capetian dynasty replaced the Carolingian. The Capetians controlled the centre of France around Paris and Orléans. But Normandy was a separate feudal state. Under Duke William of Normandy the Normans began their conquest of England in 1066.

The Capetian dynasty ruled France until 1328. It had a strong, centralized monarchy and extended French territory. But Philip VI's accession in 1328 was challenged by Edward III of England. Fighting broke out between France and England in 1337 and continued, off and on, until the French, inspired by Joan of Arc, defeated the English at Orléans in 1429, weakening their rule in France which ended at last in 1453.

A powerful monarchy gradually emerged and new territories were occupied. However, French conquests in Italy were ended when the French were defeated in the 1500s. Religious conflict between Roman Catholics and Protestant Huguenots occurred in France in the 1500s, but religious freedom for Protestants was granted by the first Bourbon monarch, Henry IV, in 1598.

The Bourbon monarchy became extremely powerful but it was overthrown by the French Revolution in 1789. In 1792 the First Republic was established, but seven years later Napoleon Bonaparte seized power. After brilliant military successes, Napoleon was finally defeated in 1815. The Bourbon monarchy was re-established. But in 1848, Louis Philippe was exiled and the Second Republic was proclaimed.

This republic was short-lived. In 1851 Louis Napoleon, nephew of Napoleon Bonaparte, took power and became emperor in 1852. In 1870-1871, France lost the Franco-Prussian War and surrendered Alsace and part of Lorraine to Germany.

A provisional republican government was set up in 1871 and the Third Republic began in 1875. France's territorial losses aroused Franco-German hostility and, in 1904, France established close relations with Britain through the Entente Cordiale. In 1907 France, with Britain and Russia, formed the Triple Entente which lined up against Germany and Austria-Hungary in 1914. France suffered greatly during World Wars I and II.

In 1946 the Fourth Republic came into being. But post-war recovery was hindered by expensive colonial wars, especially in Indo-China and later in Algeria. Successive governments failed to solve the nation's problems.

Finally, the war-time leader Charles de Gaulle was elected president in 1958 under a new constitution establishing the Fifth Republic. The chief feature of the constitution was that it greatly extended the president's powers.

The president is directly elected by universal suffrage for seven-year terms. He nominates and dismisses the prime minister and other ministers. There are two houses of parliament: the National Assembly and the Senate. The National Assembly is directly elected. It can be dissolved by the president after consultation with the prime minister. The Senate is comprised of delegates from the National Assembly, the communes (units of local government) and other groups.

The presidential elections are supervised by a nine-member constitutional council, which acts as a guardian of the constitution. Three members are nominated by the president, three by the president of the national Assembly and three by the president of the Senate.

The new constitution brought stability to France. Under President de Gaulle, the nation rapidly disengaged from colonialism and pursued an independent attitude in foreign affairs. Through the European Economic Community, France became increasingly prosperous. Under the socialist government of President Mitterand central control exercised by the *Prefect* has been devolved to local *departement* level.

Physical features and climate

The landscapes of France are very varied, and mainland France can be divided into eight main regions.

The northwest peninsula contains Brittany, which is a hilly scenic region of ancient rocks. Brittany's coast is deeply indented by drowned river valleys. In the north the region extends into western Normandy, and in the south into Anjou and La Vendée. The climate is mild and the rainfall, which occurs all the year round, supports lush grasslands which are used especially for dairy farming. Many coastal peoples are engaged in fishing or in the flourishing tourist trade.

The Paris basin includes the basins of the Seine, Somme and middle Loire rivers. The region is a synclinal depression consisting of circular belts of limestone, chalk and sandstone hills, separated by clay vales. The hills are mostly bordered by steep, outward-facing scarps, but they dip gently towards the centre of the basin, where Paris, a great route centre, straddles the Seine. The original site of Paris was an island in the Seine called the Ile de la Cité.

Within the Paris basin, there are several distinctive sub-regions. Southwest of Paris is the loam-covered, dry limestone Beauce region which is important for wheat and sheep-grazing. To the southeast, the limestone Brie plateau is covered by mostly clay soils. Brie is known for its dairy produce and sugar-beet farming. To the east, vine-growing regions include the chalk champagne district. North of Paris is a region of chalk hills where fruits and dairy products are important. In the far south, the middle Loire valley contains industrial centres that were once picturesque market towns, such as Orléans and Tours. In the north, near the Belgian frontier, there is a major industrial region, based on an extension of the Belgian coalfield into France. The largest industrial city here is Lille.

The eastern borderlands are a low, broken plateau region between the Meuse and Rhine rivers. The Vosges mountains are in the southeast of this region. In the eastern borderlands lie the vast iron ore deposits which stretch from Nancy to the Belgium-Luxembourg frontier. This region is a great industrial area. The German Ruhr area supplies coking coal for iron and steel production.

The central plateau (Massif Central) occupies the heart of France. It covers about one-sixth of the country, averages 914m (3,000ft) above sea level and winters are severe. The plateau is partly volcanic in origin and there are remains of volcanic cones, called *puys*, in the northwest. These volcanic remnants reach heights of more than 1,830m (6,000ft) above sea level. In the west and south, limestone massifs have typical karst scenery, with little surface drainage, potholes, disappearing streams, gorges and large cave networks. The thinly-populated central plateau contains the headwaters of the Dordogne, Garonne, Loire and Seine rivers.

The Rhône-Saône basin is flanked by the central plateau in the west, the Jura mountains in the northeast, and the foothills of the French Alps in the southeast. Lyon stands on the junction of the Rhône and Saône. North of Lyon, there is a rich farming region which includes the famous vineyard country of Burgundy. Summer temperatures are fairly hot but there is some summer rain. To the south of Lyon, the Rhône valley becomes increasingly dry and Mediterranean in character.

In southwestern France, the Aquitaine basin is a low-lying area that broadens to the south. It rises eastwards to the central plateau and southwards to the lofty Pyrenees. Sand dunes and a belt of sandy soils border the coast of Aquitaine (the Landes), but farther inland the plains and river valleys are fertile.

Below: *A medieval fortress towers over Rocamadour, a pilgrimage centre in France.*

Left: *The city of Dijon, in Bourgogne, France, has many outstanding buildings, some dating back to the fifteenth century.*

Above: *The river Seine and the Trocadéro, one of France's great national museums, from the world-famous Eiffel Tower, Paris.*

Mediterranean France is growing in industrial importance. Much of the coastlands west of Marseille are marshy, but rice, cattle and wine production are important activities. Oil refining and petrochemicals are among industrial activities and there is a large complex around the steel plant at Fos-sur-Mer. East of Marseille is a rich coastal belt, including the tourist Riviera region. Also on the Riviera is the small independent principality of Monaco.

Monaco covers an area of only 195 hectares (481 acres) and has a population of 27,000. The principality is taken up by the city of Monte Carlo, famous for its casino.

The French Alps rise behind the southeastern coastlands. The highest point is Mont Blanc on the Franco-Italian border. The swift-flowing streams of the French Alps are utilized for hydroelectric power.

Corsica (Corse in French) is a wild mountainous island in the Mediterranean Sea, some 14.5km (9 miles) north of the Italian island of Sardinia. Corsica covers 8,680km^2 (3,368sq.m.) and has a population of 240,000.

The climate of maritime northwestern France is mild and moist all the year round, although most of the rain falls in winter. To the east, the climate becomes more continental in character and annual temperature ranges steadily increase. To the south, the average temperatures gradually rise. The Mediterranean coastlands have hot, dry summers and mild, moist winters. The mountains and plateau regions have more severe climates than surrounding lowland areas.

Minerals

France's most important mineral resource is iron ore. The chief mining area is in Lorraine, where Europe's largest deposits occur. Although the Lorraine ore is low grade, it is easily mined. Some is exported to West Germany. The second iron ore area is around Caen in Normandy.

Coal is mined in the northeast, in Lorraine and in some areas around the central plateau. The coalfield in the northeast, an extension of the Belgian coalfield, produces mainly steam coal, which is unsuitable for metallurgical industries. The Lorraine coal, although abundant, is not of coking quality and the deposits around the central plateau are mainly of local importance. As a result, France has to import coal.

France produces some petroleum, mainly from the Landes in the southeast and some natural gas is obtained from the Lacq region in the foothills of the Pyrenees. Some bauxite and other metal ores, potash, salt and sulphur are also mined.

Industry and communications

France has always been known for its wines and quality goods, such as silks, particularly from Lyon, lace and fine porcelain (Limoges and Sèvres). Luxury goods, such as perfumes, were famous products of Paris. Today France still produces all these items and in some years is the world's leading wine producer.

Since 1945, the growth of France's heavy industry capacity has been rapid and about 30 out of every 100 working people are employed in manufacturing – more than twice as many as in farming, fishing and forestry. Economic progress in the 1960s and 1970s was spectacular, but in the 1980s France encountered many of the same problems as other Western economies.

Today France's leading industrial goods are aerospace products, cars, chemicals, engineering products and

Map 10 SOUTHERN FRANCE

BORDEAUX   46

TEMPERATURE   °C

14°

PRESSURE   mb

PRECIPITATION   mm

900mm

J F M A M J J A S O N D

LYON   ★   200

TEMPERATURE   °C

19°

PRESSURE   mb

PRECIPITATION   mm

813mm

J F M A M J J A S O N D

Projection: Conical with two standard parallels

West from Greenwich   0   East from Greenwich

1:2 500 000

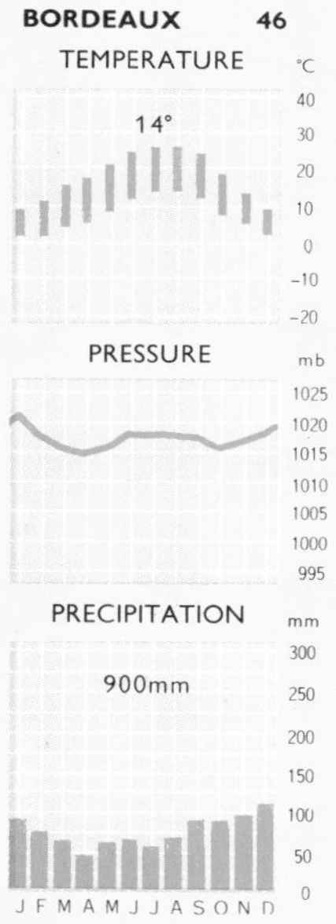

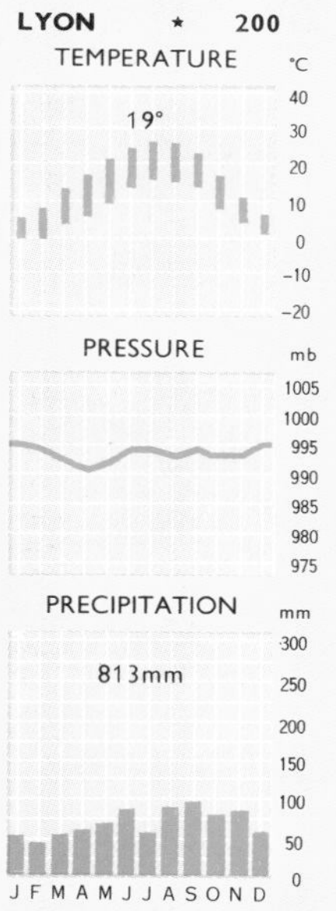

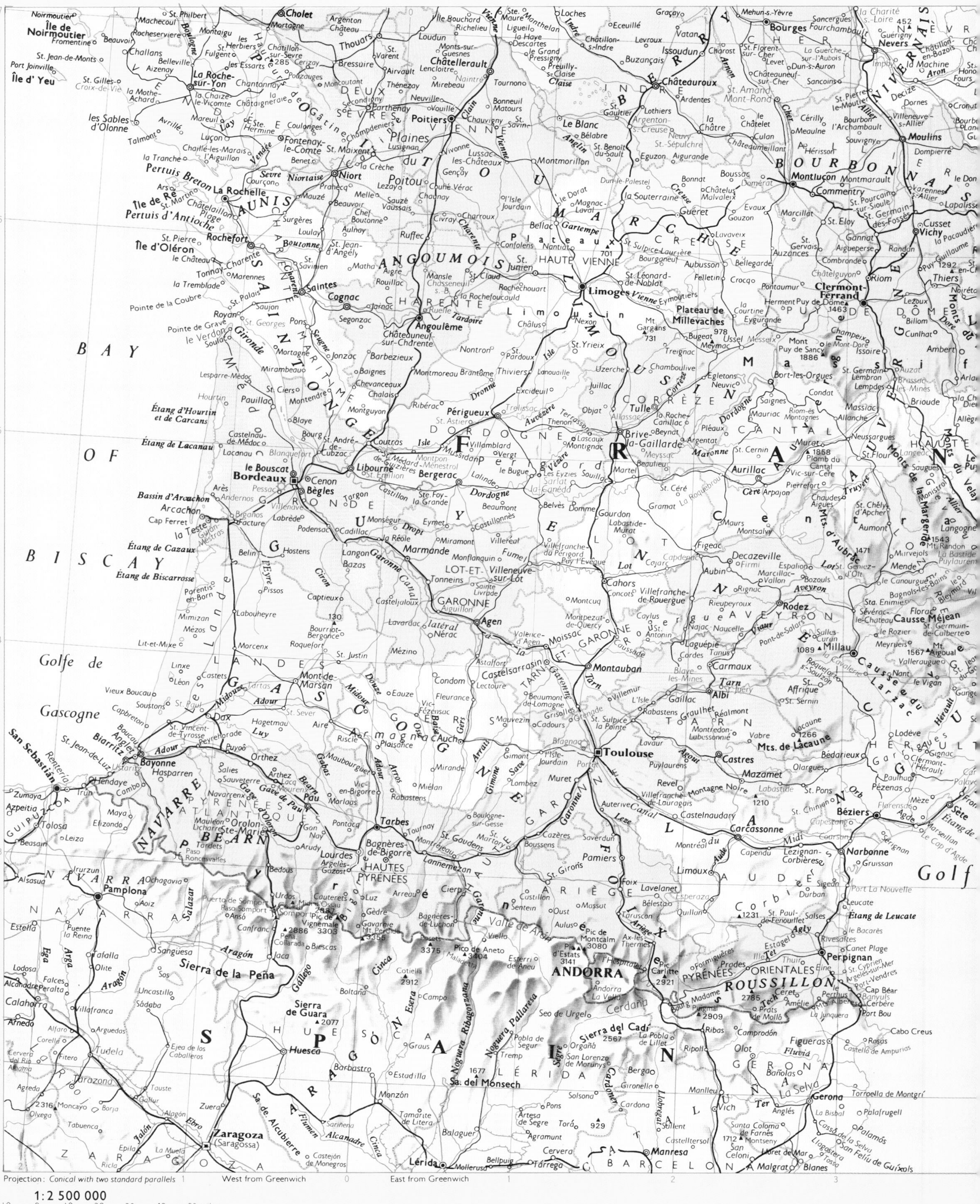

Left: *Glamorous, sophisticated St Tropez, an ancient port on the French Riviera.*

textiles. The chief industrial areas are around Paris, where traditional luxury industries thrive alongside heavy industries, on and around the mining areas, and in the major ports where imported raw materials are used. Although oil has been a major stimulus to industrial expansion, the development of hydro-electric power in the Alps, Pyrenees, Vosges and the central plateau has helped new industrial centres to arise in these and adjacent areas. France is in the forefront of nuclear power development.

France has one of the best developed transport systems in Europe, with more than 790,000km (491,000 miles) of roads and 35,600km (22,100 miles) of railways. Canals are important in the northeast and some rivers, such as the Seine below Paris, are used to transport heavy goods and materials. Navigable waterways total 7,600km (4,720 miles). The chief ports are Marseille, Le Havre and Rouen, which together handle more than half of France's seaborne trade. Dunkirk, Bordeaux, Nantes, Saint-Nazaire and Caen are also important ocean ports.

Agriculture, forestry and fishing
Because of France's differing climates, its agriculture is also varied. Only about 14 percent of the country is unproductive,

Map 11

MARSEILLE 4
TEMPERATURE °C
17°
PRESSURE mb
PRECIPITATION mm
546mm
F M A M J J A S O N D

PERPIGNAN 43
TEMPERATURE °C
16°
PRESSURE mb
PRECIPITATION mm
639 mm
J F M A M J J A S O N D

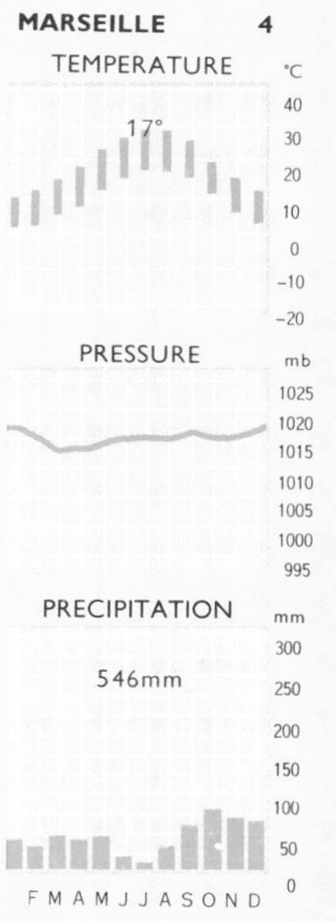

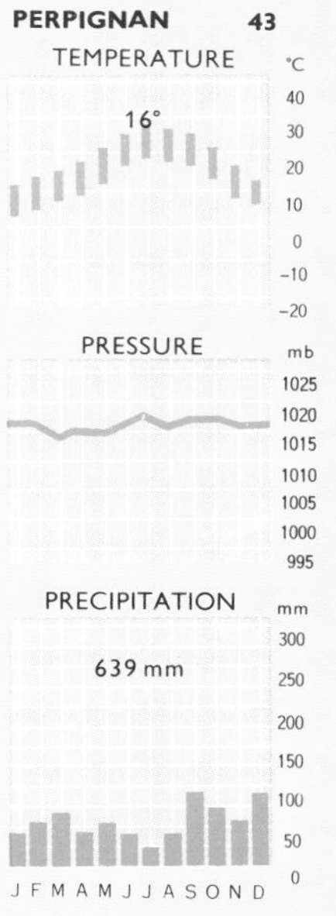

and France's chief natural resource is its fertile soil.

Cultivated fields cover 31 percent of the country, pasture 26 percent, and vineyards about 2.5 percent. Forests cover 26 percent, especially in highland areas, and timber is used to manufacture a wide range of wood products.

The chief crops are wheat, barley, maize, rice, sugar-beet, tobacco and potatoes. Many fruits, including apples, pears, plums, peaches and apricots are grown. Livestock raising is important and there are 23.5 million cattle, 11.6m pigs and 13m sheep. The chief dairy regions are in the northwest.

The chief wheatlands are in the Paris and Aquitaine basins. The leading wine-producing areas are the lower Loire valley, the lowlands of the Charente and Garonne rivers in Aquitaine, the Champagne district, the Burgundy region and the Mediterranean-facing southern slopes of the central plateau and the Languedoc plains. Brandies from Armagnac and Cognac are well-known and France produces a variety of liqueurs. Normandy is known for its cider and Alsace produces beer.

French agriculture was traditionally a peasant industry and it was relatively under-developed. Many changes have occurred in the last 25 years. Many small farms have been consolidated, fertilizers are more widely used and many farms have been mechanized. As a result, France often has agricultural surpluses, which she has tried to dispose of through the European Economic Community. However, problems have arisen because West Germany, a food importer, has wanted to protect its farmers from French competition.

Fishing is important, especially around the northwestern peninsula, where sardine canning is a thriving industry in the coastal towns, and in the Mediterranean. France has more than 75,000 fishermen and about 11,000 fishing vessels.

Trade and foreign relations

France's chief trading partners are fellow members of the EEC. Trade with the French Community (former French overseas territories), the US, and Switzerland is also important.

Despite the loss of most of its overseas empire, France has sought to re-establish its world status by seeking, through the EEC, to make Europe a united world power, independent of the super-powers, the US and the USSR. France has pursued an independent policy in foreign affairs and has tended to challenge the leadership of the West by the US. It has attempted to establish good relations with communist countries. In addition to its overseas territories, there are four overseas departments in non-metropolitan France – Martinique, Guadeloupe, Réunion and Guiana.

Map 12   THE NETHERLANDS, BELGIUM AND LUXEMBOURG

1:2 500 000

Projection: Conical with two standard parallels   East from Greenwich   COPYRIGHT. GEORGE PHILIP & SON. LTD.

UTRECHT   **3**
TEMPERATURE
16°
PRESSURE
PRECIPITATION
766 mm

BRUSSEL   ★ **100**
TEMPERATURE
16°
PRESSURE
PRECIPITATION
855mm

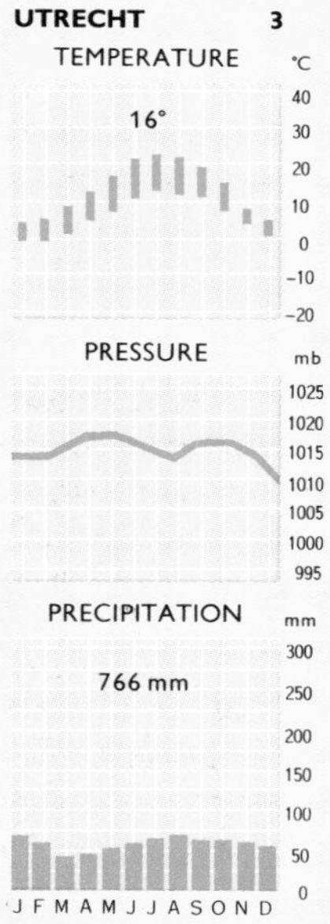

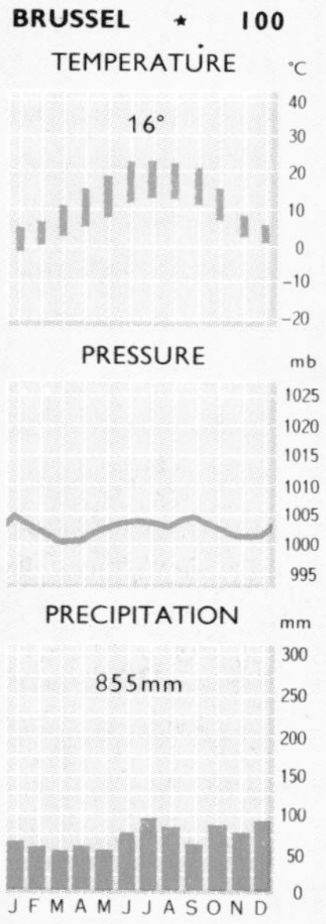

The two monarchies of Belgium and the Netherlands, with the Grand Duchy of Luxembourg, are sometimes called the Low Countries, although southeastern Belgium and much of Luxembourg contain uplands. These countries are also described as the Benelux countries after the Benelux Customs Union, established in 1947, which led to the creation of the Benelux Economic Union in 1960. Their economies have also become increasingly integrated through the EEC. They possess thriving industries and fertile farmlands and they are also centres of trade.

Right: *Luxembourg's Saxon name of Lucilinburhuc ('little fortress'), symbolized its strategic position at the crossroads of Europe.*

The Netherlands

Area: 41,548km² (16,042sq.m.).
Population: 14.5 million.
Joint capital: Amsterdam/The Hague.
Largest city: Rotterdam (1.04m).
Language: Dutch.
Ethnic group: Dutch.
Main exports: chemicals, electrical equipment, flower bulbs, machinery, meat, petroleum products.
Average temperatures: 4°C (39°F) Jan. 17°C (65°F) July.
Highest point: on the German border near Aachen, 322m (1,057ft).

The Netherlands is a delta formed from sediments deposited by rivers, including the Maas, Rhine and Scheldt. Water covers about 17 percent of the country and about two-fifths of the land is below sea level. Large, low-lying areas called *polders* have been enclosed by dykes (sea walls), drained and reclaimed from the sea. Despite more than 140 floods in the last 700 years, the Dutch people have never ceased in their struggle to enlarge their country by reclamation.

On the reclaimed land, they have practised highly efficient agriculture and, in recent years, manufacturing has developed quickly. Despite the post-war loss of its overseas empire, the Netherlands is now a prosperous, densely-populated country.

People, history and constitution

The Dutch language belongs to the Germanic group and most of the people are of Germanic origin. The country has come under Roman, Frankish (Germanic), French and Spanish influence. Largely independent from 1581, it rose to world prominence in the 17th century as a commercial and colonial power and as an artistic centre. A constitutional monarchy was established in 1815, but, in 1830, the southern part broke away to become the kingdom of Belgium.

The Netherlands, neutral in World War I, was occupied by Germany in World War II. Tremendous damage was done when the Germans were driven out, but post-war recovery was rapid.

The Netherlands has an hereditary monarchy. Its parliament consists of two chambers. The Upper or First Chamber has 75 members, elected indirectly by the provincial states. The Second Chamber has 150 directly-elected members. The seat of government is at The Hague.

Physical features and climate

The polder region, which covers 40 percent of the Netherlands, lies behind a narrow, sandy coastal strip. Although flat, this region is an attractive patchwork of fields, criss-crossed by canals. The towns, mostly old, are picturesque. Glacial deposits cover much of the east, with peat bogs in places. But much of this mostly infertile land has been reclaimed. The Netherlands has cool summers and mild, moist winters.

Mining, industry and communications

The Netherlands has little coal but some petroleum and a valuable offshore field of natural gas. Its chief industrial resource is a highly-skilled workforce with a long tradition of craftsmanship. Many of the materials needed for heavy industry are imported. Amsterdam and Rotterdam are the main industrial centres. Some industries process farm products and others use imported materials.

The country has an excellent network of roads, railways and canals. Rotterdam and its outport, Europoort, form the world's busiest port.

Agriculture and fishing

Farmland covers 62 percent of the land and two-thirds of it is pasture. Cattle-raising for butter, cheese and meat is important and the dairy industry is highly efficient. The nation has 5.4 million cattle and, with Belgium, has more cattle per square kilometre than any other country. There are also 0.7m. sheep, 10.6m. pigs and 82m. poultry. The chief crops are cereals, sugar-beet, potatoes and flower bulbs. Sea and inshore fishing are important industries.

Trade and foreign relations

The country's chief trading partners are EEC nations and the US. The Netherlands, like Belgium, is a member of West European institutions such as the EEC and NATO.

Luxembourg

Area; 2,586km^2 (998sq.m.).
Population: 365,800.
Capital: Luxembourg (79,000).
Languages: French, German, Luxembourgeois.
Ethnic groups: mixed French, Belgian, Dutch and German.
Main exports: iron and steel, farm products.
Average temperatures: 0.5°C (31°F) Jan. 17.5°C (63°F) July.
Highest point: 565m (1,854ft).

Luxembourg is a small Grand Duchy, with a Grand Duke or Duchess as head of state. It was occupied by Germany between 1940 and 1944. Luxembourg has major iron ore deposits and steel manufacturing is very important, although farming still provides a useful source of income. The Grand Duchy also earns 'invisibles' from foreign companies registered in the country, tourism and its commercial radio station.

Belgium

Area: 30,519km^2 (11,778sq.m.).
Population: 9.85 million.
Capital: Brussels (1.06m).
Languages: Dutch, French, German.
Ethnic groups: Flemish, Walloons, with some German-speaking people in the southeast.
Main exports: manufactured goods including chemicals, machinery, foodstuffs, textiles.
Average temperatures: Brussels, 4°C (39°F) Jan. 23°C (75°F) July.
Highest point: Botrange Mt., 693m (2,274ft).

Belgium is one of western Europe's most densely-populated and industrialized nations. It is a prominent member of West European institutions, including the Benelux Economic Union, the EEC, NATO, the Council of Europe and the West European Union. Brussels is the headquarters of the EEC and NATO.

People and language

Belgium's official languages are Flemish, French and German. The two major language groups are the Flemings in the north, who speak a Dutch dialect, and the French-speaking Walloons in the south. Brussels is bilingual, but language divisions have created communal conflict. To reduce conflict, the government has granted the language groups more autonomy. Most of the people are Roman Catholics.

History and constitution

Belgium declared its independence from the Netherlands in 1830. It was occupied by Germany in World Wars I and II. Since then, it has recovered quickly, despite the loss of its colonial territories, especially the Belgian Congo, now Zaïre. Belgium is a constitutional monarchy. The Senate is partly elected directly by the people and partly by provincial councils, for four-year terms. The directly-elected Chamber of Representatives also sits for four years.

Physical features and climate

Sand dunes fringe Belgium's short coastline. Behind the coastal strip is a rich, flat area which is largely reclaimed marshland. The central plains form the largest region. They include the basin of the River Scheldt and its tributaries. The Campine region near the Dutch frontier is Belgium's chief coal-mining area. The south Belgian coalfield, which has declined in recent times, extends from Mons, along the Sambre-Meuse valley, to the industrial city of Liège. South of this coalfield are the southern highlands which rise to the Ardennes. Belgium has a mild, moist climate.

Minerals, industry and communications

Belgium's large coal and iron deposits form the basis of prosperous engineering and metal-working industries. Some industries process farm products and the woollen and linen textile industries of Flanders have been important for centuries. Brussels, like Paris, is known for its luxury goods. New industries have recently been established in the port of Antwerp and other northern centres as a result of imported petroleum and the development of coal mining in the Campine. This has led to a relative decline of the southern industrial area in the Sambre-Meuse valley. Belgium has the world's greatest density of railways and a good road system.

Agriculture, forestry, fishing, trade

Only 3 percent of the active population work in farming, forestry and fishing. The chief crops are cereals, especially wheat and barley, sugar-beet and potatoes. Livestock are also important, but Belgium imports food. Forests cover nearly one-fifth of the land and forestry and fishing are both important. Belgium's chief trading partners are EEC nations and the United States.

Right: *Despite their limited power, windmills drained the several hundred polders of The Netherlands in earlier times.*

Below: *The Grand Place, at the heart of the Old Town in Brussels, Belgium's capital.*

Map 13 GERMANY AND SWITZERLAND

BERLIN * 55
TEMPERATURE °C
20°
PRESSURE mb
PRECIPITATION mm
603mm
J F M A M J J A S O N D
MÜNCHEN * 524
TEMPERATURE °C
20°
PRESSURE mb
PRECIPITATION mm
957mm
J F M A M J J A S O N D
GENÈVE * 405
TEMPERATURE °C
19°
PRESSURE mb
PRECIPITATION mm
853mm
J F M A M J J A S O N D
NORTH SEA
BALTIC SEA
1:3 000 000
miles
km
Deutsche Bucht
NORDFRIESISCHE INSELN
OSTFRIESISCHE INSELN
DENMARK
WEST GERMANY
EAST GERMANY
POLAND
CZECHOSLOVAKIA
AUSTRIA
SWITZERLAND
ITALY
FRANCE
BELGIUM
LUXEMBOURG
NETHERLANDS
YUGOSLAVIA
BERLIN
HAMBURG
MÜNCHEN (Munich)
FRANKFURT
KÖLN
DÜSSELDORF
STUTTGART
DRESDEN
LEIPZIG
Conical with two standard parallels
East from Greenwich
COPYRIGHT GEORGE PHILIP & SON LTD

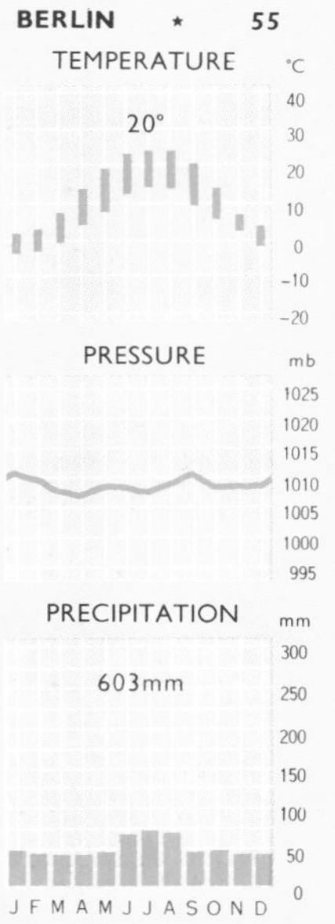

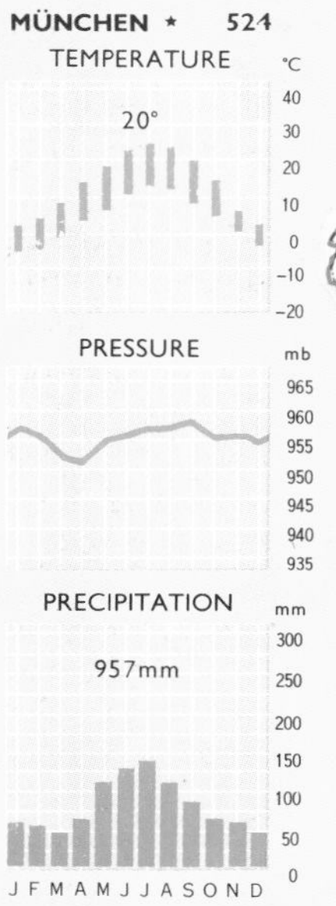

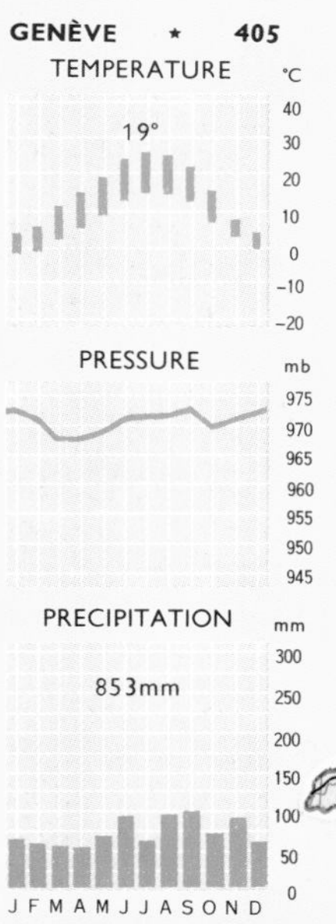

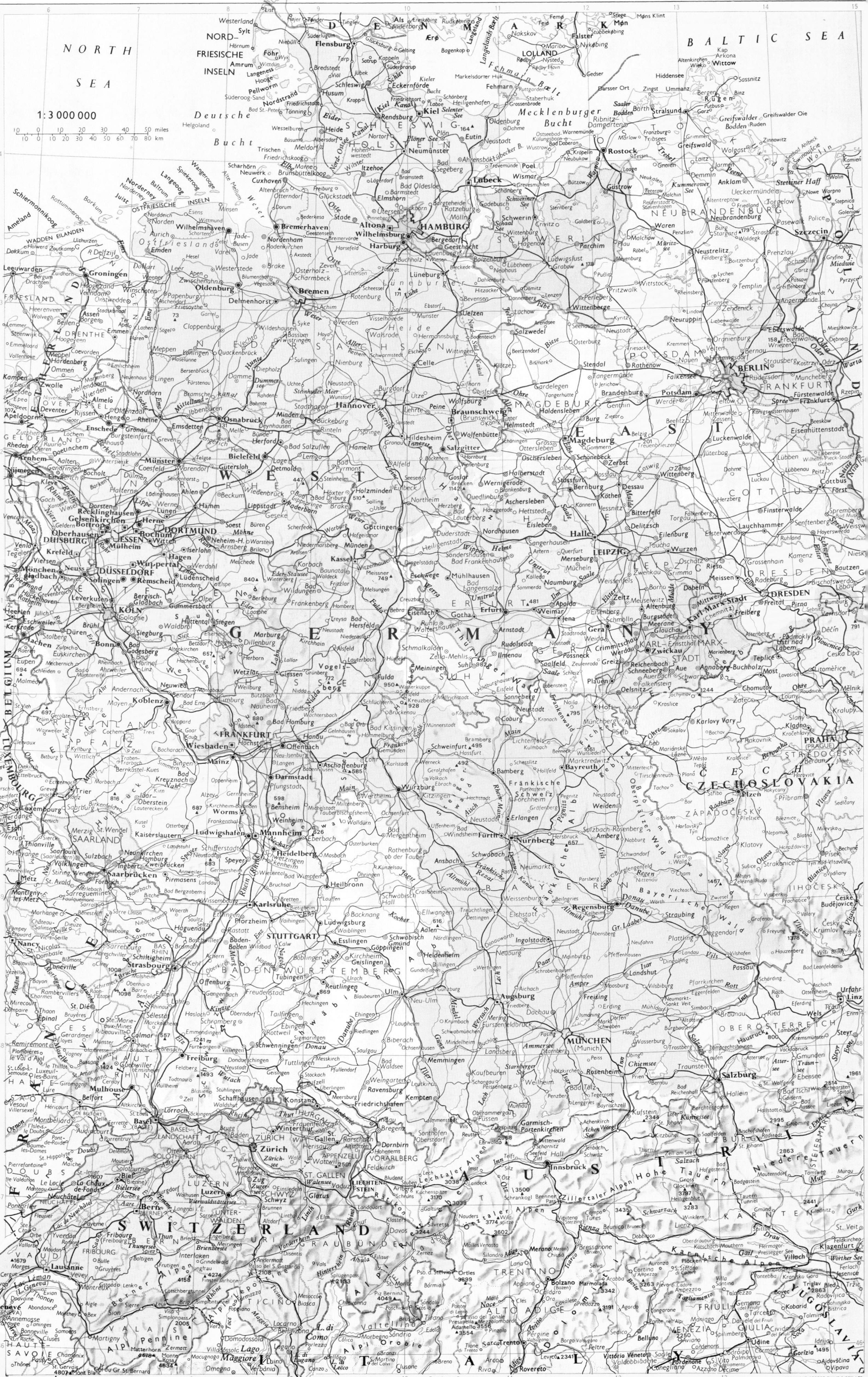

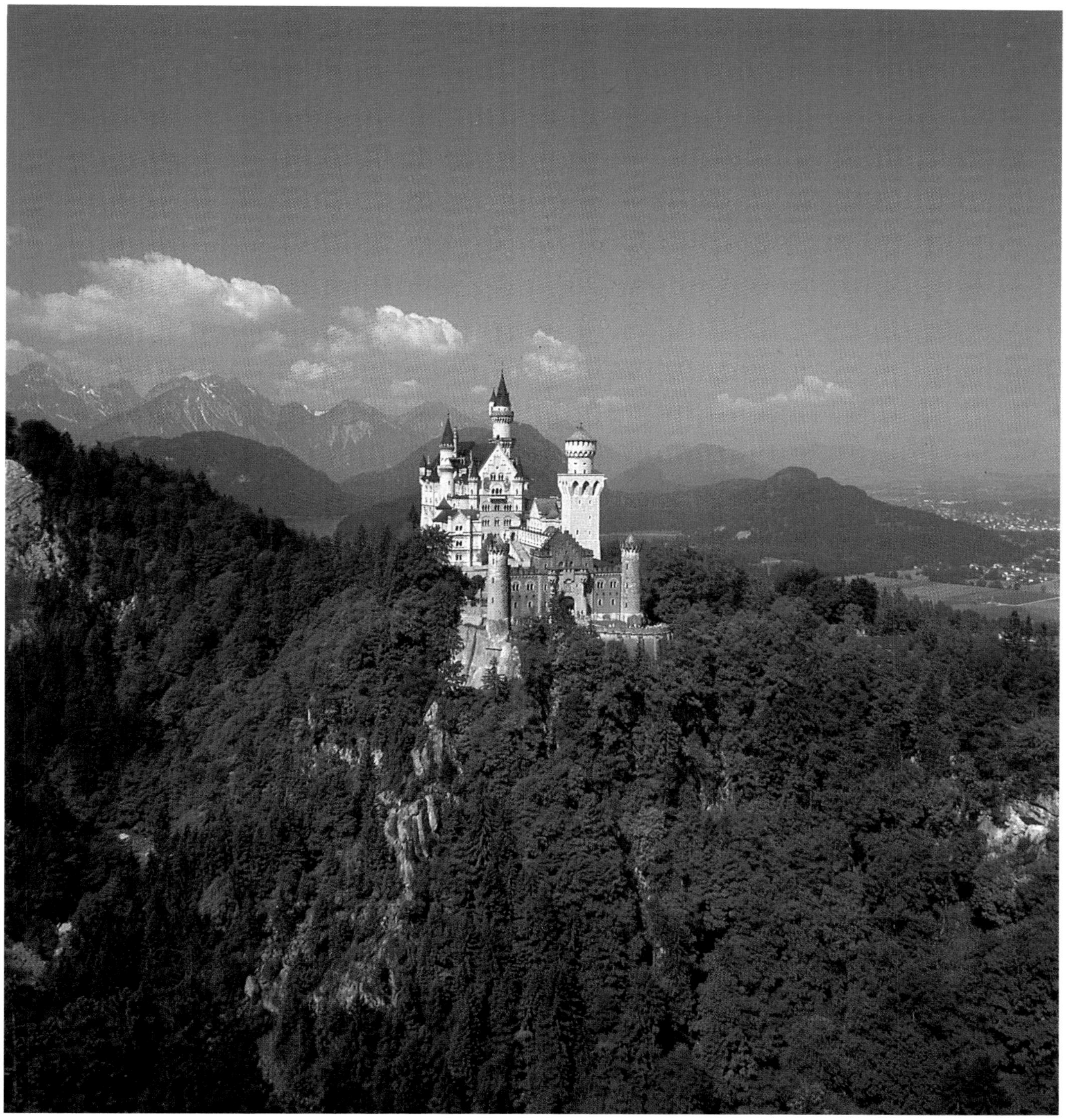

Left: *Neuschwanstein Castle, built in the late 19th century amid the dramatic beauty of West Germany's Bavarian Alps.*

Before 1800 The German people were divided into more than 300 states. But, after the defeat of Napoleon, the number of states was reduced to 39, including Prussia. Between 1814 and 1871, these states were loosely confederated. Following the success of Germany in the Franco-Prussian War (1870-1871), a federated German empire, or *Reich*, was established with the King of Prussia as its *Kaiser* (emperor). The united Germany rapidly expanded its military power, and colonized overseas territories.

In World War I, Germany, Austria-Hungary, Bulgaria and Turkey formed a powerful central European alliance. But, after their defeat in 1918, Germany lost its overseas empire, and, in Europe, it lost territory to Belgium, Czechoslovakia, Denmark, France, Lithuania and Poland.

In the 1920s, Germany suffered appalling inflation and unemployment and, finally, Adolf Hitler and the National Socialist (Nazi) party established an absolute dictatorship in 1933. Germany began to recover lost territory. It occupied the Rhineland in 1936. In 1938 German troops took Austria and, later, seized the German-speaking parts of Czechoslovakia. In 1939, Germany took the rest of Czechoslovakia and Memel from Lithuania. Finally, the German invasion of Poland on September 1, 1939, precipitated World War II.

After Germany collapsed in 1945, it lost the territories it had seized and a large area of eastern Germany was taken by Poland. The eastern border of Germany was fixed along the Oder-Neisse rivers. Some 10 million Germans were expelled from East Prussia, Poland, Czechoslovakia and other countries and these refugees went mainly to western Germany.

Germany was partitioned into American, British, French and Russian zones. Berlin, the capital, lay within the Russian zone, but it, too, was partitioned into four occupation areas. At that time, the occupation was considered to be temporary. German reunification was expected before long. By 1948 the American, British and French zones had become one unit, West Germany. But the Russians kept control of their zone.

In 1949 West Germany became a federal republic, but a communist regime was established in East Germany. Since 1949 West and East Germany have developed as separate countries. Berlin remains divided. West Berlin, comprising the former American, British and French zones, has its own government, but it is effectively part of West Germany. East Berlin is the capital of East Germany.

Both West and East Germany have made remarkable recoveries since 1945. But the methods adopted have differed greatly.

West Germany

Area: 248,687km² (96,018sq.m.).
Population: 61.42 million.
Capital: Bonn (295,000).
Largest city: West Berlin (1,870,000).
Language: German.
Ethnic group: Germans.
Main exports: cars, machinery, iron and steel, chemicals, electronics, electrical equipment, textiles, processed food.
Average temperatures: 4°C (40°F) Jan. 21°C (70°F) July.
Highest point: Zugspitze, 2,968m (9,738ft).

The German language belongs to the same family as Danish, Dutch, English, Norwegian and Swedish. Ethnically, the Germans are a mixed people, although two main types may be distinguished: the long-skulled, fair, tall, blue-eyed Nordic people; and the broader-skulled, short, sturdy, dark-haired and dark-eyed Alpine people.

The population of West Germany increased rapidly after 1945. First came about 8.5 million German refugees, most from the lost territories in the east. Later, many more East Germans entered West Germany. East German refugees totalled about two million between 1955 and 1961. Despite East German efforts to prevent emigration, an average of 21,000 people left East for West Germany each year between 1965 and 1973. Most refugees were absorbed into industrial employment. West Germany's largest cities are West Berlin (1.87m.), Hamburg (1.75m.) and München or Munich (1.28m.).

Protestants form 49 percent of the population and Roman Catholics 44.6 percent. At the end of 1985, there were about 1.8m. foreign workers employed in West Germany. These *Gastarbeiter* (guest-workers) came from Turkey, Yugoslavia, Italy, Greece, Spain and other countries.

Constitution

The *Bundesrepublik Deutschland*, or the Federal Republic of Germany, came into existence in 1949. When Britain, France and the US revoked the Occupation Statute in 1955, West Germany became an independent democratic country.

The Federal Republic is divided into *Länder* (states), each of which has its own Government. The federal government controls such matters as citizenship rights, currency, federal communications and foreign affairs.

The federal parliament consists of two houses. The members of the lower house, the *Bundestag* (Federal Diet), are elected for four-year terms. Berlin sends representatives but they have no vote. The upper house is the *Bundesrat* (Federal Council). It consists of representatives of the governments of the *Länder*. The federal president is elected by the Federal Assembly for five-year terms. This assembly consists of all the members of the *Bundestag* with an equal number of representatives from the *Länder*. The president may serve only two terms.

The government is led by the federal chancellor, who is proposed by the president and elected by the *Bundestag*. The chancellor selects federal ministers who are appointed by the president. The chief political parties are the Social Democrats, the Christian Democrats, the Free Democrats and the Greens.

Physical features and climate

West Germany has four main physical regions: the north German plain; the central uplands; south-west Germany; and the southern uplands.

The North German plain is largely covered by glacial deposits and much of it is poorly drained. In some parts the soils are infertile, especially the sandy heathlands, such as Lüneburger Heide (Lüneberg Heath). The northwest coast is deeply indented by drowned river valleys, such as those of the Elbe and the Weser.

Central Germany is a region of plateaux, low hills and block mountains. It includes the Ruhr coalfield, West Germany's chief industrial region.

Southwest Germany contains the Rhenish highlands which are divided by the Rhine (Rhein) and its tributaries. To the south, the Rhine occupies a deep trough flanked in the west by the Odenwald and Schwarzwald (Black Forest) uplands.

Southeastern Germany is an area of varied relief. It contains the limestone plateaux of the Swabian and Franconian Jura and in the south it rises to the Alps which border Austria.

The high parts of the southern uplands have a severe climate, but most of West Germany enjoys a mild climate, because it is nearer the sea.

Minerals and industry

West Germany is a major producer of coal and lignite. The chief coalfields are in the Ruhr, Saar and Aachen areas. The country produces some iron ore, potash, salt and various metals. Petroleum is also extracted, but most is imported, particularly by pipeline from the south. West Germany is a major industrial nation. Manufacturing first grew up around the coalfields and ports, but its spread to other areas has accelerated since 1958 because of the increasing use of petroleum and availability of electricity generated by coal and distributed by a grid system. Munich and Nürnberg (Nuremberg) are notable examples of major industrial areas without nearby coalfields. Machinery, electrical engineering, chemicals and textiles are all important industries in West Germany. The establishment of new industrial plant has been rapid since 1945, especially in some areas that formerly had only limited industrial capacity, such as Bavaria and Baden-Würtemberg.

West Germany's industrial revival after 1945 was based on such factors as the availability of refugee labour, a world shortage of coal and steel, and the necessity of replacing destroyed plant with new machinery. Although the country benefited from US aid, the Germans worked hard to rebuild their wealth.

West Germany is well provided with roads, railways and waterways.

Agriculture, forestry and fishing

The proportion of people engaged in farming dropped from 20 percent of the labour force in 1939 to 4 percent in 1980. More than half of the land is used for farming. The chief cereals are barley, wheat, oats and rye. Potatoes, sugar beet, wine, dairy products and meat are all important. The richest farming region is the rift valley of the middle Rhine.

Forests cover nearly 30 percent of the land and forestry, based on scientific methods, is a major industry, especially for timber used in construction. The forests have suffered badly from industrial pollution in the form of 'acid rain'. The northern ports of West Germany have sizeable fishing fleets.

Trade and foreign relations

West Germany's leading trading partners are fellow members of the EEC, the US, Switzerland and Austria. West Germany was a founder member of the European Economic Community.

Because of its position between East and West, West Germany occupies a key role in western defence strategy and it is a member of NATO. In 1970 it recognized the Oder-Neisse line as Poland's permanent frontier with East Germany and it later sought to relieve tensions with its communist neighbour through agreements on Berlin. A treaty, signed in 1972, established the basis for relations between West and East Germany.

Above: *The dark fir trees from which West Germany's Black Forest takes its name. Forestry is a major industry in Germany.*

Below: *Lying on the canalized Neckar River, Heidelberg in West Germany is a university city and centre for tourism.*

East Germany

Area: 108,333km^2 (41,817sq.m.).
Population: 16.7 million.
Capital: East Berlin (1.19m).
Language: German.
Ethnic group: Germans.
Main exports: manufactured products, chemical products, coal (lignite).
Average temperatures: 0°C (32°F) Jan. 18°C (65°F) July.
Highest point: Brocken, 1,142m (3,747ft).

The people of East Germany differ from West Germans only in their political institutions. Religion is officially discouraged. But, in the 1964 census, nearly 60 percent of East Germans were reported to be Protestants and about 8 percent Roman Catholics.

History and constitution

Following the establishment of the Federal Republic of Germany, the communist German Democratic Republic (GDR) was set up in 1949.

Today the GDR has a People's Chamber consisting of 500 deputies. The People's Chamber elects the Council of State which was set up after the office of president was abolished in 1960. The Council of State consists of a chairman, who represents the country in international law, six deputy chairmen, 18 members and a secretary. The People's Chamber also elects the Council of Ministers, the National Defence Council and Supreme Court judges. For local government, the country is divided into 14 districts.

Physical features and climate

The northern part of the GDR is a section of the North European plain. The Baltic coastline is sandy and fringed by sand bars which enclose lagoons. To the south, moraine hills alternate with lakes and marshes. Soils are low in fertility. South of the moraine belt is a flat, poorly-drained depression. The rivers

Below: *Rapid postwar reconstruction has created the modern metropolis of Frankfurt, now an international banking centre.*

occupy southeast-northwest valleys which were formed by melt water when the glaciers receded at the end of the Ice Age. Berlin is situated in one of these.

The southern part of East Germany is a hilly region enclosed by ancient upland areas. It is by far the most populous and wealthy part of the country, both agriculturally and industrially. The uplands include the Harz mountains in the east, the Thüringer Wald uplands in the southwest and the Erzgebirge in the southeast along the border with Czechoslovakia. East Germany's climate is more continental than that of West Germany and winters are distinctly colder.

Above: *Interlaken, with Mounts Eiger, Mönch and Jungfrau in the distance, is one of Switzerland's most popular resorts.*

Minerals and industry

East Germany is the world's most important lignite producer. It also has massive reserves of potash, which is used in chemical industries, and some rare metals, including antimony, arsenic and uranium. However, East Germany lacks iron ore, non-ferrous metals and petroleum. All these items are imported.

Before World War II, the economy of what is now the GDR was essentially agricultural. But today manufacturing contributes two-thirds of the country's national income. All manufacturing industries are nationalized. They produce fertilizers, chemicals, synthetic rubber, cement, textiles, shoes and iron and steel. Apart from Berlin, the chief industrial areas are in the southeast, including Karl-Marx-Stadt and Zwickau. Other industrial centres include Halle, Leipzig, Magdeburg, Stassfurt and the port of Rostock. Communications in East Germany are generally less well developed than in West Germany.

Agriculture, forestry and fishing

Agriculture has been largely collectivized and has made less progress than manufacturing since 1945. Arable farming for wheat, rye, barley, oats potatoes and sugar-beet is relatively more important than in West Germany. Livestock include 5.7m. cattle and 12.1m. pigs.

Forests cover about 27 percent of the land. Sea fishing and inland fishing, especially for carp, are important.

Trade and foreign relations

More than 68 percent of the GDR's trade is with communist countries and only 7 percent with West Germany. The GDR is a member of the communist military Warsaw Pact alliance and also of CMEA (Council for Mutual Economic Assistance).

Switzerland

Area: 41,293km^2 (15,943sq.m.).
Population: 6.6 million.
Capital: Bern (Berne) (301,000).
Languages: German, French, Italian, Romansh.
Ethnic group: Swiss nationals include German-speakers (73.5 percent), French-speakers (20.1 percent), Italian-speakers (4.5 percent), Romansh-speakers (0.9 percent), others (1.0 percent). Nearly 1m. foreigners also live in Switzerland.
Main exports: machinery, chemicals, clocks and watches, textiles, scientific instruments, dairy produce.
Average temperatures: 0°C (32°F) Jan. 18.5°C (65°F) July.
Highest point: Monte Rosa, 4,634m (15,203ft).

The Swiss are mostly people of Germanic or Latin origin. The largest group speak a dialect of German. French is spoken in the west and Italian in south-central areas. German, French and Italian are the official languages. Romansh, a Rhaeto-Romantic language related to Latin, is spoken in the southeast.

The people are divided into Roman Catholics (47.6 percent), Protestants (44.3 percent) and others (8.1 percent). The foreign residents are mostly immigrant workers, but some work for international organizations, such as agencies of the UN.

History and constitution

In 1291 the people of two forest areas, Schwyz and Uri, united with neighbouring Unterwalden and declared their independence from the Austrian rulers of the House of Hapsburg. From this beginning, a league of loosely-allied independent *cantons* (states) grew up and the league's independence was finally recognized in 1648.

France conquered the area in 1798 and established the Helvetic League, a federal republic of 19 cantons. But, after Napoleon lost power, the Swiss reverted to their previous loose alliance. In 1815 Swiss neutrality was guaranteed by the Congress of Vienna.

The country's present constitution dates from 1874. Switzerland is now a federal republic containing 23 cantons, each of which has its own government for local matters. The federal government controls such things as defence, the coining of money, the railways and the planning of national public parks.

The federal parliament consists of two houses. The *Nationalrat* (National Council) contains 200 national councillors, directly elected in proportion to the population of the cantons. The *Ständerat* (Council of State) has 46 members – two being chosen by each canton. Executive authority is vested in the *Bundesrat* (Federal Council), which is chosen by a joint session of the federal parliament. The president of the *Bundesrat* may not serve two consecutive years.

Physical features and climate

Switzerland has three distinctive regions. The Jura mountains run northeast to southwest in western Switzerland. They reach heights of about 1,520m (5,000ft) above sea level. The central plateau lies between 460 and 910m (1,500-3,000ft). Although it covers only one-quarter of the country, it contains nearly three-quarters of the population. The lofty, snow-capped Alps cover more than half of Switzerland. They contain magnificent glaceated scenery which attracts many tourists to mountain resorts. Switzerland's climate varies greatly according to the altitude. The central plateau has warm summers and cool winters, but the mountains are much colder and wetter.

Industry and agriculture

Switzerland is a highly industrialized nation. Because it lacks minerals (apart from salt deposits), it has concentrated on processing industries and metal industries, such as clock-making and precision instrument manufacture, which require few raw materials but highly-skilled labour. Yet machinery products and chemicals have become increasingly important. Processing industries produce butter, cheese, meat, sugar, textiles and tobacco. Although use of oil is increasing, most of the country's power comes from hydro-electric stations.

Because of its position in central Europe, the most important routes are north-south roads and railways which use passes such as the St Bernard or tunnels such as the St Gotthard. About six percent of the land is arable, meadows and pastures are 46 percent, forests 24 percent and unproductive land 24 percent. Livestock farming, especially for dairy products, is extremely important, with upland pastures used in summer. Wheat and other cereals, potatoes, sugar-beet and vegetables all grow in the central plateau.

Trade and foreign relations

Switzerland's main trading partners are countries of the EEC, the US and Austria. Switzerland's neutrality, stability and good government have given it a special reputation in the world. Its currency is highly respected and it is a major centre of international commerce, banking and insurance.

Map 14 | AUSTRIA, CZECHOSLOVAKIA AND HUNGARY

PRAHA ★ 262
TEMPERATURE °C

20°

PRESSURE mb

PRECIPITATION mm

411mm

J F M A M J J A S O N D

INNSBRUCK 582
TEMPERATURE °C

22°

PRESSURE mb

PRECIPITATION mm

868mm

J F M A M J J A S O N D

1:2 500 000

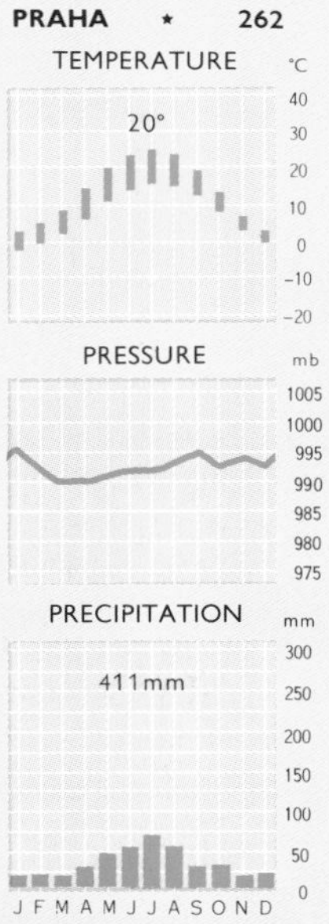

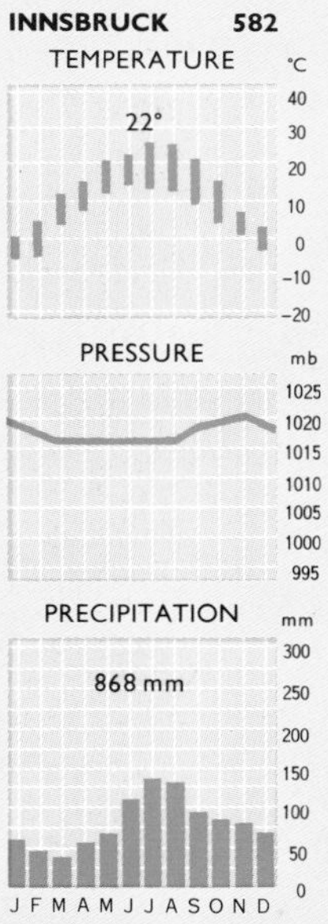

Austria

Area: 83,855km² (32,376sq.m.).
Population: 7.56 million.
Capital: Wien (Vienna) (1.5m).
Language: German.
Ethnic groups: German-speaking Austrians.
There is a small Slovene minority.
Main exports: iron and steel goods,
machinery, timber, wood pulp, paper,
chemicals.
Average temperatures: −2°C (29°F) Jan. 19°C
(67°F) July.
Highest point: Gross Glockner, 3,797m
(12,457ft).

Austria was once the centre of the great Hapsburg empire. Croats, Czechs, Hungarians, Italians, Poles, Rumanians, Ruthenians, Serbs, Slovenes and Slovaks settled there and today the population is a mixture of these ethnic groups. The official language is German and about 84 percent of the people are Roman Catholics.

From 962, Austria was part of the Holy Roman Empire. In the 1200s, Austria became a possession of the Hapsburg family and, after 1438, successive Hapsburgs served as Holy Roman Emperors. Vienna became one of the most glittering cultural centres in Europe. In 1806 the Holy Roman Empire came to an end, the ruler be-

coming the Emperor of Austria and (from 1867) the dual monarch of Austria and Hungary.

The country's power gradually declined during the 1800s. In 1919, the Austro-Hungarian empire was broken up and Czechoslovakia and Yugoslavia became separate countries. In its truncated form, Austria faced many problems and offered no resistance when Germany took it over in March 1938.

After World War II, Austria, like Germany, was divided into American, British, French and Soviet zones. Austria became independent in 1955 as a neutral federal republic. There are nine federal states, each of which has an elected provincial assembly. The

Nationalrat (national council) and the *Bundesrat* (federal council) together form the National Assembly.

Physical features and climate
Most of Austria is mountainous. The east-west Alpine ranges cover 70 percent of the country. The Alps are loftiest in the west, where winter sports attract many tourists. In the east, the Alps are more open and support rather more people than in the west. In the north, the Alps descend to a low plateau, which is crossed by the Danube. The Vienna basin in the northeast forms a small but thickly-populated lowland.

The country has a climate similar to that of Switzerland, with severe winters,

Map 15

WIEN ★ 203
TEMPERATURE °C
22°

PRESSURE mb

PRECIPITATION mm
660mm

J F M A M J J A S O N D

BUDAPEST 139
TEMPERATURE °C
25°

PRESSURE mb

PRECIPITATION mm
614 mm

J F M A M J J A S O N D

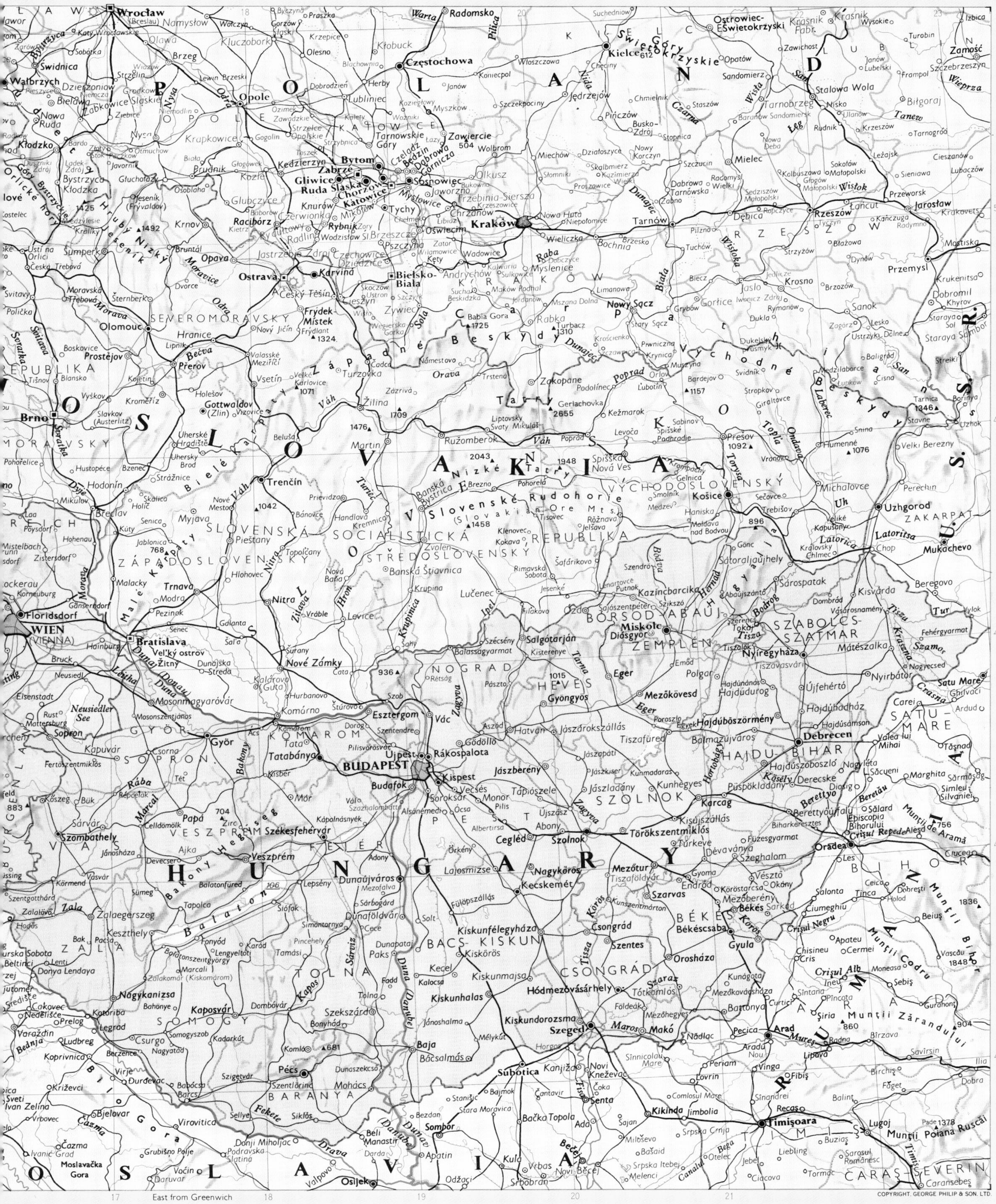

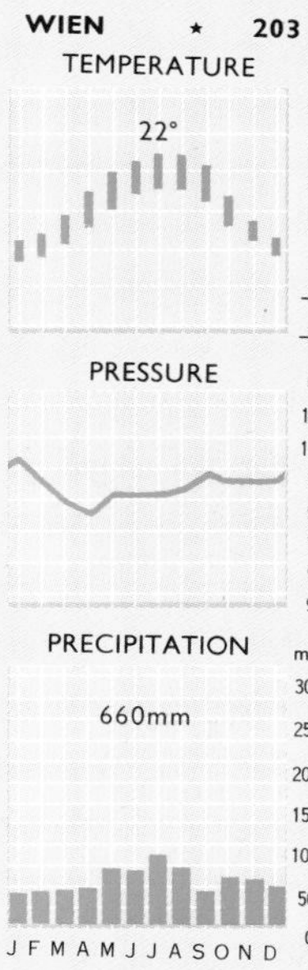

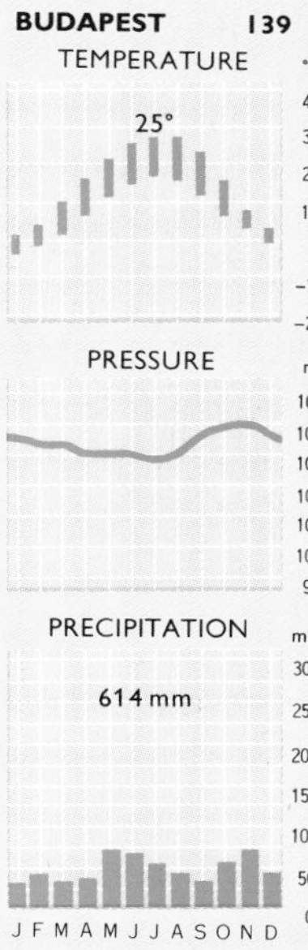

★ Pressure at station level

COPYRIGHT. GEORGE PHILIP & SON. LTD.

East from Greenwich

especially in the mountains, and warm summers in low-lying areas.

Minerals, industry and communications

Austria produces large quantities of iron ore and lignite and some magnesite, lead, zinc and petroleum. It is also a major producer of high-grade graphite.

Manufacturing is becoming increasingly important in Austria and Vienna is the chief centre. Hydro-electricity is widely used because of the shortage of coal. The chief manufacturing and power companies have been national-

Left: *A skiing and summer resort, Schwert Pill lies in the Inn valley in Austria.*

ized. Manufactured products include steel, iron and steel products, electrical machinery and textiles.

Communications are hampered by the Alps. East-west communications run along the Danube, an important waterway in the north, and along east-west valleys in the south. North-south routes are through mountain passes, such as the rail crossing at the Brenner Pass, linking Innsbruck with Italy.

Agriculture and forestry

Some farming is practised in the eastern Alps and the Alpine forelands, but the chief farming area is the Vienna basin. Only about 17 percent of Austria is cultivated and the chief crops are barley, oats, potatoes, rye and wheat. Cattle, pigs and sheep are kept in large numbers. However, Austria has to import much of its food.

Forests cover nearly 40 percent of Austria and timber-using industries produce furniture, wood pulp and paper.

Trade and foreign relations

West Germany, Italy and Switzerland are major trading partners of Austria, which is a member of the European Free Trade Association.

Austria is culturally Germanic, but it had strong historic links with eastern Europe. These links have been weakened since World War II. Neutral Austria has received much US aid and has become increasingly oriented towards the west.

Liechtenstein

Area: 160km² (62sq.m.).
Population: 27,000.
Capital: Vaduz (4,900).
Language: German.
Ethnic group: Alemannic.
Main exports: manufactured products.
Average temperatures: 0°C (32°F) Jan. 20°C (69°F) July.
Highest point: Naarkopf, 2,570m (8,432ft).

Liechtenstein is a small, neutral principality which originated in 1342, although its present frontiers were not fixed until 1434. Swiss currency is used and Liechtenstein has been part of a customs union with Switzerland since 1923. Formerly an agricultural country, Liechtenstein has become highly industrialized in the last 30 years. Light industries predominate. They manufacture an enormous variety of products.

Czechoslovakia

Area: 127,896km² (49,368sq.m.).
Population: 15.4 million.
Capital: Praha or Prague (1.19m).
Languages: Czech, Slovak.
Ethnic groups: Czechs, Moravians, Slovaks. Minorities include German-speaking peoples, mainly in Bohemia, and Magyars in Slovakia.
Main exports: machinery, industrial consumer goods, raw materials and fuels.
Average temperatures: −7°C (20°F) Jan. 19°C (67°F) July.
Highest point: Gerlachovka, 2,655m (8,711ft).

Formerly part of the Austro-Hungarian empire, Czechoslovakia became a separate state in 1918, uniting the Czechs and Slovaks in a new republic. The boundaries were fixed by treaty in 1919.

In 1938, Hitler demanded that Sudetenland, the German-speaking area, should be handed over to Germany. Britain, France, and Italy agreed to satisfy Hitler's demands in September 1938. At the same time, Poland took Teschen and Hungary took southern Slovakia. The dismemberment of the country was completed in March 1939, when Germany took what remained of the country. Bohemia and Moravia became part of Germany, Slovakia became a German puppet state and Ruthenia went to Hungary. Czechoslovakia was liberated by Soviet troops in 1945. The original frontiers were restored except for Ruthenia which went to the USSR. More than three million German-speaking people were expelled.

Elections in 1946 resulted in the communist party emerging as the largest single party. In 1948 the communists seized power. In 1968 pressure for liberalization culminated in Bulgarian, Hungarian, Polish and Soviet forces occupying Czechoslovakia. But in 1970, a 20-year Czechoslovak-Soviet friendship, co-operation and mutual assistance treaty was signed.

Today Czechoslovakia is a federal socialist republic, containing the Czech Socialist Republic and the Slovak Socialist Republic, each having equal authority.

In 1973 the Czechs, who live mainly in Bohemia and Moravia in western Czechoslovakia, accounted for 64 percent of the population. The Slovaks, who live in the east, made up another 30 percent. The remainder included Hungarians, German-speaking people, Poles, Russians and Gypsies. Nearly three-quarters of the population are Roman Catholics but as with the other countries of Eastern Europe the Church is not recognized by the state, and few nominal Catholics actually practise their religion.

Physical features and climate

In Bohemia, the rich farming basin of the River Elbe is almost enclosed by mountains. Prague stands on the Vltava, a tributary of the Elbe. To the east are the plains of Moravia. Slovakia is a forested mountainous region, except for the Danube lowlands around the river port of Bratislava. Czechoslovakia has cold winters, warm summers and moderate rainfall.

Above: *Karlovy Vary lies on the river Ohre in the Bohemian Massif in west Czechoslovakia, an area strongly influenced by western Europe and rich in minerals.*

Minerals and industry

Czechoslovakia has large deposits of hard and soft coal. Some iron ore and other metals are extracted but many raw materials are imported.

The country's manufacturing industries recovered and expanded rapidly after 1945. Today about 39 percent of employed people work in manufacturing, as opposed to 15 percent in agriculture and forestry. All industries are nationalized. Products include iron and steel, chemicals, cars, sugar, beer, textiles and shoes. The country's terrain has made communications difficult, but efforts have been made to open up less accessible highland areas.

Agriculture and forestry

About 55 percent of the land is used for farming. The chief crops are sugar-beet, potatoes, wheat, maize, oats and rye. Czechoslovakia has 5.1 million cattle and more than seven million pigs. Most farms are collectives or state farms, but private plots still exist on the collectives.

Forests of spruce, beech, pine and oak cover about 35 percent of the land. Paper-making is a major industry.

Trade and foreign relations

Some 69 percent of Czechoslovakia's trade is with communist countries. The largest non-communist trading partners are West Germany, Austria and the UK. In 1973 Czechoslovakia signed a treaty with West Germany, annulling the 1938 Munich agreement and normalizing relations.

Hungary

Area: 93,032km² (35,911sq.m.).
Population: 10.68 million.
Capital: Budapest (2.06m).
Languages: Magyar (Hungarian).
Ethnic groups: Magyars: minorities include Germans, Slovaks, Rumanians, Croats, Serbs, Gypsies.
Main exports: machinery, industrial consumer goods, raw materials, food.
Average temperatures: −1°C (30°F) Jan. 21°C (70°F) July.
Highest point: Mt Kekes, 1,015m (3,330ft).

The Magyars (Hungarians) are people of Finno-Ugric and Turkish descent, although they have mixed with local people. Some 48 percent of the people live in urban areas, the largest city by far being Budapest. Nearly 50 percent of the people are Roman Catholics, but few attend church.

Hungary was part of the Austro-Hungarian empire from 1867 until it was dismembered after World War I. In 1918 Hungary was proclaimed a republic and, in 1919, there was a brief spell of communist rule. However, Admiral Horthy re-established Hungary as a monarchy, although there was no monarch. Horthy proclaimed himself regent.

In the 1930s, Hitler supported some of Hungary's claims for the recovery of its lost territories. In 1939 and 1940, Hungary was granted areas seized by Germany, including southern Slovakia, Ruthenia and part of Transylvania. Hungary supported Germany but later tried to negotiate a separate armistice with the Allies. Germany invaded Hungary but Soviet troops drove the Germans out by 1945.

Hungary's area was reduced to its pre-1938 size. In 1948 the communists, aided by the USSR, took power. In 1956 an anti-Stalinist revolution was suppressed by Soviet troops. Today Hungary is a communist people's republic. Power is vested in the 352-member parliament, which elects the presidential council, whose chairman is the head of state.

Physical features and climate

The limestone Bakony Forest ridge separates the hilly Little Alföld in the northwest from Transdanubia in the southwest and the flat Great Alföld, or the Hungarian plain, in the east. Mountains occur only in the far north. Hot dry summers and cold winters are the chief features of the climate. Most rain falls in autumn and winter.

Minerals and industry

Hungary lacks large mineral reserves and imports much of what it needs for manufacturing. It produces some coal, lignite, bauxite and iron ore, and petroleum and natural gas deposits have been discovered.

Manufacturing has been the fastest developing sector of the economy since 1945. Food processing is important but metal, chemical and textile industries have been expanding quickly. In contrast with other COMECON members, Hungary has made great efforts to develop light, consumer goods industries in recent years. About 36 percent of employed people now work in manufacturing, and Hungarians have been an important source of skilled manpower for Soviet industry. Hungary is well provided with roads, railways and waterways.

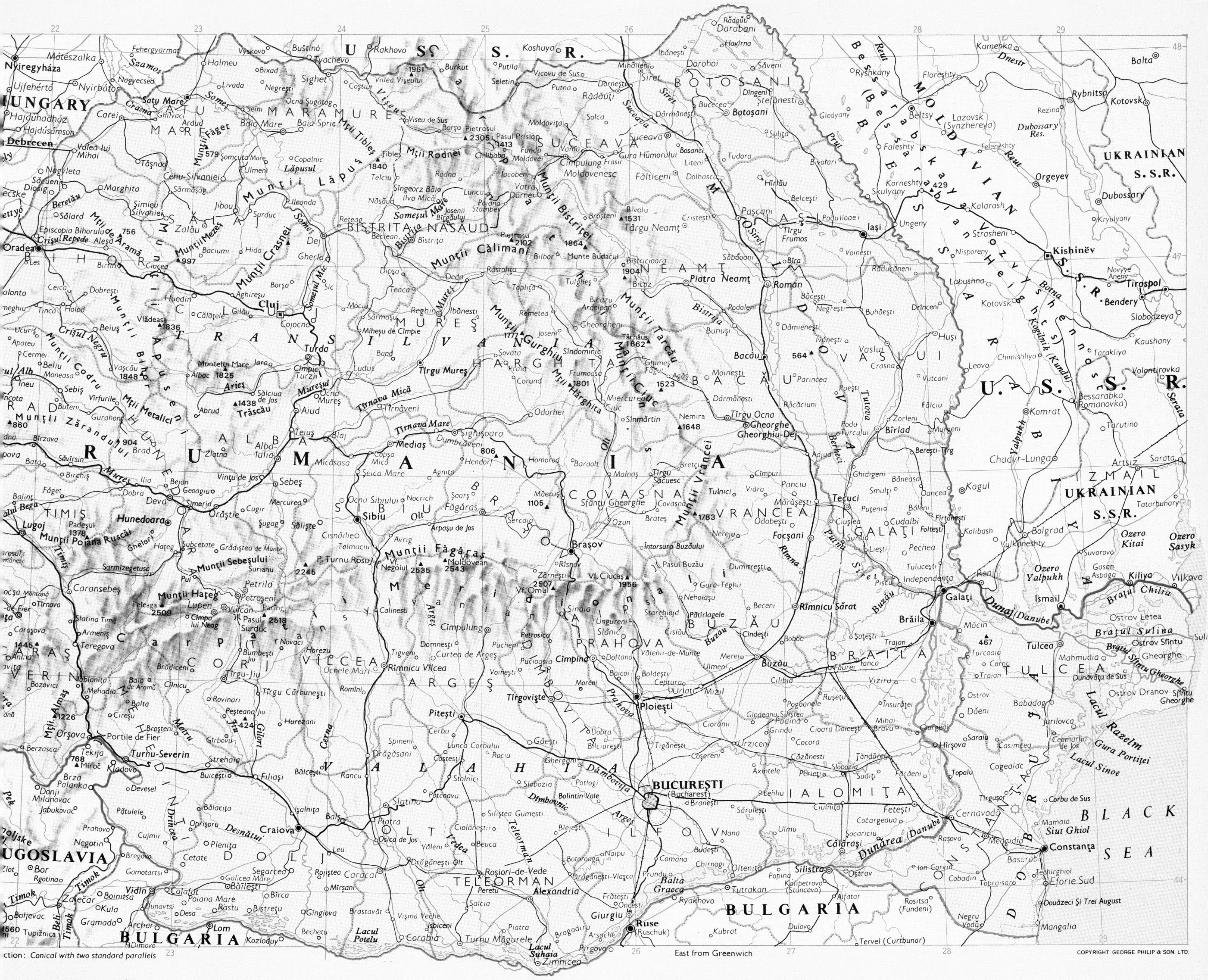

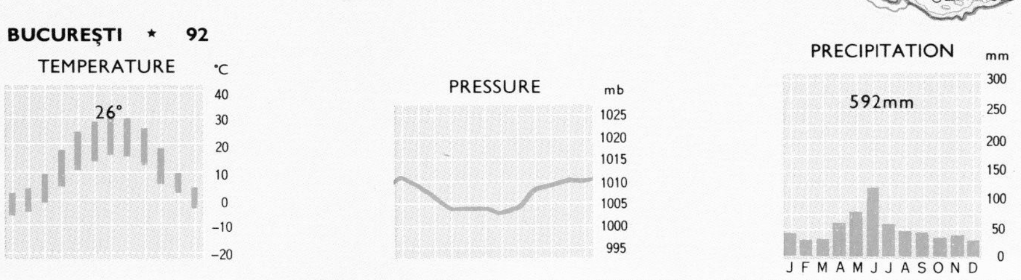

Agriculture, forestry and fishing

About 25 percent of the labour force work in agriculture. A high proportion of Hungary is farmed. Most land is collectivized or run by state farms. Hungary has nearly two million cattle, more than three million sheep and over nine million pigs. Vineyards on the northern mountain slopes produce *tokay* wines.

Forests cover 16 percent of the land. Fishing takes place on the Duna (Danube) and Tisza rivers and also in Lake Balaton.

Trade and foreign relations

Some 62 percent of Hungary's trade is with COMECON countries, especially the USSR. After the uprising in 1956, Hungary restored its close relations with the USSR.

Left: *Diosgyor, an old steel town in eastern Hungary, showing a typical contrast between old and new buildings.*

Romania

Area: 237,500km² (91,699sq.m.).
Population: 22.6 million.
Capital: Bucuresti or Bucharest (1.8m).
Languages: Romanian.
Ethnic groups: Romanian; minorities include Hungarians, Germans, Russians, Bulgarians, Turks.
Main exports: cement; cereals; equipment for oilfields; engineering and construction products; fuel oil; ships; tractors.
Average temperatures: −4°C (25°F) Jan. 24°C (75°F) July.
Highest point: Moldoveanu, 2,543m (8,343ft).

Romanians are descended from a mixture of peoples, including ancient Dacian tribesmen, Romans and some Turkish and Slavic peoples. The language is based on Latin. About 48 percent of the people live in urban areas.

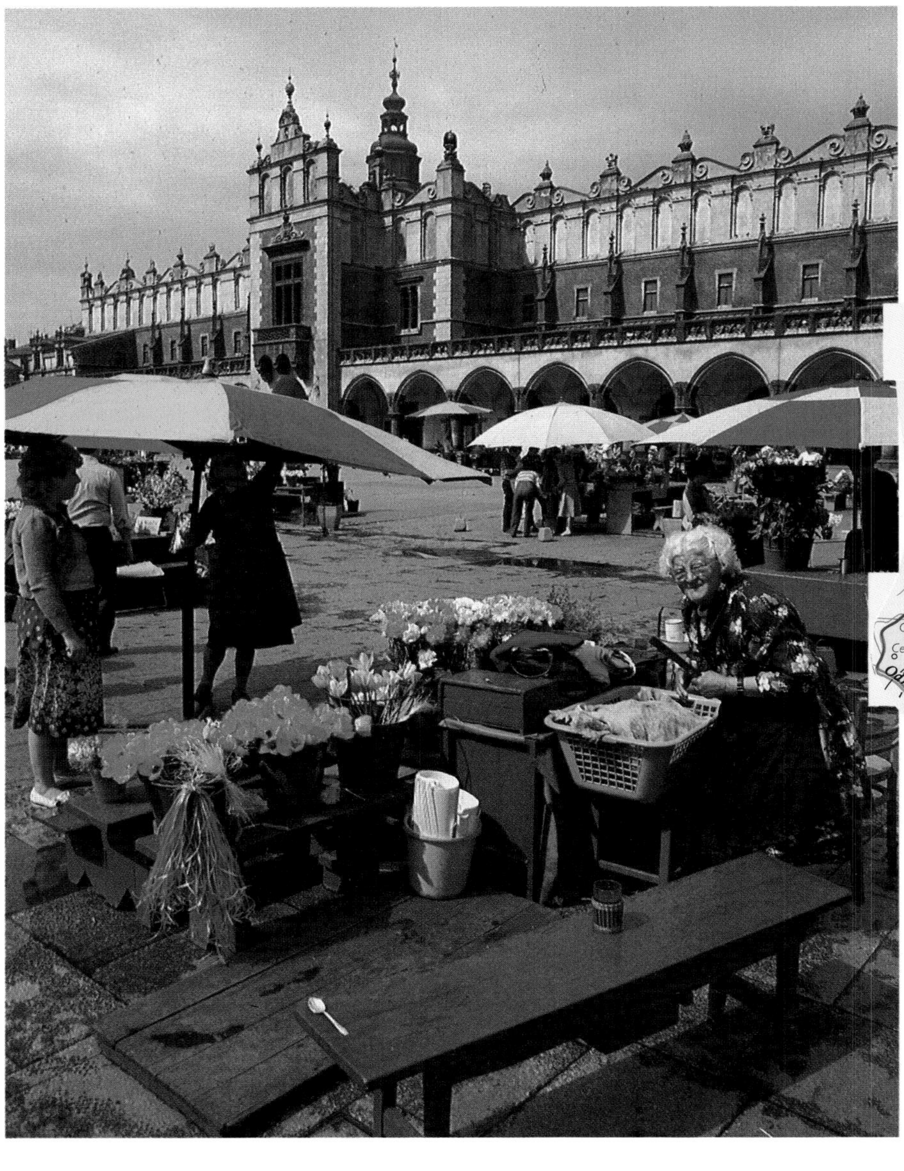

Left: *A farmstead in Transylvania, Romania, in a landscape which supports a great diversity of agriculture, from livestock raising and timber to cereal crops.*

Above: *A flower seller in the medieval town centre of Kraków, one of Poland's leading cultural centres whose walls and defensive gates are well preserved.*

Romania came into being as a monarchy following a union of Moldavia and Walachia in 1861. In World War I, Romania supported the Allies and, after the war, its territory was extended following the break-up of the Austro-Hungarian empire. In 1940 Romania lost much territory to Bulgaria, Hungary and the USSR. It finally joined the Allies in 1944.

The communists took power after World War II and King Michael was forced to abdicate in 1947. Today Romania is a socialist republic.

Physical features

Transylvania forms the heart of Romania. It consists of a central plateau ringed by the Carpathian mountains in the east, the Transylvanian Alps in the south, and the Bihor massif in the west. Transylvania is flanked by fertile plains in the west. The Walachian plains and Moldavia are in the south and east. The climate is continental with hot summers and cold winters.

Minerals and industry

Romania produces oil and natural gas, salt, lignite and various metals, but it imports large quantities of coke, iron ore and other metals.

Manufacturing has increased greatly since 1945, especially with the development of the Ploieşti oilfield and manufactures are now the most valuable exports. They include steel and steel products, chemicals, textiles and processed farm products. Consumer goods are increasing in importance. Romania's internal communications are poor.

Agriculture and forestry

Agriculture still employs about 42 percent of the labour force. The chief crops of this fertile country are maize, potatoes, sugar beet and wheat. Romania has about six million cattle, 12.5 million pigs and 17.3 million sheep. Most land is collectivized or run by state farms.

Forests cover 27 percent of the land. The pine and oak forests of Transylvania support a flourishing timber industry.

Trade and foreign relations

About 60 percent of Romania's trade is with COMECON countries. But recently Romania has been looking beyond the Soviet bloc. In the 1970s it signed trading agreements with the UK, China and the US.

Poland

Area: 312,683km² (120,628sq.m.).
Population: 37.3 million.
Capital: Warszawa or Warsaw (1.63m).
Language: Polish.
Ethnic groups: Poles; minorities include Russians, Jews, Slovaks and Lithuanians.
Main exports: coal, lignite, coke, fertilizers, ships.
Average temperatures: −1.7°C (29°F) Jan. 18.9°C (66°F) July.
Highest point: Rysy Peak, 2,503m (8,212ft).

Most Poles belong to the Western Slavic ethnic group. Although a communist country, Poland has strong religious traditions and it is estimated that 80 percent of the people are active Roman Catholics. The rest are Orthodox or Protestant. Nearly three million Jews perished at the hands of the Nazis during World War II.

Poland became an independent kingdom in 1025, but since then it has suffered many partitions and boundary changes. Twice, in 1795 and 1939, it disappeared from the map.

In World War I, the Poles were forced to fight for opposing Russian, German and Austrian armies. But in 1918, Poland became an independent republic. It contained large German, Russian, Lithuanian and Jewish communities. Following Germany's invasion of Czechoslovakia in March 1939, Hitler demanded special privileges for the Germans in Poland and transport rights through the Polish corridor – the area between East Prussia and the rest of Germany which gave Poland access to the Baltic Sea. The Germans attacked Poland in September 1939 and, despite brave resistance, the country fell. It was partitioned between Germany and the USSR.

After liberation in 1945, Poland lost territory in the east to the USSR, but gained territory from Germany. About 2.5 million Germans were expelled from Poland and another two million from East Prussia. Most of them went to West Germany. Poland's eastern border, the Oder-Neisse line, was not recognized by West Germany until 1970. The post-war communist government launched a rapid programme of industrialization, nationalization and collectivization. However, the communists were unable to break the power of the churches and collectivization was eventually abandoned. Today more than 80 percent of the farmland is privately owned. Anti-Soviet riots in 1956 led to anti-Stalinists taking control of the communist party. The 1970s and 1980s saw many challenges to the authority of the government, typified by the emergence of the trade union known as Solidarity.

Today Poland is a communist people's republic, with power effectively in the hands of the communist party. The country has a 460-member *Sejm* (parliament) and a 15-member Council of State.

Physical features and climate

Northern Poland is largely covered by glacial deposits and the soils are poor. Although poorly drained, the central lowlands are more fertile. The southern plateau, which rises above 183m (600ft), contains Poland's best farmland and most important mineral deposits, especially the Upper Silesian coalfield. In the southeast, the plateau rises up to the Carpathian mountains which border Czechoslovakia. Poland has cold winters and mild summers, although conditions become more extreme from west to east and from north to south. The average annual rainfall varies between 508 and 1,016 millimetres (20-40 inches).

Minerals and industry

Poland is Europe's leading coal exporter and a major copper producer. Poland also extracts iron ore, lead, salt and zinc.

Since 1945 Poland has become a major industrial nation. Large manufacturing centres, such as Gliwice and

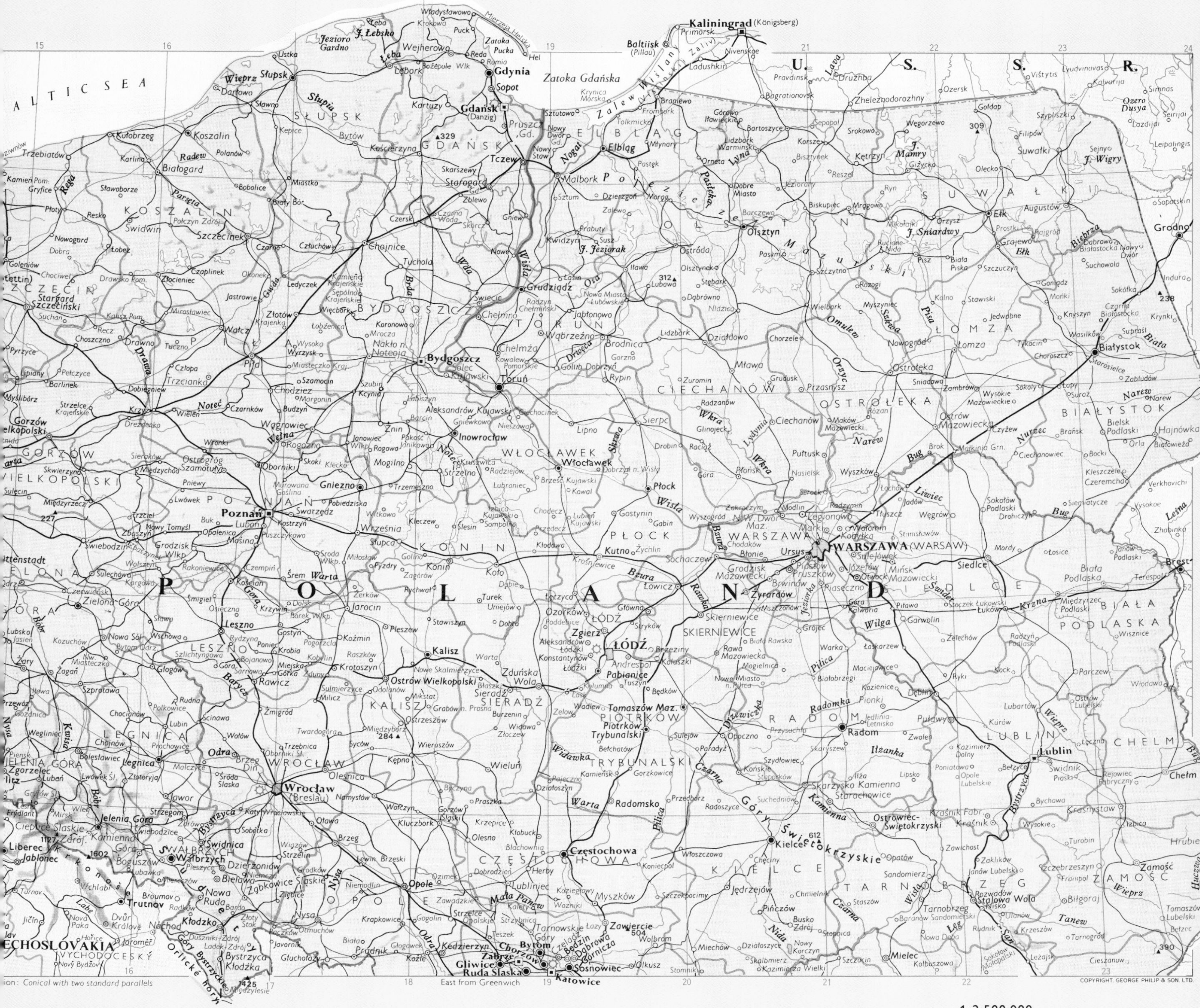

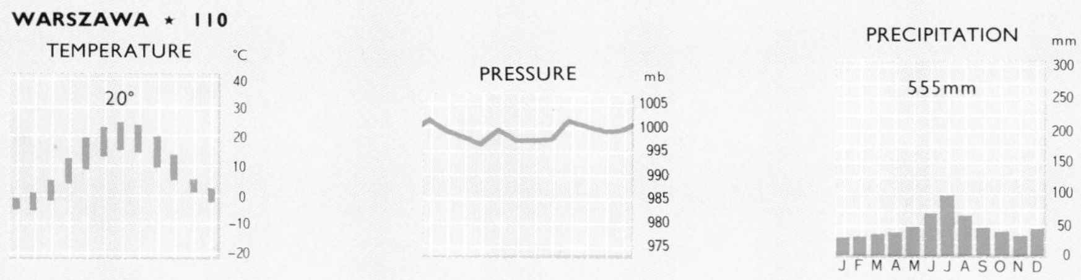

Katowice, stand on the Upper Silesian coalfield. Away from the coalfields, major industrial centres include Krakow, Lódź, Warsaw and Wroclaw. Steel and steel products, fertilizers, locomotives, metals, ships and textiles are among the varied manufactures produced.

In addition to a good road and rail network, waterways, including the rivers Odra (Oder) and Wisla (Vistula), are important lines of communication. The chief seaports, Gdánsk (Danzig), Gdynia and Szczecin (Stettin), are also centres of ship-building and other industries.

Agriculture, forestry and fishing

Before 1939 Poland depended mainly on farming, but agriculture now employs only 29 percent of the labour force. The chief crops are rye, potatoes, wheat, oats, barley and sugar-beet. Poland has 12 million cattle, 20 million pigs and 3.9 million sheep.

Forests, mostly coniferous, cover more than 25 percent of the land. Timber forms the basis of a major paper industry. In 1982 Poland had a deep-sea fishing fleet consisting of 103 vessels.

Trade and foreign relations

About 54 percent of Poland's trade is with COMECON countries, and West Germany and the UK are also important trade partners. Western companies are encouraged to set up operations in Poland, taking up to 49 percent of the shares. Trading with the USA was disrupted in 1982 after the banning of Solidarity.

Right: *Bukowina, in the Tatra Mountains, the foothills of the Carpathians, on Poland's border with Czechoslovakia.*

Map 18 WESTERN SPAIN AND PORTUGAL

LISBOA 77
TEMPERATURE
PRESSURE
PRECIPITATION
708mm

MADRID 660
TEMPERATURE
PRESSURE
PRECIPITATION
444mm

GIBRALTAR 27
TEMPERATURE
PRESSURE
PRECIPITATION
863mm

1:3 000 000

Projection: Conical with two standard parallels

West from Greenwich

COPYRIGHT: GEORGE PHILIP & SON

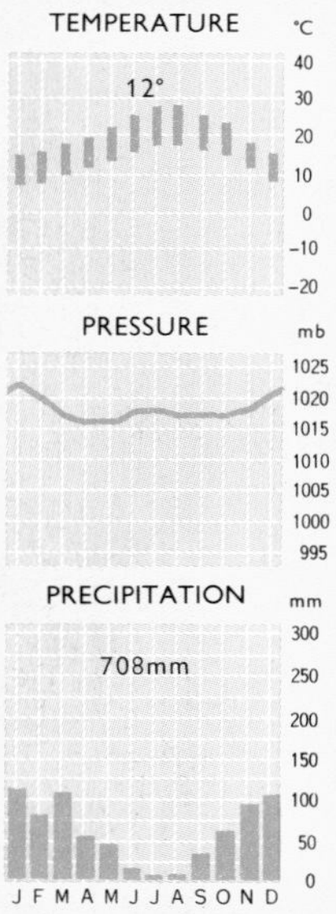

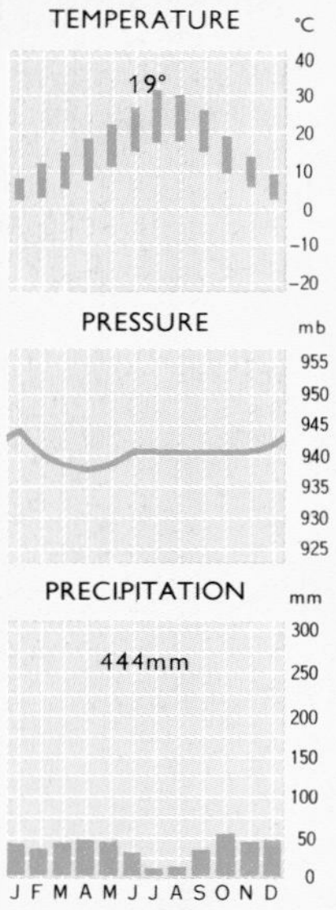

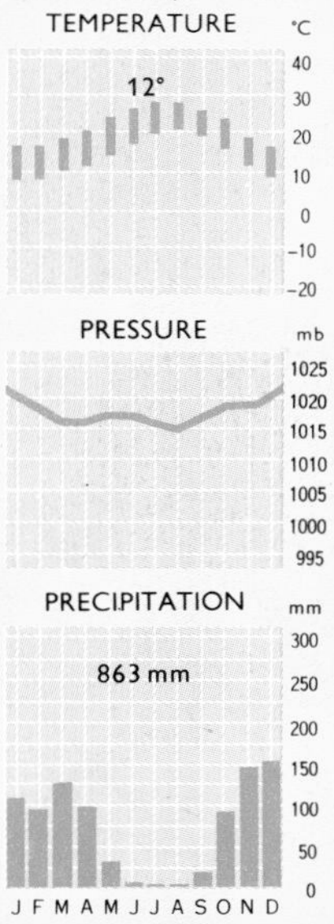

Portugal

Area: 91,985km² (35,516sq.m.).
Population: 10.3 million.
Capital: Lisboa or Lisbon (2m).
Language: Portuguese.
Ethnic group: Portuguese.
Main exports: wine, cork, textiles, wood pulp, resin, sardines.
Average temperatures: 10°C (50°F) Jan. 21°C (70°F) July.
Highest point: Malhao, 1,991m (6,532ft).

The Portuguese are a mixture of the original Iberians and later invaders, including Carthaginians, Celts, Germanic tribes, Greeks, Moors and Romans. The Portuguese language developed from Galician and is similar to Spanish.

The people are mostly Roman Catholics. Their economy depends mainly on agriculture, forestry and fishing and many people are relatively poor. The distribution of population is unbalanced with many more people living in the north than in the south. Emigration, especially to Brazil, has long been an important demographic safety valve. More recently many Portuguese workers who migrated to France have returned, as have former colonists from Africa.

History and constitution

The early history of Portugal is similar to that of Spain. But Spain recognized Portugal as an independent kingdom in 1385. In the 15th century, mainly through the activities of Prince Henry the Navigator, the Portuguese led the way to the exploration of the African coastline and the search for a sea route to India. Vasco da Gama finally reached India in 1498. Portugal's overseas empire grew quickly, including the colonization of Brazil. However, conflict with Spain and rivalry with other European powers gradually weakened Portugal and Brazil was lost in 1822.

Portugal became a republic in 1910, but this impoverished country suffered from political unrest. In 1928 Antonio de Oliveira Salazar became finance minister and, in 1932, prime minister. Effectively a dictator, Salazar remained in power until he died in 1970, when Dr Caetano succeeded him.

Wars in the overseas possessions of Portugal – Angola, Guinea-Bissau and Mozambique – were a great strain on the country's resources. Finally, in 1974, Caetano was overthrown by army officers led by General Antonio de Spinola. Political conflict between army leaders and the revived political parties caused the moderate Spinola to resign as president and he in turn went into exile in 1975.

A Supreme Revolutionary Council ruled Portugal until 1976, when democratic government returned. The SRC became the Council of the Revolution, an advisory body until it was dissolved in 1982. Portugal's continuing economic problems should be alleviated by membership of the European Economic Community (EEC) from January 1, 1986.

Physical features and climate

Northern Portugal is a westward extension of the Spanish *meseta*. It is fringed by a narrow coastal lowland. The lowlands broaden to the southwest, where the capital and chief port Lisbon stands on the estuary of the River Tejo (Tagus).

Minerals and industry

Portugal has various mineral resources which are generally under-exploited. The country produces some coal, copper, uranium, wolframite and other metals.

Efforts have been made to increase the importance of manufacturing. The chief industries are wine-making, sardine-canning and textile manufacturing, but Portugal has also to developed a steel industry. Lisbon is the chief manufacturing centre. Portugal has more than 30,000km (18,640m.) of roads and 3,500km (2,170m.) of railways. Tourism continues to grow in importance, with the Algarve region attracting large numbers of visitors.

Agriculture, forestry and fishing

Agriculture remains the basis of Portugal's economy. Wheat, maize, olives and vines are important and Portugal has about 3.5 million pigs and a million cattle.

Forests of pine, cork oak and other oaks, eucalyptus, chestnuts and other trees cover about one-third of the land. Portugal is the world's chief supplier of cork. Sardine fishing is of great importance and canned sardines are a leading export.

Trade and foreign relations

Portugal's chief trading partners are the UK, West Germany, the US and France. After the coup of 1974, Portugal recognized the USSR and COMECON countries for the first time, but trade with communist countries is small. Most of the aid that Portugal has recently received has come from EEC countries and the USA.

Right: *A house in the Algarve, southern Portugal. The migration of workers from the countryside to the towns and abroad has left rural areas economically depressed.*

Left: *Portuguese fishermen mending their nets. Although the fishing industry has prospered it is still largely traditional.*

The Azores Islands
The Cape Verde Islands
The Madeira Islands

These three island groups in the Atlantic Ocean were governed by Portugal until 1975, when the Cape Verde Islands became an independent republic. Nationalist demands for independence have also been made in the Azores and Madeira islands.

The northernmost group, the Azores, are about 2,070km (800m.) from Portugal. Administratively, they form three Portuguese districts. The Madeira Islands lie west of Morocco. The largest island, Madeira, is fertile and renowned for its wine. The Cape Verde Islands lie west of Senegal.

The **Azores Islands** consist of nine islands with an area of 2,247km² (867sq.m.) and 243,410 people, and are of great strategic value.

The **Cape Verde Islands** consist of 10 islands and five islets. They have an area of 4,033km² (1,557sq.m.) and 297,000 people. The capital is Praia.

The **Madeira Islands** cover 794km² (306sq.m.) and have 270,000 people. There are two main islands, Madeira and Porto Santo, and two uninhabited island groups, the Desertas and Selvagens.

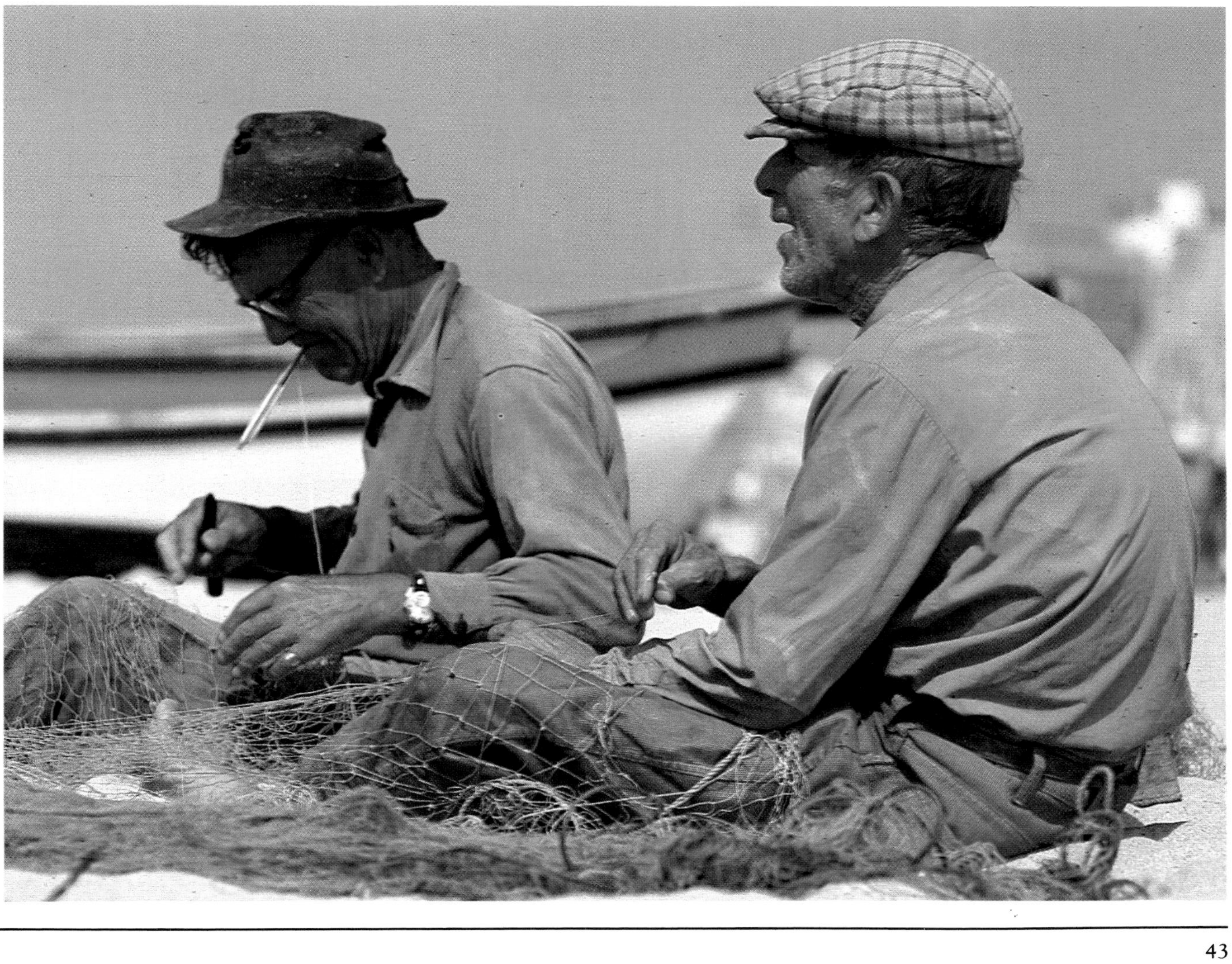

Map 19

EASTERN SPAIN

ALICANTE ★ 81
TEMPERATURE
PRESSURE
PRECIPITATION
328mm
★ Pressure at station level

BARCELONA 93
TEMPERATURE
PRESSURE
PRECIPITATION
587 mm

ZARAGOZA 237
TEMPERATURE
PRESSURE
PRECIPITATION
337 mm

1 : 3 000 000

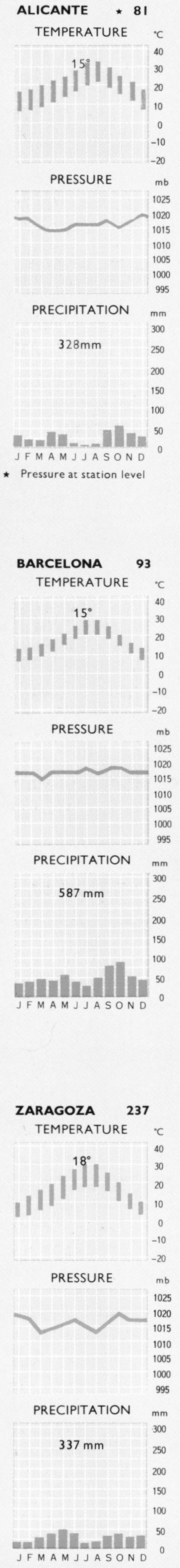

Above: *Madrid, the Spanish capital, is the highest of all European capital cities.*

Spain

Area: 504,750km^2 (194,884sq.m.), including the Balearic and Canary Islands.
Population: 38.5 million.
Capital: Madrid (3.19m).
Languages: Spanish (Castilian), Basque, Catalan, Galician.
Ethnic groups: Spaniards, Basques, Catalans, Galicians.
Main exports: manufactured goods; food (especially fruit), drink and tobacco.
Average temperatures: 5°C (41°F) Jan. 26°C (78°F) July on central plateau, but cooler in the north and warmer on southern and eastern coasts.
Highest point: Mulhacén, 3,478m (11,411ft).

The early people of Spain, the Iberians, mixed with later invaders who included Carthaginians, Celts, Germanic tribes, Moors and Romans.

The Spanish language is Castilian. There are three other languages. Basque is spoken in the Spanish provinces bordering the Bay of Biscay and the French frontier. Some Basques live in France. Basque is an ancient tongue, quite unlike French or Spanish. The Basque people are also ethnically different from Frenchmen and Spaniards. They are of medium height with narrow faces.

Two other languages, Catalan and Galician, developed from Romance languages, as did Castilian. Catalan is spoken in the northeast. It resembles the Provençal language of southern France. Galician is spoken in the northwest. It is the language from which Portuguese developed. Many Basque and Catalan-speaking people, although bilingual, have their own culture and have supported separatist policies. The state religion in Spain is Roman Catholicism.

History and constitution

From about 480 BC, Spain was held successively by the Carthaginians, the Romans and Germanic tribes. The Moors invaded Spain in AD 711 and much of the peninsula fell under Moslem influence, apart from Christian outposts in the north. The Moors left their mark on Spain and some of their superb palaces and fortresses still survive, such as at Cordoba and Granada. A Christian revival began in the 1100s and by 1276 the Moors held only Granada.

Castile emerged as the leading kingdom in the late 1300s and in 1469 Castile was united with Aragon through the marriage of Ferdinand of Aragon and Isabella of Castile. From this union, the other independent kingdoms of Spain were gradually welded into one nation.

Columbus's voyage in 1492 began the rapid emergence of Spain as a great world power. Even today, the Spanish language is spoken throughout most of Central and South America, except for Brazil. However, from the late 1500s, Spanish power gradually began to decline and Spanish sea power was finally destroyed at the Battle of Trafalgar in 1805.

By the 1900s, Spain was a poor farming country beset with many problems. In 1923 it became a dictatorship under Primo de Rivera, with the king's approval. In 1930 the king and the army brought the dictatorship to an end, but in 1931 Spain became a republic. The royal family left Spain and the nation became increasingly divided politically. Finally, the bitterly fought Civil War (1936-1939) brought General Francisco Franco to power. Franco ruled as a dictator. He restored the institution of the monarchy but there was no monarch.

However, when Franco died in 1975, his designated successor, Prince Don Juan Carlos de Borbon, became king and head of state. Democracy was introduced, and it has survived despite an attempted *coup d'état.* Spain joined the European Economic Community (EEC) in 1986.

Physical features and climate

Five-sixths of Spain is a plateau, called the *meseta.* It is bordered by mountains and generally narrow coastal plains.

Northern Spain is mountainous. Galicia in the northwest is a rugged area, resembling Brittany. The Cantabrian mountains, extending eastwards from Galicia to the French border, reach 1,800m (6,000ft) above sea level. The Pyrenees in the northeast contain peaks of more than 3,350m (11,000ft).

The Spanish *meseta* is mostly between 600 and 900m (2,000-3,000ft) above sea level. It is broken by high ridges called *sierras.* To the southeast is another mountain range which contains Spain's highest peak, Mulhacén.

The largest plains are in Andalusia and Aragon. The Andalusian plain in the southwest is rich and well-watered, whereas much of the Aragon plain in the northeast is arid. The south and east are fringed by a series of coastal plains. Several, including those around Alicante and Valencia, are fertile after irrigation. The northeast coast is rugged in places.

The entire Mediterranean coast has become a great centre for about 42 million tourists per year. Coastal regions have hot, dry summers and mild winters. The northern mountains have cool summers and mild winters with rain falling throughout the year. The interior has an almost continental climate, with a large annual temperature range.

Minerals and industry

Spain has important mineral resources, but many are only partially developed. However, Spain produces coal, lignite iron ore, lead and zinc. It also leads the world in mercury production.

Manufacturing has been steadily increasing in importance. Today about 27 percent of the workforce are in manufacturing as compared with 30 percent in agriculture and fishing. The chief industries include textiles, especially cotton and woollen goods, iron and steel, shipbuilding, paper-milling, cork and cement. Engineering industries in general are increasing. Wine-making is a major industry, especially sherry from the Jerez region in the south. The chief industrial regions are in the northwest around Bilbao and in Cataluña, especially around Spain's second city and largest port, Barcelona (1.75m.).

In some areas, communications are poorly developed and travel is difficult.

Agriculture, forestry and fishing

Agriculture is still Spain's chief activity. Cereals, especially wheat and barley, vines, maize, potatoes and vegetables are important. Typical Mediterranean crops, such as oranges and olives, flourish in areas such as the plains of Andalusia and other coastal areas. Livestock farming is a major industry. Spain has more than 11 million sheep, 11.6 million pigs and five million cattle. Sheep-raising is the chief activity on the *meseta.*

Forestry contributes about seven percent of the value of agricultural production. Fishing, especially for sardines, tunny fish and cod, is most important.

Trade and foreign relations

Spain's chief trading partners are in Western Europe. Under the Franco dictatorship Spain became politically and economically isolated from her neighbours and this created major problems. Many Spaniards left to seek work in France and West Germany. Democracy has enabled Spain to apply for EEC membership and at the same time reform its ailing economy. The admission of Spain will have a considerable effect on EEC agricultural policy.

The Balearic Islands The Canary Islands

These Spanish island groups contain popular holiday resorts. The 15 Balearic islands in the Mediterranean form a province of Spain. They include Mallorca (Majorca), the largest, Menorca (Minorca) and Ibiza. The chief tourist centres in the Canary Islands, which number 13, are Palma and Tenerife. Six of the Canary Islands are barren and uninhabited. The Canary Islands form two provinces of Spain: Santa Cruz de Tenerife (capital, Tenerife); and Las Palmas de Gran Canaria (capital, Palma).

The **Balearic Islands** have an area of 5,014km^2 (1,936sq.m.) and 685,000 people. The provincial capital is Palma de Mallorca (304,000).

The **Canary Islands** have an area of 7,273km^2 (2,808sq.m.) and 1,445,000 people.

Andorra, Gibraltar

These two small territories are both in the Iberian peninsula. They rely very much on tourism as a source of revenue.

Andorra covers an area of 465km^2 (190sq.m.) and has a population of 42,000. Its capital is Andorra la Vella. This mountainous, landlocked country nestles in the Pyrenees. France is to the north and Spain to the south. Andorrans speak Catalan, French and Spanish. Andorra is a co-principality, technically ruled by the Spanish Bishop of Urgel and the French president. In fact, French and Spanish delegations are appointed and the legislature is the General Council of the Valleys.

Gibraltar has an area of 6km^2 (2.3sq.m.) and a population of 29,000, occupying a rocky peninsula. It has been a British fortress since 1704. Spain has demanded its return but, in 1967, 99.6 percent of the people voted to remain British. The border with Spain was closed in 1969 and not fully reopened until 1985. Gibraltar has a ship repair yard and an airfield, and an important strategic position.

Map 20   NORTHERN ITALY AND WESTERN YUGOSLAVIA

MILANO   121
TEMPERATURE

PRESSURE

PRECIPITATION
1017mm.

AJACCIO   4
TEMPERATURE

PRESSURE

PRECIPITATION
672 mm

1:2 500 000

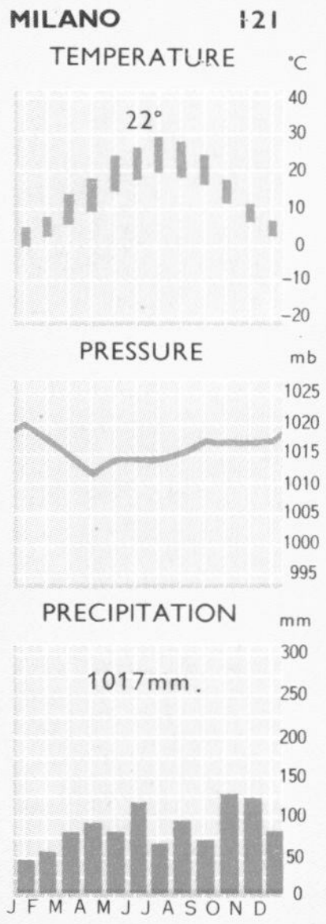

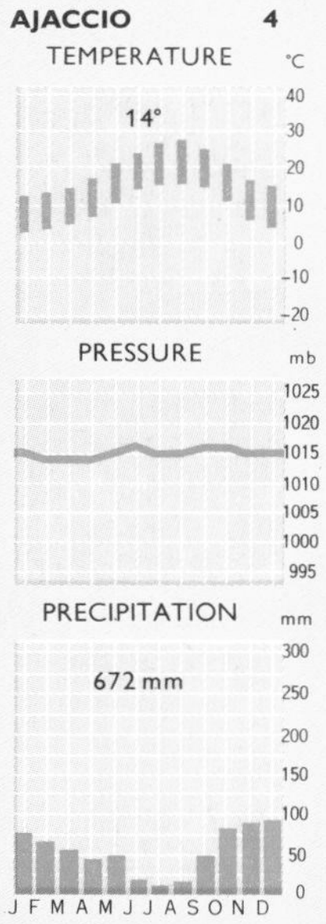

Italy

Area: 301,268km² (116,320sq.m.).
Population: 57.4 million.
Capital: Rome (2.9m).
Language: Italian.
Ethnic groups: Italian (99 percent), Germanic, Albanian.
Main exports: motor vehicles, engineering products, chemicals, clothing, textiles, wine, fruit and vegetables.
Average temperatures: 24°C (75°F) in July, 9°C (42.8°F) in January in Rome.
Highest point: Grenzgipfel Peak on Mt. Rosa 4,634m (15,203ft).

Italy is regarded as one of the most beautiful countries in the world, both for its natural surroundings and for its cultural heritage. Within its graceful peninsula, shaped like a slender boot, are snowcapped mountains, plains and valleys and a 4,313km (2,681m.) coastline ranging from golden beaches to steep cliffs.

The cities match the splendour of their natural setting. Venice, with its maze of canals, is unique. Florence, where Renaissance art reaches its greatest peak, is one of the world's best loved and most visited places. Rome combines cosmopolitan flair with echoes of past imperial grandeur.

No country has contributed more to the arts and sciences. Names such as Dante, Leonardo, Michelangelo, Machiavelli, Galileo, Columbus and Verdi all testify to Italy's signal achievements in literature, painting, sculpture, music and learning.

Physical features and climate
The Italian peninsula extends south for 1,223km (760m.). Its average width from the Mediterranean in the west to the Adriatic in the east is about 241km (150m.).

The Alps in the north separate Italy from France, Switzerland, Austria and Yugoslavia. South of the Alps lies the broad Plain of Lombardy, Italy's most densely populated region.

The Apennines begin south of the Plain. They rise more than 2,438m (8,000ft) in places and form a backbone that runs the entire length of the peninsula, continuing into Sicily. In the northwest, the Apennines include the white marble quarries of Carrara which have been worked for their beautiful stone for more than 2,000 years.

Sicily, a triangular island and the largest in the Mediterranean, lies close to the toe of the peninsula. It consists mainly of a rugged plateau surrounded by a coastal plain dotted with cities such as Palermo, Messina and Catania.

Map 21

FIRENZE ★ 51

TEMPERATURE °C
19°

PRESSURE mb

PRECIPITATION mm
825mm

J F M A M J J A S O N D

TRIESTE 11

TEMPERATURE °C
20°

PRESSURE mb

PRECIPITATION mm
1023 mm

J F M A M J J A S O N D

COPYRIGHT GEORGE PHILIP & SON LTD.

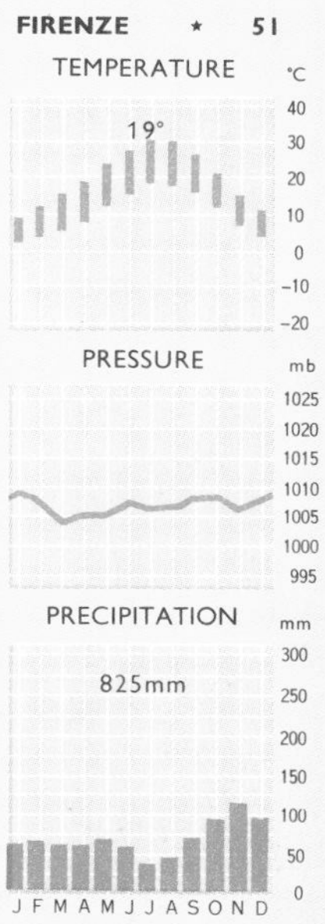

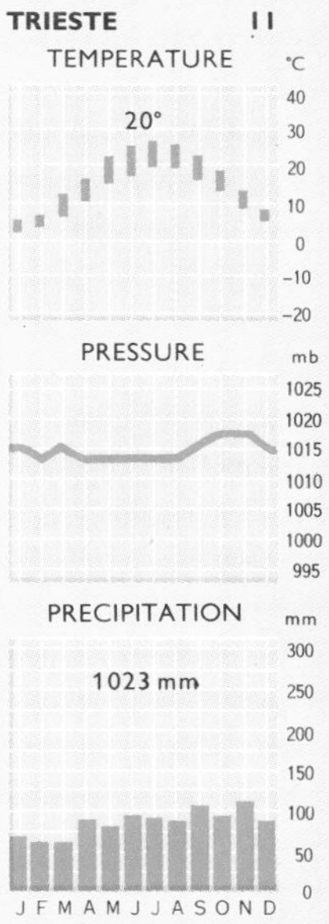

Sardinia, Italy's other main island, lying 241km (150m.) to the west, is also mountainous.

The Po flows westward across the Lombardy Plain into the Adriatic. Its delta is subject to flooding and major drainage schemes have been undertaken during this century. The Arno rises in the Apennines and flows westward through Florence and Pisa into the Mediterranean. The Tiber, the river of Rome, also flows into the Mediterranean.

Glaciers advancing south from the Alps during the last ice age scooped out huge hollows which now form the beautiful lakes of Como, Maggiore and Garda at the foot of the mountains. In central Italy, the lakes of Trasimeno, Bracciano and Bolsena fill the circular craters of dead volcanoes.

Italy still has three active volcanoes. Vesuvius, 1,277m (4,190ft) is near Naples. Stromboli, 926m (3,038ft) stands on the island of the same name between the Italian mainland and Sicily. Etna, 3,390m (11,122ft) is situated on the northeast corner of Sicily. Continuing tectonic activity has led to severe earthquakes in recent years, especially in the south.

Right: The Roman amphitheatre at Santa Maria Capua Vetere, Italy, a country rich in monuments and ancient ruins.

Above: *Italian farms, like this one near Siena in Tuscany, are usually small.*

Below: *Venice's 28 miles of canals have long appealed to the romantic imagination.*

Italy, with its long, hot summers, is generally thought of as a sunny land. However, fierce squalls called *temporali* often cause severe damage in summer. Winters, although warmer in the south, bring deep snow to high regions and temperatures drop to below freezing. The Milan region is one of the foggiest in Europe, a combination of the physical nature of its site and its industrialization.

Italy is poor in minerals, although it is a leading producer of mercury and has useful deposits of natural gas in Lombardy. Other minerals include coal, lignite, sulphur and petroleum but these are produced in modest quantities. Hydro-electric power has been developed and over two million tonnes of oil were produced in 1983.

The people

The ancestors of the Italians include the barbarians who swept into the land in the 5th century with the decline of Rome. Teutonic and Slavic people also settled in Italy. Carthaginians, Greeks, Arabs and Normans were among the earliest inhabitants of Sicily.

A small German-speaking minority lives in the Alto Adige region near the Austrian border. In the south-east there is a tiny community of Albanian-speaking people.

Milan (1.56m) is the commercial and financial centre. Every Italian city has its own highly individual history and character. Among the best known in addition to Rome, Florence and turin are Naples (1.2m), Genoa (0.75m), and Bologna (0.45m).

The cities, where the people are mainly apartment dwellers, are full of noise and movement. Rural life is enlivened by feast days celebrating some local saint or religious occasion with processions, ceremonies, fairs and carnivals. Dramatic and energetic sports, such as football and motor racing, are popular. More than 90 percent of the people are Roman Catholic.

Italian food is appreciated throughout the world, particularly the many kinds of *pasta* and the sauces that adorn them and the universally popular *pizza*.

Agriculture and industry

A major economic problem for Italy is the disparity in earnings of between the people of the industrialized north and the poor small farmers of the rural south. About two-thirds of the land is under cultivation, but less than one Italian in five now works in farming. Much of the terrain makes agriculture difficult and Italy is not self-sufficient in food. Although about a fifth of the land is forested, Italy also has to import timber.

Wheat grows throughout most of the country. Other important crops include maize, rye, barley, oats and olives. Italy is a major producer of olive oil. Vineyards occur widely. With France, Italy is one of the two leading producers of wine in the world. Fruits and vegetables are also major crops, but the meat and dairying industries are small. From mostly indifferent pastures, Italian cattle produce the milk that makes two famous cheeses: Parmesan and Gorgonzola.

Italy's chief industrial region is in the triangle formed by Turin, Milan and Genoa. Turin and Milan are centres of the motor industry. ·Fiat (Europe's second biggest producer of vehicles), Alfa Romeo, Ferrari, Maserati and Lamborghini are names known worldwide.

Italy's big oil-refining plants have encouraged the growth of petro-chemical manufactures. Other industrial products

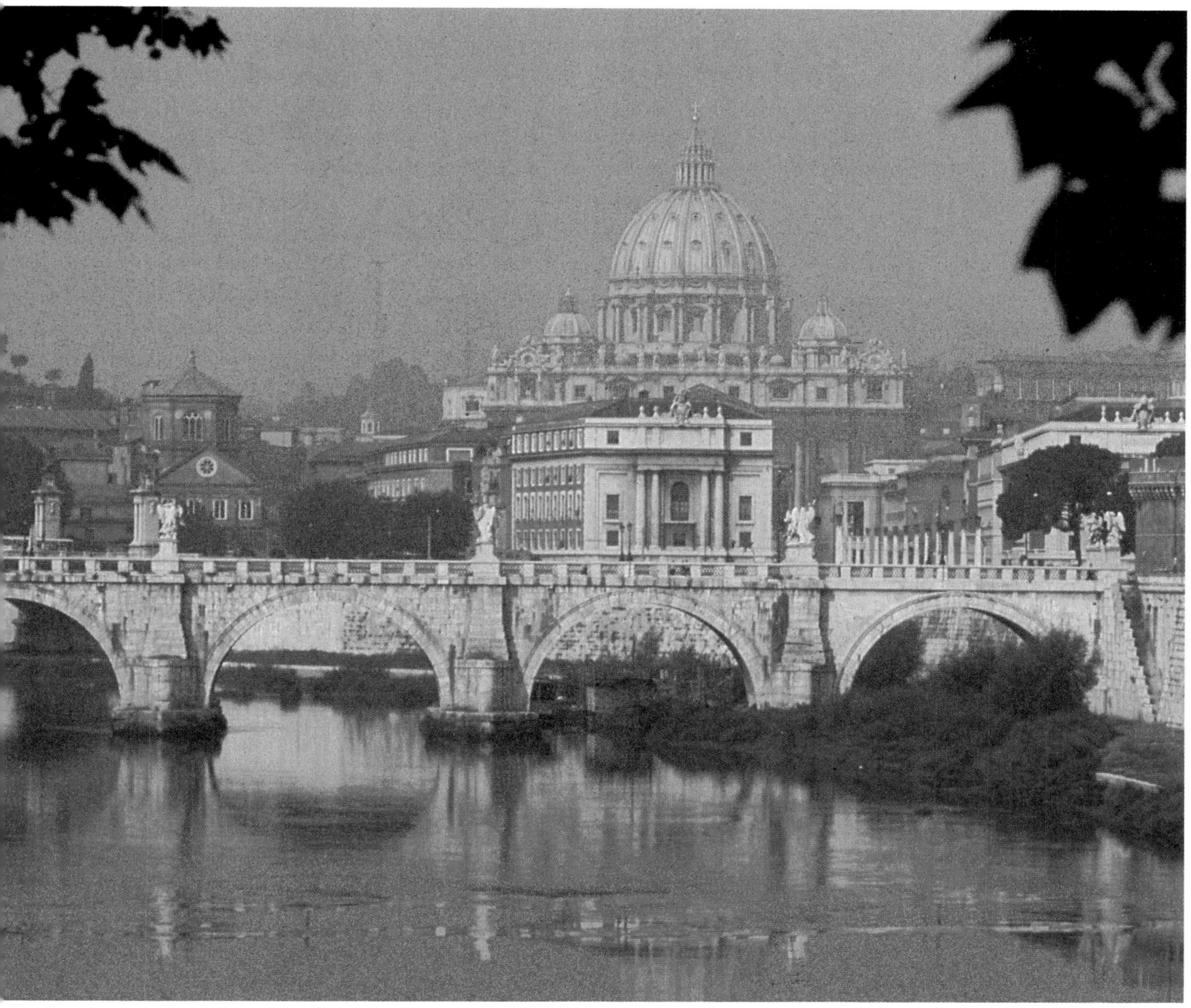

Above: *St Peter's Basilica, Rome, is on the Apostle's traditional burial site.*

Below: *Italy's vineyards produce wines to rival even those of the French.*

include textiles, computers, synthetic fibres, domestic electrical appliances and ships. Major efforts are being made to develop industry in the south, particularly petro-chemicals, steel production and light industries.

Italy is famous for its craft industries. These include the gloves and shoes of Florence's leather trade, ornate glass and delicate lace from Venice, silks from Milan and finely carved cameos from Naples.

Tourism is a major source of foreign earnings with more than 46 million visitors each year.

There are some excellent roadway systems. The Autostrada del Sol runs the length of the peninsula. Motorways connect Milan with Turin, Genoa and Venice. The major ports are Genoa, Venice, Naples, La Spezia and Cagliari in Sardinia.

Government

Italy is a republic with a president who serves for seven years. Elections are scheduled every five years for the two-chamber parliament consisting of the senate and the chamber of deputies.

Two small independent states lie within Italian territory. **Vatican City**, the smallest independent state in the world, has a population of about 1,000, most of them ecclesiastical officials. Its head of state is the Pope who is also head of the Roman Catholic Church. St Peter's, the largest church in Christendom, is situated in the Vatican, which is on the right bank of the Tiber in Rome.

San Marino, which claims to be the oldest republic in the world, is situated south-west of Rimini near the Adriatic. Traditionally dating from the 5th century, its independence was recognized by Pope Urban VIII in 1631. Tourism and the sale of postage stamps are important sources of revenue, although there is some farming and manufacture.

The arts

Italy has a unique place in the history of the arts as the birthplace of Renaissance humanism which began to develop during the 14th century with the support of prosperous merchant and banking families such as the De Medici in Florence. The pioneers were Giotto (1266-1337) in painting, Petrarch (1304-1374) in poetry and Giovanni Boccaccio (1313?-1375) in prose.

Giotto broke away from the stiff conventions of medieval religious painting. Petrarch revived the ideals of ancient Greek and Roman literature and made the Italian language into a literary vehicle. Boccaccio, with his lively tales of the *Decameron*, was the father of modern prose literature.

These three were followed by geniuses such as Leonardo da Vinci (1452-1519), painter, architect, inventor and scientist; Michelangelo (1465-1564) sculptor, painter, architect and poet; and many others who brought the High Renaissance to a peak of unsurpassed glory. Since then, Italy has made outstanding contributions in the field of music and, more recently, the cinema.

History

Italy has one of the oldest civilizations in Europe, but is one of the continent's youngest nations.

About 500 BC, the Romans began building their empire which lasted in the west until the 5th century AD. After the barbarian invasions from the north, Italy disintegrated into a collection of rival states which included duchies, principalities, city-states, and the Papal lands which occupied a third of the peninsula.

This situation, in which much of Italy was dominated by foreign powers such as Austria, France and Spain, continued until the mid-1800s. The *Risorgimento*, or resurgence of the desire for unification, began in 1860. Its philosopher was Giuseppe Mazzini. Its political architect was Count Camillo Cavour and its liberator-hero and brilliant general was Giuseppe Garibaldi.

Through the efforts of this triumvirate, Italy was declared an independent kingdom in 1861. Total unification took another decade, when the Papal lands were seized and the Pope withdrew to the Vatican.

Italy entered World War I on the side of the Allies against Austria and Germany. It suffered severe losses. In the discontent that followed, the Fascists, led by Benito Mussolini, came to power in 1922 and ruled the country until 1943.

The Fascist regime embarked on an empire-building campaign in North Africa and Abyssinia (now Ethiopia) and Italy entered World War II on the side of Germany against Britain and France.

Serious defeats in Greece and north Africa helped to topple Mussolini and the dictator was captured and executed by partisans in 1945.

In 1946 the Italian people decided in a referendum to abolish the monarchy.

Italy became a member of the United Nations in 1955, a founder member of the North Atlantic Treaty Organization in 1949 and a founder member of the European Economic Community in 1958.

Map 22 | SOUTHERN ITALY

ROMA 17
TEMPERATURE °C
17°
40
30
20
10
0
-10
-20

PRESSURE mb
1025
1020
1015
1010
1005
1000
995

PRECIPITATION mm
744mm
300
250
200
150
100
50
0
J F M A M J J A S O N D

PALERMO 31
TEMPERATURE °C
14°
40
30
20
10
0
-10
-20

PRESSURE mb
1025
1020
1015
1010
1005
1000
995

PRECIPITATION mm
512mm
300
250
200
150
100
50
0
J F M A M J J A S O N D

Projection: Conical with two standard parallels
1:2 500 000
10   0   10   20   30   40   50 miles
10   0   10 20 30 40 50 60 70 80km

East from Greenwich

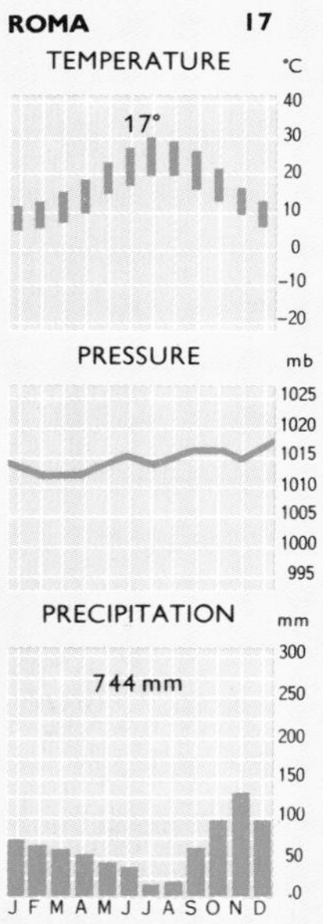

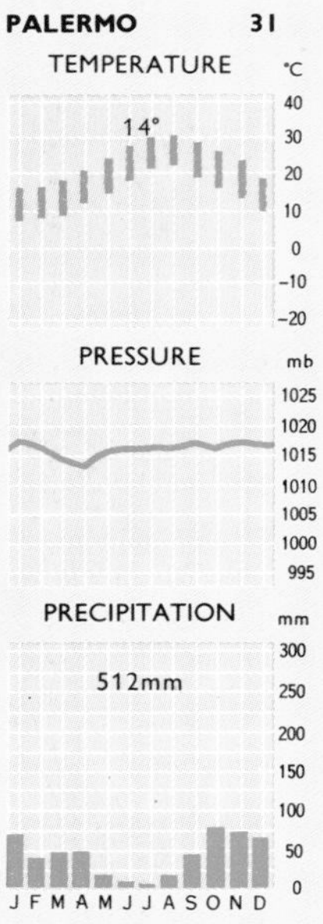

From the 1950s onward, the Italian economy developed rapidly. The country, which had once been preponderantly agricultural, became one of the Europe's most important industrial nations. Emigration to the USA was considerable in the late 19th and early 20th centuries, and since 1945 many Italians have gone to Australia or France, West Germany and Switzerland. Extensive regional development schemes are being undertaken to increase labour opportunities in the south through industrialization.

Left: *Pisa's white marble cathedral and campanile – the 'leaning tower'.*

Malta

Area: 316km² (122sq.m.).
Population: 369,189.
Capital: Valletta (14,152).
Languages: Maltese, English, Italian.
Ethnic groups: Maltese 95 percent, English, Italian.
Main exports: textiles, wine, flower seeds, potatoes, scrap metal.
Average temperatures: 12°C (53°F) Jan. 25°C (77°F) July.
Highest point: Tas-Salib, 244m (800ft).

Map 23

NAPOLI 110
TEMPERATURE °C
16°
PRESSURE mb
PRECIPITATION mm
915 mm
J F M A M J J A S O N D

MESSINA 54
TEMPERATURE °C
15°
PRESSURE mb
PRECIPITATION mm
902 mm
J F M A M J J A S O N D

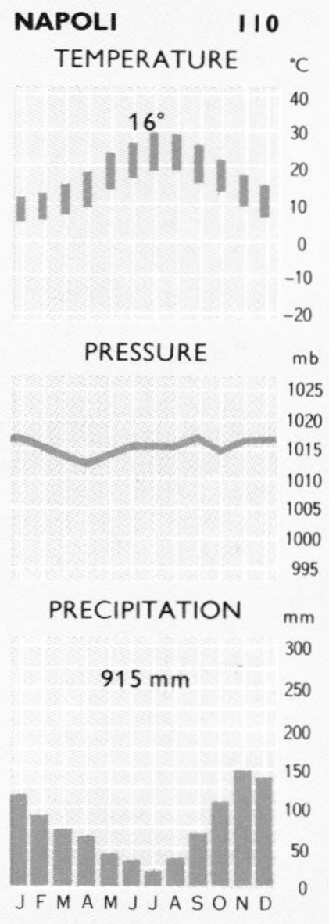

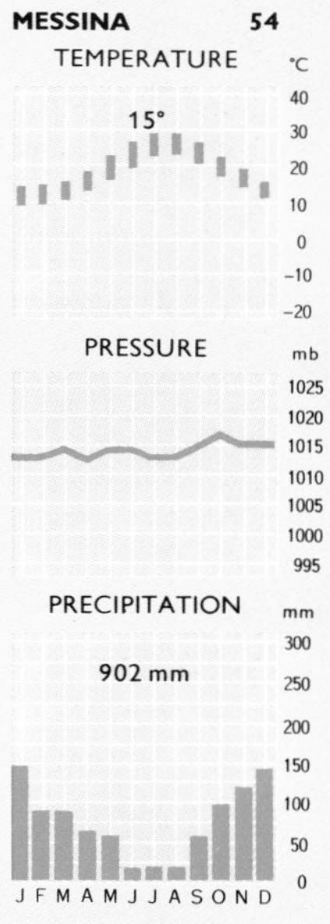

Malta is an independent state in the Mediterranean. It consists of five islands: Malta, which is the largest; Gozo, Comino and the uninhabited Comminotto and Filfla. The islands are about 92km (58m.) south of Sicily.

The landscape is hilly with cultivated terraces. The climate is Mediterranean with mild winters and warm summers, although strong westerly winds blow in autumn.

Malta's only mineral resource is limestone, used for cement manufacture.

Left: *The Grand and Marsamxett harbours of the Maltese seaport and capital, Valletta, flank Mt Sceberras, the city's nucleus.*

Lack of space and poor soil hamper agriculture and much of the food has to be imported. The country's chief assets are its fine harbour at Valletta and its strategic location as a military base and a fuelling point for shipping. The tourist trade is also an important source of foreign earnings.

The people are descended from many previous settlers: Phoenicians, Greeks, Normans, Spaniards, Arabs and Italians. Maltese is a west Arabic dialect with Italian admixtures mainly from the Sicilian dialect. Roman Catholicism is the state religion.

Malta has a workforce of a little over 120,000, of whom the majority work in

manufacture or service industries. Docks and shipping are major employers. Agriculture is boosted by part-time smallholders.

Remains dating from the stone and bronze ages and various ancient buildings testify to the antiquity of human settlement on Malta. After being ruled by Normans, the Holy Roman Empire, Spain, and France, Malta became a British colony in 1814. During World War II it became a much-bombed and beleaguered fortress for which the community was awarded the George Cross, Britain's highest decoration for civilian valour. Malta became independent in 1964.

Map 24   YUGOSLAVIA AND BULGARIA

BEOGRAD ★ 132
TEMPERATURE
°C
23°

PRESSURE
mb

PRECIPITATION
700mm

J F M A M J J A S O N D

ŠIBÉNIK   77
TEMPERATURE
°C
18°

PRESSURE
mb

PRECIPITATION
877mm

J F M A M J J A S O N D

1:2 500 000

Projection : Conical with two standard parallels   East from Greenwich

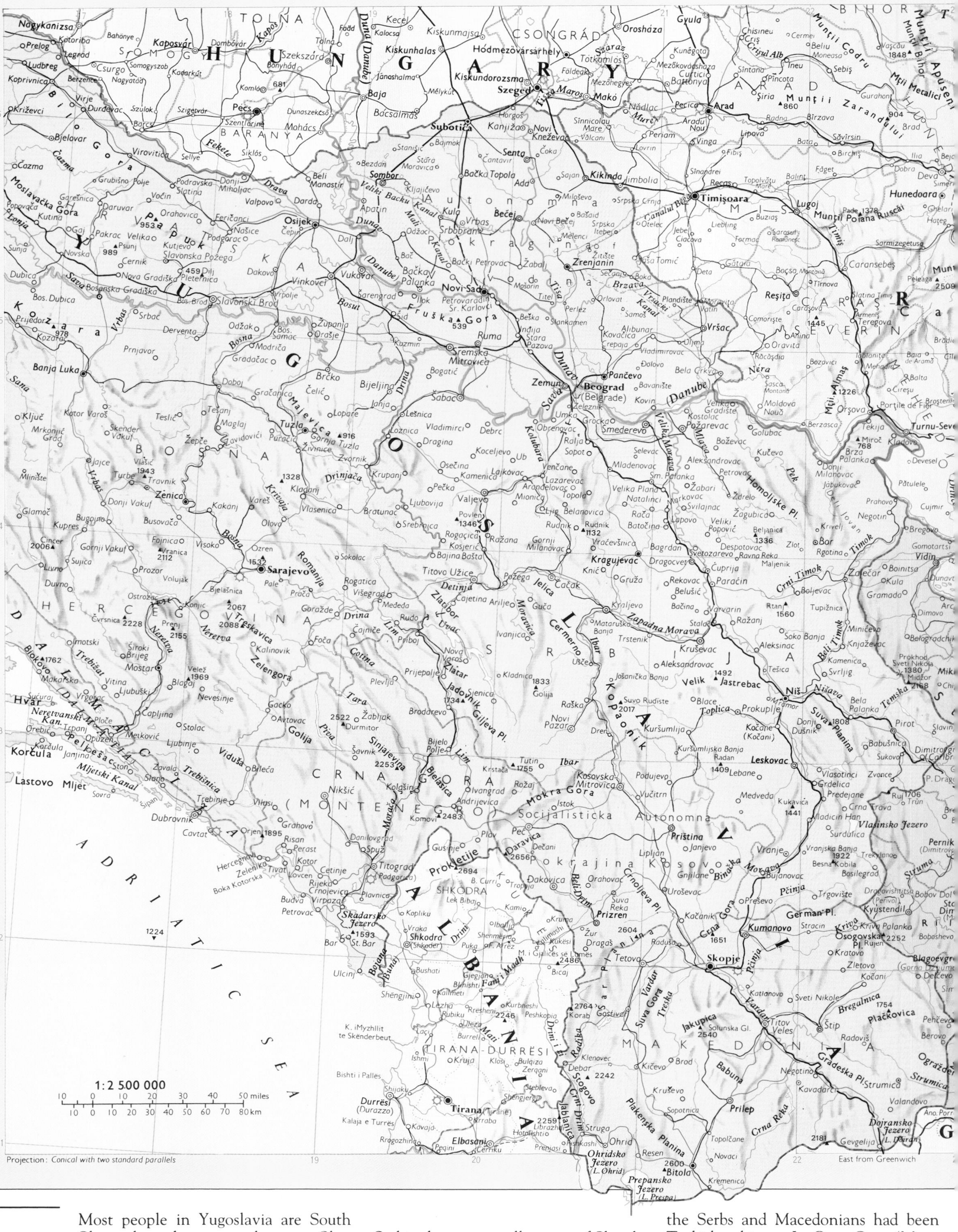

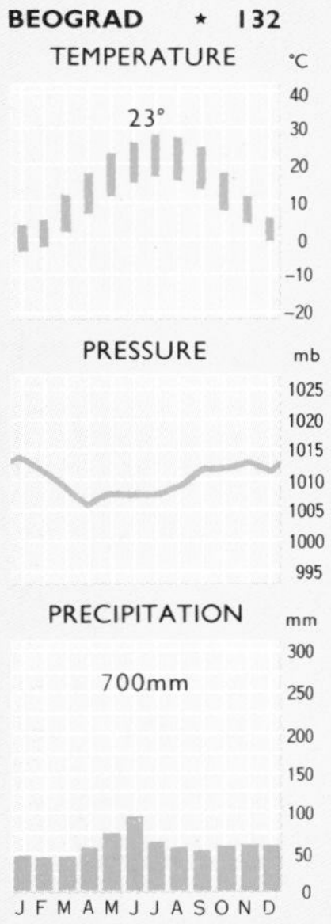

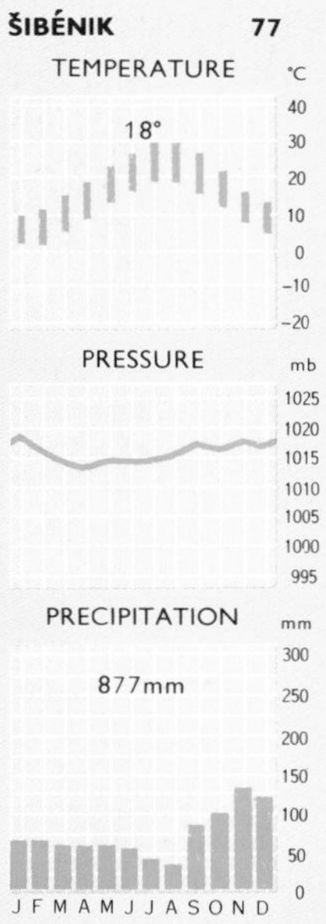

Yugoslavia

Area: 255,804km² (98,766sq.m.).
Population: 23.15 million.
Capital: Beograd or Belgrade (777,000, met. area 1.4m).
Languages: Serbo-Croat, Slovene, Macedonian, Albanian.
Ethnic groups: Serbs, Croats, Slovenes, Macedonians. Minorities include Albanians, Hungarians, Rumanians and Turks.
Main exports: machinery and metal products, non-ferrous metals, textiles, chemicals, ships, timber.
Average temperatures: 8°C (46°F) Jan. 25°C (77°F) July on coast, but cooler in inland mountain valleys.
Highest point: Triglav, 2,863m (9,393ft).

Most people in Yugoslavia are South Slavs, but there are also non-Slav minorities. The Serbs and the Croats are the largest groups. Politically divided centuries ago, they came under different influences, principally religious, but their language, Serbo-Croat, is the same. The Slovenes live in the north and speak another Slav language, while the Macedonians in the south speak a language which is close to Bulgarian.

The non-Slavs live mainly in the south and east. The largest groups are the Albanians in the south, and the Hungarians and Rumanians in the east. There are small Turkish areas in the central and southern regions and pockets of Vlachs (related to Rumanians) scattered over the country. In northeast

Serbia there are small groups of Slovaks and Ruthenes, who belong to the Western Slav group. The German minority was expelled after World War II.

The Croats and Slovenes are Roman Catholics and use the Latin alphabet. The Serbs and Macedonians are Orthodox and use the Cyrillic alphabet. The Albanians are mostly Muslims and some Muslim Serbs live in Bosnia. The other minorities are divided between Roman Catholic and Orthodox.

History and constitution
Yugoslavia was founded in 1918 as a union of the South Slavs. Before that time, the Croats and Slovenes were part of the Austro-Hungarian empire, while

the Serbs and Macedonians had been Turkish subjects. In Crna Gora (Montenegro), some Serbs had remained independent. Serbia regained its freedom in the 1800s and gradually expanded its territory.

After World War I, the Serbs of Montenegro united with the Kingdom of Serbia, and the Croats, Slovenes and Macedonians joined the new nation. For two decades there were many problems, particularly the wish of the Roman Catholic Croats for more autonomy.

In 1941 Germany and its allies, Bulgaria, Hungary and Italy, attacked Yugoslavia. The country was divided between the victors, although a semi-independent state of Croatia was established. Partisan groups fought the Germans and

Map 25

VARNA ★ 35

TEMPERATURE °C

22°

PRESSURE mb

PRECIPITATION mm

476 mm

J F M A M J J A S O N D

SOFIYA ★ 550

TEMPERATURE °C

22°

PRESSURE mb

PRECIPITATION mm

661 mm

J F M A M J J A S O N D

COPYRIGHT GEORGE PHILIP & SON LTD

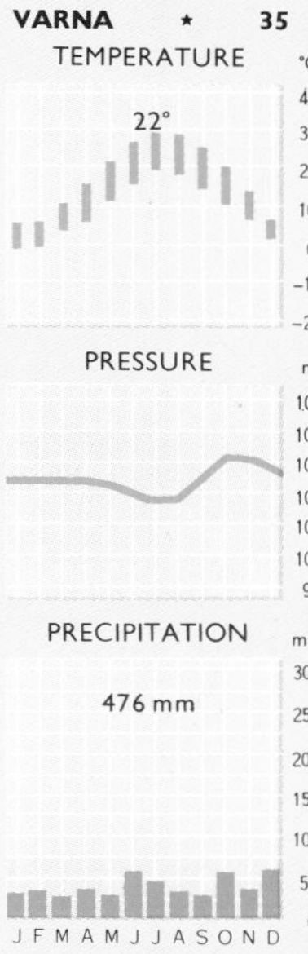

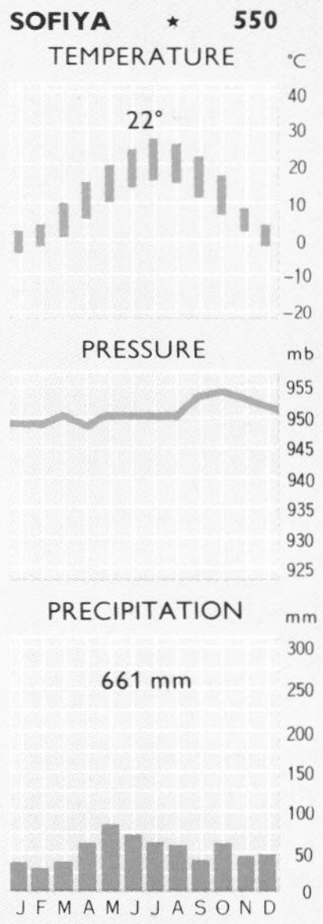

the communist leader, Josip Broz (Tito) soon took over the leadership of the resistance.

After the war, the monarchy was abolished and Yugoslavia became a socialist federal republic, notable in East Europe for its independent stance towards Russia. It contains six republics, Serbia, Croatia, Slovenia, Montenegro, Bosnia-Herzegovina and Macedonia. The Serbian republic has two autonomous provinces, Kosovo and Vojvodina. The first is the home of the Albanian minority. The other includes most of the other minorities.

Physical features and climate

The Dalmatian coast of Yugoslavia borders the Adriatic Sea. The coastline has sunk and former mountain ranges which parallel the coast now form long, narrow islands. Former valleys are now large harbours. The coast has a Mediterranean climate and it attracts more than five million tourists a year.

Inland, the Dinaric Alps run the whole length of the country. Bare limestone outcrops give rise to the characteristic *karst* landscape, which includes swallow holes, gorges and underground cave networks. Beyond the mountains, the land descends through a forested hilly zone to the interior plains. The plains have a continental climate. The

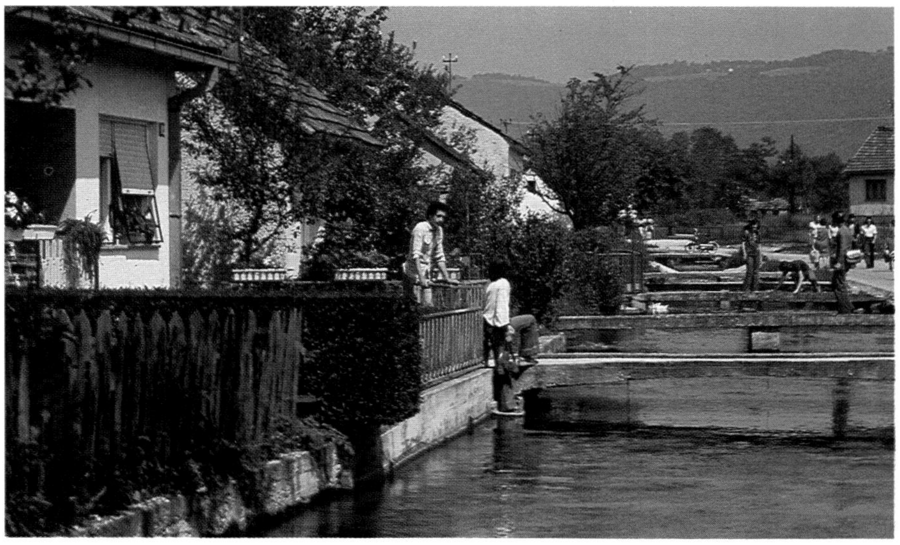

Right: *A tributary of the Danube, the Bosna in the Yugoslavian highlands is one of the country's most important rivers.*

capital, Belgrade and the second city Zagreb (1.17m) are both situated on the interior plains.

Minerals and Industry

Yugoslavia has considerable mineral resources and it produces coal, iron ore, gold, copper, lead, chrome, manganese and other minerals. Crude petroleum production is increasing.

Most industry is in the northwest. The country produces cement, chemicals, fertilizers, pig-iron, steel and textiles. Yugoslavia has extended its road system and railways since 1945. Communication with the interior is obstructed by the mountain ranges which parallel the coast.

The tourist industry, especially in the northwest coastal region, is of growing importance.

Agriculture, forestry and fishing

Agriculture is still the chief occupation of most Yugoslavs. The land produces barley, fruit, maize, rye, tobacco and wheat. Livestock farming, especially sheep and pig-raising, is important.

Timber is an important export. The country's forests are mainly beech, fir and oak. Fishing, both coastal and inland, employs a large number of people.

Trade and foreign relations

Yugoslavia's main trading partners are the USSR, West Germany and Italy. Since 1948, Yugoslavia has remained outside the two power blocs and has identified itself with the non-aligned nations. Stability in international relations was maintained despite the death of Marshal Tito in 1980. Some 600,000 Yugoslavs work abroad, mostly in northern European countries such as West Germany, and their remittances and savings are a major source of foreign currency. Inflation has been at the forefront of economic problems, as has the size of foreign debts.

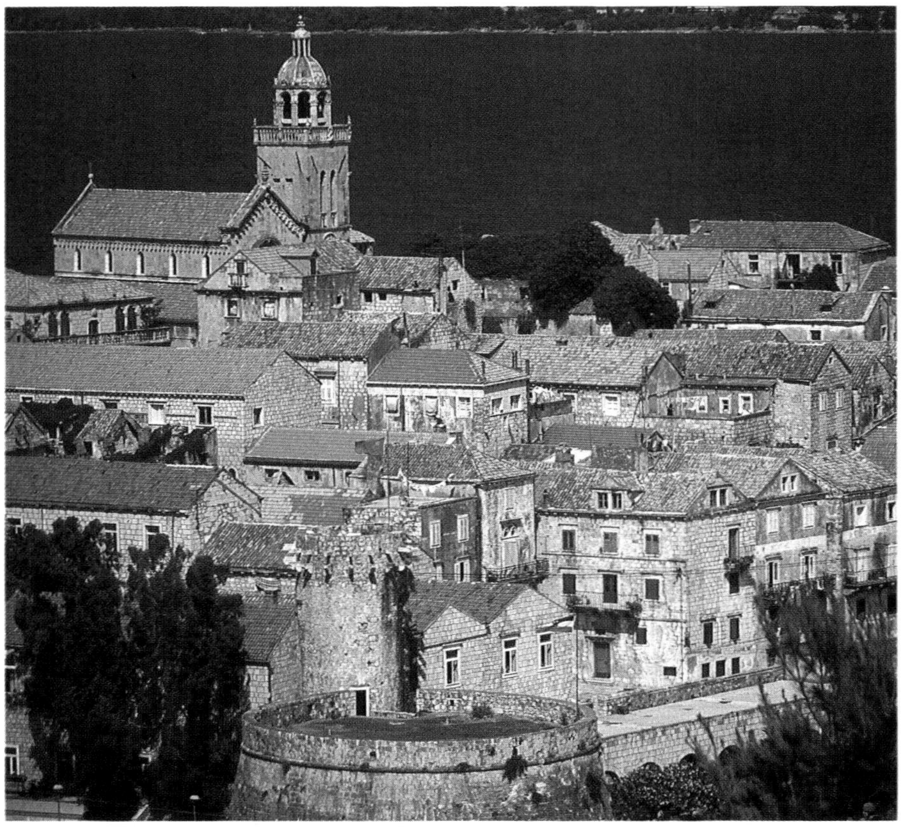

Right: *The island of Korčula, Yugoslavia, was formed when the mountain ranges of the Adriatic coast were submerged.*

Below: *The Black Sea fishing village of Nesebŭr, Bulgaria, is one of a number of picturesque seaside resorts.*

Bulgaria

Area: 110,912km² (42,823sq.m.).
Population: 8.93 million.
Capital: Sofiya or Sofia (1.08m).
Languages: Bulgarian, Turkish.
Ethnic groups: Bulgarians, Turks, Greeks, Macedonians, Armenians, Gypsies.
Main exports: food products, tobacco, iron, leather, textiles, machinery.
Average temperatures: 4°C (40°F) Jan. 21°C (70°F) July.
Highest point: Musala, 2,925m (9,592ft).

The original Bulgars were an Asian tribe who conquered, and were absorbed by, the Slavs living south of the Danube. The Bulgarian language is Slav. The so-called Pomaks are Bulgarians who became Muslims under Turkish rule.

A Bulgarian empire existed in the 10th century, but the country was then ruled by the Greeks and, later, by the Turks. After pressure from European powers, an autonomous principality was set up in the 1870s and Bulgaria became an independent kingdom in 1908. In World War I, Bulgaria fought with Germany and lost territory in 1919. It again joined Germany in 1941 and attacked Yugoslavia and Greece. The USSR occupied Bulgaria in 1944 and a people's republic was set up in 1946.

Physical features and climate

The Balkan mountains cover much of northern Bulgaria. In the far north, the land descends to the Danubian lowlands. Between the Balkan mountains and the undeveloped Rhodope mountains in the southwest is the central lowland – Bulgaria's most productive area. Bulgaria's climate is transitional between Mediterranean in the south and continental in the north.

Minerals and industry

Bulgaria has deposits of copper, iron ore, lead, manganese and zinc. Coal is also mined. Petroleum is extracted in the northeast and there is offshore drilling in the Black Sea.

About a third of the people work in manufacturing industries. All industry is nationalized and manufactured products include coke, fertilizers, steel and textiles. Hydro-electric stations provide power and the USSR has helped to build a nuclear power station on the Danube. Bulgaria has two large Black Sea ports, Varna and Burgas. It has a large merchant fleet and an extensive road and rail network. The tourist industry on the Black Sea coast is growing in importance.

Agriculture and forestry

By 1958 all farmland was collectivized, and in 1979 all state and collective farms came under the co-ordination of the National Agro-Industrial Union. The main farm products are wheat and other cereals, sunflower seeds, cotton, tobacco, fruit and vegetables and vines. Bulgaria is the world's leading supplier of attar of roses. Cattle, sheep, pigs and poultry are raised, together with large numbers of horses and asses.

Almost two-thirds of Bulgaria's forests are of hardwoods and timber production is increasing. Fishing is important for local consumption.

Trade and foreign relations

Four-fifths of Bulgaria's trade is with other COMECON countries, mostly with the USSR. Agreements allow for Soviet oil and natural gas to be piped to Bulgaria in exchange for food, clothing and electronic components. Italy is the biggest non-communist trading partner, but in 1974 Bulgaria and the UK signed a long-term economic, scientific and technological agreement. Bulgaria has a long-standing dispute with Yugoslavia over Macedonia, which is mostly in Yugoslavia; this arises because of the close similarities between Macedonians and Bulgarians.

Greece

Area: 131,957km² (50,949sq.m.).
Population: 10.1 million.
Capital: Athinai or Athens (3.03m).
Language: Greek.
Ethnic groups: Greeks with Turkish and Slav minorities.
Main exports: manufactured goods, chemicals, foodstuffs, especially fruit, tobacco, cotton, wine.
Average temperatures: 9°C (48°F) Jan. 28°C (80°F) July in Athinai.
Highest point: Oros Olimbos or Mt Olympus 2,917m (9,570ft).

Greece has a unique heritage as the cradle of the most brilliant culture of the ancient world. Classical Greek philosophy, art, literature and scientific method permeate Western civilization, and Athenian democracy has been a model for many nations. Although today one of Europe's less prosperous countries, Greece continues to exercise a powerful attraction to visitors because of the beauty of the warm Aegean islands and the vitality and exuberance of its people.

History and people

The history of ancient Greece began about 3000 BC with the rise of the Aegean (Cycladic) civilization. This reached a peak in the Minoan culture of Crete, which gave way to the warrior state of Mycenae and ended about 1100 BC with successive waves of invaders. Emigrants from mainland Greece estab-

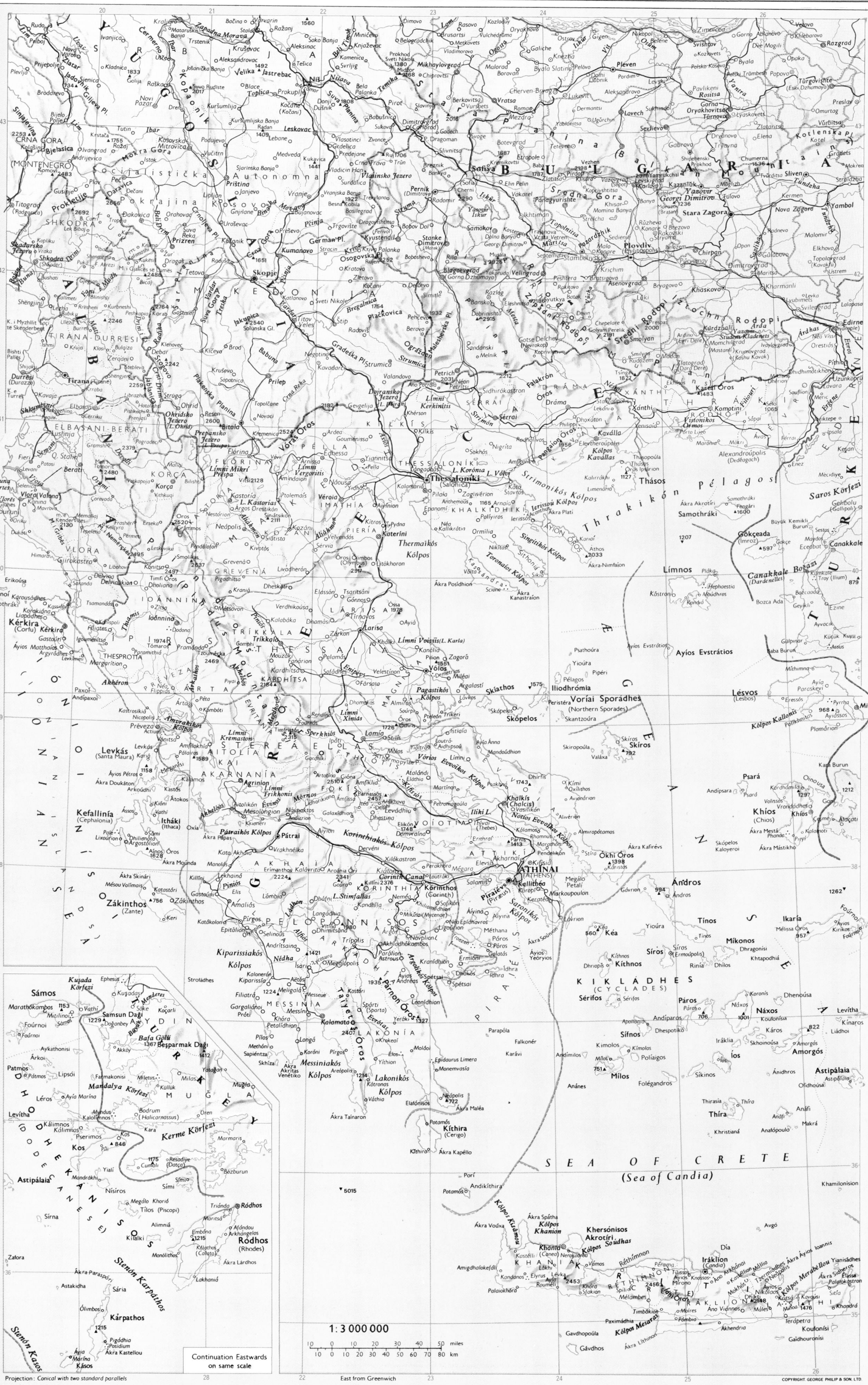
YUGOSLAVIA
BULGARIA
ALBANIA
TURKEY
MAKEDONIJA
Socijalistička Autonomna Pokrajina Kosovo
Crna Gora (Montenegro)
Sofiya
Skopje
Tiranë
Thessaloníki
Athínai (Athens)
Pátrai
Lárisa
Vólos
Kérkira (Corfu)
Ionian Sea
Aegean Sea
Thrakikón Pélagos
Kikládhes (Cyclades)
Dhodhekánisos (Dodecanese)
Rodhos (Rhodes)
Kárpathos
Kríti
Iráklion (Candia)
Sea of Crete (Sea of Candia)
Pelopónnisos
Límnos
Lésvos
Khíos
Náxos
Sámos
Kos
Kíthira (Cerigo)
1: 3 000 000
miles
km
Continuation Eastwards on same scale

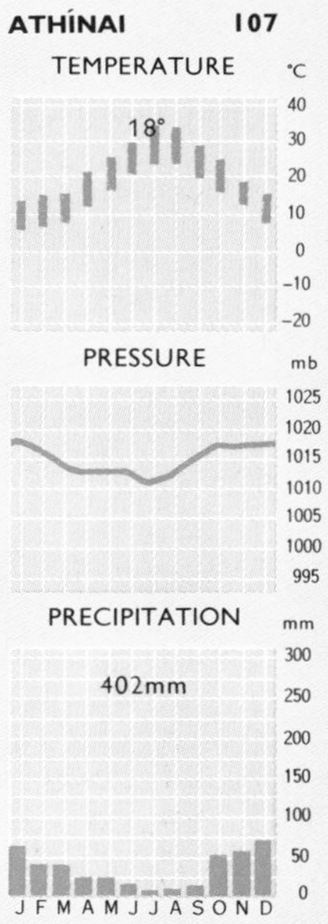
ATHÍNAI 107
TEMPERATURE °C
18°
PRESSURE mb
PRECIPITATION mm
402mm
J F M A M J J A S O N D

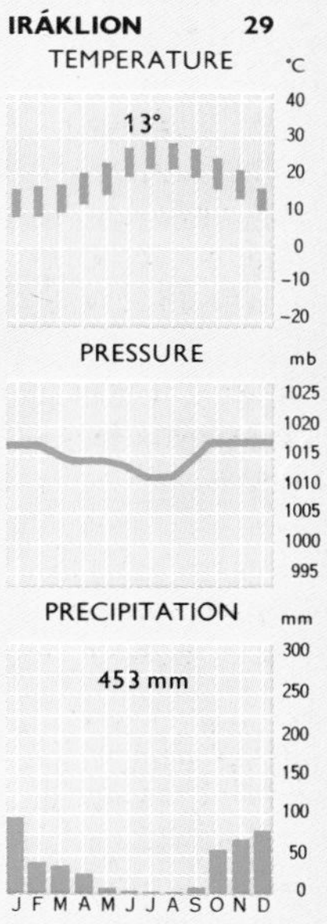
IRÁKLION 29
TEMPERATURE °C
13°
PRESSURE mb
PRECIPITATION mm
453 mm
J F M A M J J A S O N D

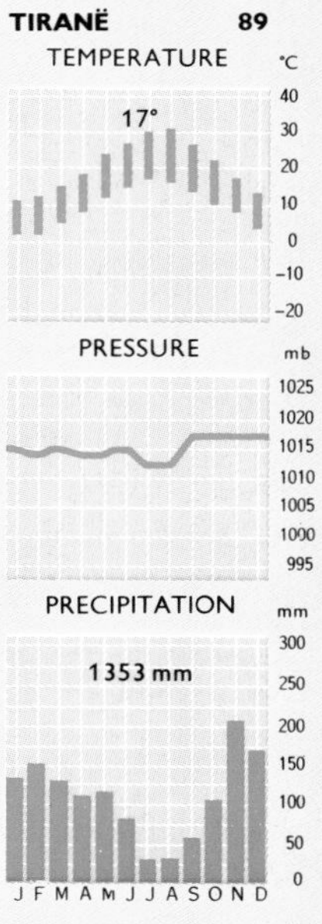
TIRANË 89
TEMPERATURE °C
17°
PRESSURE mb
PRECIPITATION mm
1353 mm
J F M A M J J A S O N D

lished many settlements throughout southern Europe on sites that were later to develop into great cities, such as Constantinople and Odessa. Trade with these colonies greatly increased the wealth and power of the mainland.

Athens emerged as the foremost Greek power with the repulse of Persian invaders. The 5th century BC saw a remarkable flowering of the arts, science and philosophy which continued even after power passed to the Spartans and Thebans. In the 4th century the rise of Macedonia culminated in Alexander the Great's conquest of the Persian empire. Roman rule was established by 146 BC and in AD 395, Greece became part of the East Roman or Byzantine empire. This fell in 1453 when the Turks took Constantinople (Istanbul).

But the spirit of Greek nationalism was never extinguished. The Greek Orthodox Church (to which 98 percent of the population belong) and the Greek language were both preserved. The spoken Greek language, *demotike*, is pronounced quite differently from ancient Greek. But today's official documents and newspapers are written in *katharevousa*, a revival of classical Greek. In 1821 the Greeks rebelled against Turkish rule and proclaimed their independence. Following a long struggle, Greek independence was ratified by treaty in 1830 and the country became a monarchy. Throughout the 1800s, Greek territory was gradually extended. Wars against Turkey in 1912 and 1913 resulted in Greece taking much of Macedonia, Crete and several Aegean islands.

Greece fought on the side of the Allies in World War I. After the war, Greece lost Smyrna to Turkey and, in 1923, there was a large transfer of population between the two countries. In 1924 Greece became a republic, but the

Above: *The Metéora monasteries are built above wild gorges on the jagged granitic peaks of mountainous mainland Greece.*

Right: *The Greek temple of Apollo on Mt Parnassus, Delphi, which the ancient Greeks believed to be the centre of the world.*

monarchy was restored in 1935. In World War II, Greece forced back Italian invaders, but fell to the Germans in 1941. After the Germans were defeated in 1944, a civil war broke out which continued until 1949.

A revolution in 1967 led to the departure of the king and the establishment of a military dictatorship. A referendum in 1973 resulted in a majority in favour of a republic. The military regime was overthrown in 1974 and, in another referendum, the Greeks voted against the restoration of the monarchy. The country is now a constitutional republic.

Physical features and climate

Makhedonia or Macedonia and Thráki or Thrace occupy northern and northeastern Greece. Behind flat coastal plains, hills rise gradually towards the mountains along the Bulgarian and Yugoslav borders. Northern Greece has a mild climate, but winters are colder than in southern Greece and damaging frosts often occur.

Most of the Greek mainland forms a peninsula, which is almost divided into two by deep gulfs. In fact, the gulfs are connected by the artificial Corinth Canal which is about 6½km (4m.) long. The northern part of the peninsula contains the rugged central Pindus mountain range, where the rainfall is heavy. West of this range lies a lower region with a Mediterranean climate. To the east lies the large alluvial plain of Thessalia, to the north of which is Greece's highest mountain, Mt Olympus. To the south of Thessalia is easterr Greece, the most famous historical region which contains Athens. This region has broken relief and a Mediterranean climate.

The southern extension of the peninsula, Peloponnisos, is mainly mountainous with a number of fertile coastal plains and valleys. Peloponnisos contains the sites of many classical cities, including Sparta. It has hot summers and mild, moist winters.

The largest Greek island is Crete. It covers 8,331km^2 (3,217sq.m.) and has a population of 502,165. Although mainly mountainous, Crete has some narrow coastal plains in the north of the island.

There are six other groups of Greek islands. In the west, the seven **Ionian islands** are rugged, although Kérkira or Corfu is a popular tourist centre. In the northeastern Aegean Sea, the **Thracian islands**, including Thasos and Samothráki are mountainous, but Limnos is mostly flat. Off the eastern coast of Greece, the **Sporádhes** are a group of small rocky islands. The **Kikládhes**, or Cyclades, contain more than 20 islands, the largest of which is Naxos. In the south, Thíra or Santorinī contains Minoan sites which were buried during a tremendous volcanic eruption. The **Eastern Aegean islands** include Lesvos or Lesbos, Khíos or Chios, and Samos. The **Dodecanese** group was acquired from Italy in 1945. These hilly islands, lying close to the Turkish mainland, include Ródhos or Rhodes.

Minerals and industry

Mining is of relatively little importance in Greece. The country has little coal, but some petroleum, iron ore and various other minerals are produced. Manufacturing has increased rapidly in recent years. For example, manufactured

products accounted for only 17 percent of Greece's exports in 1960, but they had risen to 45 percent in 1970. Many industries are concerned with processing farm products. For example, wine and olive oil are important exports. But Greece now has many varied industries, including chemical and metal industries. About 19 out of every 100 employed people work in manufacturing. Athinai, including the port of Piraievs (Piraeus) and Thessaloniki, or Salonica, are the chief manufacturing centres. Inland communications are hampered by the rugged relief, but no part of the country is more than 130km (80m.) from the sea. Sea transport has always been important and today Greece has one of the world's largest merchant navies. Many Greek ships also sail under foreign flags and shipping is an important source of revenue. Another indirect source of income comes from the expanding tourist industry. More than five million tourists visited Greece in 1981, some attracted by the mainland and island beaches, and others by the superb historical sites.

Agricultural, forestry and fishing

A quarter of all employed people work in agriculture. However, only about one-third of the country can be cultivated, the rest being too rugged. Maize, wheat and other cereals are grown for home consumption. Cotton, tobacco and typical Mediterranean crops, such as apricots, citrus fruits, grapes, melons and olives, are exported. Greece has more than eight million sheep, four million goats and nearly one million cattle.

Much of Greece's original forest has been destroyed and this has resulted in severe soil erosion in many areas. Forests now cover only about 19 percent of the country. Fishing is a more important industry than forestry and sponges are an important product.

Above: *The Acropolis, a citadel rising 500 feet above sea-level, forms the focus of Athens, capital of Greece.*

Left: *Low whitewashed walls, narrow windows and a slow pace of life characterize the villages of Greece.*

Trade and foreign relations

In January 1980 Greece joined the European Economic Community (EEC) and today its fellow members form its chief trading partners, together with the USA.

The traditional hostility with Turkey remains largely unresolved and threatens the unity of NATO. The divided island of Cyprus is still a focus for discontent. Under the socialist government of *Pasok* Greece has followed an increasingly independent line.

Albania

Area: 28,748km^2 (11,100sq.m.).
Population: 2.75 million.
Capital: Tirana (175,000).
Language: Albanian.
Ethnic groups: Albanians, Greeks, Vlachs.
Main exports: chrome ore, copper wire, crude oil, fruit, tobacco, vegetables.
Average temperatures: 4°C (40°F) Jan. 27°C (81°F) July.
Highest point: Mt Korab, 2,762m (9,063ft).

The Albanians are descendants of Illyrian tribes who lived in the Balkans before the Slavs. They are divided into two groups – the Ghegs and the Tosks. The Ghegs live north of the Shkumbini river and the Tosks to the south. There are some differences between their dialects and the official language is based on Tosk pronunciation. Albanians also live in adjacent areas in Yugoslavia and Greece. Albania has a small Greek minority in the south and groups of Vlachs are scattered in central and southern Albania. Vlachs speak a Latin language related to Rumanian.

History and constitution

When the Romans conquered the Balkans, they used Illyrians in their armies. Some Illyrians even became Roman emperors.

The Slavs later pushed the Illyrians back into what is now Albania and, later, the Turks conquered them. Most Albanians became Muslims, but there were Roman Catholic and Greek Orthodox minorities. Albanians held important positions in the Turkish empire, but their homeland was backward.

In 1913 they declared their independence, but there was no strong central ruler until a kingdom was established under King Zog I in 1925. Italian influence was very strong and Italy invaded Albania in 1939. Albania remained a monarchy under the Italian king. Partisan groups fought the Italians and communists soon dominated the resistance movement. After liberation, a communist republic was set up. By 1961 Albania had quarrelled with the USSR and China became its closest ally, but 16 years later this special relationship was also terminated. First Secretary Enver Hoxha died in 1985.

Physical features and economy

Albania is largely mountainous, but there are fertile regions in the centre. The climate is temperate. The coast is dry, but mountain areas are well-watered.

Albania has considerable mineral wealth but it has only recently begun to develop it. Coal, chromium ore and copper are worked and ferro-nickel ore output is increasing. Salt and bitumen are also produced. The oil industry is becoming important. An oil pipeline connects the central Albanian oilfields to the port of Vlora.

All industry in Albania is nationalized, even the smallest workshop. The chief industries are food processing, textiles, petroleum products and cement. The government is developing chemical and engineering industries and there is an iron and steel works at Elbasani in central Albania. The country's 253km (157m.) of railways have all been built since 1947. The 3,100km (1,926m.) of roads serve all except the mountain districts in the north where pack ponies and donkeys are still essential.

Most Albanians work in agriculture but, because of the country's wild and rugged terrain, arable land is confined mainly to the coast and the Korca basin. All land is owned by the state and farming is largely collectivized. The main crops are cotton, fruit, grains, potatoes, sugar-beet and tobacco. Livestock farming is carried out mainly on state farms.

Almost half of Albania is forested, mainly with chestnut, elm, oak, pine and walnut, and timber is a major resource. Fishing is not an important industry and catches are for local consumption.

Trade and foreign relations

Until 1977 Albania received massive aid from China. Today Albania is without close allies; its chief trading partners are communist countries other than the USSR, and Italy, France and India.

Map 27 — SCANDINAVIA AND THE BALTIC LANDS

ICELAND
on the same scale
as general map

TRONDHEIM 58
TEMPERATURE
19°
PRESSURE
PRECIPITATION
870mm

HELSINKI 46
TEMPERATURE
24°
PRESSURE
PRECIPITATION
688mm

BERGEN 43
TEMPERATURE
14°
PRESSURE
PRECIPITATION
1930mm

1:6 000 000

Projection: Conical with two standard parallels

COPYRIGHT. GEORGE PHILIP & SON.

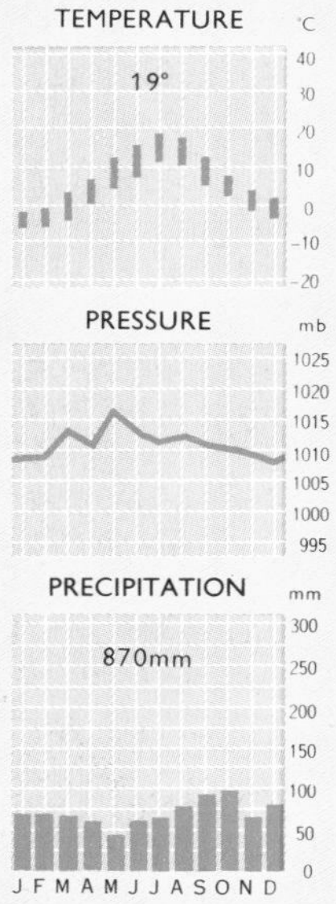

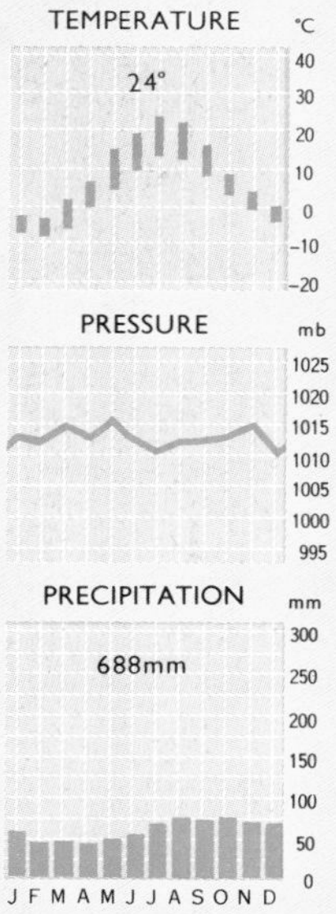

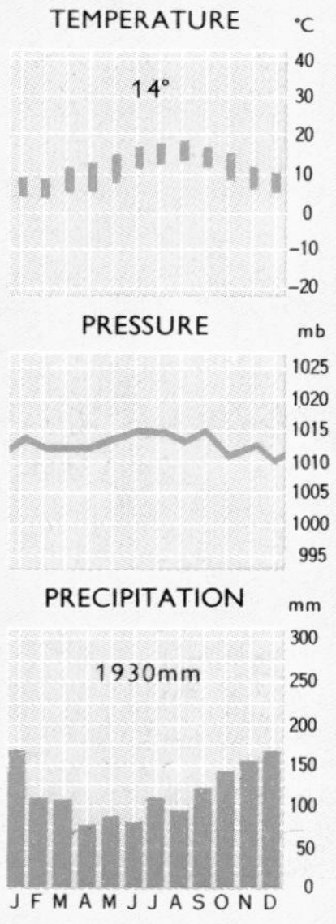

Iceland

Area: 103,000km^2 (39,770sq.m.).
Population: 238,000.
Capital: Reykjavik (87,300).
Language: Icelandic.
Ethnic groups: Norwegians, Lapps, Finns.
Main exports: fish and fish products.
Average temperatures: −1°C (30°F) Jan. 11°C (52°F) July in Reykjavik.
Highest point: Hvannadalshnukur, 2,119m (6,952ft).

The republic of Iceland is a rugged island lying 1,050km (650 miles) west of Norway in the North Atlantic Ocean just south of the Arctic Circle. Despite its northerly latitude, the warming influence of the North Atlantic Drift provides it with a comparatively temperate climate and it has a growing population that has achieved economic prosperity based on a single major export, fish.

Iceland was settled from Norway about AD 850. Its literary tradition extends back to the sagas and its parliamentary assembly, the *Althing*, has a 1,000-year history. Formerly ruled by Denmark, the country was largely self-governing from 1918 and an independent republic was established in 1944.

The island is of volcanic origin and is subject to frequent earthquakes and volcanic eruptions, one of which destroyed a large part of the fishing port of Vestmanaeyjar on Heimaey Island in 1973. Grassy coastal lowlands rise to a largely barren inland plateau with volcanic peaks, and several glaciers extend to fjords. Precipitation averages 76cm (30in) at Reykjavik. The lowlands carry sheep and dairy and beef cattle. Industries include diatomite mining and aluminium smelting, but the main industry is fishing and processing, which employ a sixth of the workforce.

Icelandic waters, where warm and cold currents mingle, are rich in cod, haddock, herring and other fish. These valuable fishing grounds have been the subject of several disputes over territorial rights. Iceland's progressive extension of its fishing limits out to 320km (200 miles) was contested by other nations who traditionally fished there, notably Britain. Iceland's aim was to protect the region from overfishing. The Iceland fleet's catch in 1982 was 766,000 tonnes.

Finland

Area: 337,000km^2 (130,000sq.m.).
Population: 4.87 million.
Capital: Helsinki (932,000).
Languages: Finnish, Swedish.
Ethnic groups: Finnish, Lappish (1.4m).
Main exports: timber and timber products, metals and machinery, textiles.
Average temperatures: 18°C (64°F) July; −6°C (21°F) Feb. in Helsinki.
Highest point: Haltiatunturi 1,328m (4,357ft).

Apart from Iceland, Finland is the most northerly country in the world. A third of its area lies within the Arctic Circle. It has some 60,000 lakes, and 80,000 islands lie along its rocky, jagged coastline. The Finns are a proud and hardy people. They have fought 42 wars against the Russians – and lost them all. After World War II, they had a reparations bill of £180 million from Moscow. Yet they have emerged with a vigorous economy and a prosperous society, though many Finns still migrate to work in Sweden.

Land and climate

Coniferous forests cover 71 percent of Finland. The landscape is heavily glaceated, and lakes and waterways cover 10 percent of the total area. Inland, water remains frozen from December to May. Most of the country is a flat low-lying plateau, dropping to a lower plain along the south and west coasts. The thousands of offshore islands make navigation difficult. In the north, Finland extends into Lapland, which rises in places to over 1,000m (3,300ft).

Economy

The economy of Finland is based largely on its forests, which contain valuable reserves of pine, spruce, birch, and fir trees – Finland's 'green gold'. The forest industries include the manufacture of cellulose, paper, board, woodpulp, plywood, and finished articles ranging from spools to furniture and prefabricated houses. A fifth of the working population is engaged in agriculture. The average farm is small. Cattle are usually raised, and the chief crops are oats, barley, wheat, rye, and potatoes. Another fifth of the work force is employed in manufacturing industries, although few plants have more than 500 workers. Metal-processing has overtaken wood-processing in the numbers employed. The foodstuff and textile industries are also important to the economy. Finland is renowned for its design, including glass, ceramics, tableware, and furniture.

A tall, fair people, the Finns place much emphasis on improving mind and body. They have produced many fine writers and musicians, including the composer Sibelius, and are well known for their sporting accomplishments, particularly athletics. More than a million Finns compete in cross-country skiing. Another national passion is the *sauna*, a steam bath that has now beome popular in many other countries.

History and constitution

The Finns call their country *Suomi*. Unlike the other Scandinavian nations, Finland is not a monarchy. The head of state is a president, and there is a one-house parliament. Finland is neither part of a western alliance, nor is it a Soviet satellite.

Finland has been fully independent only since 1917. The Finns had lived as separate clans for a thousand years before they became part of Sweden in the 12th century. The Swedes and the Russians fought many battles on Finnish land, and the Russians seized control in 1809. But Finland finally broke away from the Russian Revolution in 1917. Civil war followed but with the aid of Germany Finland was prevented from becoming a communist state. The Finns again found themselves on the German side in World War II, when the USSR attacked them. Remarkably, they survived both the war and their enormous war debts, and emerged as a proud and prosperous nation.

Top: *Volcanic rock formation north-west of Borgarnes on the west coast of Iceland.*

Right: *Heavily afforested, Finland's most important raw material is timber.*

Norway

Area: 323,886km^2 (125,053sq.m.).
Population: 4.13 million.
Capital: Oslo (447,000).
Languages: Bokmål (or Riksmål), Nynorsk (or Landsmål).
Ethnic groups: Norwegian, Lappish (20,000).
Main exports: machinery and transport equipment, metallurgical products, pulp and paper, fish and fish products, chemicals, oil.
Average temperatures: 17°C (63°F) July; −5°C (23°F) Jan. in Oslo.
Highest point: Galdhøpiggen 2,469m (8,100ft).

A long narrow country that occupies the western part of the Scandinavian Peninsula, Norway is a seafaring nation with one of the world's largest merchant marine fleets. About 80 percent of all Norwegians live within 20 kilometres (12 miles) of the sea. A proud and nationalist people, the Norwegians enjoy one of the highest standards of living in the world. And despite industrialization, they have managed to preserve the country's natural beauty – seen most strikingly in its mountains, valleys, and fjords.

Land and climate

More than a third of Norway lies within the Arctic Circle. Most of the country is a high, mountainous plateau covered by bare rock smoothed out by ancient glaciers. There are lowlands in the southeast and around Trondheim.

The most notable physical features of Norway are the fjords, the long, narrow sea inlets that indent the coast. Some 150,000 islands lie off the coast. The climate of Norway is mild for such a northerly country, especially along the west coast. There, the warm North Atlantic Drift keeps most of the seaports ice-free. Inland, it is colder, because the mountains block the warm west winds.

Right: *Built on the rocky west coast of Norway, where the bulk of the country's furniture industry is sited, Ålesund is the local centre of the Sunnmøre region, Vestlandet. Steep-walled narrow fjords cut deep into the interior mountain region.*

Below: *One of the nation's three historic urban centres, Bergen remains the most important port on the west coast of Norway despite its almost complete destruction by fire four times, the last in 1855.*

Economy

Only five percent of the land is used for agriculture or grazing. Nearly 75 percent consists of mountains and moorland. Most of the people live in the countryside, many in the small settlements scattered along the valley floors of the interior and in the small pockets of flat land to be found in the Atlantic fringe.

A land of few natural resources, Norway has built its economy on human resources. The people have harnessed the rushing streams to provide cheap and abundant hydro-electric power, they have built ships to import a wide variety of raw materials, and they have earned a reputation for the manufacture of quality goods that they can market throughout the world. The exploitation of North Sea oil has brought further economic advances.

About half of Norway's factories are in the Oslo area. Products include chemi-

Above: *The scenic beauty of the fertile cultivated plain of Dalarna in central Sweden, especially around lake Siljan, has made it a noted tourist area.*

Left: *Built on 22 islands on Lake Mälär, Sweden's capital Stockholm is one of the most beautiful in the world.*

cals, metals, processed foods, and paper and wood pulp. Fishing and forestry are also important. Much of the fish caught, chiefly cod and herring, is processed for export.

The Norwegians are an outdoor people. Skiing is the national sport, and the country boasts some 10,000 ski jumps. The leading exponents are national idols. The Norwegians have also excelled in the arts, producing such giants as the playwright Henrik Ibsen, the composer Edvard Grieg, and the expressionist painter Edvard Munch. But perhaps the most famous of all Norwegians are their explorers – Leif Eriksson, who probably discovered America some 500 years before Columbus, Fridtjof Nansen, who became a great diplomat and humanitarian, Roald Amundsen, the first man to reach the South Pole, and Thor Heyerdahl of *Kon Tiki* fame.

A constitutional monarchy, Norway has a prime minister and a one-house parliament called the *Storting*. The country was first united in about AD 872 by King Harold Fairhair. Previously, Norwegian Vikings had colonized Iceland. Norway has been fully independent only since 1905, after 686 years as an overshadowed member of Nordic unions with Sweden and Denmark.

Norway suffered greatly in World War II. Invaded by Germany in 1940, its people resisted bravely. When finally overcome, they set up a government-in-exile in Britain, and the people continued to resist the Nazis in every conceivable way. American aid helped Norway recover after the war, and the fierce independence of the people restored the country's prosperity. Active regional development programmes are aimed at developing the economic and social potential of the whole country.

Sweden

Area: 449,964km² (173,686sq.m.).
Population: 8.33 million.
Capital: Stockholm (1.6m).
Language: Swedish.
Ethnic groups: Swedish, Lappish (10,000).
Main exports: machinery and engineering products; pulp, paper, and other wood products, iron ore and steel; food products.
Average temperatures: 17°C (63°F) July; −3°C (27°F) Jan. in Stockholm.
Highest point: Mount Kebnekaise 2,117m (6,946ft).

Sweden is a land of lakes, forests, and mountains. An extended, thin country, some 1,600 kilometres (1,000 miles) long, it ranges from the gentle, rolling south with its lakes, through the vast forests, to the glacial mountains of the north. The 96,000 lakes make up nine percent of the total area; over half the land is covered with forests; and a seventh lies within the Arctic Circle. Sweden is a highly industrialized nation, and enjoys a standard of living that is one of the highest in the world.

Land and climate

The northern two-thirds of Sweden is sparsely populated. The Kölen Mountains form the northern boundary with Norway, and cutting a huge swathe through the country are the moss-carpeted forests and lichen-clad rocks. Swift rivers flow south-eastwards through this area to the Gulf of Bothnia, providing abundant hydro-electric power. Most of Sweden's people live in the southern lowlands, particularly in Skåne, the southernmost province.

Sweden has few fjords, but tens of thousands of tiny islands shelter the mainland. In winter, most of the northern coast freezes up from November to April, and in particularly severe winters nearly all the country is locked in ice. The south has comparatively mild winters, and the whole country has pleasant summers.

Economy

The economy of Sweden is based chiefly on engineering and industrial products. Natural resources include timber (pine, spruce, birch), iron ore, and water power. There is no coal, so the hydro-electric energy is supplemented by imported oil. 'Acid rain', the industrial pollution of other countries, is becoming a serious threat to Sweden's forests and lakes.

Less than six percent of Sweden's work force is employed on the land. Sweden is the world's leading producer of iron ore, and this accounts for six percent of the country's exports. The engineering industry accounts for a third of Sweden's industrial production. Products include ships, motor-cars, and agricultural machinery. Sweden produces 10 percent of the world's wood pulp, and many other timber-based products, including paper, plywood, and furniture.

History and constitution

The Swedes enjoy one of the most advanced welfare systems in the world, with free education and medical treatment and generous pensions for the needy. Sweden is a constitutional monarchy, with a prime minister and a one-house parliament called the *Riksdag*. The constitution was adopted in 1809 – only the United States has an older one. The Swedes call their country *Sverige*, 'land of the Svear'. The Roman historian Tacitus wrote about the Svear in AD 100. During the Viking period (8th-11th centuries), the Swedish Vikings went eastwards to trade and plunder. It was in the 11th century that Christianity took hold in Sweden, which was developing on the lines of a feudal kingdom. Sweden was united with Denmark and Norway in 1397. It broke away from the union in 1523 under Gustavus I, who encouraged Lutheranism, which became the state denomination in about 1540. Sweden began to expand in the late 1500s, and won many victories in the Thirty Years' War (1618-48) and again under Charles XII (reigned 1697-1718), to become one of the greatest powers in Europe. But Swedish power soon declined, with defeat by Russia in the Battle of Poltava (1709). A period of parliamentary government followed the death of Charles XII.

During the Napoleonic Wars, Sweden lost Finland to Russia, but gained Norway from Denmark (Norway eventually became independent in 1905). The Industrial Revolution came late to Sweden, and there was such poverty that nearly half a million people emigrated to the United States between 1867 and 1886. But economic progress saw Sweden emerge as an important industrial nation by 1900. Sweden remained neutral in both world wars, and further rapid progress led to prosperity, partly maintained by the immigration of workers, especially from Finland and the Mediterranean.

Right: *The waterfront at Copenhagen – cultural, industrial and trade centre, and capital of Denmark.*

Below: *Windmills have always been an important source of power in Denmark, which has few fossil fuel resources.*

Denmark

Area: 43,075km² (16,631sq.m.).
Population: 5.1 million.
Capital: København or Copenhagen (1.4m).
Language: Danish.
Ethnic groups: Danish, German (30,000).
Main exports: machinery, meat and meat products (especially bacon), chemicals, dairy products, fish.
Average temperatures: 15°C (59°F) July; –1°C (30°F) Jan. in Copenhagen.
Highest point: Yding Skovhøj 173m (568ft).

A land of small farms, lakes, and islands, Denmark is one of the world's most prosperous countries. It is the oldest kingdom and one of the most efficient agricultural countries on earth. Its engineeers are world famous and it has produced numerous Nobel prize winners including the atomic physicist Niels Bohr. Other great figures include the writer Hans Christian Andersen and the philosopher Søren Kierkegaard.

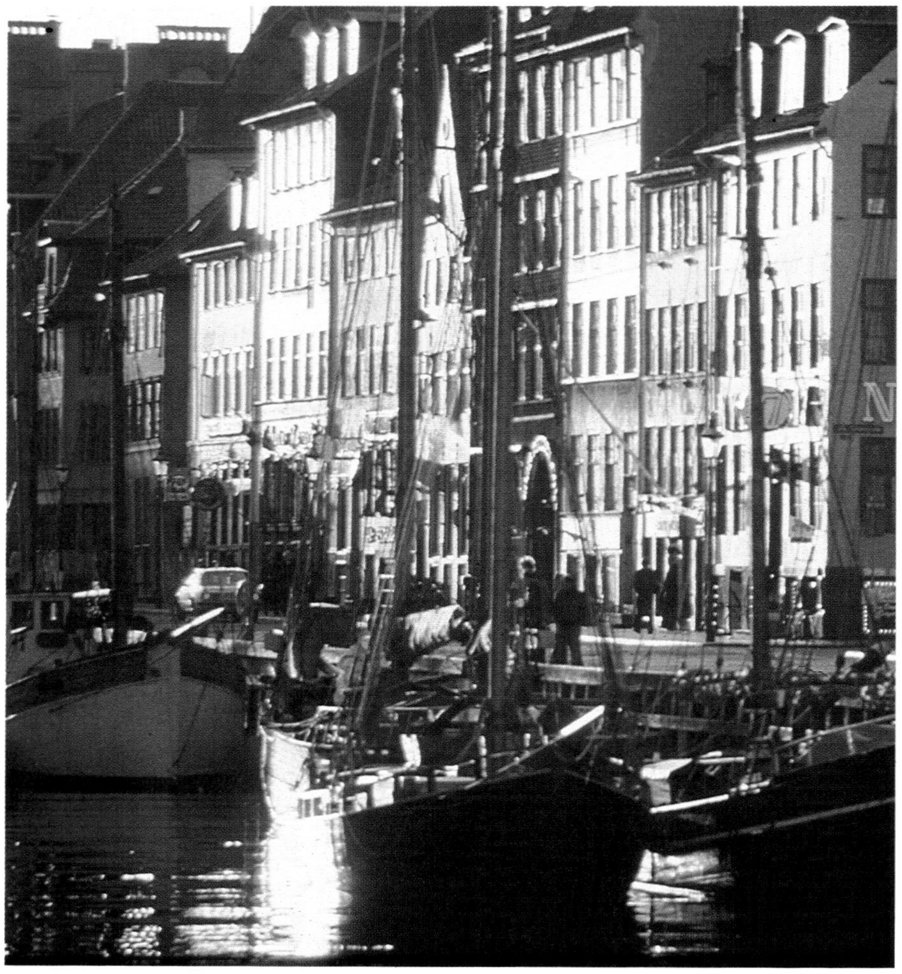

Land and climate

Denmark consists of a peninsula, Jylland (Jutland), and nearly 500 nearby islands, the largest of which is Sjaelland (Zealand). Denmark's capital, Copenhagen, lies on the east coast of Zealand, facing Sweden across a narrow strait. Jutland borders West Germany to the south. The world's largest island, Greenland, discussed in the section on the Arctic, is a self-governing province of Denmark. It lies some 2,000km (1,250m.) from Denmark, and is about 50 times as large. The Faröes, a smaller group of islands in the North Atlantic between Iceland and the British Isles, are also part of the kingdom of Denmark.

Most of Denmark is low-lying, with undulating plains. The west coast of Jutland has extensive sandy beaches, closing off inlets. Fjords are a feature of the other coasts, forming natural harbours. Most of the land in eastern Jutland is covered by morainic material deposited in ancient times by melting glaciers. Being almost surrounded by water, Denmark had a mild, damp climate.

Economy

About three-quarters of the land is used for farming. Nearly half of Denmark's industry is situated in the Copenhagen area, where more than a quarter of the people live. The country is poor in natural resources, so metals and fuel have to be imported in large quantities. Manufacturing industries based on these raw materials, however, provide important exports, particularly steel products. The country is known for the quality and beauty of its manufactured goods such as furniture and silver. Although only 10 percent of the country's labour force is engaged in agriculture, fishing, and forestry, it is for its food products that Denmark is best known. The deep moraine soils of the islands provide the best farmland. The farms are small but intensive, and scientific methods have earned the Danes a reputation as outstanding farmers. The main occupation is the raising of pigs and cattle, and the chief products are butter, cheese, bacon, and ham. The chief crop is barley, of which Denmark is one of the world's leading producers.

The population of Denmark is almost entirely Scandinavian. The only minority group, about 30,000 people of German descent, live in Jutland, along the border with Germany. The Danes have a reputation as an easy-going people, and they are among the greatest beer drinkers in the world.

History and constitution

Denmark is a constitutional monarchy, with a prime minister and one-house parliament called the *Folketing*. The constitution of Denmark is founded on the charter of 1953.

The country was settled by the Danes, a Scandinavian branch of the Teutons, in the 6th century. The Danes took part in Viking raids on western Europe for some 300 years from the 8th century. They lived in small communities at first, but were united in about 950 by King Harald Bluetooth, who introduced Christianity to the country. Danish kings ruled England from 1013 to 1042, and when Denmark, Norway, and Sweden were united in 1397, Denmark was the centre of power. In the 17th and 18th centuries, however, Denmark lost territory and power to Sweden in a series of wars. In 1814 it lost Norway to Sweden in the Napoleonic wars.

During World War II, Denmark was occupied by the Germans, but there was widespread resistance to the Nazis. After the war, American aid helped rebuild the country's economy. Manufacturing gradually overtook farming as the leading industry. One of the original members of EFTA, in 1959, Denmark joined the European Economic Community in 1973.

OSLO 94
TEMPERATURE °C
23°
PRESSURE mb
PRECIPITATION mm
730 mm

STOCKHOLM 44
TEMPERATURE °C
21°
PRESSURE mb
PRECIPITATION mm
554 mm

KØBENHAVN 13
TEMPERATURE °C
18°
PRESSURE mb
PRECIPITATION mm
603mm

1:3 000 000

Projection : Conical with two standard parallels   East from Greenwich   COPYRIGHT GEORGE PHILIP & SON LTD.

Map 29   ASIA AND EUROPEAN RUSSIA

DENSITY OF POPULATION
1 : 80 000 000

Inhabitants	per mile²	per km²
	under 2	under 1
	2 – 16	1 – 6
	16 – 32	6 – 12
	32 – 64	12 – 25
	64 – 128	25 – 50
	128 – 256	50 – 100
	256 – 512	100 – 200
	over 512	over 200

■ Towns of over 500 000 inhabitants

Projection: Bonne   East from Greenwich

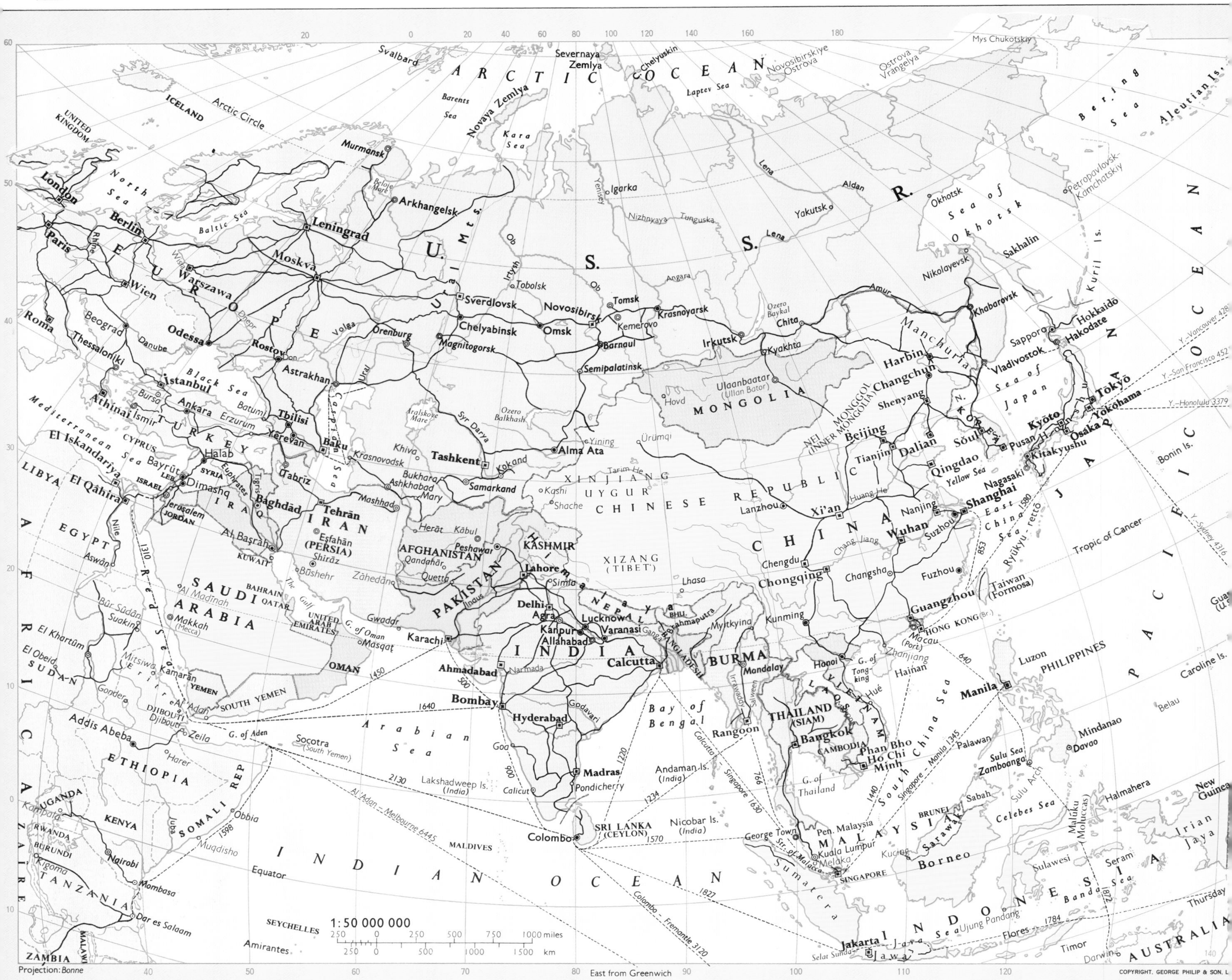

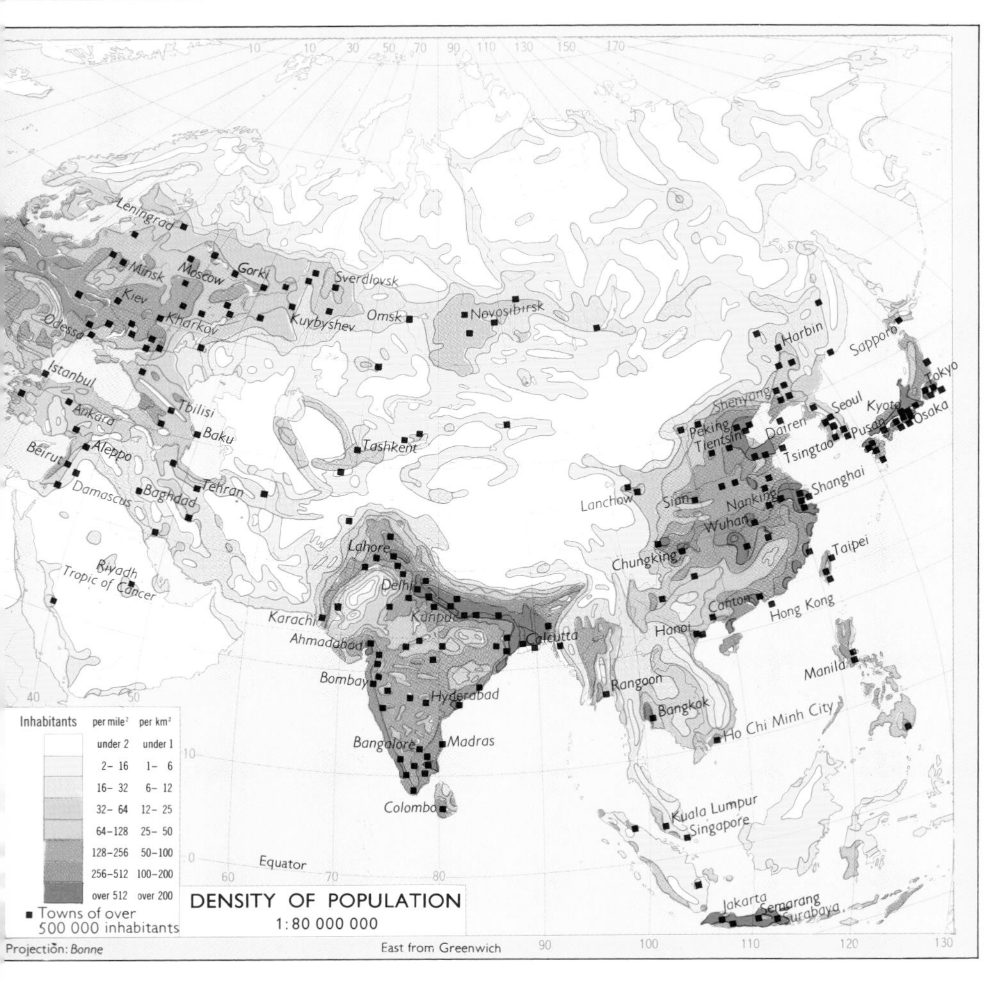

Asia is the largest, most populous and physically most diverse of the world's continents. In geographic terms it extends from the Pacific to the Mediterranean and the Ural mountains of Russia. In this book South-West Asia is discussed separately while the whole of the USSR is included in this section. Although most of the USSR's population and industry lie west of the Urals in Europe, its vast Siberian lands make up a third of the entire Asian continent. Russia was historically the only East-West route not impeded by natural barriers, and the USSR today remains the only European power to have established a physical presence in Asia.

The USSR is the largest country in the world. Before the 1917 revolution it was called Russia. Today the term 'Russia' should strictly be applied to only the largest of the USSR's constituent republics. At its widest point, between eastern Europe and the Pacific, the USSR stretches across a distance of 8,000km (5,250 miles). Its climate ranges from some of the world's lowest temperatures in the Arctic north to the blistering heat of Central Asia. Its vast agricultural and mineral resources have made it a major economic power.

Politically however, the USSR's potential dominance of Asia is chal-lenged by the rise of the People's Repub-lic of China. Between 1840 and 1945, China fell under the influence first of European powers and then of Japan. Today it is reasserting its historic posi-tion as the most influential nation of Asia. The physical contrasts between China's arid interior and the favoured eastern plains that support the bulk of its awesome population continue to present major economic problems. After a period of rigorous revolutionary socialism China is today permitting a more relaxed way of life for its citizens.

China shares with much of southern and southeastern Asia a monsoonal weather pattern that is produced by atmospheric pressure changes in Central Asia and which brings alternating periods of heavy rain and drought. The dependence of farmers on this pattern of rainfall makes southern Asia particularly vulnerable to famine following poor har-vests. It is therefore in India, Pakistan and Bangladesh that rising birthrates in recent years have put the greatest pres-sure on diminishing resources of land. Food is more abundant in South-East Asia with its rich rice-growing regions. There progress has sometimes been hampered less by rising populations than by the destructive impact of war. Two decades of fighting in Vietnam left scars which remain unhealed today. Laos and Cambodia have suffered greatly as well in the wake of war.

Despite some highly developed areas, such as Singapore, Hong Kong, and Taiwan, much of South-East Asia is poorly developed industrially. In general throughout Asia about two-thirds of the people are farmers. The notable exception is Japan, a country which has developed rapidly this century. Although still tentative in taking any diplomatic initiatives within the region, Japan has become a major source of finance and expertise throughout much of South-East Asia during the past 15 years, as well as the major trading partner for many countries of the region.

The Union of Soviet Socialist Republics

Area: 22,400,000km^2 (8,650,000sq.m.).
Population: 278 million.
Capital: Moscow (8.54m).
Language: Russian is the native tongue of 60 per cent of the people; also Ukrainian, Byelorussian, Lithuanian, Latvian, Estonian, Moldavian, Yiddish, Georgian, Armenian, Uzbek, Tatar, Kazakh, Azerbaijani and 50 others.
Ethnic groups: Russian 55 percent, Ukrainians 17 percent, Uzbeks 3.8 percent, Byelorussian 3.7 percent, Tatars 2.5 percent, Kazakhs 2.2 percent.
Main exports: oil, gas, coal, iron and manganese ore, paper, cotton, engineering products, transport equipment, watches.
Average temperatures: −11°C (13°F) Jan. 21°C (70°F) July In Moscow. −50°C (−58F) Jan. 14°C (57°F) July in Siberia. 21°C (70°F) Jan. 30°C (86°F) July, in central Asia.
Highest point: Communism Peak, 7,495m (24,590ft).

The USSR's landscape consists broadly of a large upland plateau in the east and two vast plains separated by a range of mountains extending from north to south and rising to a moderate height. Taller ranges rise along some of the border areas.

The fertile East European Plain, where nearly three-quarters of the Soviet people live, extends from the Polish border in the west to the Ural Mountains, which are traditionally regarded as the dividing line between Europe and Asia. These mountains are rich in minerals and reach their greatest height at 1,865m (6,120ft).

The West Siberian Lowland, the world's longest continuous plain, lies east of the Urals. It is bounded by the Arctic Ocean in the north and the Turan Lowland in the south.

Much of the Turan Lowland is semi-arid and the region contains two great deserts: the Kara Kum and the Kyzyl Kum.

The Central Siberian Uplands, which have important mineral deposits, lie east of the river Yenisei and rise to a height of 600m (2,000ft).

The Uplands continue into eastern Siberia where some of the peaks rise to more than 3,048m (10,000ft)

The Soviet Union's highest mountains are in the Pamir Knot on the border with Afghanistan. Communism Peak, the highest point, is in this range.

The Caucasus range, in the southwest between the Caspian and Black Seas, is the USSR's second highest with some peaks rising to 5,486m (18,000ft). Other mountainous regions are the Altai, Tien Shan and Sayan ranges along the border with China and Mongolia. These mountains rise to more than 3,048m (10,000ft) in places. The Kamchatka peninsula in eastern Asia is mountainous and volcanic.

The USSR's lowest point is the Karagiye Depression near the Caspian Sea which is 132m (433ft) below sea level.

The Caspian, covering more than 422,153km^2 (163,000sq.m.), is the largest body of inland water in the world. The USSR also has Europe's biggest lake, Lake Ladoga near Leningrad which covers 18,388km^2 (7,100sq.m.). Lake Baikal in the central Siberian Uplands is 1,737m (5,700ft) deep and the deepest fresh-water lake in the world.

Among important rivers in the USSR is the Volga which flows 3,680km (2,300m.) from the Valday Hills near Moscow into the Caspian and is the longest river in Europe. Canals link the Volga with the Baltic in the north and with the River Don near Volgograd, formerly Stalingrad. The Dnepr, or Dnieper, the third-largest river in Europe, flows into the Black Sea and is a major source of electrical energy. Siberia's main rivers – the Yenisei, Lena and Ob – are each more than 3,200km (2,000m.) long.

Climate

The Soviet Union is a land of climatic extremes. In Verkhoyansk in eastern Siberia a temperature of −90°F (−68°C) has been recorded while in central Asia July temperatures can rise to 77°F (25°C). In general, the summers are warm, but long, cold winters are characteristic of most of the country, with snow covering the ground for several months. The European Plain and the Pacific coast receive the greatest precipitation both as rain and snow with amounts ranging from 20 to 40 inches a year. The Arctic, Siberia and the desert regions receive less than 10 inches a year. Rainfall is generally light to moderate in the east.

Natural resources

The USSR's enormous natural wealth puts it in the lead in the output of certain minerals. Coal reserves are estimated at 7,800,000,000,000 tonnes and deposits are widespread although the Donets and the Kuznets basins are the main mining regions. Output rivals that of the US.

Known oil reserves total 70 billion tonnes, chiefly in the Volga and Urals regions, but with important deposits in the Caucasus. New fields have been exploited in western Siberia and Kazakhstan. Unexploited petroleum deposits, either under ground or water, are estimated at 300,000 tonnes. Production of both oil and natural gas is rising rapidly, supplying the Soviet Union with its main energy source and also being exported both to eastern and western European countries through huge pipelines.

About 40 percent of the world's reserves in iron ore are located in the USSR which leads the world in the production of this metal. Ukraine and the Urals are the chief sources. The USSR also leads in the production of manganese which is mined in Ukraine and Georgia. There are big copper deposits in the Urals, Uzbekistan, Kazakhstan and Armenia and the Altai region is rich in lead and zinc. Rarer minerals, such as titanium, are produced in Ukraine and the Urals and uranium in Uzbekistan.

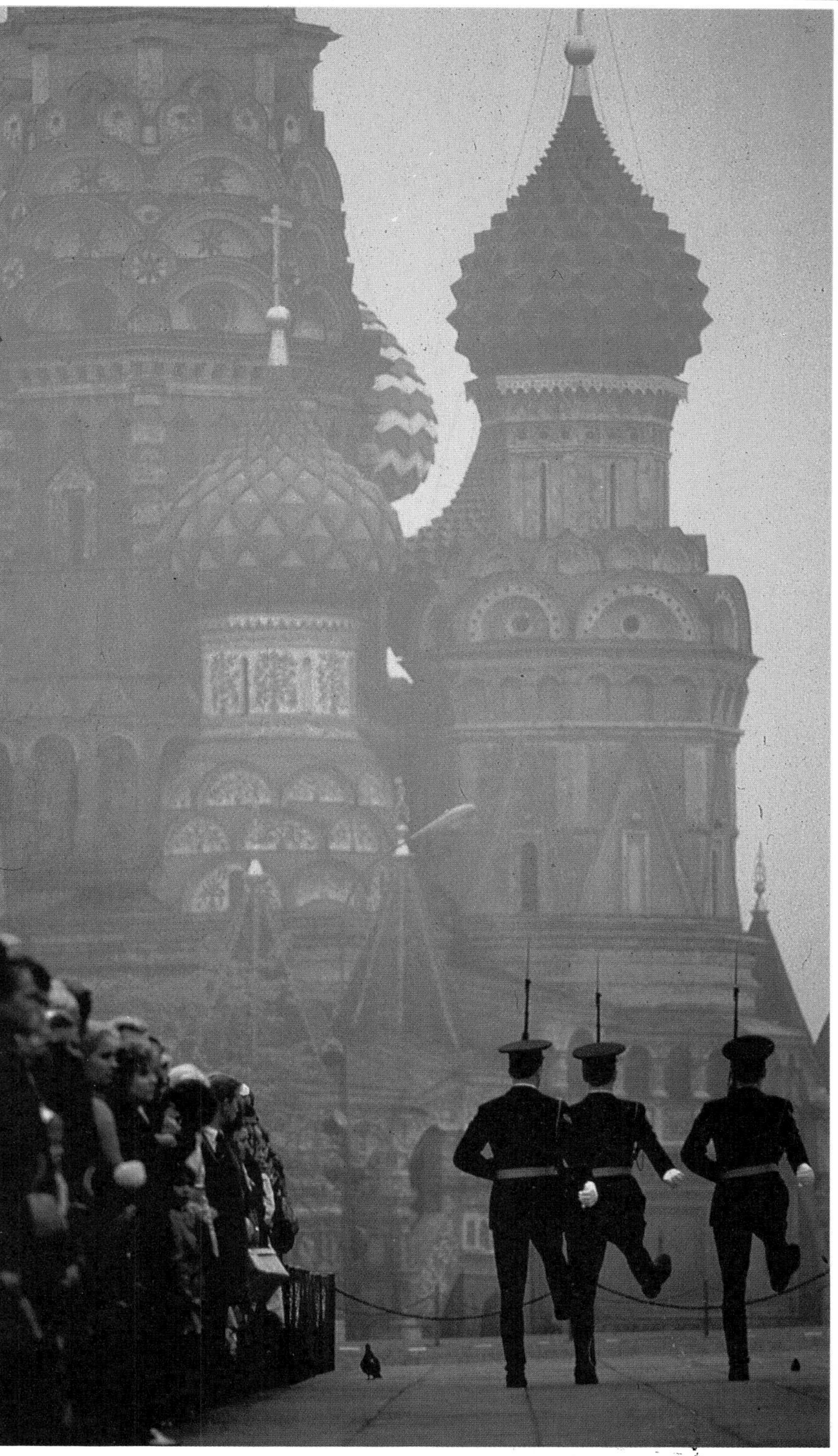

Above: *The cathedral of St Basil in Moscow's Red Square, a place of pilgrimage for Soviet citizens.*

The USSR is the world's second-largest producer of gold after South Africa. It is also a major source of precious minerals such as diamonds, beryllium and mercury.

Timber resources are an estimated 80,000,000,000m^3 (2,800,000,000,000 ft^3). The chief forest areas in Siberia and the far east are rich in furs.

Economy: agriculture

There is no private ownership in industry in the USSR and only a limited form of it in agriculture. All economic activity is carried out either as a state enterprise or as a collective or co-operative.

The economy is directed from the centre by the State Planning Commission (Gosplan) through five-year plans prepared by various state committees specializing in different sectors of the economy.

Self-employment is rare, being confined to such persons as craftsmen, highly skilled artisans, authors, actors, composers and performers of the arts.

The only significant free enterprise sector is in agriculture. In the fruit and vegetable markets of towns and cities farmers sell produce from private plots which they are allowed to cultivate under the collective farming system. Although small, these plots supply nearly half the total output of fruit and vegetables as well as considerable quantities of meat and dairy products.

Agricuture is predominantly socialized however, with two types of farm: the *kolkhoz* (collective farm) and the *sovkhoz* (state farm). Collective farms operate as a cooperative on a profit sharing basis. Apart from certain delivery obligations to the government, they have freedom in planning and decision-making.

On the state farms, where planning is under closer government control, employees are paid a wage. There are nearly 34,000 collective farms and about 15,000 state farms. The state farms are about twice as large as the collectives and average 6,000 hectares (15,000 acres). Such units might each carry 1,240 cattle, 1,600 sheep and goats and 880 pigs in mixed farming areas.

Chief crops are wheat, rye, maize, barley, oats, sugar-beet, potatoes, sunflower seeds, tea and cotton. About 25 percent of the population works on the land.

Despite its tremendous potential, Soviet agriculture has frequently suffered

Map 30   THE UNION OF SOVIET SOCIALIST REPUBLICS

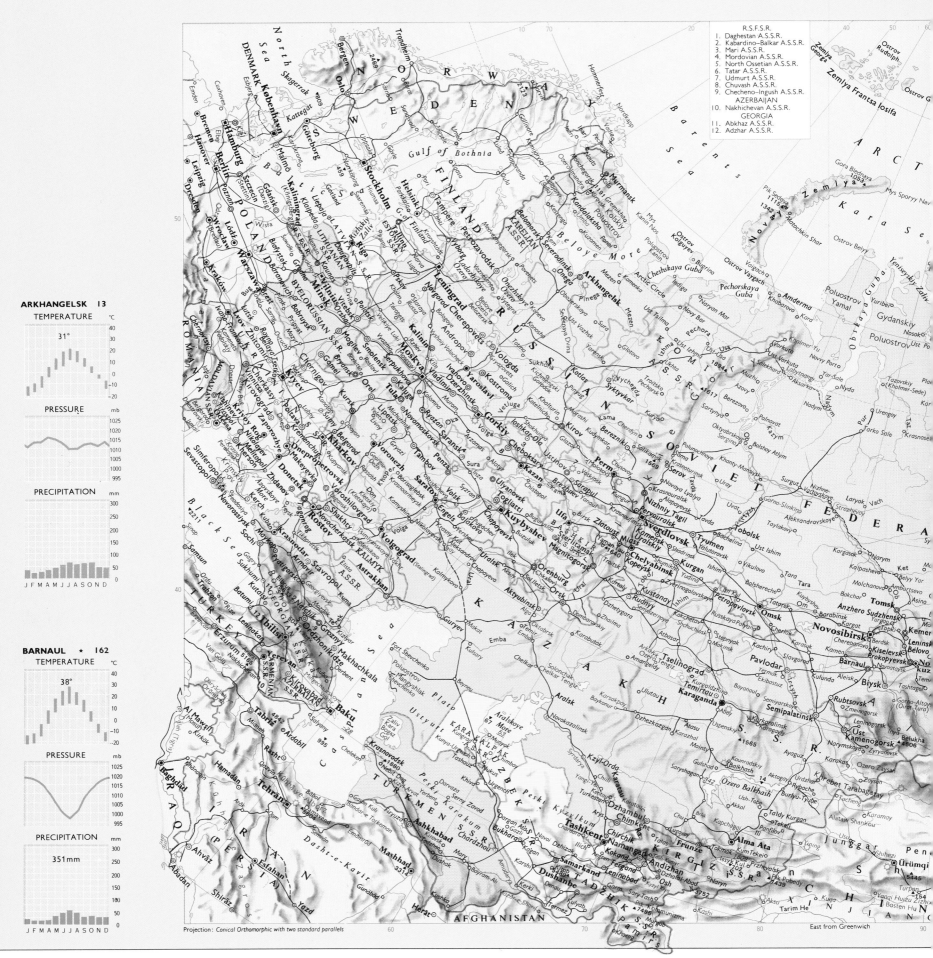

R.S.F.S.R.
1. Daghestan A.S.S.R.
2. Kabardino–Balkar A.S.S.R.
3. Mari A.S.S.R.
4. Mordovian A.S.S.R.
5. North Ossetian A.S.S.R.
6. Tatar A.S.S.R.
7. Udmurt A.S.S.R.
8. Chuvash A.S.S.R.
9. Checheno–Ingush A.S.S.R.
AZERBAIJAN
10. Nakhichevan A.S.S.R.
GEORGIA
11. Abkhaz A.S.S.R.
12. Adzhar A.S.S.R.

ARKHANGELSK 13
TEMPERATURE   °C
31°

PRESSURE   mb

PRECIPITATION   mm

J F M A M J J A S O N D

BARNAUL ★ 162
TEMPERATURE   °C
38°

PRESSURE   mb

PRECIPITATION   mm
351mm

J F M A M J J A S O N D

Projection: Conical Orthomorphic with two standard parallels   East from Greenwich

from inefficiency since it was socialized in the 1930s. This has been blamed partly on collective farmers spending more time on their small private plots and neglecting the wider needs of the collective. Weather conditions such as drought have been a periodic factor in crop failure. Reduced harvests in the 1970s forced the Soviet Union to make major grain purchases from the United States of America.

Hardly more than a quarter of the total area of the USSR is farmed. The main farming region is the European Plain, but during the 1950s the govern-ment began to develop the so-called virgin lands of central Asia. Special strains of cereal crops have also been evolved to grow in less clement climates, as in Siberia.

One of the problems facing Soviet agriculture has been migration to the cities as the country transformed itself from a backward rural nation into an industrial power. More than half the population now live in urban areas. Demand for specialized foods such as meat has been rising and Soviet farmers have found it difficult to meet. Livestock numbers are now increasing.

Left: *The mighty barrier of the Caucasus Mountains in the south of the Soviet Union.*

Industry and trade
As an industrial power the USSR is

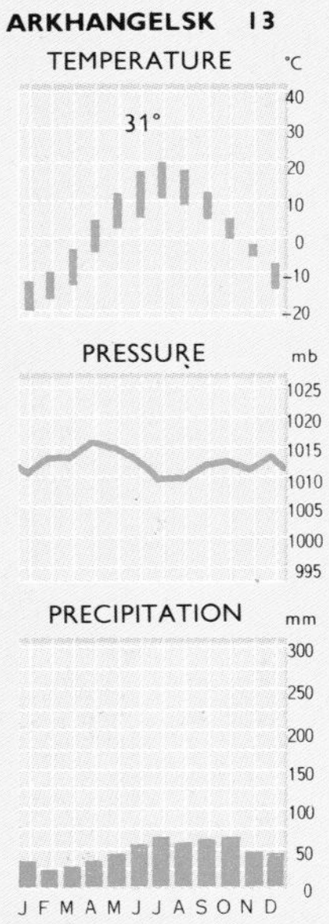

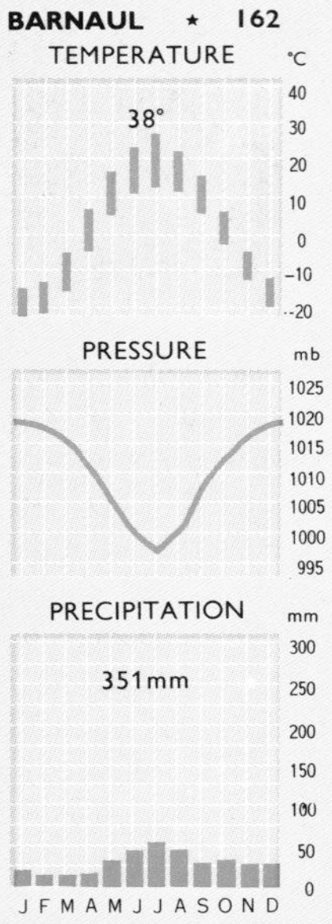

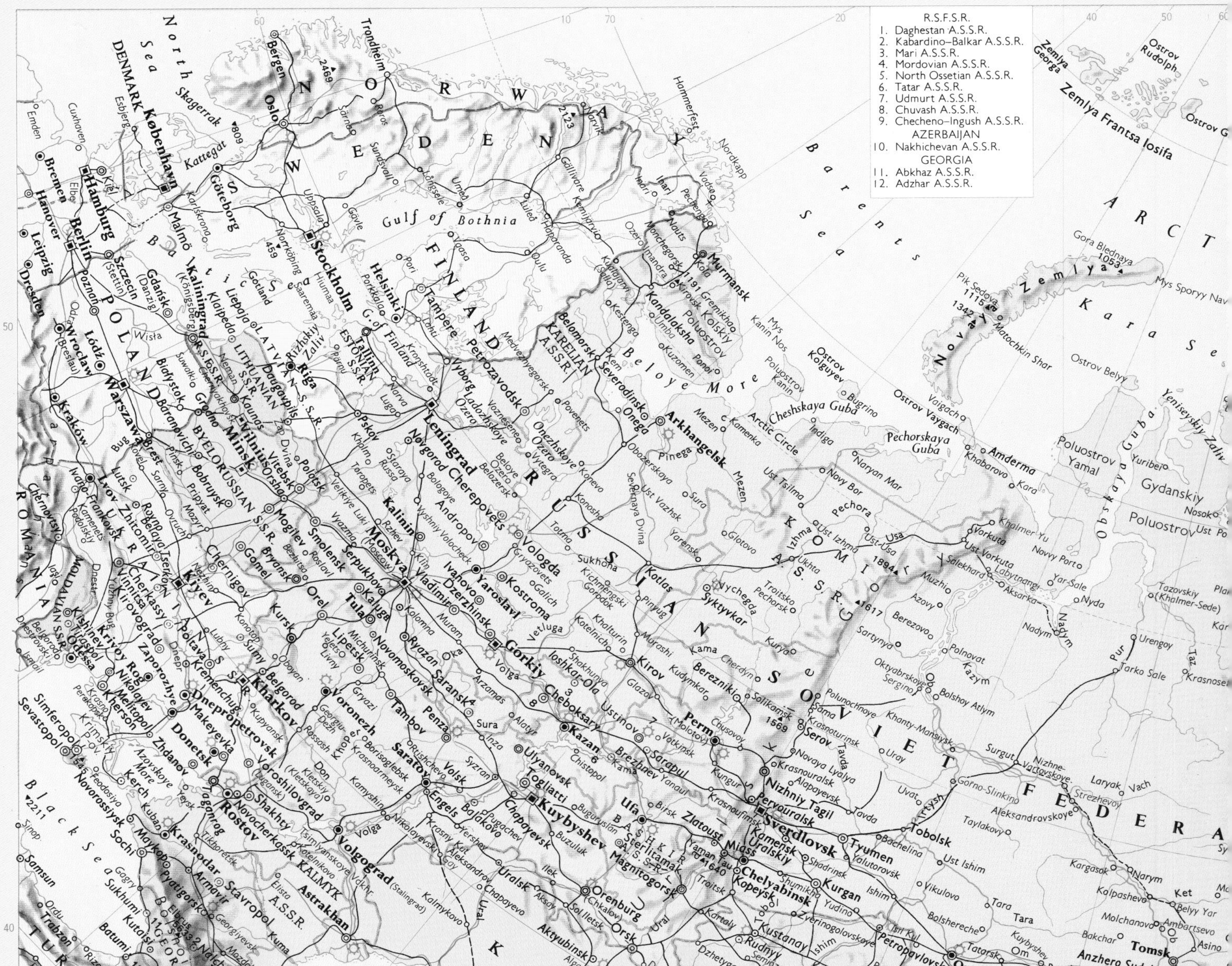

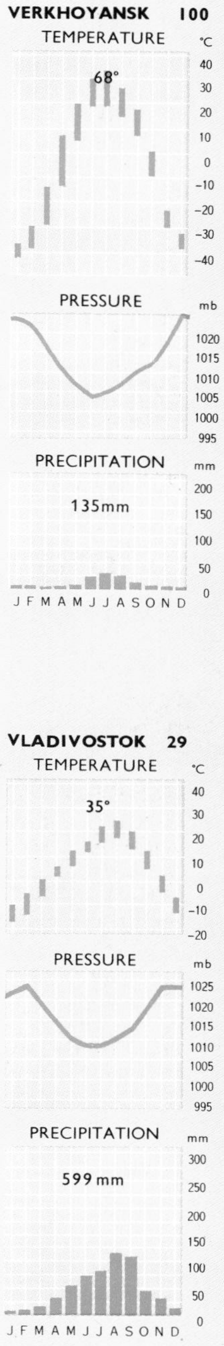

second only to the United States. After the 1917 revolution all efforts were devoted to building up heavy industry. But the period up to the end of World War II brought little improvement in the availability of consumer goods for the Soviet people despite significant advances in many other sectors of the economy.

However, from the late 1950s the government began to pay more heed to the consumer sector. The aim of the 1981-5 five-year plan has been to improve living standards and to develop industry in the Asian republics.

Industrial production still represents about 77 percent of the gross national product and 45 percent of industry is still geared to heavy engineering and non-consumer activity, such as metallurgy and chemicals. Chief products are machinery, heavy transport equipment, machine tools, plastics, synthetic fibres, chemicals and fertilizers.

In the consumer sector the USSR has greatly increased output of domestic refrigerators, washing machines, radio and television sets, textiles, cameras, clocks and watches from the 1960s onward although output cannot match demand. During this period the country also began to build up a private motor car industry with the help of Fiat of Italy.

Soviet foreign trade is significant only within a restricted area of the world and most of it is with the countries of eastern Europe which are subject to considerable Soviet influence in their own trade policies through the planning organization COMECON (Council for Mutual Economic Aid) established in 1949. Some consumer goods are exported to developing countries in Africa and Asia. Trade with the west, although increasing, is mainly in raw materials such as hides and skins, ores, gas, pretroleum and textile fibres.

The USSR has approximately 760,000km (472,000m.) of roads. The main problem facing motor transport is the sheer size of the country and the climatic extremes which reduce vast zones to frozen wastes, bog or desert. Railways are an important means of transport and there is a network of 143,300km (89,000m.). Air transport also plays an important part, especially in the remote regions of Asia.

Soviet hydroelectric potential is twice that of the United States and about 11 percent of the world's total. Most of the power comes from large schemes on the rivers Volga and Dnepr but the Yenisei, Angara, Ob and Irtysh rivers also supply considerable energy.

The people

Scores of ethnic groups make up the Soviet population, each group having its own distinctive language and culture.

The Slavs, comprising the Russians, Ukrainians and Byelorussians, form the

| Map 32 | EUROPEAN RUSSIA (CENTRAL) |

LENINGRAD 4

TEMPERATURE °C

27°

PRESSURE mb

PRECIPITATION mm

603mm

J F M A M J J A S O N D

MOSKVA ★ 156

TEMPERATURE °C

31°

PRESSURE mb

PRECIPITATION mm

624mm

J F M A M J J A S O N D

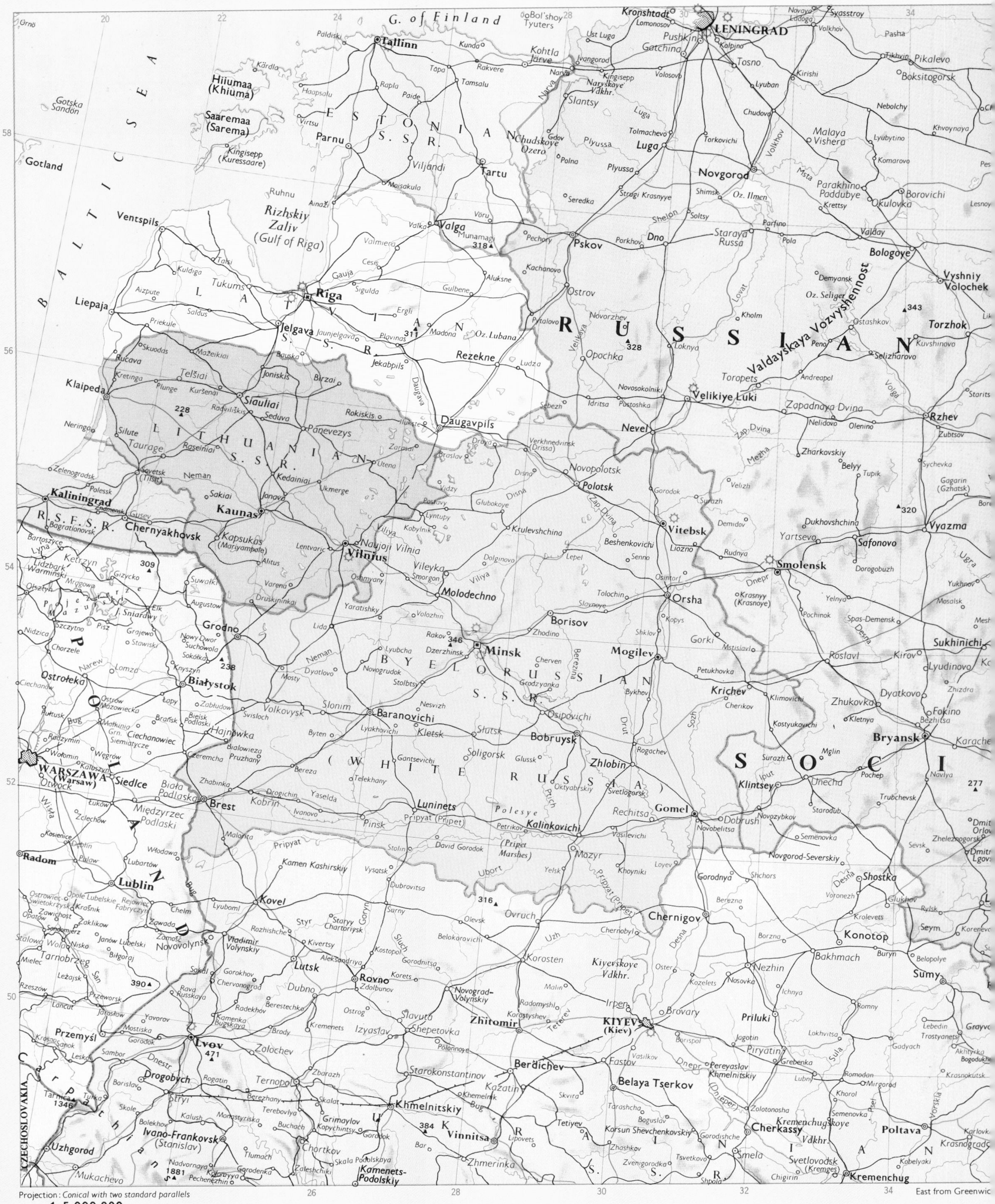

Projection : Conical with two standard parallels

1:5 000 000

20 10 0   20   40   60   80   100 miles
40 20 0   40   80   120   160 km

East from Greenwich

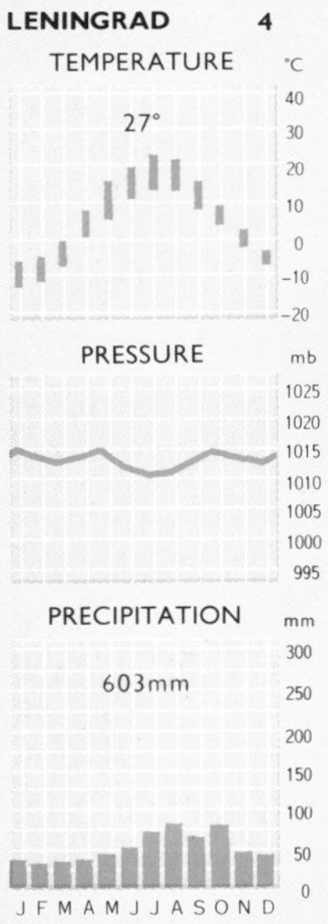

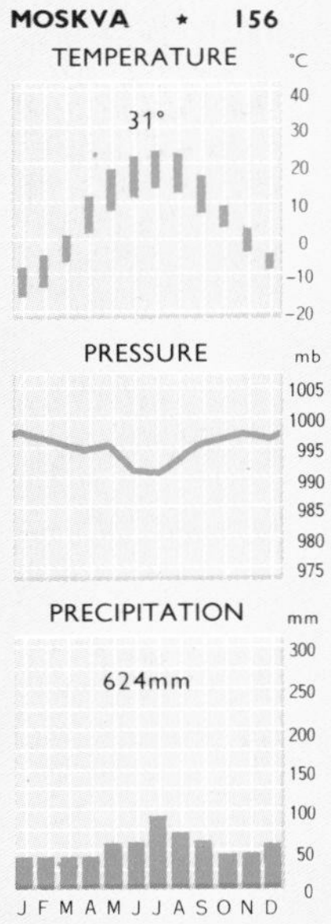

largest single group although their languages differ slightly. The Turkic peoples of central Asia are second, followed by the Tatars, the Ugro-Finnic of the Baltic, the Japhetics of the Caucasus and the Iranians of Azerbaijan, Armenia and parts of central Asia.

The government officially encourages the development of various languages and cultures, but Russian remains the most important tongue. In the Baltic regions and in some other areas where strong ethnic or cultural traditions were seen as threats to national unity, conscious efforts have been made to break up groups of peoples by forced migrations.

The Soviet constitution guarantees freedom of worship but religion is firmly separated from the state. The traditional faith of the Slavs is the Russian Orthodox Church. Lithuania is a Roman Catholic region while Estonia and Latvia are traditionally Lutheran. Most of the Turkic peoples are Muslims and there are Buddhists in eastern Asia.

Sport and athletics are extremely popular and the government gives them considerable help and encouragement. Soviet teams have distinguished themselves internationally in soccer, winter sports, especially ice hockey, and rowing.

Right: Known as 'The Venice of the North', Leningrad is a city of waterways.

Map 33

KIYEV ★ 179

TEMPERATURE °C

27°

PRESSURE mb

PRECIPITATION mm

677mm

J F M A M J J A S O N D

KUYBYSHEV 44

TEMPERATURE °C

34°

PRESSURE mb

PRECIPITATION mm

519 mm

J F M A M J J A S O N D

COPYRIGHT. GEORGE PHILIP & SON. LTD.

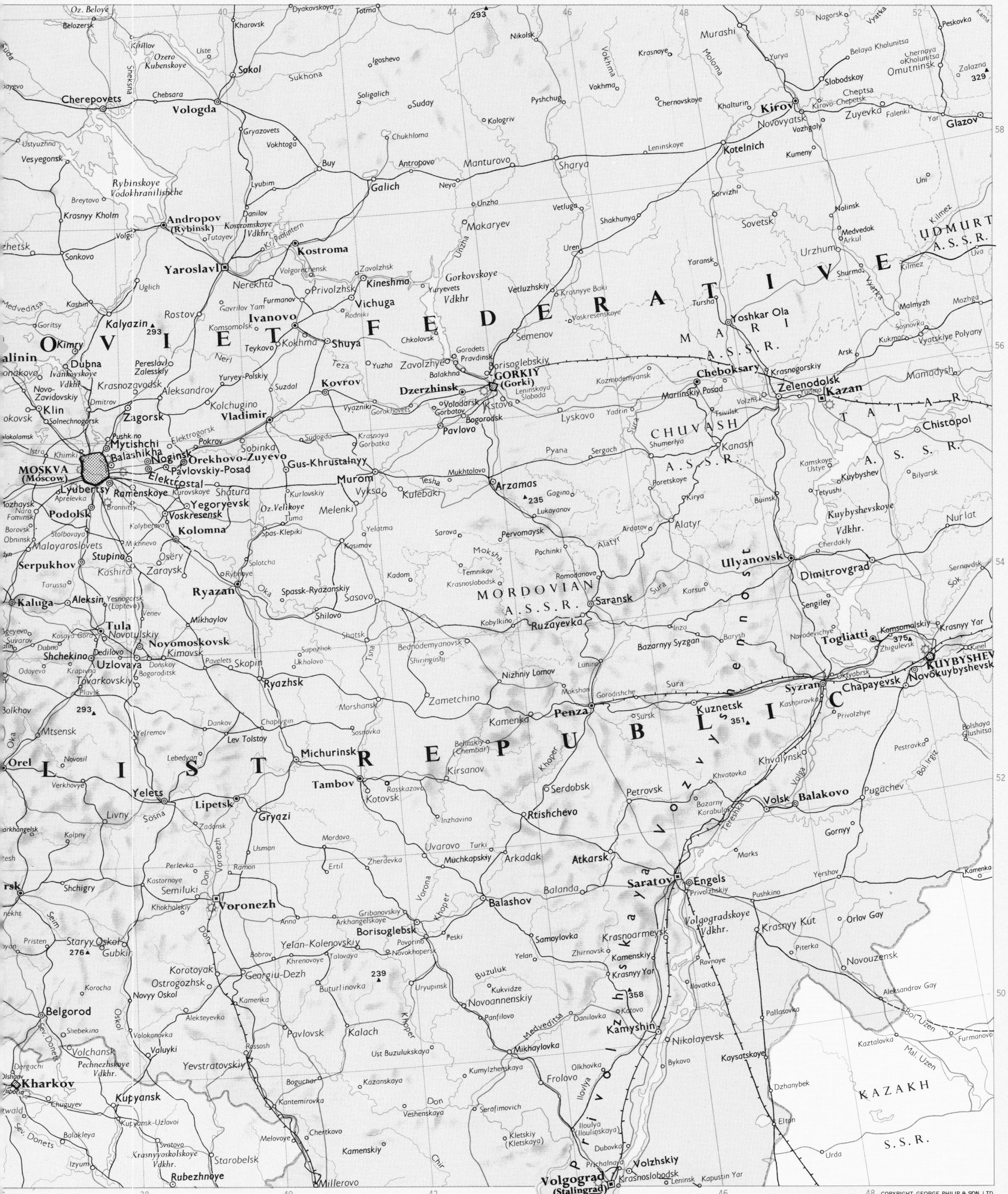

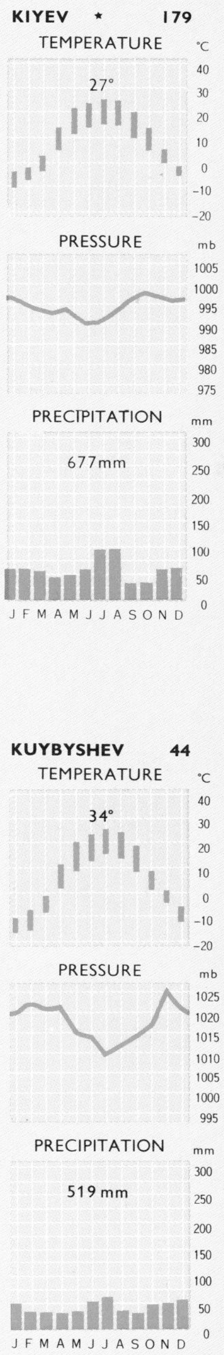

The government also encourages cultural activities. Opera and ballet are greatly appreciated with celebrated companies such as the Bolshoi in Moscow and the Kirov in Leningrad.

There is also a great literary tradition born from such classic authors as Pushkin, Tolstoy, Dostoyevsky and Chekhov. Modern literature however is expected by the government to devote itself mainly to subjects concerning the day-to-day life of the mass of the people and any departure from this to speculative philosophy or criticism of the political system is discouraged. Several writers such as Solzhenitsin and Pasternak have resisted this pressure to conform.

Government

The Soviet Union is a federation of 15 republics: Russian Federation, Armenia, Azerbaijan, Byelorussia, Estonia, Georgia, Kazakhstan, Kirgizia, Latvia, Lithuania, Moldavia, Tadzhikistan, Turkmenistan, Ukraine and Uzbekistan.

Each of the republics has its own legislature but the highest lawmaking body is the Supreme Soviet of the Soviet Union which meets in Moscow. This is a parliament which has two chambers: the Council of the Union and the Council of the Nationalities. The president of the presidium of the Supreme Soviet is also head of state.

Executive power is exercised by the Council of Ministers whose chairman is prime minister.

Effective power lies with the communist party and no other party is permitted. Party membership is granted to relatively few as a privilege and in recognition of unusual ability. The party shapes major policies which later receive the formal approval of the Supreme Soviet. The general secretary of the party's central committee is regarded as the most powerful official in Russia.

Apart from the republics, Russia has 20 autonomous republics, eight autonomous regions, 10 national districts and six territories to accommodate special ethnic groups such as Jews and German-speaking communities.

History

The Scythians were among the earliest inhabitants of Russia. In pre-Christian times they lived in the steppe region on the northern shores of the Black Sea. The Slavs, who later established their dominance, migrated from the northern forests and settled along the rivers Volga and Don. They founded the city of Novgorod in about the 9th century AD and dominated the Viking settlement of Kiev which became the major city. Christianity was introduced through Kiev's contacts with Byzantium.

Map 34 | EUROPEAN RUSSIA (SOUTH)

SIMFEROPOL 205

TEMPERATURE °C

23°

PRESSURE mb

PRECIPITATION mm

482 mm

J F M A M J J A S O N D

ODESSA 64

TEMPERATURE °C

25°

PRESSURE mb

PRECIPITATION mm

473 mm

J F M A M J J A S O N D

1:5 000 000

Projection: Conical with two standard parallels

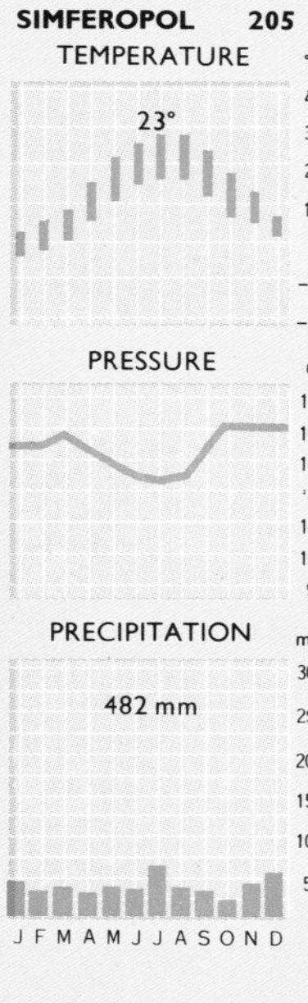

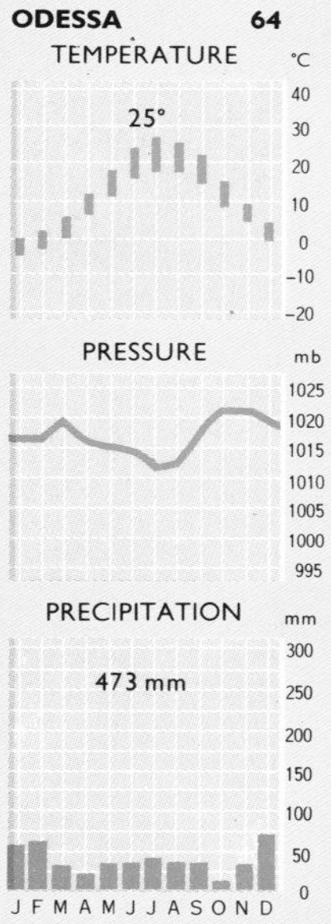

Kiev was vanquished by the Golden Horde of the Mongols in the 1200s and the new rulers set up their empire in what is now Volgograd.

Muscovy emerged as the strongest state from the 1400s. It proceeded to unite the country by conquest and the campaign reached its culmination when Ivan IV, known as 'the Terrible', defeated the Tatars and made Kazan and Astrakhan part of Russia.

Russia fell into disarray after Ivan's death. The country was invaded by Poles. Cossacks in the Don region ceaselessly tried to overthrow the tsar and palace intrigues were fomented by the lordly boyars.

Peter the Great, who became tsar in 1696, determined to curb the boyars and modernize Russia. He built the country's first navy and wrested right of way through the Baltic after a 21-year war with Sweden. Peter also built St Petersburg, now Leningrad, as part of his aim of closer relationships with Europe.

Westernization continued under Catherine the Great who reigned from 1762 to 1796. Her successful campaigns against the Turks secured for Russia access to the Black Sea.

By this time Russia had become a major power allied with Prussia, Austria and Britain against Napoleon. The French emperor invaded Russia but his armies were routed in 1812/13.

The later nineteenth century was a time of discontent and risings, but it saw imperial expansion during which Russia acquired Kazakhstan, Turkestan, Uzbekistan and other large territories in eastern Asia.

Rivalry led to war with Japan and in 1905 the Russian fleet was ignominiously sunk after sailing halfway around the world for the engagement.

The defeat accelerated the major discontent at home. In the same year there was an abortive revolution which, however, forced Tsar Nicholas II to promise a new constitution and reforms.

Meanwhile the Marxist Social Democrat Party split up into its two factions: the Bolsheviks and the Mensheviks. The Bolsheviks, led by Vladimir Ulyanov, later to call himself Lenin, were much more radical and better organized.

Russia entered World War I against Germany and Austria. The conflict sharpened the misery at home and in 1917 the tsarist system collapsed and Lenin and his Bolsheviks came to power. The Tsar and, it is believed, his family were executed.

Civil war broke out despite the intervention of British, French and American forces on the side of the counter-revolutionary 'white' Russians, the Red Army was victorious.

Lenin died in 1924. His place was soon taken by Joseph Stalin who had established himself by the late 1920s and ruthlessly eliminated his rivals.

The Soviet people rallied to the defence of their motherland in World War II. After untold suffering they drove the German invader out and established

Map 35

ASTRAKHAN ★ 18

TEMPERATURE °C
31°

PRESSURE mb

PRECIPITATION mm
196mm

J F M A M J J A S O N D

ROSTOV 77

TEMPERATURE °C
29°

PRESSURE mb

PRECIPITATION mm
579 mm

J F M A M J J A S O N D

COPYRIGHT GEORGE PHILIP & SON. LTD.

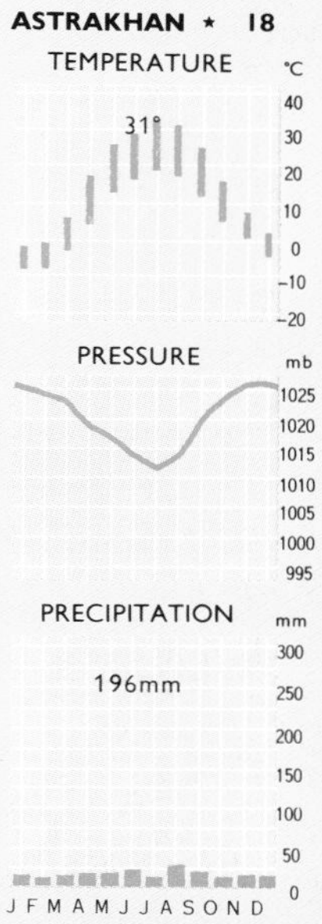

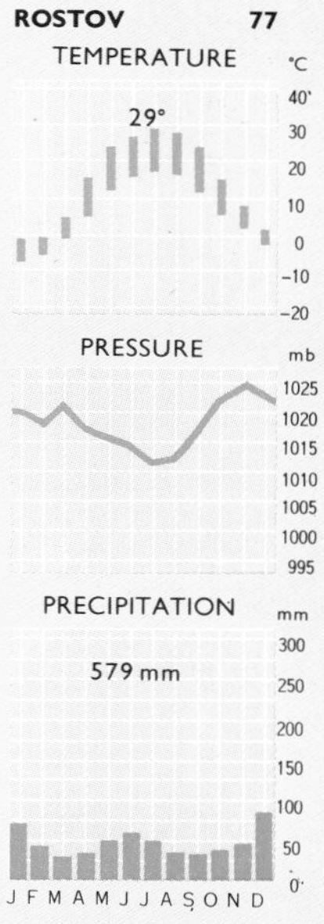

a buffer zone in the east European states.

Postwar tension between the USSR and the west led to a period of mutual suspicion and hostility known as the Cold War. However, after Stalin's death in 1953 the first signs of a thaw appeared and developed. At the same time Soviet relations with China deteriorated as the two major communist powers disagreed on the application of Marxist principles.

In 1961 Russia launched the first manned space flight and followed it with other spectacular achievements.

Relations between the USSR and the USA fluctuated during the 1970s and 80s. Observance of human rights and the ever growing arsenal of nuclear weapons were among contentious issues subjected to international negotiation.

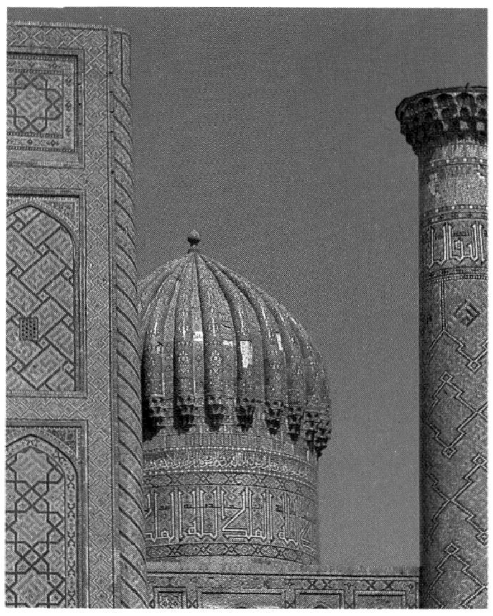

Left: *Islamic mosques, Soviet Samarkand.*

Mongolia

Mongolia is an independent republic in eastern Asia. It consists of a vast plateau, part of which is in the Gobi desert.

Mongolia lies between the USSR in the north and China in the south. The Altai Range rises 4,268m (14,000ft) in the north. The climate is extreme with severe winters and short summers. July temperatures reach 100°F (38°C) and fall to −54°F (−40°C) in January.

Three times larger than France, Mongolia is the most thinly populated country in the world with a population of about 1.9 million in an area of 1,565,000km^2 (604,250sq.m.). The capital, Ulan Bator, has about 400,000 inhabitants.

Outside the capital the Mongolian people are mainly nomadic herdsmen tending camels, sheep, goats and horses. The traditional religion is Buddhism. Chief exports are cattle, wool, hides and meat products. The country also has reserves of coal, gold, tungsten, uranium, petroleum and copper.

The state of Mongolia, founded by the great Mongol emperor Genghis Khan, emerged from Russian and Chinese domination in 1924 as an independent republic with a communist system of government similar to that of its major ally and trading partner, the USSR.

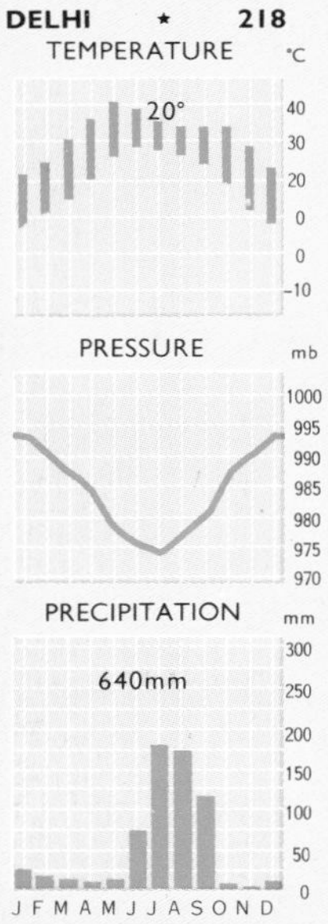

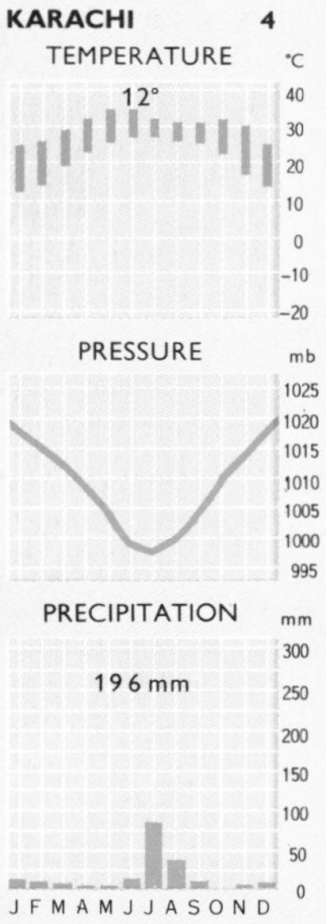

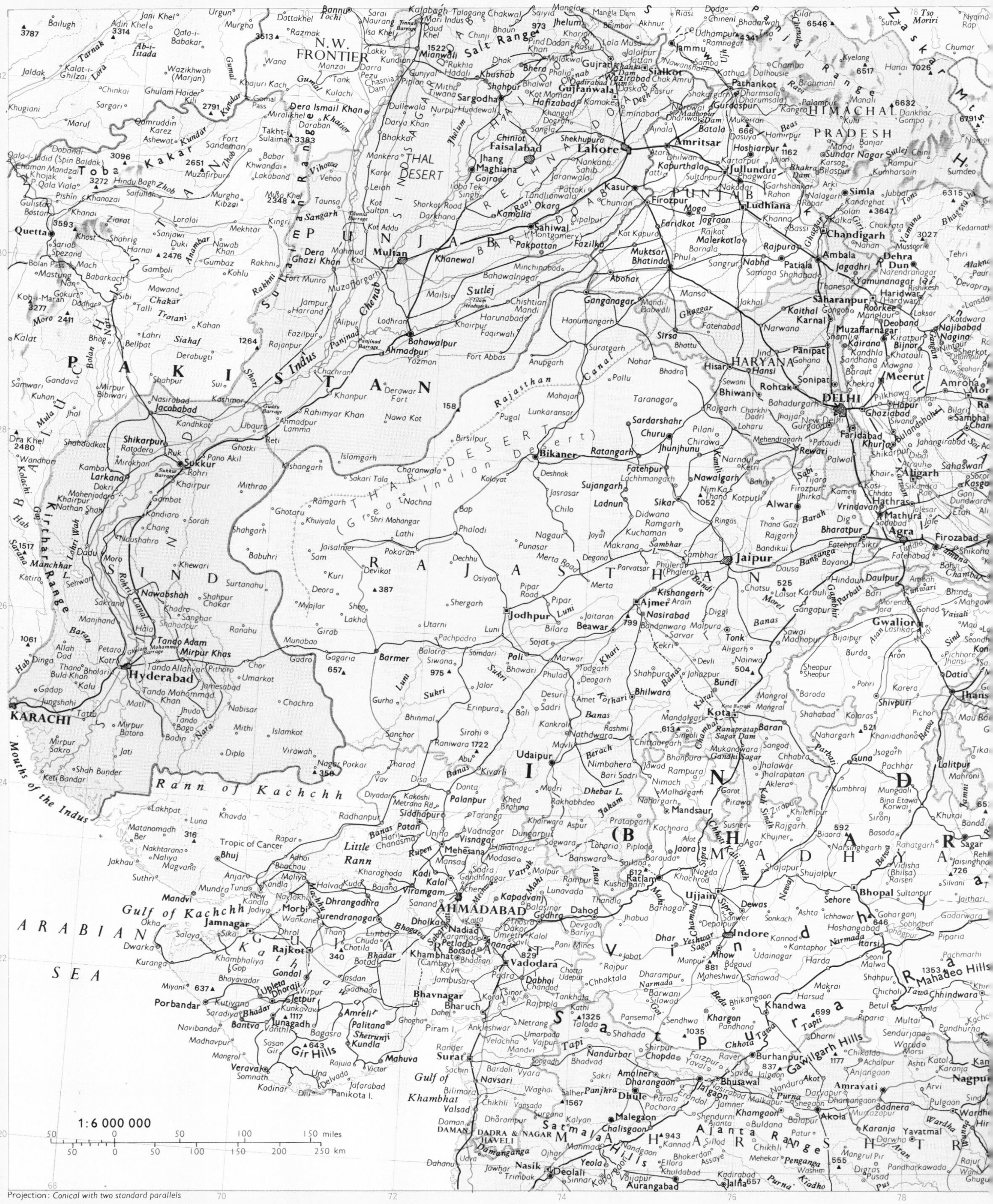

Pakistan

Area: 796,095km² (307,293sq.m.).
Population: 99 million.
Capital: Islamabad (340,000).
Largest city: Karachi (5.1m).
Languages: Punjabi, Urdu, English.
Ethnic groups: Punjabis, Sindhis, Pathans.
Main exports: cotton and leather goods, hides, skins, carpets.
Average temperatures: 19°C (66°F) Jan. 30°C (86°F) June on central plain.
Highest point: Nanga Parbat 8,125m (26,660ft).

The Islamic Republic of Pakistan was established as a home for India's large Moslem minority when British rule ended in 1947. It consisted originally of two sections 1,600km (1,000 miles) apart, but after civil war in 1971 the eastern section gained independence as Bangladesh. A country of few resources, with little more than 20 percent of its population literate, Pakistan faces formidable problems in coping with its high birthrate.

Most of the population farm or herd livestock in the eastern and central region of the Punjab, where the Indus and six other rivers irrigate a wide alluvial plain. North of the temperate upper Indus region the land rises to the towering wall of the Hindu Kush. Mountain ranges extend southward to the arid

Right: *The Hunza river in north Pakistan flows from China through the Himalayas.*

Map 37

KABUL ★ 1815

TEMPERATURE °C

28°

PRESSURE mb

PRECIPITATION mm

338mm

J F M A M J J A S O N D

CALCUTTA ★ 6

TEMPERATURE °C

11°

PRESSURE mb

PRECIPITATION mm

1600mm

J F M A M J J A S O N D

COPYRIGHT GEORGE PHILIP & SON, LTD

SOUTHERN ASIA
POLITICAL
1 : 40 000 000

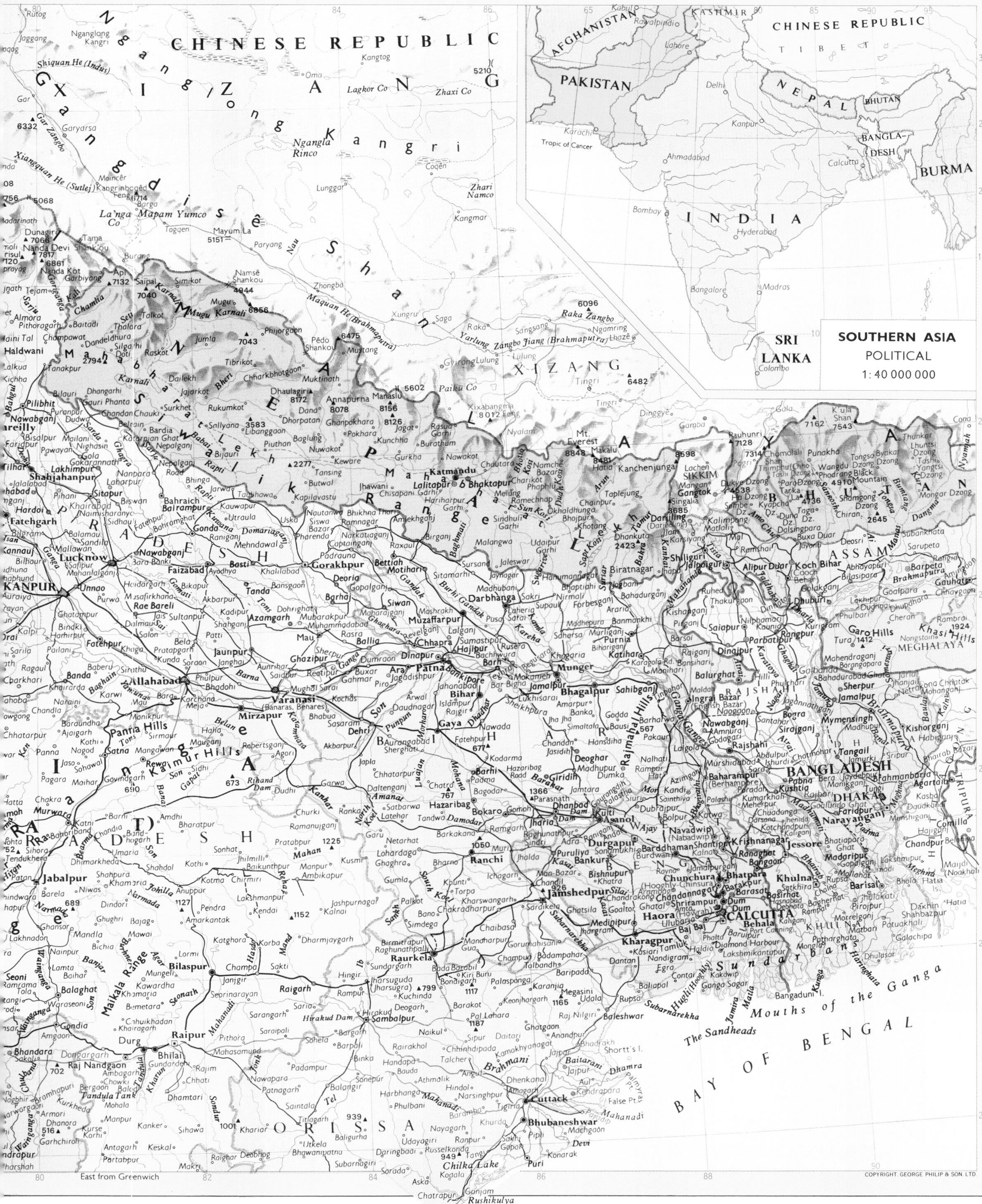

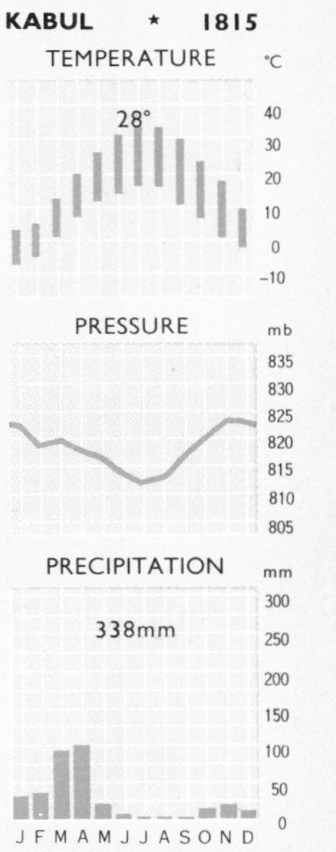

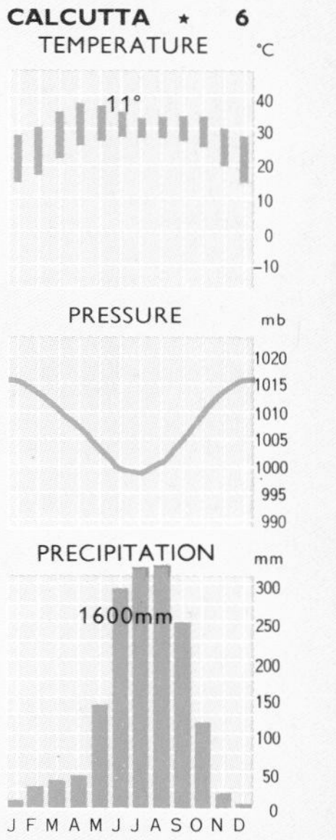

plateaus of Baluchistan to the west.

The monsoon climate is characterized by hot, dry summers with temperatures above 40°C on the plain, ending in a rainy season. From October to March, a cold dry wind blows from the northeast.

Wheat is the staple crop with cotton, sugar cane, rice and tobacco also grown. Rich fishing grounds provide vital protein in the national diet. Energy resources include a huge natural gas field at Sui, oil on the Potwar plateau and considerable hydro-electric potential. Low-grade coal seams are worked and there are iron ore deposits.

The Islamic faith, followed by nearly 90 per cent of the population, is the main cohesive force in a nation of diverse cultures and languages. Unlike India, Pakistan has been unable to pre-serve its democratic institutions in the face of military intervention. Major problems have been created by the introduction of Islamic law and the arrival of refugees from Afghanistan.

Bangladesh

Area: 143,999km² (55,598sq.m.).
Population: 101 million.
Capital: Dhaka (Dacca) (3.4m).
Languages: Bengali, Urdu, Hindi.
Ethnic groups: Bengalis, Biharis.
Main exports: jute, skins, hides.
Average temperature: 28°C (82°F).
Highest point: Mt Keokradong 1,230m (4,034ft).

Bangladesh emerged as a new nation in 1971 when the Bengali majority in East Pakistan asserted independence in a civil war that left an already undernourished population in widespread poverty. With a birthrate increasing at 2.8 percent a year and a population density of 666 per square kilometre, the country is forced to import grains, adding to the economic burden of paying for vital imports of fuel, fertilizers and machine goods.

Bangladesh occupies the largest delta in the world, a flat, fertile plain crossed by the Ganges, Brahmaputra and Meghna rivers. The monsoonal climate is generally warm and humid with high

Right: *Traditional and modern water transport at a village in the coastal riverine area of southern Bangladesh.*

Map 38 SOUTHERN INDIA AND SRI LANKA

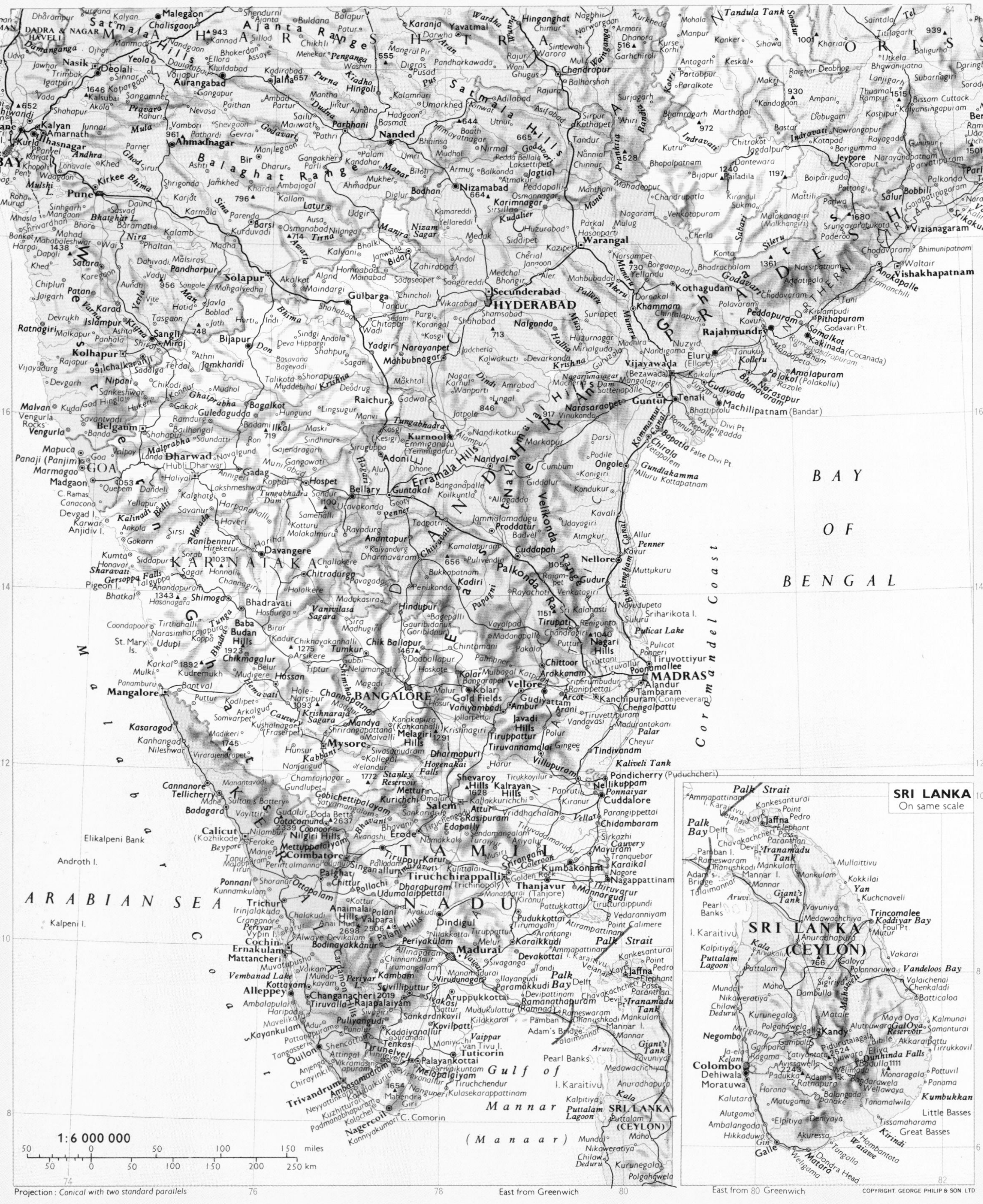

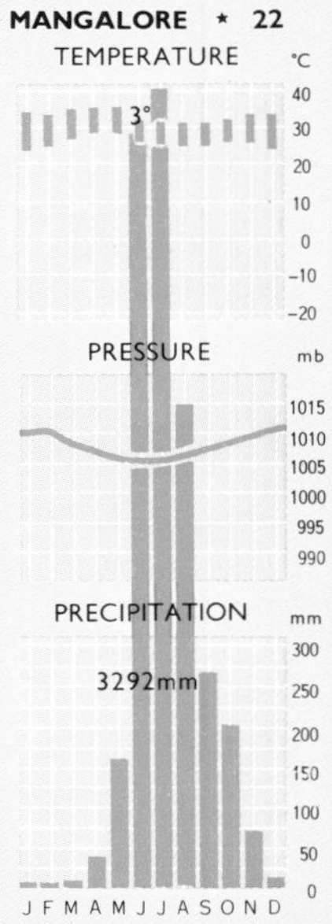

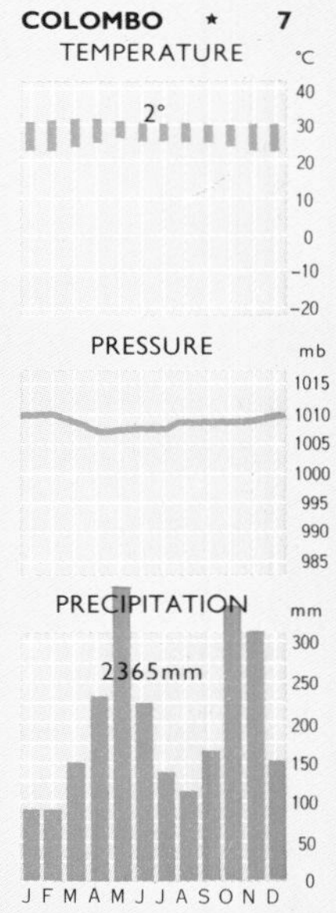

temperatures in April and heavy rain between June and October. Floods, often resulting from cyclones and tidal waves funnelled up the Bay of Bengal, menace harvests and bring starvation and death.

The population is 80 percent Moslem and overwhelmingly rural, mostly small farmers living in stilt houses and using ancient methods to produce the staple food, rice. The major cash crop, jute, accounts for half the total world supply and jute processing is the only significant export earning industry. Fishing is important and tea is also grown. The development of the economy has been hampered by political instability and by natural disasters. Exploitation of off-shore oil resources may prove an asset.

Nepal

Area: 145,391km^2 (56,136sq.m.).
Population: 16.1 million.
Capital: Katmandu (210,000).
Language: Nepali.
Ethnic groups: Nepalis, Gurkhas, Sherpas.
Main exports: cattle, hides, timber.
Average temperatures: 10°C (50°F) Jan. 24.4°C (76°F) July in Katmandu.
Highest point: Mt Everest *(Sagarmatha)* 8,848m (29,028ft).

Nepal is an independent consitutional monarchy famed as the birthplace of Gautama Buddha and the main point of access to the world's highest peak, Mt Everest (Sagarmatha). From the sub-arctic temperatures of the high Himalayas, the land falls through temperate mountain valleys to warm swampy plains (Terai) near the Indian border.

Jute and sugar cane are grown in the Terai region and forests covering more than half the country provide timber. Most of the people are illiterate subsistence farmers growing rice, maize and millet, but tourism and small industries are developing rapidly.

Bhutan

The independent Buddhist kingdom of Bhutan is a constitutional monarchy bordered by India (which controls its foreign affairs) and Tibet. It has an area of 47,000km^2 (18,147sq,m,), a population of some 1.25 million and a capital at Thimbu (15,000). From the icy peaks of the Eastern Himalayas, the land falls to sub-tropical river valleys and plains near the Indian border. The people are mainly illiterate herdsmen and farmers.

Jammu and Kashmir

Kashmir is the subject of a territorial dispute between India, which controls two-thirds of the country through a governing assembly, and Pakistan, which holds the north-western remainder. A beautiful mountainous region, it has an area of 222,237km² (85,806 sq.m.) and a population of 5.98 million, two-thirds Moslem. The capital is Srinagar (520,000) in summer and Jammu (200,000) in winter, when upland temperatures fall to freezing point. Most of the people grow rice, maize, wheat and fruit in the Vale of Kashmir or weave wool and silk in cottage industries. Mt Godwin Austen 8,611m (28,250ft) is the highest of many peaks in the Himalaya and Karakoram ranges which dominate the territory.

India

Area: 3,166,829km² (1,222,395sq.m.).
Population: 762 million.
Capital: New Delhi (5.7m).
Largest city: Calcutta (9.17m).
Languages: Hindi and English principal of 10 major languages.
Ethnic groups: Indo-Aryan, Dravidian, Mongoloid.
Main exports: tea, jute, coffee, cotton goods, hides and skins, iron ore.
Average temperatures: 29°C (85°F) June, 21°F (70°F) Jan. in Delhi.
Highest point: Nanda Devi 7,817m (25,645ft).

Above: *The ruins of an ancient stronghold known as Lion Mountain, built on a rock pillar in Sigiriya, Sri Lanka.*

Left: *Eighty percent of India's population still lives in villages, like this one in Bangalore in the south of India.*

India, although only the seventh biggest country in the world in area, has the second highest population. Culturally the centre of Hinduism, it has been deeply influenced by the 200 years of British rule that preceded its independence in 1947. During this time the railway system (fourth largest in the world), bureaucracy, language and constitutional traditions of the British established patterns that remain embedded in Indian life.

Physically, India is shut off from central Asia by the great mountain wall of the Himalayas, with many peaks rising above 7,000 metres (23,000ft). South of this arc lies a wide plain irrigated by the three immense river systems of the Indus, Ganges and Brahmaputra. This mainly flat alluvial plain supports much of India's population. The Indian Peninsula is dominated by the Deccan Plateau which rises to the Western Ghats. A narrow coastal plain lies between these hills and the Arabian Sea. East of the Eastern Ghats, a broader plain is crossed by several major rivers.

Peninsular India lies within the Tropic of Cancer and throughout the subcontinent the climate is generally warm and humid with summer temperatures rising to 38°C (100°F) or higher in the Ganges plain. The dominant climatic influences are seasonal monsoons which bring rain from June to September, particularly heavy in Assam. A drier wind brings a cool season from December to February. Hot, dry weather from March to May precedes the return of heavy rain.

Agriculture and industry

The average per capita income in India is less than $US260 a year and undernourishment affects millions. Although the country has some 182 million cattle and 62 million buffaloes, Hinduism forbids their slaughter for meat. The milk yield is low and agricultural methods are generally inefficient with little application of technology. The demand for food has led to the deforestation of much of the country and farm land covers about half the total area. But with nearly 70 percent of the population engaged in agriculture (many as sharecroppers), farm organization is inefficient and in spite of production improvements through the 'Green Revolution', staples such as rice and wheat have to be imported to bolster output.

India has large reserves of coal in the northeast and some of the world's biggest and best-grade deposits of iron ore in the east and south of the Peninsula. It also leads the world in production of mica and is second in manganese output. Bauxite is among a wide range of other mineral resources, and oil output from Assam and offshore rigs in the Gulf of Cambay is rising.

Industrial production is based on a series of five-year plans which have rapidly expanded the steel, engineering and electrical industries. About half the factory workforce is employed in the most successful industry, textiles. India is third in world production of cotton goods. Industry is concentrated mainly in the northeast, coastal west and south, with Bombay a major textiles area.

People, constitution and history

India is a democratic federal republic and member of the Commonwealth of Nations. Strongly centralized rule is exercised by the government in New Delhi, dominated since the first elections in 1952 by the Congress Party. Religion plays a crucial role in India. More than 83 percent of the population is Hindu and the laws of this faith influence both social and economic life. There are 3,000 castes, each imposing specific restrictions. Laws prohibiting unequal treatment because of caste, religion or sex are only slowly changing traditional attitudes. Despite free schooling until 14, literacy has risen to only 36 percent. With 845 languages and dialects spoken in India, the choice of Hindi as the official language (replacing English) in 1965 aroused tensions as access to the best jobs now depends on its mastery.

The Indian people are descended from the intermarriage of dark Dravidians who settled the Indus valley about 3000 BC and Aryans who invaded it about 1500 BC. Muslim and Mongol invasions after the 11th century led to the Mogul empire which disintegrated before the inroads of European traders, culminating in the rule of the British East India Company in the mid-1800s. When the British withdrew in 1947 the subcontinent was partitioned into Muslim Pakistan and Hindu India after bloody riots. India's most severe economic problem continues to be her population growth, averaging 2.5 percent, 15 million, a year.

Sri Lanka

Area: 65,610km² (25,332sq.m.).
Population: 16.4 million.
Capital: Colombo (1.4m).
Languages: Sinhala, English, Tamil.
Ethnic groups: Sinhalese (75 percent), Tamils, Moors, Burghers.
Main exports: tea, rubber, coconut products, graphite.
Average temperature: 27°C (80°F).
Highest point: Pidurutalagala 2,524m (8,281ft).

Sri Lanka, a vivid tropical island 32 kilometres (20 miles) off the southeastern coast of India, is an important shipping entrepôt and producer of tea and rubber. Its main trading partner is Britain which colonized the island in 1802 and granted it independence in 1948. Today Sri Lanka is a socialist republic increasingly torn by conflict between the Sinhalese (Buddhist) majority and the Tamil (Hindu) minority.

A low coastal plain, broad in the north, surrounds a mountainous interior and is irrigated by many narrow rivers. Sea breezes on the coast and altitude in the hills temper the tropical climate. There are dry zones in the north-east but rainfall is heavy in the south-west where most of the cash crops are grown. Sri Lanka is second only to India in tea production, but has to import much of its staple foods.

Sri Lanka has the world's biggest output of high-quality graphite and there are gemstone deposits. Forests covering 40 percent of the island are rich in ebony and other hardwoods. The waters of the Mahaweli and Amban Ganga provide crop irrigation and hydro-electric power. Sri Lanka has a fishing fleet of some 27,000 vessels.

Map 39 | THE EAST INDIES

RANGOON ★ 5
TEMPERATURE °C
2616mm

SINGAPORE 10
TEMPERATURE °C
2413mm

1:12 500 000

Projection: Mercator

East from Greenwich

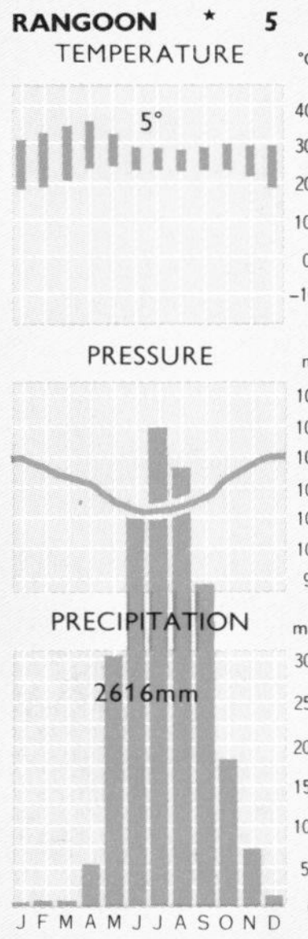

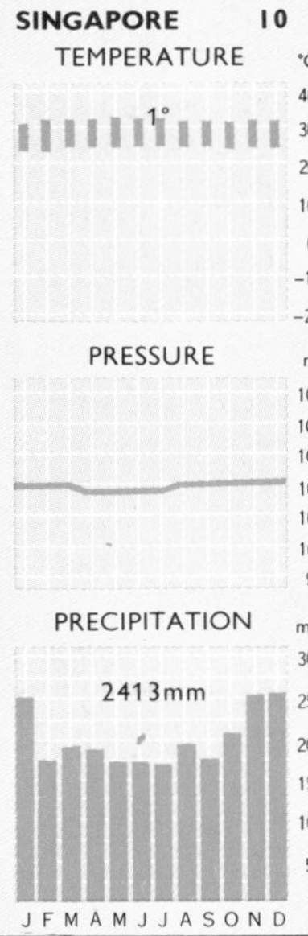

The Philippines

Area: 299,404km² (115,600sq.m.).
Population: 56.8 million.
Capital: Manila (5.92m).
Languages: Filipino (Tagalog), English, Spanish.
Ethnic groups: Malayo-Polynesian (90 percent), Chinese, Spanish, American.
Main exports: timber, copra, sugar, hemp, tobacco, electrical goods.
Average temperatures: 24°C (75°F) Jan. 28°C (82°F) June (coastal).
Highest point: Mt Apo 2,954m (9,692ft).

The only predominantly Christian nation in Asia (80 percent Roman Catholic), the Republic of the Philip-

pines comprises 730 inhabited islands and thousands of coral atolls forming a splintered triangle between Taiwan to the north and Borneo to the south. It is a country of brilliant-hued flowers, dense rainforests, swift rivers, active volcanoes and picturesque villages of raised bamboo or rattan huts amidst rice, maize, sweet potato and banana cultivations. The climate is hot and wet with frequent typhoons between June and November.

More than half of the population live by farming or fishing. The volcanic mountain chain running the length of the islands leaves only narrow coastal plains in most areas but the Philippines has achieved self-sufficiency in rice by high-yield plantations on the main island of Luzon.

Hydro-electric and geothermal power is being developed and manufacturing

Above: *Outrigger canoes on the Rio Hondo near Zamboanga in the Philippines.*

industries have been started with the aid of the USA which is the Republic's main trading partner. But most of the work-force is engaged in agricultural processing with 1.2 million in coconut production. The Philippines is the world's leading copra producer and a major supplier of abaca (Manila hemp), used in making rope. It has valuable high-quality hardwoods such as mahogany, and is the world's sixth biggest timber producer.

Independence, achieved in 1946, followed 350 years of Spanish and nearly 50 years of American control. Spanish-American cultural influence is strong. The Philippines show sharp inequalities in wealth, and this led to increasing social unrest and insurrection during the presidency of Ferdinand Marcos, which was marked by periods of martial law and

Map 40

JAVA AND MADURA

50   0   50   100   150   200 miles
50   0   50   100   150   200   250   300 km

JAKARTA   8
TEMPERATURE   °C
PRESSURE   mb
PRECIPITATION   mm
1798mm
J F M A M J J A S O N D

SANDAKAN   46
TEMPERATURE   °C
PRESSURE   mb
PRECIPITATION   mm
3142mm
J F M A M J J A S O N D

COPYRIGHT. GEORGE PHILIP & SON. LTD

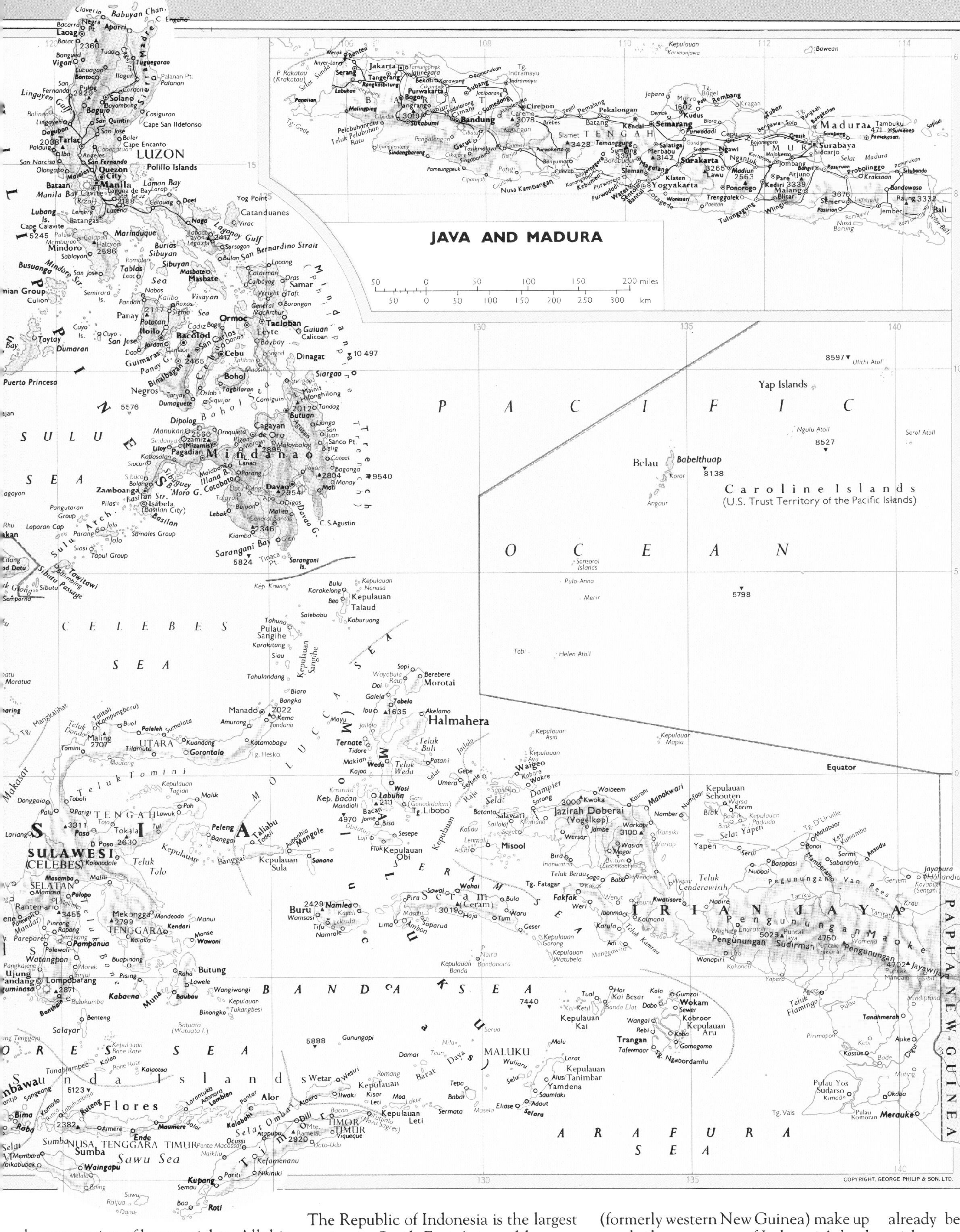

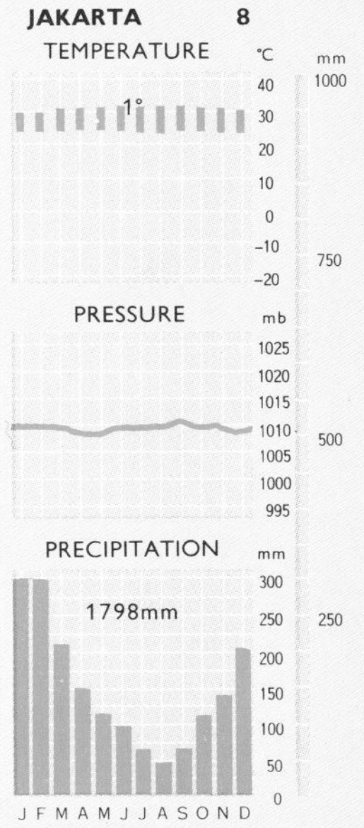

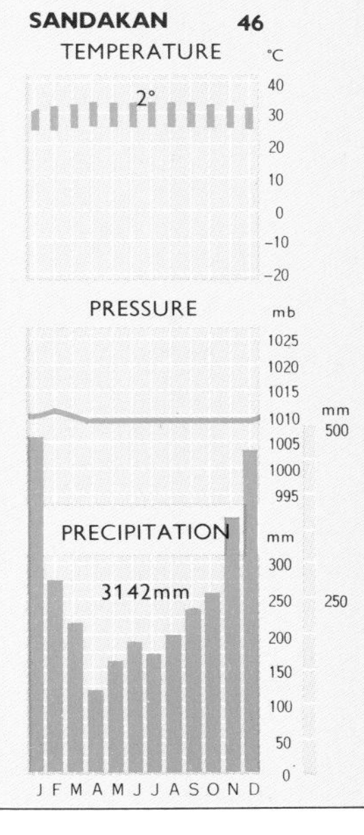

the suppression of human rights. All this ended in February 1986 with the election of the liberal, Mrs Corazon Aquino, and Marcos fled into exile.

Indonesia

Area: 1,919,400km² (741,101sq.m.).
Population: 168 million.
Capital: Jakarta (6.5m).
Languages: Bahasa Indonesian, Malayo-Polynesian dialects.
Ethnic groups: Javanese (50 percent), Sundanese, Malay, Chinese.
Main exports: oil and petroleum products, timber, rubber, coffee, tin.
Average temperature: 27°C (80°F).
Highest point: Punjak Jaya, 5,029m (16,503ft).

The Republic of Indonesia is the largest nation in South-East Asia and by population the fifth biggest in the world. Its gross national product is only about a twentieth of Japan's, however. An archipelago of more than 13,600 islands stretching from the Indian Ocean to the Pacific between the land masses of South-East Asia and Australia, it has a wet, tropical climate with a spectacular variety of wildlife. Most of the islands are mountainous, heavily forested and thinly populated. There are more than 400 volcanoes, 100 of them active. Though its population is mainly of Malay stock and is overwhelmingly Moslem, the Republic has three million Chinese who run much of its commercial life.

The three biggest islands, Kalimantan (Borneo), Sumatra and Irian Jaya (formerly western New Guinea) make up nearly three-quarters of Indonesia's land area but nearly two-thirds of the population is crammed on the most fertile rice-growing island, Java. The Indonesian government is trying to remedy this by moving people from Java to the less populated islands. In addition to the capital, Jakarta, Java has the two next biggest cities, Surabaya (2.03 million) and Bandung (1.46 million). Manufacturing industry is growing, but most of the population still depends on subsistence rice farming, though Indonesia is not yet self-sufficient in this staple crop.

Ample resources of oil, wood, coal, and hydro-electric power give Indonesia considerable industrial potential but there are transport and other difficulties in developing it. Sumatra, Kalimantan and Java have large oil fields and oil has already become the mainstay of trade with more than 480 million barrels exported annually. Tin, bauxite and nickel are important mineral products, with others yet to be developed. Production of rubber, formerly Indonesia's main export, is again rising, while teak is the most important wood in a timber industry of great potential.

After more than three centuries of Dutch control, Indonesia won independence in 1949. Since the failure of a communist coup in 1965, the country has established closer relations with the Western bloc, trading mainly with the USA, Japan and Singapore. With the consent of a People's Consultative Assembly, its president rules through an executive backed by the armed forces (275,000 strong). Literacy, now 70 percent, is being increased rapidly.

Map 41 | MAINLAND SOUTH-EAST ASIA

MANDALAY ✱ 77
TEMPERATURE ℃
11°
PRESSURE mb
PRECIPITATION mm
828mm
J F M A M J J A S O N D

BANGKOK 2
TEMPERATURE ℃
5°
PRESSURE mb
PRECIPITATION mm
1397mm
J F M A M J J A S O N D

PENINSULAR MALAYSIA AND SINGAPORE
1:6 000 000
50   0   50 miles
50   0   50 km

Projection: Conical with two standard parallels

1:10 000 000
50   0   50   100   150   200 miles
50   0   100   200   300 km

East from Greenwich

COPYRIGHT. GEORGE PHILIP & SON. LTD.

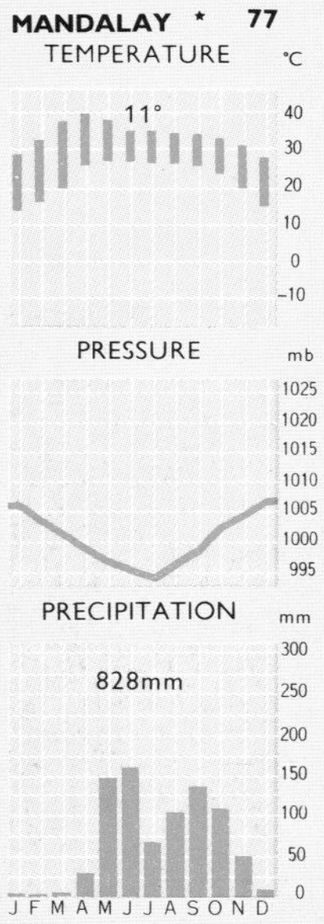

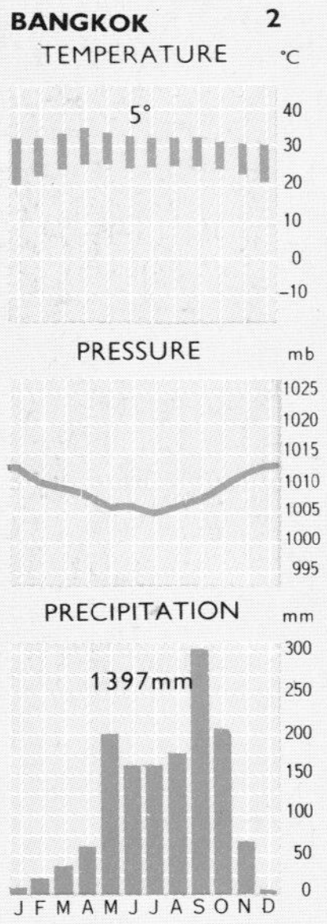

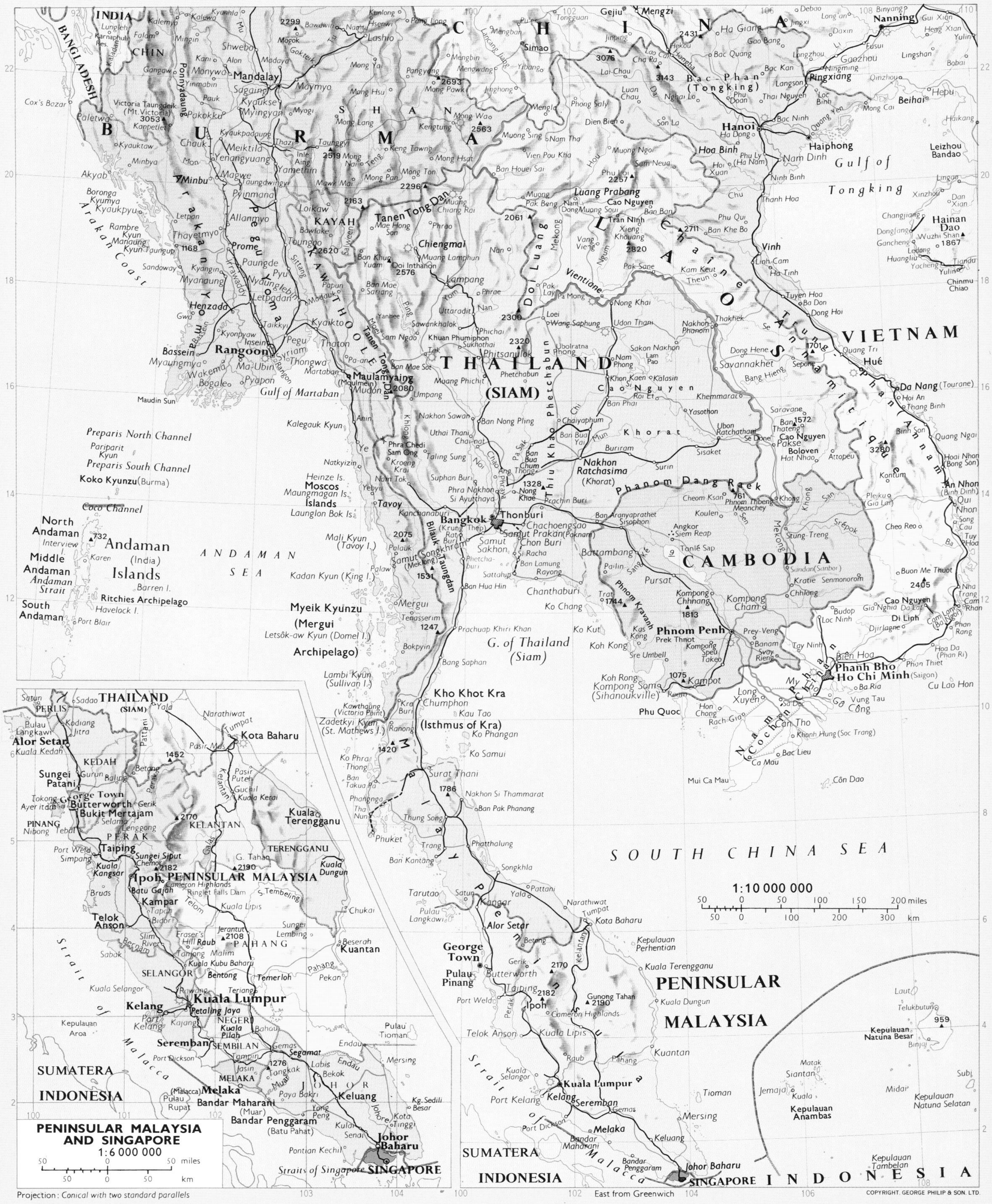

Burma

Area: 678,033km² (261,790sq.m.).
Population: 35.31 million.
Capital: Rangoon (2.46m).
Languages: Burmese and many Sino-Tibetan tongues.
Ethnic groups: Burmese, Chinese (450,000), Indian (180,000).
Main exports: rice, teak, rubber, oil, minerals.
Average temperatures: 33℃ (92°F) April, 21℃ (70°F) Dec. in Rangoon but much colder in high country.
Highest point: Gjajabi Razi 5,881m (19,295ft).

The Socialist Republic of the Union of Burma has chosen a Buddhist way to socialism and has succeeded in isolating itself from political alignments in its region. Settled originally from China and Tibet, Burma became a British province of India in 1885, won independence in 1948 and has been a one-party state since 1962. Little touched by western technology, it is a vivid green land of myriad temples and pagodas, the most famous being the 2,500-year old Shwe Dagon pagoda in Rangoon.

Upper Burma is mountainous and thickly forested with major valleys formed by rivers running to the Bay of Bengal, the longest of which is the Irrawaddy (2,012km; 1,250 miles). This river system spreads out into a wide delta west of Rangoon. In the south, a narrow swampy coastal strip hemmed in by mountains runs down into the Malay Peninsula. Burma's hot, wet climate and fertile plains make it a rich rice-growing area and four-fifths of the annual crop is exported. With tropical forests covering half the country, Burma is the world's leading supplier of teak and a major producer of bamboo. The population is 80 percent rural and apart from crafts there is little manufacturing. The opium trade has long been an important source of wealth in the interior. Oil in the Irrawaddy valley supplies all local needs. Fine jade and gemstones are among many mineral resources. Burma trades mainly with Britain, India, Indonesia and Japan.

Laos

Area: 236,800km² (91,429sq.m.).
Population: 3.8 million.
Capital: Vientiane (177,000).
Language: Lao.
Ethnic groups: Lao (56 percent), Meo, Thai, Kha, Yao.
Main exports: opium, handicrafts.
Average temperatures: 28℃ (82°F) July, 21℃ (70°F) Jan.
Highest point: Mt Bia 2,817m (9,242ft).

Laos was once known as Lan Xang – 'land of a million elephants'. It is a mountainous, humid, densely forested country cut off from its neighbouring

Above: *Wood and bamboo buildings built on piles, on Ince Lake, Burma.*

Above right: *Women threshing corn on the fertile valley plains of Thailand.*

states by the Annamese mountains in the north and east and by the broad Mekong River on the west. Laos has rich teak forests and undeveloped reserves of gold, gypsum, lead, silver, tin and zinc.

Along the Mekong, which forms the boundary with Thailand, fertile rice-growing areas support most of the population. Corn, tobacco and cotton are grown in highland areas and the Meo hill people harvest large crops of opium. Thatched houses on bamboo stilts are common in lower areas where heavy monsoon rain between May and September brings flooding. Though China is constructing a highway in the north, most of the roads are passable only in dry weather. There are no railways and the Mekong and its tributaries provide the main means of transport, but air travel is increasingly important.

Buddhist Laos was part of French Indo-China for 50 years until 1954 when it became an independent constitutional monarchy with a royal capital at Luang Prabang. Efforts to form a neutral government broke down in 1960 and a war between Royal Lao forces, backed by the United States, and the Pathet Lao, backed by North Vietnam, became a key part of the bigger conflict in Vietnam because of supply trails running through Laos. Two years after a ceasefire in 1973 the Pathet Lao took over the government and ended the monarchy.

Above: *At the edge of the Himalayan chain Thailand's river valleys are dotted with paddy fields and tropical forests.*

Vietnam

Area: 329,566km^2 (127,219sq.m.).
Population: 60.5 million.
Capital: Hanoi (2.6m).
Languages: Vietnamese, Montagnard dialects.
Ethnic groups: Vietnamese (84 percent), Montagnard (3.2 million), Chinese (800,000), Cambodian.
Main exports: coal, rubber, rice.
Average temperatures: 29°C (85°F) June, 17.4°C (63°F) Jan. in Hanoi but rarely below 26°C (79°F) in Ho Chi Minh City.
Highest point: Fan Si Pan 3,143m (10,312ft).

In the course of three bitter Indo-China wars between 1945 and 1975, Vietnam was divided in two, disrupting an economic balance between the coal-based industrial resources of the north and the rich rice-producing region of the south. Following the withdrawal of US forces in 1973 and the final defeat of the southern army in 1975, the two economies have been integrated on socialist lines.

Physically, Vietnam consists of the deltas of the Hong (Red) and Mekong rivers, linked by a narrow coastal plain with the Annamite mountain chain extending from the borders of China in the north down the western side of the country towards Ho Chi Minh City. The Hong River drains rich, densely-populated farmland protected by dykes against summer floods. To the west, the country is mountainous jungle, inhabited mainly by Montagnard tribes. Rice is grown in the middle coastal lowlands but the most fertile areas lie in the broad southern delta of the Mekong.

The years of war severely damaged the Vietnamese economy, but recovery has been assisted by international aid. Nearly three-quarters of the workforce live off the land, the chief crops being sugar cane, rice, maize, cotton and sweet potatoes. Rubber is also produced. There are stocks of two million cattle and 11.4 million pigs. Agriculture is organized on state and collective lines, and in the south urban families have been resettled to work in the countryside since the war. There are mineral reserves of coal, iron ore, manganese, bauxite, and chromite. Industries include cement, paper making and textiles. Hydro-electric power is being developed.

The Vietnamese people originally expanded southwards from China. They followed the Buddhist faith. The country was under French rule during the colonial era, and in subsequent civil wars was subjected to United States and Australian intervention. After the war Vietnam became involved in further conflicts with China and Cambodia. Vietnam today enjoys an 87 percent adult literacy rate.

Thailand

Area: 514,000km^2 (198,457sq.m.).
Population: 52.7 million.
Capital: Bangkok (5.5m).
Languages: Thai, Chinese, Malay.
Ethnic groups: Thai, Chinese (4 million), Malay, Vietnamese.
Main exports: rice, rubber, tin, maize, timber, jute.
Average temperatures: 33°C (92°F) April, 24°F (75°F) Nov. in Bangkok.
Highest point: Inthanom Peak 2,595m (8,514ft).

The fertile, densely-forested kingdom of Thailand is among the most prosperous nations of its region and the only one never colonized by Europeans. It has steep mountains in the northwest and the high, dry Khorat Plateau on the east, but most of its population is concentrated in the broad rice-growing valley formed by the Chao Phraya River which runs to the port capital of Bangkok, a crowded, cosmopolitan city built over canals. Southern Thailand is a narrow mountainous strip extending into the Malay Peninsula.

Three-quarters of the people are engaged in rice-growing and live in small villages grouped around Buddhist *wats*. Thailand exports a sixth of its 19 million tonne annual rice crop. It is the world's third largest rubber producer, mainly from plantations in the south. Thailand is also an important supplier of tin and other varied mineral resources are underdeveloped. Its silk, lacquer and handicrafts are famous. With investment from the USA and Japan, manufacturing and hydroelectric power are being developed.

Thailand's climate is dominated by heavy monsoon rain between May and September. The rail and road system is still rudimentary and water transport and fishing are important in the economy. Forests, mainly of teak, cover nearly 60 percent of the land and teem with bird and animal life; elephants are used in the timber industry.

The slim, small-boned Thai people have a distinctive and colourful culture. A large Chinese minority is active in commercial life. The Thai state was founded about 1350. A constitutional monarchy with a civilian government but a recent tradition of military rule, Thailand was strongly pro-western in the 1950s when the South-East Asia Treaty Organization headquarters was established in Bangkok. A skilful diplomatic balance is maintained with Thailand's neighbours and rural unrest, mainly in the north, has been contained.

Top: *The dinh (market) is the centre of village activity for Vietnam's overwhelmingly rural population.*

Above: *Rural dwellings in West Malaysia are of wood, with thatched roofing called* atap, *and are often surrounded by trees.*

Cambodia (Kampuchea)

Area: 181,035km² (71,000sq.m.).
Population: 16.2 million.
Capital: Phnom Penh (formerly 500,000).
Languages: Khmer, French, Chinese.
Ethnic groups: Khmer, Chinese, Vietnamese.
Main exports: formerly rubber, corn, rice.
Average temperature: 29°C (85°F).

Cambodia (Democratic Kampuchea) was once the centre of an empire controlling much of South-East Asia. Angkor Wat and other ancient Buddhist-Hindu ruins north of the Tonle Sap (Great Lake) bear witness to one thousand years of Khmer culture. A French protectorate from 1863 to 1953, Cambodia was embroiled in the Vietnam conflict in 1970 when civil war followed the dissolution of the monarchy. The victorious National United Front of Cambodia (Khmers Rouges) inaugurated a Marxist state in 1975. In 1979 the regime fell to Vietnamese invaders, and its leader, Pol Pot, commenced a guerrilla war. In 1982 a coalition was formed between opposing factions.

Bordered by low mountains, the country is predominantly flat and wet. It is dominated by the Mekong River which rises under heavy monsoon rains (May-November) and reverses the Tonle Sap river, flooding a large area around the lake. This is a crucial feature of the subsistence rice-growing and internal fishing economy on which 90 percent of the population depends. The years of war and subsequent unrest saw great hardship, atrocities carried out upon the civilian population, and a total disruption of industry and rubber production.

Malaysia

Area: 330,435km² (127,581sq.m.).
Population: 15.7 million.
Capital: Kuala Lumpur (510,000).
Languages: Bahasa Malay, English, Chinese.
Ethnic groups: Malay (45 percent), Chinese (36 percent), Indian (10 percent).
Main exports: rubber, timber, tin, palm oil, iron ore.
Average temperatures: 27°C (81°F) in West Malaysia; 31°C (88°F) in East Malaysia.
Highest point: Mt Kinabalu (Sabah) 4,101m (13,455ft).

The Federation of Malaysia is a constitutional monarchy within the Commonwealth made up of 13 states, nine of them Moslem sultanates. Two of these states – Sabah and Sarawak – are former British protectorates in northern Borneo (Eastern Malaysia) and are separated from the Malay peninsula by the South China Sea. Apart from cool highland areas, Malaysia is hot and damp with dense jungle covering much of the country, particularly in Eastern Malaysia. Sabah and Sarawak are mountainous and the coastal plains of the peninsula are also divided by central ranges. Rainfall is heavy from November to March.

Much of the population is concentrated in coastal villages and illiteracy is high. But efficient production of rubber, tin, timber and other natural resources has produced a relatively high standard of living. Malaysia is the world's leading rubber producer and supplies more than a third of the world's tin concentrates. There are oil fields off the east coast of the peninsula as well as off Sabah and Sarawak and refineries in Sarawak process oil from the neighbouring state of Brunei.

The most multi-racial nation of the region, Malaysia has coped well with tensions between the rural Malay majority and a predominantly urban, highly-skilled Chinese minority. The election of 1982 returned a National Front majority to the House of Representatives. Strong links are retained with Britain which controlled and developed the peninsula for a century and granted it independence after a long struggle against communist insurgency. Japan is now a major investor and is Malaysia's main trading partner.

Singapore

Area: 618km² (238.6sq.m.).
Population: 2.5 million.
Languages: Malay, Mandarin Chinese, Tamil, English.
Ethnic groups: Chinese (74 percent), Malay (14 percent), Indian (8 percent).
Main exports: petroleum products and oil, processed rubber, ships, electrical goods.
Average temperature: 27°C (80°F).

The tiny but dynamic island republic of Singapore, separated from the Malay peninsula by a causeway across the 1.2km-wide Johore Strait, has the highest standard of living in South-East Asia. Its wealth is based largely on the skill with which its Chinese majority has exploited a fine harbour at the crossroads of Asian sea lanes to become the world's fourth biggest port and a major trading, shipbuilding and processing entrepôt.

A former British colony, Singapore became independent within the Commonwealth in 1959. A brief political marriage with Malaysia was broken off in 1965 and the city state is a capitalist democracy strictly governed since independence by the People's Action Party.

The warm climate is tempered by sea breezes. Annual rainfall averages 241cm (95in). The low-lying, swampy terrain is intensively cultivated but much of the republic's food has to be imported. About 90 percent of the population lives in the city where shipbuilding yards, petrochemical plants, oil refineries, engineering works, mills and factories are concentrated.

Brunei

Brunei is a former oil-rich British protectorate which refused to join the Malaysian federation. It achieved independence in 1983. A sultanate surrounded by Sarawak in northern Borneo, it has an area of 5,765km² (2,226sq.m.) and a population of 214,00, mainly Malay and Chinese (25 percent). The capital is Banda Seri Begawan (pop. 37,000). Brunei has rich offshore and onshore oil fields.

Above: *China's Stone Forest, Shilin, is a maze of grey peaks and pinnacles.*

The People's Republic of China

Area: 9,597,000km² (3,704,400sq.m.).
Population: 1,042 million.
Capital: Beijing or Peking (11m).
Largest city: Shanghai (13m).
Languages: Mandarin (official) and many other Chinese dialects, chiefly Wu, Cantonese, Fukien, Hakka.
Ethnic groups: Sinitic, Mongoloid.
Main exports: agricultural products, silk and textiles, tin, molybdenum, tea.
Average temperatures: −7°C (20°F) Jan. in north and central areas but warmer in south and −23°C (−10°F) in northwest and Tibet. 27°C (80°F) in July, but hotter in deserts and cooler in the mountains.
Highest point: Mt Everest (Qongolongma) 8,848m (29,028ft).

China has the biggest population of any country (about a fifth of the world total) and the third largest land area after the USSR and Canada. Its Chinese name, Chung Kuo (Middle Kingdom) reflects its importance as the oldest independent nation, with a history stretching back more than 2,000 years. Its ancient civilization invented paper and printing, silk production, porcelain, gunpowder and the compass. In addition to its heritage of art and literature it has been the centre of the Buddhist religion, Confucianism and Taoism. Unified government emerged with the Shang dynasty about 1500 BC and under the Han dynasty (206 BC-AD 220) the Chinese empire rivalled that of Rome in extent. After a period of Mongol dominance in the 13th century, Chinese power was finally reasserted under the Chi'ing dynasty of the Manchus, who ruled from 1644 to 1911. A long period of deliberate isolation from western technology ended in the 19th century. The humiliating imposition of foreign spheres of influence gave way to the emergence of modern Chinese nationalism under Sun Yat-sen in 1921.

A bitter struggle with Japan from 1937 to 1945 was followed by a civil war that ended in the withdrawal of the Nationalist government of Chiang Kai-shek to Taiwan and the victory of the Chinese Communist Party under Mao Tse-tung in 1949. During the past 25 years China has been transformed from a backward agricultural nation into an increasingly industrial economy with a nuclear and space technology and an increasing capacity to exploit its vast mineral resources. Confrontation with the West, highlighted by the Korean War of 1950-53, and by tension over the USA's protection of Taiwan, followed by a sharp quarrel with the USSR, has given way to a more flexible international stance and to increasing participation in international affairs. China was admitted to the United Nations in 1971.

The People's Republic of China comprises 21 provinces, six self-governing regions and three special cities, Peking, Shanghai and Tientsin. The autonomous regions include Tibet, which was independent from 1914 until 1950. The country is a one-party state, strongly centralized on Peking and ruled by the Communist Party of China with nearly 40 million members. Elected people's representatives vote for candidates nominated by the party for the National People's Congress. The State Council is headed by the premier and the Chairman of the Republic is Head of State.

People and social organization

For visitors to China, the most overwhelming impression is of its teeming population and the sense of purposeful organization and energy. More than 90 percent of China's 1,042 million people live in the eastern fifth of the country There are about 30 cities with populations of more than a million, including Shanghai, one of the world's biggest cities. The rural population in the eastern sector is also dense, especially around the mouths of the Yangtze Kiang and Hwang Ho (Yellow) rivers as well as in the coastal valleys and plains and the north central plain. Although the government is encouraging late marriages and smaller families, the population is growing by about 14 million a year, putting continued pressure on social and economic resources.

Nearly a third of the people live in urban areas. Grain (rice in the south, wheat in the north) is the staple diet, supplemented with vegetables and fish. Literacy (only 50 percent in 1960) is being extended through adult education and by combining study with work in farms or factories. The close-knit pattern of life centred on the traditional Chinese extended family has been broken up to some degree and religion, especially Confucianism, is not officially encouraged. Large communities organized as cooperatives or communes have replaced individual land holdings, although some small plots are allowed. Housing ranges from modern apartments to houses of mud and straw or bamboo and clay, caves and, in Inner Mongolia, tents. Life in China is austere by western standards with few consumer goods available. The revolution resulted in massive progress being made in improving the lot of the Chinese peasant after centuries of oppression. However convulsive radical movements such as the Cultural Revolution of the 1960s did disrupt economic progress. Since the death of Mao Tse-tung in 1976 the Chinese leadership has concentrated on stability and liberalization, and a more pragmatic approach to economic problems. Foreign investment has been encouraged and special economic zones established.

Land and climate

Nearly two-thirds of China's land surface is classed as highlands or plateaux. In general the land slopes from west to east, with the two major river systems of the Yangtze Kiang and Hwang Ho flowing in a similar direction. China can be divided into three main regions.

Western (or outer) China is cut off from the Indian sub-continent in the southwest by the Himalaya Mountains. North of this towering chain the vast Tibetan Plateau extends in a series of bleak uplands, averaging 4,600m (15,000ft) in height. Most of the two million Tibetans live in the southern valleys. Beyond the Kunlun Mountains on the north of the plateau, the Takla Makan desert and Dzungarian Basin stretch westward through Sinkiang to the Tien Shan and Pamir mountains and north to the Altai mountains bordering Asian Russia and Mongolia. The Turfan Depression on the northern edge of the Takla Makan desert is 154m (505ft) below sea level. The Gobi Desert extends southward from Mongolia, part of a desert belt spreading from west to east across 3,860km (2,400 miles).

Northern China includes the rolling Manchurian Plain in the northeast and the broad North China Plain extending southward from Peking, crossed by the Hwang Ho (Yellow) River. The name Yellow River derives from the colour of its waters, which carry silt from the Loess Highlands in the west where the river in its upper reaches cuts gorges in a region of fine, wind-blown soil. Both the Manchurian Plain and the North China Plain are fertile agricultural areas.

Southern China, lying east and south of the Tsin Ling mountains, is dominated in the north by the Yangtze Kiang River, 5,800km (3,600 miles) long – the world's longest river after the Nile and the Amazon. Like the Hwang Ho, it rises in the Tibet Plateau and crosses a fertile plain. Its upper reaches, surrounded by mountains, cross another rich farming area, the Szechwan Basin. South of the Yangzte Plain, rugged hills and uplands with terraced farms extend to a smaller plain around Kwangchow (Canton).

The climate of Southern China is humid and subtropical but in the north and west harsh seasonal variations are produced by the movement of two dominant air masses. Cold, dry air moving eastward from Central Asia in winter brings temperatures as low as −34°C (−30°F), freezing the northern rivers, including the Hwang Ho, for several months. Yet in summer, desert temperatures rise to more than 38°C (100°F) as warm air blows inland from the sea, bringing eastern areas most of their annual rainfall, averaging 200cm, (80in) in coastal areas. Little moisture reaches Mongolia and Sinkiang.

Left: *A market street in Shanghai, one of the world's largest seaports and a major industrial and commercial centre.*

Below: *Agriculture in Kwangsi Chuang autonomous region in southern China.*

Agriculture, fishing and forestry

With at least two-thirds of its people engaged in agriculture, China is the third largest producer of food in the world. But because of its huge population it remains locked in a centuries-old struggle for self-sufficiency and wheat still has to be imported from countries such as Canada and Australia. Hardly more than a third of its land area can be farmed and flood, drought and erosion are constant dangers. With little modern machinery and fertilizers (apart from animal and human manure), methods of irrigation and cultivation rely heavily on muscle power. Yet China leads the world in production of rice, is second in vegetables and third in wheat, cotton, maize and tea. It has the most pigs (nearly 300 million) and 100 million sheep.

Above a seventh of the land is under intensive cultivation, mainly in the east. The South China ricelands extend to the Yangtze plain. Cotton is also grown mainly in this plain and in the North China Plain and Loess Highlands. The wheat belt extends from the Loess Highlands and North China Plain to Manchuria and the corn belt from the Yunnan Plateau to Manchuria. The northwest is the major pastoral area, with many sheep and goats. Vegetables and fruit are grown widely in the east and tea and rubber in the south.

Fish are a major protein source and China's shallow coastal waters provide a rich variety, supplemented by inland fishing. Forests cover only a tenth of the land, mainly in border areas, and China has to import some timber.

Minerals, industry and trade

Through a series of Five- and Ten-Year Plans since 1949, the government has sought to convert China into a leading industrial power, drawing on large mineral resources, many of which are still largely unexploited. With formidable transport problems, especially in the west where the road and rail system is limited, and with several organizational setbacks, this aim has been only partially achieved. Production of consumer goods is still low. But great strides have been made in heavy industry, particularly in Manchuria. China now ranks seventh in world iron and steel production.

Nearly 90 percent of energy is supplied by coal, mined chiefly north of the Yangtze in open-cast beds. China is third in world coal production and fifth in iron, mainly from low-grade deposits in

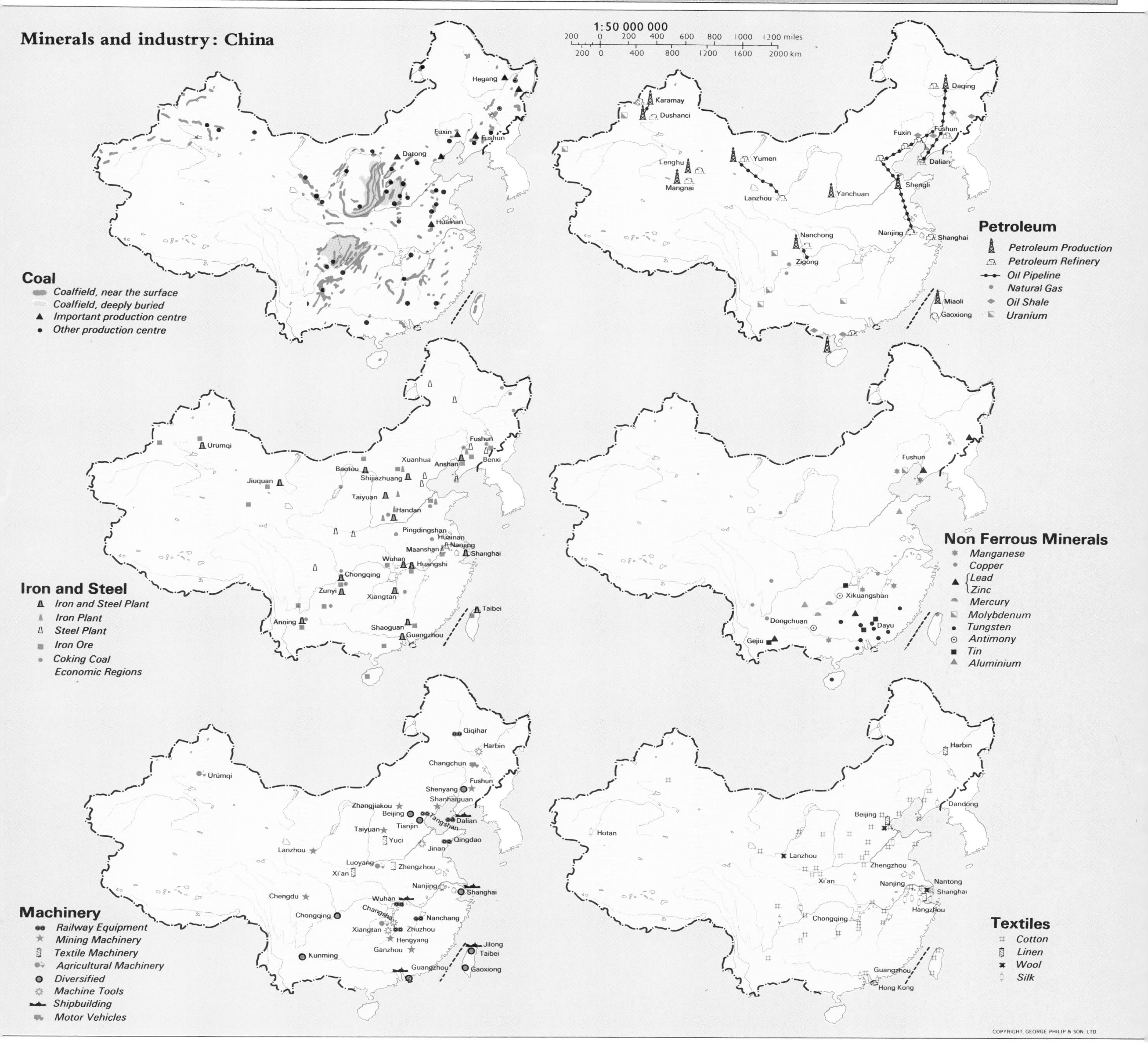

the northeast. Oil production has been developed in recent years, with over 100 million tonnes of crude oil extracted in 1982. South China has the most important deposits of other minerals, especially tungsten, antimony, tin and molybdenum, with lesser reserves of manganese, lead, copper and zinc. There is large but as yet poorly developed hydro-electric potential.

The Szechwan Basin, Manchuria, the area around Shanghai, and the other centres such as Peking, Tientsin, Chungking, Nanking and Hangchow are major industrial centres. A wide range of manufactures, from aircraft to chemicals, are produced, with textiles the biggest light industry. Handicrafts are important, making up about a quarter of manufactured goods. Until the 1960s, China traded mainly with the USSR, but its most important trading partners now are Hong Kong, Japan, the USA, Australia and the EEC, with which special trading agreements have been signed.

Taiwan

Area: 36,174km^2 (13,968sq.m.).
Population: 19.2 million.
Capital: Taipei (3m).
Languages: Mandarin and other Chinese dialects.
Ethnic groups: Chinese, Malayo-Polynesian (150,000).
Main exports: textiles, electrical and electronic equipment, plywood, canned foods.
Average temperatures: 18°C (65°F) Jan. 27°C (80°F) July.
Highest point: Yu Shan 3,997m (13,113ft).

The Republic of Taiwan lies 140km (90 miles) off the coast of China. Also known as Formosa or Nationalist China, it includes the Pescadores islands in the Taiwan Strait and the island fortresses of Quemoy and Matsu a few kilometres off the Chinese coast. Its claim to represent the government of mainland China has lost credibility since 1971 when its seat at the United Nations was transferred to the People's Republic of China. But with one of the best-balanced economies in the region, it is a prosperous, well-armed nation that shows no sign of reverting to its former status as a Chinese province.

China was forced to cede Taiwan to Japan in 1895 and regained the island only in 1945. In 1949 it became a refuge for the defeated regime of Chiang Kai-shek when about 1.5 million Chinese crossed from the mainland. Under the protection and with the economic aid of the USA, its population doubled in 20 years and since 1958 China has made no effort to regain the island by force. The presidential constitution is still based on that of the mainland in 1945 and most political and economic power is held by the new Chinese settlers. Taiwanese Chinese are engaged mainly in farming.

Most of the people live on the western coastal plain. Terraced hills rise to the dramatic Chungyang Range which is heavily forested and runs the length of the island, forming steep cliffs on the east. Swift rivers are apt to flood during the summer and winter monsoons while typhoons are common. The humid, subtropical climate suits crops such as rice, sugar cane, soyabeans, fruit and vegetables and although only a quarter of the land can be farmed, intensive cultivation produces two or three crops a year. Holdings average only 1.2 hectares (three acres) but are now being consolidated. Fishing is an important industry.

There are valuable reserves of natural gas and some coal, copper and gold deposits. But the main natural resource is timber, and forest products are a major export. The main feature of Taiwan's economy is the rapid development of manufacturing and processing industries and Taiwan is a leading exporter of clothing, textiles, electrical equipment and a wide range of other finished goods. Literacy is high and about 13 percent of the workforce is now in manufacturing. Taiwanese multi-national firms are now a major force in Southern Asia. Tourism is of growing importance.

Map 43 | EASTERN CHINA AND KOREA

HONG KONG 33
TEMPERATURE °C
13°
PRESSURE mb
PRECIPITATION mm
2161mm

HANKOW 37
TEMPERATURE °C
26°
PRESSURE mb
PRECIPITATION mm
1257mm

TIENTSIN 4
TEMPERATURE °C
32°
PRESSURE mb
PRECIPITATION mm
533mm

1:12 000 000

Projection: Lambert's Equivalent Azimuthal

East from Greenwich

COPYRIGHT GEORGE PHILIP & SON, LTD.

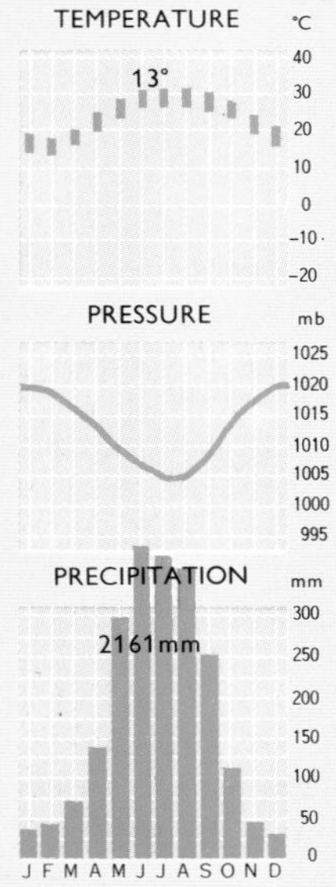

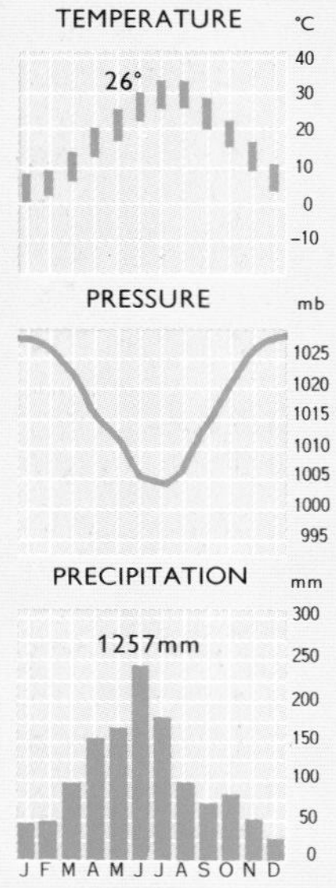

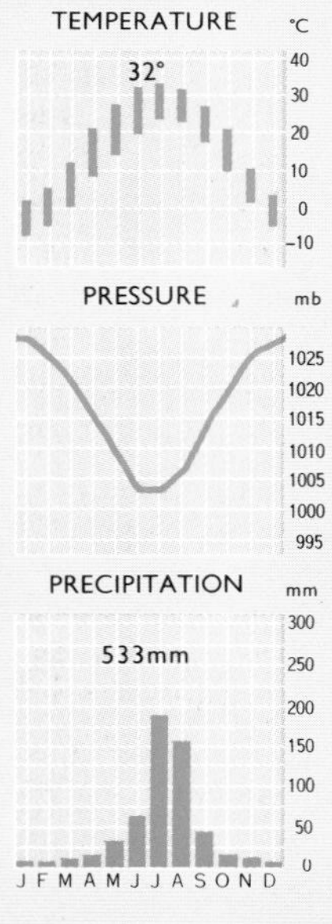

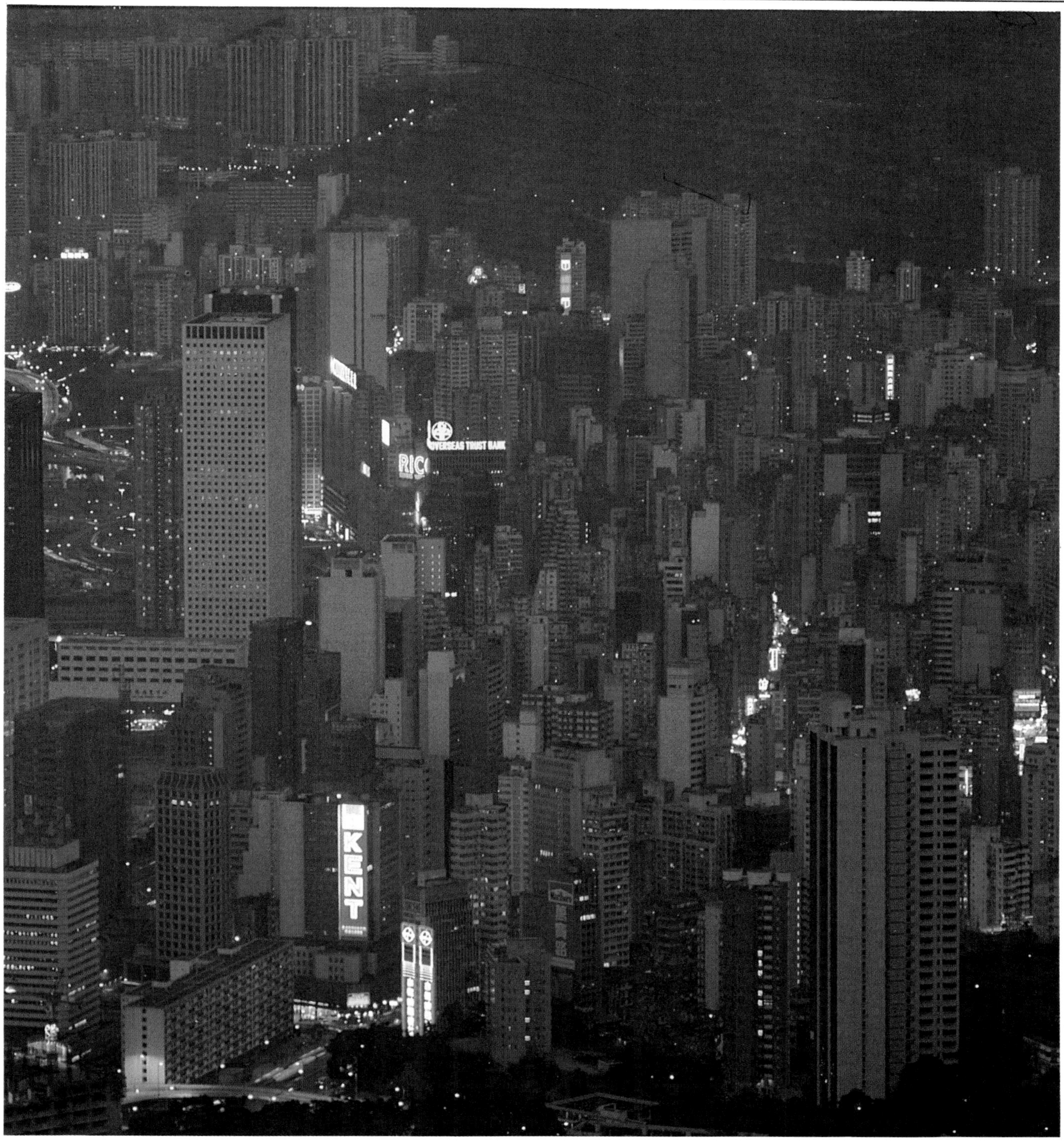

Above: *Hong Kong's cityscape is visual proof of its position in world trade.*

The Korean peninsula extends southwards from northeast China (Manchuria). Korea's long history as a unified kingdom, largely independent within China's sphere of influence, ended in 1910 when it was seized by Japan. Since Japan's defeat in 1945 the peninsula has been divided between the states now known as the Democratic People's Republic of Korea (North) and the Republic of Korea (South). As the north was primarily industrial and the south agricultural, the division was unfortunate. The communist regime in the north attacked the south in 1950, beginning a destructive war in which United Nations forces led by the USA came to the aid of the south while the USSR and China supported the north. The war reached a stalemate in 1953 and a Demilitarized Zone of 1,260km^2 (487sq.m.) now separates the two republics at about the 38th parallel. Reunification talks started in 1980, but have since come to nothing.

The peninsula divides the Sea of Japan on the east from the Yellow Sea on the west. It reaches its widest point of 515km (320 miles) near Pyongyang. The Korea Strait 192km (120 miles) wide separates Korea from Japan and there are about 3,000 islands, the largest of which, Cheju, has South Korea's highest peak, Halla-San. Mountains and rugged hills are the most characteristic land features. Ranges, highest on the east, extend down the centre of the peninsula from the Chinese border, which is formed largely by the Yalu River. The climate is monsoonal with hot humid summers but cold, dry winters that are long and quite severe, particularly in the north.

North Korea

Area: 122,098km^2 (47,130sq.m.).
Population: 20.1 million.
Capital: Pyongyang (1.5m).
Language and ethnic group: Korean.
Main exports: copper, iron ore, lead, tungsten, zinc.
Average temperatures: −3°C (26°F) Jan. 21°C (70°F) July.
Highest point: Paektu-San 2,744m (9,003ft).

The Democratic People's Republic of Korea is governed by the Korean Communist Party and has a large army (784,500) and militia (1.8 million). Apart from a small strip of coastal lowland in the northeast, the rolling northwestern plain around Pyongyang supports most of the population. Although the economy is predominantly industrial, grain output has risen rapidly under a programme of collective farming in units averaging about 300 families.

North Korea has some of the richest mineral deposits in Asia and is a leading producer of graphite, tungsten and magnesium. Coal, iron ore, lead, zinc and petroleum, together with hydroelectric power, are the basis of fast-growing industries in which most factories are government-owned. Just over half of North Korea's trade is with communist countries, notably the Soviet Union.

South Korea

Area: 98,992km^2 (38,221sq.m.).
Population: 42.7 million.
Capital: Soul, or Seoul (8.4m).
Language and Ethnic group: Korean.
Main exports: clothing, textiles, electrical equipment, cars, fish, tungsten.
Average temperatures: −2°C (28°F) Jan. 24°F (75°F) July.
Highest point: Halla-San 1,950m (6,398ft).

The Republic of Korea has a partly elective government but is under presidential rule and maintains a standing army of 540,000. As in North Korea, literacy is high. Successful efforts have been made to transform the primarily agricultural economy into a mixed one. Despite few mineral resources apart from tungsten, a strong manufacturing sector has been built up, chiefly in textiles, plywood, plastics, fertilizers, cement, electronics and, more recently, cars. This is concentrated chiefly in the Seoul area.

The rolling southwestern plain around Seoul is also an important agricultural area, as is the southern plain drained by the Naktong River. There are some 2.5 million farms, most of them covering less than a hectare (2.5 acres). Rice is the main crop, followed by beans, barley and wheat. Fishing is also important. Trade is mainly with Japan and the USA.

Hong Kong

Area: 1,066.53km^2 (412sq.m.).
Population: 5.5 million.
Capital: Victoria (700,000).
Languages: English, Chinese.
Ethnic groups: Chinese (98 percent), European.
Main exports: textiles, plastics, electronic equipment, ships.
Average temperatures: 15°C (59°F) Jan. 28°C (82°F) July.
Highest point: Tai Mo Shan 958m (3,144ft).

The British Crown colony of Hong Kong occupies a unique place in the world as the last toehold of 19th-century European influence in China. Its political viability since the revolution has depended on its usefulness to China as a key point of contact with the west. Its economic prosperity is based on a highly-skilled manufacturing workforce, trade through its magnificent free port and heavy tourist traffic (one million annually).

The colony, largely autonomous, lies near the Chu Chiang (Pearl) River on the south coast of China 145km (90m.) southeast of Canton. Together with some 240 small islands it comprises the island of Hong Kong with the business centre on its northern slopes. The Kowloon Peninsula, which is the main industrial and shopping area, and a predominantly farming area north of this on the Chinese mainland are known as the New Territories. Britain acquired Hong Kong in 1843, Kowloon in 1860 and a 99-year lease of the New Territories in 1898. Without the New Territories, the colony is not viable, so following an accord signed between the British and Chinese governments, Hong Kong will be returned to China in the year 1997.

Hong Kong has a tropical monsoon climate, wet between June and September. The hilly terrain and limited land area mean that much food has to be imported to supplement fishing and fruit and vegetable farming. Ship-building is the main heavy industry but most of the workforce is in light industry, especially textiles, plastics and electronics. Hong Kong handles a lot of China's external trade and exports 90 percent of its own manufactured products, mainly to the USA and Britain.

Macau, or **Macao,** a Portuguese enclave at the mouth of the Pearl River, 64km (40m.) west of Hong Kong, is a tourist and gambling centre comprising the city of Macau and two small islands. It has an area of 16km^2 (6sq.m.) and a population of about 300,000, mainly Chinese.

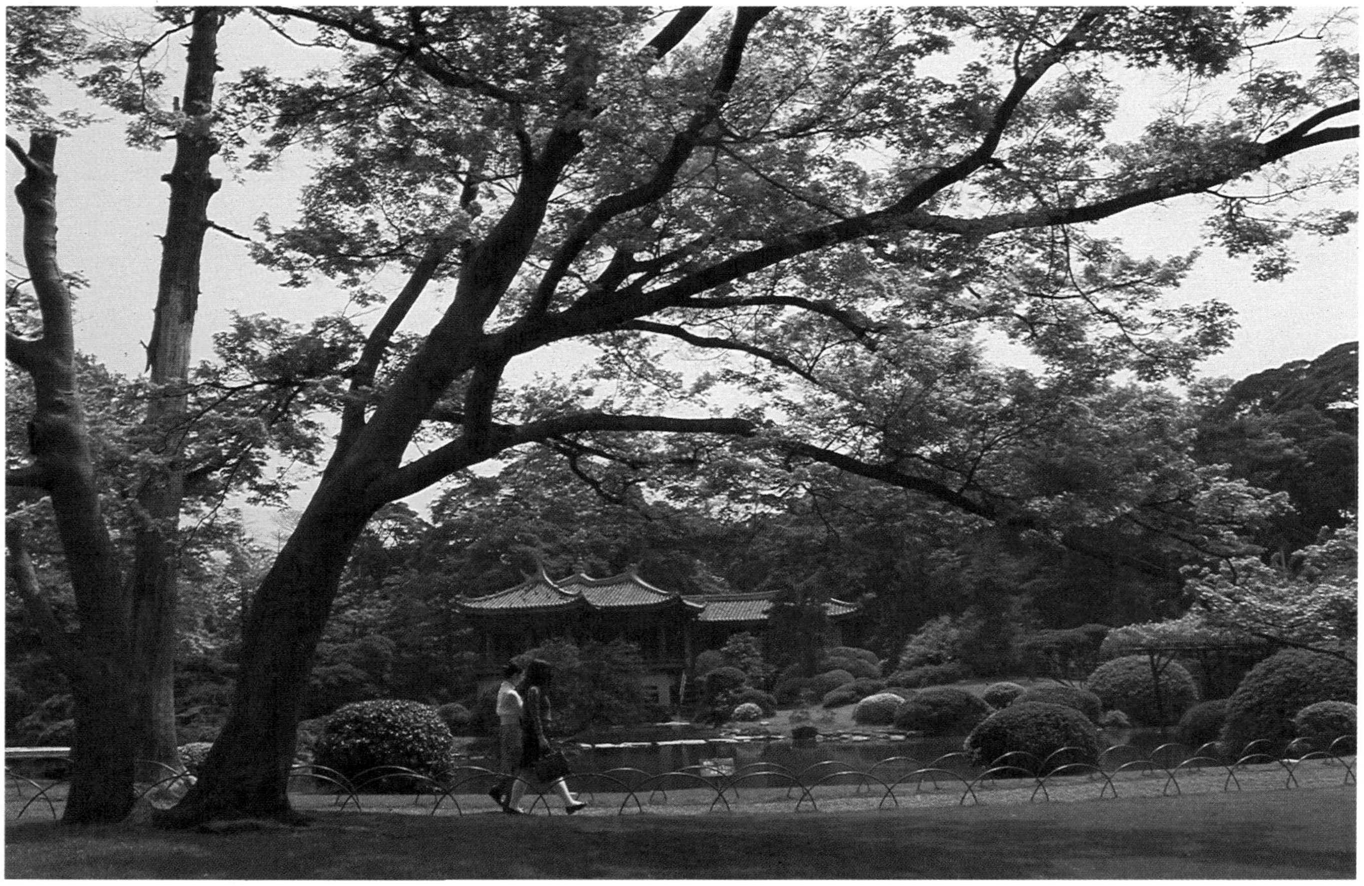

Left: *Shinjuku Gyoen Park, one of Tokyo's many beautiful parks and gardens.*

Above: *The port of Nagasaki in Japan, the world's principal ship-building nation.*

Japan

Area: 377,765km^2 (145,817sq.m.).
Population: 120 million.
Capital: Tokyo (11.7m).
Language: Japanese.
Ethnic groups: Japanese, Ainu (15,000).
Main exports: iron and steel, ships, motor-cars, electronics, optical, electrical and other machinery and appliances, chemicals, textile products, canned fish.
Average temperatures: 3°C (37°F) Jan. 26°C (78°F) Aug. in Tokyo.
Highest point: Mount Fuji 3,776m (12,388ft).

A nation once symbolized by cherry blossom, the geisha, and international isolationism, Japan now projects an image of highly efficient industrialization. Its products – cameras, hi-fi equipment, televisions, super-tankers – are familiar in most parts of the world. From a defeated, overcrowded, humiliated country at the end of World War II, it has transformed itself into one of the leading industrial nations of the world. With meagre natural resources, it has been able to do this only because of the tremendous energy and determination of its people.

Land and climate

Japan consists of four main islands and over 3,000 smaller ones. The four large islands – Hokkaido, Honshu (the largest), Shikoku and Kyushu – are strung out along the coast of eastern Asia in a great arc. They are the upper part of a great mountain range that rises from the floor of the Pacific. As a result, Japan is a rugged country, with only 15 percent of its land level enough for cultivation. About 200 of Japan's mountains are volcanoes, of which nearly 60 are active.

About 75 percent of Japan's people live on Honshu, crowded into the cities and conurbations along the southern coast. Half of Japan's population lives on only two percent of its land area. Metropolitan Tokyo, with a population of 8.35 million, is one of the largest cities in the world. Seven other Japanese cities have populations of more than a million. Honshu has several swift rivers which supply hydro-electric power, and hot springs can be found throughout the island.

Most of Japan has a moderate climate, although Hokkaido has cool summers and cold winters. Honshu has warm, humid summers, and mild winters in the south but is cold in the north. The two smaller islands have long hot summers and mild winters. All of Japan has a high rainfall. There are two seasons of heavy rain, following the pattern of the Asiatic monsoon. In the western mountains, winter snow collects to such a depth that spring floods are extremely difficult to control. Together with typhoons and tidal waves, floods claim an average of 600 victims a year.

Water is Japan's only significant natural resource. By means of thousands of irrigation channels, it helps crops grow at a remarkable rate, making possible some of the highest agricultural yields in the world. It is harnessed to produce the abundant hydro-electric power that supplies Japan's huge cities and industrial complexes.

Japan has more earthquakes than anywhere else in the world – some 1,500 a year. Most of these are barely perceptible but there is one severe earthquake on average every 2½ years. Occasionally, these are disastrous. In 1923, half of Tokyo and all of Yokohama were destroyed by an earthquake and the resulting fires.

People and culture

Japan is characterized by an almost complete identity of race, people, and nation. The only minority group is the Ainu, a Caucasoid people whose ancestors were among the first occupants of the islands. Most of the remaining Ainu, some 15,000, live on Hokkaido. The Japanese resemble the Chinese. They have yellowish skin, high cheek bones, dark oblique eyes, and straight black hair. They are, on average, shorter than the Chinese or Koreans.

There are two main religions in Japan, Shintoism and Buddhism, and many Japanese practise both. Buddhism, in particular, has played an important part in the development of art in Japan. Its best painting and sculpture shows a strong Buddhist influence. In the theatre, Japan has created two new forms of drama, noh and kabuki. It is known also for its colour printing, ceramics, silk embroidery, and flower arranging. The distinctive Japanese culture is also seen in clothing and cuisine, and particularly in domestic architecture.

In sport, the Japanese gave the world martial arts such as judo and karate, and they have their own highly ritualized form of wrestling, Sumo. They excel, too, at gymnastics and table tennis.

Economy

Some 39 percent of the work force is engaged in modern manufacturing industry. Japan leads the world in shipbuilding, motorcycle manufacture, electronics, and the production of radios, cameras, and watches, and is second in the manufacture of motor-cars and television sets. Textiles and chemicals are also important industries.

About 12 percent of Japan's labour force is employed in agriculture, forestry and fishing. Despite the shortage of arable land, Japan is self-sufficient in rice. Other important crops include potatoes, cabbage, sweet potatoes, fruit and wheat. The forests produce good-quality timber, but Japan has to import wood for its manufacturing industries.

Japan is the leading fishing nation in the world. The fish caught in greatest

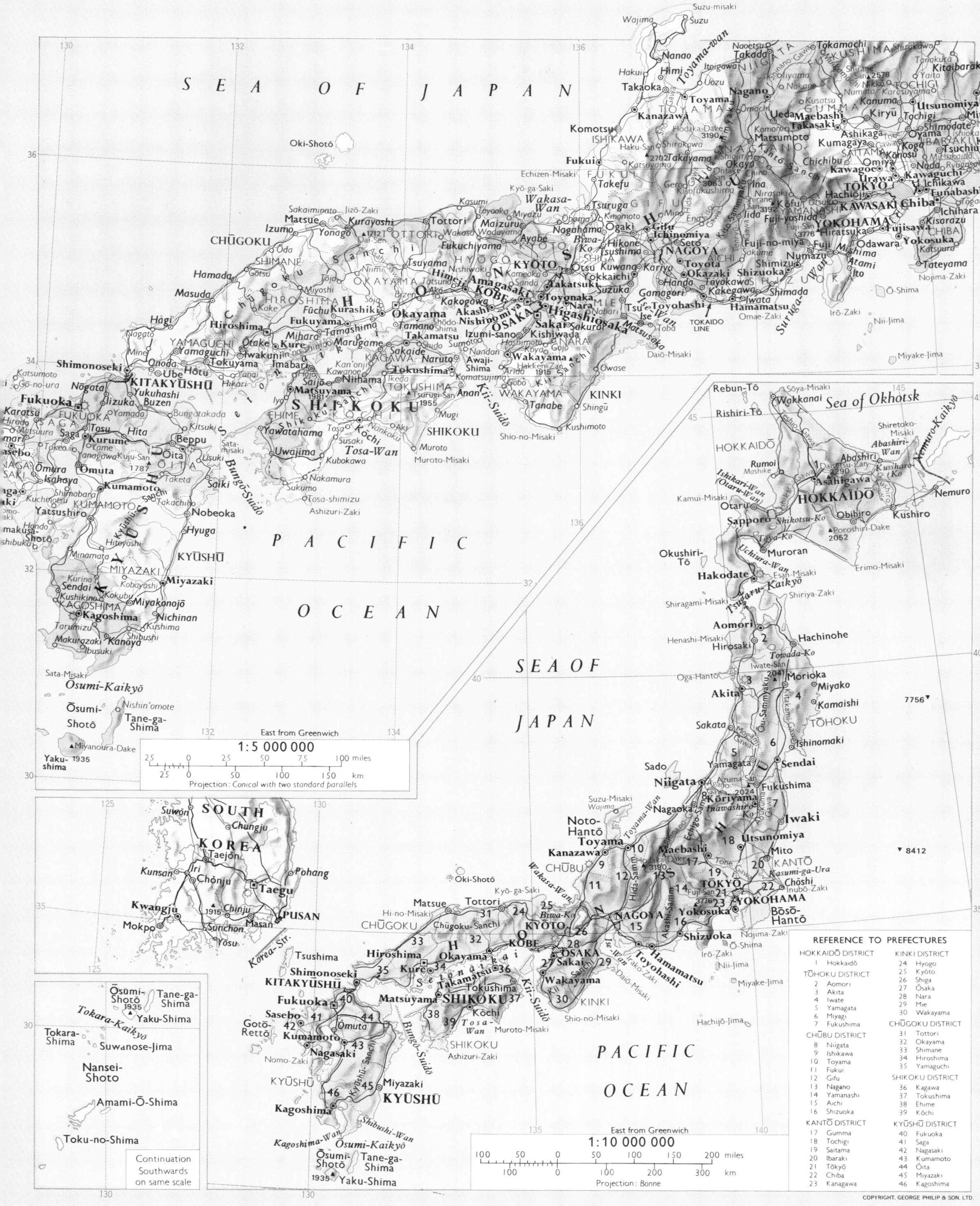

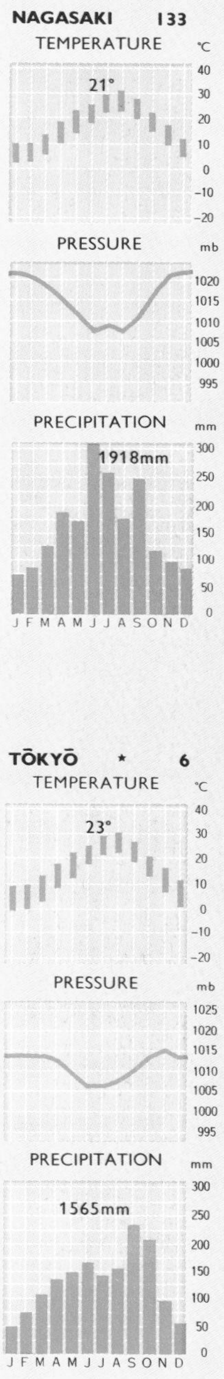

quantities are cod, haddock, mackerel and shellfish, and other catches include whales, octopus, squid and eels.

Constitution

Japan's Diet has a House of Representatives and a House of Councillors. The government is based on the 1947 constitution, formulated after Japan's defeat in World War II. Under this, the emperor has no governmental powers, and Japan renounces its sovereign right to make war.

The present Imperial Family are direct descendants of the house of Yamato, which united Japan as a nation in about AD 200. Emperors ruled with varying degrees of authority until the mid-1100s. In about 1200, a new warrior class came to power, called *shoguns* (great generals). Successive families of shoguns ruled for nearly 700 years, until the young Emperor Meiji was restored to imperial power in 1868.

For hundreds of years, Japan had followed a policy of complete seclusion from the rest of the world. It was the Americans who, in an attempt to gain power in the Pacific, forced the Japanese to open their ports to foreign ships. Commodore Matthew Perry was sent with warships in 1853 to open trade relations with Japan. He delivered a letter from the president of the United States, and returned in 1854 to sign a treaty with the reluctant Japanese.

Japan's imperialist expansion began in the 1880s. Rivalry with China led to a war (1894-95) in which Japan gained from China Formosa and a sphere of influence in Korea. With further gains from a war with Russia (1904-5), Japan became a world power. As an ally of Britain in World War I, Japan was able to seize German territory in Asia and the Pacific. But Japan followed a policy of peace until the early 1930s, when its military leaders began to take advantage of growing nationalism and anti-West feeling, provoked in part by the West's refusal to accept the Japanese as full equals. Japan seized Manchuria in 1931, and won control of other parts of China in the late 1930s. Anti-communist treaties were signed with Germany and Italy, and, with the military now in full control, the Japanese attacked American bases at Pearl Harbour in December 1941. After initial victories in World War II, Japan gradually slipped to complete defeat, but surrendered only after atom bombs had obliterated Hiroshima and Nagasaki in 1945.

American occupation forces under General Douglas MacArthur stayed until 1952, by which time Japan had a new constitution, was demilitarized, and had begun a programme of economic reform. Out of defeat, Japan grew from the mid-1950s, in less than two decades, into one of the world's major industrial powers.

Map 45 | THE NEAR AND MIDDLE EAST

JERUSALEM   757

TEMPERATURE   °C

PRESSURE   mb

PRECIPITATION   mm

528mm

J F M A M J J A S O N D

SAMSUN   40

TEMPERATURE   °C

PRESSURE   mb

PRECIPITATION   mm

739mm

J F M A M J J A S O N D

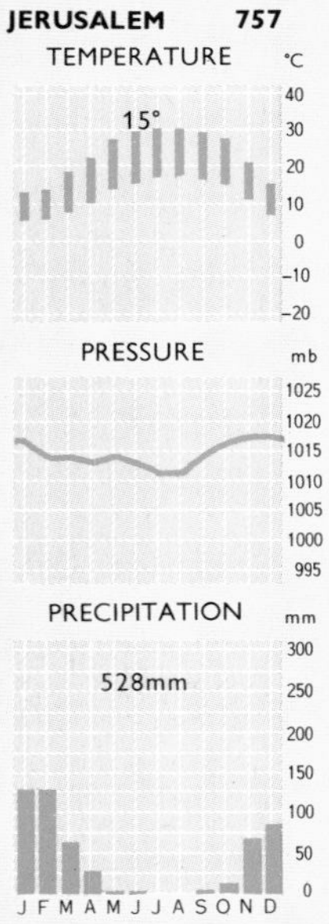

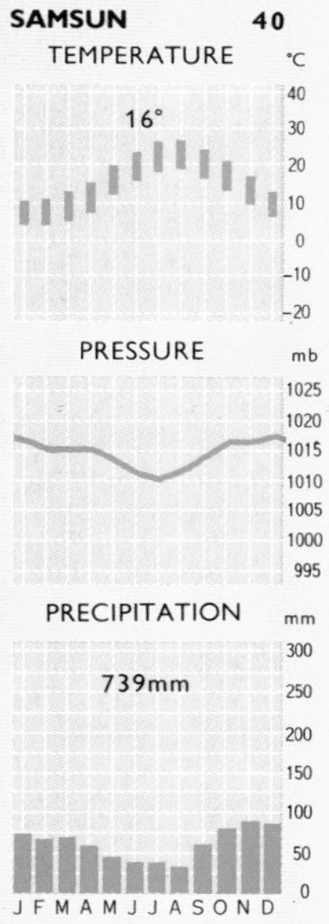

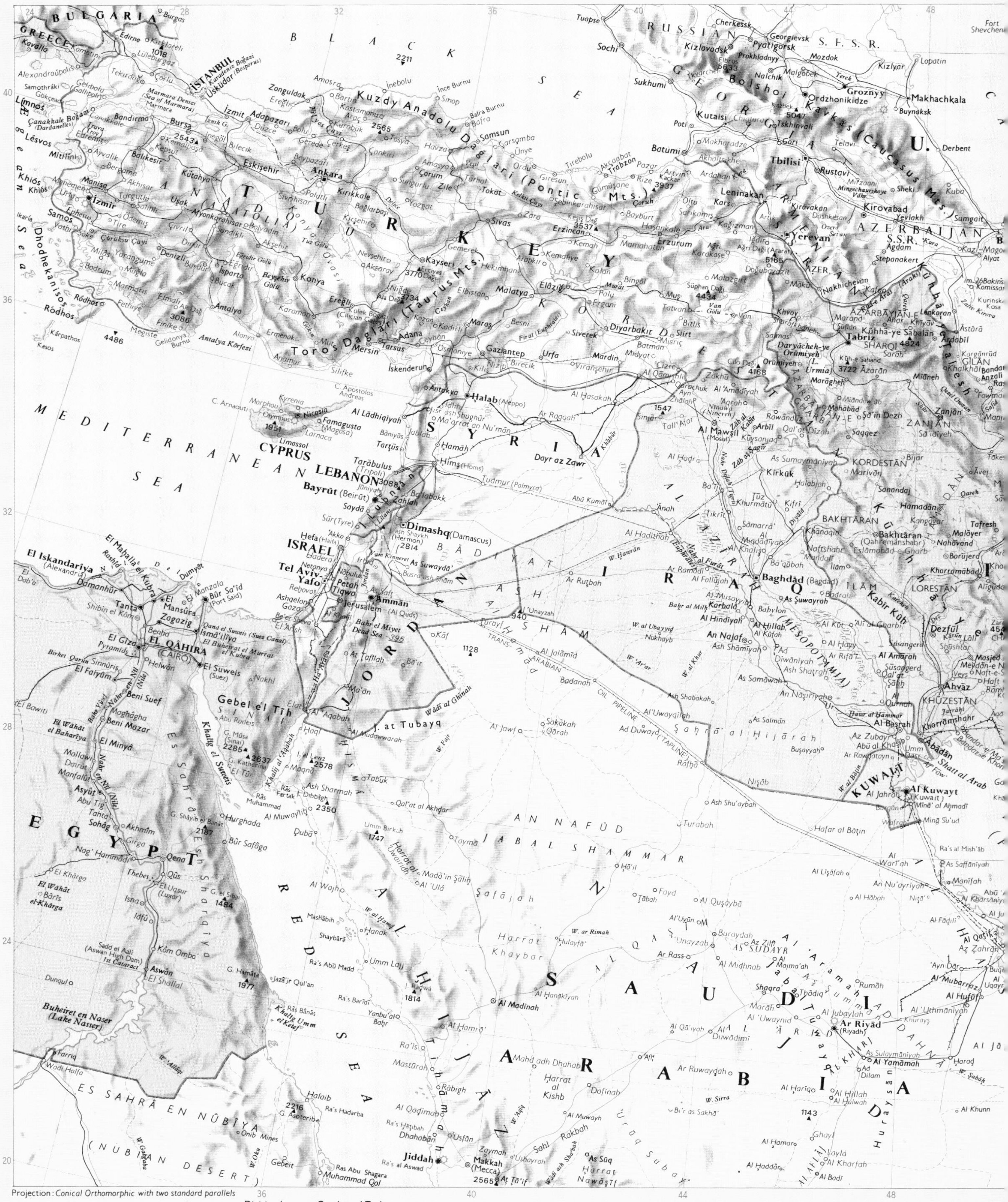

Projection: Conical Orthomorphic with two standard parallels

Division between Greeks and Turks
in Cyprus; Turks to the North.

Until recent years the Near and
Middle East was noted more for its
historical context than for its natural
resources. Today, the importance of
Arabian oil has brought it to the forefront of world affairs. But a parched environment remains a dominant feature
of the region and although industry is
developing in several countries the
majority of the people are poor farmers.

The region stretches from Turkey in
the north to the vast desert of the
Arabian peninsula in the south and to
the Hindu Kush in Afghanistan. The
region, sometimes referred to as the Near
East or the Middle East, has given birth
to three of the great world religions:
Judaism, Christianity and Islam. Religions have often given rise to unrest and

conflict in the region. From early
historic times, cultural influences have
spread from the Middle East into Europe,
North and East Africa, and the Indian
subcontinent.

Arabs form the largest population
group, together with Turks, Iranians,
Kurds, Jews and Armenians, and Arabic
is the most widely-spoken language.
Turkey was a major power in the Mediterranean regions until 1918. There
have been three chief sources of regional
strife in recent years. The first was the
creation of the state of Irael in 1948.
Palestinian refugees fled to neighbouring
states and major wars ensued over the
next three decades, engulfing Egypt,
Syria, Jordan and Lebanon. The second
was the emergence of Islamic funda-

Map 46

BAGHDĀD 34
TEMPERATURE °C

PRESSURE mb

PRECIPITATION mm
140mm

J F M A M J J A S O N D

TEHRĀN ★ 1220
TEMPERATURE °C

PRESSURE mb

PRECIPITATION mm
246mm

J F M A M J J A S O N D

1:10 000 000

100 0 100 200 300 miles
100 0 100 200 300 400 500 km

East from Greenwich

COPYRIGHT. GEORGE PHILIP & SON. LTD

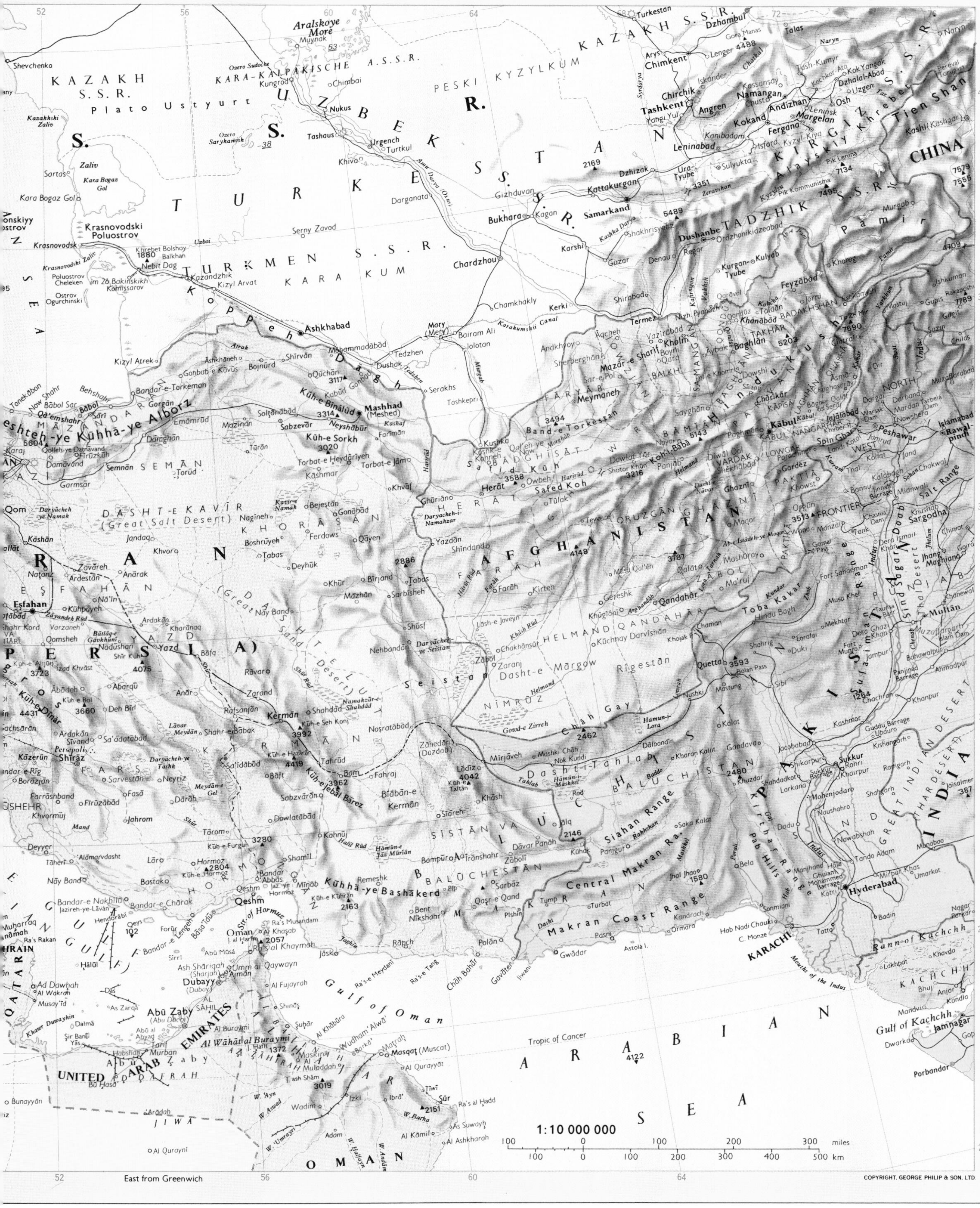

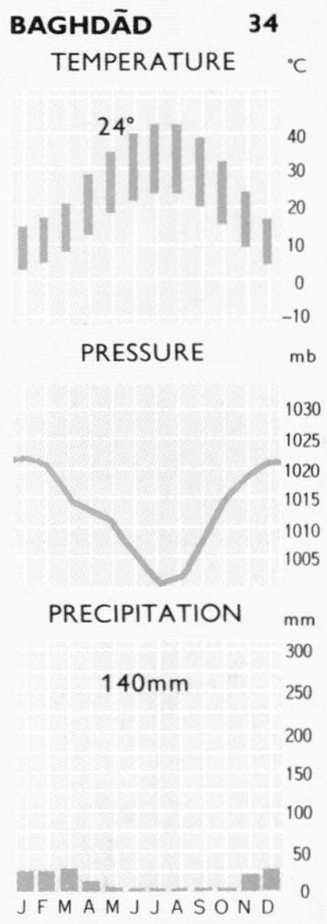

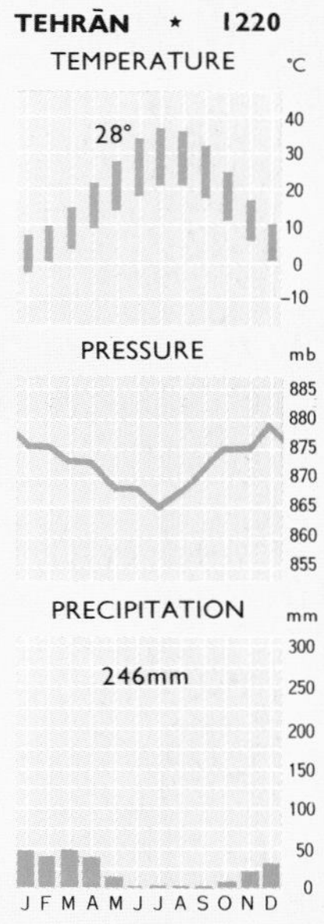

mentalism during the Iranian revolution of 1979. Iran has been at war with Iraq since 1980. The third was the 1979 Soviet intervention in Afghanistan, which resulted in a protracted guerrilla war.

As early as 1974 the Middle East was producing one-third of the world's petroleum and exporting most of it. The new power of the region was shown by the price rises imposed during the 1970s by the Organization of Petroleum Exporting Countries (OPEC). In 1982 Saudi Arabia alone produced nearly 6½ million barrels daily. By the mid 1980s, however, prices had slumped.

Left: *Galata Bridge crosses the Golden Horn to Yeni Mosque in Istanbul, Turkey.*

Turkey

Area: 779,452km² (300,947sq.m.).
Population: 52 million.
Capital: Ankara (2.2m).
Largest city: Istanbul (2.77m).
Language: Turkish.
Ethnic groups: Turks, Kurds (1.7 million), Arabs, Circassians, Armenians, Greeks.
Main exports: grains, cotton, tobacco, chromium and minerals, dried fruit and nuts, carpets.
Average temperatures: 4°C (40°F) Jan. 23°C (73°F) July on coast but much colder on plateau.
Highest point: Mt Ararat 5,165m (16,946ft).

Turkey is a large republic bridging Europe and Asia, with most of its territory forming the peninsula of Asia Minor. Its position, spanning the waterway between the Black Sea and the Mediterranean (the Bosporus, the Sea of Marmara, and the Dardanelles), has given it strategic importance. Its rich cultural heritage is centred upon the famous city of Istanbul. As Constantinople, this city was the capital of the Byzantine Empire, bastion of Graeco-Roman civilization for a thousand years. As Istanbul, it was the centre of the Moslem world, mingling Arabic and Turkish traditions. Since the 1920s, when Turkey adopted western social and economic ideas, much headway has been made in developing an industrial and

manufacturing base in a nation that remains primarily agricultural.

People and constitution

The dark-skinned Turkish people are a mixture of Asiatic, Baltic and Mediterranean stock. The Seljuk Turks took Asia Minor from the Byzantine Empire in the 11th century. After the fall of Constantinople to the Ottoman Turks in 1453, the Turkish Empire was extended to the Balkans, Central Europe, Persia and North Africa, reaching its height toward the end of the 16th century before the battle of Lepanto halted its spread into Europe. Territory was then lost steadily, although in the 19th century the European Powers propped Turkey up to hold Russia in check. The

Young Turk movement pressed for modernization from 1908 and under Mustafa Kemal gained power in 1922, abolishing the sultanate in favour of a republic, reforming the legal and educational system and ending restrictions on women such as the veil and harem. In 1947, Turkey turned to America for aid against Russian pressure, becoming a NATO member in 1952. Today, Turkey is governed by a National Security Council and a Consultative Assembly.

Land and climate

Thrace (European Turkey) has rolling plains extending to low mountains bordering Bulgaria. Anatolia (Asia Minor) is dominated by a rugged inland plateau 800-1,800m (2,600 to 6,000ft) high bordered on the north by the Pontic Mountains and on the south by the Taurus Mountains with a narrow coastal strip along the Mediterranean and a broader plain in the north. The plateau is dry with severe winters but the climate is mild and moist in coastal areas. Anatolia is prone to earthquakes.

Economy

About 60 percent of the workforce is employed in agriculture. Sheep and goats are raised on the plateau, which is also the main area for grains and sugarbeet. Cotton and fruit are grown in coastal areas and tobacco in the north.

Although carpets provide Turkey's only significant manufactured export apart from hand-crafted products, the manufacturing sector is expanding with government backing, particularly in textiles, chemicals, paper, cement and glass. With an iron and steel plant at Karabuk, heavy industry is also developing. Petroleum production from oil reserves in Raman and Garzan is rising. Turkey is also an important chromite producer and has some copper, iron, lead, zinc and silver. Its main energy source, however, is coal and lignite.

Cyprus

Area: 9,251km² (3,527sq.m.).
Population: 700,000.
Capital: Nicosia (161,000).
Languages: Greek, Turkish.
Ethnic groups: Greek (77 percent), Turkish.
Main exports: wine, fruit, asbestos, copper and iron ores, olive oil.
Average temperatures: 13°C (55°F) Jan. 27°C (80°F) July.
Highest point: Mt Olympus 1,951m (6,401ft).

The republic of Cyprus lies only 64km (40 miles) south of Turkey in the eastern Mediterranean and 97km (60 miles) west of Syria. It is an island of rugged beauty with a history of political turbulence both before and since 1960 when a struggle for *enosis* (union with Greece) led to Britain granting its former colony independence on the basis of equal rights for the Greek and Turkish communities. Tension between the Greek-speaking, Greek Orthodox majority and the Turkish Moslem minority finally erupted in civil war in 1974. A Turkish invasion was followed by a UN-supervised ceasefire. The northeastern sector declared unilaterally in 1983 that it was the independent Turkish Republic of Northern Cyprus, but failed to gain international recognition.

The three main land forms are the northern Kyrenia range, the Troodos Range, highest in the southwest, and the broad Mesaoria Plain between them. Although snow falls on the higher mountains, the winters are mild and the hot, dry summers are ideal for citrus fruits. The climate, the long coastline of rocky headlands and fine beaches and the wealth of historical sites makes tourism an important industry. About half the Cypriot people are small farmers and vine-growing is the chief industry. Mining is also carried on, mainly in the Troodos Range.

Syria

Area: 185,180km² (71,498sq.m.).
Population: 10.6 million.
Capital: Dimashq or Damascus (1.14m).
Languages: Arabic, Kurdish, Armenian, French.
Ethnic groups: Arabs, Kurds, Armenians.
Main exports: cotton, textiles, fruit, vegetables, tobacco.
Average temperatures: 0°C (32°F) Jan. 32°C (90°F) July.
Highest point: J. ash Sheikh (Mt Hermon) 2,814m (9,232ft).

Northern Syria is a land of rolling plains, whilst in the south and west are deserts. High mountains rise above the coastal plain along the Mediterranean. The coast has a mild climate with ample rainfall, but the arid interior has more extreme temperatures. Farming, especially fruit production, is the chief activity, with the help of irrigation.

The valley of the Euphrates was a cradle of civilization and Syria was the home of several ancient empires. It finally became a Roman province. Muslim Arabs conquered the area in AD 636, but Christian Crusaders ruled much of the country for two centuries. It was part of the Turkish empire until World War I. France then ruled the territory until 1946, when Syria became independent. In 1958, Syria united with Egypt in the United Arab Republic but became independent again in 1961.

A socialist republic, Syria has regularly fought against Israel in recent years. Syria also became embroiled in the affairs of Lebanon in 1975 and following the Israeli invasion of 1982.

Iraq

Area: 434,924km² (167,925sq.m.).
Population: 15.5 million.
Capital: Baghdad (3.17m).
Languages: Arabic, Kurdish.
Ethnic groups: Arabs, Kurds, Persians, Turks.
Main exports: petroleum, petroleum products, dates, hides, cement, wool.
Average temperatures: 9°C (48°F) Jan. 34°F (94°F) July.
Highest point: Zagros mountains, over 3,048m (10,000ft).

The Tigris-Euphrates region of Iraq (Mesopotamia) was a centre of ancient civilizations, including Babylonia and Assyria. Today most of Iraq is a dry, sandy plain, with swamps in the south, desert in the west and mountains in the northeast. The rainfall is low but the plains are well irrigated by the Euphrates and Tigris rivers. Many Iraqis are farmers, raising large numbers of livestock. Most farms are along the two main rivers. They produce cereals, fruit and tobacco. Iraq is one of the world's major petroleum producers.

Conquered by Muslim Arabs in the AD 600s, Iraq later became part of the Turkish empire. Britain ruled the country from 1918 until 1932, when Iraq became an independent monarchy. The army took control in 1958 and established a republic. A period of unrest followed and two more army revolts led to changes in the leadership.

Internally, Iraq has been torn by conflict with its Kurdish minority. Iraq's external relations have been marked by hostilities against Israel and against Iran. The war with Iran had been a major drain on the economy and has forced Iraq to export its oil via pipelines rather than through the Gulf.

Lebanon

Area: 10,452km² (4,036sq.m.).
Population: 2.6 million.
Capital: Beirut (702,000).
Languages: Arabic, French.
Ethnic group: Arabs.
Main exports: banking services, vegetables, tobacco, textiles, machinery.
Average temperatures: 10°C (50°F) Jan. 27°C (80°F) July.
Highest point: 3,083m (10,115ft).

Lebanon is made up of a narrow coastal plain, the Lebanon mountains which run throughout the country, and a fertile inland plain. The climate is temperate and many people are farmers, producing cereals and fruit. Manufactures include textiles, cement and processed foods. Because of the lack of minerals, commerce and trading are important.

France took an interest in the region from the 1860s because Lebanon had a Christian majority and ruled Lebanon from 1918 until 1946, when it became an independent parliamentary republic. Post-war years were marked by factional fighting between Christians and Moslems. Israel attacked Palestinian fighters based in Lebanon and in 1982 invaded the country. Atrocities and devastation became the order of the day, and when the Israelis withdraw in 1985, rival militias fought for power.

Israel

Area: 20,700km² (7,992sq.m.).
Population: 4.15 million.
Capital: Jerusalem (473,000).
Languages: Hebrew, Arabic.
Ethnic groups: Jews, Arabs (500,000).
Main exports: fruit, vegetables, textiles, engineering products, minerals, fertilizers.
Average temperatures: 7°C (45°F) Jan. 24°C (75°F) July.
Highest point: Mt Meiron 1,208m (3,963ft).

Since Israel became an independent parliamentary democracy in 1948, Israelis have worked to develop their country and establish industries. Their achievements in land reclamation and irrigation have been outstanding. Many Israelis live and work in co-operative communities, such as *kibbutzim*, where the people collectively own all property. But the Israelis have also faced a continuing struggle with the Arab world.

The land is divided into four main regions. The coast, Galilee in the north, and the Emek, south of Galilee, are fertile areas. The coast is a region of citrus fruit and vegetable production and mixed farming. Galilee's products include cereals, olives and tobacco. The Emek is a region of varied crops and it is notable for fish breeding.

The largest region, the Negev, is in the south. Formerly a barren desert,

parts of the northern Negev have been irrigated. Sisal, groundnuts, cotton and flower bulbs are cultivated on the irrigated land. The Negev has petroleum and natural gas deposits. Other minerals, including potash, bromine and salt, are mined in the Dead Sea area. Israel has a flourishing tourist industry, especially because of its Biblical sites.

The Arab-Israeli conflict

Some Jews have always lived in Palestine, but most Israelis are recent immigrants, who have been settling in the area since the 1880s. In 1948 the UN decided to partition Palestine into a Jewish and an Arab state. But this was unacceptable to the Arabs. Israel's neighbours attacked and, at the end of the conflict, Israel held all of Palestine except the central region of Samaria, part of Judea (including the Old City of Jerusalem) and the Gaza Strip along the Mediterranean coast.

Palestinian Arab refugees formed guerrilla armies in Arab lands. War broke out in 1956 and Israel temporarily occupied the Sinai region of Egypt. In a third war in 1967, Israel tok Sinai, Samaria, Jerusalem, Judea and the Golan Heights in Syria. In many of the newly-occupied zones Jewish settlements were set up, arousing local hostility and internal dissent. Palestinian guerrillas continued to be a thorn in the flesh. The Arab states made some advances in the war of 1973, and peace with Egypt ensued in 1975. Sinai was returned, and the 1978 Camp David agreement aimed to bring peace to the region. However, Israel became involved in a protracted invasion of Lebanon in 1982-5 which alienated further sections of domestic and international opinion.

Below: *A shepherd boy with his flock, in an olive grove on the hills overlooking Nazareth in Galilee, northern Israel.*

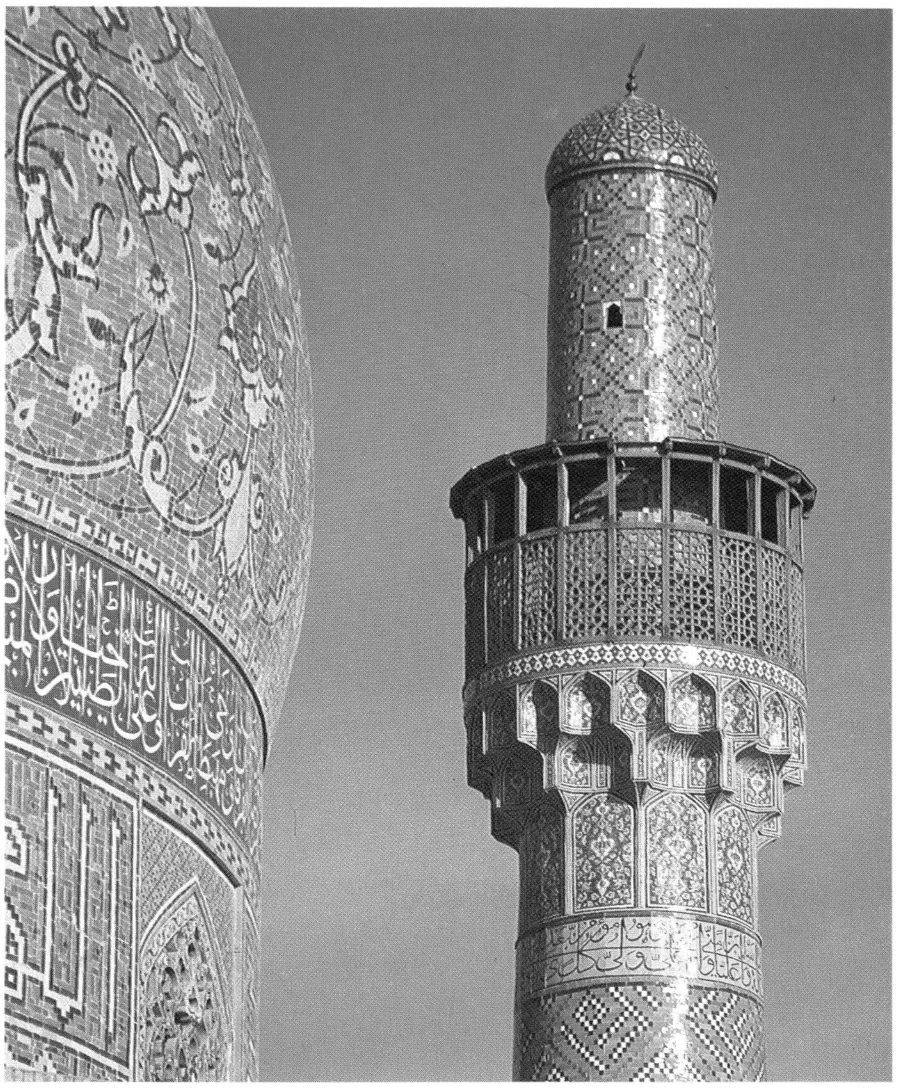

Right: *A dome and minaret in Isfahan, an Iranian city famous for its architecture.*

Jordan

Area: 95,396km^2 (36,832sq.m.).
Population: 3.5 million.
Capital: Amman (1.23m).
Languages: Arabic, Circassian.
Ethnic groups: Arabs, Circassians.
Main exports: phosphates, fruit and vegetables, hides.
Average temperatures: 7°C (45°F) Jan. 24°C (75°F) July.
Highest point: Jebel Ram 1,754m (5,755ft).

Most of Jordan consists of sandy desert and rocky plains, but uplands west of the River Jordan are fertile. This region produces most of Jordan's food. Because only a small part of Jordan can be farmed, many people work in commerce. Bedouin tribes in eastern and southern areas raise livestock. Potash, phosphates and manganese are founded in the Dead Sea area and in the southern region.

The state of Transjordan was set up by Britain after World War I. It became an independent constitutional monarchy in 1946. In 1948 Jordan fought Israel and conquered central Palestine and part of Jerusalem. It received 500,000 Palestinian refugees and Palestinians still form a major part of Jordan's population.

Israel occupied the west bank area of Jordan and Jordanian Jerusalem in 1967, depriving Jordan of its most fertile area. However, Arabs from the west bank can visit Jordan and vice versa. A dispute with Palestinian nationalists in Jordan led to heavy fighting in the 1960s. Finally, the guerrillas withdrew from Jordanian territory.

Iran

Area: 1,648,000km^2 (636,293sq.m.).
Population: 45 million.
Capital: Tehran (4.5m).
Languages: Persian, Kurdish, Turki, Baluchi.
Ethnic groups: Iranians, Kurds, Arabs, Turks.
Main exports: petroleum, petroleum products, carpets, cotton, hides, fruit, minerals.
Average temperatures: 0°C (32°F) Jan. 35°C (95°F) July.
Highest point: Qolleh ye Demavand or Mt Demavend 5,604m (18,380ft).

Iran (formerly Persia) consists mainly of high plateaux almost surrounded by mountains, with narrow lowlands along the Caspian Sea and the Gulf. The highest mountains are in the west and north. Two vast deserts lie in the east.

Farming is the main occupation and cereals, vegetables, fruit, cotton and tobacco are important. The Khuzistan lowlands in the southwest have Iran's richest petroleum deposits which make it the fourth leading world petroleum producer. Semi-nomadic tribes, such as the Baktiari, and settled groups of Kurds and Turcomans raise livestock.

Ancient Persia was powerful between 550 and 330 BC, but it fell to the armies of Alexander the Great. It was later ruled by the Parthians and the Persian Sassanid dynasty until it fell to the Muslim Arabs in the AD 600s.

Iran lost territory to Russia in the 1800s and Britain became the dominant power in the Gulf region. In 1925 the ruling dynasty was overthrown by the Pahlavi family. Mohammad Reza Pahlavi took office as Shah in 1941 after Britain and the USSR had threatened to intervene. They each retained a force in the country until after World War II. Soviet troops finally withdrew from Iranian territory in the late 1940s.

A left-wing government took office in the 1950s and nationalized the petroleum industry. The Shah left the country but was restored to power after a short time. Despite a programme of reform, the Shah's rule became unpopular, thanks to widespread corruption, westernization, and the activities of the secret police. In 1979 the Shah finally fell, and the Ayatollah Khomeini returned from exile. A fundamentalist Islamic leader, Khomeini eradicated all opposition and reintroduced traditional law. War with Iraq broke out in 1980.

Afghanistan

Area: 652,090km^2 (251,773sq.m.).
Population: 14.7 million.
Capital: Kabul (913,000).
Languages: Pushtu, Persian.
Ethnic groups: Pathans (55 percent), Tadshiks, Uzbeks.
Main exports: natural gas, lambskins, cotton, nuts, fruit, carpets.
Average temperatures: −3°C (27°F) Jan. 25°C (77°F) July in Kabul.
Highest point: 7,620m (25,000ft) in the Hindu Kush.

Afghanistan is a land-locked republic bordered by the USSR in the north, Iran in the west and Pakistan in the south and east, with a narrow corridor to China and Kashmir. Its position between Asia Minor and India made it an historic invasion route and in the 19th century the British in India regarded it as a key buffer state against Russia. Britain recognized its independence as a constitutional monarchy in 1919. Following an army coup in 1973, a presidential republic was established. This was toppled in turn in 1978. A year later Soviet troops intervened in support of the People's Democratic Party. They soon controlled the lowlands, but in the mountain passes they were continually harrassed by *muhajadin* guerrillas. About 2 million Afghanis fled south to Pakistan.

Physically, Afghanistan is dominated by the towering ranges of the Hindu Kush which slope westward across much of the country to a high plateau, mainly of sandy desert in the southwest. Most of the population is concentrated in the four river valleys of the Kabul in the east, the Helmand in the southwest, the Hari Rud in the northwest and the Amu Darya in the north.

No part of the country is less than 609m (2,000ft) above sea level and a large area above 2,500m (8,000ft) has long, severe winters. There are sharp extremes of climate elsewhere and the mountains cut Afghanistan off from the rain-bearing Indian monsoons. Average rainfall is only 30cm (12in) a year.

Afghanistan is a land of striking beauty but scanty resources. As about three-quarters of the population live by farming, the shortage of cultivated land means that the economy is precarious. Although the major crop is wheat, some grain has to be imported.

Industry is concentrated mainly on textiles with some cement and sugar works. Natural gas from Shorbaghan is sent to the USSR and Afghanistan has the world's largest deposits of the semi-precious stone lapis lazuli. Some coal, chromite and salt are mined but resources of oil, sulphur, gold, silver, lead, copper and zinc are unexploited.

Map 47   ARABIA AND THE HORN OF AFRICA

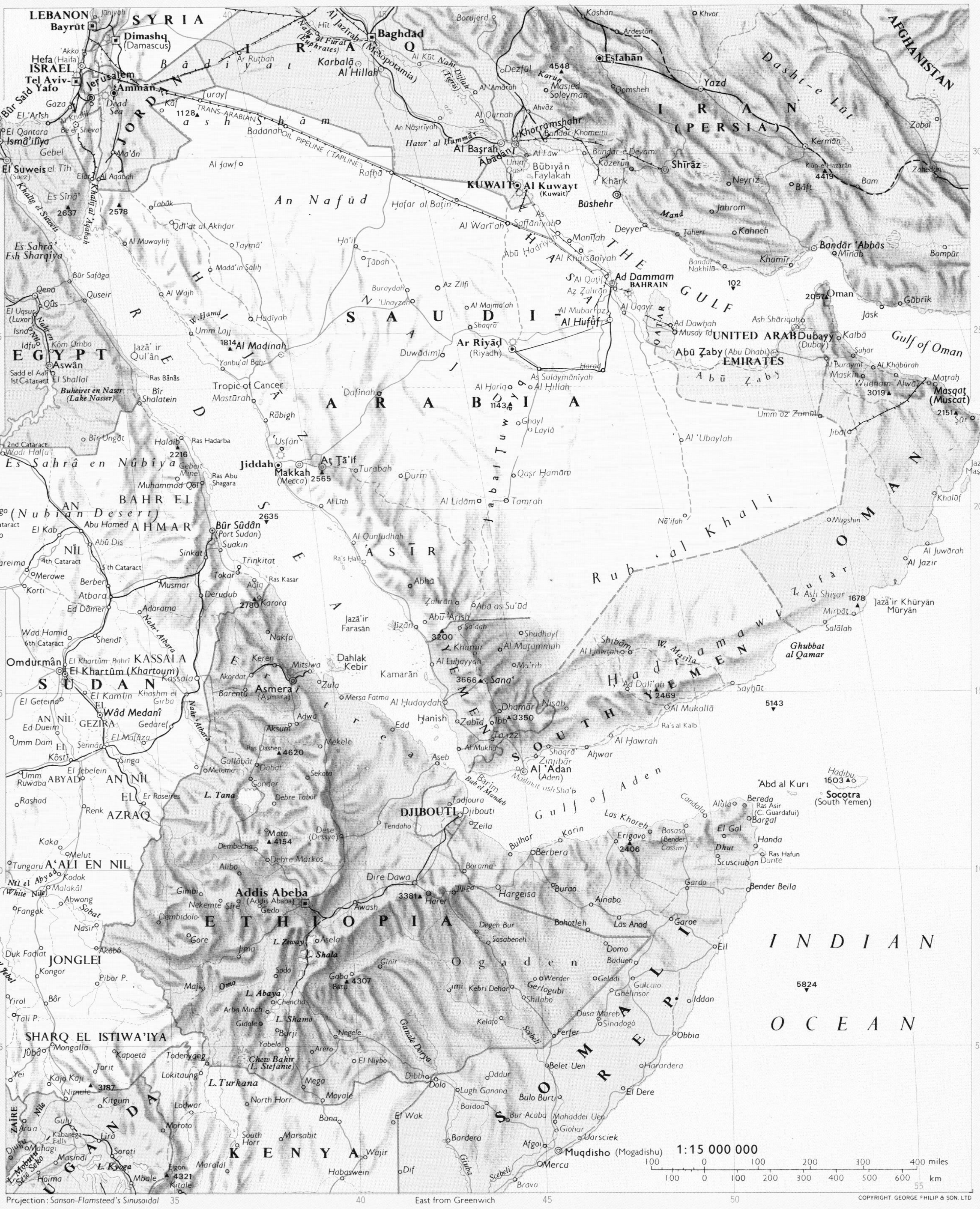

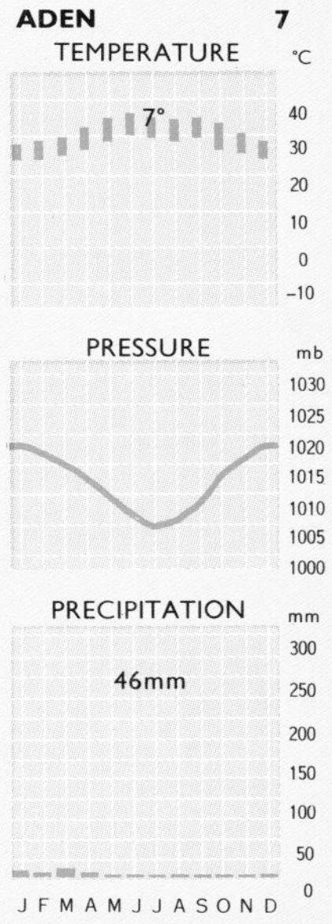

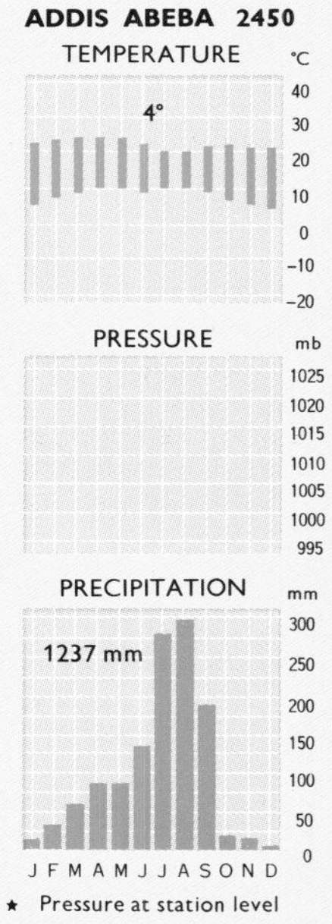

ADEN 7
TEMPERATURE °C

PRESSURE mb

PRECIPITATION mm
46mm

ADDIS ABEBA 2450
TEMPERATURE °C

PRESSURE mb

PRECIPITATION mm
1237 mm

★ Pressure at station level

1:15 000 000

Projection: Sanson-Flamsteed's Sinusoidal   East from Greenwich   COPYRIGHT GEORGE PHILIP & SON LTD

United Arab Emirates, Qatar, Kuwait, Bahrain

Once extremely poor, the small east Arabian states are now among the world's major petroleum producers and oil revenues are bringing rapid development. Other products are fish, dates and camels. The people are Muslims and mostly Arabs, but there are Baluchi, Indian and African minorities. All The states have recently brought in large numbers of migrant workers, especially from the Indian settlement. The special treaties these states once had with Britain have now lapsed and they have now become fully independent.

United Arab Emirates has an area of 92,100km² (32,300sq.m.) and 1.3 million people. Its capital is Abu Dhabi (449,000).

Qatar has an area of 11,437km² (4,415sq.m.) and 300,000 people. Its capital is Doha (190,000).

Kuwait has an area of 17,818km² (6,880sq.m.) and 1.9 million people. Its capital is Kuwait (61,000).

Bahrain has an area of 583km² (225sq.m.) and a population of 400,000. Its capital is Manama (122,000).

Right: *Bahrain's vast oil wealth is concentrated in few hands, and piped water and a modern way of life have yet to reach the rural poor.*

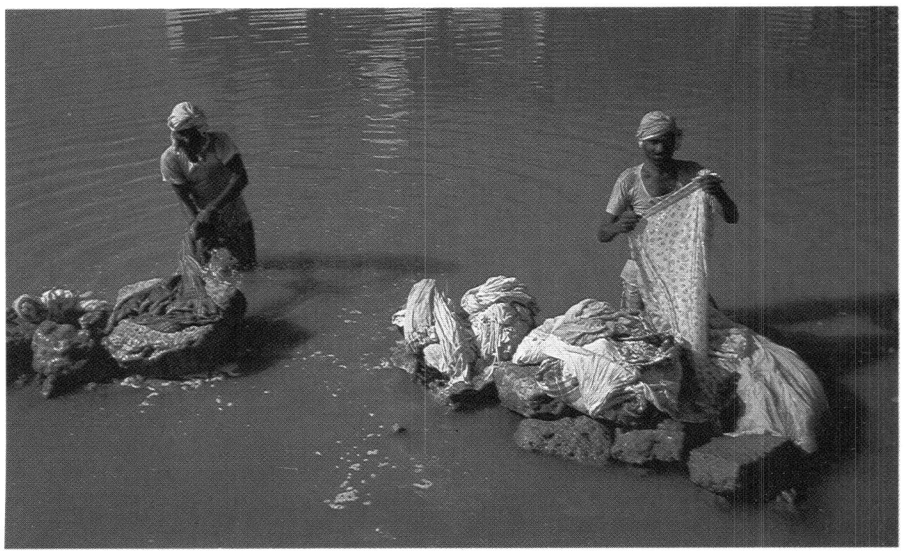

Saudi Arabia

Area: 2,400,004km² (927,000sq.m.).
Population: 11.2 million.
Capital: Riyadh (667,000).
Language: Arabic.
Ethnic group: Arabs.
Main exports: petroleum and petroleum products.
Average temperatures: 22°C (72°F) Jan. 30°F (86°F) July, with cooler winters in north.
Highest point: Asir range 3,048m (10,000ft).

Saudi Arabia occupies most of the Arabian peninsula. It has a long Red Sea coastline in the west and a substantial Gulf coastal strip lying between Kuwait and the United Arab Emirates.

The west coast is low-lying, rising to mountains behind which is a rocky, sandy interior. This desert country extends across the peninsula to the Gulf coast. A vast sand desert, known as the Rub'al Khali (empty quarter) covers the southeast of the country.

The people are Muslims and two of its cities, Makkah (Mecca) and Al Madinah (Medina), are the holiest places of Islam. The former is the birthplace of the Prophet Muhammad and the religious capital of the kingdom. Thousands of pilgrims from all over the Islamic world visit Makkah every year.

Although the government has invested heavily in agricultural development, many Saudis are Bedouins who still lead nomadic lives. Farmers produce cereals, dates, fruit, hides, honey and wool, as well as raising camels, horses and sheep.

Petroleum, first discovered in 1938, is Saudi Arabia's most important resource and provides almost all of the country's foreign earnings. In 1982 Saudi Arabia was the third largest producer of petroleum after the USA and the USSR. Crude oil is shipped abroad or to refineries on the Gulf. A pipeline carries oil to the Lebanese Mediterranean port of Sayda. Much government investment in major urban construction projects is now occurring; these include universities, hospitals and power stations. Much of the workforce is immigrant.

Originally divided into several states, Saudi Arabia was under nominal Turkish control for several centuries. Its leaders fought with the Allies in World War I and gained full independence for their lands. In 1926 the ruler of Najd (central Arabia) conquered the coastal states and founded the modern Saudi Arabian kingdom.

South Yemen

Area: 287,682km² (111,074sq.m.).
Population: 2 million.
Capital: Al'Adan or Aden (285,000).
Language: Arabic.
Ethnic group: Arabs.
Main exports: cotton, oil products, ship bunkering, fish, fish products.
Average temperatures: 25°C (77°F) Jan. 35°C (95°F) July at Al'Adan.
Highest point: in Hadhramawt, 2,469m (8,100ft).

The country called South Yemen was formerly named the Federation of South Arabia. It lies in the southeast of the Arabian peninsula and it has a long coastline along the Gulf of Aden. It borders on Yemen, Saudi Arabia and Oman. South Yemen is a mountainous country with burning hot deserts along the frontier with Saudi Arabia

The people are Muslims and most of them are farmers. The principal crops are millet, sesame and sorghum, but cotton is becoming increasingly important. Fishing is the second most important activity.

Al 'Adan was traditionally one of the region's busiest ports, ideally situated for shipping which passed through Suez. It suffered a setback during the canal's 1969-75 closure. It was a haunt of pirates until Britain took it over in 1839. The colony and the neighbouring protectorate became a federation in 1962 and, in 1967, National Liberation Front nationalists overran the sultanates and set up a republic. Civil war broke out in 1986. The country's official name is the People's Democratic Republic of Yemen.

Ethiopia

Area: 1,221,900km² (471,776sq.m.).
Population: 36 million.
Capital: Addis Ababa (1.28m).
Languages: Amharic, Galla.
Ethnic groups: Semites (Amhara, Tigre), Cushites (Galla, Somali).
Main exports: coffee, civet, hides, oil seeds, wax.
Average temperature: 17°C (63°F) on the highlands.
Highest point: Ras Dashen, 4,620m (15,158ft).

Ethiopia consists mainly of two plateaux, divided by the East African Rift Valley. The northern plateau contains mountain ranges and volcanic peaks, such as Ras Dashen. The capital Addis Ababa is on the plateau at about 2,438m (8,000ft) above sea level. The southern plateau is smaller. It descends to dry, semi-desert areas in the south-east. The plateaux are cool, well-watered and fertile and most people are farmers. The chief cash crop is coffee. Tropical forests occur in the southwest and an arid plain borders the Red Sea.

A uniquely isolated Coptic Christian state from the AD 300s, Ethiopia is the oldest independent nation in Africa. Italy occupied Ethiopia from 1936 until 1941, when it was liberated by British and Ethiopian troops. After the war, Emperor Selassie's reforms were considered by many Ethiopians to be too limited and too slow. Finally, the country became a republic after army officers deposed the emperor in 1974. The next decade saw a further *coup* and socialist domestic policies. Wars broke out with Somalia in the Ogaden region and with Eritrean secessionists. The 1980s were marked by widespread famine which shocked the conscience of the world. Refugees flocked westwards to the Sudan.

Somalia, Djibouti

The Somali Democratic Republic is mainly mountainous in the north. The south is semi-desert, with fertile areas along the Juba and Shebelle rivers. Livestock products are the chief exports, but crops are grown in the south. The republic consists of the former colonies of British and Italian Somaliland which were united after independence in 1960. In 1969 a *coup d'état* brought a military regime to power which pursued Marxist policies. Ten years later constitutional rule was re-established.

Above: *Sunni Muslims at one of the five daily prayers in Saudi Arabia, the home of Islam, a word which means 'surrender'.*

Most people in the republic of Djibouti belong to Somali clans. There are some Arabs and Europeans. The territory is mostly desert. Its economy is based on livestock.

The **Somali Democratic Republic** has an area of 637,657km² (246,201sq.m.) and a population of 6.5 million. Its capital is Mogadiscio (600,000).

Djibouti has an area of 23,000km² (8,800sq.m.) and 340,000 people. Its capital is the port of Djibouti (150,000).

Oman

Area: 278,250km² (105,000sq.m.).
Population: 1.5 million.
Capital: Muscat (80,000).
Language: Arabic.
Ethnic groups: Arabs with minorities of Baluchis, Indians and Africans.
Main exports: petroleum, dates, limes, fish, tobacco, fruit, vegetables.
Average temperature: 31°C (88°F).
Highest point: Jabal Ash Sham, 3,047m (9,997ft).

Oman is situated in southeast Arabia and has a coastline extending 1,600km (1,000m.) between the United Arab Emirates and South Yemen. Inland, Oman extends to the edge of the great Rub' al Khali desert in Saudi Arabia. A range of hills and a plateau lie behind the narrow coastal plain. The northwestern coastal plain is fertile with date gardens stretching for more than 240km (150m), but the rest of the coast is barren. In the south lies the fertile province of Dhofar. Dates are the chief export. Oil production began in 1967 and in 1982 reserves were estimated at 2,900 million barrels. Copper is also extracted and refined.

Oman was an independent state from the 11th century but was harrassed by Persia for many years. The Portuguese controlled Oman's ports for over 100 years but, by 1698, Oman was free. In the 1700s, there were internal problems until the present royal family took control. A treaty was signed with Britain in 1748. In the mid-1800s, Oman lost its overseas possessions, including Zanzibar, which established a sultanate under a member of the royal house. In 1970 the new sultan, who had deposed his father, began a programme of reform. The government had to fight a war against guerrillas to gain control of the interior.

Yemen

Area: 195,000km² (73,300sq.m.).
Population: 7.7 million.
Capital: Sana (448,000).
Language: Arabic.
Ethnic group: Arabs.
Main exports: coffee, qat (narcotic shrub).
Average temperatures: 16°C (60°F) Jan. 27°C (80°F) July.
Highest point: in the Asir range, 3,760m (12,336ft).

Yemen, officially the Yemen Arab Republic, lies in the southwest of the Arabian peninsula. The land is mountainous with a low-lying coastal belt, but is more productive agriculturally than other parts of the Arabian peninsusla.

The Yemenis are Muslims and most of them are farmers or fishermen. Millet is the chief subsistence crop. Cotton is grown along the coast and the famous 'Mokha' coffee is an important export. Qat, a shrub whose leaves are narcotic, is now the country's leading export.

In ancient times, Yemen was a wealthy and powerful state. It was ruled by religious leaders called Imams. In 1962 Imam Ahmad died: army officers deposed his son and proclaimed the country a republic. In the ensuing struggle for power, the republican forces were helped by Egypt and the royalists were aided by Saudi Arabia. By 1967 the republicans were in control. In 1978 a People's Constituent Assembly was set up, and in 1982 a General People's Congress, which is partly elected.

Map 48   AFRICA

LUANDA   59

TEMPERATURE   °C

6°

PRESSURE   mb

PRECIPITATION   mm

323mm

J F M A M J J A S O N D

ACCRA   27

TEMPERATURE   °C

4°

PRESSURE   mb

PRECIPITATION   mm

724mm

J F M A M J J A S O N D

DENSITY OF POPULATION
1 : 80 000 000
Inhabitants

per mile	per km²	per mile	per km²
under 2	under 1	32–64	12–25
2–8	1–3	64–128	25–50
8–16	3–6	128–256	50–100
16–32	6–12	over 256	over 100

• Towns of over 200 000 inhabitants

Projection: Zenithal Equidistant

1 : 40 000 000

	200	0	200	400	600	800	1000 miles
200	0	200	400	600	800	1000	1200 1400 1600 km

DJ.   Djibouti
LES.   Lesotho
O.F.S.   Orange Free State
SWAZ.   Swaziland

COPYRIGHT. GEORGE PHILIP & SON. LTD.

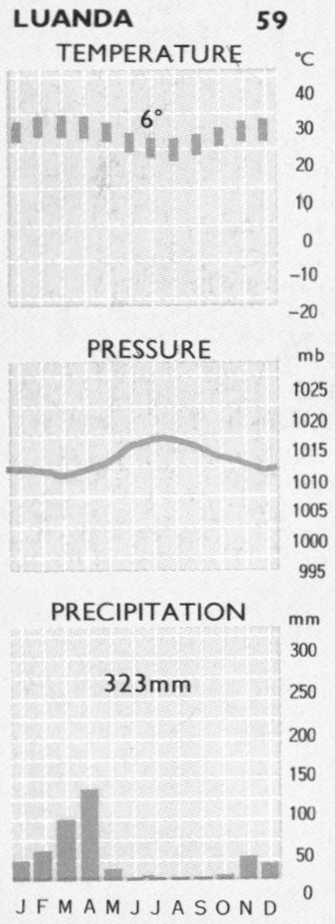

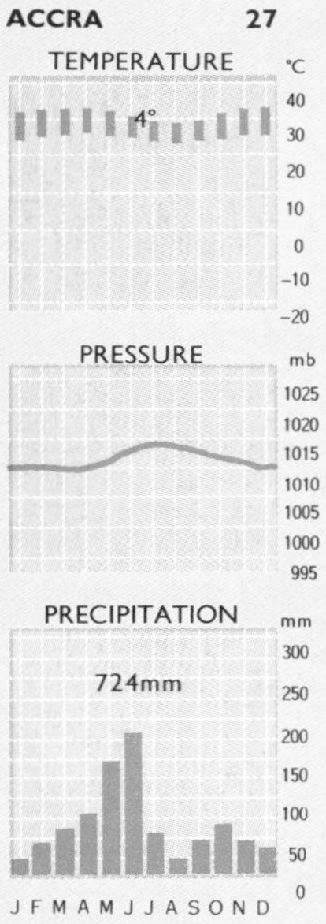

Africa today forms a large part of the developing world. The political map of the region has changed greatly since 1945 with rapid transitions from colonial status to full independence, achieved in some cases only after wars against former European rulers. Many place names, particularly those recalling colonialism, have been changed. For example, the Belgian Congo became Zaïre and its capital, Leopoldville, was renamed Kinshasa.

Since independence, economic difficulties, international interference and inter-communal strife have led to the creation of many one-party states and military governments. South Africa, the continent's most prosperous country, has a government still controlled by settlers of European origin who form only 17 percent of the population. By 1985 the South African government's policy of *apartheid*, or separate development based upon racial discrimination, was facing increasing hostility at home and abroad. In the north of the continent years of drought in the sub-Saharan region compounded political problems, and Ethiopia and Sudan suffered from famine.

Africa contains vast tracts of burning desert, large areas with unreliable rainfall and broad expanses of dense tropical forest. Because so much of the environment is hostile to man, the continent is

Right: Sisal hemp, a major Tanzanian crop, laid out in rows to dry in Illonga.

thinly populated. But in places falling mortality rates have led to population rises which have added to economic problems.

Plantation agriculture is nevertheless important and many African countries now depend for export revenue on cash crops. Ghana leads the world in cocoa production and Nigeria in palm oil exports. Other major agricultural exports include coffee, cotton and tobacco.

The main economic potential of Africa however, lies in its vast mineral reserves. Nigeria and Libya are among leading oil exporters. South Africa produces about three-quarters of the non-communist world's gold. Zaïre is the leading industrial diamond producer and Zambia is a leading copper exporter.

Above: *An oasis near Rissani on the edge of the Sahara in eastern Morocco, where the desert exerts a powerful influence.*

Right: *Apartment blocks and offices have replaced Benghazi's old buildings since Libya's discovery of oil in the 1950s.*

Morocco

Area: 458,730km² (177,070sq.m.).
Population: 24.3 million.
Capital: Rabat (596,000).
Language: Arabic.
Ethnic groups: Arabs, Berbers.
Main exports: phosphates, citrus fruits, cork, fish, timber, wool.
Average temperatures: 16°C (60°F) Jan. 22°F (72°F) July on coast.
Highest point: Mt Toubkal, 4,165m (13,665ft).

The lowlands and low plateaux facing the Atlantic Ocean are the richest and most populous parts of Morocco. The climate is equable and moist, although summer days are often hot. The largest city, Casablanca (2.4m.), is on the coast. Casablanca, Agadir, Essaouira and Safi are centres of an important fishing industry. Beyond the coastlands, a dry strip of land separates the fertile low plateaux from the high plateaux and ranges of the Atlas mountains. The mountains have an extreme climate. Summer temperatures often reach 37°C (100°F), whereas in winter temperatures plummet to −10°C (14°F).

About six out of every 10 Moroccans work in agriculture. Morocco's production of phosphates, the chief export, is second only to that of the USA. Manufacturing is increasing in importance, but unemployment is high and has led to considerable emigration to Europe.

Most of Morocco was a French protectorate between 1912 and 1956, although the north was Spanish. The country became independent in 1956 as a constitutional monarchy. The king now governs with a directly and indirectly elected chamber of 267 deputies. In the 1970s, Morocco claimed the territory of Spanish Sahara, which has large phosphate deposits. The Spaniards agreed to withdraw in early 1976, leaving Morocco occupying the north and Mauritania the south. Mauritania withdrew, but Polisario guerrillas, attempting to create a West Saharan state and backed in this by Algeria, continued to fight.

Libya

Area: 1,759,540km² (637,358sq.m.).
Population: 4 million.
Capitals: Banghazi (650,000), Tarabulus or Tripoli (980,000).
Language: Arabic.
Ethnic groups: Arabs, Berbers.
Main export: petroleum.
Average temperatures: 11°C (52°F) Jan. 29°C (85°F) July on coast.
Highest point: Picco Bette, 2,286m (7,500ft).

Most of Libya's fertile land is near the coast, especially in the west between the Tunisian border and Misratah. In places behind the coast there is a dry plateau, parts of which are fertile. The most fertile region in the east is the Al Marj (Barce) plain. Libya's chief crops are barley, groundnuts, olives, wheat and other typical Mediterranean crops. In the south, the low coastal plateaux merge into the Sahara, where settlements occur only around oases and petroleum fields. Nearly nine-tenths of Libya is desert, but it has the highest per capita income in Africa because of its petroleum exports. In 1983 Libya had established oil reserves of 21,500 million barrels.

Formerly Turkish, Libya came under Italian rule in 1912, although the east was not subdued until 1932. During World War II, Libya was the scene of several major battles. From 1943, Britain controlled the north and France the south. In 1951 Libya became an

Commercial crops: Africa

COMMERCIAL CROPS
- Cotton
- Grapes
- Groundnuts
- Oil Palm
- Rubber
- Citrus Fruits
- Cocoa
- Coffee
- Sugar Cane
- Tobacco

Minerals: Africa

MINERALS
- Aluminium
- Chromium
- Copper
- Diamonds
- Gold
- Iron
- Lead/Zinc
- Manganese
- Tin

The Copper Belt

The Rand

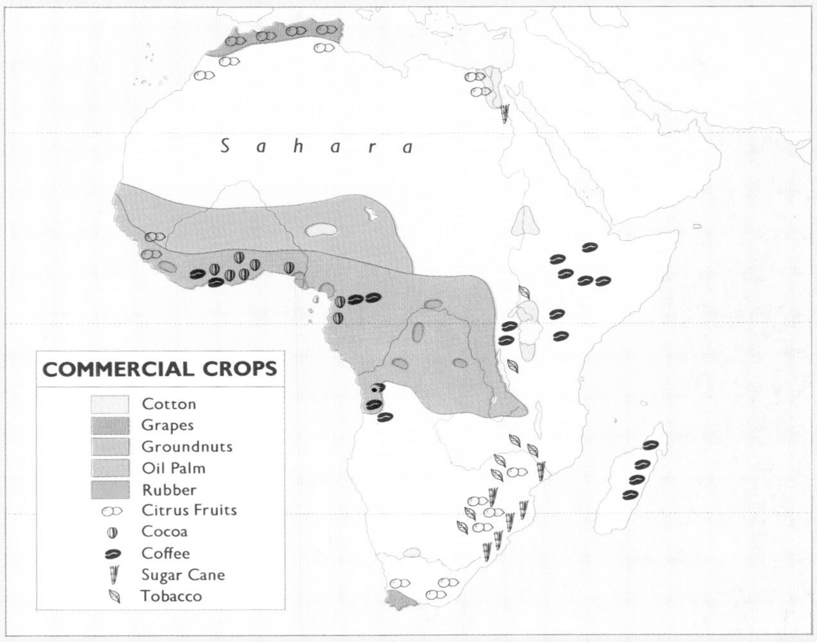

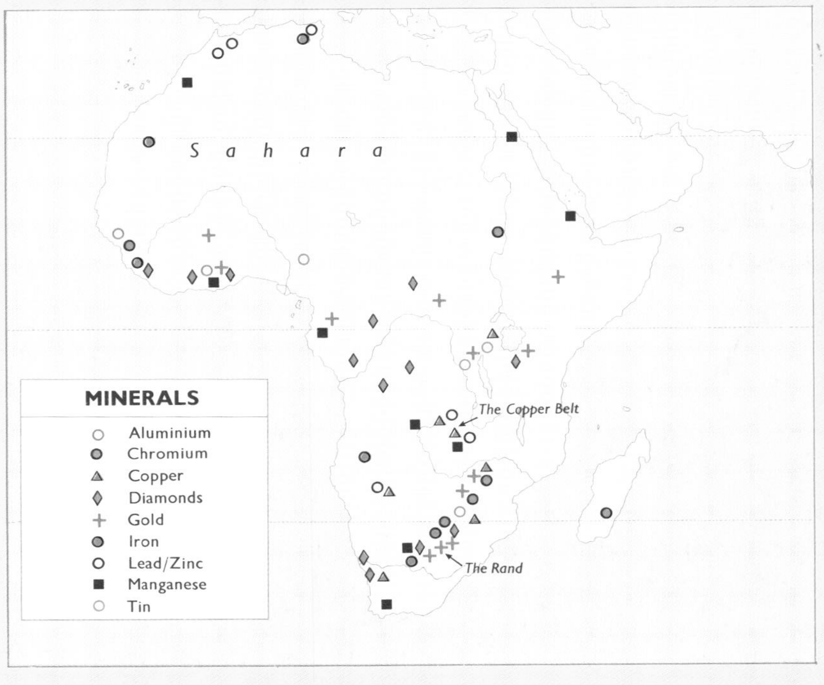

independent monarchy. Army officers deposed the monarch in 1969. They established a Revolutionary Command Council which introduced an Islamic form of socialism. Today Colonel Muammar Qadhafi remains Leader of the Revolution, but power is vested in a series of delegate congresses and committees.

Tunisia

Area: 164,150km^2 (63,170sq.m.).
Population: 7 million.
Capital: Tunis (557,000).
Languages: Arabic, French.
Ethnic groups: Arabs, Berbers.
Main exports: phosphates, agricultural products, esparto grass.
Average temperatures: 10°C (50°F) Jan. 27°C (80°F) July on coast.
Highest point: Djebel Chambi, 1,544m (5,066ft).

Lying at the eastern end of the Atlas mountains, Tunisia is a sunny country with an increasing tourist trade. Its relief is varied and the rainfall decreases from north to south – the south being desert. Tunisia's most valuable industry is mining, especially phosphates, which form 35 percent of the exports. Many of the people are farmers, although farming contributes only one-fifth of the national income. Crops include barley, dates, figs, grapes, maize, oats, olives, oranges, sorghum and wheat. Many Tunisians leave to work in France or Libya.

Tunisia won independence as a monarchy in 1956, but became a single-party presidential republic in 1957.

Algeria

Area: 2,381,741km^2 (919,590sq.m.).
Population: 21.5 million.
Capital: Alger or Algiers (1.51m.).
Languages: Arabic, French.
Ethnic groups: Arabs, Berbers.
Main exports: barley, dates, fruits, iron ore, olives, petroleum and natural gas, phosphates, wine.
Average temperatures: 16°C (60°F) Jan. (22°C (75°F) July, on the coast.
Highest point: Mt Tahat, 2,918m (9,573ft).

Although it is Africa's third largest petroleum producer and a leading producer of natural gas, Algeria is mainly a farming country. Farming is mostly confined to the Mediterranean zone and vines are the chief commercial crop. Cereals, citrus fruits and olives are also important. The inland steppes of the High Atlas are used as pasture. The thinly-populated Sahara, where petroleum and natural gas are extracted, covers most of the country.

Algeria, an Islamic nation, was a French territory from 1848 to 1962. Between 1954 and 1962, the Algerian National Liberation Front (FLN) fought with French forces. Most French settlers, who numbered about one million, returned to France in 1961-62. Algeria has had a military government since 1965. This government has established close links with the Soviet Union. Algeria is a one-party state. The FLN nominates the president and candidates for the Assembly. The country's high birth-rate and high unemployment rate have encouraged emigration.

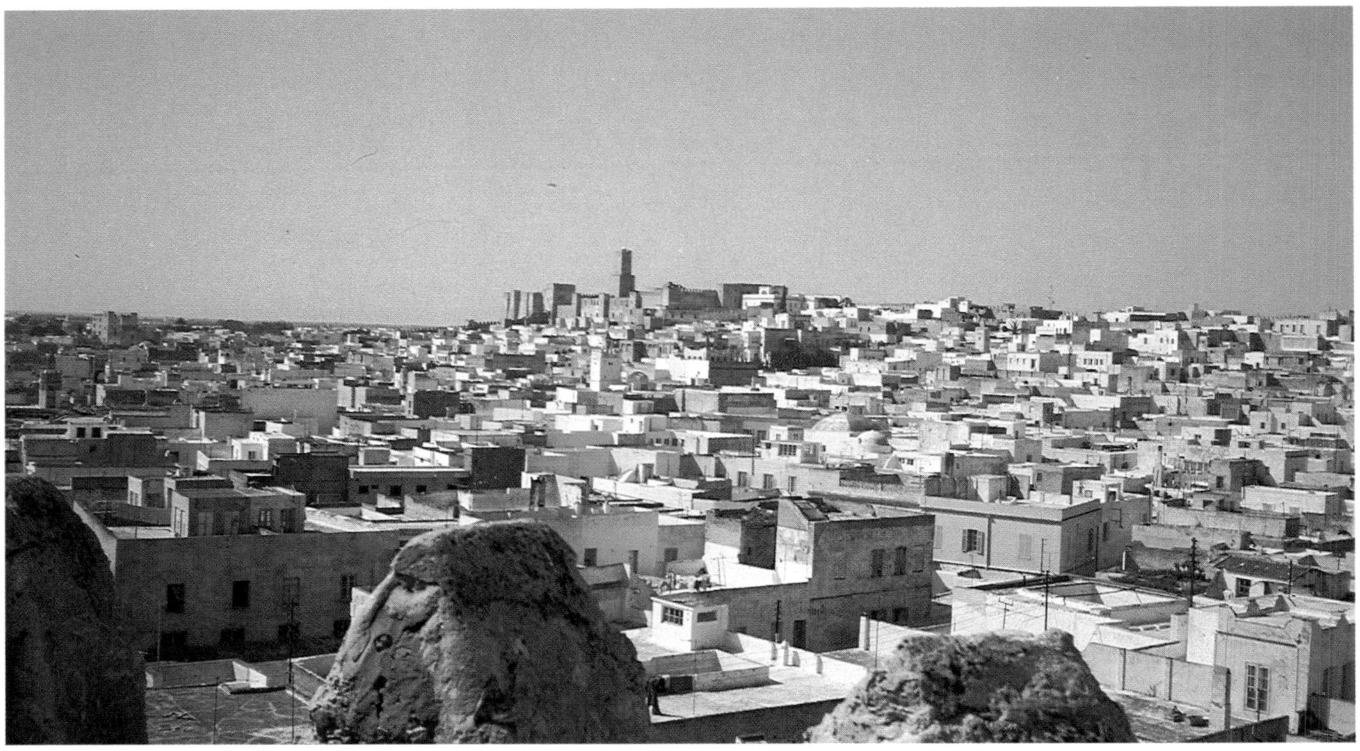

Above: *Sixth-century ramparts enclose the old town in Sousse, an important port and fishing centre on Tunisia's east coast.*

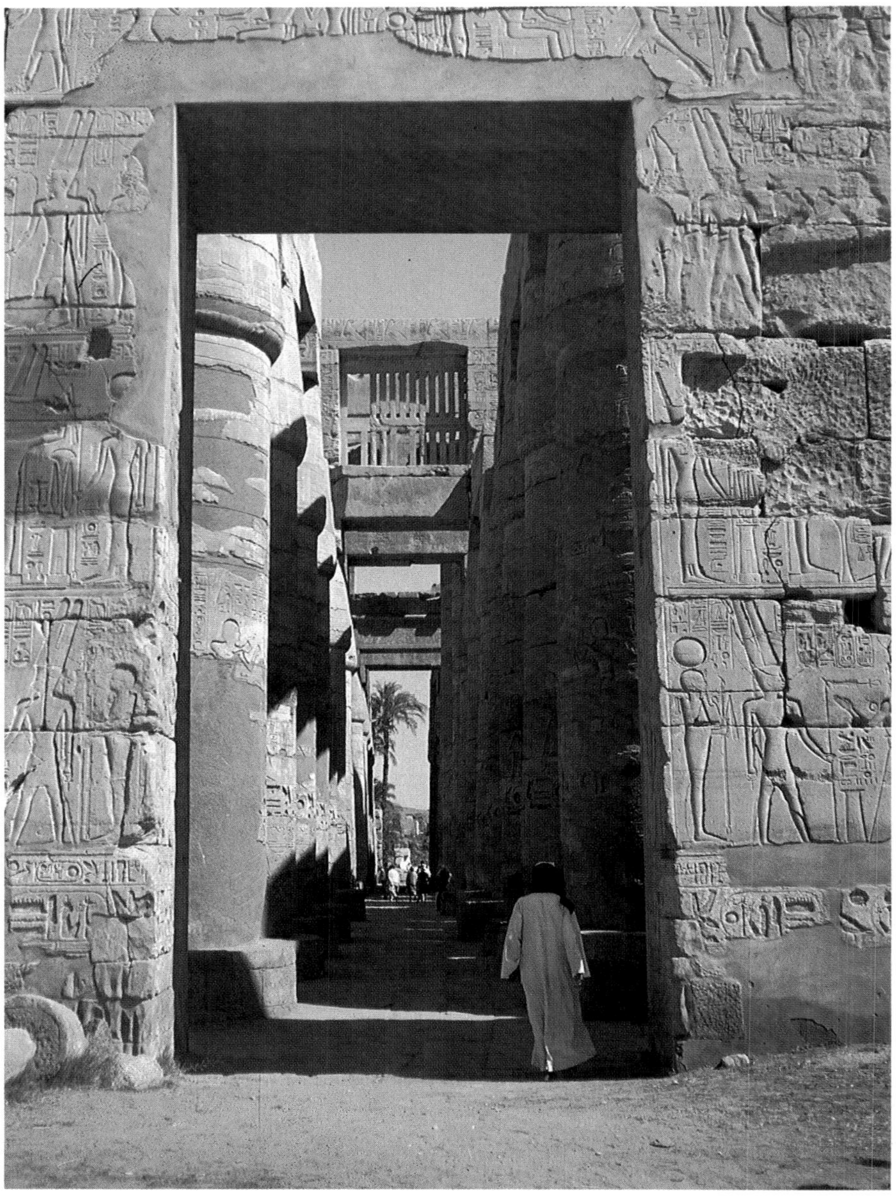

Right: *The ruins of the great temple of Amon, built by Rameses II more than 3,000 years ago, at Karnak on the east bank of the Nile in Upper Egypt.*

Egypt

Area: 1,002,000km^2 (386,900sq.m.).
Population: 48.3 million.
Capital: El Qâhira or Cairo (8.54m.).
Language: Arabic.
Ethnic groups: Arabs and some people of European and Turkish descent.
Main exports: cotton textiles and raw cotton, iron and steel, machinery, fertilizers, chemicals, vegetables.
Average temperatures: 13°C (55°F) Jan. 32°C (90°F) July.
Highest point: Gebel Katherînah, 2,637m (8,652ft).

Egyptians are mostly of Arab or Turkish descent, but there are Berber and European minorities. Most people are Sunni Muslims, although there is a Coptic Christian minority. Egypt has been an Arabic-speaking state since AD 640.

More than 95 percent of all Egyptians live in the Nile valley and farming occupies three-fifths of the people. Around the Nile delta are two of Africa's largest cities, El Qâhira or Cairo and El Iskandarîya or Alexandria (2.3m.).

Ancient Egypt, one of the world's greatest civilizations, grew up in the Nile valley. Alexander the Great conquered Egypt in 332 BC and the area later became part of the Roman Empire. Christianity was introduced and Egypt became the centre of the Coptic Church in AD 395. But after the Arab conquest of AD 640, Egypt adopted Islam and the Arabic language.

From 1517, Egypt was a province of the Ottoman (Turkish) empire. France ruled Egypt briefly between 1798 and 1801, when British and Turkish forces helped to expel them. In 1805, Mohammed Ali Pasha was appointed governor by the Turks. He began to modernize the country and, in 1841, he broke away from the Ottomans. After his death, Egypt's prosperity declined, although the Suez Canal was opened in 1869. In 1882, Britain occupied the country and held it as a protectorate between 1914 and 1922, when it became a monarchy. By 1936, British troops occupied only the Canal zone.

Conflict with Israel

In 1948-49 Egyptian forces fought against the establishment of the state of Israel. In Egypt, nationalism increased and, under Colonel Nasser, Egypt was declared a republic in 1953. Britain agreed to withdraw its troops by 1956, but in that year Nasser nationalized the Suez Canal. An abortive British-French invasion aimed at holding the Canal Zone ended after a few months.

Egypt now tried to consolidate Arab power in the Middle East by attempting political union with Syria and with Yemen, but the experiments failed. The 1960s and 1970s were dominated by conflict with Israel. The Sinai region was temporarily lost and the Suez Canal closed. In 1973 however Egypt made military advances, and Nasser's successor, Anwar as-Sadat, secured peace with Israel. Assassinated in 1981, Sadat was succeeded by Hosni Mubarak.

The President of the Arab Republic of Egypt is nominated by the 392-member People's Assembly. A *Shura*, or 210-member Consultative Council, was formed in 1980.

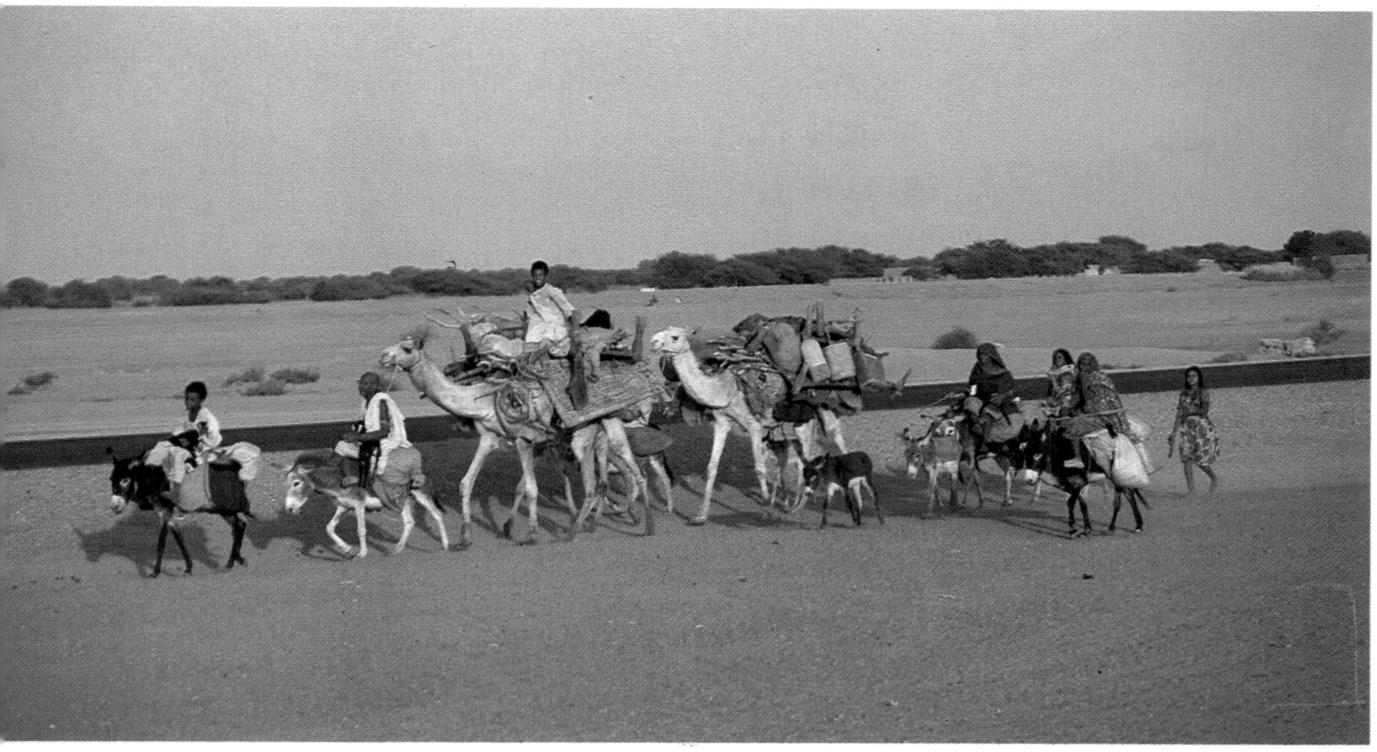

Left: *Migrating nomads with camels and goats in the arid plain of Sudan.*

Above: *Paved streets and shade trees lend Ouagadougou, capital of Burkina Faso, the appearance of a modern town.*

Physical features and climate

Most of Egypt is desert and nearly all the people live in the fertile Nile valley, which covers only three percent of the land. The upper Nile valley is narrow and lined by cliffs in places. The lower Nile valley includes the broad, thickly-populated Nile delta.

To the west of the Nile, the wind-swept desert contains the Qattara Depression, which is 133m (436ft) below sea level. To the east, highlands border the Red Sea. Egypt's highest mountains are in the Sinai peninsula. The climate of Egypt is hot and dry. The rainfall decreases from north to south between 254 and 25mm (10-1in).

Minerals and industry

Egypt has some petroleum deposits, and also phosphates and some iron ore.

In Africa, Egypt is second only to South Africa in industrial output. Industries located in the main cities are varied, including cigarettes, cotton textiles, fertilizers, iron and steel, machinery, paper, shoes and sugar refining. Much of Egypt's power comes from the Aswan High Dam. The Suez Canal is a major source of revenue. In Egypt, the Nile is used for transport and the country has 4,321km (2,685m.) of railways and 16,182km (10,055m.) of metalled highways.

Agriculture

Most Egyptians are farmers, who irrigate their small farms along the Nile. The chief commercial crop is cotton. Other crops include barley, beans, fruit, lentils, maize, millet, onions, rice, sugar-cane and wheat. Egypt has large numbers of cattle and sheep.

Trade and foreign relations

Egypt trades with both western and communist countries, exporting to the USA, the USSR, and member states of the EEC. Past foreign policies have veered between warm relations with the USSR and the USA. Peace with Israel has to some extent endangered relations between Egypt and other Arab states.

Mauritania, Western Sahara

These two largely desert or semi-desert countries face the Atlantic Ocean. Mauritania, an independent republic since 1960, has important iron ore reserves. Most of its agriculture and population are in the Senegal river valley which forms its southern border.

In 1975, Spain agreed to withdraw from Western Sahara, letting Morocco take the north, which has large deposits of phosphates, and Mauritania the south. However, an Algerian-backed Saharan nationalist group (*Frente Polisario*) resisted Moroccan and Mauritanian occupation and claimed full independence. Mauritania handed over territory to Morocco, but the fight continued. In 1982 the 'Democratic Saharan Arab Republic' was recognized by the Organization of African Unity (OAU).

Mauritania has an area of 1,030,700-km^2 (397,953sq.m.) and 1.8 million people. The capital is Nouakchott (135,000).

Spanish Sahara was called **Western Sahara** after the Spaniards withdrew in early 1976. The territory covers 266,769km^2 (102,680sq.m.) and has about 109,000 people. The capital is El Aaiún (33,000).

Mali, Niger, Chad, Burkina Faso

These landlocked nations became independent from France in 1960. Each territory has subsequently become a military republic. In Mali, Niger and Chad, the Sahara covers the north and savanna occurs in the south. Burkina Faso has a higher average annual rainfall than elsewhere but rainfall is generally unreliable. All four countries depend on agriculture and migration of many workers to the south.

Mali is a one-party state. The President and the 82-member National Assembly are elected directly. It has an area of 1,240,000km^2 (478,764sq.m.) and 7.7 million people. The capital is Bamako (404,000).

Niger, a military republic since 1974, has an area of 1,267,000km^2 (489,189 sq.m.) and 4.5 million people. The capital is Niamey (102,000).

Chad has an area of 1,186,408km^2 (458,075sq.m.) and 6.3 million people. The capital is N'Djamena (225,000). Its recent history has been one of military *coups* and of civil war.

Burkina Faso (Upper Volta) became independent in 1960. After a succession of military *coups* it changed to its current name in 1984. It has an area of 274,122km^2 (105,811sq.m.) and 6.7 million people. The capital is Ouagadougou (286,000).

Map 49   NORTHERN AFRICA

ALGER 59
TEMPERATURE
°C
13°

PRESSURE
mb

PRECIPITATION
762mm

J F M A M J J A S O N D

TOMBOUCTOU 301
TEMPERATURE
°C
13°

PRECIPITATION
231mm

J F M A M J J A S O N D

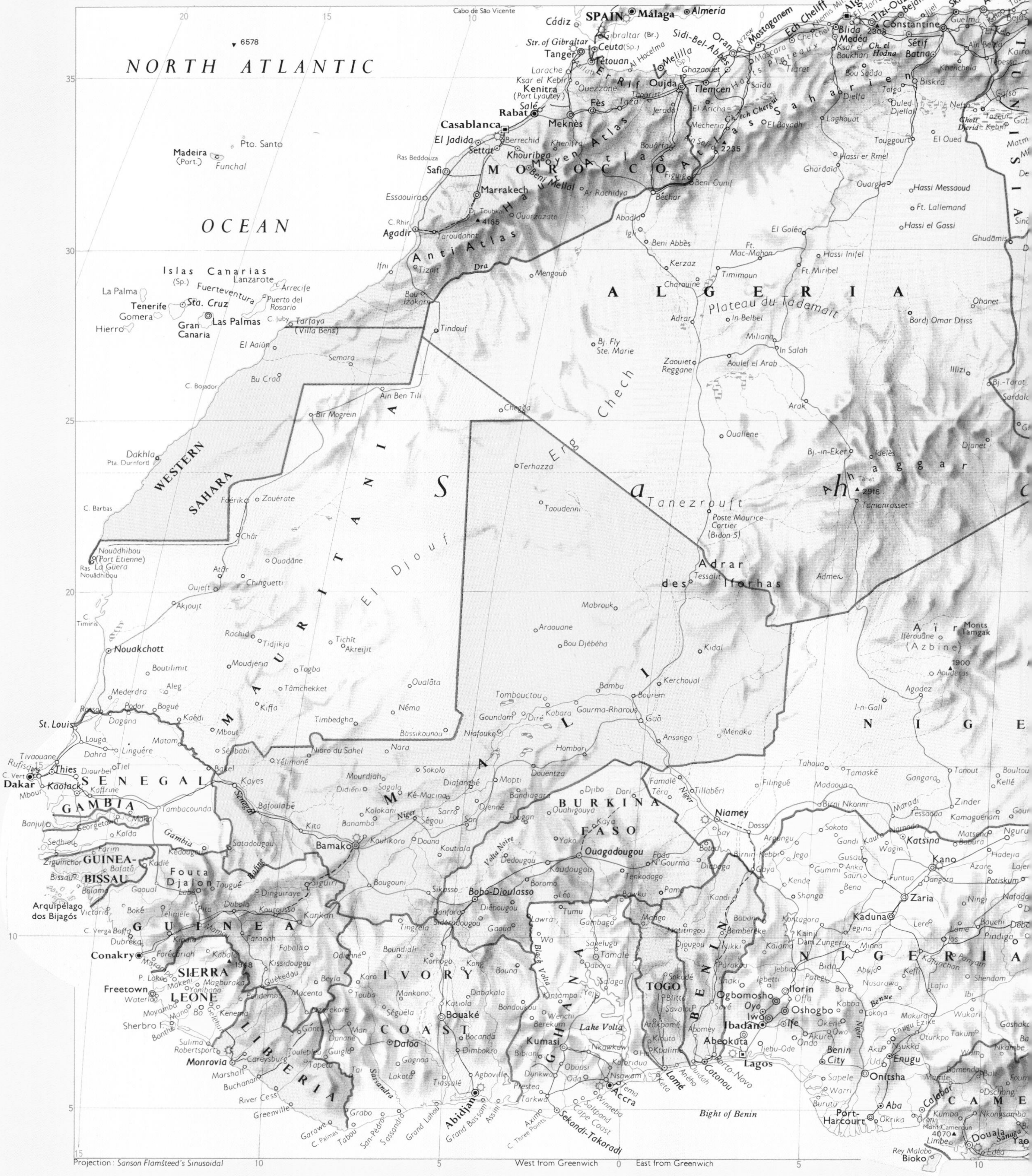

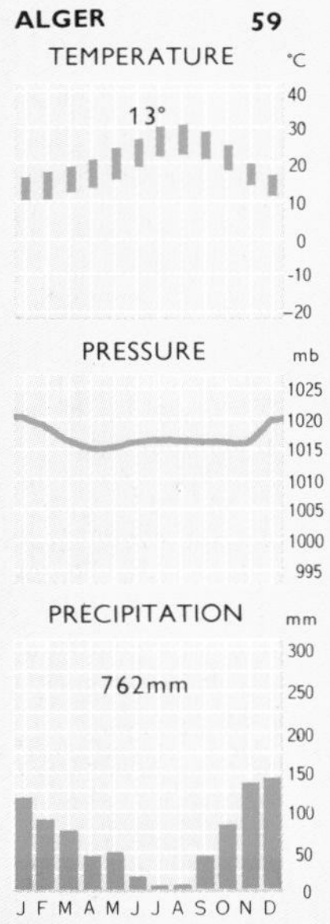

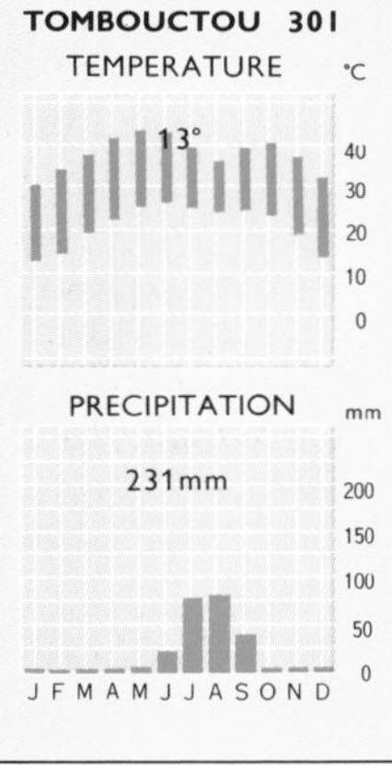

Sudan

Area: 2,505,813km² (967,494sq.m.).
Population: 21.8 million.
Capital: El Khartum or Khartoum (1.6m).
Language: Arabic.
Ethnic groups: Arabs and Nubians in the north, Black Africans in the south.
Main exports: cotton, dates, groundnuts, gum arabic, hides and skins, livestock.
Average temperatures: 16°C (60°F) Jan. 35°C (95°F) July.
Highest point: Mt Kinyeti, 3,187m (10,456ft).

Sudan is the largest African country. Much of the north is desert, which merges into grassland, savanna and forest in the south. Sudan is divided ethnically into the Muslim, Arabic-speaking north and the Black African south. Farming is Sudan's chief activity and cotton, grown under irrigation, is the main crop. A civil war from 1964-72 was followed by a period of peace under Ja'afar al-Nimeiri. In 1985, amidst growing economic and political problems, Nimeiri was overthrown.

Senegal, Gambia

Senegal, a former French territory which became independent in 1960, encloses the small former British territory of Gambia which became independent in 1965. Groundnuts are the chief exports of both countries. In 1982 the two states formed a close alliance known as the Confederation of Senegambia.

Most Senegalese are Muslims and the official language is French. Senegal is a one-party republic. Massive reserves of iron ore have been discovered.

Most Gambians are also Muslims and the official language is English. Gambia became a republic with an elected House of Representatives.

Senegal has an area of 196,192km² (75,750sq.m.) and 6.7 million people. The capital is Dakar (979,000), a major sea and air port. The Senegal river valley in the north is the most important agricultural region.

Gambia has an area of 11,295km² (4,361sq.m.) and 800,000 people. The capital is Banjul (45,000), at the mouth of the Gambia river whose valley forms the heart of the country.

Guinea, Guinea-Bissau

Guinea, a former French territory, became an independent republic in 1958. Most of the people are Muslims and the official language is French.

Map 50

EL ISKANDARIYA 32

TEMPERATURE °C
13°

PRESSURE mb
1025
1020
1015
1010
1005
1000
995

PRECIPITATION mm
178mm
300
250
200
150
100
50
J F M A M J J A S O N D

EL KHARTÛM 390

TEMPERATURE °C
10°

PRESSURE mb
1025
1020
1015
1010
1005
1000

PRECIPITATION mm
158mm
300
250
200
150
100
50
J F M A M J J A S O N D

COPYRIGHT. GEORGE PHILIP & SON. LTD.

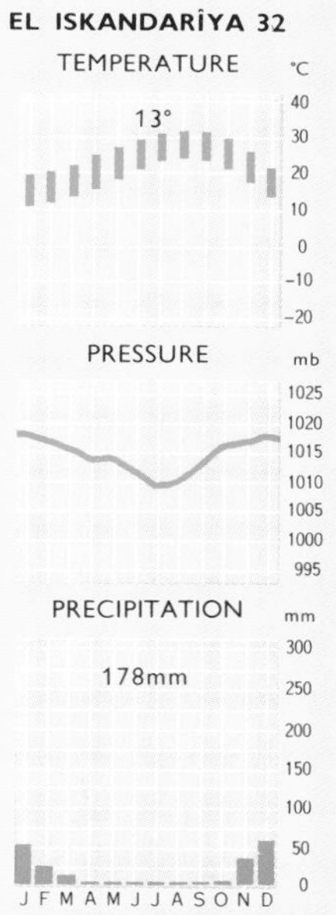

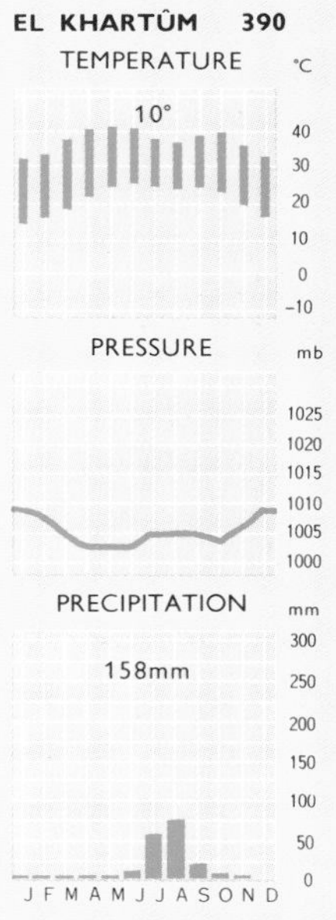

Before 1958, Guinea was an agricultural country. Today minerals, including bauxite, diamonds and iron ore, are the chief exports. Guinea has been greatly assisted by communist countries, including the USSR.

Neighbouring Guinea-Bissau, which has an economy based on farming, won independence from Portugal in 1974. This followed a long war of liberation which began in 1962. Most of the people are Muslims.

Guinea has an area of 245,857km² (94,926sq.m.) and 6.1 million people. The capital is Conakry (763,000). It has a low-lying coastal plain backed by a plateau rising to 1,500m.

Guinea-Bissau has an area of 36,125km² (13,948sq.m.) and 844,000 people. The capital is Bissau (109,000).

Sierra Leone, Liberia

The history of both of these states is linked with the slave trade. Freetown, capital of Sierra Leone, was founded in 1788 as a home for freed slaves. The modern descendants of these slaves form an important group called Creoles.

Right: *A primitive ferry brings equipment to modernize rural Sierra Leone.*

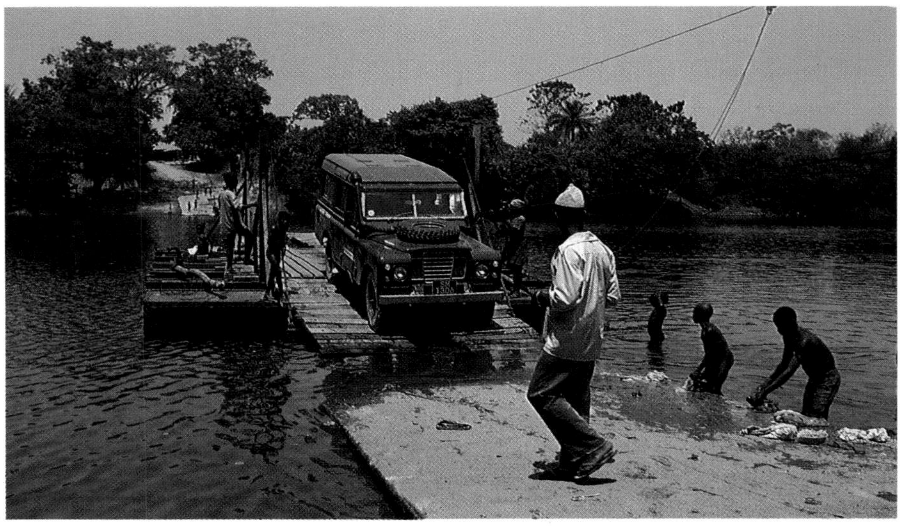

Sierra Leone was a British colony from 1808 to 1961. In 1971, it became a republic.

Free Afro-American slaves founded Monravia in 1822. Liberia became independent in 1847. For many years it remained under US influence. A *coup d'état* in 1980 brought Samuel Kanyon Doe to power.

Sierra Leone's chief exports are minerals, including diamonds and iron ore. Tropical crops are grown by the farmers, who make up more than 70 percent of the population.

Iron ore has overtaken rubber as Liberia's chief export. Liberia's large shipping fleet includes mainly foreign ships, which fly Liberia's flag. The ship owners take advantage of the low rates of taxation charged by Liberia.

Sierra Leone has an area of 73,326 km^2 (27,925sq.m.) and 3.6 million people. The capital is Freetown (316,000).

Liberia has an area of 111,369km^2 (43,000sq.m.) and 2.2 million people. The capital is Monrovia (425,000).

Ivory Coast, Ghana, Togo, Benin

These four countries extend northwards from the Gulf of Guinea. They have similar climates and vegetation. The southern forests are important for their timber and for tropical crop plantations. The northern savanna is used for grazing and for the cultivation of such crops as cotton and millet.

Ivory Coast has an area of 322,463 km^2 (124,503sq.m.) and a population of 10.1 million. The capital is Abidjan (686,000). A former French territory, Ivory Coast became independent in 1960 and later a one-party state. Coffee, cocoa and cotton are the chief exports. Industries in Abidjan process farm products, cement, paper, timber and other products. Power comes from the hydroelectric projects on the Bia, Bandama and Sassandra rivers.

Ghana has an area of 238,305km^2 (92,010sq.m.) and a population of 14.3 million. The capital is Accra (758,000). Formerly the British colony of Gold Coast, Ghana became independent in 1957, incorporating part of neighbouring Togoland. Ghana became a republic in 1960 under the presidency of Dr Kwame Nkrumah. Since then brief periods of democratic civilian rule have been interrupted by military intervention, most recently by Flight-Lt. J. Rawlings.

Ghana is the world's largest producer of cocoa, and timber is another important export. The Volta River hydroelectric scheme provides power for aluminium smelting and other industries. Some gold and diamonds are also exported.

Togo has an area of 56,000km^2 (21,622sq.m.) and 2.9 million people. The capital is Lomé (283,000). Part of former Togoland was incorporated into Ghana in 1957. The rest was ruled by France until it became independent in 1960. After years of military rule, constitutional rule was re-established in 1980.

Benin was called Dahomey until November 1975, when the name change was announced. Benin has an area of 112,622km^2 (43,483sq.m.) and a population of 4 million. The capital is Porto Novo (208,000). The country became independent from France in 1960. Between 1960 and 1972, Benin suffered five *coups*. It is now a Marxist republic. The economy is based on farming and palm oil is the chief export.

Nigeria

Area: 923,768km^2 (356,667sq.m.).
Population: 91.2 million.
Capital: Lagos (1.7m).
Languages: Hausa, Ibo, Yoruba.
Ethnic groups: about 250, including Hausa, Kanuri, Fulani, Ibo, Yoruba.
Main exports: petroleum, cocoa, cotton, groundnuts, palm kernels and oil, hides and skins, rubber, timber, tin and alloys.
Average temperature: 27°C (80°F) in the south.
Highest point: nearly 2,130m (7,000ft) on Cameroon border.

Nigeria has a larger population than any other African country, although 13 African countries cover a larger area. About 70 out of every 100 Nigerians live in rural areas. But Nigeria is unusual in Africa in having many well-developed large towns, including Lagos, Ibadan, Ogbomosho, Kano and Oshogbo.

Nigerians are divided into about 250 groups, each of which has its own language or dialect. The chief groups in the Muslim north are the Fulani, Hausa and Kanuri. Muslims make up 48 percent of the population. The people in the south are mainly Christians (34 percent of the total population) or they practise traditional religions (18 percent). The largest groups in the south are the Ibo to the east and the Yoruba to the west. Nigeria's ethnic diversity has created many problems, including the civil war of 1967-70.

History and constitution

Knowledge of Nigeria's early history is fragmentary. However, archaeologists have discovered impressive artistic cultures, such as Nok (500 BC-AD 200), Ife (after AD 1200) and Benin, which was flourishing in the late 1400s, when the Portuguese visited the area.

Britain occupied Lagos in 1861 and, gradually, British influence spread inland. In 1900 the British colony of Southern Nigeria was established, followed by the creation of a protectorate over Northern Nigeria in 1906. The North and South were merged in 1914 to form modern Nigeria.

Britain applied a policy of indirect federal rule. After 1945, Nigeria was divided into three regions, North, East and West. A central council co-ordinated the regional governments. Nigeria became independent in 1960 as a federation and in 1963 it became a republic.

Ethnic differences caused tensions, and two army *coups* occurred in 1966. Fighting also broke out between Hausas and Ibos who lived in the north. To reduce tensions, the military government split Nigeria into 12 regions, but the former Eastern Region broke away and set up a rebel republic called Biafra. A bitter war ended with Biafra's defeat in 1970. Subsequent governments, military and civilian, sought to unify the country. From 1979-83 Nigeria had a democratic government headed by President Shehu Shagari. In 1984 however a Supreme Military Council took power once again, committed to the eradication of corruption, which few denied was a long-standing problem. A further military *coup* occurred in August 1985.

Physical features and climate

Nigeria is mostly a land of low plateaux and plains. Mangrove swamps border much of the coast, which includes the delta of the great Niger River. Inland, tropical forests merge into savanna in the centre of the country. The hot, wet coast has average temperatures of about 27°C (80°F) all the year round. In the arid north, temperatures vary from season to season. Summer temperatures sometimes reach 46°C (115°F).

Minerals and industry

Nigeria possesses major petroleum deposits, which were first discovered in 1956. In 1952 Nigeria was Africa's largest petroleum producer, and the world's tenth largest. Oil revenue brought wealth, but economic problems loomed large. Attempts to build a new capital city at Abuja were frustrated by lack of finance. Nigeria has many other minerals, including some of Africa's few coal reserves.

Nigeria has varied industries, producing metal and engineering products as well as processing farm and forest products. The country has more than 4,180km (2,600m.) of railways and 108,000km (67,100m.) of maintained roads.

Agriculture, forestry and fishing

Most Nigerians work on the land. Groundnuts, palm oil, cocoa and rubber are important exports. Food crops include bananas, cassava, maize, millet, rice and yams. Large herds of cows, sheep and goats are also important.

Nigeria exports hardwoods from the southern forests, which cover about 31,000km^2 (12,000sq.m.). Fishing is carried on in and around the Niger delta and fish are a useful source of extra dietary protein.

Trade and foreign relations

Britain remains the chief trading partner of Nigeria, although the USA, the West Indies, the Netherlands and France are also important buyers of Nigerian petroleum. Nigeria has played an active role in Pan-African affairs.

Central African Republic, Congo, Gabon

With Chad, these three territories formed part of French Equatorial Africa from 1910 to 1960, when they became separate independent states. The Central African Republic was politically

Below: *The University of Ghana at Accra, blending modern and traditional West African architecture, is a far cry from the capital's overcrowded slums.*

unstable and was taken over by a military government. Both Gabon and Congo are one-party states.

Central African Republic, one of the poorest nations in Africa, has an area of 622,436km^2 (240,324sq.m.) and a population of 2.25 million. The capital is Bangui (pop. 387,000). Most of the people are subsistence farmers.

Congo has an area of 342,000km^2 (132,046sq.m.) and 1.74 million people. Its capital is Brazzaville (pop. 422,000), and its chief export is timber, with some diamonds.

Gabon has an area of 267,667km^2 (103,346sq.m.) and 1.37 million people. The capital is Libreville (pop. 350,000). A fairly prosperous African country, Gabon has large mineral resources, which form the basis of its exports, including iron ore, manganese, petroleum and uranium, and also has valuable stands of timber. Gabon retains close links with France.

Cameroon Equatorial Guinea

These neighbouring states nestle in northwestern equatorial Africa. Cameroon was created in 1961 when the southern part of the former British Cameroons joined French Cameroon (independent in 1960) to form one nation. Equatorial Guinea was Spanish until 1968. It consists of the territory of Rio Muni on the mainland and the island of Bioko (formerly Fernando Póo). Both Cameroon and Equatorial Guinea export cocoa and coffee.

Cameroon covers 465,054km^2 (179,558sq.m.) and has 9.7 million people. Its capital is Yaoundé (pop. 178,000) although the largest city is Douala (314,000). Its highest point, Mt Cameroon is 4,070m (13,354ft) high and is the wettest place in Africa with 10,160mm (400in) of rain per year. Cameroon has many ethnic groups, some numbering only 50 persons. One of the larger groups, the Fang, form the majority in Rio Muni.

Equatorial Guinea has an area of 28,051km^2 (10,830sq.m.), with a population of 398,000. Its capital is Malabo (pop. 25,000).

Below: *Traditional indigo dye pits outside the thatched mud huts and compound wall of Zaria in north central Nigeria.*

Zambia

Area: 752,620km^2 (290,586sq.m.).
Population: 6.8 million.
Capital: Lusaka (538,469).
Languages: Bemba, Nyanja, English.
Ethnic groups: Tonga, Lozi, Bemba, Ngoni.
Main exports: copper, zinc, lead, tobacco.
Average temperatures: 11-35°C (70-95°F).
Highest point: Muchinga Mts, 2,130m (7,000ft).

Land-locked Zambia stands on a savanna-covered plateau. Zambia has more than 70 ethnic groups. Most are farmers and many are at subsistence level. The country's wealth lies in mining; copper accounts for 90 percent of the exports. The Copperbelt region on the Zaïre border is Zambia's most densely-populated area, with centres at Kitwe, Mufulira and Ndola. The Kariba Dam in the south supplies power for copper smelting. Other minerals include cadmium, cobalt, lead and zinc.

Formerly the British protectorate of Northern Rhodesia, the country became independent as Zambia in 1964. It became a one-party state in 1972.

Zaïre

Area: 2,344,885km^2 (905,365sq.m.).
Population: 33.1 million.
Capital: Kinshasa (2m).
Languages: French, Swahili, Lingala.
Ethnic groups: Bakongo, Baluba, Balunda, Bamongo
Main exports: copper, zinc, cobalt, cassiterite, industrial diamonds, oil palm products, coffee, cotton.
Average temperature: 27°C (80°F) in low-lying areas.
Highest point: Ruwenzori on Ugandan border, 5,119m (16,795ft).

Formerly named Congo, Zaïre is the second largest African country, more than 1.5 times as large as the combined area of the European Economic Community. Most of Zaïre lies in the depression of the Zaïre (formerly Congo) River and its tributaries. Mountains rise in the east and south. Tropical forest covers the Zaïre basin, which is hot and wet, with savanna in the drier north and south.

Zaïre has a few pygmies, but most of the population consists of Bantu-speaking peoples. About 70 percent of the people work on farms, but the nation's wealth is based on minerals, especially copper. Zaïre is also the world's leading industrial diamond producer.

The explorer Henry Morton Stanley established the potential of Zaïre in the 1870s. From 1884, Zaïre was the personal property of King Léopold II of Belgium. After reports of ill-treatment of the people by Europeans, the Belgian government took control in 1908.

When Zaïre became independent in 1960, civil disorder and fighting broke out. From 1965, order was restored and, by the 1970s, the country was stable. Development of its massive hydro-electricity potential has included the construction of Inga Dam, near Matadi, which is one of the most impressive hydro-electric complexes in the world.

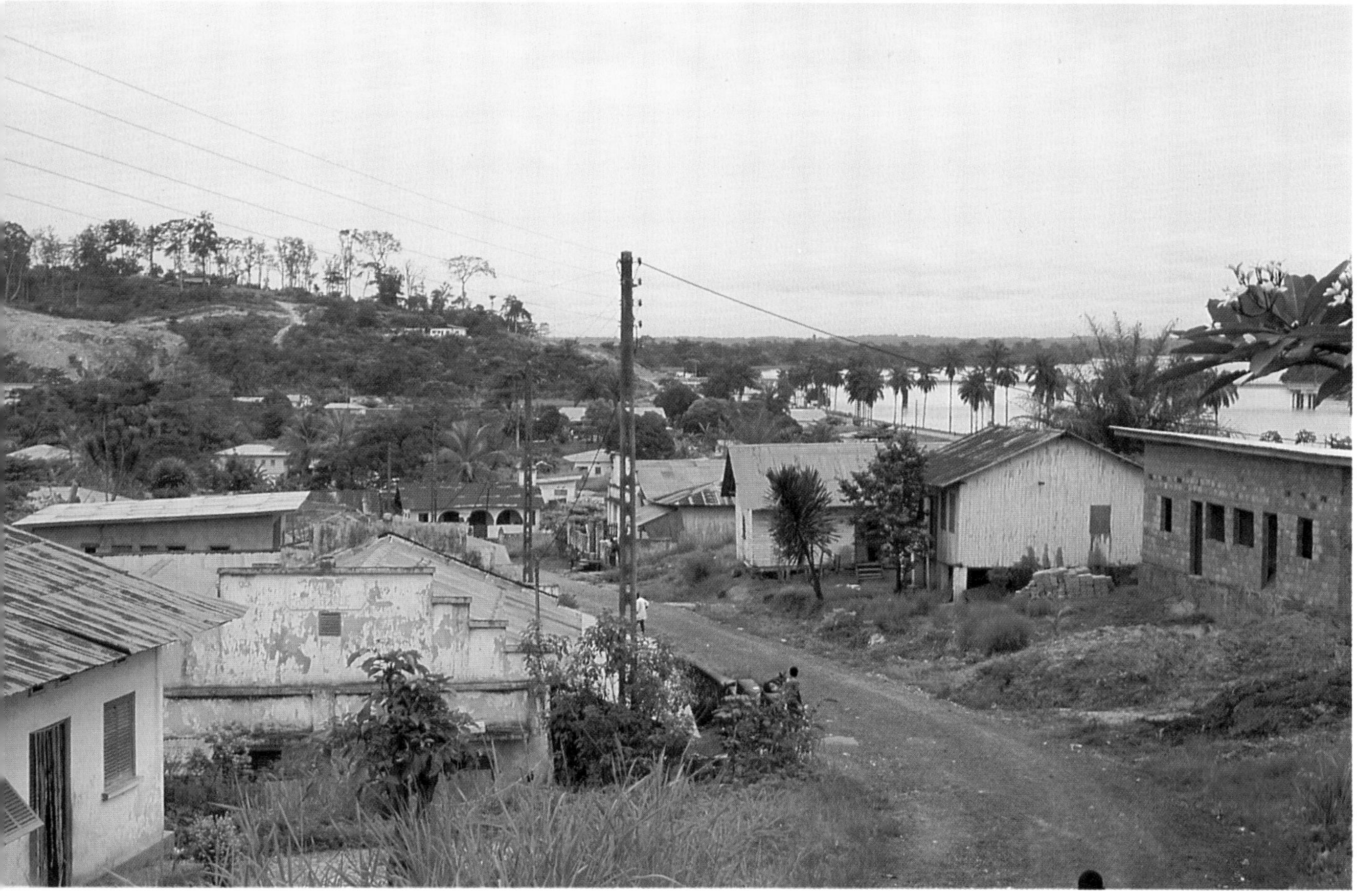

Left: *Lambaréné, a lumbering centre in western Gabon, lies on an island on the river Ogooué amid dense equatorial rain forest.*

Kenya

Area: 582,646km² (224,960sq.m.).
Population: 19.5 million.
Capital: Nairobi (1.2m).
Languages: Swahili, English.
Ethnic groups: Kikuyu, Luo, Luhya.
Main exports: coffee, tea, petroleum products.
Average temperatures: 27°C (80°F) on the coast, 10°-21°C (50°-70°F) on the plateau.
Highest point: Mt Kenya, 5,199m (17,058ft).

Rich in wildlife and superb scenery, Kenya has a fast-expanding tourist industry, which is second only to coffee as a source of revenue. Nearly half of Kenya is a high plateau. The plateau is divided by the East African Rift Valley which, in places, is flanked by walls more than 900m (3,000ft) high. Volcanic masses, such as Mt Kenya, rise above the plateau. To the north-east, the country becomes arid. The oldest human remains ever found (2.5m yrs old) were discovered in the Rift Valley.

Farming is the main occupation. The pleasant, fertile southwest plateau attracted many European settlers when Kenya became a British colony in 1920. The presence of European and Asian immigrants aggravated a land shortage among Kenya's largest ethnic group, the Kikuyu, and in 1952 the Kikuyu launched an uprising called Mau Mau. Although the rebellion was put down, Kenya became independent in 1963. A one-party state, Kenya has pursued a policy of land redistribution, Africanization and economic development. Nairobi and Mombasa have expanded rapidly, and Kenya currently has the world's highest rate of population growth.

Uganda

Area: 236,860km² (91,343sq.m.).
Population: 14.7 million.
Capital: Kampala (332,000).
Languages: English, Swahili.
Ethnic groups: Baganda, Banyoro, Batoro.
Main exports: coffee, cotton.
Average temperatures: 15°-29°C (59°-84°F).
Highest point: Mt Elgon, 4,321m (14,176ft) on Kenya border; Ruwenzori border with Zaïre, 5,199m (16,795ft).

Water, including part of Lake Victoria, covers about one-seventh of Uganda and fish are an important source of dietary protein. The economy, however, is based on farming and the rich soils support food and cash crop farming, especially coffee and cotton. Local processing industries get power from the Owen Falls hydro-electric plant. Most of Uganda is between 900 and 1,500m (3,000-5,000ft) above sea level and the climate is milder than normal for equatorial areas.

More than 40 ethnic groups live in Uganda. The largest group, the Baganda, lives in Buganda province, the richest farming region. From 1893 to 1962, Britain ruled Uganda. After independence, unrest was caused by conflict between the Baganda and the central government. President Milton Obote was overthrown by the dictatorial General Idi Amin in 1971. Amin fell from power with the Tanzanian invasion of 1979, and in 1980 Dr Obote was re-elected. He was himself overthrown for a second time in 1985, and went into exile. Three political changes and their associated conflicts have wrecked a potentially very rich economy.

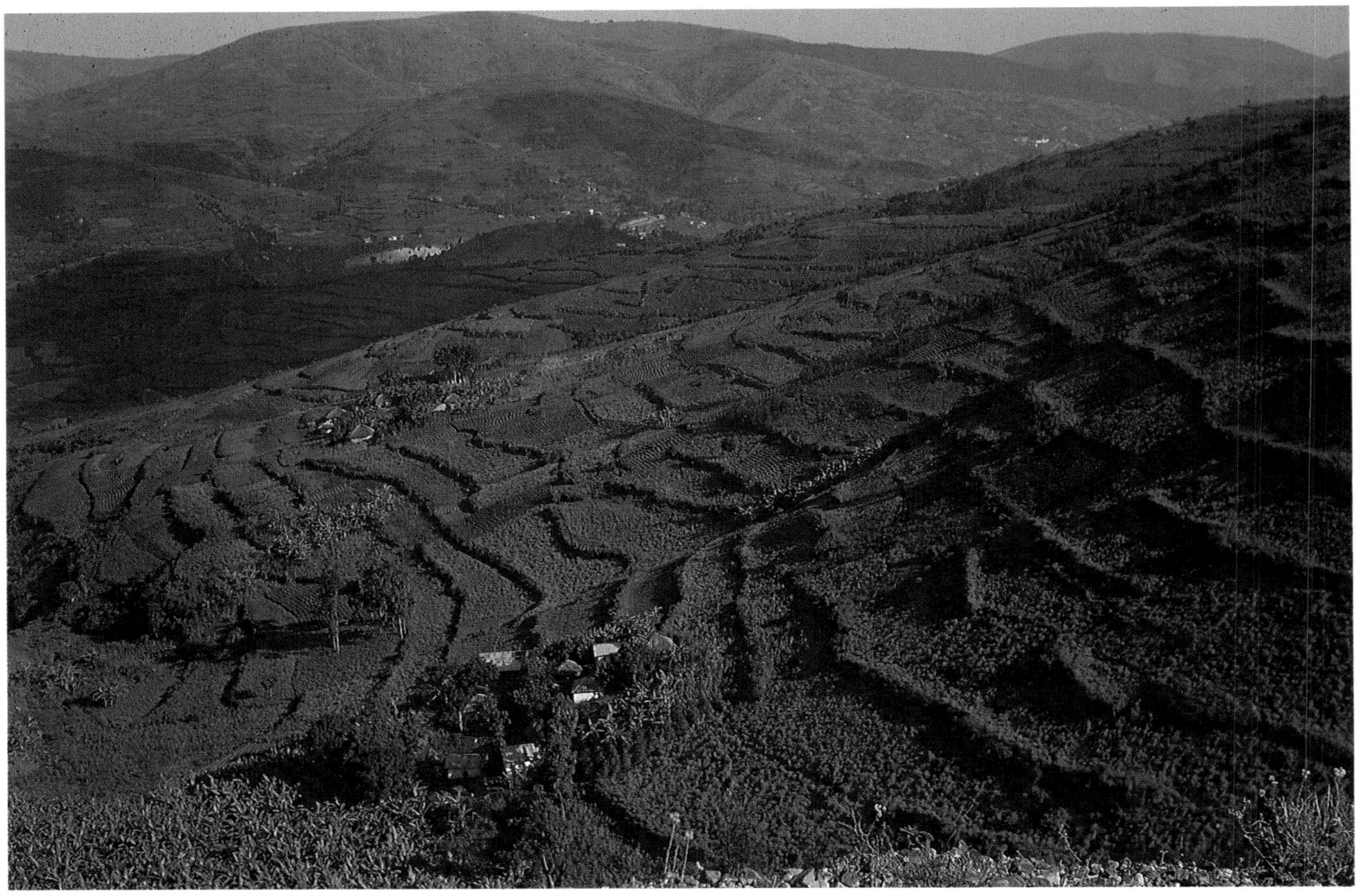

Above: *Scattered farmsteads lie among the densely terraced foothills of the fertile Virunga Mountains, in the Kigezi district of southwestern Uganda.*

Malawi

Area: 126,338km² (48,779sq.m.).
Population: 7.1 million.
Capital: Lilongwe (103,000).
Largest city: Blantyre (219,000).
Languages: English, Nyanja/Chewa.
Ethnic groups: Nyanja/Chewa, Tumbuka, Yao, Lomwe.
Main exports: tea, tobacco.
Average temperatures: 23°C (74°F) on plains, 21°C (69°F) in highlands.
Highest point: Mt Mlanje, 3,000m (9,843ft).

Malawi is a densely-populated, land-locked country. Lake Malawi (Nyasa) is in the Rift Valley in the east. The west is a tableland. Farming is the chief activity. The chief cash crops are tea and tobacco. Because of the dense population, many workers migrate to Zimbabwe, South Africa and Zambia. Formerly the British protectorate of Nyasaland, Malawi, a one-party republic, became independent in 1963.

Tanzania

Area: 945,050km² (364,886sq.m.).
Population: 21.73 million.
Capital: Dodoma (40,000).
Languages: English, Swahili.
Ethnic groups: Sukuma, Nyamwezi, Ha, Makonde, Gogo.
Main exports: sisal, coffee, cotton, pyrethrum, cloves, sugar.
Average temperatures: 26°C (78°F) on coast, 17°C (63°F) on plateau.
Highest point: Mt Kilimanjaro, 5,895m (19,340ft).

Above: *A woman with her baby harvests sugar cane in the Mbambara Tanga region of Tanzania, where collective peasant enterprises receive government support.*

Tanzania consists of mainland Tanganyika and the small offshore island territory of Zanzibar. These territories united in 1964. The mainland has a tropical coastal belt and a cooler, drier inland plateau. Africa's highest mountain, Kilimanjaro, is in the north-east.

More than 120 ethnic groups live in Tanzania and there are small European, Asian and Arab minorities. Tanzania has a farming economy, mostly subsistence, but cash crops form the bulk of the exports. A one-party state, Tanzania implemented a self-help policy called *Ujamaa*, whereby people are brought together to work in co-operative villages. Tanzania was a German colony from the 1880s to 1918, when Britain took over. Tanganyika became independent in 1961 and Zanzibar in 1963. Two of the country's main problems are unreliable rainfall in the interior and a poorly-developed communication system. The latter problem was however helped by the completion of the Tanzania-Zambia (Tan-Zam) railway.

Rwanda, Burundi

Rwanda and Burundi are small, densely-populated states in the heart of equatorial Africa. Most of the people are subsistence cultivators. Their chief export is coffee. There is a Bantu Hutu majority, with the minority Tutsi (nine percent in Rwanda and less than 15 percent in Burundi) and a few Twa (pygmies).

Called Ruanda-Urundi, the area was colonized by Germany in the late 1800s. After World War II, Belgium was mandated to govern the area until 1962, when it split into two independent nations. The Tutsi minority were feudal rulers over the Hutu. In the last 30 years, much Tutsi-Hutu conflict has occurred. The Hutu removed the Tutsi leadership of Rwanda in 1959. In Burundi, many Hutu were massacred by the Tutsi in the 1970s.

Rwanda has an area of 26,338km² (10,169sq.m.) and 6.3 million people. Its capital is Kigali (pop. 156,650).

Burundi has an area of 27,834km² (10,747sq.m.) and 4.92 million people. Its capital is Bujumbura (pop. 141,000).

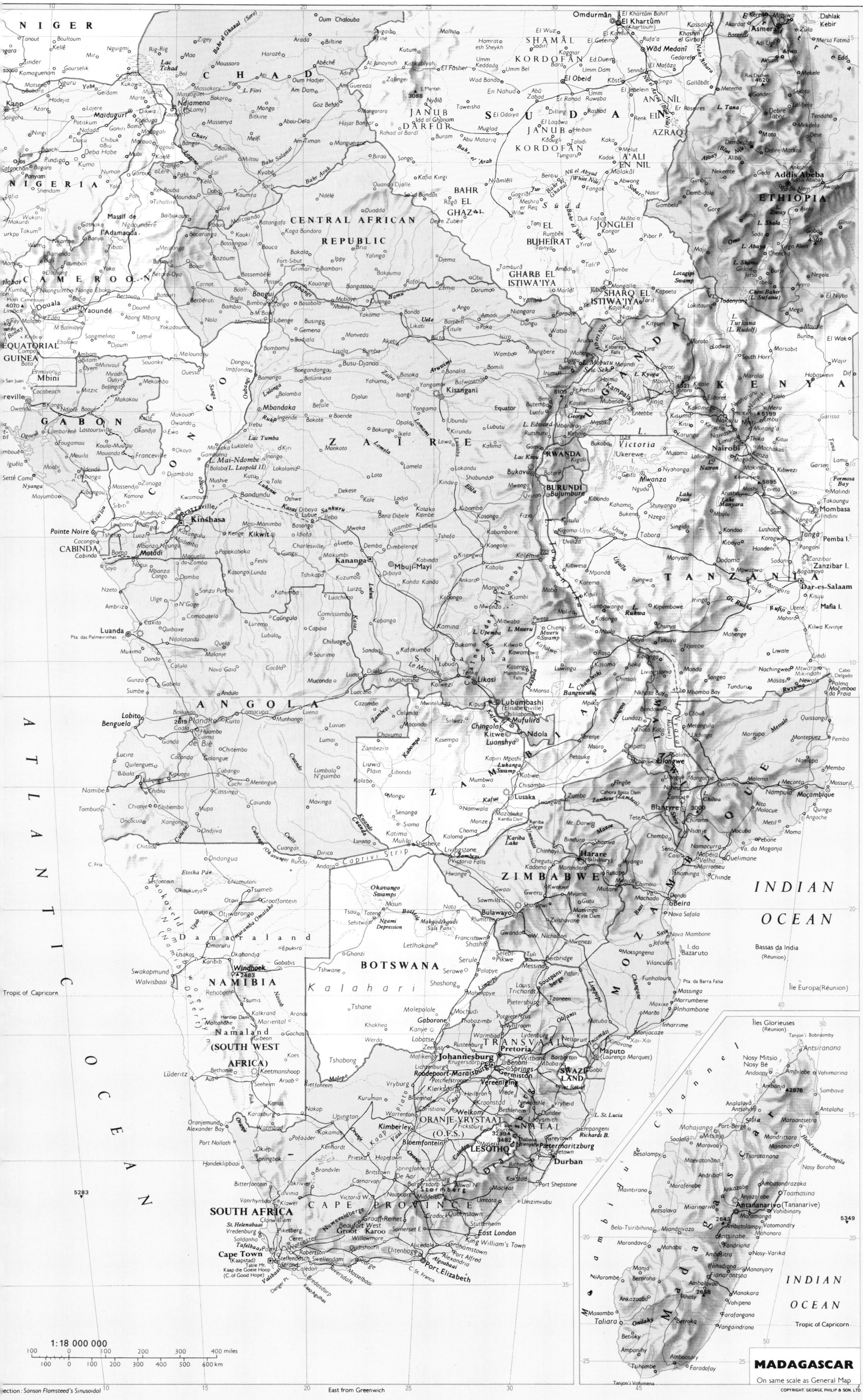
NIGER
NIGERIA
CHAD
SUDAN
ETHIOPIA
CENTRAL AFRICAN REPUBLIC
CAMEROON
EQUATORIAL GUINEA
GABON
CONGO
ZAÏRE
UGANDA
KENYA
RWANDA
BURUNDI
TANZANIA
CABINDA
ANGOLA
ZAMBIA
MALAWI
MOZAMBIQUE
ZIMBABWE
BOTSWANA
NAMIBIA (SOUTH WEST AFRICA)
SOUTH AFRICA
LESOTHO
SWAZILAND
ATLANTIC OCEAN
INDIAN OCEAN
Mozambique Channel
MADAGASCAR
On same scale as General Map
1:18 000 000
Projection: Sanson Flamsteed's Sinusoidal
East from Greenwich
COPYRIGHT GEORGE PHILIP & SON LTD.

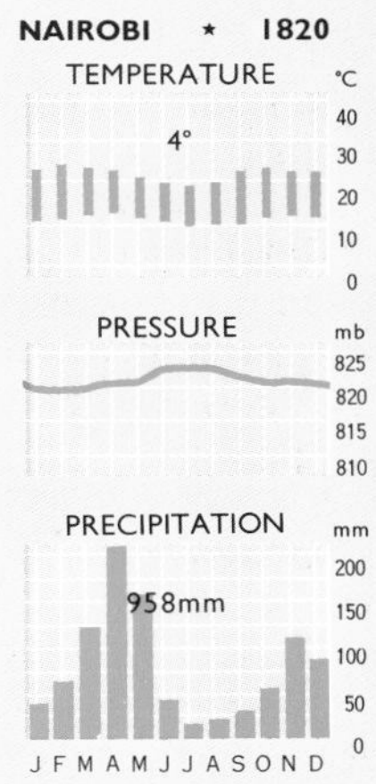
NAIROBI ★ 1820
TEMPERATURE °C
4°
PRESSURE mb
PRECIPITATION mm
958mm
J F M A M J J A S O N D

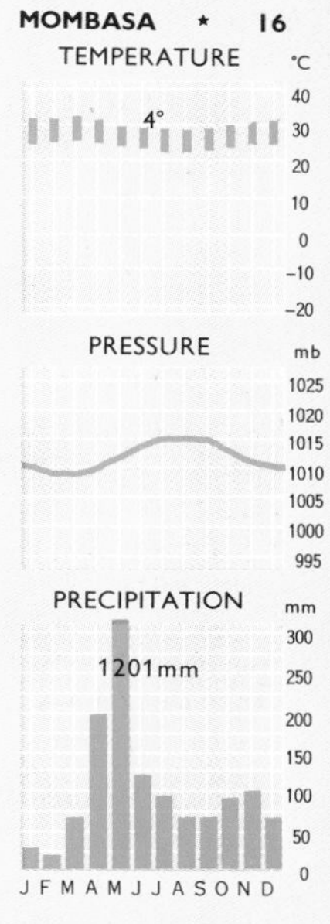
MOMBASA ★ 16
TEMPERATURE °C
4°
PRESSURE mb
PRECIPITATION mm
1201mm
J F M A M J J A S O N D

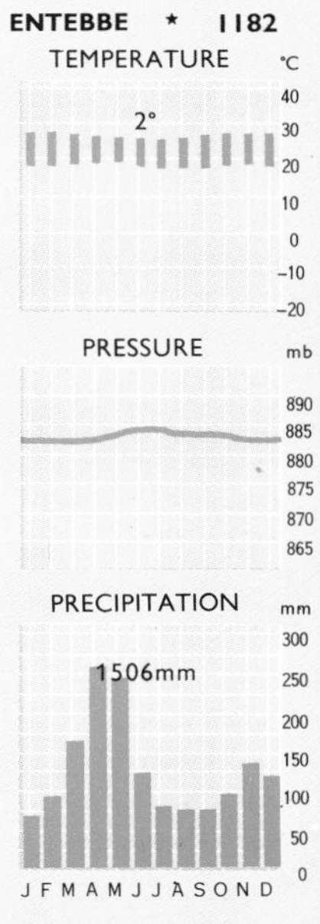
ENTEBBE ★ 1182
TEMPERATURE °C
2°
PRESSURE mb
PRECIPITATION mm
1506mm
J F M A M J J A S O N D

Left: *Harare, the capital of Zimbabwe.*

Angola, Mozambique

These former Portuguese territories became independent in 1975, following several years of guerrilla activity. The cost of the colonial wars weakened Portugal's economy and was one reason for the 1974 *coup* in Portugal which brought left-wing groups to power. Civil war in Angola erupted after the Portuguese withdrawal.

Coffee is Angola's chief crop, but diamonds, iron ore, petroleum and other minerals are produced. Mozambique's economy is based on farming, especially cashew nuts, copra, cotton, sisal, sugar and tea. The Cabora Bassa dam is a major source of power. Mozambique also derives income from its migrant labourers in South Africa and from its ports and transport facilities.

Angola has an area of 1,246,700km² (481,351sq.m.), with £9 million people. Its capital is Luanda (700,000).

Mozambique has an area of 799,380km² (308,642sq.m.), with 13.9 million people. The capital is Maputo (355,000).

Namibia

Area: 824,269km² (318,261sq.m.).
Population: 1.04 million.
Capital: Windhoek (64,700).
Languages: Afrikaans, English, Bantu languages.
Ethnic groups: Ovambos, Whites, Damaras.
Main exports: diamonds, base metals, fish products, meat.
Average temperature: 19°C (66°F) in the highlands.
Highest point: 2,483m (8,146ft).

This huge, arid and sparsely-inhabited territory (previously known as South-West Africa) contains the coastal Namib desert and part of the Kalahari semi-desert. Most people live in the central highlands where livestock raising is important. But the country's mineral resources, especially diamonds, are most important. South Africa was mandated to rule this former German territory in 1919 but refused to accept UN rulings that it should become the independent country of Namibia. In 1971 the World Court of Justice declared South African rule of the territory to be illegal. South Africa's terms of conceding independence proved unacceptable, and guerrilla war continued.

Botswana, Lesotho, Swaziland

These territories were formerly ruled by Britain. Botswana (formerly Bechuanaland) and Lesotho (Basutoland) became independent in 1966 and Swaziland in 1968. These nations are neighbours of South Africa, to which they supply many migrant labourers. Much of Botswana is semi-desert. Beef cattle raising is the chief economic activity. Livestock are important in Lesotho, but mining is increasingly significant in Swaziland.

Botswana has an area of 600,372km² (231,840sq.m.) and 1.1 million people. The capital is Gaborone (79,000).

Lesotho has an area of 30,355km² (11,720sq.m.) and 1.47 million people. Its capital is Maseru (45,000).

Swaziland has an area of 17,363km² (6,704sq.m.) and 626,000 people. Its capital is Mbabane (23,000).

Zimbabwe

Area: 390,308km² (150,699sq.m.).
Population: 8.6 million.
Capital: Harare (656,000).
Languages: English, Ndebele, Shona.
Ethnic groups: Bantu-speaking groups, including Ndebele, Shona; European and Asian minorities.
Main exports: tobacco, asbestos, copper, meat, clothing, chrome ore.
Average temperatures: Harare, 14°C (57°F) June, 21°C (70°F) Nov.
Highest point: near Mozambique border, more than 2,595m (8,514ft).

Zimbabwe is a land with a mild climate, good agricultural land and substantial mineral reserves. Settled by Europeans during the colonial era, Zimbabwe became an independent country with majority rule only after a long struggle which culminated in a guerrilla war. Today Zimbabwe is an independent republic with a government led by Robert Mugabe of the ZANU party.

People
Most Zimbabweans are Bantu-speaking Africans. The largest groups are the Ndebele in the south and the Shona in the north. Traditional hostility between these two peoples has provoked conflict since 1980. Minorities of European and Asian origin remain in the country.

History and constitution
The state of Zimbabwe was formerly known as Rhodesia. It takes its modern name from ancient ruins which indicate the presence of an advanced culture in the region during the middle ages.

From 1898 Rhodesia was governed by a British High Commissioner in South Africa, but the British settlers secured internal self-government in 1923. Between 1953 and 1963, Rhodesia was part of a federation with what is now Malawi and Zambia. After the federation was dissolved, Rhodesia failed to agree on an independence settlement with Britain that would allow early progress toward majority rule. Despite a unilateral declaration of independence by the white minority in 1965, they were finally compelled to yield. True independence and majority rule came in 1980.

Physical features and climate
Zimbabwe consists mostly of a plateau, called the *high veld*, averaging about 1,400m (4,593ft) above sea level. Lower areas, the *low veld*, include the Zambezi trough in the north and the Limpopo lowlands in the south.

Below: *Striking tribal decoration on the walls of a Ndebele village house in the Northern Transvaal, South Africa.*

The tropical climate is moderated by the altitude. Most areas have between 700 and 900mm (28-35 inches) of rain per year, although the eastern highlands are much wetter. Woodland savanna covers much of Zimbabwe.

Minerals
Mining contributes six percent of the gross domestic product. The most valuable mineral is asbestos. Coal, copper, chrome and gold are also mined.

Industry and communications
Hydro-electricity from the Kariba Dam is now the chief source of power for manufacturing which contributes 25 percent of the GDP. The chief manufacturng centres are Bulawayo and Harare.

The chief artery of communications is the Bulawayo-Harare railway. Zimbabwe's outlets to the sea are by rail through South Africa and through Mozambique to the ports of Beira and Maputo. There are 3,394km (2,109m.) of railway and 88,000km (54,680m.) of metalled and unmetalled road.

Agriculture
Agriculture accounts for 18 percent of the GDP. Tobacco is the chief cash crop and maize the main subsistence crop. Other products include citrus fruits, sugar cane and tea. Cattle farming is also important, the country supporting 5.6 million cattle. Nearly a third of the workforce are peasant farmers.

South Africa

Area: 1,123,226km^2 (433,678sq.m.).
Population: 32.5 million.
Capitals: Cape Town (1.1m), Pretoria (562,000).
Largest city: Johannesburg (1.4m).
Languages: Afrikaans, English, Bantu and Asian languages.
Ethnic groups: Black Africans, including Zulu and Xhosa, Europeans, Asians, people of mixed race.
Main exports: cereals, diamonds, fissionable materials, fruits, gold and other metals, iron and steel, machinery and vehicles, textiles.
Average temperatures: Cape Town 12.2°C (54°F) July, 22°C (71°F) Feb.; Johannesburg 10°C (51°F) June, 20°C (68°F) Jan.
Highest point: Mont aux Sources on Lesotho border, 3,299m (10,823ft).

South Africa is the most developed and industrialized nation in Africa. Its wealth is based on its rich mineral resources and its efficient farming. It produces uranium, coal, gem diamonds, asbestos, copper and about two-thirds of the world's new gold.

People
Europeans account for 17.5 percent of the population, but they control the government and the economy. About 65 percent speak Afrikaans – a language derived from Dutch. Most of the other Europeans speak English.

The largest groups of Bantu-speaking Black Africans are the Zulu and the Xhosa. Altogether Black South Africans form about 70 percent of the population, and there are also many people of mixed or Asian descent. South Africa has institutionalized racial discrimination. The policy of *apartheid* or 'separate development' aims to settle those Blacks who are not allowed to work in areas designated for Whites into 'Bantustans' or nominally independent 'homelands'. The independence of these homelands is not recognized internationally, as they are enclaves entirely dependent upon South Africa.

South Africa has a Senate and a House of Assembly, all of whose members are whites. The State President is elected for a seven-year term. Asian and 'Coloured' (mixed race) South Africans have now been allowed a degree of separate representation, but the Black majority remains disenfranchised.

History and constitution
The Dutch established the first European settlement on the site of Cape Town in 1652. Gradually, settlers called *Boers* (farmers) spread inland. From 1781 they fought a series of wars against the Bantu people, who themselves had moved southwards into the region, displacing most of the indigenous Bushmen and Hottentots.

Between 1795 and 1803, and again in 1806, the British ruled the Cape. Many Afrikaners opposed British rule and, in 1835, they began the Great Trek which led to the founding of Orange Free State and the South African Republic (now the Transvaal). The British and Afrikaners fought wars in 1880-81 and 1899-1902, which Britain won. In 1910 the Orange Free State, Transvaal, Cape Province and Natal united to form the Union of South Africa.

From 1948 onwards South African politics were dominated by the ideology of the Afrikaner National Party. Its racial policies led to withdrawal from the Commonwealth in 1961 and the establishment of a republic. By 1986 civil unrest had become a serious problem, and international opinion was becoming increasingly alienated.

Minerals: South Africa

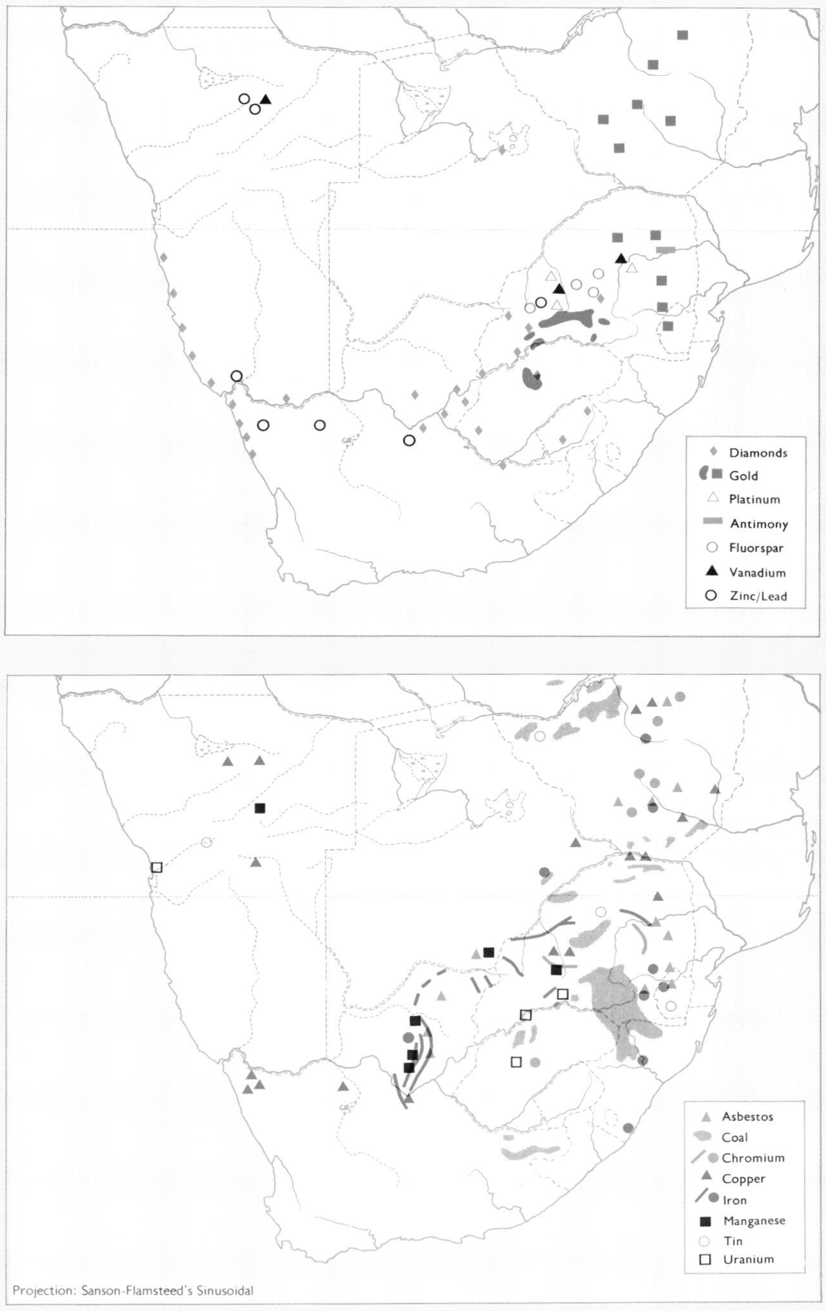

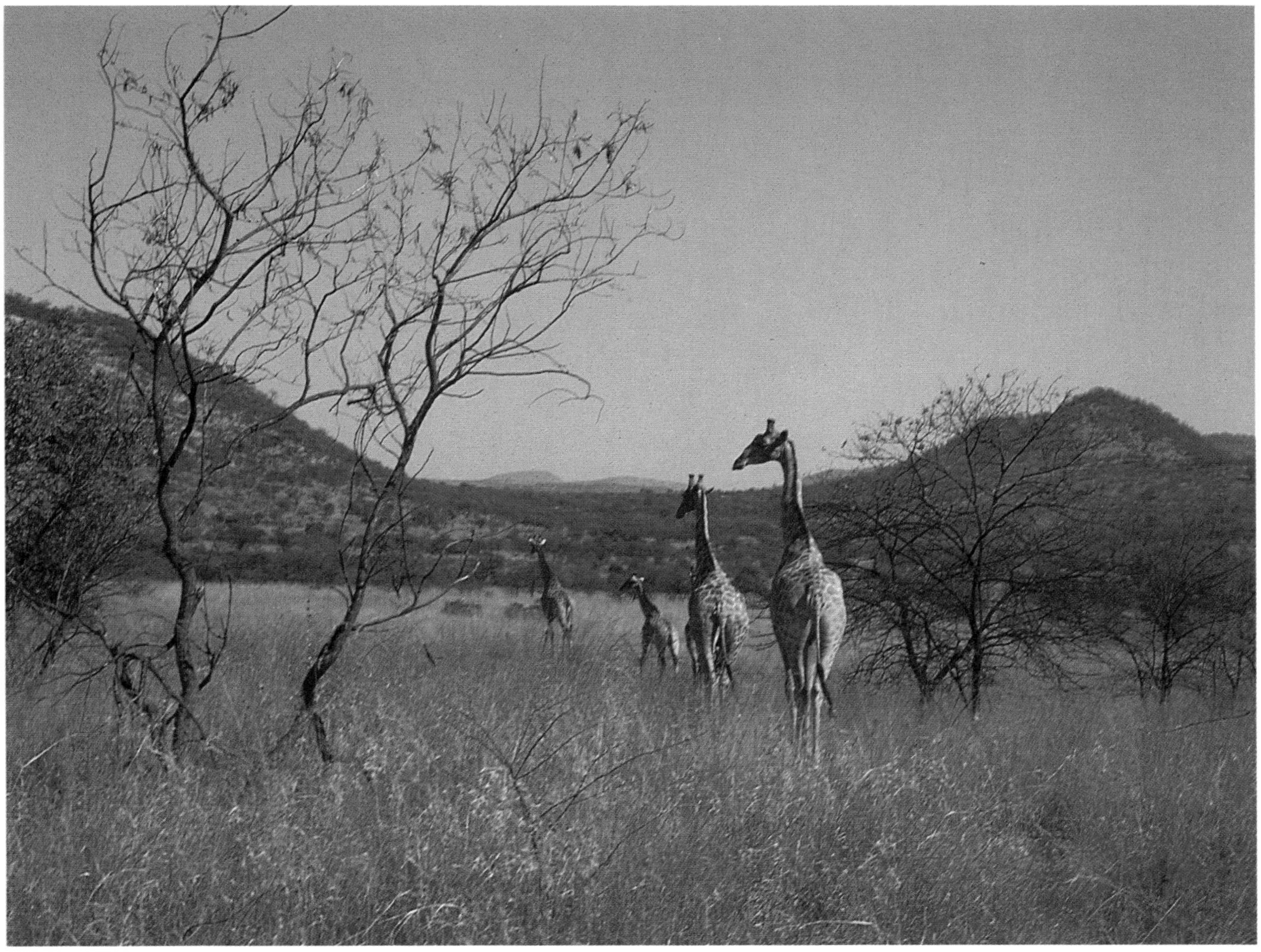

Right: *South African game reserves, such as Pilanesburg in Boputatswana, protect native animal species from extinction.*

Map 52 | SOUTHERN AFRICA

KIMBERLEY ★ 1197
TEMPERATURE °C
15°

PRESSURE mb

PRECIPITATION mm
409mm

CAPE TOWN 17
TEMPERATURE °C
9°

PRESSURE mb

PRECIPITATION mm
508mm

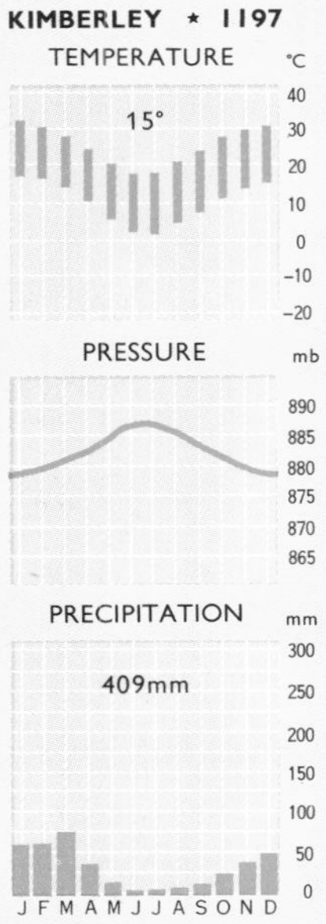

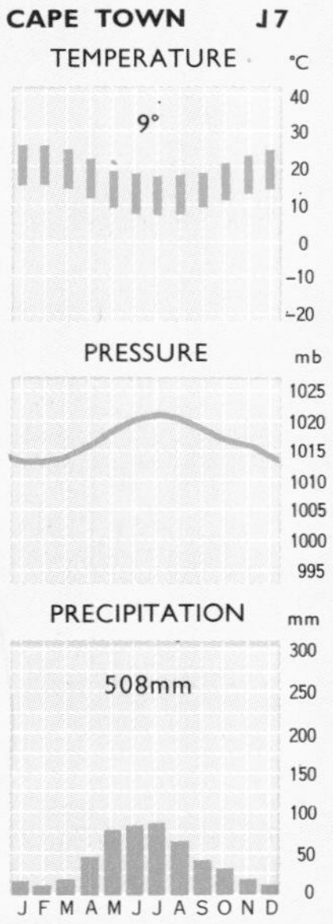

Physical features and climate
South Africa consists mainly of a plateau, more than 1,220m. (4,000ft) above sea level, bordered by steep escarpments. The chief rivers draining the plateau are the Orange and Limpopo systems. Around the plateau are mountain ranges and lower plateaux.

The climate is mostly sub-tropical, but the altitude moderates temperatures. Parts of the interior suffer from frosts. Most of the country has less than 762mm (30in) of rain per year and half of South Africa is arid or semi-arid. The south-west Cape has a pleasant Mediterranean climate. Most African savanna animals flourish in protected areas, especially in the Kruger National Park.

Minerals
Gold, South Africa's most valuable mineral, is mined around Johannesburg and in Orange Free State. South Africa produces many other metals and diamonds. Important coal mines are in the Witwatersrand and in Natal.

Industry and communications
Manufacturing is the most valuable sector of the economy. The chief industrial centres are south Transvaal, Cape Town, Durban and Port Elizabeth.

Agriculture, forestry and fishing
Agriculture, forestry and fishing employ abut 28 percent of the people. Pastoral farming, especially sheep and cattle, is extremely important. Arable farms cover only 11 percent of the land. Maize is the chief subsistence crop. Cotton, fruits, groundnuts, sugar, tobacco and vines are major cash crops. Forestry supplies most domestic requirements, and fishing is important off the west coast.

Trade and foreign relations
South Africa is an important trading nation, with Europe and America as chief business partners. In the 1970s South Africa managed to achieve a degree of *détente* with parts of Black Africa, but growing economic problems in the 1980s have been exacerbated by civil strife and international censure.

Madagascar

Area: 587,041km² (226,657sq.m.).
Population: 9.74 million.
Capital: Antananarivo (400,000).
Languages: Malagasy, French.
Ethnic groups: about 20, of which the Merina are the largest.
Main exports: cloves, coffee, vanilla, sugar.
Average temperature: 29°C (85°F) on coast, cooler highlands.
Highest point: Mt Maromokotro, 2,876m (9,436ft).

The Democratic Republic of Madagascar consists of the world's fourth largest

Map 53

1:8,000,000

DURBAN   **5**
TEMPERATURE   °C
7°
PRESSURE   mb
PRECIPITATION   mm
1008mm
J F M A M J J A S O N D

JOHANNESBURG + 1665
TEMPERATURE   °C
10°
PRESSURE   mb
PRECIPITATION   mm
709mm
J F M A M J J A S O N D

**MALAGASY
REPUBLIC**

On same scale as General Map

COPYRIGHT. GEORGE PHILIP & SON. LTD.

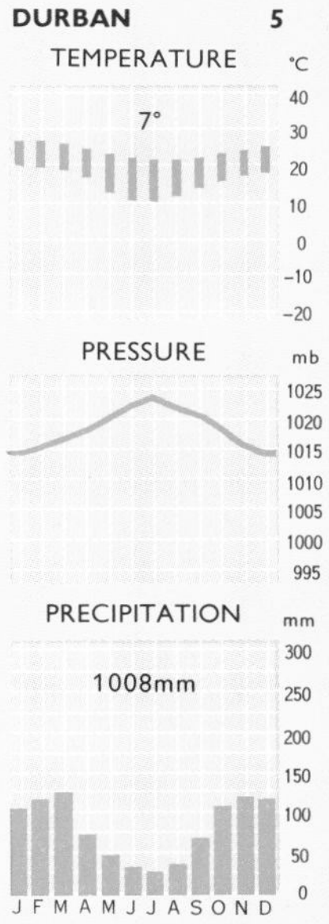

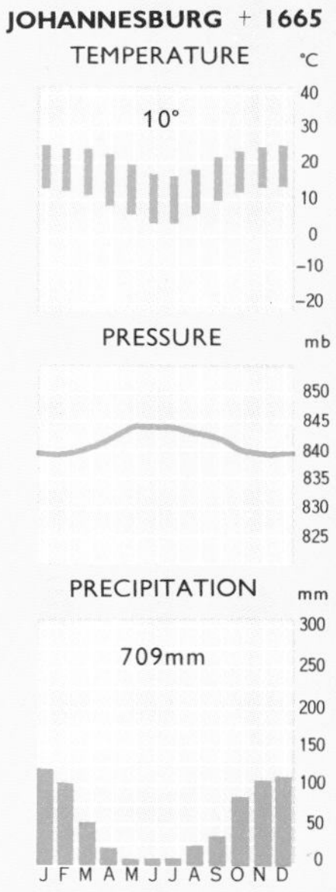

island and some smaller islands as well. The central plateau of Madagascar divides the eastern forests from the western plains. The southwest is semi-arid. The country's economy is based on farming, but only five percent of the land is cultivated. Coffee is the chief cash crop.

People from Indonesia settled in Madagascar about 1,000 years ago. They mixed with people from mainland Africa and with Arabs. The country was ruled by France between 1885 and 1960, when it became an independent republic.

Right: *Known as 'The Great Red Island' because of its red soil, Madagascar basks in a tropical climate.*

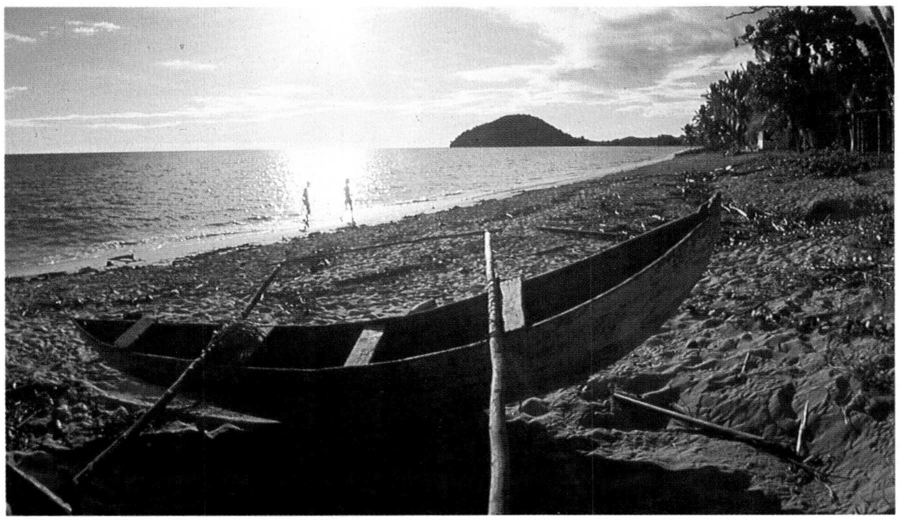

Mauritius

Mauritius, lying 800km (500 miles) east of Madagascar is a densely populated island republic within the Commonwealth with an area of 1,865km² (720sq.m.) and a population of 969,000, mainly Indian. Its warm, damp climate and volcanic soil are suited to sugar cane on which its economy is almost wholly dependent, although tourism is of growing importance.

The deepwater harbour at Port Louis handles over a million tons of shipping each year, and there is a well-orgnised internal transport system.

Map 54 | AUSTRALIA

PERTH   **60**
TEMPERATURE   °C
10°

PRESSURE   mb

PRECIPITATION   mm
881mm

J F M A M J J A S O N D

DARWIN   **30**
TEMPERATURE   °C
5°

PRESSURE   mb

PRECIPITATION   mm
1491mm

J F M A M J J A S O N D

Projection: Bonne

East from Greenwich

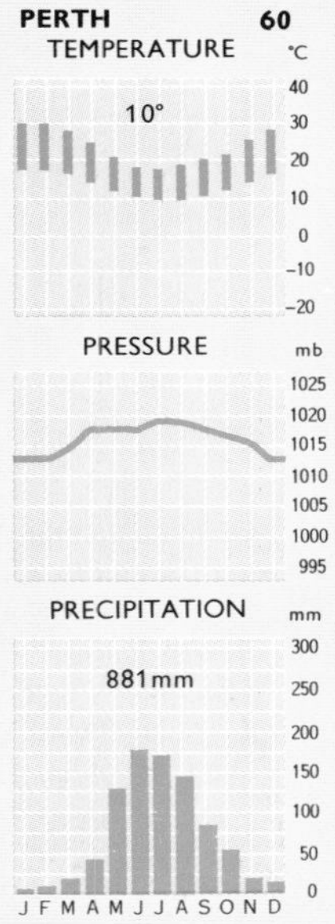

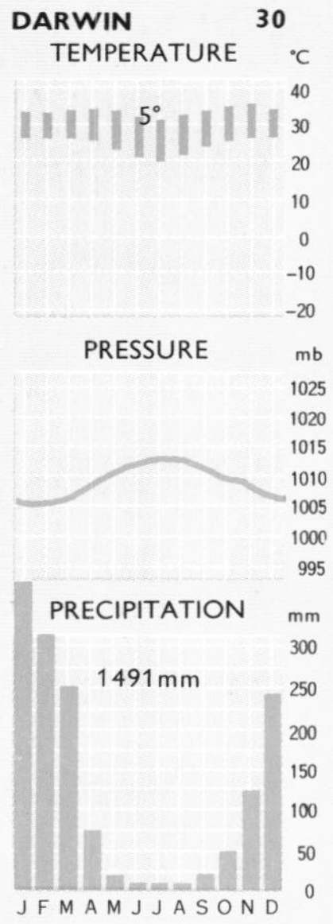

Australia, the sixth biggest continental land mass in the world, is the driest and flattest of all and the only one occupied by a single nation. From the air, much of the interior looks like a featureless red shield, burnished by sun. Only one third of the land has adequate rainfall for agriculture, but with the help of irrigation and artesian bores, two-thirds of it is farmed. Australia is also rich in minerals.

The continent is ancient in formation. Physically, it is dominated by the arid Western Plateau. Broken by several major ranges in the west and centre, this plateau rises from the Indian Ocean to an average height of 300 metres

(1,000ft) and slopes gradually eastward across two-thirds of the continent to the Central Lowlands which stretch from the Gulf of Carpentaria in the north to the Great Australian Bight in the south. From the sheep, cattle and wheat-growing country in the basin formed by the Murray River and its tributaries, the Eastern Highlands rise to the Great Dividing Range. Relatively low in Queensland, this long mountain chain reaches its greatest height in the Australian Alps and runs through Victoria to the southern island of Tasmania. East of the Great Dividing Range is a warm, moist, well-populated coastal strip.

Spanning 33 degrees of latitude (the

equivalent of the distance from Panama to Montréal), Australia has a wide climatic range with temperatures as low as −23°C (−8°F) on record. But in the south the summers are generally warm and sunny, the winters mild and damp. In the tropical north, the summer brings heavy monsoon rains and Tasmania also has high rainfall, but two-thirds of the continent receives less than 50cm (20in) of rain annually and evaporation is rapid. Apart from desert and small areas of rain forest in the north, the characteristic vegetation is scrub: mainly eucalyptus (gum) and acacia (wattle) trees and grasses which are well adapted to dry conditions.

Australia

Area: 7,682,300km² (2,965,368sq.m.).
Population: 15.8 million.
Capital: Canberra (256,000).
Largest city: Sydney (3.3m).
Language: English.
Ethnic groups: British (80 percent), Italian, Greek, Aboriginal.
Main exports: iron ore, coal and other minerals, wool, beef, wheat, sugar, dairy products.
Average temperatures: 26°C (78°F) Jan.; 16°C (62°F) July in Sydney; 32°C (90°F) Jan., 23°C (74°F) July in Darwin.
Highest point: Mt Kosciusko 2,228m (7,310ft).

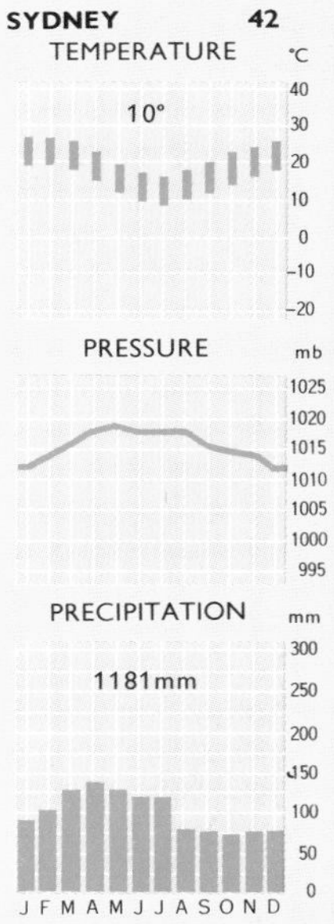

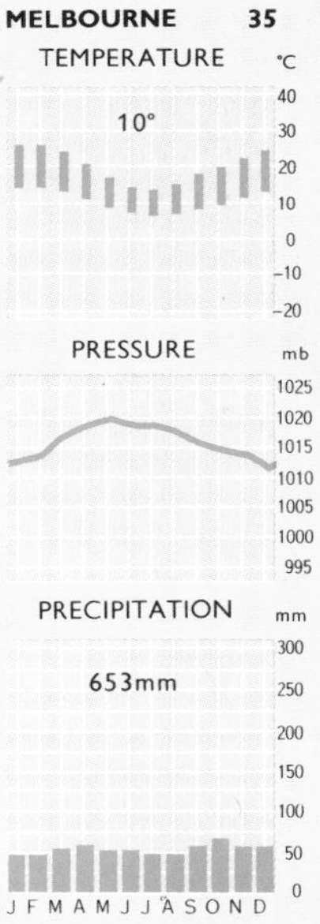

In the harsh, bright landscape of Australia, a predominantly Anglo-Saxon people have created in the past 200 years a nation with a sense of expansive destiny. Their country is as big as the entire Indian sub-continent but its wealth is shared by fewer than 16 million people. Like Americans in the 19th century, they are characteristically energetic, brashly optimistic and youthful. Nearly half the population is aged under 25. Since 1945 rapid immigration and development of mineral resources have produced an affluent society.

Though half its immigrants still come from Britain, the flavour of Australian life has been changed by an influx of large minorities from Italy, Greece, Central Europe, Holland, Poland and Turkey. There are about 140,000 Aborigines, most of them of mixed blood, but despite small numbers of Asians, Australia is overwhelmingly white. The outback (known as the 'bush'), with its isolated farming stations linked by efficient airways and radio and television services, and its dusty country towns with quiet verandahs, has left an enduring mark on Australia's self-image, but today most Australians live in cities with sprawling suburban bungalows of brick, wood and 'fibro' surrounding sophisticated urban centres.

Passionately fond of horse-racing and the outdoor life, Australians are among the world's best athletes, excelling in swimming, tennis, sailing, cricket and a wide range of other sports. They have produced outstanding writers, painters, film makers, performing artists and scientists and have a well-developed education system, increasingly orientated towards technology. They are an informal, blunt, strongly egalitarian people with a rough-and-tumble tradition of political democracy.

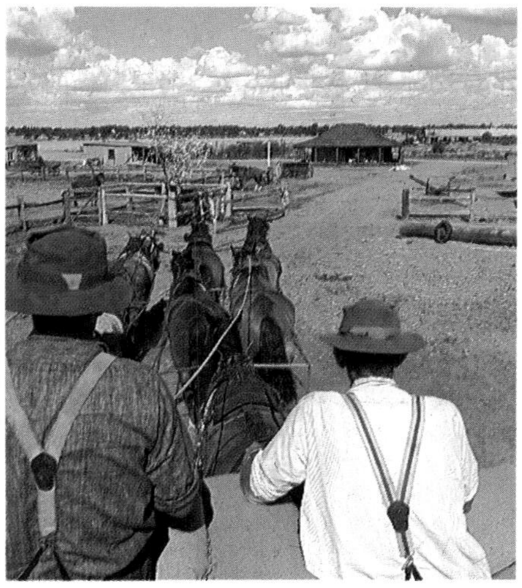

Right: *Lachland, New South Wales, a typically dry, dusty Australian settlement.*

Above: *The design for Australia's federal capital, Canberra, was decided by a competition held in 1911.*

Right: *Sheep drafting in western Victoria. Australia's Merino sheep produce outstandingly fine quality wool.*

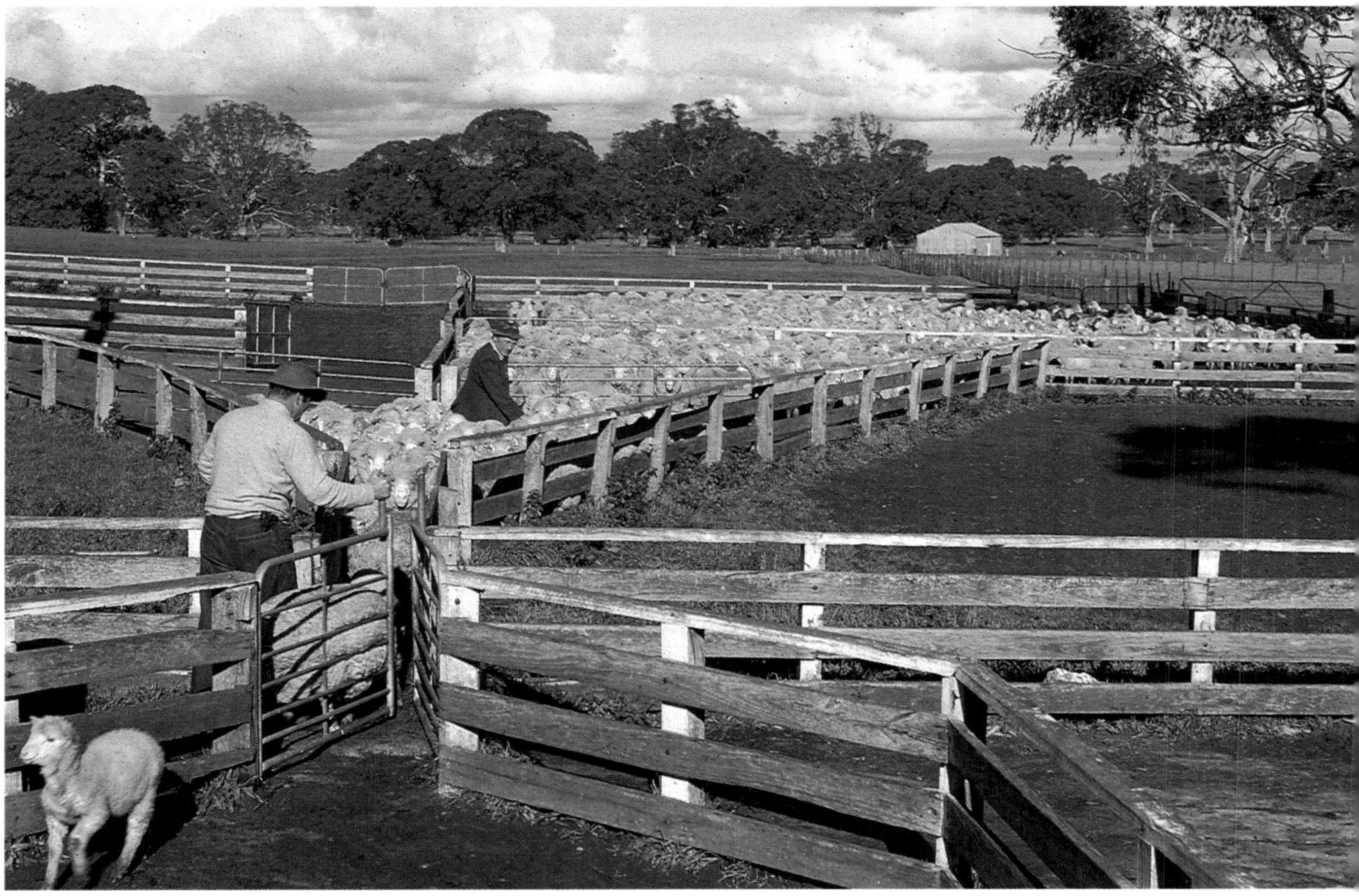

History and education

The Commonwealth of Australia is a federation of six states and two territories. Until the late 18th century it was inhabited by mainly nomadic Aborigines who occupied it for several thousand years but developed no urban settlements. They numbered about 300,000 in 1770 when Captain James Cook claimed the island continent for Britain. A penal colony was established on the inhospitable shores of Port Jackson, near Sydney, in 1778 and free settlers from Britain began arriving also. From outposts in the southwest, settlement spread out slowly as explorers crossed the Great Dividing Range and penetrated the hinterland.

The discovery of gold in new South Wales and Victoria in the 1850s brought a wave of immigration. By 1859 there were six separate colonies including Queensland, South Australia, Western Australia and the island of Tasmania. Transport advances and the development of a strong pastoral economy based on the export of wool and meat to Britain led to the uniting of the six colonies in the independent Commonwealth of Australia in 1901.

In 1927, the capital was moved from Melbourne to Canberra where an administrative centre modelled on Washington D.C. was established on an empty plain midway between the rival cities of Melbourne and Sydney. The Federal Government administers both Australian Capital Territory (the Canberra area) and the huge but sparsely-settled Northern Territory. A House of Representatives with usually 125 members and a 64-member Senate make up the Federal Parliament. The British monarch is the formal Head of State, represented by a Governor-General.

States and territories

Population is heavily concentrated in the southeast with about 40 percent of Australians living in Sydney and Melbourne. Estimated population distribution in 1982 was: New South Wales (5.3 million), Victoria (4 million), Queensland (2.5 million), South Australia (1.3 million), Western Australia (1.3 million), Tasmania (431,000), Australian Capital Territory (233,000), Northern Territory (131,000).

Sydney, capital of new South Wales, is a vibrant city built around a beautiful harbour set off by skyscrapers, the gleaming shells of its radically-designed Opera House and a steel suspension bridge 503 metres (1,650ft) long. It is the country's chief port and commercial centre as well as the focus of an industrial complex that includes the neighbouring cities of Newcastle and Wollongong. Victoria's capital, Melbourne (2.9 million) is a more urban industrial city and the financial hub of the country. Australia's third largest city, Brisbane (1.1 million), capital of the holiday state of Queens-

Above: *Part of the vast, almost uninhabited land of the great Australian Outback.*

land, is another major industrial city, as is Adelaide (969,000), capital of South Australia, a state that produces much of Australia's fine wine.

The biggest state is Western Australia with an area of 2,527,621km² (975,920sq.m.), but until the development of its vast mineral reserves in the 1960s it supported only a small population in the south-west corner. The capital, Perth (969,000) with its adjoining ports of Fremantle houses two-thirds of its population. An updated single-gauge rail link to Sydney across a distance of nearly 4,000 kilometres was completed in 1970.

The smallest state, Tasmania, is an important fruit and horticultural and mineral-producing area with its capital in the port city of Hobart (174,000). The Northern Territory's administrative centre, Darwin (60,000) is scheduled by 1988 to be linked with the south by rail, forming the first north-south transcontinental rail link. The service centre for the state's barren interior is the trim settlement of Alice Springs (20,000). Near it, at the geographical centre of the continent, rise two remarkable sandstone outcrops, the monolith of Ayers Rock and the domes of Mt Olga.

Climate and water resources
Most areas of Australia have an average of eight hours of sunshine a day. Summer temperatures often climb to 38°C (100°F) in the hottest months which are January-February in the south and November-December in the north. Torrential rain falls in the tropical north in January-March, a season known as 'the Wet'. South of the Tropic of Capri-

corn, rain is relatively infrequent in summer. In Sydney, heat waves caused by hot, dry winds blowing off the land are periodically relieved by cooler winds blowing up the east coast from the south. Winters are mild and dry in the tropical north but depressions moving up from the south of the continent bring winter rain to most of Australia's cities, and temperatures in Victoria and New South Wales fall to 10°C (50°F) or considerably lower in upland areas such as Canberra.

Some areas of Queensland and Tasmania get up to 450cm (180in) of rain a year but two-thirds of the continent must depend on irrigation or artesian water supplies. Through the plains bloom and creeks flow after rain, most of the rivers in the interior are usually dry. A feature of the interior is dry salt-encrusted lakes called playas such as Lake Eyre which covers a million square kilometres and is below sea level. Fortunately, Australia has the most extensive artesian reserves in the world. About a third of the continent is supplied by bores, 18,000 of them in the Great Artesian Basin which stretches from north central Queensland to South Australia.

Australia's main river system is the Murray and its major tributaries, the Darling and Murrumbidgee. The Murray rises in the Alps and flows to Encounter Bay near Adelaide. Its system is the basis of vast irrigation schemes in New South Wales, Victoria and South Australia. The Snowy Mountains Scheme, completed in 1972 at a cost of $A800 million, irrigates some 2,300km² (888sq.m.) and provides a hydro-electric generating capacity of nearly 4,000 megawatts. In Western Australia, the Ord River scheme in the Kimberleys will double the state's irrigated area.

Farming, forestry and fishing
Fewer than 20 percent of Australians live outside towns but it is the farms and farmers of the outback that give the nation its most distinctive character. Scattered across the face of the continent are a quarter of a million farms and their production has always been the main source of the country's export earnings. Australia has about 133 million sheep producing a third of the world's wool. Its next most important product is wheat, two-thirds of it exported. Australia is also one of the world's leading exporters of beef and veal, exporting half its annual production. It has about 20 million beef cattle. Another four million dairy cattle produce half a million tonnes of dairy products. Some 8,000 sugar cane plantations in eastern Queensland and northern New South Wales produce 2.5 million tonnes of raw sugar a year. Fruit production ranges from the main crop, apples (23 million bushels) to a wide range of tropical fruits.

Most of Australia's farms are between 200 and 2,000 hectares (500 and 5,000 acres), but about 25,000 of them are bigger than this. In the Northern Territory, some cattle stations spread over immense areas of 400,000 hectares (one million acres), carrying about 10,000 cattle. Outback sheep stations are also vast, averaging 20,000 hectares (50,000 acres) and each running about 6,000 sheep. Australia's hardy Merino breed with long fine wool makes up three-quarters of the nation's flock.

The pastoral zone, which has most of Australia's big sheep and cattle stations, runs through central Queensland and New South Wales to South Australia. East and south of this is a wheat-sheep zone, with a similar zone in the western part of Western Australia. The high rainfall zone which carries most of Australia's dairy and mixed farms is found in Victoria and Tasmania, the eastern part of New South Wales and South Australia and the south-west of Western Australia.

Queensland is the main cattle state and New South Wales the chief wool state, followed by Western Australia. Much of the Western Plateau is too dry for farming. Outback farmers maintain a tenacious struggle against the ever-present threat of drought and the bush

fires that often accompany it. Government support for farming is strong, with direct subsidies to dairy farmers and aid to other sectors.

Forestry is confined mainly to wetter areas of the east and south of the continent and Tasmania. Species of eucalyptus provide most of the country's needs for hardwood and paper but softwoods have to be imported. Radiata pine is being planted to overcome this. The fishing industry is confined mainly to meeting local needs with the biggest catch taken off Western Australia. In tropical waters, pearls are cultivated.

Minerals and energy resources
The past 30 years have seen a major shift in Australia from a mainly pastoral economy to rapid industrial development. Iron ore and coal are the chief mineral exports. Australia is also the world's leading exporter of bauxite, fourth in production of lead and zinc and an important supplier of copper, nickel, manganese, tin and silver. Oil fields, mainly offshore, already produce three-quarters of the country's crude oil needs and iron and coal resources are the basis of a significant steel industry. Investment capital for the development of these resources has come mainly from the United States, Britain and Japan, but Australia has recently adopted a policy of greater self-sufficiency, while continuing to offer tax concessions and other incentives for exploration.

Many of the most dramatic mineral finds of the past three decades have been made in Western Australia. Though Kalgoorlie has been a famous gold-producing centre since the discovery of its 'Golden Mile' in 1891, this state was for many years the least developed in the Commonwealth.. Today it is the biggest exporter of iron ore (mainly to Japan) from vast deposits in the Hamersley and Ophthalmia ranges in the northwest of the state, feeding ports at Dampier and Port Hedland. Other important deposits are at Yampi Sound and Koolyanobbing. Iron is also mined in the Middleback Ranges in South Australia, Mt Bundy and Frances Creek in the Northern Territory and in northwest Tasmania around the Savage River. Iron ore worth over one thousand million Australian dollars was mined in the country as a

Density of population: Australia

DENSITY OF POPULATION
1 : 50 000 000

Inhabitants	per mile² under 2	per km² under 1
	2- 8	1- 3
	8- 16	3- 6
	16- 32	6- 12
	32- 64	12- 25
	64-128	25- 50
	128-256	50-100
	over 256	over 100

○ Towns of 50-100 000 inhabitants
■ over 100 000

COPYRIGHT GEORGE PHILIP & SON, LTD.

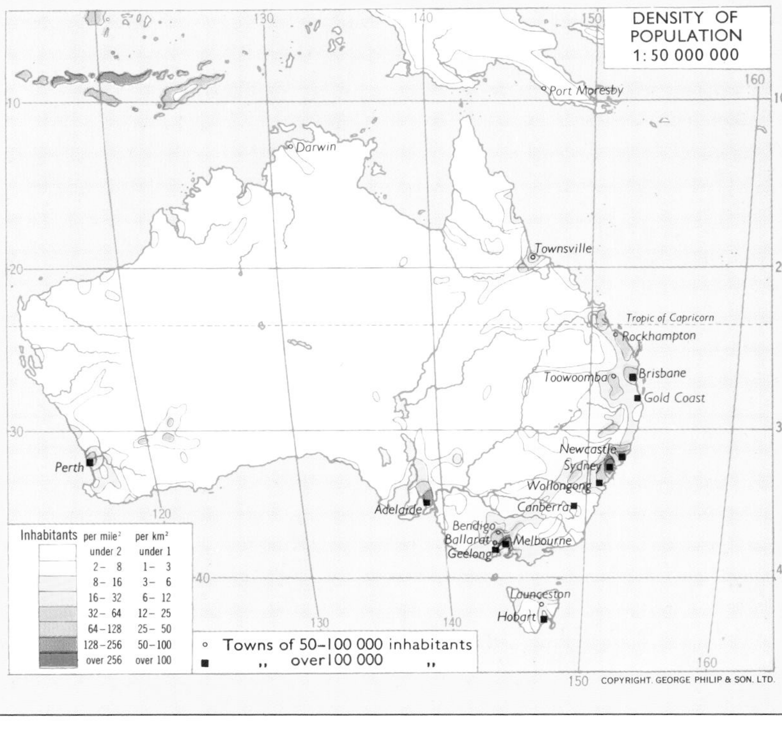

Natural vegetation: Australia

Projection: Bonne

FOREST VEGETATION

	Tropical Rain Forest ("Brush") —soft woods (palms, cypress, hoop pines), tree-ferns, lianas, epiphytes–mangrove swamps on coast.
	Eastern Sub-tropical and Temperate Rain Forest—eucalypt hardwoods (gum trees), palms, tree-ferns, epiphytes, and in Tasmania, conifers and beech
	Sub-tropical and Temperate Woodland (eucalypts, brigalow scrub)
	Evergreen Forest and Xerophilous Woodland plants { of Mediterranean type – eucalypts (in W. Australia, jarrah, karri and tuart), "maquis" scrub, bulbous and tuberous plants

——— Southern Limit of Palms

GRASS AND SCRUB VEGETATION

Tropical Savanna (grassland with scattered trees and scrub—the Queensland "Bush"—low eucalypts and brigalow scrub).
Tropical and Sub-tropical Grassland
Temperate Grassland
Seasonal Grassland
Mallee Scrub and Seasonal Grassland.
Dry Semi-desert (mulga and other scrub)
Dry Semi-desert (sand, bare rock and spinifex scrub)
Alpine, above timber line

········ Boundaries of Artesian Basins
(The so-called "Deserts" of the Old Explorers are becoming in many districts pastoral regions by boring for water in the Artesian Basins)
——— 10-inch Annual Isohyet (25 cm)
Salt Pans and Lakes

PRINCIPAL SCRUB FORMATIONS

Brigalow Mallee   Mulga

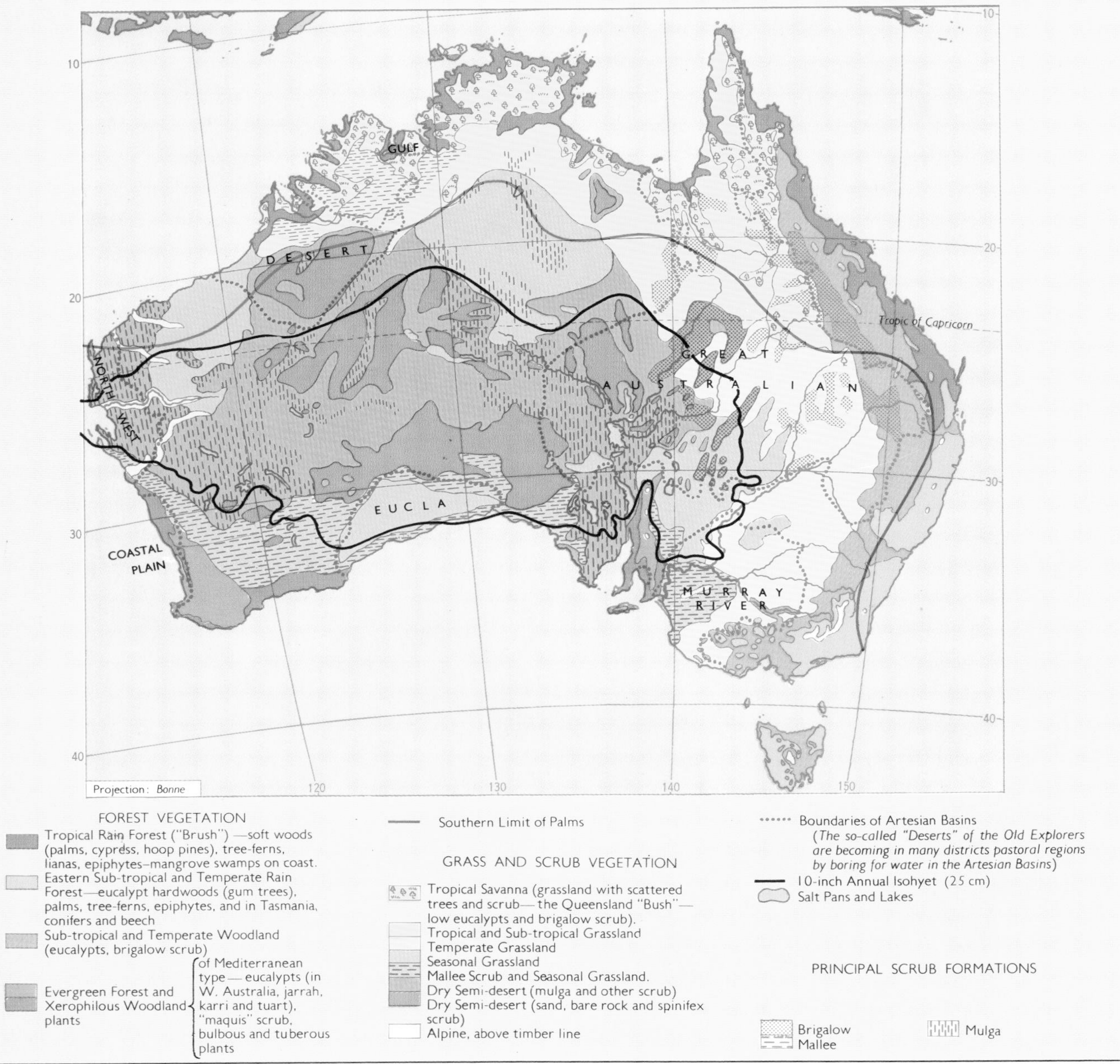

whole in 1981-2. Coal deposits worth nearly three times as much were extracted in the same period.

Mining is a major activity in the Northern Territory. Uranium deposits are being worked at Rum Jungle near Darwin and further north on the Gove peninsula, bauxite reserves are being opened up. Australia's vast bauxite deposits, notably at Weipa on Cape York Peninsula in Queensland and also in the Darling Ranges, Western Australia, supply an aluminium refinery at Glad-stone and smelters at Kurri Kurri, Point Henry and Bell Bay (Tasmania) as well as a smelter at Bluff, New Zealand.

The most important copper deposits are at Mt Isa and Mt Morgan in Queensland and Cobar, New South Wales. Mt Isa is also a major producer of lead and zinc, together with the long-established mining centre of Broken Hill in the west of New South Wales, which also produces silver.

Though Western Australia is exploiting oil and natural gas fields at Barrow Island and Dongara, Australia's major energy resources lie in the east. Queensland's Moonie field was opened in 1961 and natural gas from the same sedimentary basin is piped to Brisbane. Adelaide is supplied with natural gas from fields at Moomba and Gidgealpa. The most significant reserves of oil are offshore in the Bass Strait south of Victoria which

Below: Sydney in New South Wales is dominated by Sydney Harbour Bridge, one of the biggest single spans in the world.

processes the oil at Dutson. Most of Australia's power comes from coal-based thermal plants, though hydro-electricity is being developed, especially in Tasmania and New South Wales where a nuclear energy station has also been built.

Industry and trade
Australia has become a highly industrialized country with about a quarter of its work force engaged in manufacturing. Disruption of normal trade during World War II stimulated rapid expansion of manufacturing and there are now nearly 40,000 factories. Industrial development has been based mainly on the coal deposits of the east. Victoria recovers brown coal by open-cast methods in the Latrobe Valley while both New South Wales and Queensland have large reserves of black coal. These, together with iron ores, supply a steel industry managed by the Broken Hill Proprietary Company and its subsidiaries. A thriving automobile industry, largely overseas-owned produces upwards of 350,000 vehicles a year, including well-known Australian models such as the Holden. This and a growing ship-building industry are supplied by steelworks at Port Kembla and Newcastle near Sydney, Whyalla in South Australia and Kwinana near Fremantle. Chemical, petrochemical and textile industries are also based on local resources. Other important industries are engineering, foodstuffs and paper. However, exports of manufactured goods make up only a quarter of overseas earnings.

Australia has the twelfth biggest volume of trade in the world. Until the early 1970s, farm products, chiefly wool, wheat and meat, accounted for more than half its export income. But during the 1970s, with huge contracts for supplying iron ore and coking coal, exports of ores and refined metals became increasingly significant earners. Australia's main customers are Japan for minerals and wool, the United States for meat and Britain for a wide range of products.

The main imports are heavy machinery, electronics, transport equipment and textiles. The United States is the main supplier, followed by Britain, Japan, West Germany and Canada. Many home industries are protected by high tariffs. Trade with New Zealand is facilitated by the Australia-New Zealand Free Trade Agreement (Nafta). New Zealand is an important market for Australian cars and other manufactures and in return sells Australia pulp and paper.

External relations and territories
Australia is a member of the Commonwealth and its traditional links with Britain remain strong. But since 1945 it has turned increasingly towards the United States, its major ally in the 1951 ANZUS defence treaty. It is active diplomatically in the Pacific and South-East Asia, maintaining close relations with its largest neighbour, Indonesia and with its major trading partner, Japan. Australia governs several islands in the Indian Ocean: Christmas Island, which supplies phosphate, Cocos (Keeling) Island and the Heard and McDonald islands. Two Australian islands in the Tasman Sea are mainly tourist resorts: Norfolk Island (pop. 2,400), a former penal colony later settled by descendants of the Bounty mutineers, and coral-ringed Lord Howe Island. Australia also administered Papua New Guinea until its independence in 1975.

Gulf of Carpentaria
Cape York Peninsula
Great Barrier Reef
CORAL SEA ISLANDS TERRITORY
PAPUA NEW GUINEA
Bismarck Archipelago
Bismarck Sea
SOLOMON SEA
CORAL SEA
GREAT QUEENSLAND
AUSTRALIAN BASIN
The Great Dividing Range
NEW SOUTH WALES
SOUTH AUSTRALIA
VICTORIA
PACIFIC OCEAN
Tasman Sea
Bass Strait
TASMANIA
Cairns
Townsville
Mackay
Rockhampton
Bundaberg
BRISBANE
Newcastle
SYDNEY & Port Jackson
Wollongong
CANBERRA
MELBOURNE
ADELAIDE
Broken Hill
Mount Isa
Hobart
Launceston
Continuation Southwards
East from Greenwich
COPYRIGHT GEORGE PHILIP & SON LTD.

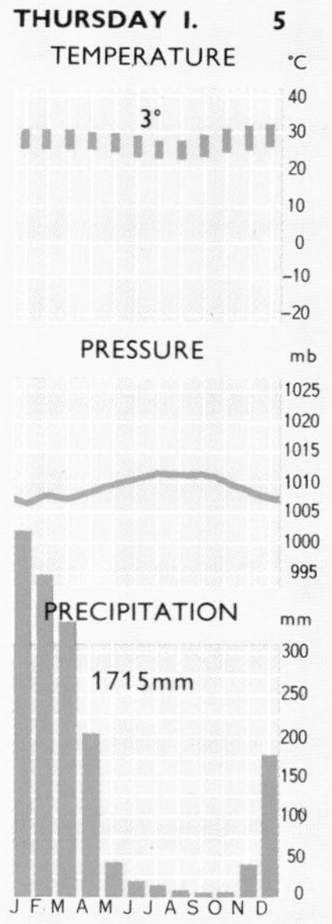
THURSDAY I. 5
TEMPERATURE
°C
3°
PRESSURE
mb
PRECIPITATION
mm
1715mm
J F M A M J J A S O N D

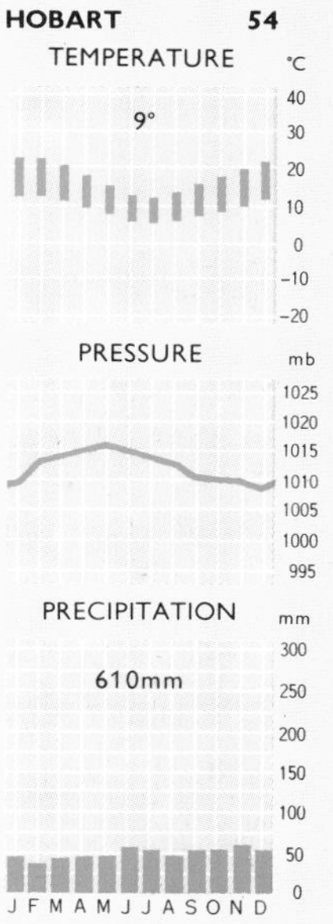
HOBART 54
TEMPERATURE
°C
9°
PRESSURE
mb
PRECIPITATION
mm
610mm
J F M A M J J A S O N D

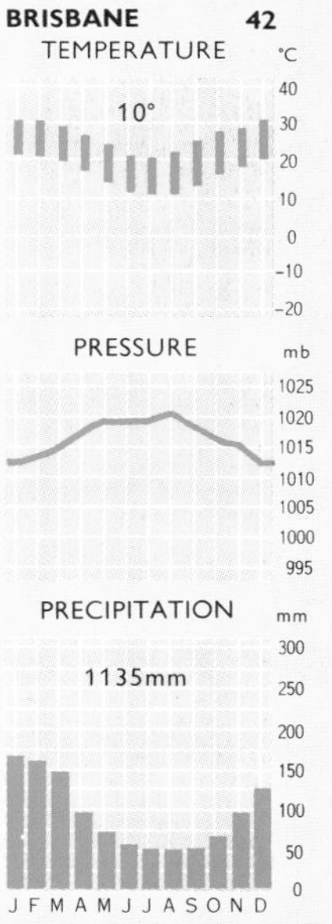
BRISBANE 42
TEMPERATURE
°C
10°
PRESSURE
mb
PRECIPITATION
mm
1135mm
J F M A M J J A S O N D

Map 57 | THE PACIFIC OCEAN

PORT MORESBY 38

TEMPERATURE °C

3°

PRESSURE mb

PRECIPITATION mm

1011mm

J F M A M J J A S O N D

TULAGI 2

TEMPERATURE °C

1°

PRESSURE mb

PRECIPITATION mm

3134mm

J F M A M J J A S O N D

Projection: Mollweide's Homolographic

East from Greenwich

Principal Shipping Routes
(Distances in Nautical Miles)

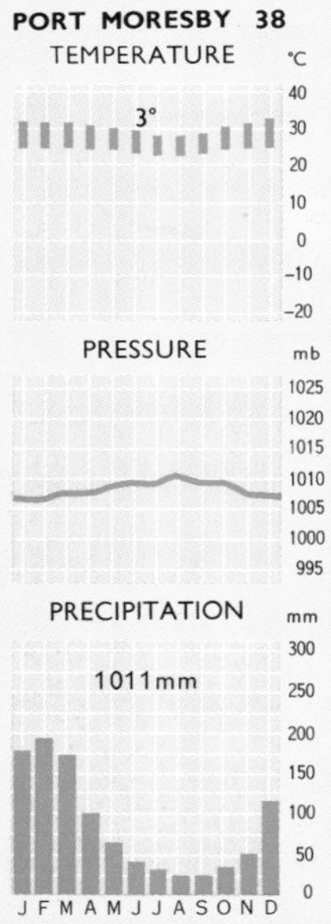

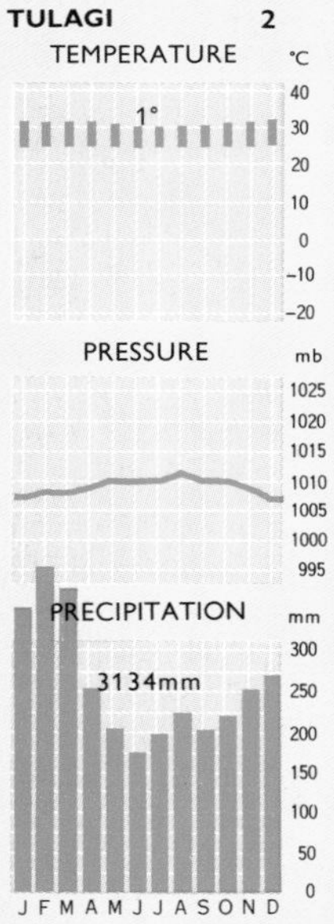

The Pacific has upwards of 20,000 islands but only two groups with substantial land areas and populations – New Zealand and Papua New Guinea. Some 3.5 million people are distributed through the other islands of Polynesia, stretching up to the US state of Hawaii, Melanesia (from New Guinea to Fiji) and Micronesia in the western Pacific. Oceania was explored in detail by Europeans only in the 18th century.

The Pacific is the greatest of the world's oceans, with an area vast enough to accommodate all the other oceans. It can belie its name with devastating winds. In the sub-tropics, westerlies prevail, while in the tropics steadier trade winds blow from the east, cooling both sides of the equator.

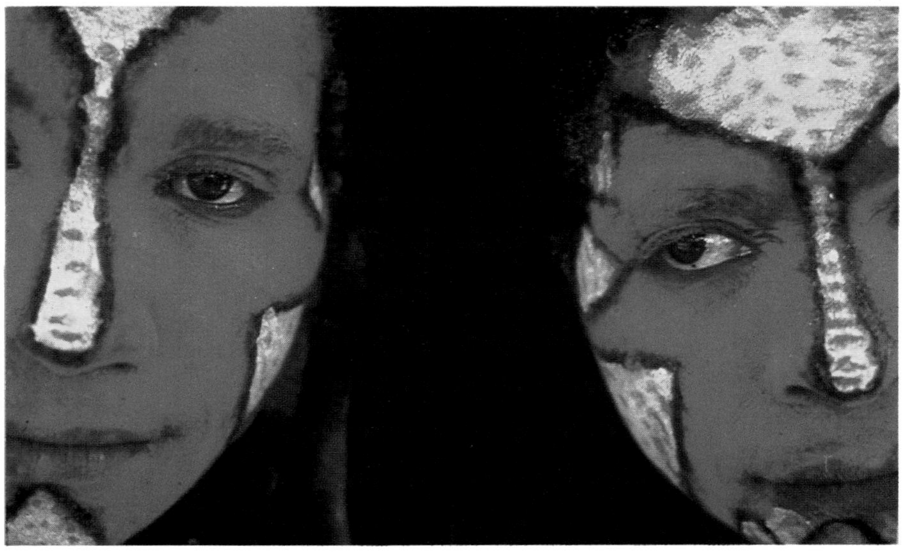

Papua New Guinea

Area: 462,840km² (178,656sq.m.).
Population: 3.26 million.
Capital: Port Moresby (124,000).
Languages: English, Pidgin, 700 tribal dialects.
Ethnic groups: Melanesian, Papuan, Negrito, Asian, European.
Main exports: copper, copra, coffee, cocoa, timber, rubber, gold.
Average temperature: 27°C (80°F) in lowlands.
Highest point: Mt Wilhelm, 4,694m (15,400ft).

Left: *The Melanesians of New Guinea use body painting for ceremonial occasions.*

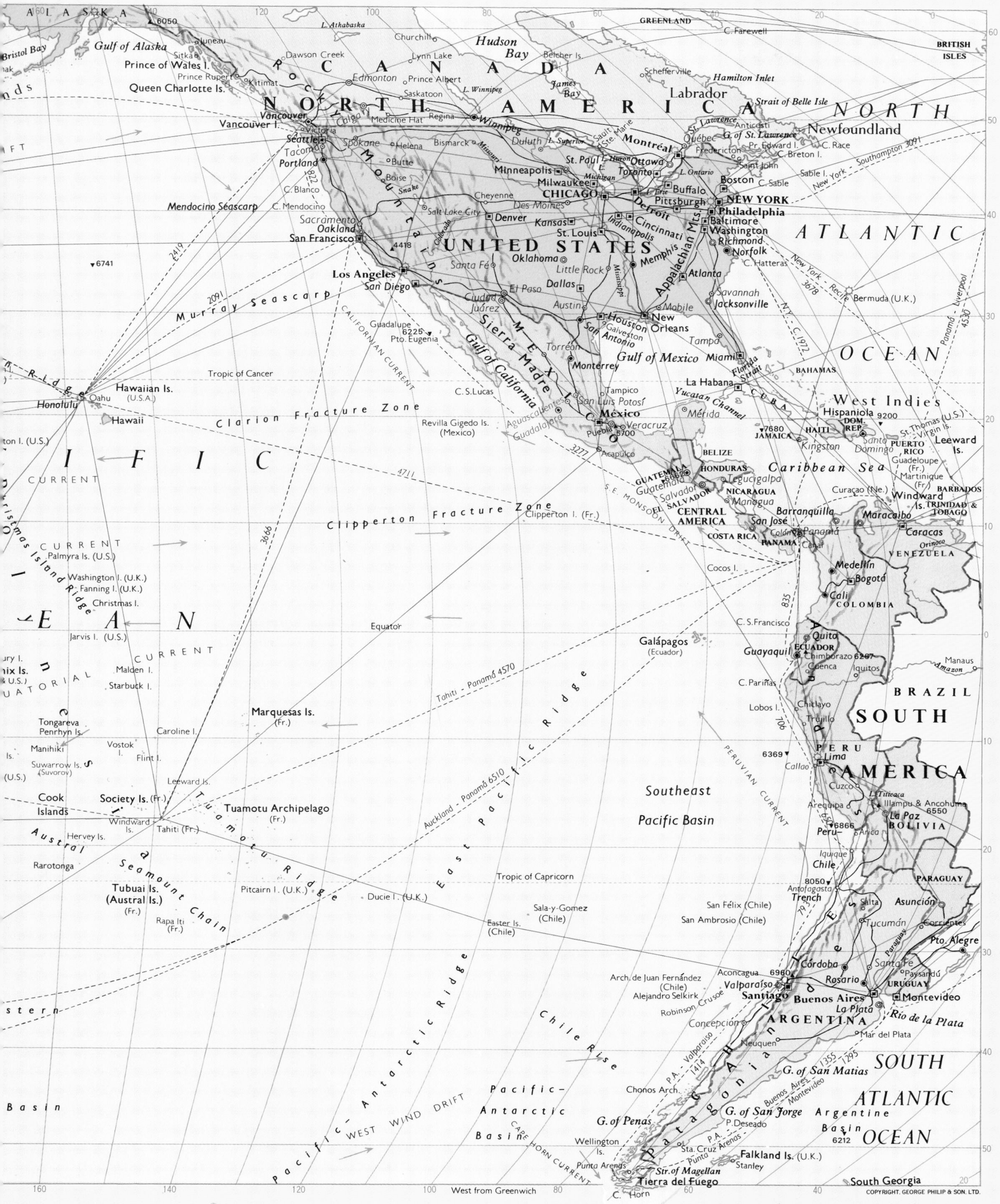

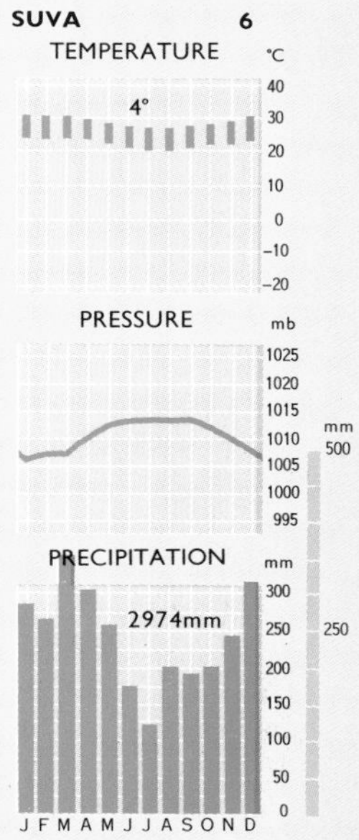

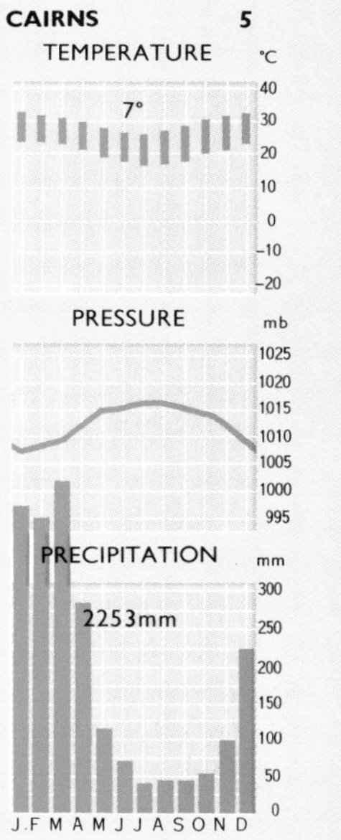

The nation of Papua New Guinea, independent since 1975, comprises the eastern half of the large island of New Guinea, the major islands of New Britain in the Bismarck Archipelago, Bougainville in the Solomons, and several smaller volcanic or coral islands. Formerly administered by Australia, the parliamentary government resisted secession moves by Bougainville whose copper mine at Panguna is becoming the major revenue earner.

Predominantly hot, humid and wet, with mangrove swamps and coastal plains rising to tropical forests in the jagged Bismarck and Owen Stanley ranges, the main island of New Guinea has areas that were explored only recently, and remnants of Stone Age head-hunting tribal cultures exist. Outside of the European-run cash crop plantations, mainly in the southeast and on New Britain, most of the people subsist on crops such as sago, yams and taro with pigs and poultry.

Polynesia, Melanesia and Micronesia

Ever since Cook and other mariners charted them, the tropical islands of Polynesia, Melanesia and Micronesia have been romanticized by Europeans enchanted by their palm-fringed beaches and simple village-based societies. Tourism is now an important local industry, especially in Polynesia. Although much of the Pacific is part of the developing world with increasing migration to towns, the economics of most islands are still based on fishing and the farming of root crops, fruit, corn, coconuts, pigs and chickens.

The peoples of Oceania probably originated in Asia. They speak a variety of Malayo-Polynesian tongues, although English is the common language (simplified to Pidgin in Melanesia) and French is spoken in Vanuatu, New Caledonia and French Polynesia. The Polynesians are taller and lighter skinned than Micronesians, who have some Asian features. Melanesians are shorter (except in Fiji), and darker.

In the tropics, average temperatures on the islands range between 21-27°C (70-80°F). There is a wet season from December to March in Polynesia and Melanesia. The bigger islands are of a high volcanic type but most are low-lying atolls with coral reefs.

Hawaii with an area of 16,755km² (6,471sq.m.) has the biggest population (965,000) and capital, Honolulu (365,000). A tourist and food-processing centre, it became the 50th state of the United States in 1959, is a major defence base and has ship-building and oil processing industries. The population is a mixture of American (40 percent), Japanese (30 percent), Polynesian (15 percent), Filipino and Chinese and is concentrated on Oahu. Hawaii itself is

Map 59 NEW ZEALAND

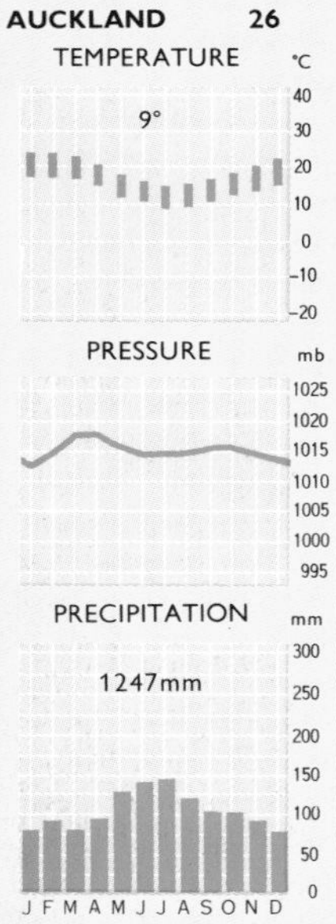

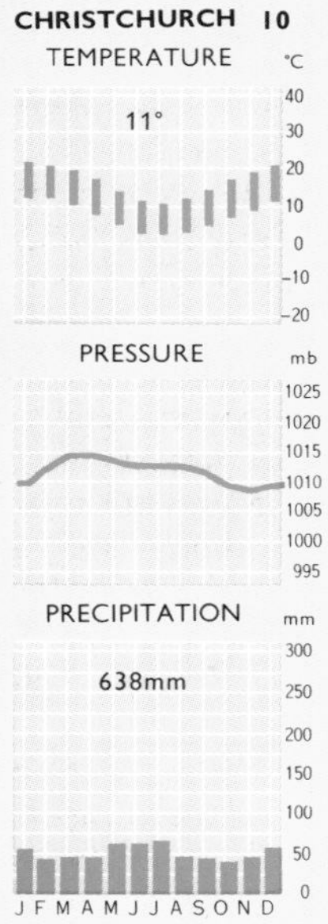

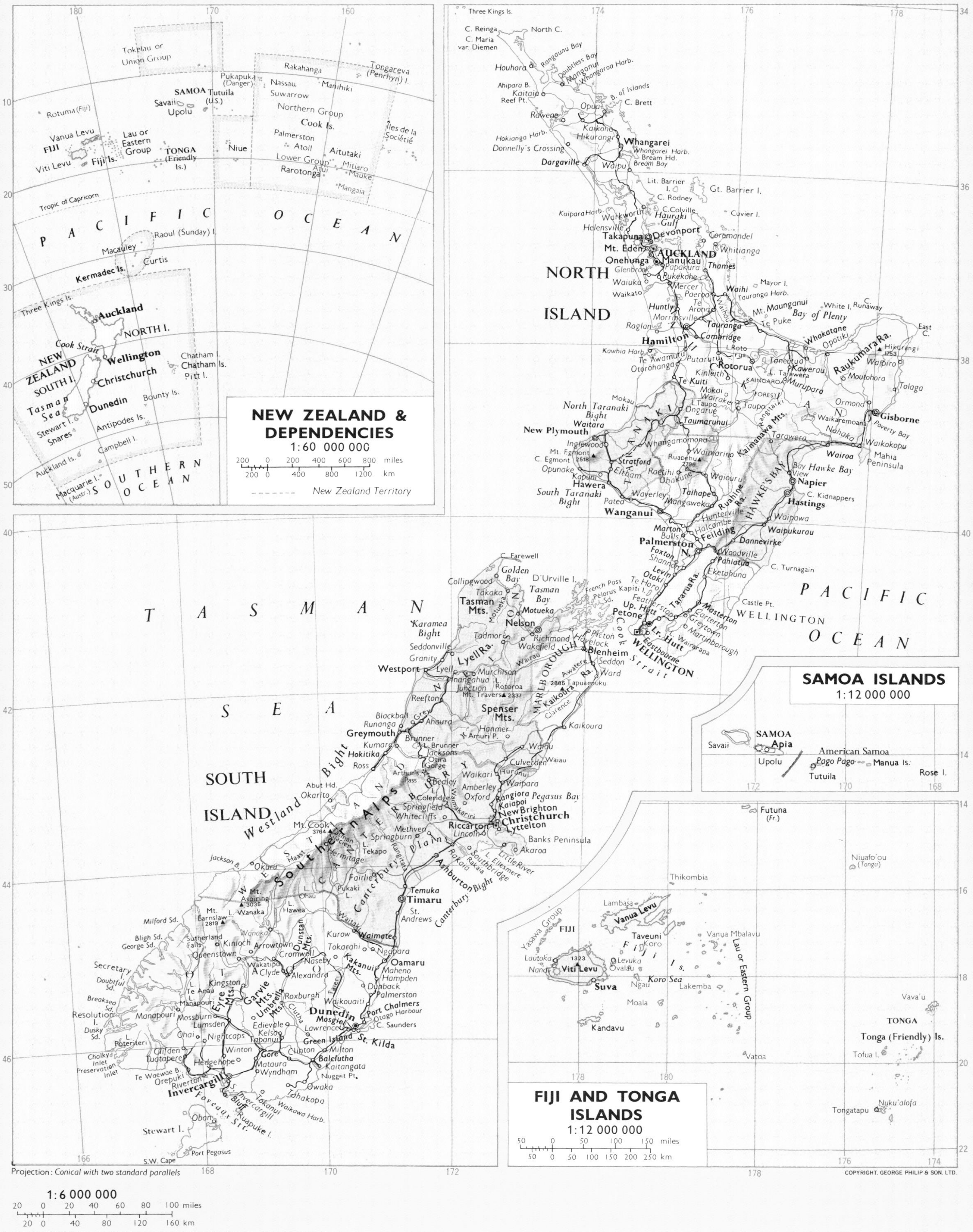

the largest of the 132 islands in the group and has a famous active volcano, Mauna Loa 4,170m (13,680ft).

The US also administers **American Samoa** (34,000), **Guam** (106,000), the most important of several strategic island bases, and the **US Trust Territory of the Pacific,** comprising the Micronesian groups of the Carolines, Marshalls and Marianas.

Fiji, with an area of 18,333km^2 (7,078sq.m.) and a population of 663,000, is the only Pacific nation with an Indian majority. A British colony until 1970, it is now an independent democracy with a capital at Suva (118,000). Fiji is an important producer of sugar and copra and has a gold mine at Vatukoula and lesser deposits of manganese, silver and copper. Land ownership is mainly in the hands of the Fijians who are slightly outnumbered by the Indian community.

Vanuatu (population 117,000), with its capital at Vila (14,000) became independent from Britain and France in 1980. **Kiribati,** the **Solomon Islands** and **Tuvalu** are also new nations, previously ruled by Britain, and the tiny colony of **Pitcairn**, famous as the hiding place of the Bounty mutineers, is administered by the British High Commissioner in New Zealand. Southeast of Pitcairn lies **Easter Island,** an isolated Chilean dependency whose massive statues carved in volcanic rock are an archaeological mystery.

New Caledonia has significant mineral deposits, chiefly nickel, chrome and iron. An overseas territory of France, it has an area of 19,103km^2 (7,375sq.m.) and a population of 146,000 with a capital at Nouméa (74,000). Recent years have seen disturbances involving French colonists and the Melanesians.

The tourist hub and centre of French influence in the Pacific is Papeete (63,000), capital of Tahiti in **French Polynesia** (148,000) which comprises the Society, Marquesas and Tubuai Islands and the Tuamotu Archipelago. Like the **Wallis and Futuna Islands,** this is also an overseas territory of France and French nuclear weapons are tested in the Tuamotu group.

Western Samoa (156,000), with a capital at Apia, became the first independent Polynesian democracy in 1962 under the guidance of New Zealand. It exports copra, bananas and cacao.

Tonga (99,000), a former British protectorate, is an independent kingdom which exports copra and bananas.

Nauru (8,000), a tiny independent Micronesian island, has become rich through vast deposits of phosphate, also mined on Banaba, and shipped to Australia, New Zealand and Japan.

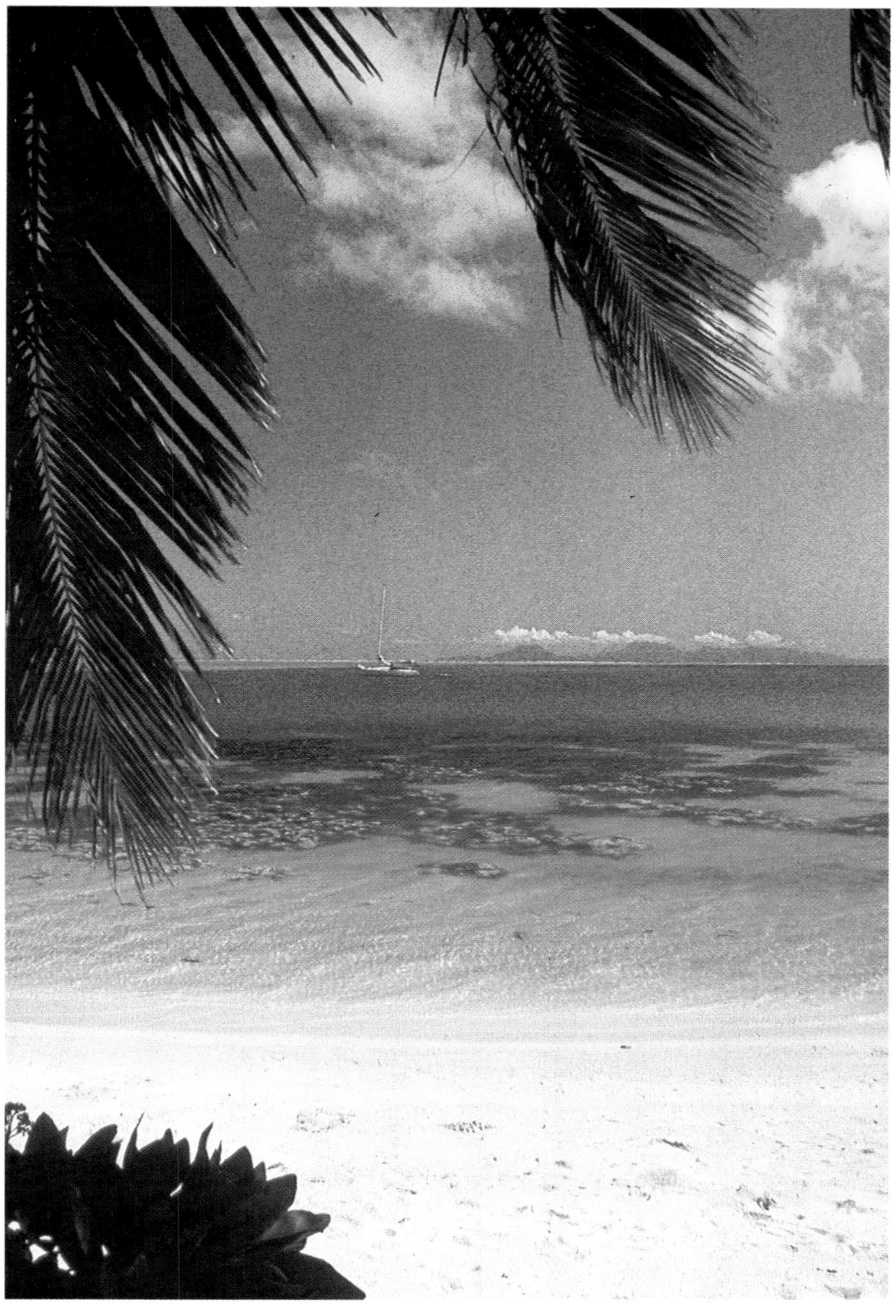

Above: *The lagoons, coral reefs and sandy beaches of French Polynesia's 130 islands have led to a booming tourist industry.*

Above right: *Forest and pastoral land by Lake Wakatipu, South Island: the source of much of New Zealand's prosperity.*

New Zealand

Area: 268,704km² (103,720sq.m.).
Population: 3.3 million.
Capital: Wellington (343,000).
Largest city: Auckland (863,000).
Languages: English, Maori.
Ethnic groups: British, Polynesian (250,000).
Main exports: dairy produce, wool, meat, forest products.
Average temperatures: 23°C (73°F) Jan., 8°C (46°F) July in Auckland but cooler in south.
Highest point: Mt Cook 3,764m (12,349ft).

New Zealand is the largest and most prosperous island nation in the South Pacific. Its people are predominantly British but there is a high rate of intermarriage with the Maori minority which makes up 10 percent of the population. A temperate climate and the application of scientific farming methods to some of the world's best grasslands have produced a strong agricultural economy supported by a wide range of manufacturing industries and an expanding industrial sector. In spite of its remoteness from its major markets, New Zealand maintains almost full employment and a high standard of living. With a land area slightly bigger than the United Kingdom's, but with a population of little more than three million, it also provides its people with an unmatched opportunity to enjoy landscapes and seascapes of striking beauty.

History, constitution and people

New Zealand is one of the world's youngest countries, historically as well as geologically. Polynesian mariners covering immense distances in open canoes reached the 'Land of the Long White Cloud' from the Society Island about the 10th century and settled it by purposeful migration in the 13th century. They found a land of forests and birds whose only mammals were two species of bats. European discovery by Abel Tasman in 1642 was not followed up until after Captain James Cook charted the coasts in 1769. Settlement by whalers, sealers and missionaries was followed by the reluctant acceptance of British sovereignty by the Maoris in the Treaty of Waitangi, 1840.

Largely self-governing from the 1860s, New Zealand pioneered much social legislation, including the earliest votes for women in 1893. The country became an independent dominion in 1907 and is a unicameral parliamentary democracy within the Commonwealth of Nations. The British monarch is the nominal Head of State represented by a Governor-General. Close cultural and trade links are retained with Britain, which remains the major source of immigration. Including Pacific Islanders, the Polynesian population numbers about 250,000, is strongly concentrated in Auckland and is well integrated into a multi-racial society. There are minorities of Yugoslav, Dutch, Chinese and Indian origin. Influenced by their isolation, New Zealanders tend to be undemonstrative, self-reliant and egalitarian, proud of their sporting record and their excellent health, educational and social services.

Physical features and climate

New Zealand lies 1,930km (1,200 miles) east of Australia. Its two main islands are divided by the narrow Cook Strait and are predominantly hilly in the north and mountainous in the south. The farthest inland point is only 130km (80 miles) from the sea.

In the North Island, the rolling northern peninsula widens south of Auckland into the Waikato basin. Both regions carry hill and lowland farms, orchards and forests. In the centre of the island a denuded pumice plateau with thermal springs surrounds several active volcanoes, the highest Mt Ruapehu 2,797m (9,175ft). The eastern ranges extend to the capital, Wellington, with mainly sheep country in the east and dairying predominating in the west.

The larger South Island is dominated by the Southern Alps which soar to permanent snowfields in the centre of the island, feeding a series of deep lakes and major rivers including the Rakaia, Waitaki and Clutha. Dense forests in the west extend into the granite mountains and deeply indented coastline of Fiordland. To the east lie the sheeplands and grain-growing region of the Canterbury Plains. South of this, the rolling Otago Plateau extends to another rich pastoral area in Southland. Stewart Island with a small fishing settlement lies across Foveaux Strait.

The climate is generally mild and moist. Except inland, where summers are hot and dry and the winters frosty, most areas are tempered by sea breezes. These become blustery around Wellington. Pressure ridges move usually from east to west, bringing high rainfall to some southwestern areas but moderate rainfall elsewhere.

The vegetation is mainly evergreen, with beech and native fern in upland areas. In addition to its beaches and national parks, scenic grandeurs such as the 580m (1,904ft) Sutherland Falls and remnants of giant kauri forests, New Zealand's introduced wildlife, including deer, pigs, trout and salmon, make it attractive to sporting tourists.

Agriculture, forestry and fishing

New Zealand's prosperity is based on its earnings from grasslands which are often fertilized by aerial top-dressing and which carry some 70 million sheep and eight million cattle. Although only a third of the land is farmed, sheep flocks produce more than 380,000 tonnes of wool a year and provide a dual income through the production of fat lambs and mutton. The best sheep country is in Canterbury and Southland in the South Island and in Manawatu, Hawkes Bay and South Auckland in the North Island. Some high country sheep farms

Above: *Wellington, New Zealand's capital, surrounds a fine natural harbour.*

Left: *Arrowtown is still nostalgic for New Zealand's rollicking gold-rush days.*

in Otago and Canterbury cover 20,000 hectares (50,000 acres) each, but the average is 450 hectares (1,125 acres).

A highly efficient dairy industry, organized on cooperative lines, produces export earnings that rival those of meat. Butter and cheese head a wide range of products. The richest dairy farms are in the North Island, particularly Taranaki, the Waikato, the Hauraki Plains and the Bay of Plenty. Over half the cattle are for beef production. Wheat, barley, corn and sugar-beet are grown, chiefly in the South Island. Fruit production is also important, with apples and pears from Nelson and Hawkes Bay providing the main export crops. Central Otago, Gisborne and Northland are other fruit-growing areas. New Zealand's improving white wines come mainly from Auckland and Hawkes Bay.

A third of the country is forested and large plantations of exotic radiata pine, chiefly in the Rotorua-Bay of Plenty area, are the basis of a pulp and paper industry that provides New Zealand's only major manufactured exports. More than 2.3 million cubic metres of timber are cut annually. Fishing is underdeveloped but a range of seafood delicacies includes crayfish tails packed for export.

Minerals, industry, trade and territories

Despite their agricultural economy, most New Zealanders live in towns and work in secondary or service industries. Under import and tariff protection, a range of small-scale manufacturing has been fostered with strong electrical, transport, woodworking, machinery, textiles, chemicals and plastics sectors in addition to the major freezing and food-processing sector. Industry is heavily concentrated around Auckland with its fine gulf port. Christchurch, with a port at Lyttleton, and Lower Hutt with a port at Wellington are also important. There are specialist ports at Tauranga and Whangarei.

Mineral resources are scarce, apart from several coal deposits, mainly in the Waikato and Westland, natural gas at Kapuni and offshore in Taranaki. But an iron and steel industry at Glenbrook near Auckland is based on rich ironsands on the west coast of the North Island. Cheap hydro-electricity from the southern lakes provides power for an aluminium smelter at Bluff using Australian bauxite. Hydro-electricity from the Waikato, Clutha and Waitaki rivers is the main source of energy. There is a geothermal field at Wairakei.

New Zealand's trade in agricultural products, sold mainly to Britain and the USA, earns nearly 90 percent of export income. Major imports are heavy machinery and transport equipment, metals, fuels, chemicals and textiles. Air New Zealand flies the Pacific and there is an extensive network of internal airways. New Zealand administers the Tokelau islands and handles defence and foreign affairs for Niue and the Cook Islands, self-governing territories which, like New Zealand itself, are rapidly expanding their tourist industry.

Antarctica

Antarctica is the fifth largest continent in the world and the coldest and bleakest of all the land masses. Its area of 13,200,000km^2 (5,100,000sq.m.) is extended in midwinter (June) by pack ice stretching out for several hundred kilometres. A temperature of −88.3°C (−126.9°F) was registered near the South Pole – the lowest ever recorded. Although fossil plants indicate that vegetation once grew, the continent is now a desolate land, locked in ice and swept by freezing winds. Coastal areas warm up in summer but temperatures remain below freezing point.

Glaciers grind down long valleys from the Transantarctic Mountains which divide the continent into East Antarctica, facing the Indian Ocean and Africa, and West Antarctica, facing the Pacific. These mountains extend along the Antarctic Peninsula and rise to a high point of 5,140m (16,846ft) in the Vinson Massif. Much of East Antarctica is a high plateau, more than 1,800m (6,000ft) above sea level, consisting of ancient rock covered by ice up to 2,700m (9,000ft) thick. In West Antarctica the icecap is even thicker – up to 4,270m (14,000ft) and there are two immense bays, the Ross Sea and the Weddell Sea.

Sub-Glacial Limits (at Sea Level) of Polar Basins

LITTLE AMERICA
TEMPERATURE
Range 41.1°C

PRESSURE
M.S.L.

Little America 78°34′S. 163°56′W.

MAWSON ★ 14
TEMPERATURE   °C
18°
PRESSURE   mb
PRECIPITATION   mm
362 mm

MELCHIOR   8
TEMPERATURE   °C
10°
PRESSURE   mb
PRECIPITATION   mm
1115 mm

Antarctic Explorers
- Cook 1772–75
- Bellingshausen 1819–21
- Weddell 1820–24
- Biscoe 1831–32
- D'Urville 1839–40
- Shackleton 1907–9
- Wilkes 1839–40
- Ross 1840–43
- Gerlache 1898–99
- Scott 1910–12
- Amundsen 1911–12
- Mawson 1911–14
- Byrd 1928–30 (by air)
- Byrd (U.S. Antarctic Service) 1939–41,1946–47(bases, Stonington I. & Little America)
- Trans-Antarctic Route 1958
- Soviet Expedition 1959
- Scott (N.Z.) Permanent Bases

Seas open all year
Extreme limits of drift-ice
Seas covered by pack-ice in Spring
Ice caps and permanent ice shelf

Progress of Exploration
Coasts explored between 1800 and 1850
Coasts explored since 1900
+ Byrd 1926 Highest latitudes reached by explorers with date

ion: Zenithal Equidistant

COPYRIGHT. GEORGE PHILIP & SON. LTD.

1:35 000 000

200   0   200   400   600   800 miles
400   0   400   800   1200 km

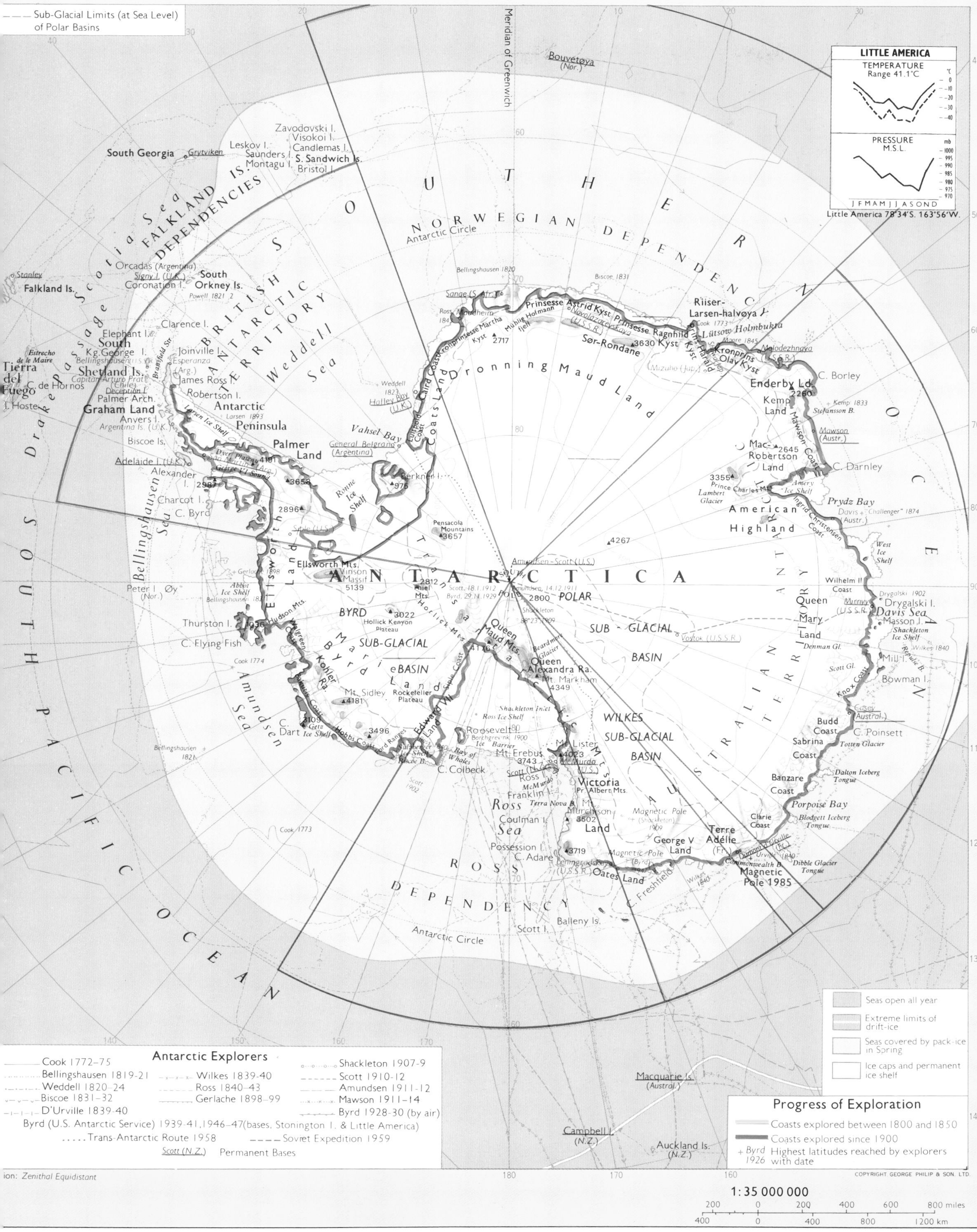

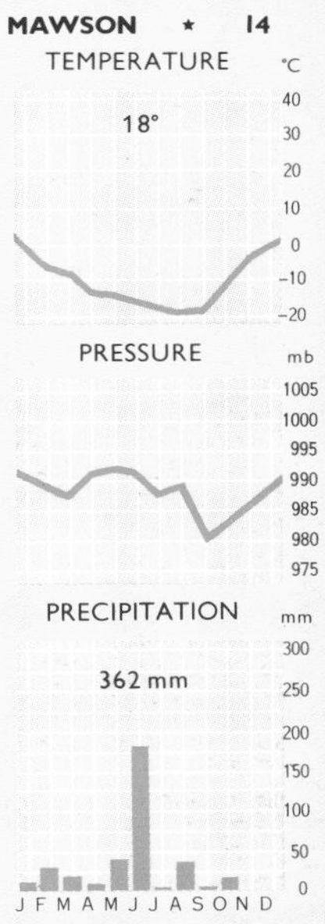

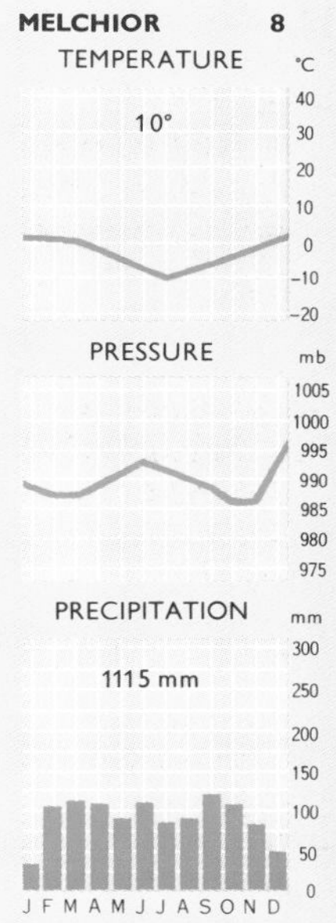

The coasts are rich in sea life and the region's only significant, but controlled, industry is whaling, carried on by Japan and other nations. East Antarctica has coal deposits and possibly oil and gas. Territorial claims to parts of Antarctica by Argentina, Australia, Britain, Chile, France, Norway and New Zealand have been deferred until 1989. The USSR and the USA are also active in the region and the USA maintains four permanent stations in Operation Deep Freeze (supplied from Christchurch, New Zealand). At McMurdo Sound near the active volcano Mt Erebus – 3,749m (12,448ft) – nuclear energy provides comfortable living quarters

alongside a 2,400m (8,000ft) runway.

Once called Terra Incognita Australis, Antarctica was visited by whalers from 1821 and exploration began in 1838. Roald Amundsen and four other Norwegians reached the South Pole on December 14, 1911, followed 35 days later by a British team, under Robert F. Scott, which perished on its return journey. The American Richard E. Byrd carried out extensive exploration from the 1920s and permanent bases were set up when an extensive joint research programme was carried out in 1958.

Right: *Antarctica – the earth's coldest, remotest and most unspoiled continent.*

Map 61 | NORTH AMERICA

NEW YORK · 96
TEMPERATURE °C
24°
PRESSURE mb
PRECIPITATION mm
1092mm

SEATTLE * 38
TEMPERATURE °C
13°
PRESSURE mb
PRECIPITATION mm
848mm

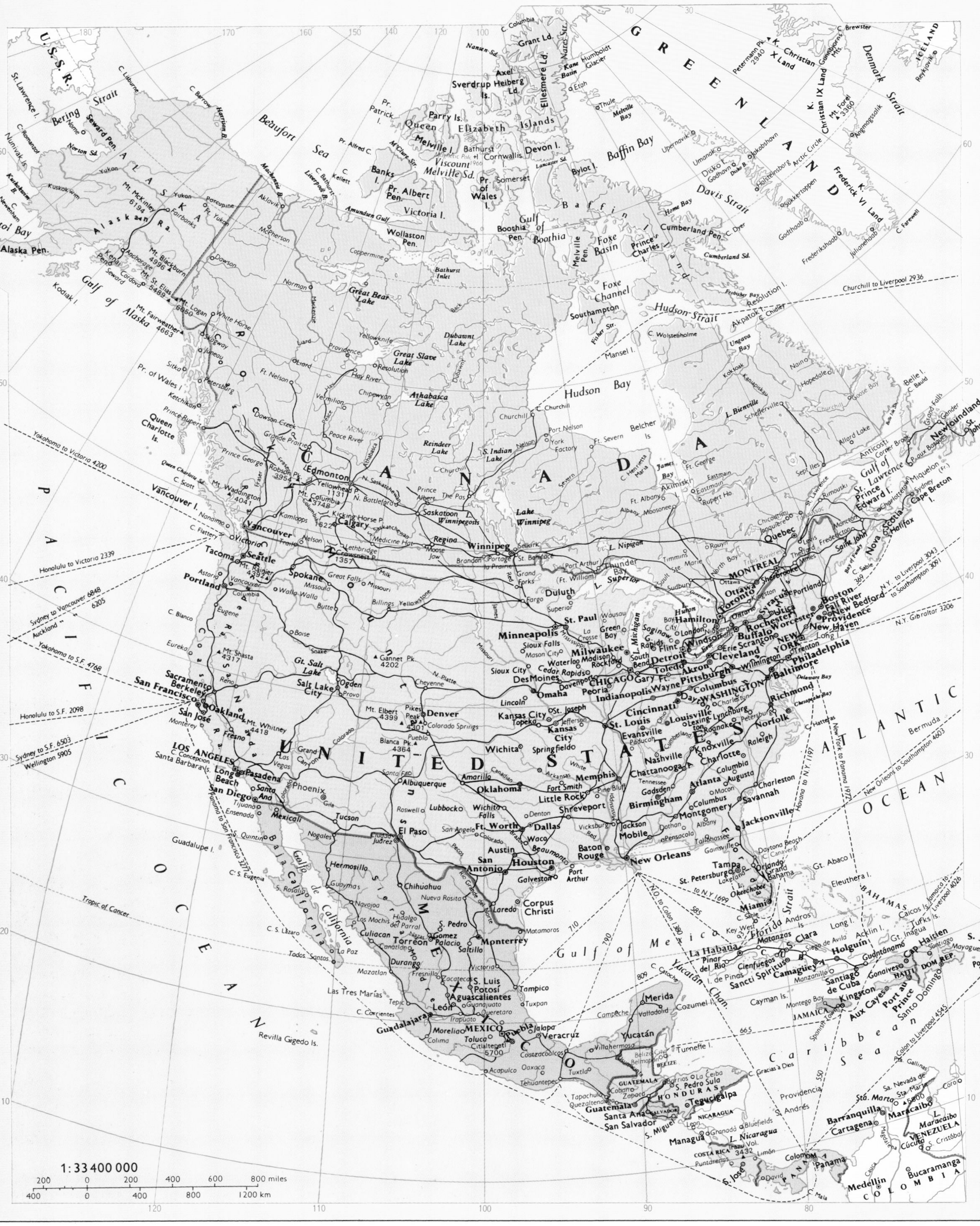

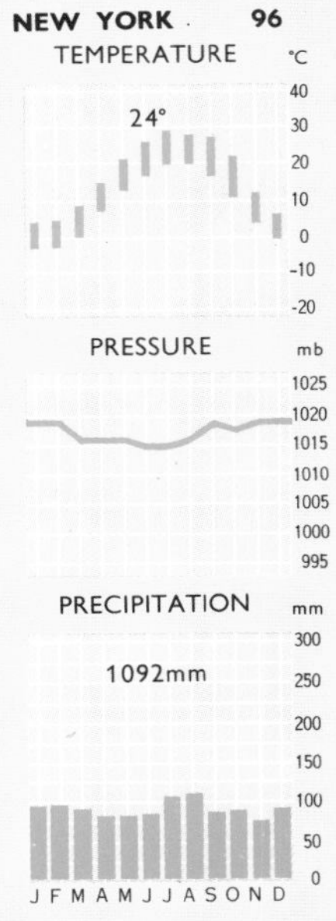

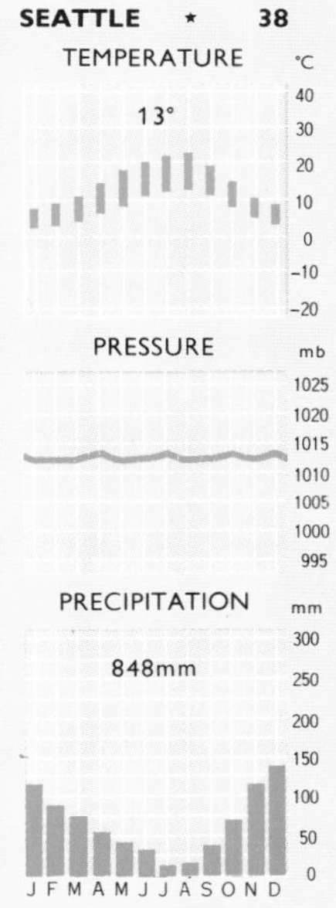

N orth America, including Canada, the United States, Mexico, Alaska, and Greenland, but excluding Central America and the West Indies, is the third largest continent after Asia and Africa. It has an area of more than 24.4m km² (9.42m sq.m.) and an estimated population of nearly 344 million.

The continent is shaped roughly like an inverted triangle, with its broad base spanning the frozen wastes of the Arctic in the north and its apex dipping into the tropical waters of the Gulf of Mexico in the southeast. From north to south the greatest distance is about 6,400km (4,000 miles), and from east to west about 7,900km (4,900 miles). It is flanked on the west by the Pacific Ocean, on the east by the Atlantic and

the Gulf of Mexico, on the north by the Arctic Ocean, and on the south it borders Belize and Guatemala.

North America's terrain exhibits almost every kind of surface from permanently ice-covered wastelands and scorching deserts to magnificent forests and lush, grass-covered plains. High mountains, huge rivers, lakes, and waterfalls, and incalculable deposits of mineral wealth all form part of the varied scene and add to the abundant natural resources of the continent.

There are three major regions distinguished by their widely differing landforms. The Western Highlands or Cordillera runs down the Pacific coast from Alaska through Mexico. The system is made up of the Rocky Moun-

tains, the Alaska Range, the St Elias Mountains, the Cascade Range, the Sierra Nevada, and the Sierra Madre. The Rockies extend for more than 4,800km (3,000 miles), and their high ridge, known as the Continental Divide, separates the river systems that flow to opposite sides of North America. The mountains are high and rugged, with many exceeding 4,270m (14,000ft).

The second major upland rises in the east of the continent, and is known as the Appalachian Highlands. This is made up of several mountain ranges and broad plateaux that are nowhere as high as the Western Highlands The Laurentian, Adirondack, and northern ranges of the Appalachian Mountains make up the northern part of the system. The

Appalachians continue southwards through the eastern United States.

The third landform covers the middle of the continent in the form of an immense plain that is 2,400km (1,500 miles) wide in places, and is drained by several large river systems. Among these are the Missouri-Mississippi in the south, the Great Lakes – St Lawrence in the centre, and the Mackenzie, and the Red-Nelson-Saskatchewan in the north.

Temperatures vary greatly over this huge land mass, and often reach extremes. A temperature of 57°C (134°F) has been recorded in Death Valley, in California. At the other end of the scale, the air temperature in the upper Yukon once fell to −63°C (−82°F). On the east, the temperature is influenced by

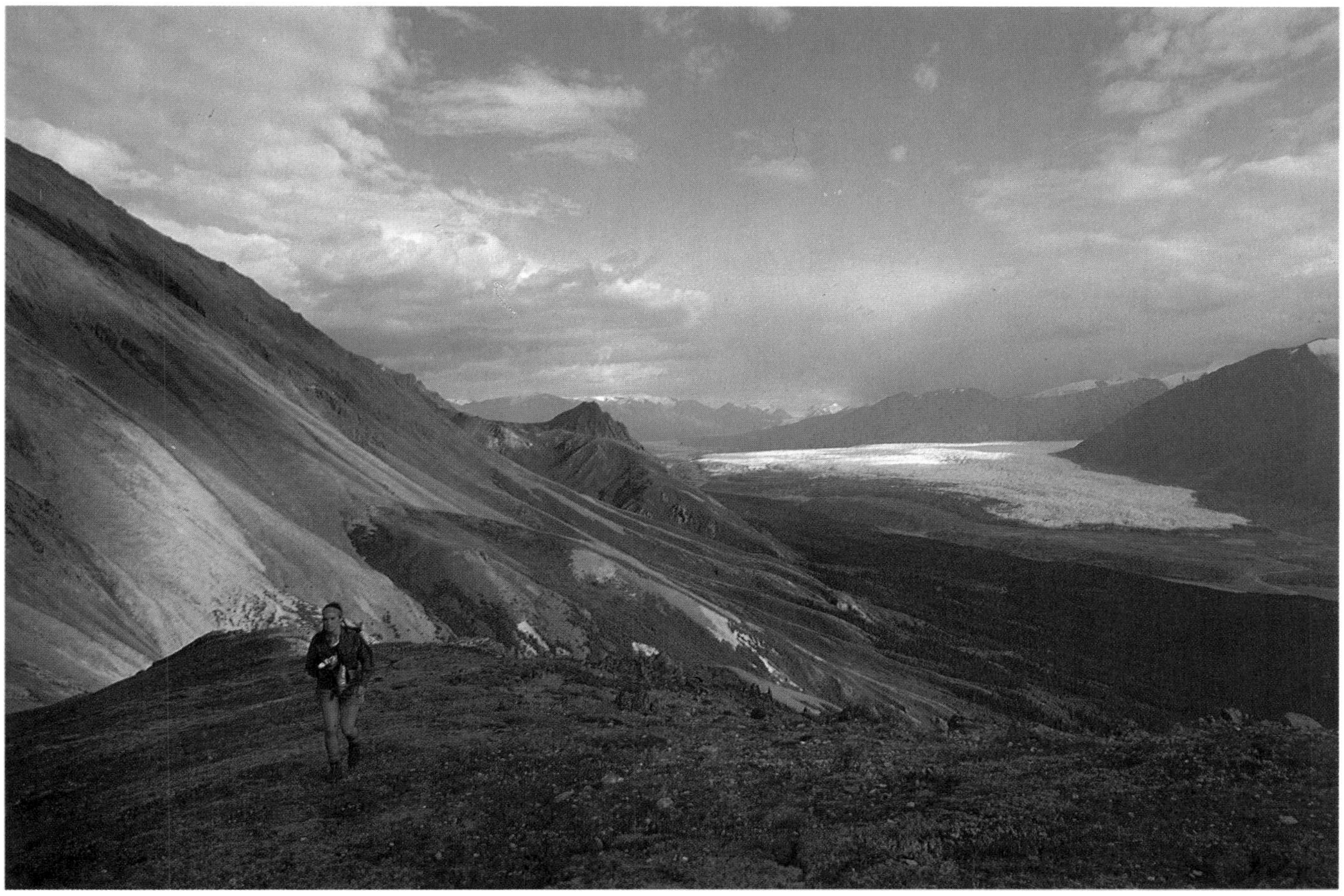

Left: *Donsek Glacier in Canada, where vast tracts of land have an Arctic climate.*

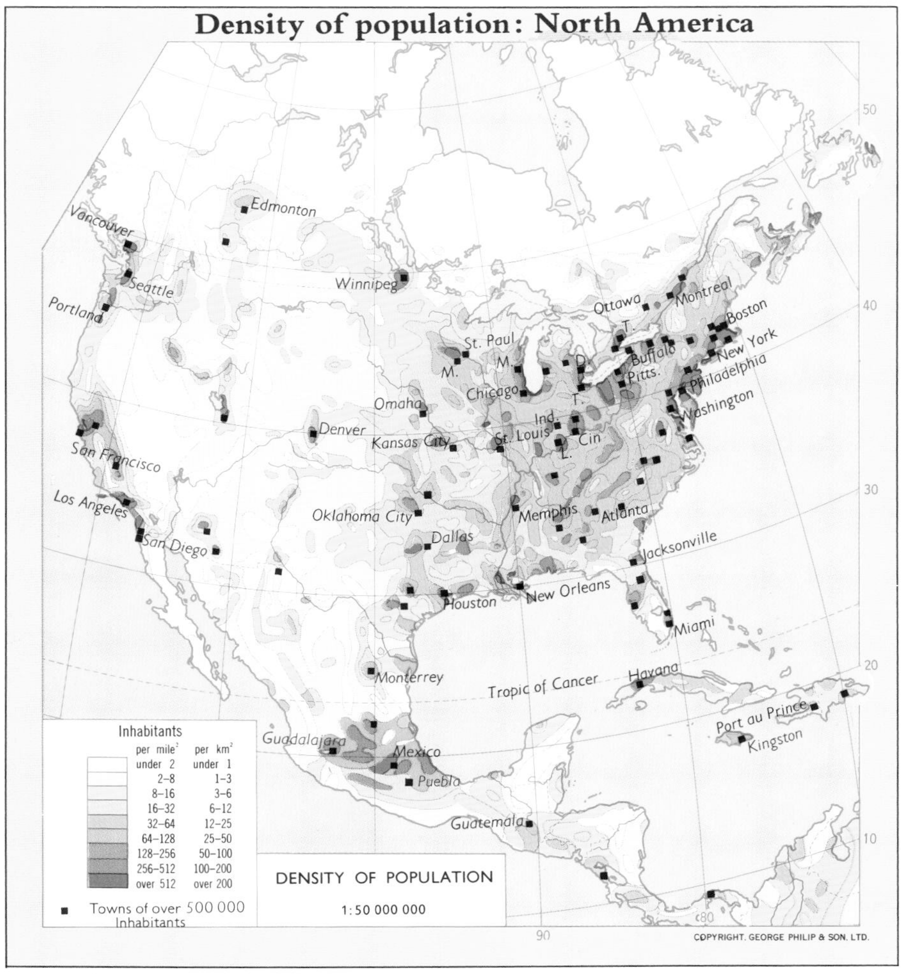

the warm Gulf Stream and the cold Labrador Current. Rainfall generally is heavy on the coasts and often meagre in the interior.

Vegetation varies widely with climate and soil. In the far north trees are unknown, but moss, lichens, and a few stunted, hardy plants grow here and there during the brief summer weeks. Farther south, huge forests cover great parts of Canada and eastern and western regions of the United States. More than 1,000 kinds of trees have been counted, including the giant redwoods of California, some of which are more than 3,000 years old. Desert vegetation is found in parts of the south.

It seems likely that about 30,000 years ago nomadic people from Asia crossed a land bridge that existed at that time between Siberia and Alaska. They were the ancestors of the North American Indians. The Eskimos arrived much later, again possibly from Asia, probably about 6,000 years ago. After Christopher Columbus alerted Europeans to the existence of North America in 1492, the continent was invaded at various times, mainly by Spanish, English, and French explorers. As settlements expanded, warfare broke out between the three nationalities, while the original inhabitants, the Amerindian peoples, were steadily eliminated by all three.

Hawaii, the 50th state of the United States, is described in the article on Oceania. Mexico and Greenland are also described separately.

Canada

Area: 9,976,139km² (3,851,809sq.m.).
Population: 25.4 million.
Capital: Ottawa (718,000).
Largest city: Toronto (3m).
Languages: English, French.
Ethnic groups: British, French, Amerindian, Eskimo.
Main exports: lumber, paper, metals, machinery, aluminium, wood pulp, petroleum.
Average temperatures: 18°C (0°F) Jan., 18°C (65°F) July in Winnipeg, but considerably less severe winters in coastal states, especially in the southwest.
Highest point: Mt Logan (Yukon Territory), 6,050m (19,850ft).

Canada, a land of long, harsh winters and mild summers, is the largest country in area in the Western Hemisphere and the second largest in the world after the USSR. Most of its great potential wealth still lies untapped in its huge forests and river systems and in mineral deposits deep underground. The people of this young nation are scattered patchily over the vast land, but most of them live within 320km (200m.) of the United States border in the south. Huge stretches in the north are completely uninhabited.

The predominant cultures are British (about 45 percent) and French (about 30 percent) in origin. Other Europeans make up about 20 percent and the remainder of the people are Amerindians and Eskimos.

French-speaking Canadians have to a great extent retained their customs, Roman Catholic religion, and culture, as well as their language. The culture of the English-speaking communities is less definite because by no means all their members are of English stock.

All parliamentary business is carried on in both English and French. The federal courts also use both languages, and stamps and banknotes are printed in English and French. But in Québec, the official language has been French since 1974.

Most Canadian Indians live on government reserves. They include members of the Algonkian, Huron, Iroquois, and Salish groups, and by 1981 numbered about 368,000, with a steadily increasing population.

Canada's 25,000 Eskimos, who live in the far north between Alaska and Greenland, are also increasing in numbers. Traditionally they have hunted and fished in the frozen wastelands. But, particularly from the late 1960s onwards, many have found well-paid jobs with mining, transport, and petroleum companies.

Canadians are often energetic and self-reliant, with a passionate love of the outdoors. Hunting is a favourite recreation. The Canadian outdoor image has been reinforced by the colourful Royal Canadian Mounted Police (the 'Mounties'), the country's national law enforcement department.

History and constitution

The first recorded landing by a European on Canadian soil was made in 1497 by John Cabot, an Italian-born explorer sailing in the service of King Henry VII of England. Some 37 years later, the French explorer Jacques Cartier landed on the Gaspé Peninsula and sailed up the St Lawrence River, naming his discovery New France. Soon an intense rivalry developed between the French and the English.

In the early 1600s another French explorer, Samuel de Champlain, arrived in the St Lawrence region and founded Québec, the first permanent settlement

Below: *A lively, thriving cosmopolitan city, Toronto, Ontario, still has vestiges of the original, rather sedate provincial town.*

Map 62 EASTERN CANADA

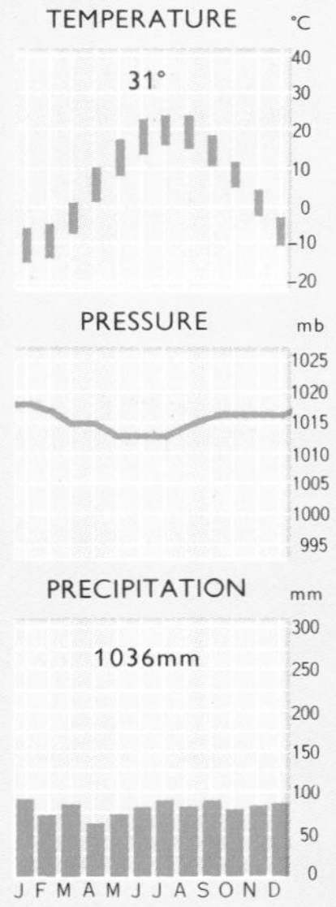

in Canada. He also greatly extended the area and influence of New France.

Fighting between the French and English dragged on sporadically until the fall of Québec in 1759, when French Canada finally came under British rule. In 1867, the British North America Act established the Dominion of Canada.

Today, Canada is an independent, self-governing, constitutional monarchy, and a member of the Commonwealth of Nations. Its nominal head of state is the British monarch, who is represented by a Governor-General. The nation consists of a federation of 10 provinces and two territories. The provinces are: Alberta, British Columbia, Manitoba, New Brunswick, Newfoundland, Nova Scotia, Ontario, Prince Edward Island, Québec, and Saskatchewan; and the territories are the Northwest Territories and Yukon Territory.

Each province is self-governing, and the territories have some self-government. Parliament, which meets in Ottawa, is made up of 104 members of the Senate, appointed by the Governor General, and 282 members of the House of Commons, elected by the people. The head of government is the prime minister, who is the leader of the majority party in the House of Commons. Voters in national elections must be Canadian citizens at least 18 years old.

Land and climate

Canada covers the whole of the northern half of North America except for Greenland and Alaska. It stretches 4,627km (2,875m.) from north to south, and 5,187km (3,223m.) from east to west.

The land falls into seven major natural regions: the Appalachian Highlands, an ancient system of low mountains that covers Newfoundland, the Gaspé Peninsula of Québec, New Brunswick, Prince Edward Island, and Nova Scotia; the Great Lakes-St Lawrence Lowland, which is the most heavily populated and industrialized region in Canada; the Canadian Shield, beneath whose ancient rocks lies a vast storehouse of mineral wealth; the Hudson Bay Lowland, a low-lying, swampy region on the southwestern shore of Hudson Bay; the Interior Plains, which cover much of the Prairie Provinces (Manitoba, Alberta, Saskatchewan) and part of north-eastern British Columbia, where Canada's great wheat belt is located; the Western Mountain region or Cordillera, which consists of two major mountain ranges – the Rockies and the Coast Mountains; and the Arctic Islands, almost all of which lie within the Arctic Circle.

Canada is abundantly supplied with rivers and lakes, and holds about one-third of all the fresh water on earth. However, pollution is now a major problem. The principal rivers are the Mackenzie, the St Lawrence, and the Fraser, although large areas of the country are also drained by the Columbia and the Yukon, parts of whose courses flow through the United States.

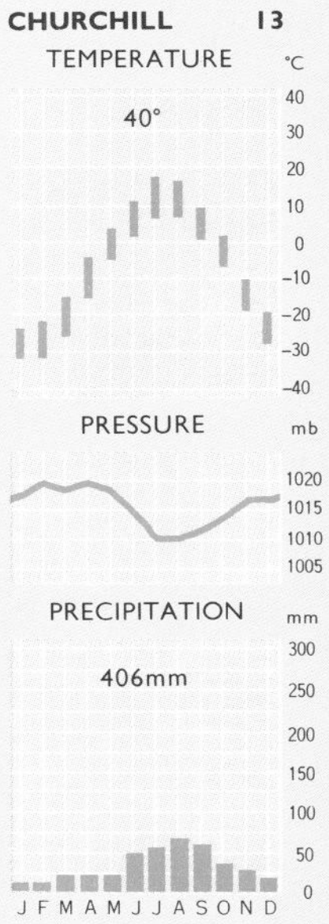

Canada shares four of the Great Lakes (Ontario, Erie, Huron, and Superior) with the United States.

Canada has a continental climate that ranges from freezing cold to blistering heat. Northern Canada has long, cold winters and relatively short, cool summers with the warmest region in southwestern Ontario.

Provinces and cities

The two largest and most heavily populated provinces are Ontario and Québec. Ontario (8.6m) contains the main industrial centres. Its capital, Toronto (3m), is a busy port on Lake Ontario and has become the largest city in Canada. Ottawa (718,000), the federal capital, is also in Ontario. Québec Province (6.4m) is the centre of French-speaking Canada and is another leading industrial region. Its capital, Québec, or Québec City (576,000) is the unofficial capital of French Canada. Montréal (2.8m) is the province's largest city and the second largest city in Canada. Located on the St Lawrence Seaway about 1,600km (1,000m.) from the Atlantic, it is one of the world's largest inland ports.

British Columbia (2.7m) is the third largest province, and includes Vancouver Island on which its capital city, Victoria (pop. 233,000), stands. Van-

Left: *The breadth and quantity of flow give Niagara Falls, Ontario, a grandeur and beauty attested to by more than four million visitors annually.*

Map 64 | WESTERN CANADA

DAWSON 324

TEMPERATURE ℃

PRESSURE mb

PRECIPITATION mm
320mm

J F M A M J J A S O N D

Projection: Lambert's Equivalent Azimuthal

West from Greenwich

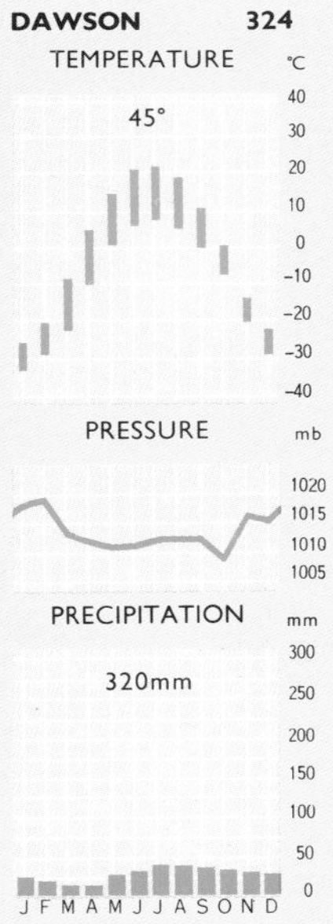

couver (1.3m) on the mainland, is the largest city and port. The province boasts spectacular mountain and coastal scenery, and is strongly British in character.

The Prairie Provinces contain a huge wheat belt that helps to feed not only Canada but also much of the rest of the world, and large petroleum reserves are another asset in these provinces.

Farming, fishing and forestry

About nine-tenths of Canada's farm produce comes from the Great Lakes-St Lawrence Lowland and the Interior Plains. Grain crops, especially wheat, predominate. Livestock – dairy and beef cattle, poultry, pigs, and sheep – are a valuable source of farm income. Beef

cattle ranches are found mainly in Alberta, whereas dairy herds are grazed mainly in the Great Lakes-St Lawrence Lowlands and parts of British Columbia. Vegetables and fruit flourish in the sunshine of British Columbia and on the Ontario peninsula, but they are also grown in a multitude of smallholdings in Prince Edward Island.

Canada has two of the world's greatest fishing grounds. These are the Grand Banks (cod, haddock, mackerel, herring, lobster) off the northeastern shores of Newfoundland and Nova Scotia, and

Right: *Much of Canada is a land of dense forest, myriad lakes and bare rock. Many of the country's rich natural resources have yet to be tapped.*

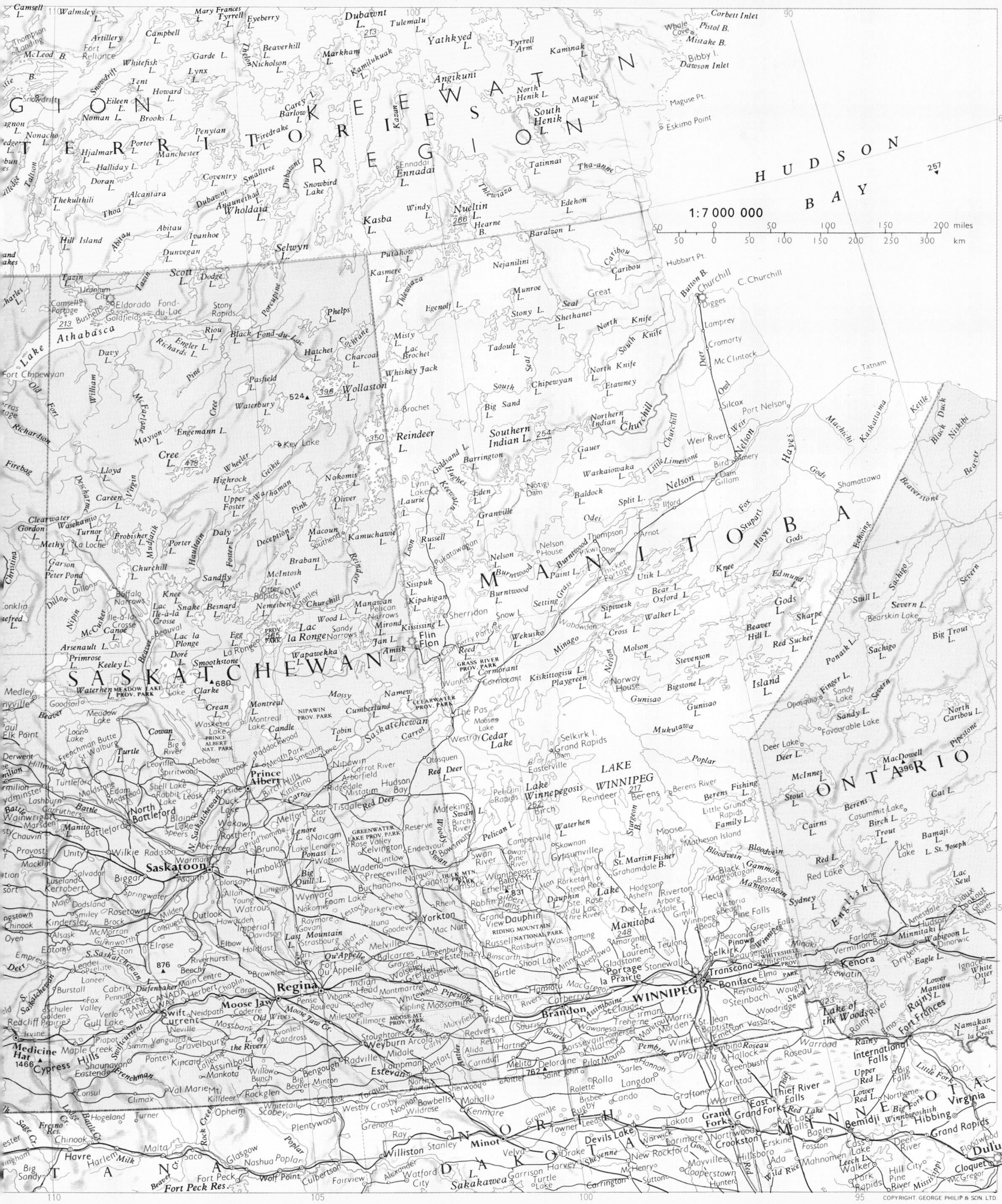

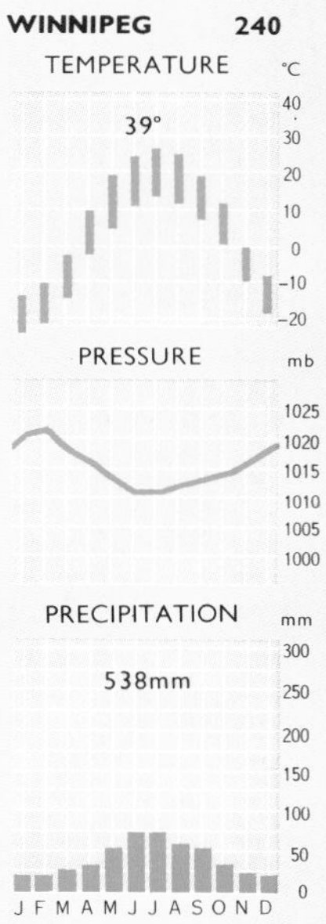

the coastal waters that fringe the shores of British Columbia (salmon, halibut, shellfish). Canada's many rivers and lakes yield huge quantities of salmon, trout, perch, pike, and other species.

About half of Canada's land surface is forested. The softwood trees such as tamarack, balsam fir, and spruce supply wood pulp that is manufactured into more than half the world's newsprint. Other wood products are also made.

Minerals and energy resources

Canada is the world's largest producer of asbestos, which comes mainly from eastern Québec. It is also a leading producer of uranium, found chiefly in Ontario and northern Saskatchewan. The Western Interior Plains are particularly rich in oil, natural gas, bituminous sands, coal, gypsum, and potash. Iron ore comes from parts of Ontario, Newfoundland, Québec, and British Columbia. The Canadian Shield is known to hold important deposits of gold, silver, copper, lead, iron, zinc, uranium, platinum, and nickel.

Canada's immense water resources have encouraged the building of hydro-electric plants that today make the nation one of the world's leading producers of hydro-electric power. About 66 percent of this power is generated in Ontario and Québec.

Industry and trade

Manufacturing is Canada's most important activity. More than 66 percent of the country's products are manufactured. The major products are processed food, transport equipment, electronic goods and machinery. Other important industries include the manufacture of paper and paper products and the processing of primary metals, chemical products and wood products.

Trade and relations

Canada's principal trade partners (imports and exports) in order of importance are the United States, Britain, Japan and West Germany. Canada exports about 40 percent of its products and imports about the same proportion of the goods it needs. Two-thirds of its exports go to the United States. They include cars and parts, lumber, petroleum, aluminium, newsprint and whisky. It imports from the United States slightly more than it exports, including chemicals, plastics, iron and steel, computers, and cars and parts. To Britain, Canada exports wheat and tobacco as well as manufactured items. The opening of the St Lawrence Seaway (shared by Canada and the United States) in 1959 enabled ocean-going ships to reach the Great Lakes ports and brought a boom in Canadian trade, especially with Europe.

During the long premiership of Pierre Trudeau, Canada loosened its traditional trading ties with the United States, Britain and other European countries and established commercial links with China, the Soviet Union, and various South American nations.

Left: *Washington's Capitol, home of the Senate and the House of Representatives.*

The United States of America

Area: 9,363,123km^2 (3,615,122sq.m.).
Population: 239 million.
Capital: Washington, D.C. (4.13m).
Largest city: New York City (7.07m).
Language: English.
Ethnic groups: British, Irish, Continental Europeans, Hispanics Jewish, Negroes, Amerindians, Asians.
Main exports: transport equipment and machinery, food, live animals, raw materials, chemicals, computers, electronic goods.
Average temperatures: −2°C (29°F) Jan., 22°C (72°F) July in Boston, Mass; 19°C (67°F) Jan., 28°C (83°F) July in Miami, Florida.
Highest point: Mt McKinley (Alaska), 6,194m (20,320ft).

The United States (often shortened to USA or US) is the fourth largest country in the world. This huge and varied land is one of the richest and most powerful nations and the majority of its peoples enjoy the highest standards of living on earth.

Only the Soviet Union, Canada and China are larger in area, and only China, India, and the Soviet Union have larger populations. Of the estimated 239 million people living in the United States in 1985, more than 24 million were blacks, about eight million were of Hispanic origin, and about 80,000 were Amerindians.

The nation today is a melting pot of dozens of different races. The Indians and Eskimos had already been living there for thousands of years when the first English settlers arrived in the 1600s and proceeded to colonize Virginia and New England, which today is made up of the states of Connecticut, Massachusetts, Rhode Island, Vermont, New Hampshire, and Maine.

The English were followed by others: Spaniards who went to what is now California and Florida, Dutch to New York, Germans to Pennsylvania, and French to Louisiana. Later, hundreds of thousands of Negroes were shipped from Africa to work as slaves on the plantations of the southern states. Rapid European immigration during the 19th century reached a peak in the period 1900-10.

After World War II there was another great influx of people, most of them homeless Jews and other European refugees. Today, the largest immigrant groups are Italians, Germans, Poles, and Russians. Almost all of them are well integrated into American life but they still retain a degree of individuality and culture in matters of worship, food, and traditional festivals.

There is complete freedom of worship in the United States. The majority of the people are Christians and about five percent Jews. There are also minority Islamic groups and followers of eastern religions. There are more Protestants than any other Christians, but Roman Catholics form the largest single Christian denomination.

Education is compulsory up to about the age of 16. Public schools are free, and run by state and local authorities. Churches and private individuals and agencies run a number of private educational establishments. The educational system is divided into primary (elementary), secondary (high school), and higher education. The last includes colleges, technical schools, and universities. More than 99 percent of American adults can read and write. In 1954 the Supreme Court ruled that racial segregation in the public schools was unconstitutional, and since that time there has been a gradual but steady integration of black and white schoolchildren throughout the country, in spite of some violent opposition initially.

Americans in general are prosperous, optimistic, and extrovert. Although family ties are strong, they have a tradition based on the equality of all and the feeling of independence associated with this conviction. This may account in part for the energetic and restless nature of the typical American, who works and plays hard and has a passion for novelty. Among favourite outdoor activities are hunting, fishing, golf, baseball, and football.

History and constitution

The first white settlements in what is now the United States were established by the Spaniards in Florida in 1565. The first permanent English settlement was made at Jamestown, Virginia, in 1607. Thirteen years later, the Pilgrim Fathers travelled across the Atlantic in the *Mayflower* and landed at Plymouth, Massachusetts. They were Separatist Puritans who fled from religious persecution in England.

In 1682 English and Welsh Quakers founded Pennsylvania, named after their leader, William Penn. By 1760, 13 colonies had been established, stretching from Georgia in the south to Massachusetts in the north. The one-and-a-half million British subjects who lived in them were mainly of English, Scottish, German, Dutch, and Swedish extraction. For many years they were threatened by the French, who pushed southwards from the Great Lakes region of Canada as far as Louisiana. But by the end of the Seven Years War in 1763, the French had been permanently defeated and British rule established.

Below: *The World Trade Center buildings, an international financial symbol, in New York's financial centre, Manhattan.*

In the 1770s, the colonists began to rebel against British rule, rejecting 'taxation without representation'. The first fighting in what became known as the War of American Independence (called by Americans the War of the Revolution) broke out near Boston in 1775. In 1776 the colonies (New Hampshire, Massachusetts, Rhode Island, Connecticut, New York, New Jersey, Pennsylvania, Delaware, Virginia, North Carolina, South Carolina, Maryland, and Georgia) declared themselves 'free and independent states'. Under the brilliant leadership of George Washington they defeated the British armies. Britain recognized the newly independent states by the Treaty of Paris in 1783.

The constitution as drawn up in 1787 and Washington was elected the first president of the new republic in 1789. In 1803 Louisiana was purchased from the French, and in 1819 Florida was bought from Spain. War broke out with Britain again in 1812 but lasted only two years. As a result of a war with Mexico (1846-48), the United States gained Texas, California, Utah, and New Mexico.

In 1861 the Civil War began between 11 of the southern states (the Confederates) and the northern states (the Union). The war was fought mainly over the rights of the southern states to own and employ Negro slaves and to secede from the Union. The Confederate president was Jefferson Davis; the Union was led by Abraham Lincoln.

The war ended in 1865 with the defeat of the Confederates, the end of slavery, and a deep-rooted bitterness between the North and the South.

American intervention in World War I on the Allied side in 1917 proved decisive for eventual victory but was followed by post-war isolationism in the United States. The Great Depression, which began in 1929, hit the United States hard. President Franklin D. Roosevelt, elected in 1933, finally led his country out of its crisis with his dynamic New Deal policies.

The United States entered World War II in December 1941, shouldering almost the whole burden of the war in the Pacific, and assuming a major role in the conflict against Germany and Italy. The Axis powers collapsed in 1945, Japan surrendering only after the Americans had dropped atomic bombs on Hiroshima and Nagasaki. Further military involvement in Korea (1950-53) and Vietnam (1964-73) left most Americans war-weary and disillusioned.

A milestone in space technology was achieved with the lunar landing of two American astronauts in 1969, followed by more ambitious explorations of the Moon. But these triumphs were soon to be overshadowed by the Watergate scandal of 1974 when President Richard Nixon resigned rather than face possible impeachment for alleged political improprieties. He was succeeded by his Vice-President, Gerald Ford. After a period of liberalism under President Jimmy Carter, the USA returned to conservative values, electing former film actor Ronald Reagan to the presidency.

The United States today is a federal republic of 50 states, plus the District of Columbia, an area of 179km^2 (695 sq.m.) which makes up Washington, the nation's capital.

Government is exercised on three

LAKE SUPERIOR
ONTARIO
QUÉBEC
CANADA
LAKE HURON
LAKE ERIE
LAKE ONTARIO
MICHIGAN
WISCONSIN
ILLINOIS
INDIANA
OHIO
PENNSYLVANIA
NEW YORK
NEW JERSEY
MARYLAND
DELAWARE
WEST VIRGINIA
VIRGINIA
KENTUCKY
TENNESSEE
NORTH CAROLINA
SOUTH CAROLINA
GEORGIA
ALABAMA
MISSISSIPPI
FLORIDA
MASS.
CONN.
NEW HAMPSHIRE
MAINE
CHICAGO
MILWAUKEE
DETROIT
TORONTO
BUFFALO
CLEVELAND
PITTSBURGH
PHILADELPHIA
NEW YORK
BOSTON
MONTREAL
BALTIMORE
WASHINGTON D.C.
CINCINNATI
GULF OF MEXICO
ATLANTIC OCEAN
BAHAMAS
Continuation Eastwards On same scale
1:7 000 000
miles
km
Projection: Alber's Equal Area with two standard parallels
West from Greenwich
COPYRIGHT. GEORGE PHILIP & SON. LTD

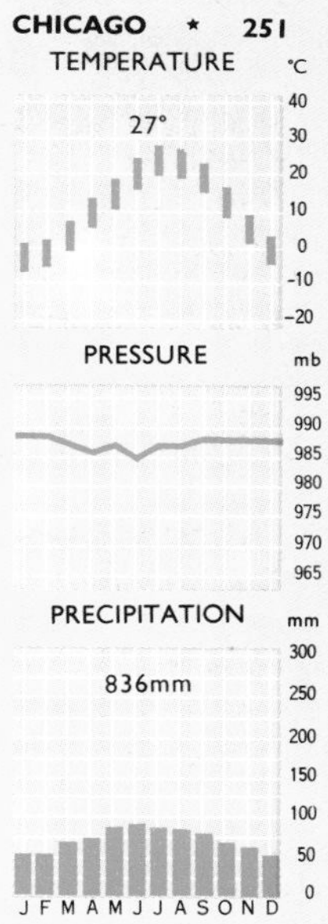
CHICAGO • 251
TEMPERATURE
°C
27°
PRESSURE
mb
PRECIPITATION
mm
836mm
J F M A M J J A S O N D

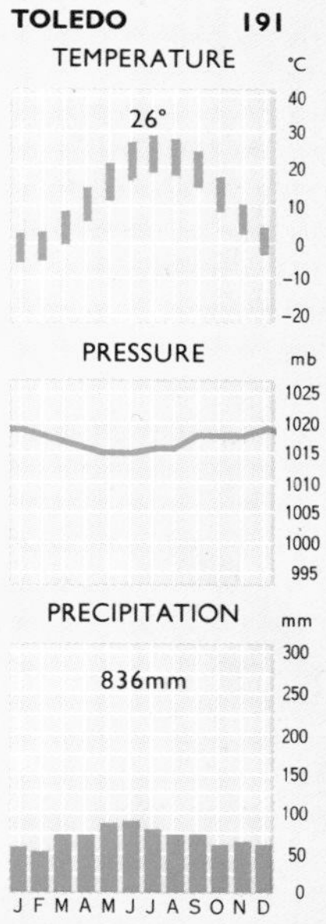
TOLEDO 191
TEMPERATURE
°C
26°
PRESSURE
mb
PRECIPITATION
mm
836mm
J F M A M J J A S O N D

Map 67 | THE MIDDLE UNITED STATES

ST. LOUIS ★ 173
TEMPERATURE °C
26°
PRESSURE mb
PRECIPITATION mm
1001mm
J F M A M J J A S O N D

NEW ORLEANS ★ 2
TEMPERATURE °C
16°
PRESSURE mb
PRECIPITATION mm
1458mm
J F M A M J J A S O N D

DENVER ★ 1610
TEMPERATURE °C
23°
PRESSURE mb
PRECIPITATION mm
358mm
J F M A M J J A S O N D

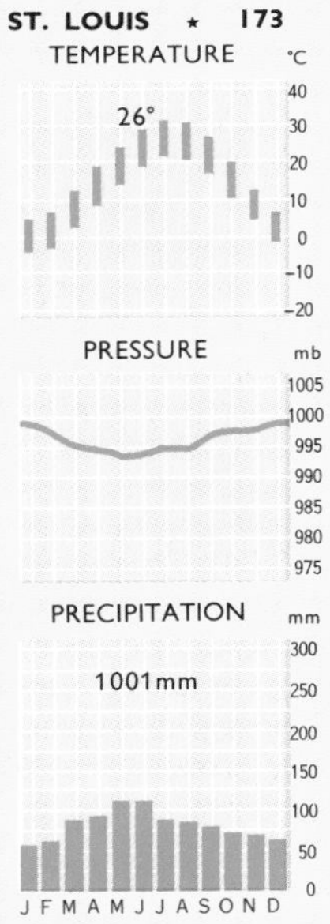

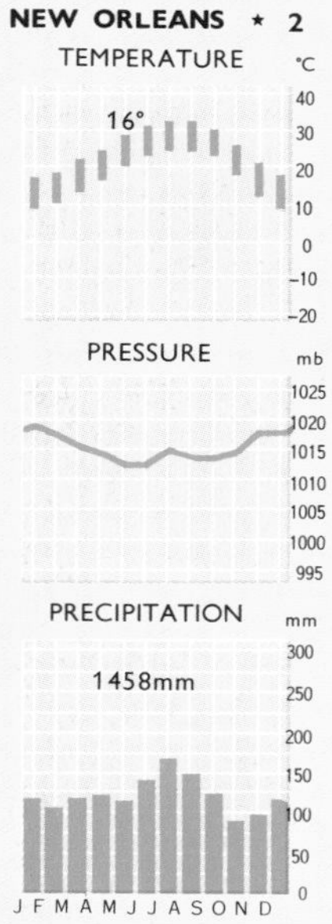

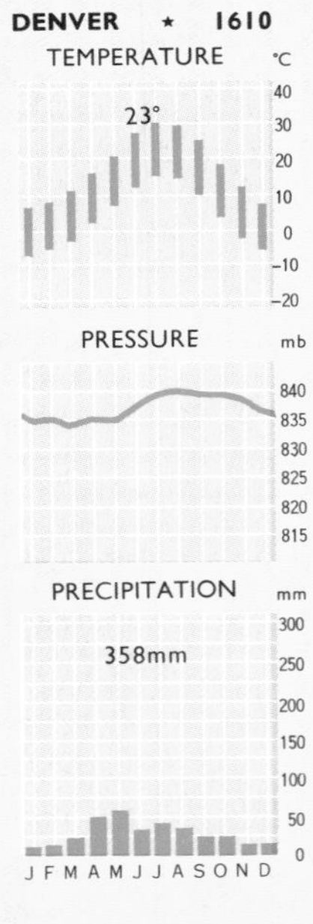

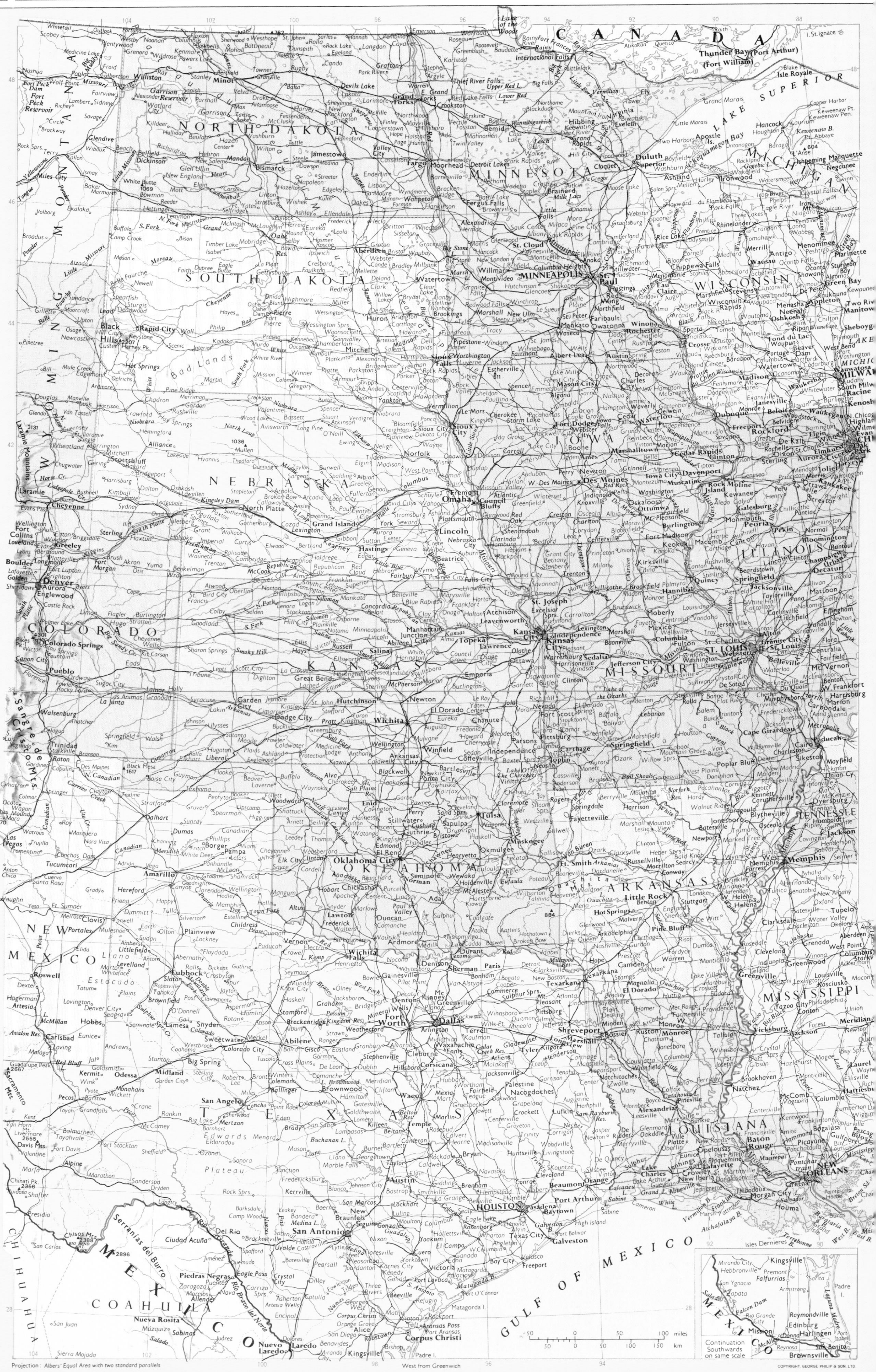

Projection: Albers' Equal Area with two standard parallels

West from Greenwich

COPYRIGHT GEORGE PHILIP & SON, LTD.

Continuation Southwards on same scale

levels: national, state, and local. The national or federal government has three main branches – executive, legislative, and judicial. Each branch is usually independent of the other two and can exercise certain checks and balances. The chief executive is the president. He is elected for a four-year term and cannot serve more than two terms. The legislative branch is the Congress, which is made up of the Senate and the House of Representatives. The Senate consists of 100 members (two from each state) who are elected for six-year terms. The House of Representatives has 435 members, who are elected for two years. The numbers from each state vary according to their respective populations.

The judicial branch consists of the Supreme Court, made up of a chief justice and eight associate justices; some 90 federal district courts; and 11 courts of appeal.

At the state level, each state also has its own executive (the governor), legislative, and judicial branches.

The two main political parties are the Democrats and the Republicans. Distinctions between the two are not always clear-cut, but the Democratic party tends to be the party of the 'small man', with popular support in the South. The Republican Party tends to favour 'big business', with corresponding support in the North.

Land and climate

The United States occupies the central portion of the North American continent. It is bordered by Canada on the north, the Pacific Ocean on the west, Mexico on the southwest, the Caribbean Sea on the south, and the Atlantic Ocean on the east. The land extends 2,575km (1,598m.) from the Canadian border to the Gulf of Mexico, and more than 4,800km (nearly 3,000m.) from the Atlantic to the Pacific. The state of Alaska, lying northwest of Canada, the island state of Hawaii, and various outlying regions add further to the nation's immense size.

There are three main physical regions: the western mountains, the eastern highlands, and the vast plains in between. Fringing the Pacific Ocean in the west is the Pacific Mountain System. The westernmost part of the system is known as the Pacific Coastal Region – a chain of low mountains and deep valleys. Eastward of this is the rugged Cascade Range running from Canada to northern California, and its southern continuation, the Sierra Nevada.

Inwards from the Pacific Mountain System are the Intermountain Plateaux. These are, for the most part, dry upland regions sometimes carved up by deep gorges. The magnificent Rocky Mountains rise to the east of the Intermountain Plateaux. They are high, rugged, and in many places heavily forested. They are also rich in minerals.

In the extreme east of the country, the Coastal Plain extends from Massachusetts to the Gulf of Mexico, along the Atlantic coast. Low and often swampy, the plain varies between 120km (75m.) and 480km (300m.) in width. Inland from the Coastal Plain are the Appalachian Highlands, which extend from the Gulf of St Lawrence to Alabama. These highlands consist of very ancient, worn rocks whose highest peaks do not quite reach 2,400m (7,000ft).

Two contiguous regions – the Central Lowland, which stretches westwards from the Appalachians, and the Great Plains, which lie to the west of the Central Lowlands – cover the central part of the country. These two enormous regions jointly make up about half the area of the United States, and stretch from the Great Lakes to the Gulf of Mexico. They include some of the most fertile agricultural land in the world.

Fresh water is generally abundant in the United States except for a few desert regions in parts of the west and southwest. The largest drainage system is that of the Missouri-Mississippi-Ohio. These rivers, with their tributaries, flow southwards through the central plains and empty into the Gulf of Mexico. The Columbia in the northwest of the country, and the Colorado in the southwest, are the two most important rivers that empty into the Pacific. During its course, the Colorado has carved out a huge gash in the earth's surface more than 1.6km (1m.) deep; the Grand Canyon, as it is called, is one of the wonders of the world.

Most of the short, swift rivers that flow into the Atlantic rise in the Appalachians; they include the Hudson, Delaware, and Potomac. Many rivers have been harnessed to provide hydroelectric power, water for irrigation, and waterways for transport.

The Great Lakes lie on the Canadian border. Only one of them – Lake Michigan – lies wholly within the United States; the other four are shared with Canada. On the border, too, are the famous and picturesque Niagara Falls. One of the two falls is American, the other Canadian. Their enormous water power has been harnessed for industrial and domestic use.

Right: *Glacier Bay in the Alexander Archipelago of southern Alaska – a huge unexplored land of untapped resources.*

Below: *Once an inland sea floor, the fertile soil of the flat and seemingly endless Kansas plain supports 86,000 farms.*

The country's climate varies widely according to latitude and physical features. Parts of the plateaux and mountains in the southwest are almost completely rainless, yet other regions fringing the Gulf of Mexico receive more than 150cm (60in) of rain a year, as do the coasts of northern California, Washington, and Oregon. Permanent snow lies on some parts of the Rockies and in Alaska, while southern California, Florida, and Hawaii bask in an almost subtropical climate. New England has very cold winters and hot summers. In the Central Lowland plains, the absence of mountain barriers leaves the wind unobstructed, and unpredictable air currents can change the weather with great suddenness. Parts of the south are also subject to hurricanes, which cut destructive swathes inland from the Caribbean.

States and cities

The United States has traditionally been divided into ten great political, economic and social regions. The oldest, in terms of settlement and history, is New England, where much of the nation's industry is located. A region renowned for its wealth and density of population is New York, the 'Empire State'. New York City is by far the largest city in the country and is a centre of banking, trade, shipping, and transport. A third region is made up of Pennsylvania, New Jersey, and Delaware – the so-called Middle Atlantic States. This is a region that has valuable agricultural land, as well as immense deposits of iron and coal. It includes the cities of Pittsburgh, with its great steelworks, and Philadelphia, a centre which blends tradition with industries such as chemicals and textiles.

The Middle West includes Ohio, Indiana, Illinois, Michigan, and Wisconsin. The iron ore of Michigan lies at the heart of its vast industry, although farming is also important. The nation's second largest city, Chicago, stands at the crossroads of major land, air, and sea routes and is one of North America's great grain and stock markets. Also in this region is Detroit, the motor vehicle manufacturing capital of the country and of the world.

Above: *Los Angeles, the semitropical, southern Californian metropolis of palm trees, oil wealth and show business, on a clear day.*

Minnesota, Iowa, North and South Dakota, Nebraska, and Kansas are known collectively as the Prairie States. They are the country's granary, producing enough maize and wheat to feed not only America but much of the rest of the world. The Mountain States of Montana, Wyoming, Colorado, New Mexico, Utah, Nevada, Arizona, and Idaho are a mixture of pastureland, mining areas, and stretches of desert.

California, Oregon, Washington, Alaska, and Hawaii are known as the Pacific States. California is a noted holiday and tourist region, boasting the film capital of the world in Los Angeles. The city is the nation's third largest and is a major centre of oil production and refining, and of aircraft manufacture. Alaska and Hawaii were the 49th and 50th states respectively to join the Union, both in 1959. Alaska, easily the largest of all the states, was purchased from Russia for $7.2m in 1867 – less than two cents an acre.

The South is made up of the states of Virginia, North and South Carolina, Alabama, Georgia, Mississippi, Louisiana, and Florida. Subtropical produce such as tobacco, cotton, and rice are the staple crops. The South is now a major industrial region. Texas, the richest and second biggest state, where everything seems larger than life-size, and Oklahoma, make up the South-West. This is the legendary home of the American cowboy. But today the region's incalculable wealth is derived mainly from oil. The Border States make up the last major division. They comprise the remaining states – Arkansas, Kentucky, Maryland, Missouri, Tennessee, and West Virginia – that stand between and divide the great economic areas. Kentucky's 'blue grass' feeds some of the country's finest bloodstock, while Nashville in Tennessee is the home of 'country music', a major pillar of the recording business.

Farming, forestry and fishing

There are some three million farms in the United States, averaging about 400 acres each. Together they make the nation the largest single agricultural producer in the world. After supplying domestic needs, American farmers have a large surplus for export.

Corn (maize) is grown in the so-called 'corn belt' of the Mid-West, where the fertile soil and equable climate are ideal. The United States grows nearly half the world's total corn crop.

Wheat grows in all areas except those with extremes of climate. Kansas (for winter wheat), North and South Dakota, Minnesota, and Montana produce the main harvests.

The 'cotton belt' of the South is the largest cotton-producing region in the world. Dairy farming is carried on mainly along parts of the North Pacific coast and in the northeast of the country. Fruit of various kinds is grown in many regions. California, Florida, and southwestern Arizona are the principal citrus crop areas; apples come from New York, Washington, and California; and sheltered mountain slopes in many areas produce grapes, plums, pears, peaches and cherries.

Livestock rearing is confined mainly to the western states such as Texas, Arizona, and New Mexico. There, cattle, sheep, and horses graze on millions of acres of range land.

More than half the United States was once covered with huge forests. But for many generations lumberjacks have been felling more trees than foresters have been planting. As a result, the lumber industry has moved steadily westwards from the Atlantic coast until today it is centred on the Pacific coast forests.

Fish forms an important part of the American diet. The two oceans, together with the Gulf of Mexico and the Great Lakes, yield an average of about three million tons of fish and other seafood a year.

Minerals and energy resources

The United States produces more crude petroleum than any other country – it amounts to about one-fifth of the world's entire output, and is easily the most valuable of the nation's minerals. The search for new oilfields never ceases, and in the late 1960s a major strike was made in the north of Alaska, and transport problems in that inhospitable terrain had to be overcome. Natural gas, most of it from Texas, is the next most important resource.

Coal is another valuable mineral – the United States is the second largest producer after the Soviet Union. Although the nation's largest deposits lie in Alaska, Illinois, and Montana, almost all the coal that is actually mined comes from the nine states east of the Mississippi, with Kentucky and West Virginia leading the others.

The country is also rich in iron ore (Michigan, Minnesota, and Wisconsin), copper (most of which comes from Arizona), and has substantial deposits of gold and silver. Promising strikes led to famous gold rushes – in California in 1849, Alaska at the turn of the century, and in other parts of the country at various times.

A resource that has helped to make the United States one of the richest nations on earth is its fertile soil. The different varieties give ample evidence of their fertility, from the rich, dark brown soil of the prairies to the alluvial deposits of the great Mississippi Valley. These soils support an almost endless variety of food crops, decorative plants, and forest trees.

The United States was a pioneer in the development of nuclear energy for use in wartime, but the nation is also well advanced in the building of nuclear power plants for peaceful uses – as potential large-scale producers of electrical power.

Industry and trade

The United States is the world's leading manufacturing nation. Most of its industry is located north of the Ohio River and east of the Mississippi, but the south and west coasts are growing rapidly in importance. Food processing is the most valuable industry, followed by transport equipment, electronics, chemicals, machinery, and metal products. California, Wisconsin, Michigan, New Jersey, and New York lead in the food processing and packaging industries. The computer and electronics industry is centred in California and New England.

More iron and steel is produced in the United States than anywhere else on earth. Pennsylvania leads among the states, with a work force running into hundreds of thousands. Paper manufacture is another industry in which the United States has a clear lead over the rest of the world. The states which have the most timber for this industry are Oregon, Washington, Maine, and Wisconsin.

There is also a flourishing American textile industry. Carpets come mainly from Philadelphia; woollen goods from Massachusetts, Rhode Island, and Pennsylvania; and cotton goods are produced principally by Alabama, Georgia, and North and South Carolina.

Most Americans firmly believe that the great growth and wealth of their manufacturing industry stems from the lively spirit of competition inherent in free enterprise allied to a minimum of government interference.

The chief imports of the United States are basic raw materials such as tin, manganese, nickel, bauxite, and crude oil. In spite of the nation's enormous wealth, its share of world trade declined perceptibly in the late 1960s and early 1970s, although it still carried on a greater volume of international trade than any other single country. Canada is the main trading partner, followed by Japan, West Germany and Great Britain.

External relations

The fiasco of the Vietnam War caused widespread disillusionment in the USA, but it did not herald a new era of isolationism.

Relations with the People's Republic of China improved rapidly from the 1970s onwards. The Cold War with the USSR also began to thaw in the 1970s, but Soviet intervention in Afghanistan and the election of Ronald Reagan to the US presidency halted the improvement in relations. US fear of communism in Central America led to support for the *contras*, military insurgents attempting to overthrow the democratically elected Sandinista government of Nicaragua.

In the Middle East, President Carter secured peace between Israel and Egypt, but fell from office largely as a result of his failure to resolve a hostage crisis with the Khomeini regime in Iran. Some years later, President Reagan faced similar problems in Lebanon. By 1985 the Reagan administration's policy of 'constructive engagement' with the Republic of South Africa was coming under increasing fire from liberal opinion within the USA, and limited economic sanctions against that country were introduced by Reagan.

Relations with fellow NATO members and the member states of the EEC remained very close and were helped in the 1980s by the mutual conservatism of European and American governments. US nuclear policies proved less popular with many in Europe, and the introduction of Cruise missiles to US bases in Western Europe was accomplished only against determined opposition.

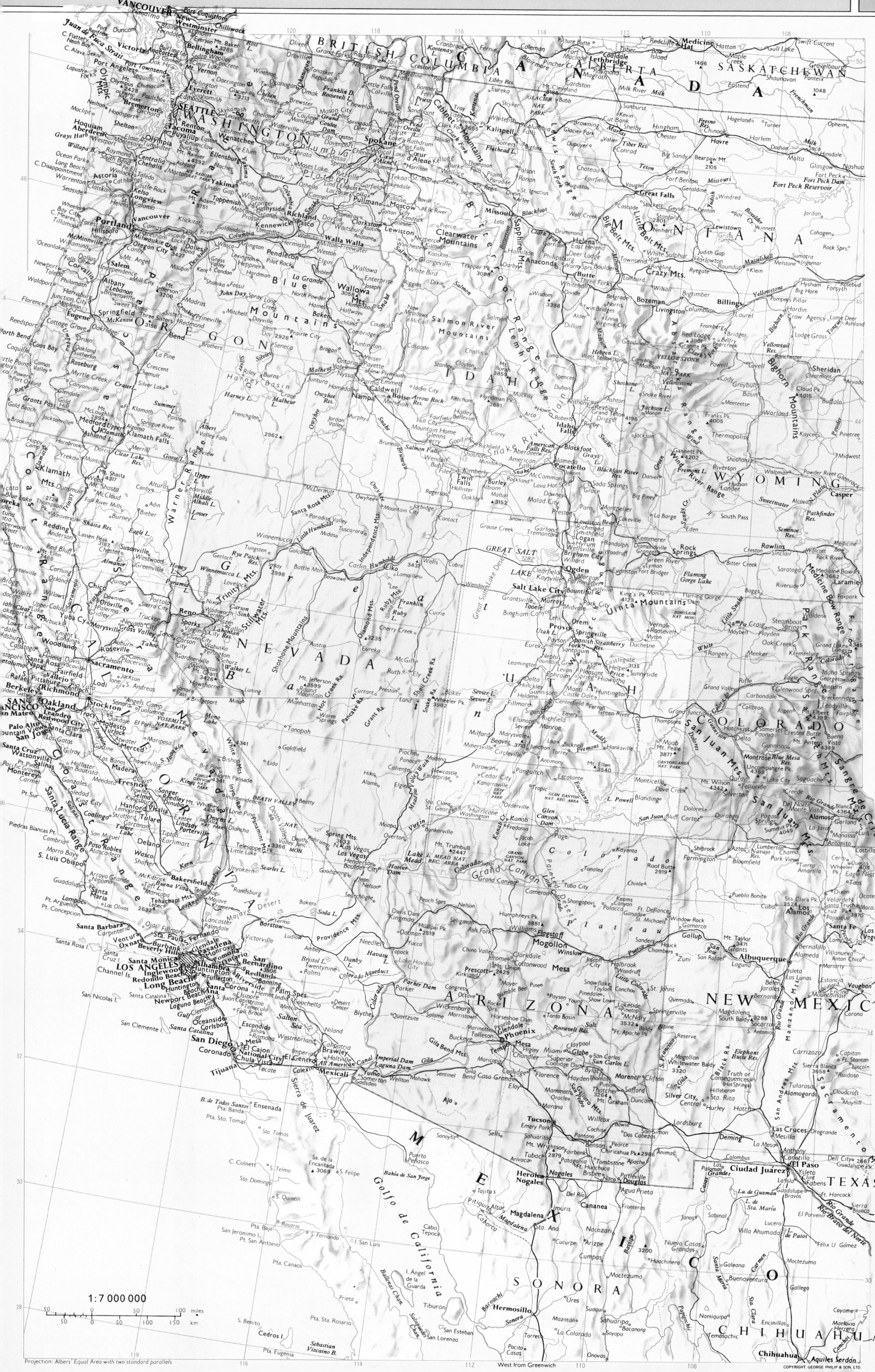
BRITISH COLUMBIA
CANADA
ALBERTA
SASKATCHEWAN
WASHINGTON
OREGON
IDAHO
MONTANA
WYOMING
NEVADA
UTAH
COLORADO
CALIFORNIA
ARIZONA
NEW MEXICO
TEXAS
MEXICO
SONORA
CHIHUAHUA
Great Basin
Colorado Plateau
Golfo de California
1:7 000 000
miles
km
Projection: Albers' Equal Area with two standard parallels
West from Greenwich
COPYRIGHT, GEORGE PHILIP & SON, LTD.

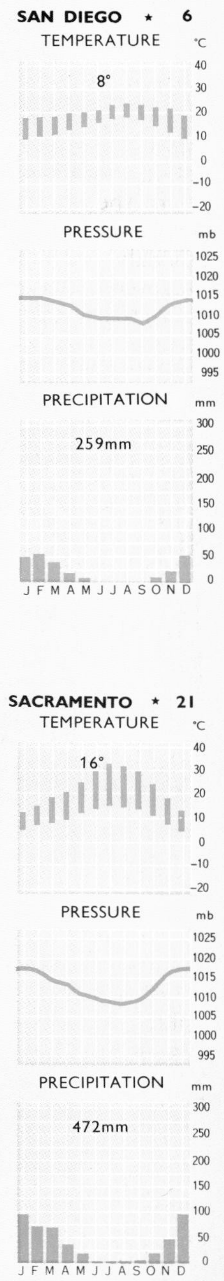
SAN DIEGO 6
TEMPERATURE
°C
8°
PRESSURE
mb
PRECIPITATION
mm
259mm
J F M A M J J A S O N D
SACRAMENTO 21
TEMPERATURE
°C
16°
PRESSURE
mb
PRECIPITATION
mm
472mm
J F M A M J J A S O N D

In 1492, Christopher Columbus was convinced he had reached India by sailing westwards round the globe. As a result, he gave the name West Indies to the lush green islands that dotted the warm Caribbean Sea where he made his landfall. He had actually touched the fringe of a vast New World that stretched almost from pole to pole.

In the wake of Columbus came the *conquistadores*, Spanish conquerors who quickly established themselves on the mainland that formed a mountainous barrier between the Caribbean and the Pacific Ocean. That region, lying between the southwestern United States in the north and South America, is today made up of Mexico and Central America. Mexico is properly part of North America, whereas Central America forms a narrow land bridge linking North and South America.

This bridge extends more than 1,600 kilometres (1,000 miles) from Mexico to Colombia. Most of the countries that make up the region have coastlines on both the Pacific in the west and the Caribbean Sea, part of the Atlantic, in the east.

In 1823, Guatemala, El Salvador, Honduras, Nicaragua and Costa Rica broke free from Spanish rule to form the United Provinces. This federation lasted only 15 years but those five countries, together with Belize and Panama comprise the region now known as Central America.

The Caribbean coastal plains are generally hot, humid and heavily forested. Behind them rise the central highlands. These in turn slope down to the Pacific coastal plains, which are usually rather narrow with less rainfall than on the east. Earthquakes, volcanic eruptions and hurricanes blowing in from the Caribbean sometimes devastate large areas. The climate is tropical and varies more with altitude than with the seasons.

The most valuable resources of central America are forests of fine hardwood trees, rich volcanic soil and potential mineral wealth. Most of the people work on farms and plantations where bananas, coffee and cacao are the main crops.

The people themselves are largely a mixture of Indians (the original inhabitants) and Europeans, mainly Spaniards. Spanish is the official language except in Belize, where English is spoken.

English is also widely spoken in the West Indies – a loose term for the scattered string of islands in the Caribbean Sea. These form a 3,200-kilometre (2,000-mile) crescent stretching almost from the tip of Florida to the waters off the Venezuelan coast. The islands are usually classified in three main groups: the Bahamas in the north, the Greater Antilles near the centre and the Lesser Antilles in the southeast. The Greater Antilles include the large islands of Cuba, Puerto Rico, Jamaica and Hispaniola (Haiti and the Dominican Republic). The Lesser Antilles comprises the Windward Islands, Leeward Islands, Barbados, Trinidad and Tobago, and the Netherlands Antilles.

Originally the home of Amerindian peoples, the islands were colonized by Europeans and peopled with slaves they transported from Africa. The Spanish, French, British and Dutch were all major powers in the region.

Independence came first in the larger islands, such as Cuba and Haiti, and later to many of the smaller islands: St Christopher (St Kitts)-Nevis for example became fully independent in 1983. Some islands still remain colonies or overseas departments of other countries, or to other kinds of association: the Commonwealth of Puerto Rico, for instance, is an outlying territory of the USA.

Since the Spanish-American War the USA has been politically involved in the Caribbean, and as recently as 1983 led an invasion of Grenada. Since the 1959 revolution Cuba has been an ally of the USSR and this has caused considerable tension in the region.

Below: *Guatamalan Indians, wearing the colourful handwoven clothes of the local textile industry, sell traditional wood carvings at Chichicastenango market.*

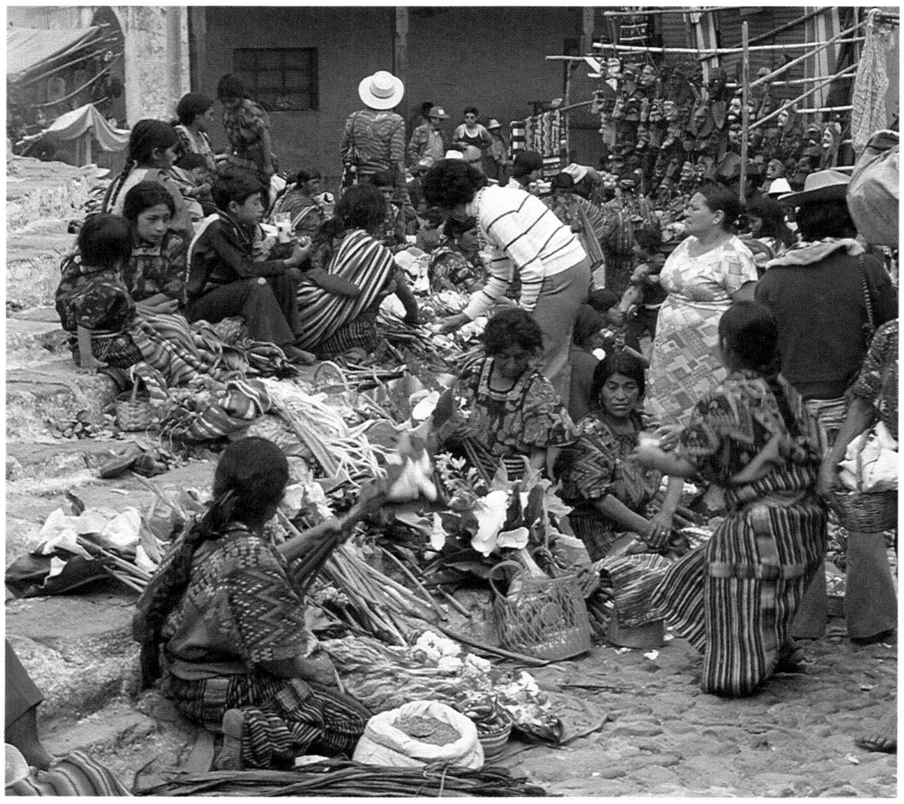

Left: *Remains of a palace of the great Mayan civilization at Palenque, Mexico.*

Mexico

Area: 1,958,201km^2 (756,198sq.m.).
Population: 79.79 million.
Capital: Mexico City (14m).
Languages: Spanish, Indian languages.
Ethnic groups: Mestizo (mixed race) 75 percent, Amerindian 15 per cent, European 10 percent.
Main exports: oil, cotton, sugar, coffee, sulphur, silver, shrimps.
Average temperatures: 24°C (75°F) lowlands, 18°C (64°F) central plateau, 15°C (59°F) mountains.
Highest point: Mt Orizaba (Citlaltepetl), 5,760m (18,898ft).

The United Mexican States, to give the country its official name, is a Latin American republic that shares a 2,491-kilometre (1,549-mile) border in the north with the United States. Mexico's western shores are washed by the Pacific, while its eastern coast lies on the Gulf of Mexico and the Caribbean Sea. On the southeast it borders Guatemala and Belize.

Mexico is a vast, rugged land of bold and striking contrasts. From the air, it looks like a lump of badly crumpled parchment.

Lower (Baja) California is a narrow peninsula, 1,223 kilometres (760 miles) long, separated for most of its length from the Mexico mainland by the Gulf of California. It is a sparsely populated region of mountains and deserts.

Mexico's mountains are made up mostly of two ranges. In the west, the Sierra Madre Occidental runs northwards to the US border. In the east, the Sierra Madre Oriental skirts the shores of the Gulf of Mexico. The two ranges unite near the middle of the country to form a spectacular jumble of towering peaks and countless volcanoes. Earthquakes are common and in 1985 much of the central part of Mexico City was destroyed.

Between the two Sierra Madre ranges lies the central plateau. The southern part of this region is fertile and temperate. As a result, two-thirds of the people live there. The tropical peninsula of Yucatán, in the southeast, is a limestone plain whose surface features range from steaming swamps to forested hills.

About 30 percent of the population is engaged in farming, fishing, breeding livestock, and forestry. The birthrate is high but the country is self-sufficient in cereals, vegetables, and fruit. Though still the largest producer of silver in the world, Mexico's main minerals are oil, copper, mercury, zinc, lead, iron and sulphur. Another important source of income is tourism. Pre-Columbian archaeological treasures help attract more than four million visitors to Mexico a year.

The first Spaniards arrived in the land that is now Mexico in 1517, when the Aztecs were the leading civilization in the region. By the mid-1500s, the invaders under Hernán Cortés had conquered the whole country. Mexico was unable to free itself from Spanish rule until 1821. It remains a predominantly Roman Catholic nation.

Today, Mexico is a federal democracy under a powerful presidency. In spite of rapid industrial development based on

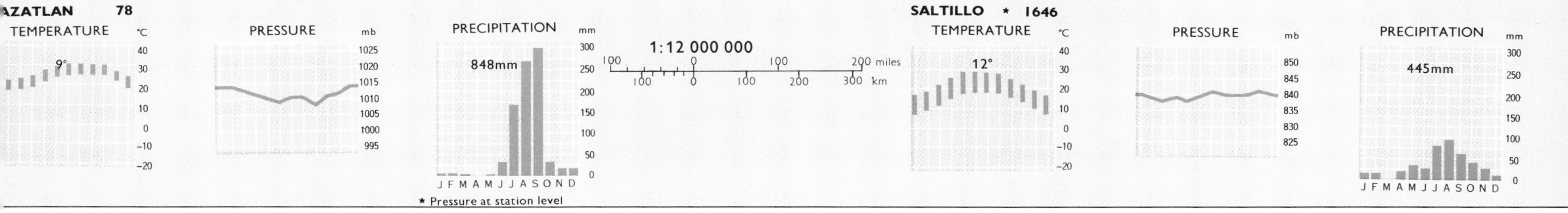

local oil resources and increasing prosperity in urban areas, Mexico still faces many economic problems and has a mounting national debt.

Guatemala

Guatemala is the most northerly of the Central American republics, and the third largest. On the east it is bordered by Belize, the Caribbean Sea, Honduras, and El Salvador; on the north and west by Mexico; and on the south by the Pacific Ocean. It has an area of 108,889km^2 (42,042sq.m.) and a population of 8 million. The capital and largest city is Guatemala City, with 1.33 million inhabitants.

Guatemala has more pure-blooded Indians, descendants of the Mayas, than any other Central American nation. They form the largest and poorest section of the community. A smaller section is made up of wealthy landowners who live on huge estates very much in the old colonial style. Most of the country's wealth has traditionally been based on coffee, sugar and cotton. Political changes have generally been violent.

Belize

Belize, formerly British Honduras, became fully independent in 1981, despite Guatemalan claims to its territory. It lies on the east coast of the region, bordered on the north by Mexico, on the west and south by Guatemala, and on the east by the Caribbean Sea. Its area is 22,965km^2 (8,867sq.m.), and its population is 158,000. The capital, built inland in 1970 to protect it from frequent hurricanes is Belmopan (3,000). The former capital and largest city is Belize City (39,000).

Honduras

Honduras is a sparsely populated land of mountains and forests. It is the second largest of the Central American republics, and the world's third largest producer of bananas. It is bordered on the north and northeast by the Caribbean Sea, on the west by El Salvador and the Pacific, and on the South and southeast by Nicaragua. Its area is 112,088km^2 (43,277sq.m.) and it has a population of 4.14 million. The capital and largest city is Tegucigalpa (532,000).

El Salvador

El Salvador is the smallest of the Central American republics, and one of the most densely populated. It is the only country that has no coastline on the Caribbean. Its area is 21,393km^2 (8,260sq.m.) with a population of 5.3 million. The capital and largest city is San Salvador (884,000). The economy is based mainly on coffee and cotton.

Nicaragua

Nicaragua, the largest of the Central American nations, stretches from the Pacific to the Caribbean, which flank it west and east, respectively. Honduras lies to the north and Costa Rica to the south. Its area is 148,000km^2 (50,193sq.m.), and it has 2.9 million inhabitants. The capital and largest city is Managua (615,000). In 1979 the government of General Somoza was overthrown by left-wing 'Sandinista' revolutionaries. Elections held in 1984 consolidated the Sandinistas' power base. Cotton, bananas, timber and sugar are the main exports.

Right: *Owned by the USA, the Panama Canal connects the Atlantic and Pacific.*

Costa Rica

Costa Rica is unusual on several counts. It has the highest literacy rate in Latin America, a high per capita income, and no standing armed forces. Nicaragua lies to the north and Panama to the south. A climber on the summit of Irazú volcano can see both the Pacific coast in the west and the Caribbean in the east. Costa Rica has an area of 51,100km^2 (19,344sq.m.) and a population of 2.4 million. The capital and largest city is San José (245,000).

Panama

Panama is a narrow, snake-like strip of land linking Central and South America. It has an area of 75,650km^2 (29,209sq.m.) and a population of 1.97 million. The capital and largest city is Panama City (389,000).

Panama exports bananas, shrimps and cocoa. The Panama Canal Area, a narrow strip flanking the Panama Canal, is one of the world's most important waterways. Previously known as the Canal Zone, this area was under US jurisdiction until 1979. The USA maintains military and operational facilities until 1999.

Cuba

Area: 114,524km^2 (44,218sq.m.).
Population: 10 million.
Capital: Havana (1.9m).
Language: Spanish.
Ethnic groups: European (73 percent), Negro and Mestizo (27 percent).
Main exports: sugar, nickel, tobacco, shrimps.
Average temperatures: Nov.-April 21°C (70°F), May-Oct. 27°C (81°F).
Highest point: Pico Turquino, 2,132m (6,500ft).

Cuba is the largest island in the Caribbean. It has several low mountain ranges, but mostly it is a land of fertile plains, valleys, and gentle hills. It has two principal river systems, one flowing north and west, the other flowing south.

Cuba is the world's second-biggest producer and the leading exporter of sugar and sugar cane. Another highly important crop is tobacco, and Cuban cigars are world famous. Cuba has now developed a wide range of industries.

In 1959, a young revolutionary lawyer, Fidel Castro, overthrew the harsh, dictatorial regime of Fulgencio Batista. Castro then turned Cuba into a socialist state modelled on the Soviet Union. The United States severed diplomatic relations with Cuba, which now depends heavily on its Soviet ally for assistance.

Puerto Rico

Puerto Rico is a commonwealth of the United States with internal self-government but without federal representation. Its area is only 8,897km^2 (3,435sq.m.), but it has a population of 3.3 million. The capital and largest city is San Juan (515,500). English and Spanish are the official languages. Most of the people are Mestizos (of mixed Negro-Spanish descent). The mountainous, dry, but fertile island is a favourite with US holidaymakers. Before World War II, Puerto Rico was an impoverished island with many of its inhabitants emigrating to New York City in search of work. But a postwar programme of economic expansion labelled 'Operation Bootstrap' has increased manufacturing and sugar processing, which ranks second to tourism as the main dollar-earning industry.

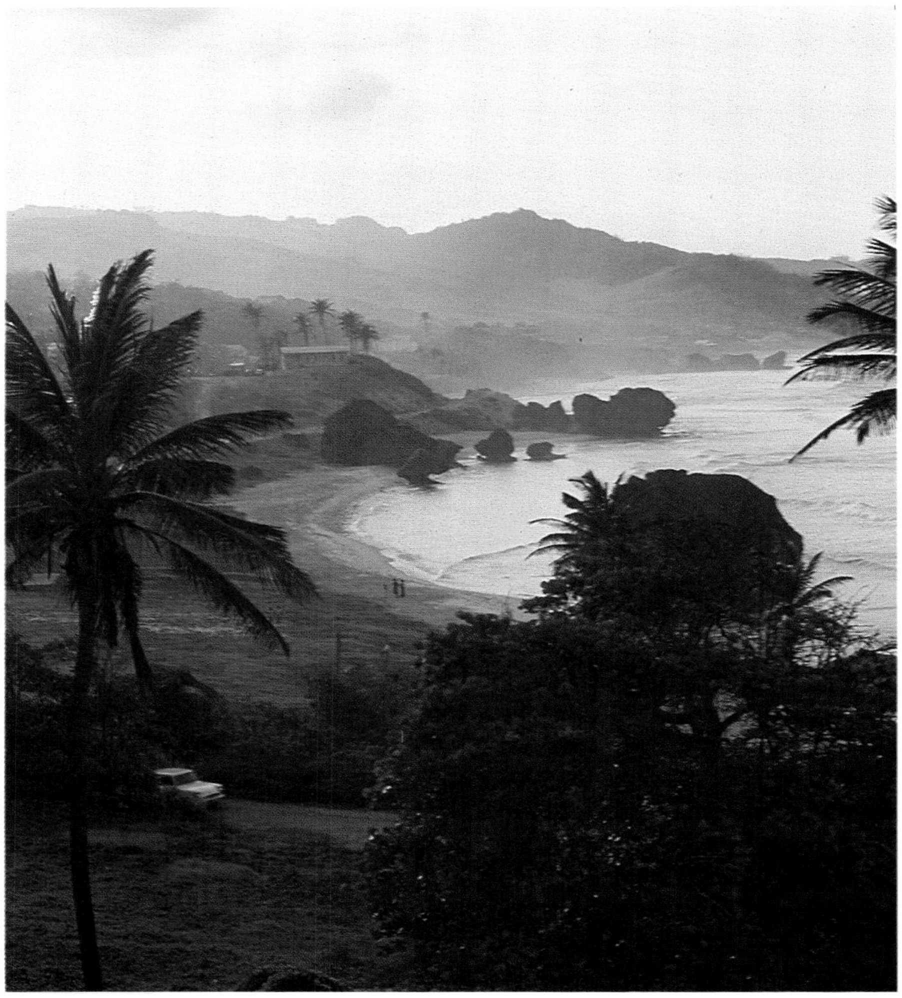

Above: *The east coast of Barbados, also known as 'Little England' because of its close ties with Britain.*

The Bahamas

The Bahamas are an archipelago of 700 islands and about 2,000 rocks and cays, but fewer than 30 of the islands are inhabited. They cover a land area of 13,864km^2 (5,353sq.m.), and have a population of 228,000. Nassau (135,000), on New Providence Island, is the capital and largest city. Tourism is the main industry.

Jamaica

Jamaica is a wildly beautiful, mountainous, densely crowded island that relies heavily on tourism for its income. Its area is 11,425km^2 (4,411sq.m.) and it has 2.3 million inhabitants mainly of Negro descent. Kingston (644,000) is the capital and largest city. Although primarily an agricultural country growing sugar, bananas, cocoa, coffee and fruits, Jamaica is one of the world's largest producers of bauxite. British influence remains strong and Jamaica is the largest Caribbean member of the Commonwealth.

Haiti

Haiti forms the western part of the island of Hispaniola, which it shares with the Dominican Republic. It has an area of 27,750km^2 (10,741sq.m.) and 5.8 million inhabitants. Port-au-Prince (459,000) is the capital and largest city. Most of the people are descended from African slaves whose rebellions against France established the first Negro republic in the early 1800s. The official language is French but most people speak Creole or one of several African dialects. With a history of despotic government and voodoo practice, the economy and social life are primitive and overcrowding reduces agriculture to subsistence level. However, a number of industries have been established, largely with American capital. The Duvalier family which had ruled since 1957 was overthrown in 1986.

The Dominican Republic

The Dominican Republic occupies the eastern and much larger portion of the island of Hispaniola, with Haiti on its western frontier. It has an area of 48,442km^2 (18,700sq.m.) and a population of 6.3 million. The capital and largest city is Santo Domingo (817,000). Spanish is the official language. Most of the people are of mixed Spanish and Negro descent. Sugar and coffee are the chief exports. Until 1966 the Dominican Republic had a depressing history of violence and revolution.

The Leeward Islands

These comprise the US Virgin Islands, the British Virgin Islands, St Christopher (Kitts)-Nevis, Anguilla, Antigua and Barbuda, Redonda, Montserrat, and Dominica, Guadeloupe, Marie-Galante, St Barthélemy, Les Saintes, Désirade, and the northern part of St Martin, and part of the Netherlands Antilles, made up of St Eustatius, Saba, and the southern part of St Martin.

Right: *The sheltered harbour of St Johns, the principal town in Antigua.*

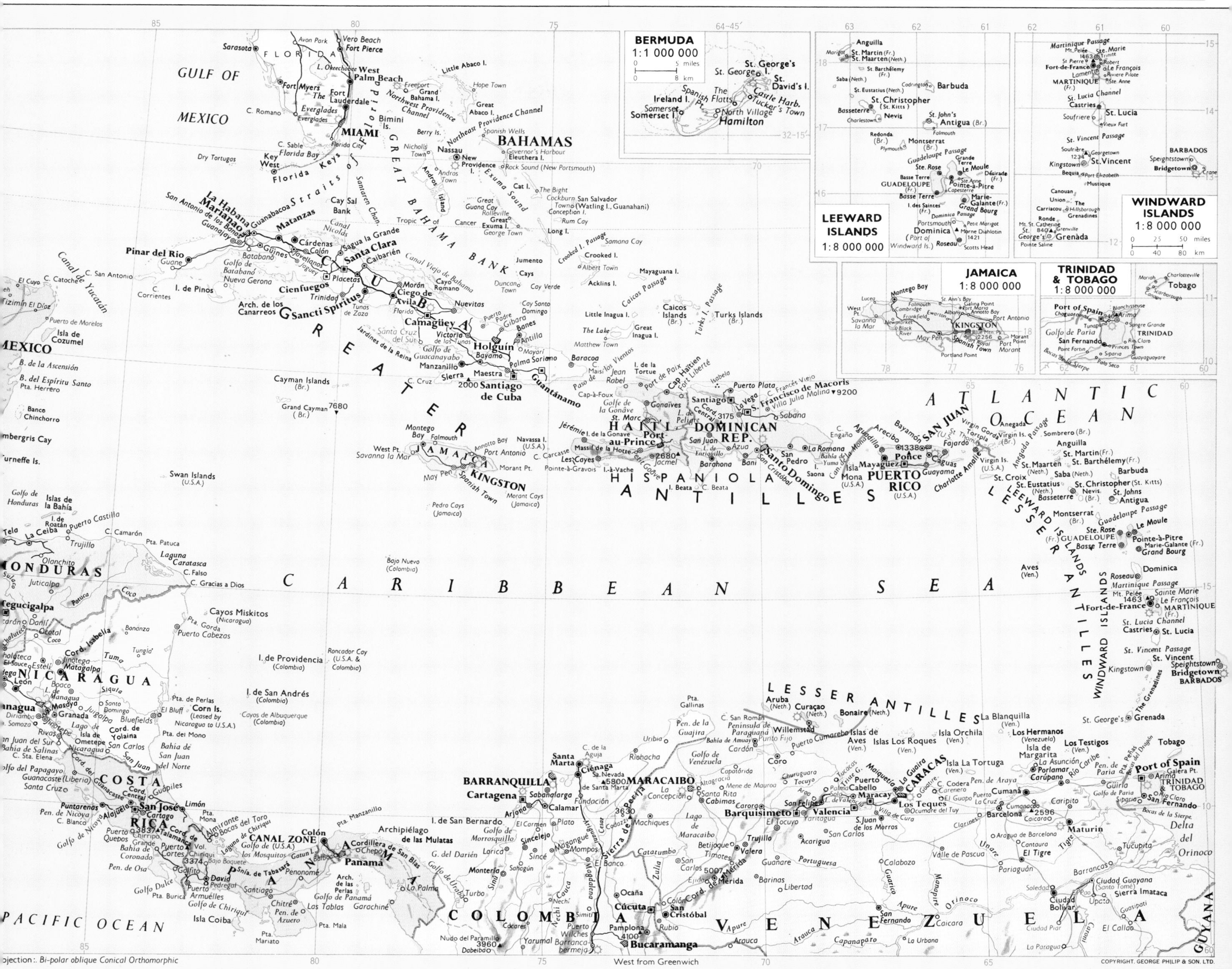

1:12 000 000

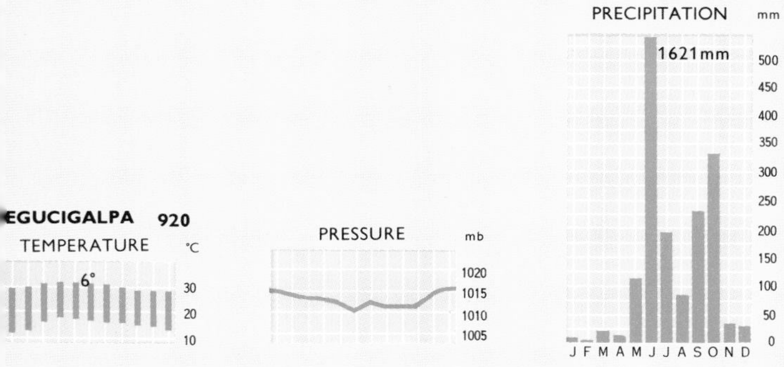

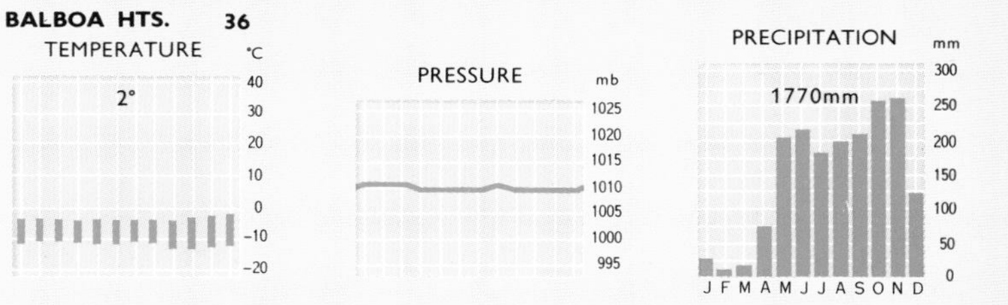

The Windward Islands

These are made up of St Lucia and St Vincent, Grenada (independent), Martinique (French), and 600 islets and reefs between Grenada and St Vincent called the Grenadines.

Barbados

Barbados, the most easterly of the Caribbean islands, is a coral island. Since being granted independence by Britain in 1966, it has greatly expanded its tourist industry. It has an area of 431km^2 (166sq.m.) and a population of 252,000. The capital and only large town is Bridgetown.

Trinidad and Tobago

Trinidad and Tobago consists of the large island of Trinidad and the smaller island of Tobago lying 11 kilometres (seven miles) northeast of the Venezuelan coast. Its area is 5,128km^2 (1,980sq.m.) and its population is 1.16 million. Port-of-Spain (56,000) is the capital and largest city. The population is mostly Negro, but there is a large East Indian minority. Most of the revenue comes from petroleum.

MAP 71 | SOUTH AMERICA

LIMA 120
TEMPERATURE
8°

PRESSURE

PRECIPITATION
41mm

RIO DE JANEIRO 61
TEMPERATURE
6°

PRESSURE

PRECIPITATION
1082mm

Projection: Lambert's Equivalent Azimuthal

COPYRIGHT. GEORGE PHILIP & SON. LTD.

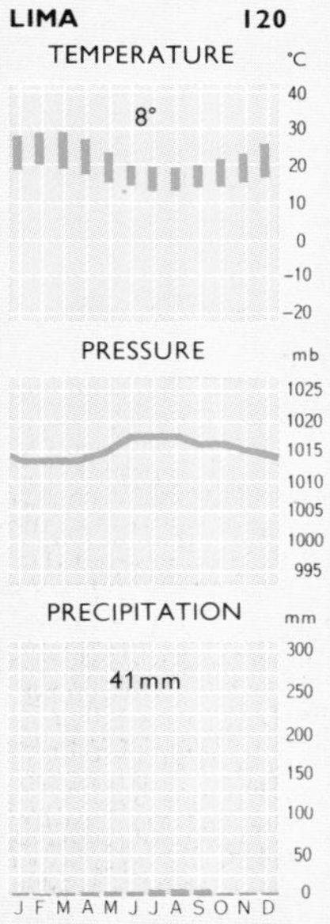

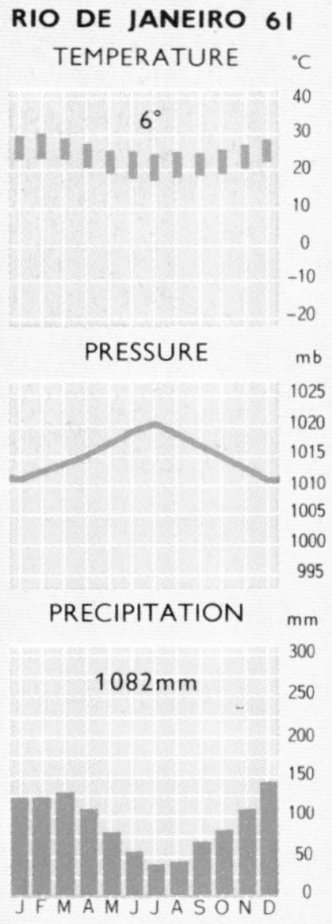

South America is the fourth largest of the continents. Because of its length and topography, it experiences a great range of climatic conditions and has a greater variety of peoples and cultures than any other continent. In the case of many Amerindian tribes, the way of life is little removed from that of the Stone Age. Yet in some of the large cities such as Buenos Aires, Rio de Janeiro, and São Paulo, the culture is as sophisticated as anywhere in the world.

South America can be conveniently divided into three main areas: the young Andes Mountains in the west, the ancient, weathered Brazilian and Guiana Highlands in the east, and the immense interior lowland lying between.

The Andes are so high and rugged that, until the advent of air travel, they proved to be an almost impassable barrier between east and west and seriously hindered the development of the continent. A series of parallel ranges runs all the way from northern Colombia to the southern tip of Tierra del Fuego. Many of the peaks are active volcanoes.

The Brazilian Highlands make up the oldest part of South America. They extend eastwards into the 'bulge' of Brazil, and southwards from the Amazon basin to the borders of Uruguay. For the most part they are gentle, well-watered hills whose fertile soil encourages the growth of coffee and cotton in favoured locations. The Guiana Highlands run across southeastern Venezuela, skirt the southern region of the Guianas, and

enter northeastern Brazil. The dense forests that grow there are still largely unexplored.

The interior lowland stretches from the Amazon basin to the Rio de la Plata. It includes the tropical rain forests of the Amazon, the *llanos* or grassy plains of the lower Orinoco, and the plains of southern Bolivia, Paraguay and Argentina. These last plains, in their northern parts, are inhospitable and wild, and are known as the Gran Chaco; but farther south they merge with the Argentine Pampa, one of the most fertile regions of the continent. The three great river systems are those of the Orinoco, which flows northeastwards through Venezuela into the Atlantic; the Amazon which starts about 160 kilometres (100 miles)

from the Pacific and flows for 6,400 kilometres (4,000 miles) before emptying into the Atlantic; and the system of the Rio de la Plata which with its tributaries drains part of Bolivia, Brazil, Paraguay, and Uruguay.

Although South America experiences almost every kind of climate, there are few of the extremes found in North America or Asia, for example. The highest temperatures are reached in northern Argentina, and the coldest in Tierra del Fuego, which faces Antarctica. The Peru or 'Humboldt' current has a cooling effect on the Pacific coast, while the Brazil Current warms most of the Atlantic coast. Westerly winds from Antarctica bring cold air to much of the southern part of the continent.

Colombia

Area: 1,138,914km² (439,737sq.m.).
Population: 29.4 million.
Capital: Bogotá (4.5m).
Language: Spanish.
Ethnic groups: mixed Negro, Indian, and European stock.
Main exports: coffee, petroleum, emeralds, agricultural products.
Average temperature: varies with altitude from subtropical heat to permanent snow.
Highest point: Pico Cristóbal Colón, 5,775m (18,947ft).

Colombia is the fourth largest country in South America and the only one with a coastline on both sides of the continent. The Pacific Ocean lies on the west, the Isthmus of Panama on the northwest, and the Caribbean Sea on the north. To the south are Peru and Ecuador, to the southeast Brazil, and Venezuela lies to the northeast.

From the border with Ecuador almost to the shores of the Caribbean Sea, four great mountain ranges run parallel across the country between Bogotá and the Pacific. Most people live in the high, narrow, fertile valleys that divide the mountain ranges. These mountains have traditionally formed a serious barrier to transport and communications and, as a result, the country's internal development and unification have been slow. Today, air transport forms a vital link between isolated communities.

Huge grassy plains, called *llanos*, cover parts of the south and east of the country. These eventually give way to the steaming equatorial rain forests of the Amazon basin. Colombia's largest river is the Magdalena which flows northwards for 1,600km (1,000 miles) to empty into the Caribbean. The valley of the Cauca, its main tributary, is a fertile farming region.

Colombia's main products are crude petroleum, coffee, bananas, gold, and emeralds. It supplies nearly all the world's emeralds. Although most people

Below: *Caracas sprawls over a mountain-rimmed valley in Venezuela's highlands.*

are of mixed ancestry, there are also about 400 tribes of Amerindians.

The nation is a presidential democracy. After a period of anarchy and bitter civil war from 1948 to 1958, the country entered an era of relative stability. But it was soon faced with grave inflation, unemployment, and a staggering population growth of 600,000 a year.

Venezuela

Area: 912,050km² (352,145sq.m.).
Population: 17.3 million.
Capital: Caracas (2.6m).
Language: Spanish.
Ethnic groups: Mestizo (65 percent), European (21 percent), Negro (7 percent), Amerindian (2 percent).
Main exports: petroleum and petroleum products, iron ore.
Average temperature: varies with altitude, 21°C (69°F) at 900m (3,000ft).
Highest point: Pico Bolivar, 1,877m (6,000ft).

Venezuela lies on the northern coast of South America, with the Caribbean Sea forming its northern border. Colombia lies to the west, Brazil to the south, and Guyana to the east.

As a result of its petroleum deposits, Venezuela is the richest country in South America. Its name means 'Little Venice' in Spanish. The Spanish explorers who first set foot in the region in 1499 called it this after finding an Indian village on stilts in the middle of Lake Maracaibo that reminded them of Venice.

Venezuela can be divided into four main regions. The Andean or Venezuelan Highlands, a spur of the Andes, run across the northwestern corner of the country. The second region is made up of the Maracaibo Lowlands – a hot, humid region surrounding Lake Maracaibo. This is a huge, shallow, freshwater lake that is open to the sea. The nation's life-giving petroleum is taken from the lake's bed and shores. A third region, called the Guyana Highlands, rises to the south of the River Orinoco. It is a wild, sparsely populated area that covers more than half the country. Finally, the *llanos* (grassy plains) of the Orinoco occupy a vast central plain.

The Orinoco itself, 2,560km (1,600 miles) long, is the eighth longest river in the world. Venezuela also claims the highest waterfall in the world, Angel Falls, with a drop of 979m (3,212ft).

Venezuela's major resource is petroleum, and it exports more oil than any other country in Latin America. But supplies are expected to run out by the end of this century, so Venezuelans are rapidly developing new resources. These include especially iron, but also bauxite, asbestos, asphalt, and nickel. Cattle are reared on the *llanos*, but most farmers produce only enough food for themselves and their families.

After gaining its independence from Spain in 1811, Venezuela endured more than 100 years of violence and dictatorships. But following agrarian reform and a new constitution adopted in 1961, general elections have been more democratic.

Below: *A smallholding in the central cordillera of Colombia, a country which depends almost entirely on coffee production, despite rich gold, silver and industrial mineral deposits.*

Density of population: South America

DENSITY OF POPULATION
1:80 000 000

Inhabitants per km²
under 1
1–3
3–6
6–12
12–25
25–50
over 50
■ Towns of over 200 000 inhabitants

COPYRIGHT. GEORGE PHILIP & SON. LTD.

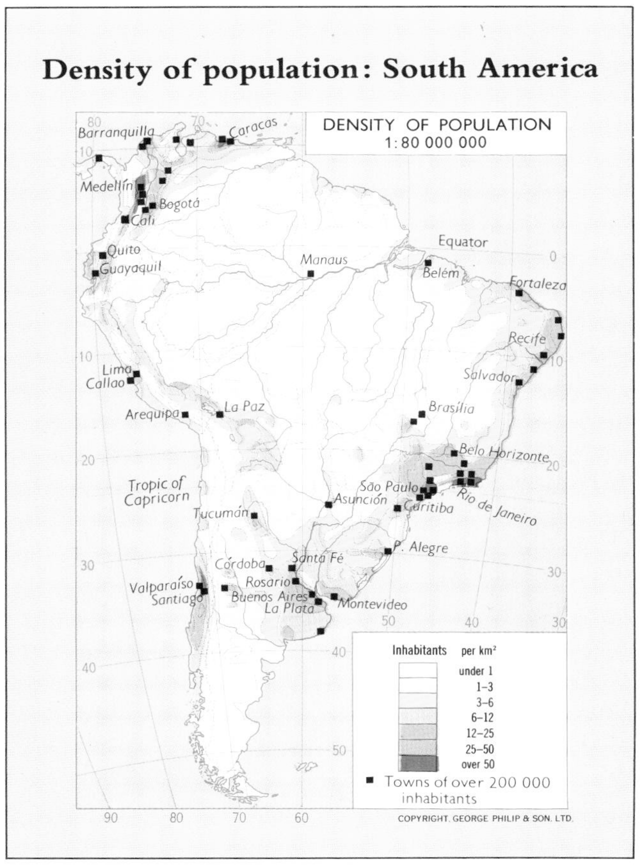

Map 72 | SOUTH AMERICA (NORTH)

LA PAZ ★ 3658

TEMPERATURE °C
4°

PRESSURE mb

PRECIPITATION mm
574mm

JFMAMJJASOND

QUITO ★ 2850

TEMPERATURE °C
1°

PRESSURE mb

PRECIPITATION mm
1123mm

JFMAMJJASOND

1:16 000 000

Projection: Sanson-Flamsteed's Sinusoidal

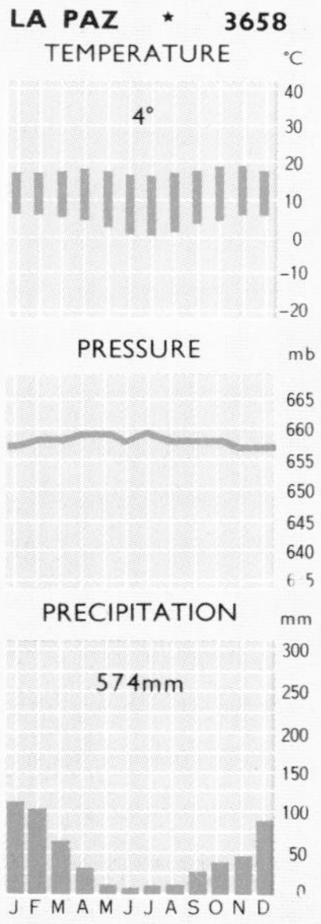

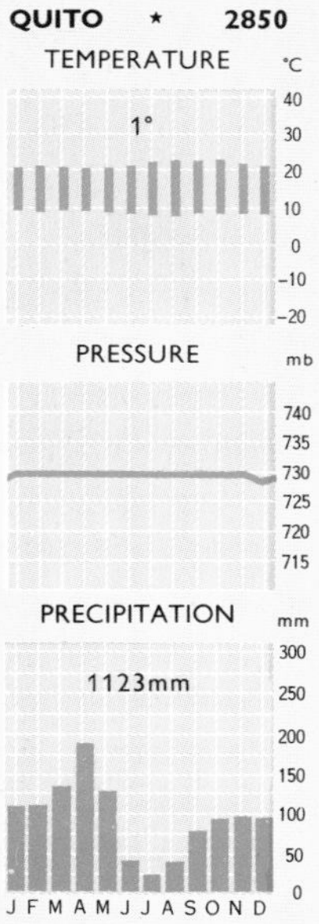

Guyana

Area: 214,969km² (83,000sq.m.).
Population: 965,000.
Capital: Georgetown (188,000).
Language: English.
Ethnic groups: Chinese, Indonesian, Negro, mixed, Amerindian.
Main exports: sugar, bauxite, alumina, manganese, rice.
Average temperature: 27°C (80°F).
Highest point: Mt Roraima, 2,810m (9,219ft).

Guyana, formerly British Guiana, is located on the northeast coast of South America. It is bordered by the Atlantic Ocean, Venezuela, Brazil, and Surinam.

More than three-quarters of the land area is made up of equatorial rain forest. To the west and south of this region is a belt of grassy plains where cattle are reared. The third section is a strip of coastland on the Atlantic. Almost all the people live in this coastal strip, in spite of its humid climate and flat, swampy terrain.

Guyana is the fourth largest producer of bauxite in the world. It gained its independence from Britain in 1966 and became a republic in 1970. The country was initially developed as a sugar growing colony and sugar cane, with rice, continues to be the main crop. Guyana has been involved in a number of territorial disputes with Venezuela and Surinam.

Above: *The cathedral in Guyana's capital, Georgetown, a city which lies below sea-level and is protected by dykes.*

Surinam

Surinam, formerly Dutch Guiana, is one of the three small states on the northeast coast of South America known collectively as the Guianas. It is flanked by Guyana on the west and French Guiana on the east. To the north lies the Atlantic Ocean, and to the south is Brazil. The country has an area of 163,820km² (63,235sq.m.) and a population of 370,000. The capital and largest city is Paramaribo (68,000).

Surinam was an autonomous part of the Netherlands until 1975. Like the other Guianas, it is a tropical country with a low, flat, swampy plain on the

Map 73

CARACAS 1042
TEMPERATURE °C
3°
PRESSURE mb
PRECIPITATION mm
833mm
J F M A M J J A S O N D

BOGOTÁ ★ 2645
TEMPERATURE °C
1°
PRESSURE mb
PRECIPITATION mm
1059mm
J F M A M J J A S O N D

COPYRIGHT. GEORGE PHILIP & SON, LTD.

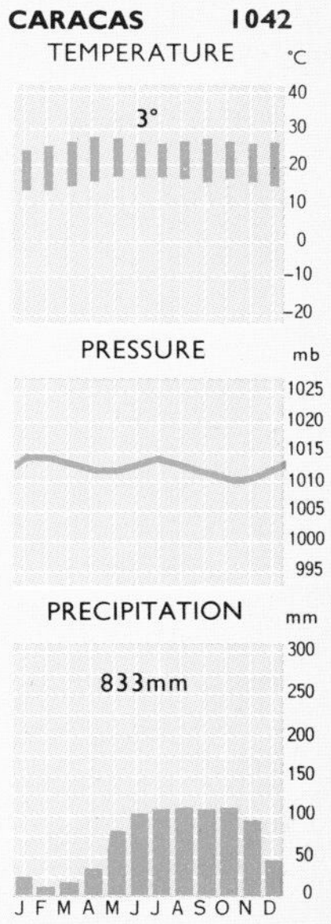

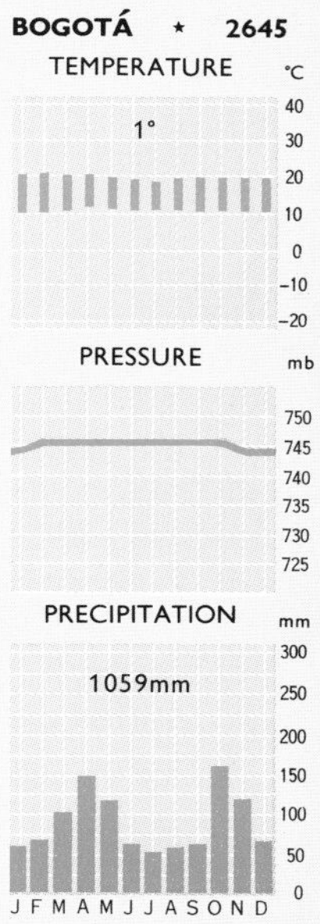

coast. Inland there are dense forests, plateaux, and low mountains. Very little of the land is cultivated, but there are large, high-grade deposits of bauxite which is the main export. Almost half the people are Negroes, but there are substantial minorities of Indonesian and Chinese. Dutch is the official language, but English, Chinese, and local dialects are widely spoken.

French Guiana

French Guiana is the smallest and most sparsely populated of the Guianas. It is located on the northeast coast of South America and bordered on the north by the Atlantic Ocean, on the west by Surinam, and on the south and east by Brazil. It has an area of 83,533km² (32,252sq.m.), and a population of 79,000. The capital and largest city is Cayenne (38,000).

French Guiana is an overseas department of France. Most of the people are Negroes who live in the coastal lowlands. The land is hardly developed at all, apart from a little forestry.

The French penal colony of Devil's Island, an island off the coast of French Guiana, was notorious for its brutality. It was closed in 1944.

The European Space Agency's Ariane rocket, used for delivering satellites into Earth orbit, is launched from a site in French Guiana.

Ecuador

Area: 283,561km² (109,484sq.m.).
Population: 8.9 million.
Capital: Quito (1.1m).
Largest city: Guayaquil (1.3m).
Languages: Spanish, Quechua.
Ethnic groups: Indian (40 percent), Mestizo (40 percent), European (10 percent), Negro (10 percent).
Main exports: bananas, sugar cane, coffee, cocoa.
Average temperature: varies with altitude, from tropical lowlands to snow-capped peaks.
Highest point: Mt Chimborazo, 6,272m (20,577ft).

Ecuador is one of the smallest countries in South America. It is located on the northwestern coast of the continent. It gets its name (which means 'equator' in Spanish), from the fact that the country straddles the equator. Its neighbours are Colombia on the north and Peru on the east and south. The Pacific Ocean lies on the west.

Ecuador is a mountainous country, with two main ranges of the Andes running from northeast to southwest for about 680 kilometres (425 miles). Most of the inhabitants live in the fertile central valley that divides the ranges. There are more than 30 volcanoes, a number of them active. Among them is Cotopaxi, 5,896 metres (19,344ft) high, the highest active volcano in the world.

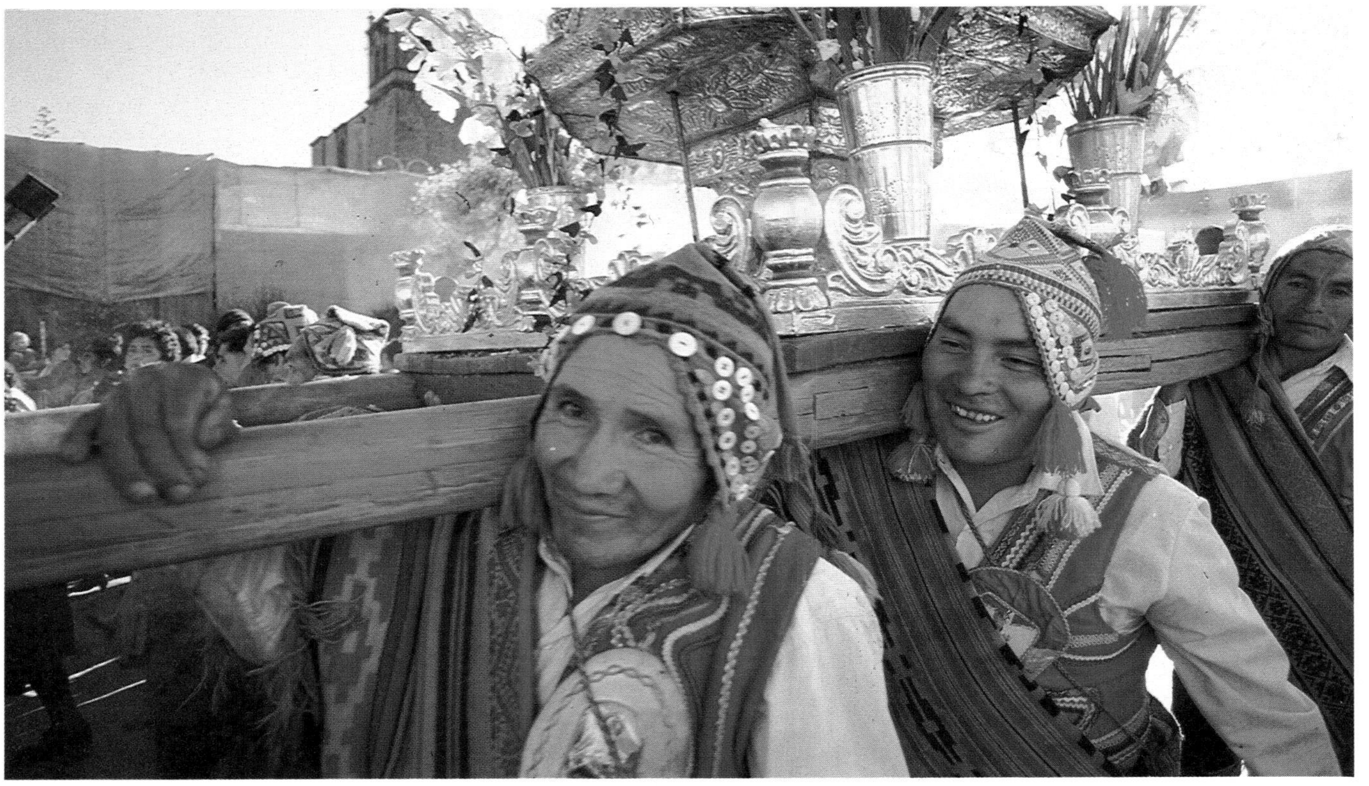

Above: *Quechua Indians, adapting Catholic festivals to suit older practices, celebrate Corpus Christi in Cuzco, Peru.*

Right: *From a small Indian settlement, São Paulo, Brazil, has grown into the world's largest industrial centre.*

The Galápagos Islands, an offshore group, some 960 kilometres (600 miles) from the mainland, are also part of Ecuador.

Some of the rivers flow westwards down the mountain slopes into the Pacific, while the rest flow eastwards to form part of the Amazon system. A narrow, low-lying swampy plain fringes the Pacific Ocean in the west. To the east of the mountains is another sparsely populated stretch of lowlands, but these are densely forested.

The main products are bananas, coffee, cocoa, sugar, oil, and straw ('Panama') hats. Ecuador is the largest exporter of bananas in the world, but oil exports are increasing and may soon provide the country's main income.

Ecuador has potential wealth, based on its mineral resources. But internal divisions resulting from political differences, social inequalities, and geographical obstacles have kept the country largely undeveloped.

Peru

Area: 1,285,216km^2 (496,225sq.m.).
Population: 19.5 million.
Capital: Lima (5.3m).
Languages: Spanish, Quechua, Aymara.
Ethnic groups: Indian (46 percent), Mestizo (43 percent), European (11 per cent).
Main exports: copper, fishmeal, silver, iron.
Average temperature: coast, 25°C (77°F), elsewhere dependent on altitude.
Highest point: Mt Huascarán, 6,767m (22,205ft).

Peru, a land of deserts, mountains, and jungles, is the third largest country in South America. It lies on the west coast of the continent and is bordered on the northwest by Ecuador, on the northeast by Colombia, on the east by Brazil, on the southeast by Bolivia, on the south by Chile, and on the west by the Pacific Ocean.

Peru has a 2,253-kilometre (1,400-mile) coastline on the Pacific. Between the sea and the Andes in the hinterland is a long, narrow, desert coastal stretch with fertile oasis areas. Several ranges of the Andes running north and south form the backbone of the country. These are divided by deep valleys. The eastern slopes of the mountains descend into jungle-clad plains, a region in some parts little explored.

Peru's two longest rivers, the Marañón and Ucayali, flow from the eastern side of the Andes to form the headwaters of the Amazon. On the west, more than 50 short rivers tumble down the mountains across the coastal plains and into the ocean.

The climate is almost tropical in many of the valleys, but it grows colder with altitude. The Humboldt Current cools the Peruvian shores as it sweeps northwards and also brings rich fishing resources. With an annual catch exceeding 10 million tonnes, Peru has become one of the world's leading fishing nations.

Peru also has great mineral wealth. Among the most important minerals are antimony, copper, bismuth, gold, zinc, silver, and lead. The chemical industry and the processing of fertilizers are also important. Agricultural products include sugar, cotton, wool, and coffee, and irrigation is important on the coastal plain.

Military rule was replaced by a democratically elected government in 1980. Although Spanish is the official language, Quechua, descended from the language of the ancient Incas, is still widely spoken.

Brazil

Area: 8,511,965km^2 (3,286,488sq.m.).
Population: 138.4 million.
Capital: Brasília (763,000).
Largest city: São Paulo (13m).
Language: Portuguese.
Ethnic groups: European (62 percent), mixed race (26 percent), Negro (11 percent).
Main exports: coffee, soya beans, cotton, timber, iron ore.
Average temperatures: vary with latitude and altitude; NE Brazil, 38°C (100°F); Belo Horizonte (lat. 20°S), 20°C (68°F).
Highest point: Pico da Bandeira, 2,890m (9,482ft).

Brazil is a country of superlatives. It is the largest country in South America, both in area and population, and the fifth largest country in the world. It covers almost half of South America, and much of it has remained unexplored until recently. It possesses the world's greatest river system – that of the Amazon – and some of the world's largest forests. It grows more coffee than any other country, and its countless varieties of flora and fauna have never been fully catalogued. The capital, Brasília, which superseded Rio de Janeiro in 1960, is considered one of the world's architectural showpieces.

Brazil sprawls over the northeastern and much of the central part of South America. It is bordered by French Guiana, Surinam, Guyana, and Venezuela on the north, Colombia on the northwest, Peru, Bolivia, Paraguay, and Argentina on the west, Uruguay on the south, and the Atlantic Ocean on the east and northeast.

The land falls naturally into three main regions. The northern part is made up of the hot, humid, heavily-forested region of the Amazon basin and the Brazilian Highlands, near the border with Venezuela. Strenuous government efforts are being made to open up Amazonia. In the northeast there is an extremely hot region of scrubland where catastrophic droughts are common. A series of plateaux criss-crossed by fertile river valleys make up the central and southern parts of the country. About 50 percent of the people, 75 percent of the agriculture, and 80 percent of the mining and manufacturing industries are located in this pleasant and healthy part of the country. Recently industrialized, the economy of Brazil enjoys a high rate of investment, and this is reflected in the equally high rate of urban growth. The city of São Paulo is the largest industrial centre in the region.

Brazil can claim some of the world's greatest rivers. The Amazon, which is navigable for its entire length within Brazil (3,158km, 1,962 miles), discharges more water than any river on earth. Other great waterways are the Negro, Madeira, São Francisco, Tocantíns, and Panama.

The construction of the trans-Amazonian highway has greatly stimulated exploitation of the rain forest, and vast areas are being felled for their valuable timber and the land grassed down for cattle ranching. This development is the cause of worldwide concern

Left: *Rio de Janeiro, Brazil's capital, overlooking Botafogo Bay and Sugar Loaf.*

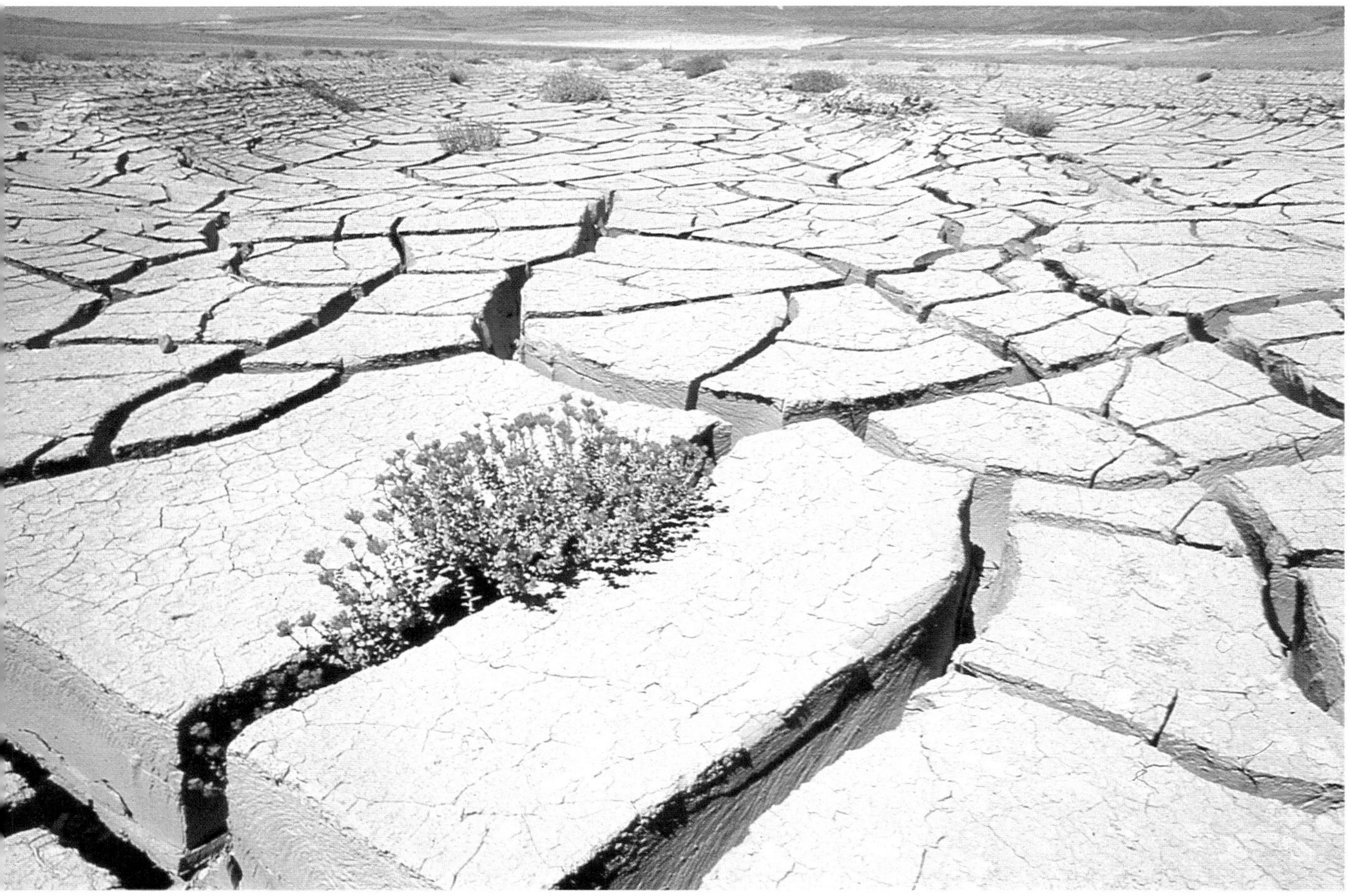

Above: *After nine months without rain little survives in Chile's Alacama Desert.*

among environmentalists, who believe that the destruction of the forest could have ecological implications for the world as a whole.

Most of Brazil's vast mineral wealth remains untapped, but it already supplies much of the world's quartz crystal, sheet mica, beryl, columbium, manganese, and iron ore. The country also has valuable deposits of gold, diamonds, nickel, and oil.

Brazil was originally claimed for Portugal in 1500. Some 300 years later it became a monarchy independent of Portugal, and finally became a republic in 1889. In 1964 the civilian government was overthrown by a military junta. Democratic elections were held in 1984. Following the death of the president-elect, vice-president José Sarnay took office.

Bolivia

Area: 1,098,581km^2 (424,565sq.m.).
Population: 6.2 million.
Capital: (actual) La Paz (881,000), (legal) Sucre (80,000).
Languages: Spanish, Quechea, Aymara, and other Amerindian dialects.
Ethnic groups: Amerindian (63 percent), Mestizo (22 percent), European (15 percent).
Main exports: silver, tin, petroleum, tungsten.
Average temperature: varies mainly between night and day; at La Paz (annual) 9°C (47°F).
Highest point: Mt Tocorpuri, 6,754m (22,162ft).

Bolivia is a large landlocked country in the heart of the continent. It is bordered by Brazil on the north and east, by Paraguay and Argentina on the south, and by Peru and Chile on the west. Bolivia straddles the Andes Mountains where some of the highest peaks in the whole system are found. Between two parallel ranges in the west lies the Altiplano, a huge, high, bleak plateau that forms the main physical feature of the country, and where most of the people live. Forested lowlands stretch across the northern and eastern parts of the country, and these merge with scrub and desert farther south.

Lake Titicaca, the highest navigable inland body of water in the world, lies on the border with Peru at a height of 3,810 metres (12,507ft).

The climate is hot in western regions and generally cooler in the east. The rainy season lasts from December to February.

Bolivia, in spite of huge deposits of tin and silver, is the poorest nation in South America. This is largely a result of a drastic fall in tin exports in the face of lower-cost production elsewhere, and the many labour problems that occurred in the mines. Most of the labour force is made up of Quechua and Aymara Indians, who live in harsh and monotonous life. Food shortages and official price rises have sparked off revolt and civil unrest. Bolivia does have large petroleum resources, producing over 8 million barrels in 1981.

Chile

Area: 756,626km^2 (292,072sq.m.).
Population: 11.7 million.
Capital: Santiago (4.1m).
Language: Spanish.
Ethnic groups: Mestizo (68 percent), European (30 percent), Amerindian (2 percent).
Main exports: copper, fertilizer, iron ore, molybdenum, silver, pulp and paper.
Average temperatures: vary according to zone – central zone 20°C (68°F) January, 5°C (41°F) August.
Highest point: Mt Ojos del Salado, 6,885m (22,589ft).

Chile runs down the west coast of South America, a long, narrow ribbon of land that stretches about 4,500 kilometres (2,800 miles) from the borders of Peru nearly to the Antarctic. The land is sandwiched between the Andes in the east and the Pacific in the west, and is never more than 400 kilometres (250 miles) wide at any point. Peru lies to the north, and Chile's eastern neighbours are Bolivia and Argentina.

Chile's extreme length covers many geographical zones, and each has its own climate. The far south is made up of desolate forests, fjords, islands, and glaciers, ending at Cape Horn, the stormy tip of South America. To the north of this region is a wonderland of immense lakes, forests, mountains, and rivers, which is the nation's favourite holiday resort. In the centre of the country is Chile's heartland, where most of the people live. This is a fertile region, warmed by summer sun and watered by winter rains. The basis of its prosperity, however, is industrial. Still farther north most of the vegetation peters out in semi-desert, and in the extreme north true desert takes over.

The 150,000 pure-blooded Araucanian Indians who live in the south of the country are the descendants of the only large group of Amerindians who were never completely conquered, either by the Incas or the Spaniards.

In spite of possessing the world's largest reserves of copper, and being the leading producer of iodine, Chile suffered catastrophic inflation in the late 1960s. In 1970, Salvador Allende, a Marxist, became President. He died three years later when the military seized power. General Augusto Pinochet's regime has since met with widespread resistance from trade unionists.

Above: *The Iguazú Falls lie on a tributary of the Rio de la Plata in Argentina.*

Left: *The Lopez Palace, built on the bank of the Paraguay river at Asunción.*

Paraguay

Area: 406,752km² (157,048sq.m.).
Population: 3.6 million.
Capital: Asunción (794,000).
Languages: Spanish, Guaraní.
Ethnic groups: Mestizo (95 percent), European (5 percent).
Main exports: meat products, quebracho extract, yerba maté (Paraguayan tea), cotton.
Average temperature: 24°C (74°F) throughout the year.
Highest point: Paraná plateau, 600m (1,968ft).

Paraguay, completely landlocked in the heart of the continent, is surrounded by Argentina, Bolivia, and Brazil. The land is cut in two by the River Paraguay, which, with the Paraná, forms two great arteries to the sea by way of the estuary of the Río de la Plata.

To the west of the River Paraguay is the Chaco, an inhospitable region of scrub, jungle, and swamps. To the east are gently rolling grasslands that rise to a forested plateau. Almost all the inhabitants live in this latter region. There they enjoy a subtropical climate with mild, fairly dry winters.

Paraguay, a military dictatorship, has fought and lost two disastrous wars against her neighbours during the last 100 years. Resources are few and most of the inhabitants are extremely poor. Many emigrate to Argentina to work. Most of the exports are agricultural products, including the extract of *quebracho* ('axe-breaker'), an extremely hard wood, used in tanning.

Although Spanish is the official language, the country is virtually bilingual, for most people also speak Guaraní, the language of the conquered Amerindians. Cattle ranching is the only major industry.

Argentina

Area: 2,776,889km² (1,072,163sq.m.).
Population: $».6 million.
Capital: Buenos Aires (9m).
Language: Spanish.
Ethnic groups: European (97 percent).
Main exports: grain, meat, wool, hides.
Average temperatures: (the Pampa) 21°C (70°F) January, 10°C (50°F) July.
Highest point: Mt Aconcagua, 6,960m (22,835ft).

Argentina is the second largest country in South America, after Brazil, both in area and population. It covers most of the southern and southeastern part of the continent, stretching from the tropics in the north almost to ice-bound Antarctica in the south.

The country is bordered on the north by Paraguay and Bolivia, on the northeast by Uruguay and Brazil, on the east and south by the South Atlantic, and on the west by Chile. Argentina shares the large island of Tierra del Fuego in the extreme south with Chile.

The Gran Chaco, a region of wooded plains, lies in the north of the country. To the south and southwest of Buenos Aires (the largest city in the southern hemisphere) is the prosperous heart of Argentina, the Pampa. This vast, almost treeless expanse of fertile grassland is where millions of beef cattle and sheep are reared. In the Andean region to the west of the Pampa, orchards of citrus fruits and vineyards flourish in the shadow of the mountains. Argentina's mines are also located there. Patagonia, a bleak, windy plateau, lies to the south. There the main occupations are sheep farming and drilling for oil.

Aconcagua, Argentina's highest point, is also the highest peak in the western hemisphere. The two most important rivers are the Paraná and Uruguay. They flow into the broad estuary of the Río de la Plata, on whose banks stands two imposing capital cities Buenos Aires Montevigo.

The climate varies with the zone. In the north, the winters are mild but the summers are humid and hot. Large areas of the extreme northwest are semi-desert. In the central region, the weather is mild all the year round, while in Patagonia winters are cold and summers are hot.

Besides exporting more beef than any other country, Argentina is one of the leading exporters of sheep and wool. Other important agricultural products include wheat, cotton, rye, barley, alfalfa, oats, linseed, fruit, sugar, and cotton. Mining produces quantities of coal, zinc, lead, copper, iron, silver, and gold, while oil production is on the increase. Meat processing and canning is the principal export industry.

There are almost no descendants of the original Amerindian inhabitants. Most of the people are of Spanish or Italian ancestry, and about a third of the country's population lives in Buenos Aires and its suburbs.

Argentina's post-World War II history has been one of political turmoil. In 1946 Juan Domingo Perón became president, but nine years later was overthrown and exiled to Spain. After a number of governments, both civilian and military, had risen and fallen, Perón returned in 1973, only to die the following year. His widow succeeded him and inherited a country torn by strife. The military seized power three years later.

Argentina's invasion of the Falkland Islands (*Islas Malvinas*) in 1982 led to war with Britain and the downfall of General Galtieri and his military junta. The following year saw a return to democracy with the election of Raúl Alfonsin's Radical Civil Union party.

Uruguay

Area: 177,508km² (66,536sq.m.).
Population: 3 million.
Capital: Montevideo (1.3m).
Language: Spanish.
Ethnic groups: European (90 percent), Mestizo (10 percent).
Main exports: wool, meat, hides.
Average temperatures: 23°C (73°F) January. 10°C (50°F) June.
Highest point: Cuchilla Grande range, 600m (2,000ft).

Uruguay, the smallest republic in South America, lies on the southeast coast of the continent. It is bordered by Argentina on the south and west, and by Brazil on the north and northeast. The Atlantic Ocean washes its southeastern shores.

PUNTA ARENAS 8

TEMPERATURE   °C
9°   40
                     30
                     20
                     10
                      0
                    −10
                    −20

PRESSURE   mb
                    1025
                    1020
                    1015
                    1010
                    1005
                    1000
                     995

PRECIPITATION   mm
366mm   300
                     250
                     200
                     150
                     100
                      50
                       0
J F M A M J J A S O N D

BUENOS AIRES 27

TEMPERATURE   °C
                     40
14°   30
                     20
                     10
                      0
                    −10
                    −20

PRESSURE   mb
                    1025
                    1020
                    1015
                    1010
                    1005
                    1000
                     995

PRECIPITATION   mm
950mm   300
                     250
                     200
                     150
                     100
                      50
                       0
J F M A M J J A S O N D

1:16 000 000

100 50 0   100   200   300 miles
100   0   100 200 300 400   km

Projection: Sanson-Flamsteed's Sinusoidal

West from Greenwich

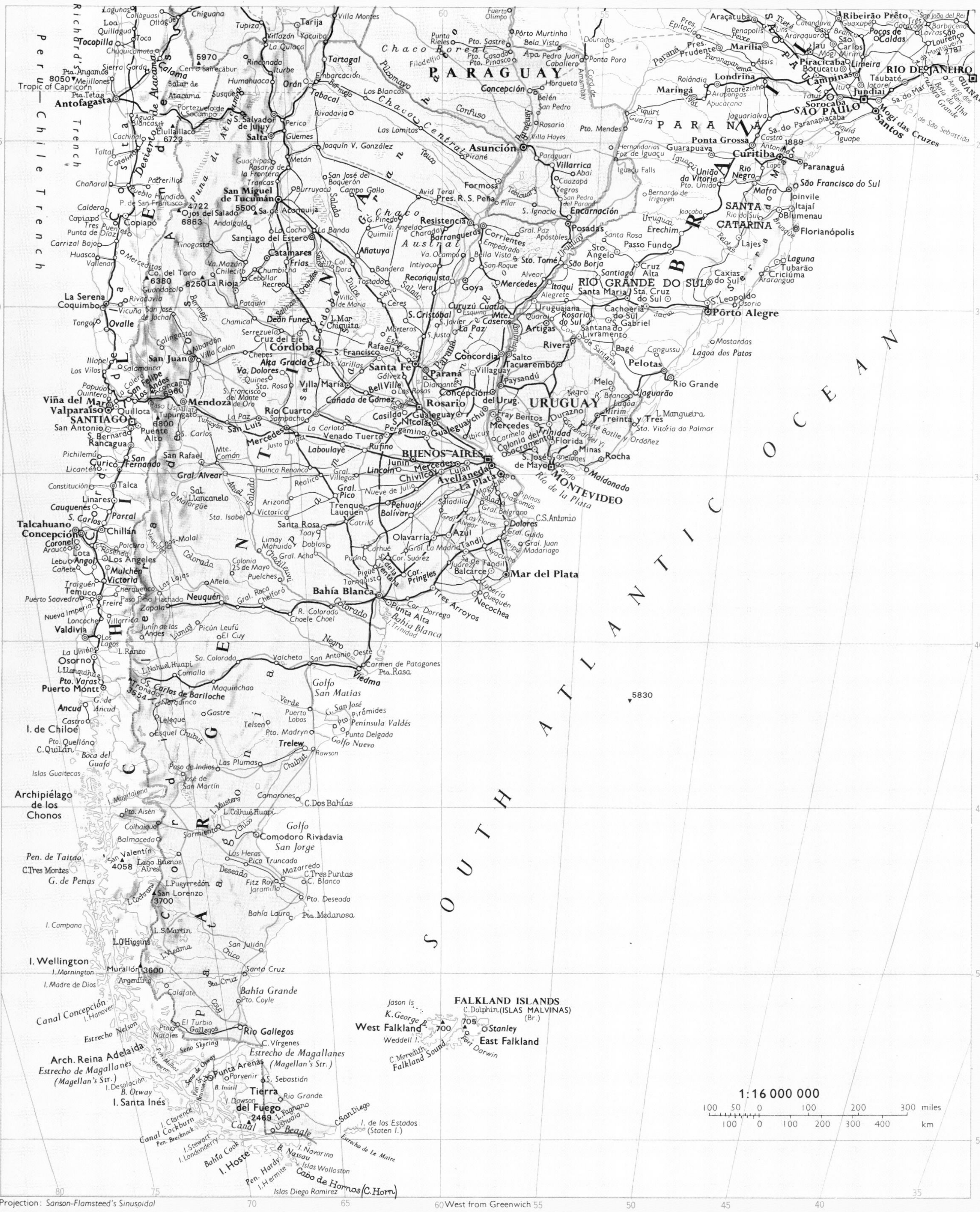

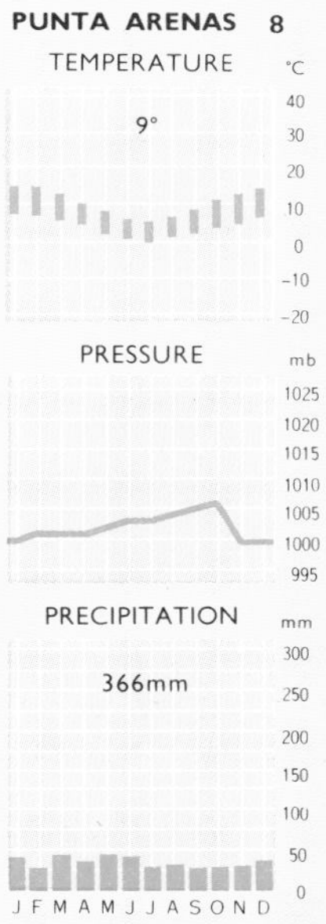

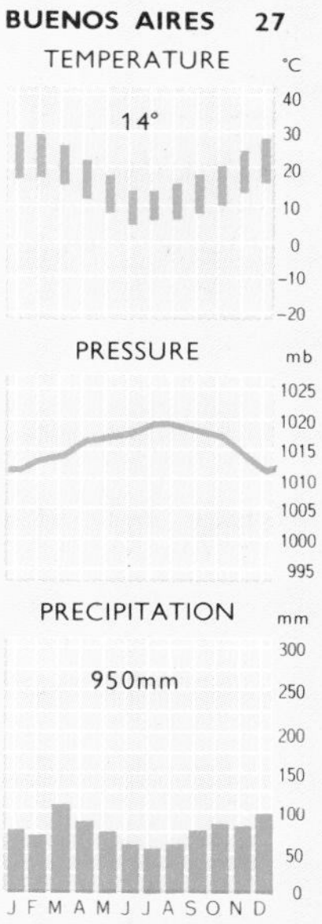

Uruguay is a land of rolling, grassy hills, broad plains, and numerous streams. A unique feature of the country is that there is no great physical contrast between one part and another, and that virtually the whole of the land is populated. The River Uruguay and the Río de la Plata separate the country from Argentina. The Negro, flowing through the middle of the country, is another important river. The pleasant, healthy climate, with ample, well-distributed rainfall, resembles the climate of the Mediterranean region.

Uruguay's excellent climate and its fertile soil are its main resources. The principal industry is agriculture, and there are more cattle and sheep in Uruguay than people. The rearing of livestock takes up 90 percent of the land. Cattle are herded on the open range by cowboys called *gauchos*.

Almost all the people are of European descent, mainly Spanish and Italian, and Montevideo is the only large city.

Uruguay pioneered social democracy in South America and before World War II was regarded as the most stable of all Latin American republics. But in the 1960s and 1970s the overburdened social system began to break down. Widespread strikes and urban terrorism brought suspension of parliament in 1973. However in 1984 elections were held again, and Julio Maria Sanguinetti became president.

Right: *A gaucho herding cattle in Uruguay.*

Index to text

Note: This index covers references in the text only. Place names are covered by the Index to Maps on pages 146-176. The numerals in italic type indicate that the subject is given in an illustration.

A

Abaca (Manila hemp) 76
Aborigines 109
'Acid rain' pollution 34, 61
The Acropolis 57
Act of Union (1707) 17
Aegean (Cycladic) civilization 54
Aegean islands 56
Agricultural products
  Africa 94; Argentine exports 142; Australian staples *110*, 111; Canadian pastoral and arable 124; China 82; Cuban sugar and tobacco 134; Denmark 62; Egypt 97; France 28, 29; Guyanan sugar and rice 138; Honduran bananas 133; Indian subcontinent 75; Israel 90; Italy *48*; Jamaica 134; Japan 86; Libya 95; Nepalese subsistence farming 74; Mozambique 104; Netherlands 31; New Zealand *117*, 118; Nigeria 100; Oceania 115; Peru 140; Romania 40; South African pastoral and arable 106; South Korea 85; Syria 90; Taiwanese multiple cropping 83; Tanzanian sugar cane *102*; Tunisia 96; Ugandan cotton and coffee *102*; United States 130; Uruguayan livestock 143; U.S.S.R. 65; Vietnam 79, 80; Yemeni millet 93; Zimbabwe tobacco and maize 105
Ahmad, *Imam* 93
Air travel
  Arctic routes 15; Laos 79; Soviet Asia 67
Al Marj (Barce) plain 95
Albania
  invasions and liberation 57; people and language 57
Alexander the Great 56, 91, 96
Alfonsin, Raúl, Argentine Radical Civil Union party 142
Algerian National Liberation Front (FLN) 96
Algonkian Indians 121
Allende, Salvador, president of Chile 142
Alsace region of France 26
  language 24
Altai Mountains 65, 71, 82
Althing, Icelandic parliament 59
American Civil War 126
Amerindians 121, 132, 136, 142
Amin, *General* Idi, Ugandan president 102
Amundsen, Roald 61, 119
Anderson, Hans Christian 62
Andes mountains 136, 139, 141
Andorran people and languages 45
Angkor Wat 80
Annamese mountains 79
Antarctic discovery and exploration 119
ANZUS Australia/New Zealand/US defence treaty 112
apartheid 94, 105, 130
Apennines 46
Aquino, *Mrs* Corazon 77
Aquitaine basin 26
Arab-Israeli wars 90, 91, 96, 130
Araucanian Indians 142
Arctic 14
  strategic defence 15; transportation *15*
Arctic Circle 14
Arctic limit 14
Ariane rocket launch site 139
Artesian wells, Australia 111
Aswan High Dam 97
Atlas mountains 95, 96
Australian-administered territories 112
Australian history and education 110
Austrian Alps 36
Austrian people and language 36
Austro-Hungarian empire 38, 40, 52
Autostrada del Sol 49
Aymara Indians 141
Azores islands, demands for independence 43

B

Baktiari, semi-nomadic tribe 91
Basque language 24, 45
Bass Strait oil exploitation 112
Batista, Fulgencio 134
Bay of Bengal offshore oil exploration 74
Baykal, Lake 65
Beauce region of France 26
Bedouin tribes 91, 93
Belgian cession from Holland (1830) 31
Belgian people and languages 31
Belize-Guatamalan territorial claims 133
Benelux countries 17, 30
Benelux Customs Union (1947) 30
Benin Nigerian culture 100
Bihor Massif 40
Black Sea offshore oil 54
Boccaccio, Giovanni 49
Boers (farmers) South Africa 105
Bohr, Niels 62
Bolsheviks 70
Bonaparte, Louis Napoleon 26
Bonaparte, Napoleon 26, 33, 70
Bounty HMS, mutineers 112, 116
Bourbon monarchy of France 26
Brazilian deforestation 140
Brenner Pass 37
Breton language 24
British Camp, Iron Age hill fort *20*
British Commonwealth of Nations 18, 75, 80, 107, 112, 122
British East India Company 75
British North American Act, 1867 122
Broz, Josip *see* Tito *Marshal*
Buddhism 71, 81, 86
Bulgarian people and language 54
Bundesrat, West German Federal Council 33
Bundestag, West German Federal Diet 33
Byrd, Richard E. 119
Byzantine empire 80

C

Cabora Bassa dam 104
Cabot, John 121
Caesar, Julius 26
Caetano, *Dr* 43
Cambrian Mountains 20
Cameroon ethnic groups 101
Canadian French-English rivalry 122
Canadian people and languages 121
Canadian provinces and cities 123
Canadian Shield mineral deposits 122, 125
Cape Province 105
Cape Verde Islands independence (1975) 43
Capetian dynasty of France 26
Carlos, *Prince* Don Juan 45
Carolingian dynasty of France 26
Carpathian mountains 40
Carrara marble quarries 46
Carter, Jimmy, US president 126, 130
Cartier, Jacques 121
Caspian Sea 16, 65
Castro, Fidel 134
Catalan language 24, 45
Catherine the Great 70
Caucasus mountain range 65, 68
Cavour, *Count* Camillo 49
Central American peoples and languages 132
Central Lowlands of Scotland 18, 22
Central Siberian Uplands mineral deposits 65
The Chaco of Paraguay 142
Chamber of Representatives, Belgian 31
Champlain, Samuel de 121
Channel Islands 17
Charlemagne 26
Charles XII, King of Sweden 72
Charles the Bald 26
Cheviot Hills (UK) 18
Chiang Kai-shek 81, 83
Chinese people and languages 81
Christianity
  Byzantine contacts 69; Middle East origin 88
Chungyang Range 83
Climate and relief
  Afghanistan 91; Albania 57; Antarctica 118; Arabian peninsula 93; Argentina 142; Australia 108, 111; Austria 36; Bangladesh 73; Belgium 31; Bhutan 74; Bolivia 141; Brazil 140; Bulgaria 54; Burma 78; Cambodia (Kampuchea) 80; Canada 122; Central America 132; Chile 142; China 82; Cuba 134; Cyprus 90; Czechoslovakia *38*; Denmark *62*; East Germany 34; Ecuador 139, 140; Egypt 97; Ethiopia 93; Europe 16; Finland 59; France 26, 27; Great Britain 18; Greece and Greek islands 56; Greenland 15; Hong Kong 85; Hungary 38; Iceland 59; Indian peninsula 75; Indonesia 77; Iraq 90; Ireland *22*, 23; Israel 90, 91; Italy 46; Ivory Coast, Ghana, Togo and Benin 100; Japan 86; Kashmir 75; Kenya 102; Korean peninsula 85; Lebanon 90; Libya 95; Madagascar *107*; Malaysia 80; Malta 51; Mexico 132; Mongolia 71; Morocco 95; Nepal 74; Netherlands 31; New Zealand 117; Nigeria 100; North America 120; Norway 60; Oman 93; Pakistan 72, 73; Papua New Guinea 115; Paraguay 142; Peru 140; The Philippines 76; Poland 40; Portugal 43; Romania 40; Singapore island 80; South Africa 106; South America 136; Spain 45; Sri Lanka 75; Surinam 138, 139; Sweden 61; Switzerland 35; Syria 90; Taiwan 83; Tanzania 102; Thailand 79; Tunisia 96; Turkey 90; Uganda 102; United States 129; Uruguay 143; USSR 65; Venezuela 137; Vietnam 79; West Germany 33; Yemen 93; Yugoslavia 53; Zaïre 101; Zimbabwe 104
Clovis (Frankish king) 26
CMEA (Council for Mutual Economic Assistance) 35
'Cod war' 59
Cold War 16, 71, 130
Columbus, Christopher 45, 46, 61, 121, 132
COMECON 17, 39, 40, 41, 54, 67
Comino (Malta) 51
Comminotto (Malta) 51
Communist Party of China 81
Confederation of Senegambia 98
Confucianism 81, 82
Congress of Vienna (1815) 35
Congress Party of India 75
Conquistadores 132
Consultative Assembly of Turkey 90
Cook, *Captain* James 110, 115, 117
Coptic Church 93, 96
Corsica 27
Cortés, Hernán 132
Costa Rican literacy 134
Council of Ministers (USSR) 69
Council of State, German Democratic Republic 34
Council of State, Poland 40
Council of State, Switzerland 35
Council of the Nationalities (USSR) 69
Council of the Union (USSR) 69
Creoles 99, 134
Crown Colonies and Protectorates 22, 85, 96, 100, 101, 102
Crusaders in Syria 90
Cryolite 15
Cultural Revolution (1960s), China 82
Cypriot peoples and languages 90
Cyprus: Greek-Turkish tensions 57, 90
Czech people and languages 38
Czech Socialist Republic 38
Czechoslovakia: invasion by USSR (1968) 38

D

Dante Alighieri 46
Davis, Jefferson, Confederate president 126
Deccan plateau 75
Demilitarized Zone of Korea 85
Desertas (Madeira Islands) 43
Deserts
  Alacama, Chile *141*; Gobi 71, 82; Kara Kum 65; Kyzyl Kum 65; Namib 104; Negev irrigation 90, 91; Rub'al Khali 93; Sahara 96
Devil's Island, French penal colony 139
Dinaric Alps 53
Dodecanese island group 56
Doe, Samuel Kanyon, Liberian president 100
Dominican people and language 134
Donets basin (USSR) 65
Donsek glacier *121*
Dutch language and people 31
Dzungarian Basin 82

E

Earthquakes 47, 86, 90, 132
East African Rift Valley 93, 102
East Anglian landscape 20
East European Plain 65, 66
Eastern Ghats 75
Edward III, King of England 26
EEC (European Economic Community) 17, 18, 24, 29, 43, 45, 49, 57, 62
EFTA (European Free Trade Association) 38, 62
Elbrus, Mt. 16
enosis (Cypriot union with Greece) 90
Entente Cordiale 26
Eriksson, Leif 61
Eskimos 14, 15, 121
Everest, Mt. 74

F

Falkland Islands conflict 22, 142
Faröes 62
Federal Council of Switzerland 35
Federal Republic of Germany, *Bundesrepublik Deutschland* 33
  chancellor and political parties 33; election of president 33
Ferdinand of Aragon 45
Filfla (Malta) 51
Finnish history and constitution 59
Flemings of Belgium 31
Folketing Danish parliament 62
Ford, Gerald, US president 126
Forestation in UK 21
France
  election of president 26; Seven Years War (1756-63) in N. America 126
Franco, *General* Francisco 45
Franco-Prussian War (1870-71) 33
Frente Polisario Saharan nationalists 95, 97

G

Galician language 45
Galileo Galilei 46
Galtieri *General* 142
Gama, Vasco da 43
Garibaldi, Giuseppe 49
Gaul 26
Gaulle, Charles de 26
Gautama Buddha 74
General Council of the Valleys, Andorra 45
General People's Congress of Yemen 93
Genghis Khan 71
George Cross 51
Geothermal power 76, 118
German Democratic Republic: history and constitution 34
German invasion of Czechoslovakia 38
German language and people 33
German political history 33
Gibraltar sovereignty referendum (1967) 45
Giotto (Ambrogio de Bondone) 49
Gobi desert 71, 82
Godwin Austen, Mt. 75
Golan Heights 91
Golden Horde of the Mongols 70
'Golden Mile' Kalgoorlie 111
Gozo (Malta) 51
Grampian mountains 18
Grand Canyon 129
Great Depression (1929-33) 126
Great Dividing Range of Australia 108
Great European Plain 16
'Great Trek' by Afrikaners 105
Greek nationalism 56
Greek revolution (1967) 56
Grieg, Eduard 61
Guarani language 142
Guatemalan peoples 133
Gulf of Cambay oil exploitation 75
Gulf Stream 121
Gustavus I, King of Sweden 62

H

Hapsburg empire 36
Hapsburg, House of 35
Harald Bluetooth, King of Denmark 62
Harold Fairhair, King of Norway 61
Hebrides: cession by Norway (1266)
Helvetic League 35
Henry VII, King of England 121
Henry the Navigator 43
Heyerdahl, Thor 61
Himalayas 75, 82
Hindu Kush 72, 91
Hinduism 75
Hitler, Adolf 33, 38
Horthy, *Admiral*, regent of Hungary 38
House of Assembly, South Africa 105
House of Commons, Canadian Parliament 122
House of Councillors, of Japanese Diet 87
House of Representatives, Australian Federal Parliament 110
House of Representatives, Malaysia 80
House of Representatives, of Japanese Diet 87
House of Representatives, US Congress 129
Houses of Parliament (UK) 18
Hoxha, Enver, Albanian First Secretary 57
Humboldt Current 136, 140
Humboldt Glacier 15
Hungarian annexations in Slovakia 38
Hungarian Revolution (1956) 38
Huron Indians 121
Hydro-electric power 28, 35, 37, 48, 54, 60, 61, 65, 67, 73, 75, 76, 77, 79, 83, 85, 86, 100, 101, 102, 111, 112, 118, 125, 129

I

Ibiza 45
Ibsen, Henrik 61
Iceland: Viking colonization 61
Icelandic territorial waters 59
Ife (AD 1200-) Nigerian culture 100
Immigrant workers
  Finns in Sweden 59, 62; *Gastarbeiter* in West Germany 33, 45, 54; in Australia 109; in France 25, 45, 96; Malawi reservoir 102; Moroccans in Europe 95; Mozambiquans in S. Africa 104; Saudi Arabian workforce 93; Tunisians in Libya 96
India
  'Green Revolution' 75; Kashmir territorial dispute 74
Indian people and languages 75
The Industrial Revolution 16, 17, 62
Inga Dam, nr. Matadi, Zaïre 101
Inuit people *see* Eskimos
Ionian islands 56
IRA (Irish Republican Army) 18, 22
Iran-Iraq war 90
Iranian Revolution (1979) 89
Iranians 68
Irish Civil War (1922-3) 22
Irish Language and people 22
Iroquois Indians 121
Isabella of Castile 45
Islam *71*, 88, 93, 96
  legal problems of Pakistan 73
Isle of Man 17
Italian people and language 48
Italy
  abolition of monarchy (1946) 49; artistic inheritance 46, 49; two-chamber parliament 49
Ivan IV 'the Terrible' 70

J

Japanese Imperial Family 87
Japanese people and culture 86
Japhetic peoples (Caucasus) 68
Joan d'Arc 26
Jordanian people and languages 91
Judaism 88

K

Kabuki drama of Japan 86
Kamchatka peninsular 65
Karagiye depression 65
Karakoram range 75
Kariba Dam, Zambia 101, 105
Karst landscape 53
Kemal, Mustafa [Ataturk] 90
Khmer culture, Cambodia 80
Khmers Rouges *see* National United Front of Cambodia
Khomeini, Ayatollah 91, 130
Khorat plateau 79
Khuzistan lowlands 91

Index

Kibbutzim Israeli co-operative communities 90
Kierkegaard, Søren 62
Kikládhes (Cyclades) island group 56
Kölen Mountains 61
Kolkhoz collective farm (USSR) 65
Korean War (1950-53) 81, 85, 126
Kruger National Park 106
Kunlun mountains 82
Kurds 90, 91
Kuznets basin (USSR) 65
Kyrenia mountains 90

L

Labrador Current 121
Lacq region of France: natural gas extraction 27
Ladoga, Lake 65
Lake District of England *17*, 20
Landes 26
  onshore oil exploitation 27
Landlocked African states 97, 98, 101, 102
Lapplanders 14, 59
Lebanese Moslem-Christian conflict 90
Leeward Islands composition 134
Lenin (Vladimir Ulyanov) 70
Leonardo da Vinci *see* Vinci, Leonardo da
Leopold II, King of the Belgians 101
Lepanto, battle of 89
Lincoln, Abraham 126
'Little Venice' Venezuela 137
Llanos, grassy plains 136, 137
Llywelyn ap Gruffydd 17
Loess Highlands (N. China) 82
Lutheranism in Sweden 62

M

MacArthur, *General* Douglas 87
Machiavelli, Niccolo 46
Madeira Islands demands for independence 43
Magna Carta 17
Malay peoples and languages 80
Mallorca (Majorca) 45
Maltese archaeological remains 51
Maltese people and language 51
Manchurian Plain 82
Manufacturing industries
  Albania 57; Australia 112; Belgium 31; Canada 125; Chilean iodine production 142; China 83; Czechoslovakia 38; Denmark 62; East Germany 35; Egypt 97; Finland 59; France 27; Ghana 100; Greece 57; Hawaii 115; Hong Kong 85; Hungary 38; Icelandic aluminium smelting 59; India 75; Indonesia 77; Ireland 23; Italy 48; Japan 86; Liechtenstein 38; Maltese diversification 51; Nigeria 100; Norway 60, 61; Poland 41; Romania 40; South Africa 106; South Korea 85; Spain 45; Sweden 61; Switzerland 35; Taiwan 83; Turkish developments 90; United Kingdom 21; United States 129, 130; USSR 67; Vietnamese cement, paper and textiles 79; West Germany 34
Mao Tse-tung 81
Maoris 117
Marcos, Ferdinand, Philippines president 76
Marxist Social Democrat Party 70
Massif Centrale (France) 26
Matsu island (Taiwan) 83
Mau Mau 102
Mayflower 126
Mazzini, Giuseppe 49
Medici, De (of Florence) 49
Mekong delta 79
Menorca (Minorca) 45
Mensheviks 70
Merovingian dynasty of France 26
Mesaoria Plain 90
Meseta, Spain 43, 45
Meteorology
  Arctic regions 15; Asian monsoon patterns 64
Mexican history 132
Michael, King of Romania, abdication (1947) 40
Michelangelo 46, 49
Middle Eastern people and languages 88
Midlands plain (UK) minerals 20
Mineral resources
  antimony 83, 140; asbestos 105, 125, 137; asphalt 137; bauxite 75, 77, 79, 99, 111, 112, 118, 134, 137, 138; beryllium 65, 141; bismuth 140; bitumen 57, 125; bromine 91; chalk 20; china clay 20; chromite 54, 57, 79, 90, 91, 105, 116; coal 14, 20, 27, 31, 34, 38, 40, 43, 45, 48, 54, 56, 57, 65, 75, 77, 79, 82, 85, 90, 91, 100, 105, 106, 111, 118, 125, 130, 142; columbian 141; copper 14, 40, 43, 54, 57, 65, 83, 90, 91, 93, 94, 101, 105, 111, 112, 116, 125, 130, 132, 140, 142; cryolite 15; diamonds 65, 94, 99, 100, 101, 104, 106, 141; diatomite 59; gemstones 75, 78, 137; gold 14, 54, 65, 79, 91, 94, 100, 105, 106, 116, 125, 130, 140, 141, 142; graphite 37, 75, 85; gypsum 79, 125; iron ore 14, 20, 27, 31, 34, 37, 38, 40, 45, 54, 56, 61, 65, 75, 79, 82, 85, 90, 97, 98, 99, 100, 111, 116, 118, 125, 130, 132, 137, 141, 142; jade 78; lapis lazuli 91; lead 14, 37, 40, 45, 54, 65, 79, 83, 85, 90, 91, 111, 112, 125, 132, 140, 142; lignite 34, 35, 37, 38, 40, 45, 48, 90; limestone 20, 51; magnesite 37, 85; manganese 54, 65, 75, 79, 83, 91, 111, 116, 141; mercury 45, 48, 65, 132; mica 75, 141; molybdenum 83, nickel 14, 57, 77, 111, 116, 125, 137, 141; nitrates 142; oil and natural gas 27, 37, 40, 54, 56, 57, 65, 73, 74, 75, 77, 78, 80, 83, 85, 89, 90, 91, 92, 93, 94, 95, 96, 97, 100, 111, 112, 118, 125, 130, 132, 135, 137, 141, 142; phosphates 91, 95, 96, 97, 116; platinum 125; potash 35, 91, 125; quartz crystal 141; salt 40, 57, 91; silver 79, 90, 91, 111, 112, 116, 125, 130, 132, 140, 142; sulphur 48, 91, 132; thorium 14, tin 77, 79, 80, 83, 111; titanium 65; tungsten 83, 85; uranium 14, 43, 65, 105, 112, 125; wolframite 43, zinc 37, 40, 45, 54, 65, 79, 83, 85, 90, 91, 111, 112, 125, 132, 140, 142
Minoan culture of Crete 54
Mogul empire 75
Mohammed Ali Pasha 96
Moldavian union with Walachia (1861) 40
Monaco, area and population 27
Mubarak, Hosni 96
Mugabe, Robert, prime minister Zimbabwe 104
Muhammad, Prophet 93
Munch, Eduard 61
Muslim Arabs 91
Mussolini, Benito 49
Mycenae, warrior state 54

N

NAFTA (New Zealand-Australian Free Trade Agreement) 112
Namib Desert 104
Nansen, Fridtjof 61
Napoleon *see* Bonaparte
Napoleonic Wars: Danish loss of Norway 62; Swedish territorial gains and losses 62
Nasser, *Colonel* Abdul 96
Natal, Union of South Africa 105
National Assembly of Austria 36
National Assembly of France 26
National Assembly of Mali 97
National Council of Switzerland 35
National People's Congress of China 81
National Security Council of Turkey 90
National Socialist Party of Germany 33
National United Front of Cambodia (Khmers Rouges) 80
NATO North Atlantic Treaty Organisation 16, 31, 34, 49, 57, 90
Natural resources
  Albanian collectivization 57; Antarctic whaling 119; Arctic region 14; Argentina 142; Australian water 111; Austrian farming 37; Belgium 31; Bulgarian National Agro-Industrial Union 54; Burmese teak and bamboo 78; Canadian forestry 125; Congo timber 101; Czechoslovakia 38; East Germany 35; Ecuador 140; Fiji 116; Finnish forestry 59; France 28; Ghanaian cocoa 94, 100; Greece 57; Hungary 39; Indonesian teak and rubber 77; Ireland 23; Italy 48, Ivory Coast 100; Japanese water utilization 86; Laos 79; Malaysian rubber production 80; Mauritian sugar cane 107; Mexico 132; Nepal 74; Nigeria 94, 100; North Korea 85; Pakistan 73; Philippines copra and hardwoods 76; Poland 41; Portugal 43; Romania 40; Saudi Arabia 93; Somali livestock products 93; Spain 45; Sri Lankan tea, hardwoods and rubber 75; Sweden 61; Switzerland 35; Taiwanese timber 83; Tanzanian sisal hemp 94; Thai rubber production 80; Turkey 90; Ugandan lake fisheries 102; United Kingdom 21; US lumber industry 130; USSR virgin lands policy 66; Vietnam 79; West Germany 34; Yemeni cotton, coffee and Qat 93; Yugoslavia 54
Nautilus USS 15
Netherlands: neutrality in World War I 31; parliament 31
New Territories (Hong Kong) 85
Niagara Falls *123*, 129
Nicholas II, Tsar of Russia 70
Nigerian Civil War (1967-70) 100
Nigerian peoples and languages 100
Nimeiri, Ja'afar al-, President of Sudan 96
Nixon, Richard, US president 126
Nkrumah, *Dr* Kwame, Ghanaian president 100
Noh drama of Japan 86
Nok (500 BC-AD 200) Nigerian culture 100
Norsemen, Greenland settlement 15
North American Indians 121
North Atlantic Drift 20, 23, 59, 60
North China Plain 82
North Sea oil and gas exploitation 18, 21, 31, 60
Northern Ireland, Roman Catholic minority 18
Northern tree line 14
Norwegian artists and explorers 61
Nuclear power 22, 28, 54, 112, 130
Nuclear weapons: against Japan 126; testing sites 116

O

OAU Organization of African Unity 97
Obote, *Dr* Milton, Ugandan President 102
Oceania peoples and languages 115
Oder-Neisse Line 33, 34, 40
OPEC Organization of Petroleum Exporting Countries 89
'Operation Bootstrap' in Puerto Rico 134
'Operation Deep Freeze' US Antarctic station 119
Orange Free State foundation 105
Ord River irrigation scheme 111
Orkney, cession by Norway (1468) 17
Ottoman Turks 89
Owen Falls, Ugandan hydro-electricity 102

P

Pahlavi, Mohammad Reza 91
Pakistan people and languages 73; Kashmir territorial dispute 74
Pamir Mountains 82
Pampa, Argentina 136
Panama Canal Area (*formerly* Zone) *134*
Paris basin 26
Parthians 91
Pathet Lao 79
Pearl Harbour, Japanese attack (Dec '41) 87
Peary, Robert E. 14
Penn, William 126
Pennines 18
People's Action Party of Singapore 80
People's Chamber of GDR 34
People's Consultative Assembly of Indonesia 77
Perón, Eva 142
Perón, Juan Domingo, president of Argentina 142
Perry, *Commodore* Matthew 87
Pescadores islands 83
Peter the Great 70
Petrarch, Francisco Petrarca 49
Pilanesburg Game Reserve, South Africa *105*
Pilgrim Fathers (1620) 126
Pinochet, *General* Augusto 142
Plain of Lombardy 46
playa, salt encrusted lake 111
Ploesti oilfield 40
Pol Pot, Khmers Rouges leader 80
polders (Netherlands) *31*
Polish annexation of Teschen (Czechoslovakia) 38
Polish Corridor 33, 40
Polish national identity 40
Poltava, battle of (1709) 62
Pontic Mountains 90
Population trends
  Australia 110, 111; Bangladesh birthrate 73; Canada 121; China 82; Colombia 137; European 16; in France 25; Iceland 59; Indian growth problem 75; Indonesian redistribution 77; Italian emigration 50; Japanese distribution 86; Kenyan growth 101; Mexico 132; Mongolian nomads 71; New Zealand 117; Oceania 114, 115; Pakistan birth rate 72; Portuguese emigration 43; Swedish 19th and 20thC emigration 62; Taiwan since 1949 83; US immigration 126; USSR country to city migration 66; in West Germany 33; worldwide 10
Port and harbour facilities
  Al 'Adan, South Yemen 93; Australia 111; France 28; Hong Kong free port 85; Italy 49; Japan 86; Malta *51*; Mauritius, Port Louis 107; Mozambique 104, 105; Netherlands 31; New Zealand *118*; Poland 41; St Lawrence Seaway and Great Lakes 125, 129; Singapore 80; South Africa 105; United Kingdom 20
Portuguese colonization of Brazil 43, 141
Portuguese people and language 43
Prussia, King (*Kaiser*) of 33

Q

Qadhafi, *Colonel* Muammar 96
Qat, narcotic shrub 93
Qattara Depression 97
quebracho 'axe-breaker' hardwood 142
Quechua Indian people and language *140*, 141
Quemoy island (Taiwan) 83

R

Rawlings, *Flight-Lt.* J., Ghana 100
Reagan, Ronald, US president 126, 130
'Red Army' 70
Renaissance art in Italy 46, 49
Renaissance humanism 49
Revolutionary Command Council of Libya 96
Rhône-Saône basin 26
Riksdag Swedish parliament 62
Risorgimento, Italian unification 49
Rivera, Primo de 45
Riviera, French 27
Romanian people and language 39
Roosevelt, Franklin D., president of USA 126
Royal Canadian Mounted Police 121
Rub 'al Khali desert 93
Russo-Japanese War (1904-5) 70, 87

S

Sadat, Anwar as- 96
Sahara Desert 96
St Bernard tunnel 35
St Gothard tunnel 35
St Lawrence Seaway 125
Salazar, Antonio de Oliveira 43
Salish Indians 121
San Marino 49
Sandinista government, Nicaragua 130, 133
Sanguinetti, Julio Maria, president of Uruguay 143
Sarnay, José, president of Brazil 141
Sassanid dynasty of Persia 91
Scott, Robert F. 119
Scythians 69
Sea-fishing industry
  Canada 124; China 82; France 26, 29; Greek specialization 57; Icelandic exports 59; Japan 86; Netherlands 31; Nigeria 100; Oceania 115; Peru 140; Portugal 43; South Korea 85; Spain 45; Sri Lanka 75; United Kingdom *20*, 21; United States 130; West Germany 34; Yugoslavia 54
Sejm (Polish parliament) 40
Selassie, Emperor of Ethiopia 93
Seljuk Turks 89
Selvagens (Madeira Islands) 43
Senate, Australian Federal Parliament 110
Senate, of Belgium 31
Senate, Canadian Parliament 122
Senate, of France 26
Senate, of South Africa 105
Senate, US Congress 129
Shetland Islands, cession by Norway (1468) 17
Shagari, Shehu Nigerian president 100
Shintoism 86
shipping flags of convenience 100
Shura Consultative Council of Egypt 96
Sibelius, Jan 59
Siberian Uplands 65
Sierras, Spain 45
Slave trade 99
Slavs' migration 69
Slovak Socialist Republic 38
Snowy Mountains [irrigation] Scheme 111
South African people and languages 105
South China Sea oil and gas exploitation 80
South-East Asia Treaty Organization 80
Southern Uplands of Scotland 18
Sovkhoz state farm (USSR) 65
Space exploration 71, 126
Spanish-American War 132
Spanish Civil War (1936-39) 45
Spanish people and language 45
Spanish Sahara, Moroccan guerrilla war 95, 97
Spinola, *General* Antonio de 43
Sporádhes island group 56
Sri Lanka: Sinhalese-Tamil conflict 75
Stalin, Joseph 70
Stanley, Henry Morton (19thC explorer) 101
State Council of PRC 81
State Planning Commission (Gosplan) USSR 65
Storting, Norwegian parliament 61
Sudanese ethnic groups 98
Suez Canal 96, 97
Sumo wrestling 86
Sunni Muslims 93, 96
Supreme Court of USA 129
Supreme Revolutionary Council of Portugal 43
Supreme Soviet of the Soviet Union 69
Surinam peoples and languages 139
Sutherland Falls, New Zealand 117
Swedish people and culture 61, 62
Swedish welfare system 61, 62
Swiss Alps *35*
Swiss neutrality 35
Swiss people and languages 35
Szechwan Basin 82

T

Tacitus 62
Takla Makan desert 82
Taoism 81
Tartars 68, 70
Tasman, Abel 117
Taurus Mountains 90
temporali summer squalls 48
Thirty Years War (1618-1648), Swedish participation
Thracian islands 56
Tibetan Plateau 82
Titicaca, Lake 141
Tito, *Marshal* (Josip Broz) 53, 54
Tourism 22, 23, 26, 31, *35*, *37*, 45, 49, 51, 53, 57, 74, 85, 90, 91, 96, 102, 115, 132, 134, 135
Trade and external affairs
  Albania 57; Algeria 96; Argentina 142; Australia 112; Austria 38; Bulgaria 54; Burma 78; Canada 125; China 83, 130; Czechoslovakia 38; East Germany 35; Egypt 97; France 29; Gabon 101; Greece 57; Guinea 99; Hong Kong 85; Hungary 39; Indonesia 77; Ireland 23; Liberian iron ore and rubber 100; Malaysia 80; Mongolia 71; Morocco 95; Nigeria 100; North Korea 85; Norwegian merchant marine 60; Poland 41; Portugal 43; Romanian trading agreements 40; South Africa 106; South Korea 85; Spain 45; Switzerland 35; Taiwan 83; Thailand 80; United Kingdom 22, 41; USA 41, 130; USSR 67; West Germany 34, 41; Yugoslavia 54
Trafalgar, battle of (1805) 45
Transdanubia region (Hungary) 38
Transportation systems
  Albanian developments 57; Bangladesh coastal riverine *73*; China 82; French 28; Greek maritime 57; Egyptian road, rail and waterway 97; Italian roadways 49; Laotian waterways 79; Netherlands 31; New Zealand air links 118; Poland 41; South American waterways 136, 140; Tanzania-Zambia (Tan-Zam) Railway 102; United States 129; USSR air transport 67, pipelines 65, railway network 67, roads 67, waterways 65; Zimbabwe: Bulawayo-Harare rail link 105
Transylvanian Alps 40
Treaty of Paris (1783) 126
Treaty of Waitangi (1840) 117
Triple Entente 26
Troodos mountains 90
Trudeau, Pierre, Canadian premier 125
Trust territories of the Pacific 116
Tundra 14
Turan Lowland 65
Turcomans 91
Turfan Depression (W. China) 82
Turkic peoples of Central Asia 68
Turkish people and constitution 89
Tutsi-Hutu conflicts 102

U

Ugandan people and languages 102
Ugro-Finnish peoples 68
Ujamaa, Tanzanian self-help policy 102
Ulyanov, Vladimir (Lenin) 70
Unilateral Declaration of Independence, Rhodesia 104
United Nations
  Chinese admission (1971) 81, 83; Italian membership 49; Korean War (1950-53) 81, 85; Namibian independence 104; Palestine partition (1948) 91
Upper Silesian coalfield 40
Ural Mountains, mineral deposits 65
Urban VIII, pope 49
US
  people and language 126; commonwealth countries 134; states and cities 129
USSR
  first manned space flight (1961) 71; ideological rift with China 71; peoples and languages 67, 68; sport and cultural activities 68

V

Vale of Kashmir *75*
Vasco de Gama *see* Gama, Vasco da
Vatican *49*
Verdi, Giuseppi 46
Vietnam War (1964-73) 126, 130
Vietnamese people and languages 79
Vikings
  colonization 61, setlement of Kiev 69; trade and plunder 62
Vinci, Leonardo da 46, 49
Vlachs 57
volcanoes
  Cotopaxi 139; Etna 47; Heimaey Island 59; Indonesian 77; Japanese 86; Mauna Loa, Hawaii 116; Minoan sites on Thira 56; Mt. Erebus 119; Mt. Ruapehu, New Zealand 117; Stromboli 47; Vesuvius 47
Volga, river 16
Volta hydroelectric scheme 100

W

Walachia, union with Moldavia (1861) 40
Walloons of Belgium 31
War of American Independence 126
Warsaw Pact 17, 35
Washington, George 126
Wats, Buddhist temples 80
West Siberian Lowland 65
Western Ghats 75
Wien basin 36
William of Normandy 26
Wind power 62
Windward Islands, composition 135
World Court of Justice 104

YZ

Yakut (people of Siberia) 14
Yamato, House of 87
Yangzte Plain 82
Yogoslavia: abolition of monarchy 53; peoples and languages 52
Yunnan Plateau 82
Zambian ethnics groups 101
Zimbabwe people and languages 104
Zog I, King of Albania 57

Index to maps

The number in dark type which follows each name in the index refers to the map number where that feature or place will be found.

The geographical co-ordinates which follow the place name are sometimes only approximate but are close enough for the place name to be located.

An open square □ signifies that the name refers to an administrative division of a country while a solid square ■ follows the name of a country.

Rivers have been indexed to their mouth or to where they join another river. All rivers are followed by the symbol →.

The alphabetic order of names composed of two or more words is governed primarily by the first word and then by the second. This is an example of the rule:

East Tawas
Eastbourne
Easter Is.
Eastern Ghats
Eastleigh

Names composed of a proper name (Mexico) and a description (Gulf of) are positioned alphabetically by the proper name. If the same word occurs in the name of a town and a geographical feature, the town name is listed first followed by the name or names of the geographical features.

Names beginning with M', Mc are all indexed as if they were spelled Mac.

Names composed of the definite article (Le, La, Les, L') and a proper name are usually alphabetized by the proper name:

Havre, Le
Spezia, La
Wash, The

If the same place name occurs twice or more in the index and the places are in different countries, they will be followed by the country and be in the latter's alphabetical order:

Boston, U.K.
Boston, U.S.A.

If the same place name occurs two or more times in the index and all are in the same country, each is followed by the name of the administrative subdivision in which it is located. The names are placed in the alphabetical order of the subdivisions. For example:

Columbus, Ga., U.S.A.
Columbus, Miss., U.S.A.
Columbus, Ohio, U.S.A.

If there is a mixture of these situations, the primary order is fixed by the alphabetical sequence of the countries and the secondary order by that of the country subdivisions:

Rochester, U.K.
Rochester, Minn., U.S.A.
Rochester, N.Y., U.S.A.

Below is a list of abbreviations used in the index.

A.S.S.R. – Autonomous Soviet Socialist Republic
Ala. – Alabama
Arch. – Archipelago
Ariz. – Arizona
Ark. – Arkansas
B. – Baie, Bahia, Bay, Boca, Bucht, Bugt
B.C. – British Columbia
Br. – British
C. – Cabo, Cap, Cape
Calif. – California
Chan. – Channel
Col. – Colombia
Colo. – Colorado
Conn. – Connecticut
Cord. – Cordillera
D.C. – District of Columbia
Del. – Delaware
Dep. – Dependency
Des. – Desert
Dist. – District
Dom. Rep. – Dominican Republic
E. – East
Fd. – Fjord
Fed. – Federal, Federation
Fla. – Florida
Fr. – France, French
G. – Golfe, Golfo, Gulf, Guba
Ga. – Georgia
Gt. – Great
Hts. – Heights
I.(s) – Ile, Ilha, Insel, Isla, Island(s)
Ill. – Illinois
Ind. – Indiana
K. – Kap, Kapp
Kans. – Kansas
Ky. – Kentucky
L. – Lac, Lacul, Lago, Lagoa, Lake, Limni, Loch, Lough
La. – Louisiana
Ld. – Land
Mad. P. – Madhya Pradesh
Man. – Manitoba
Mass. – Massachusetts
Md. – Maryland
Mich. – Michigan
Minn. – Minnesota
Miss. – Mississippi
Mo. – Missouri
Mont. – Montana
Mt.(s) – Mont, Monta, Monti, Muntii, Montaña, Mount, Mountain(s)
N. – North, Northern
N.B. – New Brunswick
N.C. – North Carolina
N. Dak. – North Dakota
N.H. – New Hampshire
N.J. – New Jersey
N. Mex. – New Mexico
N.S. – Nova Scotia
N.S.W. – New South Wales
N.Y. – New York
N.Z. – New Zealand
Nat. Park – National Park
Nebr. – Nebraska
Neth. – Netherlands
Nev. – Nevada
Nfld. – Newfoundland
Nic. – Nicaragua
Nig. – Nigeria
Okla. – Oklahoma
Ont. – Ontario
Oreg. – Oregon
P. – Pass, Paso, Pasul
Pa. – Pennsylvania
Pak. – Pakistan
Pass. – Passage
Pen. – Peninsula
Pk. – Peak
Plat. – Plateau
Prov. – Province, Provincial
Pt. – Point
Pta. – Ponta, Punta
Pte. – Pointe
Qué. – Québec
R. – Rio, River
R.S.F.S.R. – Russian Soviet Federative Socialist Republic
Ra.(s) – Range(s)
Rep. – Republic
Res. – Reserve, Reservoir
S. – South
S. Africa – South Africa
S.C. – South Carolina
S. Dak. – South Dakota
S.S.R. – Soviet Socialist Republic
Sa. – Serra, Sierra
Sask. – Saskatchewan
Scot. – Scotland
Sd. – Sound
Sp. – Spain, Spanish
St. – Saint
Str. – Strait, Stretto
Tenn. – Tennessee
Terr. – Territory
Tex. – Texas
U.K. – United Kingdom
U.S.A. – United States of America
U.S.S.R. – Union of Soviet Socialist Republics
Ut. P. – Uttar Pradesh
Va. – Virginia
Vic. – Victoria
Vt. – Vermont
Wash. – Washington
W. – West
W. Va. – West Virginia
Wis. – Wisconsin
Wyo. – Wyoming
Yug. – Yugoslavia

A

Aachen **13** 50 47N 6 4 E
Aalborg = Ålborg **28** 57 2N 9 54 E
Aalen **13** 48 49N 10 6 E
A'âli en Nîl □ **50** 9 30N 31 30 E
Aalsmeer **12** 52 17N 4 43 E
Aalst **12** 50 56N 4 2 E
Aalten **12** 51 56N 6 35 E
Aarau **13** 47 23N 8 4 E
Aare → **13** 47 33N 8 14 E
Aarhus = Århus **28** 56 8N 10 11 E
Aarschot **12** 50 59N 4 49 E
Aba **49** 5 10N 7 19 E
Ābādān **45** 30 22N 48 20 E
Ābādeh **46** 31 8N 52 40 E
Abadla **49** 31 2N 2 45W
Abai **74** 25 58 S 55 54W
Abakan **31** 53 40N 91 10 E
Abancay **72** 13 35 S 72 55W
Abariringa **57** 2 50 S 171 40W
Abashiri **44** 44 0N 144 15 E
Abashiri-Wan **44** 44 0N 144 30 E
Abaya, L. **50** 6 30N 37 50 E
Abbay = Nîl el Azraq → **50** 15 38N 32 31 E
Abbeville, France **9** 50 6N 1 49 E
Abbeville, U.S.A. **66** 34 12N 82 21W
Abd al Kūrī **47** 12 5N 52 20 E
Abéché **50** 13 50N 20 35 E
Åbenrå **28** 55 3N 9 25 E
Abeokuta **49** 7 3N 3 19 E
Aberaeron **5** 52 15N 4 16W
Aberayron = Aberaeron **5** 52 15N 4 16W
Aberdare **5** 51 43N 3 27W
Aberdeen, U.K. **6** 57 9N 2 6W
Aberdeen, S. Dak., U.S.A. **67** 45 30N 98 30W
Aberdeen, Wash., U.S.A. **68** 47 0N 123 50W
Aberdovey **5** 52 33N 4 3W
Aberfeldy **6** 56 37N 3 50W
Abergavenny **5** 51 49N 3 1W
Aberystwyth **5** 52 25N 4 6W
Abidjan **49** 5 26N 3 58W
Abilene **67** 32 22N 99 40W
Abingdon **5** 51 40N 1 17W
Abitibi L. **62** 48 40N 79 40W
Abkhaz A.S.S.R. □ **35** 43 0N 41 0 E
Abkit **31** 64 10N 157 10 E
Åbo **27** 60 28N 22 15 E
Abohar **36** 30 10N 74 10 E
Aboméy **49** 7 10N 2 5 E
Abondance **11** 46 18N 6 43 E
Abong-Mbang **51** 4 0N 13 8 E
Abou-Deïa **50** 11 20N 19 20 E
Aboyne **6** 57 4N 2 48W
Abrantes **18** 39 24N 8 7W
Abreschviller **9** 48 39N 7 6 E
Abrets, Les **11** 45 32N 5 35 E
Abri **50** 20 50N 30 27 E
Abrud **15** 46 19N 23 5 E
Abruzzi □ **21** 42 15N 14 0 E
Absaroka Ra. **68** 44 40N 110 0W
Abū al Khaşīb **45** 30 25N 48 0 E
Abū 'Alī **45** 27 20N 49 27 E
Abu 'Arīsh **47** 16 53N 42 48 E
Abu Dhabi = Abū Z̧āby **46** 24 28N 54 22 E
Abû Dis **50** 19 12N 33 38 E
Abu Hamed **50** 19 32N 33 13 E
Abu Matariq **50** 10 59N 26 9 E
Abu Tig **50** 27 4N 31 15 E
Abû Zabad **50** 12 25N 29 10 E
Abū Z̧āby **46** 24 28N 54 22 E
Abuja **49** 9 16N 7 2 E
Abunā **72** 9 40 S 65 20W
Abunā → **72** 9 41 S 65 20W
Abwong **50** 9 2N 32 14 E
Acámbaro **69** 20 2N 100 44W
Acaponeta **69** 22 30N 105 22W
Acapulco **69** 16 51N 99 56W
Acatlán **69** 18 10N 98 3W
Acayucan **69** 17 57N 94 55W
Accous **10** 43 0N 0 36W
Accra **49** 5 35N 0 6W
Accrington **5** 53 46N 2 22W
Achalpur **36** 21 22N 77 32 E
Achill **7** 53 56N 9 55W
Achill Hd. **7** 53 59N 10 15W
Achill I. **7** 53 58N 10 5W
Achill Sound **7** 53 53N 9 55W
Achinsk **31** 56 20N 90 20 E
Acland, Mt. **55** 24 50 S 148 20 E
Aconcagua, Cerro **74** 32 39 S 70 0W
Aconquija, Mt. **74** 27 0 S 66 0W
Açores, Is. dos = Azores **1** 38 44N 29 0W
Acre = 'Akko **45** 32 55N 35 4 E
Acre □ **72** 9 1 S 71 0W
Ad Dawhah **46** 25 15N 51 35 E
Ada **67** 34 50N 96 45W
Adaja → **18** 41 32N 4 52W
Adamaoua, Massif de l' **50** 7 20N 12 20 E
Adamawa Highlands = Adamaoua, Massif de l' **50** 7 20N 12 20 E
Adamello, Mt. **20** 46 10N 10 34 E
Adams, Mt. **68** 46 10N 121 28W
Adam's Bridge **38** 9 15N 79 40 E
Adam's Peak **38** 6 48N 80 30 E
Adana **45** 37 0N 35 16 E
Adapazarı **45** 40 48N 30 25 E
Adarama **50** 17 10N 34 52 E
Adavale **56** 25 52 S 144 32 E
Adda → **20** 45 8N 9 53 E
Addis Ababa = Addis Abeba **50** 9 2N 38 42 E
Addis Abeba **50** 9 2N 38 42 E
Addis Alem **50** 9 0N 38 17 E
Addu Atoll **29** 0 30 S 73 0 E
Adelaide **56** 34 52 S 138 30 E
Aden = Al 'Adan **47** 12 45N 45 0 E
Aden, G. of **47** 12 30N 47 30 E
Adi Ugri **50** 14 58N 38 48 E
Adieu, C. **54** 32 0 S 132 10 E
Adige → **21** 45 9N 12 20 E
Adilabad **38** 19 33N 78 20 E
Adirondack Mts. **66** 44 0N 74 15W
Admer **49** 20 21N 5 27 E
Admiralty G. **54** 14 20 S 125 55 E
Admiralty Is. **56** 2 0 S 147 0 E
Adoni **38** 15 33N 77 18W
Adour → **10** 43 32N 1 32W
Adra **19** 36 43N 3 3W
Adrano **23** 37 40N 14 49 E
Adrar **49** 27 51N 0 11W
Adré **50** 13 40N 22 20 E
Adrī **50** 27 32N 13 2 E
Adrian **66** 41 55N 84 0W
Adriatic Sea **4** 43 0N 16 0 E
Adwa **50** 14 15N 38 52 E
Adzhar A.S.S.R. □ **35** 42 0N 42 0 E
Ægean Sea **4** 37 0N 25 0 E
Aerht'ai Shan **42** 46 40N 92 45 E
Afars & Issas, Terr. of = Djibouti ■ **47** 12 0N 43 0 E
Afghanistan ■ **46** 33 0N 65 0 E
Afgoi **47** 2 7N 44 59 E
Afuá **73** 0 15 S 50 20W
Afyonkarahisar **45** 38 45N 30 33 E
Agadez **49** 16 58N 7 59 E
Agadir **49** 30 28N 9 55W
Agano → **44** 37 57N 139 8 E
Agapa **31** 71 27N 89 15 E
Agboville **49** 5 55N 4 15W
Agde **10** 43 19N 3 28 E
Agde, C. d' **10** 43 16N 3 28 E
Agen **10** 44 12N 0 38 E
Aginskoye **31** 51 6N 114 32 E
Agly → **10** 42 46N 3 3 E
Agon **8** 49 2N 1 34W
Agout → **10** 43 47N 1 41 E
Agra **36** 27 17N 77 58 E
Agri → **23** 40 13N 16 44 E
Ağri Daği **45** 39 50N 44 15 E
Agrigento **22** 37 19N 13 33 E
Agrinion **26** 38 37N 21 27 E
Água Clara **73** 20 25 S 52 45W
Agua Prieta **69** 31 18N 109 34W
Aguadas **72** 5 40N 75 38W
Aguadilla **70** 18 27N 67 10W
Aguas Blancas **74** 24 15 S 69 55W
Aguascalientes **69** 21 53N 102 18W
Aguascalientes □ **69** 22 0N 102 30W
Aguilas **19** 37 23N 1 35W
Agulhas, C. **52** 34 52 S 20 0 E
Ahaggar **49** 23 0N 6 30 E
Ahiri **38** 19 30N 80 0 E
Ahlen **13** 51 45N 7 52 E
Ahmadabad **36** 23 0N 72 40 E
Ahmadnagar **38** 19 7N 74 46 E
Ahmadpur **36** 29 12N 71 10 E
Ahvāz **45** 31 20N 48 40 E
Ahvenanmaa = Åland **27** 60 15N 20 0 E
Ahwar **47** 13 30N 46 40 E
Aichi □ **44** 35 0N 137 15 E
Aigle, L' **8** 48 46N 0 38 E
Aignay-le-Duc **9** 47 40N 4 43 E
Aigoual, Mt. **10** 44 8N 3 35 E
Aigre **10** 45 54N 0 1 E
Aigueperse **10** 46 3N 3 13 E
Aigues → **11** 44 7N 4 43 E
Aigues-Mortes **11** 43 35N 4 12 E
Aigues-Mortes, G. d' **11** 43 31N 4 3 E
Aiguilles **11** 44 47N 6 51 E
Aiguillon **10** 44 18N 0 21 E
Aiguillon-sur-Mer, L' **10** 46 20N 1 18W
Aigurande **10** 46 27N 1 49 E
Aiken **66** 33 34N 81 50W
Aillant-sur-Tholon **9** 47 52N 3 20 E
Ailly-sur-Noye **9** 49 45N 2 20 E

Index

Ailsa Craig **6** 55 15N 5 7W
Aim **31** 59 0N 133 55 E
Aimorés **73** 19 30 S 41 4W
Ain □ **11** 46 5N 5 20 E
Ain → **11** 45 45N 5 11 E
Aïn Beïda **49** 35 50N 7 29 E
Aïn Ben Tili **49** 25 59N 9 27W
Aïn-Sefra **49** 32 47N 0 37W
Ainabo **47** 9 0N 46 25 E
Aïr **49** 18 30N 8 0 E
Airaines **9** 49 58N 1 55 E
Airdrie **6** 55 53N 3 57W
Aire →, France **9** 49 18N 4 49 E
Aire →, U.K. **5** 53 42N 0 55W
Aire-sur-la-Lys **9** 50 37N 2 22 E
Aire-sur-l'Adour **10** 43 42N 0 15W
Airvault **8** 46 50N 0 8W
Aisne □ **9** 49 42N 3 40 E
Aisne → **9** 49 26N 2 50 E
Aiud **25** 46 19N 23 44 E
Aix-en-Provence **11** 43 32N 5 27 E
Aix-la-Chapelle = Aachen **13** 50 47N 6 4 E
Aix-les-Bains **11** 45 41N 5 53 E
Aixe-sur-Vienne **10** 45 47N 1 9 E
Áíyina **26** 37 45N 23 26 E
Aiyion **26** 38 15N 22 5 E
Aizenay **8** 46 44N 1 38W
Ajaccio **11** 41 55N 8 40 E
Ajaccio, G. d' **11** 41 52N 8 40 E
Ajanta Ra. **38** 20 28N 75 50 E
Ajdâbiyah **50** 30 54N 20 4 E
Ajmer **36** 26 28N 74 37 E
Akashi **44** 34 45N 135 0 E
Akershus fylke □ **28** 60 0N 11 10 E
Aketi **51** 2 38N 23 47 E
Akhelóös → **26** 38 36N 21 14 E
Akhisar **45** 38 56N 27 48 E
Akhmîm **50** 26 31N 31 47 E
Akimiski I. **62** 52 50N 81 30W
Akita **44** 39 45N 140 7 E
Akjoujt **49** 19 45N 14 15W
'Akko **45** 32 55N 35 4 E
Akobo → **50** 7 48N 33 3 E
Akola **36** 20 42N 77 2 E
Akordat **50** 15 30N 37 40 E
Akranes **27** 64 19N 21 58W
Akreïjit **49** 18 19N 9 11W
Akron **66** 41 7N 81 31W
Akrotíri, Ákra **26** 40 26N 25 27 E
Aksaray **45** 38 25N 34 2 E
Aksarka **30** 66 31N 67 50 E
Akşehir **45** 38 18N 31 30 E
Aksenovo Zilovskoye **31** 53 20N 117 40 E
Aksum **50** 14 5N 38 40 E
Aktyubinsk **30** 50 17N 57 10 E
Aku **49** 6 40N 7 18 E
Akure **49** 7 15N 5 5 E
Akureyri **27** 65 40N 18 6W
Al 'Adan **47** 12 45N 45 0 E
Al Amādīyah **45** 37 5N 43 30 E
Al Amārah **45** 31 55N 47 15 E
Al 'Aqabah **45** 29 31N 35 0 E
Al Başrah **45** 30 30N 47 50 E
Al Bu'ayrāt **50** 31 24N 15 44 E
Al Ḩadīthah **45** 31 28N 37 8 E
Al Hāmad **45** 31 30N 39 30 E
Al Ḩasakah **45** 36 35N 40 45 E
Al Ḩawrah **47** 13 50N 47 35 E
Al Ḩawţah **47** 16 5N 48 20 E
Al Ḩayy **45** 32 5N 46 5 E
Al Ḩijāz **47** 26 0N 37 30 E
Al Ḩillah **45** 32 30N 44 25 E
Al Hindīyah **45** 32 30N 44 10 E
Al Hoceïma **49** 35 8N 3 58W
Al Ḩudaydah **47** 14 50N 43 0 E
Al Hūfuf **45** 25 25N 49 45 E
Al Irq **50** 29 5N 21 35 E
Al Jāfūrah **45** 25 0N 50 15 E
Al Jaghbūb **50** 29 42N 24 38 E
Al Jawf **50** 24 10N 23 24 E
Al Jazirah, Asia **45** 33 30N 44 0 E
Al Jazirah, Libya **50** 26 10N 21 20 E
Al Junaynah **50** 13 27N 22 45 E
Al Khalīl **45** 31 32N 35 6 E
Al Khalūf **47** 20 30N 58 13 E
Al Kufrah **50** 24 17N 23 15 E
Al Kūt **45** 32 30N 46 0 E
Al Kuwayt **45** 29 30N 47 30 E
Al Lādhiqīyah **45** 35 30N 35 45 E
Al Lidām **47** 20 33N 44 45 E
Al Luḩayyah **47** 15 45N 42 40 E
Al Madīnah **47** 24 35N 39 52 E
Al Manāmāh **46** 26 10N 50 30 E
Al Marj **50** 32 25N 20 30 E
Al Mawşil **45** 36 15N 43 5 E
Al Mubarraz **45** 25 30N 49 40 E
Al Muḩarraq **46** 26 15N 50 40 E
Al Mukallā **47** 14 33N 49 2 E
Al Mukhā **47** 13 18N 43 15 E
Al Qaşabát **50** 32 39N 14 1 E
Al Qaţīf **45** 26 35N 50 0 E
Al Qaţrūn **50** 24 56N 15 3 E
Al Quds = Jerusalem **45** 31 47N 35 10 E
Al Qurnah **45** 31 1N 47 25 E
Al Uqaylah ash Sharqīgah **50** 30 12N 19 10 E
Al 'Uthmānīyah **45** 25 5N 49 22 E
Alabama □ **66** 33 0N 87 0W
Alabama → **66** 31 8N 87 57W
Alagoas □ **73** 9 0 S 36 0W
Alagoinhas **73** 12 7 S 38 20W
Alajuela **70** 10 2N 84 8W
Álamos **69** 27 1N 108 56W
Alamosa **68** 37 30N 106 0W
Åland **27** 60 15N 20 0 E
Alandur **38** 13 0N 80 15 E
Alapayevsk **30** 57 52N 61 42 E
Alaska □ **61** 65 0N 150 0W
Alaska, G. of **61** 58 0N 145 0W
Alatyr **33** 54 45N 46 35 E
Alba **20** 44 41N 8 1 E
Alba Iulia **25** 46 8N 23 39 E
Albacete **19** 39 0N 1 50W
Albania ■ **26** 41 0N 20 0 E
Albany, Australia **54** 35 1 S 117 58 E
Albany, Ga., U.S.A. **66** 31 40N 84 10W
Albany, N.Y., U.S.A. **66** 42 35N 73 47W
Albany, Oreg., U.S.A. **68** 44 41N 123 0W
Albany → **62** 52 17N 81 31W
Albarracín, Sierra de **19** 40 30N 1 30W
Albatross B. **56** 12 45 S 141 30 E
Albemarle **66** 35 27N 80 15W
Albemarle Sd. **66** 36 0N 76 30W
Alberche → **18** 39 58N 4 46W
Albert **9** 50 0N 2 38 E
Albert, L. = Mobutu Sese Seko, L. **51** 1 30N 31 0 E
Albert Lea **67** 43 32N 93 20W
Albert Nile → **51** 3 36N 32 2 E
Alberta □ **64** 54 40N 115 0W
Albertville = Kalemie **51** 5 55 S 29 9 E
Albertville **11** 45 40N 6 22 E
Albi **10** 43 56N 2 9 E
Albion **66** 42 15N 84 45W
Ålborg **28** 57 2N 9 54 E
Alborz, Reshteh-ye Kūhhā-ye **46** 36 0N 52 0 E
Albuquerque **68** 35 5N 106 47W
Alburquerque **18** 39 15N 6 59W
Albury **56** 36 3 S 146 56 E
Alcalá de Henares **19** 40 28N 3 22W
Alcalá la Real **18** 37 27N 3 57W
Alcamo **22** 37 59N 12 55 E
Alcaníz **19** 41 2N 0 8W
Alcântara, Brazil **73** 2 20 S 44 30W
Alcántara, Spain **18** 39 41N 6 57W
Alcaraz, Sierra de **19** 38 40N 2 20W
Alcaudete **18** 37 35N 4 5W
Alcázar de San Juan **19** 39 24N 3 12W
Alcira **19** 39 9N 0 30W
Alcobaça **18** 39 32N 9 0W
Alcoy **19** 38 43N 0 30W
Aldabra Is. **2** 9 22 S 46 28 E
Aldan **31** 58 40N 125 30 E
Aldan → **31** 63 28N 129 35 E
Aldeburgh **5** 52 9N 1 35 E
Alderney **8** 49 42N 2 12W
Aldershot **5** 51 15N 0 43W
Aleg **49** 17 3N 13 55W
Alejandro Selkirk, I. **58** 33 50 S 80 15W
Aleksandrovsk-Sakhalinskiy **31** 50 50N 142 20 E
Aleksandrovskiy Zavod **31** 50 40N 117 50 E
Alençon **8** 48 27N 0 4 E
Aleppo = Ḩalab **45** 36 10N 37 15 E
Aléria **11** 42 5N 9 26 E
Alès **11** 44 9N 4 5 E
Alessándria **20** 44 54N 8 37 E
Ålesund **27** 62 28N 6 12 E
Alet-les-Bains **10** 42 59N 2 14 E
Aleutian Is. **57** 52 0N 175 0W
Aleutian Trench **57** 48 0N 180 0 E
Alexander B. **52** 28 36 S 16 33 E
Alexander City **66** 32 58N 85 57W
Alexandria = El Iskandarîya **50** 31 0N 30 0 E
Alexandria, Canada **64** 52 35N 122 27W
Alexandria, S. Africa **52** 33 38 S 26 28 E
Alexandria, La., U.S.A. **67** 31 20N 92 30W
Alexandria, Va., U.S.A. **66** 38 47N 77 1W
Alexandrina, L. **56** 35 25 S 139 10 E
Alexandroúpolis **26** 40 50N 25 54 E
Alexis Creek **64** 52 10N 123 20W
Alford **6** 57 13N 2 42W
Alfreton **5** 53 6N 1 22W
Alga **30** 49 53N 57 20 E
Algarve **18** 36 58N 8 20W
Algeciras **18** 36 9N 5 28W
Algemesí **19** 39 11N 0 27W
Alger **49** 36 42N 3 8 E
Algeria ■ **49** 28 30N 2 0 E
Alghero **22** 40 34N 8 20 E
Algiers = Alger **49** 36 42N 3 8 E
Algoa B. **52** 33 50 S 25 45 E
Alhama de Murcia **19** 37 51N 1 25W
Alhambra **68** 34 2N 118 10W
Aliákmon → **26** 40 30N 22 36 E
Alibo **50** 9 52N 37 5 E
Alicante **19** 38 23N 0 30W
Alice Springs **54** 23 40 S 133 50 E
Aligarh **36** 27 55N 78 10 E
Alingsås **28** 57 56N 12 31 E
Alipur **36** 29 25N 70 55 E
Alipur Duar **37** 26 30N 89 35 E
Aliquippa **66** 40 38N 80 18W
Aliwal North **52** 30 45 S 26 45 E
Aljustrel **18** 37 55N 8 10W
Alkmaar **12** 52 37N 4 45 E
All American Canal **68** 32 45N 115 0W
Allahabad **37** 25 25N 81 58 E
Allakh-Yun **31** 60 50N 137 5 E
Allanche **10** 45 14N 2 57 E
Allassac **10** 45 15N 1 29 E
Allegheny → **66** 40 27N 80 0W
Allegheny Mts. **66** 38 0N 80 0W
Allègre **10** 45 12N 3 41 E
Allen, Bog of **7** 53 15N 7 0W
Allen, L. **7** 54 12N 8 5W
Allende **69** 28 20N 100 51W
Allentown **66** 40 36N 75 30W
Alleppey **38** 9 30N 76 28 E
Aller → **13** 52 57N 9 10 E
Allevard **11** 45 24N 6 5 E
Allier □ **10** 46 25N 3 0 E
Allier → **9** 46 57N 3 4 E
Alloa **6** 56 7N 3 49W
Allos **11** 44 15N 6 38 E
Alma, Canada **63** 48 35N 71 40W
Alma, U.S.A. **66** 43 25N 84 40W
Alma Ata **30** 43 15N 76 57 E
Almada **18** 38 40N 9 9W
Almadén **18** 38 49N 4 52W
Almansa **19** 38 51N 1 5W
Almanzor, Pico de **18** 40 15N 5 18W
Almanzora → **19** 37 14N 1 46W
Almazán **19** 41 30N 2 30W
Almelo **12** 52 22N 6 42 E
Almendralejo **18** 38 41N 6 26W
Almería **19** 36 52N 2 27W
Almirante **70** 9 10N 82 30W
Almora **37** 29 38N 79 40 E
Alnwick **5** 55 25N 1 42W
Alor **40** 8 15 S 124 30 E
Alor Setar **41** 6 7N 100 22 E
Alpena **62** 45 6N 83 24W
Alpes-de-Haute-Provence □ **11** 44 8N 6 10 E
Alpes-Maritimes □ **11** 43 55N 7 10 E
Alpha **56** 23 39 S 146 37 E
Alsace **9** 48 15N 7 25 E
Alsask **65** 51 21N 109 59W
Alsásua **19** 42 54N 2 10W
Alsten **27** 65 58N 12 40 E
Alta **27** 69 57N 23 10 E
Alta Gracia **74** 31 40 S 64 30W
Altaelva → **27** 69 46N 23 45 E
Altafjorden **27** 70 5N 23 5 E
Altagracia **72** 10 45N 71 30W
Altai = Aerht'ai Shan **42** 46 40N 92 45 E
Altamaha → **66** 31 19N 81 17W
Altamira **73** 3 12 S 52 10W
Altkirch **9** 47 37N 7 15 E
Altmühl → **13** 48 54N 11 54 E
Alto Molocue **51** 15 50 S 37 35 E
Alton **67** 38 55N 90 5W
Altona **13** 53 32N 9 56 E
Altoona **66** 40 32N 78 24W
Altun Shan **42** 38 30N 88 0 E
Alùla **47** 11 50N 50 45 E
Alvarado **69** 18 46N 95 46W
Alvesta **28** 56 54N 14 35 E
Älvsborgs län □ **28** 58 30N 12 30 E
Älvsbyn **27** 65 40N 21 0 E
Alwar **36** 27 38N 76 34 E
Alxa Zuoqi **42** 38 50N 105 40 E
Alyangula **55** 13 55 S 136 30 E
Alyaskitovyy **31** 64 45N 141 30 E
Alyata **35** 39 58N 49 25 E
Alyth **6** 56 38N 3 15W
Alzey **13** 49 48N 8 4 E
Am Dam **50** 12 40N 20 35 E
Am-Timan **50** 11 0N 20 10 E
Amadeus, L. **54** 24 54 S 131 0 E
Amâdi, Sudan **50** 5 29N 30 25 E
Amadi, Zaïre **51** 3 40N 26 40 E
Amagasaki **44** 34 42N 135 20 E
Amakusa-Shotō **44** 32 15N 130 10 E
Amalner **36** 21 5N 75 5 E
Amapá **73** 2 5N 50 50W
Amapá □ **73** 1 40N 52 0W
Amarillo **67** 35 14N 101 46W
Amaro, Mt. **21** 42 5N 14 6 E
Amasya **45** 40 40N 35 50 E
Amatitlán **69** 14 29N 90 38W
Amazon = Amazonas → **72** 0 5 S 50 0W
Amazonas → **72** 0 5 S 50 0W
Ambala **36** 30 23N 76 56 E
Ambalavao **53** 21 50 S 46 56 E
Ambam **51** 2 20N 11 15 E
Ambanja **53** 13 40 S 48 27 E
Ambarchik **31** 69 40N 162 20 E
Ambato **72** 1 5 S 78 42W
Ambatolampy **53** 19 20 S 47 35 E
Ambatondrazaka **53** 17 55 S 48 28 E
Ambérieu-en-Bugey **11** 45 57N 5 20 E
Ambert **10** 45 33N 3 44 E
Ambikapur **37** 23 15N 83 15 E
Ambilobé **53** 13 10 S 49 3 E
Ambleside **5** 54 26N 2 58W
Ambo **72** 10 5 S 76 10W
Ambon **40** 3 35 S 128 20 E
Ambositra **53** 20 31 S 47 25 E
Amboyna I. **39** 7 50N 112 50 E
Ambriz **51** 7 48 S 13 8 E
Amderma **30** 69 45N 61 30 E
Ameca **69** 20 33N 104 2W
Ameca → **69** 20 41N 105 18W
Ameland **12** 53 27N 5 45 E
Amélie-les-Bains-Palalda **10** 42 29N 2 41 E
Amen **31** 68 45N 180 0 E
American Samoa ■ **58** 14 20 S 170 40W
Americus **66** 32 0N 84 10W
Amersfoort **12** 52 9N 5 23 E
Ames **67** 42 0N 93 40W
Amga **31** 60 50N 132 0 E
Amga → **31** 62 38N 134 32 E
Amgu **31** 45 45N 137 15 E
Amgun → **31** 52 56N 139 38 E
Amherst **63** 45 48N 64 8W
Amherstburg **62** 42 6N 83 6W
Amiata, Mte. **21** 42 54N 11 40 E
Amiens **9** 49 54N 2 16 E
Amirante Is. **2** 6 0 S 53 0 E
Amlwch **5** 53 24N 4 21W
'Ammān **45** 31 57N 35 52 E
Ammanford **5** 51 48N 4 0W
Amorgós **26** 36 50N 25 57 E
Amos **62** 48 35N 78 5W
Amoy = Xiamen **43** 24 25N 118 4 E
Ampanihy **53** 24 40 S 44 45 E
Amravati **36** 20 55N 77 45 E
Amreli **36** 21 35N 71 17 E
Amritsar **36** 31 35N 74 57 E
Amroha **36** 28 53N 78 30 E
Amrum **13** 54 37N 8 21 E
Amsterdam, Neth. **12** 52 23N 4 54 E
Amsterdam, U.S.A. **66** 42 58N 74 10W
Amsterdam, I. **2** 37 30 S 77 30 E
Amudarya → **30** 43 40N 59 0 E
Amund Ringnes I. **3** 78 20N 96 25W
Amundsen Sea **60** 72 0 S 115 0W
Amur → **31** 52 56N 141 10 E
Amursk **31** 50 14N 136 54 E
Amurzet **31** 47 50N 131 5 E
An Najaf **45** 32 3N 44 15 E
An Nāşirīyah **45** 31 0N 46 15 E
An Nhon **41** 13 55N 109 7 E
An Nîl □ **50** 19 30N 33 0 E
An Nîl el Abyad □ **50** 14 0N 32 15 E
An Nîl el Azraq □ **50** 12 30N 34 30 E
An Nu'ayrīyah **45** 27 30N 48 30 E
An Uaimh **7** 53 39N 6 40W
Anabar → **31** 73 8N 113 36 E
Anaconda **68** 46 7N 113 0W
Anacortes **68** 48 30N 122 40W
Anadolu **45** 38 0N 30 0 E
Anadyr **31** 64 35N 177 20 E
Anadyr → **31** 64 55N 176 5 E
Anadyrskiy Zaliv **31** 64 0N 180 0 E
Anaheim **68** 33 50N 118 0W
Anakapalle **38** 17 42N 83 6 E
Analalava **53** 14 35 S 48 0 E
Anamur **45** 36 8N 32 58 E
Anan **44** 33 54N 134 40 E
Anápolis **73** 16 15 S 48 50W
Anārak **46** 33 25N 53 40 E
Anatolia = Anadolu **45** 38 0N 30 0 E
Añatuya **74** 28 20 S 62 50W
Anaye **50** 19 15N 12 50 E
Ancenis **8** 47 21N 1 10W
Anchorage **61** 61 10N 149 50W
Ancohuma, Nevada **72** 16 0 S 68 50W
Ancona **21** 43 37N 13 30 E
Ancud **74** 42 0 S 73 50W
Ancud, G. de **74** 42 0 S 73 0W
Åndalsnes **27** 62 35N 7 43 E
Andalucía □ **18** 37 35N 5 0W
Andalusia **66** 31 19N 86 30W
Andaman Is. **41** 12 30N 92 30 E
Andaman Sea **41** 13 0N 96 0 E
Andaman Str. **41** 12 15N 92 20 E
Andara **52** 18 2 S 21 9 E
Andelot **9** 48 15N 5 18 E
Andelys, Les **8** 49 15N 1 25 E
Andenne **12** 50 30N 5 5 E
Andernos-les-Bains **10** 44 44N 1 6W
Anderson, Ind., U.S.A. **66** 40 5N 85 40W
Anderson, S.C., U.S.A. **66** 34 32N 82 40W
Andes, Cord. de los **72** 20 0 S 68 0W
Andfjorden **27** 69 10N 16 20 E
Andhra Pradesh □ **38** 16 0N 79 0 E
Andikíthira **26** 35 52N 23 15 E
Andizhan **30** 41 10N 72 0 E
Andoany **53** 13 25 S 48 16 E
Andorra ■ **19** 42 30N 1 30 E
Andorra La Vella **19** 42 31N 1 32 E
Andover **5** 51 13N 1 29W
Ándria **23** 41 13N 16 17 E
Andriba **53** 17 30 S 46 58 E
Andropov **33** 58 5N 38 50 E
Ándros **26** 37 50N 24 57 E
Andros I. **70** 24 30N 78 0W
Andújar **18** 38 3N 4 5W
Andulo **51** 11 25 S 16 45 E
Aného **49** 6 12N 1 34 E
Aneto, Pico de **19** 42 37N 0 40 E
Angara → **31** 58 30N 97 0 E
Angarsk **31** 52 30N 104 0 E
Ånge **27** 62 31N 15 35 E
Ängelholm **28** 56 15N 12 58 E
Angels Camp **68** 38 8N 120 30W
Ångermanälven → **27** 62 40N 18 0 E
Angers **8** 47 30N 0 35W
Angerville **9** 48 19N 2 0 E
Ängesån → **27** 66 50N 22 15 E
Angkor **41** 13 22N 103 50 E
Anglesey **5** 53 17N 4 20W
Anglet **10** 43 29N 1 31W
Anglin → **10** 46 42N 0 52 E
Anglure **9** 48 35N 3 50 E
Angmagssalik **3** 65 40N 37 20W
Ango **51** 4 10N 26 5 E
Angol **74** 37 56 S 72 45W
Angola ■ **51** 12 0 S 18 0 E
Angoulême **10** 45 39N 0 10 E
Angoumois **10** 45 50N 0 25 E
Angren **30** 41 1N 70 12 E
Anguilla **70** 18 14N 63 5W
Angus, Braes of **6** 56 51N 3 10W
Anholt **28** 56 42N 11 33 E
Anhui □ **43** 32 0N 117 0 E
Anin **41** 15 36N 97 50 E
Anjidiv I. **38** 14 40N 74 10 E
Anjou **8** 47 20N 0 15W
Anjozorobe **53** 18 22 S 47 52 E
Anju **43** 39 36N 125 40 E
Anka **49** 12 13N 5 58 E
Ankang **43** 32 40N 109 1 E
Ankara **45** 40 0N 32 54 E
Ankazoabo **53** 22 18 S 44 31 E
Ankazobe **53** 18 20 S 47 10 E
Ankoro **51** 6 45 S 26 55 E
Ann Arbor **66** 42 17N 83 45W
Annaba **49** 36 50N 7 46 E
Annalee → **7** 54 3N 7 15W
Annam = Trung-Phan **41** 16 0N 108 0 E
Annamitique, Chaîne **41** 17 0N 106 0 E
Annan **6** 55 0N 3 17W
Annan → **6** 54 58N 3 18W
Annapolis **66** 39 0N 76 30W
Annecy **11** 45 55N 6 8 E
Annecy, L. d' **11** 45 52N 6 10 E
Annemasse **11** 46 12N 6 16 E
Anniston **66** 33 45N 85 50W
Annonay **11** 45 15N 4 40 E
Annot **11** 43 58N 6 38 E
Annotto Bay **70** 18 17N 77 3W
Anqing **43** 30 30N 117 3 E
Ansbach **13** 49 17N 10 34 E
Anse, L' **62** 46 47N 88 28W
Anshun **43** 26 18N 105 57 E
Ansirabe **53** 19 55 S 47 2 E
Anson B. **54** 13 20 S 130 6 E
Ansongo **49** 15 25N 0 35 E
Anstruther **6** 56 14N 2 40W
Antabamba **72** 14 40 S 73 0W
Antakya **45** 36 14N 36 10 E
Antalaha **53** 14 57 S 50 20 E
Antalya **45** 36 52N 30 45 E
Antalya Körfezi **45** 36 15N 31 30 E
Antananarivo **53** 18 55 S 47 31 E
Antarctic Pen. **60** 67 0 S 60 0W
Antarctica **60** 90 0 S 0 0 E
Antequera **18** 37 5N 4 33W
Anti Atlas **49** 30 0N 8 30W
Antibes **11** 43 34N 7 6 E
Antibes, C. d' **11** 43 31N 7 7 E
Anticosti, I. d' **63** 49 30N 63 0W
Antifer, C. d' **8** 49 41N 0 10 E
Antigo **62** 45 8N 89 5W
Antigua, Guat. **69** 14 34N 90 41W
Antigua, W. Indies **70** 17 0N 61 50W
Antigua & Barbuda ■ **70** 17 20N 61 48W
Antilla **70** 20 40N 75 50W
Antioch **68** 38 7N 121 45W
Antioche, Pertuis d' **10** 46 6N 1 20W
Antioquia **72** 6 40N 75 55W
Antipodes Is. **57** 49 45 S 178 40 E
Antofagasta **74** 23 50 S 70 30W
Antongila, Helodrano **53** 15 30 S 49 50 E
Antrain **8** 48 28N 1 30W
Antrim **7** 54 43N 6 13W
Antrim □ **7** 54 55N 6 20W
Antrim, Mts. of **7** 54 57N 6 8W
Antsalova **53** 18 40 S 44 37 E
Antsiranana **53** 12 25 S 49 20 E
Antsohihy **53** 14 50 S 47 59 E
Antwerp = Antwerpen **12** 51 13N 4 25 E
Antwerpen **12** 51 13N 4 25 E
Antwerpen □ **12** 51 15N 4 40 E
Anupgarh **36** 29 10N 73 10 E
Anuradhapura **38** 8 22N 80 28 E
Anvers = Antwerpen **12** 51 13N 4 25 E
Anxious B. **54** 33 24 S 134 45 E
Anyang **42** 36 5N 114 21 E
Anzhero-Sudzhensk **30** 56 10N 86 0 E
Ánzio **22** 41 28N 12 37 E
Aomori **44** 40 45N 140 45 E
Aosta **20** 45 43N 7 20 E
Aoudéras **49** 17 45N 8 20 E
Aoulef el Arab **49** 26 55N 1 2 E
Apalachee B. **66** 30 0N 84 0W
Apalachicola **66** 29 40N 85 0W
Apalachicola → **66** 29 40N 85 0W
Aparri **40** 18 22N 121 38 E
Apatzingan **69** 19 5N 102 21W
Apeldoorn **12** 52 13N 5 57 E
Apennines **20** 44 20N 10 20 E
Apia **57** 13 50 S 171 50W
Apizaco **69** 19 25N 98 9W
Aplao **72** 16 0 S 72 40W
Apolo **72** 14 30 S 68 30W
Apostle Is. **62** 47 0N 90 30W
Apostolos Andreas, C. **45** 35 42N 34 35 E
Appalachian Mts. **66** 38 0N 80 0W
Appennini **23** 41 0N 15 0 E
Appleby **5** 54 35N 2 29W
Appleton **67** 44 17N 88 25W
Apt **11** 43 53N 5 24 E
Apulia = Púglia □ **23** 41 0N 16 30 E
Apure → **72** 7 37N 66 25W
Aqîq **50** 18 14N 38 12 E
Aquidauana **73** 20 30 S 55 50W
Áquila, L' **21** 42 21N 13 24 E
Aquiles Serdán **69** 28 36N 105 53W
Ar Rachidiya **49** 31 58N 4 20W
Ar Riyāḑ **47** 24 41N 46 42 E
Ar Ruţbah **45** 33 0N 40 15 E
Ara **37** 25 35N 84 32 E
'Arab, Bahr el → **50** 8 50N 29 30 E
Arab, Shatt al **45** 30 0N 48 31 E
Arabia **47** 25 0N 45 0 E
Arabian Desert = Es Sahrâ' Esh Sharqîya **50** 27 30N 32 30 E
Arabian Gulf = Gulf, The **46** 27 0N 50 0 E
Arabian Sea **29** 16 0N 65 0 E
Aracaju **73** 10 55 S 37 4W
Aracati **73** 4 30 S 37 44W
Araçatuba **73** 21 10 S 50 30W
Aracena **18** 37 53N 6 38W
Arad **16** 46 10N 21 20 E
Arada **50** 15 0N 20 20 E
Arafura Sea **40** 9 0 S 135 0 E
Aragón □ **19** 41 25N 1 0W
Aragón → **19** 42 13N 1 44W
Araguacema **73** 8 50 S 49 20W
Araguaia → **73** 5 21 S 48 41W
Araguari **73** 18 38 S 48 11W
Arak, Algeria **49** 25 20N 3 45 E
Arāk, Iran **45** 34 0N 49 40 E
Aral Sea = Aralskoye More **30** 44 30N 60 0 E
Aralsk **30** 46 50N 61 20 E
Aralskoye More **30** 44 30N 60 0 E
Aramac **56** 22 58 S 145 14 E
Aran I. **7** 55 0N 8 30W
Aran Is. **7** 53 5N 9 42W
Aranjuez **18** 40 1N 3 40W
Aranos **52** 24 9 S 19 7 E
Araouane **49** 18 55N 3 30W
Araraquara **73** 21 50 S 48 0W
Ararat **56** 37 16 S 143 0 E
Ararat, Mt. = Ağri Daği **45** 39 50N 44 15 E
Aras, Rūd-e → **45** 39 10N 47 10 E
Araya, Pen. de **72** 10 40N 64 0W
Arbatax **22** 39 57N 9 42 E
Arbaza **31** 52 40N 92 30 E
Arbīl **45** 36 15N 44 5 E
Arbois **9** 46 55N 5 46 E
Arbresle, L' **11** 45 50N 4 36 E
Arbroath **6** 56 34N 2 35W
Arc **9** 47 28N 5 34 E
Arc → **11** 45 34N 6 12 E
Arcachon **10** 44 40N 1 10W
Arcachon, Bassin d' **10** 44 42N 1 10W
Arcadia **66** 27 20N 81 50W
Archangel = Arkhangelsk **30** 64 40N 41 0 E
Archer → **56** 13 28 S 141 41 E
Arcila = Asilah **49** 35 29N 6 0W
Arcis-sur-Aube **9** 48 32N 4 10 E

Arcos **19** 41 12N 2 16W
Arcot **38** 12 53N 79 20 E
Arcs, Les **11** 43 27N 6 29 E
Arctic Ocean **3** 78 0N 160 0W
Arda → **25** 41 40N 26 29 E
Ardabīl **45** 38 15N 48 18 E
Ardèche □ **11** 44 42N 4 16 E
Ardèche → **11** 44 16N 4 39 E
Ardee **7** 53 51N 6 32W
Ardennes **12** 50 0N 5 10 E
Ardennes □ **9** 49 35N 4 40 E
Ardentes **9** 46 45N 1 50 E
Ardgour **6** 56 45N 5 25W
Ardmore **67** 34 10N 97 5W
Ardnacrusha **7** 52 43N 8 38W
Ardnamurchan, Pt. of **6** 56 44N 6 14W
Ardres **9** 50 50N 2 0 E
Ardrossan **6** 55 39N 4 50W
Ards □ **7** 54 35N 5 30W
Ards Pen. **7** 54 30N 5 25W
Arecibo **70** 18 29N 66 42W
Arendal **28** 58 28N 8 46 E
Arequipa **72** 16 20 S 71 30W
Arero **50** 4 41N 38 50 E
Arès **10** 44 47N 1 8W
Arévalo **18** 41 3N 4 43W
Arezzo **21** 43 28N 11 50 E
Argelès-Gazost **10** 43 0N 0 6W
Argelès-sur-Mer **10** 42 34N 3 1 E
Argens → **11** 43 24N 6 44 E
Argent-sur-Sauldre **9** 47 33N 2 25 E
Argentan **8** 48 45N 0 1W
Argentário, Mte. **21** 42 23N 11 11 E
Argentat **10** 45 6N 1 56 E
Argenteuil **9** 48 57N 2 14 E
Argentière-la-Bessée, L' **11** 44 47N 6 33 E
Argentina ■ **74** 35 0 S 66 0W
Argentino, L. **74** 50 10 S 73 0W
Argenton-Château **8** 46 59N 0 27W
Argenton-sur-Creuse **10** 46 36N 1 30 E
Argeş □ **25** 45 0N 24 45 E
Argeş → **25** 44 30N 25 50 E
Argo **50** 19 28N 30 30 E
Argolikós Kólpos **26** 37 20N 22 52 E
Argonne **9** 49 10N 5 0 E
Árgos **26** 37 40N 22 43 E
Argostólion **26** 38 12N 20 33 E
Argun → **31** 53 20N 121 28 E
Argungu **49** 12 40N 4 31 E
Århus **28** 56 8N 10 11 E
Arica, Chile **72** 18 32 S 70 20W
Arica, Colombia **72** 2 0 S 71 50W
Arid, C. **54** 34 1 S 123 10 E
Ariège □ **10** 42 56N 1 30 E
Ariège → **10** 43 30N 1 25 E
Arima **70** 10 38N 61 17W
Ario de Rosales **69** 19 12N 101 43W
Aripuanã **72** 9 25 S 60 30W
Aripuanã → **72** 5 7 S 60 25W
Ariquemes **72** 9 55 S 63 6W
Arisaig **6** 56 55N 5 50W
Aristazabal I. **64** 52 40N 129 10W
Ariza **44** 41 19N 2 3W
Arizona □ **68** 34 20N 111 30W
Arjeplog **27** 66 3N 18 2 E
Arjona **72** 10 14N 75 22W
Arka **31** 60 15N 142 0 E
Arkadelphia **67** 34 5N 93 0W
Arkaig, L. **6** 56 58N 5 10W
Arkansas □ **67** 35 0N 92 30W
Arkansas → **67** 33 48N 91 4W
Arkansas City **67** 37 4N 97 3W
Arkhangelsk **30** 64 40N 41 0 E
Arklow **7** 52 48N 6 10W
Arkticheskiy, Mys **31** 81 10N 95 0 E
Arlanc **10** 45 25N 3 42 E
Arlanzón → **18** 42 3N 4 17W
Arles **11** 43 41N 4 40 E
Arlington, Va., U.S.A. **66** 38 52N 77 5W
Arlington, Wash., U.S.A. **68** 48 11N 122 4W
Arlon **12** 49 42N 5 49 E
Armagh **7** 54 22N 6 40W
Armagh □ **7** 54 18N 6 37W
Armagnac **10** 43 50N 0 10 E
Armançon → **9** 47 59N 3 30 E
Armavir **35** 45 2N 41 7 E
Armenia **72** 4 35N 75 45W
Armenian S.S.R. □ **35** 40 0N 44 0 E
Armentières **9** 50 40N 2 50 E
Armidale **56** 30 30 S 151 40 E
Armstrong, B.C., Canada **64** 50 25N 119 10W
Armstrong, Ont., Canada **62** 50 18N 89 4W
Arnaouti, C. **45** 35 6N 32 17 E
Arnarfjörður **27** 65 48N 23 40W
Arnay-le-Duc **9** 47 10N 4 27 E
Árnes **27** 66 1N 21 31W
Arnhem **12** 51 58N 5 55 E
Arnhem, C. **55** 12 20 S 137 30 E
Arnhem B. **54** 12 20 S 136 10 E
Arnhem Land **54** 13 10 S 134 30 E
Arno → **20** 43 41N 10 17 E
Arnon → **9** 47 13N 2 1 E
Arnøy **27** 70 9N 20 40 E
Arnprior **62** 45 26N 76 21W
Aroab **52** 26 41 S 19 39 E
Aron → **10** 46 50N 3 28 E
Arpajon **9** 48 36N 2 15 E
Arpajon-sur-Cère **10** 44 53N 2 28 E
Arran **6** 55 34N 5 12W
Arras **9** 50 17N 2 46 E
Arrats → **10** 44 6N 0 52 E
Arreau **10** 42 54N 0 22 E
Arrecife **49** 28 57N 13 37W
Arrée, Mts. d' **8** 48 26N 3 55W
Arriaga **69** 16 14N 93 54W
Arromanches-les-Bains **8** 49 20N 0 38W
Arros → **10** 43 40N 0 2W
Arrou **8** 48 6N 1 8 E
Arrow, L. **7** 54 3N 8 20W
Ars-en-Ré **10** 46 12N 1 31W
Ars-sur-Moselle **9** 49 5N 6 4 E
Árta **26** 39 8N 21 2 E
Artemovsk, R.S.F.S.R., U.S.S.R. **31** 54 45N 93 35 E
Artemovsk, Ukraine S.S.R., U.S.S.R. **34** 48 35N 38 0 E
Artenay **9** 48 5N 1 50 E
Arthez-de-Béarn **10** 43 29N 0 38W
Artigas **74** 30 20 S 56 30W
Artois **9** 50 20N 2 30 E
Artvin **34** 41 14N 41 44 E
Aru, Kepulauan **40** 6 0 S 134 30 E
Arua **51** 3 1N 30 58 E
Aruanã **73** 14 54 S 51 10W
Aruba **70** 12 30N 70 0W
Arudy **10** 43 7N 0 28W
Arusha **51** 3 20 S 36 40 E
Aruwimi → **51** 1 13N 23 36 E
Arve → **11** 46 11N 6 8 E
Arvida **63** 48 25N 71 14W
Arvidsjaur **27** 65 35N 19 10 E
Arvika **28** 59 40N 12 36 E
Arys **30** 42 26N 68 48 E
Arzamas **33** 55 27N 43 55 E
Arzew **49** 35 50N 0 23W
'As Saffānīyah **45** 28 5N 48 50 E
As Samāwah **45** 31 15N 45 15 E
As Sumaymānīyah **45** 35 35N 45 29 E
As Suwaydā' **45** 32 40N 36 30 E
As Şuwayrah **45** 32 55N 45 0 E
Asahigawa **44** 43 46N 142 22 E
Asansol **37** 23 40N 87 1 E
Asbestos **63** 45 47N 71 58W
Ascension I. **1** 8 0 S 14 15W
Aschaffenburg **13** 49 58N 9 8 E
Áscoli Piceno **21** 42 51N 13 34 E
Aseb **47** 13 0N 42 40 E
Asela **50** 8 0N 39 0 E
Asfeld **9** 49 27N 4 5 E
Ash Shām, Bādiyat **45** 32 0N 40 0 E
Ash Shāmīyah **45** 31 55N 44 35 E
Ash Shāriqah **46** 25 23N 55 26 E
Ash Shaţrah **45** 31 30N 46 10 E
Ashburton → **54** 21 40 S 114 56 E
Ashby-de-la-Zouch **5** 52 45N 1 29W
Ashcroft **64** 50 40N 121 20W
Asheboro **66** 35 43N 79 46W
Asheville **66** 35 39N 82 30W
Ashford **5** 51 8N 0 53 E
Ashikaga **44** 36 28N 139 29 E
Ashizuri-Zaki **44** 32 44N 133 0 E
Ashkhabad **30** 38 0N 57 50 E
Ashland, Ky., U.S.A. **66** 38 25N 82 40W
Ashland, Oreg., U.S.A. **68** 42 10N 122 38W
Ashland, Wis., U.S.A. **62** 46 40N 90 52W
Ashmore Reef **54** 12 14 S 123 5 E
Ashq'elon **45** 31 42N 34 35 E
Ashtabula **66** 41 52N 80 50W
Ashton-under-Lyne **5** 53 30N 2 8W
Ashuanipi, L. **63** 52 45N 66 15W
Asifabad **38** 19 20N 79 24 E
Asilah **49** 35 29N 6 0W
Asinara, G. dell' **22** 41 0N 8 30 E
Asinara I. **22** 41 5N 8 15 E
'Asīr □ **47** 18 40N 42 30 E
Asir, Ras **47** 11 55N 51 10 E
Askersund **28** 58 53N 14 55 E
Askja **27** 65 3N 16 48W
Asmara = Asmera **50** 15 19N 38 55 E
Asmera **50** 15 19N 38 55 E
Aso **44** 33 0N 131 5 E
Aspres-sur-Buëch **11** 44 32N 5 44 E
Asse **12** 50 24N 4 10 E
Assen **12** 53 0N 6 35 E
Assini **49** 5 9N 3 17W
Assiniboia **65** 49 40N 105 59W
Assiniboine → **65** 49 53N 97 8W
Assisi **21** 43 4N 12 36 E
Assynt, L. **6** 58 25N 5 15W
Astaffort **10** 44 4N 0 40 E
Asti **20** 44 54N 8 11 E
Astipálaia **26** 36 32N 26 22 E
Astorga **18** 42 29N 6 8W
Astoria **68** 46 16N 123 50W
Astrakhan **35** 46 25N 48 5 E
Asturias **18** 43 15N 6 0W
Asunción **74** 25 10 S 57 30W
Aswân **50** 24 4N 32 57 E
Aswân High Dam = Sadd el Aali **50** 23 54N 32 54 E
Asyût **50** 27 11N 31 4 E
At Ţafīlah **45** 30 45N 35 30 E
At Ta'if **47** 21 5N 40 27 E
Atacama, Desierto de **74** 24 0 S 69 20W
Atacama, Salar de **74** 23 30 S 68 20W
Atakpamé **49** 7 31N 1 13 E
Atalaya **72** 10 45 S 73 50W
Atami **44** 35 5N 139 4 E
Atâr **49** 20 30N 13 5W
Atara **31** 63 10N 129 10 E
Atbara **50** 17 42N 33 59 E
'Atbara → **50** 17 40N 33 56 E
Atchafalaya B. **67** 29 30N 91 20W
Atchison **67** 39 40N 95 10W
Ath **12** 50 38N 3 47 E
Athabasca **64** 54 45N 113 20W
Athabasca → **61** 58 40N 110 50W
Athabasca, L. **61** 59 15N 109 15W
Athboy **7** 53 37N 6 55W
Athenry **7** 53 18N 8 45W
Athens = Athínai **26** 37 58N 23 46 E
Athens, Ala., U.S.A. **66** 34 49N 86 58W
Athens, Ga., U.S.A. **66** 33 56N 83 24W
Athens, Ohio, U.S.A. **66** 39 25N 82 6W
Athens, Tenn., U.S.A. **66** 35 45N 84 38W
Athens, Tex., U.S.A. **67** 32 11N 95 48W
Atherton **56** 17 17 S 145 30 E
Athínai **26** 37 58N 23 46 E
Athlone **7** 53 26N 7 57W
Atholl, Forest of **6** 56 51N 3 50W
Áthos **26** 40 9N 24 22 E
Athy **7** 53 0N 7 0W
Ati **50** 13 13N 18 20 E
Atico **72** 16 14 S 73 40W
Atka **31** 60 50N 151 48 E
Atlanta **66** 33 50N 84 24W
Atlantic **67** 41 25N 95 0W
Atlantic City **66** 39 25N 74 25W
Atlantic Ocean **1** 0 0 20 0W
Atlas Mts. = Haut Atlas **49** 32 30N 5 0W
Atlin **64** 59 31N 133 41W
Atmore **66** 31 2N 87 30W
Attawapiskat → **62** 52 57N 82 18W
Attichy **9** 49 25N 3 3 E
Attigny **9** 49 28N 4 35 E
Attleboro **66** 41 56N 71 18W
Attur **38** 11 35N 78 30 E
Åtvidaberg **28** 58 12N 16 0 E
Aubagne **11** 43 17N 5 37 E
Aube □ **9** 48 15N 4 10 E
Aube → **9** 48 34N 3 43 E
Aubenas **11** 44 37N 4 24 E
Aubenton **9** 49 50N 4 12 E
Aubigny-sur-Nère **9** 47 30N 2 24 E
Aubin **10** 44 33N 2 15 E
Aubrac, Mts. d' **10** 44 40N 3 2 E
Auburn, Ala., U.S.A. **66** 32 37N 85 30W
Auburn, N.Y., U.S.A. **66** 42 57N 76 39W
Aubusson **10** 45 57N 2 11 E
Auch **10** 43 39N 0 36 E
Auchel **9** 50 30N 2 29 E
Auckland **59** 36 52 S 174 46 E
Auckland Is. **57** 50 40 S 166 5 E
Aude □ **10** 43 8N 2 28 E
Aude → **10** 43 13N 3 14 E
Auderville **8** 49 43N 1 57W
Audierne **8** 48 1N 4 34W
Audincourt **9** 47 30N 6 50 E
Augathella **56** 25 48 S 146 35 E
Augsburg **13** 48 22N 10 54 E
Augusta, Italy **23** 37 14N 15 12 E
Augusta, Ga., U.S.A. **66** 33 29N 81 59W
Augusta, Maine, U.S.A. **63** 44 20N 69 46W
Augustów **17** 53 51N 23 0 E
Augustus, Mt. **54** 24 20 S 116 50 E
Aulnay **10** 46 2N 0 22W
Aulne → **8** 48 17N 4 16W
Aulnoye-Aymeries **9** 50 12N 3 50 E
Ault **8** 50 8N 1 26 E
Aulus-les-Bains **10** 42 49N 1 19 E
Aumale **9** 49 46N 1 46 E
Aumont-Aubrac **10** 44 43N 3 17 E
Aunis **10** 46 5N 0 50W
Aups **11** 43 37N 6 15 E
Aurangabad, Bihar, India **37** 24 45N 84 18 E
Aurangabad, Maharashtra, India **38** 19 50N 75 23 E
Auray **8** 47 40N 2 59W
Aurillac **10** 44 55N 2 26 E
Aurora, Colo., U.S.A. **67** 39 44N 104 55W
Aurora, Ill., U.S.A. **67** 41 42N 88 12W
Aus **52** 26 35 S 16 12 E
Aust-Agder fylke □ **27** 58 55N 7 40 E
Austerlitz = Slavkov **15** 49 10N 16 52 E
Austin, Minn., U.S.A. **67** 43 37N 92 59W
Austin, Tex., U.S.A. **67** 30 20N 97 45W
Austin, L. **54** 27 40 S 118 0 E
Austral Downs **55** 20 30 S 137 45 E
Australia ■ **2** 23 0 S 135 0 E
Australian Alps **56** 36 30 S 148 30 E
Australian Cap. Terr. □ **56** 35 30 S 149 0 E
Australian Dependency □ **60** 73 0 S 90 0 E
Austria ■ **14** 47 0N 14 0 E
Austvågøy **27** 68 20N 14 40 E
Auterive **10** 43 21N 1 29 E
Authie → **9** 50 22N 1 38 E
Authon-du-Perche **8** 48 12N 0 54 E
Autlán **69** 19 40N 104 30W
Autun **9** 46 58N 4 17 E
Auvergne **10** 45 20N 3 15 E
Auvergne, Mts. d' **10** 45 20N 2 55 E
Auvézére → **10** 45 12N 0 50 E
Auxerre **9** 47 48N 3 32 E
Auxi-le-Château **9** 50 15N 2 8 E
Auxonne **9** 47 10N 5 20 E
Auzances **10** 46 2N 2 30 E
Auzat-sur-Allier **10** 45 27N 3 19 E
Avallon **9** 47 30N 3 53 E
Avalon Pen. **63** 47 30N 53 20W
Aveiro, Brazil **73** 3 10 S 55 5W
Aveiro, Portugal **18** 40 37N 8 38W
Avellaneda **74** 34 50 S 58 10W
Avellino **23** 40 54N 14 46 E
Aversa **23** 40 58N 14 11 E
Aves, I. de **70** 15 45N 63 55W
Avesnes-sur-Helpe **9** 50 8N 3 55 E
Avesta **28** 60 9N 16 10 E
Aveyron □ **10** 44 22N 2 45 E
Aveyron → **10** 44 5N 1 16 E
Avignon **11** 43 57N 4 50 E
Ávila **18** 40 39N 4 43W
Avilés **18** 43 35N 5 57W
Avize **9** 48 59N 4 0 E
Avoca **7** 52 52N 6 13W
Avon □ **5** 51 30N 2 40W
Avon →, Avon, U.K. **5** 51 30N 2 43W
Avon →, Hants., U.K. **5** 50 44N 1 45W
Avon →, Warwick, U.K. **5** 52 0N 2 9W
Avon, Îles **55** 19 37 S 158 17 E
Avonmouth **5** 51 30N 2 42W
Avranches **8** 48 40N 1 20W
Avre → **8** 48 47N 1 22 E
Awash **47** 9 1N 40 10 E
Awbārī **50** 26 46N 12 57 E
Awe, L. **6** 56 15N 5 15W
Awjilah **50** 29 8N 21 7 E
Ax-les-Thermes **10** 42 44N 1 50 E
Axarfjörður **27** 66 15N 16 45W
Axel Heiberg I. **3** 80 0N 90 0W
Axim **49** 4 51N 2 15W
Axminster **5** 50 47N 3 1W
Aÿ **9** 49 3N 4 0 E
Ayabe **44** 35 20N 135 20 E
Ayacucho **72** 13 0 S 74 0W
Ayamonte **18** 37 12N 7 24W
Ayan **31** 56 30N 138 16 E
Ayers Rock **54** 25 23 S 131 5 E
Ayíos Evstrátios **26** 39 34N 24 58 E
Aylesbury **5** 51 48N 0 49W
Ayon, Ostrov **31** 69 50N 169 0 E
Ayr, Australia **56** 19 35 S 147 25 E
Ayr, U.K. **6** 55 28N 4 37W
Ayr → **6** 55 29N 4 40W
Ayre, Pt. of **5** 54 27N 4 21W
Aytos **25** 42 42N 27 16 E
Ayutla **69** 16 58N 99 17W
Az Zahrān **45** 26 10N 50 7 E
Az Zubayr **45** 30 20N 47 50 E
Azamgarh **37** 26 5N 83 13 E
Azare **49** 11 55N 10 10 E
Azay-le-Rideau **8** 47 16N 0 30 E
Azbine = Aïr **49** 18 30N 8 0 E
Azerbaijan S.S.R. □ **35** 40 20N 48 0 E
Azores **1** 38 44N 29 0W
Azov **35** 47 3N 39 25 E
Azov Sea = Azovskoye More **34** 46 0N 36 30 E
Azovskoye More **34** 46 0N 36 30 E
Azúa de Compostela **70** 18 25N 70 44W
Azuaga **18** 38 16N 5 39W
Azuero, Pen. de **70** 7 30N 80 30W
Azul **74** 36 42 S 59 43W

B

Baarle Nassau **12** 51 27N 4 56 E
Baarn **12** 52 12N 5 17 E
Bāb el Māndeb **47** 12 35N 43 25 E
Babahoyo **72** 1 40 S 79 30W
Babana **49** 10 31N 3 46 E
Babine L. **64** 54 48N 126 0W
Bābol **46** 36 40N 52 50 E
Babura **49** 12 51N 8 59 E
Babylon **45** 32 40N 44 30 E
Bac Ninh **41** 21 13N 106 4 E
Bac Phan **41** 22 0N 105 0 E
Bac Quang **41** 22 30N 104 48 E
Bacabal **73** 4 15 S 44 45W
Bacău **25** 46 35N 26 55 E
Baccarat **9** 48 28N 6 42 E
Backnang **13** 48 57N 9 26 E
Backstairs Passage **55** 35 40 S 138 5 E
Bacolod **40** 10 40N 122 57 E
Bacqueville-en-Caux **8** 49 47N 1 0 E
Bad Ems **13** 50 22N 7 44 E
Bad Godesberg **13** 50 41N 7 4 E
Bad Hersfeld **13** 50 52N 9 42 E
Bad Homburg **13** 50 17N 8 33 E
Bad Ischl **14** 47 44N 13 38 E
Bad Kissingen **13** 50 11N 10 5 E
Bad Kreuznach **13** 49 47N 7 47 E
Bad Lands **67** 43 40N 102 10W
Bad Lauterberg **13** 51 38N 10 29 E
Bad Mergentheim **13** 49 29N 9 47 E
Bad Nauheim **13** 50 24N 8 45 E
Bad Oldesloe **13** 53 48N 10 22 E
Bad Pyrmont **13** 51 59N 9 15 E
Bad Salzuflen **13** 52 8N 8 44 E
Bad Waldsee **13** 47 56N 9 46 E
Bad Wildungen **13** 51 7N 9 10 E
Bad Wimpfen **13** 49 12N 9 10 E
Badagara **38** 11 35N 75 40 E
Badajoz **18** 38 50N 6 59W
Badakhshān □ **46** 36 30N 71 0 E
Badalona **19** 41 26N 2 15 E
Badampahar **36** 22 10N 86 10 E
Badarinath **37** 30 45N 79 30 E
Baden **15** 48 1N 16 13 E
Baden-Baden **13** 48 45N 8 15 E
Baden-Württemberg □ **13** 48 40N 9 0 E
Badgastein **14** 47 7N 13 9 E
Bādghīsāt □ **46** 35 0N 63 0 E
Badin **36** 24 38N 68 54 E
Baduen **47** 7 15N 47 40 E
Badulla **38** 7 1N 81 7 E
Baeza **19** 37 57N 3 25W
Bafatá **49** 12 8N 14 40W
Baffin B. **3** 72 0N 64 0W
Baffin I. **61** 68 0N 75 0W
Bafia **49** 4 40N 11 10 E
Bafing → **49** 13 49N 10 50W
Bafoulabé **49** 13 50N 10 55W
Bafra **45** 41 34N 35 54 E
Bāft **46** 29 15N 56 38 E
Bafwasende **51** 1 3N 27 5 E
Bagamoyo **51** 6 28 S 38 55 E
Bagdarin **31** 54 26N 113 36 E
Bagé **74** 31 20 S 54 15W
Bagenalstown = Muine Bheag **7** 52 42N 6 57W
Baghdād **45** 33 20N 44 30 E
Baghlān **46** 36 12N 69 0 E
Baghlān □ **46** 36 0N 68 30 E
Bagnères-de-Bigorre **10** 43 5N 0 9 E
Bagnères-de-Luchon **10** 42 47N 0 38 E
Bagnoles-de-l'Orne **8** 48 32N 0 25W
Bagnols-sur-Cèze **11** 44 10N 4 36 E
Bahamas ■ **70** 24 0N 75 0W
Baharampur **37** 24 2N 88 27 E
Bahawalpur **36** 29 24N 71 40 E
Bahía = Salvador **73** 13 0 S 38 30W
Bahía □ **73** 12 0 S 42 0W
Bahía Blanca **74** 38 35 S 62 13W
Bahr el Ahmar □ **50** 20 0N 35 0 E
Bahr el Ghazâl □ **50** 7 0N 28 0 E
Bahr Salamat → **50** 9 20N 18 0 E
Bahraich **37** 27 38N 81 37 E
Bahrain ■ **46** 26 0N 50 35 E
Baia Mare **15** 47 40N 23 35 E
Baïbokoum **50** 7 46N 15 43 E
Baidoa **47** 3 8N 43 30 E
Baie Comeau **63** 49 12N 68 10W
Baie-St-Paul **63** 47 28N 70 32W
Baignes-Ste.-Radegonde **10** 45 23N 0 25W
Baigneux-les-Juifs **9** 47 31N 4 39 E
Ba'ījī **45** 35 0N 43 30 E
Baikal, L. = Baykal, Oz. **31** 53 0N 108 0 E
Baile Atha Cliath = Dublin **7** 53 20N 6 18W
Bailleul **9** 50 44N 2 41 E
Bailundo **51** 12 10 S 15 50 E
Baimuru **56** 7 35 S 144 51 E
Bain-de-Bretagne **8** 47 50N 1 40W
Bainbridge **66** 30 53N 84 34W
Bairnsdale **56** 37 48 S 147 36 E
Baïsole → **10** 43 26N 0 25 E
Baitadi **37** 29 35N 80 25 E
Baiyin **42** 36 45N 104 14 E
Baja **15** 46 12N 18 59 E
Baja California **69** 31 10N 115 12W
Baja California Norte □ **69** 30 0N 115 0W
Baja California Sur □ **69** 25 50N 111 50W
Bakala **50** 6 15N 20 20 E
Bakel **49** 14 56N 12 20W
Baker **68** 44 50N 117 55W
Baker I. **57** 0 10N 176 35W
Baker Mt. **68** 48 50N 121 49W
Baker's Dozen Is. **62** 56 45N 78 45W
Bakersfield **68** 35 25N 119 0W
Bākhtarān **45** 34 23N 47 0 E
Bakkafjörður **27** 66 2N 14 48W
Bakkagerði **27** 65 31N 13 49W
Bakony Forest = Bakony Hegység **15** 47 10N 17 30 E
Bakony Hegység **15** 47 10N 17 30 E
Bakouma **50** 5 40N 22 56 E
Baku **35** 40 25N 49 45 E
Bala, L. = Tegid, L. **5** 52 53N 3 38W
Balabac, Str. **39** 7 53N 117 5 E
Balabakk **45** 34 0N 36 10 E
Balaghat **36** 21 49N 80 12 E
Balaghat Ra. **38** 18 50N 76 30 E
Balaguer **19** 41 50N 0 50 E
Balaklava **34** 44 30N 33 30 E
Balakovo **33** 52 4N 47 55 E
Balashov **33** 51 30N 43 10 E
Balaton **15** 46 50N 17 40 E
Balboa **70** 9 0N 79 30W
Balbriggan **7** 53 35N 6 10W
Balcarce **74** 38 0 S 58 10W
Balchik **25** 43 28N 28 11 E
Baleares, Is. **19** 39 30N 3 0 E
Balearic Is. = Baleares, Is. **19** 39 30N 3 0 E
Baleshwar **36** 21 35N 87 3 E
Bali, Cameroon **49** 5 54N 10 0 E
Bali, Indonesia **39** 8 20 S 115 0 E
Balikesir **45** 39 35N 27 58 E
Balikpapan **39** 1 10 S 116 55 E
Balkan Mts. = Stara Planina **25** 43 15N 23 0 E
Balkh □ **46** 36 30N 67 0 E
Balkhash **30** 46 50N 74 50 E
Balkhash, Ozero **30** 46 0N 74 50 E
Ballachulish **6** 56 40N 5 10W
Ballarat **56** 37 33 S 143 50 E
Ballard, L. **54** 29 20 S 120 10 E
Ballater **6** 57 2N 3 2W
Ballina, Australia **56** 28 50 S 153 31 E
Ballina, Mayo, Ireland **7** 54 7N 9 10W
Ballina, Tipp., Ireland **7** 52 49N 8 27W
Ballinasloe **7** 53 20N 8 12W
Ballinrobe **7** 53 36N 9 13W
Ballinskelligs B. **7** 51 46N 10 11W
Ballon **8** 48 10N 0 14 E
Ballycastle **7** 55 12N 6 15W
Ballymena **7** 54 53N 6 18W
Ballymena □ **7** 54 53N 6 18W
Ballymoney **7** 55 5N 6 30W
Ballymoney □ **7** 55 5N 6 23W
Ballyshannon **7** 54 30N 8 10W
Balmaceda **74** 46 0 S 71 50W
Balmoral **6** 57 3N 3 13W
Balonne → **56** 28 47 S 147 56 E
Balrampur **37** 27 30N 82 20 E
Balranald **56** 34 38 S 143 33 E
Balsas → **69** 17 55N 102 10W
Balta **34** 48 2N 29 45 E
Baltic Sea **27** 56 0N 20 0 E
Baltimore, Ireland **7** 51 29N 9 22W
Baltimore, U.S.A. **66** 39 18N 76 37W
Balygychan **31** 63 56N 154 12 E
Bama **50** 11 33N 13 41 E
Bamako **49** 12 34N 7 55W
Bamba **49** 17 5N 1 24W
Bambari **50** 5 40N 20 35 E
Bamberg **13** 49 54N 10 53 E
Bambili **51** 3 40N 26 0 E
Bamenda **49** 5 57N 10 11 E
Bāmīān □ **46** 35 0N 67 0 E
Ban Aranyaprathet **41** 13 41N 102 30 E
Ban Houei Sai **41** 20 22N 100 32 E
Ban Khe Bo **41** 19 10N 104 39 E
Ban Khun Yuam **41** 18 49N 97 57 E
Ban Nong Pling **41** 15 40N 100 10 E
Ban Phai **41** 16 4N 102 44 E
Banaba **57** 0 45 S 169 50 E
Banalia **51** 1 32N 25 5 E
Banamba **49** 13 29N 7 22W
Banbridge **7** 54 21N 6 17W
Banbridge □ **7** 54 21N 6 16W
Banbury **5** 52 4N 1 21W
Banchory **6** 57 3N 2 30W
Bancroft **62** 45 3N 77 51W
Banda **36** 25 30N 80 26 E
Banda, Kepulauan **40** 4 37 S 129 50 E

Index

Banda Aceh **39** 5 35N 95 20 E
Banda Sea **40** 6 0 S 130 0 E
Bandār 'Abbās **46** 27 15N 56 15 E
Bandar-e Anzalī **45** 37 30N 49 30 E
Bandar-e Khomeyni **45** 30 30N 49 5 E
Bandar-e Lengeh **46** 26 35N 54 58 E
Bandar-e Nakhīlū **46** 26 58N 53 30 E
Bandar-e Torkeman **46** 37 0N 54 10 E
Bandar Seri Begawan **39** 4 52N 115 0 E
Bandawe **51** 11 58 S 34 5 E
Bandeira, Pico da **73** 20 26 S 41 47W
Bandiagara **49** 14 12N 3 29W
Bandırma **45** 40 20N 28 0 E
Bandon **7** 51 44N 8 45W
Bandon → **7** 51 40N 8 41W
Bandundu **51** 3 15 S 17 22 E
Bandung **40** 6 54 S 107 36 E
Banes **70** 21 0N 75 42W
Banff, Canada **64** 51 10N 115 34W
Banff, U.K. **6** 57 40N 2 32W
Banfora **49** 10 40N 4 40W
Bangalore **38** 12 59N 77 40 E
Bangassou **51** 4 55N 23 7 E
Bangeta, Mt. **56** 6 21 S 147 3 E
Banggai **40** 1 40 S 123 30 E
Banghāzī **50** 32 11N 20 3 E
Bangka, Selat **39** 2 30 S 105 30 E
Bangkok **41** 13 45N 100 35 E
Bangladesh ■ **37** 24 0N 90 0 E
Bangor, N. Ireland, U.K. **7** 54 40N 5 40W
Bangor, Wales, U.K. **5** 53 13N 4 9W
Bangor, U.S.A. **63** 44 48N 68 42W
Bangui **51** 4 23N 18 35 E
Bangweulu, L. **51** 11 0 S 30 0 E
Bani **70** 18 16N 70 22W
Banī Walīd **50** 31 36N 13 53 E
Banīnah **50** 32 0N 20 12 E
Banja Luka **24** 44 49N 17 11 E
Banjarmasin **39** 3 20 S 114 35 E
Banjul **49** 13 28N 16 40W
Bankipore **37** 25 35N 85 10 E
Banks I., B.C., Canada **64** 53 20N 130 0W
Banks I., N.W.T., Canada **3** 73 15N 121 30W
Banks I., Papua N. G. **56** 10 10 S 142 15 E
Banks Pen. **59** 43 45 S 173 15 E
Bankura **37** 23 11N 87 18 E
Bann →, Down, U.K. **7** 54 30N 6 31W
Bann →, Londonderry, U.K. **7** 55 10N 6 34W
Bannalec **8** 47 57N 3 42W
Banning **68** 33 58N 116 52W
Bannockburn **6** 56 5N 3 55W
Banon **11** 44 2N 5 38 E
Banská Bystrica **15** 48 46N 19 14 E
Banská Štiavnica **15** 48 25N 18 55 E
Banswara **36** 23 32N 74 24 E
Bantry **7** 51 40N 9 28W
Bantry, B. **7** 51 35N 9 50W
Banyo **49** 6 52N 11 45 E
Banyuls-sur-Mer **10** 42 28N 3 8 E
Baoding **42** 38 50N 115 28 E
Baoji **43** 34 20N 107 5 E
Baotou **42** 40 32N 110 2 E
Bapatla **38** 15 55N 80 30 E
Bapaume **9** 50 7N 2 50 E
Ba'qūbah **45** 33 45N 44 50 E
Bar **24** 42 8N 19 8 E
Bar Harbor **63** 44 15N 68 20W
Bar-le-Duc **9** 48 47N 5 10 E
Bar-sur-Aube **9** 48 14N 4 40 E
Bar-sur-Seine **9** 48 7N 4 20 E
Baraboo **67** 43 28N 89 46W
Baracoa **70** 20 20N 74 30W
Barahona **70** 18 13N 71 7W
Barakpur **37** 22 44N 88 30 E
Baran **36** 25 9N 76 40 E
Baranof I. **64** 57 0N 135 10W
Baranovichi **32** 53 10N 26 0 E
Barbacoas **72** 1 45N 78 0W
Barbados ■ **70** 13 0N 59 30W
Barberton **53** 25 42 S 31 2 E
Barbezieux **10** 45 28N 0 9W
Barbuda I. **70** 17 30N 61 40W
Barca, La **69** 20 17N 102 34W
Barcaldine **56** 23 43 S 145 6 E
Barcarès, Le **10** 42 47N 3 2 E
Barcelona, Spain **19** 41 21N 2 10 E
Barcelona, Venezuela **72** 10 10N 64 40W
Barcelonette **11** 44 23N 6 40 E
Barcelos **72** 1 0 S 63 0W
Barcoo → **56** 25 30 S 142 50 E
Barddhaman **37** 23 14N 87 39 E
Bardera **47** 2 20N 42 27 E
Bardia **50** 31 45N 25 0 E
Bardsey I. **5** 52 46N 4 47W
Bareilly **37** 28 22N 79 27 E
Barentin **8** 49 33N 0 58 E
Barenton **8** 48 38N 0 50W
Barents Sea **3** 73 0N 39 0 E
Barentu **50** 15 2N 37 35 E
Barfleur **8** 49 40N 1 17W
Barfleur, Pte. de **8** 49 42N 1 16W
Bargal **47** 11 25N 51 0 E
Barguzin **31** 53 37N 109 37 E
Barhi **37** 24 15N 85 25 E
Bari **23** 41 6N 16 52 E
Bari Doab **36** 30 20N 73 0 E
Barīm **47** 12 39N 43 25 E
Barinas **72** 8 36N 70 15W
Bârîs **50** 24 42N 30 31 E
Barisal **37** 22 45N 90 20 E
Barito → **39** 4 0 S 114 50 E
Barjac **11** 44 20N 4 22 E
Barjols **11** 43 34N 6 2 E
Barkly Tableland **55** 17 50 S 136 40 E
Barlee, L. **54** 29 15 S 119 30 E
Barletta **23** 41 20N 16 17 E
Barmer **36** 25 45N 71 20 E
Barmouth **5** 52 44N 4 3W
Barnard Castle **5** 54 33N 1 55W
Barnaul **30** 53 20N 83 40 E
Barnet **5** 51 37N 0 15W
Barneveld **12** 52 7N 5 36 E
Barneville-Cartevert **8** 49 23N 1 46W
Barney, Mt. **55** 28 17 S 152 44 E
Barnsley **5** 53 33N 1 29W
Barnstaple **5** 51 5N 4 3W
Baro **49** 8 35N 6 18 E
Baroda = Vadodara **36** 22 20N 73 10 E
Barquísimeto **72** 10 4N 69 19W
Barr **9** 48 25N 7 28 E
Barra **6** 57 0N 7 30W
Barra, Sd. of **6** 57 4N 7 25W
Barra Falsa, Pta. da **53** 22 58 S 35 37 E
Barra Hd. **6** 56 47N 7 40W
Barranca **72** 10 45 S 77 50W
Barrancabermeja **72** 7 0N 73 50W
Barrancas **72** 8 55N 62 5W
Barrancos **18** 38 10N 6 58W
Barranqueras **74** 27 30 S 59 0W
Barranquilla **72** 11 0N 74 50W
Barre **62** 44 15N 72 30W
Barreiro **18** 38 40N 9 6W
Barreiros **73** 8 49 S 35 12W
Barrême **11** 43 57N 6 23 E
Barrhead **64** 54 10N 114 24W
Barrie **62** 44 24N 79 40W
Barrier Ra. **55** 31 0 S 141 30 E
Barrington Tops **56** 32 6 S 151 28 E
Barrow → **7** 52 10N 6 57W
Barrow Creek **54** 21 30 S 133 55 E
Barrow I. **54** 20 45 S 115 20 E
Barrow-in-Furness **5** 54 8N 3 15W
Barrow Ra. **54** 26 0 S 127 40 E
Barrow Str. **3** 74 20N 95 0W
Barry **5** 51 23N 3 19W
Barry's Bay **62** 45 29N 77 41W
Barsi **38** 18 10N 75 50 E
Barstow **68** 34 58N 117 2W
Bartica **72** 6 25N 58 40W
Bartle Frere, Mt. **56** 17 27 S 145 50 E
Bartlesville **67** 36 50N 95 58W
Barton-upon-Humber **5** 53 41N 0 27W
Bartow **66** 27 53N 81 49W
Bas-Rhin □ **9** 48 40N 7 30 E
Basankusa **51** 1 5N 19 50 E
Basel **13** 47 35N 7 35 E
Bashkir A.S.S.R. □ **30** 54 0N 57 0 E
Basilaki I. **56** 10 35 S 151 0 E
Basilan **40** 6 35N 122 0 E
Basildon **5** 51 34N 0 29 E
Basilicata □ **23** 40 30N 16 0 E
Basingstoke **5** 51 15N 1 5W
Baskerville C. **54** 17 10 S 122 15 E
Basle = Basel **13** 47 35N 7 35 E
Basoka **51** 1 16N 23 40 E
Basongo **51** 4 15 S 20 20 E
Basque, Pays **10** 43 15N 1 20W
Basque Provinces = Vascongadas □ **19** 42 50N 2 45W
Basra = Al Başrah **45** 30 30N 47 50 E
Bass Rock **6** 56 5N 2 40W
Bass Str. **56** 39 15 S 146 30 E
Bassano **64** 50 48N 112 20W
Bassano del Grappa **21** 45 45N 11 45 E
Basse-Terre **70** 16 0N 61 40W
Bassée, La **9** 50 31N 2 49 E
Bassein **41** 16 45N 94 30 E
Basseterre **70** 17 17N 62 43W
Bassigny **9** 48 0N 5 30 E
Bassikounou **49** 15 55N 6 1W
Bastar **38** 19 15N 81 40 E
Bastelica **11** 42 1N 9 3 E
Basti **37** 26 52N 82 55 E
Bastia **11** 42 40N 9 30 E
Bastide-Puylaurent, La **10** 44 35N 3 55 E
Bastogne **12** 50 1N 5 43 E
Bata **51** 1 57N 9 50 E
Batabanó **70** 22 40N 82 20W
Batagoy **31** 67 38N 134 38 E
Batalha **18** 39 40N 8 50W
Batamay **31** 63 30N 129 15 E
Batang **42** 30 1N 99 0 E
Batangafo **50** 7 25N 18 20 E
Batavia **66** 43 0N 78 10W
Batchelor **54** 13 4 S 131 1 E
Bateman's B. **56** 35 40 S 150 12 E
Batesville **67** 35 48N 91 40W
Bath, U.K. **5** 51 22N 2 22W
Bath, Maine, U.S.A. **63** 43 50N 69 49W
Bath, N.Y., U.S.A. **66** 42 20N 77 17W
Bathgate **6** 55 54N 3 38W
Bathurst = Banjul **49** 13 28N 16 40W
Bathurst, Australia **56** 33 25 S 149 31 E
Bathurst, Canada **63** 47 37N 65 43W
Bathurst, C. **3** 70 34N 128 0W
Bathurst B. **56** 14 16 S 144 25 E
Bathurst I., Australia **54** 11 30 S 130 10 E
Bathurst I., Canada **3** 76 0N 100 30W
Batman **45** 37 55N 41 5 E
Batna **49** 35 34N 6 15 E
Baton Rouge **67** 30 30N 91 5W
Batopilas **69** 27 1N 107 44W
Batouri **51** 4 30N 14 25 E
Battambang **41** 13 7N 103 12 E
Batticaloa **38** 7 43N 81 45 E
Battle **5** 50 55N 0 30 E
Battle Creek **66** 42 20N 85 6W
Battle Harbour **63** 52 16N 55 35W
Battleford **65** 52 45N 108 15W
Batu **47** 6 55N 39 45 E
Batu Gajah **41** 4 28N 101 3 E
Batumi **35** 41 30N 41 30 E
Bauchi **49** 10 22N 9 48 E
Baud **8** 47 52N 3 1W
Baugé **8** 47 31N 0 8W
Baule, La **8** 47 17N 2 24W
Baume-les-Dames **9** 47 22N 6 22 E
Bauru **73** 22 10 S 49 0W
Baux-de-Provence, Les **11** 43 45N 4 51 E
Bavaria = Bayern □ **13** 49 7N 11 30 E
Bawean **39** 5 46 S 112 35 E
Bawku **49** 11 3N 0 19W
Bay City **66** 43 35N 83 51W
Bay Shore **66** 40 44N 73 15W
Bayamo **70** 20 20N 76 40W
Bayamón **70** 18 24N 66 10W
Bayan Har Shan **42** 34 0N 98 0 E
Bayern □ **13** 49 7N 11 30 E
Bayeux **8** 49 17N 0 42W
Bayfield **62** 43 34N 81 42W
Baykal, Oz. **31** 53 0N 108 0 E
Baykit **31** 61 50N 95 50 E
Baykonur **30** 47 48N 65 50 E
Bayon **9** 48 30N 6 20 E
Bayonne **10** 43 30N 1 28W
Bayreuth **13** 49 56N 11 35 E
Bayrūt **45** 33 53N 35 31 E
Baytown **67** 29 42N 94 57W
Baza **19** 37 30N 2 47W
Bazaruto, I. do **53** 21 40 S 35 28 E
Bazas **10** 44 27N 0 13W
Beachy Head **5** 50 44N 0 16 E
Beaconsfield **55** 41 11 S 146 48 E
Beagle, Canal **74** 55 0 S 68 30W
Béar, C. **10** 42 31N 3 8 E
Bear I. **7** 51 38N 9 50W
Béarn **10** 43 20N 0 30W
Beatrice, C. **55** 14 20 S 136 55 E
Beaucaire **11** 43 48N 4 39 E
Beauce, Plaine de la **9** 48 10N 1 45 E
Beaufort **66** 32 25N 80 40W
Beaufort Sea **3** 72 0N 140 0W
Beaufort West **52** 32 18 S 22 36 E
Beaugency **9** 47 47N 1 38 E
Beauharnois **62** 45 20N 73 52W
Beaujeu **11** 46 10N 4 35 E
Beaulieu-sur-Dordogne **10** 44 58N 1 50 E
Beaulieu-sur-Mer **11** 43 42N 7 20 E
Beauly **6** 57 29N 4 27W
Beauly → **6** 57 26N 4 28W
Beaumaris **5** 53 16N 4 7W
Beaumetz-lès-Loges **9** 50 15N 2 38 E
Beaumont, France **10** 44 45N 0 46 E
Beaumont, U.S.A. **67** 30 5N 94 8W
Beaumont-de-Lomagne **10** 43 53N 1 0 E
Beaumont-le-Roger **8** 49 4N 0 47 E
Beaumont-sur-Oise **9** 49 9N 2 17 E
Beaumont-sur-Sarthe **8** 48 13N 0 8 E
Beaune **9** 47 2N 4 50 E
Beaune-la-Rolande **9** 48 4N 2 25 E
Beaupréau **8** 47 12N 0 59W
Beauséjour **65** 50 5N 96 35W
Beausset, Le **11** 43 12N 5 48 E
Beauvais **9** 49 25N 2 8 E
Beauval **65** 55 9N 107 37W
Beauvoir-sur-Mer **8** 46 55N 2 2W
Beauvoir-sur-Niort **10** 46 12N 0 30W
Beaver → **65** 55 26N 107 45W
Beaver Falls **66** 40 44N 80 20W
Beaverlodge **64** 55 11N 119 29W
Beawar **36** 26 3N 74 18 E
Beccles **5** 52 27N 1 33 E
Bečej **24** 45 36N 20 3 E
Béchar **49** 31 38N 2 18W
Beckley **66** 37 50N 81 8W
Bédarieux **10** 43 37N 3 10 E
Bédarrides **11** 44 2N 4 54 E
Bedford, U.K. **5** 52 8N 0 29W
Bedford, U.S.A. **66** 38 50N 86 30W
Bedford □ **5** 52 4N 0 28W
Bedford, C. **56** 15 14 S 145 21 E
Bedourie **56** 24 30 S 139 30 E
Be'er Sheva' **45** 31 15N 34 48 E
Beersheba = Be'er Sheva' **45** 31 15N 34 48 E
Beeston **5** 52 55N 1 11W
Befale **51** 0 25N 20 45 E
Bega **56** 36 41 S 149 51 E
Bégard **8** 48 38N 3 18W
Bègles **10** 44 45N 0 35W
Behbehān **45** 30 30N 50 15 E
Bei'an **42** 48 10N 126 20 E
Beibei **43** 29 47N 106 22 E
Beihai **43** 21 28N 109 6 E
Beijing **42** 39 55N 116 20 E
Beilen **12** 52 52N 6 27 E
Beira **51** 19 50 S 34 52 E
Beirut = Bayrūt **45** 33 53N 35 31 E
Beitbridge **51** 22 12 S 30 0 E
Beja, Portugal **18** 38 2N 7 53W
Béja, Tunisia **49** 36 43N 9 12 E
Bejaia **49** 36 42N 5 2 E
Békéscsaba **15** 46 40N 21 5 E
Bela **37** 25 50N 82 0 E
Bela Crkva **24** 44 55N 21 27 E
Bélâbre **10** 46 34N 1 8 E
Belau Is. **57** 7 30N 134 30 E
Belaya Tserkov **32** 49 45N 30 10 E
Belcher Is. **62** 56 15N 78 45W
Belém **73** 1 20 S 48 30W
Bélesta **10** 42 55N 1 56 E
Belet Uen **47** 4 30N 45 5 E
Belev **33** 53 50N 36 5 E
Belfast, U.K. **7** 54 35N 5 56W
Belfast, U.S.A. **63** 44 30N 69 0W
Belfast □ **7** 54 35N 5 56W
Belfast, L. **7** 54 40N 5 50W
Belfort **9** 47 38N 6 50 E
Belgaum **38** 15 55N 74 35 E
Belgium ■ **12** 50 30N 5 0 E
Belgorod **33** 50 35N 36 35 E
Belgorod-Dnestrovskiy **34** 46 11N 30 23 E
Belgrade = Beograd **24** 44 50N 20 37 E
Beli Drim → **24** 42 6N 20 25 E
Belin-Béliet **10** 44 29N 0 47W
Belinga **51** 1 10N 13 2 E
Belitung **39** 3 10 S 107 50 E
Belize ■ **69** 17 0N 88 30W
Belize City **69** 17 25N 88 0W
Belkovskiy, Ostrov **31** 75 32N 135 44 E
Bell Ville **74** 32 40 S 62 40W
Bella Coola **64** 52 25N 126 40W
Bellac **10** 46 7N 1 3 E
Bellaire **66** 40 1N 80 46W
Bellary **38** 15 10N 76 56 E
Belle Glade **66** 26 43N 80 38W
Belle-Ile **8** 47 20N 3 10W
Belle Isle **63** 51 57N 55 25W
Belle Isle, Str. of **63** 51 30N 56 30W
Belle-Isle-en-Terre **8** 48 33N 3 23W
Belledonne, Chaîne de **11** 45 20N 6 10 E
Bellefontaine **66** 40 20N 83 45W
Bellegarde **9** 47 59N 2 26 E
Bellegarde-en-Marche **10** 45 59N 2 18 E
Bellegarde-sur-Valserine **11** 46 4N 5 50 E
Bellême **8** 48 22N 0 34 E
Belleville, Canada **62** 44 10N 77 23W
Belleville, France **11** 46 7N 4 45 E
Belleville, U.S.A. **67** 38 30N 90 0W
Belleville-sur-Vie **8** 46 46N 1 25W
Bellevue **64** 49 35N 114 22W
Belley **11** 45 46N 5 41 E
Bellingham **64** 48 45N 122 27W
Bellingshausen Sea **60** 66 0 S 80 0W
Bellinzona **13** 46 11N 9 1 E
Bellona Reefs **55** 21 26 S 159 0 E
Belluno **21** 46 8N 12 13 E
Bélmez **18** 38 17N 5 17W
Belmopan **69** 17 18N 88 30W
Belmullet **7** 54 13N 9 58W
Belo Horizonte **73** 19 55 S 43 56W
Belo-Tsiribihina **53** 19 40 S 44 30 E
Belogorsk **31** 51 0N 128 20 E
Beloit **67** 42 35N 89 0W
Belomorsk **30** 64 35N 34 30 E
Belovo **30** 54 30N 86 0 E
Beloye More **30** 66 30N 38 0 E
Beloye Ozero **30** 45 15N 46 50 E
Belozersk **33** 60 0N 37 30 E
Beltsy **34** 47 48N 28 0 E
Belturbet **7** 54 6N 7 28W
Belukha **30** 49 50N 86 50 E
Belvès **10** 44 46N 1 0 E
Belyando → **56** 21 38 S 146 50 E
Belyy, Ostrov **30** 73 30N 71 0 E
Bembéréke **49** 10 11N 2 43 E
Bemidji **67** 47 30N 94 50W
Ben Cruachan **6** 56 26N 5 8W
Ben Dearg **6** 57 47N 4 58W
Ben Gardane **50** 33 11N 11 11 E
Ben Hope **6** 58 24N 4 36W
Ben Lawers **6** 56 33N 4 13W
Ben Lomond, Australia **56** 41 38 S 147 42 E
Ben Lomond, U.K. **6** 56 12N 4 39W
Ben Macdhui **6** 57 4N 3 40W
Ben Mhor **6** 57 16N 7 21W
Ben More, Central, U.K. **6** 56 23N 4 31W
Ben More, Strathclyde, U.K. **6** 56 26N 6 2W
Ben More Assynt **6** 58 7N 4 51W
Ben Nevis **6** 56 48N 5 0W
Ben Vorlich **6** 56 22N 4 15W
Ben Wyvis **6** 57 40N 4 35W
Bena **49** 11 20N 5 50 E
Bena Dibele **51** 4 4 S 22 50 E
Benalla **56** 36 30 S 146 0 E
Benares = Varanasi **37** 25 22N 83 0 E
Bénat, C. **11** 43 5N 6 22 E
Benbecula **6** 57 26N 7 21W
Bencubbin **54** 30 48 S 117 52 E
Bend **68** 44 2N 121 15W
Bender Beila **47** 9 30N 50 48 E
Bendery **34** 46 50N 29 30 E
Bendigo **56** 36 40 S 144 15 E
Bénestroff **9** 48 54N 6 45 E
Benet **10** 46 22N 0 35W
Benevento **23** 41 7N 14 45 E
Benfeld **9** 48 22N 7 34 E
Bengal, Bay of **29** 15 0N 90 0 E
Bengbu **43** 32 58N 117 20 E
Benghazi = Banghāzī **50** 32 11N 20 3 E
Benguela **51** 12 37 S 13 25 E
Beni **51** 0 30N 29 27 E
Beni → **72** 10 23 S 65 24W
Beni Abbès **49** 30 5N 2 5W
Beni Mazâr **50** 28 32N 30 44 E
Beni Mellal **49** 32 21N 6 21W
Beni Ounif **49** 32 0N 1 10W
Beni Suef **50** 29 5N 31 6 E
Benidorm **19** 38 33N 0 9W
Benin ■ **49** 10 0N 2 0 E
Benin, Bight of **49** 5 0N 3 0 E
Benin City **49** 6 20N 5 31 E
Benjamin Constant **72** 4 40 S 70 15W
Bennett, Ostrov **31** 76 21N 148 56 E
Bennettsville **66** 34 38N 79 39W
Bénodet **8** 47 53N 4 7W
Benoni **53** 26 11 S 28 18 E
Bensheim **13** 49 40N 8 38 E
Bentinck I. **56** 17 3 S 139 35 E
Benton **67** 34 30N 92 35W
Benue → **49** 7 48N 6 46 E
Benxi **42** 41 20N 123 48 E
Beograd **24** 44 50N 20 37 E
Beppu **44** 33 15N 131 30 E
Berau, Teluk **40** 2 30 S 132 30 E
Berber **50** 18 0N 34 0 E
Berbera **47** 10 30N 45 2 E
Berbérati **51** 4 15N 15 40 E
Berdichev **34** 49 57N 28 30 E
Berdyansk **34** 46 45N 36 50 E
Bereda **47** 11 45N 51 0 E
Berekum **49** 7 29N 2 34W
Berezina → **32** 52 33N 30 14 E
Berezniki **30** 59 24N 56 46 E
Bérgamo **20** 45 42N 9 40 E
Bergedorf **13** 53 28N 10 12 E
Bergen, Neth. **12** 52 40N 4 43 E
Bergen, Norway **27** 60 23N 5 20 E
Bergen-op-Zoom **12** 51 30N 4 18 E
Bergerac **10** 44 51N 0 30 E
Bergisch-Gladbach **13** 50 59N 7 9 E
Bergues **9** 50 58N 2 24 E
Bergum **12** 53 13N 5 59 E
Berhala, Selat **39** 1 0 S 104 15 E
Berhampur **38** 19 15N 84 54 E
Bering Sea **57** 58 0N 167 0 E
Bering Str. **3** 66 0N 170 0W
Beringen **12** 51 3N 5 14 E
Beringovskiy **31** 63 3N 179 19 E
Berja **19** 36 50N 2 56W
Berkeley, U.K. **5** 51 41N 2 28W
Berkeley, U.S.A. **68** 37 52N 122 20W
Berkshire □ **5** 51 30N 1 20W
Berlin, Germany **13** 52 32N 13 24 E
Berlin, U.S.A. **63** 44 29N 71 10W
Bermuda ■ **1** 32 45N 65 0W
Bern **13** 46 57N 7 28 E
Bernay **8** 49 5N 0 35 E
Berne = Bern **13** 46 57N 7 28 E
Bernier I. **54** 24 50 S 113 12 E
Bernkastel-Kues **13** 49 55N 7 4 E
Beroroha **53** 21 40 S 45 10 E
Beroun **14** 49 57N 14 5 E
Berre, Étang de **11** 43 27N 5 5 E
Berrechid **49** 33 18N 7 36W
Berry **9** 46 50N 2 0 E
Bertincourt **9** 50 5N 2 58 E
Bertoua **51** 4 30N 13 45 E
Berufjörður **27** 64 48N 14 29W
Berwick-upon-Tweed **5** 55 47N 2 0W
Berwyn Mts. **5** 52 54N 3 26W
Besalampy **53** 16 43 S 44 29 E
Besançon **9** 47 15N 6 0 E
Bessèges **11** 44 18N 4 8 E
Bessemer **66** 33 25N 86 57W
Bessin **8** 49 18N 1 0W
Bessines-sur-Gartempe **10** 46 6N 1 22 E
Bethanien **52** 26 31 S 17 8 E
Bethlehem, S. Africa **53** 28 14 S 28 18 E
Bethlehem, U.S.A. **66** 40 39N 75 24W
Béthune **9** 50 30N 2 38 E
Béthune → **8** 49 53N 1 9 E
Betioky **53** 23 48 S 44 20 E
Beton-Bazoches **9** 48 42N 3 15 E
Betroka **53** 23 16 S 46 0 E
Betsiamites **63** 48 56N 68 40W
Bettiah **37** 26 48N 84 33 E
Betul **36** 21 58N 77 59 E
Beuil **11** 44 6N 6 59 E
Beuvron → **8** 47 29N 1 15 E
Beverley, Australia **54** 32 9 S 116 56 E
Beverley, U.K. **5** 53 52N 0 26W
Beverly Hills **68** 34 4N 118 29W
Beverwijk **12** 52 28N 4 38 E
Beyla **49** 8 30N 8 38W
Beynat **10** 45 8N 1 44 E
Beyneu **30** 45 10N 55 3 E
Beyşehir Gölü **45** 37 40N 31 45 E
Bezhitsa **32** 53 19N 34 17 E
Béziers **10** 43 20N 3 12 E
Bhadrakh **36** 21 10N 86 30 E
Bhadravati **38** 13 49N 75 40 E
Bhagalpur **37** 25 10N 87 0 E
Bhakra Dam **36** 31 30N 76 45 E
Bhandara **36** 21 5N 79 42 E
Bhanrer Ra. **36** 23 40N 79 45 E
Bharat = India ■ **2** 20 0N 78 0 E
Bharatpur **36** 27 15N 77 30 E
Bhatpara **37** 22 50N 88 25 E
Bhavnagar **36** 21 45N 72 10 E
Bhawanipatna **38** 19 55N 80 10 E
Bhilwara **36** 25 25N 74 38 E
Bhima → **38** 16 25N 77 17 E
Bhimavaram **38** 16 30N 81 30 E
Bhind **36** 26 30N 78 46 E
Bhiwandi **38** 19 20N 73 0 E
Bhiwani **36** 28 50N 76 9 E
Bhola **37** 22 45N 90 35 E
Bhopal **36** 23 20N 77 30 E
Bhubaneshwar **36** 20 15N 85 50 E
Bhuj **36** 23 15N 69 49 E
Bhusaval **36** 21 3N 75 46 E
Bhutan ■ **37** 27 25N 90 30 E
Biafra, B. of = Bonny, Bight of **51** 3 30N 9 20 E
Biała Podlaska **17** 52 4N 23 6 E
Białystok **17** 53 10N 23 10 E
Biarritz **10** 43 29N 1 33W
Bibala **51** 14 44 S 13 24 E
Biberach **13** 48 5N 9 49 E
Bibiani **49** 6 30N 2 8W
Biche, L. la **64** 54 50N 112 3W
Bida **49** 9 3N 5 58 E
Bidar **38** 17 55N 77 35 E
Biddeford **66** 43 30N 70 28W
Bideford **5** 51 1N 4 13W
Bié, Planalto de **51** 12 0 S 16 0 E
Bieber **68** 41 4N 121 6W
Biel **13** 47 8N 7 14 E
Bielé Karpaty **15** 49 5N 18 0 E
Bielefeld **13** 52 2N 8 31 E
Biella **20** 45 33N 8 3 E
Bielsko-Biała **15** 49 50N 19 2 E
Bien Hoa **41** 10 57N 106 49 E
Bienne = Biel **13** 47 8N 7 14 E
Bienville, L. **62** 55 5N 72 40W
Big Cypress Swamp **66** 26 12N 81 10W
Big Rapids **66** 43 42N 85 27W
Big Spring **67** 32 10N 101 25W
Big Stone Gap **66** 36 52N 82 45W
Big Trout L. **62** 53 40N 90 0W
Biganos **10** 44 39N 0 59W
Biggar, Canada **65** 52 4N 108 0W
Biggar, U.K. **6** 55 38N 3 31W
Bighorn → **68** 46 9N 107 28W
Bighorn Mts. **68** 44 30N 107 30W
Bigorre **10** 43 10N 0 5 E
Bihać **21** 44 49N 15 57 E
Bihar **37** 25 5N 85 40 E
Bihar □ **37** 25 0N 86 0 E
Bijagós, Arquipélago dos **49** 11 15N 16 10W
Bijapur, Karnataka, India **38** 16 50N 75 55 E
Bijapur, Mad. P., India **38** 18 50N 80 50 E
Bijeljina **24** 44 46N 19 17 E
Bijnor **36** 29 27N 78 11 E
Bikaner **36** 28 2N 73 18 E
Bikin **31** 46 50N 134 20 E
Bikini Atoll **57** 12 0N 167 30 E
Bilara **36** 26 14N 73 53 E
Bilaspur **37** 22 2N 82 15 E

Bilauk Taungdan **41** 13 0N 99 0 E
Bilbao **19** 43 16N 2 56W
Bíldudalur **27** 65 41N 23 36W
Bilibino **31** 68 3N 166 20 E
Bilir **31** 65 40N 131 20 E
Billingham **5** 54 36N 1 18W
Billings **68** 45 43N 108 29W
Billiton Is. = Belitung **39** 3 10 S 107 50 E
Billom **10** 45 43N 3 20 E
Bilma **50** 18 50N 13 30 E
Biloela **56** 24 24 S 150 31 E
Biloxi **67** 30 24N 88 53W
Biltine **50** 14 40N 20 50 E
Bimbo **51** 4 15N 18 33 E
Bina-Etawah **36** 24 13N 78 14 E
Bīnālūd, Kūh-e **46** 36 30N 58 30 E
Binche **12** 50 26N 4 10 E
Bindura **51** 17 18 S 31 18 E
Bingen **13** 49 57N 7 53 E
Bingham **63** 45 5N 69 50W
Bingham Canyon **68** 40 31N 112 10W
Binghamton **66** 42 9N 75 54W
Bioko **49** 3 30N 8 40 E
Bir Autrun **50** 18 15N 26 40 E
Bir Mogrein **49** 25 10N 11 25W
Bîr Ungât **50** 22 8N 33 48 E
Birao **50** 10 20N 22 47 E
Bird I. **55** 22 10 S 155 28 E
Birdlip **5** 51 50N 2 7W
Birdsville **56** 25 51 S 139 20 E
Birdum **54** 15 39 S 133 13 E
Birkenhead **5** 53 24N 3 1W
Bîrlad **25** 46 15N 27 38 E
Birmingham, U.K. **5** 52 30N 1 55W
Birmingham, U.S.A. **66** 33 31N 86 50W
Birmitrapur **36** 22 24N 84 46 E
Birni Nkonni **49** 13 55N 5 15 E
Birnin Kebbi **49** 12 32N 4 12 E
Birobidzhan **31** 48 50N 132 50 E
Birr **7** 53 7N 7 55W
Birsk **30** 55 25N 55 30 E
Biscarrosse et de Parentis, Étang de **10** 44 21N 1 10W
Biscay, B. of **4** 45 0N 2 0W
Bischwiller **9** 48 46N 7 50 E
Biscostasing **62** 47 18N 82 9W
Bishop Auckland **5** 54 40N 1 40W
Bishop's Stortford **5** 51 52N 0 11 E
Biskra **49** 34 50N 5 44 E
Bismarck **67** 46 49N 100 49W
Bismarck Arch. **56** 2 30 S 150 0 E
Bismarck Sea **56** 4 10 S 146 50 E
Bispfors **27** 63 1N 16 37 E
Bissau **49** 11 45N 15 45W
Bistriţa **15** 47 9N 24 35 E
Bistriţa → **15** 46 30N 26 57 E
Bitam **51** 2 5N 11 25 E
Bitche **9** 49 2N 7 25 E
Bitkine **50** 11 59N 18 13 E
Bitola **24** 41 5N 21 10 E
Bitter L. = Buheirat-Murrat-el-Kubra **50** 30 15N 32 40 E
Bitterfontein **52** 31 1 S 18 32 E
Bitterroot Range **68** 46 0N 114 20W
Biu **50** 10 40N 12 3 E
Biwa-Ko **44** 35 15N 136 10 E
Biysk **30** 52 40N 85 0 E
Bizerte **49** 37 15N 9 50 E
Bjargtangar **27** 65 30N 24 30W
Bjelovar **24** 45 56N 16 49 E
Bjørnøya **3** 74 30N 19 0 E
Black → **41** 21 15N 105 20 E
Black Diamond **64** 50 45N 114 14W
Black Forest = Schwarzwald **13** 48 0N 8 0 E
Black Hills **67** 44 0N 103 50W
Black Mt. = Mynydd Du **5** 51 45N 3 45W
Black Mts. **5** 51 52N 3 5W
Black Sea **34** 43 30N 35 0 E
Black Volta → **49** 8 41N 1 33W
Blackall **56** 24 25 S 145 45 E
Blackburn **5** 53 44N 2 30W
Blackpool **5** 53 48N 3 3W
Blacksod B. **7** 54 6N 10 0W
Blackstone Ra. **54** 26 0 S 129 0 E
Blackwater →, Ireland **7** 51 55N 7 50W
Blackwater →, U.K. **7** 54 31N 6 35W
Blackwell **67** 36 55N 97 20W
Blaenau Ffestiniog **5** 53 0N 3 57W
Blagodarnoye **35** 45 7N 43 37 E
Blagoveshchensk **31** 50 20N 127 30 E
Blain **8** 47 29N 1 45W
Blainville-sur-l'Eau **9** 48 33N 6 23 E
Blair Athol **56** 22 42 S 147 31 E
Blair Atholl **6** 56 46N 3 50W
Blairgowrie **6** 56 36N 3 20W
Blairmore **64** 49 40N 114 25W
Blâmont **9** 48 35N 6 50 E
Blanc, Le **10** 46 37N 1 3 E
Blanc, Mont **11** 45 48N 6 50 E
Blanca Peak **68** 37 35N 105 29W
Blanche L., S. Austral., Australia **56** 29 15 S 139 40 E
Blanche L., W. Austral., Australia **54** 22 25 S 123 17 E
Blanco, C. **68** 42 50N 124 40W
Blanda → **27** 65 20N 19 40W
Blandford Forum **5** 50 52N 2 10W
Blangy-sur-Bresle **9** 49 55N 1 37 E
Blankenberge **12** 51 20N 3 9 E
Blanquefort **10** 44 55N 0 38W
Blantyre **51** 15 45 S 35 0 E
Blarney **7** 51 57N 8 35W
Blaydon **5** 54 56N 1 47W
Blaye **10** 45 8N 0 40W
Blaye-les-Mines **10** 44 1N 2 8 E
Blaze, Pt. **54** 12 56 S 130 11 E
Bleiburg **14** 46 35N 14 49 E
Blekinge län □ **28** 56 20N 15 20 E
Bléone → **11** 44 5N 6 0 E
Bletchley **5** 51 59N 0 44W
Bleymard, Le **10** 44 30N 3 42 E
Blida **49** 36 30N 2 49 E
Blind River **62** 46 10N 82 58W
Blitar **40** 8 5 S 112 11 E
Blitta **49** 8 23N 1 6 E
Bloemfontein **52** 29 6 S 26 7 E
Bloemhof **52** 27 38 S 25 32 E
Blois **8** 47 35N 1 20 E
Blönduós **27** 65 40N 20 12W
Bloody Foreland **7** 55 10N 8 18W
Bloomington, Ill., U.S.A. **67** 40 27N 89 0W
Bloomington, Ind., U.S.A. **66** 39 10N 86 30W
Bloomsburg **66** 41 0N 76 30W
Blue Mts., Australia **55** 33 40 S 150 0 E
Blue Mts., Oreg., U.S.A. **68** 45 15N 119 0W
Blue Mts., Pa., U.S.A. **66** 40 30N 76 30W
Blue Mud B. **55** 13 30 S 136 0 E
Blue Nile = Nîl el Azraq → **50** 15 38N 32 31 E
Blue Ridge Mts. **66** 36 30N 80 15W
Blue Stack Mts. **7** 54 46N 8 5W
Bluefield **66** 37 18N 81 14W
Bluefields **70** 12 20N 83 50W
Blumenau **74** 27 0 S 49 0W
Blyth **5** 55 8N 1 32W
Bo **49** 7 55N 11 50W
Bo Hai **42** 39 0N 120 0 E
Boa Vista **72** 2 48N 60 30W
Boaco **70** 12 29N 85 35W
Bobbili **38** 18 35N 83 30 E
Bobcaygeon **62** 44 33N 78 33W
Böblingen **13** 48 41N 9 1 E
Bobo-Dioulasso **49** 11 8N 4 13W
Bóbr → **17** 52 4N 15 4 E
Bobraomby, Tanjon' i **53** 12 40 S 49 10 E
Bobruysk **32** 53 10N 29 15 E
Bôca do Acre **72** 8 50 S 67 27W
Boca Raton **66** 26 21N 80 5W
Bocanda **49** 7 5N 4 31W
Bocaranga **50** 7 0N 15 35 E
Bocas del Toro **70** 9 15N 82 20W
Bocholt **13** 51 50N 6 35 E
Bochum **13** 51 28N 7 12 E
Bocognano **11** 42 5N 9 4 E
Boda **51** 4 19N 17 26 E
Bodaybo **31** 57 50N 114 0 E
Boden **27** 65 50N 21 42 E
Bodensee **13** 47 35N 9 25 E
Bodhan **38** 18 40N 77 44 E
Bodmin **5** 50 28N 4 44W
Bodmin Moor **5** 50 33N 4 36W
Bodrog → **15** 48 15N 21 35 E
Boën **11** 45 44N 4 0 E
Boende **51** 0 24 S 21 12 E
Boffa **49** 10 16N 14 3W
Bogalusa **67** 30 50N 89 55W
Bogan → **56** 29 59 S 146 17 E
Boggeragh Mts. **7** 52 2N 8 55W
Bognor Regis **5** 50 47N 0 40W
Bogong, Mt. **56** 36 47 S 147 17 E
Bogor **40** 6 36 S 106 48 E
Bogorodskoye **31** 52 22N 140 30 E
Bogota **72** 4 34N 74 0W
Bogra **37** 24 51N 89 22 E
Boguchany **31** 58 40N 97 30 E
Bogué **49** 16 45N 14 10W
Bohain-en-Vermandois **9** 49 59N 3 28 E
Bohemian Forest = Böhmerwald **13** 49 30N 12 40 E
Böhmerwald **13** 49 30N 12 40 E
Bohol **40** 9 50N 124 10 E
Bohol Sea **40** 9 0N 124 0 E
Bohotleh **47** 8 20N 46 25 E
Boileau, C. **54** 17 40 S 122 7 E
Boise **68** 43 43N 116 9W
Boise City **67** 36 45N 102 30W
Boissevain **65** 49 15N 100 5W
Bojador C. **49** 26 0N 14 30W
Bojana → **24** 41 52N 19 22 E
Boké **49** 10 56N 14 17W
Boknafjorden **27** 59 14N 5 40 E
Bokoro **50** 12 25N 17 14 E
Bokote **51** 0 12 S 21 8 E
Bokungu **51** 0 35 S 22 50 E
Bol **50** 13 30N 15 0 E
Bolama **49** 11 30N 15 30W
Bolaños → **69** 21 12N 104 5W
Bolbec **8** 49 30N 0 30 E
Bolesławiec **17** 51 17N 15 37 E
Bolívar **74** 36 15 S 60 53W
Bolivia ■ **72** 17 6 S 64 0W
Bollène **11** 44 18N 4 45 E
Bollnäs **28** 61 21N 16 24 E
Bolobo **51** 2 6 S 16 20 E
Bologna **21** 44 30N 11 20 E
Bologne **9** 48 10N 5 8 E
Bologoye **32** 57 55N 34 0 E
Bolomba **51** 0 35N 19 0 E
Boloven, Cao Nguyen **41** 15 10N 106 30 E
Bolsena, L. di **21** 42 35N 11 55 E
Bolshevik, Ostrov **31** 78 30N 102 0 E
Bolshoi Kavkas **35** 42 50N 44 0 E
Bolshoy Anyuy → **31** 68 30N 160 49 E
Bolshoy Begichev, Ostrov **31** 74 20N 112 30 E
Bolshoy Lyakhovskiy, Ostrov **31** 73 35N 142 0 E
Bolsward **12** 53 3N 5 32 E
Bolton **5** 53 35N 2 26W
Bolzano **21** 46 30N 11 20 E
Boma **51** 5 50 S 13 4 E
Bombala **56** 36 56 S 149 15 E
Bombay **38** 18 55N 72 50 E
Bomboma **51** 2 25N 18 55 E
Bomili **51** 1 45N 27 5 E
Bomongo **51** 1 27N 18 21 E
Bomu → **51** 4 40N 22 30 E
Bon, C. **50** 37 1N 11 2 E
Bonaire **70** 12 10N 68 15W
Bonaparte Archipelago **54** 14 0 S 124 30 E
Bonavista **63** 48 40N 53 5W
Bondo **51** 3 55N 23 53 E
Bondoukou **49** 8 2N 2 47W
Bo'ness **6** 56 0N 3 38W
Bongandanga **51** 1 24N 21 3 E
Bongor **50** 10 35N 15 20 E
Bonifacio **11** 41 24N 9 10 E
Bonifacio, Bouches de **22** 41 12N 9 15 E
Bonin Is. **57** 27 0N 142 0 E
Bonn **13** 50 43N 7 6 E
Bonnat **10** 46 20N 1 54 E
Bonnétable **8** 48 11N 0 25 E
Bonneuil-Matours **8** 46 41N 0 34 E
Bonneval **8** 48 11N 1 24 E
Bonneville **11** 46 4N 6 24 E
Bonnie Rock **54** 30 29 S 118 22 E
Bonny, Bight of **51** 3 30N 9 20 E
Bonny-sur-Loire **9** 47 33N 2 50 E
Bonnyville **65** 54 20N 110 45W
Bonthe **49** 7 30N 12 33W
Boom **12** 51 6N 4 20 E
Boone **67** 42 5N 93 53W
Boonville **66** 38 3N 87 13W
Boothia, Gulf of **3** 71 0N 90 0W
Bootle, Cumbria, U.K. **5** 54 17N 3 24W
Bootle, Merseyside, U.K. **5** 53 28N 3 1W
Booué **51** 0 5 S 11 55 E
Bôr, Sudan **50** 6 10N 31 40 E
Bor, Yugoslavia **24** 44 8N 22 7 E
Borama **47** 9 55N 43 7 E
Borås **28** 57 43N 12 56 E
Borāzjān **46** 29 22N 51 10 E
Bordeaux **10** 44 50N 0 36W
Borden I. **3** 78 30N 111 30W
Borders □ **6** 55 35N 2 50W
Bordertown **56** 36 19 S 140 45 E
Borðeyri **27** 65 12N 21 6W
Bordj Fly Ste. Marie **49** 27 19N 2 32W
Bordj-in-Eker **49** 24 9N 5 3 E
Bordj Omar Driss **49** 28 10N 6 40 E
Bordj-Tarat **49** 25 55N 9 3 E
Borgarnes **27** 64 32N 21 55W
Børgefjellet **27** 65 20N 13 45 E
Borger, Neth. **12** 52 54N 6 44 E
Borger, U.S.A. **67** 35 40N 101 20W
Borgholm **28** 56 52N 16 39 E
Borisoglebsk **33** 51 27N 42 5 E
Borisov **32** 54 17N 28 28 E
Borja **72** 4 20 S 77 40W
Borkou **50** 18 15N 18 50 E
Borlänge **28** 60 29N 15 26 E
Borneo **39** 1 0N 115 0 E
Bornholm **28** 55 10N 15 0 E
Borogontsy **31** 62 42N 131 8 E
Boromo **49** 11 45N 2 58W
Borovichi **32** 58 25N 33 55 E
Borroloola **55** 16 4 S 136 17 E
Bort-les-Orgues **10** 45 24N 2 29 E
Borth **5** 52 29N 4 3W
Borujerd **45** 33 55N 48 50 E
Borzya **31** 50 24N 116 31 E
Bosa **22** 40 17N 8 32 E
Bosanska Gradiška **24** 45 10N 17 15 E
Bosaso **47** 11 12N 49 18 E
Boscastle **5** 50 42N 4 42W
Boshan **42** 36 28N 117 49 E
Bosna → **24** 45 4N 18 29 E
Bosna i Hercegovina □ **24** 44 0N 18 0 E
Bōsō-Hantō **44** 35 20N 140 20 E
Bosobolo **51** 4 15N 19 50 E
Bosporus = Karadeniz Boğazı **45** 41 10N 29 10 E
Bossangoa **50** 6 35N 17 30 E
Bossekop **27** 69 57N 23 15 E
Bossembélé **50** 5 25N 17 40 E
Bossier City **67** 32 28N 93 48W
Bosso **50** 13 43N 13 19 E
Bossut C. **54** 18 42 S 121 35 E
Bosten Hu **42** 41 55N 87 40 E
Boston, U.K. **5** 52 59N 0 2W
Boston, U.S.A. **66** 42 20N 71 0W
Bothnia, G. of **27** 63 0N 20 0 E
Botletle → **52** 20 10 S 23 15 E
Botoşani **15** 47 42N 26 41 E
Botswana ■ **52** 22 0 S 24 0 E
Bottrop **13** 51 34N 6 59 E
Botucatu **73** 22 55 S 48 30W
Bou Djébéha **49** 18 25N 2 45W
Bou Izakarn **49** 29 12N 9 46W
Bouaké **49** 7 40N 5 2W
Bouar **51** 6 0N 15 40 E
Bouârfa **49** 32 32N 1 58 E
Bouca **50** 6 45N 18 25 E
Boucau **10** 43 32N 1 29W
Bouches-du-Rhône □ **11** 43 37N 5 2 E
Bougainville C. **54** 13 57 S 126 4 E
Bougouni **49** 11 30N 7 20W
Bouillon **12** 49 44N 5 3 E
Boulder **67** 40 3N 105 10W
Boulia **56** 22 52 S 139 51 E
Bouligny **9** 49 17N 5 45 E
Boulogne → **8** 47 12N 1 47W
Boulogne-sur-Gesse **10** 43 18N 0 38 E
Boulogne-sur-Mer **9** 50 42N 1 36 E
Bouloire **8** 47 59N 0 45 E
Boultoum **49** 14 45N 10 25 E
Bouna **49** 9 10N 3 0W
Boundiali **49** 9 30N 6 20W
Bounty I. **57** 48 0 S 178 30 E
Bourbon-Lancy **10** 46 37N 3 45 E
Bourbon-l'Archambault **10** 46 36N 3 4 E
Bourbonnais **10** 46 28N 3 0 E
Bourbonne-les-Bains **9** 47 54N 5 45 E
Bourem **49** 17 0N 0 24W
Bourg **10** 45 3N 0 34W
Bourg-Argental **11** 45 18N 4 32 E
Bourg-de-Péage **11** 45 2N 5 3 E
Bourg-en-Bresse **11** 46 13N 5 12 E
Bourg-St.-Andéol **11** 44 23N 4 39 E
Bourg-St.-Maurice **11** 45 35N 6 46 E
Bourganeuf **10** 45 57N 1 45 E
Bourges **9** 47 9N 2 25 E
Bourget, L. du **11** 45 44N 5 52 E
Bourgneuf, B. de **8** 47 3N 2 10W
Bourgneuf-en-Retz **8** 47 2N 1 58W
Bourgneuf-la-Fôret, Le **8** 48 10N 0 59W
Bourgogne **9** 47 0N 4 50 E
Bourgoin-Jallieu **11** 45 36N 5 17 E
Bourgueil **8** 47 17N 0 10 E
Bourke **56** 30 8 S 145 55 E
Bournemouth **5** 50 43N 1 53W
Bourriot-Bergonce **10** 44 7N 0 14W
Bouscat, Le **10** 44 53N 0 37W
Boussac **10** 46 22N 2 13 E
Boussens **10** 43 12N 0 58 E
Bousso **50** 10 34N 16 52 E
Boutilimit **49** 17 45N 14 40W
Bouvet I. = Bouvetøya **1** 54 26 S 3 24 E
Bouvetøya **1** 54 26 S 3 24 E
Bouzonville **9** 49 17N 6 32 E
Bovigny **12** 50 12N 5 55 E
Bowen **56** 20 0 S 148 16 E
Bowland, Forest of **5** 54 0N 2 30W
Bowling Green, Ky., U.S.A. **66** 37 0N 86 25W
Bowling Green, Ohio, U.S.A. **66** 41 22N 83 40W
Bowling Green, C. **56** 19 19 S 147 25 E
Bowmanville **62** 43 55N 78 41W
Bowmore **6** 55 45N 6 18W
Bowral **56** 34 26 S 150 27 E
Boxtel **12** 51 36N 5 20 E
Boyle **7** 53 58N 8 19W
Boyne → **7** 53 43N 6 15W
Boyne City **62** 45 13N 85 1W
Bozeman **68** 45 40N 111 0W
Bozen = Bolzano **21** 46 30N 11 20 E
Bozouls **10** 44 28N 2 43 E
Bozoum **50** 6 25N 16 35 E
Brabant □ **12** 50 46N 4 30 E
Brač **21** 43 20N 16 40 E
Bracadale, L. **6** 57 20N 6 30W
Bracciano, L. di **21** 42 8N 12 11 E
Bracebridge **62** 45 2N 79 19W
Brach **50** 27 31N 14 20 E
Bracieux **9** 47 30N 1 30 E
Bräcke **27** 62 45N 15 26 E
Brad **15** 46 10N 22 50 E
Bradenton **66** 27 25N 82 35W
Bradford, U.K. **5** 53 47N 1 45W
Bradford, U.S.A. **66** 41 58N 78 41W
Bradshaw **55** 15 21 S 130 16 E
Braga **18** 41 35N 8 25W
Bragança, Brazil **73** 1 0 S 47 2W
Bragança, Portugal **18** 41 48N 6 50W
Brahmanbaria **37** 23 58N 91 15 E
Brahmani → **36** 20 39N 86 46 E
Brahmaputra → **37** 24 2N 90 59 E
Braich-y-pwll **5** 52 47N 4 46W
Brăila **25** 45 19N 27 59 E
Braintree **5** 51 53N 0 34 E
Brakel **13** 51 49N 5 5 E
Brampton **62** 43 45N 79 45W
Branco → **72** 1 20 S 61 50W
Brandenburg **13** 52 24N 12 33 E
Brandon **65** 49 50N 99 57W
Brandon, Mt. **7** 52 15N 10 15W
Brandon B. **7** 52 17N 10 8W
Brandvlei **52** 30 25 S 20 30 E
Braniewo **17** 54 25N 19 50 E
Brańsk **17** 52 45N 22 50 E
Brantford **62** 43 10N 80 15W
Brantôme **10** 45 22N 0 39 E
Brasil, Planalto **73** 18 0 S 46 30W
Brasília **73** 15 47 S 47 55 E
Braşov **25** 45 38N 25 35 E
Brassac-les-Mines **10** 45 24N 3 20 E
Brasschaat **12** 51 19N 4 27 E
Brassey, Banjaran **39** 5 0N 117 15 E
Brasstown Bald, Mt. **66** 34 54N 83 45W
Bratislava **15** 48 10N 17 7 E
Bratsk **31** 56 10N 101 30 E
Brattleboro **66** 42 53N 72 37W
Braunschweig **13** 52 17N 10 28 E
Braunton **5** 51 6N 4 9W
Brava **47** 1 20N 44 8 E
Bravo del Norte → **69** 25 57N 97 9W
Brawley **68** 32 58N 115 30W
Bray **7** 53 12N 6 6W
Bray, Pays de **9** 49 46N 1 26 E
Bray-sur-Seine **9** 48 25N 3 14 E
Brazil **66** 39 32N 87 8W
Brazil ■ **73** 10 0 S 50 0W
Brazilian Highlands = Brasil, Planalto **73** 18 0 S 46 30W
Brazos → **67** 28 53N 95 23W
Brazzaville **51** 4 9 S 15 12 E
Brčko **24** 44 54N 18 46 E
Breadalbane **6** 56 30N 4 15W
Brechin **6** 56 44N 2 40W
Brecon **5** 51 57N 3 23W
Brecon Beacons **5** 51 53N 3 27W
Breda **12** 51 35N 4 45 E
Bredasdorp **52** 34 33 S 20 2 E
Bregenz **13** 47 30N 9 45 E
Bréhal **8** 48 53N 1 30W
Bréhat, I. de **8** 48 51N 3 0W
Breiðafjörður **27** 65 15N 23 15W
Breil-sur-Roya **11** 43 56N 7 31 E
Bremen **13** 53 4N 8 47 E
Bremerhaven **13** 53 34N 8 35 E
Bremerton **68** 47 30N 122 38W
Brenham **67** 30 5N 96 27W
Brenner Pass **13** 47 0N 11 30 E
Brent **5** 51 33N 0 18W
Brentwood **5** 51 37N 0 19 E
Bréscia **20** 45 33N 10 13 E
Breskens **12** 51 23N 3 33 E
Breslau = Wrocław **17** 51 5N 17 5 E
Bresle → **8** 50 4N 1 22 E
Bresles **9** 49 25N 2 13 E
Bressanone **21** 46 43N 11 40 E
Bressay I. **6** 60 10N 1 5W
Bresse **9** 46 50N 5 10 E
Bresse, La **9** 48 0N 6 53 E
Bressuire **8** 46 51N 0 30W
Brest, France **8** 48 24N 4 31W
Brest, U.S.S.R. **32** 52 10N 23 40 E
Bretagne **8** 48 0N 3 0W
Bretçu **25** 46 7N 26 18 E
Breteuil, Eure, France **8** 48 50N 0 53 E
Breteuil, Oise, France **9** 49 38N 2 18 E
Breton, Pertuis **10** 46 17N 1 25W
Breton Sd. **67** 29 40N 89 12W
Brewer **63** 44 43N 68 50W
Brewster **68** 48 10N 119 51W
Brewster, Kap **3** 70 7N 22 0W
Brewton **66** 31 9N 87 2W
Brezhnev **30** 55 42N 52 19 E
Bria **50** 6 30N 21 58 E
Briançon **11** 44 54N 6 39 E
Briare **9** 47 38N 2 45 E
Bribie I. **56** 27 0 S 152 58 E
Bricquebec **8** 49 28N 1 38W
Bridgend **5** 51 30N 3 35W
Bridgeport **66** 41 12N 73 12W
Bridgeton **66** 39 29N 75 10W
Bridgetown, Australia **54** 33 58 S 116 7 E
Bridgetown, Barbados **70** 13 0N 59 30W
Bridgewater **63** 44 25N 64 31W
Bridgewater, C. **56** 38 23 S 141 23 E
Bridgnorth **5** 52 33N 2 25W
Bridgwater **5** 51 7N 3 0W
Bridlington **5** 54 6N 0 11W
Bridport **5** 50 43N 2 45W
Brie, Plaine de la **9** 48 35N 3 10 E
Brie-Comte-Robert **9** 48 40N 2 35 E
Briec **8** 48 6N 4 0W
Brienne-le-Château **9** 48 24N 4 30 E
Brienon-sur-Armançon **9** 47 59N 3 38 E
Briey **9** 49 14N 5 57 E
Brig **13** 46 18N 7 59 E
Brigg **5** 53 33N 0 30W
Brigham City **68** 41 30N 112 1W
Brighton **5** 50 50N 0 9W
Brignogan-Plage **8** 48 40N 4 20W
Brignoles **11** 43 25N 6 5 E
Bríndisi **23** 40 39N 17 55 E
Brionne **8** 49 11N 0 43 E
Brioude **10** 45 18N 3 24 E
Briouze **8** 48 42N 0 23W
Brisbane **56** 27 25 S 153 2 E
Bristol, U.K. **5** 51 26N 2 35W
Bristol, Conn., U.S.A. **66** 41 44N 72 57W
Bristol, Tenn., U.S.A. **66** 36 36N 82 11W
Bristol Channel **5** 51 18N 4 30W
Bristow **67** 35 55N 96 28W
British Antarctic Territory □ **60** 66 0 S 45 0W
British Columbia □ **64** 55 0N 125 15W
British Guiana = Guyana ■ **72** 5 0N 59 0W
British Honduras = Belize ■ **69** 17 0N 88 30W
British Isles **4** 55 0N 4 0W
Britstown **52** 30 37 S 23 30 E
Brittany = Bretagne **8** 48 0N 3 0W
Brive-la-Gaillarde **10** 45 10N 1 32 E
Brlik **30** 44 0N 74 5 E
Brno **15** 49 10N 16 35 E
Broad B. **6** 58 14N 6 16W
Broad Haven **7** 54 20N 9 55W
Broad Law **6** 55 30N 3 22W
Broad Sd. **56** 22 0 S 149 45 E
Broads, The **5** 52 45N 1 30 E
Broadsound Ra. **55** 22 50 S 149 30 E
Brocken **13** 51 48N 10 40 E
Brockton **66** 42 8N 71 2W
Brockville **62** 44 35N 75 41W
Brod **24** 41 35N 21 17 E
Brodick **6** 55 34N 5 9W
Broglie **8** 49 0N 0 30 E
Broken Hill = Kabwe **51** 14 30 S 28 29 E
Broken Hill **56** 31 58 S 141 29 E
Bromfield **5** 52 25N 2 45W
Bromley **5** 51 20N 0 5 E
Brønderslev **28** 57 16N 9 57 E
Brookhaven **67** 31 40N 90 25W
Brooks **64** 50 35N 111 55W
Broom, L. **6** 57 55N 5 15W
Broome **54** 18 0 S 122 15 E
Broons **8** 48 20N 2 16W
Brora **6** 58 0N 3 50W
Brora → **6** 58 4N 3 52W
Brosna → **7** 53 8N 8 0W
Brou **8** 48 13N 1 11 E
Broughty Ferry **6** 56 29N 2 50W
Brouwershaven **12** 51 45N 3 55 E
Brown Willy **5** 50 35N 4 34W
Brownsville **67** 25 56N 97 25W
Brownwood **67** 31 45N 99 0W
Bruay-en-Artois **9** 50 29N 2 33 E
Bruce, Mt. **54** 22 37 S 118 8 E
Bruche → **9** 48 34N 7 43 E
Bruchsal **13** 49 9N 8 39 E
Bruck an der Leitha **15** 48 1N 16 47 E
Brue → **5** 51 10N 2 59W
Bruges = Brugge **12** 51 13N 3 13 E
Brugge **12** 51 13N 3 13 E
Brühl **13** 50 49N 6 51 E
Brûlon **8** 47 58N 0 15W
Brumath **9** 48 43N 7 40 E
Brunei = Bandar Seri Begawan **39** 4 52N 115 0 E
Brunei ■ **39** 4 50N 115 0 E
Bruno **65** 52 20N 105 30W
Brunswick = Braunschweig **13** 52 17N 10 28 E
Brunswick, Ga., U.S.A. **66** 31 10N 81 30W
Brunswick, Maine, U.S.A. **63** 43 53N 69 50W
Brunswick B. **54** 15 15 S 124 50 E

Bruny I. 56 43 20 S 147 15 E
Brussel 12 50 51N 4 21 E
Brussels = Bruxelles 12 50 51N 4 21 E
Bruxelles 12 50 51N 4 21 E
Bruyères 9 48 10N 6 40 E
Bryan, Ohio, U.S.A. 66 41 30N 84 30W
Bryan, Tex., U.S.A. 67 30 40N 96 27W
Bryansk 32 53 13N 34 25 E
Bryne 27 58 44N 5 38 E
Bu Craa 49 26 45N 12 50W
Bucaramanga 72 7 0N 73 0W
Buchan 6 57 32N 2 8W
Buchan Ness 6 57 29N 1 48W
Buchanan 49 5 57N 10 2W
Buchanan, L. 54 25 33 S 123 2 E
Buchans 63 48 50N 56 52W
Bucharest =
Bucureşti 25 44 27N 26 10 E
Bückeburg 13 52 16N 9 2 E
Buckhannon 66 39 2N 80 10W
Buckhaven 6 56 10N 3 2W
Buckie 6 57 40N 2 58W
Buckingham, Canada 62 45 37N 75 24W
Buckingham, U.K. 5 52 0N 0 59W
Buckingham □ 5 51 50N 0 55W
Buckingham B. 55 12 10 S 135 40 E
Buckland Newton 5 50 45N 2 25W
Bucquoy 9 50 9N 2 43 E
Bucureşti 25 44 27N 26 10 E
Bucyrus 66 40 48N 83 0W
Budapest 15 47 29N 19 5 E
Budaun 36 28 5N 79 10 E
Bude 5 50 49N 4 33W
Budennovsk 34 44 50N 44 10 E
Búðareyri 27 65 2N 14 13W
Búðir 27 64 49N 23 23W
Budjala 51 2 50N 19 40 E
Buenaventura,
Colombia 72 3 53N 77 4W
Buenaventura,
Mexico 69 29 51N 107 29W
Buenos Aires 74 34 30 S 58 20W
Buffalo 66 42 55N 78 50W
Bug →, Poland 17 52 31N 21 5 E
Bug →, U.S.S.R. 34 46 59N 31 58 E
Buga 72 4 0N 76 15W
Bugeat 10 45 36N 1 55 E
Bugue, Le 10 44 55N 0 56 E
Buguruslan 30 53 39N 52 26 E
Buheirat-Murrat-el-
Kubra 50 30 15N 32 40 E
Builth Wells 5 52 10N 3 26W
Buir Nur 42 47 50N 117 42 E
Buis-les-Baronnies 11 44 17N 5 16 E
Bujumbura 51 3 16 S 29 18 E
Bukachacha 31 52 55N 116 50 E
Bukama 51 9 10 S 25 50 E
Bukavu 51 2 20 S 28 52 E
Bukene 51 4 15 S 32 48 E
Bukhara 30 39 48N 64 25 E
Bukit Mertajam 41 5 22N 100 28 E
Bukittinggi 39 0 20 S 100 20 E
Bukoba 51 1 20 S 31 49 E
Bulandshahr 36 28 28N 77 51 E
Bulawayo 51 20 7 S 28 32 E
Bulgaria ■ 25 42 35N 25 30 E
Bulhar 47 10 25N 44 30 E
Bull Shoals L. 67 36 40N 93 5W
Bullfinch 54 30 58 S 119 3 E
Bulloo → 56 28 43 S 142 30 E
Bully-les-Mines 9 50 27N 2 44 E
Bulo Burti 47 3 50N 45 33 E
Bulolo 56 7 10 S 146 40 E
Bulun 31 70 37N 127 30 E
Bumba 51 2 13N 22 30 E
Buna 51 2 58N 39 30 E
Bunbah, Khalīj 50 32 20N 23 15 E
Bunbury 54 33 20 S 115 35 E
Buncrana 7 55 8N 7 28W
Bundaberg 56 24 54 S 152 22 E
Bundi 36 25 30N 75 35 E
Bundoran 7 54 24N 8 17W
Bungo-Suidō 44 33 0N 132 15 E
Bunia 51 1 35N 30 20 E
Buorkhaya, Mys 31 71 50N 132 40 E
Buqbua 50 31 29N 25 29 E
Bur Acaba 47 3 12N 44 20 E
Bûr Safâga 50 26 43N 33 57 E
Bûr Sa'îd 50 31 16N 32 18 E
Bûr Sûdân 50 19 32N 37 9 E
Burao 47 9 32N 45 32 E
Burbank 68 34 9N 118 23W
Burdur 45 37 45N 30 22 E
Bure → 5 52 38N 1 45 E
Bureya → 31 49 27N 129 30 E
Burgas 25 42 33N 27 29 E
Burgdorf 13 52 27N 10 0 E
Burgenland □ 15 47 20N 16 20 E
Burgersdorp 52 31 0 S 26 20 E
Burgos 19 42 21N 3 41W
Burgsteinfurt 13 52 9N 7 23 E
Burgsvik 28 57 3N 18 19 E
Burgundy =
Bourgogne 9 47 0N 4 50 E
Burhou 8 49 45N 2 15W
Burin 63 47 1N 55 14W
Burji 50 5 29N 37 51 E
Burketown 56 17 45 S 139 33 E
Burkina Faso ■ 49 12 0N 1 0W
Burlington, Canada 62 43 18N 79 45W
Burlington, Iowa,
U.S.A. 67 40 50N 91 5W
Burlington, N.C.,
U.S.A. 66 36 7N 79 27W
Burlington, N.J.,
U.S.A. 66 40 5N 74 50W
Burlington, Vt.,
U.S.A. 66 44 27N 73 14W
Burma ■ 41 21 0N 96 30 E
Burnett → 55 24 45 S 152 23 E
Burnie 56 41 4 S 145 56 E
Burnley 5 53 47N 2 15W
Burns 68 43 40N 119 4W
Burns Lake 64 54 20N 125 45W
Burra 56 33 40 S 138 55 E
Burry Port 5 51 41N 4 17W
Bursa 45 40 15N 29 5 E
Burton-upon-Trent 5 52 48N 1 39W
Buru 40 3 30 S 126 30 E
Burundi ■ 51 3 15 S 30 0 E
Burutu 49 5 20N 5 29 E
Bury 5 53 36N 2 19W
Bury St. Edmunds 5 52 15N 0 42 E
Buryat A.S.S.R. □ 31 53 0N 110 0 E
Businga 51 3 16N 20 59 E
Buskerud fylke □ 28 60 13N 9 0 E
Bussang 9 47 50N 6 50 E
Busselton 54 33 42 S 115 15 E
Bussum 12 52 16N 5 10 E
Bustard Hd. 55 24 0 S 151 48 E
Busto Arsizio 20 45 40N 8 50 E
Busu-Djanoa 51 1 43N 21 23 E
Buta 51 2 50N 24 53 E
Butare 51 2 31 S 29 52 E
Butaritari 57 3 30N 174 0 E
Bute 6 55 48N 5 2W
Butembo 51 0 9N 29 18 E
Butler 66 40 52N 79 52W
Butte 68 46 0N 112 31W
Butterworth 41 5 24N 100 23 E
Butuan 40 8 57N 125 33 E
Butung 40 5 0 S 122 45 E
Buturlinovka 33 50 50N 40 35 E
Buxton 5 53 16N 1 54W
Buxy 9 46 44N 4 40 E
Buy 33 58 28N 41 28 E
Buyaga 31 59 50N 127 0 E
Buzançais 8 46 54N 1 25 E
Buzău 25 45 10N 26 50 E
Buzău → 25 45 10N 27 20 E
Buzen 44 33 35N 131 5 E
Buzi → 51 19 50 S 34 43 E
Buzuluk 30 52 48N 52 12 E
Buzzards Bay 66 41 45N 70 38W
Bydgoszcz 17 53 10N 18 0 E
Byelorussian
S.S.R. □ 32 53 30N 27 0 E
Byron, C. 55 28 38 S 153 40 E
Byrranga, Gory 31 75 0N 100 0 E
Byske 27 64 57N 21 11 E
Byske älv → 27 64 57N 21 13 E
Bytom 17 50 25N 18 54 E

C

Caála 51 12 46 S 15 30 E
Cabimas 72 10 23N 71 25W
Cabinda 51 5 33 S 12 11 E
Cabinda □ 51 5 0 S 12 30 E
Cabinet Mts. 68 48 0N 115 30W
Cabo Pantoja 72 1 0 S 75 10W
Cabonga, Réservoir 62 47 20N 76 40W
Cabora Bassa Dam 51 15 20 S 32 50 E
Caborca 69 30 40N 112 10W
Cabot Strait 63 47 15N 59 40W
Cabrera, I. 19 39 8N 2 57 E
Cabri 65 50 35N 108 25W
Cabriel → 19 39 14N 1 3W
Čačak 24 43 54N 20 20 E
Cáceres 18 39 26N 6 23W
Cache Bay 62 46 22N 80 0W
Cachoeira 73 12 30 S 39 0W
Cachoeira de
Itapemirim 73 20 51 S 41 7W
Cachoeira do Sul 74 30 3 S 52 53W
Cacólo 51 10 9 S 19 21 E
Caconda 51 13 48 S 15 8 E
Cacongo 51 5 11 S 12 5 E
Cadarache 11 43 41N 5 43 E
Cader Idris 5 52 43N 3 56W
Cadillac, Canada 62 48 14N 78 23W
Cadillac, France 10 44 38N 0 20W
Cadillac, U.S.A. 66 44 16N 85 25W
Cádiz 18 36 30N 6 20W
Cádiz, G. de 18 36 40N 7 0W
Cadours 10 43 44N 1 2 E
Caen 8 49 10N 0 22W
Caernarfon 5 53 8N 4 17W
Caernarfon B. 5 53 4N 4 40W
Caernarvon =
Caernarfon 5 53 8N 4 17W
Caerphilly 5 51 34N 3 13W
Cagayan de Oro 40 8 30N 124 40 E
Cágliari 22 39 15N 9 6 E
Cágliari, G. di 22 39 8N 9 10 E
Cagnes-sur-Mer 11 43 40N 7 9 E
Caguas 70 18 14N 66 4W
Caha Mts. 7 51 45N 9 40W
Caher 7 52 23N 7 56W
Cahersiveen 7 51 57N 10 13W
Cahore Pt. 7 52 34N 6 11W
Cahors 10 44 27N 1 27 E
Cahuapanas 72 5 15 S 77 0W
Caia 51 17 51 S 35 24 E
Caibarién 70 22 30N 79 30W
Caicos Is. 70 21 40N 71 40W
Cairn Gorm 6 57 7N 3 40W
Cairn Toul 6 57 3N 3 44W
Cairngorm Mts. 6 57 6N 3 42W
Cairns 56 16 57 S 145 45 E
Cairo = El Qâhira 50 30 1N 31 14 E
Cairo 67 37 0N 89 10W
Caithness, Ord of 6 58 9N 3 37W
Caiundo 51 15 50 S 17 28 E
Cajamarca 72 7 5 S 78 28W
Cajarc 10 44 29N 1 50 E
Calabar 49 4 57N 8 20 E
Calabozo 72 9 0N 67 28W
Calábria □ 23 39 24N 16 30 E
Calahorra 19 42 18N 1 59W
Calais, France 9 50 57N 1 56 E
Calais, U.S.A. 63 45 11N 67 20W
Calais, Pas de 9 51 0N 1 20 E
Calama, Brazil 72 8 0 S 62 50W
Calama, Chile 74 22 30 S 68 55W
Calamar 72 10 15N 74 55W
Calamian Group 40 11 50N 119 55 E
Calamocha 19 40 50N 1 17W
Calatayud 19 41 20N 1 40W
Calca 72 13 22 S 72 0W
Calcutta 37 22 36N 88 24 E
Calder → 5 53 44N 1 21W
Caldwell 68 43 45N 116 42W
Caledon 52 34 14 S 19 26 E
Caledon → 52 30 31 S 26 5 E
Caledon B. 55 12 45 S 137 0 E
Calella 19 41 37N 2 40 E
Calenzana 11 42 31N 8 51 E
Calf of Man 5 54 4N 4 48W
Calgary 64 51 0N 114 10W
Cali 72 3 25N 76 35W
Calicut 38 11 15N 75 43 E
California □ 68 37 25N 120 0W
California, G. de 69 28 0N 112 0W
Callabonna, L. 56 29 40 S 140 5 E
Callac 8 48 25N 3 27W
Callan 7 52 33N 7 25W
Callander 6 56 15N 4 14W
Callao 72 12 0 S 77 0W
Calne 5 51 26N 2 0W
Caltagirone 23 37 13N 14 30 E
Caltanissetta 23 37 30N 14 3 E
Calulo 51 10 1 S 14 56 E
Calunda 51 12 7 S 23 36 E
Calvados □ 8 49 5N 0 15W
Calvi 11 42 34N 8 45 E
Calvinia 52 31 28 S 19 45 E
Cam → 5 52 21N 0 16 E
Cam Lam 41 11 54N 109 10 E
Cam Ranh 41 11 54N 109 12 E
Camabatela 51 8 20 S 15 26 E
Camacupa 51 11 58 S 17 22 E
Camagüey 70 21 20N 78 0W
Camaná 72 16 30 S 72 50W
Camarat, C. 11 43 12N 6 41 E
Camaret 8 48 16N 4 37W
Camargue 11 43 34N 4 34 E
Camarones 74 44 50 S 65 40W
Cambay = Khambhat 36 22 23N 72 33 E
Cambo-les-Bains 10 43 22N 1 23W
Cambodia ■ 41 12 15N 105 0 E
Camborne 5 50 13N 5 18W
Cambrai 9 50 11N 3 14 E
Cambrian Mts. 5 52 25N 3 52W
Cambridge, Canada 62 43 23N 80 15W
Cambridge, U.K. 5 52 13N 0 8 E
Cambridge, Mass.,
U.S.A. 66 42 20N 71 8W
Cambridge, Md.,
U.S.A. 66 38 33N 76 2W
Cambridge, Ohio,
U.S.A. 66 40 1N 81 35W
Cambridge Gulf 54 14 55 S 128 15 E
Cambridgeshire □ 5 52 12N 0 7 E
Camden, Ark.,
U.S.A. 67 33 40N 92 50W
Camden, N.J.,
U.S.A. 66 39 57N 75 7W
Camden, S.C.,
U.S.A. 66 34 17N 80 34W
Camembert 8 48 53N 0 10 E
Cameroon ■ 50 6 0N 12 30 E
Cameroun, Mt. 49 4 13N 9 10 E
Cametá 73 2 12 S 49 30W
Caminha 18 41 50N 8 50W
Camiri 72 20 3 S 63 31W
Camissombo 51 8 7 S 20 38 E
Camocim 73 2 55 S 40 50W
Camooweal 56 19 56 S 138 7 E
Campagna 23 40 40N 15 5 E
Campania □ 23 40 50N 14 45 E
Campbell I. 57 52 30 S 169 0 E
Campbell River 64 50 5N 125 20W
Campbellton 63 47 57N 66 43W
Campbeltown 6 55 25N 5 36W
Campeche 69 19 51N 90 32W
Campeche □ 69 19 0N 90 30W
Campeche, B. de 69 20 0N 94 0W
Camperville 65 51 59N 100 9W
Campina Grande 73 7 20 S 35 47W
Campinas 73 22 50 S 47 0W
Campo 51 2 22N 9 50 E
Campo Grande 73 20 25 S 54 40W
Campobasso 23 41 34N 14 40 E
Campos 73 21 50 S 41 20W
Camrose 64 53 0N 112 50W
Can Tho 41 10 2N 105 46 E
Canada ■ 61 60 0N 100 0W
Cañada de Gómez 74 32 40 S 61 30W
Çanakkale Boğazi 26 40 0N 26 0 E
Cananea 69 30 57N 110 18W
Canarias, Is. 49 28 30N 16 0W
Canary Is. =
Canarias, Is. 49 28 30N 16 0W
Canaveral, C. 66 28 28N 80 31W
Canberra 56 35 15 S 149 8 E
Cancale 8 48 40N 1 50W
Canche → 9 50 31N 1 39 E
Candala 47 11 30N 49 58 E
Candé 8 47 34N 1 0W
Candia = Iráklion 26 35 20N 25 12 E
Canet-Plage 10 42 41N 3 2 E
Cangas 18 42 16N 8 47W
Çankırı 45 40 40N 33 37 E
Canmore 64 51 7N 115 18W
Canna 6 57 3N 6 33W
Cannanore 38 11 53N 75 27 E
Cannes 11 43 32N 7 0 E
Canning Basin 54 19 50 S 124 0 E
Cannock 5 52 42N 2 2W
Canora 65 51 40N 102 30W
Canourgue, Le 10 44 26N 3 13 E
Canso 63 45 20N 61 0W
Cantabria □ 18 43 10N 4 0W
Cantabrian Mts. =
Cantábrica,
Cordillera 18 43 0N 5 10W
Cantábrica,
Cordillera 18 43 0N 5 10W
Cantal □ 10 45 5N 2 45 E
Cantal, Plomb du 10 45 3N 2 45 E
Canterbury 5 51 17N 1 5 E
Canterbury Plains 59 43 55 S 171 22 E
Canton = Guangzhou 43 23 5N 113 10 E
Canton, Ill., U.S.A. 67 40 32N 90 0W
Canton, Miss.,
U.S.A. 67 32 40N 90 1W
Canton, Ohio,
U.S.A. 66 40 47N 81 22W
Canutama 72 6 30 S 64 20W
Cap-Chat 63 49 6N 66 40W
Cap-de-la-Madeleine 62 46 22N 72 31W
Cap-Haïtien 70 19 40N 72 20W
Capaia 51 8 27 S 20 13 E
Capbreton 10 43 39N 1 26W
Capdenac 10 44 34N 2 5 E
Cape Barren I. 56 40 25 S 148 15 E
Cape Breton I. 63 46 0N 60 30W
Cape Coast 49 5 5N 1 15W
Cape Fear → 66 34 30N 78 25W
Cape Girardeau 67 37 20N 89 30W
Cape May 66 39 1N 74 53W
Cape Montague 63 46 5N 62 25W
Cape Province □ 52 32 0 S 23 0 E
Cape Town 52 33 55 S 18 22 E
Cape Verde Is. ■ 1 17 10N 25 20W
Cape York Peninsula 56 12 0 S 142 30 E
Capella, Mt. 56 5 4 S 141 8 E
Capelle, La 9 49 59N 3 50 E
Capendu 10 43 11N 2 31 E
Capestang 10 43 20N 3 2 E
Capraia 20 43 2N 9 50 E
Caprera 22 41 12N 9 28 E
Capri 23 40 34N 14 15 E
Capricorn, C. 55 23 30 S 151 13 E
Caprivi Strip 52 18 0 S 23 0 E
Captieux 10 44 18N 0 16W
Caquetá → 72 1 15 S 69 15W
Caracal 25 44 8N 24 22 E
Caracas 72 10 30N 66 55W
Caransebeş 15 45 28N 22 18 E
Carantec 8 48 40N 3 55W
Caratinga 73 19 50 S 42 10W
Caravaca 19 38 8N 1 52W
Carballo 18 43 13N 8 41W
Carberry 65 49 50N 99 25W
Carbonara, C. 22 39 8N 9 30 E
Carbondale 67 37 45N 89 10W
Carbonear 63 47 42N 53 13W
Carbonia 22 39 10N 8 30 E
Carcassonne 10 43 13N 2 20 E
Cardamon Hills 38 9 30N 77 15 E
Cárdenas, Cuba 70 23 0N 81 30W
Cárdenas, Mexico 69 21 0N 99 40W
Cardiff 5 51 28N 3 11W
Cardigan 5 52 6N 4 41W
Cardigan B. 5 52 30N 4 30W
Cardona 19 41 56N 1 40 E
Cardston 64 49 15N 113 20W
Carei 15 47 40N 22 29 E
Carentan 8 49 19N 1 15W
Carey, L. 54 29 0 S 122 15 E
Careysburg 49 6 34N 10 30W
Cargados Garajos 2 17 0 S 59 0 E
Cargèse 11 42 7N 8 35 E
Carhaix-Plouguer 8 48 18N 3 36W
Caribbean Sea 70 15 0N 75 0W
Cariboo Mts. 64 53 0N 121 0W
Caribou 63 46 55N 68 0W
Caribou Mts. 64 59 12N 115 40W
Carignan 9 49 38N 5 10 E
Carinhanha 73 14 15 S 44 46W
Carinthia □ =
Kärnten □ 14 46 52N 13 30 E
Carlingford, L. 7 54 0N 6 5W
Carlisle, U.K. 5 54 54N 2 55W
Carlisle, U.S.A. 66 40 12N 77 10W
Carlit, Pic 10 42 35N 1 55 E
Carlow 7 52 50N 6 58W
Carlow □ 7 52 43N 6 50W
Carlsbad, Calif.,
U.S.A. 68 33 11N 117 25W
Carlsbad, N. Mex.,
U.S.A. 67 32 20N 104 14W
Carlyle 65 49 40N 102 20W
Carman 65 49 30N 98 0W
Carmarthen 5 51 52N 4 20W
Carmarthen B. 5 51 40N 4 30W
Carmaux 10 44 3N 2 10 E
Carmel-by-the-Sea 68 36 38N 121 55W
Carmona 18 37 28N 5 42W
Carnarvon, Australia 54 24 51 S 113 42 E
Carnarvon, S. Africa 52 30 56 S 22 8 E
Carndonagh 7 55 15N 7 16W
Carnegie, L. 54 26 5 S 122 30 E
Carnic Alps =
Karnische Alpen 14 46 36N 13 0 E
Carnot 51 4 59N 15 56 E
Carnot B. 54 17 20 S 121 30 E
Carnsore Pt. 7 52 10N 6 20W
Carolina, La 18 38 17N 3 38W
Caroline I. 58 9 15 S 150 3W
Caroline Is. 57 8 0N 150 0 E
Carpathians, Mts. 15 49 30N 21 0 E
Carpaţii Meridionali 25 45 30N 25 0 E
Carpentaria, G. of 55 14 0 S 139 0 E
Carpentras 11 44 3N 5 2 E
Carrara 20 44 5N 10 7 E
Carrauntoohill, Mt. 7 52 0N 9 49W
Carrick-on-Shannon 7 53 57N 8 7W
Carrick-on-Suir 7 52 22N 7 30W
Carrickfergus 7 54 43N 5 50W
Carrickfergus □ 7 54 43N 5 49W
Carrickmacross 7 54 0N 6 43W
Carroll 67 42 2N 94 55W
Carrollton 66 33 36N 85 5W
Carron → 6 57 30N 5 30W
Carron, L. 6 57 22N 5 35W
Carrouges 8 48 34N 0 10W
Carse of Gowrie 6 56 30N 3 10W
Carson City 68 39 12N 119 46W
Carstairs 6 55 42N 3 41W
Cartagena, Colombia 72 10 25N 75 33W
Cartagena, Spain 19 37 38N 0 59W
Cartago, Colombia 72 4 45N 75 55W
Cartago, C. Rica 70 9 50N 85 52W
Carteret 8 49 23N 1 47W
Cartersville 66 34 11N 84 48W
Carthage 67 37 10N 94 20W
Cartier I. 54 12 31 S 123 29 E
Cartwright 63 53 41N 56 58W
Caruaru 73 8 15 S 35 55W
Carúpano 72 10 39N 63 15W
Caruthersville 67 36 10N 89 40W
Carvin 9 50 30N 2 57 E
Casablanca 49 33 36N 7 36W
Casale Monferrato 20 45 8N 8 28 E
Casas Grandes 69 30 22N 107 57W
Cascade Ra. 68 47 0N 121 30W
Caserta 23 41 5N 14 20 E
Cashel 7 52 31N 7 53W
Casilda 74 33 10 S 61 10W
Casino 56 28 52 S 153 3 E
Casiquiare → 72 2 1N 67 7W
Casma 72 9 30 S 78 20W
Caspe 19 41 14N 0 1W
Casper 68 42 52N 106 20W
Caspian Sea 30 43 0N 50 0 E
Casquets 8 49 46N 2 15W
Cassel 9 50 48N 2 30 E
Cassiar Mts. 64 59 30N 130 30W
Cassinga 51 15 5 S 16 4 E
Cassis 11 43 14N 5 32 E
Casteljaloux 10 44 19N 0 6 E
Castellammare del
Golfo 22 38 2N 12 53 E
Castellammare di
Stábia 23 40 47N 14 29 E
Castellane 11 43 50N 6 31 E
Castellón de la Plana 19 39 58N 0 3W
Castelnau-de-Médoc 10 45 2N 0 48W
Castelnaudary 10 43 20N 1 58 E
Castelo Branco 18 39 50N 7 31W
Castelsarrasin 10 44 2N 1 7 E
Castelvetrano 22 37 40N 12 46 E
Castets 10 43 52N 1 6W
Castilla La Nueva 18 39 45N 3 20W
Castilla La Vieja 18 41 55N 4 0W
Castilla y Leon □ 18 42 0N 5 0W
Castillon, Barr. de 11 43 53N 6 33 E
Castillon-en-
Couserans 10 42 56N 1 1 E
Castillon-la-Bataille 10 44 51N 0 2W
Castillonès 10 44 39N 0 37 E
Castle Douglas 6 54 57N 3 57W
Castlebar 7 53 52N 9 17W
Castleblaney 7 54 7N 6 44W
Castlegar 64 49 20N 117 40W
Castlemaine 56 37 2 S 144 12 E
Castlereagh 7 53 47N 8 30W
Castlereagh □ 7 54 33N 5 53W
Castlereagh → 56 30 12 S 147 32 E
Castlereagh B. 54 12 10 S 135 10 E
Castletown 5 54 4N 4 40W
Castletown
Bearhaven 7 51 40N 9 54W
Castor 64 52 15N 111 50W
Castres 10 43 37N 2 13 E
Castries 70 14 0N 60 50W
Castro 74 42 30 S 73 50W
Castro del Río 18 37 41N 4 29W
Cat I. 70 24 30N 75 30W
Catacáos 72 5 20 S 80 45W
Catalonia =
Cataluña □ 19 41 40N 1 15 E
Cataluña □ 19 41 40N 1 15 E
Catamarca 74 28 30 S 65 50W
Catanduanes 40 13 50N 124 20 E
Catánia 23 37 31N 15 4 E
Catanzaro 23 38 54N 16 38 E
Catastrophe C. 54 34 59 S 136 0 E
Cateau, Le 9 50 7N 3 32 E
Cato I. 55 23 15 S 155 32 E
Catoche, C. 69 21 35N 87 5W
Catskill Mts. 66 42 15N 74 15W
Cauca → 72 8 54N 74 28W
Caucasus Mts. =
Bolshoi Kavkas 35 42 50N 44 0 E
Caudebec-en-Caux 8 49 30N 0 42 E
Caudry 9 50 7N 3 22 E
Caulnes 8 48 18N 2 10W
Caúngula 51 8 26 S 18 38 E
Cauquenes 74 36 0 S 72 22W
Caussade 10 44 10N 1 33 E
Causse-Méjean 10 44 18N 3 42 E
Cauterets 10 42 52N 0 8W
Caux, Pays de 8 49 38N 0 35 E
Cavaillon 11 43 50N 5 2 E
Cavalaire-sur-Mer 11 43 10N 6 33 E
Cavalerie, La 10 44 0N 3 10 E
Cavallo, I. de 11 41 22N 9 16 E
Cavan 7 54 0N 7 22W
Cavan □ 7 53 58N 7 10W
Caxias 73 4 55 S 43 20W
Caxias do Sul 74 29 10 S 51 10W
Caxito 51 8 30 S 13 30 E
Cayenne 73 5 0N 52 18W
Cayes, Les 70 18 15N 73 46W
Cayeux-sur-Mer 9 50 10N 1 30 E
Caylus 10 44 15N 1 47 E
Cayman Is. 70 19 40N 80 30W
Cazaux et de
Sanguinet, Étang
de 10 44 29N 1 10W
Cazères 10 43 13N 1 5 E
Cazombo 51 11 54 S 22 56 E
Ceanannus Mor 7 53 42N 6 53W
Ceará = Fortaleza 73 3 45 S 38 35W
Ceará □ 73 5 0 S 40 0W
Cebu 40 10 18N 123 54 E
Cedar → 67 41 17N 91 21W
Cedar Falls 67 42 39N 92 29W
Cedar L. 65 53 10N 100 0W
Cedar Rapids 67 42 0N 91 38W
Cedartown 66 34 1N 85 15W
Ceduna 54 32 7 S 133 46 E
Cefalù 23 38 3N 14 1 E
Cegléd 15 47 11N 19 47 E
Cehegín 19 38 6N 1 48W
Ceiba, La 70 15 40N 86 50W
Celaya 69 20 31N 100 37W
Celbridge 7 53 20N 6 33W
Celebes =
Sulawesi □ 40 2 0 S 120 0 E
Celebes Sea 40 3 0N 123 0 E
Celje 21 46 16N 15 18 E
Celle 13 52 37N 10 4 E

Cenis, Col du Mont 11 45 15N 6 55 E
Center 67 31 50N 94 10W
Centerville 67 40 45N 92 57W
Central □ 6 56 10N 4 30W
Central, Cordillera 72 5 0N 75 0W
Central African Republic ■ 51 7 0N 20 0 E
Central Ra. 56 5 0 S 143 0 E
Centralia 67 38 32N 89 5W
Cephalonia = Kefallinía 26 38 20N 20 30 E
Ceram Sea = Seram Sea 40 2 30 S 128 30 E
Cerbère 10 42 26N 3 10 E
Cerbicales, Is. 11 41 33N 9 22 E
Cère → 10 44 55N 1 49 E
Ceres 52 33 21 S 19 18 E
Céret 10 42 30N 2 42 E
Cerignola 23 41 17N 15 53 E
Cérilly 10 46 37N 2 50 E
Cerisiers 9 48 8N 3 30 E
Cerizay 8 46 50N 0 40W
Cerknica 21 45 48N 14 21 E
Cernavodă 25 44 22N 28 3 E
Cernay 9 47 44N 7 10 E
Cerritos 69 22 26N 100 17W
Cervera 19 41 40N 1 16 E
Cervera del Río Alhama 19 42 2N 1 58W
Cervione 11 42 20N 9 29 E
Cesena 21 44 9N 12 14 E
České Budějovice 14 48 55N 14 25 E
Ceskomoravská Vrchovina 14 49 30N 15 40 E
Český Těšin 15 49 45N 18 39 E
Cessnock 56 32 50 S 151 21 E
Cetinje 24 42 23N 18 59 E
Ceuta 49 35 52N 5 18W
Cévennes 10 44 10N 3 50 E
Ceylon = Sri Lanka ■ 38 7 30N 80 50 E
Cèze → 11 44 6N 4 43 E
Chabeuil 11 44 54N 5 3 E
Chablais 11 46 20N 6 36 E
Chablis 9 47 47N 3 48 E
Chachapoyas 72 6 15 S 77 50W
Chachoengsao 41 13 42N 101 5 E
Chad ■ 50 15 0N 17 15 E
Chad, L. = Tchad, L. 50 13 30N 14 30 E
Chadan 31 51 17N 91 35 E
Chagda 31 58 45N 130 38 E
Chagny 9 46 57N 4 45 E
Chāh Bahār 46 25 20N 60 40 E
Chaillé-les-Marais 10 46 25N 1 2W
Chaise-Dieu, La 10 45 18N 3 42 E
Chaize-le-Vicomte, La 8 46 40N 1 18W
Chakradharpur 37 22 45N 85 40 E
Chakwal 36 32 56N 72 53 E
Chala 72 15 48 S 74 20W
Chalais 10 45 16N 0 3 E
Chalhuanca 72 14 15 S 73 15W
Chalindrey 9 47 43N 5 26 E
Chalisgaon 38 20 30N 75 10 E
Challans 8 46 50N 1 52W
Challapata 72 18 53 S 66 50W
Chalon-sur-Saône 9 46 48N 4 50 E
Chalonnes-sur-Loire 8 47 20N 0 45W
Châlons-sur-Marne 9 48 58N 4 20 E
Châlus 10 45 39N 0 58 E
Chamba, India 36 32 35N 76 10 E
Chamba, Tanzania 51 11 37 S 37 0 E
Chambal → 37 26 29N 79 15 E
Chambersburg 66 39 53N 77 41W
Chambéry 11 45 34N 5 55 E
Chambon-Feugerolles, Le 11 45 24N 4 19 E
Chambri L. 56 4 15 S 143 10 E
Chamonix-Mont-Blanc 11 45 55N 6 51 E
Champagne 9 48 40N 4 20 E
Champagne, Plaine de 9 49 0N 4 30 E
Champagnole 9 46 45N 5 55 E
Champaign 67 40 8N 88 14W
Champaubert 9 48 50N 3 45 E
Champdeniers 10 46 29N 0 25W
Champeix 10 45 37N 3 8 E
Champion B. 54 28 44 S 114 36 E
Champlain, L. 66 44 30N 73 20W
Chañaral 74 26 23 S 70 40W
Chandigarh 36 30 43N 76 47 E
Chandpur 37 23 8N 90 45 E
Chandrapur 38 19 57N 79 25 E
Chang Jiang → 43 31 48N 121 10 E
Changanacheri 38 9 25N 76 31 E
Changane → 53 24 30 S 33 30 E
Changchun 42 43 57N 125 17 E
Changde 43 29 4N 111 35 E
Changsha 43 28 12N 113 0 E
Changzhi 42 36 10N 113 6 E
Changzhou 43 31 47N 119 58 E
Channapatna 38 12 40N 77 15 E
Channel Is. 8 49 30N 2 40W
Channel-Port aux Basques 63 47 30N 59 9W
Chantada 18 42 36N 7 46W
Chanthaburi 41 12 38N 102 12 E
Chantilly 9 49 12N 2 29 E
Chantonnay 8 46 40N 1 3W
Chanute 67 37 45N 95 25W
Chao Phraya → 41 13 32N 100 36 E
Chapala, L. de 69 20 15N 103 0W
Chapayevo 35 50 25N 51 10 E
Chapayevsk 33 53 0N 49 40 E
Chapel Hill 66 35 53N 79 3W
Chapelle d'Angillon, La 9 47 21N 2 25 E
Chapelle-Glain, La 8 47 38N 1 11W
Chapleau 62 47 50N 83 24W
Châr 49 21 32N 12 45 E
Chara 31 56 54N 118 20 E
Charagua 72 19 45 S 63 10W
Charaña 72 17 30 S 69 25W
Chard 5 50 52N 2 59W
Chardzhou 30 39 6N 63 34 E
Charente □ 10 45 50N 0 16 E
Charente → 10 45 57N 1 5W
Charente-Maritime □ 10 45 45N 0 45W
Chari → 50 12 58N 14 31 E
Chārīkār 46 35 0N 69 10 E
Charité-sur-Loire, La 9 47 10N 3 1 E
Charleroi 12 50 24N 4 27 E
Charles, C. 66 37 10N 75 59W
Charles City 67 43 2N 92 41W
Charleston, S.C., U.S.A. 66 32 47N 79 56W
Charleston, W. Va., U.S.A. 66 38 24N 81 36W
Charlesville 51 5 27 S 20 59 E
Charleville 56 26 24 S 146 15 E
Charleville-Mézières 9 49 44N 4 40 E
Charlieu 11 46 10N 4 10 E
Charlotte, Mich., U.S.A. 66 42 36N 84 48W
Charlotte, N.C., U.S.A. 66 35 16N 80 46W
Charlotte Amalie 70 18 22N 64 56W
Charlotte Harbor 66 26 58N 82 4W
Charlotte Waters 54 25 56 S 134 54 E
Charlottenburg 13 52 31N 13 15 E
Charlottesville 66 38 1N 78 30W
Charlottetown 63 46 14N 63 8W
Charlton 67 40 59N 93 20W
Charlton I. 62 52 0N 79 20W
Charmes 9 48 22N 6 17 E
Charolles 11 46 27N 4 16 E
Chârost 9 46 58N 2 7 E
Charouine 49 29 0N 0 15W
Charroux 10 46 9N 0 25 E
Charters Towers 56 20 5 S 146 13 E
Chartre-sur-le-Loir, La 8 47 44N 0 34 E
Chartres 8 48 29N 1 30 E
Chascomús 74 35 30 S 58 0W
Chasovnya-Uchurskaya 31 57 15N 132 50 E
Chasseneuil-sur-Bonnieure 10 45 52N 0 29 E
Châtaigneraie, La 10 46 39N 0 44W
Château-Arnoux 11 44 6N 6 0 E
Château-Chinon 9 47 4N 3 56 E
Château-d'Oléron, Le 10 45 54N 1 12W
Château-du-Loir 8 47 40N 0 25 E
Château-Gontier 8 47 50N 0 48W
Château-la-Vallière 8 47 30N 0 20 E
Château-Landon 9 48 8N 2 40 E
Château-Porcien 9 49 31N 4 13 E
Château-Renault 8 47 36N 0 56 E
Château-Salins 9 48 50N 6 30 E
Château-Thierry 9 49 3N 3 20 E
Châteaubourg 8 48 7N 1 25W
Châteaubriant 8 47 43N 1 23W
Châteaudun 8 48 3N 1 20 E
Châteaugiron 8 48 3N 1 30W
Châteaulin 8 48 11N 4 8W
Châteaumeillant 10 46 35N 2 12 E
Châteauneuf-du-Faou 8 48 11N 3 50W
Châteauneuf-en-Thymerais 8 48 35N 1 13 E
Châteauneuf-sur-Charente 10 45 36N 0 3W
Châteauneuf-sur-Cher 9 46 52N 2 18 E
Châteauneuf-sur-Loire 9 47 52N 2 13 E
Châteaurenard, Bouches-du-Rhône, France 11 43 53N 4 51 E
Châteaurenard, Loiret, France 9 47 56N 2 55 E
Châteauroux 9 46 50N 1 40 E
Châtelaillon-Plage 10 46 5N 1 5W
Châtelaudren 8 48 33N 2 59W
Châtelet, Le 10 46 38N 2 16 E
Châtelet-en-Brie, Le 9 48 31N 2 48 E
Châtelguyon 10 45 55N 3 4 E
Châtellerault 8 46 50N 0 30 E
Châtelus-Malvaleix 10 46 18N 2 1 E
Chatham, N.B., Canada 63 47 2N 65 28W
Chatham, Ont., Canada 62 42 24N 82 11W
Chatham, U.K. 5 51 22N 0 32 E
Chatham Is. 57 44 0 S 176 40W
Châtillon-Coligny 9 47 50N 2 51 E
Châtillon-en-Bazois 9 47 3N 3 39 E
Châtillon-en-Diois 11 44 41N 5 29 E
Châtillon-sur-Indre 8 46 59N 1 10 E
Châtillon-sur-Loire 9 47 35N 2 44 E
Châtillon-sur-Marne 9 49 6N 3 44 E
Châtillon-sur-Seine 9 47 50N 4 33 E
Chatrapur 36 19 22N 85 2 E
Châtre, La 10 46 35N 2 0 E
Chattahoochee → 66 30 43N 84 51W
Chattanooga 66 35 2N 85 17W
Chaudanne, Barr. de 11 43 51N 6 32 E
Chaudes-Aigues 10 44 51N 3 1 E
Chauffailles 11 46 13N 4 20 E
Chaulnes 9 49 48N 2 47 E
Chaumont 9 48 7N 5 8 E
Chaumont-en-Vexin 9 49 16N 1 53 E
Chaumont-sur-Loire 8 47 29N 1 11 E
Chaunay 10 46 13N 0 9 E
Chauny 9 49 37N 3 12 E
Chausey, Is. 8 48 52N 1 49W
Chaussin 9 46 59N 5 22 E
Chauvigny 8 46 34N 0 39 E
Chaux-de-Fonds, La 13 47 7N 6 50 E
Chaves 18 41 45N 7 32W
Chavuma 51 13 4 S 22 40 E
Chazelles-sur-Lyon 11 45 39N 4 22 E
Cheb 14 50 9N 12 28 E
Cheboksary 33 56 8N 47 12 E
Cheboygan 62 45 38N 84 29W
Chech, Erg 49 25 0N 2 15W
Checheno-Ingush A.S.S.R. □ 35 43 30N 45 29 E
Chef-Boutonne 10 46 7N 0 4W
Chegdomyn 31 51 7N 133 1 E
Chegga 49 25 27N 5 40W
Chegutu 51 18 10 S 30 14 E
Chehalis 68 46 44N 122 59W
Cheiron, Mt. 11 43 49N 6 58 E
Cheju Do 43 33 29N 126 34 E
Cheleken 30 39 26N 53 7 E
Chelforó 74 39 0 S 66 33W
Chelkar Tengiz, Solonchak 30 48 0N 62 30 E
Chelles 9 48 52N 2 33 E
Chełm 17 51 8N 23 30 E
Chełmno 17 53 20N 18 30 E
Chelmsford 5 51 44N 0 29 E
Chelmża 17 53 10N 18 39 E
Cheltenham 5 51 55N 2 5W
Chelyabinsk 30 55 10N 61 24 E
Chemainus 64 48 55N 123 42W
Chemillé 8 47 14N 0 45W
Chemnitz = Karl-Marx-Stadt 13 50 50N 12 55 E
Chemult 68 43 14N 121 47W
Chen, Gora 31 65 16N 141 50 E
Chenab → 36 30 23N 71 2 E
Chencha 50 6 15N 37 32 E
Chengde 42 40 59N 117 58 E
Chengdu 42 30 38N 104 2 E
Cheo Reo 41 13 25N 108 28 E
Cher □ 9 47 10N 2 30 E
Cher → 8 47 21N 0 29 E
Cherbourg 8 49 39N 1 40W
Cherchell 49 36 35N 2 12 E
Cherdyn 30 60 24N 56 29 E
Cheremkhovo 31 53 8N 103 1 E
Cherepovets 33 59 5N 37 55 E
Chergui, Chott ech 49 34 21N 0 25 E
Cherkassy 34 49 27N 32 4 E
Chernigov 32 51 28N 31 20 E
Chernogorsk 31 53 49N 91 18 E
Chernovtsy 34 48 15N 25 52 E
Chernoye 31 70 30N 89 10 E
Chernyakhovsk 30 54 36N 21 48 E
Chernyshovskiy 31 63 0N 112 30 E
Cherokee 67 42 40N 95 30W
Cherskiy 31 68 45N 161 18 E
Cherskogo Khrebet 31 65 0N 143 0 E
Cherwell → 5 51 46N 1 18W
Chesapeake 66 36 43N 76 15W
Chesapeake Bay 66 38 0N 76 12W
Cheshire □ 5 53 14N 2 30W
Cheshskaya Guba 30 67 20N 47 0 E
Chesne, Le 9 49 30N 4 45 E
Chester, U.K. 5 53 12N 2 53W
Chester, Pa., U.S.A. 66 39 54N 75 20W
Chester, S.C., U.S.A. 66 34 44N 81 13W
Chesterfield 5 53 14N 1 26W
Chesterfield, Îles 57 19 52 S 158 15 E
Chetumal 69 18 30N 88 18W
Chevanceaux 10 45 18N 0 14W
Cheviot, The 5 55 29N 2 8W
Cheviot Hills 5 55 20N 2 30W
Chew Bahir 50 4 40N 36 50 E
Cheyenne 67 41 9N 104 49W
Cheyenne → 67 44 40N 101 15W
Cheylard, Le 11 44 55N 4 25 E
Chhapra 37 25 48N 84 44 E
Chhatarpur 37 24 55N 79 35 E
Chhindwara 36 22 2N 78 59 E
Chiang Mai 41 18 47N 98 59 E
Chiange 51 15 35 S 13 40 E
Chiapa → 69 16 42N 93 0W
Chiapas □ 69 16 30N 92 30W
Chiba 44 35 30N 140 7 E
Chiba □ 44 35 30N 140 20 E
Chibemba 51 15 48 S 14 8 E
Chibia 51 15 10 S 13 42 E
Chibougamau 62 49 56N 74 24W
Chibuk 50 10 52N 12 50 E
Chicago 67 41 53N 87 40W
Chicago Heights 66 41 29N 87 37W
Chichagof I. 64 58 0N 136 0W
Chichester 5 50 50N 0 47W
Chichibu 44 36 5N 139 10 E
Chickasha 67 35 0N 98 0W
Chiclana de la Frontera 18 36 26N 6 9W
Chiclayo 72 6 42 S 79 50W
Chico 68 39 45N 121 54W
Chicopee 66 42 6N 72 37W
Chicoutimi 63 48 28N 71 5W
Chidambaram 38 11 20N 79 45 E
Chidley, C. 3 60 23N 64 26W
Chiengi 51 8 45 S 29 10 E
Chiengmai = Chiang Mai 41 18 47N 98 59 E
Chiers → 9 49 39N 5 0 E
Chiese → 20 45 8N 10 25 E
Chieti 21 42 22N 14 10 E
Chihli, G. of = Bo Hai 42 39 0N 120 0 E
Chihuahua 69 28 38N 106 5W
Chihuahua □ 69 28 30N 106 0W
Chiili 30 44 20N 66 15 E
Chik Bollapur 38 13 25N 77 45 E
Chikmagalur 38 13 15N 75 45 E
Chilapa 69 17 40N 99 11W
Childers 56 25 15 S 152 17 E
Chile ■ 74 35 0 S 72 0W
Chililabombwe 51 12 18 S 27 43 E
Chilka L. 36 19 40N 85 25 E
Chillagoe 56 17 7 S 144 33 E
Chillán 74 36 40 S 72 10W
Chillicothe, Mo., U.S.A. 67 39 45N 93 30W
Chillicothe, Ohio, U.S.A. 66 39 20N 82 58W
Chilliwack 64 49 10N 121 54W
Chiloé, I. de 74 42 30 S 73 50W
Chilpancingo 69 17 30N 99 30W
Chiltern Hills 5 51 44N 0 42W
Chiluage 51 9 30 S 21 50 E
Chilwa, L. 51 15 15 S 35 40 E
Chimay 12 50 3N 4 20 E
Chimborazo 72 1 29 S 78 55W
Chimbote 72 9 0 S 78 35W
Chimkent 30 42 18N 69 36 E
Chimoio 51 19 4 S 33 30 E
China ■ 29 30 0N 110 0 E
Chinandega 70 12 35N 87 12W
Chincha Alta 72 13 25 S 76 7W
Chinchón 19 40 9N 3 26W
Chinde 51 18 35 S 36 30 E
Chingola 51 12 31 S 27 53 E
Chinguetti 49 20 25N 12 24W
Chinhoyi 51 17 20 S 30 8 E
Chiniot 36 31 45N 73 0 E
Chinju 43 35 12N 128 2 E
Chinnampo 43 38 52N 125 10 E
Chinon 8 47 10N 0 15 E
Chinsali 51 10 30 S 32 2 E
Chióggia 21 45 13N 12 15 E
Chíos = Khíos 26 38 27N 26 9 E
Chipata 51 13 38 S 32 28 E
Chippenham 5 51 27N 2 7W
Chippewa Falls 67 44 55N 91 22W
Chiquián 72 10 10 S 77 0W
Chiquimula 69 14 51N 89 37W
Chiquinquira 72 5 37N 73 50W
Chirala 38 15 50N 80 26 E
Chirchik 30 41 29N 69 35 E
Chisamba 51 14 55 S 28 20 E
Chistopol 33 55 25N 50 38 E
Chita 31 52 0N 113 35 E
Chitembo 51 13 30 S 16 50 E
Chitré 70 7 59N 80 27W
Chittaurgarh 36 24 52N 74 38 E
Chittoor 38 13 15N 79 5 E
Chiusi 21 43 1N 11 58 E
Chivasso 20 45 10N 7 52 E
Chivilcoy 74 34 55 S 60 0W
Chkalov = Orenburg 30 51 45N 55 6 E
Choisy-le-Roi 9 48 45N 2 24 E
Choix 69 26 43N 108 17W
Chojnice 17 53 42N 17 32 E
Chokurdakh 31 70 38N 147 55 E
Cholet 8 47 4N 0 52W
Choluteca 70 13 20N 87 14W
Choma 51 16 48 S 26 59 E
Chomutov 14 50 28N 13 23 E
Chon Buri 41 13 21N 101 1 E
Chongjin 43 41 47N 129 50 E
Chŏngju 43 36 39N 127 27 E
Chongqing 43 29 35N 106 25 E
Chŏnju 43 35 50N 127 4 E
Chonos, Arch. de los 74 45 0 S 75 0W
Chorley 5 53 39N 2 39W
Chorzów 17 50 18N 18 57 E
Chōshi 44 35 45N 140 51 E
Choszczno 17 53 7N 15 25 E
Chotila 36 22 23N 71 15 E
Christchurch, N.Z. 59 43 33 S 172 47 E
Christchurch, U.K. 5 50 44N 1 33W
Christiana 52 27 52 S 25 8 E
Christmas I. = Kiritimati 58 1 58N 157 27W
Christmas I. 57 10 30 S 105 40 E
Chu 30 43 36N 73 42 E
Chūbu □ 44 36 45N 137 30 E
Chubut → 74 43 20 S 65 5W
Chudskoye, Oz. 32 58 13N 27 30 E
Chūgoku □ 44 35 0N 133 0 E
Chūgoku-Sanchi 44 35 0N 133 0 E
Chukotskiy Khrebet 31 68 0N 175 0 E
Chukotskoye More 31 68 0N 175 0W
Chula Vista 68 32 39N 117 8W
Chulman 31 56 52N 124 52 E
Chulucanas 72 5 8 S 80 10W
Chumikan 31 54 40N 135 10 E
Chumphon 41 10 35N 99 14 E
Chuna → 31 57 47N 94 37 E
Chunchŏn 43 37 58N 127 44 E
Chungking = Chongqing 43 29 35N 106 25 E
Chunya 51 8 30 S 33 27 E
Chuquibamba 72 15 47 S 72 44W
Chur 13 46 52N 9 32 E
Churchill → 63 53 19N 60 10W
Churchill Falls 63 53 36N 64 19W
Churchill Pk. 64 58 10N 125 10W
Churu 36 28 20N 74 50 E
Chusovoy 30 58 15N 57 40 E
Chuvash A.S.S.R. □ 33 55 30N 47 0 E
Cicero 67 41 48N 87 48W
Ciechanów 17 52 52N 20 38 E
Ciego de Avila 70 21 50N 78 50W
Ciénaga 72 11 1N 74 15W
Cienfuegos 70 22 10N 80 30W
Cierp 10 42 55N 0 40 E
Cieszyn 15 49 45N 18 35 E
Cieza 19 38 17N 1 23W
Cimone, Mte. 20 44 10N 10 40 E
Cimpina 25 45 10N 25 45 E
Cimpulung 25 45 17N 25 3 E
Cinca → 19 41 26N 0 21 E
Cincinnati 66 39 10N 84 26W
Ciney 12 50 18N 5 5 E
Cinto, Mte. 11 42 24N 8 54 E
Ciotat, La 11 43 10N 5 37 E
Circleville 66 39 35N 82 57W
Cirebon 40 6 45 S 108 32 E
Cirencester 5 51 43N 1 59W
Cirey-sur-Vezouze 9 48 35N 6 57 E
Ciron → 10 44 36N 0 18W
Citlaltépetl, Volcán 69 19 1N 97 16W
Ciudad Bolívar 72 8 5N 63 36W
Ciudad Camargo, Chihuahua, Mexico 69 27 40N 105 10W
Ciudad Camargo, Tamaulipas, Mexico 69 26 19N 98 50W
Ciudad de Valles 69 21 59N 99 1W
Ciudad del Carmen 69 18 38N 91 50W
Ciudad Guayana 72 8 0N 62 30W
Ciudad Guzmán 69 19 41N 103 29W
Ciudad Juárez 69 31 44N 106 29W
Ciudad Madero 69 22 16N 97 50W
Ciudad Mante 69 22 44N 98 57W
Ciudad Obregón 69 27 29N 109 56W
Ciudad Real 18 38 59N 3 55W
Ciudad Rodrigo 18 40 35N 6 32W
Ciudad Victoria 69 23 44N 99 8W
Civitanova Marche 21 43 18N 13 41 E
Civitavécchia 21 42 6N 11 46 E
Civray 10 46 10N 0 17 E
Çivril 45 38 20N 29 43 E
Cizre 45 37 19N 42 10 E
Clacton-on-Sea 5 51 47N 1 10 E
Clain → 8 46 47N 0 33 E
Claire, L. 64 58 35N 112 5W
Clairvaux-les-Lacs 11 46 35N 5 45 E
Clamecy 9 47 28N 3 30 E
Clanwilliam 52 32 11 S 18 52 E
Clara 7 53 20N 7 38W
Clare □ 7 52 20N 9 0W
Clare → 7 53 22N 9 5W
Clare I. 7 53 48N 10 0W
Claremont 66 43 23N 72 20W
Claremore 67 36 40N 95 37W
Claremorris 7 53 45N 9 0W
Clarence → 56 29 25 S 153 22 E
Clarence Str. 54 12 0 S 131 0 E
Claresholm 64 50 0N 113 33W
Clarke, I. 56 40 32 S 148 10 E
Clarksburg 66 39 18N 80 21W
Clarksdale 67 34 12N 90 33W
Clarkston 68 46 28N 117 2W
Clarksville 66 36 32N 87 20W
Clayette, La 11 46 17N 4 19 E
Clear, C. 7 51 26N 9 30W
Clear I. 7 51 26N 9 30W
Clearwater, Canada 64 51 38N 120 2W
Clearwater, U.S.A. 66 27 58N 82 45W
Clearwater, Mts. 68 46 20N 115 30W
Cleburne 67 32 18N 97 25W
Cleethorpes 5 53 33N 0 2W
Cleeve Cloud 5 51 56N 2 0W
Clelles 11 44 50N 5 38 E
Clermont, Australia 55 22 49 S 147 39 E
Clermont, France 9 49 23N 2 24 E
Clermont-en-Argonne 9 49 5N 5 4 E
Clermont-Ferrand 10 45 46N 3 4 E
Clermont-l'Hérault 10 43 38N 3 26 E
Clerval 9 47 25N 6 30 E
Clervaux 12 50 4N 6 2 E
Cléry-St.-André 9 47 50N 1 46 E
Cleveland, Miss., U.S.A. 67 33 43N 90 43W
Cleveland, Ohio, U.S.A. 66 41 28N 81 43W
Cleveland, Tenn., U.S.A. 66 35 9N 84 52W
Cleveland, Tex., U.S.A. 67 30 18N 95 0W
Cleveland □ 5 54 35N 1 8 E
Cleveland, C. 56 19 11 S 147 1 E
Clew B. 7 53 54N 9 50W
Clifden 7 53 30N 10 2W
Clifton Forge 66 37 49N 79 51W
Clinton, B.C., Canada 64 51 6N 121 35W
Clinton, Ont., Canada 62 43 37N 81 32W
Clinton, Iowa, U.S.A. 67 41 50N 90 12W
Clinton, Mass., U.S.A. 66 42 26N 71 40W
Clinton, Mo., U.S.A. 67 38 20N 93 46W
Clinton, S.C., U.S.A. 66 34 30N 81 54W
Clipperton, I. 58 10 18N 109 13W
Clisson 8 47 5N 1 16W
Cloates, Pt. 54 22 43 S 113 40 E
Clonakilty 7 51 37N 8 53W
Clonakilty B. 7 51 33N 8 50W
Cloncurry 56 20 40 S 140 28 E
Clones 7 54 10N 7 13W
Clonmel 7 52 22N 7 42W
Cloppenburg 13 52 50N 8 3 E
Clovis 67 34 20N 103 10W
Cloyes-sur-le-Loir 8 48 0N 1 14 E
Cluj-Napoca 15 46 47N 23 38 E
Cluny 11 46 26N 4 38 E
Cluses 11 46 5N 6 35 E
Clwyd □ 5 53 5N 3 20W
Clwyd → 5 53 20N 3 30W
Clyde → 6 55 56N 4 29W
Clyde, Firth of 6 55 20N 5 0W
Clydebank 6 55 54N 4 25W
Coahuila □ 69 27 20N 102 0W
Coaldale 64 49 45N 112 35W
Coalinga 68 36 10N 120 21W
Coalville 5 52 43N 1 21W
Coast Mts. 64 55 0N 129 0W
Coast Ranges 68 41 0N 123 0W
Coastal Plains Basin 54 30 10 S 115 30 E
Coatbridge 6 55 52N 4 2W
Coatepeque 69 14 46N 91 55W
Coatzacoalcos 69 18 9N 94 25W
Cobalt 62 47 25N 79 42W
Cobán 69 15 30N 90 21W
Cobar 56 31 27 S 145 48 E
Cóbh 7 51 50N 8 18W
Cobourg 62 43 58N 78 10W
Cobourg Pen. 54 11 20 S 132 15 E
Cóbué 51 12 0 S 34 58 E
Coburg 13 50 15N 10 58 E
Cochabamba 72 17 26 S 66 10W
Cochin 38 9 59N 76 22 E
Cochin China = Nam-Phan 41 10 30N 106 0 E
Cochran 66 32 25N 83 23W
Cochrane 62 49 0N 81 0W
Cockatoo I. 54 16 6 S 123 37 E
Cockburn, Canal 74 54 30 S 72 0W
Coco → 70 15 0N 83 8W
Coco Chan. 41 13 50N 93 25 E
Cocobeach 51 0 59N 9 34 E
Cocos I. 58 5 25N 87 55W
Cocos Is. 2 12 10 S 96 55 E
Cod, C. 66 42 8N 70 10W
Codajás 72 3 55 S 62 0W
Codó 73 4 30 S 43 55W
Coen 56 13 52 S 143 12 E
Coesfeld 13 51 56N 7 10 E
Cœur d'Alene 68 47 45N 116 51W
Coevorden 12 52 40N 6 44 E
Coffeyville 67 37 0N 95 40W
Coffs Harbour 56 30 16 S 153 5 E
Coghinas → 22 40 55N 8 48 E
Cognac 10 45 41N 0 20W
Cohoes 66 42 47N 73 42W

Coiba, I. 70 7 30N 81 40W
Coihaique 74 45 30 S 71 45W
Coimbatore 38 11 2N 76 59 E
Coimbra 18 40 15N 8 27W
Coín 18 36 40N 4 48W
Cojimies 72 0 20N 80 0W
Cojutepequé 69 13 41N 88 54W
Colac 56 38 21 S 143 35 E
Colchester 5 51 54N 0 55 E
Coldstream 6 55 39N 2 14W
Coleman 64 49 40N 114 30W
Coleman → 56 15 6 S 141 38 E
Coleraine 7 55 8N 6 40W
Coleraine □ 7 55 8N 6 40 E
Colesberg 52 30 45 S 25 5 E
Coligny 11 46 23N 5 21 E
Colima 69 19 14N 103 43W
Colima □ 69 19 10N 104 0W
Coll 6 56 40N 6 35W
College Park 66 33 42N 84 27W
Collie 54 33 22 S 116 8 E
Collier B. 54 16 10 S 124 15 E
Collingwood 62 44 29N 80 13W
Collinsville 56 20 30 S 147 56 E
Collonges 11 46 9N 5 52 E
Collooney 7 54 11N 8 28W
Colmar 9 48 5N 7 20 E
Colmars 11 44 11N 6 39 E
Colne 5 53 51N 2 11W
Cologne = Köln 13 50 56N 6 58 E
Colombey-les-Belles 9 48 32N 5 54 E
Colombey-les-Deux-Églises 9 48 13N 4 50 E
Colômbia 73 20 10 S 48 40W
Colombia ■ 72 3 45N 73 0W
Colombo 38 6 56N 79 58 E
Colón, Cuba 70 22 42N 80 54W
Colón, Panama 70 9 20N 79 54W
Colonia 74 34 25 S 57 50W
Colonsay 6 56 4N 6 12W
Colorado □ 68 37 40N 106 0W
Colorado →, Argentina 74 39 50 S 62 8W
Colorado →, U.S.A. 68 34 45N 114 40W
Colorado Plateau 68 36 40N 110 30W
Colorado Springs 67 38 55N 104 50W
Columbia, Miss., U.S.A. 67 31 16N 89 50W
Columbia, Mo., U.S.A. 67 38 58N 92 20W
Columbia, S.C., U.S.A. 66 34 0N 81 0W
Columbia, Tenn., U.S.A. 66 35 40N 87 0W
Columbia → 68 46 15N 124 5W
Columbia, C. 3 83 0N 70 0W
Columbia, District of □ 66 38 55N 77 0W
Columbia Basin 68 47 30N 118 30W
Columbretes, Is. 19 39 50N 0 50 E
Columbus, Ga., U.S.A. 66 32 30N 84 58W
Columbus, Ind., U.S.A. 66 39 14N 85 55W
Columbus, Miss., U.S.A. 66 33 30N 88 26W
Columbus, Ohio, U.S.A. 66 39 57N 83 1W
Colwyn Bay 5 53 17N 3 44W
Comácchio 21 44 41N 12 10 E
Combeaufontaine 9 47 38N 5 54 E
Comblain-au-Pont 12 50 29N 5 35 E
Combles 9 50 0N 2 50 E
Combourg 8 48 25N 1 46W
Combronde 10 45 58N 3 5 E
Comeragh Mts. 7 52 17N 7 35W
Comilla 37 23 28N 91 10 E
Comitán 69 16 18N 92 9W
Commentry 10 46 20N 2 46 E
Commercy 9 48 43N 5 34 E
Communism Pk. = Kommunizma, Pik 30 39 0N 72 2 E
Como 20 45 48N 9 5 E
Como, L. di 20 46 5N 9 17 E
Comodoro Rivadavia 74 45 50 S 67 40W
Comorin, C. 38 8 3N 77 40 E
Comoro Is. ■ 2 12 10 S 44 15 E
Comox 64 49 42N 124 55W
Compiègne 9 49 24N 2 50 E
Côn Dao 41 8 45N 106 45 E
Conakry 49 9 29N 13 49W
Concarneau 8 47 52N 3 56W
Conceição da Barra 73 18 35 S 39 45W
Concepción, Argentina 74 27 20 S 65 35W
Concepción, Chile 74 36 50 S 73 0W
Concepción, Est. de 74 50 30 S 74 55W
Concepción del Oro 69 24 38N 101 25W
Concepción del Uruguay 74 32 35 S 58 20W
Conchos → 69 29 35N 104 25W
Concord, Calif., U.S.A. 68 37 59N 122 2W
Concord, N.C., U.S.A. 66 35 28N 80 35W
Concord, N.H., U.S.A. 66 43 12N 71 30W
Concordia 74 31 20 S 58 2W
Concots 10 44 26N 1 40 E
Condamine 64 26 56 S 150 9 E
Condamine → 55 27 7 S 149 48 E
Condat 10 45 21N 2 46 E
Condé-sur-l'Escaut 9 50 26N 3 34 E
Condé-sur-Noireau 8 48 51N 0 33W
Condom 10 43 57N 0 22 E
Conflans-en-Jarnisy 9 49 10N 5 52 E
Confolens 10 46 2N 0 40 E
Congleton 5 53 10N 2 12W
Congo = Zaïre → 51 6 4 S 12 24 E
Congo (Kinshasa) = Zaïre ■ 51 3 0 S 23 0 E
Congo ■ 51 1 0 S 16 0 E
Conn, L. 7 54 3N 9 15W
Connacht 7 53 23N 8 40W
Conneaut 66 41 55N 80 32W
Connecticut □ 66 41 40N 72 40W
Connecticut → 66 41 17N 72 21W
Connemara 7 53 29N 9 45W
Connerré 8 48 3N 0 30 E
Conon → 6 57 33N 4 28W
Cononbridge 6 57 32N 4 30W
Conquet, Le 8 48 21N 4 46W
Constance, L. = Bodensee 13 47 35N 9 25 E
Constanţa 25 44 14N 28 38 E
Constantina 18 37 51N 5 40W
Constantine 49 36 25N 6 42 E
Contai 37 21 54N 87 46 E
Contamana 72 7 19 S 74 55W
Contes 11 43 49N 7 19 E
Contres 8 47 24N 1 26 E
Contrexéville 9 48 10N 5 53 E
Conway = Conwy → 5 53 18N 3 50W
Conway, N.H., U.S.A. 63 43 58N 71 8W
Conway, S.C., U.S.A. 66 33 49N 79 2W
Conwy 5 53 17N 3 50W
Conwy → 5 53 18N 3 50W
Coober Pedy 54 29 1 S 134 43 E
Cook, Mt. 59 43 36 S 170 9 E
Cook Is. 58 17 0 S 160 0W
Cook Strait 59 41 15 S 174 29 E
Cookeville 66 36 12N 85 30W
Cookstown 7 54 40N 6 43W
Cookstown □ 7 54 40N 6 43W
Cooktown 56 15 30 S 145 16 E
Coolgardie 54 30 55 S 121 8 E
Cooma 56 36 12 S 149 8 E
Coonamble 56 30 56 S 148 27 E
Coondapoor 38 13 42N 74 40 E
Coopers Cr. → 56 28 29 S 137 46 E
Coorong, The 55 35 50 S 139 20 E
Coos Bay 68 43 26N 124 7W
Cootamundra 56 34 36 S 148 1 E
Cootehill 7 54 5N 7 5W
Copenhagen = København 28 55 41N 12 34 E
Copiapó 74 27 30 S 70 20W
Copper Cliff 62 46 28N 81 4W
Coquet → 5 55 18N 1 45W
Coquimbo 74 30 0 S 71 20W
Corabia 25 43 48N 24 30 E
Coracora 72 15 5 S 73 45W
Coral Gables 66 25 45N 80 16W
Coral Sea 57 15 0 S 150 0 E
Coral Sea Islands Terr. 55 20 0 S 155 0 E
Corato 23 41 12N 16 22 E
Corbeil-Essonnes 9 48 36N 2 26 E
Corbie 9 49 54N 2 30 E
Corbières 10 42 55N 2 35 E
Corbigny 9 47 16N 3 40 E
Corbin 66 37 0N 84 3W
Corby 5 52 49N 0 31W
Corcubión 18 42 56N 9 12W
Cordele 66 31 55N 83 49W
Cordes 10 44 5N 1 57 E
Córdoba, Argentina 74 31 20 S 64 10W
Córdoba, Mexico 69 18 53N 96 56W
Córdoba, Spain 18 37 50N 4 50W
Córdoba, Sierra de 74 31 10 S 64 25W
Corfu = Kérkira 26 39 38N 19 50 E
Corigliano Cálabro 23 39 36N 16 31 E
Corinth = Kórinthos 26 37 56N 22 55 E
Corinth 66 34 54N 88 30W
Corinth, G. of = Korinthiakós Kólpos 26 38 16N 22 30 E
Corinto, Brazil 73 18 20 S 44 30W
Corinto, Nic. 70 12 30N 87 10W
Cork 7 51 54N 8 30W
Cork □ 7 51 50N 8 50W
Cork Harbour 7 51 46N 8 16W
Corlay 8 48 20N 3 5W
Çorlu 45 41 11N 27 49 E
Corner Brook 63 48 57N 57 58W
Corner Inlet 55 38 45 S 146 20 E
Cornwall 62 45 2N 74 44W
Cornwall □ 5 50 26N 4 40W
Cornwallis I. 3 75 8N 95 0W
Coro 72 11 25N 69 41W
Coroatá 73 4 8 S 44 0W
Corocoro 72 17 15 S 68 28W
Coroico 72 16 0 S 67 50W
Coromandel Coast 38 12 30N 81 0 E
Corona 68 33 49N 117 36W
Coronado 68 32 45N 117 9W
Coronel 74 37 0 S 73 10W
Coronel Pringles 74 38 0 S 61 30W
Corozal 69 9 19N 75 18W
Corps 11 44 50N 5 56 E
Corpus Christi 67 27 50N 97 28W
Corrèze □ 10 45 20N 1 45 E
Corrèze → 10 45 10N 1 28 E
Corrib, L. 7 53 5N 9 10W
Corrientes 74 27 30 S 58 45W
Corrientes, C., Colombia 72 5 30N 77 34W
Corrientes, C., Cuba 70 21 43N 84 30W
Corrientes, C., Mexico 69 20 25N 105 42W
Corse 11 42 0N 9 0 E
Corse, C. 11 43 1N 9 25 E
Corse-du-Sud □ 11 41 45N 9 0 E
Corsica = Corse 11 42 0N 9 0 E
Corsicana 67 32 5N 96 30W
Corte 11 42 19N 9 11 E
Cortland 66 42 35N 76 11W
Cortona 21 43 16N 12 0 E
Çorum 45 40 30N 34 57 E
Corumbá 72 19 0 S 57 30W
Coruña, La 18 43 20N 8 25W
Corunna = Coruña, La 18 43 20N 8 25W
Corvallis 68 44 36N 123 15W
Cosamaloapan 69 18 23N 95 50W
Cosenza 23 39 17N 16 14 E
Coshocton 66 40 17N 81 51W
Cosne-sur-Loire 9 47 24N 2 54 E
Cossé-le-Vivien 8 47 57N 0 54W
Cosson → 8 47 30N 1 15 E
Costa Blanca 19 38 25N 0 10W
Costa Brava 19 41 30N 3 0 E
Costa del Sol 18 36 30N 4 30W
Costa Dorada 19 40 45N 1 15 E
Costa Rica ■ 70 10 0N 84 0W
Cotagaita 72 20 45 S 65 40W
Côte d'Azur 11 43 25N 7 10 E
Côte d'Or 9 47 10N 4 50 E
Côte-d'Or □ 9 47 30N 4 50 E
Côte-St.-André, La 11 45 24N 5 15 E
Cotentin 8 49 15N 1 30W
Côtes de Meuse 9 49 15N 5 22 E
Côtes-du-Nord □ 8 48 25N 2 40W
Cotonou 49 6 20N 2 25 E
Cotopaxi, Vol. 72 0 40 S 78 30W
Cotswold Hills 5 51 42N 2 10W
Cottbus 13 51 44N 14 20 E
Coubre, Pte. de la 10 45 42N 1 15W
Couches 9 46 53N 4 30 E
Couëron 8 47 13N 1 44W
Couesnon → 8 48 38N 1 32W
Couhé 10 46 17N 0 11 E
Coulanges-sur-Yonne 9 47 31N 3 33 E
Coulommiers 9 48 50N 3 3 E
Coulonges-sur-l'Autize 10 46 29N 0 36W
Council Bluffs 67 41 20N 95 50W
Courçon 10 46 15N 0 50W
Couronne, C. 11 43 19N 5 3 E
Cours-la-Ville 11 46 7N 4 19 E
Coursan 10 43 14N 3 4 E
Courseulles-sur-Mer 8 49 20N 0 29W
Courtine-le-Trucq, La 10 45 41N 2 15 E
Courtrai = Kortrijk 12 50 50N 3 17 E
Courville-sur-Eure 8 48 28N 1 15 E
Coutances 8 49 3N 1 28W
Couterne 8 48 30N 0 25W
Coutras 10 45 3N 0 8W
Coventry 5 52 25N 1 31W
Covilhã 18 40 17N 7 31W
Covington, Ga., U.S.A. 66 33 36N 83 50W
Covington, Ky., U.S.A. 66 39 5N 84 30W
Cowal, L. 56 33 40 S 147 25 E
Cowan, L. 54 31 45 S 121 45 E
Cowdenbeath 6 56 7N 3 20W
Cowes 5 50 45N 1 18W
Cowra 56 33 49 S 148 42 E
Coxim 73 18 30 S 54 55W
Cracow = Kraków 15 50 4N 19 57 E
Cradock 52 32 8 S 25 36 E
Craiova 25 44 21N 23 48 E
Cranbrook 64 49 30N 115 46W
Craon 8 47 50N 0 58W
Craonne 9 49 27N 3 46 E
Craponne-sur-Arzon 10 45 19N 3 51 E
Crateús 73 5 10 S 40 39W
Crato 73 7 10 S 39 25W
Crau, La 11 43 32N 4 40 E
Crawfordsville 66 40 2N 86 51W
Crawley 5 51 7N 0 10W
Crazy Mts. 68 46 14N 110 30W
Crécy-en-Brie 9 48 50N 2 53 E
Crécy-en-Ponthieu 9 50 15N 1 53 E
Cree → 6 54 51N 4 24W
Creil 9 49 15N 2 29 E
Cremona 20 45 8N 10 2 E
Crépy 9 49 35N 3 32 E
Crépy-en-Valois 9 49 14N 2 54 E
Cres 21 44 58N 14 25 E
Crescent City 68 41 45N 124 12W
Crest 11 44 44N 5 2 E
Creston, Canada 64 49 10N 116 31W
Creston, U.S.A. 67 41 0N 94 20W
Crestview 66 30 45N 86 35W
Crete = Kriti 26 35 15N 25 0 E
Creus, C. 19 42 20N 3 19 E
Creuse □ 10 46 10N 2 0 E
Creuse → 10 47 0N 0 34 E
Creusot, Le 9 46 48N 4 24 E
Crèvecœur-le-Grand 9 49 37N 2 5 E
Crewe 5 53 6N 2 28W
Criciúma 74 28 40 S 49 23W
Crieff 6 56 22N 3 50W
Crimea = Krymskiy P-ov. 34 45 0N 34 0 E
Crinan 6 56 6N 5 34W
Crişul Negru → 15 46 38N 22 26 E
Crna Gora 24 42 10N 21 30 E
Crna Gora □ 24 42 40N 19 20 E
Crna Reka → 24 41 33N 21 59 E
Croaghpatrick 7 53 46N 9 40W
Crocker I. 54 11 12 S 132 32 E
Crockett 67 31 20N 95 30W
Crocodile Is. 54 12 3 S 134 58 E
Crocq 10 45 52N 2 21 E
Croisette, C. 11 43 14N 5 22 E
Croisic, Le 8 47 18N 2 30W
Croisic, Pte. du 8 47 19N 2 31W
Cromarty 6 57 40N 4 2W
Cromer 5 52 56N 1 18 E
Cronat 9 46 43N 3 40 E
Crooked I. 70 22 50N 74 10W
Cross Fell 5 54 44N 2 29W
Cross L. 65 54 45N 97 30W
Crosse, La 67 43 48N 91 13W
Crosshaven 7 51 48N 8 19W
Crotone 23 39 5N 17 6 E
Crow Hd. 7 51 34N 10 9W
Crowley 67 30 15N 92 20W
Crowsnest Pass 64 49 40N 114 40W
Croydon, Australia 56 18 13 S 142 14 E
Croydon, U.K. 5 51 18N 0 5W
Crozet Is. 2 46 27 S 52 0 E
Crozon 8 48 15N 4 30W
Cruz, C. 70 19 50N 77 50W
Cruz Alta 74 28 45 S 53 40W
Cruz del Eje 74 30 45 S 64 50W
Cruzeiro do Sul 72 7 35 S 72 35W
Csongrád 15 46 43N 20 12 E
Cu Lao Hon 41 10 54N 108 18 E
Cuamba 51 14 45 S 36 22 E
Cuando → 51 17 30 S 23 15 E
Cuba ■ 70 22 0N 79 0W
Cubango → 52 18 50 S 22 25 E
Cuchi 51 14 37 S 16 58 E
Cucuí 72 1 12N 66 50W
Cúcuta 72 7 54N 72 31W
Cuddalore 38 11 46N 79 45 E
Cuddapah 38 14 30N 78 47 E
Cue 54 27 25 S 117 54 E
Cuenca, Ecuador 72 2 50 S 79 9W
Cuenca, Spain 19 40 5N 2 10W
Cuenca, Serranía de 19 39 55N 1 50W
Cuernavaca 69 18 55N 99 15W
Cuers 11 43 14N 6 5 E
Cuevas del Almanzora 19 37 18N 1 58W
Cuevo 72 20 15 S 63 30W
Cuiabá 73 15 30 S 56 0W
Cuillin Hills 6 57 14N 6 15W
Cuillin Sd. 6 57 4N 6 20W
Cuima 51 13 25 S 15 45 E
Cuiseaux 11 46 30N 5 22 E
Cuito → 52 18 1 S 20 48 E
Cuitzeo, L. de 69 19 55N 101 5W
Culan 10 46 34N 2 20 E
Culebra, Sierra de la 18 41 55N 6 20W
Culiacán 69 24 48N 107 24W
Cullen 6 57 45N 2 50W
Cullera 19 39 9N 0 17W
Culloden Moor 6 57 29N 4 7W
Culoz 11 45 47N 5 46 E
Culver, Pt. 54 32 54 S 124 43 E
Cumaná 72 10 30N 64 5W
Cumberland, Canada 64 49 40N 125 0W
Cumberland, U.S.A. 66 39 40N 78 43W
Cumberland → 66 36 15N 87 0W
Cumberland Is. 56 20 35 S 149 10 E
Cumberland Plateau 66 36 0N 84 30W
Cumbria □ 5 54 35N 2 55W
Cumbrian Mts. 5 54 30N 3 0W
Cumbum 38 15 40N 79 10 E
Cumnock 6 55 27N 4 18W
Cunene → 52 17 20 S 11 50 E
Cúneo 20 44 23N 7 31 E
Cunlhat 10 45 38N 3 32 E
Cunnamulla 56 28 2 S 145 38 E
Cupar 6 56 20N 3 0W
Curaçao 70 12 10N 69 0W
Curaray → 72 2 20 S 74 5W
Cure → 9 47 40N 3 41 E
Curicó 74 34 55 S 71 20W
Curitiba 74 25 20 S 49 10W
Curtis I. 56 23 35 S 151 10 E
Curuá → 73 5 23 S 54 22W
Curuçá 73 0 43 S 47 50W
Curuzú Cuatiá 74 29 50 S 58 5W
Cushing 67 35 59N 96 46W
Cusihuiriáchic 69 28 14N 106 50W
Cusset 10 46 8N 3 28 E
Cuthbert 66 31 47N 84 47W
Cuttack 36 20 25N 85 57 E
Cuvier, C. 54 23 14 S 113 22 E
Cuxhaven 13 53 51N 8 41 E
Cuyahoga Falls 66 41 8N 81 30W
Cuzco, Bolivia 72 20 0 S 66 50W
Cuzco, Peru 72 13 32 S 72 0W
Cwmbran 5 51 39N 3 0W
Cyclades = Kikládhes 26 37 20N 24 30 E
Cypress Hills 65 49 40N 109 30W
Cyprus ■ 45 35 0N 33 0 E
Cyrenaica 50 27 0N 23 0 E
Czechoslovakia ■ 15 49 0N 17 0 E
Częstochowa 17 50 49N 19 7 E

D

Da → 41 21 15N 105 20 E
Da Hinggan Ling 42 48 0N 121 0 E
Da Nang 41 16 4N 108 13 E
Da Yunhe → 43 34 25N 120 5 E
Daba Shan 43 32 0N 109 0 E
Dabakala 49 8 15N 4 20W
Dąbie 17 53 27N 14 45 E
Dabola 49 10 50N 11 5W
Daboya 49 9 30N 1 20W
Dabrowa Tarnówska 15 50 10N 20 59 E
Dacca = Dhaka 37 23 43N 90 26 E
Dacca □ = Dhaka □ 37 24 25N 90 25 E
Dadanawa 72 2 50N 59 30W
Dadra and Nagar Haveli □ 36 20 5N 73 0 E
Dadu 36 26 45N 67 45 E
Dagana 49 16 30N 15 35W
Daghestan A.S.S.R. □ 35 42 30N 47 0 E
Dahlak Kebir 47 15 50N 40 10 E
Dahod 36 22 50N 74 15 E
Dahomey = Benin ■ 49 10 0N 2 0 E
Dahra 49 15 22N 15 30W
Daingean 7 53 18N 7 15W
Daiō-Misaki 44 34 15N 136 45 E
Dairût 50 27 34N 30 43 E
Dajarra 56 21 42 S 139 30 E
Dakar 49 14 34N 17 29W
Dakhla 49 23 50N 15 53W
Dakhla, El Wâhât el- 50 25 30N 28 50 E
Dakhovskaya 35 44 13N 40 13 E
Đakovica 24 42 22N 20 26 E
Dalandzadgad 42 43 27N 104 30 E
Dalbeattie 6 54 55N 3 50W
Dalby 56 27 10 S 151 17 E
Dalhousie 63 48 5N 66 26W
Dali 42 25 40N 100 10 E
Dalian 42 38 50N 121 40 E
Daliang Shan 42 28 0N 102 45 E
Dalkeith 6 55 54N 3 5W
Dallas, Oreg., U.S.A. 68 45 0N 123 15W
Dallas, Tex., U.S.A. 67 32 50N 96 50W
Dalmacija □ 24 43 20N 17 0 E
Dalmatia = Dalmacija □ 24 43 20N 17 0 E
Dalmellington 6 55 20N 4 25W
Dalneretchensk 31 45 50N 133 40 E
Daloa 49 7 0N 6 30W
Dalrymple, Mt. 55 21 1 S 148 39 E
Dalton 66 34 47N 84 58W
Dalvík 27 65 58N 18 32W
Daly → 54 13 35 S 130 19 E
Daly Waters 54 16 15 S 133 24 E
Daman 36 20 25N 72 57 E
Damanhûr 50 31 0N 30 30 E
Damaraland 52 21 0 S 17 0 E
Damascus = Dimashq 45 33 30N 36 18 E
Damāvand 46 35 47N 52 0 E
Damāvand, Qolleh-ye 46 35 56N 52 10 E
Damba 51 6 44 S 15 20 E
Damietta = Dumyât 50 31 24N 31 48 E
Dammarie 8 48 20N 1 30 E
Dammartin-en-Goële 9 49 3N 2 41 E
Damme 13 52 32N 8 12 E
Damoh 37 23 50N 79 28 E
Dampier 54 20 41 S 116 42 E
Dampier Arch. 54 20 38 S 116 32 E
Dampier Downs 54 18 24 S 123 5 E
Dampier Str. 56 5 50 S 148 0 E
Damville 8 48 51N 1 5 E
Damvillers 9 49 20N 5 21 E
Danbury 66 41 23N 73 29W
Dandeldhura 37 29 20N 80 35 E
Dandong 42 40 10N 124 20 E
Danger Is. = Pukapuka 58 10 53 S 165 49W
Danger Pt. 52 34 40 S 19 17 E
Dangora 49 11 30N 8 7 E
Dangriga 69 17 0N 88 13W
Danilov 33 58 16N 40 13 E
Dannemora 28 60 12N 17 51 E
Dansville 66 42 32N 77 41W
Dante 47 10 25N 51 16 E
Danube → 25 45 20N 29 40 E
Danville, Ill., U.S.A. 66 40 10N 87 40W
Danville, Ky., U.S.A. 66 37 40N 84 45W
Danville, Va., U.S.A. 66 36 40N 79 20W
Danzig = Gdańsk 17 54 22N 18 40 E
Daoulas 8 48 22N 4 17W
Dar es Salaam 51 6 50 S 39 12 E
Daraj 49 30 10N 10 28 E
Darbhanga 37 26 15N 85 55 E
Dardanelles = Çanakkale Boğazi 26 40 0N 26 0 E
Dârfûr 50 13 40N 24 0 E
Dargan Ata 30 40 29N 62 10 E
Darién, G. del 72 9 0N 77 0W
Darjeeling = Darjiling 37 27 3N 88 18 E
Darjiling 37 27 3N 88 18 E
Darling → 56 34 4 S 141 54 E
Darling Ra. 54 32 30 S 116 0 E
Darlington 5 54 33N 1 33W
Darłowo 17 54 25N 16 25 E
Darmstadt 13 49 51N 8 40 E
Darnah 50 32 40N 22 35 E
Darnétal 8 49 25N 1 10 E
Darney 9 48 5N 6 2 E
Darror → 47 10 30N 50 0 E
Dart → 5 50 24N 3 36W
Dartmoor 5 50 36N 4 0W
Dartmouth, Canada 63 44 40N 63 30W
Dartmouth, U.K. 5 50 21N 3 35W
Daru 56 9 3 S 143 13 E
Darwha 36 20 15N 77 45 E
Darwin 54 12 25 S 130 51 E
Dasht-e Kavīr 46 34 30N 55 0 E
Dasht-e Lūt 46 31 30N 58 0 E
Dasht-e Mārgow 46 30 40N 62 30 E
Datia 36 25 39N 78 27 E
Datong 42 40 6N 113 18 E
Daugava → 32 57 4N 24 3 E
Daugavpils 32 55 53N 26 32 E
Daulpur 36 26 45N 77 59 E
Dauphin 65 51 9N 100 5W
Dauphiné 11 45 15N 5 25 E
Davangere 38 14 25N 75 55 E
Davao 40 7 0N 125 40 E
Davenport 67 41 30N 90 40W
Davenport Ra. 54 20 28 S 134 0 E
David 70 8 30N 82 30W
Davis Str. 61 65 0N 58 0W
Davos 13 46 48N 9 49 E
Dawson → 55 23 25 S 149 45 E
Dawson Creek 64 55 45N 120 15W
Dax 10 43 44N 1 3W
Dayr az Zawr 45 35 20N 40 5 E
Dayton, Ohio, U.S.A. 66 39 45N 84 10W
Dayton, Wash., U.S.A. 68 46 20N 118 10W
Daytona Beach 66 29 14N 81 0W
De Aar 52 30 39 S 24 0 E
De Grey 54 20 12 S 119 12 E
De Land 66 29 1N 81 19W
De Ridder 67 30 48N 93 15W
De Soto 67 38 7N 90 33W
Deakin 54 30 46 S 128 0 E
Deal 5 51 13N 1 25 E
Dean, Forest of 5 51 50N 2 35W
Deán Funes 74 30 20 S 64 20W
Dease → 64 59 56N 128 32W
Dease Lake 64 58 25N 130 6W
Death Valley 68 36 19N 116 52W
Deauville 8 49 23N 0 2 E
Deba Habe 49 10 14N 11 20 E
Debar 24 41 31N 20 30 E
Debre Markos 50 10 20N 37 40 E
Debre Tabor 50 11 50N 38 26 E
Debrecen 15 47 33N 21 42 E
Decatur, Ala., U.S.A. 66 34 35N 87 0W
Decatur, Ga., U.S.A. 66 33 47N 84 17W
Decatur, Ill., U.S.A. 67 39 50N 89 0W
Decazeville 10 44 34N 2 15 E
Deccan 38 18 0N 79 0 E
Decize 9 46 50N 3 28 E
Dédougou 49 12 30N 3 25W
Dee →, Scotland, U.K. 6 57 4N 2 7W

Place	Page	Lat.	Long.
Dee →, Wales, U.K.	**5**	53 15N	3 7W
Deepdale	**54**	21 42 S	116 10 E
Deer Lake	**63**	49 11N	57 27W
Defiance	**66**	41 20N	84 20W
Degeh Bur	**47**	8 11N	43 31 E
Deh Bīd	**46**	30 39N	53 11 E
Dehibat	**49**	32 0N	10 47 E
Dehra Dun	**36**	30 20N	78 4 E
Deinze	**12**	50 59N	3 32 E
Dej	**15**	47 10N	23 52 E
Dekese	**51**	3 24 S	21 24 E
Delano	**68**	35 48N	119 13W
Delaware □	**66**	39 0N	75 40W
Delaware →	**66**	39 20N	75 25W
Delft	**12**	52 1N	4 22 E
Delfzijl	**12**	53 20N	6 55 E
Delgado, C.	**51**	10 45 S	40 40 E
Delgo	**50**	20 6N	30 40 E
Delhi	**36**	28 38N	77 17 E
Delice →	**45**	39 45N	34 15 E
Delicias	**69**	28 13N	105 28W
Delle	**9**	47 30N	7 2 E
Delmenhorst	**13**	53 3N	8 37 E
Delong, Ostrova	**31**	76 40N	149 20 E
Delray Beach	**66**	26 27N	80 4W
Demanda, Sierra de la	**19**	42 15N	3 0W
Demba	**51**	5 28 S	22 15 E
Dembecha	**50**	10 32N	37 30 E
Dembidolo	**50**	8 34N	34 50 E
Demer →	**12**	50 57N	4 42 E
Demopolis	**66**	32 30N	87 48W
Den Burg	**12**	53 3N	4 47 E
Den Haag = 's-Gravenhage	**12**	52 7N	4 17 E
Den Helder	**12**	52 57N	4 45 E
Den Oever	**12**	52 56N	5 2 E
Denain	**9**	50 20N	3 22 E
Denau	**30**	38 16N	67 54 E
Denbigh	**5**	53 12N	3 26W
Dendermonde	**12**	51 2N	4 5 E
Denham	**54**	25 56 S	113 31 E
Denham Ra.	**56**	21 55 S	147 46 E
Denia	**19**	38 49N	0 8 E
Deniliquin	**56**	35 30 S	144 58 E
Denison	**67**	33 50N	96 40W
Denison Range	**55**	28 30 S	136 5 E
Denizli	**45**	37 42N	29 2 E
Denmark	**54**	34 59 S	117 25 E
Denmark ■	**28**	55 30N	9 0 E
Denmark Str.	**1**	66 0N	30 0W
Denton	**67**	33 12N	97 10W
D'Entrecasteaux Is.	**56**	9 0 S	151 0 E
D'Entrecasteaux Pt.	**54**	34 50 S	115 57 E
Denver	**67**	39 45N	105 0W
Deoghar	**37**	24 30N	86 42 E
Deolali	**38**	19 58N	73 50 E
Deoria	**37**	26 31N	83 48 E
Deputatskiy	**31**	69 18N	139 54 E
Dera Ghazi Khan	**36**	30 5N	70 43 E
Dera Ismail Khan	**36**	31 50N	70 50 E
Derbent	**34**	42 5N	48 15 E
Derby, Australia	**54**	17 18 S	123 38 E
Derby, U.K.	**5**	52 55N	1 28W
Derby □	**5**	52 55N	1 28W
Derg →	**7**	54 42N	7 26W
Derg, L.	**7**	53 0N	8 20W
Derry = Londonderry	**7**	55 0N	7 20W
Derryveagh Mts.	**7**	55 0N	8 40W
Derudub	**50**	17 31N	36 7 E
Derval	**8**	47 40N	1 41W
Derwent →, Derby, U.K.	**5**	52 53N	1 17W
Derwent →, N. Yorks., U.K.	**5**	53 45N	0 57W
Derwent Water, L.	**5**	54 35N	3 9W
Des Moines	**67**	41 35N	93 37W
Des Moines →	**67**	40 23N	91 25W
Descartes	**10**	46 59N	0 42 E
Deschutes →	**68**	45 30N	121 0W
Dese	**47**	11 5N	39 40 E
Desna →	**32**	50 33N	30 32 E
Despeñaperros, Paso	**19**	38 24N	3 30W
Dessau	**13**	51 49N	12 15 E
Desvres	**9**	50 40N	1 48 E
Detmold	**13**	51 55N	8 50 E
Detroit	**66**	42 23N	83 5W
Deurne, Belgium	**12**	51 12N	4 24 E
Deurne, Neth.	**12**	51 27N	5 49 E
Deutsche Bucht	**13**	54 10N	7 51 E
Deux-Sèvres □	**8**	46 35N	0 20W
Deva	**15**	45 53N	22 55 E
Devakottai	**38**	9 55N	78 45 E
Deventer	**12**	52 15N	6 10 E
Deveron →	**6**	57 40N	2 31W
Devizes	**5**	51 21N	2 0W
Devon I.	**3**	75 10N	85 0W
Devonport, Australia	**56**	41 10 S	146 22 E
Devonport, U.K.	**5**	50 23N	4 11W
Devonshire □	**5**	50 50N	3 40W
Dewas	**36**	22 59N	76 3 E
Dewsbury	**5**	53 42N	1 38W
Dezfūl	**45**	32 20N	48 30 E
Dezhneva, Mys	**31**	66 5N	169 40W
Dhahran = Az Ẓahrān	**45**	26 10N	50 7 E
Dhaka	**37**	23 43N	90 26 E
Dhaka □	**37**	24 25N	90 25 E
Dhamar	**47**	14 30N	44 20 E
Dhamtari	**36**	20 42N	81 35 E
Dhanbad	**37**	23 50N	86 30 E
Dhankuta	**37**	26 55N	87 40 E
Dhar	**36**	22 35N	75 26 E
Dharmapuri	**38**	12 10N	78 10 E
Dharwad	**38**	15 22N	75 15 E
Dhaulagiri	**37**	28 39N	83 28 E
Dhenkanal	**36**	20 45N	85 35 E
Dhidhimótikhon	**26**	41 22N	26 29 E
Dhikti	**26**	35 8N	25 22 E
Dhírfis	**26**	38 40N	23 54 E
Dhodhekánisos	**26**	36 35N	27 0 E
Dhrol	**36**	22 33N	70 25 E
Dhuburi	**37**	26 2N	89 59 E
Dhula	**47**	15 10N	47 30 E
Dhule	**36**	20 58N	74 50 E
Di Linh, Cao Nguyen	**41**	11 30N	108 0 E
Diafarabé	**49**	14 9N	4 57W
Diamantina	**73**	18 17 S	43 40W
Diamantina →	**56**	26 45 S	139 10 E
Diamantino	**73**	14 30 S	56 30W
Diamond Harbour	**37**	22 11N	88 14 E
Diapaga	**49**	12 5N	1 46 E
Dibaya	**51**	6 30 S	22 57 E
Dibaya-Lubue	**51**	4 12 S	19 54 E
Dibbi	**47**	4 10N	41 52 E
Didiéni	**49**	13 53N	8 6W
Didsbury	**64**	51 35N	114 10W
Die	**11**	44 47N	5 22 E
Diébougou	**49**	11 0N	3 15W
Diefenbaker L.	**65**	51 0N	106 55W
Diego Garcia	**2**	7 50 S	72 50 E
Diekirch	**12**	49 52N	6 10 E
Diélette	**8**	49 33N	1 52W
Dieppe	**8**	49 54N	1 4 E
Dieren	**12**	52 3N	6 6 E
Diest	**12**	50 58N	5 4 E
Dieulefit	**11**	44 32N	5 4 E
Dieuze	**9**	48 49N	6 43 E
Differdange	**12**	49 31N	5 54 E
Digby	**63**	44 38N	65 50W
Digne	**11**	44 5N	6 12 E
Digoin	**10**	46 29N	3 58 E
Digranes	**27**	66 4N	14 44 E
Dijlah, Nahr →	**45**	31 0N	47 25 E
Dijon	**9**	47 20N	5 0 E
Diksmuide	**12**	51 2N	2 52 E
Dikwa	**50**	12 4N	13 30 E
Dilling	**50**	12 3N	29 35 E
Dillon	**66**	34 26N	79 20W
Dilolo	**51**	10 28 S	22 18 E
Dimashq	**45**	33 30N	36 18 E
Dimbokro	**49**	6 45N	4 46W
Dimitrovgrad, Bulgaria	**25**	42 5N	25 35 E
Dimitrovgrad, U.S.S.R.	**33**	54 14N	49 39 E
Dinajpur	**37**	25 33N	88 43 E
Dinan	**8**	48 28N	2 2W
Dinant	**12**	50 16N	4 55 E
Dinara Planina	**21**	44 0N	16 30 E
Dinard	**8**	48 38N	2 6W
Dinaric Alps = Dinara Planina	**21**	44 0N	16 30 E
Dindigul	**38**	10 25N	78 0 E
Dingle	**7**	52 9N	10 17W
Dingle B.	**7**	52 3N	10 20W
Dinguiraye	**49**	11 18N	10 49W
Dingwall	**6**	57 36N	4 26W
Dinosaur National Monument	**68**	40 30N	108 58W
Dinuba	**68**	36 31N	119 22W
Diourbel	**49**	14 39N	16 12W
Diré	**49**	16 20N	3 25W
Dire Dawa	**47**	9 35N	41 45 E
Diriamba	**70**	11 51N	86 19W
Dirk Hartog I.	**54**	25 50 S	113 5 E
Dirranbandi	**56**	28 33 S	148 17 E
Disa	**36**	24 18N	72 10 E
Disappointment L.	**54**	23 20 S	122 40 E
Disaster B.	**56**	37 15 S	150 0 E
Discovery B.	**56**	38 10 S	140 40 E
Disko	**3**	69 45N	53 30W
Disko Bugt	**3**	69 10N	52 0W
District of Columbia □	**66**	38 55N	77 0W
Diu	**36**	20 45N	70 58 E
Dives →	**8**	49 18N	0 7W
Dives-sur-Mer	**8**	49 18N	0 8W
Divnoye	**35**	45 55N	43 21 E
Dixon	**67**	41 50N	89 30W
Dixon Entrance	**64**	54 30N	132 0W
Diyarbakir	**45**	37 55N	40 18 E
Djado	**50**	21 4N	12 14 E
Djambala	**51**	2 32 S	14 30 E
Djanet	**49**	24 35N	9 32 E
Djaul I.	**56**	2 58 S	150 57 E
Djawa = Jawa	**40**	7 0 S	110 0 E
Djelfa	**49**	34 40N	3 15 E
Djema	**51**	6 3N	25 15 E
Djenné	**49**	14 0N	4 30W
Djerid, Chott	**49**	33 42N	8 30 E
Djibo	**49**	14 9N	1 35W
Djibouti	**47**	11 30N	43 5 E
Djibouti ■	**47**	12 0N	43 0 E
Djolu	**51**	0 35N	22 5 E
Djougou	**49**	9 40N	1 45 E
Djoum	**51**	2 41N	12 35 E
Djourab	**50**	16 40N	18 50 E
Djugu	**51**	1 55N	30 35 E
Djúpivogur	**27**	64 39N	14 17W
Dmitriya Lapteva, Proliv	**31**	73 0N	140 0 E
Dnepr →	**34**	46 30N	32 18 E
Dneprodzerzhinsk	**34**	48 32N	34 37 E
Dnepropetrovsk	**34**	48 30N	35 0 E
Dnestr →	**34**	46 18N	30 17 E
Dnieper = Dnepr →	**34**	46 30N	32 18 E
Dniester = Dnestr →	**34**	46 18N	30 17 E
Doba	**50**	8 40N	16 50 E
Dobbyn	**56**	19 44 S	139 59 E
Dobruja	**25**	44 30N	28 15 E
Dodecanese = Dhodhekánisos	**26**	36 35N	27 0 E
Dodge City	**67**	37 42N	100 0W
Dodoma	**51**	6 8 S	35 45 E
Doetinchem	**12**	51 59N	6 18 E
Doi Luang	**41**	18 30N	101 0 E
Dokkum	**12**	53 20N	5 59 E
Dol-de-Bretagne	**8**	48 34N	1 47W
Dolbeau	**63**	48 53N	72 18W
Dole	**9**	47 7N	5 31 E
Dolgellau	**5**	52 44N	3 53W
Dolgelley = Dolgellau	**5**	52 44N	3 53W
Dollart	**12**	53 20N	7 10 E
Dolomites = Dolomiti	**21**	46 30N	11 40 E
Dolomiti	**21**	46 30N	11 40 E
Dolores	**74**	36 20 S	57 40W
Dombarovskiy	**30**	50 46N	59 32 E
Dombasle-sur-Meurthe	**9**	48 38N	6 21 E
Dombes	**11**	46 0N	5 0 E
Domburg	**12**	51 34N	3 30 E
Domérat	**10**	46 21N	2 32 E
Domfront	**8**	48 37N	0 40W
Dominica ■	**70**	15 20N	61 20W
Dominican Rep. ■	**70**	19 0N	70 30W
Domme	**10**	44 48N	1 12 E
Domo	**47**	7 50N	47 10 E
Dompaire	**9**	48 14N	6 14 E
Dompierre-sur-Besbre	**10**	46 31N	3 41 E
Domrémy-la-Pucelle	**9**	48 26N	5 40 E
Don →, England, U.K.	**5**	53 41N	0 51W
Don →, Scotland, U.K.	**6**	57 14N	2 5W
Don →, U.S.S.R.	**35**	47 4N	39 18 E
Don Benito	**18**	38 53N	5 51W
Donaghadee	**7**	54 38N	5 32W
Donau →	**15**	48 10N	17 0 E
Donauwörth	**13**	48 42N	10 47 E
Doncaster	**5**	53 31N	1 9W
Dondo, Angola	**51**	9 45 S	14 25 E
Dondo, Mozam.	**51**	19 33 S	34 46 E
Dondra Head	**38**	5 55N	80 40 E
Donegal	**7**	54 39N	8 8W
Donegal □	**7**	54 53N	8 0W
Donegal B.	**7**	54 30N	8 35W
Donets →	**35**	47 33N	40 55 E
Donetsk	**34**	48 0N	37 45 E
Dongara	**54**	29 14 S	114 57 E
Donges	**8**	47 18N	2 4W
Dongola	**50**	19 9N	30 22 E
Dongou	**51**	2 0N	18 5 E
Dongting Hu	**42**	29 18N	112 45 E
Donjon, Le	**10**	46 22N	3 48 E
Dønna	**27**	66 6N	12 30 E
Donzère	**11**	44 28N	4 43 E
Donzère-Mondragon, Barr. de	**11**	44 13N	4 42 E
Donzy	**9**	47 20N	3 6 E
Doon →	**6**	55 26N	4 41W
Dora, L.	**54**	22 0 S	123 0 E
Dora Báltea →	**20**	45 11N	8 5 E
Dorada, La	**72**	5 30N	74 40W
Dorat, Le	**10**	46 14N	1 5 E
Dorchester	**5**	50 42N	2 28W
Dordogne □	**10**	45 5N	0 40 E
Dordogne →	**10**	45 2N	0 36W
Dordrecht	**12**	51 48N	4 39 E
Dore →	**10**	45 50N	3 35 E
Dore, Mts.	**10**	45 32N	2 50 E
Dori	**49**	14 3N	0 2W
Dornes	**9**	46 48N	3 18 E
Dornoch	**6**	57 52N	4 0W
Dornoch Firth	**6**	57 52N	4 0W
Dorohoi	**15**	47 56N	26 30 E
Dorre I.	**54**	25 13 S	113 12 E
Dorris	**68**	41 59N	121 58W
Dorset □	**5**	50 48N	2 25W
Dortmund	**13**	51 32N	7 28 E
Doruma	**51**	4 42N	27 33 E
Dosso	**49**	13 0N	3 13 E
Dothan	**66**	31 10N	85 25W
Douai	**9**	50 21N	3 4 E
Douala	**49**	4 0N	9 45 E
Douarnenez	**8**	48 6N	4 21W
Doubs □	**9**	47 10N	6 20 E
Doubs →	**9**	46 53N	5 1 E
Doubtful Sd.	**59**	45 20 S	166 49 E
Doudeville	**8**	49 43N	0 47 E
Doué-la-Fontaine	**8**	47 11N	0 16W
Douentza	**49**	14 58N	2 48W
Douglas, U.K.	**5**	54 9N	4 29W
Douglas, Ariz., U.S.A.	**68**	31 21N	109 30W
Douglas, Ga., U.S.A.	**66**	31 32N	82 52W
Doulevant-le-Château	**9**	48 23N	4 55 E
Doullens	**9**	50 10N	2 20 E
Doumé	**51**	4 15N	13 25 E
Dounreay	**6**	58 34N	3 44W
Dourados	**73**	22 9 S	54 50W
Dourdan	**9**	48 30N	2 1 E
Douro →	**18**	41 8N	8 40W
Douvaine	**11**	46 19N	6 16 E
Douze →	**10**	43 54N	0 30W
Dove →	**5**	52 51N	1 36W
Dover, U.K.	**5**	51 7N	1 19 E
Dover, Del., U.S.A.	**66**	39 10N	75 31W
Dover, N.H., U.S.A.	**66**	43 12N	70 51W
Dover, Pt.	**54**	32 32 S	125 32 E
Dover, Str. of	**8**	51 0N	1 30 E
Dovey →	**5**	52 32N	4 0W
Dovrefjell	**27**	62 15N	9 33 E
Down □	**7**	54 20N	6 0W
Downham Market	**5**	52 36N	0 22 E
Downpatrick	**7**	54 20N	5 43W
Downpatrick Hd.	**7**	54 20N	9 21W
Draa, Oued →	**49**	28 40N	11 10W
Drac →	**11**	45 12N	5 42 E
Drachten	**12**	53 7N	6 5 E
Dragoman, Prokhod	**24**	43 0N	22 53 E
Draguignan	**11**	43 32N	6 27 E
Drake Passage	**60**	58 0 S	68 0W
Drakensberg	**53**	31 0 S	28 0 E
Dráma	**26**	41 9N	24 10 E
Drammen	**28**	59 42N	10 12 E
Drangajökull	**27**	66 9N	22 15W
Drau = Drava →	**24**	45 33N	18 55 E
Drava →	**24**	45 33N	18 55 E
Draveil	**9**	48 41N	2 25 E
Drayton Valley	**64**	53 12N	114 58W
Drenthe □	**12**	52 52N	6 40 E
Dresden	**13**	51 2N	13 45 E
Dreux	**8**	48 44N	1 23 E
Driffield	**5**	54 0N	0 25W
Drina →	**24**	44 53N	19 21 E
Drøbak	**28**	59 39N	10 39 E
Drogheda	**7**	53 45N	6 20W
Drogobych	**32**	49 20N	23 30 E
Droichead Nua	**7**	53 11N	6 50W
Droitwich	**5**	52 16N	2 10W
Drôme □	**11**	44 38N	5 15 E
Drôme →	**11**	44 46N	4 46 E
Dronne →	**10**	45 2N	0 9W
Dronning Maud Land	**60**	72 30 S	12 0 E
Dropt →	**10**	44 35N	0 6W
Drumheller	**64**	51 25N	112 40W
Drummond Ra.	**56**	23 45 S	147 10 E
Drummondville	**62**	45 55N	72 25W
Druzhina	**31**	68 14N	145 18 E
Dryden	**65**	49 47N	92 50W
Drysdale →	**54**	13 59 S	126 51 E
Dschang	**49**	5 32N	10 3 E
Du Bois	**66**	41 8N	78 46W
Du Quoin	**67**	38 0N	89 10W
Dubai = Dubayy	**46**	25 18N	55 20 E
Dubayy	**46**	25 18N	55 20 E
Dubbo	**56**	32 11 S	148 35 E
Dublin, Ireland	**7**	53 20N	6 18W
Dublin, U.S.A.	**66**	32 30N	82 34W
Dublin □	**7**	53 24N	6 20W
Dublin B.	**7**	53 18N	6 5W
Dubovka	**35**	49 5N	44 50 E
Dubréka	**49**	9 46N	13 31W
Dubrovnik	**24**	42 39N	18 6 E
Dubrovskoye	**31**	58 55N	111 10 E
Dubuque	**67**	42 30N	90 41W
Duchess	**56**	21 20 S	139 50 E
Ducie I.	**58**	24 40 S	124 48W
Duderstadt	**13**	51 30N	10 15 E
Dudinka	**31**	69 30N	86 13 E
Dudley	**5**	52 30N	2 5W
Duero →	**18**	41 8N	8 40W
Dufftown	**6**	57 26N	3 9W
Duifken Pt.	**56**	12 33 S	141 38 E
Duisburg	**13**	51 27N	6 42 E
Duku	**49**	10 43N	10 43 E
Duluth	**67**	46 48N	92 10W
Dum Hadjer	**50**	13 18N	19 41 E
Dumbarton	**6**	55 58N	4 35W
Dumfries	**6**	55 4N	3 37W
Dumfries & Galloway □	**6**	55 0N	4 0W
Dümmersee	**13**	52 30N	8 21 E
Dumyât	**50**	31 24N	31 48 E
Dun Laoghaire	**7**	53 17N	6 9W
Dun-le-Palestel	**10**	46 18N	1 39 E
Dun-sur-Auron	**9**	46 53N	2 33 E
Dunaföldvár	**15**	46 50N	18 57 E
Dunărea →	**25**	45 20N	29 40 E
Dunbar	**6**	56 0N	2 32W
Dunblane	**6**	56 10N	3 58W
Duncan, Canada	**64**	48 45N	123 40W
Duncan, U.S.A.	**67**	34 25N	98 0W
Duncan Pass.	**41**	11 0N	92 30 E
Dundalk	**7**	54 1N	6 25W
Dundalk Bay	**7**	53 55N	6 15W
Dundas	**62**	43 17N	79 59W
Dundas, L.	**54**	32 35 S	121 50 E
Dundas Str.	**54**	11 15 S	131 35 E
Dundee, S. Africa	**53**	28 11 S	30 15 E
Dundee, U.K.	**6**	56 29N	3 0W
Dundrum	**7**	54 17N	5 50W
Dundrum B.	**7**	54 12N	5 40W
Dunedin	**59**	45 50 S	170 33 E
Dunfermline	**6**	56 5N	3 28W
Dungannon	**7**	54 30N	6 47W
Dungannon □	**7**	54 30N	6 55W
Dungarvan	**7**	52 6N	7 40W
Dungarvan Bay	**7**	52 5N	7 35W
Dungeness	**5**	50 54N	0 59 E
Dungu	**51**	3 40N	28 32 E
Dunhuang	**42**	40 8N	94 36 E
Dunières	**11**	45 13N	4 20 E
Dunkeld	**6**	56 34N	3 36W
Dunkerque	**9**	51 2N	2 20 E
Dunkery Beacon	**5**	51 15N	3 37W
Dunkirk = Dunkerque	**9**	51 2N	2 20 E
Dunkirk	**66**	42 30N	79 18W
Dunkwa	**49**	6 0N	1 47W
Dúnleary = Dun Laoghaire	**7**	53 17N	6 9W
Dunmanus B.	**7**	51 31N	9 50W
Dunmore	**66**	41 27N	75 38W
Dunmore Hd.	**7**	52 10N	10 35W
Dunn	**66**	35 18N	78 36W
Dunnet Hd.	**6**	58 38N	3 22W
Dunoon	**6**	55 57N	4 56W
Dunqul	**50**	23 26N	31 37 E
Duns	**6**	55 47N	2 20W
Dunsmuir	**68**	41 10N	122 18W
Dunstable	**5**	51 53N	0 31W
Durack Range	**54**	16 50 S	127 40 E
Durance →	**11**	43 55N	4 45 E
Durango	**19**	43 13N	2 40W
Durango □	**69**	24 50N	104 50W
Durant	**67**	34 0N	96 25W
Durazno	**74**	33 25 S	56 31W
Durban, France	**10**	42 59N	2 49 E
Durban, S. Africa	**53**	29 49 S	31 1 E
Düren	**13**	50 48N	6 30 E
Durg	**36**	21 15N	81 22 E
Durham, U.K.	**5**	54 47N	1 34W
Durham, U.S.A.	**66**	36 0N	78 55W
Durham □	**5**	54 42N	1 45W
Durness	**6**	58 34N	4 45W
Durrësi	**26**	41 19N	19 28 E
Durtal	**8**	47 40N	0 18W
Dusa Mareb	**47**	5 30N	46 15 E
Dushanbe	**30**	38 33N	68 48 E
Düsseldorf	**13**	51 15N	6 46 E
Duyun	**43**	26 18N	107 29 E
Duzce	**45**	40 50N	31 10 E
Dvina, Sev. →	**30**	64 32N	40 30 E
Dwarka	**36**	22 18N	69 8 E
Dyersburg	**67**	36 2N	89 20W
Dyfed □	**5**	52 0N	4 30W
Dzamin Üüd	**42**	43 50N	111 58 E
Dzerzhinsk, Byelorussian S.S.R., U.S.S.R.	**32**	53 40N	27 1 E
Dzerzhinsk, R.S.F.S.R., U.S.S.R.	**33**	56 14N	43 30 E
Dzhalal-Abad	**30**	40 56N	73 0 E
Dzhalinda	**31**	53 26N	124 0 E
Dzhambul	**30**	42 54N	71 22 E
Dzhankoi	**34**	45 40N	34 20 E
Dzhardzhan	**31**	68 10N	124 10 E
Dzhelinde	**31**	70 0N	114 20 E
Dzhetygara	**30**	52 11N	61 12 E
Dzhezkazgan	**30**	47 44N	67 40 E
Dzhikimde	**31**	59 1N	121 47 E
Dzhizak	**30**	40 6N	67 50 E
Dzhugdzur, Khrebet	**31**	57 30N	138 0 E
Dzuumod	**42**	47 45N	106 58 E

E

Place	Page	Lat.	Long.
Eagle River	**62**	45 55N	89 17W
Ealing	**5**	51 30N	0 19W
Earn →	**6**	56 20N	3 19W
Earn, L.	**6**	56 23N	4 14W
Easley	**66**	34 52N	82 35W
East Angus	**63**	45 30N	71 40W
East C.	**59**	37 42 S	178 35 E
East Chicago	**66**	41 40N	87 30W
East China Sea	**42**	30 5N	126 0 E
East Falkland	**74**	51 30 S	58 30W
East Germany ■	**13**	52 0N	12 0 E
East Indies	**39**	0 0	120 0 E
East Kilbride	**6**	55 46N	4 10W
East Liverpool	**66**	40 39N	80 35W
East London	**53**	33 0 S	27 55 E
East Orange	**66**	40 46N	74 13W
East Pakistan = Bangladesh ■	**37**	24 0N	90 0 E
East Point	**66**	33 40N	84 28W
East Retford	**5**	53 19N	0 55W
East St. Louis	**67**	38 37N	90 4W
East Siberian Sea	**31**	73 0N	160 0 E
East Sussex □	**5**	51 0N	0 20 E
Eastbourne	**5**	50 46N	0 18 E
Easter Islands	**58**	27 0 S	109 0W
Eastern Ghats	**38**	14 0N	78 50 E
Eastleigh	**5**	50 58N	1 21W
Eastmain	**62**	52 10N	78 30W
Eastmain →	**62**	52 27N	78 26W
Easton	**66**	40 41N	75 15W
Eau Claire	**67**	44 46N	91 30W
Eauze	**10**	43 53N	0 7 E
Ebbw Vale	**5**	51 47N	3 12W
Eberbach	**13**	49 27N	8 59 E
Eberswalde	**13**	52 49N	13 50 E
Ebingen	**13**	48 13N	9 1 E
Eboli	**23**	40 39N	15 2 E
Ebolowa	**51**	2 55N	11 10 E
Ebro →	**19**	40 43N	0 54 E
Ech Cheliff	**49**	36 10N	1 20 E
Échelles, Les	**11**	45 26N	5 46 E
Echternach	**12**	49 49N	6 25 E
Echuca	**54**	36 10 S	144 20 E
Ecija	**18**	37 30N	5 10W
Eckernförde	**13**	54 26N	9 50 E
Écommoy	**8**	47 50N	0 17 E
Écos	**9**	49 9N	1 35 E
Écouché	**8**	48 42N	0 10W
Ecuador ■	**72**	2 0 S	78 0W
Écueillé	**8**	47 5N	1 21 E
Ed Dâmer	**50**	17 27N	34 0 E
Ed Debba	**50**	18 0N	30 51 E
Ed Dueim	**50**	14 0N	32 10 E
Edam, Canada	**65**	53 11N	108 46W
Edam, Neth.	**12**	52 31N	5 3 E
Eday	**6**	59 11N	2 47W
Edd	**47**	14 0N	41 38 E
Eddrachillis B.	**6**	58 16N	5 10W
Eddystone	**5**	50 11N	4 16W
Ede	**12**	52 4N	5 40 E
Édea	**49**	3 51N	10 9 E
Eden →	**5**	54 57N	3 2W
Edenderry	**7**	53 21N	7 3W
Ederstausee	**13**	51 11N	9 0 E
Edge Hill	**5**	52 7N	1 28W
Edgeøya	**3**	77 45N	22 30 E
Edhessa	**26**	40 48N	22 5 E
Edinburg	**67**	26 22N	98 10W
Edinburgh	**6**	55 57N	3 12W
Edirne	**25**	41 40N	26 34 E
Edmonton	**64**	53 30N	113 30W
Edmundston	**63**	47 23N	68 20W
Edson	**64**	53 35N	116 28W
Edward, L.	**51**	0 25 S	29 40 E
Edwards Plateau	**67**	30 30N	101 5W
Eekloo	**12**	51 11N	3 33 E
Effingham	**66**	39 8N	88 30W
Égadi, Ísole	**22**	37 55N	12 16 E
Eger	**15**	47 53N	20 27 E
Egersund	**27**	58 26N	6 1 E
Égletons	**10**	45 24N	2 3 E
Egmont, Mt.	**59**	39 17 S	174 5 E
Eğridir Gölü	**45**	37 53N	30 50 E
Éguzon	**10**	46 27N	1 33 E
Egvekinot	**31**	66 19N	179 50W
Egypt ■	**50**	28 0N	31 0 E
Ehime □	**44**	33 30N	132 40 E
Eifel	**13**	50 10N	6 45 E
Eigg	**6**	56 54N	6 10W
Eighty Mile Beach	**54**	19 30 S	120 40 E
Eil	**47**	8 0N	49 50 E
Eil, L.	**6**	56 50N	5 15W
Einasleigh	**56**	18 32 S	144 5 E
Einbeck	**13**	51 48N	9 50 E
Eindhoven	**12**	51 26N	5 30 E
Eire ■	**7**	53 0N	8 0W
Eiríksjökull	**27**	64 46N	20 24W
Eirunepé	**72**	6 35 S	69 53W
Eisenach	**13**	50 58N	10 18 E
Eisenerz	**14**	47 32N	14 54 E
Ekimchan	**31**	53 0N	133 0W
El Aaiún	**49**	27 9N	13 12W
El Alamein	**50**	30 48N	28 58 E
El Aricha	**49**	34 13N	1 10W
El 'Arîsh	**50**	31 8N	33 50 E
El Asnam = Ech Cheliff	**49**	36 10N	1 20 E
El Bawiti	**50**	28 25N	28 45 E
El Bayadh	**49**	33 40N	1 1 E
El Buheirat □	**50**	7 0N	30 0 E
El Cajon	**68**	32 49N	117 0W

Index

El Callao 72 7 18N 61 50W
El Centro 68 32 50N 115 40W
El Cerro 72 17 30 S 61 40W
El Dere 47 3 50N 47 8 E
El Djouf 49 20 0N 11 30 E
El Dorado, Ark.,
U.S.A. 67 33 10N 92 40W
El Dorado, Kans.,
U.S.A. 67 37 55N 96 56W
El Escorial 18 40 35N 4 7W
El Faiyûm 50 29 19N 30 50 E
El Fâsher 50 13 33N 25 26 E
El Ferrol 18 43 29N 8 15W
El Fuerte 69 26 25N 108 39W
El Gal 47 10 58N 50 20 E
El Geteina 50 14 50N 32 27 E
El Gezira □ 50 15 0N 33 0 E
El Giza 50 30 0N 31 10 E
El Goléa 49 30 30N 2 50 E
El Harrach 49 36 45N 3 5 E
El Iskandarîya 50 31 0N 30 0 E
El Jadida 49 33 11N 8 17W
El Jebelein 50 12 40N 32 55 E
El Kab 50 19 27N 32 46 E
El Kala 49 36 50N 8 30 E
El Kamlin 50 15 3N 33 11 E
El Kef 49 36 12N 8 47 E
El Khandaq 50 18 30N 30 30 E
El Khârga 50 25 30N 30 33 E
El Khartûm 50 15 31N 32 35 E
El Khartûm Bahrî 50 15 40N 32 31 E
El Laqâwa 50 11 25N 29 1 E
El Mafâza 50 13 38N 34 30 E
El Mahalla el Kubra 50 31 0N 31 0 E
El Mansûra 50 31 0N 31 19 E
El Minyâ 50 28 7N 30 33 E
El Obeid 50 13 8N 30 10 E
El Odaiya 50 12 8N 28 12 E
El Oro 69 27 15N 103 30W
El Oued 49 33 20N 6 58 E
El Paso 68 31 50N 106 30W
El Progreso 69 15 26N 87 51W
El Qâhira 50 30 1N 31 14 E
El Qantara 50 30 51N 32 20 E
El Qasr 50 25 44N 28 42 E
El Reno 67 35 30N 98 0W
El Salvador ■ 69 13 50N 89 0W
El Shallal 50 24 0N 32 53 E
El Suweis 50 29 58N 32 31 E
El Tigre 72 8 44N 64 15W
El Turbio 74 51 45 S 72 5W
El Uqsur 50 25 41N 32 38 E
El Wak 51 2 49N 40 56 E
El Wuz 50 15 0N 30 7 E
Elat 45 29 30N 34 56 E
Elâzığ 45 38 37N 39 14 E
Elba 20 42 48N 10 15 E
Elbasani 26 41 9N 20 9 E
Elbe → 14 53 50N 9 0 E
Elbert, Mt. 68 39 5N 106 27W
Elberton 66 34 7N 82 51W
Elbeuf 8 49 17N 1 2 E
Elbląg 17 54 10N 19 25 E
Elbrus 35 43 21N 42 30 E
Elburg 12 52 26N 5 50 E
Elburz Mts. =
Alborz, Reshteh-ye
Kūhhā-ye 46 36 0N 52 0 E
Elche 19 38 15N 0 42W
Elcho I. 55 11 55 S 135 45 E
Eldorado 69 24 20N 107 22W
Eldorado Springs 67 37 54N 93 59W
Eldoret 51 0 30N 35 17 E
Eleuthera 70 25 0N 76 20W
Elgin, U.K. 6 57 39N 3 20W
Elgin, Ill., U.S.A. 67 42 0N 88 20W
Elgin, Oreg., U.S.A. 68 45 37N 118 0W
Elgon, Mt. 51 1 10N 34 30 E
Elista 35 46 16N 44 14 E
Elizabeth, Australia 56 34 42 S 138 41 E
Elizabeth, U.S.A. 66 40 37N 74 12W
Elizabeth City 66 36 18N 76 16W
Elizabethton 66 36 20N 82 13W
Elizabethtown 66 37 40N 85 54W
Elk Point 65 53 54N 110 55W
Elkhart 66 41 42N 85 55W
Elkhovo 25 42 10N 26 40 E
Elkins 66 38 53N 79 53W
Elko 68 40 50N 115 50W
Ellef Ringnes I. 3 78 30N 102 2W
Ellensburg 68 47 0N 120 30W
Ellesmere I. 3 79 30N 80 0W
Ellesworth Land 60 76 0 S 89 0W
Ellice Is. = Tuvalu ■ 57 8 0 S 178 0 E
Elliot Lake 62 46 25N 82 35W
Ellon 6 57 21N 2 5W
Ellwangen 13 48 57N 10 9 E
Elmhurst 67 41 52N 87 58W
Elmira 66 42 8N 76 49W
Elmshorn 13 53 44N 9 40 E
Elne 10 42 36N 2 58 E
Éloyes 9 48 6N 6 36 E
Elrose 65 51 12N 108 0W
Elsinore = Helsingør 28 56 2N 12 35 E
Eluru 38 16 48N 81 8 E
Elvas 18 38 50N 7 10W
Elven 8 47 44N 2 36W
Elverum 28 60 53N 11 34 E
Elwood 66 40 20N 85 50W
Ely, U.K. 5 52 24N 0 16 E
Ely, U.S.A. 68 39 10N 114 50W
Elyria 66 41 22N 82 8W
Emāmrūd 46 36 30N 55 0 E
Emba → 30 46 38N 53 14 E
Embrun 11 44 34N 6 30 E
Embu 51 0 32 S 37 38 E
Emden 13 53 22N 7 12 E
Emerald 56 23 32 S 148 10 E
Emilia-Romagna □ 20 44 33N 10 40 E
Emmeloord 12 52 44N 5 46 E
Emmen 12 52 48N 6 57 E
Emmerich 13 51 50N 6 12 E
Empalme 69 27 58N 110 51W
Empangeni 53 28 50 S 31 52 E
Emporia 66 36 41N 77 32W
Ems → 13 52 37N 9 26 E
Emsdetten 13 52 11N 7 31 E
En Nahud 50 12 45N 28 25 E
Enard B. 6 58 5N 5 20W
Encarnación 74 27 15 S 55 50W
Encarnación de Díaz 69 21 31N 102 14W
Encontrados 72 9 3N 72 14W
Encounter B. 56 35 45 S 138 45 E
Endeavour Str. 56 10 45 S 142 0 E
Enderbury I. 57 3 8 S 171 5W
Enderby 64 50 35N 119 10W
Enderby Land 60 66 0 S 53 0 E
Endicott 66 42 6N 76 2W
Enewatak 57 11 30N 162 15 E
Enez 26 40 45N 26 5 E
Enfield 5 51 39N 0 4W
Engadin 13 46 45N 10 10 E
Engaño, C. 70 18 30N 68 20W
Engels 33 51 28N 46 6 E
Enggano 39 5 20 S 102 40 E
Enghien 12 50 37N 4 2 E
England □ 4 53 0N 2 0W
Englewood 67 39 40N 105 0W
English Bazar =
Ingraj Bazar 37 24 58N 88 10 E
English Channel 5 50 0N 2 0W
Enid 67 36 26N 97 52W
Enkhuizen 12 52 42N 5 17 E
Enna 23 37 34N 14 15 E
Ennedi 50 17 15N 22 0 E
Ennis 7 52 51N 8 59W
Enniscorthy 7 52 30N 6 35W
Enniskillen 7 54 20N 7 40W
Ennistimon 7 52 56N 9 18W
Enns → 14 48 14N 14 32 E
Enontekiö 27 68 23N 23 37 E
Enriquillo, L. 70 18 20N 72 5W
Enschede 12 52 13N 6 53 E
Ensenada 69 31 52N 116 37W
Ensisheim 9 47 50N 7 20 E
Entebbe 51 0 4N 32 28 E
Enterprise 68 45 30N 117 18W
Entre Ríos □ 74 30 30 S 58 30W
Entrecasteaux, Pt. d' 54 34 50 S 115 56 E
Enugu 49 6 20N 7 30 E
Enugu Ezike 49 7 0N 7 29 E
Envermeu 8 49 53N 1 15 E
Enz → 13 49 1N 9 6 E
Eólie, I. 23 38 30N 14 50 E
Epe 12 52 21N 5 59 E
Épernay 9 49 3N 3 56 E
Épernon 9 48 35N 1 40 E
Ephesus 45 37 50N 27 33 E
Épinac-les-Mines 9 46 59N 4 31 E
Épinal 9 48 10N 6 27 E
Epping 5 51 42N 0 8 E
Epukiro 52 21 40 S 19 9 E
Equatorial Guinea ■ 51 2 0N 8 0 E
Er Rahad 50 12 45N 30 32 E
Er Rif 49 35 1N 4 1W
Er Roseires 50 11 55N 34 30 E
Erāwadī Myit → =
Irrawaddy → 41 15 50N 95 6 E
Ercha 31 69 45N 147 20 E
Ercıyaş Dağı 45 38 30N 35 30 E
Erdre → 8 47 13N 1 32W
Erechim 74 27 35 S 52 15W
Ereğli 45 41 15N 31 30 E
Eresma → 18 41 26N 40 45W
Erfurt 13 50 58N 11 2 E
Erğene → 25 41 1N 26 22 E
Ergeni
Vozvyshennost 35 47 0N 44 0 E
Eriboll, L. 6 58 28N 4 41W
Érice 22 38 4N 12 34 E
Erie 66 42 10N 80 7W
Erie, L. 62 42 15N 81 0W
Erigavo 47 10 35N 47 20 E
Erímanthos 26 37 57N 21 50 E
Erimo-misaki 44 41 50N 143 15 E
Eritrea □ 50 14 0N 38 30 E
Erlangen 13 49 35N 11 0 E
Ermelo 12 52 18N 5 35 E
Erne → 7 54 30N 8 16W
Erne, Lough 7 54 26N 7 46W
Ernée 8 48 18N 0 56W
Erode 38 11 24N 77 45 E
Erquy 8 48 38N 2 29W
Erquy, C. d' 8 48 39N 2 29W
Erramala Hills 38 15 30N 78 15 E
Errigal, Mt. 7 55 2N 8 8W
Erris Hd. 7 54 19N 10 0W
Erstein 9 48 25N 7 38 E
Ervy-le-Châtel 9 48 2N 3 55 E
Erzgebirge 13 50 25N 13 0 E
Erzin 31 50 15N 95 10 E
Erzincan 45 39 46N 39 30 E
Erzurum 45 39 57N 41 15 E
Es Sahrâ' Esh
Sharqîya 50 27 30N 32 30 E
Es Sînâ' 50 29 0N 34 0 E
Esan-Misaki 44 41 40N 141 10 E
Esbjerg 28 55 29N 8 29 E
Escanaba 62 45 44N 87 5W
Esch-sur-Alzette 12 49 32N 6 0 E
Eschwege 13 51 10N 10 3 E
Eschweiler 13 50 49N 6 14 E
Escondido 68 33 9N 117 4W
Escuintla 69 14 20N 90 48W
Eşfahān 46 33 0N 53 0 E
Esh Shamâlîya □ 50 19 0N 29 0 E
Esk →,
Dumf. & Gall.,
U.K. 6 54 58N 3 4W
Esk →, N. Yorks.,
U.K. 5 54 27N 0 36W
Eskifjörður 27 65 3N 13 55W
Eskilstuna 28 59 22N 16 32 E
Eskişehir 45 39 50N 30 35 E
Esla → 18 41 29N 6 3W
Eslāmābād-e Gharb 45 34 10N 46 30 E
Esmeraldas 72 1 0N 79 40W
Espalion 10 44 32N 2 47 E
Espanola 62 46 15N 81 46W
Esperance 54 33 45 S 121 55 E
Esperance B. 54 33 48 S 121 55 E
Espéraza 10 42 56N 2 14 E
Espichel, C. 18 38 22N 9 16W
Espinhaço, Serra do 73 17 30 S 43 30W
Espírito Santo □ 73 20 0 S 40 45W
Essaouira 49 31 32N 9 42W
Essarts, Les 8 46 47N 1 12W
Essen, Belgium 12 51 28N 4 28 E
Essen, W. Germany 13 51 28N 6 59 E
Essequibo → 72 6 50N 58 30W
Essex □ 5 51 48N 0 30 E
Esslingen 13 48 43N 9 19 E
Essonne □ 9 48 30N 2 20 E
Estados, I. de Los 74 54 40 S 64 30W
Estagel 10 42 47N 2 40 E
Estelí 70 13 9N 86 22W
Esternay 9 48 44N 3 33 E
Estevan 65 49 10N 102 59W
Estherville 67 43 25N 94 50W
Estissac 9 48 16N 3 48 E
Estonian S.S.R. □ 32 58 30N 25 30 E
Estoril 18 38 42N 9 23W
Estrada, La 18 42 43N 8 27W
Estrêla, Serra da 18 40 10N 7 45W
Esztergom 15 47 47N 18 44 E
Étables-sur-Mer 8 48 38N 2 51W
Étain 9 49 13N 5 38 E
Étampes 9 48 26N 2 10 E
Étang-sur-Arroux 11 46 51N 4 11 E
Étaples 9 50 30N 1 39 E
Etawah 36 26 48N 79 6 E
Ethiopia ■ 47 8 0N 40 0 E
Etive, L. 6 56 30N 5 12W
Etna 23 37 45N 15 0 E
Etosha Pan 52 18 40 S 16 30 E
Étrépagny 9 49 18N 1 36 E
Étretat 8 49 42N 0 12 E
Ettlingen 13 48 58N 8 25 E
Ettrick Water 6 55 31N 2 55W
Etzatlán 69 20 46N 104 5W
Eu 8 50 3N 1 26 E
Euboea = Évvoia 26 38 30N 24 0 E
Eucla Basin 54 31 19 S 126 9 E
Euclid 66 41 32N 81 31W
Eufaula, Ala.,
U.S.A. 66 31 55N 85 11W
Eufaula, Okla.,
U.S.A. 67 35 20N 95 33W
Eugene 68 44 0N 123 8W
Eupen 12 50 37N 6 3 E
Euphrates = Furāt,
Nahr al → 45 31 0N 47 25 E
Eure □ 8 49 10N 1 0 E
Eure → 8 49 18N 1 12 E
Eure-et-Loir □ 8 48 22N 1 30 E
Eureka, Canada 3 80 0N 85 56W
Eureka, Calif.,
U.S.A. 68 40 50N 124 0W
Eureka, Nev.,
U.S.A. 68 39 32N 116 2W
Europa, Picos de 18 43 10N 4 49W
Europa, Pta. de 18 36 3N 5 21W
Europoort 12 51 57N 4 10 E
Euskirchen 13 50 40N 6 45 E
Eutin 13 54 7N 10 38 E
Eutsuk L. 64 53 20N 126 45W
Evanston 67 42 0N 87 40W
Evansville 66 38 0N 87 35W
Évaux-les-Bains 10 46 12N 2 29 E
Evensk 31 62 12N 159 30 E
Everard, L. 54 31 30 S 135 0 E
Everard Ras. 54 27 5 S 132 28 E
Everest, Mt. 37 28 5N 86 58 E
Everett 68 48 0N 122 10W
Everglades 66 26 0N 80 30W
Everglades Nat. Park. 66 25 27N 80 53W
Evesham 5 52 6N 1 57W
Évian-les-Bains 11 46 24N 6 35 E
Evinayong 51 1 26N 10 35 E
Évisa 11 42 15N 8 48 E
Évora 18 38 33N 7 57W
Évreux 8 49 0N 1 8 E
Évron 8 48 10N 0 24W
Évvoia 26 38 30N 24 0 E
Évvoia □ 26 38 40N 23 40 E
Ewe, L. 6 57 49N 5 38W
Ewo 51 0 48 S 14 45 E
Excelsior Springs 67 39 20N 94 10W
Excideuil 10 45 20N 1 4 E
Exe → 5 50 38N 3 27W
Exeter 5 50 43N 3 31W
Exmes 8 48 45N 0 10 E
Exmoor 5 51 10N 3 59W
Exmouth, Australia 54 21 54 S 114 10 E
Exmouth, U.K. 5 50 37N 3 26W
Exmouth G. 54 22 15 S 114 15 E
Expedition Range 56 24 30 S 149 12 E
Extremadura □ 18 39 30N 6 5W
Eyasi, L. 51 3 30 S 35 0 E
Eyemouth 6 55 53N 2 5W
Eygurande 10 45 40N 2 26 E
Eyjafjörður 27 66 15N 18 30W
Eymet 10 44 40N 0 25 E
Eymoutiers 10 45 40N 1 45 E
Eyrarbakki 27 63 52N 21 9W
Eyre 54 32 15 S 126 18 E
Eyre, L. 55 29 30 S 137 26 E
Eyre Cr. → 56 26 40 S 139 0 E
Eyre Pen. 54 33 30 S 137 17 E
Eyzies-de-Tayac-
Sireuil, Les 10 44 56N 1 1 E

F

Fabriano 21 43 20N 12 52 E
Facatativá 72 4 49N 74 22W
Fachi 49 18 6N 11 34 E
Facture 10 44 39N 0 58W
Fada 50 17 13N 21 34 E
Fada-n-Gourma 49 12 10N 0 30 E
Faddeyevskiy, Ostrov 31 76 0N 150 0 E
Faenza 21 44 17N 11 53 E
Făgăras 25 45 48N 24 58 E
Fagersta 28 60 1N 15 46 E
Fagnières 9 48 58N 4 20 E
Fair Hd. 7 55 14N 6 10W
Fairbanks 61 64 50N 147 50W
Fairfield, Ala.,
U.S.A. 66 33 30N 87 0W
Fairfield, Calif.,
U.S.A. 68 38 14N 122 1W
Fairfield, Tex.,
U.S.A. 67 31 40N 96 0W
Fairmont, Minn.,
U.S.A. 67 43 37N 94 30W
Fairmont, W. Va.,
U.S.A. 66 39 29N 80 10W
Fairview 64 56 5N 118 25W
Faisalabad 36 31 30N 73 5 E
Faizabad 37 26 45N 82 10 E
Fajardo 70 18 20N 65 39W
Falaise 8 48 54N 0 12W
Falkenberg 28 56 54N 12 30 E
Falkirk 6 56 0N 3 47W
Falkland Is. 74 51 30 S 59 0W
Falkland Is.
Dependency □ 60 57 0 S 40 0W
Falköping 28 58 12N 13 33 E
Fall River 66 41 45N 71 5W
Falls City 67 40 0N 95 40W
Falmouth, Jamaica 70 18 30N 77 40W
Falmouth, U.K. 5 50 9N 5 5W
False B. 52 34 15 S 18 40 E
Falster 28 54 45N 11 55 E
Falsterbo 28 55 23N 12 50 E
Falun 28 60 37N 15 37 E
Famagusta 45 35 8N 33 55 E
Fandriana 53 20 14 S 47 21 E
Fannich, L. 6 57 40N 5 0W
Fano 21 43 50N 13 0 E
Faradje 51 3 50N 29 45 E
Faradofay 53 25 2 S 47 0 E
Farafangana 53 22 49 S 47 50 E
Farâh 46 32 20N 62 7 E
Farâh □ 46 32 25N 62 10 E
Faranah 49 10 3N 10 45W
Farasān, Jazā'ir 47 16 45N 41 55 E
Fareham 5 50 52N 1 11W
Farewell, C. 59 40 29 S 172 43 E
Farewell C. = Farvel,
Kap 3 59 48N 43 55W
Fargo 67 46 52N 96 40W
Farim 49 12 27N 15 9W
Farnborough 5 51 17N 0 46W
Farne Is. 5 55 38N 1 37W
Faro 18 37 2N 7 55W
Faroe Is. 4 62 0N 7 0W
Farquhar, C. 54 23 50 S 113 36 E
Farrar → 6 57 30N 4 30W
Farrukhabad-cum-
Fatehgarh 37 27 30N 79 32 E
Fars □ 46 29 30N 55 0 E
Fársala 26 39 17N 22 23 E
Farsund 27 58 5N 6 55 E
Farvel, Kap 3 59 48N 43 55W
Fāryāb □ 46 36 0N 65 0 E
Fastnet Rock 7 51 22N 9 37W
Fatehgarh 37 27 25N 79 35 E
Fatehpur, Raj., India 36 28 0N 74 40 E
Fatehpur, Ut. P.,
India 37 25 56N 81 13 E
Faucille, Col de la 11 46 22N 6 2 E
Faulquemont 9 49 3N 6 36 E
Fauquembergues 9 50 36N 2 5 E
Fauske 27 67 17N 15 25 E
Favara 22 37 19N 13 39 E
Favignana 22 37 56N 12 18 E
Faxaflói 27 64 29N 23 0W
Faya-Largeau 50 17 58N 19 6 E
Fayence 11 43 38N 6 42 E
Fayetteville, Ark.,
U.S.A. 67 36 0N 94 5W
Fayetteville, N.C.,
U.S.A. 66 35 0N 78 58W
Fazilka 36 30 27N 74 2 E
Fdérik 49 22 40N 12 45W
Feale → 7 52 26N 9 40W
Fear, C. 66 33 51N 78 0W
Feather → 68 38 47N 121 36W
Fécamp 8 49 45N 0 22 E
Fehmarn 13 54 26N 11 10 E
Fehmarn Bælt 13 54 35N 11 20 E
Feira de Santana 73 12 15 S 38 57W
Feldkirch 13 47 15N 9 37 E
Felixstowe 5 51 58N 1 22 E
Felletin 10 45 53N 2 11 E
Femunden 27 62 10N 11 53 E
Fengjie 43 31 5N 109 36 E
Feni Is. 56 4 0 S 153 40 E
Fenit 7 52 17N 9 51W
Feno, C. de 11 41 58N 8 33 E
Fens, The 5 52 45N 0 2 E
Feodosiya 34 45 2N 35 28 E
Fère, La 9 49 39N 3 21 E
Fère-Champenoise 9 48 45N 4 0 E
Fère-en-Tardenois 9 49 10N 3 30 E
Ferfer 47 5 4N 45 9 E
Fergana 30 40 23N 71 19 E
Fergusson I. 56 9 30 S 150 45 E
Fermanagh □ 7 54 21N 7 40W
Fermoy 7 52 4N 8 18W
Fernando de Noronha 73 4 0 S 33 10W
Fernando Póo =
Bioko 49 3 30N 8 40 E
Fernie 64 49 30N 115 5W
Ferrara 21 44 50N 11 36 E
Ferret, C. 10 44 38N 1 15W
Ferrette 9 47 30N 7 20 E
Ferrières 9 48 5N 2 48 E
Ferté-Bernard, La 8 48 10N 0 40 E
Ferté-Macé, La 8 48 35N 0 22W
Ferté-St.-Aubin, La 9 47 42N 1 57 E
Ferté-sous-Jouarre,
La 9 48 56N 3 8 E
Ferté-Vidame, La 8 48 37N 0 53 E
Fès 49 34 0N 5 0W
Feshi 51 6 8 S 18 10 E
Fetlar 6 60 36N 0 52W
Feurs 11 45 45N 4 13 E
Feyzābād 46 37 7N 70 33 E
Fezzan 50 27 0N 15 0 E
Ffestiniog 5 52 58N 3 56W
Fianarantsoa 53 21 26 S 47 5 E
Fianga 50 9 55N 15 9 E
Fichtelgebirge 13 50 10N 12 0 E
Ficksburg 53 28 51 S 27 53 E
Fife □ 6 56 13N 3 2W
Fife Ness 6 56 17N 2 35W
Figeac 10 44 37N 2 2 E
Figueira da Foz 18 40 7N 8 54W
Figueras 19 42 18N 2 58 E
Figuig 49 32 5N 1 11W
Fiji ■ 57 17 20 S 179 0 E
Filey 5 54 13N 0 18W
Filiatrá 26 37 9N 21 35 E
Filipstad 28 59 43N 14 9 E
Findhorn → 6 57 38N 3 38W
Findlay 66 41 0N 83 41W
Fingõe 51 14 55 S 31 50 E
Finistère □ 8 48 20N 4 0W
Finisterre, C. 18 42 50N 9 19W
Finke → 54 27 0 S 136 10 E
Finland ■ 30 63 0N 27 0 E
Finland, G. of 27 60 0N 26 0 E
Finlay → 64 57 0N 125 10W
Finn → 7 54 50N 7 55W
Finnmark fylke □ 27 69 30N 25 0 E
Finucane I. 54 20 19 S 118 30 E
Fiora → 21 42 20N 11 35 E
Firenze 21 43 47N 11 15 E
Firmi 10 44 33N 2 19 E
Firminy 11 45 23N 4 18 E
Firozabad 36 27 10N 78 25 E
Firozpur 36 30 55N 74 40 E
Fish → 52 28 7 S 17 10 E
Fishguard 5 51 59N 4 59W
Fismes 9 49 20N 3 40 E
Fitchburg 66 42 35N 71 47W
Fitri, L. 50 12 50N 17 28 E
Fitzgerald 66 31 45N 83 16W
Fitzroy → 54 17 31 S 123 35 E
Fitzroy Crossing 54 18 9 S 125 38 E
Fizi 51 4 17 S 28 55 E
Flagstaff 68 35 10N 111 40W
Flamborough Hd. 5 54 8N 0 4W
Flaming Gorge Res. 68 41 15N 109 30W
Flandre Occidental □ 12 51 0N 3 0 E
Flandre Orientale □ 12 51 0N 4 0 E
Flandres, Plaines des 12 51 10N 3 15 E
Flåsjön 27 64 5N 15 40 E
Flatey,
Barðastrandarsýsla,
Iceland 27 66 10N 17 52W
Flatey,
Suður-þingeyjarsýsla,
Iceland 27 65 22N 22 56W
Flathead L. 68 47 50N 114 0W
Flattery, C. 68 48 21N 124 43W
Flavy-le-Martel 9 49 43N 3 12 E
Flèche, La 8 47 42N 0 4W
Fleetwood 5 53 55N 3 1W
Flensburg 13 54 46N 9 28 E
Flers 8 48 47N 0 33W
Fletton 5 52 34N 0 13W
Fleurance 10 43 52N 0 40 E
Flin Flon 65 54 46N 101 53W
Flinders → 56 17 36 S 140 36 E
Flinders B. 54 34 19 S 115 19 E
Flinders I. 56 40 0 S 148 0 E
Flinders Ranges 56 31 30 S 138 30 E
Flint, U.K. 5 53 15N 3 7W
Flint, U.S.A. 66 43 5N 83 40W
Flint → 66 30 52N 84 38W
Flint, I. 58 11 26 S 151 48W
Flixecourt 9 50 0N 2 5 E
Flodden 5 55 37N 2 8W
Flora 66 38 40N 88 30W
Florac 10 44 20N 3 37 E
Florence = Firenze 21 43 47N 11 15 E
Florence, Ala.,
U.S.A. 66 34 50N 87 40W
Florence, S.C.,
U.S.A. 66 34 12N 79 44W
Florennes 12 50 15N 4 35 E
Florensac 10 43 23N 3 28 E
Florenville 12 49 40N 5 19 E
Flores, Guat. 69 16 59N 89 50W
Flores, Indonesia 40 8 35 S 121 0 E
Flores Sea 39 6 30 S 124 0 E
Floriano 73 6 50 S 43 0W
Florianópolis 74 27 30 S 48 30W
Florida 74 34 7 S 56 10W
Florida □ 66 28 30N 82 0W
Florida, Straits of 70 25 0N 80 0W
Florø 27 61 35N 5 1 E
Flushing = Vlissingen 12 51 26N 3 34 E
Fly → 56 8 25 S 143 0 E
Foam Lake 65 51 40N 103 32W
Fóggia 23 41 28N 15 31 E
Föhr 13 54 40N 8 30 E
Foix 10 42 58N 1 38 E
Folda,
Nord-Trøndelag,
Norway 27 64 41N 10 50 E
Folda, Nordland,
Norway 27 67 38N 14 50 E
Folkestone 5 51 5N 1 11 E
Follette, La 66 36 23N 84 9W
Fond du Lac 67 43 46N 88 26W
Fontaine-Française 9 47 32N 5 21 E
Fontainebleau 9 48 24N 2 40 E
Fonte Boa 72 2 33 S 66 0W
Fontenay-le-Comte 10 46 28N 0 48W
Fontur 27 66 23N 14 32W
Foochow = Fuzhou 43 26 5N 119 16 E
Forbach 9 49 10N 6 52 E
Forbes 56 33 22 S 148 0 E
Forcalquier 11 43 58N 5 47 E
Forécariah 49 9 28N 13 10W
Forel, Mt. 3 66 52N 36 55W
Forestburg 64 52 35N 112 1W
Forestville 63 48 48N 69 2W

Forez, Mts. du **10** 45 40N 3 50 E
Forfar **6** 56 40N 2 53W
Forges-les-Eaux **9** 49 37N 1 30 E
Forlì **21** 44 14N 12 2 E
Formby Pt. **5** 53 33N 3 7W
Formentera **19** 38 43N 1 27 E
Formiguères **10** 42 37N 2 5 E
Formosa = Taiwan ■ **43** 23 30N 121 0 E
Formosa **74** 26 15 S 58 10W
Formosa Bay **51** 2 40 S 40 20 E
Forres **6** 57 37N 3 38W
Forrest City **67** 35 0N 90 50W
Forsayth **56** 18 33 S 143 34 E
Fort Albany **62** 52 15N 81 35W
Fort Augustus **6** 57 9N 4 40W
Fort-Coulonge **62** 45 50N 76 45W
Fort-de-France **70** 14 36N 61 2W
Fort Dodge **67** 42 29N 94 10W
Fort Frances **65** 48 36N 93 24W
Fort George **62** 53 50N 79 0W
Fort Kent **63** 47 12N 68 30W
Fort Lallemand **49** 31 13N 6 17 E
Fort Lauderdale **66** 26 10N 80 5W
Fort Liard **64** 60 14N 123 30W
Fort Mackay **64** 57 12N 111 41W
Fort Macleod **64** 49 45N 113 30W
Fort MacMahon **49** 29 43N 1 45 E
Fort McMurray **64** 56 44N 111 7W
Fort Madison **67** 40 39N 91 20W
Fort Miribel **49** 29 25N 2 55 E
Fort Myers **66** 26 39N 81 51W
Fort Nelson **64** 58 50N 122 44W
Fort Nelson → **64** 59 32N 124 0W
Fort Payne **66** 34 25N 85 44W
Fort Peck L. **68** 47 40N 107 0W
Fort Pierce **66** 27 29N 80 19W
Fort Portal **51** 0 40N 30 20 E
Fort Providence **64** 61 3N 117 40W
Fort Qu'Appelle **65** 50 45N 103 50W
Fort Resolution **64** 61 10N 113 40W
Fort Rupert **62** 51 30N 78 40W
Fort St. James **64** 54 30N 124 10W
Fort St. John **64** 56 15N 120 50W
Fort Sandeman **36** 31 20N 69 31 E
Fort Saskatchewan **64** 53 40N 113 15W
Fort Scott **67** 37 50N 94 40W
Fort Severn **62** 56 0N 87 40W
Fort Shevchenko **35** 43 40N 51 20 E
Fort-Sibut **50** 5 46N 19 10 E
Fort Simpson **64** 61 45N 121 15W
Fort Smith, Canada **64** 60 0N 111 51W
Fort Smith, U.S.A. **67** 35 25N 94 25W
Fort Valley **66** 32 33N 83 52W
Fort Vermilion **64** 58 24N 116 0W
Fort Wayne **66** 41 5N 85 10W
Fort William **6** 56 48N 5 8W
Fort Worth **67** 32 45N 97 25W
Fortaleza **73** 3 45 S 38 35W
Forth, Firth of **6** 56 5N 2 55W
Fortrose **6** 57 35N 4 10W
Fortuna **68** 40 38N 124 8W
Fos-sur-Mer **11** 43 26N 4 56 E
Foshān **43** 23 4N 113 5 E
Fougamou **51** 1 16 S 10 30 E
Fougères **8** 48 21N 1 14W
Foul Pt. **38** 8 35N 81 18 E
Foulness I. **5** 51 36N 0 55 E
Foulness Pt. **5** 51 36N 0 59 E
Foumban **49** 5 45N 10 50 E
Fourchambault **9** 47 0N 3 3 E
Fourmies **9** 50 1N 4 2 E
Fours **9** 46 50N 3 42 E
Fouta Djalon **49** 11 20N 12 10W
Foveaux Str. **59** 46 42 S 168 10 E
Fowey **5** 50 20N 4 39W
Fownhope **5** 52 0N 2 37W
Foxe Basin **3** 66 0N 77 0W
Foyle, Lough **7** 55 6N 7 8W
Foynes **7** 52 37N 9 5W
Franca **73** 20 33 S 47 30W
Francavilla Fontana **23** 40 32N 17 35 E
France ■ **8** 47 0N 3 0 E
Franceville **51** 1 40 S 13 32 E
Franche-Comté **9** 46 50N 5 55 E
Francistown **53** 21 7 S 27 33 E
François **70** 14 38N 60 57W
François L. **64** 54 0N 125 30W
Franeker **12** 53 12N 5 33 E
Frankfort, Ind., U.S.A. **66** 40 20N 86 33W
Frankfort, Ky., U.S.A. **66** 38 12N 84 52W
Frankfurt am Main **13** 50 7N 8 40 E
Frankfurt an der Oder **13** 52 50N 14 31 E
Fränkische Alb **13** 49 20N 11 30 E
Fränkische Rezal → **13** 49 11N 11 1 E
Franklin, La., U.S.A. **67** 29 45N 91 30W
Franklin, N.H., U.S.A. **66** 43 28N 71 39W
Franklin, W. Va., U.S.A. **66** 38 38N 79 21W
Franz **62** 48 25N 84 30W
Fraser → **64** 49 7N 123 11W
Fraser I. **56** 25 15 S 153 10 E
Fraserburgh **6** 57 41N 2 0W
Frasne **9** 46 50N 6 10 E
Fray Bentos **74** 33 10 S 58 15W
Fredericia **28** 55 34N 9 45 E
Frederick **66** 39 25N 77 23W
Frederick Reef **55** 20 58 S 154 23 E
Fredericksburg **66** 38 16N 77 29W
Fredericton **63** 45 57N 66 40W
Frederikshavn **28** 57 28N 10 31 E
Fredrikstad **28** 59 13N 10 57 E
Freeling, Mt. **54** 22 35 S 133 6 E
Freeport, Bahamas **70** 26 30N 78 47W
Freeport, Ill., U.S.A. **67** 42 18N 89 40W
Freeport, N.Y., U.S.A. **66** 40 39N 73 35W
Freetown **49** 8 30N 13 17W
Fréhel, C. **8** 48 40N 2 20W
Freiberg **13** 50 55N 13 20 E
Freiburg **13** 48 0N 7 52 E
Freistadt **14** 48 30N 14 30 E
Fréjus **11** 43 25N 6 44 E
Fremantle **54** 32 7 S 115 47 E
Fremont, Calif., U.S.A. **68** 37 32N 122 1W
Fremont, Nebr., U.S.A. **67** 41 30N 96 30W
French Guiana ■ **73** 4 0N 53 0W
French Polynesia □ **58** 20 0 S 145 0 E
French Terr. of Afars & Issas = Djibouti ■ **47** 12 0N 43 0 E
Fresnay-sur-Sarthe **8** 48 17N 0 1 E
Fresnillo **69** 23 10N 102 53W
Fresno **68** 36 47N 119 50W
Freudenstadt **13** 48 27N 8 25 E
Frévent **9** 50 15N 2 17 E
Freycinet Pen. **56** 42 10 S 148 25 E
Freyming-Merlebach **9** 49 8N 6 48 E
Fria, C. **52** 18 0 S 12 0 E
Frías **74** 28 40 S 65 5W
Friedberg **13** 50 21N 8 46 E
Friedrichshafen **13** 47 39N 9 29 E
Friendly, Is. = Tonga ■ **57** 19 50 S 174 30W
Friesland □ **12** 53 5N 5 50 E
Friuli-Venezia Giulia □ **21** 46 0N 13 0 E
Frobisher L. **65** 56 20N 108 15W
Frohavet **27** 63 50N 9 35 E
Frome **5** 51 16N 2 17W
Frome, L. **56** 30 45 S 139 45 E
Front Range **68** 40 0N 105 40W
Front Royal **66** 38 55N 78 10W
Frontera **69** 18 32N 92 38W
Frontignan **10** 43 27N 3 45 E
Frosinone **22** 41 38N 13 20 E
Frostburg **66** 39 43N 78 57W
Frostisen **27** 68 14N 17 10 E
Frouard **9** 48 47N 6 8 E
Frøya **27** 63 43N 8 40 E
Fruges **9** 50 30N 2 8 E
Frunze **30** 42 54N 74 46 E
Frutal **73** 20 0 S 49 0W
Frýdek-Místek **15** 49 40N 18 20 E
Fuchū **44** 34 34N 133 14 E
Fuente Ovejuna **18** 38 15N 5 25W
Fuentes de Oñoro **18** 40 33N 6 52W
Fuerte → **69** 25 54N 109 22W
Fuerteventura **49** 28 30N 14 0W
Fugløysund **27** 70 15N 20 20 E
Fuji **44** 35 9N 138 39 E
Fuji-no-miya **44** 35 10N 138 40 E
Fuji-San **44** 35 22N 138 44 E
Fujian □ **43** 26 0N 118 0 E
Fujisawa **44** 35 22N 139 29 E
Fukuchiyama **44** 35 19N 135 9 E
Fukui **44** 36 0N 136 10 E
Fukui □ **44** 36 0N 136 12 E
Fukuoka **44** 33 39N 130 21 E
Fukuoka □ **44** 33 30N 131 0 E
Fukushima **44** 37 44N 140 28 E
Fukuyama **44** 34 35N 133 20 E
Fulda **13** 50 32N 9 41 E
Fulda → **13** 51 27N 9 40 E
Fullerton **68** 33 52N 117 58W
Fulton, Mo., U.S.A. **67** 38 50N 91 55W
Fulton, N.Y., U.S.A. **66** 43 20N 76 22W
Fumay **9** 50 0N 4 40 E
Fumel **10** 44 30N 0 58 E
Funabashi **44** 35 45N 140 0 E
Funafuti **57** 8 30 S 179 0 E
Funchal **49** 32 38N 16 54W
Fundación **72** 10 31N 74 11W
Fundão **18** 40 8N 7 30W
Fundy, B. of **63** 45 0N 66 0W
Funtua **49** 11 30N 7 18 E
Furāt, Nahr al → **45** 31 0N 47 25 E
Furneaux Group **56** 40 10 S 147 50 E
Furness, Pen. **5** 54 12N 3 10W
Fürth **13** 49 29N 11 0 E
Füssen **13** 47 35N 10 43 E
Futuna **57** 14 25 S 178 20 E
Fuxin **42** 42 5N 121 48 E
Fuzhou **43** 26 5N 119 16 E
Fylde **5** 53 50N 2 58W
Fyn **28** 55 20N 10 30 E
Fyne, L. **6** 56 0N 5 20W

G

Gabas → **10** 43 46N 0 42W
Gabela **51** 11 0 S 14 24 E
Gabès **49** 33 53N 10 2 E
Gabès, G. de **50** 34 0N 10 30 E
Gabon ■ **51** 0 10 S 10 0 E
Gaborone **52** 24 45 S 25 57 E
Gabrovo **25** 42 52N 25 19 E
Gacé **8** 48 49N 0 20 E
Gachsārān **46** 30 15N 50 45 E
Gadag **38** 15 30N 75 45 E
Gadarwara **36** 22 50N 78 50 E
Gadhada **36** 22 0N 71 35 E
Gadsden **66** 34 1N 86 0W
Gadwal **38** 16 10N 77 50 E
Gaffney **66** 35 3N 81 40W
Gafsa **49** 34 24N 8 43 E
Gagnoa **49** 6 56N 5 16W
Gagnon **63** 51 50N 68 5W
Gaillac **10** 43 54N 1 54 E
Gaillon **8** 49 10N 1 20 E
Gainesville, Fla., U.S.A. **66** 29 38N 82 20W
Gainesville, Ga., U.S.A. **66** 34 17N 83 47W
Gainesville, Tex., U.S.A. **67** 33 40N 97 10W
Gainsborough **5** 53 23N 0 46W
Gairdner L. **54** 31 30 S 136 0 E
Gairloch, L. **6** 57 43N 5 45W
Galangue **51** 13 42 S 16 9 E
Galápagos **58** 0 0 89 0W
Galas → **41** 4 55N 101 57 E
Galashiels **6** 55 37N 2 50W
Galaţi **15** 45 27N 28 2 E
Galatina **23** 40 10N 18 10 E
Galcaio **47** 6 30N 47 30 E
Galdhøpiggen **28** 61 38N 8 18 E
Galesburg **67** 40 57N 90 23W
Galich **33** 58 23N 42 12 E
Galicia □ **18** 42 43N 7 45W
Gallabat **50** 12 58N 36 11 E
Gallardon **9** 48 32N 1 42 E
Gallatin **66** 36 24N 86 27W
Galle **38** 6 5N 80 10 E
Gállego → **19** 41 39N 0 51W
Galley Hd. **7** 51 32N 8 56W
Gallinas, Pta. **72** 12 28N 71 40W
Gallipoli = Gelibolu **26** 40 28N 26 43 E
Gallípoli **23** 40 8N 18 0 E
Gällivare **27** 67 9N 20 40 E
Galloway **6** 55 0N 4 25W
Galloway, Mull of **6** 54 38N 4 50W
Galty Mts. **7** 52 22N 8 10W
Galtymore **7** 52 22N 8 12W
Galveston **67** 29 15N 94 48W
Galveston B. **67** 29 30N 94 50W
Galway **7** 53 16N 9 4W
Galway □ **7** 53 16N 9 3W
Galway B. **7** 53 10N 9 20W
Gambaga **49** 10 30N 0 28W
Gambela **50** 8 14N 34 38 E
Gambia ■ **49** 13 25N 16 0W
Gambia → **49** 13 28N 16 34W
Gamboma **51** 1 55 S 15 52 E
Gan **10** 43 12N 0 27W
Gand = Gent **12** 51 2N 3 42 E
Ganda **51** 13 3 S 14 35 E
Gandak → **37** 25 39N 85 13 E
Gandava **36** 28 32N 67 32 E
Gander **63** 48 58N 54 35W
Gandhi Sagar **36** 24 40N 75 40 E
Gandi **49** 12 55N 5 49 E
Ganga → **37** 23 20N 90 30 E
Ganganagar **36** 29 56N 73 56 E
Gangara **49** 14 35N 8 29 E
Ganges = Ganga → **37** 23 20N 90 30 E
Ganges **10** 43 56N 3 42 E
Gangtok **37** 27 20N 88 37 E
Gannat **10** 46 7N 3 11 E
Gansu □ **42** 36 0N 104 0 E
Ganta **49** 7 15N 8 59W
Gantheaume B. **54** 27 40 S 114 10 E
Ganzhou **43** 25 51N 114 56 E
Gaoua **49** 10 20N 3 8W
Gaoual **49** 11 45N 13 25W
Gaoxiong **43** 22 38N 120 18 E
Gap **11** 44 33N 6 5 E
Garachiné **70** 8 0N 78 12W
Garanhuns **73** 8 50 S 36 30W
Garawe **49** 4 35N 8 0W
Garberville **68** 40 11N 123 50W
Gard **47** 9 30N 49 6 E
Gard □ **11** 44 2N 4 10 E
Gard → **11** 43 51N 4 37 E
Garda, L. di **20** 45 40N 10 40 E
Gardanne **11** 43 27N 5 27 E
Garden City **67** 38 0N 100 45W
Garden Grove **68** 33 47N 117 55W
Gardēz **46** 33 37N 69 9 E
Gargan, Mt. **10** 45 37N 1 39 E
Gargano, Mte. **23** 41 43N 15 43 E
Garigliano → **22** 41 13N 13 44 E
Garland **68** 41 47N 112 10W
Garm **30** 39 0N 70 20 E
Garmsār **46** 35 20N 52 25 E
Garoe **47** 8 25N 48 33 E
Garonne → **10** 45 2N 0 36W
Garonne, Canal Latéral à la → **10** 44 15N 0 18 E
Garoua **50** 9 19N 13 21 E
Garrigue **10** 43 40N 4 0 E
Garrison Res. = Sakakawea, L. **67** 47 30N 102 0W
Garry → **6** 56 47N 3 47W
Garsen **51** 2 20 S 40 5 E
Gartempe → **10** 46 47N 0 49 E
Garwa = Garoua **50** 9 19N 13 21 E
Gary **66** 41 35N 87 20W
Garzón **72** 2 10N 75 40W
Gascogne **10** 43 45N 0 20 E
Gascony = Gascogne **10** 43 45N 0 20 E
Gascoyne → **54** 24 52 S 113 37 E
Gashaka **49** 7 20N 11 29 E
Gaspé **63** 48 52N 64 30W
Gaspé, C. de **63** 48 48N 64 7W
Gaspé, Pén. de **63** 48 45N 65 40W
Gastonia **66** 35 17N 81 10W
Gastre **74** 42 20 S 69 15W
Gata, C. de **19** 36 41N 2 13W
Gata, Sierra de **18** 40 20N 6 45W
Gateshead **5** 54 57N 1 37W
Gâtinais **9** 48 5N 2 40 E
Gâtine, Hauteurs de **10** 46 35N 0 45W
Gauhati **37** 26 10N 91 45 E
Gaula → **27** 63 21N 10 14 E
Gavarnie **10** 42 44N 0 1W
Gävleborgs län □ **28** 61 30N 16 15 E
Gavray **8** 48 55N 1 20W
Gawilgarh Hills **36** 21 15N 76 45 E
Gawler **56** 34 30 S 138 42 E
Gawler Ranges **54** 32 30 S 135 45 E
Gaxun Nur **42** 42 22N 100 30 E
Gaya, India **37** 24 47N 85 4 E
Gaya, Niger **49** 11 52N 3 28 E
Gaylord **62** 45 1N 84 41W
Gayndah **56** 25 35 S 151 32 E
Gaza **50** 31 30N 34 28 E
Gaziantep **45** 37 6N 37 23 E
Gdańsk **17** 54 22N 18 40 E
Gdańska, Zatoka **17** 54 30N 19 20 E
Gdov **32** 58 48N 27 55 E
Gdynia **17** 54 35N 18 33 E
Gebeit Mine **50** 21 3N 36 29 E
Gedaref **50** 14 2N 35 28 E
Gèdre **10** 42 47N 0 2 E
Gedser **28** 54 35N 11 55 E
Geelong **56** 38 10 S 144 22 E
Geesthacht **13** 53 25N 10 20 E
Geidam **50** 12 57N 11 57 E
Geili **50** 16 1N 32 37 E
Geislingen **13** 48 37N 9 51 E
Geita **51** 2 48 S 32 12 E
Gejiu **42** 23 20N 103 10 E
Gela **23** 37 6N 14 18 E
Geladi **47** 6 59N 46 30 E
Gelderland □ **12** 52 5N 6 10 E
Geldermalsen **12** 51 53N 5 17 E
Geldrop **12** 51 25N 5 32 E
Geleen **12** 50 57N 5 49 E
Gelehun **49** 8 20N 11 40W
Gelibolu **26** 40 28N 26 43 E
Gelsenkirchen **13** 51 30N 7 5 E
Gembloux **12** 50 34N 4 43 E
Gemena **51** 3 13N 19 48 E
Gençay **10** 46 23N 0 23 E
Gendringen **12** 51 52N 6 21 E
General Alvear **74** 35 0 S 67 40W
General Pico **74** 35 45 S 63 50W
Geneva = Genève **13** 46 12N 6 9 E
Geneva **66** 42 53N 77 0W
Geneva, L. = Léman, Lac **13** 46 26N 6 30 E
Genève **13** 46 12N 6 9 E
Gengenbach **13** 48 25N 8 0 E
Genil → **18** 37 42N 5 19W
Génissiat, Barr. de **11** 46 1N 5 48 E
Genk **12** 50 58N 5 32 E
Genlis **9** 47 11N 5 12 E
Gennargentu, Mti. del **22** 40 0N 9 10 E
Gennep **12** 51 41N 5 59 E
Gennes **8** 47 20N 0 17W
Genoa = Génova **20** 44 24N 8 56 E
Génova **20** 44 24N 8 56 E
Génova, G. di **20** 44 0N 9 0 E
Gent **12** 51 2N 3 42 E
Geographe B. **54** 33 30 S 115 15 E
Geographe Chan. **54** 24 30 S 113 0 E
George **52** 33 58 S 22 29 E
George → **63** 58 49N 66 10W
George, L. **51** 0 5N 30 10 E
George Town **41** 5 25N 100 15 E
Georgetown, Australia **55** 18 17 S 143 33 E
Georgetown, Canada **62** 43 40N 79 56W
Georgetown, Gambia **49** 13 30N 14 47W
Georgetown, Guyana **72** 6 50N 58 12W
Georgetown, U.S.A. **66** 33 22N 79 15W
Georgia □ **66** 32 0N 82 0W
Georgian B. **62** 45 15N 81 0W
Georgian S.S.R. □ **35** 42 0N 43 0 E
Georgievsk **35** 44 12N 43 28 E
Georgina → **56** 23 30 S 139 47 E
Georgiu-Dezh **33** 51 3N 39 30 E
Gera **13** 50 53N 12 11 E
Geraardsbergen **12** 50 45N 3 53 E
Geraldton, Australia **54** 28 48 S 114 32 E
Geraldton, Canada **62** 49 44N 86 59W
Gérardmer **9** 48 3N 6 50 E
Gereshk **46** 31 47N 64 35 E
Gerlogubi **47** 6 53N 45 3 E
Germany, East ■ **4** 52 0N 12 0 E
Germany, West ■ **4** 52 0N 9 0 E
Germiston **53** 26 15 S 28 10 E
Gerona **19** 41 58N 2 46 E
Gers □ **10** 43 35N 0 30 E
Gers → **10** 44 9N 0 39 E
Gettysburg **66** 39 47N 77 18W
Gévaudan **10** 44 40N 3 40 E
Gex **11** 46 21N 6 3 E
Geysir **27** 64 19N 20 18W
Ghaghara → **37** 25 45N 84 40 E
Ghana ■ **49** 8 0N 1 0W
Ghanzi **52** 21 50 S 21 34 E
Gharb el Istiwa'iya □ **50** 5 0N 30 0 E
Ghardaïa **49** 32 20N 3 37 E
Gharyān **50** 32 10N 13 0 E
Ghat **49** 24 59N 10 11 E
Ghazal, Bahr el →, Chad **50** 13 0N 15 47 E
Ghazâl, Bahr el →, Sudan **50** 9 31N 30 25 E
Ghazaouet **49** 35 8N 1 50W
Ghaziabad **36** 28 42N 77 26 E
Ghazipur **37** 25 38N 83 35 E
Ghaznī **46** 33 30N 68 28 E
Ghaznī □ **46** 32 10N 68 20 E
Ghèlinsor **47** 6 28N 46 39 E
Ghent = Gent **12** 51 2N 3 42 E
Ghisonaccia **11** 42 1N 9 26 E
Ghisoni **11** 42 7N 9 12 E
Ghowr □ **46** 34 0N 64 20 E
Ghugus **38** 19 58N 79 12 E
Giant's Causeway **7** 55 15N 6 30W
Giarabub = Al Jaghbūb **50** 29 42N 24 38 E
Giarre **23** 37 44N 15 10 E
Gibara **70** 21 9N 76 11W
Gibraltar **18** 36 7N 5 22W
Gibraltar, Str. of **18** 35 55N 5 40W
Gibson Desert **54** 24 0 S 126 0 E
Gidole **50** 5 40N 37 25 E
Gien **9** 47 40N 2 36 E
Giessen **13** 50 34N 8 40 E
Gifu **44** 35 30N 136 45 E
Gifu □ **44** 35 40N 137 0 E
Gigha **6** 55 42N 5 45W
Gignac **10** 43 39N 3 32 E
Gijón **18** 43 32N 5 42W
Gila → **68** 32 43N 114 33W
Gīlān □ **45** 37 0N 50 0 E
Gilbert → **56** 16 35 S 141 15 E
Gilbert Is. = Kiribati ■ **57** 1 0N 176 0 E
Gilford I. **64** 50 40N 126 30W
Gilgandra **56** 31 43 S 148 39 E
Gillingham **5** 51 23N 0 34 E
Gimbi **50** 9 3N 35 42 E
Gimone → **10** 44 0N 1 6 E
Gimont **10** 43 38N 0 52 E
Ginir **47** 7 6N 40 40 E
Giohar **47** 2 48N 45 30 E
Gióna, Óros **26** 38 38N 22 14 E
Gippsland **55** 37 45 S 147 15 E
Girardot **72** 4 18N 74 48W
Girdle Ness **6** 57 9N 2 2W
Giresun **45** 40 55N 38 30 E
Girga **50** 26 17N 31 55 E
Giridih **37** 24 10N 86 21 E
Giromagny **9** 47 45N 6 50 E
Gironde □ **10** 44 45N 0 30W
Gironde → **10** 45 32N 1 7W
Girvan **6** 55 15N 4 50W
Gisborne **59** 38 39 S 178 5 E
Gisenyi **51** 1 41 S 29 15 E
Gisors **9** 49 15N 1 47 E
Gitega **51** 3 26 S 29 56 E
Giuba → **47** 1 30N 42 35 E
Giurgiu **25** 43 52N 25 57 E
Givet **9** 50 8N 4 49 E
Givors **11** 45 35N 4 45 E
Givry **9** 46 41N 4 46 E
Giza = El Gîza **50** 30 0N 31 10 E
Gizhiga **31** 62 3N 160 30 E
Gizhiginskaya, Guba **31** 61 0N 158 0 E
Giźycko **17** 54 2N 21 48 E
Gjirokastra **26** 40 7N 20 10 E
Gjøvik **28** 60 47N 10 43 E
Glace Bay **63** 46 11N 59 58W
Gladstone **56** 23 52 S 151 16 E
Gláma **27** 65 48N 23 0W
Glåma → **28** 59 12N 10 57 E
Glasgow, U.K. **6** 55 52N 4 14W
Glasgow, U.S.A. **66** 37 2N 85 55W
Glastonbury **5** 51 9N 2 42W
Glazov **33** 58 9N 52 40 E
Glen Affric **6** 57 15N 5 0W
Glen Canyon Nat. Recreation Area **68** 37 30N 111 0W
Glen Coe **5** 56 40N 5 0W
Glen Garry **6** 57 3N 5 7W
Glen Innes **56** 29 44 S 151 44 E
Glen Mor **6** 57 12N 4 37 E
Glen Moriston **6** 57 10N 4 58W
Glen Orchy **6** 56 27N 4 52W
Glen Spean **6** 56 53N 4 40W
Glénans, Is. de **8** 47 42N 4 0W
Glendale **68** 34 7N 118 18W
Glengarriff **7** 51 45N 9 33W
Glenns Ferry **68** 43 0N 115 15W
Glenrothes **6** 56 12N 3 11W
Glens Falls **66** 43 20N 73 40W
Glenties **7** 54 48N 8 18W
Gliwice **17** 50 22N 18 41 E
Głogów **17** 51 37N 16 5 E
Glorieuses, Is. **53** 11 30 S 47 20 E
Glossop **5** 53 27N 1 56W
Gloucester **5** 51 52N 2 15W
Gloucestershire □ **5** 51 44N 2 10W
Gloversville **66** 43 5N 74 18W
Glückstadt **13** 53 46N 9 28 E
Gmünd **14** 48 45N 15 0 E
Gmunden **14** 47 55N 13 48 E
Gniezno **17** 52 30N 17 35 E
Gnowangerup **54** 33 58 S 117 59 E
Go Cong **41** 10 22N 106 40 E
Goa **38** 15 33N 73 59 E
Goa □ **38** 15 33N 73 59 E
Goalpara **37** 26 10N 90 40 E
Goat Fell **6** 55 37N 5 11W
Goba, Ethiopia **47** 7 1N 39 59 E
Goba, Mozam. **53** 26 15 S 32 13 E
Gobabis **52** 22 30 S 19 0 E
Gobi **42** 44 0N 111 0 E
Gochas **52** 24 59 S 18 55 E
Godavari → **38** 16 25N 82 18 E
Godavari Point **38** 17 0N 82 20 E
Godbout **63** 49 20N 67 38W
Goderich **62** 43 45N 81 41W
Goderville **8** 49 38N 0 22 E
Godhavn **3** 69 15N 53 38W
Godhra **36** 22 49N 73 40 E
Gods L. **65** 54 40N 94 15W
Godthåb **3** 64 10N 51 35W
Goeie Hoop, Kaap die = Good Hope, C. of **52** 34 24 S 18 30 E
Goeree **12** 51 50N 4 0 E
Goes **12** 51 30N 3 55 E
Gogama **62** 47 35N 81 43W
Goiânia **73** 16 43 S 49 20W
Goiás □ **73** 12 10 S 48 0W
Gojra **36** 31 10N 72 40 E
Golchikha **3** 71 45N 83 30 E
Golden Gate **68** 37 54N 122 30W
Golden Hinde **64** 49 40N 125 44W
Golden Vale **7** 52 33N 8 17W
Goldfield **68** 37 45N 117 13W
Goldsboro **66** 35 24N 77 59W
Golęniów **17** 53 35N 14 50 E
Golo → **11** 42 31N 9 32 E
Golspie **6** 57 58N 3 58W
Goma **51** 2 11 S 29 18 E
Gomel **32** 52 28N 31 0 E
Gomera **49** 28 7N 17 14W
Gómez Palacio **69** 25 34N 103 30W
Gonābād **46** 34 15N 58 45 E
Gonaïves **70** 19 20N 72 42W
Gonda **37** 27 9N 81 58 E
Gonder **50** 12 39N 37 30 E
Gondia **36** 21 23N 80 10 E
Gondrecourt-le-Château **9** 48 31N 5 30 E
Goniri **50** 11 30N 12 15 E
Good Hope, C. of **52** 34 24 S 18 30 E
Goodenough I. **56** 9 20 S 150 15 E
Goole **5** 53 42N 0 52W
Goondiwindi **56** 28 30 S 150 21 E
Goor **12** 52 13N 6 33 E
Goose Bay **63** 53 15N 60 20W
Göppingen **13** 48 42N 9 40 E
Gorakhpur **37** 26 47N 83 23 E
Gordon Downs **54** 18 48 S 128 33 E
Goré, Chad **50** 7 59N 16 31 E
Gore, Ethiopia **50** 8 12N 35 32 E
Gorey **7** 52 41N 6 18W
Gorinchem **12** 51 50N 4 59 E
Gorízia **21** 45 56N 13 37 E

Index

Gorkiy 33 56 20N 44 0 E
Gorkovskoye Vdkhr. 33 57 2N 43 4 E
Görlitz 13 51 10N 14 59 E
Gorlovka 34 48 19N 38 5 E
Gorna Oryakhovitsa 25 43 7N 25 40 E
Goroka 56 6 7 S 145 25 E
Gorron 8 48 25N 0 50W
Gort 7 53 4N 8 50W
Gorzów Wielkopolski 17 52 43N 15 15 E
Goslar 13 51 55N 10 23 E
Gospič 21 44 35N 15 23 E
Gosport 5 50 48N 1 8W
Göteborg 28 57 43N 11 59 E
Gotha 13 50 56N 10 42 E
Gotland 28 57 30N 18 33 E
Göttingen 13 51 31N 9 55 E
Gottwaldov 15 49 14N 17 40 E
Gouda 12 52 1N 4 42 E
Gough I. 1 40 10 S 9 45W
Gouin, Rés. 62 48 35N 74 40W
Goulburn 56 34 44 S 149 44 E
Goulburn Is. 54 11 40 S 133 20 E
Gounou-Gaya 50 9 38N 15 31 E
Gourdon 10 44 44N 1 23 E
Gouri 50 19 36N 19 36 E
Gourma Rharous 49 16 55N 1 50W
Gournay-en-Bray 9 49 29N 1 44 E
Gouzon 10 46 12N 2 14 E
Gove 55 12 25 S 136 55 E
Governador Valadares 73 18 15 S 41 57W
Governor's Harbour 70 25 10N 76 14W
Gower, The 5 51 35N 4 10W
Gowna, L. 7 53 52N 7 35W
Gowrie, Carse of 6 56 30N 3 10W
Goya 74 29 10 S 59 10W
Goz Beïda 50 12 10N 21 20 E
Graaff-Reinet 52 32 13 S 24 32 E
Gračac 21 44 18N 15 57 E
Graçay 9 47 10N 1 50 E
Gracias a Dios, C. 70 15 0N 83 10W
Grado 18 43 23N 6 4W
Graénalon, L. 27 64 10N 17 20W
Grafton 56 29 38 S 152 58 E
Grafton, C. 55 16 51 S 146 0 E
Graham 66 36 5N 79 22W
Graham I. 64 53 40N 132 30W
Graham Land 60 65 0 S 64 0W
Grahamstown 52 33 19 S 26 31 E
Gramat 10 44 48N 1 43 E
Grampian □ 6 57 0N 3 0W
Grampian Mts. 6 56 50N 4 0W
Gran Canaria 49 27 55N 15 35W
Gran Chaco 74 25 0 S 61 0W
Gran Paradiso 20 45 33N 7 17 E
Gran Sasso d'Italia 21 42 25N 13 30 E
Granada, Nic. 70 11 58N 86 0W
Granada, Spain 19 37 10N 3 35W
Granard 7 53 47N 7 30W
Granby 62 45 25N 72 45W
Grand Bank 63 47 6N 55 48W
Grand Bassam 49 5 10N 3 49W
Grand Canyon 68 36 3N 112 9W
Grand Cayman 70 19 20N 81 20W
Grand-Combe, La 11 44 13N 4 2 E
Grand Coulee Dam 68 48 0N 118 50W
Grand Falls 63 48 56N 55 40W
Grand Forks, Canada 64 49 0N 118 30W
Grand Forks, U.S.A. 67 48 0N 97 3W
Grand-Fougeray 8 47 44N 1 43W
Grand Island 67 40 59N 98 25W
Grand Lahou 49 5 10N 5 0W
Grand-Lieu, L. de 8 47 6N 1 40W
Grand-Lucé, Le 8 47 52N 0 28 E
Grand Mère 62 46 36N 72 40W
Grand Portage 67 47 58N 89 41W
Grand-Pressigny, Le 8 46 55N 0 48 E
Grand Rapids, Canada 65 53 12N 99 19W
Grand Rapids, U.S.A. 66 42 57N 86 40W
Grand Teton 68 43 54N 111 50W
Grand View 65 51 10N 100 42W
Grande →, Bolivia 72 15 51 S 64 39W
Grande →, Brazil 73 20 6 S 51 4W
Grande, B. 74 50 30 S 68 20W
Grande, La 68 45 15N 118 0W
Grande, La → 62 53 50N 79 0W
Grande Baleine, R. de la → 62 55 16N 77 47W
Grande de Santiago → 69 21 36N 105 26W
Grande-Motte, La 11 43 23N 4 5 E
Grande Prairie 64 55 10N 118 50W
Grande-Rivière 63 48 26N 64 30W
Grande Sauldre → 9 47 27N 2 5 E
Grandpré 9 49 20N 4 50 E
Grandvilliers 9 49 40N 1 57 E
Grange, La 66 33 4N 85 0W
Grangemouth 6 56 1N 3 43W
Granite City 67 38 45N 90 3W
Granja de Torrehermosa 18 38 19N 5 35W
Granollers 19 41 39N 2 18 E
Grant, Mt. 68 38 34N 118 48W
Grantham 5 52 55N 0 39W
Grantown-on-Spey 6 57 19N 3 36W
Grants Pass 68 42 30N 123 22W
Granville 8 48 50N 1 35W
Grass Valley 68 39 18N 121 0W
Grasse 11 43 38N 6 56 E
Graulhet 10 43 45N 1 59 E
Grave, Pte. de 10 45 34N 1 4W
Gravelbourg 65 49 50N 106 35W
Gravelines 9 51 0N 2 10 E
's-Gravenhage 12 52 7N 4 17 E
Gravesend 5 51 25N 0 22 E
Gravone → 11 41 58N 8 45 E
Gray 9 47 22N 5 35 E
Grayling 66 44 40N 84 42W
Graz 14 47 4N 15 27 E
Great Abaco I. 70 26 25N 77 10W
Great Australia Basin 55 26 0 S 140 0 E
Great Australian Bight 54 33 30 S 130 0 E
Great Bahama Bank 70 23 15N 78 0W
Great Barrier I. 59 36 11 S 175 25 E
Great Barrier Reef 56 18 0 S 146 50 E
Great Basin 68 40 0N 116 30W
Great Bear L. 61 65 30N 120 0W
Great Blasket I. 7 52 5N 10 30W
Great Dividing Ra. 55 23 0 S 146 0 E
Great Exuma I. 70 23 30N 75 50W
Great Falls 68 47 27N 111 12W
Great Inagua I. 70 21 0N 73 20W
Great Indian Desert = Thar Desert 36 28 0N 72 0 E
Great Karoo 52 31 55 S 21 0 E
Great Lake 56 41 50 S 146 40 E
Great Orme's Head 5 53 20N 3 52W
Great Ouse → 5 52 47N 0 22 E
Great Ruaha → 51 7 56 S 37 52 E
Great Salt Lake 68 41 0N 112 30W
Great Salt Lake Desert 68 40 20N 113 50W
Great Sandy Desert 54 21 0 S 124 0 E
Great Slave L. 64 61 23N 115 38W
Great Smoky Mts. Nat. Park 66 35 39N 83 30W
Great Stour = Stour → 5 51 15N 1 20 E
Great Victoria Desert 54 29 30 S 126 30 E
Great Wall 42 38 30N 109 30 E
Great Whernside 5 54 9N 1 59W
Great Yarmouth 5 52 40N 1 45 E
Greater Antilles 70 17 40N 74 0W
Greater London □ 5 51 30N 0 5W
Greater Manchester □ 5 53 30N 2 15W
Gredos, Sierra de 18 40 20N 5 0W
Greece ■ 26 40 0N 23 0 E
Greeley 67 40 30N 104 40W
Green →, Ky., U.S.A. 66 37 54N 87 30W
Green →, Utah, U.S.A. 68 38 11N 109 53W
Green Bay 67 44 30N 88 0W
Green Is. 56 4 35 S 154 10 E
Greenfield 66 42 38N 72 38W
Greenland ■ 3 66 0N 45 0W
Greenland Sea 3 73 0N 10 0W
Greenock 6 55 57N 4 46W
Greenore 7 54 2N 6 8W
Greenore Pt. 7 52 15N 6 20W
Greensboro 66 36 7N 79 46W
Greenville, Liberia 49 5 1N 9 6W
Greenville, Ala., U.S.A. 66 31 50N 86 37W
Greenville, Mich., U.S.A. 66 43 12N 85 14W
Greenville, Miss., U.S.A. 67 33 25N 91 0W
Greenville, N.C., U.S.A. 66 35 37N 77 26W
Greenville, S.C., U.S.A. 66 34 54N 82 24W
Greenville, Tenn., U.S.A. 66 36 13N 82 51W
Greenwich 5 51 28N 0 0 E
Greenwood, Miss., U.S.A. 67 33 30N 90 4W
Greenwood, S.C., U.S.A. 66 34 13N 82 13W
Gregory, L. 56 28 55 S 139 0 E
Gregory Lake 54 20 10 S 127 30 E
Gregory Ra. 56 19 30 S 143 40 E
Gremikha 30 67 50N 39 40 E
Grenada 67 33 45N 89 50W
Grenada ■ 70 12 10N 61 40W
Grenade 10 43 47N 1 17 E
Grenen 28 57 44N 10 40 E
Grenoble 11 45 12N 5 42 E
Grenville, C. 56 12 0 S 143 13 E
Gréoux-les-Bains 11 43 45N 5 52 E
Gretna Green 6 55 0N 3 3W
Grevenmacher 12 49 41N 6 26 E
Grey, C. 55 13 0 S 136 35 E
Grey Range 55 27 0 S 143 30 E
Grey Res. 63 48 20N 56 30W
Greytown 53 29 1 S 30 36 E
Griffin 66 33 17N 84 14W
Griffith 56 34 18 S 146 2 E
Grim, C. 55 40 45 S 144 45 E
Grimari 50 5 43N 20 6 E
Grimsby 5 53 35N 0 5W
Grímsey 27 66 33N 18 0W
Grimshaw 64 56 10N 117 40W
Grimstad 27 58 22N 8 35 E
Grinnell 67 41 45N 92 43W
Gris-Nez, C. 9 50 52N 1 35 E
Grisolles 10 43 49N 1 19 E
Grodno 32 53 42N 23 52 E
Grodzisk Wielkopolski 17 52 15N 16 22 E
Groix 8 47 38N 3 29W
Groix, I. de 8 47 38N 3 28W
Grójec 17 51 50N 20 58 E
Gronau 13 52 13N 7 2 E
Grong 27 64 25N 12 8 E
Groningen 12 53 15N 6 35 E
Groningen □ 12 53 16N 6 40 E
Groote Eylandt 55 14 0 S 136 40 E
Grootfontein 52 19 31 S 18 6 E
Grosne → 11 46 42N 4 56 E
Gross Glockner 14 47 5N 12 40 E
Grosseto 20 42 45N 11 7 E
Grouard Mission 64 55 33N 116 9W
Grouin, Pte. du 8 48 43N 1 51W
Groznyy 35 43 20N 45 45 E
Grudziądz 17 53 30N 18 47 E
Gruissan 10 43 8N 3 7 E
Gryazi 33 52 30N 39 58 E
Gryazovets 30 58 50N 40 20 E
Guadalajara, Mexico 69 20 40N 103 20W
Guadalajara, Spain 19 40 37N 3 12W
Guadalcanal 57 9 32 S 160 12 E
Guadalete → 18 36 35N 6 13W
Guadalhorce → 18 36 41N 4 27W
Guadalquivir → 18 36 47N 6 22W
Guadalupe, Sierra de 18 39 28N 5 30W
Guadalupe Bravos 69 31 23N 106 7W
Guadalupe I. 58 29 0N 118 50W
Guadarrama, Sierra de 18 41 0N 4 0W
Guadeloupe ■ 70 16 20N 61 40W
Guadiana → 18 37 14N 7 22W
Guadix 19 37 18N 3 11W
Guaíra 74 24 5 S 54 10W
Guajará-Mirim 72 10 50 S 65 20W
Gualeguay 74 33 10 S 59 14W
Gualeguaychú 74 33 3 S 59 31W
Guam 57 13 27N 144 45 E
Guanabacoa 70 23 8N 82 18W
Guanacaste, Cordillera del 70 10 40N 85 4W
Guanahani = San Salvador 70 24 0N 74 40W
Guanajay 70 22 56N 82 42W
Guanajuato 69 21 1N 101 15W
Guanajuato □ 69 21 0N 101 0W
Guanare 72 8 42N 69 12W
Guangdong □ 43 23 0N 113 0 E
Guangxi Zhuangzu Zizhiqu □ 43 24 0N 109 0 E
Guangzhou 43 23 5N 113 10 E
Guantánamo 70 20 10N 75 14W
Guaporé → 72 11 55 S 65 4W
Guaqui 72 16 41 S 68 54W
Guarapuava 74 25 20 S 51 30W
Guarda 18 40 32N 7 20W
Guardafui, C. = Asir, Ras 47 11 55N 51 10 E
Guatemala 69 14 40N 90 22W
Guatemala ■ 69 15 40N 90 30W
Guaviare → 72 4 3N 67 44W
Guayama 70 17 59N 66 7W
Guayaquil 72 2 15 S 79 52W
Guayaquil, G. de 72 3 10 S 81 0W
Guaymas 69 27 56N 110 54W
Gudivada 38 16 30N 81 3 E
Gudur 38 14 12N 79 55 E
Guebwiller 9 47 55N 7 12 E
Guecho 19 43 21N 2 59W
Guékédou 49 8 40N 10 5W
Guelma 49 36 25N 7 29 E
Guelph 62 43 35N 80 20W
Guéméné-Penfao 8 47 38N 1 50W
Guéméné-sur-Scorff 8 48 4N 3 13W
Guer 8 47 54N 2 8W
Güera, La 49 20 51N 17 0W
Guérande 8 47 20N 2 26W
Guerche-de-Bretagne, La 8 47 57N 1 16W
Guerche-sur-l'Aubois, La 9 46 58N 2 56 E
Guéréda 50 14 31N 22 5 E
Guéret 10 46 11N 1 51 E
Guérigny 9 47 6N 3 10 E
Guernica 19 43 19N 2 40W
Guernsey 8 49 30N 2 35W
Guerrero □ 69 17 40N 100 0W
Gueugnon 11 46 36N 4 4 E
Guiglo 49 6 45N 7 30W
Guildford 5 51 14N 0 34W
Guilin 43 25 18N 110 15 E
Guillaumes 11 44 5N 6 52 E
Guillestre 11 44 39N 6 40 E
Guilvinec 8 47 48N 4 17W
Guimarães 73 2 9 S 44 42W
Guinea ■ 49 10 20N 11 30W
Guinea, Gulf of 2 3 0N 2 30 E
Guinea-Bissau ■ 49 12 0N 15 0W
Güines 70 22 50N 82 0W
Guingamp 8 48 34N 3 10W
Guipavas 8 48 26N 4 29W
Guiscard 9 49 40N 3 1 E
Guise 9 49 52N 3 35 E
Guiyang 43 26 32N 106 40 E
Guizhou □ 43 27 0N 107 0 E
Gujan-Mestras 10 44 38N 1 4W
Gujarat □ 36 23 20N 71 0 E
Gujranwala 36 32 10N 74 12 E
Gujrat 36 32 40N 74 2 E
Gulbarga 38 17 20N 76 50 E
Gulf, The 46 27 0N 50 0 E
Gulf Basin 54 15 20 S 129 0 E
Gulfport 67 30 21N 89 3W
Gull Lake 65 50 10N 108 29W
Gulu 51 2 48N 32 17 E
Gumma □ 44 36 30N 138 20 E
Gummersbach 13 51 2N 7 32 E
Gummi 49 12 4N 5 9 E
Gümüsane 45 40 30N 39 30 E
Guna 36 24 40N 77 19 E
Gungu 51 5 43 S 19 20 E
Gunnedah 56 30 59 S 150 15 E
Guntakal 38 15 11N 77 27 E
Guntersville 66 34 18N 86 16W
Guntur 38 16 23N 80 30 E
Günz → 13 48 27N 10 16 E
Gunza 51 10 50 S 13 50 E
Gurdaspur 36 32 5N 75 31 E
Gurgaon 36 28 27N 77 1 E
Gurkha 37 28 5N 84 40 E
Gurupi → 73 1 13 S 46 6W
Guryev 35 47 5N 52 0 E
Gusau 49 12 12N 6 40 E
Güstrow 13 53 47N 12 12 E
Gütersloh 13 51 54N 8 25 E
Guthrie 67 35 55N 97 30W
Guyana ■ 72 5 0N 59 0W
Guyenne 10 44 30N 0 40 E
Gwaai 51 19 15 S 27 45 E
Gwalior 36 26 12N 78 10 E
Gwanda 51 20 55 S 29 0 E
Gweebarra B. 7 54 52N 8 21W
Gweedore 7 55 4N 8 15W
Gwent □ 5 51 45N 2 55W
Gweru 51 19 28 S 29 45 E
Gwydir → 56 29 27 S 149 48 E
Gwynedd □ 5 53 0N 4 0W
Gyaring Hu 42 34 50N 97 40 E
Gydanskiy P-ov. 30 70 0N 78 0 E
Gympie 56 26 11 S 152 38 E
Gyoda 44 36 10N 139 30 E
Gyöngyös 15 47 48N 20 0 E
Györ 15 47 41N 17 40 E
Gypsumville 65 51 45N 98 40W

H

Ha 'Arava → 45 30 50N 35 20 E
Ha Giang 41 22 50N 104 59 E
Haapamäki 27 62 18N 24 28 E
Haarlem 12 52 23N 4 39 E
Habana, La 70 23 8N 82 22W
Habaswein 51 1 2N 39 30 E
Hachijō-Jima 44 33 5N 139 45 E
Hachinohe 44 40 30N 141 29 E
Hachiōji 44 35 40N 139 20 E
Hadarba, Ras 50 22 4N 36 51 E
Haddington 6 55 57N 2 48W
Hadejia 49 12 30N 10 5 E
Hadera 45 32 27N 34 55 E
Hadramawt 47 15 30N 49 30 E
Hadrians Wall 5 55 0N 2 30W
Haeju 43 38 3N 125 45 E
Hafizabad 36 32 5N 73 40 E
Hafnarfjörður 27 64 4N 21 57W
Haft-Gel 45 31 30N 49 32 E
Hafun, Ras 47 10 29N 51 30 E
Hagen 13 51 21N 7 29 E
Hagerstown 66 39 39N 77 46W
Hagetmau 10 43 39N 0 37W
Hagfors 28 60 3N 13 45 E
Hagi, Iceland 27 65 28N 23 25W
Hagi, Japan 44 34 30N 131 22 E
Hags Hd. 7 52 57N 9 30W
Hague, C. de la 8 49 44N 1 56W
Haguenau 9 48 49N 7 47 E
Haifa = Hefa 45 32 46N 35 0 E
Haikou 43 20 1N 110 16 E
Hailar 42 49 10N 119 38 E
Haileybury 62 47 30N 79 38W
Hailuoto 27 65 3N 24 45 E
Hainan 43 19 0N 110 0 E
Hainan Dao 43 19 0N 109 30 E
Hainaut □ 12 50 30N 4 0 E
Haiphong 41 20 47N 106 41 E
Haiti ■ 70 19 0N 72 30W
Haiya Junction 50 18 20N 36 21 E
Hajar Bangar 50 10 40N 22 45 E
Hajdúböszörmény 15 47 40N 21 30 E
Hakken-Zan 44 34 10N 135 54 E
Hakodate 44 41 45N 140 44 E
Halab 45 36 10N 37 15 E
Halaib 50 22 12N 36 30 E
Halberstadt 13 51 53N 11 2 E
Halden 28 59 9N 11 23 E
Haldwani 37 29 31N 79 30 E
Hali 47 18 30N 41 30 E
Halifax, Canada 63 44 38N 63 35W
Halifax, U.K. 5 53 43N 1 51W
Halifax B. 56 18 50 S 147 0 E
Hallands län □ 28 56 50N 12 50 E
Halle, Belgium 12 50 44N 4 13 E
Halle, Germany 13 51 29N 12 0 E
Hällefors 28 59 47N 14 31 E
Hällnäs 27 64 19N 19 36 E
Halls Creek 54 18 16 S 127 38 E
Halmahera 40 0 40N 128 0 E
Halmstad 28 56 41N 12 52 E
Halq el Oued 50 36 53N 10 18 E
Hals 28 56 59N 10 18 E
Hälsingborg = Helsingborg 28 56 3N 12 42 E
Ham 9 49 45N 3 4 E
Hamada 44 34 56N 132 4 E
Hamadān 45 34 52N 48 32 E
Hamadān □ 45 35 0N 49 0 E
Hamāh 45 35 5N 36 40 E
Hamamatsu 44 34 45N 137 45 E
Hamar 28 60 48N 11 7 E
Hamarøy 27 68 5N 15 38 E
Hamburg 13 53 32N 9 59 E
Hämeenlinna 27 61 0N 24 28 E
Hameln 13 52 7N 9 24 E
Hamersley Ra. 54 22 0 S 117 45 E
Hamhung 43 39 54N 127 30 E
Hamilton, Australia 56 37 45 S 142 2 E
Hamilton, Bermuda 70 32 15N 64 45W
Hamilton, Canada 62 43 15N 79 50W
Hamilton, N.Z. 59 37 47 S 175 19 E
Hamilton, U.K. 6 55 47N 4 2W
Hamilton, U.S.A. 66 39 20N 84 35W
Hamm 13 51 40N 7 49 E
Hammerfest 27 70 39N 23 41 E
Hammond, Ind., U.S.A. 66 41 40N 87 30W
Hammond, La., U.S.A. 67 30 32N 90 30W
Hampshire □ 5 51 3N 1 20W
Hampshire Downs 5 51 10N 1 10W
Hampton 66 37 4N 76 18W
Hampton Harbour 54 20 30 S 116 30 E
Hampton Tableland 54 32 0 S 127 0 E
Hamrat esh Sheykh 50 14 38N 27 55 E
Hanau 13 50 8N 8 56 E
Hancock, Mich., U.S.A. 62 47 10N 88 40W
Hancock, Minn., U.S.A. 67 45 26N 95 46W
Handa, Japan 44 34 53N 137 0 E
Handa, Somalia 47 10 37N 51 2 E
Handan 42 36 35N 114 28 E
Handeni 51 5 25 S 38 2 E
Haney 64 49 12N 122 40W
Hanford 68 36 23N 119 39W
Hangayn Nuruu 42 47 30N 100 0 E
Hangö 27 59 50N 22 57 E
Hangu 42 39 18N 117 53 E
Hangzhou 43 30 18N 120 11 E
Hanish J. 47 13 45N 42 46 E
Hanko 27 59 59N 22 57 E
Hann, Mt. 54 16 0 S 126 0 E
Hanna 64 51 40N 111 54W
Hannibal 67 39 42N 91 22W
Hannover 13 52 23N 9 43 E
Hanoi 41 21 5N 105 55 E
Hanover, N.H., U.S.A. 63 43 43N 72 17W
Hanover, Pa., U.S.A. 66 39 46N 76 59W
Hansi 36 29 10N 75 57 E
Hanson Range 54 27 0 S 136 30 E
Hanzhong 43 33 10N 107 1 E
Haora 37 22 37N 88 20 E
Haparanda 27 65 52N 24 8 E
Hapur 36 28 45N 77 45 E
Harardera 47 4 33N 47 38 E
Harare 51 17 43 S 31 2 E
Harbin 42 45 48N 126 40 E
Harbour Breton 63 47 29N 55 50W
Harbour Grace 63 47 40N 53 22W
Harburg 13 53 27N 9 58 E
Hardangerfjorden 27 60 15N 6 0 E
Hardenberg 12 52 34N 6 37 E
Harderwijk 12 52 21N 5 38 E
Hardoi 37 27 26N 80 6 E
Harer 47 9 20N 42 8 E
Harfleur 8 49 30N 0 10 E
Hargeisa 47 9 30N 44 2 E
Hargshamn 28 60 12N 18 30 E
Hari → 39 1 16 S 104 5 E
Haridwar 36 29 58N 78 9 E
Haringhata → 37 22 0N 89 58 E
Harīrūd → 46 34 20N 62 30 E
Harlech 5 52 52N 4 7W
Harlingen, Neth. 12 53 11N 5 25 E
Harlingen, U.S.A. 67 26 20N 97 50W
Harney Basin 68 43 30N 119 0W
Härnösand 27 62 38N 18 0 E
Harriman 66 36 0N 84 35W
Harris 6 57 50N 6 55W
Harris, Sd. of 6 57 44N 7 6W
Harris L. 54 31 10 S 135 10 E
Harrisburg, Ill., U.S.A. 66 37 42N 88 30W
Harrisburg, Pa., U.S.A. 66 40 18N 76 52W
Harrison 67 36 10N 93 4W
Harrison, C. 63 54 55N 57 55W
Harrisonburg 66 38 28N 78 52W
Harrogate 5 53 59N 1 32W
Harrow 5 51 35N 0 15W
Harstad 27 68 48N 16 30 E
Hartford 66 41 47N 72 41W
Hartland Pt. 5 51 2N 4 32W
Hartlepool 5 54 42N 1 11W
Hartsville 66 34 23N 80 2W
Harvey 67 41 40N 87 40W
Harwich 5 51 56N 1 18 E
Haryana □ 36 29 0N 76 10 E
Harz 13 51 40N 10 40 E
Hasparren 10 43 24N 1 18W
Hasselt 12 50 56N 5 21 E
Hassi Inifel 49 29 50N 3 41 E
Hassi Messaoud 49 31 43N 6 8 E
Hastings, N.Z. 59 39 39 S 176 52 E
Hastings, U.K. 5 50 51N 0 36 E
Hastings, U.S.A. 67 40 34N 98 22W
Hatches Creek 54 20 56 S 135 12 E
Hathras 36 27 36N 78 6 E
Hatteras, C. 66 35 10N 75 30W
Hattiesburg 67 31 20N 89 20W
Hatvan 15 47 40N 19 45 E
Haugesund 27 59 23N 5 13 E
Hauraki Gulf 59 36 35 S 175 5 E
Haut Atlas 49 32 30N 5 0W
Haut-Rhin □ 9 48 0N 7 15 E
Haute-Corse □ 11 42 30N 9 30 E
Haute-Garonne □ 10 43 30N 1 30 E
Haute-Loire □ 10 45 5N 3 50 E
Haute-Marne □ 9 48 10N 5 20 E
Haute-Saône □ 9 47 45N 6 10 E
Haute-Savoie □ 11 46 0N 6 20 E
Haute-Vienne □ 10 45 50N 1 10 E
Hautes-Alpes □ 11 44 42N 6 20 E
Hautes-Pyrénées □ 10 43 0N 0 10 E
Hauteville-Lompnès 11 45 58N 5 36 E
Hautmont 9 50 15N 3 55 E
Hauts-de-Seine □ 9 48 52N 2 15 E
Hauts Plateaux 49 35 0N 1 0 E
Havana = Habana, La 70 23 8N 82 22W
Havant 5 50 51N 0 59W
Havelange 12 50 23N 5 15 E
Havelock 62 44 26N 77 53W
Haverfordwest 5 51 48N 4 59W
Haverhill 66 42 50N 71 2W
Havering 5 51 33N 0 20 E
Havlíčkův Brod 14 49 36N 15 33 E
Havre 68 48 34N 109 40W
Havre, Le 8 49 30N 0 5 E
Hawaiian Is. 58 20 30N 156 0W
Hawick 6 55 25N 2 48W
Hawke B. 59 39 25 S 177 20 E
Hawker 55 31 59 S 138 22 E
Hawkesbury 62 45 37N 74 37W
Hawkesbury → 55 33 30 S 151 10 E
Hawthorne 68 38 31N 118 37W
Hay 56 34 30 S 144 51 E
Hay → 56 25 14 S 138 0 E
Hay-on-Wye 5 52 4N 3 9W
Hay River 64 60 51N 115 44W
Hayange 9 49 20N 6 2 E
Haye-du-Puits, La 8 49 17N 1 33W
Hayward's Heath 5 51 0N 0 5W
Hazard 66 37 18N 83 10W
Hazaribag 37 23 58N 85 26 E
Hazebrouck 9 50 42N 2 31 E
Hazelton 64 55 20N 127 42W
Hazleton 66 40 58N 76 0W
Head of Bight 54 31 30 S 131 25 E
Healdsburg 68 38 33N 122 51W
Heanor 5 53 1N 1 20W
Heard I. 2 53 0 S 74 0 E
Hearst 62 49 40N 83 41W
Hebei □ 42 39 0N 116 0 E
Hebrides 6 57 30N 7 0W
Hebron = Al Khalīl 45 31 32N 35 6 E
Hecate Str. 64 53 10N 130 30W
Hechuan 43 30 2N 106 12 E
Hédé, France 8 48 18N 1 49W
Hede, Sweden 27 62 23N 13 30 E
Hedemora 28 60 18N 15 58 E
Heemstede 12 52 22N 4 37 E
Heerde 12 52 24N 6 2 E
Heerenveen 12 52 57N 5 55 E
Heerlen 12 50 55N 6 0 E
Hefa 45 32 46N 35 0 E

Hefei 43 31 52N 117 18 E
Hegang 42 47 20N 130 19 E
Heide 13 54 10N 9 7 E
Heidelberg 13 49 23N 8 41 E
Heidenheim 13 48 40N 10 10 E
Heilbron 53 27 16 S 27 59 E
Heilbronn 13 49 8N 9 13 E
Heilongjiang □ 42 48 0N 126 0 E
Heinola 27 61 13N 26 2 E
Heinze Is. 41 14 25N 97 45 E
Hejaz = Al Ḥijāz 47 26 0N 37 30 E
Hekimhan 45 38 50N 38 0 E
Hekla 27 63 56N 19 35W
Helena, Ark., U.S.A. 67 34 30N 90 35W
Helena, Mont., U.S.A. 68 46 40N 112 0W
Helensburgh 6 56 0N 4 44W
Helgoland 13 54 10N 7 51 E
Hellendoorn 12 52 24N 6 27 E
Hellevoetsluis 12 51 50N 4 8 E
Hellín 19 38 31N 1 40W
Helmand → 46 31 12N 61 34 E
Helmond 12 51 29N 5 41 E
Helmsdale 6 58 7N 3 40W
Helmstedt 13 52 16N 11 0 E
Helsingborg 28 56 3N 12 42 E
Helsingfors 27 60 15N 25 3 E
Helsingør 28 56 2N 12 35 E
Helsinki 27 60 15N 25 3 E
Helston 5 50 7N 5 17W
Helvellyn 5 54 31N 3 1W
Helwân 50 29 50N 31 20 E
Hempstead 66 30 5N 96 5W
Hemse 28 57 15N 18 22 E
Henan □ 43 34 0N 114 0 E
Henares → 19 40 24N 3 30W
Hendaye 10 43 23N 1 47W
Henderson 66 36 20N 78 25W
Hendersonville 66 35 21N 82 28W
Hengelo 12 52 3N 6 19 E
Hénin-Beaumont 9 50 25N 2 58 E
Hennebont 8 47 49N 3 19W
Henrichemont 9 47 20N 2 30 E
Henrietta, Ostrov 31 77 6N 156 30 E
Henrietta Maria C. 62 55 9N 82 20W
Héraðsflói 27 65 42N 14 12W
Héraðsvötn → 27 65 45N 19 25W
Herāt 46 34 20N 62 7 E
Herāt □ 46 35 0N 62 0 E
Hérault □ 10 43 34N 3 15 E
Hérault → 10 43 17N 3 26 E
Herbault 8 47 36N 1 8 E
Herbiers, Les 8 46 52N 1 1W
Herbignac 8 47 27N 2 18W
Hercegnovi 24 42 30N 18 33 E
Herðubreið 27 65 11N 16 21W
Hereford 5 52 4N 2 42W
Hereford and Worcester □ 5 52 10N 2 30W
Herentals 12 51 12N 4 51 E
Herford 13 52 7N 8 40 E
Héricourt 9 47 32N 6 45 E
Hérisson 10 46 32N 2 42 E
Herm 8 49 30N 2 28W
Herment 10 45 45N 2 24 E
Hermosillo 69 29 4N 110 58W
Hernad → 15 47 56N 21 8 E
Herne 13 51 33N 7 12 E
Herne Bay 5 51 22N 1 8 E
Herning 28 56 8N 8 58 E
Heron Bay 62 48 40N 86 25W
Herrera 18 37 26N 4 55W
Herrin 67 37 50N 89 0W
Herstal 12 50 40N 5 38 E
Hertford 5 51 47N 0 4W
Hertford □ 5 51 51N 0 5W
's-Hertogenbosch 12 51 42N 5 17 E
Hervey B. 55 25 0 S 152 52 E
Hesdin 9 50 21N 2 0 E
Hessen □ 13 50 40N 9 20 E
Hève, C. de la 8 49 30N 0 5 E
Hexham 5 54 58N 2 7W
Heysham 5 54 5N 2 53W
Hi-no-Misaki 44 35 26N 132 38 E
Hialeach 66 25 49N 80 17W
Hibbing 67 47 30N 93 0W
Hickory 66 35 46N 81 17W
Hicks Pt. 55 37 49 S 149 17 E
Hida-Sammyaku 44 36 30N 137 40 E
Hidalgo □ 69 20 30N 99 0W
Hidalgo del Parral 69 26 56N 105 40W
Hierro 49 27 44N 18 0 E
Higashiōsaka 44 34 40N 135 37 E
High Point 66 35 57N 79 58W
High Prairie 64 55 30N 116 30W
High River 64 50 30N 113 50W
High Wycombe 5 51 37N 0 45W
Highland □ 6 57 30N 5 0W
Highland Park 66 42 10N 87 50W
Hiiumaa 32 58 50N 22 45 E
Ḥijārah, Ṣaḥrā' al 45 30 25N 44 30 E
Ḥijāz □ 47 24 0N 40 0 E
Hikone 44 35 15N 136 10 E
Hildesheim 13 52 9N 9 55 E
Hillegom 12 52 18N 4 35 E
Hillingdon 5 51 33N 0 29W
Hillsboro 68 45 31N 123 0W
Hillston 56 33 30 S 145 31 E
Hilversum 12 52 14N 5 10 E
Himachal Pradesh □ 36 31 30N 77 0 E
Himalaya, Mts. 37 29 0N 84 0 E
Himeji 44 34 50N 134 40 E
Himi 44 36 50N 137 0 E
Ḥimṣ 45 34 40N 36 45 E
Hinchinbrook I. 56 18 20 S 146 15 E
Hinckley 5 52 33N 1 21W
Hindu Kush 46 36 0N 71 0 E
Hindupur 38 13 49N 77 32 E
Hines Creek 64 56 20N 118 40W
Hinganghat 36 20 30N 78 52 E
Hingoli 38 19 41N 77 15 E
Hinlopenstretet 3 79 35N 18 40 E
Hinton 66 37 40N 80 51W
Hippolytushoef 12 52 54N 4 58 E
Hirakud Dam 36 21 32N 83 45 E
Hiratsuka 44 35 19N 139 21 E
Hirosaki 44 40 34N 140 28 E
Hiroshima 44 34 24N 132 30 E
Hiroshima □ 44 34 50N 133 0 E
Hirson 9 49 55N 4 4 E
Hisar 36 29 12N 75 45 E
Hispaniola 70 19 0N 71 0W
Hita 44 33 20N 130 58 E
Hitachi 44 36 36N 140 39 E
Hitchin 5 51 57N 0 16W
Hitoyoshi 44 32 13N 130 45 E
Hitra 27 63 30N 8 45 E
Hjälmaren 28 59 18N 15 40 E
Hjørring 28 57 29N 9 59 E
Hńak 3 70 40N 52 10W
Ho 49 6 37N 0 27 E
Ho Chi Minh City = Phanh Bho Ho Chi Minh 41 10 58N 106 40 E
Hoa Binh 41 20 50N 105 20 E
Hobart 56 42 50 S 147 21 E
Hoboken 12 51 11N 4 21 E
Hobro 28 56 39N 9 46 E
Hoburgen 28 56 55N 18 7 E
Hockenheim 13 49 18N 8 33 E
Hódmezövásárhely 15 46 28N 20 22 E
Hodna, Chott el 49 35 30N 5 0 E
Hodonín 15 48 50N 17 10 E
Hœdic, I. de 8 47 20N 2 53W
Hoek van Holland 12 52 0N 4 7 E
Hof, Germany 13 50 18N 11 55 E
Hof, Iceland 27 64 33N 14 40W
Höfðakaupstaður 27 65 50N 20 19W
Hofsjökull 27 64 49N 18 48W
Hofsós 27 65 53N 19 26W
Hōfu 44 34 3N 131 34 E
Hoh Xil Shan 42 35 0N 89 0 E
Hohe Venn 12 50 30N 6 5 E
Hohhot 42 40 52N 111 40 E
Hokitika 59 42 42 S 171 0 E
Hokkaidō □ 44 43 30N 143 0 E
Holderness 5 53 45N 0 5W
Holguín 70 20 50N 76 20W
Holland 66 42 47N 86 7W
Holly Springs 67 34 45N 89 25W
Hollywood, Calif., U.S.A. 68 34 7N 118 25W
Hollywood, Fla., U.S.A. 66 26 0N 80 9W
Hólmavík 27 65 42N 21 40W
Holmsund 27 63 41N 20 20 E
Holroyd → 56 14 10 S 141 36 E
Holstebro 28 56 22N 8 37 E
Holsworthy 5 50 48N 4 21W
Holt 27 63 33N 19 48W
Holwerd 12 53 22N 5 54 E
Holy I., England, U.K. 5 55 42N 1 48W
Holy I., Wales, U.K. 5 53 17N 4 37W
Holyhead 5 53 18N 4 38W
Holyoke 66 42 14N 72 37W
Holzminden 13 51 49N 9 31 E
Hombori 49 15 20N 1 38W
Homburg 13 49 19N 7 21 E
Home Hill 56 19 43 S 147 25 E
Homs = Ḥimṣ 45 34 40N 36 45 E
Hondeklipbaai 52 30 19 S 17 17 E
Honduras ■ 70 14 40N 86 30W
Honduras, G. de 69 16 50N 87 0W
Honfleur 8 49 25N 0 13 E
Hong Kong ■ 43 22 11N 114 14 E
Hongha → 41 22 0N 104 0 E
Hongshui He → 43 23 48N 109 30 E
Honiara 57 9 27 S 159 57 E
Honiton 5 50 48N 3 11W
Honolulu 58 21 19N 157 52W
Honshū 44 36 0N 138 0 E
Hood, Pt. 54 34 23 S 119 34 E
Hood Mt. 68 45 24N 121 41W
Hoogeveen 12 52 44N 6 30 E
Hoogezand 12 53 11N 6 45 E
Hooghly → = Hughli → 37 21 56N 88 4 E
Hook Hd. 7 52 8N 6 57W
Hook of Holland = Hoek van Holland 12 52 0N 4 7 E
Hoorn 12 52 38N 5 4 E
Hoover Dam 68 36 0N 114 45W
Hope, Canada 64 49 25N 121 25 E
Hope, U.S.A. 67 33 40N 93 36W
Hope Town 70 26 35N 76 57W
Hopedale 63 55 28N 60 13W
Hopelchén 69 19 46N 89 51W
Hopetoun 54 33 57 S 120 7 E
Hopetown 52 29 34 S 24 3 E
Hopkinsville 66 36 52N 87 26W
Hoquiam 68 46 50N 123 55W
Hordaland fylke □ 27 60 25N 6 15 E
Horden Hills 54 20 40 S 130 20 E
Hormoz 46 27 35N 55 0 E
Hormuz Str. 46 26 30N 56 30 E
Horn, Austria 14 48 39N 15 40 E
Horn, Ísafjarðarsýsla, Iceland 27 66 28N 22 28W
Horn, Suður-Múlasýsla, Iceland 27 65 10N 13 31W
Horn, Cape = Hornos, C. de 74 55 50 S 67 30W
Horn Head 7 55 13N 8 0W
Hornavan 27 66 15N 17 30 E
Horncastle 5 53 13N 0 8W
Hornell 66 42 23N 77 41W
Hornos, C. de 74 55 50 S 67 30W
Hornoy 9 49 50N 1 54 E
Hornsea 5 53 55N 0 10W
Horqin Youyi Qianqi 42 46 5N 122 3 E
Horsens 28 55 52N 9 51 E
Horsham, Australia 56 36 44 S 142 13 E
Horsham, U.K. 5 51 4N 0 20W
Horten 28 59 25N 10 32 E
Hoshangabad 36 22 45N 77 45 E
Hoshiarpur 36 31 30N 75 58 E
Hospet 38 15 15N 76 20 E
Hospitalet de Llobregat 19 41 21N 2 6 E
Hoste, I. 74 55 0 S 69 0W
Hostens 10 44 30N 0 40W
Hot Springs 67 34 30N 93 0W
Hotagen 27 63 50N 14 30 E
Hoting 27 64 8N 16 15 E
Houat, I. de 8 47 24N 2 58W
Houdan 9 48 48N 1 35 E
Houffalize 12 50 8N 5 48 E
Houghton 62 47 9N 88 39W
Houghton-le-Spring 5 54 51N 1 28W
Houlton 66 46 5N 67 50W
Houma 67 29 35N 90 44W
Hourtin 10 45 11N 1 4W
Hourtin-Carcans, Étang d' 10 45 10N 1 6W
Houston, Canada 64 54 25N 126 39W
Houston, U.S.A. 67 29 50N 95 20W
Houtman Abrolhos 54 28 43 S 113 48 E
Hovd 42 48 2N 91 37 E
Hove 5 50 50N 0 10W
Howe, C. 56 37 30 S 150 0 E
Howrah = Haora 37 22 37N 88 20 E
Howth Hd. 7 53 21N 6 0W
Hoy I. 6 58 50N 3 15W
Hrádec Králové 14 50 15N 15 50 E
Hron → 15 47 49N 18 45 E
Hrvatska 21 45 20N 16 0 E
Hua Hin 41 12 34N 99 58 E
Huacho 72 11 10 S 77 35W
Huainan 43 32 38N 116 58 E
Huallaga → 72 5 0 S 75 30W
Huambo 51 12 42 S 15 54 E
Huancane 72 15 10 S 69 44W
Huancavelica 72 12 50 S 75 5W
Huancayo 72 12 5 S 75 12W
Huanchaca 72 20 15 S 66 40W
Huang Hai = Yellow Sea 43 35 0N 123 0 E
Huangshi 43 30 10N 115 3 E
Huánuco 72 9 55 S 76 15W
Huaraz 72 9 30 S 77 32W
Huascarán 72 9 8 S 77 36W
Huasco 74 28 30 S 71 15W
Huatabampo 69 26 50N 109 38W
Huautla 69 17 51N 100 5W
Hubei □ 43 31 0N 112 0 E
Hückelhoven-Ratheim 13 51 6N 6 13 E
Huddersfield 5 53 38N 1 49W
Hudiksvall 28 61 43N 17 10 E
Hudson 66 42 15N 73 46W
Hudson → 66 40 42N 74 2W
Hudson Bay 65 52 51N 102 23W
Hudson Str. 61 62 0N 70 0W
Hudson's Hope 64 56 0N 121 54W
Hue 41 16 30N 107 35 E
Huehuetenango 69 15 20N 91 28W
Huelgoat 8 48 22N 3 46W
Huelva 18 37 18N 6 57W
Huesca 19 42 8N 0 25W
Hugh → 54 25 1 S 134 1 E
Hughenden 56 20 52 S 144 10 E
Hughli → 37 21 56N 88 4 E
Huila, Nevado del 72 3 0N 76 0W
Huinca Renancó 74 34 51 S 64 22W
Huisne → 8 47 59N 0 11 E
Huixtla 69 15 9N 92 28W
Hull, Canada 62 45 25N 75 44W
Hull, U.K. 5 53 45N 0 20W
Hull → 5 53 43N 0 25W
Hulst 12 51 17N 4 2 E
Hulun Nur 42 49 0N 117 30 E
Humaitá 72 27 2 S 58 31W
Humber → 5 53 40N 0 10W
Humberside □ 5 53 50N 0 30W
Humboldt, Canada 65 52 15N 105 9W
Humboldt, U.S.A. 67 35 50N 88 55W
Humboldt → 68 40 2N 118 31W
Humboldt Gletscher 3 79 30N 62 0W
Hume, L. 56 36 0 S 147 0 E
Hūn 50 29 2N 16 0 E
Húnaflói 27 65 50N 20 50W
Hunedoara 15 45 40N 22 50 E
Hungary ■ 15 47 20N 19 20 E
Hŭngnam 43 39 49N 127 45 E
Hunsrück 13 49 30N 7 0 E
Hunstanton 5 52 57N 0 30 E
Hunte → 13 52 30N 8 19 E
Hunter I. 56 40 30 S 144 45 E
Huntingdon 5 52 20N 0 11W
Huntington, Ind., U.S.A. 66 40 52N 85 30W
Huntington, W. Va., U.S.A. 66 38 20N 82 30W
Huntington Beach 68 33 40N 118 0W
Huntly 6 57 27N 2 48W
Huntsville, Canada 62 45 20N 79 14W
Huntsville, Ala., U.S.A. 66 34 45N 86 35W
Huntsville, Tex., U.S.A. 67 30 45N 95 35W
Huon, G. 56 7 0 S 147 30 E
Huonville 56 43 0 S 147 5 E
Huron, L. 62 45 0N 83 0W
Hurricane 68 37 10N 113 12W
Húsavík 27 66 3N 17 21W
Huskvarna 28 57 47N 14 15 E
Husum 13 54 27N 9 3 E
Hutchinson 67 38 3N 97 59W
Hüttental 13 50 52N 8 1 E
Huy 12 50 31N 5 15 E
Hvammur 27 65 13N 21 49W
Hvar 21 43 11N 16 28 E
Hvítá 27 64 40N 21 5W
Hvítá → 27 64 0N 20 58W
Hvítárvatn 27 64 37N 19 50W
Hwange 51 18 18 S 26 30 E
Hyderabad, India 38 17 22N 78 29 E
Hyderabad, Pakistan 36 25 23N 68 24 E
Hyères 11 43 8N 6 9 E
Hyères, Is. d' 11 43 0N 6 20 E
Hyōgo □ 44 35 15N 135 0 E
Hythe 5 51 4N 1 5 E
Hyvinkää 27 60 38N 24 50 E

I

I-n-Gall 49 16 51N 7 1 E
Iaşi 15 47 10N 27 40 E
Ibadan 49 7 22N 3 58 E
Ibagué 72 4 20N 75 20W
Ibar → 24 43 43N 20 45 E
Ibaraki □ 44 36 10N 140 10 E
Ibarra 72 0 21N 78 7W
Ibi 49 8 15N 9 44 E
Ibiza 19 38 54N 1 26 E
Icá 72 14 0 S 75 48W
Iça → 72 2 55 S 67 58W
Iceland ■ 27 65 0N 19 0W
Icha 31 55 30N 156 0 E
Ichchapuram 38 19 10N 84 40 E
Ichihara 44 35 28N 140 5 E
Ichikawa 44 35 44N 139 55 E
Ichinomiya 44 35 18N 136 48 E
Idaho □ 68 44 10N 114 0W
Idaho Falls 68 43 30N 112 1W
Idar-Oberstein 13 49 43N 7 19 E
Idd el Ghanam 50 11 30N 24 19 E
Iddan 47 6 10N 48 55 E
Idehan 50 27 10N 11 30 E
Idehan Marzūq 50 24 50N 13 51 E
Idelès 49 23 50N 5 53 E
Idfû 50 25 0N 32 49 E
Ídhi Óros 26 35 15N 24 45 E
Ídhra 26 37 20N 23 28 E
Idiofa 51 4 55 S 19 42 E
Ieper 12 50 51N 2 53 E
Ierápetra 26 35 0N 25 44 E
Ierzu 22 39 48N 9 32 E
Ifanadiana 53 21 19 S 47 39 E
Ife 49 7 30N 4 31 E
Ifni 49 29 29N 10 12W
Iforas, Adrar des 49 19 40N 1 40 E
Igarka 31 67 30N 86 33 E
Igbetti 49 8 44N 4 8 E
Iggesund 28 61 39N 17 10 E
Iglésias 22 39 19N 8 27 E
Igli 49 30 25N 2 19W
Iguaçu → 74 25 36 S 54 36W
Iguaçu, Cat. del 74 25 41 S 54 26W
Iguaçu Falls = Iguaçu, Cat. del 74 25 41 S 54 26W
Iguala de la Independencia 69 18 21N 99 32W
Igualada 19 41 37N 1 37 E
Iguéla 51 2 0 S 9 16 E
Ihosy 53 22 24 S 46 8 E
Ii 27 65 19N 25 22 E
Iida 44 35 35N 137 50 E
Iijoki → 27 65 20N 25 20 E
Iisalmi 27 63 32N 27 10 E
Iizuka 44 33 38N 130 42 E
Ijebu-Ode 49 6 47N 3 58 E
IJmuiden 12 52 28N 4 35 E
IJssel → 12 52 35N 5 50 E
IJsselmeer 12 52 45N 5 20 E
Ikaría 26 37 35N 26 10 E
Ikela 51 1 6 S 23 6 E
Iki 44 33 45N 129 42 E
Ilanskiy 31 56 14N 96 3 E
Île-Bouchard, L' 8 47 7N 0 26 E
Île-de-France 9 49 0N 2 20 E
Ile-Rousse, L' 11 42 38N 8 57 E
Ilebo 51 4 17 S 20 55 E
Ilek 30 51 32N 53 21 E
Ilek → 30 51 30N 53 22 E
Ilfracombe, Australia 56 23 30 S 144 30 E
Ilfracombe, U.K. 5 51 13N 4 8W
Ilhéus 73 14 49 S 39 2W
Ili → 30 45 53N 77 10 E
Ilich 30 40 50N 68 27 E
Iliodhrómia 26 39 12N 23 50 E
Ilkeston 5 52 59N 1 19W
Ille-et-Vilaine □ 8 48 10N 1 30W
Ille-sur-Têt 10 42 40N 2 38 E
Illiers-Combray 8 48 18N 1 15 E
Illinois □ 67 40 15N 89 30W
Illinois → 67 38 55N 90 28W
Ilmen, Oz. 32 58 15N 31 10 E
Ilo 72 17 40 S 71 20W
Iloilo 40 10 45N 122 33 E
Ilorin 49 8 30N 4 35 E
Imabari 44 34 4N 133 0 E
Imandra, Oz. 30 67 45N 33 0 E
Imari 44 33 15N 129 52 E
Imeni Poliny Osipenko 31 52 30N 136 29 E
Imi 47 6 28N 42 10 E
Immingham 5 53 37N 0 12W
Imola 21 44 20N 11 42 E
Impéria 20 43 52N 8 0 E
Imperial 65 51 21N 105 28W
Imperial Dam 68 32 50N 114 30W
Impfondo 51 1 40N 18 0 E
Imphy 10 46 55N 3 16 E
In Belbel 49 27 55N 1 12 E
In Salah 49 27 10N 2 32 E
Ina 44 35 50N 138 0 E
Ina-Bonchi 44 35 45N 137 58 E
Iñapari 72 11 0 S 69 40W
Inari 27 68 54N 27 5 E
Inarijärvi 27 69 0N 28 0 E
Inca 19 39 43N 2 54 E
Inchon 43 37 27N 126 40 E
Incomáti → 53 25 46 S 32 43 E
Incudine, L' 11 41 50N 9 12 E
Indalsälven → 27 62 36N 17 30 E
Independence, Kans., U.S.A. 67 37 10N 95 43W
Independence, Mo., U.S.A. 67 39 3N 94 25W
Independence Fjord 3 82 10N 29 0W
India ■ 2 20 0N 78 0 E
Indian → 66 27 59N 80 34W
Indian Harbour 63 54 27N 57 13W
Indian Head 65 50 30N 103 41W
Indian Ocean 2 5 0 S 75 0 E
Indiana 66 40 38N 79 9W
Indiana □ 66 40 0N 86 0W
Indianapolis 66 39 42N 86 10W
Indiga 30 67 50N 48 50 E
Indigirka → 31 70 48N 148 54 E
Indonesia ■ 39 5 0 S 115 0 E
Indore 36 22 42N 75 53 E
Indravati → 38 19 20N 80 20 E
Indre □ 9 46 50N 1 39 E
Indre → 8 47 16N 0 11 E
Indre-et-Loire □ 8 47 20N 0 40 E
Indus → 36 24 20N 67 47 E
İnebolu 45 41 55N 33 40 E
İnegöl 45 40 5N 29 31 E
Ingende 51 0 12 S 18 57 E
Ingersoll 62 43 4N 80 55W
Ingham 56 18 43 S 146 10 E
Ingleborough 5 54 11N 2 23W
Inglewood 68 33 58N 118 21W
Ingólfshöfði 27 63 48N 16 39W
Ingolstadt 13 48 45N 11 26 E
Ingraj Bazar 37 24 58N 88 10 E
Ingulec 34 47 42N 33 14 E
Inhambane 53 23 54 S 35 30 E
Inhaminga 51 18 26 S 35 0 E
Inharrime 53 24 30 S 35 0 E
Inishbofin 7 53 35N 10 12W
Inishmore 7 53 8N 9 45W
Inishowen 7 55 14N 7 15W
Injune 56 25 53 S 148 32 E
Inn → 13 48 35N 13 28 E
Inner Hebrides 6 57 0N 6 30W
Inner Mongolia = Nei Monggol Zizhiqu □ 42 42 0N 112 0 E
Inner Sound 6 57 30N 5 55W
Innerste → 13 52 45N 9 40 E
Innisfail, Australia 56 17 33 S 146 5 E
Innisfail, Canada 64 52 0N 113 57W
Innsbruck 13 47 16N 11 23 E
Inny → 7 53 30N 7 50W
Inongo 51 1 55 S 18 30 E
Inowrocław 17 52 50N 18 12 E
Inquisivi 72 16 50 S 67 10W
Insein 41 16 50N 96 5 E
Interlaken 9 46 41N 7 50 E
International Falls 67 48 36N 93 25W
Inveraray 6 56 13N 5 5W
Inverbervie 6 56 50N 2 17W
Invercargill 59 46 24 S 168 24 E
Inverell 56 29 45 S 151 8 E
Invergordon 6 57 41N 4 10W
Inverness 6 57 29N 4 12W
Inverurie 6 57 15N 2 21W
Investigator Group 54 34 45 S 134 20 E
Investigator Str. 56 35 30 S 137 0 E
Inza 33 53 55N 46 25 E
Ioánnina □ 26 39 39N 20 57 E
Iola 67 38 0N 95 20W
Iona 6 56 20N 6 25W
Ionian Is. = Iónioi Nísoi 26 38 40N 20 0 E
Ionian Sea 4 37 30N 17 30 E
Iónioi Nísoi 26 38 40N 20 0 E
Íos 26 36 41N 25 20 E
Iowa □ 67 42 18N 93 30W
Iowa City 67 41 40N 91 35W
Iowa Falls 67 42 30N 93 15W
Ipiales 72 0 50N 77 37W
Ípiros □ 26 39 30N 20 30 E
Ipoh 41 4 35N 101 5 E
Ippy 50 6 5N 21 7 E
Ipswich, Australia 56 27 35 S 152 40 E
Ipswich, U.K. 5 52 4N 1 9 E
Iquique 72 20 19 S 70 5W
Iquitos 72 3 45 S 73 10W
Iracoubo 73 5 30N 53 10W
Iráklion 26 35 20N 25 12 E
Iran ■ 46 33 0N 53 0 E
Irapuato 69 20 41N 101 28W
Iraq ■ 45 33 0N 44 0 E
Irbid 45 32 35N 35 48 E
Irebu 51 0 40 S 17 46 E
Ireland ■ 7 53 0N 8 0W
Ireland's Eye 7 53 25N 6 4W
Iret 31 60 3N 154 20 E
Irian Jaya □ 40 4 0 S 137 0 E
Iringa 51 7 48 S 35 43 E
Iriri → 73 3 52 S 52 37W
Irish Republic ■ 7 53 0N 8 0W
Irish Sea 5 54 0N 5 0W
Irkineyeva 31 58 30N 96 49 E
Irkutsk 31 52 18N 104 20 E
Iroise, Mer d' 8 48 15N 4 45W
Iron Gate = Portile de Fier 25 44 42N 22 30 E
Iron Knob 56 32 46 S 137 8 E
Iron Mountain 62 45 49N 88 4W
Ironbridge 5 52 38N 2 29W
Ironton 66 38 35N 82 40W
Ironwood 62 46 30N 90 10W
Iroquois Falls 62 48 46N 80 41W
Irrawaddy → 41 15 50N 95 6 E
Irtysh → 30 61 4N 68 52 E
Irumu 51 1 32N 29 53 E
Irún 19 43 20N 1 52W
Irvine 6 55 37N 4 40W
Irvinestown 7 54 28N 7 38W
Is-sur-Tille 9 47 30N 5 8 E
Isaac → 56 22 55 S 149 20 E
Ísafjarðardjúp 27 66 10N 23 0W
Ísafjörður 27 66 5N 23 9W
Isangi 51 0 52N 24 10 E
Isar → 13 48 49N 12 58 E
Isbergues 9 50 36N 2 28 E
Íschia 22 40 45N 13 51 E
Ise 44 34 25N 136 45 E
Ise-Wan 44 34 43N 136 43 E
Isère □ 11 45 15N 5 40 E
Isère → 11 44 59N 4 51 E
Iserlohn 13 51 22N 7 40 E
Ishikari-Wan 44 43 25N 141 1 E
Ishikawa □ 44 36 30N 136 30 E
Ishinomaki 44 38 32N 141 20 E
Ishpeming 62 46 30N 87 40W
Isigny-sur-Mer 8 49 19N 1 6W
Isiolo 51 0 24N 37 33 E
Isiro 51 2 53N 27 40 E
İskenderun 45 36 32N 36 10 E

Isla → 6 56 32N 3 20W
Islamabad 46 33 40N 73 10 E
Island L. 65 53 47N 94 25W
Island Pond 63 48 25N 56 23W
Islay 6 55 46N 6 10W
Isle → 10 44 55N 0 15W
Isle-Adam, L' 9 49 6N 2 14 E
Isle-Jourdain, L', Gers, France 10 43 36N 1 5 E
Isle-Jourdain, L', Vienne, France 10 46 13N 0 31 E
Isle of Wight □ 5 50 40N 1 20W
Isle Royale 62 48 0N 88 50W
Isle-sur-le-Doubs, L' 9 47 26N 6 34 E
Ismail 34 45 22N 28 46 E
Ismâ'ilîya 50 30 37N 32 18 E
Isna 50 25 17N 32 30 E
İsparta 45 37 47N 30 30 E
İspica 23 36 47N 14 53 E
Israel ■ 45 32 0N 34 50 E
Issoire 10 45 32N 3 15 E
Issoudun 9 46 57N 2 0 E
Issyk-Kul, Ozero 30 42 25N 77 15 E
İstanbul 45 41 0N 29 0 E
Istra 21 45 10N 14 0 E
Istres 11 43 31N 4 59 E
Istria = Istra 21 45 10N 14 0 E
Itabuna 73 14 48 S 39 16W
Itaituba 73 4 10 S 55 50W
Itajaí 74 27 50 S 48 39W
Italy ■ 4 42 0N 13 0 E
Itaquí 74 29 8 S 56 30W
Itchen → 5 50 57N 1 20W
Ithaca 66 42 25N 76 30W
Itháki 26 38 25N 20 40 E
Ito 44 34 58N 139 5 E
Iton → 8 49 9N 1 12 E
Ituaçu 73 13 50 S 41 18W
Ituiutaba 73 19 0 S 49 25W
Iturup, Ostrov 31 45 0N 148 0 E
Itzehoe 13 53 56N 9 31 E
Ivalo 27 68 38N 27 35 E
Ivalojoki → 27 68 40N 27 40 E
Ivanhoe 56 32 56 S 144 20 E
Ivano-Frankovsk 34 48 40N 24 40 E
Ivanovo, Byelorussian S.S.R., U.S.S.R. 30 52 7N 25 29 E
Ivanovo, R.S.F.S.R., U.S.S.R. 33 57 5N 41 0 E
Ivory Coast ■ 49 7 30N 5 0W
Ivrea 20 45 30N 7 52 E
Iwaki 44 37 3N 140 55 E
Iwakuni 44 34 15N 132 8 E
Iwata 44 34 42N 137 51 E
Iwate-San 44 39 51N 141 0 E
Iwo 49 7 39N 4 9 E
Ixiamas 72 13 50 S 68 5W
Ixtepec 69 16 34N 95 6W
Ixtlán 69 20 11N 102 24W
Izamal 69 20 56N 89 1W
Izegem 12 50 55N 3 12 E
Izhevsk = Ustinov 30 56 51N 53 14 E
İzmir 45 38 25N 27 8 E
İzmit 45 40 45N 29 50 E
Izumi-sano 44 34 23N 135 18 E
Izumo 44 35 20N 132 46 E

J

Jabalpur 37 23 9N 79 58 E
Jablonec 14 50 43N 15 10 E
Jaca 19 42 35N 0 33W
Jacarèzinho 74 23 5 S 50 0W
Jackson, Mich., U.S.A. 66 42 18N 84 25W
Jackson, Miss., U.S.A. 67 32 20N 90 10W
Jackson, Tenn., U.S.A. 66 35 40N 88 50W
Jacksonville, Fla., U.S.A. 66 30 15N 81 38W
Jacksonville, Ill., U.S.A. 67 39 42N 90 15W
Jacksonville, N.C., U.S.A. 66 34 50N 77 29W
Jacksonville, Tex., U.S.A. 67 31 58N 95 19W
Jacmel 70 18 14N 72 32W
Jacobabad 36 28 20N 68 29 E
Jacques Cartier, Dét. de 63 50 0N 63 30W
Jadebusen 13 53 30N 8 15 E
Jādū 50 32 0N 12 0 E
Jaén, Peru 72 5 25 S 78 40W
Jaén, Spain 18 37 44N 3 43W
Jaffa = Tel Aviv-Yafo 45 32 4N 34 48 E
Jaffna 38 9 45N 80 2 E
Jagadhri 36 30 10N 77 20 E
Jagdalpur 38 19 3N 82 0 E
Jagst → 13 49 14N 9 11 E
Jagtial 38 18 50N 79 0 E
Jaguariaíva 74 24 10 S 49 50W
Jagüey Grande 70 22 35N 81 7W
Jahrom 46 28 30N 53 31 E
Jaipur 36 27 0N 75 50 E
Jakarta 40 6 9 S 106 49 E
Jakobstad 27 63 40N 22 43 E
Jalalabad 46 34 30N 70 29 E
Jalapa, Guat. 69 14 39N 89 59W
Jalapa, Mexico 69 17 43N 92 49W
Jalgaon, Maharashtra, India 36 21 2N 76 31 E
Jalgaon, Maharashtra, India 36 21 0N 75 42 E
Jalisco □ 69 20 20N 103 40W
Jalna 38 19 48N 75 38 E
Jalón → 19 41 47N 1 4W
Jalpaiguri 37 26 32N 88 46 E
Jaluit I. 57 6 0N 169 30 E
Jamaica ■ 70 18 10N 77 30W
Jamalpur, Bangla. 37 24 52N 89 56 E
Jamalpur, India 37 25 18N 86 28 E
Jambi 39 1 38 S 103 30 E
James → 67 42 52N 97 18W
James B. 62 51 30N 80 0W
James Range 54 24 10 S 132 30 E
Jamestown, Australia 56 33 10 S 138 32 E
Jamestown, N. Dak., U.S.A. 67 46 54N 98 42W
Jamestown, N.Y., U.S.A. 66 42 5N 79 18W
Jamkhandi 38 16 30N 75 15 E
Jammu 36 32 43N 74 54 E
Jamnagar 36 22 30N 70 6 E
Jamshedpur 37 22 44N 86 12 E
Jämtlands län □ 27 62 40N 13 50 E
Jan Mayen Is. 3 71 0N 9 0W
Janesville 67 42 39N 89 1W
Januária 73 15 25 S 44 25W
Janub Dârfûr □ 50 11 0N 25 0 E
Janub Kordofân □ 50 12 0N 30 0 E
Janville 9 48 10N 1 50 E
Janzé 8 47 55N 1 28W
Jaora 36 23 40N 75 10 E
Japan ■ 44 36 0N 136 0 E
Japan, Sea of 44 40 0N 135 0 E
Japan Trench 57 32 0N 142 0 E
Jarama → 19 40 2N 3 39W
Jargeau 9 47 50N 2 1 E
Jarnac 10 45 40N 0 11W
Jarny 9 49 9N 5 53 E
Jarosław 15 50 2N 22 42 E
Jarso 50 5 15N 37 30 E
Jarvis I. 58 0 15 S 159 55W
Jarwa 37 27 38N 82 30 E
Jäsk 46 25 38N 57 45 E
Jasło 15 49 45N 21 30 E
Jasper, Canada 64 52 55N 118 5W
Jasper, U.S.A. 66 33 48N 87 16W
Jászberény 15 47 30N 19 55 E
Jataí 73 17 58 S 51 48W
Játiva 19 39 0N 0 32W
Jaú 73 22 10 S 48 30W
Jaunpur 37 25 46N 82 44 E
Java = Jawa 40 7 0 S 110 0 E
Java Sea 39 4 35 S 107 15 E
Java Trench 57 10 0 S 110 0W
Javron 8 48 25N 0 25W
Jawa 40 7 0 S 110 0 E
Jayanti 37 26 45N 89 40 E
Jean Rabel 70 19 50N 73 5W
Jeanette, Ostrov 31 76 43N 158 0 E
Jebba 49 9 9N 4 48 E
Jebel, Bahr el → 50 9 30N 30 25 E
Jedburgh 6 55 28N 2 33W
Jedda = Jiddah 47 21 29N 39 10 E
Jędrzejów 17 50 35N 20 15 E
Jeetze → 13 53 9N 11 6 E
Jefferson, Mt. 68 44 45N 121 50W
Jefferson City 67 38 34N 92 10W
Jeffersonville 66 38 20N 85 42W
Jega 49 12 15N 4 23 E
Jelenia Góra 17 50 50N 15 45 E
Jelgava 32 56 41N 23 49 E
Jemeppe 12 50 37N 5 30 E
Jena 13 50 56N 11 33 E
Jenkins 66 37 13N 82 41W
Jennings 67 30 10N 92 45W
Jequié 73 13 51 S 40 5W
Jequitinhonha 73 16 30 S 41 0W
Jerada 49 34 17N 2 10W
Jérémie 70 18 40N 74 10W
Jerez de García Salinas 69 22 39N 103 0W
Jerez de la Frontera 18 36 41N 6 7W
Jerez de los Caballeros 18 38 20N 6 45W
Jerome 63 47 37N 82 14W
Jersey, I. 8 49 13N 2 7W
Jersey City 66 40 41N 74 8W
Jerseyville 67 39 5N 90 20W
Jerusalem 45 31 47N 35 10 E
Jervis B. 56 35 8 S 150 46 E
Jessore 37 23 10N 89 10 E
Jeypore 38 18 50N 82 38 E
Jhalawar 36 24 40N 76 10 E
Jhang Maghiana 36 31 15N 72 22 E
Jhansi 36 25 30N 78 36 E
Jhelum 36 33 0N 73 45 E
Jhelum → 36 31 20N 72 10 E
Jhunjhunu 36 28 10N 75 30 E
Jiamusi 42 46 40N 130 26 E
Ji'an 43 27 6N 114 59 E
Jiangmen 43 22 32N 113 0 E
Jiangsu □ 43 33 0N 120 0 E
Jiangxi □ 43 27 30N 116 0 E
Jian'ou 43 27 3N 118 17 E
Jiao Xian 42 36 18N 120 1 E
Jiaozuo 43 35 16N 113 12 E
Jiaxing 43 30 49N 120 45 E
Jiayi 43 23 30N 120 24 E
Jiddah 47 21 29N 39 10 E
Jihlava 14 49 28N 15 35 E
Jihlava → 14 48 55N 16 36 E
Jijel 49 36 52N 5 50 E
Jijiga 47 9 20N 42 50 E
Jilin 42 43 44N 126 30 E
Jiloca → 19 41 21N 1 39W
Jilong 43 25 8N 121 42 E
Jima 50 7 40N 36 47 E
Jiménez 69 27 8N 104 54W
Jinan 42 36 38N 117 1 E
Jingdezhen 43 29 20N 117 11 E
Jining, Nei Mongol Zizhiqu, China 42 41 5N 113 0 E
Jining, Shandong, China 43 35 22N 116 34 E
Jinja 51 0 25N 33 12 E
Jinotega 70 13 6N 85 59W
Jinotepe 70 11 50N 86 10W
Jinshi 43 29 40N 111 50 E
Jinzhou 42 41 5N 121 3 E
Jipijapa 72 1 0 S 80 40W
Jiquilpan de Juárez 69 19 59N 102 43W
Jisr ash Shughūr 45 35 49N 36 18 E
Jiu → 25 44 40N 23 25 E
Jiujiang 43 29 42N 115 58 E
Jixi 42 45 20N 130 50 E
João Pessoa 73 7 10 S 34 52W
Jobourg, Nez de 8 49 41N 1 57W
Jodhpur 36 26 23N 73 8 E
Jœuf 9 49 12N 6 0 E
Jofane 53 21 15 S 34 18 E
Jogjakarta = Yogyakarta 40 7 49 S 110 22 E
Johannesburg 53 26 10 S 28 2 E
John o' Groats 6 58 39N 3 3W
Johnson City, N.Y., U.S.A. 66 42 7N 75 57W
Johnson City, Tenn., U.S.A. 66 36 18N 82 21W
Johnston, L. 54 32 25 S 120 30 E
Johnston I. 58 17 10N 169 8W
Johnstown, N.Y., U.S.A. 66 43 1N 74 20W
Johnstown, Pa., U.S.A. 66 40 19N 78 53W
Johor □ 41 2 5N 103 20 E
Johor Baharu 41 1 28N 103 46 E
Joigny 9 47 58N 3 20 E
Joinvile 74 26 15 S 48 55 E
Joinville 9 48 27N 5 10 E
Jokkmokk 27 66 35N 19 50 E
Jökulsá á Dal → 27 65 40N 14 16W
Jökulsá Fjöllum → 27 66 10N 16 30W
Joliet 67 41 30N 88 0W
Joliette 62 46 3N 73 24W
Jolo 40 6 0N 121 0 E
Jones Sound 3 76 0N 85 0W
Jonesboro 67 35 50N 90 45W
Jonglei □ 50 7 30N 32 30 E
Jönköping 28 57 45N 14 10 E
Jönköpings län □ 28 57 30N 14 30 E
Jonquière 63 48 27N 71 14W
Jonzac 10 45 27N 0 28W
Joplin 67 37 0N 94 31W
Jordan ■ 45 31 0N 36 0 E
Jordan → 45 31 48N 35 32 E
Jörn 27 65 4N 20 1 E
Jos 49 9 53N 8 51 E
José de San Martín 74 44 4 S 70 26W
Joseph Bonaparte G. 54 14 35 S 128 50 E
Josselin 8 47 57N 2 33W
Jostedal 27 61 35N 7 15 E
Jotunheimen 28 61 35N 8 25 E
Jowzjān □ 46 36 10N 66 0 E
Joyeuse 11 44 29N 4 16 E
Juan de Fuca Str. 68 48 15N 124 0W
Juan de Nova 53 17 3 S 43 45 E
Juan Fernández, Arch. de 58 33 50 S 80 0W
Juàzeiro 73 9 30 S 40 30W
Juàzeiro do Norte 73 7 10 S 39 18W
Juby, C. 49 28 0N 12 59W
Júcar → 19 39 5N 0 10W
Juchitán de Zaragoza 69 16 26N 95 1W
Jugoslavia = Yugoslavia ■ 24 44 0N 20 0 E
Juillac 10 45 20N 1 19 E
Juiz de Fora 73 21 43 S 43 19W
Juli 72 16 10 S 69 25W
Julia Creek 56 20 39 S 141 44 E
Juliaca 72 15 25 S 70 10W
Julianehåb 3 60 43N 46 0W
Jullundur 36 31 20N 75 40 E
Jumet 12 50 27N 4 25 E
Jumilla 19 38 28N 1 19W
Jumla 37 29 15N 82 13 E
Jumna = Yamuna → 37 25 30N 81 53 E
Junagadh 36 21 30N 70 30 E
Junction B. 54 11 52 S 133 55 E
Jundah 56 24 46 S 143 2 E
Jundiaí 74 24 30 S 47 0W
Juneau 61 58 20N 134 20W
Junee 56 34 53 S 147 35 E
Junggar Pendi 42 44 30N 86 0 E
Junín 74 34 33 S 60 57W
Jur, Nahr el → 50 8 45N 29 15 E
Jura 6 56 0N 5 50W
Jura □ 9 46 47N 5 45 E
Jura, Mts. 11 46 40N 6 5 E
Jura, Sd. of 6 55 57N 5 45W
Jurado 72 7 7N 77 46W
Juruá → 72 2 37 S 65 44W
Juruena 72 13 0 S 58 10W
Juruena → 72 7 20 S 58 3W
Jussey 9 47 50N 5 55 E
Juticalpa 70 14 40N 86 12W
Jutland = Jylland 28 56 25N 9 30 E
Juventud, I. de la 70 21 40N 82 40W
Juvigny-sous-Andaine 8 48 32N 0 30W
Juvisy-sur-Orge 9 48 42N 2 22 E
Juzennecourt 9 48 10N 4 58 E
Jylland 28 56 25N 9 30 E
Jyväskylä 27 62 14N 25 50 E

K

Kaap Plateau 52 28 30 S 24 0 E
Kaapkruis 52 21 55 S 13 57 E
Kaapstad = Cape Town 52 33 55 S 18 22 E
Kabala 49 9 38N 11 37W
Kabale 51 1 15 S 30 0 E
Kabalo 51 6 0 S 27 0 E
Kabambare 51 4 41 S 27 39 E
Kabara 49 16 40N 2 50W
Kabardino-Balkar-A.S.S.R. □ 35 43 30N 43 30 E
Kabarega Falls 51 2 15N 31 30 E
Kabba 49 7 50N 6 3 E
Kabīr Kūh 45 33 0N 47 30 E
Kabkabīyah 50 13 50N 24 0 E
Kabompo → 51 14 10 S 23 11 E
Kabongo 51 7 22 S 25 33 E
Kābul 46 34 28N 69 11 E
Kābul □ 46 34 30N 69 0 E
Kabwe 51 14 30 S 28 29 E
Kachchh, Gulf of 36 22 50N 69 15 E
Kachchh, Rann of 36 24 0N 70 0 E
Kackar 35 40 45N 41 10 E
Kadan Kyun 41 12 30N 98 20 E
Kadina 56 34 0 S 137 43 E
Kadoma 51 18 20 S 29 52 E
Kâdugli 50 11 0N 29 45 E
Kaduna 49 10 30N 7 21 E
Kaédi 49 16 9N 13 28W
Kaelé 50 10 7N 14 27 E
Kaesŏng 43 37 58N 126 35 E
Kāf 45 31 25N 37 29 E
Kafakumba 51 9 38 S 23 46 E
Kafanchan 49 9 40N 8 20 E
Kaffrine 49 14 8N 15 36W
Kafia Kingi 50 9 20N 24 25 E
Kafirévs, Ákra 26 38 9N 24 38 E
Kafulwe 51 9 0 S 29 1 E
Kaga Bandoro 50 7 0N 19 10 E
Kagan 30 39 43N 64 33 E
Kagawa □ 44 34 15N 134 0 E
Kagoshima 44 31 35N 130 33 E
Kagoshima □ 44 31 30N 130 30 E
Kagoshima-Wan 44 31 25N 130 40 E
Kahama 51 4 8 S 32 30 E
Kahemba 51 7 18 S 18 55 E
Kai, Kepulauan 40 5 55 S 132 45W
Kaiama 49 9 36N 4 1 E
Kaieteur Falls 72 5 1N 59 10W
Kainji Res. 49 10 1N 4 40 E
Kaipara Harbour 59 36 25 S 174 14 E
Kairouan 49 35 45N 10 5 E
Kaiserslautern 13 49 30N 7 43 E
Kajaani 27 64 17N 27 46 E
Kajabbi 56 20 0 S 140 1 E
Kajo Kaji 50 3 58N 31 40 E
Kaka 50 10 38N 32 10 E
Kakabeka Falls 62 48 24N 89 37W
Kakamega 51 0 20N 34 46 E
Kakegawa 44 34 45N 138 1 E
Kakhovka 34 46 40N 33 15 E
Kakhovskoye Vdkhr. 34 47 5N 34 16 E
Kakinada 38 16 57N 82 11 E
Kakogawa 44 34 46N 134 51 E
Kalabagh 36 33 0N 71 28 E
Kalabáka 26 39 42N 21 39 E
Kalabo 51 14 58 S 22 40 E
Kalach 33 50 22N 41 0 E
Kalahari 52 24 0 S 21 30 E
Kalakan 31 55 15N 116 45 E
Kalamata 26 37 3N 22 10 E
Kalamazoo 66 42 20N 85 35W
Kalamazoo → 66 42 40N 86 12W
Kalemie 51 5 55 S 29 9 E
Kálfafellsstaður 27 64 11N 15 53W
Kalgoorlie-Boulder 54 30 40 S 121 22 E
Kaliakra, Nos 25 43 21N 28 30 E
Kalima 51 2 33 S 26 32 E
Kálimnos 26 37 0N 27 0 E
Kalinin 33 56 55N 35 55 E
Kaliningrad 32 54 42N 20 32 E
Kalispell 68 48 10N 114 22W
Kalisz 17 51 45N 18 8 E
Kaliua 51 5 5 S 31 48 E
Kalix → 27 65 50N 23 11 E
Kalkrand 52 24 1 S 17 35 E
Kallsjön 27 63 38N 13 0 E
Kalmar 28 56 40N 16 20 E
Kalmyk A.S.S.R. □ 35 46 5N 46 1 E
Kalmykovo 35 49 0N 51 47 E
Kalocsa 15 46 32N 19 0 E
Kalomo 51 17 0 S 26 30 E
Kaluga 33 54 35N 36 10 E
Kalundborg 28 55 41N 11 5 E
Kalutara 38 6 35N 80 0 E
Kama → 30 55 45N 52 0 E
Kamaishi 44 39 20N 142 0 E
Kamandorskiye Ostrava 31 55 0N 167 0 E
Kamaran 47 15 21N 42 35 E
Kamchatka, P-ov. 31 57 0N 160 0 E
Kamenets-Podolskiy 34 48 45N 26 10 E
Kamenjak, Rt 21 44 47N 13 55 E
Kamensk-Shakhtinskiy 35 48 23N 40 20 E
Kamensk Uralskiy 30 56 25N 62 2 E
Kamenskoye 31 62 45N 165 30 E
Kamina 51 8 45 S 25 0 E
Kamloops 64 50 40N 120 20W
Kampala 51 0 20N 32 30 E
Kampar 41 4 18N 101 9 E
Kampen 12 52 33N 5 53 E
Kampot 41 10 36N 104 10 E
Kampuchea = Cambodia ■ 41 12 15N 105 0 E
Kamsack 65 51 34N 101 54W
Kamyshin 33 50 10N 45 24 E
Kanaaupscow 62 54 2N 76 30W
Kanagawa □ 44 35 20N 139 20 E
Kananga 51 5 55 S 22 18 E
Kanash 33 55 30N 47 32 E
Kanawha → 66 38 50N 82 8W
Kanazawa 44 36 30N 136 38 E
Kanchenjunga 37 27 50N 88 10 E
Kanchipuram 38 12 52N 79 45 E
Kanda Kanda 51 6 52 S 23 48 E
Kandalaksha 30 67 9N 32 30 E
Kandi 49 11 7N 2 55 E
Kandla 36 23 0N 70 10 E
Kandy 38 7 18N 80 43 E
Kane Basin 3 79 1N 73 0W
Kane Bassin 3 79 30N 68 0W
Kangar 41 6 27N 100 12 E
Kangaroo I. 56 35 45 S 137 0 E
Kangerdlugsuak 3 68 10N 32 20W
Kangnŭng 43 37 45N 128 54 E
Kango 51 0 11N 10 5 E
Kaniapiskau → 63 56 40N 69 30W
Kaniapiskau L. 63 54 10N 69 55W
Kanin, P-ov. 30 68 0N 45 0 E
Kanin Nos, Mys 30 68 45N 43 20 E
Kankakee 67 41 6N 87 50W
Kankakee → 66 41 23N 88 16W
Kankan 49 10 23N 9 15W
Kanker 38 20 10N 81 40 E
Kankunskiy 31 57 37N 126 8 E
Kannapolis 66 35 32N 80 37W
Kannauj 37 27 3N 79 56 E
Kano 49 12 2N 8 30 E
Kanowna 54 30 32 S 121 31 E
Kanoya 44 31 25N 130 50 E
Kanpur 37 26 28N 80 20 E
Kansas □ 67 38 40N 98 0W
Kansas City, Kans., U.S.A. 67 39 0N 94 40W
Kansas City, Mo., U.S.A. 67 39 3N 94 30W
Kansk 31 56 20N 95 37 E
Kanturk 7 52 10N 8 55W
Kanuma 44 36 34N 139 42 E
Kanye 52 25 0 S 25 28 E
Kaohsiung = Gaoxiong 43 22 38N 120 18 E
Kaokoveld 52 19 15 S 14 30 E
Kaolack 49 14 5N 16 8W
Kapanga 51 8 30 S 22 40 E
Kapfenberg 14 47 26N 15 18 E
Kapiri Mposhi 51 13 59 S 28 43 E
Kāpīsā □ 46 35 0N 69 20 E
Kapoeta 50 4 50N 33 35 E
Kaposvár 15 46 25N 17 47 E
Kapuas → 39 0 25 S 109 20 E
Kapuskasing 62 49 25N 82 30W
Kara Bogaz Gol, Zaliv 30 41 0N 53 30 E
Kara Kalpak A.S.S.R. □ 30 43 0N 60 0 E
Kara Kum = Karakum, Peski 30 39 30N 60 0 E
Kara Sea 30 75 0N 70 0 E
Karabük 45 41 12N 32 37 E
Karabutak 30 49 59N 60 14 E
Karachi 36 24 53N 67 0 E
Karad 38 17 15N 74 10 E
Karadeniz Boğazı 45 41 10N 29 10 E
Karaganda 30 49 50N 73 10 E
Karaginskiy, Ostrov 31 58 45N 164 0 E
Karaikal 38 10 59N 79 50 E
Karaikkudi 38 10 0N 78 45 E
Karaj 46 35 48N 51 0 E
Karakum, Peski 30 39 30N 60 0 E
Karalon 31 57 5N 115 50 E
Karaman 45 37 14N 33 13 E
Karasburg 52 28 0 S 18 44 E
Karasjok 27 69 27N 25 30 E
Karasuk 30 53 44N 78 2 E
Karatau 30 43 10N 70 28 E
Karatau, Khrebet 30 43 30N 69 30 E
Karbalā 45 32 36N 44 3 E
Karcag 15 47 19N 20 57 E
Karda 31 55 0N 103 16 E
Kardhítsa 26 39 23N 21 54 E
Karelian A.S.S.R. □ 30 65 30N 32 30 E
Karen 41 12 49N 92 53 E
Kariba Dam 51 16 30 S 28 35 E
Kariba Gorge 51 16 30 S 28 50 E
Kariba L. 51 16 40 S 28 25 E
Karibib 52 22 0 S 15 56 E
Karimnagar 38 18 26N 79 10 E
Karimunjawa, Kepulauan 39 5 50 S 110 30 E
Karin 47 10 50N 45 52 E
Kariya 44 34 58N 137 1 E
Karkar I. 56 4 40 S 146 0 E
Karkinitskiy Zaliv 34 45 56N 33 0 E
Karl-Marx-Stadt 13 50 50N 12 55 E
Karlovac 21 45 31N 15 36 E
Karlovy Vary 14 50 13N 12 51 E
Karlsborg 28 58 33N 14 33 E
Karlshamn 28 56 10N 14 51 E
Karlskoga 28 59 22N 14 33 E
Karlskrona 28 56 10N 15 35 E
Karlsruhe 13 49 3N 8 23 E
Karlstad 28 59 23N 13 30 E
Karnal 36 29 42N 77 2 E
Karnali → 37 29 0N 83 20 E
Karnataka □ 38 13 15N 77 0 E
Karnische Alpen 14 46 36N 13 0 E
Kärnten □ 14 46 52N 13 30 E
Karonga 51 9 57 S 33 55 E
Karora 50 17 44N 38 15 E
Kárpathos 26 35 37N 27 10 E
Kars 34 40 40N 43 5 E
Karshi 30 38 53N 65 48 E
Karsun 33 54 14N 46 57 E
Kartaly 30 53 3N 60 40 E
Karungu 51 0 50 S 34 10 E
Karur 38 10 59N 78 2 E
Kasai → 51 3 30 S 16 10 E
Kasama 51 10 16 S 31 9 E
Kasanga 51 8 30 S 31 10 E
Kasangulu 51 4 33 S 15 15 E
Kasaragod 38 12 30N 74 58 E
Kasempa 51 13 30 S 25 44 E
Kasenga 51 10 20 S 28 45 E
Kāshān 46 34 5N 51 30 E
Kashi 42 39 30N 76 2 E
Kāshmar 46 35 16N 58 26 E
Kashmir 29 34 0N 76 0 E
Kasimov 33 54 55N 41 20 E
Kaskinen 27 62 22N 21 15 E
Kaskö 27 62 22N 21 15 E
Kasongo 51 4 30 S 26 33 E
Kasongo Lunda 51 6 35 S 16 49 E
Kásos 26 35 20N 26 55 E
Kassala 50 15 30N 36 0 E
Kassalâ □ 50 15 20N 36 26 E
Kassel 13 51 19N 9 32 E
Kastoría 26 40 30N 21 19 E
Kasulu 51 4 37 S 30 5 E
Kasur 36 31 5N 74 25 E
Kata 31 58 46N 102 40 E
Katako Kombe 51 3 25 S 24 20 E
Katangi 36 21 56N 79 50 E
Katangli 31 51 42N 143 14 E
Katanning 54 33 40 S 117 33 E
Katherine 54 14 27 S 132 20 E
Kathiawar 36 22 20N 71 0 E
Katihar 37 25 34N 87 36 E
Katima Mulilo 52 17 28 S 24 13 E
Katiola 49 8 10N 5 10W
Katmandu 37 27 45N 85 20 E

Katoomba 56 33 41 S 150 19 E
Katowice 17 50 17N 19 5 E
Katrine, L. 6 56 15N 4 30W
Katrineholm 28 59 9N 16 12 E
Katsina 49 13 0N 7 32 E
Katsuura 44 35 10N 140 20 E
Kattegatt 28 57 0N 11 20 E
Katwijk-aan-Zee 12 52 12N 4 24 E
Kaufbeuren 13 47 50N 10 37 E
Kaukauna 66 44 20N 88 13W
Kaukonen 27 67 31N 24 53 E
Kauliranta 27 66 27N 23 41 E
Kaunas 32 54 54N 23 54 E
Kaura Namoda 49 12 37N 6 33 E
Kautokeino 27 69 0N 23 4 E
Kavacha 31 60 16N 169 51 E
Kavali 38 14 55N 80 1 E
Kavála 26 40 57N 24 28 E
Kavieng 56 2 36 S 150 51 E
Kavkaz, Bolshoi 35 42 50N 44 0 E
Kawagoe 44 35 55N 139 29 E
Kawaguchi 44 35 52N 139 45 E
Kawambwa 51 9 48 S 29 3 E
Kawardha 37 22 0N 81 17 E
Kawasaki 44 35 35N 139 42 E
Kaya 49 13 4N 1 10W
Kayes 49 14 25N 11 30W
Kayseri 45 38 45N 35 30 E
Kazachinskoye 31 56 16N 107 36 E
Kazachye 31 70 52N 135 58 E
Kazakh S.S.R. □ 34 50 0N 70 0 E
Kazan 33 55 48N 49 3 E
Kazanlŭk 25 42 38N 25 20 E
Kāzerūn 46 29 38N 51 40 E
Kazumba 51 6 25 S 22 5 E
Ké-Macina 49 13 58N 5 22W
Kéa 26 37 35N 24 22 E
Kebnekaise 27 67 53N 18 33 E
Kebri Dehar 47 6 45N 44 17 E
Kecskemét 15 46 57N 19 42 E
Kedah □ 41 5 50N 100 40 E
Kediri 40 7 51 S 112 1 E
Kédougou 49 12 35N 12 10W
Keeling Is. = Cocos Is. 2 12 10 S 96 55 E
Keene 66 42 57N 72 17W
Keeper Hill 7 52 46N 8 17W
Keer-Weer, C. 56 14 0 S 141 32 E
Keetmanshoop 52 26 35 S 18 8 E
Keewatin 65 49 46N 94 34W
Kefallinía 26 38 20N 20 30 E
Keffi 49 8 55N 7 43 E
Keflavík 27 64 2N 22 35W
Kehl 13 48 34N 7 50 E
Keighley 5 53 52N 1 54W
Keith 6 57 33N 2 58W
Kekri 36 26 0N 75 10 E
Kël 31 69 30N 124 10 E
Kelang 41 3 2N 101 26 E
Kelantan □ 41 5 10N 102 0 E
Kelantan → 41 6 13N 102 14 E
Kelibia 50 36 50N 11 3 E
Kellé 51 0 8 S 14 38 E
Kellerberrin 54 31 36 S 117 38 E
Kellett C. 3 72 0N 126 0W
Kelloselkä 27 66 56N 28 53 E
Kells = Ceanannus Mor 7 53 42N 6 53W
Kélo 50 9 10N 15 45 E
Kelowna 64 49 50N 119 25W
Kelso, U.K. 6 55 36N 2 27W
Kelso, U.S.A. 68 46 10N 122 57W
Keluang 41 2 3N 103 18 E
Kelvington 65 52 10N 103 30W
Kem 30 65 0N 34 38 E
Kemerovo 30 55 20N 86 5 E
Kemi 27 65 44N 24 34 E
Kemijärvi 27 66 43N 27 22 E
Kemijoki → 27 65 47N 24 32 E
Kempsey 56 31 1 S 152 50 E
Kempten 13 47 42N 10 18 E
Kendal 5 54 19N 2 44W
Kende 49 11 30N 4 12 E
Kendrapara 36 20 35N 86 30 E
Kenema 49 7 50N 11 14W
Kenge 51 4 50 S 17 4 E
Kenhardt 52 29 19 S 21 12 E
Kenitra 49 34 15N 6 40W
Kenmare 7 51 52N 9 35W
Kenmare → 7 51 40N 10 0W
Kenn Reef 55 21 12 S 155 46 E
Kennet → 5 51 24N 0 58W
Kennewick 68 46 11N 119 2W
Kenogami → 62 51 6N 84 28W
Kenora 65 49 47N 94 29W
Kenosha 67 42 33N 87 48W
Kent 66 41 8N 81 20W
Kent □ 5 51 12N 0 40 E
Kentau 30 43 32N 68 36 E
Kentucky □ 66 37 20N 85 0W
Kentucky → 66 38 41N 85 11W
Kentville 63 45 6N 64 29W
Kenya ■ 51 1 0N 38 0 E
Kenya, Mt. 51 0 10 S 37 18 E
Keokuk 67 40 25N 91 24W
Keppel B. 55 23 21 S 150 55 E
Kepsut 45 39 40N 28 9 E
Kerala □ 38 11 0N 76 15 E
Kerang 56 35 40 S 143 55 E
Kerch 34 45 20N 36 20 E
Kerchoual 49 17 12N 0 20 E
Keren 50 15 45N 38 28 E
Kerguelen 2 48 15 S 69 10 E
Kericho 51 0 22 S 35 15 E
Kerki 30 37 50N 65 12 E
Kérkira 26 39 38N 19 50 E
Kerkrade 12 50 53N 6 4 E
Kermadec Is. 57 30 0 S 178 15W
Kermadec Trench 57 30 30 S 176 0W
Kermān 46 30 15N 57 1 E
Kermān □ 46 30 0N 57 0 E
Kermānshāh = Bākhtarān 45 34 23N 47 0 E
Kerrobert 65 52 0N 109 11W
Kerry □ 7 52 7N 9 35W
Kerry Hd. 7 52 26N 9 56W
Kerulen → 42 48 48N 117 0 E
Kerzaz 49 29 29N 1 37W
Keski-Suomen lääni □ 27 62 0N 25 30 E
Kestenga 30 66 0N 31 50 E
Keswick 5 54 35N 3 9W
Keta 49 5 49N 1 0 E
Kettering 5 52 24N 0 44W
Kewanee 67 41 18N 89 55W
Keweenaw B. 62 46 56N 88 23W
Keweenaw Pen. 67 47 30N 88 0W
Keyser 66 39 26N 79 0W
Kezhma 31 58 59N 101 9 E
Khabarovsk 31 48 30N 135 5 E
Khakhea 52 24 48 S 23 22 E
Khalkhāl 45 37 37N 48 32 E
Khalkís 26 38 27N 23 42 E
Khalmer Yu 30 67 58N 65 1 E
Khalturin 33 58 40N 48 50 E
Khambat, G. of 36 20 45N 72 30 E
Khambhat 36 22 23N 72 33 E
Khamir 47 16 0N 44 0 E
Khānābād 46 36 45N 69 5 E
Khānaqīn 45 34 23N 45 25 E
Khandwa 36 21 49N 76 22 E
Khandyga 31 62 42N 135 35 E
Khanewal 36 30 20N 71 55 E
Khaniá 26 35 30N 24 4 E
Khanion Kólpos 26 35 33N 23 55 E
Khanka, Ozero 31 45 0N 132 24 E
Khapcheranga 31 49 42N 112 24 E
Kharagpur 37 22 20N 87 25 E
Kharda 38 18 40N 75 34 E
Khârga, El Wâhât el 50 25 10N 30 35 E
Kharkov 34 49 58N 36 20 E
Kharovsk 33 59 56N 40 13 E
Khartoum = El Khartûm 50 15 31N 32 35 E
Khashm el Girba 50 14 59N 35 58 E
Khaskovo 25 41 56N 25 30 E
Khatanga 31 72 0N 102 20 E
Khatanga → 31 72 55N 106 0 E
Khatangskiy, Zaliv 3 66 0N 112 0 E
Khatyrka 31 62 3N 175 15 E
Khenchela 49 35 28N 7 11 E
Khenifra 49 32 58N 5 46W
Kherson 34 46 35N 32 35 E
Kheta → 31 71 54N 102 6 E
Khilok 31 51 30N 110 45 E
Khíos 26 38 27N 26 9 E
Khmelnitskiy 34 49 23N 27 0 E
Kholm, Afghan. 46 36 45N 67 40 E
Kholm, U.S.S.R. 32 57 10N 31 15 E
Kholmsk 31 47 40N 142 5 E
Khon Kaen 41 16 30N 102 47 E
Khonu 31 66 30N 143 12 E
Khoper → 33 49 30N 42 20 E
Khorāsān □ 46 34 0N 58 0 E
Khorat, Cao Nguyen 41 15 30N 102 50 E
Khorog 30 37 30N 71 36 E
Khorramābād 45 33 30N 48 25 E
Khorrāmshahr 45 30 29N 48 15 E
Khouribga 49 32 58N 6 57W
Khulna 37 22 45N 89 34 E
Khūrīyā Mūrīyā, Jazā 'ir 47 17 30N 55 58 E
Khushab 36 32 20N 72 20 E
Khūzestān □ 45 31 0N 49 0 E
Khvor 46 33 45N 55 0 E
Khvoy 45 38 35N 45 0 E
Kibangou 51 3 26 S 12 22 E
Kibombo 51 3 57 S 25 53 E
Kibondo 51 3 35 S 30 45 E
Kibwesa 51 6 30 S 29 58 E
Kibwezi 51 2 27 S 37 57 E
Kichiga 31 59 50N 163 5 E
Kicking Horse Pass 64 51 28N 116 16W
Kidal 49 18 26N 1 22 E
Kidderminster 5 52 24N 2 13W
Kiel 13 54 16N 10 8 E
Kiel Kanal = Nord-Ostsee Kanal 13 54 15N 9 40 E
Kielce 17 50 52N 20 42 E
Kiev = Kiyev 32 50 30N 30 28 E
Kiffa 49 16 37N 11 24W
Kigali 51 1 59 S 30 4 E
Kigoma-Ujiji 51 4 55 S 29 36 E
Kii-Suidō 44 33 40N 135 0 E
Kikinda 24 45 50N 20 30 E
Kikládhes 26 37 20N 24 30 E
Kikwit 51 5 0 S 18 45 E
Kildare 7 53 10N 6 50W
Kildare □ 7 53 10N 6 50W
Kilimanjaro 51 3 7 S 37 20 E
Kilindini 51 4 4 S 39 40 E
Kilis 45 36 50N 37 10 E
Kilkee 7 52 41N 9 40W
Kilkenny 7 52 40N 7 17W
Kilkenny □ 7 52 35N 7 15W
Kilkieran B. 7 53 18N 9 45W
Killala 7 54 13N 9 12W
Killala B. 7 54 20N 9 12W
Killaloe 7 52 48N 8 28W
Killarney, Canada 65 49 10N 99 40W
Killarney, Ireland 7 52 2N 9 30W
Killarney, Lakes of 7 52 0N 9 30W
Killary Harbour 7 53 38N 9 52W
Killiecrankie, Pass of 6 56 44N 3 46W
Killin 6 56 28N 4 20W
Killíni 26 37 54N 22 25 E
Killybegs 7 54 38N 8 26W
Kilmarnock 6 55 36N 4 30W
Kilosa 51 6 48 S 37 0 E
Kilrush 7 52 39N 9 30W
Kilwa Kivinje 51 8 45 S 39 25 E
Kimba 55 33 8 S 136 23 E
Kimbe B. 56 5 15 S 150 30 E
Kimberley, Australia 54 16 20 S 127 0 E
Kimberley, Canada 64 49 40N 115 59W
Kimberley, S. Africa 52 28 43 S 24 46 E
Kimry 33 56 55N 37 15 E
Kinabalu 39 6 3N 116 14 E
Kinbasket L. 64 52 0N 118 10W
Kincardine 62 44 10N 81 40W
Kindersley 65 51 30N 109 10W
Kindia 49 10 0N 12 52W
Kindu 51 2 55 S 25 50 E
Kineshma 33 57 30N 42 5 E
King George Is. 62 57 20N 80 30W
King George Sd. 54 35 5 S 118 0 E
King I., Australia 56 39 50 S 144 0 E
King I., Canada 64 52 10N 127 40W
King Leopold Ranges 54 17 30 S 125 45 E
King Sd. 54 16 50 S 123 20 E
King William's Town 52 32 51 S 27 22 E
Kingaroy 56 26 32 S 151 51 E
Kingman 68 35 12N 114 2W
Kings Canyon National Park 68 37 0N 118 35W
King's Lynn 5 52 45N 0 25 E
Kingsbridge 5 50 17N 3 46W
Kingscourt 7 53 55N 6 48W
Kingsport 66 36 33N 82 36W
Kingston, Canada 62 44 14N 76 30W
Kingston, Jamaica 70 18 0N 76 50W
Kingston, U.S.A. 66 41 55N 74 0W
Kingston South East 56 36 51 S 139 55 E
Kingston-upon-Thames 5 51 23N 0 20W
Kingstown 70 13 10N 61 10W
Kingsville, Canada 62 42 2N 82 45W
Kingsville, U.S.A. 67 27 30N 97 53W
Kingussie 6 57 5N 4 2W
Kinistino 65 52 57N 105 2W
Kinkala 51 4 18 S 14 49 E
Kinnairds Hd. 6 57 40N 2 0W
Kinross 6 56 13N 3 25W
Kinsale 7 51 42N 8 31W
Kinsale, Old Hd. of 7 51 37N 8 32W
Kinshasa 51 4 20 S 15 15 E
Kinston 66 35 18N 77 35W
Kintampo 49 8 5N 1 41W
Kintyre 6 55 30N 5 35W
Kintyre, Mull of 6 55 17N 5 55W
Kiparissía 26 37 15N 21 40 E
Kiparissiakós Kólpos 26 37 25N 21 25 E
Kipembawe 51 7 38 S 33 27 E
Kipili 51 7 28 S 30 32 E
Kippure 7 53 11N 6 23W
Kipushi 51 11 48 S 27 12 E
Kirchheim 13 48 38N 9 20 E
Kirensk 31 57 50N 107 55 E
Kirgiz S.S.R. □ 30 42 0N 75 0 E
Kiri 51 1 29 S 19 25 E
Kiribati ■ 57 1 0N 176 0 E
Kırıkkale 45 39 51N 33 32 E
Kirillov 33 59 51N 38 14 E
Kiritimati 58 1 58N 157 27W
Kirkcaldy 6 56 7N 3 10W
Kirkcudbright 6 54 50N 4 3W
Kirkee 38 18 34N 73 56 E
Kirkenes 27 69 40N 30 5 E
Kirkintilloch 6 55 57N 4 10W
Kirkjubæjarklaustur 27 63 47N 18 4W
Kirkland Lake 62 48 9N 80 2W
Kırklareli 25 41 44N 27 15 E
Kirksville 67 40 8N 92 35W
Kirkūk 45 35 30N 44 21 E
Kirkwall 6 58 59N 2 59W
Kirov 30 58 35N 49 40 E
Kirovabad 35 40 45N 46 20 E
Kirovakan 35 40 48N 44 30 E
Kirovograd 34 48 35N 32 20 E
Kirovsk 30 67 48N 33 50 E
Kirovskiy 31 54 27N 155 42 E
Kirriemuir 6 56 41N 3 0W
Kirsanov 33 52 35N 42 40 E
Kirthar Range 36 27 0N 67 0 E
Kiruna 27 67 52N 20 15 E
Kirundu 51 0 50 S 25 35 E
Kiryū 44 36 24N 139 20 E
Kisangani 51 0 35N 25 15 E
Kisarazu 44 35 23N 139 55 E
Kiselevsk 30 54 5N 86 39 E
Kishanganj 37 26 3N 88 14 E
Kishangarh 36 27 50N 70 30 E
Kishinev 34 47 0N 28 50 E
Kishiwada 44 34 28N 135 22 E
Kisii 51 0 40 S 34 45 E
Kisiju 51 7 23 S 39 19 E
Kiskörös 15 46 37N 19 20 E
Kiskunfélegyháza 15 46 42N 19 53 E
Kiskunhalas 15 46 28N 19 37 E
Kislovodsk 35 43 50N 42 45 E
Kiso-Sammyaku 44 35 45N 137 45 E
Kissidougou 49 9 5N 10 0W
Kisumu 51 0 3 S 34 45 E
Kita 49 13 5N 9 25W
Kitab 30 39 7N 66 52 E
Kitakami-Gawa → 44 38 25N 141 19 E
Kitakyūshū 44 33 50N 130 50 E
Kitale 51 1 0N 35 0 E
Kitchener 62 43 27N 80 29W
Kitgum 51 3 17N 32 52 E
Kíthira 26 36 9N 23 0 E
Kíthnos 26 37 26N 24 27 E
Kitimat 64 54 3N 128 38W
Kitinen → 27 67 34N 26 40 E
Kitui 51 1 17 S 38 0 E
Kitwe 51 12 54 S 28 13 E
Kitzingen 13 49 44N 10 9 E
Kivalo 27 66 18N 26 0 E
Kivu, L. 51 1 48 S 29 0 E
Kiyev 32 50 30N 30 28 E
Kiyevskoye Vdkhr. 32 51 0N 30 0 E
Kızıl Irmak → 34 39 15N 36 0 E
Kizlyar 35 43 51N 46 40 E
Kladno 14 50 10N 14 7 E
Klagenfurt 14 46 38N 14 20 E
Klaipeda 32 55 43N 21 10 E
Klamath → 68 41 40N 124 4W
Klamath Falls 68 42 20N 121 50W
Klamath Mts. 68 41 20N 123 0W
Klatovy 14 49 23N 13 18 E
Klawer 52 31 44 S 18 36 E
Kleena Kleene 64 52 0N 124 59W
Klerksdorp 52 26 53 S 26 38 E
Kletskaïa Kletskiy 30 49 20N 43 0 E
Kleve 13 51 46N 6 10 E
Klin 30 56 20N 36 48 E
Kłodzko 17 50 28N 16 38 E
Klouto 49 6 57N 0 44 E
Klyuchevskaya, Guba 31 55 50N 160 30 E
Knaresborough 5 54 1N 1 29W
Knighton 5 52 21N 3 2W
Knob, C. 54 34 32 S 119 16 E
Knockmealdown Mts. 7 52 16N 8 0W
Knokke 12 51 20N 3 17 E
Knossos 26 35 16N 25 10 E
Knoxville, Iowa, U.S.A. 67 41 20N 93 5W
Knoxville, Tenn., U.S.A. 66 35 58N 83 57W
Ko Chang 41 12 0N 102 20 E
Ko Kut 41 11 40N 102 32 E
Kobarid 21 46 15N 13 30 E
Kobayashi 44 31 56N 130 59 E
Kōbe 44 34 45N 135 10 E
København 28 55 41N 12 34 E
Koblenz 13 50 21N 7 36 E
Kobroor, Kepulauan 40 6 10 S 134 30 E
Kočani 24 41 55N 22 25 E
Kočevje 21 45 39N 14 50 E
Koch Bihar 37 26 22N 89 29 E
Kocheya 31 52 32N 120 42 E
Kōchi 44 33 30N 133 35 E
Kōchi □ 44 33 40N 133 30 E
Koes 52 26 0 S 19 15 E
Koforidua 49 6 3N 0 17W
Kōfu 44 35 40N 138 30 E
Koh-i-Bābā 46 34 30N 67 0 E
Kokand 30 40 30N 70 57 E
Kokchetav 30 53 20N 69 25 E
Kokkola 27 63 50N 23 8 E
Koko Kyunzu 41 14 10N 93 25 E
Kokomo 66 40 30N 86 6W
Kokstad 53 30 32 S 29 29 E
Kokuora 31 71 35N 144 50 E
Kola 30 68 45N 33 8 E
Kola Pen. = Kolskiy Poluostrov 30 67 30N 38 0 E
Kolar 38 13 12N 78 15 E
Kolar Gold Fields 38 12 58N 78 16 E
Kolari 27 67 20N 23 48 E
Kolarovgrad 25 43 18N 26 55 E
Kolda 49 12 55N 14 57W
Kolding 28 55 30N 9 29 E
Kole 51 3 16 S 22 42 E
Kolguyev, Ostrov 30 69 20N 48 30 E
Kolhapur 38 16 43N 74 15 E
Kolín 14 50 2N 15 9 E
Köln 13 50 56N 6 58 E
Koło 17 52 14N 18 40 E
Kołobrzeg 17 54 10N 15 35 E
Kolokani 49 13 35N 7 45W
Kolomna 33 55 8N 38 45 E
Kolomyya 34 48 31N 25 2 E
Kolskiy Poluostrov 30 67 30N 38 0 E
Kolwezi 51 10 40 S 25 25 E
Kolyma → 31 69 30N 161 0 E
Kolymskoye, Okhotsko 31 63 0N 157 0 E
Komárno 15 47 49N 18 5 E
Komatsu 44 36 25N 136 30 E
Komi A.S.S.R. □ 30 64 0N 55 0 E
Kommunizma, Pik 30 39 0N 72 2 E
Komono 51 3 15 S 13 20 E
Komotini 26 41 9N 25 26 E
Kompong Cham 41 12 0N 105 30 E
Kompong Chhnang 41 12 20N 104 35 E
Kompong Som 41 10 38N 103 30 E
Komsomolets, Ostrov 31 80 30N 95 0 E
Komsomolsk 31 50 30N 137 0 E
Konarhá □ 46 35 30N 71 3 E
Konch 36 26 0N 79 10 E
Kondakovo 31 69 36N 152 0 E
Kondoa 51 4 55 S 35 50 E
Kondratyevo 31 57 22N 98 15 E
Konduga 50 11 35N 13 26 E
Kong 49 8 54N 4 36W
Kong, Koh 41 11 20N 103 0 E
Kong Christian IX.s Land 3 68 0N 36 0W
Kong Christian X.s Land 3 74 0N 29 0W
Kong Franz Joseph Fd. 3 73 20N 24 30W
Kong Frederik IX.s Land 3 67 0N 52 0W
Kong Frederik VI.s Kyst 3 63 0N 43 0W
Kong Frederik VIII.s Land 3 78 30N 26 0W
Kong Oscar Fjord 3 72 20N 24 0W
Kongolo 51 5 22 S 27 0 E
Kongor 50 7 1N 31 27 E
Kongsberg 28 59 39N 9 39 E
Kongsvinger 28 60 12N 12 2 E
Konin 17 52 12N 18 15 E
Konjic 24 43 42N 17 58 E
Konosha 30 61 0N 40 5 E
Konotop 32 51 12N 33 7 E
Końskie 17 51 15N 20 23 E
Kontagora 49 10 23N 5 27 E
Konya 45 37 52N 32 35 E
Konya Ovasi 45 38 30N 33 0 E
Konza 51 1 45 S 37 7 E
Koolan I. 54 16 0 S 123 45 E
Kootenay L. 64 49 45N 116 50W
Kopaonik Planina 24 43 10N 21 50 E
Kópavogur 27 64 6N 21 55W
Koper 21 45 31N 13 44 E
Kopervik 27 59 17N 5 17 E
Kopeysk 30 55 7N 61 37 E
Köping 28 59 31N 16 3 E
Kopparbergs län □ 28 61 20N 14 15 E
Koppeh Dāgh 46 38 0N 58 0 E
Korab 24 41 44N 20 40 E
Korbach 13 51 17N 8 50 E
Korça 26 40 37N 20 50 E
Korce = Korça 26 40 37N 20 50 E
Korčula 21 42 57N 17 8 E
Kordestān □ 45 36 0N 47 0 E
Korea Bay 42 39 0N 124 0 E
Korhogo 49 9 29N 5 28W
Korinthiakós Kólpos 26 38 16N 22 30 E
Kórinthos 26 37 56N 22 55 E
Kōriyama 44 37 24N 140 23 E
Koro, Ivory C. 49 8 32N 7 30W
Koro, Mali 49 14 1N 2 58W
Korogwe 51 5 5 S 38 25 E
Körös → 15 46 43N 20 12 E
Korsakov 31 46 36N 142 42 E
Korshunovo 31 58 37N 110 10 E
Korti 50 18 6N 31 33 E
Kortrijk 12 50 50N 3 17 E
Koryakskiy Khrebet 31 61 0N 171 0 E
Kos 26 36 50N 27 15 E
Kościan 17 52 5N 16 40 E
Kosciusko 67 33 3N 89 34W
Kosciusko, Mt. 56 36 27 S 148 16 E
Kosha 50 20 50N 30 30 E
Košice 15 48 42N 21 15 E
Kosovska-Mitrovica 24 42 54N 20 52 E
Kôstî 50 13 8N 32 43 E
Kostroma 33 57 50N 40 58 E
Kostrzyn 17 52 24N 17 14 E
Koszalin 17 53 50N 16 8 E
Kota 36 25 14N 75 49 E
Kota Baharu 41 6 7N 102 14 E
Kota Kinabalu 39 6 0N 116 4 E
Kotelnich 33 58 20N 48 10 E
Kotelnikovo 30 47 38N 43 8 E
Kotelnyy, Ostrov 31 75 10N 139 0 E
Kotka 27 60 28N 26 58 E
Kotlas 30 61 15N 47 0 E
Kotor 24 42 25N 18 47 E
Kotri 36 25 22N 68 22 E
Kottayam 38 9 35N 76 33 E
Kotuy → 31 71 54N 102 6 E
Kouango 51 5 0N 20 10 E
Koudougou 49 12 10N 2 20W
Kouilou → 51 4 10 S 12 5 E
Kouki 51 7 22N 17 3 E
Koula Moutou 51 1 15 S 12 25 E
Koulikoro 49 12 40N 7 50W
Koumra 50 8 50N 17 35 E
Kouroussa 49 10 45N 9 45W
Kousseri 50 12 0N 14 55 E
Koutiala 49 12 25N 5 23W
Kovel 32 51 10N 24 20 E
Kovrov 33 56 25N 41 25 E
Kowloon 43 22 20N 114 15 E
Kozáni 26 40 19N 21 47 E
Kozhikode = Calicut 38 11 15N 75 43 E
Kpalimé 49 6 57N 0 44 E
Kra, Isthmus of = Kra, Kho Khot 41 10 15N 99 30 E
Kra, Kho Khot 41 10 15N 99 30 E
Kragerø 28 58 52N 9 25 E
Kragujevac 24 44 2N 20 56 E
Kraków 15 50 4N 19 57 E
Kraljevo 24 43 44N 20 41 E
Kramatorsk 34 48 50N 37 30 E
Kramfors 27 62 55N 17 48 E
Kraskino 31 42 44N 130 48 E
Kraśnik 17 50 55N 22 5 E
Krasnoarmeysk 30 51 0N 45 42 E
Krasnodar 35 45 5N 39 0 E
Krasnoperekopsk 30 46 0N 33 54 E
Krasnoturinsk 30 59 46N 60 12 E
Krasnoufimsk 30 56 57N 57 46 E
Krasnouralsk 30 58 21N 60 3 E
Krasnovodsk 30 40 0N 52 52 E
Krasnoyarsk 31 56 8N 93 0 E
Krasnyy Yar 35 46 43N 48 23 E
Kratie 41 12 32N 106 10 E
Kravanh, Phnom 41 12 0N 103 32 E
Krefeld 13 51 20N 6 32 E
Kremenchug 34 49 5N 33 25 E
Kremenchugskoye Vdkhr. 34 49 20N 32 30 E
Kremnica 15 48 45N 18 50 E
Kribi 51 2 57N 9 56 E
Krishna → 38 15 57N 80 59 E
Krishnanagar 37 23 24N 88 33 E
Kristiansand 27 58 9N 8 1 E
Kristianstad 28 56 2N 14 9 E
Kristiansund 27 63 7N 7 45 E
Kristiinankaupunki 27 62 16N 21 21 E
Kristinehamn 28 59 18N 14 13 E
Kristinestad 27 62 16N 21 21 E
Kríti 26 35 15N 25 0 E
Krivoy Rog 34 47 51N 33 20 E
Krk 21 45 8N 14 40 E
Kronobergs län □ 28 56 45N 14 30 E
Kronshtadt 32 60 5N 29 45 E
Kroonstad 52 27 43 S 27 19 E
Kropotkin, R.S.F.S.R., U.S.S.R. 31 59 0N 115 30 E
Kropotkin, R.S.F.S.R., U.S.S.R. 35 45 28N 40 28 E
Krosno 15 49 42N 21 46 E
Krotoszyn 17 51 42N 17 23 E
Krugersdorp 53 26 5 S 27 46 E
Krung Thep = Bangkok 41 13 45N 100 35 E
Kruševac 24 43 35N 21 28 E
Krymskiy P-ov. 34 45 0N 34 0 E
Ksar el Boukhari 49 35 51N 2 52 E
Ksar el Kebir 49 35 0N 6 0W
Kuala Dungun 41 4 45N 103 25 E
Kuala Kangsar 41 4 46N 100 56 E
Kuala Lipis 41 4 10N 102 3 E
Kuala Lumpur 41 3 9N 101 41 E
Kuala Pilah 41 2 45N 102 15 E
Kuala Trengganu 41 5 20N 103 8 E
Kuantan 41 3 49N 103 20 E
Kuba 35 41 21N 48 32 E
Kuban → 34 45 20N 37 30 E
Kucing 39 1 33N 110 25 E
Kudymkar 30 59 1N 54 39 E
Kufstein 13 47 35N 12 11 E
Kūh-e-Jebāl Bārez 46 29 0N 58 0 E
Kūh-e Sorkh 46 35 30N 58 45 E
Kūhhā-ye-Bashākerd 46 26 45N 59 0 E
Kūhhā-ye Sabalān 45 38 15N 47 45 E
Kuito 51 12 22 S 16 55 E
Kukawa 50 12 58N 13 27 E
Kulasekarappattinam 38 8 20N 78 0 E
Kulsary 30 46 59N 54 1 E
Kulunda 30 52 35N 78 57 E

Kulyab **30** 37 55N 69 50 E
Kuma → **35** 44 55N 47 0 E
Kumagaya **44** 36 9N 139 22 E
Kumamoto **44** 32 45N 130 45 E
Kumamoto □ **44** 32 55N 130 55 E
Kumanovo **24** 42 9N 21 42 E
Kumasi **49** 6 41N 1 38W
Kumba **49** 4 36N 9 24 E
Kumla **28** 59 8N 15 10 E
Kumo **49** 10 1N 11 12 E
Kunashir, Ostrov **31** 44 0N 146 0 E
Kungsbacka **28** 57 30N 12 5 E
Kungur **30** 57 25N 56 57 E
Kunlun Shan **42** 36 0N 86 30 E
Kunming **42** 25 1N 102 41 E
Kunsan **43** 35 59N 126 45 E
Kununurra **54** 15 40 S 128 50 E
Kuopio **27** 62 53N 27 35 E
Kuopion lääni □ **27** 63 25N 27 10 E
Kupa → **21** 45 28N 16 24 E
Kupang **40** 10 19 S 123 39 E
Kupyansk **30** 49 52N 37 35 E
Kura → **35** 39 50N 49 20 E
Kurashiki **44** 34 40N 133 50 E
Kurayoshi **44** 35 26N 133 50 E
Kure **44** 34 14N 132 32 E
Kurgan **30** 55 26N 65 18 E
Kuria Maria Is. = Khūriyā Mūriyā, Jazā 'ir **47** 17 30N 55 58 E
Kuril Is. = Kurilskiye Ostrova **31** 45 0N 150 0 E
Kuril Trench **57** 44 0N 153 0 E
Kurilsk **31** 45 14N 147 53 E
Kurilskiye Ostrova **31** 45 0N 150 0 E
Kurmuk **50** 10 33N 34 21 E
Kurnool **38** 15 45N 78 0 E
Kursk **33** 51 42N 36 11 E
Kuršumlija **24** 43 9N 21 19 E
Kuruman **52** 27 28 S 23 28 E
Kurume **44** 33 15N 130 30 E
Kurunegala **38** 7 30N 80 23 E
Kurya **31** 61 15N 108 10 E
Kushiro **44** 43 0N 144 25 E
Kushiro → **44** 42 59N 144 23 E
Kushka **30** 35 20N 62 18 E
Kushtia **37** 23 55N 89 5 E
Kustanay **30** 53 10N 63 35 E
Kütahya **45** 39 30N 30 2 E
Kutaisi **35** 42 19N 42 40 E
Kutaraja = Banda Aceh **39** 5 35N 95 20 E
Kutch, Gulf of = Kachchh, Gulf of **36** 22 50N 69 15 E
Kutch, Rann of = Kachchh, Rann of **36** 24 0N 70 0 E
Kutno **17** 52 15N 19 23 E
Kutu **51** 2 40 S 18 11 E
Kutum **50** 14 10N 24 40 E
Kuwait = Al Kuwayt **45** 29 30N 47 30 E
Kuwait ■ **45** 29 30N 47 30 E
Kuwana **44** 35 0N 136 43 E
Kuybyshev **33** 53 8N 50 6 E
Kuybyshevskoye Vdkhr. **33** 55 2N 49 30 E
Kuyumba **31** 60 58N 96 59 E
Kuznetsk **33** 53 12N 46 40 E
Kvænangen **27** 70 5N 21 15 E
Kvarner **21** 44 50N 14 10 E
Kvarnerič **21** 44 43N 14 37 E
Kwakoegron **73** 5 12N 55 25W
Kwando → **52** 18 27 S 23 32 E
Kwangju **43** 35 9N 126 54 E
Kwekwe **51** 18 58 S 29 48 E
Kwinana New Town **54** 32 15 S 115 47 E
Kyabé **50** 9 30N 19 0 E
Kyakhta **31** 50 30N 106 25 E
Kyle Dam **51** 20 15 S 31 0 E
Kyle of Lochalsh **6** 57 17N 5 43W
Kyō-ga-Saki **44** 35 45N 135 15 E
Kyoga, L. **51** 1 35N 33 0 E
Kyōto **44** 35 0N 135 45 E
Kyōto □ **44** 35 15N 135 45 E
Kyren **31** 51 45N 101 45 E
Kyrenia **45** 35 20N 33 20 E
Kystatyam **31** 67 20N 123 10 E
Kytal Ktakh **31** 65 30N 123 40 E
Kyulyunken **31** 64 10N 137 5 E
Kyūshū **44** 33 0N 131 0 E
Kyūshū-Sanchi **44** 32 35N 131 17 E
Kyustendil **24** 42 16N 22 41 E
Kyusyur **31** 70 39N 127 15 E
Kyzyl **31** 51 50N 94 30 E
Kyzyl-Kiya **30** 40 16N 72 8 E
Kyzylkum, Peski **30** 42 30N 65 0 E
Kzyl-Orda **30** 44 48N 65 28 E

L

Labastide-Murat **10** 44 39N 1 33 E
Labastide-Rouairoux **10** 43 28N 2 39 E
Labe = Elbe → **14** 53 50N 9 0 E
Labé **49** 11 24N 12 16W
Labouheyre **10** 44 13N 0 55W
Laboulaye **74** 34 10 S 63 30W
Labrador, Coast of □ **3** 53 20N 61 0W
Lábrea **72** 7 15 S 64 51W
Labrède **10** 44 41N 0 32W
Lac La Biche **64** 54 45N 111 58W
Lacanau **10** 44 58N 1 5W
Lacanau, Étang de **10** 44 58N 1 7W
Lacaune **10** 43 43N 2 40 E
Lacaune, Mts. de **10** 43 43N 2 50 E
Laccadive Is. = Lakshadweep Is. **29** 10 0N 72 30 E
Lacepede Is. **54** 16 55 S 122 0 E
Lachine **62** 45 30N 73 40W
Lachlan → **56** 34 22 S 143 55 E
Lachute **62** 45 39N 74 21W
Lackawanna **66** 42 49N 78 50W
Lacombe **64** 52 30N 113 44W
Laconia **63** 43 32N 71 30W
Lacq **10** 43 25N 0 35W
Ladoga, L. = Ladozhskoye Ozero **30** 61 15N 30 30 E
Ladon **9** 48 0N 2 30 E
Ladozhskoye Ozero **30** 61 15N 30 30 E
Ladysmith, Canada **64** 49 0N 123 49W
Ladysmith, S. Africa **53** 28 32 S 29 46 E
Lae **56** 6 40 S 147 2 E
Læsø **28** 57 15N 10 53 E
Lafayette, Ind., U.S.A. **66** 40 25N 86 54W
Lafayette, La., U.S.A. **67** 30 18N 92 0W
Lafia **49** 8 30N 8 34 E
Lagan → **7** 54 35N 5 55W
Lagarfljót → **27** 65 40N 14 18W
Laghmān □ **46** 34 20N 70 0 E
Laghouat **49** 33 50N 2 59 E
Lagnieu **11** 45 55N 5 20 E
Lagny **9** 48 52N 2 44 E
Lagos, Nigeria **49** 6 25N 3 27 E
Lagos, Portugal **18** 37 5N 8 41W
Lagos de Moreno **69** 21 21N 101 55W
Lagrange **54** 18 45 S 121 43 E
Laguépie **10** 44 8N 1 57 E
Laguna **74** 28 30 S 48 50W
Laguna Beach **68** 33 31N 117 52W
Lagunas, Chile **72** 21 0 S 69 45W
Lagunas, Peru **72** 5 10 S 75 35W
Lahn → **13** 50 52N 8 35 E
Laholm **28** 56 30N 13 2 E
Lahore **36** 31 32N 74 22 E
Lahr **13** 48 20N 7 52 E
Lahti **27** 60 58N 25 40 E
Laï **50** 9 25N 16 18 E
Laignes **9** 47 50N 4 20 E
Lairg **6** 58 1N 4 24W
Laja, R. de la → **69** 20 55N 100 46W
Lajere **49** 12 10N 11 25 E
Lajes **74** 27 48 S 50 20W
Lake Cargelligo **56** 33 15 S 146 22 E
Lake Charles **67** 30 15N 93 10W
Lake City, Fla., U.S.A. **66** 30 10N 82 40W
Lake City, S.C., U.S.A. **66** 33 51N 79 44W
Lake Worth **66** 26 36N 80 3W
Lakeland **66** 28 0N 82 0W
Lakewood **66** 41 28N 81 50W
Laki **27** 64 4N 18 14W
Lakonikós Kólpos **26** 36 40N 22 40 E
Lakota **49** 5 50N 5 30W
Laksefjorden **27** 70 45N 26 50 E
Lakselv **27** 70 2N 24 56 E
Lakshadweep Is. **29** 10 0N 72 30 E
Lalibela **50** 12 2N 39 2 E
Lalín **18** 42 40N 8 5W
Lalinde **10** 44 50N 0 44 E
Lamastre **11** 44 59N 4 35 E
Lamballe **8** 48 29N 2 31W
Lambaréné **51** 0 41 S 10 12 E
Lambay I. **7** 53 30N 6 0W
Lambesc **11** 43 39N 5 16 E
Lambi Kyun **41** 10 50N 98 20 E
Lame **49** 10 30N 9 20 E
Lamego **18** 41 5N 7 52W
Lamía **26** 38 55N 22 26 E
Lammermuir Hills **6** 55 50N 2 40W
Lamon Bay **40** 14 30N 122 20 E
Lampa **72** 15 22 S 70 22W
Lampang **41** 18 16N 99 32 E
Lampaul **8** 48 28N 5 7W
Lampeter **5** 52 6N 4 6W
Lamu **51** 2 16 S 40 55 E
Lanark **6** 55 40N 3 48W
Lancashire □ **5** 53 40N 2 30W
Lancaster, U.K. **5** 54 3N 2 48W
Lancaster, U.S.A. **66** 40 4N 76 19W
Lancaster Sd. **3** 74 13N 84 0W
Lanchow = Lanzhou **42** 36 1N 103 52 E
Lanciano **21** 42 15N 14 22 E
Landau **13** 49 12N 8 7 E
Landeck **13** 47 9N 10 34 E
Landen **12** 50 45N 5 3 E
Landerneau **8** 48 28N 4 17W
Landes **10** 44 0N 1 0W
Landes □ **10** 43 57N 0 48W
Landivisiau **8** 48 31N 4 6W
Landrecies **9** 50 7N 3 40 E
Land's End **5** 50 4N 5 43W
Landsberg **13** 48 3N 10 52 E
Landskrona **28** 55 53N 12 50 E
Lanett **66** 33 0N 85 15W
Langeac **10** 45 7N 3 29 E
Langeais **8** 47 20N 0 24 E
Langen **13** 49 59N 8 40 E
Langeoog **13** 53 44N 7 33 E
Langholm **6** 55 9N 2 59W
Langjökull **27** 64 39N 20 12W
Langlade **63** 46 50N 56 20W
Langogne **10** 44 43N 3 50 E
Langon **10** 44 33N 0 16W
Langøya **27** 68 45N 14 50 E
Langres **9** 47 52N 5 20 E
Langres, Plateau de **9** 47 45N 5 3 E
Languedoc **10** 43 58N 4 0 E
Lannemezan **10** 43 8N 0 23 E
Lannilis **8** 48 35N 4 32W
Lannion **8** 48 46N 3 29W
Lanouaille **10** 45 24N 1 9 E
Lansing **66** 42 47N 84 40W
Lanslebourg-Mont-Cenis **11** 45 17N 6 52 E
Lanzarote **49** 29 0N 13 40W
Lanzhou **42** 36 1N 103 52 E
Laois □ **7** 53 0N 7 20W
Laon **9** 49 33N 3 35 E
Laona **62** 45 32N 88 41W
Laos ■ **41** 17 45N 105 0 E
Lapalisse **10** 46 15N 3 38 E
Lapeer **66** 43 3N 83 20W
Lapi □ **27** 67 0N 27 0 E
Lappland **27** 68 7N 24 0 E
Laptev Sea **31** 76 0N 125 0 E
Larache **49** 35 10N 6 5W
Laragne-Montéglin **11** 44 18N 5 49 E
Laramie **67** 41 20N 105 38W
Laredo **67** 27 34N 99 29W
Largentière **11** 44 34N 4 18 E
Largs **6** 55 48N 4 51W
Lárisa **26** 39 49N 22 28 E
Larnaca **45** 35 0N 33 35 E
Larne **7** 54 52N 5 50W
Laroquebrou **10** 44 58N 2 12 E
Larrimah **54** 15 35 S 133 12 E
Larvik **28** 59 4N 10 0 E
Laryak **30** 61 15N 80 0 E
Larzac, Causse du **10** 43 50N 3 17 E
Las Anod **47** 8 26N 47 19 E
Las Cruces **68** 32 18N 106 50W
Las Khoreh **47** 11 10N 48 20 E
Las Lajas **74** 38 30 S 70 25W
Las Palmas **49** 28 7N 15 26W
Las Vegas **68** 36 10N 115 5W
Lassay **8** 48 27N 0 30W
Lassen Pk. **68** 40 29N 121 31W
Lastoursville **51** 0 55 S 12 38 E
Lastovo **21** 42 46N 16 55 E
Latacunga **72** 0 50 S 78 35W
Latakia = Al Lādhiqīyah **45** 35 30N 35 45 E
Latina **22** 41 26N 12 53 E
Latouche Treville, C. **54** 18 27 S 121 49 E
Latvian S.S.R. □ **32** 56 50N 24 0 E
Lauchhammer **13** 51 35N 13 48 E
Lauenburg **13** 53 23N 10 33 E
Laugarbakki **27** 65 20N 20 55W
Launceston, Australia **56** 41 24 S 147 8 E
Launceston, U.K. **5** 50 38N 4 21W
Laune → **7** 52 5N 9 40W
Launglon Bok **41** 13 50N 97 54 E
Laura **55** 15 32 S 144 32 E
Laurel **67** 31 41N 89 9W
Laurencekirk **6** 56 50N 2 30W
Laurens **66** 34 32N 82 2W
Laurinburg **66** 34 50N 79 25W
Laurium **62** 47 14N 88 26W
Lausanne **13** 46 32N 6 38 E
Laut Ketil, Kepulauan **39** 4 45 S 115 40 E
Lauzon **63** 46 48N 71 10W
Laval **8** 48 4N 0 48W
Lavandou, Le **11** 43 8N 6 22 E
Lavardac **10** 44 12N 0 20 E
Lavaur **10** 43 40N 1 49 E
Lavelanet **10** 42 57N 1 51 E
Laverton **54** 28 44 S 122 29 E
Lavrentiya **31** 65 35N 171 0W
Lávrion **26** 37 40N 24 4 E
Lawrence, Kans., U.S.A. **67** 39 0N 95 10W
Lawrence, Mass., U.S.A. **66** 42 40N 71 9W
Lawrenceburg **66** 35 12N 87 19W
Lawton **67** 34 33N 98 25W
Laxford, L. **6** 58 25N 5 10W
Layon → **8** 47 20N 0 45W
Laysan I. **58** 25 30N 167 0W
Lazio □ **21** 42 10N 12 30 E
Lea → **5** 51 30N 0 10W
Leader **65** 50 50N 109 30W
Leadhills **6** 55 25N 3 47W
Leamington, Canada **62** 42 3N 82 36W
Leamington, U.K. **5** 52 18N 1 32W
Learmonth **54** 22 13 S 114 10 E
Leavenworth **67** 39 25N 95 0W
Lebanon, Mo., U.S.A. **67** 37 40N 92 40W
Lebanon, Oreg., U.S.A. **68** 44 31N 122 57W
Lebanon, Pa., U.S.A. **66** 40 20N 76 28W
Lebanon, Tenn., U.S.A. **66** 36 15N 86 20W
Lebanon ■ **45** 34 0N 36 0 E
Lebrija **18** 36 53N 6 5W
Lecce **23** 40 20N 18 10 E
Lecco **20** 45 50N 9 27 E
Lech → **13** 48 44N 10 56 E
Lectoure **10** 43 56N 0 38 E
Łeczyca **17** 52 5N 19 15 E
Ledbury **5** 52 3N 2 25W
Leduc **64** 53 15N 113 30W
Lee → **7** 51 50N 8 30W
Leeds **5** 53 48N 1 34W
Leek **5** 53 7N 2 2W
Leer **13** 53 13N 7 29 E
Leesburg **66** 28 47N 81 52W
Leeton **56** 34 33 S 146 23 E
Leeuwarden **12** 53 15N 5 48 E
Leeuwin, C. **54** 34 20 S 115 9 E
Leeward Is., Atl. Oc. **70** 16 30N 63 30W
Leeward Is., Pac. Oc. **58** 16 0 S 147 0W
Lefroy, L. **54** 31 21 S 121 40 E
Leghorn = Livorno **20** 43 32N 10 18 E
Legnica **17** 51 12N 16 10 E
Lehrte **13** 52 22N 9 58 E
Leicester **5** 52 39N 1 9W
Leicester □ **5** 52 40N 1 10W
Leichhardt → **55** 17 35 S 139 48 E
Leiden **12** 52 9N 4 30 E
Leie → **12** 51 2N 3 45 E
Leinster □ **7** 53 0N 7 10W
Leinster, Mt. **7** 52 38N 6 47W
Leipzig **13** 51 20N 12 23 E
Leiria **18** 39 46N 8 53W
Leith **6** 55 59N 3 10W
Leith Hill **5** 51 10N 0 23W
Leitrim **7** 54 0N 8 5W
Leitrim □ **7** 54 8N 8 0W
Lek → **12** 51 54N 4 35 E
Leleque **74** 42 28 S 71 0W
Lelystad **12** 52 30N 5 25 E
Léman, Lac **13** 46 26N 6 30 E
Lemhi Ra. **68** 44 30N 113 30W
Lemmer **12** 52 51N 5 43 E
Lempdes **10** 45 22N 3 17 E
Lemvig **28** 56 33N 8 20 E
Lena → **31** 72 52N 126 40 E
Lencloître **8** 46 50N 0 20 E
Lengerich **13** 52 12N 7 50 E
Leninabad **30** 40 17N 69 37 E
Leninakan **35** 40 47N 43 50 E
Leningrad **32** 59 55N 30 20 E
Leninsk **35** 48 40N 45 15 E
Leninsk-Kuznetskiy **30** 54 44N 86 10 E
Leninskoye **31** 47 56N 132 38 E
Lenoir City **66** 35 40N 84 20W
Lens **9** 50 26N 2 50 E
Lensk **31** 60 48N 114 55 E
Lentini **23** 37 18N 15 0 E
Leoben **14** 47 22N 15 5 E
Leominster, U.K. **5** 52 15N 2 43W
Leominster, U.S.A. **66** 42 32N 71 45W
Léon, France **10** 43 53N 1 18W
León, Mexico **69** 21 7N 101 40W
León, Nic. **70** 12 20N 86 51W
León, Spain **18** 42 38N 5 34W
León □ **18** 42 40N 5 55W
León, Montañas de **18** 42 30N 6 18W
Leonora **54** 28 49 S 121 19 E
Leopoldsburg **12** 51 7N 5 13 E
Lepel **32** 54 50N 28 40 E
Lepikha **31** 64 45N 125 55 E
Léré **50** 9 39N 14 13 E
Lérida **19** 41 37N 0 39 E
Lérins, Is. de **11** 43 31N 7 3 E
Lérouville **9** 48 44N 5 30 E
Lerwick **6** 60 10N 1 10W
Lesbos, I. = Lésvos **26** 39 10N 26 20 E
Leskovac **24** 43 0N 21 58 E
Lesneven **8** 48 35N 4 20W
Lesotho ■ **53** 29 40 S 28 0 E
Lesozavodsk **31** 45 30N 133 29 E
Lesparre-Médoc **10** 45 18N 0 57W
Lessay **8** 49 14N 1 30W
Lesse → **12** 50 15N 4 54 E
Lesser Antilles **70** 15 0N 61 0W
Lesser Slave L. **64** 55 30N 115 25W
Lessines **12** 50 42N 3 50 E
Lésvos **26** 39 10N 26 20 E
Leszno **17** 51 50N 16 30 E
Letchworth **5** 51 58N 0 13W
Lethbridge **64** 49 45N 112 45W
Leti, Kepulauan **40** 8 10 S 128 0 E
Leticia **72** 4 9 S 70 0W
Letsôk-aw Kyun **41** 11 30N 98 25 E
Letterkenny **7** 54 57N 7 42W
Leucate **10** 42 56N 3 3 E
Leucate, Étang de **10** 42 50N 3 0 E
Leuven **12** 50 52N 4 42 E
Leuze **12** 50 36N 3 37 E
Levanger **27** 63 45N 11 19 E
Levant, I. du **11** 43 3N 6 28 E
Leven **6** 56 12N 3 0W
Leven, L. **6** 56 12N 3 22W
Levens **11** 43 50N 7 12 E
Leveque C. **54** 16 20 S 123 0 E
Leverkusen **13** 51 2N 6 59 E
Levet **9** 46 56N 2 22 E
Levie **11** 41 40N 9 7 E
Levier **9** 46 58N 6 8 E
Lévis **63** 46 48N 71 9W
Levkás **26** 38 40N 20 43 E
Levkôsia = Nicosia **45** 35 10N 33 25 E
Levroux **9** 46 59N 1 38 E
Lewes **5** 50 53N 0 2 E
Lewis **6** 58 10N 6 40W
Lewis, Butt of **6** 58 30N 6 12W
Lewis Ra. **68** 48 15N 114 0W
Lewisporte **63** 49 15N 55 3W
Lewiston, Idaho, U.S.A. **68** 46 25N 117 0W
Lewiston, Maine, U.S.A. **66** 44 3N 70 10 E
Lexington, Ky., U.S.A. **66** 38 6N 84 30W
Lexington, Mo., U.S.A. **67** 39 7N 93 55W
Lexington, N.C., U.S.A. **66** 35 50N 80 13W
Lexington, Oreg., U.S.A. **68** 45 29N 119 46W
Lexington Park **66** 38 16N 76 27W
Leyre → **10** 44 39N 1 1W
Leyte **40** 11 0N 125 0 E
Lezay **10** 46 15N 0 1 E
Lézignan-Corbières **10** 43 13N 2 43 E
Lezoux **10** 45 49N 3 21 E
Lhazê **42** 29 5N 87 38 E
Lianyungang **43** 34 40N 119 11 E
Liaoyuan **42** 42 58N 125 2 E
Liard → **64** 61 51N 121 18W
Libenge **51** 3 40N 18 55 E
Liberal **67** 37 4N 101 0W
Liberec **14** 50 47N 15 7 E
Liberia ■ **49** 6 30N 9 30W
Libertad, La **69** 29 55N 112 41W
Libonda **51** 14 28 S 23 12 E
Libourne **10** 44 55N 0 14W
Libramont **12** 49 55N 5 23 E
Libreville **51** 0 25N 9 26 E
Libya ■ **50** 27 0N 17 0 E
Licata **22** 37 6N 13 55 E
Lichfield **5** 52 40N 1 50W
Lichtenburg **52** 26 8 S 26 8 E
Lichtenfels **13** 50 7N 11 4 E
Lidköping **28** 58 31N 13 14 E
Liechtenstein ■ **13** 47 8N 9 35 E
Liège **12** 50 38N 5 35 E
Liège □ **12** 50 32N 5 35 E
Lienz **14** 46 50N 12 46 E
Liepaja **32** 56 30N 21 0 E
Lier **12** 51 7N 4 34 E
Liévin **9** 50 24N 2 47 E
Liffey → **7** 53 21N 6 20W
Lifford **7** 54 50N 7 30W
Liffré **8** 48 12N 1 30W
Ligny-en-Barrois **9** 48 36N 5 20 E
Ligny-le-Châtel **9** 47 54N 3 45 E
Ligueil **8** 47 2N 0 49 E
Liguria □ **20** 44 30N 9 0 E
Ligurian Sea **20** 43 20N 9 0 E
Lihir Group **56** 3 0 S 152 35 E
Lihou Reefs and Cays **55** 17 25 S 151 40 E
Likasi **51** 10 55 S 26 48 E
Likati **51** 3 20N 24 0 E
Lille **9** 50 38N 3 3 E
Lille Bælt **28** 55 20N 9 45 E
Lillebonne **8** 49 30N 0 32 E
Lillehammer **28** 61 8N 10 30 E
Lillers **9** 50 35N 2 28 E
Lillesand **27** 58 15N 8 23 E
Lilleshall **5** 52 45N 2 22W
Lillestrøm **28** 59 58N 11 5 E
Lillooet **64** 50 44N 121 57W
Lilongwe **51** 14 0 S 33 48 E
Lima, Peru **72** 12 0 S 77 0W
Lima, U.S.A. **66** 40 42N 84 5W
Limassol **45** 34 42N 33 1 E
Limavady **7** 55 3N 6 58W
Limavady □ **7** 55 0N 6 55W
Limbe **49** 4 1N 9 10 E
Limburg **13** 50 22N 8 4 E
Limburg □, Belgium **12** 51 2N 5 25 E
Limburg □, Neth. **12** 51 20N 5 55 E
Limeira **73** 22 35 S 47 28W
Limerick **7** 52 40N 8 38W
Limerick □ **7** 52 30N 8 50W
Limfjorden **28** 56 55N 9 0 E
Limia → **18** 41 41N 8 50W
Limmen Bight **54** 14 40 S 135 35 E
Límnos **26** 39 50N 25 5 E
Limoges **10** 45 50N 1 15 E
Limón **70** 10 0N 83 2W
Limousin **10** 45 30N 1 30 E
Limousin, Plateaux du **10** 45 45N 1 15 E
Limoux **10** 43 4N 2 12 E
Limpopo → **53** 25 5 S 33 30 E
Limuru **51** 1 2 S 36 35 E
Linares, Chile **74** 35 50 S 71 40W
Linares, Mexico **69** 24 50N 99 40W
Linares, Spain **19** 38 10N 3 40W
Lincoln, Argentina **74** 34 55 S 61 30W
Lincoln, U.K. **5** 53 14N 0 32W
Lincoln, Ill., U.S.A. **67** 40 10N 89 20W
Lincoln, Maine, U.S.A. **63** 45 27N 68 29W
Lincoln, Nebr., U.S.A. **67** 40 50N 96 42W
Lincoln □ **5** 53 14N 0 32W
Lincoln Sea **3** 84 0N 55 0W
Lincoln Wolds **5** 53 20N 0 5W
Lindau **13** 47 33N 9 41 E
Lindi **51** 9 58 S 39 38 E
Lindsay, Canada **62** 44 22N 78 43W
Lindsay, U.S.A. **68** 36 14N 119 6W
Línea de la Concepción, La **18** 36 15N 5 23W
Lingen **13** 52 32N 7 21 E
Lingga, Kepulauan **39** 0 10 S 104 30 E
Linguéré **49** 15 25N 15 5W
Linköping **28** 58 28N 15 36 E
Linlithgow **6** 55 58N 3 38W
Linnhe, L. **6** 56 36N 5 25W
Linxia **42** 35 36N 103 10 E
Linz **14** 48 18N 14 18 E
Lion, G. du **10** 43 0N 4 0 E
Lion-d'Angers, Le **8** 47 37N 0 43W
Lípari, Is. **23** 38 30N 14 50 E
Lipetsk **33** 52 37N 39 35 E
Lippe → **13** 51 39N 6 38 E
Lippstadt **13** 51 40N 8 19 E
Lira **51** 2 17N 32 57 E
Liria **19** 39 37N 0 35W
Lisala **51** 2 12N 21 38 E
Lisboa **18** 38 42N 9 10W
Lisbon = Lisboa **18** 38 42N 9 10W
Lisburn **7** 54 30N 6 9W
Liscannor, B. **7** 52 57N 9 24W
Lisianski I. **57** 26 2N 174 0W
Lisieux **8** 49 10N 0 12 E
Lisle-sur-Tarn **10** 43 52N 1 49 E
Lismore, Australia **56** 28 44 S 153 21 E
Lismore, Ireland **7** 52 8N 7 58W
Lisse **12** 52 16N 4 33 E
Lista **27** 58 7N 6 39 E
Listowel **7** 52 27N 9 30W
Lit-et-Mixe **10** 44 2N 1 15W
Litchfield **67** 39 10N 89 40W
Lithgow **56** 33 25 S 150 8 E
Líthinon, Ákra **26** 34 55N 24 44 E
Lithuanian S.S.R. □ **32** 55 30N 24 0 E
Litoměřice **14** 50 33N 14 10 E
Little Andaman I. **41** 10 40N 92 15 E
Little Current **62** 45 55N 82 0W
Little Falls **66** 43 3N 74 50W
Little Minch **6** 57 35N 6 45W
Little Missouri → **67** 47 30N 102 25W
Little Ouse → **5** 52 25N 0 50 E
Little Rock **67** 34 41N 92 10W
Littlehampton **5** 50 48N 0 32W
Liuwa Plain **51** 14 20 S 22 30 E
Liuzhou **43** 24 22N 109 22 E
Livarot **8** 49 0N 0 9 E
Liverpool, Australia **56** 33 54 S 150 58 E
Liverpool, Canada **63** 44 5N 64 41W
Liverpool, U.K. **5** 53 25N 3 0W
Liverpool Plains **56** 31 15 S 150 15 E
Liverpool Ra. **56** 31 50 S 150 30 E
Livingston, Guat. **69** 15 50N 88 50W
Livingston, U.S.A. **67** 30 44N 94 54W
Livingstone **51** 17 46 S 25 52 E
Livingstonia **51** 10 38 S 34 5 E
Livny **33** 52 30N 37 30 E
Livonia **66** 42 25N 83 23W
Livorno **20** 43 32N 10 18 E
Livron-sur-Drôme **11** 44 46N 4 51 E
Liwale **51** 9 48 S 37 58 E
Lizard Pt. **5** 49 57N 5 11W
Ljubljana **21** 46 4N 14 33 E
Ljungan → **27** 62 18N 17 23 E
Ljungby **28** 56 49N 13 55 E
Ljusdal **28** 61 46N 16 3 E
Ljusnan → **28** 61 12N 17 8 E
Ljusne **28** 61 13N 17 7 E
Llandeilo **5** 51 53N 4 0W
Llandovery **5** 51 59N 3 49W
Llandrindod Wells **5** 52 15N 3 23W
Llandudno **5** 53 19N 3 51W
Llanelli **5** 51 41N 4 11W
Llanes **18** 43 25N 4 50W
Llangollen **5** 52 58N 3 10W
Llanidloes **5** 52 28N 3 31W

Llano Estacado 67 34 0N 103 0W
Llanos 72 5 0N 71 35W
Llobregat → 19 41 19N 2 9 E
Lloret de Mar 19 41 41N 2 53 E
Lloydminster 65 53 17N 110 0W
Lobatse 52 25 12 S 25 40 E
Lobito 51 12 18 S 13 35 E
Loc Ninh 41 11 50N 106 34 E
Locarno 13 46 10N 8 47 E
Lochaber 6 56 55N 5 0W
Lochcarron 6 57 25N 5 30W
Lochem 12 52 9N 6 26 E
Loches 8 47 7N 1 0 E
Lochgelly 6 56 7N 3 18W
Lochgilphead 6 56 2N 5 37W
Lochinver 6 58 9N 5 15W
Lochnagar 6 56 57N 3 14W
Lochy → 6 56 52N 5 3W
Lock Haven 66 41 7N 77 31W
Lockerbie 6 55 7N 3 21W
Lockport 66 43 12N 78 42W
Locminé 8 47 54N 2 51W
Locronan 8 48 7N 4 15W
Loctudy 8 47 50N 4 12W
Lodève 10 43 44N 3 19 E
Lodhran 36 29 32N 71 30 E
Lodi 68 38 12N 121 16W
Lodja 51 3 30 S 23 23 E
Lodwar 51 3 10N 35 40 E
Łódź 17 51 45N 19 27 E
Lofoten 27 68 30N 15 0 E
Logan, Utah, U.S.A. 68 41 45N 111 50W
Logan, W. Va., U.S.A. 66 37 51N 81 59W
Logansport 66 40 45N 86 21W
Logroño 19 42 28N 2 27W
Lohardaga 37 23 27N 84 45 E
Lohr 13 50 0N 9 35 E
Loimaa 27 60 50N 23 5 E
Loir → 8 47 33N 0 32W
Loir-et-Cher □ 8 47 40N 1 20 E
Loire □ 11 45 40N 4 5 E
Loire → 8 47 16N 2 10W
Loire-Atlantique □ 8 47 25N 1 40W
Loiret □ 9 47 55N 2 30 E
Loja, Ecuador 72 3 59 S 79 16W
Loja, Spain 18 37 10N 4 10W
Lokandu 51 2 30 S 25 45 E
Lokeren 12 51 6N 3 59 E
Lokitaung 51 4 12N 35 48 E
Lokka 27 67 55N 27 35 E
Løkken Verk 27 63 7N 9 43 E
Lokoja 49 7 47N 6 45 E
Lokolama 51 2 35 S 19 50 E
Loliondo 51 2 2 S 35 39 E
Lolland 28 54 45N 11 30 E
Lom 25 43 48N 23 12 E
Lomami → 51 0 46N 24 16 E
Lombardia □ 20 45 35N 9 45 E
Lombardy = Lombardia □ 20 45 35N 9 45 E
Lombez 10 43 29N 0 55 E
Lombok 39 8 45 S 116 30 E
Lomé 49 6 9N 1 20 E
Lomela 51 2 19 S 23 15 E
Lomela → 51 0 15 S 20 40 E
Lomié 51 3 13N 13 38 E
Lomond, L. 6 56 8N 4 38W
Lompoc 68 34 41N 120 32W
Łomza 17 53 10N 22 2 E
Londa 38 15 30N 74 30 E
Londe-les-Maures, La 11 43 8N 6 14 E
Londinières 8 49 50N 1 25 E
London, Canada 62 42 59N 81 15W
London, U.K. 5 51 30N 0 5W
London, Greater □ 5 51 30N 0 5W
Londonderry 7 55 0N 7 20W
Londonderry □ 7 55 0N 7 20W
Londonderry, C. 54 13 45 S 126 55 E
Londrina 74 23 18 S 51 10W
Long Beach 68 33 46N 118 12W
Long Eaton 5 52 54N 1 16W
Long I., Bahamas 70 23 20N 75 10W
Long I., Papua N. G. 56 5 20 S 147 5 E
Long I., U.S.A. 66 40 50N 73 20W
Long Range Mts. 63 49 30N 57 30W
Long Xuyen 41 10 19N 105 28 E
Longa, Proliv 3 70 0N 175 0 E
Longeau 9 47 47N 5 20 E
Longford 7 53 43N 7 50W
Longford □ 7 53 42N 7 45W
Longlac 62 49 45N 86 25W
Longone → 50 10 0N 15 40 E
Longreach 56 23 28 S 144 14 E
Longtown 5 51 58N 2 59W
Longué-Jumelles 8 47 22N 0 8W
Longueau 9 49 52N 2 21 E
Longuyon 9 49 27N 5 35 E
Longview, Tex., U.S.A. 67 32 30N 94 45W
Longview, Wash., U.S.A. 68 46 9N 122 58W
Longwy 9 49 30N 5 46 E
Löningen 13 52 43N 7 44 E
Lons-le-Saunier 9 46 40N 5 31 E
Loop Hd. 7 52 34N 9 55W
Lopatina, G. 31 50 47N 143 10 E
Lopez, C. 51 0 47 S 8 40 E
Lopphavet 27 70 27N 21 15 E
Lorain 66 41 28N 82 55W
Loralai 36 30 20N 68 41 E
Lorca 19 37 41N 1 42W
Lord Howe I. 57 31 33 S 159 6 E
Lorengau 56 2 1 S 147 15 E
Loreto 21 43 26N 13 36 E
Lorgues 11 43 28N 6 22 E
Lorient 8 47 45N 3 23W
Lorn 6 56 26N 5 10W
Lorn, Firth of 6 56 20N 5 40W
Lörrach 13 47 36N 7 38 E
Lorraine 9 48 30N 6 0 E
Los Alamos 68 35 57N 106 17W
Los Andes 74 32 50 S 70 40W
Los Angeles, Chile 74 37 28 S 72 23W
Los Angeles, U.S.A. 68 34 0N 118 10W
Los Angeles Aqueduct 68 35 25N 118 0W
Los Hermanos 70 11 45N 84 25W
Los Mochis 69 25 45N 108 57W
Los Testigos 70 11 23N 63 6W
Loshkalakh 31 62 45N 147 20 E
Lošinj 21 44 30N 14 30 E
Lossiemouth 6 57 43N 3 17W
Lot □ 10 44 39N 1 40 E
Lot → 10 44 18N 0 20 E
Lot-et-Garonne □ 10 44 22N 0 30 E
Lota 74 37 5 S 73 10W
Lothian □ 6 55 50N 3 0W
Lothiers 9 46 42N 1 33 E
Loubomo 51 4 9 S 12 47 E
Loudéac 8 48 11N 2 47W
Loudun 8 47 0N 0 5 E
Loué 8 47 59N 0 9W
Loue → 9 47 1N 5 28 E
Louga 49 15 45N 16 5W
Loughborough 5 52 46N 1 11W
Loughrea 7 53 11N 8 33W
Loughros More B. 7 54 48N 8 30W
Louhans 11 46 38N 5 12 E
Louis Trichardt 53 23 1 S 29 43 E
Louis XIV, Pte. 62 54 37N 79 45W
Louisbourg 63 45 55N 60 0W
Louise I. 64 52 55N 131 50W
Louisiade Arch. 56 11 10 S 153 0 E
Louisiana □ 67 30 50N 92 0W
Louisville, Ky., U.S.A. 66 38 15N 85 45W
Louisville, Miss., U.S.A. 67 33 7N 89 3W
Loulay 10 46 3N 0 30W
Loulé 18 37 9N 8 0W
Loupe, La 8 48 29N 1 1 E
Lourdes 10 43 6N 0 3W
Lourenço-Marques = Maputo 53 25 58 S 32 32 E
Louroux-Béconnais, Le 8 47 30N 0 55W
Louth, Ireland 7 53 47N 6 33W
Louth, U.K. 5 53 23N 0 0 E
Louth □ 7 53 55N 6 30W
Louvain = Leuven 12 50 52N 4 42 E
Louvière, La 12 50 27N 4 10 E
Louviers 8 49 12N 1 10 E
Lovisa 27 60 28N 26 12 E
Low Rocky Pt. 55 42 59 S 145 29 E
Lowell 66 42 38N 71 19W
Lower California = Baja California 69 31 10N 115 12W
Lower Saxony = Niedersachsen □ 13 52 45N 9 0 E
Lowestoft 5 52 29N 1 44 E
Łowicz 17 52 6N 19 55 E
Loxton 56 34 28 S 140 31 E
Loyalty Is. = Loyauté, Is. 57 21 0 S 167 30 E
Loyauté, Is. 57 21 0 S 167 30 E
Lozère □ 10 44 35N 3 30 E
Luachimo 51 7 23 S 20 48 E
Luacono 51 11 15 S 21 37 E
Lualaba → 51 0 26N 25 20 E
Luan Chau 41 21 38N 103 24 E
Luanda 51 8 50 S 13 15 E
Luang Prabang 41 19 52N 102 10 E
Luangwa 51 15 35 S 30 16 E
Luangwa → 51 14 25 S 30 25 E
Luanshya 51 13 3 S 28 28 E
Luapula → 51 9 26 S 28 33 E
Luarca 18 43 32N 6 32W
Luashi 51 10 50 S 23 36 E
Luau 51 10 40 S 22 10 E
Lubalo 51 9 10 S 19 15 E
Lubbock 67 33 40N 101 53W
Lübeck 13 53 52N 10 41 E
Lübecker Bucht 13 54 3N 11 0 E
Lubefu 51 4 47 S 24 27 E
Lublin 17 51 12N 22 38 E
Lubnān, J. 45 33 50N 35 45 E
Lubny 30 50 3N 32 58 E
Lubumbashi 51 11 40 S 27 28 E
Lubutu 51 0 45 S 26 30 E
Luc, Le 11 43 23N 6 21 E
Luc-en-Diois 11 44 36N 5 28 E
Lucca 20 43 50N 10 30 E
Luce Bay 6 54 45N 4 48W
Lucena 18 37 27N 4 31W
Lučenec 15 48 18N 19 42 E
Lucerne = Luzern 13 47 3N 8 18 E
Lucira 51 14 0 S 12 35 E
Lucknow 37 26 50N 81 0 E
Luçon 10 46 28N 1 10W
Lüda = Dalian 42 38 50N 121 40 E
Lüdenscheid 13 51 13N 7 37 E
Lüderitz 52 26 41 S 15 8 E
Ludhiana 36 30 57N 75 56 E
Ludington 66 43 58N 86 27W
Ludlow 5 52 23N 2 42W
Ludvika 28 60 8N 15 14 E
Ludwigsburg 13 48 53N 9 11 E
Ludwigshafen 13 49 27N 8 27 E
Luebo 51 5 21 S 21 23 E
Lufira → 51 9 30 S 27 0 E
Lufkin 67 31 25N 94 40W
Luga 32 58 40N 29 55 E
Lugano 13 46 0N 8 57 E
Lugh Ganana 47 3 48N 42 34 E
Lugnaquilla 7 52 58N 6 28W
Lugo 18 43 2N 7 35W
Lugovoye 30 42 55N 72 43 E
Luiana 52 17 25 S 22 59 E
Luiza 51 7 40 S 22 30 E
Luján 74 34 45 S 59 5W
Lukanga Swamp 51 14 30 S 27 40 E
Lukenie → 51 3 0 S 18 50 E
Lukolela 51 1 10 S 17 12 E
Lule älv → 27 65 35N 22 10 E
Luleå 27 65 35N 22 10 E
Lüleburgaz 45 41 23N 27 22 E
Lulonga → 51 1 0N 18 10 E
Lulua → 51 4 30 S 20 30 E
Lumai 51 13 13 S 21 25 E
Lumbala N'guimbo 51 14 18 S 21 18 E
Lumberton 66 34 37N 78 59W
Lumbres 9 50 40N 2 5 E
Lundazi 51 12 20 S 33 7 E
Lundy 5 51 10N 4 41W
Lune → 5 54 0N 2 51W
Lüneburg 13 53 15N 10 23 E
Lüneburg Heath = Lüneburger Heide 13 53 0N 10 0 E
Lüneburger Heide 13 53 0N 10 0 E
Lunel 11 43 39N 4 9 E
Lünen 13 51 36N 7 31 E
Lunéville 9 48 36N 6 30 E
Luni 36 26 0N 73 6 E
Lūni → 36 24 41N 71 14 E
Luofu 51 0 10 S 29 15 E
Luoyang 43 34 40N 112 26 E
Luozi 51 4 54 S 14 0 E
Lure 9 47 40N 6 30 E
Luremo 51 8 30 S 17 50 E
Lurgan 7 54 28N 6 20W
Lusaka 51 15 28 S 28 16 E
Lusambo 51 4 58 S 23 28 E
Lushoto 51 4 47 S 38 20 E
Lusignan 10 46 26N 0 8 E
Lusigny-sur-Barse 9 48 16N 4 15 E
Lussac-les-Châteaux 10 46 24N 0 43 E
Luton 5 51 53N 0 24W
Lutsk 32 50 50N 25 15 E
Luxembourg 12 49 37N 6 9 E
Luxembourg □ 12 49 58N 5 30 E
Luxembourg ■ 12 50 0N 6 0 E
Luxeuil-les-Bains 9 47 49N 6 24 E
Luxor = El Uqsur 50 25 41N 32 38 E
Luy → 10 43 39N 1 9W
Luy-de-Béarn → 10 43 39N 0 48W
Luy-de-France → 10 43 39N 0 48W
Luz-St.-Sauveur 10 42 53N 0 0 E
Luzern 13 47 3N 8 18 E
Luzhou 43 28 52N 105 20 E
Luziânia 73 16 20 S 48 0W
Luzon 40 16 0N 121 0 E
Luzy 9 46 47N 3 58 E
Lvov 32 49 50N 24 0 E
Lyakhovskiye, Ostrova 31 73 40N 141 0 E
Lyallpur = Faisalabad 36 31 30N 73 5 E
Lycksele 27 64 38N 18 40 E
Lydenburg 53 25 10 S 30 29 E
Lyell I. 64 52 40N 131 35W
Lyme Regis 5 50 44N 2 57W
Lymington 5 50 46N 1 32W
Lynchburg 66 37 23N 79 10W
Lynn 66 42 28N 70 57W
Lynn Lake 65 56 51N 101 3W
Lynton 5 51 14N 3 50W
Lyon 11 45 46N 4 50 E
Lyonnais 11 45 45N 4 15 E
Lyons = Lyon 11 45 46N 4 50 E
Lys → 9 50 39N 2 24 E

M

Ma'ān 45 30 12N 35 44 E
Ma'anshan 43 31 44N 118 29 E
Ma'arrat an Nu'mān 45 35 43N 36 43 E
Maas → 12 51 45N 4 32 E
Maaseik 12 51 6N 5 45 E
Maassluis 12 51 56N 4 16 E
Maastricht 12 50 50N 5 40 E
Mablethorpe 5 53 21N 0 14 E
Mabrouk 49 19 29N 1 15W
McAlester 67 34 57N 95 46W
Macao = Macau ■ 43 22 16N 113 35 E
Macapá 73 0 5N 51 4W
McArthur → 55 15 54 S 136 40 E
McArthur River 55 16 27 S 136 7 E
Macau 73 5 0 S 36 40W
Macau ■ 43 22 16N 113 35 E
McBride 64 53 20N 120 19W
Macclesfield 5 53 16N 2 9W
McClure Str. 1 75 0N 119 0W
McComb 67 31 13N 90 30W
McDermitt 68 42 0N 117 45W
McDonald Is. 2 54 0 S 73 0 E
Macdonald L. 54 23 30 S 129 0 E
Macdonnell Ranges 54 23 40 S 133 0 E
Macduff 6 57 40N 2 30W
Macedonia = Makedhonía □ 26 40 39N 22 0 E
Macedonia = Makedonija □ 24 41 53N 21 40 E
Maceió 73 9 40 S 35 41W
Macenta 49 8 35N 9 32W
Macerata 21 43 19N 13 28 E
Macfarlane, L. 55 32 0 S 136 40 E
Macgillycuddy's Reeks 7 52 2N 9 45W
Machakos 51 1 30 S 37 15 E
Machala 72 3 20 S 79 57W
Machattie, L. 56 24 50 S 139 48 E
Machecoul 8 47 0N 1 49W
Machevna 31 61 20N 172 20 E
Machilipatnam 38 16 12N 81 8 E
Machine, La 9 46 54N 3 27 E
Machiques 72 10 4N 72 34W
Machynlleth 5 52 36N 3 51W
McIlwraith Ra. 56 13 50 S 143 20 E
Macintyre → 56 28 37 S 150 47 E
Mackay 56 21 8 S 149 11 E
Mackay, L. 54 22 30 S 129 0 E
McKeesport 66 40 21N 79 50W
Mackenzie →, Australia 56 23 38 S 149 46 E
Mackenzie →, Canada 61 69 10N 134 20W
McKinley, Mt. 3 63 2N 151 0W
McKinley Sea 3 84 0N 10 0W
McKinney 67 33 10N 96 40W
Maclean 56 29 26 S 153 16 E
Maclear 53 31 2 S 28 23 E
Macleay → 56 30 56 S 153 0 E
McLennan 64 55 42N 116 50W
McLeod L. 54 24 9 S 113 47 E
MacLeod Lake 64 54 58N 123 0W
McMinnville, Oreg., U.S.A. 68 45 16N 123 11W
McMinnville, Tenn., U.S.A. 66 35 43N 85 45W
McMurdo Sd. 60 77 0 S 170 0 E
Macomb 67 40 25N 90 40W
Mâcon, France 11 46 19N 4 50 E
Macon, U.S.A. 66 32 50N 83 37W
Macondo 51 12 37 S 23 46 E
Macquarie → 55 30 5 S 147 30 E
Macquarie Is. 57 54 36 S 158 55 E
Macroom 7 51 54N 8 57W
Madagali 50 10 56N 13 33 E
Madagascar ■ 53 20 0 S 47 0 E
Madama 50 22 0N 13 40 E
Madang 56 5 12 S 145 49 E
Madaoua 49 14 5N 6 27 E
Madaripur 37 23 19N 90 15 E
Maddalena 22 41 15N 9 23 E
Madeira 49 32 50N 17 0W
Madeira → 72 3 22 S 58 45W
Madeleine, Is. de la 63 47 30N 61 40W
Madera 68 37 0N 120 1W
Madha 38 18 0N 75 30 E
Madhya Pradesh □ 36 21 50N 81 0 E
Madikeri 38 12 30N 75 45 E
Madimba 51 5 0 S 15 0 E
Madīnat ash Sha'b 47 12 50N 45 0 E
Madingou 51 4 10 S 13 33 E
Madison, Fla., U.S.A. 66 30 29N 83 39W
Madison, Ind., U.S.A. 66 38 42N 85 20W
Madison, Wis., U.S.A. 67 43 5N 89 25W
Madisonville 66 37 20N 87 30W
Madiun 40 7 38 S 111 32 E
Madley 5 52 3N 2 51W
Madon → 9 48 36N 6 6 E
Madras, India 38 13 8N 80 19 E
Madras, U.S.A. 68 44 40N 121 10W
Madre, L., Mexico 69 25 0N 97 30W
Madre, L., U.S.A. 67 26 0N 97 40W
Madre de Dios → 72 10 59 S 66 8W
Madre del Sur, Sa. 69 17 0N 100 0W
Madre Occidental, Sa. 69 25 0N 105 0W
Madre Oriental, Sa. 69 22 0N 99 30W
Madrid 18 40 25N 3 45W
Madura, Selat 40 7 30 S 113 20 E
Madurai 38 9 55N 78 10 E
Madurantakam 38 12 30N 79 50 E
Mae Rim 41 18 54N 98 57 E
Maebashi 44 36 24N 139 4 E
Maesteg 5 51 36N 3 40W
Maestra, Sierra 70 20 15N 77 0W
Maestrazgo, Mts. del 19 40 30N 0 25W
Maevatanana 53 16 56 S 46 49 E
Mafeking 65 52 40N 101 10W
Mafia I. 51 7 45 S 39 50 E
Mafikeng 52 25 50 S 25 38 E
Mafra, Brazil 74 26 10 S 50 0W
Mafra, Portugal 18 38 55N 9 20W
Magadan 31 59 38N 150 50 E
Magadi 51 1 54 S 36 19 E
Magallanes, Estrecho de 74 52 30 S 75 0W
Magangué 72 9 14N 74 45W
Magburaka 49 8 47N 12 0W
Magdalena, Bolivia 72 13 13 S 63 57W
Magdalena, Mexico 69 30 38N 110 57W
Magdalena → 72 11 6N 74 51W
Magdeburg 13 52 8N 11 36 E
Magee, I. 7 54 48N 5 44W
Magelang 40 7 29 S 110 13 E
Magellan's Str. = Magallanes, Estrecho de 74 52 30 S 75 0W
Maggiore, L. 20 46 0N 8 35 E
Magherafelt 7 54 44N 6 37W
Magnac-Laval 10 46 13N 1 11 E
Magnetic Pole (North) 3 76 12N 100 12W
Magnitogorsk 30 53 27N 59 4 E
Magny-en-Vexin 9 49 9N 1 47 E
Magog 63 45 18N 72 9W
Magosa = Famagusta 45 35 8N 33 55 E
Magrath 64 49 25N 112 50W
Mahābād 45 36 50N 45 45 E
Mahabo 53 20 23 S 44 40 E
Mahagi 51 2 20N 31 0 E
Mahajanga 53 15 40 S 46 25 E
Mahakam → 39 0 35 S 117 17 E
Mahalapye 52 23 1 S 26 51 E
Maḩallāt 46 33 55N 50 30 E
Mahanadi → 36 20 20N 86 25 E
Mahanoro 53 19 54 S 48 48 E
Maharashtra □ 38 20 30N 75 30 E
Mahbubnagar 38 16 45N 77 59 E
Mahdia 50 35 28N 11 0 E
Mahenge 51 8 45 S 36 41 E
Mahesana 36 23 39N 72 26 E
Mahia Pen. 59 39 9 S 177 55 E
Mahón 19 39 53N 4 16 E
Mahone Bay 63 44 30N 64 20W
Mai-Ndombe, L. 51 2 0 S 18 20 E
Maîche 9 47 16N 6 48 E
Maidenhead 5 51 31N 0 42W
Maidstone 5 51 16N 0 31 E
Maiduguri 50 12 0N 13 20 E
Maignelay 9 49 32N 2 30 E
Maijdi 37 22 48N 91 10 E
Maikala Ra. 36 22 0N 81 0 E
Mailly-le-Camp 9 48 41N 4 12 E
Main →, Germany 13 50 0N 8 18 E
Main →, U.K. 7 54 49N 6 20W
Maine 8 48 0N 0 0 E
Maine □ 66 45 20N 69 0W
Maine → 7 52 10N 9 40W
Maine-et-Loire □ 8 47 31N 0 30W
Mainland, Orkney, U.K. 6 59 0N 3 10W
Mainland, Shetland, U.K. 6 60 15N 1 22W
Maintenon 9 48 35N 1 35 E
Maintirano 53 18 3 S 44 1 E
Mainz 13 50 0N 8 17 E
Maiquetía 72 10 36N 66 57W
Maisi, Pta. de 70 20 10N 74 10W
Maisse 9 48 24N 2 21 E
Maitland 56 32 33 S 151 36 E
Maiz, Is. del 70 12 15N 83 4W
Maizuru 44 35 25N 135 22 E
Maji 50 6 12N 35 30 E
Majorca, I. = Mallorca 19 39 30N 3 0 E
Maka 49 13 40N 14 10W
Makarikari = Makgadikgadi Salt Pans 52 20 40 S 25 45 E
Makarovo 31 57 40N 107 45 E
Makasar = Ujung Pandang 40 5 10 S 119 20 E
Makasar, Selat 40 1 0 S 118 20 E
Makat 30 47 39N 53 19 E
Makedhonía □ 26 40 39N 22 0 E
Makedonija □ 24 41 53N 21 40 E
Makeni 49 8 55N 12 5W
Makeyevka 34 48 0N 38 0 E
Makgadikgadi Salt Pans 52 20 40 S 25 45 E
Makhachkala 35 43 0N 47 30 E
Makindu 51 2 18 S 37 50 E
Makkah 47 21 30N 39 54 E
Maklakovo 31 58 16N 92 29 E
Makó 15 46 14N 20 33 E
Makokou 51 0 40N 12 50 E
Makoua 51 0 5 S 15 50 E
Makumbi 51 5 50 S 20 43 E
Makurazaki 44 31 15N 130 20 E
Makurdi 49 7 43N 8 35 E
Mal B. 7 52 50N 9 30W
Malabar Coast 38 11 0N 75 0 E
Malacca, Str. of 39 3 0N 101 0 E
Málaga 18 36 43N 4 23W
Málaga □ 18 36 38N 4 58W
Malakâl 50 9 33N 31 40 E
Malamyzh 31 50 0N 136 50 E
Malang 40 7 59 S 112 45 E
Malanje 51 9 36 S 16 17 E
Mälaren 28 59 30N 17 10 E
Malatya 45 38 25N 38 20 E
Malawi ■ 51 13 0 S 34 0 E
Malawi, L. 51 12 30 S 34 30 E
Malay Pen. 41 7 25N 100 0 E
Malāyer 45 34 19N 48 51 E
Malaysia ■ 39 5 0N 110 0 E
Malbaie, La 63 47 40N 70 10W
Malbork 17 54 3N 19 1 E
Malcolm 54 28 51 S 121 25 E
Maldegem 12 51 14N 3 26 E
Malden I. 58 4 3 S 155 1W
Maldives ■ 29 7 0N 73 0 E
Maldonado 74 35 0 S 55 0W
Malé Karpaty 15 48 30N 17 20 E
Maléa, Ákra 26 36 28N 23 7 E
Malegaon 36 20 30N 74 38 E
Malema 51 14 57 S 37 20 E
Malesherbes 9 48 15N 2 24 E
Malestroit 8 47 49N 2 25W
Malgomaj 27 64 40N 16 30 E
Malha 50 15 8N 25 10 E
Mali ■ 49 17 0N 3 0W
Mali Kyun 41 13 0N 98 20 E
Malindi 51 3 12 S 40 5 E
Malines = Mechelen 12 51 2N 4 29 E
Mallacoota Inlet 56 37 34 S 149 40 E
Mallaig 6 57 0N 5 50W
Mallawi 50 27 44N 30 44 E
Mallemort 11 43 43N 5 11 E
Mallorca 19 39 30N 3 0 E
Mallow 7 52 8N 8 40W
Malmberget 27 67 11N 20 40 E
Malmédy 12 50 25N 6 2 E
Malmö 28 55 36N 12 59 E
Malmöhus län □ 28 55 45N 13 30 E
Malone 62 44 50N 74 19W
Malta ■ 4 35 50N 14 30 E
Maltahöhe 52 24 55 S 17 0 E
Malton 5 54 9N 0 48W
Maluku 40 1 0 S 127 0 E
Malvan 38 16 2N 73 30 E
Malvern, U.K. 5 52 7N 2 19W
Malvern, U.S.A. 67 34 22N 92 50W
Malvern Hills 5 52 0N 2 19W
Malvinas, Is. = Falkland Is. 74 51 30 S 59 0W
Malyy Lyakhovskiy, Ostrov 31 74 7N 140 36 E
Mama 31 58 18N 112 54 E
Mamaia 25 44 18N 28 37 E
Mambilima Falls 51 10 31 S 28 45 E
Mamers 8 48 21N 0 22 E
Mamfe 49 5 50N 9 15 E
Mamoré → 72 10 23 S 65 53W
Mamou 49 10 15N 12 0W
Man 49 7 30N 7 40W
Man, I. of 5 54 15N 4 30W
Mana 73 5 45N 53 55W
Manacapuru 72 3 16 S 60 37W
Manacor 19 39 34N 3 13 E
Manado 40 1 29N 124 51 E
Managua 70 12 6N 86 20W
Manakara 53 22 8 S 48 1 E
Manam I. 56 4 5 S 145 0 E
Mananara 53 16 10 S 49 46 E
Mananjary 53 21 13 S 48 20 E
Manaus 72 3 0 S 60 0W
Mancha, La 19 39 10N 2 54W
Manche □ 8 49 10N 1 20W
Manchester, U.K. 5 53 30N 2 15W
Manchester, U.S.A. 66 42 58N 71 29W
Manda 51 10 30 S 34 40 E
Mandal 27 58 2N 7 25 E
Mandalay 41 22 0N 96 4 E
Mandale = Mandalay 41 22 0N 96 4 E
Mandelieu-la-Napoule 11 43 34N 6 57 E
Mandi 36 31 39N 76 58 E
Mandimba 51 14 20 S 35 40 E
Mandla 37 22 39N 80 30 E

Mandritsara 53 15 50 S 48 49 E
Mandsaur 36 24 3N 75 8 E
Mandvi 36 22 51N 69 22 E
Mandya 38 12 30N 77 0 E
Manfalût 50 27 20N 30 52 E
Manfredónia 23 41 40N 15 55 E
Mangalia 25 43 50N 28 35 E
Mangalore 38 12 55N 74 47 E
Mango 49 10 20N 0 30 E
Mangoche 51 14 25 S 35 16 E
Mangole 40 1 50 S 125 55 E
Mangueigne 50 10 30N 21 15 E
Mangyshlak P-ov. 30 44 30N 52 30 E
Manica 53 18 58 S 32 59 E
Manicoré 72 5 48 S 61 16W
Manicouagan → 63 49 30N 68 30W
Manihiki 58 10 24 S 161 1W
Manila 40 14 40N 121 3 E
Manisa 45 38 38N 27 30 E
Manistee 66 44 15N 86 20W
Manistique 62 45 59N 86 18W
Manitoba □ 65 55 30N 97 0W
Manitoba, L. 65 51 0N 98 45W
Manitoulin I. 62 45 40N 82 30W
Manitowoc 67 44 8N 87 40W
Manizales 72 5 5N 75 32W
Manja 53 21 26 S 44 20 E
Manjacaze 53 24 45 S 34 0 E
Manjhand 36 25 50N 68 10 E
Manjil 45 36 46N 49 30 E
Manjimup 54 34 15 S 116 6 E
Manjra → 38 18 49N 77 52 E
Mankato 67 44 8N 93 59W
Mankono 49 8 1N 6 10W
Manmad 38 20 18N 74 28 E
Mannar 38 9 1N 79 54 E
Mannar, G. of 38 8 30N 79 0 E
Mannar I. 38 9 5N 79 45 E
Mannheim 13 49 28N 8 29 E
Mano 49 8 3N 12 2W
Manombo 53 22 57 S 43 28 E
Manono 51 7 15 S 27 25 E
Manosque 11 43 49N 5 47 E
Manouane, L. 63 50 45N 70 45W
Manresa 19 41 48N 1 50 E
Mans, Le 8 48 0N 0 10 E
Mansa 51 11 13 S 28 55 E
Mansfield, U.K. 5 53 8N 1 12W
Mansfield, U.S.A. 66 40 45N 82 30W
Mansle 10 45 52N 0 12 E
Manta 72 1 0 S 80 40W
Mantes-la-Jolie 9 49 0N 1 41 E
Manthani 38 18 40N 79 35 E
Manthelan 8 47 9N 0 47 E
Mantiqueira, Serra da 73 22 0 S 44 0W
Mántova 20 45 20N 10 42 E
Mänttä 27 62 0N 24 40 E
Mantua = Mántova 20 45 20N 10 42 E
Manu 72 12 10 S 70 51W
Manuae 58 19 30 S 159 0W
Manus I. 56 2 0 S 147 0 E
Manyara, L. 51 3 40 S 35 50 E
Manych-Gudilo, Oz. 35 46 24N 42 38 E
Manyoni 51 5 45 S 34 55 E
Manzai 36 32 12N 70 15 E
Manzanares 19 39 0N 3 22W
Manzanillo, Cuba 70 20 20N 77 31W
Manzanillo, Mexico 69 19 3N 104 20W
Manzhouli 42 49 35N 117 25 E
Mao 50 14 4N 15 19 E
Mapimí 69 25 49N 103 51W
Maple 65 43 51N 79 31W
Maputo 53 25 58 S 32 32 E
Maquinchao 74 41 15 S 68 50W
Mar, Serra do 74 25 30 S 49 0W
Mar Chiquita, L. 74 30 40 S 62 50W
Mar del Plata 74 38 0 S 57 30W
Marabá 73 5 20 S 49 5W
Maracaibo 72 10 40N 71 37W
Maracaibo, L. de 72 9 40N 71 30W
Maracay 72 10 15N 67 28W
Marādah 50 29 15N 19 15 E
Maradi 49 13 29N 7 20 E
Marajó, I. de 73 1 0 S 49 30W
Maralal 51 1 0N 36 38 E
Maralinga 54 30 13 S 131 32 E
Marampa 49 8 45N 12 28W
Maranhão = São Luís 73 2 39 S 44 15W
Maranhão □ 73 5 0 S 46 0W
Maranoa → 56 27 50 S 148 37 E
Marañón → 72 4 30 S 73 35W
Marão 53 24 18 S 34 2 E
Maraş 45 37 37N 36 53 E
Marathón 26 38 11N 23 58 E
Marbella 18 36 30N 4 57W
Marble Bar 54 21 9 S 119 44 E
Marburg 13 50 49N 8 36 E
March 5 52 33N 0 5 E
Marche 10 46 5N 1 20 E
Marche □ 21 43 22N 13 10 E
Marche-en-Famenne 12 50 14N 5 19 E
Marcigny 11 46 17N 4 2 E
Marcillat-en-Combraille 10 46 12N 2 38 E
Marck 9 50 57N 1 57 E
Marckolsheim 9 48 10N 7 30 E
Marcus 57 24 0N 153 45 E
Mardin 45 37 20N 40 43 E
Maree L. 6 57 40N 5 30W
Mareeba 56 16 59 S 145 28 E
Maremma 20 42 45N 11 15 E
Marennes 10 45 49N 1 7W
Mareuil-sur-Lay 10 46 32N 1 14W
Margarita 69 9 20N 79 55W
Margate 5 51 23N 1 24 E
Margeride, Mts. de la 10 44 43N 3 38 E
Mari, A.S.S.R. □ 33 56 30N 48 0 E
Maria I. 54 14 52 S 135 45 E
Maria van Diemen, C. 59 34 29 S 172 40 E
Mariana Trench 57 13 0N 145 0 E
Marianao 70 23 8N 82 24W
Marianna 66 30 45N 85 15W
Ma'rib 47 15 25N 45 21 E
Maribor 21 46 36N 15 40 E
Maridi 50 4 55N 29 25 E
Marie-Galante 70 15 56N 61 16W
Mariehamn 27 60 5N 19 55 E
Marienberg 12 52 30N 6 35 E
Marienbourg 12 50 6N 4 31 E
Mariental 52 24 36 S 18 0 E
Mariestad 28 58 43N 13 50 E
Marietta, Ga., U.S.A. 66 34 0N 84 30W
Marietta, Ohio, U.S.A. 66 39 27N 81 27W
Marignane 11 43 25N 5 13 E
Marília 73 22 13 S 50 0W
Marín 18 42 23N 8 42W
Marinel, Le 51 10 25 S 25 17 E
Marinette 66 45 4N 87 40W
Maringá 74 23 26 S 52 2W
Marion, Ill., U.S.A. 67 37 45N 88 55W
Marion, Ind., U.S.A. 66 40 35N 85 40W
Marion, Ohio, U.S.A. 66 40 38N 83 8W
Marion Reef 56 19 10 S 152 17 E
Maritimes, Alpes 11 44 10N 7 10 E
Maritsa → 25 42 15N 24 0 E
Marken 12 52 26N 5 12 E
Market Drayton 5 52 55N 2 30W
Market Harborough 5 52 29N 0 55W
Markham I. 3 84 0N 0 45W
Markovo 31 64 40N 169 40 E
Marks 33 51 45N 46 50 E
Marlborough Downs 5 51 25N 1 55W
Marle 9 49 43N 3 47 E
Marlin 67 31 25N 96 50W
Marmagao 38 15 25N 73 56 E
Marmande 10 44 30N 0 10 E
Marmara, Sea of = Marmara Denizi 45 40 45N 28 15 E
Marmara Denizi 45 40 45N 28 15 E
Marmaris 45 36 50N 28 14 E
Marmolada, Mte. 21 46 25N 11 55 E
Marnay 9 47 16N 5 48 E
Marne □ 9 48 50N 4 10 E
Marne → 9 48 48N 2 24 E
Maroantsetra 53 15 26 S 49 44 E
Marondera 51 18 5 S 31 42 E
Maronne → 10 45 5N 1 56 E
Maroua 50 10 40N 14 20 E
Marovoay 53 16 6 S 46 39 E
Marquesas Is. 58 9 30 S 140 0W
Marquette 62 46 30N 87 21W
Marquise 9 50 50N 1 40 E
Marrakech 49 31 9N 8 0W
Marree 56 29 39 S 138 1 E
Marromeu 53 18 15 S 36 25 E
Marrupa 51 13 8 S 37 30 E
Marsá Matrûh 50 31 19N 27 9 E
Marsá Susah 50 32 52N 21 59 E
Marsabit 51 2 18N 38 0 E
Marsala 22 37 48N 12 25 E
Marseillan 10 43 23N 3 31 E
Marseille 11 43 18N 5 23 E
Marseilles = Marseille 11 43 18N 5 23 E
Marshall, Liberia 49 6 8N 10 22W
Marshall, Minn., U.S.A. 67 44 25N 95 45W
Marshall, Mo., U.S.A. 67 39 8N 93 15W
Marshall, Tex., U.S.A. 67 32 29N 94 20W
Marshall Is. 57 9 0N 171 0 E
Marshalltown 67 42 5N 92 56W
Marshfield 67 44 42N 90 10W
Marstrand 28 57 53N 11 35 E
Marte 50 12 23N 13 46 E
Martel 10 44 57N 1 37 E
Martelange 12 49 49N 5 43 E
Martha's Vineyard 66 41 25N 70 35W
Martigné-Ferchaud 8 47 50N 1 20W
Martigues 11 43 24N 5 4 E
Martinique 70 14 40N 61 0W
Martinsburg 66 39 30N 77 57W
Martinsville, Ind., U.S.A. 66 39 29N 86 23W
Martinsville, Va., U.S.A. 66 36 41N 79 52W
Martos 18 37 44N 3 58W
Marugame 44 34 15N 133 40 E
Marvejols 10 44 33N 3 19 E
Marwar 36 25 43N 73 45 E
Mary 30 37 40N 61 50 E
Mary Kathleen 56 20 44 S 139 48 E
Maryborough = Port Laoise 7 53 2N 7 20W
Maryborough, Queens., Australia 56 25 31 S 152 37 E
Maryborough, Vic., Australia 56 37 0 S 143 44 E
Maryland □ 66 39 10N 76 40W
Maryport 5 54 43N 3 30W
Marysville 68 39 14N 121 40W
Maryville 66 35 50N 84 0W
Marzūq 50 25 53N 13 57 E
Masaka 51 0 21 S 31 45 E
Masan 43 35 11N 128 32 E
Masasi 51 10 45 S 38 52 E
Masaya 70 12 0N 86 7W
Mascara 49 35 26N 0 6 E
Mascota 69 20 32N 104 49W
Maseru 52 29 18 S 27 30 E
Mashhad 46 36 20N 59 35 E
Masi 27 69 26N 23 40 E
Masi Manimba 51 4 40 S 17 54 E
Masindi 51 1 40N 31 43 E
Masisea 72 8 35 S 74 22W
Masjed Soleyman 45 31 55N 49 18 E
Mask, L. 7 53 36N 9 24W
Mason City 67 43 9N 93 12W
Masqat 46 23 37N 58 36 E
Massa 20 44 2N 10 7 E
Massachusetts □ 66 42 25N 72 0W
Massaguet 50 12 28N 15 26 E
Massakory 50 13 0N 15 49 E
Massangena 53 21 34 S 33 0 E
Massat 10 42 53N 1 21 E
Massawa = Mitsiwa 50 15 35N 39 25 E
Massena 66 44 52N 74 55W
Massénya 50 11 21N 16 9 E
Massiac 10 45 15N 3 11 E
Massif Central 10 45 30N 3 0 E
Massillon 66 40 47N 81 30W
Massinga 53 23 15 S 35 22 E
Masuda 44 34 40N 131 51 E
Masvingo 51 20 8 S 30 49 E
Matachewan 62 47 56N 80 39W
Matadi 51 5 52 S 13 31 E
Matagalpa 70 13 0N 85 58W
Matagami, L. 62 49 50N 77 40W
Matam 49 15 34N 13 17W
Matamoros, Coahuila, Mexico 69 25 32N 103 15W
Matamoros, Puebla, Mexico 69 18 2N 98 17W
Ma'ţan as Sarra 50 21 45N 22 0 E
Matane 63 48 50N 67 33W
Matanzas 70 23 0N 81 40W
Matapan, C. = Taínaron, Ákra 26 36 22N 22 27 E
Matara 38 5 58N 80 30 E
Matarani 72 77 0 S 72 10W
Mataranka 54 14 55 S 133 4 E
Matehuala 69 23 39N 100 39W
Matera 23 40 40N 16 37 E
Matha 10 45 52N 0 20W
Mathura 36 27 30N 77 40 E
Matlock 5 53 8N 1 32W
Matmata 49 33 37N 9 59 E
Mato Grosso □ 73 14 0 S 55 0W
Mato Grosso, Planalto do 73 15 0 S 59 57W
Matosinhos 18 41 11N 8 42W
Matour 11 46 19N 4 29 E
Matsue 44 35 25N 133 10 E
Matsumoto 44 36 15N 138 0 E
Matsusaka 44 34 34N 136 32 E
Matsuyama 44 33 45N 132 45 E
Mattagami → 62 50 43N 81 29W
Mattancheri 38 9 50N 76 15 E
Mattawa 62 46 20N 78 45W
Matterhorn 13 45 58N 7 39 E
Matucana 72 11 55 S 76 25W
Maturín 72 9 45N 63 11W
Mau Ranipur 36 25 16N 79 8 E
Maubeuge 9 50 17N 3 57 E
Maubourguet 10 43 29N 0 1 E
Mauléon-Licharre 10 43 14N 0 54W
Maun 52 20 0 S 23 26 E
Maungmagan Kyunzu 41 14 0N 97 48 E
Maure-de-Bretagne 8 47 53N 1 58W
Maures 11 43 15N 6 15 E
Mauriac 10 45 13N 2 19 E
Maurice L. 54 29 30 S 131 0 E
Mauritania ■ 49 20 50N 10 0W
Mauritius ■ 2 20 0 S 57 0 E
Mauron 8 48 9N 2 18W
Maurs 10 44 43N 2 12 E
Mauvezin 10 43 44N 0 53 E
Mauzé-sur-le-Mignon 10 46 12N 0 41W
Mavinga 51 15 50 S 20 21 E
Maxixe 53 23 54 S 35 17 E
May Pen 70 17 58N 77 15W
Maya → 31 54 31N 134 41 E
Mayagüez 70 18 12N 67 9W
Mayen 13 50 18N 7 10 E
Mayenne 8 48 20N 0 38W
Mayenne □ 8 48 10N 0 40W
Mayenne → 8 47 30N 0 32W
Mayerthorpe 64 53 57N 115 8W
Mayfield 66 36 45N 88 40W
Maykop 35 44 35N 40 25 E
Maynooth 7 53 22N 6 38W
Mayo □ 7 53 47N 9 7W
Maysville 66 38 39N 83 46W
Mayya 31 61 44N 130 18 E
Mazabuka 51 15 52 S 27 44 E
Mazagán = El Jadida 49 33 11N 8 17W
Mazamet 10 43 30N 2 20 E
Mazán 72 3 30 S 73 0W
Mazar-e Sharif 46 36 41N 67 0 E
Mazarredo 74 47 10 S 66 50W
Mazarrón 19 37 38N 1 19W
Mazatenango 69 14 35N 91 30W
Mazatlán 69 23 13N 106 25W
Mazoe → 51 16 20 S 33 30 E
Mbabane 53 26 18 S 31 6 E
Mbaïki 51 3 53N 18 1 E
Mbala 51 8 46 S 31 24 E
Mbale 51 1 8N 34 12 E
Mbalmayo 51 3 33N 11 33 E
Mbamba Bay 51 11 13 S 34 49 E
Mbandaka 51 0 1N 18 18 E
Mbanza Ngungu 51 5 12 S 14 53 E
Mbarara 51 0 35 S 30 40 E
Mbeya 51 8 54 S 33 29 E
Mbini □ 51 1 30N 10 0 E
Mbour 49 14 22N 16 54W
Mbout 49 16 1N 12 38W
Mbuji-Mayi 51 6 9 S 23 40 E
Mbulu 51 3 45 S 35 30 E
Mchinji 51 13 47 S 32 58 E
Mead, L. 68 36 1N 114 44W
Meadville 66 41 39N 80 9W
Meander River 64 59 2N 117 42W
Meath □ 7 53 32N 6 40W
Meaulne 10 46 36N 2 36 E
Meaux 9 48 58N 2 50 E
Mecca = Makkah 47 21 30N 39 54 E
Mechelen 12 51 2N 4 29 E
Mecheria 49 33 35N 0 18W
Mecklenburger Bucht 13 54 20N 11 40 E
Meconta 51 14 59 S 39 50 E
Meda → 54 17 20 S 123 50 E
Medan 39 3 40N 98 38 E
Medéa 49 36 12N 2 50 E
Medellín 72 6 15N 75 35W
Medemblik 12 52 46N 5 8 E
Mederdra 49 17 0N 15 38W
Medford 68 42 20N 122 52W
Mediaş 25 46 9N 24 22 E
Medicine Bow Ra. 68 41 10N 106 25W
Medicine Hat 65 50 0N 110 45W
Medina = Al Madīnah 47 24 35N 39 52 E
Medina 66 41 9N 81 50W
Medina del Campo 18 41 18N 4 55W
Medina-Sidonia 18 36 28N 5 57W
Medinipur 37 22 25N 87 21 E
Mediterranean Sea 4 35 0N 15 0 E
Médoc 10 45 10N 0 50W
Medley 65 54 25N 110 16W
Medveditsa → 33 49 35N 42 41 E
Medvezhi, Ostrava 31 71 0N 161 0 E
Medvezhyegorsk 30 63 0N 34 25 E
Medway → 5 51 28N 0 45 E
Meekatharra 54 26 32 S 118 29 E
Meerut 36 29 1N 77 42 E
Mega 50 3 57N 38 19 E
Mégantic, L. 63 45 32N 70 53W
Mégara 26 37 58N 23 22 E
Megève 11 45 51N 6 37 E
Mehadia 25 44 56N 22 23 E
Meharry, Mt. 54 22 59 S 118 35 E
Mehun-sur-Yèvre 9 47 10N 2 13 E
Mei Xian 43 24 16N 116 6 E
Meissen 13 51 10N 13 29 E
Mékambo 51 1 2N 13 50 E
Mekdela 50 11 24N 39 10 E
Meknès 49 33 57N 5 33W
Mekong → 41 9 30N 106 15 E
Melagiri Hills 38 12 20N 77 30 E
Melaka 41 2 15N 102 15 E
Melaka □ 41 2 15N 102 15 E
Melanesia 57 4 0 S 155 0 E
Melbourne 56 37 50 S 145 0 E
Melchor Muzquiz 69 27 53N 101 31W
Meldorf 13 54 5N 9 5 E
Mêle-sur-Sarthe, Le 8 48 31N 0 22 E
Melfi 50 11 0N 17 59 E
Melfort 65 52 50N 104 37W
Melilla 49 35 21N 2 57W
Melitopol 34 46 50N 35 22 E
Melk 14 48 13N 15 20 E
Mellansel 27 63 25N 18 17 E
Melle 10 46 14N 0 10W
Mellerud 28 58 41N 12 28 E
Mellish Reef 55 17 25 S 155 50 E
Melo 74 32 20 S 54 10W
Melrose 6 53 35N 2 44W
Melton Mowbray 5 52 46N 0 52W
Melun 9 48 32N 2 39 E
Melut 50 10 30N 32 13 E
Melville 65 50 55N 102 50W
Melville, C. 56 14 11 S 144 30 E
Melville B. 55 12 0 S 136 45 E
Melville I., Australia 54 11 30 S 131 0 E
Melville I., Canada 3 75 30N 112 0W
Memba 51 14 11 S 40 30 E
Memmingen 13 47 59N 10 12 E
Memphis, Tenn., U.S.A. 67 35 7N 90 0W
Memphis, Tex., U.S.A. 67 34 45N 100 30W
Menai Strait 5 53 14N 4 10W
Ménaka 49 15 59N 2 18 E
Menam = Chao Phraya → 41 13 32N 100 36 E
Menasha 66 44 13N 88 27W
Mende 10 44 31N 3 30 E
Mendip Hills 5 51 17N 2 40W
Mendocino 68 39 26N 123 50W
Mendocino, C. 68 40 26N 124 25W
Mendoza 74 32 50 S 68 52W
Menen 12 50 47N 3 7 E
Menfi 22 37 36N 12 57 E
Menindee 56 32 20 S 142 25 E
Menominee 67 45 9N 87 39W
Menongue 51 14 48 S 17 52 E
Menorca 19 40 0N 4 0 E
Mentawai, Kepulauan 39 2 0 S 99 0 E
Menton 11 43 50N 7 29 E
Menzies 54 29 40 S 120 58 E
Meppel 12 52 42N 6 12 E
Meppen 13 52 41N 7 20 E
Merabéllou, Kólpos 26 35 10N 25 50 E
Merano 21 46 40N 11 10 E
Merca 47 1 48N 44 50 E
Merced 68 37 18N 120 30W
Mercedes, Buenos Aires, Argentina 74 34 40 S 59 30W
Mercedes, Corrientes, Argentina 74 29 10 S 58 5W
Mercedes, San Luis, Argentina 74 33 40 S 65 21W
Mercedes, Uruguay 74 33 12 S 58 0W
Merdrignac 8 48 11N 2 27W
Méréville 9 48 20N 2 5 E
Mergui Arch. = Myeik Kyunzu 41 11 30N 97 30 E
Mérida, Mexico 69 20 58N 89 37W
Mérida, Spain 18 38 55N 6 25W
Mérida, Venezuela 72 8 24N 71 8W
Meriden 66 41 33N 72 47W
Meridian 66 32 20N 88 42W
Merksem 12 51 16N 4 25 E
Merlerault, Le 8 48 41N 0 16 E
Merowe 50 18 29N 31 46 E
Merredin 54 31 28 S 118 18 E
Merrick 6 55 8N 4 30W
Merritt 64 50 10N 120 45W
Mersa Fatma 47 14 57N 40 17 E
Mersch 12 49 44N 6 7 E
Mersey → 5 53 20N 2 56W
Merseyside □ 5 53 25N 2 55W
Mersin 45 36 51N 34 36 E
Merthyr Tydfil 5 51 45N 3 23W
Mértola 18 37 40N 7 40 E
Méru, France 9 49 13N 2 8 E
Meru, Kenya 51 0 3N 37 40 E
Merville 9 50 38N 2 38 E
Méry-sur-Seine 9 48 31N 3 54 E
Merzig 13 49 26N 6 37 E
Mesa 68 33 20N 111 56W
Mesa, La 68 32 48N 117 5W
Meshra er Req 50 8 25N 29 18 E
Meslay-du-Maine 8 47 58N 0 33W
Mesolóngion 26 38 21N 21 28 E
Mesopotamia = Al Jazirah 45 33 30N 44 0 E
Mesquite 68 36 47N 114 6W
Messac 8 47 49N 1 50W
Messina, Italy 23 38 10N 15 32 E
Messina, S. Africa 53 22 20 S 30 0 E
Messina, Str. di 23 38 5N 15 35 E
Messíni 26 37 4N 22 1 E
Messiniakós, Kólpos 26 36 45N 22 5 E
Mesta → 25 41 30N 24 0 E
Meta → 72 6 12N 67 28W
Metairie 67 29 59N 90 9W
Metán 74 25 30 S 65 0W
Metangula 51 12 40 S 34 50 E
Metema 50 12 56N 36 13 E
Metil 51 16 24 S 39 0 E
Metropolis 67 37 10N 88 47W
Metz 9 49 8N 6 10 E
Meulan 9 49 0N 1 55 E
Meung-sur-Loire 9 47 50N 1 40 E
Meurthe → 9 48 47N 6 9 E
Meurthe-et-Moselle □ 9 48 52N 6 0 E
Meuse □ 9 49 8N 5 25 E
Meuse → 12 50 45N 5 41 E
Mexborough 5 53 29N 1 18W
Mexia 67 31 38N 96 32W
Mexicali 69 32 40N 115 29W
México, Mexico 69 19 20N 99 10W
Mexico, U.S.A. 67 39 10N 91 55W
México □ 69 19 20N 99 30W
Mexico ■ 69 20 0N 100 0W
Meymac 10 45 32N 2 10 E
Meyrargues 11 43 38N 5 32 E
Meyrueis 10 44 12N 3 27 E
Meyssac 10 45 3N 1 40 E
Mèze 10 43 27N 3 36 E
Mezen 30 65 50N 44 20 E
Mezen → 30 66 11N 43 59 E
Mézenc, Mt. 11 44 54N 4 11 E
Mézidon 8 49 5N 0 1W
Mézilhac 11 44 49N 4 21 E
Mézin 10 44 4N 0 16 E
Mezőkövesd 15 47 49N 20 35 E
Mézos 10 44 5N 1 10W
Mezőtúr 15 47 0N 20 41 E
Mhow 36 22 33N 75 50 E
Miahuatlán 69 16 21N 96 36W
Miami 66 25 45N 80 15W
Miami Beach 66 25 49N 80 6W
Miandrivazo 53 19 31 S 45 29 E
Mīāneh 45 37 30N 47 40 E
Mianwali 36 32 38N 71 28 E
Miaoli 43 24 37N 120 49 E
Miarinarivo 53 18 57 S 46 55 E
Miass 30 54 59N 60 6 E
Michigan □ 66 44 40N 85 40W
Michigan, L. 62 44 0N 87 0W
Michigan City 66 41 42N 86 56W
Michikamau L. 63 54 20N 63 10W
Michipicoten 62 47 55N 84 55W
Michoacán □ 69 19 0N 101 50W
Michurinsk 33 52 58N 40 27 E
Micronesia 57 11 0N 160 0 E
Mid Glamorgan □ 5 51 40N 3 25W
Middelburg, Neth. 12 51 30N 3 36 E
Middelburg, S. Africa 52 31 30 S 25 0 E
Middle Andaman I. 41 12 30N 92 30 E
Middlesboro 66 36 36N 83 43W
Middlesbrough 5 54 35N 1 14W
Middleton 63 44 57N 65 4W
Middletown, Conn., U.S.A. 66 41 37N 72 40W
Middletown, N.Y., U.S.A. 66 41 28N 74 28W
Middletown, Ohio, U.S.A. 66 39 29N 84 25W
Midi, Canal du → 10 43 45N 1 21 E
Midi d'Ossau, Pic du 10 42 50N 0 26W
Midland, Canada 62 44 45N 79 50W
Midland, Mich., U.S.A. 66 43 37N 84 17W
Midland, Tex., U.S.A. 67 32 0N 102 3W
Midleton 7 51 52N 8 12W
Midou → 10 43 54N 0 30W
Midouze → 10 43 48N 0 51W
Midway Is. 57 28 13N 177 22W
Mie □ 44 34 30N 136 10 E
Międzychód 17 52 35N 15 53 E
Międzyrzec Podlaski 17 51 58N 22 45 E
Miélan 10 43 27N 0 19 E
Miercurea Ciuc 25 46 21N 25 48 E
Mieres 18 43 18N 5 48W
Migennes 9 47 58N 3 31 E
Mihara 44 34 24N 133 5 E
Mikínai 26 37 43N 22 46 E
Mikkeli 27 61 43N 27 15 E
Mikkeli □ 27 62 0N 28 0 E
Míkonos 26 37 30N 25 25 E
Mikura-Jima 44 33 52N 139 36 E
Milagro 72 2 11 S 79 36W
Milan = Milano 20 45 28N 9 10 E
Milano 20 45 28N 9 10 E
Milâs 45 37 20N 27 50 E
Milazzo 23 38 13N 15 13 E
Mildura 56 34 13 S 142 9 E
Miles 56 26 40 S 150 9 E
Milford 66 38 52N 75 27W
Milford Haven 5 51 43N 5 2W
Milford Haven, B. 5 51 40N 5 10W
Milḩ, Ras al 50 31 54N 25 6 E
Miliana 49 27 20N 2 32 E
Millau 10 44 8N 3 4 E
Millevaches, Plateau de 10 45 45N 2 0 E
Millicent 56 37 34 S 140 21 E
Millinocket 66 45 45N 68 45W
Milltown Malbay 7 52 51N 9 25W
Millville 66 39 22N 75 0W
Milly-la-Forêt 9 48 24N 2 28 E
Mílos 26 36 44N 24 25 E
Milton 6 57 18N 4 32W
Milton Keynes 5 52 3N 0 42W
Miltou 50 10 14N 17 26 E
Milwaukee 67 43 9N 87 58W
Milwaukie 68 45 27N 122 39W
Mimizan 10 44 12N 1 13W

Minamata 44 32 10N 130 30 E
Minas 74 34 20 S 55 10W
Minas de Rio Tinto 18 37 42N 6 35W
Minas Gerais □ 73 18 50 S 46 0W
Minatitlán 69 17 59N 94 31W
Mindanao 40 8 0N 125 0 E
Mindanao Sea = Bohol Sea 40 9 0N 124 0 E
Mindanao Trench 57 8 0N 128 0 E
Mindel → 13 48 31N 10 23 E
Minden, Germany 13 52 18N 8 45 E
Minden, U.S.A. 67 32 40N 93 20W
Mindoro 40 13 0N 121 0 E
Mindoro Strait 40 12 30N 120 30 E
Mindouli 51 4 12 S 14 28 E
Minehead 5 51 12N 3 29W
Mingan 63 50 20N 64 0W
Mingechaurskoye Vdkhr. 35 40 56N 47 20 E
Minigwal L. 54 29 31 S 123 14 E
Minna 49 9 37N 6 30 E
Minneapolis 67 44 58N 93 20W
Minnedosa 65 50 14N 99 50W
Minnesota □ 67 46 40N 94 0W
Miño → 18 41 52N 8 40W
Minorca = Menorca 19 40 0N 4 0 E
Minot 67 48 10N 101 15W
Minquiers, Les 8 48 58N 2 8W
Minsk 32 53 52N 27 30 E
Mińsk Mazowiecki 17 52 10N 21 33 E
Minusinsk 31 53 50N 91 20 E
Minvoul 51 2 9N 12 8 E
Miquelon, I. 63 47 2N 56 20W
Mir 50 14 5N 11 59 E
Miraj 38 16 50N 74 45 E
Miramas 11 43 33N 4 59 E
Mirambeau 10 45 23N 0 35W
Miramont-de-Guyenne 10 44 37N 0 21 E
Miranda de Ebro 19 42 41N 2 57W
Mirande 10 43 31N 0 25 E
Mirbāṭ 47 17 0N 54 45 E
Mirebeau, Côte-d'Or, France 9 47 25N 5 20 E
Mirebeau, Vienne, France 8 46 49N 0 10 E
Mirecourt 9 48 20N 6 10 E
Mirnyy 31 62 33N 113 53 E
Mirpur Khas 36 25 30N 69 0 E
Mirzapur 37 25 10N 82 34 E
Miscou I. 63 47 57N 64 31W
Mishawaka 66 41 40N 86 8W
Mishima 44 35 10N 138 52 E
Misima I. 56 10 40 S 152 45 E
Miskitos, Cayos 70 14 26N 82 50W
Miskolc 15 48 7N 20 50 E
Misool 40 1 52 S 130 10 E
Misrātah 50 32 24N 15 3 E
Missinaibi → 62 50 43N 81 29W
Mission 67 26 15N 98 20W
Mission City 64 49 10N 122 15W
Mississippi □ 67 33 0N 90 0W
Mississippi → 67 29 0N 89 15W
Mississippi, Delta of the 67 29 15N 90 30W
Missoula 68 46 52N 114 0W
Missouri □ 67 38 25N 92 30W
Missouri → 67 38 50N 90 8W
Mistassini L. 62 51 0N 73 30W
Mistretta 23 37 56N 14 20 E
Mitchell, Australia 56 26 29 S 147 58 E
Mitchell, U.S.A. 67 43 40N 98 0W
Mitchell → 56 15 12 S 141 35 E
Mitchelstown 7 52 16N 8 18W
Mito 44 36 20N 140 30 E
Mitsinjo 53 16 1 S 45 52 E
Mitsiwa 50 15 35N 39 25 E
Mittelland Kanal 13 52 23N 7 45 E
Mitú 72 1 8N 70 3W
Mitumba, Chaîne des 51 7 0 S 27 30 E
Mitwaba 51 8 2 S 27 17 E
Mitzic 51 0 45N 11 40 E
Miyagi □ 44 38 15N 140 45 E
Miyake-Jima 44 34 0N 139 30 E
Miyako 44 39 40N 141 59 E
Miyakonojō 44 31 40N 131 5 E
Miyazaki 44 31 56N 131 30 E
Miyazaki □ 44 32 30N 131 30 E
Miyazu 44 35 35N 135 10 E
Mizdah 50 31 30N 13 0 E
Mizen Hd., Cork, Ireland 7 51 27N 9 50W
Mizen Hd., Wicklow, Ireland 7 52 52N 6 4W
Mjölby 28 58 20N 15 10 E
Mjøsa 28 60 48N 11 0 E
Mladá Boleslav 14 50 27N 14 53 E
Mława 17 53 9N 20 25 E
Mmabatho 52 25 49 S 25 30 E
Mo i Rana 27 66 15N 14 7 E
Moabi 51 2 24 S 10 59 E
Moba 51 7 0 S 29 48 E
Mobaye 51 4 25N 21 5 E
Mobayi 51 4 15N 21 8 E
Moberley 67 39 25N 92 25W
Mobile 66 30 41N 88 3W
Mobutu Sese Seko, L. 51 1 30N 31 0 E
Moçambique 51 15 3 S 40 42 E
Moçâmedes = Namibe 51 15 7 S 12 11 E
Mochudi 52 24 27 S 26 7 E
Mocimboa da Praia 51 11 25 S 40 20 E
Moctezuma → 69 21 59N 98 34W
Mocuba 51 16 54 S 36 57 E
Modane 11 45 12N 6 40 E
Módena 20 44 39N 10 55 E
Modesto 68 37 43N 121 0W
Módica 23 36 52N 14 45 E
Moe 56 38 12 S 146 19 E
Moei → 41 17 25N 98 10 E
Moëlan-sur-Mer 8 47 49N 3 38W
Moengo 73 5 45N 54 20W
Moffat 6 55 20N 3 27W
Mogadishu = Muqdisho 47 2 2N 45 25 E
Mogami → 44 38 45N 140 0 E
Mogi das Cruzes 74 23 31 S 46 11W
Mogilev 32 53 55N 30 18 E
Mogilev-Podolskiy 34 48 20N 27 40 E
Mogocha 31 53 40N 119 50 E
Mohács 15 45 58N 18 41 E
Mohoro 51 8 6 S 39 8 E
Moidart, L. 6 56 47N 5 40W
Mointy 30 47 10N 73 18 E
Moirans 11 45 20N 5 33 E
Moirans-en-Montagne 11 46 26N 5 43 E
Moisie 63 50 12N 66 1W
Moisie → 63 50 14N 66 5W
Moissac 10 44 7N 1 5 E
Moïssala 50 8 21N 17 46 E
Mojave Desert 68 35 0N 116 30W
Mol 12 51 11N 5 5 E
Mold 5 53 10N 3 10W
Moldavian S.S.R. □ 34 47 0N 28 0 E
Molde 27 62 45N 7 9 E
Molepolole 52 24 28 S 25 28 E
Molfetta 23 41 12N 16 35 E
Moline 67 41 30N 90 30W
Moliro 51 8 12 S 30 30 E
Molise □ 21 41 45N 14 30 E
Mollendo 72 17 0 S 72 0W
Mölndal 28 57 40N 12 3 E
Molopo → 52 27 30 S 20 13 E
Molotov = Perm 30 58 0N 57 10 E
Moloundou 51 2 8N 15 15 E
Molsheim 9 48 33N 7 29 E
Molucca Sea 40 4 0 S 124 0 E
Moluccas = Maluku 40 1 0 S 127 0 E
Moma 51 16 47 S 39 4 E
Mombasa 51 4 2 S 39 43 E
Momchilgrad 25 41 33N 25 23 E
Mompós 72 9 14N 74 26W
Møn 28 54 57N 12 15 E
Mona, Canal de la 70 18 30N 67 45W
Monach Is. 6 57 32N 7 40W
Monaco ■ 11 43 46N 7 23 E
Monadhliath Mts. 6 57 10N 4 4W
Monaghan 7 54 15N 6 58W
Monaghan □ 7 54 10N 7 0W
Monastier-sur-Gazeille, Le 10 44 57N 3 59 E
Monastir 50 35 50N 10 49 E
Moncayo, Sierra del 19 41 48N 1 50W
Mönchengladbach 13 51 12N 6 23 E
Monchique 18 37 19N 8 38W
Monclova 69 26 50N 101 30W
Moncontour 8 48 22N 2 38W
Moncoutant 10 46 43N 0 35W
Moncton 63 46 7N 64 51W
Mondego → 18 40 9N 8 52W
Mondoví 20 44 23N 7 49 E
Mondragon 11 44 13N 4 44 E
Monessen 66 40 9N 79 50W
Monestier-de-Clermont 11 44 55N 5 38 E
Monêtier-les-Bains, Le 11 44 58N 6 30 E
Monflanquin 10 44 32N 0 47 E
Monforte 18 39 6N 7 25W
Mongalla 50 5 8N 31 42 E
Mongers, L. 54 29 25 S 117 5 E
Mongo 50 12 14N 18 43 E
Mongolia ■ 42 47 0N 103 0 E
Mongororo 50 12 3N 22 26 E
Mongu 51 15 16 S 23 12 E
Monistrol-d'Allier 10 44 58N 3 38 E
Monistrol-sur-Loire 11 45 17N 4 11 E
Monkoto 51 1 38 S 20 35 E
Monmouth, U.K. 5 51 48N 2 43W
Monmouth, U.S.A. 67 40 50N 90 40W
Monópoli 23 40 57N 17 18 E
Monqoumba 51 3 33N 18 40 E
Monroe, La., U.S.A. 67 32 32N 92 4W
Monroe, Mich., U.S.A. 66 41 55N 83 26W
Monroe, N.C., U.S.A. 66 35 2N 80 37W
Monrovia, Liberia 49 6 18N 10 47W
Monrovia, U.S.A. 68 34 7N 118 1W
Mons 12 50 27N 3 58 E
Monségur 10 44 38N 0 4 E
Mont-de-Marsan 10 43 54N 0 31W
Mont-Dore, Le 10 45 35N 2 49 E
Mont Laurier 62 46 35N 75 30W
Mont-St.-Michel, Le 8 48 40N 1 30W
Mont-sous-Vaudrey 9 46 58N 5 36 E
Montagnac 10 43 29N 3 28 E
Montague 68 41 47N 122 30W
Montague Sd. 54 14 28 S 125 20 E
Montaigu 8 46 59N 1 18W
Montalbán 19 40 50N 0 45W
Montana □ 68 47 0N 110 0W
Montargis 9 47 59N 2 43 E
Montauban 10 44 0N 1 21 E
Montbard 9 47 38N 4 20 E
Montbéliard 9 47 31N 6 48 E
Montbrison 11 45 36N 4 3 E
Montcalm, Pic de 10 42 40N 1 25 E
Montceau-les-Mines 9 46 40N 4 23 E
Montchanin 11 46 47N 4 30 E
Montcornet 9 49 40N 4 1 E
Montcuq 10 44 21N 1 13 E
Montdidier 9 49 38N 2 35 E
Monte Bello Is. 54 20 30 S 115 45 E
Monte-Carlo 11 43 46N 7 23 E
Monte Caseros 74 30 10 S 57 50W
Monte Sant' Ángelo 23 41 42N 15 59 E
Monte Santu, C. di 22 40 5N 9 42 E
Montebourg 8 49 30N 1 20W
Montego Bay 70 18 30N 78 0W
Montélimar 11 44 33N 4 45 E
Montemorelos 69 25 11N 99 42W
Montendre 10 45 16N 0 26W
Montenegro = Crna Gora □ 24 42 40N 19 20 E
Montepuez 51 13 8 S 38 59 E
Montereau-Fault-Yonne 9 48 22N 2 57 E
Monterey 68 36 35N 121 57W
Montería 72 8 46N 75 53W
Monterrey 69 25 40N 100 30W
Montes Claros 73 16 30 S 43 50W
Montevideo, Uruguay 74 34 50 S 56 11W
Montevideo, U.S.A. 67 44 55N 95 40W
Montfaucon 9 49 16N 5 8 E
Montfaucon-en-Velay 11 45 11N 4 20 E
Montfort 8 48 9N 1 58W
Montfort-l'Amaury 9 48 47N 1 49 E
Montgenèvre 11 44 56N 6 43 E
Montgomery, U.K. 5 52 34N 3 9W
Montgomery, U.S.A. 66 32 20N 86 20W
Montguyon 10 45 12N 0 12W
Montier-en-Der 9 48 30N 4 45 E
Montignac 10 45 4N 1 10 E
Montigny 9 49 7N 6 10 E
Montigny-sur-Aube 9 47 57N 4 45 E
Montijo 18 38 52N 6 39W
Montilla 18 37 36N 4 40W
Montlhéry 9 48 39N 2 15 E
Montluçon 10 46 22N 2 36 E
Montmagny 63 46 58N 70 34W
Montmarault 10 46 19N 2 57 E
Montmédy 9 49 30N 5 20 E
Montmélian 11 45 30N 6 4 E
Montmirail 9 48 51N 3 30 E
Montmoreau-St.-Cybard 10 45 23N 0 8 E
Montmorency 63 46 53N 71 11W
Montmorillon 10 46 26N 0 50 E
Montmort 9 48 55N 3 49 E
Monto 56 24 52 S 151 6 E
Montoir-sur-le-Loir 8 47 45N 0 52 E
Montoro 18 38 1N 4 27W
Montpelier 62 44 15N 72 38W
Montpellier 10 43 37N 3 52 E
Montpezat-de-Quercy 10 44 15N 1 30 E
Montpon-Ménestérol 10 45 0N 0 11 E
Montréal, Canada 62 45 31N 73 34W
Montréal, France 10 43 13N 2 8 E
Montredon-Labessonnié 10 43 45N 2 18 E
Montréjeau 10 43 6N 0 35 E
Montrésor 8 47 10N 1 10 E
Montreuil 9 50 27N 1 45 E
Montreuil-Bellay 8 47 8N 0 9W
Montreux 13 46 26N 6 55 E
Montrevault 8 47 17N 1 2W
Montrevel-en-Bresse 11 46 21N 5 8 E
Montrichard 8 47 20N 1 10 E
Montrose, U.K. 6 56 43N 2 28W
Montrose, U.S.A. 68 38 30N 107 52W
Monts-sur-Guesnes 8 46 55N 0 13 E
Montsalvy 10 44 41N 2 30 E
Montsauche 9 47 13N 4 2 E
Montserrat 70 16 40N 62 10W
Monveda 51 2 52N 21 30 E
Monze 51 16 17 S 27 29 E
Monzón 19 41 52N 0 10 E
Moonie → 56 29 19 S 148 43 E
Moore, L. 54 29 50 S 117 35 E
Moorfoot Hills 6 55 44N 3 8W
Moose Jaw 65 50 24N 105 30W
Moosehead L. 63 45 34N 69 40W
Moosomin 65 50 9N 101 40W
Moosonee 62 51 17N 80 39W
Mopeia Velha 51 17 30 S 35 40 E
Mopti 49 14 30N 4 0W
Mora 28 61 2N 14 38 E
Moradabad 36 28 50N 78 50 E
Morafenobe 53 17 50 S 44 53 E
Moramanga 53 18 56 S 48 12 E
Morar L. 6 56 57N 5 40W
Moratuwa 38 6 45N 79 55 E
Morava → 15 48 10N 16 59 E
Moravian Hts. = Ceskomoravská Vrchovina 14 49 30N 15 40 E
Morawhanna 72 8 30N 59 40W
Moray Firth 6 57 50N 3 30W
Morbihan □ 8 47 55N 2 50W
Morcenx 10 44 0N 0 55W
Mordelles 8 48 5N 1 52W
Morden 65 49 15N 98 10W
Mordovian A.S.S.R.□ 33 54 20N 44 30 E
Møre og Romsdal fylke □ 27 62 30N 8 0 E
Morecambe 5 54 5N 2 52W
Morecambe B. 5 54 7N 3 0W
Moree 56 29 28 S 149 54 E
Morehead City 66 34 46N 76 44W
Morelia 69 19 42N 101 7W
Morella 19 40 35N 0 5W
Morelos □ 69 18 45N 99 0W
Morena, Sierra 18 38 20N 4 0W
Moresby I. 64 52 30N 131 40W
Morestel 11 45 40N 5 28 E
Moret-sur-Loing 9 48 22N 2 58 E
Moreton B. 55 27 10 S 153 10 E
Moreton I. 56 27 10 S 153 25 E
Moreuil 9 49 46N 2 30 E
Morez 11 46 31N 6 2 E
Morgan City 67 29 40N 91 15W
Morganton 66 35 46N 81 48W
Morgantown 66 39 39N 79 58W
Morgat 8 48 15N 4 32W
Morhange 9 48 55N 6 38 E
Morioka 44 39 45N 141 8 E
Morlaàs 10 43 21N 0 18W
Morlaix 8 48 36N 3 52W
Mormant 9 48 37N 2 52 E
Mornington I. 56 16 30 S 139 30 E
Moro G. 40 6 30N 123 0 E
Morocco ■ 49 32 0N 5 50W
Morogoro 51 6 50 S 37 40 E
Moroleón 69 20 8N 101 12W
Morombe 53 21 45 S 43 22 E
Morón 70 22 8N 78 39W
Morón de la Frontera 18 37 6N 5 28W
Morondava 53 20 17 S 44 17 E
Morotai 40 2 10N 128 30 E
Moroto 51 2 28N 34 42 E
Morpeth 5 55 11N 1 41W
Morrilton 67 35 10N 92 45W
Morrinhos 73 17 45 S 49 10W
Morris 65 49 25N 97 22W
Morristown 66 36 18N 83 20W
Morrumbene 53 23 31 S 35 16 E
Morshansk 33 53 28N 41 50 E
Mortagne → 9 48 33N 6 27 E
Mortagne-au-Perche 8 48 31N 0 33 E
Mortagne-sur-Gironde 10 45 28N 0 47W
Mortagne-sur-Sèvre 8 46 59N 0 57W
Mortain 8 48 40N 0 57W
Morteau 9 47 3N 6 35 E
Mortes, R. das → 73 11 45 S 50 44W
Morvan 9 47 5N 4 0 E
Morvern 6 56 38N 5 44W
Morwell 56 38 10 S 146 22 E
Moscos Is. 41 14 0N 97 30 E
Moscow = Moskva 33 55 45N 37 35 E
Moscow 68 46 45N 116 59W
Mosel → 12 50 22N 7 36 E
Moselle = Mosel → 12 50 22N 7 36 E
Moselle □ 9 48 59N 6 33 E
Moshi 51 3 22 S 37 18 E
Mosjøen 27 65 51N 13 12 E
Moskenesøya 27 67 58N 13 0 E
Moskenstraumen 27 67 47N 12 45 E
Moskva 33 55 45N 37 35 E
Moskva → 33 55 5N 38 51 E
Mosquera 72 2 35N 78 24W
Mosquitos, G. de los 70 9 15N 81 10W
Moss 28 59 27N 10 40 E
Mossaka 51 1 15 S 16 45 E
Mosselbaai 52 34 11 S 22 8 E
Mossendjo 51 2 55 S 12 42 E
Mossman 55 16 21 S 145 15 E
Mossoró 73 5 10 S 37 15W
Mossuril 51 14 58 S 40 42 E
Most 14 50 31N 13 38 E
Mostaganem 49 35 54N 0 5 E
Mostar 24 43 22N 17 50 E
Mosul = Al Mawṣil 45 36 15N 43 5 E
Motala 28 58 32N 15 1 E
Mothe-Achard, La 8 46 37N 1 40W
Motherwell 6 55 48N 4 0W
Motihari 37 26 30N 84 55 E
Motte, La 11 44 20N 6 3 E
Motte-Chalançon, La 11 44 30N 5 21 E
Motul 69 21 6N 89 17W
Mouanda 51 1 28 S 13 7 E
Moúdhros 26 39 50N 25 18 E
Moudjeria 49 17 50N 12 28W
Mouila 51 1 50 S 11 0 E
Moule 70 16 20N 61 22W
Moulins 10 46 35N 3 19 E
Moulmein 41 16 30N 97 40 E
Moultrie 66 31 11N 83 47W
Moundou 50 8 40N 16 10 E
Moundsville 66 39 53N 80 43W
Mount Airy 66 36 31N 80 37W
Mount Barker 54 34 38 S 117 40 E
Mount Carmel 66 38 20N 87 48W
Mount Darwin 51 16 47 S 31 38 E
Mount Enid 54 21 42 S 116 26 E
Mount Forest 62 43 59N 80 43W
Mount Gambier 56 37 50 S 140 46 E
Mount Isa 56 20 42 S 139 26 E
Mount Lofty Ra. 55 34 35 S 139 5 E
Mount Magnet 54 28 2 S 117 47 E
Mount Morgan 56 23 40 S 150 25 E
Mount Nicholas 54 22 54 S 120 27 E
Mount Pearl 63 47 31N 52 47W
Mount Pleasant, Mich., U.S.A. 66 43 35N 84 47W
Mount Pleasant, Tex., U.S.A. 67 33 5N 95 0W
Mount Robson 64 52 56N 119 15W
Mount Sterling 66 38 0N 84 0W
Mount Vernon, Ill., U.S.A. 67 38 17N 88 57W
Mount Vernon, N.Y., U.S.A. 66 40 57N 73 49W
Mount Vernon, Wash., U.S.A. 68 48 25N 122 20W
Mount Whaleback 54 23 18 S 119 44 E
Mountain City 68 41 54N 116 0W
Mountain View 68 37 26N 122 5W
Mountmellick 7 53 7N 7 20W
Moura 72 1 32 S 61 38W
Mourdi, Dépression du 50 18 10N 23 0 E
Mourdiah 49 14 35N 7 25W
Mourenx-Ville-Nouvelle 10 43 22N 0 38W
Mourmelon-le-Grand 9 49 8N 4 22 E
Mourne → 7 54 45N 7 39W
Mourne Mts. 7 54 10N 6 0W
Mouscron 12 50 45N 3 12 E
Moussoro 50 13 41N 16 35 E
Mouthe 9 46 44N 6 12 E
Moûtiers 11 45 29N 6 32 E
Mouy 9 49 18N 2 20 E
Moville 7 55 11N 7 3W
Moy → 7 54 5N 8 50W
Moyale, Ethiopia 47 3 34N 39 4 E
Moyale, Kenya 51 3 30N 39 0 E
Moyamba 49 8 4N 12 30W
Moyen Atlas 49 33 0N 5 0W
Moyle □ 7 55 10N 6 15W
Moyyero → 31 68 44N 103 42 E
Mozambique = Moçambique 51 15 3 S 40 42 E
Mozambique ■ 51 19 0 S 35 0 E
Mozambique Chan. 53 17 30 S 42 30 E
Mozdok 35 43 45N 44 48 E
Mozyr 32 52 0N 29 15 E
Mpanda 51 6 23 S 31 1 E
Mpika 51 11 51 S 31 25 E
Mpwapwa 51 6 23 S 36 30 E
Msaken 50 35 49N 10 33 E
Msoro 51 13 35 S 31 50 E
Mtwara-Mikindani 51 10 15 S 40 2 E
Mu Us Shamo 42 39 0N 109 0 E
Muaná 73 1 25 S 49 15W
Muang Chiang Rai 41 19 52N 99 50 E
Mubende 51 0 33N 31 22 E
Mubi 50 10 18N 13 16 E
Muck 6 56 50N 6 15W
Muconda 51 10 31 S 21 15 E
Mucuri 73 18 0 S 39 36W
Mudanjiang 42 44 38N 129 30 E
Mudgee 56 32 32 S 149 31 E
Mufulira 51 12 32 S 28 15 E
Muğla 45 37 15N 28 22 E
Mugu 37 29 45N 82 30 E
Muhammad Qol 50 20 53N 37 9 E
Muine Bheag 7 52 42N 6 57W
Mukden = Shenyang 42 41 48N 123 27 E
Muktsar 36 30 30N 74 30 E
Mulchén 74 37 45 S 72 20W
Mulde → 13 51 10N 12 48 E
Mulgrave 63 45 38N 61 31W
Mulhacén 19 37 4N 3 20W
Mülheim 13 51 26N 6 53 E
Mulhouse 9 47 40N 7 20 E
Mull 6 56 27N 6 0W
Mullaittvu 38 9 15N 80 49 E
Muller, Pegunungan 39 0 30N 113 30 E
Mullet Pen. 7 54 10N 10 2W
Mullewa 54 28 29 S 115 30 E
Mullingar 7 53 31N 7 20W
Multan 36 30 15N 71 36 E
Mumbwa 51 15 0 S 27 0 E
Muna 40 5 0 S 122 30 E
München 13 48 8N 11 33 E
München-Gladbach = Mönchengladbach 13 51 12N 6 23 E
Muncie 66 40 10N 85 20W
Münden 13 51 25N 9 42 E
Mundo Novo 73 11 50 S 40 29W
Mungbere 51 2 36N 28 28 E
Munger 37 25 23N 86 30 E
Mungindi 56 28 58 S 149 1 E
Munhango 51 12 10 S 18 38 E
Munich = München 13 48 8N 11 33 E
Munising 62 46 25N 86 39W
Munku-Sardyk 31 51 45N 100 20 E
Munster, France 9 48 2N 7 8 E
Münster, Germany 13 51 58N 7 37 E
Munster □ 7 52 20N 8 40W
Muonio 27 67 57N 23 40 E
Mupa 51 16 5 S 15 50 E
Muqdisho 47 2 2N 45 25 E
Mur-de-Bretagne 8 48 12N 3 0W
Murallón, Cuerro 74 49 48 S 73 30W
Murang'a 51 0 45 S 37 9 E
Murashi 33 59 30N 49 0 E
Murat 10 45 7N 2 53 E
Murchison → 54 27 45 S 114 0 E
Murchison Falls = Kabarega Falls 51 2 15N 31 30 E
Murchison Ra. 54 20 0 S 134 10 E
Murcia 19 38 20N 1 10W
Murcia □ 19 37 50N 1 30W
Mure, La 11 44 55N 5 48 E
Mureş → 15 46 15N 20 13 E
Mureşul = Mureş → 15 46 15N 20 13 E
Muret 10 43 30N 1 20 E
Murfreesboro 66 35 50N 86 21W
Murgab 30 38 10N 74 2 E
Murgon 56 26 15 S 151 54 E
Müritz See 13 53 25N 12 40 E
Murmansk 30 68 57N 33 10 E
Muro 11 42 34N 8 54 E
Muro, C. de 11 41 44N 8 37 E
Murom 33 55 35N 42 3 E
Muroran 44 42 25N 141 0 E
Muroto-Misaki 44 33 15N 134 10 E
Murphysboro 67 37 50N 89 20W
Murray 66 36 40N 88 20W
Murray → 56 35 20 S 139 22 E
Murray Bridge 56 35 6 S 139 14 E
Murrumbidgee → 56 34 43 S 143 12 E
Murwara 37 23 46N 80 28 E
Murwillumbah 56 28 18 S 153 27 E
Mürzzuschlag 14 47 36N 15 41 E
Muş 45 38 45N 41 30 E
Musa Khel 36 30 59N 69 52 E
Musala 25 42 13N 23 37 E
Muscat = Masqat 46 23 37N 58 36 E
Muscat & Oman = Oman ■ 47 23 0N 58 0 E
Muscatine 67 41 25N 91 5W
Musgrave Ras. 54 26 0 S 132 0 E
Mushie 51 2 56 S 16 55 E
Musi → 39 2 20 S 104 56 E
Muskegon 66 43 15N 86 17W
Muskegon → 66 43 25N 86 0W
Muskegon Hts. 66 43 12N 86 17W
Muskogee 67 35 50N 95 25W
Musmar 50 18 13N 35 40 E
Musoma 51 1 30 S 33 48 E
Musselburgh 6 55 57N 3 3W
Mussidan 10 45 2N 0 22 E
Mussoorie 36 30 27N 78 6 E
Mustang 37 29 10N 83 55 E
Muswellbrook 56 32 16 S 150 56 E
Mût 50 25 28N 28 58 E
Mutaray 31 60 56N 101 0 E
Mutare 51 18 58 S 32 38 E
Muttaburra 56 22 38 S 144 29 E
Muxima 51 9 33 S 13 58 E
Muy, Le 11 43 28N 6 34 E
Muya 31 56 27N 115 50 E
Muzaffarnagar 36 29 26N 77 40 E
Muzaffarpur 37 26 7N 85 23 E
Muzillac 8 47 35N 2 30W
Mvuma 51 19 16 S 30 30 E
Mwanza, Tanzania 51 2 30 S 32 58 E
Mwanza, Zaïre 51 7 55 S 26 43 E
Mweelrea 7 53 37N 9 48W
Mweka 51 4 50 S 21 34 E
Mwenezi 51 21 15 S 30 48 E
Mwenga 51 3 1 S 28 28 E
Mweru, L. 51 9 0 S 28 40 E
Mwinilunga 51 11 43 S 24 25 E
My Tho 41 10 29N 106 23 E
Mycenae = Mikínai 26 37 43N 22 46 E
Myeik Kyunzu 41 11 30N 97 30 E
Mymensingh 37 24 45N 90 24 E
Myndd Du 5 51 45N 3 45W
Mýrdalsjökull 27 63 40N 19 6W
Myrtle Point 68 43 0N 124 4W
Mysore 38 12 17N 76 41 E
Mysore □ = Karnataka □ 38 13 15N 77 0 E
Mývatn 27 65 36N 17 0W

N

Naantali 27 60 29N 22 2 E
Naas 7 53 12N 6 40W
Nabeul 50 36 30N 10 44 E
Nablus = Nābulus 45 32 14N 35 15 E
Nābulus 45 32 14N 35 15 E
Nachingwea 51 10 23 S 38 49 E
Nacogdoches 67 31 33N 94 39W
Nacozari 69 30 24N 109 39W
Nadiad 36 22 41N 72 56 E
Nadym 30 65 35N 72 42 E
Nafada 49 11 8N 11 20 E
Nagano 44 36 40N 138 10 E
Nagano □ 44 36 15N 138 0 E
Nagaoka 44 37 27N 138 51 E
Nagappattinam 38 10 46N 79 51 E
Nagasaki 44 32 47N 129 50 E
Nagasaki □ 44 32 50N 129 40 E
Nagaur 36 27 15N 73 45 E
Nagercoil 38 8 12N 77 26 E
Nagornyy 31 55 58N 124 57 E
Nagoya 44 35 10N 136 50 E
Nagpur 36 21 8N 79 10 E
Nagykanizsa 15 46 28N 17 0 E
Nagykörös 15 47 5N 19 48 E
Nahanni Butte 64 61 2N 123 31W
Nahāvand 45 34 10N 48 22 E
Nahe → 13 49 58N 7 57 E
Naicam 65 52 30N 104 30W
Nā'ifah 47 19 59N 50 46 E
Nain 63 56 34N 61 40W
Naintré 8 46 46N 0 29 E
Nairn 6 57 35N 3 54W
Nairobi 51 1 17 S 36 48 E
Naivasha 51 0 40 S 36 30 E
Najac 10 44 14N 1 58 E
Najafābād 46 32 40N 51 15 E
Najibabad 36 29 40N 78 20 E
Nakamura 44 33 0N 133 0 E
Nakfa 50 16 40N 38 32 E
Nakhichevan A.S.S.R. □ 30 39 14N 45 30 E
Nakhodka 31 42 53N 132 54 E
Nakhon Phanom 41 17 23N 104 43 E
Nakhon Ratchasima 41 14 59N 102 12 E
Nakhon Sawan 41 15 35N 100 10 E
Nakhon Si Thammarat 41 8 29N 100 0 E
Nakina 62 50 10N 86 40W
Nakskov 28 54 50N 11 8 E
Nakuru 51 0 15 S 36 4 E
Nalchik 35 43 30N 43 33 E
Nalgonda 38 17 6N 79 15 E
Nallamalai Hills 38 15 30N 78 50 E
Nalón → 18 43 32N 6 4W
Nālūt 50 31 54N 11 0 E
Nam Co 42 30 30N 90 45 E
Nam Dinh 41 20 25N 106 5 E
Nam-Phan 41 10 30N 106 0 E
Nam Tha 41 20 58N 101 30 E
Nam Tok 41 14 21N 99 4 E
Namacurra 53 17 30 S 36 50 E
Namaland 52 24 30 S 17 0 E
Namangan 30 41 0N 71 40 E
Namapa 51 13 43 S 39 50 E
Nambour 56 26 32 S 152 58 E
Namib Desert = Namibwoestyn 52 22 30 S 15 0 E
Namibe 51 15 7 S 12 11 E
Namibia ■ 52 22 0 S 18 9 E
Namibwoestyn 52 22 30 S 15 0 E
Nampa 68 43 34N 116 34W
Nampula 51 15 6 S 39 15 E
Namsen → 27 64 27N 11 42 E
Namsos 27 64 29N 11 30 E
Namtay 31 62 43N 129 37 E
Namucha Shank'ou 37 30 0N 82 28 E
Namur 12 50 27N 4 52 E
Namur □ 12 50 17N 5 0 E
Namutoni 52 18 49 S 16 55 E
Namwala 51 15 44 S 26 30 E
Nanaimo 64 49 10N 124 0W
Nanango 56 26 40 S 152 0 E
Nanao 44 37 0N 137 0 E
Nanchang 43 28 42N 115 55 E
Nanchong 43 30 43N 106 2 E
Nancy 9 48 42N 6 12 E
Nanda Devi 37 30 23N 79 59 E
Nanded 38 19 10N 77 20 E
Nandurbar 36 21 20N 74 15 E
Nandyal 38 15 30N 78 30 E
Nanga-Eboko 51 4 41N 12 22 E
Nangarhár □ 46 34 20N 70 0 E
Nangis 9 48 33N 3 0 E
Nanjing 43 32 2N 118 47 E
Nanping 43 26 38N 118 10 E
Nansei-Shotō 44 26 0N 128 0 E
Nansen Sd. 3 81 0N 91 0W
Nant 10 44 1N 3 18 E
Nantes 8 47 12N 1 33W
Nanteuil-le-Haudouin 9 49 9N 2 48 E
Nantiat 10 46 1N 1 11 E
Nanticoke 66 41 12N 76 1W
Nanton 64 50 21N 113 46W
Nantua 11 46 10N 5 35 E
Nanuque 73 17 50 S 40 21W
Nanyuki 51 0 2N 37 4 E
Náo, C. de la 19 38 44N 0 14 E
Naoetsu 44 37 12N 138 10 E
Napa 68 38 18N 122 17W
Napier 59 39 30 S 176 56 E
Naples = Nápoli 23 40 50N 14 17 E
Napo → 72 3 20 S 72 40W
Nápoli 23 40 50N 14 17 E
Nara, Japan 44 34 40N 135 49 E
Nara, Mali 49 15 10N 7 20W
Nara □ 44 34 30N 136 0 E
Naracoorte 56 36 58 S 140 45 E
Narasapur 38 16 26N 81 40 E
Narayanganj 37 23 40N 90 33 E
Narayanpet 38 16 45N 77 30 E
Narbonne 10 43 11N 3 0 E
Nardò 23 40 10N 18 0 E
Narmada → 36 21 38N 72 36 E
Narrabri 56 30 19 S 149 46 E
Narrandera 56 34 42 S 146 31 E
Narrogin 54 32 58 S 117 14 E
Narromine 56 32 12 S 148 12 E
Narsimhapur 36 22 54N 79 14 E
Narva 32 59 23N 28 12 E
Narvik 27 68 28N 17 26 E
Naryan-Mar 30 68 0N 53 0 E
Narym 30 59 0N 81 30 E
Naryn 30 41 26N 75 58 E
Nasa 27 66 29N 15 23 E
Nasarawa 49 8 32N 7 41 E
Naser, Buheirat en 50 23 0N 32 30 E
Nashua 66 42 50N 71 25W
Nashville 66 36 12N 86 46W
Nasik 38 19 58N 73 50 E
Nasirabad 36 26 15N 74 45 E
Nassau 70 25 0N 77 20W
Nasser, L. = Naser, Buheirat en 50 23 0N 32 30 E
Nässjö 28 57 39N 14 42 E
Nata 52 20 12 S 26 12 E
Natal 73 5 47 S 35 13W
Natal □ 53 28 30 S 30 30 E
Natashquan 63 50 14N 61 46W
Natashquan → 63 50 7N 61 50W
Natchez 67 31 35N 91 25W
Natchitoches 67 31 47N 93 4W
Nathdwara 36 24 55N 73 50 E
National City 68 32 39N 117 7W
Natitingou 49 10 20N 1 26 E
Natron, L. 51 2 20 S 36 0 E
Natuna Besar, Kepulauan 39 4 0N 108 15 E
Natuna Selatan, Kepulauan 39 2 45N 109 0 E
Naturaliste, C. 54 33 32 S 115 0 E
Naturaliste Channel 54 25 20 S 113 0 E
Naucelle 10 44 13N 2 20 E
Nauru ■ 57 1 0 S 166 0 E
Nauru Is. 57 0 32 S 166 55 E
Nauta 72 4 31 S 73 35W
Nautla 69 20 20N 96 50W
Navadwip 37 23 34N 88 20 E
Navalcarnero 18 40 17N 4 5W
Navan = An Uaimh 7 53 39N 6 40W
Navarra □ 19 42 40N 1 40W
Navarrenx 10 43 20N 0 45W
Naver → 6 58 34N 4 15W
Navoi 30 40 9N 65 22 E
Navojoa 69 27 0N 109 30W
Návpaktos 26 38 23N 21 50 E
Návplion 26 37 33N 22 50 E
Navsari 36 20 57N 72 59 E
Nawabshah 36 26 15N 68 25 E
Nawakot 37 27 55N 85 10 E
Nawalgarh 36 27 50N 75 15 E
Náxos 26 37 8N 25 25 E
Nay 10 43 10N 0 18W
Näy Band 46 27 20N 52 40 E
Nayakhan 31 61 56N 159 0 E
Nayarit □ 69 22 0N 105 0W
Naze, The 5 51 53N 1 19 E
Ncheu 51 14 50 S 34 47 E
Ndélé 50 8 25N 20 36 E
Ndendé 51 2 22 S 11 23 E
Ndjamena 50 12 10N 14 59 E
Ndjolé 51 0 10 S 10 45 E
Ndola 51 13 0 S 28 34 E
Neagh, Lough 7 54 35N 6 25W
Neath 5 51 39N 3 49W
Nebraska □ 67 41 30N 100 0W
Nebraska City 67 40 40N 95 52W
Nébrodi, Monti 22 37 55N 14 50 E
Neches → 67 29 55N 93 52W
Neckar → 13 49 31N 8 26 E
Necochea 74 38 30 S 58 50W
Needles, The 5 50 39N 1 35W
Neenah 66 44 10N 88 30W
Neepawa 65 50 15N 99 30W
Nefta 49 33 53N 7 50 E
Negele 47 5 20N 39 36 E
Negeri Sembilan □ 41 2 45N 102 10 E
Negombo 38 7 12N 79 50 E
Negotin 24 44 16N 22 37 E
Negra, Pta. 72 6 6 S 81 10W
Negro →, Argentina 74 41 2 S 62 47W
Negro →, Brazil 72 3 0 S 60 0W
Negros 40 9 30N 122 40 E
Nehbandān 46 31 35N 60 5 E
Neheim-Hüsten 13 51 27N 7 58 E
Nei Monggol Zizhiqu □ 42 42 0N 112 0 E
Neijiang 43 29 35N 104 55 E
Neiva 72 2 56N 75 18W
Nekemte 50 9 4N 36 30 E
Neksø 28 55 4N 15 8 E
Nelkan 31 57 40N 136 4 E
Nellore 38 14 27N 79 59 E
Nelma 31 47 39N 139 0 E
Nelson, Canada 64 49 30N 117 20W
Nelson, U.K. 5 53 50N 2 14W
Nelson → 65 54 33N 98 2W
Nelspruit 53 25 29 S 30 59 E
Néma 49 16 40N 7 15W
Neman → 32 55 25N 21 10 E
Nemours 9 48 16N 2 40 E
Nemunas = Neman → 32 55 25N 21 10 E
Nemuro 44 43 20N 145 35 E
Nemuro-Kaikyō 44 43 30N 145 30 E
Nemuy 31 55 40N 136 9 E
Nenagh 7 52 52N 8 11W
Nene → 5 52 38N 0 13 E
Neosho 67 36 56N 94 28W
Neosho → 67 35 59N 95 10W
Nepal ■ 37 28 0N 84 30 E
Nepalganj 37 28 5N 81 40 E
Nephin 7 54 1N 9 21W
Nérac 10 44 8N 0 21 E
Nerchinsk 31 52 0N 116 39 E
Nerchinskiy Zavod 31 51 20N 119 40 E
Neretva → 24 43 1N 17 27 E
Nerva 18 37 42N 6 30W
Nes 27 65 53N 17 24W
Neskaupstaður 27 65 9N 13 42W
Nesle 9 49 45N 2 53 E
Nesque → 11 43 59N 4 59 E
Ness, Loch 6 57 15N 4 30W
Nesttun 27 60 19N 5 21 E
Netanya 45 32 20N 34 51 E
Nète → 12 51 7N 4 14 E
Nether Stowey 5 51 0N 3 10W
Netherbury 5 50 46N 2 45W
Netherdale 56 21 10 S 148 33 E
Netherlands ■ 12 52 0N 5 30 E
Netherlands Antilles ■ 70 12 15N 69 0W
Nettancourt 9 48 51N 4 57 E
Netzahualcoyotl, Presa 69 17 10N 93 30W
Neu-Isenburg 13 50 3N 8 42 E
Neu-Ulm 13 48 23N 10 2 E
Neubrandenburg 13 53 33N 13 17 E
Neuchâtel 13 47 0N 6 55 E
Neuchâtel, Lac de 13 46 53N 6 50 E
Neuf-Brisach 9 48 1N 7 30 E
Neufchâteau, Belgium 12 49 50N 5 25 E
Neufchâteau, France 9 48 21N 5 40 E
Neufchâtel-en-Bray 8 49 44N 1 26 E
Neufchâtel-sur-Aisne 9 49 26N 4 1 E
Neuillé-Pont-Pierre 8 47 33N 0 33 E
Neuilly-St.-Front 9 49 10N 3 15 E
Neumünster 13 54 4N 9 58 E
Neung-sur-Beuvron 9 47 30N 1 50 E
Neunkirchen 13 49 23N 7 12 E
Neuquén 74 38 55 S 68 0 E
Neuruppin 13 52 56N 12 48 E
Neuse → 66 35 5N 76 30W
Neusiedler See 15 47 50N 16 47 E
Neuss 13 51 12N 6 39 E
Neussargues-Moissac 10 45 9N 3 0 E
Neustadt, Bayern, Germany 13 49 34N 10 37 E
Neustadt, Bayern, Germany 13 50 23N 11 0 E
Neustadt, Rhld-Pfz., Germany 13 49 21N 8 10 E
Neustrelitz 13 53 22N 13 4 E
Neuvic 10 45 23N 2 16 E
Neuville-aux-Bois 9 48 4N 2 3 E
Neuville-de-Poitou 10 46 41N 0 15 E
Neuville-sur-Saône 11 45 52N 4 51 E
Neuvy-le-Roi 8 47 36N 0 36 E
Neuvy-St.-Sépulchre 10 46 35N 1 48 E
Neuvy-sur-Barangeon 9 47 20N 2 15 E
Neuwied 13 50 26N 7 29 E
Nevada 67 37 51N 94 22W
Nevada □ 68 39 20N 117 0W
Nevada, Sierra, Spain 19 37 3N 3 15W
Nevada, Sierra, U.S.A. 68 39 0N 120 30W
Nevada City 68 39 20N 121 0W
Nevada de Sta. Marta, Sa. 72 10 55N 73 50W
Nevanka 31 56 31N 98 55 E
Nevers 9 47 0N 3 9 E
New Albany 66 38 20N 85 50W
New Amsterdam 72 6 15N 57 36W
New Bedford 66 41 40N 70 52W
New Bern 66 35 8N 77 3W
New Britain, Papua N. G. 56 5 50 S 150 20 E
New Britain, U.S.A. 66 41 41N 72 47W
New Brunswick 66 40 30N 74 28W
New Brunswick □ 63 46 50N 66 30W
New Caledonia = Nouvelle Calédonie 57 21 0 S 165 0 E
New Castile = Castilla La Nueva 18 39 45N 3 20W
New Castle, Ind., U.S.A. 66 39 55N 85 23W
New Castle, Pa., U.S.A. 66 41 0N 80 20W
New Delhi 36 28 37N 77 13 E
New England Ra. 56 30 20 S 151 45 E
New Forest 5 50 53N 1 40W
New Glasgow 63 45 35N 62 36W
New Guinea 57 4 0 S 136 0 E
New Hampshire □ 66 43 40N 71 40W
New Hanover 56 2 30 S 150 10 E
New Haven 66 41 20N 72 54W
New Hebrides = Vanuatu ■ 57 15 0 S 168 0 E
New Iberia 67 30 2N 91 54W
New Ireland 56 3 20 S 151 50 E
New Jersey □ 66 40 30N 74 10W
New Kensington 66 40 36N 79 43W
New London 66 41 23N 72 8W
New Mexico □ 68 34 30N 106 0W
New Norfolk 56 42 46 S 147 2 E
New Orleans 67 30 0N 90 5W
New Philadelphia 66 40 29N 81 25W
New Plymouth 59 39 4 S 174 5 E
New Providence 70 25 25N 78 35W
New Radnor 5 52 15N 3 10W
New Ross 7 52 24N 6 58W
New Siberian Is. = Novosibirskiye Ostrava 31 75 0N 142 0 E
New South Wales □ 56 33 0 S 146 0 E
New Ulm 67 44 15N 94 30W
New Waterford 63 46 13N 60 4W
New Westminster 64 49 13N 122 55W
New York □ 66 42 40N 76 0W
New York City 66 40 45N 74 0W
New Zealand ■ 57 40 0 S 176 0 E
Newala 51 10 58 S 39 18 E
Newark, N.J., U.S.A. 66 40 41N 74 12W
Newark, N.Y., U.S.A. 66 43 2N 77 10W
Newark, Ohio, U.S.A. 66 40 5N 82 24W
Newark-on-Trent 5 53 6N 0 48W
Newberry, Mich., U.S.A. 62 46 20N 85 32W
Newberry, S.C., U.S.A. 66 34 17N 81 37W
Newburgh 66 41 30N 74 1W
Newbury 5 51 24N 1 19W
Newburyport 66 42 48N 70 50W
Newcastle, Australia 56 33 0 S 151 46 E
Newcastle, Canada 63 47 1N 65 38W
Newcastle, S. Africa 53 27 45 S 29 58 E
Newcastle, U.K. 7 54 13N 5 54W
Newcastle Emlyn 5 52 2N 4 29W
Newcastle Ra. 55 15 45 S 130 15 E
Newcastle-under-Lyme 5 53 2N 2 15W
Newcastle-upon-Tyne 5 54 59N 1 37W
Newcastle Waters 54 17 30 S 133 28 E
Newdegate 54 33 6 S 119 0 E
Newfoundland □ 63 53 0N 58 0W
Newham 5 51 31N 0 2 E
Newhaven 5 50 47N 0 4 E
Newmarket, Ireland 7 52 13N 9 0W
Newmarket, U.K. 5 52 15N 0 23 E
Newnan 66 33 22N 84 48W
Newport, Gwent, U.K. 5 51 35N 3 0W
Newport, I. of W., U.K. 5 50 42N 1 18W
Newport, Salop, U.K. 5 52 47N 2 22W
Newport, Ark., U.S.A. 67 35 38N 91 15W
Newport, Ky., U.S.A. 66 39 5N 84 23W
Newport, Oreg., U.S.A. 68 44 41N 124 2W
Newport, R.I., U.S.A. 66 41 13N 71 19W
Newport, Vt., U.S.A. 63 44 57N 72 17W
Newport Beach 68 33 40N 117 58W
Newport News 66 37 2N 76 30W
Newquay 5 50 24N 5 6W
Newry 7 54 10N 6 20W
Newry & Mourne □ 7 54 10N 6 15W
Newton, Iowa, U.S.A. 67 41 40N 93 3W
Newton, Mass., U.S.A. 66 42 21N 71 10W
Newton Abbot 5 50 32N 3 37W
Newton Stewart 6 54 57N 4 30W
Newtonmore 6 57 4N 4 7W
Newtown 5 52 31N 3 19W
Newtownabbey 7 54 40N 5 55W
Newtownabbey □ 7 54 45N 6 0W
Newtownards 7 54 37N 5 40W
Nexon 10 45 41N 1 11 E
Neya 33 58 21N 43 49 E
Nezhin 32 51 5N 31 55 E
Ngami Depression 52 20 30 S 22 46 E
Ngoring Hu 42 34 55N 97 5 E
Ngudu 51 2 58 S 33 25 E
Nguigmi 50 14 20N 13 20 E
Nguru 49 12 56N 10 29 E
Nha Trang 41 12 16N 109 10 E
Niafounké 49 16 0N 4 5W
Niagara Falls, Canada 62 43 7N 79 5W
Niagara Falls, U.S.A. 66 43 5N 79 0W
Niamey 49 13 27N 2 6 E
Niangara 51 3 42N 27 50 E
Nias 39 1 0N 97 30 E
Nicaragua ■ 70 11 40N 85 30W
Nicaragua, L. de 70 12 0N 85 30W
Nicastro 23 39 0N 16 18 E
Nice 11 43 42N 7 14 E
Nichinan 44 31 38N 131 23 E
Nicosia 45 35 10N 33 25 E
Nicoya, Pen. de 70 9 45N 85 40W
Nidd → 5 54 1N 1 32W
Nied → 9 49 23N 6 40 E
Niederbronn-les-Bains 9 48 57N 7 39 E
Niedersachsen □ 13 52 45N 9 0 E
Nieuw Nickerie 73 6 0N 56 59W
Nieuwpoort 12 51 8N 2 45 E
Nièvre □ 9 47 10N 3 40 E
Niger ■ 49 17 30N 10 0 E
Niger → 49 5 33N 6 33 E
Nigeria ■ 49 8 30N 8 0 E
Nii-Jima 44 34 20N 139 15 E
Niigata 44 37 58N 139 0 E
Niihama 44 33 55N 133 16 E
Nijkerk 12 52 13N 5 30 E
Nijmegen 12 51 50N 5 52 E
Nijverdal 12 52 22N 6 28 E
Nikel 27 69 24N 30 12 E
Nikki 49 9 58N 3 12 E
Nikkō 44 36 45N 139 35 E
Nikolayev 35 46 58N 32 0 E
Nikolayevsk 33 50 0N 45 35 E
Nikolayevsk-na-Amur 31 53 8N 140 44 E
Nikolskoye 31 55 12N 166 0 E
Nikopol 34 47 35N 34 25 E
Nîl, Nahr en → 50 30 10N 31 6 E
Nîl el Abyad → 50 15 38N 32 31 E
Nîl el Azraq → 50 15 38N 32 31 E
Nile = Nîl, Nahr en → 50 30 10N 31 6 E
Niles 66 41 8N 80 40W
Nimach 36 24 30N 74 56 E
Nîmes 11 43 50N 4 23 E
Nimneryskiy 31 57 50N 125 10 E
Nimule 51 3 32N 32 3 E
Nīnawá 45 36 25N 43 10 E
Ninety Mile Beach, The 55 38 15 S 147 24 E
Nineveh = Nīnawá 45 36 25N 43 10 E
Ningbo 43 29 51N 121 28 E
Ningde 43 26 38N 119 23 E
Ningxia Huizu Zizhiqu □ 42 38 0N 106 0 E
Ninove 12 50 51N 4 2 E
Niobrara → 67 42 45N 98 0W
Nioro du Sahel 49 15 15N 9 30W
Niort 10 46 19N 0 29W
Nipawin 65 53 20N 104 0W
Nipigon 62 49 0N 88 17W
Nipigon, L. 62 49 50N 88 30W
Nipissing L. 62 46 20N 80 0W
Nirmal 38 19 3N 78 20 E
Nirmali 37 26 20N 86 35 E
Niš 24 43 19N 21 58 E
Nişāb 47 14 25N 46 29 E
Nishinomiya 44 34 45N 135 20 E
Niterói 73 22 52 S 43 0W
Nith → 6 55 20N 3 5W
Nitra 15 48 19N 18 4 E
Nitra → 15 47 46N 18 10 E
Niue I. 58 19 2 S 169 54W
Nivelles 12 50 35N 4 20 E
Nivernais 9 47 0N 3 20 E
Nizamabad 38 18 45N 78 7 E
Nizhne Kolymsk 31 68 34N 160 55 E
Nizhneangarsk 31 55 47N 109 30 E
Nizhneudinsk 31 54 54N 99 3 E
Nizhnevartovsk 30 60 56N 76 38 E
Nizhneyansk 31 71 26N 136 4 E
Nizhniy Tagil 30 57 55N 59 57 E
Nizhnyaya Tunguska → 31 64 20N 93 0 E
Nizké Tatry 15 48 55N 20 0 E
Njombe 51 9 20 S 34 50 E
Nkambe 49 6 35N 10 40 E
Nkawkaw 49 6 36N 0 49W
Nkhata Bay 51 11 33 S 34 16 E
Nkhota Kota 51 12 56 S 34 15 E
Nkongsamba 49 4 55N 9 55 E
Nobeoka 44 32 36N 131 41 E
Nocera Inferiore 23 40 45N 14 37 E
Nogales, Mexico 69 31 20N 110 56W
Nogales, U.S.A. 68 31 33N 110 56W
Nōgata 44 33 48N 130 44 E
Nogent-en-Bassigny 9 48 1N 5 20 E
Nogent-le-Rotrou 8 48 20N 0 50 E
Nogent-sur-Seine 9 48 30N 3 30 E
Noginsk 31 64 30N 90 50 E
Nogoa → 56 23 40 S 147 55 E
Noi → 41 14 50N 100 15 E
Noire, Mt. 8 48 11N 3 40W
Noirétable 10 45 48N 3 46 E
Noirmoutier, I. de 8 46 58N 2 10W
Noirmoutier-en-l'Ile 8 47 0N 2 14W
Nokhtuysk 31 60 0N 117 45 E
Nola 51 3 35N 16 4 E
Nolay 9 46 58N 4 35 E
Nonancourt 8 48 47N 1 11 E
Nonant-le-Pin 8 48 42N 0 12 E
Nong Khae 41 14 29N 100 53 E
Nong Khai 41 17 50N 102 46 E
Nonoava 69 27 28N 106 44W
Nontron 10 45 31N 0 40 E
Nonza 11 42 47N 9 21 E
Noord Brabant □ 12 51 40N 5 0 E
Noord Holland □ 12 52 30N 4 45 E
Noordbeveland 12 51 35N 3 50 E
Noordoostpolder 12 52 45N 5 45 E
Noordwijk aan Zee 12 52 14N 4 26 E
Nootka I. 64 49 32N 126 42W
Nóqui 51 5 55 S 13 30 E
Noranda 62 48 20N 79 0W
Nord □ 9 50 15N 3 30 E
Nord-Ostsee Kanal 13 54 15N 9 40 E
Nord-Süd Kanal 13 53 0N 10 32 E
Nord-Trøndelag fylke □ 27 64 20N 12 0 E
Nordaustlandet 3 79 14N 23 0 E
Nordegg 64 52 29N 116 5W
Norden 13 53 35N 7 12 E
Nordenham 13 53 29N 8 28 E
Norderney 13 53 42N 7 15 E
Nordfriesische Inseln 13 54 40N 8 20 E
Nordhorn 13 52 27N 7 4 E
Nordkapp, Norway 27 71 10N 25 44 E
Nordkapp, Svalbard 3 80 31N 20 0 E
Nordland fylke □ 27 65 40N 13 0 E
Nordrhein-Westfalen □ 13 51 45N 7 30 E
Nordstrand 13 54 27N 8 50 E
Nordvik 31 74 2N 111 32 E
Nore → 7 52 40N 7 20W
Norfolk 66 36 40N 76 15W
Norfolk □ 5 52 39N 1 0 E
Norfolk Broads 5 52 30N 1 15 E
Norfolk I. 57 28 58 S 168 3 E
Norilsk 31 69 20N 88 6 E
Norman 67 35 12N 97 30W
Norman → 56 17 28 S 140 49 E
Normanby → 56 14 23 S 144 10 E
Normanby I. 56 10 55 S 151 5 E
Normandie 8 48 45N 0 10 E
Normandie, Collines de 8 48 45N 0 45W
Normandin 62 48 49N 72 31W
Normandy = Normandie 8 48 45N 0 10 E
Normanton 56 17 40 S 141 10 E
Norquinco 74 41 51 S 70 55W
Norrbotten □ 27 66 30N 22 30 E
Norrby 27 64 55N 18 15 E
Nørresundby 28 57 5N 9 52 E
Norristown 66 40 9N 75 21W
Norrköping 28 58 37N 16 11 E
Norrland □ 27 66 50N 18 0 E
Norrtälje 28 59 46N 18 42 E
Norsk 31 52 30N 130 0 E
North Andaman I. 41 13 15N 92 40 E
North Battleford 65 52 50N 108 17W
North Bay 62 46 20N 79 30W
North Bend 68 43 28N 124 14W
North Berwick 6 56 4N 2 44W
North C. 59 34 23 S 173 4 E
North Carolina □ 66 35 30N 80 0W
North Channel, Br. Is. 6 55 0N 5 30W
North Channel, Canada 62 46 0N 83 0W
North Dakota □ 67 47 30N 100 0W
North Down □ 7 54 40N 5 45W
North Downs 5 51 17N 0 30 E
North Esk → 6 56 44N 2 25W
North Foreland 5 51 22N 1 28 E
North Frisian Is. = Nordfriesische Inseln 13 54 40N 8 20 E
North I. 59 38 0 S 175 0 E
North Korea ■ 43 40 0N 127 0 E
North Minch 6 58 5N 5 55W
North Ossetian A.S.S.R. □ 35 43 30N 44 30 E

North Platte **67** 41 10N 100 50W
North Platte → **67** 41 15N 100 45W
North Pole **3** 90 0N 0 0 E
North Ronaldsay **6** 59 20N 2 30W
North Saskatchewan → **65** 53 15N 105 5W
North Sea **4** 56 0N 4 0 E
North Sentinel I. **41** 11 35N 92 15 E
North Stradbroke I. **55** 27 35 S 153 28 E
North Sydney **63** 46 12N 60 15W
North Thompson → **64** 50 40N 120 20W
North Tonawanda **66** 43 5N 78 50W
North Tyne → **5** 54 59N 2 7W
North Uist **6** 57 40N 7 15W
North Vancouver **64** 49 25N 123 3W
North Walsham **5** 52 49N 1 22 E
North West Basin **54** 25 45 S 115 0 E
North West C. **54** 21 45 S 114 9 E
North West Frontier □ **36** 34 0N 71 0 E
North West Highlands **6** 57 35N 5 2W
North West River **63** 53 30N 60 10W
North York Moors **5** 54 25N 0 50W
North Yorkshire □ **5** 54 15N 1 25W
Northallerton **5** 54 20N 1 26W
Northam **54** 31 35 S 116 42 E
Northampton, Australia **54** 28 27 S 114 33 E
Northampton, U.K. **5** 52 14N 0 54W
Northampton, U.S.A. **66** 42 22N 72 31W
Northampton □ **5** 52 16N 0 55W
Northeim **13** 51 42N 10 0 E
Northern Circars **38** 17 30N 82 30 E
Northern Ireland □ **7** 54 45N 7 0W
Northern Marianas **57** 17 0N 145 0 E
Northern Territory □ **54** 16 0 S 133 0 E
Northfield **67** 44 30N 93 10W
Northumberland □ **5** 55 12N 2 0W
Northumberland, C. **56** 38 5 S 140 40 E
Northumberland Str. **63** 46 20N 64 0W
Northwich **5** 53 16N 2 30W
Norwalk **66** 41 9N 73 25W
Norway ■ **4** 63 0N 11 0 E
Norwegian Dependency □ **60** 66 0 S 15 0 E
Norwegian Sea **1** 66 0N 1 0 E
Norwich **5** 52 38N 1 17 E
Noss Hd. **6** 58 29N 3 4W
Nossob → **52** 26 55 S 20 45 E
Nosy Boraha **53** 16 50 S 49 55 E
Nosy Varika **53** 20 35 S 48 32 E
Noto **23** 36 52N 15 4 E
Notre Dame B. **63** 49 45N 55 30W
Nottaway → **62** 51 22N 78 55W
Nottingham **5** 52 57N 1 10W
Nottingham □ **5** 53 10N 1 0W
Nouâdhibou **49** 20 54N 17 0W
Nouâdhibou, Ras **49** 20 50N 17 0W
Nouakchott **49** 18 9N 15 58W
Nouméa **57** 22 17 S 166 30 E
Noupoort **52** 31 10 S 24 57 E
Nouveau Comptoir **62** 53 0N 78 49W
Nouvelle Calédonie **57** 21 0 S 165 0 E
Nouzonville **9** 49 48N 4 44 E
Nova Friburgo **73** 22 16 S 42 30W
Nova Gaia **51** 10 10 S 17 35 E
Nova Granada **73** 20 30 S 49 20W
Nova Lisboa = Huambo **51** 12 42 S 15 54 E
Nova Mambone **53** 21 0 S 35 3 E
Nova Scotia □ **63** 45 10N 63 0W
Nova Sofala **53** 20 7 S 34 42 E
Novara **20** 45 27N 8 36 E
Novaya Lyalya **30** 59 10N 60 35 E
Novaya Sibir, Ostrov **31** 75 10N 150 0 E
Novaya Zemlya **30** 75 0N 56 0 E
Novgorod **32** 58 30N 31 25 E
Novgorod-Severskiy **32** 52 2N 33 10 E
Novi Pazar **25** 43 25N 27 15 E
Novi Sad **24** 45 18N 19 52 E
Novocherkassk **35** 47 27N 40 5 E
Novokuybyshevsk **33** 53 7N 49 58 E
Novokuznetsk **30** 53 45N 87 10 E
Novomoskovsk **33** 54 5N 38 15 E
Novorossiysk **34** 44 43N 37 46 E
Novorybnoye **31** 72 50N 105 50 E
Novoshakhtinsk **35** 47 46N 39 58 E
Novosibirsk **30** 55 0N 83 5 E
Novosibirskiye Ostrava **31** 75 0N 142 0 E
Novouzensk **33** 50 32N 48 17 E
Novska **24** 45 19N 17 0 E
Nowra **56** 34 53 S 150 35 E
Nowy Sącz **15** 49 40N 20 41 E
Nowy Tomyśl **17** 52 19N 16 10 E
Noyant **8** 47 30N 0 6 E
Noyers **9** 47 40N 4 0 E
Noyon **9** 49 34N 3 0 E
Nozay **8** 47 34N 1 38W
Nsanje **51** 16 55 S 35 12 E
Nsawam **49** 5 50N 0 24W
Nsukka **49** 6 51N 7 29 E
Nûbîya, Es Sahrâ En **50** 21 30N 33 30 E
Nueva Gerona **70** 21 53N 82 49W
Nueva Rosita **69** 27 57N 101 13W
Nuevitas **70** 21 30N 77 20W
Nuevo Laredo **69** 27 30N 99 30W
Nuevo Leon □ **69** 25 40N 100 0W
Nuits-St.-Georges **9** 47 10N 4 56 E
Nukheila **50** 19 1N 26 21 E
Nukus **30** 42 20N 59 7 E
Nullarbor Plain **54** 30 45 S 129 0 E
Numan **50** 9 29N 12 3 E
Numata **44** 36 45N 139 4 E
Numazu **44** 35 7N 138 51 E
Nuneaton **5** 52 32N 1 29W
Nunspeet **12** 52 21N 5 45 E
Nuremburg = Nürnberg **13** 49 26N 11 5 E
Nürnberg **13** 49 26N 11 5 E
Nuwakot **37** 28 10N 83 55 E
Nuweveldberge **52** 32 10 S 21 45 E
Nuyts, Pt. **54** 35 4 S 116 38 E
Nuyts Arch. **54** 32 35 S 133 20 E
Nyahanga **51** 2 20 S 33 37 E
Nyahururu **51** 0 2N 36 27 E
Nyainqentanglha Shan **42** 30 0N 90 0 E
Nyâlâ **50** 12 2N 24 58 E
Nyasa, L. = Malawi, L. **51** 12 30 S 34 30 E
Nybro **28** 56 44N 15 55 E
Nyeri **51** 0 23 S 36 56 E
Nyíregyháza **15** 47 58N 21 47 E
Nykarleby **27** 63 22N 22 31 E
Nykøbing **28** 54 56N 11 52 E
Nyköping **28** 58 45N 17 0 E
Nylstroom **53** 24 42 S 28 22 E
Nynäshamn **28** 58 54N 17 57 E
Nyons **11** 44 22N 5 10 E
Nysa **17** 50 30N 17 22 E
Nysa → **17** 52 4N 14 46 E
Nyurba **31** 63 17N 118 28 E
Nzega **51** 4 10 S 33 12 E
N'Zérékoré **49** 7 49N 8 48W
Nzeto **51** 7 10 S 12 52 E

O

Ō-Shima **44** 34 44N 139 24 E
Oahe L. **67** 45 30N 100 25W
Oak Hill **66** 38 0N 81 7W
Oak Park **67** 41 55N 87 45W
Oak Ridge **66** 36 1N 84 12W
Oakengates **5** 52 42N 2 29W
Oakham **5** 52 40N 0 43W
Oakland **68** 37 50N 122 18W
Oakridge **68** 43 47N 122 31W
Oamaru **59** 45 5 S 170 59 E
Oaxaca **69** 17 2N 96 40W
Oaxaca □ **69** 17 0N 96 30W
Ob → **30** 66 45N 69 30 E
Oba **62** 49 4N 84 7W
Oban **6** 56 25N 5 30W
Obbia **47** 5 25N 48 30 E
Oberhausen **13** 51 28N 6 50 E
Obernai **9** 48 28N 7 30 E
Oberstdorf **13** 47 25N 10 16 E
Obihiro **44** 42 56N 143 12 E
Objat **10** 45 16N 1 24 E
Obluchye **31** 49 1N 131 4 E
Obo **51** 5 20N 26 32 E
Oboyan **30** 51 13N 36 37 E
Obozerskaya **30** 63 20N 40 15 E
Obskaya Guba **30** 69 0N 73 0 E
Obuasi **49** 6 17N 1 40W
Ocala **66** 29 11N 82 5W
Ocampo **69** 28 11N 108 23W
Ocaña, Colombia **72** 8 15N 73 20W
Ocaña, Spain **19** 39 55N 3 30W
Occidental, Cordillera **72** 5 0N 76 0W
Ocean, I. = Banaba **57** 0 45 S 169 50 E
Ocean City **66** 39 18N 74 34W
Oceanside **68** 33 13N 117 26W
Ochil Hills **6** 56 14N 3 40W
Oconee → **66** 31 58N 82 32W
Oconto **66** 44 52N 87 53W
Ocotlán **69** 20 21N 102 46W
Octeville **8** 49 38N 1 40W
Ódáðahraun **27** 65 5N 17 0W
Odawara **44** 35 20N 139 6 E
Odda **27** 60 3N 6 35 E
Oddur **47** 4 11N 43 52 E
Ödemiş **45** 38 15N 28 0 E
Odense **28** 55 22N 10 23 E
Odenwald **13** 49 40N 9 0 E
Oder → **17** 53 33N 14 38 E
Odessa, U.S.A. **67** 31 51N 102 23W
Odessa, U.S.S.R. **34** 46 30N 30 45 E
Odienné **49** 9 30N 7 34W
Odorheiul Secuiesc **25** 46 21N 25 21 E
Odra → **17** 53 33N 14 38 E
Odžak **24** 45 3N 18 18 E
Ofanto → **23** 41 22N 16 13 E
Offa **49** 8 13N 4 42 E
Offaly □ **7** 53 15N 7 30W
Offenbach **13** 50 6N 8 46 E
Offenburg **13** 48 29N 7 56 E
Offranville **8** 49 52N 1 1 E
Ofotfjorden **27** 68 27N 16 40 E
Ōgaki **44** 35 21N 136 37 E
Ogbomosho **49** 8 1N 4 11 E
Ogden **68** 41 13N 112 1W
Ogdensburg **66** 44 40N 75 27W
Oglio → **20** 45 2N 10 39 E
Ognon → **9** 47 16N 5 28 E
Ogooué → **51** 1 0 S 9 0 E
Ogowe = Ogooué → **51** 1 0 S 9 0 E
Ohanet **49** 28 44N 8 46 E
Ohey **12** 50 26N 5 8 E
Ohio □ **66** 40 20N 14 10 E
Ohio → **66** 38 0N 86 0W
Ohre → **14** 50 30N 14 10 E
Ohridsko, Jezero **24** 41 8N 20 52 E
Oil City **66** 41 26N 79 40W
Oise □ **9** 49 28N 2 30 E
Oise → **9** 49 0N 2 4 E
Ōita **44** 33 14N 131 36 E
Ōita □ **44** 33 15N 131 30 E
Ojos del Salado, Cerro **74** 27 0 S 68 40W
Oka → **30** 56 20N 43 59 E
Okahandja **52** 22 0 S 16 59 E
Okahukura **57** 38 48 S 175 14 E
Okandja **51** 0 35 S 13 45 E
Okanogan → **68** 48 6N 119 43W
Okaukuejo **52** 19 10 S 16 0 E
Okavango Swamps **52** 18 45 S 22 45 E
Okaya **44** 36 0N 138 10 E
Okayama **44** 34 40N 133 54 E
Okayama □ **44** 35 0N 133 50 E
Okazaki **44** 34 57N 137 10 E
Okeechobee, L. **66** 27 0N 80 50W
Okefenokee Swamp **66** 30 50N 82 15W
Okehampton **5** 50 44N 4 1W
Okene **49** 7 32N 6 11 E
Oker → **13** 52 30N 10 22 E
Okha **31** 53 40N 143 0 E
Okhotsk **31** 59 20N 143 10 E
Okhotsk, Sea of **31** 55 0N 145 0 E
Okhotskiy Perevoz **31** 61 52N 135 35 E
Okhotsko Kolymskoye **31** 63 0N 157 0 E
Oki-Shotō **44** 36 5N 133 15 E
Okiep **52** 29 39 S 17 53 E
Oklahoma □ **67** 35 20N 97 30W
Oklahoma City **67** 35 25N 97 30W
Okmulgee **67** 35 38N 96 0W
Okrika **49** 4 40N 7 10 E
Oktabrsk **30** 49 28N 57 25 E
Oktyabrskoy Revolyutsii, Os. **31** 79 30N 97 0 E
Oktyabrskoye **30** 62 28N 66 3 E
Okushiri-Tō **44** 42 15N 139 30 E
Ólafsfjörður **27** 66 4N 18 39W
Ólafsvík **27** 64 53N 23 43W
Olanchito **70** 15 30N 86 30W
Öland **28** 56 45N 16 38 E
Olargues **10** 43 34N 2 53 E
Olavarría **74** 36 55 S 60 20W
Ólbia **22** 40 55N 9 30 E
Old Castile = Castilla La Vieja **18** 41 55N 4 0W
Old Castle **7** 53 46N 7 10W
Old Town **63** 45 0N 68 41W
Oldbury **5** 51 38N 2 30W
Oldenburg, Niedersachsen, Germany **13** 53 10N 8 10 E
Oldenburg, Schleswig-Holstein, Germany **13** 54 16N 10 53 E
Oldenzaal **12** 52 19N 6 53 E
Oldham **5** 53 33N 2 8W
Olds **64** 51 50N 114 10W
Olekma → **31** 60 22N 120 42 E
Olekminsk **31** 60 25N 120 30 E
Olenek **31** 68 28N 112 18 E
Olenek → **31** 73 0N 120 10 E
Oléron, I. d' **10** 45 55N 1 15W
Oleśnica **17** 51 13N 17 22 E
Olga **31** 43 50N 135 14 E
Olga, Mt. **54** 25 20 S 130 50 E
Olgastretet **3** 78 35N 25 0 E
Olifants → **53** 23 57 S 31 58 E
Ólimbos, Óros **26** 40 6N 22 23 E
Oliveira **73** 20 39 S 44 50W
Olivenza **18** 38 41N 7 9W
Oliver **64** 49 13N 119 37W
Ollagüe **72** 21 15 S 68 10W
Olney **66** 38 40N 88 0W
Olomouc **15** 49 38N 17 12 E
Oloron, Gave d' → **10** 43 33N 1 5W
Oloron-Ste.-Marie **10** 43 11N 0 38W
Olovyannaya **31** 50 58N 115 35 E
Oloy → **31** 66 29N 159 29 E
Olsztyn **17** 53 48N 20 29 E
Olt → **25** 43 50N 24 40 E
Olteniţa **25** 44 7N 26 42 E
Olympia, Greece **26** 37 39N 21 39 E
Olympia, U.S.A. **68** 47 0N 122 58W
Olympic Mts. **68** 47 50N 123 45W
Olympus, Mt. = Ólimbos, Óros **26** 40 6N 22 23 E
Olympus, Mt. **68** 47 52N 123 40W
Ōmachi **44** 36 30N 137 50 E
Omagh **7** 54 36N 7 20W
Omagh □ **7** 54 35N 7 15W
Omaha **67** 41 15N 96 0W
Omak **68** 48 24N 119 31W
Oman ■ **47** 23 0N 58 0 E
Oman, G. of **46** 24 30N 58 30 E
Omaruru **52** 21 26 S 16 0 E
Omboué **51** 1 35 S 9 15 E
Ombrone → **20** 42 39N 11 0 E
Omdurmân **50** 15 40N 32 28 E
Ōmiya **44** 35 54N 139 38 E
Ommen **12** 52 31N 6 26 E
Omo → **50** 6 25N 36 10 E
Omolon → **31** 68 42N 158 36 E
Omsk **30** 55 0N 73 12 E
Omsukchan **31** 62 32N 155 48 E
Omul, Vf. **25** 45 27N 25 29 E
Ōmura **44** 32 56N 130 0 E
Omuramba Omatako → **51** 17 45 S 20 25 E
Ōmuta **44** 33 0N 130 26 E
Oncócua **52** 16 30 S 13 25 E
Onda **19** 39 55N 0 17W
Ondangua **52** 17 57 S 16 4 E
Ondo **49** 7 4N 4 47 E
Öndverðarnes **27** 64 52N 24 0W
Onega **30** 64 0N 38 10 E
Onega, G. of = Onezhskaya Guba **30** 64 30N 37 0 E
Onega, L. = Onezhskoye Ozero **30** 62 0N 35 30 E
Oneida **66** 43 5N 75 40W
Onekotan, Ostrov **31** 49 25N 154 45 E
Onezhskaya Guba **30** 64 30N 37 0 E
Onezhskoye Ozero **30** 62 0N 35 30 E
Ongole **38** 15 33N 80 2 E
Onguren **31** 53 38N 107 36 E
Onilahy → **53** 23 34 S 43 45 E
Onitsha **49** 6 6N 6 42 E
Onoda **44** 34 2N 131 25 E
Onslow **54** 21 40 S 115 12 E
Onslow B. **66** 34 20N 77 20W
Onstwedde **12** 53 2N 7 4 E
Ontake-San **44** 35 53N 137 29 E
Ontario **68** 34 2N 117 40W
Ontario □ **62** 52 0N 88 10W
Ontario, L. **62** 43 40N 78 0W
Oodnadatta **54** 27 33 S 135 30 E
Ooldea **54** 30 27 S 131 50 E
Oost-Vlaanderen □ **12** 51 5N 3 50 E
Oostende **12** 51 15N 2 50 E
Oosterhout **12** 51 39N 4 47 E
Oosterschelde **12** 51 33N 4 0 E
Ootacamund **38** 11 30N 76 44 E
Opala, U.S.S.R. **31** 51 58N 156 30 E
Opala, Zaïre **51** 0 40 S 24 20 E
Opanake **38** 6 35N 80 40 E
Opava **15** 49 57N 17 58 E
Opelousas **67** 30 35N 92 7W
Ophthalmia Ra. **54** 23 15 S 119 30 E
Opole **17** 50 42N 17 58 E
Oporto = Porto **18** 41 8N 8 40W
Opp **66** 31 19N 86 13W
Oppland fylke □ **28** 61 15N 9 40 E
Or, Le Mont d' **9** 46 45N 6 18 E
Oradea **15** 47 2N 21 58 E
Öræfajökull **27** 64 2N 16 39W
Orai **37** 25 58N 79 30 E
Oraison **11** 43 55N 5 55 E
Oran, Algeria **49** 35 45N 0 39W
Oran, Argentina **74** 23 10 S 64 20W
Orange, Australia **56** 33 15 S 149 7 E
Orange, France **11** 44 8N 4 47 E
Orange, U.S.A. **67** 30 10N 93 50W
Orange → = Oranje → **52** 28 41 S 16 28 E
Orange, C. **73** 4 20N 51 30W
Orange Free State □ **52** 28 30 S 27 0 E
Orangeburg **66** 33 35N 80 53W
Oranje → **52** 28 41 S 16 28 E
Oranje Vrystaat □ = Orange Free State □ **52** 28 30 S 27 0 E
Oranjemund **52** 28 38 S 16 29 E
Oraşul Stalin = Braşov **25** 45 38N 25 35 E
Orb → **10** 43 15N 3 18 E
Orbec **8** 49 1N 0 23 E
Orbetello **21** 42 26N 11 11 E
Orbost **56** 37 40 S 148 29 E
Orchies **9** 50 28N 3 14 E
Ord → **54** 15 33 S 138 15 E
Ord, Mt. **54** 17 20 S 125 34 E
Ordos = Mu Us Shamo **42** 39 0N 109 0 E
Ordu **45** 40 55N 37 53 E
Ordzhonikidze **35** 43 0N 44 35 E
Ore Mts. = Erzgebirge **13** 50 25N 13 0 E
Örebro **28** 59 20N 15 18 E
Örebro län □ **28** 59 27N 15 0 E
Oregon □ **68** 44 0N 121 0W
Oregon City **68** 45 21N 122 35W
Orekhovo-Zuyevo **33** 55 50N 38 55 E
Orel **33** 52 57N 36 3 E
Orenburg **30** 51 45N 55 6 E
Orense **18** 42 19N 7 55W
Orford Ness **5** 52 6N 1 31 E
Orgon **11** 43 47N 5 3 E
Oriental, Cordillera **72** 6 0N 73 0W
Origny-Ste.-Benoîte **9** 49 50N 3 30 E
Orihuela **19** 38 7N 0 55W
Orillia **62** 44 40N 79 24W
Orinoco → **72** 9 15N 61 30W
Orissa □ **36** 20 0N 84 0 E
Oristano **22** 39 54N 8 35 E
Oristano, G. di **22** 39 50N 8 22 E
Crizaba **69** 18 51N 97 6W
Orkanger **27** 63 18N 9 52 E
Orkla → **27** 63 18N 9 51 E
Orkney □ **6** 59 0N 3 0W
Orkney Is. **6** 59 0N 3 0W
Orland **68** 39 46N 122 12W
Orlando **66** 28 30N 81 25W
Orléanais **9** 48 0N 2 0 E
Orléans **9** 47 54N 1 52 E
Orlik **31** 52 30N 99 55 E
Ornans **9** 47 7N 6 10 E
Orne □ **8** 48 40N 0 5 E
Orne → **8** 49 18N 0 15W
Örnsköldsvik **27** 63 17N 18 40 E
Orocué **72** 4 48N 71 20W
Orotukan **31** 62 16N 151 42 E
Oroville **68** 39 31N 121 30W
Orsha **32** 54 30N 30 25 E
Orsk **30** 51 12N 58 34 E
Orşova **25** 44 41N 22 25 E
Ortegal, C. **18** 43 43N 7 52W
Orthez **10** 43 29N 0 48W
Ortigueira **18** 43 40N 7 50W
Ortles **20** 46 31N 10 33 E
Ortona **21** 42 21N 14 24 E
Orūmīyeh **45** 37 40N 45 0 E
Orūmīyeh, Daryācheh-ye **45** 37 50N 45 30 E
Oruro **72** 18 0 S 67 9W
Oruzgān □ **46** 33 30N 66 0 E
Orvault **8** 47 17N 1 38W
Orvieto **21** 42 43N 12 8 E
Orwell → **5** 52 2N 1 12 E
Oryakhovo **25** 43 40N 23 57 E
Osage → **67** 38 35N 91 57W
Ōsaka **44** 34 40N 135 30 E
Osaka □ **44** 34 30N 135 30 E
Osceola **67** 35 40N 90 0W
Osh **30** 40 37N 72 49 E
Oshawa **62** 43 50N 78 50W
Oshkosh, Nebr., U.S.A. **67** 41 27N 102 20W
Oshkosh, Wis., U.S.A. **66** 44 3N 88 35W
Oshogbo **49** 7 48N 4 37 E
Oshwe **51** 3 25 S 19 28 E
Osijek **24** 45 34N 18 41 E
Oskaloosa **67** 41 18N 92 40W
Oskarshamn **28** 57 15N 16 27 E
Oslo **28** 59 55N 10 45 E
Oslofjorden **28** 59 20N 10 35 E
Osmanabad **38** 18 5N 76 10 E
Osmaniye **45** 37 5N 36 10 E
Osnabrück **13** 52 16N 8 2 E
Osorno **74** 40 25 S 73 0W
Osprey Reef **56** 13 52 S 146 36 E
Oss **12** 51 46N 5 32 E
Ossa, Mt. **56** 41 52 S 146 3 E
Óssa, Oros **26** 39 47N 22 42 E
Osse → **10** 44 7N 0 17 E
Ossora **31** 59 20N 163 13 E
Oste → **13** 53 30N 9 12 E
Ostend = Oostende **12** 51 15N 2 50 E
Östergötlands län □ **28** 58 35N 15 45 E
Osterholz-Scharmbeck **13** 53 14N 8 48 E
Östersund **27** 63 10N 14 38 E
Østfold fylke □ **28** 59 25N 11 25 E
Ostfriesische Inseln **13** 53 45N 7 15 E
Ostfriesland **13** 53 20N 7 30 E
Ostrava **15** 49 51N 18 18 E
Ostróda **17** 53 42N 19 58 E
Ostrołeka **17** 53 4N 21 32 E
Ostrów Mazowiecka **17** 52 50N 21 51 E
Ostrów Wielkopolski **17** 51 36N 17 44 E
Ostrowiec-Świętokrzyski **17** 50 55N 21 22 E
Ōsumi-Kaikyō **44** 30 55N 131 0 E
Osuna **18** 37 14N 5 8W
Oswego **66** 43 29N 76 30W
Oswestry **5** 52 52N 3 3W
Ōtake **44** 34 12N 132 13 E
Otaru **44** 43 10N 141 0 E
Otavi **52** 19 40 S 17 24 E
Otjiwarongo **52** 20 30 S 16 33 E
Otranto **23** 40 9N 18 28 E
Otranto, C. d' **23** 40 7N 18 30 E
Otranto, Str. of **23** 40 15N 18 40 E
Ōtsu **44** 35 0N 135 50 E
Ottawa, Canada **62** 45 27N 75 42W
Ottawa, U.S.A. **67** 38 40N 95 6W
Ottawa → = Outaouais → **62** 45 27N 74 8W
Otter Rapids, Ont., Canada **62** 50 11N 81 39W
Otter Rapids, Sask., Canada **65** 55 38N 104 44W
Ottumwa **67** 41 0N 92 25W
Oturkpo **49** 7 16N 8 8 E
Otway, C. **56** 38 52 S 143 30 E
Otwock **17** 52 5N 21 20 E
Ötztaler Alpen **13** 46 45N 11 0 E
Ouachita → **67** 31 38N 91 49W
Ouachita Mts. **67** 34 50N 94 30W
Ouadâne **49** 20 50N 11 40W
Ouadda **50** 8 15N 22 20 E
Ouagadougou **49** 12 25N 1 30W
Ouallene **49** 24 41N 1 11 E
Ouanda Djallé **50** 8 55N 22 53 E
Ouango **51** 4 19N 22 30 E
Ouargla **49** 31 59N 5 16 E
Ouarzazate **49** 30 55N 6 50W
Oubangi → **51** 0 30 S 17 50 E
Ouche → **9** 47 6N 5 16 E
Ouddorp **12** 51 50N 3 57 E
Oude Rijn → **12** 52 12N 4 24 E
Oudenaarde **12** 50 50N 3 37 E
Oudon **8** 47 22N 1 19W
Oudtshoorn **52** 33 35 S 22 14 E
Ouessant, I. d' **8** 48 28N 5 6W
Ouesso **51** 1 37N 16 5 E
Ouezzane **49** 34 51N 5 35W
Ouidah **49** 6 25N 2 0 E
Ouistreham **8** 49 17N 0 18W
Oujda **49** 34 41N 1 55W
Oujeft **49** 20 2N 13 0W
Ouled Djellal **49** 34 28N 5 2 E
Oulu **27** 65 1N 25 29 E
Oulu □ **27** 65 10N 27 20 E
Oulujärvi **27** 64 25N 27 15 E
Oulujoki → **27** 65 1N 25 30 E
Oum Chalouba **50** 15 48N 20 46 E
Ounianga-Kébir **50** 19 4N 20 29 E
Ounianga Sérir **50** 18 54N 20 51 E
Our → **12** 49 55N 6 5 E
Ourcq → **9** 49 1N 3 1 E
Ourthe → **12** 50 29N 5 35 E
Ouse →, E. Sussex, U.K. **5** 50 43N 0 3 E
Ouse →, N. Yorks., U.K. **5** 54 3N 0 7 E
Oust **10** 42 52N 1 13 E
Oust → **8** 47 35N 2 6W
Outaouais → **62** 45 27N 74 8W
Outer Hebrides **6** 57 30N 7 40W
Outjo **52** 20 5 S 16 7 E
Outlook **65** 51 30N 107 0W
Outreau **9** 50 40N 1 36 E
Ouvèze → **11** 43 59N 4 51 E
Ouyen **56** 35 1 S 142 22 E
Ouzouer-le-Marché **9** 47 54N 1 32 E
Ovalle **74** 30 33 S 71 18W
Ovar **18** 40 51N 8 40W
Overflakkee **12** 51 44N 4 10 E
Overijssel □ **12** 52 25N 6 35 E
Overpelt **12** 51 12N 5 20 E
Övertorneå **27** 66 23N 23 38 E
Oviedo **18** 43 25N 5 50W
Ovruch **30** 51 25N 28 45 E
Owase **44** 34 7N 136 12 E
Owatonna **67** 44 3N 93 10W
Owen Sound **62** 44 35N 80 55W
Owen Stanley Range **56** 8 30 S 147 0 E
Owendo **51** 0 17N 9 30 E
Owensboro **66** 37 40N 87 5W
Owo **49** 7 10N 5 39 E
Owosso **66** 43 0N 84 10W
Owyhee → **68** 43 46N 117 2W
Ox Mts. **7** 54 6N 9 0W
Oxelösund **28** 58 43N 17 15 E
Oxford, U.K. **5** 51 45N 1 15W
Oxford, U.S.A. **66** 36 19N 78 36W
Oxford □ **5** 51 45N 1 15W
Oxford L. **65** 54 51N 95 37W
Oxnard **68** 34 10N 119 14W
Oyama **44** 36 18N 139 48 E
Oyem **51** 1 34N 11 31 E
Oykel → **6** 57 55N 4 26W
Oymyakon **31** 63 25N 142 44 E
Oyo **49** 7 46N 3 56 E
Oyonnax **11** 46 16N 5 40 E
Ozamis **40** 8 15N 123 50 E
Ozark **66** 31 29N 85 39W
Ozark Plateau **67** 37 20N 91 40W
Ozarks, L. of **67** 38 10N 92 40W

P

Paarl 52 33 45 S 18 56 E
Paatsi → 27 68 55N 29 0 E
Pabna 37 24 1N 89 18 E
Pacaraima, Sierra 72 4 0N 62 30W
Pacasmayo 72 7 20 S 79 35W
Pacaudière, La 10 46 11N 3 52 E
Pachuca 69 20 10N 98 40W
Pacific Ocean 57 10 0N 140 0W
Padang 39 1 0 S 100 20 E
Paderborn 13 51 42N 8 44 E
Pádova 21 45 24N 11 52 E
Padro, Mte. 11 42 28N 8 59 E
Padstow 5 50 33N 4 57W
Padua = Pádova 21 45 24N 11 52 E
Paducah 66 37 0N 88 40W
Pag 21 44 30N 14 50 E
Pagastikós Kólpos 26 39 15N 23 0 E
Pagny-sur-Moselle 9 48 59N 6 0 E
Pahang □ 41 3 30N 102 45 E
Paignton 5 50 26N 3 33W
Päijänne, L. 27 61 30N 25 30 E
Paimbœuf 8 47 17N 2 0W
Paimpol 8 48 48N 3 4W
Painesville 66 41 42N 81 18W
Painted Desert 68 36 0N 111 30W
Pais Vasco □ 19 43 0N 2 30W
Paisley 6 55 51N 4 27W
Paita 72 5 11 S 81 9W
Pak Sane 41 18 22N 103 39 E
Pakistan ■ 36 30 0N 70 0 E
Pakse 41 15 5N 105 52 E
Paktīā □ 46 33 0N 69 15 E
Pala 50 9 25N 15 5 E
Palagruža 21 42 24N 16 15 E
Palais, Le 8 47 20N 3 10W
Palam 38 19 0N 77 0 E
Palamós 19 41 50N 3 10 E
Palampur 36 32 10N 76 30 E
Palana 31 59 10N 159 59 E
Palani Hills 38 10 14N 77 33 E
Palanpur 36 24 10N 72 25 E
Palapye 52 22 30 S 27 7 E
Palatka, U.S.A. 66 29 40N 81 40W
Palatka, U.S.S.R. 31 60 6N 150 54 E
Palawan 39 9 30N 118 30 E
Palayankottai 38 8 45N 77 45 E
Palazzo, Pte. 11 42 28N 8 30 E
Palembang 39 3 0 S 104 50 E
Palencia 18 42 1N 4 34W
Palermo 22 38 8N 13 20 E
Palestine 67 31 42N 95 35W
Palghat 38 10 46N 76 42 E
Pali 36 25 50N 73 20 E
Palitana 36 21 32N 71 49 E
Palizada 69 18 15N 92 5W
Palk Bay 38 9 30N 79 15 E
Palk Strait 38 10 0N 79 45 E
Palm Is. 56 18 40 S 146 35 E
Palm Springs 68 33 51N 116 35W
Palma 51 10 46 S 40 29 E
Palma, B. de 19 39 30N 2 39 E
Palma, La, Canary Is. 49 28 40N 17 50W
Palma, La, Panama 70 8 15N 78 0W
Palma, La, Spain 18 37 21N 6 38W
Palma de Mallorca 19 39 35N 2 39 E
Palma Soriano 70 20 15N 76 0W
Palmas, C. 49 4 27N 7 46W
Pálmas, G. di 22 39 0N 8 30 E
Palmeirinhas, Pta. das 51 9 2 S 12 57 E
Palmer → 54 24 46 S 133 25 E
Palmer Land 60 73 0 S 60 0W
Palmerston, C. 55 21 32 S 149 29 E
Palmerston North 59 40 21 S 175 39 E
Palmi 23 38 21N 15 51 E
Palmira 72 3 32N 76 16W
Palmyra = Tudmur 45 34 36N 38 15 E
Palmyra Is. 58 5 52N 162 5W
Palo Alto 68 37 25N 122 8W
Palos, C. de 19 37 38N 0 40W
Pama 49 11 19N 0 44 E
Pamiers 10 43 7N 1 39 E
Pamirs 30 37 40N 73 0 E
Pamlico Sd. 66 35 20N 76 0W
Pampa 67 35 35N 100 58W
Pampas 74 35 0 S 63 0W
Pamplona 19 42 48N 1 38W
Panaca 68 37 51N 114 23W
Panaji 38 15 25N 73 50 E
Panamá 70 9 0N 79 25W
Panama ■ 70 8 48N 79 55W
Panamá, G. de 70 8 4N 79 20W
Panama Canal 69 9 10N 79 37W
Panama City 66 30 10N 85 41W
Panay 40 11 10N 122 30 E
Pančevo 24 44 52N 20 41 E
Pancorbo, Paso 19 42 32N 3 5W
Pandharpur 38 17 41N 75 20 E
Pangani 51 5 25 S 38 58 E
Pangkalpinang 39 2 0 S 106 0 E
Panna 37 24 40N 80 15 E
Pantelleria 22 36 52N 12 0 E
Pánuco 69 22 3N 98 10W
Panyam 49 9 27N 9 8 E
Paoua 50 7 9N 16 20 E
Papá 15 47 22N 17 30 E
Papenburg 13 53 7N 7 25 E
Papua, Gulf of 56 9 0 S 144 50 E
Papua New Guinea ■ 56 8 0 S 145 0 E
Pará = Belém 73 1 20 S 48 30W
Pará □ 73 3 20 S 52 0W
Paraburdoo 54 23 14 S 117 32 E
Paracatu 73 17 10 S 46 50W
Paradip 36 20 15N 86 35 E
Paragua, La 72 6 50N 63 20W
Paraguay ■ 74 23 0 S 57 0W
Paraguay → 74 27 18 S 58 38W
Paraíba = João Pessoa 73 7 10 S 34 52W
Paraíba □ 73 7 0 S 36 0W
Parainen 27 60 18N 22 18 E
Parakou 49 9 25N 2 40 E
Paramaribo 73 5 50N 55 10W
Paramushir, Ostrov 31 50 24N 156 0 E
Paraná 74 31 45 S 60 30W
Paraná □ 74 24 30 S 51 0W
Paraná → 74 33 43 S 59 15W
Paranaguá 74 25 30 S 48 30W
Paranaíba → 73 20 6 S 51 4W
Paray-le-Monial 11 46 27N 4 7 E
Parbhani 36 19 8N 76 52 E
Pardubice 14 50 3N 15 45 E
Parecis, Serra dos 72 13 0 S 60 0W
Paren 31 62 30N 163 15 E
Parent 62 47 55N 74 35W
Parentis-en-Born 10 44 21N 1 4W
Parfuri 53 22 28 S 31 17 E
Paria, G. de 70 10 20N 62 0W
Parika 72 6 50N 58 20W
Parintins 73 2 40 S 56 50W
Pariparit Kyun 41 14 55 S 93 45 E
Paris, France 9 48 50N 2 20 E
Paris, Tenn., U.S.A. 66 36 20N 88 20W
Paris, Tex., U.S.A. 67 33 40N 95 30W
Paris, Ville de □ 9 48 50N 2 20 E
Park Range 68 40 0N 106 30W
Parker 68 34 8N 114 16W
Parkersburg 66 39 18N 81 31W
Parkes, A.C.T., Australia 55 35 18 S 149 8 E
Parkes, N.S.W., Australia 56 33 9 S 148 11 E
Parma 20 44 50N 10 20 E
Parnaguá 73 10 10 S 44 38W
Parnaíba 73 2 54 S 41 47W
Parnaíba → 73 3 0 S 41 50W
Parnassós 26 38 35N 22 30 E
Pärnu 32 58 28N 24 33 E
Paroo → 55 31 28 S 143 32 E
Paroo Chan. 55 30 50 S 143 35 E
Páros 26 37 5N 25 12 E
Parpaillon 11 44 30N 6 40 E
Parral 74 36 10 S 71 52W
Parras 69 25 30N 102 20W
Parrett → 5 51 7N 2 58W
Parry Is. 3 77 0N 110 0W
Parry Sound 62 45 20N 80 0W
Parsons 67 37 20N 95 17W
Parthenay 8 46 38N 0 16W
Paruro 72 13 45 S 71 50W
Parvān □ 46 35 0N 69 0 E
Parvatipuram 38 18 50N 83 25 E
Pas-de-Calais □ 9 50 30N 2 10 E
Pasadena, Calif., U.S.A. 68 34 5N 118 9W
Pasadena, Tex., U.S.A. 67 29 45N 95 14W
Pasaje 72 3 23 S 79 50W
Pascagoula 67 30 21N 88 30W
Pasco 68 46 10N 119 0W
Pasco, Cerro de 72 10 45 S 76 10W
Pasley, C. 54 33 52 S 123 35 E
Paso Robles 68 35 40N 120 45W
Passage West 7 51 52N 8 20W
Passau 13 48 34N 13 27 E
Passero, C. 23 36 42N 15 8 E
Passo Fundo 74 28 10 S 52 20W
Passy 11 45 55N 6 41 E
Pasto 72 1 13N 77 17W
Patagonia 74 45 0 S 69 0W
Patay 9 48 2N 1 40 E
Patchogue 66 40 46N 73 1W
Pategi 49 8 50N 5 45 E
Paternò 23 37 34N 14 53 E
Paterson 66 40 55N 74 10W
Pathankot 36 32 18N 75 45 E
Patiala 36 30 23N 76 26 E
Pátmos 26 37 21N 26 36 E
Patna 37 25 35N 85 12 E
Patos, L. dos 74 31 20 S 51 0 E
Patos de Minas 73 18 35 S 46 32W
Pátrai 26 38 14N 21 47 E
Pátraikós, Kólpos 26 38 17N 21 30 E
Patti 23 38 8N 14 57 E
Patuakhali 37 22 20N 90 25 E
Patuca → 70 15 50N 84 18W
Pátzcuaro 69 19 32N 101 36W
Pau 10 43 19N 0 25W
Pau, Gave de → 10 43 33N 1 12W
Pauillac 10 45 11N 0 46W
Paulhan 10 43 33N 3 28 E
Paulistana 73 8 9 S 41 9W
Paulo Afonso 73 9 21 S 38 15W
Pavia 20 45 10N 9 10 E
Pavlodar 30 52 33N 77 0 E
Pavlograd 34 48 30N 35 52 E
Pavlovo, Gorkiy, U.S.S.R. 33 55 58N 43 5 E
Pavlovo, Yakut A.S.S.R., U.S.S.R. 31 63 5N 115 25 E
Pavlovsk 33 50 26N 40 5 E
Pawtucket 66 41 51N 71 22W
Payette 68 44 0N 117 0W
Paysandú 74 32 19 S 58 8W
Paz, La, Argentina 74 30 50 S 59 45W
Paz, La, Bolivia 72 16 20 S 68 10W
Paz, La, Mexico 69 24 10N 110 18W
Pazardzhik 25 42 12N 24 20 E
Peace → 64 59 0N 111 25W
Peace River 64 56 15N 117 18W
Peak, The 5 53 24N 1 53W
Peak Range 56 22 50 S 148 20 E
Peary Land 3 82 40N 33 0W
Pebane 51 17 10 S 38 8 E
Pebas 72 3 10 S 71 46W
Peč 24 42 40N 20 17 E
Pechenga 30 69 30N 31 25 E
Pechora → 30 68 13N 54 15 E
Pechorskaya Guba 30 68 40N 54 0 E
Pecos → 67 29 42N 102 30W
Pécs 15 46 5N 18 15 E
Pedro Afonso 73 9 0 S 48 10W
Pedro Juan Caballero 74 22 30 S 55 40W
Peebles 6 55 40N 3 12W
Peekskill 66 41 18N 73 57W
Peel 5 54 14N 4 40W
Pegu 41 17 20N 96 29 E
Pehuajó 74 35 45 S 62 0W
Peine 13 52 19N 10 12 E
Peip'ing = Beijing 42 39 55N 116 20 E
Pekalongan 40 6 53 S 109 40 E
Pekan 41 3 30N 103 25 E
Pekanbaru 39 0 30N 101 15 E
Pekin 67 40 35N 89 40W
Peking = Beijing 42 39 55N 116 20 E
Pelat, Mt. 11 44 16N 6 42 E
Peleaga 15 45 22N 22 55 E
Peleng 40 1 20 S 123 30 E
Pelkosenniemi 27 67 6N 27 28 E
Pellworm 13 54 30N 8 40 E
Peloponnese = Pelopónnisos □ 26 37 10N 22 0 E
Pelopónnisos □ 26 37 10N 22 0 E
Peloro, C. 23 38 15N 15 40 E
Pelotas 74 31 42 S 52 23W
Pelvoux, Massif de 11 44 52N 6 20 E
Pematangsiantar 39 2 57N 99 5 E
Pemba I. 51 5 0 S 39 45 E
Pemberton 54 34 30 S 116 0 E
Pembroke, Canada 62 45 50N 77 7W
Pembroke, U.K. 5 51 41N 4 57W
Pen-y-Ghent 5 54 10N 2 15W
Peña de Francia, Sierra de 18 40 32N 6 10W
Peñalara, Pico 18 40 51N 3 57W
Penang = Pinang 41 5 25N 100 15 E
Peñarroya-Pueblonuevo 18 38 19N 5 16W
Peñas, C. de 18 43 42N 5 52W
Penas, G. de 74 47 0 S 75 0W
Pend Oreille, L. 68 48 0N 116 30W
Pendembu 49 9 7N 12 14W
Pendleton 68 45 35N 118 50W
Penetanguishene 62 44 50N 79 55W
Peniche 18 39 19N 9 22W
Penicuik 6 55 50N 3 14W
Peninsular Malaysia □ 41 4 0N 102 0 E
Penmarch 8 47 49N 4 21W
Penmarch, Pte. de 8 47 48N 4 22W
Penner → 38 14 35N 80 10 E
Pennines 5 54 50N 2 20W
Pennsylvania □ 66 40 50N 78 0W
Penola 56 37 25 S 140 21 E
Penong 54 31 59 S 133 5 E
Penonomé 70 8 31N 80 21W
Penrhyn Is. 58 9 0 S 158 30W
Penrith, Australia 56 33 43 S 150 38 E
Penrith, U.K. 5 54 40N 2 45W
Pensacola 66 30 30N 87 10W
Penticton 64 49 30N 119 38W
Pentland 56 20 32 S 145 25 E
Pentland Firth 6 58 43N 3 10W
Pentland Hills 6 55 48N 3 25W
Penza 33 53 15N 45 5 E
Penzance 5 50 7N 5 32W
Penzhino 31 63 30N 167 55 E
Penzhinskaya Guba 31 61 30N 163 0 E
Peoria 67 40 40N 89 40W
Perak □ 41 5 0N 101 0 E
Perche 8 48 31N 1 1 E
Perche, Collines du 8 48 30N 0 40 E
Percy 8 48 55N 1 11W
Perdido, Mte. 19 42 40N 0 5 E
Perdu, Mt. 19 42 40N 0 5 E
Pereira 72 4 49N 75 43W
Perekop 34 46 10N 33 42 E
Pereyaslav Khmelnitskiy 32 50 3N 31 28 E
Pergamino 74 33 52 S 60 30W
Péribonca → 63 48 45N 72 5W
Périers 8 49 11N 1 25W
Périgord 10 45 0N 0 40 E
Périgueux 10 45 10N 0 42 E
Perlis □ 41 6 30N 100 15 E
Perm 30 58 0N 57 10 E
Pernambuco = Recife 73 8 0 S 35 0W
Pernambuco □ 73 8 0 S 37 0W
Péronne 9 49 55N 2 57 E
Perpignan 10 42 42N 2 53 E
Perros-Guirec 8 48 49N 3 28W
Perry, Iowa, U.S.A. 67 41 48N 94 5W
Perry, Okla., U.S.A. 67 36 20N 97 20W
Persepolis 46 29 55N 52 50 E
Persia = Iran ■ 46 33 0N 53 0 E
Persian Gulf = Gulf, The 46 27 0N 50 0 E
Perth, Australia 54 31 57 S 115 52 E
Perth, Canada 62 44 55N 76 15W
Perth, U.K. 6 56 24N 3 27W
Perth Amboy 66 40 31N 74 16W
Perthus, Le 10 42 30N 2 53 E
Pertuis 11 43 42N 5 30 E
Peru 66 40 42N 86 0W
Peru ■ 72 8 0 S 75 0W
Peru-Chile Trench 58 20 0 S 72 0W
Perúgia 21 43 6N 12 24 E
Pervomaysk 34 48 10N 30 46 E
Pervouralsk 30 56 55N 60 0 E
Pésaro 21 43 55N 12 53 E
Pescara 21 42 28N 14 13 E
Peshawar 46 34 2N 71 37 E
Pessac 10 44 48N 0 37W
Petah Tiqwa 45 32 6N 34 53 E
Petaling Jaya 41 3 4N 101 42 E
Petaluma 68 38 13N 122 39W
Petange 12 49 33N 5 55 E
Petatlán 69 17 31N 101 16W
Petauke 51 14 14 S 31 20 E
Peterborough, Australia 56 32 58 S 138 51 E
Peterborough, Canada 62 44 20N 78 20W
Peterborough, U.K. 5 52 35N 0 14W
Peterhead 6 57 30N 1 49W
Petersburg 66 37 17N 77 26W
Petit Goâve 70 18 27N 72 51W
Petitsikapau, L. 63 54 37N 66 25W
Petlad 36 22 30N 72 45 E
Petoskey 62 45 22N 84 57W
Petra, Ostrova 3 76 15N 118 30 E
Petreto-Bicchisano 11 41 47N 8 58 E
Petrich 25 41 24N 23 13 E
Petrolia 62 42 54N 82 9W
Petrolina 73 9 24 S 40 30W
Petropavlovsk 30 54 53N 69 13 E
Petropavlovsk-Kamchatskiy 31 53 3N 158 43 E
Petrópolis 73 22 33 S 43 9W
Petroşeni 25 45 28N 23 20 E
Petrovaradin 24 45 16N 19 55 E
Petrovsk 33 52 22N 45 19 E
Petrovsk-Zabaykalskiy 31 51 20N 108 55 E
Petrozavodsk 30 61 41N 34 20 E
Pevek 31 69 41N 171 19 E
Peyrehorade 10 43 34N 1 7W
Peyruis 11 44 1N 5 56 E
Pézenas 10 43 28N 3 24 E
Pforzheim 13 48 53N 8 43 E
Pfungstadt 13 49 47N 8 36 E
Phalodi 36 27 12N 72 24 E
Phalsbourg 9 48 46N 7 15 E
Phan Rang 41 11 34N 109 0 E
Phangan, Ko 41 9 45N 100 0 E
Phanh Bho Ho Chi Minh 41 10 58N 106 40 E
Phenix City 66 32 30N 85 0W
Philadelphia 66 40 0N 75 10W
Philippeville 12 50 12N 4 33 E
Philippines ■ 40 12 0N 123 0 E
Phillip, I. 56 38 30 S 145 12 E
Phitsanulok 41 16 50N 100 12 E
Phnom Penh 41 11 33N 104 55 E
Phoenix 68 33 30N 112 10W
Phoenix Is. 57 3 30 S 172 0W
Phra Chedi Sam Ong 41 15 16N 98 23 E
Phuket 41 7 52N 98 22 E
Piacenza 20 45 2N 9 42 E
Pialba 56 25 20 S 152 45 E
Piana 11 42 15N 8 34 E
Piatra Neamţ 15 46 56N 26 21 E
Piauí □ 73 7 0 S 43 0W
Piave → 21 45 32N 12 44 E
Piazza Ármerina 23 37 21N 14 20 E
Pibor Post 50 6 47N 33 3 E
Picardie 9 49 50N 3 0 E
Picardie, Plaine de 9 50 0N 2 0 E
Picayune 67 30 31N 89 40W
Picquigny 9 49 56N 2 10 E
Picton 59 41 18 S 174 3 E
Pictou 63 45 41N 62 42W
Pidurutalagala 38 7 10N 80 50 E
Piedad, La 69 20 20N 102 1W
Piedmont = Piemonte □ 20 45 0N 7 30 E
Piedmont Plateau 66 34 0N 81 30W
Piedras Negras 69 28 42N 100 31W
Piemonte □ 20 45 0N 7 30 E
Pierre Benite, Barrage 11 45 42N 4 49 E
Pierre-de-Bresse 11 46 54N 5 13 E
Pierrefeu-du-Var 11 43 13N 6 9 E
Pierrefonds 9 49 20N 3 0 E
Pierrefontaine-les-Varans 9 47 14N 6 32 E
Pierrefort 10 44 55N 2 50 E
Pierrelatte 11 44 23N 4 43 E
Piet Retief 53 27 1 S 30 50 E
Pietermaritzburg 53 29 35 S 30 25 E
Pietersburg 53 23 54 S 29 25 E
Pietrosul 15 47 35N 24 43 E
Piketberg 52 32 55 S 18 40 E
Pikeville 66 37 30N 82 30W
Pilbara 54 21 15 S 118 16 E
Pilcomayo → 74 25 21 S 57 42W
Pilibhit 37 28 40N 79 50 E
Pílos 26 36 55N 21 42 E
Pimba 55 31 18 S 136 46 E
Pimenta Bueno 72 11 35 S 61 10W
Pinang 41 5 25N 100 15 E
Pinang □ 41 5 20N 100 20 E
Pinar del Río 70 22 26N 83 40W
Pinaroo 55 35 17 S 140 53 E
Pinawa 65 50 9N 95 50W
Pincher Creek 64 49 30N 113 57W
Pindiga 49 9 58N 10 53 E
Pindos Óros 26 40 0N 21 0 E
Pindus Mts. = Pindos Óros 26 40 0N 21 0 E
Pine Bluff 67 34 10N 92 0W
Pine Creek 54 13 50 S 132 10 E
Pine Pass 64 55 25N 122 42W
Pine Point 64 60 50N 114 28W
Pinega → 30 64 8N 46 54 E
Pinerolo 20 44 47N 7 21 E
Pinetown 53 29 48 S 30 54 E
Pineville 67 31 22N 92 30W
Piney 9 48 22N 4 21 E
Ping → 41 15 42N 100 9 E
Pingdong 43 22 39N 120 30 E
Pingxiang 43 22 6N 106 46 E
Pinhel 18 40 50N 7 1W
Piniós → 26 39 55N 22 10 E
Pinjarra 54 32 37 S 115 52 E
Pinsk 32 52 10N 26 1 E
Pinyug 30 60 5N 48 0 E
Piombino 20 42 54N 10 30 E
Pioner, Os. 31 79 50N 92 0 E
Piotrków Trybunalski 17 51 23N 19 43 E
Pipriac 8 47 49N 1 58W
Piqua 66 40 10N 84 10W
Piracicaba 73 22 45 S 47 40W
Piræus = Piraiévs 26 37 57N 23 42 E
Piraiévs 26 37 57N 23 42 E
Pirapora 73 17 20 S 44 56W
Pírgos 26 37 40N 21 27 E
Piriac-sur-Mer 8 47 22N 2 33W
Pirin Planina 25 41 40N 23 30 E
Pirineos 19 42 40N 1 0 E
Pirmasens 13 49 12N 7 30 E
Pirot 24 43 9N 22 39 E
Pisa 20 43 43N 10 23 E
Pisagua 72 19 40 S 70 15W
Pisco 72 13 50 S 76 12W
Písek 14 49 19N 14 10 E
Pissos 10 44 19N 0 49W
Pistóia 20 43 57N 10 53 E
Pisuerga → 18 41 33N 4 52W
Pitcairn I. 58 25 5 S 130 5W
Pite älv → 27 65 20N 21 25 E
Piteå 27 65 20N 21 25 E
Piteşti 25 44 52N 24 54 E
Pithapuram 38 17 10N 82 15 E
Pithiviers 9 48 10N 2 13 E
Pitlochry 6 56 43N 3 43W
Pitt I. 64 53 30N 129 50W
Pittsburg, Kans., U.S.A. 67 37 21N 94 43W
Pittsburg, Tex., U.S.A. 67 32 59N 94 58W
Pittsburgh 66 40 25N 79 55W
Pittsfield 66 42 28N 73 17W
Piura 72 5 15 S 80 38W
Pizzo 23 38 44N 16 10 E
Placentia 63 47 20N 54 0W
Placentia B. 63 47 0N 54 40W
Placerville 68 38 47N 120 51W
Placetas 70 22 15N 79 44W
Plainfield 66 40 37N 74 28W
Plainview 67 34 10N 101 40W
Plaisance 10 43 36N 0 3 E
Pláka 26 40 0N 25 24 E
Plancoët 8 48 32N 2 13W
Plasencia 18 40 3N 6 8W
Plaster Rock 63 46 53N 67 22W
Plata, La 74 35 0 S 57 55W
Plata, Río de la 74 34 45 S 57 30W
Platani → 22 37 23N 13 16 E
Platí, Ákra 26 40 27N 24 0 E
Platte → 67 39 16N 94 50W
Plattsburg 62 44 41N 73 30W
Plauen 13 50 29N 12 9 E
Pleasantville 66 39 25N 74 30W
Pléaux 10 45 8N 2 13 E
Plélan-le-Grand 8 48 0N 2 7W
Plémet-la-Pierre 8 48 11N 2 36W
Pléneuf-Val-André 8 48 35N 2 32W
Plenty, Bay of 59 37 45 S 177 0 E
Plessisville 63 46 14N 71 47W
Plestin-les-Grèves 8 48 40N 3 39W
Pleven 25 43 26N 24 37 E
Plevlja 24 43 21N 19 21 E
Ploemeur 8 47 44N 3 26W
Ploërmel 8 47 55N 2 26W
Ploieşti 25 44 57N 26 5 E
Plombières-les-Bains 9 47 58N 6 27 E
Plöner See 13 54 10N 10 22 E
Plouaret 8 48 37N 3 28W
Plouay 8 47 55N 3 21W
Ploudalmézeau 8 48 34N 4 41W
Plougasnou 8 48 42N 3 49W
Plouha 8 48 41N 2 57W
Plouhinec 8 48 0N 4 29W
Plovdiv 25 42 8N 24 44 E
Plumtree 51 20 27 S 27 55 E
Pluvigner 8 47 46N 3 1W
Plymouth 5 50 23N 4 9W
Plymouth Sd. 5 50 20N 4 10W
Plynlimon = Pumlumon Fawr 5 52 29N 3 47W
Plzen 14 49 45N 13 22 E
Po → 20 44 57N 12 4 E
Pobeda 31 65 12N 146 12 E
Pobedino 31 49 51N 142 49 E
Pobedy Pik 30 40 45N 79 58 E
Pocatello 68 42 50N 112 25W
Pochutla 69 15 50N 96 31W
Poços de Caldas 73 21 50 S 46 33W
Podensac 10 44 40N 0 22W
Podkamennaya Tunguska → 31 61 50N 90 13 E
Podolsk 33 55 25N 37 30 E
Podor 49 16 40N 15 2W
Pofadder 52 29 10 S 19 22 E
Point Edward 62 43 0N 82 30W
Point Pedro 38 9 50N 80 15 E
Point Stephens 55 32 38 S 152 12 E
Pointe-à-Pitre 70 16 10N 61 30W
Pointe Noire 51 4 48 S 11 53 E
Poissy 9 48 55N 2 2 E
Poitiers 8 46 35N 0 20 E
Poitou 10 46 40N 0 10W
Poitou, Seuil du 10 46 30N 0 1W
Poix de Picardie 9 49 47N 2 0 E
Poix-Terron 9 49 38N 4 38 E
Pokrovsk 31 61 29N 126 12 E
Poland ■ 17 52 0N 20 0 E
Polden Hills 5 51 7N 2 50W
Polesye 32 52 0N 28 10 E
Poligny 9 46 50N 5 42 E
Polillo Is. 40 14 56N 122 0 E
Políyiros 26 40 23N 23 25 E
Pollachi 38 10 35N 77 0 E
Polotsk 32 55 30N 28 50 E
Poltava 34 49 35N 34 35 E
Polynesia 58 10 0 S 162 0W
Pombal 18 39 55N 8 40W
Pomona 68 34 2N 117 49W
Pompano Beach 66 26 12N 80 6W
Pompey 9 48 46N 6 6 E
Ponape 57 6 55N 158 10 E
Ponca City 67 36 40N 97 5W
Ponce 70 18 1N 66 37W
Poncin 11 46 6N 5 25 E
Pondicherry 38 11 59N 79 50 E
Ponferrada 18 42 32N 6 35W
Ponnani 38 10 45N 75 59 E
Ponoi → 30 66 59N 41 17 E
Ponoka 64 52 42N 113 40W
Pons 10 45 35N 0 34W
Pont-à-Mousson 9 48 54N 6 1 E
Pont-Audemer 8 49 21N 0 30 E
Pont-Aven 8 47 51N 3 47W
Pont-de-Roide 9 47 23N 6 45 E
Pont-de-Salars 10 44 18N 2 44 E
Pont-de-Vaux 9 46 26N 4 56 E
Pont-de-Veyle 11 46 17N 4 53 E
Pont-l'Abbé 8 47 52N 4 15W
Pont-l'Évêque 8 49 18N 0 11 E
Pont-St.-Esprit 11 44 16N 4 40 E
Pont-sur-Yonne 9 48 18N 3 10 E
Ponta Grossa 74 25 7 S 50 10W
Ponta Pora 73 22 20 S 55 35W
Pontacq 10 43 11N 0 8W
Pontailler-sur-Saône 9 47 13N 5 25 E

Pontarlier 9 46 54N 6 20 E
Pontaubault 8 48 40N 1 20W
Pontaumur 10 45 52N 2 40 E
Pontcharra 11 45 26N 6 1 E
Pontchartrain, L. 67 30 12N 90 0W
Pontchâteau 8 47 25N 2 5W
Ponte-Leccia 11 42 28N 9 13 E
Pontedera 20 43 40N 10 37 E
Pontefract 5 53 42N 1 19W
Pontevedra 18 42 26N 8 40W
Pontiac 66 42 40N 83 20W
Pontianak 39 0 3 S 109 15 E
Pontine Is. =
Ponziane, Isole 22 40 55N 13 0 E
Pontivy 8 48 5N 2 58W
Pontoise 9 49 3N 2 5 E
Pontorson 8 48 34N 1 30W
Pontrieux 8 48 42N 3 10W
Ponts-de-Cé, Les 8 47 25N 0 30W
Pontypool 5 51 42N 3 1W
Pontypridd 5 51 36N 3 21W
Ponziane, Isole 22 40 55N 13 0 E
Poole 5 50 42N 1 58W
Pooley I. 64 52 45N 128 15W
Poona = Pune 38 18 29N 73 57 E
Poopó, L. de 72 18 30 S 67 35W
Popayán 72 2 27N 76 36W
Poperinge 12 50 51N 2 42 E
Popigay 31 72 1N 110 39 E
Poplar Bluff 67 36 45N 90 22W
Popocatépetl, Volcán 69 19 2N 98 38W
Popokabaka 51 5 41 S 16 40 E
Popondetta 56 8 48 S 148 17 E
Porbandar 36 21 44N 69 43 E
Porcher I. 64 53 50N 130 30W
Pori 27 61 29N 21 48 E
Porjus 27 66 57N 19 50 E
Porkkala 27 59 59N 24 26 E
Pornic 8 47 7N 2 5W
Poronaysk 31 49 13N 143 0 E
Poroshiri-Dake 44 42 41N 142 52 E
Porquerolles, I. de 11 43 0N 6 13 E
Porretta, Passo di 20 44 2N 10 56 E
Porsangen 27 70 40N 25 40 E
Port Alberni 64 49 40N 124 50W
Port Alfred, Canada 63 48 18N 70 53W
Port Alfred, S. Africa 52 33 36 S 26 55 E
Port Angeles 68 48 7N 123 30W
Port Antonio 70 18 10N 76 30W
Port Arthur,
Australia 56 43 7 S 147 50 E
Port Arthur, U.S.A. 67 30 0N 94 0W
Port-au-Prince 70 18 40N 72 20W
Port Augusta 56 32 30 S 137 50 E
Port Augusta West 56 32 29 S 137 29 E
Port Bergé Vaovao 53 15 33 S 47 40 E
Port Blair 41 11 40N 92 30 E
Port Bradshaw 55 12 30 S 137 20 E
Port-Cartier 63 50 2N 66 50W
Port Colborne 62 42 50N 79 10W
Port Coquitlam 64 49 15N 122 45W
Port Darwin,
Australia 54 12 24 S 130 45 E
Port Darwin,
Falk. Is. 74 51 50 S 59 0W
Port Davey 56 43 16 S 145 55 E
Port-de-Bouc 11 43 24N 4 59 E
Port-de-Paix 70 19 50N 72 50W
Port Elgin 62 44 25N 81 25W
Port Elizabeth 52 33 58 S 25 40 E
Port Ellen 6 55 38N 6 10W
Port-en-Bessin 8 49 21N 0 45W
Port Erin 5 54 5N 4 45W
Port Etienne =
Nouâdhibou 49 20 54N 17 0W
Port Fairy 56 38 22 S 142 12 E
Port-Gentil 51 0 40 S 8 50 E
Port Glasgow 6 55 57N 4 40W
Port Harcourt 49 4 40N 7 10 E
Port Hawkesbury 63 45 36N 61 22W
Port Hedland 54 20 25 S 118 35 E
Port Hope 62 43 56N 78 20W
Port Huron 66 43 0N 82 28W
Port Jackson 55 33 50 S 151 18 E
Port-Joinville 8 46 45N 2 23W
Port-la-Nouvelle 10 43 1N 3 3 E
Port Laoise 7 53 2N 7 20W
Port-Leucate 10 42 53N 3 3 E
Port Lincoln 54 34 42 S 135 52 E
Port Loko 49 8 48N 12 46W
Port Louis 8 47 42N 3 22W
Port Macquarie 56 31 25 S 152 25 E
Port Morant 70 17 54N 76 19W
Port Moresby 56 9 24 S 147 8 E
Port Musgrave 56 11 55 S 141 50 E
Port-Navalo 8 47 34N 2 54W
Port Nolloth 52 29 17 S 16 52 E
Port of Spain 70 10 40N 61 31W
Port Phillip B. 56 38 10 S 144 50 E
Port Pirie 56 33 10 S 138 1 E
Port Said = Bûr Sa'îd 50 31 16N 32 18 E
Port-St.-Louis-du-
Rhône 11 43 23N 4 49 E
Port Shepstone 53 30 44 S 30 28 E
Port Simpson 64 54 30N 130 20W
Port Stanley 62 42 40N 81 10W
Port Sudan = Bûr
Sûdân 50 19 32N 37 9 E
Port-sur-Saône 9 47 42N 6 2 E
Port Talbot 5 51 35N 3 48W
Port Townsend 68 48 7N 122 50W
Port-Vendres 10 42 32N 3 8 E
Portadown 7 54 27N 6 26W
Portage La Prairie 65 49 58N 98 18W
Portalegre 18 39 19N 7 25W
Portalegre □ 18 39 20N 7 40W
Portarlington 7 53 10N 7 10W
Porte, La 66 41 36N 86 43W
Porterville 68 36 5N 119 0W
Porthcawl 5 51 28N 3 42W
Portile de Fier 25 44 42N 22 30 E
Portimão 18 37 8N 8 32W
Portland, Australia 56 38 20 S 141 35 E
Portland, Maine,
U.S.A. 63 43 40N 70 15W
Portland, Oreg.,
U.S.A. 68 45 35N 122 40W
Portland, Bill of 5 50 31N 2 27W
Portland, C. 55 40 46 S 148 0 E
Portland, I. of 5 50 32N 2 25W
Porto, France 11 42 16N 8 42 E
Porto, Portugal 18 41 8N 8 40W
Porto, G. de 11 42 17N 8 34 E
Pôrto Alegre 74 30 5 S 51 10W
Porto Empédocle 22 37 18N 13 30 E
Pôrto Mendes 74 24 30 S 54 15W
Porto Novo 49 6 23N 2 42 E
Porto Santo 49 33 45N 16 25W
Pôrto Seguro 73 16 26 S 39 5W
Porto Tórres 22 40 50N 8 23 E
Porto-Vecchio 11 41 35N 9 16 E
Pôrto Velho 72 8 46 S 63 54W
Portoferráio 20 42 50N 10 20 E
Portoscuso 22 39 12N 8 22 E
Portovíejo 72 1 7 S 80 28W
Portpatrick 6 54 50N 5 7W
Portree 6 57 25N 6 11W
Portrush 7 55 13N 6 40W
Portsall 8 48 37N 4 45W
Portsmouth, Domin. 70 15 34N 61 27W
Portsmouth, U.K. 5 50 48N 1 6W
Portsmouth, N.H.,
U.S.A. 66 43 5N 70 45W
Portsmouth, Ohio,
U.S.A. 66 38 45N 83 0W
Portsmouth, Va.,
U.S.A. 66 36 50N 76 20W
Portsoy 6 57 41N 2 41W
Porttipahta 27 68 5N 26 40 E
Portugal ■ 18 40 0N 7 0W
Portuguese-Guinea =
Guinea-Bissau ■ 49 12 0N 15 0W
Portuguese Timor ■
= Timor 40 9 0 S 125 0 E
Portumna 7 53 5N 8 12W
Porvenir 74 53 10 S 70 16W
Porvoo 27 60 24N 25 40 E
Posadas 74 27 30 S 55 50W
Possel 51 5 5N 19 10 E
Poste-de-la-Baleine 62 55 17N 77 45W
Poste Maurice Cortier 49 22 14N 1 2 E
Potchefstroom 52 26 41 S 27 7 E
Potenza 23 40 40N 15 50 E
Potgietersrus 53 24 10 S 28 55 E
Poti 35 42 10N 41 38 E
Potiskum 49 11 39N 11 2 E
Potomac → 66 38 0N 76 23W
Potosí 72 19 38 S 65 50W
Potsdam, Germany 13 52 23N 13 4 E
Potsdam, U.S.A. 62 44 40N 74 59W
Pottsville 66 40 39N 76 12W
Pouancé 8 47 44N 1 10W
Pouce Coupé 64 55 40N 120 10W
Poughkeepsie 66 41 40N 73 57W
Pouilly-sur-Loire 9 47 17N 2 57 E
Poulaphouca Res. 7 53 8N 6 30W
Pouldu, Le 8 47 41N 3 36W
Pourri, Mt. 11 45 32N 6 52 E
Pouzauges 8 46 47N 0 50W
Povenets 30 62 50N 34 50 E
Póvoa de Varzim 18 41 25N 8 46W
Powder → 67 46 47N 105 12W
Powell, L. 68 37 25N 110 45W
Powell Creek 54 18 6 S 133 46 E
Powell River 64 49 50N 124 35W
Powys □ 5 52 20N 3 20W
Poyarkovo 31 49 36N 128 41 E
Požarevac 24 44 35N 21 18 E
Poznań 17 52 25N 16 55 E
Pozoblanco 18 38 23N 4 51W
Prachuap Khiri Khan 41 11 49N 99 48 E
Pradelles 10 44 46N 3 52 E
Prades 10 42 38N 2 23 E
Prague = Praha 14 50 5N 14 22 E
Praha 14 50 5N 14 22 E
Prahecq 10 46 19N 0 26W
Praid 25 46 32N 25 10 E
Prainha, Amazonas,
Brazil 72 7 10 S 60 30W
Prainha, Pará, Brazil 73 1 45 S 53 30W
Prairie du Chien 67 43 1N 91 9W
Prato 20 43 53N 11 5 E
Prats-de-Mollo-la-
Preste 10 42 25N 2 27 E
Pravia 18 43 30N 6 12W
Pré-en-Pail 8 48 28N 0 12W
Préfailles 8 47 9N 2 11W
Premier Downs 54 30 30 S 126 30 E
Prepansko Jezero 26 40 55N 21 0 E
Přerov 15 49 28N 17 27 E
Presidencia Roque
Saenz Peña 74 26 45 S 60 30W
Presidente Prudente 73 22 5 S 51 25W
Prespa, L. =
Prepansko Jezero 26 40 55N 21 0 E
Presque Isle 66 46 40N 68 0W
Prestbury 5 51 54N 2 2W
Presteigne 5 52 17N 3 0W
Preston 5 53 46N 2 42W
Preston, C. 54 20 51 S 116 12 E
Prestonpans 6 55 58N 3 0W
Prestwick 6 55 30N 4 38W
Pretoria 53 25 44 S 28 12 E
Preuilly-sur-Claise 8 46 51N 0 56 E
Préveza 26 38 57N 20 47 E
Pribilof Is. 3 56 0N 170 0W
Příbram 14 49 41N 14 2 E
Prichard 66 30 47N 88 5W
Prieska 52 29 40 S 22 42 E
Prikaspiyskaya
Nizmennost 35 47 0N 48 0 E
Prilep 24 41 21N 21 37 E
Priluki 32 50 30N 32 24 E
Prince Albert 65 53 15N 105 50W
Prince Alfred C. 3 74 20N 124 40W
Prince Edward I. □ 63 46 20N 63 20W
Prince Edward Is. 2 45 15 S 39 0 E
Prince George 64 53 55N 122 50W
Prince of Wales I. 3 73 0N 99 0W
Prince of Wales Is. 55 10 40 S 142 10 E
Prince Patrick I. 3 77 0N 120 0W
Prince Regent Inlet 3 73 0N 90 0W
Prince Rupert 64 54 20N 130 20W
Princess Charlotte B. 56 14 25 S 144 0 E
Princess Royal I. 64 53 0N 128 40W
Princeton 64 49 27N 120 30W
Principe da Beira 72 12 20 S 64 30W
Pripet = Pripyat → 32 51 20N 30 9 E
Pripet Marshes =
Polesye 32 52 0N 28 10 E
Pripyat → 32 51 20N 30 9 E
Priština 24 42 40N 21 13 E
Privas 11 44 45N 4 37 E
Privolzhskaya
Vozvyshennost 33 51 0N 46 0 E
Prizren 24 42 13N 20 45 E
Proddatur 38 14 45N 78 30 E
Progreso 69 21 17N 89 40W
Prokopyevsk 30 54 0N 86 45 E
Propriano 11 41 41N 8 52 E
Proserpine 56 20 21 S 148 36 E
Prostějov 15 49 30N 17 9 E
Provence 11 43 40N 5 46 E
Providence 66 41 50N 71 28W
Provideniya 31 64 23N 173 18W
Provins 9 48 33N 3 15 E
Provo 68 40 16N 111 37W
Pruszków 17 52 9N 20 49 E
Prut → 25 46 3N 28 10 E
Prydz B. 60 69 0 S 74 0 E
Przemyśl 15 49 50N 22 45 E
Przeworsk 15 50 6N 22 32 E
Przhevalsk 30 42 30N 78 20 E
Pskov 32 57 50N 28 25 E
Pucallpa 72 8 25 S 74 30W
Pudukkottai 38 10 28N 78 47 E
Puebla 69 19 3N 98 12W
Puebla □ 69 18 50N 98 0W
Pueblo 67 38 20N 104 40W
Puelches 74 38 5 S 65 51W
Puente Alto 74 33 32 S 70 35W
Puente-Genil 18 37 22N 4 47W
Puerto Armuelles 70 8 20N 82 51W
Puerto Ayacucho 72 5 40N 67 35W
Puerto Barrios 69 15 40N 88 32W
Puerto Cabello 72 10 28N 68 1W
Puerto Cabezas 70 14 0N 83 30W
Puerto Castilla 70 16 0N 86 0W
Puerto Cortes,
C. Rica 70 8 55N 84 0W
Puerto Cortés, Hond. 69 15 51N 88 0W
Puerto de Santa
María 18 36 36N 6 13W
Puerto del Rosario 49 28 30N 13 52W
Puerto Heath 72 12 34 S 68 39W
Puerto La Cruz 72 10 13N 64 38W
Puerto Lobos 74 42 0 S 65 3W
Puerto Maldonado 72 12 30 S 69 10W
Puerto Montt 74 41 28 S 73 0W
Puerto Padre 70 21 13N 76 35W
Puerto Pinasco 74 22 36 S 57 50W
Puerto Plata 70 19 48N 70 45W
Puerto Quepos 70 9 29N 84 6W
Puerto Rico ■ 70 18 15N 66 45W
Puerto Vallarta 69 20 37N 105 15W
Puertollano 18 38 43N 4 7W
Pugachev 33 52 0N 48 49 E
Puget Sd. 68 47 15N 122 30W
Puget-Théniers 11 43 58N 6 53 E
Púglia □ 23 41 0N 16 30 E
Puigcerdá 19 42 24N 1 50 E
Puisaye, Collines de
la 9 47 37N 3 20 E
Puiseaux 9 48 11N 2 30 E
Pukapuka 58 10 53 S 165 49W
Pula 22 39 0N 9 0 E
Pulaski, Tenn.,
U.S.A. 66 35 10N 87 0W
Pulaski, Va., U.S.A. 66 37 4N 80 49W
Pulicat, L. 38 13 40N 80 15 E
Pullman 68 46 49N 117 10W
Pumlumon Fawr 5 52 29N 3 47W
Punakha 37 27 42N 89 52 E
Punata 72 17 32 S 65 50W
Pune 38 18 29N 73 57 E
Punjab □, India 36 31 0N 76 0 E
Punjab □, Pakistan 36 30 0N 72 0 E
Puno 72 15 55 S 70 3W
Punta Alta 74 38 53 S 62 4W
Punta Arenas 74 53 10 S 71 0W
Punta Gorda 69 16 10N 88 45W
Puntarenas 70 10 0N 84 50W
Punto Fijo 72 11 50N 70 13W
Puquio 72 14 45 S 74 10W
Pur → 30 67 31N 77 55 E
Purbeck, Isle of 5 50 40N 2 5W
Puri 36 19 50N 85 58 E
Purmerend 12 52 30N 4 58 E
Purnia 37 25 45N 87 31 E
Pursat 41 12 34N 103 50 E
Puruliya 37 23 17N 86 24 E
Purus → 72 3 42 S 61 28W
Pusan 43 35 5N 129 0 E
Pushchino 31 54 10N 158 0 E
Pushkino 33 51 16N 47 0 E
Putignano 23 40 50N 17 5 E
Putorana, Gory 31 69 0N 95 0 E
Putten 12 52 16N 5 36 E
Putumayo → 72 3 7 S 67 58W
Puy, Le 10 45 3N 3 52 E
Puy-de-Dôme 10 45 46N 2 57 E
Puy-de-Dôme □ 10 45 40N 3 5 E
Puy-Guillaume 10 45 57N 3 29 E
Puy-l'Évêque 10 44 31N 1 9 E
Puyallup 68 47 10N 122 22W
Puylaurens 10 43 35N 2 0 E
Pweto 51 8 25 S 28 51 E
Pwllheli 5 52 54N 4 26W
Pyasina → 31 73 30N 87 0 E
Pyatigorsk 35 44 2N 43 6 E
Pyŏngyang 43 39 0N 125 30 E
Pyramid L. 68 40 0N 119 30W
Pyrénées 10 42 45N 0 18 E
Pyrénées-
Atlantiques □ 10 43 10N 0 50W
Pyrénées-
Orientales □ 10 42 35N 2 26 E

Q

Qādib 47 12 35N 54 2 E
Qā'emshahr 46 36 30N 52 55 E
Qahremānshahr =
Bākhtarān 45 34 23N 47 0 E
Qaidam Pendi 42 37 0N 95 0 E
Qamar, Ghubbat al 47 16 20N 52 30 E
Qamruddin Karez 36 31 45N 68 20 E
Qandahār 46 31 32N 65 30 E
Qāra 50 29 38N 26 30 E
Qaṣr-e Qand 46 26 15N 60 45 E
Qasr Farâfra 50 27 0N 28 1 E
Qatar ■ 46 25 30N 51 15 E
Qattâra, Munkhafed
el 50 29 30N 27 30 E
Qāyen 46 33 40N 59 10 E
Qazvin 45 36 15N 50 0 E
Qena 50 26 10N 32 43 E
Qeshm 46 26 55N 56 10 E
Qila Saifullāh 36 30 45N 68 17 E
Qilian Shan 42 38 30N 96 0 E
Qingdao 42 36 5N 120 20 E
Qinghai □ 42 36 0N 98 0 E
Qinghai Hu 42 36 40N 100 10 E
Qinhuangdao 42 39 56N 119 30 E
Qiqihar 42 47 26N 124 0 E
Qizān 47 17 0N 42 20 E
Qom 46 34 40N 51 0 E
Qomsheh 46 32 0N 51 55 E
Qondūz □ 46 36 50N 68 50 E
Qu Xian 43 30 48N 106 58 E
Quang Ngai 41 15 13N 108 58 E
Quantock Hills 5 51 8N 3 10W
Quanzhou 43 24 55N 118 34 E
Quarré-les-Tombes 9 47 21N 4 0 E
Quatsino 64 50 30N 127 40W
Queanbeyan 56 35 17 S 149 14 E
Québec 63 46 52N 71 13W
Québec □ 63 50 0N 70 0W
Queen Charlotte 64 53 15N 132 2W
Queen Charlotte Is. 64 53 20N 132 10W
Queen Charlotte Str. 64 51 0N 128 0W
Queen Elizabeth Is. 1 76 0N 95 0W
Queens Chan. 54 15 0 S 129 30 E
Queenscliff 56 38 16 S 144 39 E
Queensland □ 56 22 0 S 142 0 E
Queenstown,
Australia 56 42 4 S 145 35 E
Queenstown,
S. Africa 52 31 52 S 26 52 E
Quela 51 9 10 S 16 56 E
Quelimane 51 17 53 S 36 58 E
Quelpart = Cheju Do 43 33 29N 126 34 E
Querétaro 69 20 36N 100 23W
Querétaro □ 69 21 0N 99 55W
Quesnel 64 53 0N 122 30W
Quesnoy, Le 9 50 15N 3 38 E
Questembert 8 47 40N 2 28W
Quetta 36 30 15N 66 55 E
Quezaltenango 69 14 50N 91 30W
Quezon City 40 14 38N 121 0 E
Qui Nhon 41 13 40N 109 13 E
Quibaxe 51 8 24 S 14 27 E
Quibdo 72 5 42N 76 40W
Quiberon 8 47 29N 3 9W
Quilengues 51 14 12 S 14 12 E
Quillabamba 72 12 50 S 72 50W
Quillan 10 42 53N 2 10 E
Quillebeuf-sur-Seine 8 49 28N 0 30 E
Quilon 38 8 50N 76 38 E
Quilpie 56 26 35 S 144 11 E
Quimper 8 48 0N 4 9W
Quimperlé 8 47 53N 3 33W
Quincy, Calif.,
U.S.A. 68 39 56N 121 0W
Quincy, Fla., U.S.A. 66 30 34N 84 34W
Quincy, Ill., U.S.A. 67 39 55N 91 20W
Quincy, Mass.,
U.S.A. 66 42 14N 71 0W
Quinga 51 15 49 S 40 15 E
Quingey 9 47 7N 5 52 E
Quintana Roo □ 69 19 40N 88 30W
Quintanar de la
Orden 19 39 36N 3 5W
Quintanar de la
Sierra 19 41 57N 2 55W
Quintin 8 48 26N 2 56W
Quipungo 51 14 37 S 14 40 E
Quissac 11 43 55N 4 0 E
Quissanga 51 12 24 S 40 28 E
Quitman 66 30 49N 83 35W
Quito 72 0 15 S 78 35W
Quixadá 73 4 55 S 39 0W
Quorn 56 32 25 S 138 0 E
Qûs 50 25 55N 32 50 E
Quseir 50 26 7N 34 16 E

R

Raahe 27 64 40N 24 28 E
Raasay 6 57 25N 6 4W
Raasay, Sd. of 6 57 30N 6 8W
Rabastens 10 43 50N 1 43 E
Rabastens-de-Bigorre 10 43 23N 0 9 E
Rabat 49 34 2N 6 48W
Rabaul 56 4 24 S 152 18 E
Race, C. 63 46 40N 53 5W
Rach Gia 41 10 5N 105 5 E
Racine 67 42 41N 87 51W
Rădăuţi 15 47 50N 25 59 E
Radium Hill 55 32 30 S 140 42 E
Radium Hot Springs 64 50 35N 116 2W
Radnor Forest 5 52 17N 3 10W
Radolfzell 13 47 44N 8 58 E
Radom 17 51 23N 21 12 E
Radomir 24 42 37N 23 4 E
Radomsko 17 51 5N 19 28 E
Radstock 5 51 17N 2 25W
Radstock, C. 54 33 12 S 134 20 E
Radville 65 49 30N 104 15W
Rae 64 62 50N 116 3W
Rae Bareli 37 26 18N 81 20 E
Raeren 12 50 41N 6 7 E
Raeside, L. 54 29 20 S 122 0 E
Rafaela 74 31 10 S 61 30W
Rafai 51 4 59N 23 58 E
Rafsanjān 46 30 30N 56 5 E
Ragusa 23 36 56N 14 42 E
Rahad al Bardī 50 11 20N 23 40 E
Raichur 38 16 10N 77 20 E
Raigarh 36 21 56N 83 25 E
Rainier, Mt. 68 46 50N 121 50W
Rainy L. 65 48 42N 93 10W
Rainy River 65 48 43N 94 29W
Raipur 36 21 17N 81 45 E
Rajahmundry 38 17 1N 81 48 E
Rajapalaiyam 38 9 25N 77 35 E
Rajasthan □ 36 26 45N 73 30 E
Rajasthan Canal 36 28 0N 72 0 E
Rajgarh 36 24 2N 76 45 E
Rajkot 36 22 15N 70 56 E
Rajojooseppi 27 68 25N 28 30 E
Rajpipla 36 21 50N 73 30 E
Rajshahi 37 24 22N 88 39 E
Rajshahi □ 37 25 0N 89 0 E
Raleigh 66 35 47N 78 39W
Raleigh B. 66 34 50N 76 15W
Ramanathapuram 38 9 25N 78 55 E
Rambervillers 9 48 20N 6 38 E
Rambouillet 9 48 39N 1 50 E
Ramechhap 37 27 25N 86 10 E
Ramgarh, Bihar,
India 37 23 40N 85 35 E
Ramgarh, Raj., India 36 27 30N 70 36 E
Rampur 36 28 50N 79 5 E
Rampur Hat 37 24 10N 87 50 E
Ramsey 5 54 20N 4 21W
Ramsgate 5 51 20N 1 25 E
Ramtek 36 21 20N 79 15 E
Ramu → 56 4 0 S 144 41 E
Ranaghat 37 23 15N 88 35 E
Rancagua 74 34 10 S 70 50W
Rance → 8 48 34N 1 59W
Rance, Barrage de la 8 48 30N 2 3W
Ranchi 37 23 19N 85 27 E
Randan 10 46 2N 3 21 E
Randers 28 56 29N 10 1 E
Råne älv → 27 65 50N 22 20 E
Rangoon 41 16 45N 96 20 E
Ranibennur 38 14 35N 75 30 E
Raniganj 37 23 40N 87 5 E
Rannoch, L. 6 56 41N 4 20W
Rannoch Moor 6 56 38N 4 48W
Raon l'Étape 9 48 24N 6 50 E
Rapa Iti 58 27 35 S 144 20W
Rapid City 67 44 0N 103 0W
Rarotonga 58 21 30 S 160 0W
Ra's al-Unuf 50 30 25N 18 15 E
Ras Bânâs 50 23 57N 35 59 E
Ras Dashen 51 13 8N 38 26 E
Râs Timirist 49 19 21N 16 30W
Rasa, Punta 74 40 50 S 62 15W
Rashad 50 11 55N 31 0 E
Rashîd 50 31 21N 30 22 E
Rasht 45 37 20N 49 40 E
Rason, L. 54 28 45 S 124 25 E
Rastatt 13 48 50N 8 12 E
Ratangarh 36 28 5N 74 35 E
Rath Luirc 7 52 21N 8 40W
Rathdrum 7 52 57N 6 13W
Rathkeale 7 52 32N 8 57W
Rathlin I. 7 55 18N 6 14W
Rathlin O'Birne I. 7 54 40N 8 50W
Ratlam 36 23 20N 75 0 E
Ratnagiri 38 16 57N 73 18 E
Rattray Hd. 6 57 38N 1 50W
Ratzeburg 13 53 41N 10 46 E
Raub 41 3 47N 101 52 E
Raufarhöfn 27 66 27N 15 57W
Rauma 27 61 10N 21 30 E
Ravenna 21 44 28N 12 15 E
Ravensburg 13 47 48N 9 38 E
Ravenshoe 56 17 37 S 145 29 E
Ravensthorpe 54 33 35 S 120 2 E
Ravi → 36 30 35N 71 49 E
Rawalpindi 46 33 38N 73 8 E
Rawlinna 54 30 58 S 125 28 E
Rawlins 68 41 50N 107 20W
Rawlinson Range 54 24 40 S 128 30 E
Ray, C. 63 47 33N 59 15W
Rayadurg 38 14 40N 76 50 E
Rayagada 38 19 15N 83 20 E
Raychikhinsk 31 49 46N 129 25 E
Raymond 64 49 30N 112 35W
Raz, Pte. du 8 48 2N 4 47W
Razgrad 25 43 33N 26 34 E
Ré, I. de 10 46 12N 1 30W
Reading, U.K. 5 51 27N 0 57W
Reading, U.S.A. 66 40 20N 75 53W
Réalmont 10 43 48N 2 10 E
Rebais 9 48 50N 3 10 E
Rebiana 50 24 12N 22 10 E
Rebun-Tō 44 45 23N 141 2 E
Recherche, Arch. of
the 54 34 15 S 122 50 E
Recife 73 8 0 S 35 0W
Recklinghausen 13 51 36N 7 10 E
Reconquista 74 29 10 S 59 45W
Recreo 74 29 25 S 65 10W
Red →, Minn.,
U.S.A. 67 48 10N 97 0W
Red →, Tex.,
U.S.A. 67 31 0N 91 40W
Red Bluff 68 40 11N 122 11W
Red Deer 64 52 20N 113 50W
Red Lake 65 51 3N 93 49W
Red Oak 67 41 0N 95 10W
Red Sea 47 25 0N 36 0 E
Red Tower Pass =
Turnu Rosu Pasul 25 45 33N 24 17 E
Red Wing 67 44 32N 92 35W
Redbridge 5 51 35N 0 7 E
Redcar 5 54 37N 1 4W
Redcliff 65 50 10N 110 50W
Redding 68 40 30N 122 25W
Redditch 5 52 18N 1 57W
Redlands 68 34 0N 117 11W

Redon 8 47 40N 2 6W
Redondela 18 42 15N 8 38W
Redondo 18 38 39N 7 37W
Redruth 5 50 14N 5 14W
Redwater 64 53 55N 113 6W
Redwood City 68 37 30N 122 15W
Ree, L. 7 53 35N 8 0W
Reedley 68 36 36N 119 27W
Regensburg 13 49 1N 12 7 E
Réggio di Calábria 23 38 7N 15 38 E
Réggio nell' Emilia 20 44 42N 10 38 E
Regina 65 50 27N 104 35W
Rehoboth 52 23 15 S 17 4 E
Rehovot 45 31 54N 34 48 E
Rei-Bouba 50 8 40N 14 15 E
Reichenbach 13 50 36N 12 19 E
Reidsville 66 36 21N 79 40W
Reigate 5 51 14N 0 11W
Reims 9 49 15N 4 1 E
Reina Adelaida, Arch. 74 52 20 S 74 0W
Rekinniki 31 60 51N 163 40 E
Rémalard 8 48 26N 0 47 E
Remanso 73 9 41 S 42 4W
Remich 12 49 32N 6 22 E
Remiremont 9 48 0N 6 36 E
Remoulins 11 43 55N 4 35 E
Remscheid 13 51 11N 7 12 E
Rendsburg 13 54 18N 9 41 E
Rene 31 66 2N 179 25W
Renfrew, Canada 62 45 30N 76 40W
Renfrew, U.K. 6 55 52N 4 24W
Renk 50 11 50N 32 50 E
Renkum 12 51 58N 5 43 E
Renmark 56 34 11 S 140 43 E
Rennes 8 48 7N 1 41W
Rennes, Bassin de 8 48 0N 1 30W
Reno 68 39 30N 119 50W
Reno → 21 44 37N 12 17 E
Réole, La 10 44 35N 0 1W
Republic 62 46 25N 87 59W
Republican → 67 39 3N 96 48W
Repulse B. 55 20 31 S 148 45 E
Requena, Peru 72 5 5 S 73 52W
Requena, Spain 19 39 30N 1 4W
Resistencia 74 27 30 S 59 0W
Retalhuleu 69 14 33N 91 46W
Rethel 9 49 30N 4 20 E
Réthímnon 26 35 18N 24 30 E
Retiers 8 47 55N 1 23W
Réunion 2 22 0 S 56 0 E
Reutlingen 13 48 28N 9 13 E
Revel 10 43 28N 2 0 E
Revelstoke 64 51 0N 118 10W
Revigny-sur-Ornain 9 48 49N 4 59 E
Revilla Gigedo, Is. 58 18 40N 112 0W
Revin 9 49 55N 4 39 E
Rewa 37 24 33N 81 25 E
Rewari 36 28 15N 76 40 E
Rey Malabo 49 3 45N 8 50 E
Reykjahlið 27 65 40N 16 55W
Reykjanes 27 63 48N 22 40W
Reykjavík 27 64 10N 21 57 E
Reynolds Ra. 54 22 30 S 133 0 E
Reynosa 69 26 5N 98 18W
Rhayader 5 52 19N 3 30W
Rheden 12 52 0N 6 3 E
Rhein → 12 51 52N 6 20 E
Rhein-Main-Donau-Kanal → 13 49 1N 11 27 E
Rheine 13 52 17N 7 25 E
Rheinland-Pfalz □ 13 50 0N 7 0 E
Rheydt 13 51 10N 6 24 E
Rhin = Rhein → 12 51 52N 6 20 E
Rhinau 9 48 19N 7 43 E
Rhine = Rhein → 12 51 52N 6 20 E
Rhinelander 62 45 38N 89 29W
Rhode Island □ 66 41 38N 71 37W
Rhodes = Ródhos 26 36 15N 28 10 E
Rhodesia = Zimbabwe ■ 51 19 0 S 30 0 E
Rhodope Mts. = Rhodopi Planina 25 41 40N 24 20 E
Rhodopi Planina 25 41 40N 24 20 E
Rhondda 5 51 39N 3 30W
Rhône □ 11 45 54N 4 35 E
Rhône → 11 43 28N 4 42 E
Rhum 6 57 0N 6 20W
Rhyl 5 53 19N 3 29W
Rhymney 5 51 32N 3 7W
Riachão 73 7 20 S 46 37W
Rians 11 43 37N 5 44 E
Riau, Kepulauan 39 0 30N 104 20 E
Ribadeo 18 43 35N 7 5W
Ribble → 5 54 13N 2 20W
Ribe 28 55 19N 8 44 E
Ribeauvillé 9 48 10N 7 20 E
Ribécourt 9 49 30N 2 55 E
Ribeirão Prêto 73 21 10 S 47 50W
Ribemont 9 49 47N 3 27 E
Ribérac 10 45 15N 0 20 E
Riberalta 72 11 0 S 66 0W
Riceys, Les 9 47 59N 4 22 E
Richelieu 8 47 0N 0 20 E
Richland 68 46 15N 119 15W
Richmond, Australia 56 20 43 S 143 8 E
Richmond, S. Africa 53 29 51 S 30 18 E
Richmond, N. Yorks., U.K. 5 54 24N 1 43W
Richmond, Surrey, U.K. 5 51 28N 0 18W
Richmond, Calif., U.S.A. 68 37 58N 122 21W
Richmond, Ind., U.S.A. 66 39 50N 84 50W
Richmond, Ky., U.S.A. 66 37 40N 84 20W
Richmond, Va., U.S.A. 66 37 33N 77 27W
Richwood 66 38 17N 80 32W
Ridgeway 66 42 56 S 147 16 E
Ried 14 48 14N 13 30 E
Rieti 21 42 23N 12 50 E
Rieupeyroux 10 44 19N 2 12 E
Riez 11 43 49N 6 6 E
Rifstangi 27 66 32N 16 12W
Rig Rig 50 14 13N 14 25 E
Riga 32 56 53N 24 8 E
Riga, G. of = Rīgas Jūras Līcis 32 57 40N 23 45 E
Rīgas Jūras Līcis 32 57 40N 23 45 E
Rīgestān □ 46 30 15N 65 0 E
Rignac 10 44 25N 2 16 E
Rigolet 63 54 10N 58 23W
Riihimäki 27 60 45N 24 48 E
Rijeka 21 45 20N 14 21 E
Rijn → 12 52 12N 4 21 E
Rijssen 12 52 19N 6 30 E
Rijswijk 12 52 4N 4 22 E
Rímini 21 44 3N 12 33 E
Rîmnicu Sărat 25 45 26N 27 3 E
Rîmnicu Vîlcea 25 45 9N 24 21 E
Rimouski 63 48 27N 68 30W
Rineanna 7 52 42N 85 7W
Ringkøbing 28 56 5N 8 15 E
Ringvassøy 27 69 56N 19 15 E
Rinía 26 37 23N 25 13 E
Rinteln 13 52 11N 9 3 E
Rio Branco 72 9 58 S 67 49W
Rio Claro 70 10 20N 61 25W
Río Cuarto 74 33 10 S 64 25W
Rio de Janeiro 73 23 0 S 43 12W
Rio de Janeiro □ 73 22 50 S 43 0W
Río Gallegos 74 51 35 S 69 15W
Río Grande 74 32 0 S 52 20W
Rio Grande → 67 25 57N 97 9W
Rio Grande do Norte □ 73 5 40 S 36 0W
Rio Grande do Sul □ 74 30 0 S 53 0W
Río Mulatos 72 19 40 S 66 50W
Río Muni = Mbini □ 51 1 30N 10 0 E
Rio Negro 74 26 0 S 50 0W
Rio Verde 73 17 50 S 51 0W
Riobamba 72 1 50 S 78 45W
Ríohacha 72 11 33N 72 55W
Rioja, La 74 29 20 S 67 0W
Rioja, La □ 19 42 20N 2 20W
Riom 10 45 54N 3 7 E
Riom-ès-Montagnes 10 45 17N 2 39 E
Rion-des-Landes 10 43 55N 0 56W
Ríosucio 72 7 27N 77 7W
Rioz 9 47 26N 6 5 E
Ripon 5 54 8N 1 31W
Riscle 10 43 39N 0 5W
Rishiri-Tō 44 45 11N 141 15 E
Risle → 8 49 26N 0 23 E
Risør 28 58 43N 9 13 E
Ritchies Archipelago 41 12 5N 94 0 E
Riva Bella 8 49 17N 0 18W
Rivas 70 11 30N 85 50W
Rive-de-Gier 11 45 32N 4 37 E
Riverdsale 52 34 7 S 21 15 E
Riverhead 66 40 53N 72 40W
Riverina 55 35 30 S 145 20 E
Riverside 68 34 0N 117 22W
Riverton 65 51 1N 97 0W
Rives 11 45 21N 5 31 E
Rivesaltes 10 42 47N 2 50 E
Rivière-du-Loup 63 47 50N 69 30W
Riyadh = Ar Riyāḍ 47 24 41N 46 42 E
Rizzuto, C. 23 38 54N 17 5 E
Rjukan 28 59 54N 8 33 E
Roag, L. 6 58 10N 6 55W
Roanne 11 46 3N 4 4 E
Roanoke, Ala., U.S.A. 66 33 9N 85 23W
Roanoke, Va., U.S.A. 66 37 19N 79 55W
Roanoke → 66 35 56N 76 43W
Roanoke Rapids 66 36 28N 77 42W
Robe → 7 53 38N 9 10W
Robertson 52 33 46 S 19 50 E
Robertsport 49 6 45N 11 26W
Robeson Ch. 3 82 0N 61 30W
Robinson Crusoe I. 58 33 38 S 78 52W
Robinson Ranges 54 25 40 S 119 0 E
Robla, La 18 42 50N 5 41W
Roblin 65 51 14N 101 21W
Roboré 72 18 10 S 59 45W
Robson, Mt. 64 53 10N 119 10W
Roca, C. da 18 38 40N 9 31W
Rocha 74 34 30 S 54 25W
Rochdale 5 53 36N 2 10W
Roche-Bernard, La 8 47 31N 2 19W
Roche-Canillac, La 10 45 12N 1 57 E
Roche-sur-Yon, La 8 46 40N 1 25W
Rochechouart 10 45 50N 0 49 E
Rochefort, Belgium 12 50 9N 5 12 E
Rochefort, France 10 45 56N 0 57W
Rochefort-en-Terre 8 47 42N 2 22W
Rochefoucauld, La 10 45 44N 0 24 E
Rochelle, La 10 46 10N 1 9W
Rocheservière 8 46 57N 1 30W
Rochester, U.K. 5 51 22N 0 30 E
Rochester, Minn., U.S.A. 67 44 1N 92 28W
Rochester, N.H., U.S.A. 66 43 19N 70 57W
Rochester, N.Y., U.S.A. 66 43 10N 77 40W
Rock Hill 66 34 55N 81 2W
Rock Island 67 41 30N 90 35W
Rock Sprs. 68 41 40N 109 10W
Rockford 67 42 20N 89 0W
Rockglen 65 49 11N 105 57W
Rockhampton 56 23 22 S 150 32 E
Rockingham Forest 5 52 28N 0 42W
Rockland 63 44 6N 69 6W
Rocky Mount 66 35 55N 77 48W
Rocky Mountain House 64 52 22N 114 55W
Rocky Mts. 64 55 0N 121 0W
Rocky Pt. 54 33 30 S 123 57 E
Rocroi 9 49 55N 4 30 E
Roda, La 19 39 13N 2 15W
Rødbyhavn 28 54 39N 11 22 E
Rodez 10 44 21N 2 33 E
Ródhos 26 36 15N 28 10 E
Rodriguez 2 19 45 S 63 20 E
Roe → 7 55 10N 6 59W
Roebourne 54 20 44 S 117 9 E
Roebuck B. 54 18 5 S 122 20 E
Roermond 12 51 12N 6 0 E
Roeselare 12 50 57N 3 7 E
Rogaland fylke □ 27 59 12N 6 20 E
Rogers 67 36 20N 94 5W
Rogliano 11 42 57N 9 30 E
Rohan 8 48 4N 2 45W
Rohrbach-lès-Bitche 9 49 3N 7 15 E
Rohri 36 27 45N 68 51 E
Rohtak 36 28 55N 76 43 E
Roisel 9 49 58N 3 6 E
Rojo, C. 69 21 33N 97 20W
Rolla 67 37 56N 91 42W
Roma, Australia 56 26 32 S 148 49 E
Roma, Italy 22 41 54N 12 30 E
Romaine → 63 50 18N 63 47W
Roman, Bulgaria 25 43 8N 23 54 E
Roman, Romania 15 46 57N 26 55 E
Roman, U.S.S.R. 31 66 4N 112 14 E
Romana, La 70 18 27N 68 57W
Romanche → 11 45 5N 5 43 E
Romania ■ 25 46 0N 25 0 E
Romans-sur-Isère 11 45 3N 5 3 E
Rome = Roma 22 41 54N 12 30 E
Rome, Ga., U.S.A. 66 34 20N 85 0W
Rome, N.Y., U.S.A. 66 43 14N 75 29W
Romenay 11 46 30N 5 1 E
Romilly-sur-Seine 9 48 31N 3 44 E
Romney Marsh 5 51 0N 1 0 E
Romorantin-Lanthenay 9 47 21N 1 45 E
Romsdalen 27 62 25N 8 0 E
Rona 6 57 33N 6 0W
Ronda 18 36 46N 5 12W
Rondane 28 61 57N 9 50 E
Rondônia □ 72 11 0 S 63 0W
Rong, Koh 41 10 45N 103 15 E
Ronge, L. la 65 55 6N 105 17W
Ronse 12 50 45N 3 35 E
Roorkee 36 29 52N 77 59 E
Roosendaal 12 51 32N 4 29 E
Roper → 54 14 43 S 135 27 E
Roquefort 10 44 2N 0 20W
Roquemaure 11 44 3N 4 48 E
Roquevaire 11 43 20N 5 36 E
Roraima □ 72 2 0N 61 30W
Roraima, Mt. 72 5 10N 60 40W
Røros 27 62 35N 11 23 E
Rosa 51 9 33 S 31 15 E
Rosa, Monte 13 45 57N 7 53 E
Rosans 11 44 24N 5 29 E
Rosario, Argentina 74 33 0 S 60 40W
Rosário, Brazil 73 3 0 S 44 15W
Rosario, Mexico 69 22 58N 105 53W
Rosario, Paraguay 74 24 30 S 57 35W
Rosário do Sul 74 30 15 S 54 55W
Rosas 19 42 19N 3 10 E
Roscoff 8 48 44N 4 0W
Roscommon 7 53 38N 8 11W
Roscommon □ 7 53 40N 8 15W
Roscrea 7 52 58N 7 50W
Roseau, Domin. 70 15 20N 61 24W
Roseau, U.S.A. 67 48 51N 95 46W
Roseburg 68 43 10N 123 20W
Rosenberg 67 29 30N 95 48W
Rosendaël 9 51 3N 2 24 E
Rosenheim 13 47 51N 12 9 E
Rosetown 65 51 35N 107 59W
Roseville 68 38 46N 121 17W
Rosières-en-Santerre 9 49 49N 2 42 E
Roskilde 28 55 38N 12 3 E
Roslavl 32 53 57N 32 55 E
Rosporden 8 47 57N 3 50W
Ross Dependency □ 60 70 0 S 170 5W
Ross on Wye 5 51 55N 2 34W
Rossan Pt. 7 54 42N 8 47W
Rossland 64 49 6N 117 50W
Rosslare 7 52 17N 6 23W
Rosso 49 16 40N 15 45W
Rossosh 35 50 15N 39 28 E
Røssvatnet 27 65 45N 14 5 E
Rosthern 65 52 40N 106 20W
Rostock 13 54 4N 12 9 E
Rostov, Don, U.S.S.R. 35 47 15N 39 45 E
Rostov, Moskva, U.S.S.R. 33 57 14N 39 25 E
Rostrenen 8 48 14N 3 21W
Roswell 67 33 26N 104 32W
Rosyth 6 56 2N 3 26W
Rotenburg 13 53 6N 9 24 E
Rothenburg ob der Tauber 13 49 21N 10 11 E
Rother → 5 50 59N 0 40 E
Rotherham 5 53 26N 1 21W
Rothes 6 57 31N 3 12W
Rothesay 6 55 50N 5 3W
Roto 56 33 0 S 145 30 E
Rotorua 59 38 9 S 176 16 E
Rotterdam 12 51 55N 4 30 E
Rottumeroog 12 53 33N 6 34 E
Rottweil 13 48 9N 8 38 E
Rotuma 57 12 25 S 177 5 E
Roubaix 9 50 40N 3 10 E
Rouen 8 49 27N 1 4 E
Rouillac 10 45 47N 0 4W
Round Mt. 56 30 26 S 152 16 E
Rousay 6 59 10N 3 2W
Roussillon, Isère, France 11 45 24N 4 49 E
Roussillon, Pyrénées-Or., France 10 42 30N 2 35 E
Rouyn 62 48 20N 79 0W
Rovaniemi 27 66 29N 25 41 E
Rovereto 20 45 53N 11 3 E
Rovigo 21 45 4N 11 48 E
Rovinj 21 45 5N 13 40 E
Rovno 32 50 40N 26 10 E
Rovuma → 51 10 29 S 40 28 E
Rowley Shoals 54 17 30 S 119 0 E
Royan 10 45 37N 1 2W
Roye 9 49 42N 2 48 E
Rozay-en-Brie 9 48 41N 2 58 E
Rozoy-sur-Serre 9 49 42N 4 8 E
Rtishchevo 33 55 16N 43 50 E
Ruapehu 59 39 17 S 175 35 E
Rub' al Khali 47 18 0N 48 0 E
Rubh a' Mhail 6 55 55N 6 10W
Rubha Hunish 6 57 42N 6 20W
Rubicone → 21 44 8N 12 28 E
Rubio 72 7 43N 72 22W
Rubtsovsk 30 51 30N 81 10 E
Rudnogorsk 31 57 15N 103 42 E
Rudnyy 30 52 57N 63 7 E
Rudolf, Ostrov 30 81 45N 58 30 E
Rue 9 50 15N 1 40 E
Ruelle 10 45 41N 0 14 E
Rufa'a 50 14 44N 33 22 E
Ruffec 10 46 2N 0 12 E
Rufiji → 51 7 50 S 39 15 E
Rufino 74 34 20 S 62 50W
Rufisque 49 14 40N 17 15W
Rugby 5 52 23N 1 16W
Rügen 13 54 22N 13 25 E
Rugles 8 48 50N 0 40 E
Ruhr → 13 51 25N 6 44 E
Rukwa L. 51 8 0 S 32 20 E
Rum Jungle 54 13 0 S 130 59 E
Rumania = Romania ■ 25 46 0N 25 0 E
Rumbêk 50 6 54N 29 37 E
Rumford 63 44 30N 70 30W
Rumilly 11 45 53N 5 56 E
Rumoi 44 43 56N 141 39W
Runcorn 5 53 20N 2 44W
Rungwa 51 6 55 S 33 32 E
Rupat 39 1 45N 101 40 E
Rupert → 62 51 29N 78 45W
Rusape 51 18 35 S 32 8 E
Ruse 25 43 48N 25 59 E
Rushden 5 52 17N 0 37W
Russell 65 50 50N 101 20W
Russellkonda 36 19 57N 84 42 E
Russellville, Ala., U.S.A. 66 34 30N 87 44W
Russellville, Ark., U.S.A. 67 35 15N 93 8W
Russian S.F.S.R. □ 31 62 0N 105 0 E
Russkoye Ustie 3 71 0N 149 0 E
Rustenburg 52 25 41 S 27 14 E
Ruston 67 32 30N 92 58W
Rutherglen 6 55 50N 4 11W
Rutland I. 41 11 25N 92 40 E
Rutshuru 51 1 13 S 29 25 E
Ruurlo 12 52 5N 6 24 E
Ruwenzori 51 0 30N 29 55 E
Ružomberok 15 49 3N 19 17 E
Rwanda ■ 51 2 0 S 30 0 E
Ryan, L. 6 55 0N 5 2W
Ryazan 33 54 40N 39 40 E
Ryazhsk 33 53 45N 40 3 E
Rybache 30 46 40N 81 20 E
Rybinsk = Andropov 33 58 5N 38 50 E
Rybinskoye Vdkhr. 33 58 30N 38 25 E
Ryde 5 50 44N 1 9W
Rye 5 50 57N 0 46 E
Rye → 5 54 12N 0 53W
Rypin 17 53 3N 19 25 E
Ryūkyū Is. = Nansei-Shotō 44 26 0N 128 0 E
Rzeszów 15 50 5N 21 58 E
Rzhev 32 56 20N 34 20 E

S

Sa Dec 41 10 20N 105 46 E
Saale → 13 51 57N 11 56 E
Saar → 9 49 41N 6 32 E
Saarbrücken 13 49 15N 6 58 E
Saarburg 13 49 36N 6 32 E
Saaremaa 32 58 30N 22 30 E
Saariselkä 27 68 16N 28 15 E
Saarland □ 9 49 15N 7 0 E
Saarlouis 13 49 19N 6 45 E
Sabadell 19 41 28N 2 7 E
Sabah □ 39 6 0N 117 0 E
Sábana de la Mar 70 19 7N 69 24W
Sabáudia 22 41 17N 13 2 E
Sabhah 50 27 9N 14 29 E
Sabinas 69 27 51N 101 7W
Sabinas Hidalgo → 69 26 50N 99 35W
Sable, C. 63 43 29N 65 38W
Sable I. 63 44 0N 60 0W
Sablé-sur-Sarthe 8 47 50N 0 20W
Sables-d'Olonne, Les 10 46 30N 1 45W
Sabolev 31 54 20N 155 30 E
Sabzevār 46 36 15N 57 40 E
Saco 63 43 30N 70 27W
Sacramento 68 38 33N 121 30 E
Sacramento → 68 38 3N 121 56W
Sacramento Mts. 68 32 30N 105 30W
Sádaba 19 42 19N 1 12W
Sadani 51 5 58 S 38 35 E
Sadd el Aali 50 23 54N 32 54 E
Sado 44 38 0N 138 25 E
Sado, Shima 44 38 15N 138 30 E
Safed Koh 46 34 0N 70 0 E
Säffle 28 59 8N 12 55 E
Saffron Walden 5 52 2N 0 15 E
Safi 49 32 18N 9 20W
Saga 44 33 15N 130 16 E
Saga □ 44 33 15N 130 20 E
Sagala 49 14 9N 6 38W
Saginaw 66 43 26N 83 55W
Saginaw B. 66 43 50N 83 40W
Sagone 11 42 7N 8 42 E
Sagone, G. de 11 42 4N 8 40 E
Sagra, La 19 37 57N 2 35W
Sagres 18 37 0N 8 58W
Sagua la Grande 70 22 50N 80 10W
Saguenay → 63 48 22N 71 0W
Sagunto 19 39 42N 0 18W
Sahagún 18 42 18N 5 2W
Sahara 49 23 0N 5 0 E
Saharanpur 36 29 58N 77 33 E
Saharien, Atlas 49 33 30N 1 0 E
Sahiwal 36 30 45N 73 8 E
Sahuaripa 69 29 3N 109 14W
Saibai I. 56 9 25 S 142 40 E
Sa'id Bundas 50 8 24N 24 48 E
Saïda 49 34 50N 0 11 E
Saignes 10 45 20N 2 31 E
Saigon = Phanh Bho Ho Chi Minh 41 10 58N 106 40 E
Saijō 44 33 55N 133 11 E
Saiki 44 32 58N 131 51 E
Saillans 11 44 42N 5 12 E
Ṣa'in Dezh 45 36 40N 46 25 E
St. Abb's Head 6 55 55N 2 10W
St.-Affrique 10 43 57N 2 53 E
St.-Agrève 11 45 0N 4 23 E
St.-Aignan 8 47 16N 1 22 E
St. Albans, U.K. 5 51 44N 0 19W
St. Albans, U.S.A. 62 44 49N 73 7W
St. Alban's Head 5 50 34N 2 3W
St. Albert 64 53 37N 113 32W
St.-Amand-en-Puisaye 9 47 32N 3 5 E
St.-Amand-les-Eaux 9 50 27N 3 25 E
St.-Amand-Mont-Rond 10 46 43N 2 30 E
St.-Amarin 9 47 54N 7 0 E
St.-Amour 11 46 26N 5 21 E
St.-André-de-Cubzac 10 44 59N 0 26W
St.-André-de-l'Eure 8 48 54N 1 16 E
St.-André-les-Alpes 11 43 58N 6 30 E
St. Andrews 6 56 20N 2 48W
St. Anne 8 49 43N 2 11W
St.-Antonin-Noble-Val 10 44 10N 1 45 E
St. Asaph 5 53 15N 3 27W
St.-Astier 10 45 8N 0 31 E
St.-Aubin-du-Cormier 8 48 15N 1 26W
St-Augustin-Saguenay 63 51 13N 58 38W
St. Augustine 66 29 52N 81 20W
St. Austell 5 50 20N 4 48W
St.-Avold 9 49 6N 6 43 E
St. Bee's Hd. 5 54 30N 3 38 E
St.-Benoît-du-Sault 10 46 26N 1 24 E
St.-Bernard, Col du Petit 11 45 41N 6 51 E
St. Boniface 65 49 53N 97 5W
St.-Bonnet 11 44 40N 6 5 E
St.-Brévin-les-Pins 8 47 14N 2 10W
St.-Brice-en-Coglès 8 48 25N 1 22W
St. Brides B. 5 51 48N 5 15W
St.-Brieuc 8 48 30N 2 46W
St.-Calais 8 47 55N 0 45 E
St.-Cast-le-Guildo 8 48 37N 2 18W
St. Catharines 62 43 10N 79 15W
St. Catherine's Pt. 5 50 34N 1 18W
St.-Céré 10 44 51N 1 54 E
St.-Cernin 10 45 5N 2 25 E
St.-Chamond 11 45 28N 4 31 E
St. Charles 67 38 46N 90 30W
St.-Chély-d'Apcher 10 44 48N 3 17 E
St.-Chinian 10 43 25N 2 56 E
St. Christopher-Nevis ■ 70 17 20N 62 40W
St.-Ciers-sur-Gironde 10 45 17N 0 37W
St.-Claud 10 45 54N 0 28 E
St.-Claude 11 46 22N 5 52 E
St. Cloud 67 45 30N 94 11W
St. Croix 70 17 45N 64 45W
St.-Cyr-sur-Mer 11 43 11N 5 43 E
St. David's 5 51 54N 5 16W
St. David's Head 5 51 55N 5 16W
St.-Denis 9 48 56N 2 22 E
St.-Denis-d'Orques 8 48 2N 0 17W
St.-Dié 9 48 17N 6 56 E
St.-Dizier 9 48 38N 4 56 E
St.-Égrève 11 45 14N 5 41 E
St. Elias, Mt. 64 60 14N 140 50W
St.-Eloy-les-Mines 10 46 10N 2 51 E
St.-Émilion 10 44 53N 0 9W
St.-Étienne 11 45 27N 4 22 E
St.-Étienne-de-Tinée 11 44 16N 6 56 E
St-Félicien 62 48 40N 72 25W
St.-Florent 11 42 41N 9 18 E
St.-Florent-sur-Cher 9 46 59N 2 15 E
St.-Florentin 9 48 0N 3 45 E
St.-Flour 10 45 2N 3 6 E
St.-Fons 11 45 42N 4 52 E
St. Francis, C. 52 34 14 S 24 49 E
St.-Fulgent 8 46 50N 1 10W
St.-Gaudens 10 43 6N 0 44 E
St.-Gengoux-le-National 11 46 37N 4 40 E
St.-Geniez-d'Olt 10 44 27N 2 58 E
St. George, Australia 56 28 1 S 148 30 E
St. George, Bermuda 70 32 24N 64 42W
St-Georges 12 50 37N 5 20 E
St.-Georges, Fr. Gui. 73 4 0N 52 0W
St. George's, Grenada 70 12 5N 61 43W
St. George's Channel, Papua N. G. 56 4 10 S 152 20 E
St. George's Channel, U.K. 7 52 0N 6 0W
St.-Georges-de-Didonne 10 45 36N 1 0W
St.-Germain-de-Calberte 10 44 13N 3 48 E
St.-Germain-des-Fossés 10 46 12N 3 26 E
St.-Germain-du-Plain 9 46 42N 4 58 E
St.-Germain-en-Laye 9 48 54N 2 6 E
St.-Germain-Laval 11 45 50N 4 1 E
St.-Germain-Lembron 10 45 27N 3 14 E
St.-Gervais-d'Auvergne 10 46 4N 2 50 E
St.-Gervais-les-Bains 11 45 53N 6 42 E
St.-Gildas, Pte. de 8 47 8N 2 14W
St.-Gilles 11 43 40N 4 26 E
St.-Gilles-Croix-de-Vie 10 46 41N 1 55W
St.-Girons 10 42 59N 1 8 E
St.-Gualtier 8 46 39N 1 26 E
St.-Guénolé 8 47 49N 4 23W
St. Helena 1 15 55 S 5 44W
St. Helena B. 52 32 40 S 18 10 E
St. Helens, U.K. 5 53 28N 2 44W
St. Helens, U.S.A. 68 45 55N 122 50W
St. Helens, Mt. 68 46 12N 122 11W
St. Helier 8 49 11N 2 6W

St.-Hilaire-du-Harcouët 8 48 35N 1 5W
St.-Hippolyte 9 47 19N 6 50 E
St.-Hippolyte-du-Fort 10 43 58N 3 52 E
St.-Honoré-les-Bains 9 46 54N 3 50 E
St-Hubert 12 50 2N 5 23 E
St-Hyacinthe 62 45 40N 72 58W
St. Ives, Cambs., U.K. 5 52 20N 0 5W
St. Ives, Cornwall, U.K. 5 50 13N 5 29W
St.-James 8 48 31N 1 20W
St-Jean 62 45 20N 73 20W
St.-Jean-d'Angély 10 45 57N 0 31W
St.-Jean-de-Bournay 11 45 30N 5 9 E
St.-Jean-de-Luz 10 43 23N 1 39W
St.-Jean-de-Maurienne 11 45 16N 6 21 E
St.-Jean-de-Monts 8 46 47N 2 4W
St.-Jean-du-Gard 10 44 7N 3 52 E
St.-Jean-en-Royans 11 45 1N 5 18 E
St-Jérôme 62 45 47N 74 0W
St. John 63 45 20N 66 8W
St. John's 63 47 35N 52 40W
St. John's → 63 30 20N 81 30W
St. Johnsbury 63 44 25N 72 1W
St. Joseph, Mich., U.S.A. 66 42 5N 86 30W
St. Joseph, Mo., U.S.A. 67 39 46N 94 50W
St. Joseph, L. 62 51 10N 90 35W
St.-Juéry 10 43 57N 2 12 E
St.-Julien-Chapteuil 11 45 2N 4 4 E
St.-Julien-du-Sault 9 48 1N 3 17 E
St.-Julien-en-Genevois 11 46 9N 6 5 E
St.-Junien 10 45 53N 0 55 E
St.-Just-en-Chaussée 9 49 30N 2 25 E
St.-Just-en-Chevalet 10 45 55N 3 50 E
St.-Justin 10 43 59N 0 14W
St.-Laurent-du-Pont 11 45 23N 5 45 E
St.-Laurent-en-Grandvaux 11 46 35N 5 58 E
St. Lawrence 63 46 54N 55 23W
St. Lawrence → 63 49 30N 66 0W
St. Lawrence, Gulf of 63 48 25N 62 0W
St. Leonard 63 47 12N 67 58W
St.-Léonard-de-Noblat 10 45 49N 1 29 E
St.-Lô 8 49 7N 1 5W
St-Louis 49 16 8N 16 27W
St. Louis 67 38 40N 90 12W
St.-Loup-sur-Semouse 9 47 53N 6 16 E
St. Lucia ■ 70 14 0N 60 50W
St. Lucia, L. 53 28 5S 32 30 E
St. Maarten 70 18 0N 63 5W
St.-Maixent-l'École 10 46 24N 0 12W
St.-Malo 8 48 39N 2 1W
St.-Malo, G. de 8 48 50N 2 30W
St.-Mandrier-sur-Mer 11 43 4N 5 57 E
St.-Marc 70 19 10N 72 41W
St.-Marcellin 11 45 9N 5 20 E
St.-Marcouf, Is. 8 49 30N 1 10W
St.-Martin, I. 70 18 0N 63 0W
St.-Martin-de-Ré 10 46 12N 1 21W
St.-Martin-Vésubie 11 44 4N 7 15 E
St.-Martory 10 43 9N 0 56 E
St. Mary Pk. 56 31 32S 138 34 E
St. Marys, Australia 56 41 35S 148 11 E
St. Mary's, U.K. 5 49 55N 6 17W
St. Marys, U.S.A. 66 41 27N 78 33W
St.-Mathieu, Pte. de 8 48 20N 4 45W
St.-Maur-des-Fossés 9 48 48N 2 30 E
St.-Médard-de-Guizières 10 45 1N 0 4W
St.-Méen-le-Grand 8 48 11N 2 12W
St. Michael's Mt. 5 50 7N 5 30W
St.-Michel-de-Maurienne 11 45 12N 6 28 E
St.-Mihiel 9 48 54N 5 32 E
St.-Nazaire 8 47 17N 2 12W
St. Neots 5 52 14N 0 16W
St.-Nicolas-de-Port 9 48 38N 6 18 E
St.-Omer 9 50 45N 2 15 E
St.-Palais-sur-Mer 10 45 38N 1 5W
St.-Pardoux-la-Rivière 10 45 29N 0 45 E
St. Pascal 63 47 32N 69 48W
St. Paul, Ind. Oc. 2 30 40S 77 34 E
St. Paul, U.S.A. 67 44 54N 93 5W
St. Paul, I. 63 47 12N 60 9W
St.-Paul-de-Fenouillet 10 42 48N 2 30 E
St.-Paul-lès-Dax 10 43 44N 1 3W
St.-Péray 11 44 57N 4 50 E
St.-Père-en-Retz 8 47 11N 2 2W
St. Peter Port 8 49 27N 2 31W
St. Petersburg 66 27 45N 82 40W
St.-Philbert-de-Grand-Lieu 8 47 2N 1 39W
St.-Pierre-d'Oléron 10 45 57N 1 19W
St.-Pierre-Église 8 49 40N 1 24W
St.-Pierre-en-Port 8 49 48N 0 30 E
St.-Pierre et Miquelon □ 63 46 55N 56 10W
St.-Pierre-le-Moûtier 9 46 47N 3 7 E
St.-Pierre-sur-Dives 8 49 2N 0 1W
St.-Pol-de-Léon 8 48 41N 4 0W
St.-Pol-sur-Mer 9 51 1N 2 20 E
St.-Pol-sur-Ternoise 9 50 23N 2 20 E
St.-Pons 10 43 30N 2 45 E
St.-Pourçain-sur-Sioule 10 46 18N 3 18 E
St.-Quay-Portrieux 8 48 39N 2 51W
St.-Quentin 9 49 50N 3 16 E
St.-Rambert-d'Albon 11 45 17N 4 49 E
St.-Raphaël 11 43 25N 6 46 E
St.-Rémy-de-Provence 11 43 48N 4 50 E
St.-Renan 8 48 26N 4 37W
St.-Saëns 8 49 41N 1 16 E
St.-Sauveur-en-Puisaye 9 47 37N 3 12 E
St.-Sauveur-le-Vicomte 8 49 23N 1 32W
St.-Savin 10 46 34N 0 53 E
St.-Savinien 10 45 53N 0 42W
St.-Seine-l'Abbaye 9 47 26N 4 47 E
St.-Sernin-sur-Rance 10 43 54N 2 35 E
St.-Servan-sur-Mer 8 48 38N 2 0W
St.-Sever 10 43 45N 0 35W
St.-Sever-Calvados 8 48 50N 1 3W
St.-Sulpice 10 43 46N 1 41 E
St.-Sulpice-Laurière 10 46 3N 1 29 E
St.-Syprien 10 42 37N 3 2 E
St.-Thégonnec 8 48 31N 3 57W
St. Thomas, Canada 62 42 45N 81 10W
St. Thomas, W. Indies 70 18 21N 64 55W
St.-Tropez 11 43 17N 6 38 E
St.-Vaast-la-Hougue 8 49 35N 1 17W
St.-Valéry-en-Caux 8 49 52N 0 43 E
St.-Valéry-sur-Somme 9 50 11N 1 38 E
St.-Vallier 11 45 11N 4 50 E
St.-Vallier-de-Thiey 11 43 42N 6 51 E
St.-Varent 8 46 53N 0 13W
St. Vincent, G. 56 35 0S 138 0 E
St. Vincent and the Grenadines ■ 70 13 0N 61 10W
St.-Vincent-de-Tyrosse 10 43 39N 1 19W
St-Vith 12 50 17N 6 9 E
St.-Yrieix-la-Perche 10 45 31N 1 12 E
Ste.-Adresse 8 49 31N 0 5 E
Ste Anne de Beaupré 63 47 2N 70 58W
Ste.-Enimie 10 44 22N 3 26 E
Ste.-Foy-la-Grande 10 44 50N 0 13 E
Ste.-Hermine 10 46 32N 1 4W
Ste.-Livrade-sur-Lot 10 44 24N 0 36 E
Ste.-Marie 70 14 48N 61 1W
Ste.-Marie-aux-Mines 9 48 15N 7 12 E
Ste.-Maure-de-Touraine 8 47 7N 0 37 E
Ste.-Maxime 11 43 19N 6 39 E
Ste.-Menehould 9 49 5N 4 54 E
Ste.-Mère-Église 8 49 24N 1 19W
Ste.-Rose 70 16 20N 61 45W
Ste. Rose du lac 65 51 4N 99 30W
Saintes 10 45 45N 0 37W
Stes.-Maries-de-la-Mer 11 43 26N 4 26 E
Saintonge 10 45 40N 0 50W
Saitama □ 44 36 25N 139 30 E
Sajama 72 18 7S 69 0W
Sakai 44 34 30N 135 30 E
Sakakawea, L. 67 47 30N 102 0W
Sakata 44 38 55N 139 50 E
Sakhalin 31 51 0N 143 0 E
Sakhalinskiy Zaliv 31 54 0N 141 0 E
Sala 28 59 58N 16 35 E
Sala-y-Gómez 58 26 28S 105 28W
Salaberry-de-Valleyfield 62 45 15N 74 8W
Salado →, Argentina 74 31 40S 60 41W
Salado →, Mexico 69 26 52N 99 19W
Salaga 49 8 31N 0 31W
Salālah 47 16 56N 53 59 E
Salamanca, Spain 18 40 58N 5 39W
Salamanca, U.S.A. 66 42 10N 78 42W
Salamis 26 37 56N 23 30 E
Salbris 9 47 25N 2 3 E
Salcombe 5 50 14N 3 47W
Saldaña 18 42 32N 4 48W
Saldanha 52 33 0S 17 58 E
Sale, Australia 56 38 6S 147 6 E
Salé, Morocco 49 34 3N 6 48W
Sale, U.K. 5 53 26N 2 19W
Salekhard 30 66 30N 66 35 E
Salem, India 38 11 40N 78 11 E
Salem, Mass., U.S.A. 66 42 29N 70 53W
Salem, Oreg., U.S.A. 68 45 0N 123 0W
Salem, Va., U.S.A. 66 37 19N 80 8W
Salernes 11 43 34N 6 15 E
Salerno 23 40 40N 14 44 E
Salford 5 53 30N 2 17W
Salies-de-Béarn 10 43 28N 0 56W
Salina, Italy 23 38 35N 14 50 E
Salina, U.S.A. 67 38 50N 97 40W
Salina Cruz 69 16 10N 95 12W
Salinas, Ecuador 72 2 10S 80 58W
Salinas, U.S.A. 68 36 40N 121 41W
Salinas → 68 36 45N 121 48W
Salinas Grandes 74 30 0S 65 0W
Salins-les-Bains 9 46 58N 5 52 E
Salisbury = Harare 51 17 43S 31 2 E
Salisbury, U.K. 5 51 4N 1 48W
Salisbury, Md., U.S.A. 66 38 20N 75 38W
Salisbury, N.C., U.S.A. 66 35 20N 80 29W
Salisbury Plain 5 51 13N 1 50W
Salle, La 67 41 20N 89 6W
Salles-Curan 10 44 11N 2 48 E
Salmon → 68 45 51N 116 46W
Salmon Arm 64 50 40N 119 15W
Salmon River Mts. 68 45 0N 114 30W
Salo 27 60 22N 23 10 E
Salon-de-Provence 11 43 39N 5 6 E
Salonica = Thessaloníki 26 40 38N 22 58 E
Salonta 15 46 49N 21 42 E
Salop = Shropshire □ 5 52 36N 2 45W
Salses 10 42 50N 2 55 E
Salsk 35 46 28N 41 30 E
Salso → 23 37 6N 13 55 E
Salt Lake City 68 40 45N 111 58W
Salta 74 24 57S 65 25W
Saltcoats 6 55 38N 4 47W
Saltee Is. 7 52 7N 6 37W
Saltfjorden 27 67 15N 14 10 E
Salthólmavík 27 65 24N 21 57W
Saltillo 69 25 25N 101 0W
Salto 74 31 27S 57 50W
Salton Sea 68 33 20N 115 50W
Saltpond 49 5 15N 1 3W
Salûm 50 31 31N 25 7 E
Salûm, Khâlig el 50 31 30N 25 9 E
Salur 38 18 27N 83 18 E
Saluzzo 20 44 39N 7 29 E
Salvador 73 13 0S 38 30W
Salween → 41 16 31N 97 37 E
Salzburg 14 47 48N 13 2 E
Salzburg □ 14 47 15N 13 0 E
Salzgitter 13 52 13N 10 22 E
Sam Neua 41 20 29N 104 0 E
Sama 30 60 12N 60 22 E
Sama de Langreo 18 43 18N 5 40W
Samagaltai 31 50 36N 95 3 E
Samangán □ 46 36 15N 68 3 E
Samar 40 12 0N 125 0 E
Samarkand 30 39 40N 66 55 E
Sāmarrā 45 34 12N 43 52 E
Samatan 10 43 29N 0 55 E
Sambalpur 36 21 28N 84 4 E
Sambava 53 14 16S 50 10 E
Sambhal 36 28 35N 78 37 E
Sambhar 36 26 52N 75 6 E
Sambre → 12 50 27N 4 52 E
Same 51 4 2S 37 38 E
Samer 9 50 38N 1 44 E
Samoëns 11 46 5N 6 45 E
Sámos 26 37 45N 26 50 E
Samothráki 26 40 28N 25 28 E
Samsun 45 41 15N 36 22 E
Samut Prakan 41 13 32N 100 40 E
Samut Sakhon 41 13 31N 100 13 E
Samut Songkhram → 41 13 24N 100 1 E
San 49 13 15N 4 57W
San → 15 50 45N 21 51 E
San Ambrosio 58 26 28S 79 53W
San Andreas 68 38 0N 120 39W
San Andrés Tuxtla 69 18 27N 95 13W
San Angelo 67 31 30N 100 30W
San Antonio, Chile 74 33 40S 71 40W
San Antonio, U.S.A. 67 29 30N 98 30W
San Antonio, C., Argentina 74 36 15S 56 40W
San Antonio, C., Cuba 70 21 50N 84 57W
San Antonio de los Baños 70 22 54N 82 31W
San Antonio Oeste 74 40 40S 65 0W
San Benedetto 20 45 2N 10 57 E
San Bernardino 68 34 7N 117 18W
San Bernardino Str. 40 13 0N 125 0 E
San Bernardo 74 33 40S 70 50W
San Blas, C. 66 29 40N 85 12W
San Carlos, Chile 74 36 10S 72 0W
San Carlos, Mexico 69 29 1N 100 51W
San Carlos, Nic. 70 11 12N 84 50W
San Carlos de Bariloche 74 41 10S 71 25W
San Clemente I. 68 32 53N 118 30W
San Cristóbal, Argentina 74 30 20S 61 10W
San Cristóbal, Dom. Rep. 70 18 25N 70 6W
San Cristóbal, Venezuela 72 16 50N 92 40W
San Cristóbal de las Casas 69 16 45N 92 38W
San Diego 68 32 43N 117 10W
San Felipe, Chile 74 32 43S 70 42W
San Felipe, Colombia 72 1 55N 67 6W
San Felíu de Guíxols 19 41 45N 3 1 E
San Félix 58 26 23S 80 0W
San Fernando, Chile 74 34 30S 71 0W
San Fernando, Mexico 69 30 0N 115 10W
San Fernando, Spain 18 36 28N 6 17W
San Fernando, Trin. & Tob. 70 10 20N 61 30W
San Fernando, U.S.A. 68 34 15N 118 29W
San Fernando de Apure 72 7 54N 67 15W
San Francisco 68 37 47N 122 30W
San Francisco de Macorís 70 19 19N 70 15W
San Francisco del Oro 69 26 52N 105 51W
San Gabriel 74 0 36N 77 49W
San Gottardo, Paso del 13 46 33N 8 33 E
San Ignacio 72 16 20S 60 55W
San Joaquin → 68 37 4N 121 51W
San Jorge, G. 74 46 0S 66 0W
San Jorge, G. de 19 40 50N 0 55W
San José, Bolivia 72 17 53S 60 50W
San José, C. Rica 70 10 0N 84 2W
San Jose, U.S.A. 68 37 20N 121 53W
San José de Mayo 74 34 27S 56 40W
San José del Cabo 69 23 3N 109 41W
San José del Guaviare 72 2 35N 72 38W
San Juan, Argentina 74 31 30S 68 30W
San Juan, Dom. Rep. 70 18 49N 71 12W
San Juan, Puerto Rico 70 18 28N 66 8W
San Juan → 70 10 56N 83 42W
San Juan, C. 51 1 5N 9 20 E
San Juan de los Morros 72 9 55N 67 21W
San Juan Mts. 68 38 30N 108 30W
San Julián 74 49 15S 67 45W
San Leandro 68 37 40N 122 6W
San Lorenzo 72 1 15N 78 50W
San Lucas, C. 69 22 50N 110 0W
San Luis 74 33 20S 66 20W
San Luis de la Paz 69 21 18N 100 31W
San Luis Obispo 68 35 21N 120 38W
San Luis Potosí 69 22 9N 100 59W
San Luis Potosí □ 69 22 30N 100 30W
San Marcos 69 14 59N 91 52W
San Marino ■ 21 43 56N 12 25 E
San Mateo 68 37 32N 122 19W
San Matías 72 16 25S 58 20W
San Matías, G. 74 41 30S 64 0W
San Miguel 69 13 30N 88 12W
San Miguel de Tucumán 74 26 50S 65 20W
San-Pédro 49 4 50N 6 33W
San Pedro → 69 21 45N 105 30W
San Pedro de las Colonias 69 25 45N 102 59W
San Pedro de Macorís 70 18 30N 69 18W
San Pedro Sula 69 15 30N 88 0W
San Rafael, Argentina 74 34 40S 68 21W
San Rafael, U.S.A. 68 37 59N 122 32W
San Remo 20 43 48N 7 47 E
San Roque 74 28 25S 58 45W
San Salvador, Bahamas 70 24 0N 74 40W
San Salvador, El Salv. 69 13 40N 89 10W
San Salvador de Jujuy 74 24 10S 64 48W
San Sebastián 19 43 17N 1 58W
San Valentin, Mte. 74 46 30S 73 30W
San Vicente de la Barquera 18 43 23N 4 29W
Sana' 47 15 27N 44 12 E
Sana → 21 45 3N 16 23 E
Sanaga → 49 3 35N 9 38 E
Sanandaj 45 35 18N 47 1 E
Sanary-sur-Mer 11 43 7N 5 49 E
Sancergues 9 47 10N 2 54 E
Sancerre 9 47 20N 2 50 E
Sancerrois, Coll. du 9 47 20N 2 40 E
Sancoins 9 46 47N 2 55 E
Sancti-Spíritus 70 21 52N 79 33W
Sancy, Puy de 10 45 32N 2 50 E
Sanday 6 59 15N 2 30W
Sandnes 27 58 50N 5 45 E
Sandness 6 60 18N 1 38W
Sandoa 51 9 41S 23 0 E
Sandomierz 17 50 40N 21 43 E
Sandover → 55 21 43S 136 32 E
Sandpoint 68 48 20N 116 34W
Sandringham 5 52 50N 0 30 E
Sandstone 54 27 59S 119 16 E
Sandusky 66 41 25N 82 40W
Sandviken 28 60 38N 16 46 E
Sandy C., Queens., Australia 55 24 42S 153 15 E
Sandy C., Tas., Australia 56 41 25S 144 45 E
Sandy Lake 65 53 0N 93 15W
Sanford, Fla., U.S.A. 66 28 45N 81 20W
Sanford, Maine, U.S.A. 63 43 28N 70 47W
Sanford, N.C., U.S.A. 66 35 30N 79 10W
Sanford → 54 27 22S 115 53 E
Sanga → 51 1 5S 17 0 E
Sanga-Tolon 31 61 50N 149 40 E
Sangamner 38 19 37N 74 15 E
Sangar 31 64 2N 127 31 E
Sangay 72 2 0S 78 20W
Sangihe, P. 40 3 45N 125 30 E
Sangli 38 16 55N 74 33 E
Sangmélina 51 2 57N 12 1 E
Sangonera → 19 37 59N 1 4W
Sangre de Cristo Mts. 68 37 0N 105 0W
Sanguinaires, Is. 11 41 51N 8 36 E
Sankt Moritz 13 46 30N 9 50 E
Sankt Wendel 13 49 27N 7 9 E
Sankuru → 51 4 17S 20 25 E
Sanlúcar de Barrameda 18 36 46N 6 21W
Sannicandro Gargánico 23 41 50N 15 34 E
Sanok 15 49 35N 22 10 E
Sanquhar 6 55 21N 3 56W
Sanshui 43 23 10N 112 56 E
Santa Ana, Bolivia 72 13 50S 65 40W
Santa Ana, Mexico 69 30 33N 111 7W
Santa Ana, U.S.A. 68 33 48N 117 55W
Santa Bárbara, Mexico 69 26 48N 105 49W
Santa Barbara, U.S.A. 68 34 25N 119 40W
Santa Catalina I. 68 33 20N 118 30W
Santa Catarina □ 74 27 25S 48 30W
Santa Clara, Cuba 70 22 20N 80 0W
Santa Clara, U.S.A. 68 37 21N 122 0W
Santa Clotilde 72 2 33S 73 45W
Santa Cruz, Bolivia 72 17 43S 63 10W
Santa Cruz, U.S.A. 68 36 55N 122 1W
Santa Cruz, Is. 57 10 30S 166 0 E
Santa Cruz de Tenerife 49 28 28N 16 15W
Santa Cruz del Sur 70 20 44N 78 0W
Santa Cruz do Sul 74 29 42S 52 25W
Santa Fe, Argentina 74 31 35S 60 41W
Santa Fe, U.S.A. 68 35 40N 106 0W
Santa Inés, I. 74 54 0S 73 0W
Santa Lucia Range 68 36 0N 121 20W
Santa Maria, Brazil 74 29 40S 53 48W
Santa Maria, U.S.A. 68 34 58N 120 29W
Santa Maria da Vitória 73 13 24S 44 12W
Santa Maria di Leuca, C. 23 39 48N 18 20 E
Santa Marta 72 11 15N 74 13W
Santa Maura = Levkás 26 38 40N 20 43 E
Santa Monica 68 34 0N 118 30W
Santa Rosa, Argentina 74 36 40S 64 17W
Santa Rosa, U.S.A. 68 38 26N 122 43W
Santa Rosa I., Calif., U.S.A. 68 34 0N 120 6W
Santa Rosa I., Fla., U.S.A. 66 30 23N 87 0W
Santa Rosalía 69 27 19N 112 17W
Santana do Livramento 74 30 55S 55 30W
Santander 18 43 27N 3 51W
Santander Jiménez 69 24 13N 98 28W
Santarém, Brazil 73 2 25S 54 42W
Santarém, Portugal 18 39 12N 8 42W
Santiago, Brazil 74 29 11S 54 52W
Santiago, Chile 74 33 24S 70 40W
Santiago, Panama 70 8 0N 81 0W
Santiago de Compostela 18 42 52N 8 37W
Santiago de Cuba 70 20 0N 75 49W
Santiago de los Cabelleros 70 19 30N 70 40W
Santiago del Estero 74 27 50S 64 15W
Santiago Ixcuintla 69 21 50N 105 11W
Santo Amaro 73 12 30S 38 43W
Santo Ângelo 74 28 15S 54 15W
Santo Domingo 70 18 30N 69 59W
Santo Tomé 74 28 40S 56 5W
Santoña 18 43 29N 3 27W
Santos 74 24 0S 46 20W
Sanvignes-les-Mines 9 46 40N 4 18 E
Sanza Pombo 51 7 18S 15 56 E
São Borja 74 28 39S 56 0W
São Carlos 73 22 0S 47 50W
São Francisco → 73 10 30S 36 24W
São Francisco do Sul 74 26 15S 48 36W
São João del Rei 73 21 8S 44 15W
São José do Rio Prêto 73 20 50S 49 20W
São Leopoldo 74 29 50S 51 10W
São Lourenço 73 22 7S 45 3W
São Luís 73 2 39S 44 15W
São Paulo 74 23 32S 46 37W
São Paulo □ 73 22 0S 49 0W
Sao Paulo, I. 1 0 50N 31 40W
São Paulo de Olivença 72 3 27S 68 48W
São Roque, C. de 73 5 30S 35 16W
São Tomé & Principe ■ 2 0 12N 6 39 E
São Vicente, C. de 18 37 0N 9 0W
Saône → 11 45 44N 4 50 E
Saône-et-Loire □ 9 46 30N 4 50 E
Sapele 49 5 50N 5 40 E
Sapporo 44 43 0N 141 21 E
Sapulpa 67 36 0N 96 0W
Saqqez 45 36 15N 46 20 E
Sar Planina 24 42 10N 21 0 E
Sarajevo 24 43 52N 18 26 E
Saranac Lake 62 44 20N 74 10W
Sarangani B. 40 6 0N 125 13 E
Sarangarh 36 21 30N 83 5 E
Saransk 33 54 10N 45 10 E
Sarapul 30 56 28N 53 48 E
Sarasota 66 27 20N 82 30W
Saratoga Springs 66 43 5N 73 47W
Saratov 33 51 30N 46 2 E
Sarawak □ 39 2 0N 113 0 E
Sardalas 49 25 50N 10 34 E
Sardarshahr 36 28 30N 74 29 E
Sardegna 22 39 57N 9 0 E
Sardinia = Sardegna 22 39 57N 9 0 E
Sargodha 36 32 10N 72 40 E
Sarh 50 9 5N 18 23 E
Sārī 46 36 30N 53 4 E
Sarina 56 21 22S 149 13 E
Sark 8 49 25N 2 20W
Sarlat-la-Canéda 10 44 54N 1 13 E
Sarmiento 74 45 35S 69 5W
Sarnia 62 42 58N 82 23W
Sarny 32 51 17N 26 40 E
Saronikós Kólpos 26 37 45N 23 45 E
Saros Körfezi 26 40 30N 26 15 E
Sarpsborg 28 59 16N 11 12 E
Sarralbe 9 49 0N 7 1 E
Sarre = Saar → 9 49 41N 6 32 E
Sarre, La 62 48 45N 79 15W
Sarre-Union 9 48 57N 7 4 E
Sarrebourg 9 48 43N 7 3 E
Sarreguemines 9 49 5N 7 4 E
Sarro 49 13 40N 5 15W
Sartène 11 41 38N 8 58 E
Sarthe □ 8 47 58N 0 10 E
Sarthe → 8 47 33N 0 31W
Sartilly 8 48 45N 1 28W
Sary-Tash 30 39 44N 73 15 E
Sarzeau 8 47 31N 2 48W
Sasabeneh 47 7 59N 44 43 E
Sasaram 37 24 57N 84 5 E
Sasebo 44 33 10N 129 43 E
Saskatchewan □ 65 54 40N 106 0W
Saskatchewan → 65 53 37N 100 40W
Saskatoon 65 52 10N 106 38W
Saskylakh 31 71 55N 114 1 E
Sasovo 33 54 25N 41 55 E
Sassandra 49 5 0N 6 8W
Sassandra → 49 4 58N 6 5W
Sássari 22 40 44N 8 33 E
Sata-Misaki 44 30 59N 130 40 E
Satadougou 49 12 25N 11 25W
Satara 38 17 44N 73 58 E
Satmala Hills 38 20 15N 74 40 E
Satna 37 24 35N 80 50 E
Sátoraljaújhely 15 48 25N 21 41 E
Satpura Ra. 36 21 25N 76 10 E
Sattahip 41 12 41N 100 54 E
Satu Mare 15 47 46N 22 55 E
Sauðarkrókur 27 65 45N 19 40W
Saudi Arabia ■ 47 26 0N 44 0 E
Sauerland 13 51 0N 8 0 E
Saugues 10 44 58N 3 32 E
Saujon 10 45 41N 0 55W
Saulieu 9 47 17N 4 14 E
Sault 11 44 6N 5 24 E
Sault Ste. Marie, Canada 62 46 30N 84 20W
Sault Ste. Marie, U.S.A. 62 46 27N 84 22W
Saumur 8 47 15N 0 5W
Saurbær, Borgarfjarðarsýsla, Iceland 27 64 24N 21 35W
Saurbær, Eyjafjarðarsýsla, Iceland 27 65 27N 18 13W
Sauri 49 11 42N 6 44 E
Sauveterre-de-Béarn 10 43 24N 0 57W
Sauzé-Vaussais 10 46 8N 0 8 E
Sava → 24 44 50N 20 26 E
Savalou 49 7 57N 1 58 E
Savanna la Mar 70 18 10N 78 10W
Savannah 66 32 4N 81 4W
Savannah → 66 32 2N 80 53W
Savannakhet 41 16 30N 104 49 E
Savanur 38 14 59N 75 21 E
Savé 49 8 2N 2 29 E
Save →, France 10 43 47N 1 17 E
Save →, Mozam. 53 21 16S 34 0 E
Savelugu 49 9 38N 0 54W
Savenay 8 47 20N 1 55W

Saverdun **10** 43 14N 1 34 E
Saverne **9** 48 43N 7 20 E
Savigny-sur-Braye **8** 47 53N 0 49 E
Savoie □ **11** 45 26N 6 25 E
Savona **20** 44 19N 8 29 E
Sawai Madhopur **36** 26 0N 76 25 E
Sawankhalok **41** 17 19N 99 50 E
Sawara **44** 35 55N 140 30 E
Sawatch Mts. **68** 38 30N 106 30W
Sawel, Mt. **7** 54 48N 7 5W
Sawmills **51** 19 30 S 28 2 E
Sawu Sea **40** 9 30 S 121 50 E
Say **49** 13 8N 2 22 E
Sayan, Vostochnyy **31** 54 0N 96 0 E
Sayan, Zapadnyy **31** 52 30N 94 0 E
Saydā **45** 33 35N 35 25 E
Sayḩut **47** 15 12N 51 10 E
Sayula **69** 19 52N 103 36W
Sazan **26** 40 30N 19 20 E
Săzava → **14** 49 53N 14 24 E
Scaër **8** 48 2N 3 42W
Scafell Pikes **5** 54 26N 3 14W
Scalpay **6** 57 51N 6 40W
Scandinavia **27** 64 0N 12 0 E
Scapa Flow **6** 58 52N 3 6W
Scarborough **5** 54 17N 0 24W
Schagen **12** 52 49N 4 48 E
Schefferville **63** 54 48N 66 50W
Schelde → **12** 51 15N 4 16 E
Schenectady **66** 42 50N 73 58W
Scheveningen **12** 52 6N 4 16 E
Schiedam **12** 51 55N 4 25 E
Schiermonnikoog **12** 53 30N 6 15 E
Schifferstadt **13** 49 22N 8 23 E
Schiltigheim **9** 48 35N 7 45 E
Schio **21** 45 42N 11 21 E
Schirmeck **9** 48 29N 7 12 E
Schleswig **13** 54 32N 9 34 E
Schleswig-Holstein □ **13** 54 10N 9 40 E
Schouwen **12** 51 43N 3 45 E
Schramberg **13** 48 12N 8 24 E
Schreiber **62** 48 45N 87 20W
Schwabach **13** 49 19N 11 3 E
Schwäbisch Gmünd **13** 48 49N 9 48 E
Schwäbisch Hall **13** 49 7N 9 45 E
Schwäbische Alb **13** 48 30N 9 30 E
Schwarzwald **13** 48 0N 8 0 E
Schweinfurt **13** 50 3N 10 12 E
Schwerin **13** 53 37N 11 22 E
Schwetzingen **13** 49 22N 8 35 E
Schwyz **13** 47 2N 8 39 E
Sciacca **22** 37 30N 13 3 E
Scilla **23** 38 18N 15 44 E
Scilly, Isles of **5** 49 55N 6 15W
Scone **6** 56 25N 3 26W
Scoresbysund **3** 70 20N 23 0W
Scotia Sea **60** 56 5 S 56 0W
Scotland □ **6** 57 0N 4 0W
Scott Reef **54** 14 0 S 121 50 E
Scottsbluff **67** 41 55N 103 35W
Scottsdale **56** 41 9 S 147 31 E
Scranton **66** 41 22N 75 41W
Scunthorpe **5** 53 35N 0 38W
Scusciuban **47** 10 18N 50 12 E
Seaforth **62** 43 35N 81 25W
Searcy **67** 35 15N 91 45W
Seattle **68** 47 41N 122 15W
Seaview Ra. **56** 18 40 S 145 45 E
Sebastián Vizcaíno, B. **69** 28 0N 114 30W
Sebastopol = Sevastopol **34** 44 35N 33 30 E
Sebring **66** 27 30N 81 26W
Sebuku, Teluk **39** 4 0N 118 10 E
Sechura, Desierto de **72** 6 0 S 80 30W
Seclin **9** 50 33N 3 2 E
Secondigny **8** 46 37N 0 26W
Secunderabad **38** 17 28N 78 30 E
Sedalia **67** 38 40N 93 18W
Sedan **9** 49 43N 4 57 E
Sedhiou **49** 12 44N 15 30W
Seeheim **52** 26 50 S 17 45 E
Sées **8** 48 38N 0 10 E
Seg-ozero **32** 63 0N 33 10 E
Segamat **41** 2 30N 102 50 E
Segonzac **10** 45 36N 0 14W
Ségou **49** 13 30N 6 16W
Segovia **18** 40 57N 4 10W
Segré **8** 47 40N 0 52W
Segre → **19** 41 40N 0 43 E
Séguéla **49** 7 55N 6 40W
Segura → **19** 38 6N 0 54W
Sehitwa **52** 20 30 S 22 30 E
Sehore **36** 23 10N 77 5 E
Seiland **27** 70 25N 23 15 E
Seille → **11** 46 31N 4 57 E
Sein, I. de **8** 48 2N 4 52W
Seinäjoki → **27** 62 40N 22 45 E
Seine → **8** 49 26N 0 26 E
Seine, B. de la **8** 49 40N 0 40W
Seine-et-Marne □ **9** 48 45N 3 0 E
Seine-Maritime □ **8** 49 40N 1 0 E
Seine-St.-Denis □ **9** 48 58N 2 24 E
Seistan **46** 30 50N 61 0 E
Sekondi-Takoradi **49** 4 58N 1 45W
Selangor □ **41** 3 10N 101 30 E
Selby **5** 53 47N 1 5W
Sele → **23** 40 27N 14 58 E
Selemdzha → **31** 51 42N 128 53 E
Selenter See **13** 54 19N 10 26 E
Sélestat **9** 48 16N 7 26 E
Sélibabi **49** 15 10N 12 15W
Selîma, El Wâhât el **50** 21 22N 29 19 E
Selkirk, Canada **65** 50 10N 96 55W
Selkirk, U.K. **6** 55 33N 2 50W
Selkirk Mts. **64** 51 15N 117 40W
Selles-sur-Cher **9** 47 16N 1 33 E
Sellières **9** 46 50N 5 32 E
Selma, Ala., U.S.A. **66** 32 30N 87 0W
Selma, Calif., U.S.A. **68** 36 39N 119 39W
Selma, N.C., U.S.A. **66** 35 32N 78 15W
Selongey **9** 47 36N 5 11 E
Selsey Bill **5** 50 44N 0 47W
Seltz **9** 48 54N 8 4 E
Sélune → **8** 48 38N 1 22W
Selvas **72** 6 30 S 67 0W
Selwyn **56** 21 32 S 140 30 E
Selwyn Ra. **56** 21 10 S 140 0 E
Seman → **26** 40 45N 19 50 E
Semarang **40** 7 0 S 110 26 E
Seminole **67** 35 15N 96 45W
Semiozernoye **30** 52 22N 64 8 E
Semipalatinsk **30** 50 30N 80 10 E
Semmering Pass **14** 47 41N 15 45 E
Semnān **46** 35 55N 53 25 E
Semnān □ **46** 36 0N 54 0 E
Semois → **12** 49 53N 4 44 E
Semur-en-Auxois **9** 47 30N 4 20 E
Senanga **52** 16 2 S 23 14 E
Sendai, Kagoshima, Japan **44** 31 50N 130 20 E
Sendai, Miyagi, Japan **44** 38 15N 140 53 E
Senegal ■ **49** 14 30N 14 30W
Senegal → **49** 15 48N 16 32W
Senhor-do-Bonfim **73** 10 30 S 40 10W
Senigállia **21** 43 42N 13 12 E
Senj **21** 45 0N 14 58 E
Senja **27** 69 25N 17 30 E
Senlis **9** 49 13N 2 35 E
Sennâr **50** 13 30N 33 35 E
Senneterre **62** 48 25N 77 15W
Senonches **8** 48 34N 1 2 E
Sens **9** 48 11N 3 15 E
Senta **24** 45 55N 20 3 E
Seo de Urgel **19** 42 22N 1 23 E
Seoul = Sŏul **43** 37 31N 126 58 E
Sepik → **56** 3 49 S 144 30 E
Sept-Îles **63** 50 13N 66 22W
Sequoia Nat. Park **68** 36 30N 118 30W
Seraing **12** 50 35N 5 32 E
Seram **40** 3 10 S 129 0 E
Seram Sea **40** 2 30 S 128 30 E
Serbia = Srbija □ **24** 43 30N 21 0 E
Serdobsk **33** 52 28N 44 10 E
Seremban **41** 2 43N 101 53 E
Serena, La **74** 29 55 S 71 10W
Serenje **51** 13 14 S 30 15 E
Sergipe □ **73** 10 30 S 37 30W
Sérifontaine **9** 49 20N 1 45 E
Sérignan **10** 43 17N 3 17 E
Sermaize-les-Bains **9** 48 47N 4 54 E
Serny Zavod **30** 39 59N 58 50 E
Serov **30** 59 29N 60 35 E
Serowe **52** 22 25 S 26 43 E
Serpukhov **33** 54 55N 37 28 E
Sérrai **26** 41 5N 23 31 E
Serre-Ponçon, L. de **11** 44 22N 6 20 E
Serres **11** 44 26N 5 43 E
Serule **52** 21 57 S 27 20 E
Sesfontein **52** 19 7 S 13 39 E
Sesheke **52** 17 29 S 24 13 E
Sestao **19** 43 18N 3 0W
Sète **10** 43 25N 3 42 E
Sétif **49** 36 9N 5 26 E
Seto **44** 35 14N 137 6 E
Setonaikai **44** 34 20N 133 30 E
Settat **49** 33 0N 7 40W
Setté-Cama **51** 2 32 S 9 45 E
Settle **5** 54 5N 2 18W
Setúbal **18** 38 30N 8 58W
Setúbal, B. de **18** 38 40N 8 56W
Seugne → **10** 45 42N 0 32W
Sevan, Ozero **34** 40 30N 45 20 E
Sevastopol **34** 44 35N 33 30 E
Seven Sisters **64** 54 56N 128 10W
Sévérac-le-Château **10** 44 20N 3 5 E
Severn →, Canada **62** 56 2N 87 36W
Severn →, U.K. **5** 51 35N 2 38W
Severnaya Zemlya **31** 79 0N 100 0 E
Severo-Kurilsk **31** 50 40N 156 8 E
Severo-Yeniseyskiy **31** 60 22N 93 1 E
Severodinsk **30** 64 27N 39 58 E
Sevilla **18** 37 23N 6 0W
Sèvre-Nantaise → **8** 47 12N 1 33W
Sèvre-Niortaîse → **10** 46 28N 0 50W
Seychelles ■ **2** 5 0 S 56 0 E
Seyðisfjörður **27** 65 16N 14 0W
Seymchan **31** 62 54N 152 30 E
Seyne **11** 44 21N 6 22 E
Seyne, La **11** 43 7N 5 52 E
Seyssel **11** 45 57N 5 50 E
Sézanne **9** 48 40N 3 40 E
Sfax **50** 34 49N 10 48 E
Sfîntu Gheorghe **25** 45 52N 25 48 E
Shaanxi □ **43** 35 0N 109 0 E
Shaba □ **51** 8 0 S 25 0 E
Shabunda **51** 2 40 S 27 16 E
Shache **42** 38 20N 77 10 E
Shadrinsk **30** 56 5N 63 32 E
Shaftesbury **5** 51 0N 2 12W
Shahdād **46** 30 30N 57 40 E
Shahdadkot **36** 27 50N 67 55 E
Shahḩāt **50** 32 48N 21 54 E
Shahrig **36** 30 15N 67 40 E
Shajapur **36** 23 27N 76 21 E
Shakhty **35** 47 40N 40 16 E
Shakhunya **33** 57 40N 46 46 E
Shaki **49** 8 41N 3 21 E
Shala, L. **50** 7 30N 38 30 E
Shamâl Dârfûr □ **50** 15 0N 25 0 E
Shamâl Kordofân □ **50** 15 0N 30 0 E
Shamo, L. **50** 5 45N 37 30 E
Shamokin **66** 40 47N 76 33W
Shamva **51** 17 20 S 31 32 E
Shandong □ **42** 36 0N 118 0 E
Shanghai **43** 31 15N 121 26 E
Shangqiu **43** 34 26N 115 36 E
Shangrao **43** 28 25N 117 59 E
Shangshui **43** 33 42N 114 35 E
Shannon **3** 75 10N 18 30W
Shannon → **7** 52 35N 9 30W
Shantar, Ostrov Bolshoy **31** 55 9N 137 40 E
Shantou **43** 23 18N 116 40 E
Shantung = Shandong □ **42** 36 0N 118 0 E
Shanxi □ **42** 37 0N 112 0 E
Shaoguan **43** 24 48N 113 35 E
Shaoxing **43** 30 0N 120 35 E
Shaoyang **43** 27 14N 111 25 E
Shapinsay **6** 59 2N 2 50W
Shaqrā' **47** 13 22N 45 44 E
Sharjah = Ash Shāriqah **46** 25 23N 55 26 E
Shark B. **54** 25 55 S 113 32 E
Sharon **66** 41 18N 80 30W
Sharq el Istiwa'iya □ **50** 5 0N 33 0 E
Sharya **33** 58 22N 45 20 E
Shashi, Botswana **53** 21 15 S 27 27 E
Shashi, China **43** 30 25N 112 14 E
Shasta, Mt. **68** 41 30N 122 12W
Shasta L. **68** 40 50N 122 15W
Shaunavon **65** 49 35N 108 25W
Shaw → **54** 20 21 S 119 17 E
Shawano **66** 44 45N 88 38W
Shawinigan **62** 46 35N 72 50W
Shawnee **67** 35 15N 97 0W
Shebele, Wabi → **47** 2 0N 44 0 E
Sheboygan **67** 43 46N 87 45W
Sheelin, Lough **7** 53 48N 7 20W
Sheep Haven **7** 55 12N 7 55W
Sheerness **5** 51 26N 0 47 E
Sheffield **5** 53 23N 1 28W
Shekhupura **36** 31 42N 73 58 E
Shelburne **63** 43 47N 65 20W
Shelburne B. **55** 11 50 S 142 50 E
Shelby **66** 35 18N 81 34W
Shelbyville, Ind., U.S.A. **66** 39 30N 85 42W
Shelbyville, Tenn., U.S.A. **66** 35 30N 86 25W
Shelikhova, Zaliv **31** 59 30N 157 0 E
Shellharbour **56** 34 31 S 150 51 E
Shelling Rocks **7** 51 45N 10 35W
Shelton **68** 47 15N 123 6W
Shemakha **35** 40 38N 48 37 E
Shenandoah **67** 40 50N 95 25W
Shenandoah → **66** 39 19N 77 44W
Shendam **49** 8 49N 9 30 E
Shendî **50** 16 46N 33 22 E
Shenyang **42** 41 48N 123 27 E
Shepparton **56** 36 23 S 145 26 E
Sherborne **5** 50 56N 2 31W
Sherbro I. **49** 7 30N 12 40W
Sherbrooke **63** 45 28N 71 57W
Sheridan **68** 44 50N 107 0W
Sherman **67** 33 40N 96 35W
Sherridon **65** 55 8N 101 5W
Sherwood Forest **5** 53 5N 1 5W
Shetland □ **6** 60 30N 1 30W
Shetland Is. **6** 60 30N 1 30W
Shibām **47** 16 0N 48 36 E
Shibushi **44** 31 25N 131 8 E
Shiel, L. **6** 56 48N 5 32W
Shiga □ **44** 35 20N 136 0 E
Shigaib **50** 15 5N 23 35 E
Shijiazhuang **42** 38 2N 114 28 E
Shikarpur **36** 27 57N 68 39 E
Shikoku **44** 33 30N 133 30 E
Shikoku □ **44** 33 30N 133 30 E
Shikoku-Sanchi **44** 33 30N 133 30 E
Shilabo **47** 6 22N 44 32 E
Shiliguri **37** 26 45N 88 25 E
Shilka **31** 52 0N 115 55 E
Shilka → **31** 53 20N 121 26 E
Shillelagh **7** 52 46N 6 32W
Shimabara **44** 32 48N 130 20 E
Shimada **44** 34 49N 138 10 E
Shimane □ **44** 35 0N 132 30 E
Shimanovsk **31** 52 15N 127 30 E
Shimizu **44** 35 0N 138 30 E
Shimodate **44** 36 20N 139 55 E
Shimoga **38** 13 57N 75 32 E
Shimonoseki **44** 33 58N 131 0 E
Shin, L. **6** 58 7N 4 30W
Shin-Tone → **44** 35 44N 140 51 E
Shinano → **44** 36 50N 138 30 E
Shingū **44** 33 40N 135 55 E
Shinyanga **51** 3 45 S 33 27 E
Shio-no-Misaki **44** 33 25N 135 45 E
Shīrāz **46** 29 42N 52 30 E
Shire → **51** 17 42 S 35 19 E
Shiriya-Zaki **44** 41 25N 141 30 E
Shisur **47** 17 30N 54 0 E
Shivpuri **36** 25 26N 77 42 E
Shizuoka **44** 35 0N 138 24 E
Shizuoka □ **44** 35 15N 138 40 E
Shkodra **26** 42 6N 19 20 E
Shkumbini → **26** 41 5N 19 50 E
Shmidt, O. **31** 81 0N 91 0 E
Shoeburyness **5** 51 31N 0 49 E
Shologontsy **31** 66 13N 114 0 E
Shoshone **68** 43 0N 114 27W
Shoshone Mts. **68** 39 30N 117 30W
Shoshong **52** 22 56 S 26 31 E
Shreveport **67** 32 30N 93 50W
Shrewsbury **5** 52 42N 2 45W
Shrirampur **37** 22 44N 88 21 E
Shropshire □ **5** 52 36N 2 45W
Shumikha **30** 55 10N 63 15 E
Shurugwi **51** 19 40 S 30 0 E
Sialkot **36** 32 32N 74 30 E
Siam = Thailand ■ **41** 16 0N 102 0 E
Sian = Xi'an **43** 34 15N 109 0 E
Siauliai **32** 55 56N 23 15 E
Šibenik **21** 43 48N 15 54 E
Siberia **3** 60 0N 100 0 E
Siberut **39** 1 30 S 99 0 E
Sibi **36** 29 30N 67 54 E
Sibiti **51** 3 38 S 13 19 E
Sibiu **25** 45 45N 24 9 E
Sichuan □ **43** 31 0N 104 0 E
Sicilia **23** 37 30N 14 30 E
Sicily = Sicilia **23** 37 30N 14 30 E
Sicuani **72** 14 21 S 71 10W
Siddipet **38** 18 0N 78 51 E
Sidéradougou **49** 10 42N 4 12W
Sîdi Barrâni **50** 31 38N 25 58 E
Sidi-bel-Abbès **49** 35 13N 0 39W
Sidlaw Hills **6** 56 32N 3 10W
Sidmouth **5** 50 40N 3 13W
Sidney **64** 48 39N 123 24W
Sidon = Saydā **45** 33 35N 35 25 E
Sidra, G. of = Surt, Khalīj **50** 31 40N 18 30 E
Siedlce **17** 52 10N 22 20 E
Siegburg **13** 50 48N 7 12 E
Siegen **13** 50 52N 8 2 E
Siena **21** 43 20N 11 20 E
Sierck-les-Bains **9** 49 26N 6 20 E
Sierra Leone ■ **49** 9 0N 12 0W
Sífnos **26** 37 0N 24 45 E
Sigean **10** 43 2N 2 58 E
Sighetu-Marmatiei **15** 47 57N 23 52 E
Sighişoara **25** 46 12N 24 50 E
Siglufjörður **27** 66 12N 18 55W
Signy-l'Abbaye **9** 49 40N 4 25 E
Sigtuna **28** 59 36N 17 44 E
Sigüenza **19** 41 3N 2 40W
Siguiri **49** 11 31N 9 10W
Sihanoukville = Kompong Som **41** 10 38N 103 30 E
Siirt **45** 37 57N 41 55 E
Sikar **36** 27 33N 75 10 E
Sikasso **49** 11 18N 5 35W
Sikeston **67** 36 52N 89 35W
Sikhote Alin, Khrebet **31** 46 0N 136 0 E
Síkinos **26** 36 40N 25 8 E
Sikkim □ **37** 27 50N 88 30 E
Sil → **18** 42 27N 7 43W
Silgarhi Doti **37** 29 15N 81 0 E
Siling Co **42** 31 50N 89 20 E
Silistra **25** 44 6N 27 19 E
Siljan **28** 60 55N 14 45 E
Silkeborg **28** 56 10N 9 32 E
Sillé-le-Guillaume **8** 48 10N 0 8W
Simcoe **62** 42 50N 80 20W
Simenga **31** 62 42N 108 25 E
Simeulue **39** 2 45N 95 45 E
Simferopol **34** 44 55N 34 3 E
Simi Valley **68** 34 16N 118 47W
Simikot **37** 30 0N 81 50 E
Simla **36** 31 2N 77 9 E
Simojärvi **27** 66 5N 27 3 E
Simojoki → **27** 65 35N 25 1 E
Simplon Pass **13** 46 15N 8 0 E
Simpson Desert **55** 25 0 S 137 0 E
Simushir, Ostrov **31** 46 50N 152 30 E
Sinadogo **47** 5 50N 47 0 E
Sinai = Es Sînâ' **50** 29 0N 34 0 E
Sinaloa □ **69** 25 0N 107 30W
Sinaloa de Levya **69** 25 50N 108 20W
Sīnāwan **49** 31 0N 10 37 E
Sincelejo **72** 9 18N 75 24W
Sinclair Mills **64** 54 5N 121 40W
Sind □ **36** 26 0N 69 0 E
Sind Sagar Doab **36** 32 0N 71 30 E
Sines **18** 37 56N 8 51W
Singa **50** 13 10N 33 57 E
Singapore ■ **41** 1 17N 103 51 E
Singapore, Straits of **41** 1 15N 104 0 E
Singen **13** 47 45N 8 50 E
Singida **51** 4 49 S 34 48 E
Singitikós Kólpos **26** 40 6N 24 0 E
Singleton **56** 32 33 S 151 0 E
Singleton, Mt. **54** 29 27 S 117 15 E
Sinkat **50** 18 55N 36 49 E
Sinni → **23** 40 9N 16 42 E
Sinnuris **50** 29 26N 30 31 E
Sinskoye **31** 61 8N 126 48 E
Sint Niklaas **12** 51 10N 4 9 E
Sint Truiden **12** 50 48N 5 10 E
Sintra **18** 38 47N 9 25W
Sinŭiju **43** 40 5N 124 24 E
Sioma **52** 16 25 S 23 28 E
Sion **13** 46 14N 7 20 E
Sioux City **67** 42 32N 96 25W
Sioux Falls **67** 43 35N 96 40W
Sioux Lookout **65** 50 10N 91 50W
Siping **42** 43 8N 124 21 E
Sipora **39** 2 18 S 99 40 E
Sir Edward Pellew Group **55** 15 40 S 137 10 E
Siracusa **23** 37 4N 15 17 E
Sirajganj **37** 24 25N 89 47 E
Siret → **15** 47 58N 26 5 E
Sirohi **36** 24 52N 72 53 E
Sironj **36** 24 5N 77 39 E
Síros **26** 37 28N 24 57 E
Sirsa **36** 29 33N 75 4 E
Sisak **21** 45 30N 16 21 E
Sissonne **9** 49 34N 3 51 E
Sisteron **11** 44 12N 5 57 E
Sitapur **37** 27 38N 80 45 E
Sitges **19** 41 17N 1 47 E
Sittard **12** 51 0N 5 52 E
Siuri **37** 23 50N 87 34 E
Sivas **45** 39 43N 36 58 E
Siverek **45** 37 50N 39 19 E
Sivrihisar **45** 39 30N 31 35 E
Sîwa **50** 29 11N 25 31 E
Siwalik Range **37** 28 0N 83 0 E
Siwan **37** 26 13N 84 21 E
Sizewell **5** 52 13N 1 38 E
Sjælland **28** 55 30N 11 30 E
Skagafjörður **27** 65 54N 19 35W
Skagerrak **28** 57 30N 9 0 E
Skagway **64** 59 23N 135 20W
Skaidi **27** 70 26N 24 30 E
Skara **28** 58 25N 13 30 E
Skaraborgs län □ **28** 58 20N 13 30 E
Skeena → **64** 54 9N 130 5W
Skegness **5** 53 9N 0 20 E
Skellefte älv → **27** 64 45N 21 10 E
Skellefteå **27** 64 45N 20 58 E
Skelleftehamn **27** 64 47N 20 59 E
Skerries, The **5** 53 27N 4 40W
Skibbereen **7** 51 33N 9 16W
Skiddaw **5** 54 39N 3 9W
Skien **28** 59 12N 9 35 E
Skierniewice **17** 51 58N 20 10 E
Skikda **49** 36 50N 6 58 E
Skipton **5** 53 57N 2 1W
Skíros **26** 38 55N 24 34 E
Skive **28** 56 33N 9 2 E
Skjálfandafljót → **27** 65 59N 17 25W
Skjálfandi **27** 66 5N 17 30W
Skoghall **28** 59 20N 13 30 E
Skopje **24** 42 1N 21 32 E
Skovorodino **31** 54 0N 125 0 E
Skowhegan **63** 44 49N 69 40W
Skull **7** 51 32N 9 40W
Skwierzyna **17** 52 33N 15 30 E
Skye **6** 57 15N 6 10W
Slaney → **7** 52 52N 6 45W
Slatina **25** 44 28N 24 22 E
Slave → **64** 61 18N 113 39W
Slavkov **15** 49 10N 16 52 E
Slavyansk **34** 48 55N 37 36 E
Sleaford **5** 53 0N 0 22W
Sleat, Sd. of **6** 57 5N 5 47W
Sliedrecht **12** 51 50N 4 45 E
Slieve Aughty **7** 53 4N 8 30W
Slieve Bloom **7** 53 4N 7 40W
Slieve Donard **7** 54 10N 5 57W
Slieve Gullion **7** 54 8N 6 26W
Slieve Mish **7** 52 12N 9 50W
Slievenamon **7** 52 25N 7 37W
Sligo **7** 54 17N 8 28W
Sligo □ **7** 54 10N 8 35W
Sligo B. **7** 54 20N 8 40W
Sliven **25** 42 42N 26 19 E
Slochteren **12** 53 12N 6 48 E
Slough **5** 51 30N 0 35W
Slovakia = Slovensko □ **15** 48 30N 19 0 E
Slovenija □ **21** 45 58N 14 30 E
Slovenské Rudohorie **15** 48 45N 20 0 E
Slovensko □ **15** 48 30N 19 0 E
Sluis **12** 51 18N 3 23 E
Slyne Hd. **7** 53 25N 10 10W
Slyudyanka **31** 51 40N 103 40 E
Smara **49** 32 9N 8 16W
Smederevo **24** 44 40N 20 57 E
Smidovich **31** 48 36N 133 49 E
Smith Sund **3** 78 30N 74 0W
Smithers **64** 54 45N 127 10W
Smithfield **66** 35 31N 78 16W
Smiths Falls **62** 44 55N 76 0W
Smoky → **64** 56 10N 117 21W
Smøla **27** 63 23N 8 3 E
Smolensk **32** 54 45N 32 0 E
Smolikas, Óros **26** 40 9N 20 58 E
Smolyan **25** 41 36N 24 38 E
Smyrna = İzmir **45** 38 25N 27 8 E
Snaefell **5** 54 18N 4 26W
Snæfellsjökull **27** 64 49N 23 46W
Snake → **68** 46 12N 119 2W
Snake River Plain **68** 43 13N 113 0W
Sneek **12** 53 2N 5 40 E
Snizort, L. **6** 57 33N 6 28W
Snøhetta **27** 62 19N 9 16 E
Snowdon **5** 53 4N 4 8W
Snowy → **56** 37 46 S 148 30 E
Snyder **67** 32 45N 100 57W
Soalala **53** 16 6 S 45 20 E
Sobat, Nahr → **50** 9 22N 31 33 E
Sobral **69** 3 50 S 40 20W
Sochi **35** 43 35N 39 40 E
Société, Is. de la **58** 17 0 S 151 0W
Society Is. = Société, Is. de la **58** 17 0 S 151 0W
Socotra **47** 12 30N 54 0 E
Söderhamn **28** 61 18N 17 10 E
Söderköping **28** 58 31N 16 20 E
Södermanlands län □ **28** 59 10N 16 30 E
Södertälje **28** 59 12N 17 39 E
Sodiri **50** 14 27N 29 0 E
Sodo **50** 7 0N 37 41 E
Soest, Germany **13** 51 34N 8 7 E
Soest, Neth. **12** 52 9N 5 19 E
Sofia = Sofiya **25** 42 45N 23 20 E
Sofia → **53** 15 27 S 47 23 E
Sofiiski **31** 52 15N 133 59 E
Sofiya **25** 42 45N 23 20 E
Sognefjorden **27** 61 10N 5 50 E
Sohâg **50** 26 33N 31 43 E
Soignies **12** 50 35N 4 5 E
Soissons **9** 49 25N 3 19 E
Sōja **44** 34 40N 133 45 E
Söke **45** 37 48N 27 28 E
Sokodé **49** 9 0N 1 11 E
Sokol **33** 59 30N 40 5 E
Sokółka **17** 53 25N 23 30 E
Sokolo **49** 14 53N 6 8W
Sokoto **49** 13 2N 5 16 E
Sol Iletsk **30** 51 10N 55 0 E
Solapur **38** 17 43N 75 56 E
Soledad, Colombia **72** 10 55N 74 46W
Soledad, Venezuela **72** 8 10N 63 34W
Solent, The **5** 50 45N 1 25W
Solenzara **11** 41 53N 9 23 E
Solesmes **9** 50 10N 3 30 E
Solfonn **27** 60 2N 6 57 E
Soligalich **33** 59 5N 42 10 E
Solikamsk **30** 59 38N 56 50 E
Solimões → = Amazonas → **72** 0 5 S 50 0W
Solingen **13** 51 10N 7 4 E
Sollefteå **27** 63 12N 17 20 E
Sóller **19** 39 46N 2 43 E
Sologne **9** 47 40N 1 45 E
Sololá **69** 14 49N 91 10 E
Solomon Is. ■ **57** 6 0 S 155 0 E
Solomon Sea **56** 7 0 S 150 0 E
Solothurn **13** 47 13N 7 32 E
Solţānābād **46** 36 29N 58 5 E
Soltau **13** 52 59N 9 50 E
Solunska Glava **24** 41 44N 21 31 E
Solway Firth **5** 54 45N 3 38W
Solwezi **51** 12 11 S 26 21 E
Somali Rep. ■ **47** 7 0N 47 0 E
Sombernon **9** 47 20N 4 40 E
Sombor **24** 45 46N 19 9 E
Sombrerete **69** 23 38N 103 39W
Somerset, Bermuda **70** 32 16N 64 55W
Somerset, U.S.A. **66** 37 5N 84 40W
Somerset □ **5** 51 9N 3 0W
Somerset East **52** 32 42 S 25 35 E
Somerset I. **3** 73 30N 93 0W
Someş → **15** 47 15N 23 45 E
Somme □ **9** 50 0N 2 20 E
Somme → **9** 50 11N 1 38 E
Somme, B. de la **8** 50 14N 1 33 E
Sommepy-Tahure **9** 49 15N 4 31 E
Sommesous **9** 48 44N 4 12 E
Sommières **11** 43 47N 4 6 E
Somport, Puerto de **19** 42 48N 0 31W
Sønderborg **28** 54 55N 9 49 E

Sonepur **36** 20 55N 83 50 E
Songea **51** 10 40 S 35 40 E
Songeons **9** 49 32N 1 50 E
Songkhla **41** 7 13N 100 37 E
Sonipat **36** 29 0N 77 5 E
Sonora □ **69** 29 20N 110 40W
Sonthofen **13** 47 31N 10 16 E
Soochow = Suzhou **43** 31 19N 120 38 E
Sopot **17** 54 27N 18 31 E
Sop's Arm **63** 49 46N 56 56W
Sør-Trøndelag fylke □ **27** 63 0N 10 0 E
Sorata **72** 15 50 S 68 40W
Sorel **62** 46 0N 73 10W
Sorgues **11** 44 1N 4 53 E
Soria **19** 41 43N 2 32W
Sorocaba **74** 23 31 S 47 27W
Soroti **51** 1 43N 33 35 E
Sørøya **27** 70 40N 22 30 E
Sørøysundet **27** 70 25N 23 0 E
Sorrento **23** 40 38N 14 23 E
Sorsele **27** 65 31N 17 30 E
Sorsogon **40** 13 0N 124 0 E
Sosnovka **31** 54 9N 109 35 E
Sosnowiec **17** 50 20N 19 10 E
Sospel **11** 43 52N 7 27 E
Sotteville-lès-Rouen **8** 49 24N 1 5 E
Souanké **51** 2 10N 14 3 E
Soúdhas, Kólpos **26** 35 25N 24 10 E
Souillac **10** 44 53N 1 29 E
Sŏul **43** 37 31N 126 58 E
Soulac-sur-Mer **10** 45 30N 1 7W
Soultz-sous-Forêts **9** 48 57N 7 52 E
Sources, Mt. aux **53** 28 45 S 28 50 E
Sourdeval **8** 48 43N 0 55W
Souris, Man., Canada **65** 49 40N 100 20W
Souris, P.E.I., Canada **63** 46 21N 62 15W
Sousse **50** 35 50N 10 38 E
Soustons **10** 43 45N 1 19W
Souterraine, La **10** 46 15N 1 30 E
South Africa, Rep. of ■ **51** 32 0 S 17 0 E
South Australia □ **54** 32 0 S 139 0 E
South Bend **66** 41 38N 86 20W
South Carolina □ **66** 33 45N 81 0W
South Charleston **66** 38 20N 81 40W
South China Sea **57** 10 0N 113 0 E
South Dakota □ **67** 45 0N 100 0W
South Downs **5** 50 53N 0 10W
South East C. **56** 43 40 S 146 50 E
South Esk → **6** 56 44N 3 3W
South Foreland **5** 51 7N 1 23 E
South Georgia **71** 54 30 S 37 0W
South Glamorgan □ **5** 51 30N 3 20W
South Haven **66** 42 22N 86 20W
South Horr **51** 2 12N 36 56 E
South I. **59** 44 0 S 170 0 E
South Korea ■ **43** 36 0N 128 0 E
South Molton **5** 51 1N 3 50W
South Nahanni → **64** 61 3N 123 21W
South Orkney Is. **60** 63 0 S 45 0W
South Passage **54** 26 7 S 113 9 E
South Platte → **67** 41 7N 100 42W
South Porcupine **62** 48 30N 81 12W
South Ronaldsay **6** 58 46N 2 58W
South Sandwich Is. **1** 57 0 S 27 0W
South Sentinel I. **41** 11 1N 92 16 E
South Shetland Is. **60** 62 0 S 59 0W
South Shields **5** 54 59N 1 26W
South Tyne → **5** 54 46N 2 25W
South Uist **6** 57 20N 7 15W
South West Africa = Namibia ■ **52** 22 0 S 18 9 E
South West Cape **59** 47 16 S 167 31 E
South Yemen ■ **47** 15 0N 48 0 E
South Yorkshire □ **5** 53 30N 1 20W
Southampton **5** 50 54N 1 23W
Southampton I. **3** 64 30N 84 0W
Southend-on-Sea **5** 51 32N 0 42 E
Southern Alps **59** 43 41 S 170 11 E
Southern Cross **54** 31 12 S 119 15 E
Southern Ocean **2** 62 0 S 60 0 E
Southern Uplands **6** 55 30N 3 3W
Southport, Australia **56** 27 58 S 153 25 E
Southport, U.K. **5** 53 38N 3 1W
Southwold **5** 52 19N 1 41 E
Soutpansberg **53** 23 0 S 29 30 E
Souvigny **10** 46 33N 3 10 E
Sovetsk, Lithuania, U.S.S.R. **32** 55 6N 21 50 E
Sovetsk, R.S.F.S.R., U.S.S.R. **33** 57 38N 48 53 E
Sovetskaya Gavan **31** 48 50N 140 0 E
Soviet Union ■ = Union of Soviet Socialist Republics ■ **31** 60 0N 100 0 E
Sōya-Misaki **44** 45 30N 142 0 E
Soyo **51** 6 8 S 12 11 E
Sozh → **32** 51 57N 30 48 E
Spa **12** 50 29N 5 53 E
Spain ■ **4** 40 0N 5 0W
Spalding **5** 52 47N 0 9W
Spandau **13** 52 35N 13 7 E
Spanish Town **70** 18 0N 76 57W
Sparks **68** 39 30N 119 45W
Sparta = Spárti **26** 37 5N 22 25 E
Sparta **67** 43 55N 90 47W
Spartanburg **66** 35 0N 82 0W
Spárti **26** 37 5N 22 25 E
Spartivento, C., Calabria, Italy **23** 37 56N 16 4 E
Spartivento, C., Sard., Italy **22** 38 52N 8 50 E
Spassk-Dalniy **31** 44 40N 132 48 E
Spátha, Akra **26** 35 42N 23 43 E
Speightstown **70** 13 15N 59 39W
Spencer **67** 43 5N 95 19W
Spencer, C. **56** 35 20 S 136 53 E
Spencer G. **56** 34 0 S 137 20 E
Sperrin Mts. **7** 54 50N 7 0W
Spessart **13** 50 10N 9 20 E
Spey → **6** 57 26N 3 25W
Speyer **13** 49 19N 8 26 E
Spézia, La **20** 44 8N 9 50 E
Spinazzola **23** 40 58N 16 5 E
Spithead **5** 50 43N 1 5W
Spitzbergen = Svalbard **3** 78 0N 17 0 E
Split **21** 43 31N 16 26 E
Splügenpass **13** 46 30N 9 20 E
Spokane **68** 47 45N 117 25W
Spoleto **21** 42 46N 12 47 E
Sporyy Navolok, Mys **30** 75 50N 68 40 E
Spratly, I. **39** 8 20N 112 0 E
Spree → **13** 52 32N 13 13 E
Spring Mts. **68** 36 20N 115 43W
Springbok **52** 29 42 S 17 54 E
Springfield, Ill., U.S.A. **67** 39 48N 89 40W
Springfield, Mass., U.S.A. **66** 42 8N 72 37W
Springfield, Mo., U.S.A. **67** 37 15N 93 20W
Springfield, Ohio, U.S.A. **66** 39 58N 83 48W
Springfield, Oreg., U.S.A. **68** 44 2N 123 0W
Springfield, Tenn., U.S.A. **66** 36 35N 86 55W
Springfield, Vt., U.S.A. **66** 43 20N 72 30W
Springfontein **52** 30 15 S 25 40 E
Springhill **63** 45 40N 64 4W
Springs **53** 26 13 S 28 25 E
Springsure **56** 24 8 S 148 6 E
Spurn Hd. **5** 53 34N 0 8 E
Squamish **64** 49 45N 123 10W
Srbija □ **24** 43 30N 21 0 E
Sredinnyy Khrebet **31** 57 0N 160 0 E
Sredne Tambovskoye **31** 50 55N 137 45 E
Srednekolymsk **31** 67 27N 153 40 E
Srednevilyuysk **31** 63 50N 123 5 E
Srepok → **41** 13 33N 106 16 E
Sretensk **31** 52 10N 117 40 E
Sri Lanka ■ **38** 7 30N 80 50 E
Srikakulam **38** 18 14N 83 58 E
Stade **13** 53 35N 9 31 E
Staðarhólskirkja **27** 65 23N 21 58W
Stadlandet **27** 62 10N 5 10 E
Stadskanaal **12** 53 4N 6 55 E
Stafafell **27** 64 25N 14 52W
Staffa **6** 56 26N 6 21W
Stafford **5** 52 49N 2 9W
Stafford □ **5** 52 53N 2 10W
Staines **5** 51 26N 0 30W
Stakhanov **35** 48 35N 38 40 E
Stalingrad = Volgograd **35** 48 40N 44 25 E
Stalybridge **5** 53 29N 2 4W
Stamford, U.K. **5** 52 39N 0 29W
Stamford, U.S.A. **66** 41 5N 73 30W
Stanke Dimitrov **24** 42 17N 23 9 E
Stanley, Canada **65** 55 24N 104 22W
Stanley, Falk. Is. **74** 51 40 S 59 51W
Stanovoy Khrebet **31** 55 0N 130 0 E
Stanthorpe **56** 28 36 S 151 59 E
Stara Planina **25** 43 15N 23 0 E
Stara Zagora **25** 42 26N 25 39 E
Staraya Russa **32** 57 58N 31 23 E
Starbuck I. **58** 5 37 S 155 55W
Staritsa **32** 56 33N 35 0 E
Starkville **66** 33 26N 88 48W
Starogard **17** 53 59N 18 30 E
Start Pt. **5** 50 13N 3 38W
Staryy Kheydzhan **31** 60 0N 144 50 E
State College **66** 40 47N 77 49W
Staten, I. = Estados, I. de Los **74** 54 40 S 64 30W
Statesboro **66** 32 26N 81 46W
Statesville **66** 35 48N 80 51W
Staunton **66** 38 7N 79 4W
Stavanger **27** 58 57N 5 40 E
Stavelot **12** 50 23N 5 55 E
Staveren **12** 52 53N 5 22 E
Stavern **28** 59 0N 10 1 E
Stavropol **35** 45 5N 42 0 E
Stawell **56** 37 5 S 142 47 E
Steenvoorde **9** 50 48N 2 33 E
Steenwijk **12** 52 47N 6 7 E
Steep Pt. **54** 26 8 S 113 8 E
Stefanie L. = Chew Bahir **50** 4 40N 36 50 E
Steiermark □ **14** 47 26N 15 0 E
Steigerwald **13** 49 45N 10 30 E
Steinbach **65** 49 32N 96 40W
Steinfort **12** 49 39N 5 55 E
Steinhuder Meer **13** 52 48N 9 20 E
Steinkjer **27** 63 59N 11 31 E
Stellarton **63** 45 32N 62 30W
Stellenbosch **52** 33 58 S 18 50 E
Stendal **13** 52 36N 11 50 E
Stensele **27** 65 3N 17 8 E
Stephenville **63** 48 31N 58 35W
Sterling **67** 41 45N 89 45W
Sterlitamak **30** 53 40N 56 0 E
Stettin = Szczecin **17** 53 27N 14 27 E
Stettler **64** 52 19N 112 40W
Steubenville **66** 40 21N 80 39W
Stevens Port **67** 44 32N 89 34W
Stewart **64** 55 56N 129 57W
Stewart I. **59** 46 58 S 167 54 E
Steyr **14** 48 3N 14 25 E
Stikine → **64** 56 40N 132 30W
Stillwater, Minn., U.S.A. **67** 45 3N 92 47W
Stillwater, Okla., U.S.A. **67** 36 5N 97 3W
Stillwater Ra. **68** 39 45N 118 6W
Štip **24** 41 42N 22 10 E
Stirling **6** 56 7N 3 57W
Stirling Ra. **54** 34 23 S 118 0 E
Stockerau **15** 48 24N 16 12 E
Stockholm **28** 59 20N 18 3 E
Stockport **5** 53 25N 2 11W
Stockton **68** 38 0N 121 20W
Stockton-on-Tees **5** 54 34N 1 20W
Stoke-on-Trent **5** 53 1N 2 11W
Stokkseyri **27** 63 50N 21 2W
Stokksnes **27** 64 14N 14 58W
Stolac **24** 43 8N 17 59 E
Stolberg **13** 50 48N 6 13 E
Stolbovaya **31** 64 50N 153 50 E
Stolbovoy, Ostrov **31** 56 44N 163 14 E
Stonehaven **6** 56 58N 2 11W
Stonewall **65** 50 10N 97 19W
Stora Lulevatten **27** 67 10N 19 30 E
Stora Sjöfallet **27** 67 29N 18 40 E
Storavan **27** 65 45N 18 10 E
Store Bælt **28** 55 20N 11 0 E
Støren **27** 63 3N 10 18 E
Storm B. **56** 43 10 S 147 30 E
Storm Lake **67** 42 35N 95 11W
Stormberge **52** 31 16 S 26 17 E
Stornoway **6** 58 12N 6 23W
Storsjön **27** 62 50N 13 8 E
Storuman **27** 65 5N 17 10 E
Stour →, Dorset, U.K. **5** 50 48N 2 7W
Stour →, Hereford & Worcs., U.K. **5** 52 25N 2 13W
Stour →, Kent, U.K. **5** 51 15N 1 20 E
Stour →, Suffolk, U.K. **5** 51 55N 1 5 E
Stourbridge **5** 52 28N 2 8W
Stowmarket **5** 52 11N 1 0 E
Strabane **7** 54 50N 7 28W
Strabane □ **7** 54 45N 7 25W
Strahan **56** 42 9 S 145 20 E
Stralsund **13** 54 17N 13 5 E
Strand **52** 34 9 S 18 48 E
Strangford, L. **7** 54 30N 5 37W
Stranraer **6** 54 54N 5 0W
Strasbourg **9** 48 35N 7 42 E
Stratford **62** 43 23N 81 0W
Stratford-on-Avon **5** 52 12N 1 42W
Strath Spey **6** 57 15N 3 40W
Strathclyde □ **6** 56 0N 4 50W
Strathmore **6** 56 40N 3 4W
Strathpeffer **6** 57 35N 4 32W
Strathy Pt. **6** 58 35N 4 0W
Stratton **5** 51 41N 1 45W
Straumnes **27** 66 26N 23 8W
Streaky Bay **54** 32 48 S 134 13 E
Streator **66** 41 9N 88 52W
Strelka **31** 58 5N 93 3 E
Strickland → **56** 7 35 S 141 36 E
Strómboli **23** 38 48N 15 12 E
Stromeferry **6** 57 20N 5 33W
Stromness **6** 58 58N 3 18W
Ströms vattudal **27** 64 15N 14 55 E
Strömstad **28** 58 55N 11 15 E
Strömsund **27** 63 51N 15 33 E
Stronsay **6** 59 8N 2 38W
Stroud **5** 51 44N 2 12W
Struer **28** 56 30N 8 35 E
Strumica **24** 41 28N 22 41 E
Strzelecki Cr. → **56** 29 37 S 139 59 E
Stuart L. **64** 54 30N 124 30W
Stuart Range **54** 29 10 S 134 56 E
Stung Treng **41** 13 31N 105 58 E
Sturgeon Bay **66** 44 52N 87 20W
Sturgeon Falls **62** 46 25N 79 57W
Sturt Cr. → **54** 20 8 S 127 24 E
Stutterheim **52** 32 33 S 27 28 E
Stuttgart, Germany **13** 48 46N 9 10 E
Stuttgart, U.S.A. **67** 34 30N 91 33W
Stykkishólmur **27** 65 2N 22 40W
Suakin **50** 19 8N 37 20 E
Subotica **24** 46 6N 19 49 E
Suceava **15** 47 38N 26 16 E
Suchitoto **69** 13 56N 89 0W
Suck → **7** 53 17N 8 18W
Sucre **72** 19 0 S 65 15W
Sudan ■ **50** 15 0N 30 0 E
Sudbury, Canada **62** 46 30N 81 0W
Sudbury, U.K. **5** 52 2N 0 44 E
Sûdd **50** 8 20N 30 0 E
Sudetan Mts. = Sudety **15** 50 20N 16 45 E
Sudety **15** 50 20N 16 45 E
Sueca **19** 39 12N 0 21W
Suez = El Suweis **50** 29 58N 32 31 E
Suez, G. of = Suweis, Khalîg el **50** 28 40N 33 0 E
Suffolk **66** 36 47N 76 33W
Suffolk □ **5** 52 16N 1 0 E
Suhbaatar **42** 50 17N 106 10 E
Suippes **9** 49 8N 4 30 E
Suir → **7** 52 15N 7 10W
Sukhona → **30** 60 30N 45 0 E
Sukhumi **35** 43 0N 41 0 E
Sukkur **36** 27 42N 68 54 E
Sulaiman Range **36** 30 30N 69 50 E
Sulawesi □ **40** 2 0 S 120 0 E
Sulima **49** 6 58N 11 32W
Sulina **25** 45 10N 29 40 E
Sulitälma **27** 67 17N 17 28 E
Sulitjelma **27** 67 9N 16 3 E
Sullana **72** 4 52 S 80 39W
Sullivan **66** 39 5N 87 26W
Sully-sur-Loire **9** 47 45N 2 20 E
Sulphur Springs **67** 33 5N 95 36W
Sultanpur **37** 26 18N 82 4 E
Sulu Arch. **40** 6 0N 121 0 E
Sulu Sea **40** 8 0N 120 0 E
Suluq **50** 31 44N 20 14 E
Sulzbach **13** 49 18N 7 4 E
Sumatera □ **39** 0 40N 100 20 E
Sumba **40** 9 45 S 119 35 E
Sumbawa **39** 8 26 S 117 30 E
Sumbe **51** 11 10 S 13 48 E
Sumburgh Hd. **6** 59 52N 1 17W
Summerland **64** 49 32N 119 41W
Summerside **63** 46 24N 63 47W
Sumperk **15** 49 59N 17 0 E
Sumter **66** 33 55N 80 22W
Sumy **32** 50 57N 34 50 E
Sunart, L. **6** 56 42N 5 43W
Sunbury **66** 40 50N 76 46W
Sunda, Selat **39** 6 20 S 105 30 E
Sunda Is. **57** 5 0 S 105 0 E
Sundarbans, The **37** 22 0N 89 0 E
Sundargarh **36** 22 4N 84 5 E
Sunderland **5** 54 54N 1 22W
Sundsvall **27** 62 23N 17 17 E
Sungei Patani **41** 5 38N 100 29 E
Sungei Siput **41** 4 51N 101 6 E
Sungurlu **45** 40 12N 34 21 E
Sunnyside **68** 46 24N 120 2W
Sunnyvale **68** 37 23N 122 2W
Suntar **31** 62 15N 117 30 E
Supaul **37** 26 10N 86 40 E
Superior **67** 46 45N 92 5W
Superior, L. **62** 47 40N 87 0W
Suphan Dağı **45** 38 54N 42 48 E
Sūr **45** 22 34N 59 32 E
Sura → **33** 56 6N 46 0 E
Surabaya **40** 7 17 S 112 45 E
Surakarta **40** 7 35 S 110 48 E
Surat **36** 21 12N 72 55 E
Surat Thani **41** 9 6N 99 20 E
Suratgarh **36** 29 18N 73 55 E
Sûre → **12** 49 44N 6 31 E
Surgères **10** 46 7N 0 47W
Surgut **30** 61 14N 73 20 E
Suriapet **38** 17 10N 79 40 E
Surin **41** 14 50N 103 34 E
Surinam ■ **73** 4 0N 56 0W
Surrey □ **5** 51 16N 0 30W
Surt **50** 31 11N 16 39 E
Surt, Khalīj **50** 31 40N 18 30 E
Surtsey **27** 63 20N 20 30W
Suruga-Wan **44** 34 45N 138 30 E
Susa **20** 45 8N 7 3 E
Susanino **31** 52 50N 140 14 E
Susanville **68** 40 28N 120 40W
Susquehanna → **66** 39 33N 76 5W
Susuman **31** 62 47N 148 10 E
Sutherland Pt. **55** 28 15 S 153 35 E
Sutlej → **36** 29 23N 71 3 E
Sutton-in-Ashfield **5** 53 7N 1 20W
Suva **57** 18 6 S 178 30 E
Suva Planina **24** 43 10N 22 5 E
Suwałki **17** 54 8N 22 59 E
Suwannee → **66** 29 18N 83 9W
Suwanose-Jima **44** 29 38N 129 43 E
Suwarrow Is. **58** 15 0 S 163 0W
Suweis, Khalîg el **50** 28 40N 33 0 E
Suzdal **33** 56 29N 40 26 E
Suze-sur-Sarthe, La **8** 47 53N 0 2 E
Suzhou **43** 31 19N 120 38 E
Suzu-Misaki **44** 37 31N 137 21 E
Suzuka **44** 34 55N 136 36 E
Svalbard **3** 78 0N 17 0 E
Svalbarð **27** 66 12N 15 43W
Svanvik **27** 69 25N 30 3 E
Svappavaara **27** 67 40N 21 3 E
Svartisen **27** 66 40N 13 50 E
Svendborg **28** 55 4N 10 35 E
Sverdlovsk **30** 56 50N 60 30 E
Sverdrup Is. **3** 79 0N 97 0W
Svishtov **25** 43 36N 25 23 E
Svobodnyy **31** 51 20N 128 0 E
Svolvær **27** 68 15N 14 34 E
Swain Reefs **56** 21 45 S 152 20 E
Swakopmund **52** 22 37 S 14 30 E
Swale → **5** 54 5N 1 20W
Swan → **54** 32 3 S 115 45 E
Swan Hill **56** 35 20 S 143 33 E
Swan Hills **64** 54 42N 115 24W
Swan Is. **70** 17 22N 83 57W
Swan River **65** 52 10N 101 16W
Swanage **5** 50 36N 1 59W
Swansea **5** 51 37N 3 57W
Swaziland ■ **53** 26 30 S 31 30 E
Sweden ■ **27** 57 0N 15 0 E
Sweetwater **67** 32 30N 100 28W
Swellendam **52** 34 1 S 20 26 E
Świdnica **17** 50 50N 16 30 E
Świebodzin **17** 52 15N 15 31 E
Swift Current **65** 50 20N 107 45W
Swilly, L. **7** 55 12N 7 35W
Swindon **5** 51 33N 1 47W
Świnoujście **17** 53 54N 14 16 E
Switzerland ■ **13** 46 30N 8 0 E
Swords **7** 53 27N 6 15W
Sydney, Australia **56** 33 53 S 151 10 E
Sydney, Canada **63** 46 7N 60 7W
Sydney Mines **63** 46 18N 60 15W
Sydprøven **3** 60 30N 45 35W
Syktyvkar **30** 61 45N 50 40 E
Sylacauga **66** 33 10N 86 15W
Sylarna **27** 63 2N 12 13 E
Sylt **13** 54 50N 8 20 E
Sylvan Lake **64** 52 20N 114 3W
Syracuse **66** 43 4N 76 11W
Syrdarya → **30** 46 3N 61 0 E
Syria ■ **45** 35 0N 38 0 E
Syul'dzhyukyor **31** 63 14N 113 32 E
Syzran **33** 53 12N 48 30 E
Szczecin **17** 53 27N 14 27 E
Szczecinek **17** 53 43N 16 41 E
Szechwan = Sichuan □ **43** 31 0N 104 0 E
Szeged **15** 46 16N 20 10 E
Székesfehérvár **15** 47 15N 18 25 E
Szekszárd **15** 46 22N 18 42 E
Szentes **15** 46 39N 20 21 E
Szolnok **15** 47 10N 20 15 E
Szombathely **15** 47 14N 16 38 E

T

Tabacal **74** 23 15 S 64 15W
Tabar Is. **56** 2 50 S 152 0 E
Tabarka **49** 36 56N 8 46 E
Tabasco □ **69** 18 0N 92 40W
Taber **64** 49 47N 112 8W
Tablas **40** 12 25N 122 2 E
Table B. = Tafelbaai **52** 33 35 S 18 25 E
Table Mt. **52** 34 0 S 18 22 E
Tábor **14** 49 25N 14 39 E
Tabora **51** 5 2 S 32 50 E
Tabou **49** 4 30N 7 20W
Tabrīz **45** 38 7N 46 20 E
Tacna **72** 18 0 S 70 20W
Tacoma **68** 47 15N 122 30W
Tacuarembó **74** 31 45 S 56 0W
Tademaït, Plateau du **49** 28 30N 2 30 E
Tadjoura **47** 11 50N 42 55 E
Tadoussac **63** 48 11N 69 42W
Tadzhik S.S.R. □ **30** 35 30N 70 0 E
Taegu **43** 35 50N 128 37 E
Taejŏn **43** 36 20N 127 28 E
Tafalla **19** 42 30N 1 41W
Tafelbaai **52** 33 35 S 18 25 E
Taga Dzong **37** 27 5N 89 55 E
Taganrog **35** 47 12N 38 50 E
Tagish **64** 60 19N 134 16W
Tagliamento → **21** 45 38N 13 5 E
Tagua, La **72** 0 3N 74 40W
Tagula I. **56** 11 30 S 153 30 E
Tagus = Tajo → **18** 38 40N 9 24W
Tahat **49** 23 18N 5 33 E
Tahiti **58** 17 37 S 149 27W
Tahoe, L. **68** 39 0N 120 9W
Tahoua **49** 14 57N 5 16 E
Tahta **50** 26 44N 31 32 E
Taï **49** 5 55N 7 30W
Taibei **43** 25 4N 121 29 E
Taidong **43** 22 43N 121 9 E
Tailfingen **13** 48 15N 9 1 E
Taimyr, Oz. **31** 74 20N 102 0 E
Tain **6** 57 49N 4 4W
Tainan **43** 23 17N 120 18 E
Taínaron, Ákra **26** 36 22N 22 27 E
T'aipei = Taibei **43** 25 4N 121 29 E
Taiping **41** 4 51N 100 44 E
Taitao, Pen. de **74** 46 30 S 75 0W
Taivalkoski **27** 65 33N 28 12 E
Taiwan ■ **43** 23 30N 121 0 E
Taïyetos Óros **26** 37 0N 22 23 E
Taiyuan **42** 37 52N 112 33 E
Taizhong **43** 24 12N 120 35 E
Ta'izz **47** 13 35N 44 2 E
Tajo → **18** 38 40N 9 24W
Tājūrā **50** 32 51N 13 21 E
Tak **41** 16 52N 99 8 E
Takada **44** 37 7N 138 15 E
Takamatsu **44** 34 20N 134 5 E
Takanabe **44** 32 8N 131 30 E
Takaoka **44** 36 47N 137 0 E
Takasaki **44** 36 20N 139 0 E
Takatsuki **44** 34 51N 135 37 E
Takaungu **51** 3 38 S 39 52 E
Takayama **44** 36 18N 137 11 E
Takefu **44** 35 50N 136 10 E
Takhār □ **46** 36 40N 70 0 E
Takla Landing **64** 55 30N 125 50W
Takum **49** 7 18N 9 36 E
Talara **72** 4 38 S 81 18 E
Talas **30** 42 30N 72 13 E
Talaud, Kepulauan **40** 4 30N 127 10 E
Talavera de la Reina **18** 39 55N 4 46W
Talbert, Sillon de **8** 48 53N 3 5W
Talbot, C. **54** 13 48 S 126 43 E
Talca **74** 35 28 S 71 40W
Talcahuano **74** 36 40 S 73 10W
Talcher **36** 21 0N 85 18 E
Ţalesh, Kūhhā-ye **45** 39 0N 48 30 E
Tali Post **50** 5 55N 30 44 E
Taliabu **40** 1 45 S 125 0 E
Tall 'Afar **45** 36 22N 42 27 E
Talladega **66** 33 28N 86 2W
Tallahassee **66** 30 25N 84 15W
Tallering Pk. **54** 28 6 S 115 37 E
Tallinn **32** 59 22N 24 48 E
Tallulah **67** 32 25N 91 12W
Talmont **10** 46 27N 1 37W
Talodi **50** 10 35N 30 22 E
Tamale **49** 9 22N 0 50W
Tamano **44** 34 29N 133 59 E
Tamanrasset **49** 22 50N 5 30 E
Tamar → **5** 50 33N 4 15W
Tamaské **49** 14 49N 5 43 E
Tamaulipas □ **69** 24 0N 98 45W
Tambacounda **49** 13 45N 13 40W
Tambov **33** 52 45N 41 28 E
Tamburâ **50** 5 40N 27 25 E
Tâmchekket **49** 17 25N 10 40W
Tamega → **18** 41 5N 8 21W
Tamgak, Mts. **49** 19 12N 8 35 E
Tamil Nadu □ **38** 11 0N 77 0 E
Tammisaari **27** 60 0N 23 26 E
Tamo Abu, Pegunungan **39** 3 10N 115 0 E
Tampa **66** 27 57N 82 38W
Tampa B. **66** 27 40N 82 40W
Tampere **27** 61 30N 23 50 E
Tampico **69** 22 20N 97 50W
Tamworth, Australia **56** 31 7 S 150 58 E
Tamworth, U.K. **5** 52 38N 1 41W
Tana **27** 70 26N 28 14 E
Tana →, Kenya **51** 2 32 S 40 31 E
Tana →, Norway **27** 70 30N 28 23 E
Tana, L. **50** 13 5N 37 30 E
Tanafjorden **27** 70 45N 28 25 E
Tanami Desert **54** 18 50 S 132 0 E
Tananarive = Antananarivo **53** 18 55 S 47 31 E
Tánaro → **20** 45 1N 8 47 E
Tancarville **8** 49 29N 0 28 E
Tandil **74** 37 15 S 59 6W
Tando Adam **36** 25 45N 68 40 E
Tane-ga-Shima **44** 30 30N 131 0 E
Tanezrouft **49** 23 9N 0 11 E
Tanga **51** 5 5 S 39 2 E
Tanga Is. **56** 3 20 S 153 15 E
Tanganyika, L. **51** 6 40 S 30 0 E
Tanger **49** 35 50N 5 49W
Tanggula Shan **42** 32 40N 92 10 E
Tangier = Tanger **49** 35 50N 5 49W
Tangshan **42** 39 38N 118 10 E
Tanimbar, Kepulauan **40** 7 30 S 131 30 E
Taninges **11** 46 7N 6 36 E
Tannu-Ola **31** 51 0N 94 0 E
Tanout **49** 14 50N 8 55 E
Tanta **50** 30 45N 30 57 E
Tanus **10** 44 8N 2 19 E
Tanzania ■ **51** 6 40 S 34 0 E
Taoudenni **49** 22 40N 3 55W
Taourirt **49** 34 25N 2 53W
Tapachula **69** 14 54N 92 17W

Tapajós → 73 2 24 S 54 41W
Tapeta 49 6 29N 8 52W
Tapi → 36 21 8N 72 41 E
Tara →, U.S.S.R. 30 56 42N 74 36 E
Tara →, Yugoslavia 24 43 21N 18 51 E
Tarabagatay, Khrebet 30 48 0N 83 0 E
Tarābulus, Lebanon 45 34 31N 35 50 E
Tarābulus, Libya 50 32 49N 13 7 E
Taranga Hill 36 24 0N 72 40 E
Táranto 23 40 30N 17 11 E
Táranto, G. di 23 40 0N 17 15 E
Tarapoto 72 6 30 S 76 20W
Tarare 11 45 54N 4 26 E
Tarascon 11 43 48N 4 39 E
Tarascon-sur-Ariège 10 42 50N 1 36 E
Tarauacá 72 8 6 S 70 48W
Taravo → 11 41 42N 8 49 E
Tarbat Ness 6 57 52N 3 48W
Tarbert, Strathclyde, U.K. 6 55 55N 5 25W
Tarbert, W. Isles, U.K. 6 57 54N 6 49W
Tarbes 10 43 15N 0 3 E
Tarcoola 54 30 44 S 134 36 E
Tardets-Sorholus 10 43 8N 0 52W
Tardoire → 10 45 52N 0 14 E
Taree 56 31 50 S 152 30 E
Tarentaise 11 45 30N 6 35 E
Tarfaya 49 27 55N 12 55W
Targon 10 44 44N 0 16W
Tarifa 18 36 1N 5 36W
Tarija 72 21 30 S 64 40W
Tarim Basin = Tarim Pendi 42 40 0N 84 0 E
Tarim Pendi 42 40 0N 84 0 E
Tarkhankut, Mys 34 45 25N 32 30 E
Tarko Sale 30 64 55N 77 50 E
Tarkwa 49 5 20N 2 0W
Tarn □ 10 43 49N 2 8 E
Tarn → 10 44 5N 1 6 E
Tarn-et-Garonne □ 10 44 8N 1 20 E
Tarnów 15 50 3N 21 0 E
Tarnowskie Góry 17 50 27N 18 54 E
Taroom 56 25 36 S 149 48 E
Taroudannt 49 30 30N 8 52W
Tarragona 19 41 5N 1 17 E
Tarrasa 19 41 34N 2 1 E
Tarso Emissi 50 21 27N 18 36 E
Tarsus 45 36 58N 34 55 E
Tartagal 74 22 30 S 63 50W
Tartas 10 43 50N 0 49W
Tartu 32 58 20N 26 44 E
Tarṭūs 45 34 55N 35 55 E
Tarutao, Ko 41 6 33N 99 40 E
Tasāwah 50 26 0N 13 30 E
Taschereau 62 48 40N 78 40W
Tash-Kumyr 30 41 40N 72 10 E
Tashkent 30 41 20N 69 10 E
Tåsjön 27 64 15N 16 0 E
Taskan 31 62 59N 150 20 E
Tasman Pen. 56 43 10 S 148 0 E
Tasman Sea 57 36 0 S 160 0 E
Tasmania □ 56 42 0 S 146 30 E
Tatar A.S.S.R. □ 30 55 30N 51 30 E
Tatarsk 30 55 14N 76 0 E
Tateyama 44 35 0N 139 50 E
Tatry 15 49 20N 20 0 E
Tatta 36 24 42N 67 55 E
Taubaté 74 23 0 S 45 36W
Tauern 14 47 15N 12 40 E
Taunton, U.K. 5 51 1N 3 7W
Taunton, U.S.A. 66 41 54N 71 6W
Taunus 13 50 15N 8 20 E
Taupo, L. 59 38 46 S 175 55 E
Taurianova 23 38 22N 16 1 E
Taurus Mts. = Toros Dagları 45 37 0N 35 0 E
Tavda 30 58 7N 65 8 E
Tavda → 30 59 20N 63 28 E
Taverny 9 49 2N 2 13 E
Taveta 51 3 23 S 37 37 E
Tavignano → 11 42 7N 9 33 E
Tavira 18 37 8N 7 40W
Tavistock 5 50 33N 4 9W
Tavoy 41 14 2N 98 12 E
Taw → 5 17 37 S 177 55 E
Tawas City 66 44 16N 83 31W
Tay → 6 56 37N 3 38W
Tay, Firth of 6 56 25N 3 8W
Tay, L. 6 56 30N 4 10W
Tayabamba 72 8 15 S 77 16W
Taymyr, Poluostrov 31 75 0N 100 0 E
Tayport 6 56 27N 2 52W
Tayshet 31 55 58N 98 1 E
Tayside □ 6 56 25N 3 30W
Taz → 30 67 32N 78 40 E
Taza 49 34 16N 4 6W
Tbilisi 35 41 43N 44 50 E
Tchad = Chad ■ 50 15 0N 17 15 E
Tchad, L. 50 13 30N 14 30 E
Tchibanga 51 2 45 S 11 0 E
Te Anau, L. 59 45 15 S 167 45 E
Tébessa 49 35 22N 8 8 E
Tech → 10 42 36N 3 3 E
Tecuala 69 22 23N 105 27W
Tecuci 25 45 51N 27 27 E
Tees → 5 54 36N 1 25W
Teesside 5 54 37N 1 13W
Tefé 72 3 25 S 64 50W
Tegal 40 6 52 S 109 8 E
Tegelen 12 51 20N 6 9 E
Tegid, L. 5 52 53N 3 38W
Tegina 49 10 5N 6 11 E
Tegucigalpa 70 14 5N 87 14W
Tehachapi 68 35 11N 118 29W
Tehachapi Mts. 68 35 0N 118 40W
Tehrān 46 35 44N 51 30 E
Tehuacán 69 18 27N 97 23W
Tehuantepec 69 16 21N 95 13W
Tehuantepec, G. de 69 16 0N 94 50W
Tehuantepec, Istmo de 69 17 0N 94 30W
Teifi → 5 52 4N 4 14W
Teign → 5 50 41N 3 42W
Teignmouth 5 50 33N 3 30W
Teil, Le 11 44 33N 4 40 E
Teilleul, Le 8 48 32N 0 53W
Tejo → 18 38 40N 9 24W
Tekax 69 20 12N 89 17W
Tekeli 30 44 50N 79 0 E
Tekirdağ 45 40 58N 27 30 E
Tekkali 38 18 37N 84 15 E
Tel Aviv-Yafo 45 32 4N 34 48 E
Tela 70 15 40N 87 28W
Telavi 35 42 0N 45 30 E
Telegraph Cr. → 64 58 0N 131 10W
Telemark fylke □ 28 59 25N 8 30 E
Teles Pires → 72 7 21 S 58 3W
Telford 5 52 42N 2 31W
Télimélé 49 10 54N 13 2W
Tell City 66 38 0N 86 44W
Tellicherry 38 11 45N 75 30 E
Tema 49 5 41N 0 0 E
Teme → 5 52 23N 2 15W
Temerloh 41 3 27N 102 25 E
Temirtau 30 50 5N 72 56 E
Temosachic 69 28 57N 107 51W
Tempe 68 33 26N 111 59W
Temple 67 31 5N 97 22W
Temple B. 56 12 15 S 143 3 E
Templemore 7 52 48N 7 50W
Temuco 74 38 45 S 72 40W
Tenali 38 16 15N 80 35 E
Tenancingo 69 19 0N 99 33W
Tenango 69 19 7N 99 33W
Tenay 11 45 55N 5 31 E
Tenby 5 51 40N 4 42W
Tenda, Col di 11 44 7N 7 36 E
Tendaho 47 11 48N 40 54 E
Tende 11 44 5N 7 35 E
Tenerife 49 28 15N 16 35W
Teng Xian 43 35 5N 117 10 E
Tenkasi 38 8 55N 77 20 E
Tenke 51 10 32 S 26 7 E
Tenkodogo 49 11 54N 0 19W
Tennant Creek 54 19 30 S 134 15 E
Tennessee □ 66 36 0N 86 30W
Tennessee → 66 37 4N 88 34W
Tenryū-Gawa → 44 35 39N 137 48 E
Tenterfield 56 29 0 S 152 0 E
Teófilo Otoni 73 17 50 S 41 30W
Tepic 69 21 30N 104 54W
Teplice 14 50 40N 13 48 E
Ter → 19 42 0N 3 12 E
Ter Apel 12 52 53N 7 5 E
Téra 49 14 0N 0 45 E
Teraina, I. 58 4 43N 160 25W
Téramo 21 42 40N 13 40 E
Terek → 34 44 0N 47 30 E
Terengganu □ 41 4 55N 103 0 E
Teresina 73 5 9 S 42 45W
Tergnier 9 49 40N 3 17 E
Terhazza 49 23 38N 5 22W
Termez 30 37 15N 67 15 E
Términos, L. de 69 18 37N 91 33W
Térmoli 21 42 0N 15 0 E
Terneuzen 12 51 20N 3 50 E
Terney 31 45 3N 136 37 E
Terni 21 42 34N 12 38 E
Terrace 64 54 30N 128 35W
Terracina 22 41 17N 13 12 E
Terralba 22 39 42N 8 38 E
Terrasson-la-Villedieu 10 45 8N 1 18 E
Terre Haute 66 39 28N 87 24W
Terrell 67 32 44N 96 19W
Territoire de Belfort □ 9 47 40N 6 55 E
Terschelling 12 53 25N 5 20 E
Teruel 19 40 22N 1 8W
Tervola 27 66 6N 24 49 E
Tešanj 24 44 38N 17 59 E
Teshio-Gawa → 44 44 53N 141 45 E
Teslin 64 60 10N 132 43W
Tessalit 49 20 12N 1 0 E
Tessaoua 49 13 47N 7 56 E
Test → 5 51 7N 1 30W
Teste, La 10 44 37N 1 8W
Têt → 10 42 44N 3 2 E
Tete 51 16 13 S 33 33 E
Teteven 25 42 58N 24 17 E
Tétouan 49 35 35N 5 21W
Tetovo 24 42 1N 21 2 E
Teuco → 74 25 35 S 60 11W
Tevere → 21 41 44N 12 14 E
Teviot → 6 55 21N 2 51W
Tewkesbury 5 51 59N 2 8W
Texarkana, Ark., U.S.A. 67 33 25N 94 0W
Texarkana, Tex., U.S.A. 67 33 25N 94 3W
Texas □ 67 31 40N 98 30W
Texas City 67 29 20N 94 55W
Texel 12 53 5N 4 50 E
Teziutlán 69 19 49N 97 21W
Thabana Ntlenyana 53 29 30 S 29 16 E
Thabazimbi 53 24 40 S 27 21 E
Thailand ■ 41 16 0N 102 0 E
Thailand, G. of 41 11 30N 101 0 E
Thame → 5 51 35N 1 8W
Thames 59 37 7 S 175 34 E
Thames → 5 51 30N 0 35 E
Thane 38 19 12N 72 59 E
Thanet, I. of 5 51 21N 1 20 E
Thanh Hoa 41 19 48N 105 46 E
Thanh Pho Ho Chi Minh = Phanh Bho Ho Chi Minh 41 10 58N 106 40 E
Thanjavur 38 10 48N 79 12 E
Thann 9 47 48N 7 5 E
Thaon-les-Vosges 9 48 15N 6 24 E
Thar Desert 36 28 0N 72 0 E
Tharad 36 24 30N 71 44 E
Thargomindah 56 27 58 S 143 46 E
Thásos 26 40 40N 24 40 E
Thau, Bassin de 10 43 23N 3 36 E
The Dalles 68 45 40N 121 11W
The English Company's Is. 55 11 50 S 136 32 E
The Granites 54 20 35 S 130 21 E
The Grenadines, Is. 70 12 40N 61 20W
The Hague = 's-Gravenhage 12 52 7N 4 17 E
The Hamilton → 54 26 40 S 135 19 E
The Macumba → 55 27 52 S 137 12 E
The Pas 65 53 45N 101 15W
Thebes = Thívai 26 38 19N 23 19 E
Theil, Le 8 48 16N 0 42 E
Thénezay 8 46 44N 0 2W
Thenon 10 45 9N 1 4 E
Theodore 55 24 55 S 150 3 E
Thérain → 9 49 15N 2 27 E
Thermaïkos Kólpos 26 40 15N 22 45 E
Thermopylae P. 26 38 48N 22 35 E
Thessalía □ 26 39 30N 22 0 E
Thessalon 62 46 20N 83 30W
Thessaloníki 26 40 38N 22 58 E
Thessaloniki, Gulf of = Thermaïkos Kólpos 26 40 15N 22 45 E
Thetford 5 52 25N 0 44 E
Thetford Mines 63 46 8N 71 18W
Thiberville 8 49 8N 0 27 E
Thicket Portage 65 55 19N 97 42W
Thiérache 9 49 51N 3 45 E
Thiers 10 45 52N 3 33 E
Thies 49 14 50N 16 51W
Thika 51 1 1 S 37 5 E
Thillot, Le 9 47 53N 6 46 E
Thimphu 37 27 31N 89 45 E
þingvallavatn 27 64 11N 21 9W
Thionville 9 49 20N 6 10 E
Thíra 26 36 23N 25 27 E
Thirsk 5 54 15N 1 20W
Thistle I. 54 35 0 S 136 8 E
Thívai 26 38 19N 23 19 E
Thiviers 10 45 25N 0 54 E
Thizy 11 46 2N 4 18 E
þjórsá → 27 63 47N 20 48W
Thoissey 11 46 12N 4 48 E
Thomaston 66 32 54N 84 20W
Thomasville, Ga., U.S.A. 66 30 50N 84 0W
Thomasville, N.C., U.S.A. 66 35 55N 80 4W
Thomson → 56 25 11 S 142 53 E
Thon Buri 41 13 43N 100 29 E
Thônes 11 45 54N 6 18 E
Thonon-les-Bains 11 46 22N 6 29 E
þórisvatn 27 64 20N 18 55W
þorlákshöfn 27 63 51N 21 22W
Thornaby on Tees 5 54 36N 1 19W
þórshöfn 27 66 12N 15 20W
Thouarcé 8 47 17N 0 30W
Thouars 8 46 58N 0 15W
Thrace = Thráki □ 26 41 9N 25 30 E
Thráki □ 26 41 9N 25 30 E
Three Hills 64 51 43N 113 15W
Three Points, C. 49 4 42N 2 6W
Throssell Ra. 54 22 3 S 121 43 E
Thueyts 11 44 41N 4 9 E
Thuin 12 50 20N 4 17 E
Thuir 10 42 38N 2 45 E
Thule 3 77 40N 69 0W
Thun 13 46 45N 7 38 E
Thunder B. 62 45 0N 83 20W
Thunder Bay 62 48 20N 89 15W
Thunkar 37 27 55N 91 0 E
Thüringer Wald 13 50 35N 11 0 E
Thurles 7 52 40N 7 53W
Thursday I. 55 10 30 S 142 3 E
Thurso 6 58 34N 3 31W
Thury-Harcourt 8 48 59N 0 30W
Tian Shan 42 43 0N 84 0 E
Tianjin 42 39 8N 117 10 E
Tianshui 43 34 32N 105 40 E
Tiaret 49 35 20N 1 21 E
Tiassalé 49 5 58N 4 57W
Tibati 50 6 22N 12 30 E
Tiber = Tevere → 21 41 44N 12 14 E
Tibesti 50 21 0N 17 30 E
Tibet = Xizang □ 42 32 0N 88 0 E
Tibooburra 55 29 26 S 142 1 E
Tichît 49 18 21N 9 29W
Ticino □ 13 46 20N 8 45 E
Ticino → 20 45 9N 9 14 E
Ticul 69 20 24N 89 32W
Tidjikja 49 18 29N 11 35W
Tiel, Neth. 12 51 53N 5 26 E
Tiel, Senegal 49 14 55N 15 5W
Tielt 12 51 0N 3 20 E
Tienen 12 50 48N 4 57 E
Tientsin = Tianjin 42 39 8N 117 10 E
Tierra de Campos 18 42 10N 4 50W
Tierra del Fuego, I. Gr. de 74 54 0 S 69 0W
Tiétar → 18 39 50N 6 1W
Tiffin 66 41 8N 83 10W
Tifton 66 31 28N 83 32W
Tigil 31 57 49N 158 40 E
Tignish 63 46 58N 64 2W
Tigris = Dijlah, Nahr → 45 31 0N 47 25 E
Tih, Gebel el 50 29 32N 33 26 E
Tijuana 69 32 32N 117 1W
Tikamgarh 36 24 44N 78 50 E
Tikhoretsk 35 45 56N 40 5 E
Tiksi 31 71 40N 128 45 E
Tilburg 12 51 31N 5 6 E
Tilbury 5 51 27N 0 24 E
Tilichiki 31 60 27N 166 5 E
Till → 5 55 35N 2 3W
Tillabéri 49 14 28N 1 28 E
Tillsonburg 62 42 53N 80 44W
Tílos 26 36 27N 27 27 E
Tilt → 6 56 50N 3 50W
Timaru 59 44 23 S 171 14 E
Timbedgha 49 16 17N 8 16W
Timbuktu = Tombouctou 49 16 50N 3 0W
Timimoun 49 29 14N 0 16 E
Timişoara 16 45 43N 21 15 E
Timmins 62 48 28N 81 25W
Timok → 24 44 10N 22 40 E
Timor 40 9 0 S 125 0 E
Timor Sea 55 10 0 S 127 0 E
Tinaca Pt. 40 5 30N 125 25 E
Tinchebray 8 48 47N 0 45W
Tindouf 49 27 42N 8 10W
Tinée → 11 43 55N 7 11 E
Tinjoub 49 29 45N 5 40W
Tinnoset 28 59 55N 9 3 E
Tinogasta 74 28 5 S 67 32W
Tínos 26 37 33N 25 8 E
Tioman, Pulau 41 2 50N 104 10 E
Tipperary 7 52 28N 8 10W
Tipperary □ 7 52 37N 7 55W
Tipton 5 52 32N 2 4W
Tirana 26 41 18N 19 49 E
Tiraspol 34 46 55N 29 35 E
Tire 45 38 5N 27 50 E
Tirebolu 45 40 58N 38 45 E
Tiree 6 56 31N 6 55W
Tîrgovişte 25 44 55N 25 27 E
Tîrgu-Jiu 25 45 5N 23 19 E
Tîrgu Mureş 25 46 31N 24 38 E
Tirodi 36 21 40N 79 44 E
Tirol □ 14 47 3N 10 43 E
Tirso → 22 39 52N 8 33 E
Tiruchchirappalli 38 10 45N 78 45 E
Tirunelveli 38 8 45N 77 45 E
Tirupati 38 13 45N 79 25 E
Tiruvannamalai 38 12 15N 79 5 E
Tisdale 65 52 50N 104 0W
Tisza → 15 46 8N 20 2 E
Tit-Ary 31 71 55N 127 2 E
Titicaca, L. 72 15 30 S 69 30W
Titograd 24 42 30N 19 19 E
Titov Veles 24 41 46N 21 47 E
Titovo Užice 24 43 55N 19 50 E
Titule 51 3 15N 25 31 E
Tivaouane 49 14 56N 16 45W
Tiverton 5 50 54N 3 30W
Tívoli 21 41 58N 12 45 E
Tizi-Ouzou 49 36 42N 4 3 E
Tizimín 69 21 9N 88 9W
Tiznit 49 29 48N 9 45W
Tjeggelvas 27 66 37N 17 45 E
Tlaxcala □ 69 19 25N 98 10W
Tlaxiaco 69 17 18N 97 40W
Tlemcen 49 34 52N 1 21W
Tmassah 50 26 19N 15 51 E
Toamasina 53 18 10 S 49 25 E
Toba 44 34 30N 136 51 E
Toba Kakar 36 31 30N 69 0 E
Tobago 70 11 10N 60 30W
Tobermory 6 56 37N 6 4W
Tobol 30 52 40N 62 39 E
Tobolsk 30 58 15N 68 10 E
Tocantins → 73 1 45 S 49 10W
Toccoa 66 34 32N 83 17W
Tochigi 44 36 25N 139 45 E
Tochigi □ 44 36 45N 139 45 E
Tocopilla 74 22 5 S 70 10W
Todenyang 51 4 35N 35 56 E
Todos Santos 69 23 27N 110 13W
Togba 49 17 26N 10 12W
Togliatti 33 53 32N 49 24 E
Togo ■ 49 8 30N 1 35 E
Toinya 50 6 17N 29 46 E
Tokaj 15 48 8N 21 27 E
Tokar 50 18 27N 37 56 E
Tokara Kaikyō 44 30 0N 130 0 E
Tokat 45 40 22N 36 35 E
Tokelau Is. 57 9 0 S 171 45W
Tokmak 30 42 49N 75 15 E
Tokushima 44 34 4N 134 34 E
Tokushima □ 44 34 15N 134 0 E
Tokuyama 44 34 3N 131 50 E
Tōkyō 44 35 45N 139 45 E
Tōkyō □ 44 35 40N 139 30 E
Tolbukhin 25 43 37N 27 49 E
Toledo, Spain 18 39 50N 4 2W
Toledo, U.S.A. 66 41 37N 83 33W
Toledo, Montes de 18 39 33N 4 20W
Tolga 49 34 40N 5 22 E
Toliara 53 23 21 S 43 40 E
Tolima, Vol. 72 4 40N 75 19W
Tolo 51 2 55 S 18 34 E
Tolosa 19 43 8N 2 5W
Toluca 69 19 20N 99 40W
Tom Price 54 22 40 S 117 48 E
Tomar 18 39 36N 8 25W
Tomaszów Mazowiecki 17 51 30N 19 57 E
Tombé 50 5 53N 31 40 E
Tombigbee → 66 31 4N 87 58W
Tombouctou 49 16 50N 3 0W
Tombua 52 15 55 S 11 55 E
Tomelloso 19 39 10N 3 2W
Tomini, Teluk 40 0 10 S 122 0 E
Tommot 31 59 4N 126 20 E
Tomnavoulin 6 57 19N 3 18W
Tomsk 30 56 30N 85 5 E
Tonalá 69 16 4N 93 45W
Tonantins 72 2 45 S 67 45W
Tonawanda 66 43 0N 78 54W
Tonbridge 5 51 12N 0 18 E
Tong Xian 42 39 55N 116 35 E
Tonga ■ 57 19 50 S 174 30W
Tonga Trench 57 18 0 S 175 0W
Tongareva 58 9 0 S 158 0W
Tongchuan 43 35 6N 109 3 E
Tongeren 12 50 47N 5 28 E
Tonghua 42 41 42N 125 58 E
Tongking, G. of 41 20 0N 108 0 E
Tongue 6 58 29N 4 25W
Tongue → 67 46 24N 105 52W
Tonk 36 26 6N 75 54 E
Tonlé Sap 41 13 0N 104 0 E
Tonnay-Charente 10 45 56N 0 55W
Tonneins 10 44 23N 0 19 E
Tonnerre 9 47 51N 3 59 E
Tonopah 68 38 4N 117 12W
Tønsberg 28 59 19N 10 25 E
Toora-Khem 31 52 28N 96 17 E
Toowoomba 56 27 32 S 151 56 E
Topeka 67 39 3N 95 40W
Toppenish 68 46 27N 120 16W
Tor Bay 54 35 5 S 117 50 E
Torbay 5 50 26N 3 31W
Tordesillas 18 41 30N 5 0W
Torey 31 50 33N 104 50 E
Torfajökull 27 63 54N 19 0W
Torhout 12 51 5N 3 7 E
Torigni-sur-Vire 8 49 3N 0 58W
Torino 20 45 4N 7 40 E
Torit 50 4 27N 32 31 E
Tormes → 18 41 18N 6 29W
Torne älv → 27 65 50N 24 12 E
Torneträsk 27 68 24N 19 15 E
Tornio 27 65 50N 24 12 E
Tornionjoki → 27 65 50N 24 12 E
Toro, Cerro del 74 29 10 S 69 50W
Toronîos Kólpos 26 40 5N 23 30 E
Toronto 62 43 39N 79 20W
Toropets 32 56 30N 31 40 E
Tororo 51 0 45N 34 12 E
Toros Dagları 45 37 0N 35 0 E
Torquay 5 50 27N 3 31W
Torre Annunziata 23 40 45N 14 26 E
Tôrre de Moncorvo 18 41 12N 7 8W
Torrelavega 18 43 20N 4 5W
Torremolinos 18 36 38N 4 30W
Torrens, L. 56 31 0 S 137 50 E
Torreón 69 25 33N 103 26W
Torres Strait 56 9 50 S 142 20 E
Torres Vedras 18 39 5N 9 15W
Torrevieja 19 37 59N 0 42W
Torridge → 5 50 51N 4 10W
Torridon, L. 6 57 35N 5 50W
Torrington 66 41 50N 73 9W
Tortosa 19 40 49N 0 31 E
Tortosa, C. 19 40 41N 0 52 E
Toruń 17 53 0N 18 39 E
Tory I. 7 55 17N 8 12W
Tosa-Wan 44 33 15N 133 30 E
Toscana 20 43 30N 11 5 E
Tostado 74 29 15 S 61 50W
Toteng 52 20 22 S 22 58 E
Tôtes 8 49 41N 1 3 E
Totma 33 60 0N 42 40 E
Totnes 5 50 26N 3 41W
Totonicapán 69 14 58N 91 12W
Tottori 44 35 30N 134 15 E
Tottori □ 44 35 30N 134 12 E
Touba 49 8 22N 7 40W
Toubkal, Djebel 49 31 0N 8 0W
Toucy 9 47 44N 3 15 E
Tougan 49 13 11N 2 58W
Touggourt 49 33 6N 6 4 E
Tougué 49 11 25N 11 50W
Toul 9 48 40N 5 53 E
Toulepleu 49 6 32N 8 24W
Toulon 11 43 10N 5 55 E
Toulouse 10 43 37N 1 27 E
Toummo 50 22 45N 14 8 E
Touques → 8 49 22N 0 8 E
Touquet-Paris-Plage, Le 9 50 30N 1 36 E
Tour-du-Pin, La 11 45 33N 5 27 E
Touraine 8 47 20N 0 30 E
Tourcoing 9 50 42N 3 10 E
Tournai 12 50 35N 3 25 E
Tournan-en-Brie 9 48 44N 2 46 E
Tournay 10 43 13N 0 13 E
Tournon 11 45 4N 4 50 E
Tournon-St.-Martin 8 46 45N 0 58 E
Tournus 11 46 35N 4 54 E
Tours 8 47 22N 0 40 E
Townshend, C. 55 22 18 S 150 30 E
Townshend I. 56 22 10 S 150 31 E
Townsville 56 19 15 S 146 45 E
Towson 66 39 26N 76 34W
Toyama 44 36 40N 137 15 E
Toyama □ 44 36 45N 137 30 E
Toyama-Wan 44 37 0N 137 30 E
Toyohashi 44 34 45N 137 25 E
Toyokawa 44 34 48N 137 27 E
Toyonaka 44 34 50N 135 28 E
Toyooka 44 35 35N 134 48 E
Toyota 44 35 3N 137 7 E
Tozeur 49 33 56N 8 8 E
Trabzon 34 41 0N 39 45 E
Tracy 68 37 46N 121 27W
Trafalgar, C. 18 36 10N 6 2W
Trail 64 49 5N 117 40W
Tralee 7 52 16N 9 42W
Tralee B. 7 52 17N 9 55W
Tramore 7 52 10N 7 10W
Tran Ninh, Cao Nguyen 41 19 30N 103 10 E
Tranås 28 58 3N 14 59 E
Tranche-sur-Mer, La 8 46 20N 1 27W
Trangan 40 6 40 S 134 20 E
Trani 23 41 17N 16 24 E
Transcona 65 49 55N 97 0W
Transilvania 25 46 19N 25 0 E
Transvaal □ 52 25 0 S 29 0 E
Transylvania = Transilvania 25 46 19N 25 0 E
Trápani 22 38 1N 12 30 E
Traralgon 56 38 12 S 146 34 E
Trasimeno, L. 21 43 10N 12 5 E
Traverse City 66 44 45N 85 39W
Travnik 24 44 17N 17 39 E
Trébbia → 20 45 4N 9 41 E
Trebinje 24 42 44N 18 22 E
Třeboň 14 48 59N 14 48 E
Tredegar 5 51 47N 3 16W
Tregaron 5 52 14N 3 56W
Trégastel-Plage 8 48 49N 3 31W
Tréguier 8 48 47N 3 16W
Trégunc 8 47 51N 3 51W
Treignac 10 45 32N 1 48 E
Treinta y Tres 74 33 16 S 54 17W
Trelew 74 43 10 S 65 20W
Trélissac 10 45 11N 0 47 E
Trelleborg 28 55 20N 13 10 E
Trélon 9 50 5N 4 6 E
Tremblade, La 10 45 46N 1 8W
Tremp 19 42 10N 0 52 E
Trenque Lauquen 74 36 5 S 62 45W
Trent → 5 53 33N 0 44W
Trentino-Alto Adige □ 20 46 30N 11 0 E
Trento 20 46 5N 11 8 E
Trenton, Canada 62 44 10N 77 34W
Trenton, Mo., U.S.A. 67 40 5N 93 37W

Trenton, N.J., U.S.A. **66** 40 15N 74 41W
Trepassey **63** 46 43N 53 25W
Tréport, Le **8** 50 3N 1 20 E
Tres Arroyos **74** 38 26 S 60 20W
Três Lagoas **73** 20 50 S 51 43W
Tres Montes, C. **74** 46 50 S 75 30W
Tres Puntas, C. **74** 47 0 S 66 0W
Trets **11** 43 27N 5 41 E
Treviso **21** 45 40N 12 15 E
Trévoux **11** 45 57N 4 47 E
Triaucourt-en-Argonne **9** 48 59N 5 2 E
Tribulation, C. **56** 16 5 S 145 29 E
Trichur **38** 10 30N 76 18 E
Trier **13** 49 45N 6 37 E
Trieste **21** 45 39N 13 45 E
Trieux → **8** 48 43N 3 9W
Triglav **21** 46 21N 13 50 E
Tríkkala **26** 39 34N 21 47 E
Trim **7** 53 34N 6 48W
Trincomalee **38** 8 38N 81 15 E
Trindade, I. **1** 20 20 S 29 50W
Trinidad, Bolivia **72** 14 46 S 64 50W
Trinidad, Colombia **72** 5 25N 71 40W
Trinidad, Cuba **70** 21 48N 80 0W
Trinidad, Uruguay **74** 33 30 S 56 50W
Trinidad, U.S.A. **67** 37 15N 104 30W
Trinidad & Tobago ■ **70** 10 30N 61 20W
Trinity → **67** 30 30N 95 0W
Trinity B., Australia **55** 16 30 S 146 0 E
Trinity B., Canada **63** 48 20N 53 10W
Trinity Mts. **68** 40 20N 118 50W
Trinkitat **50** 18 45N 37 51 E
Tripoli = Tarābulus, Lebanon **45** 34 31N 35 50 E
Tripoli = Tarābulus, Libya **50** 32 49N 13 7 E
Trípolis **26** 37 31N 22 25 E
Tristan da Cunha **1** 37 6 S 12 20W
Trivandrum **38** 8 41N 77 0 E
Trnava **15** 48 23N 17 35 E
Trobriand Is. **56** 8 30 S 151 0 E
Troglav **21** 43 56N 16 36 E
Trois-Riviéres **62** 46 25N 72 34W
Troitsk **30** 54 10N 61 35 E
Troitsko Pechorsk **30** 62 40N 56 10 E
Trölladyngja **27** 64 54N 17 16W
Trollhättan **28** 58 17N 12 20 E
Troms fylke □ **27** 68 56N 19 0 E
Tromsø **27** 69 40N 18 56 E
Trondheim **27** 63 36N 10 25 E
Trondheimsfjorden **27** 63 35N 10 30 E
Troon **6** 55 33N 4 40W
Trossachs, The **6** 56 14N 4 24W
Trostan **7** 55 4N 6 10W
Trotternish **6** 57 32N 6 15W
Trout L. **64** 60 40N 121 40W
Trouville-sur-Mer **8** 49 21N 0 5 E
Trowbridge **5** 51 18N 2 12W
Troy, Ala., U.S.A. **66** 31 50N 85 58W
Troy, N.Y., U.S.A. **66** 42 45N 73 39W
Troyes **9** 48 19N 4 3 E
Trucial States = United Arab Emirates ■ **46** 23 50N 54 0 E
Trujillo, Hond. **70** 16 0N 86 0W
Trujillo, Peru **72** 8 6 S 79 0W
Trujillo, Spain **18** 39 28N 5 55W
Trujillo, Venezuela **72** 9 22N 70 38W
Truk **57** 7 25N 151 46 E
Trun **8** 48 50N 0 2 E
Trung-Phan **41** 16 0N 108 0 E
Truro, Canada **63** 45 21N 63 14W
Truro, U.K. **5** 50 17N 5 2W
Trutnov **14** 50 37N 15 54 E
Truyère → **10** 44 38N 2 34 E
Tsaratanana **53** 16 47 S 47 39 E
Tsau **52** 20 8 S 22 22 E
Tselinograd **30** 51 10N 71 30 E
Tshabong **52** 26 2 S 22 29 E
Tshane **52** 24 5 S 21 54 E
Tshela **51** 4 57 S 13 4 E
Tshikapa **51** 6 28 S 20 48 E
Tshofa **51** 5 13 S 25 16 E
Tshwane **52** 22 24 S 22 1 E
Tsimlyanskoye Vdkhr. **35** 48 0N 43 0 E
Tsingtao = Qingdao **42** 36 5N 120 20 E
Tskhinvali **35** 42 14N 44 1 E
Tsna → **33** 54 55N 41 58 E
Tsu **44** 34 45N 136 25 E
Tsuchiura **44** 36 5N 140 15 E
Tsugaru-Kaikyō **44** 41 35N 141 0 E
Tsumeb **52** 19 9 S 17 44 E
Tsumis **52** 23 39 S 17 29 E
Tsuruga **44** 35 45N 136 2 E
Tsushima **44** 34 20N 129 20 E
Tuam **7** 53 30N 8 50W
Tuamotu Arch. **58** 17 0 S 144 0W
Tuapse **35** 44 5N 39 10 E
Tubarão **74** 28 30 S 49 0W
Tübingen **13** 48 31N 9 4 E
Tubruq **50** 32 7N 23 55 E
Tubuaeran I. **58** 3 51N 159 22W
Tubuai Is. **58** 25 0 S 150 0W
Tucacas **72** 10 48N 68 19W
Tucson **68** 32 14N 110 59W
Tucumcari **67** 35 12N 103 45W
Tucupita **72** 9 2N 62 3W
Tucuruí **73** 3 42 S 49 44W
Tudela **19** 42 4N 1 39W
Tudmur **45** 34 36N 38 15 E
Tugur **31** 53 44N 136 45 E
Tūkrah **50** 32 30N 20 37 E
Tukuyu **51** 9 17 S 33 35 E
Tula, Mexico **69** 23 0N 99 43W
Tula, U.S.S.R. **33** 54 13N 37 38 E
Tulare **68** 36 15N 119 26W
Tulcán **72** 0 48N 77 43W
Tulcea **25** 45 13N 28 46 E
Tuli **51** 21 58 S 29 13 E
Tullahoma **66** 35 23N 86 12W
Tullamore **7** 53 17N 7 30W
Tulle **10** 45 16N 1 46 E
Tullins **11** 45 18N 5 29 E
Tullow **7** 52 48N 6 45W
Ţulmaythah **50** 32 40N 20 55 E
Tulsa **67** 36 10N 96 0W
Tulua **72** 4 6N 76 11W
Tulun **31** 54 32N 100 35 E
Tuma → **70** 13 6N 84 35W
Tumaco **72** 1 50N 78 45W
Tumatumari **72** 5 20N 58 55W
Tumba, L. **51** 0 50 S 18 0 E
Túmbes **72** 3 37 S 80 27W
Tumkur **38** 13 18N 77 6 E
Tummel, L. **6** 56 43N 3 55W
Tumu **49** 10 56N 1 56W
Tumucumaque, Serra **73** 2 0N 55 0W
Tumut **56** 35 16 S 148 13 E
Tunbridge Wells **5** 51 7N 0 16 E
Tunduru **51** 11 8 S 37 25 E
Tundzha → **25** 41 40N 26 35 E
Tungabhadra → **38** 15 57N 78 15 E
Tungaru **50** 10 9N 30 52 E
Tungnafellsjökull **27** 64 45N 17 55W
Tunguska, Nizhnyaya → **31** 65 48N 88 4 E
Tunguska, Podkamennaya → **31** 61 36N 90 18 E
Tunis **49** 36 50N 10 11 E
Tunisia ■ **49** 33 30N 9 10 E
Tunja **72** 5 33N 73 25W
Tunnsjøen **27** 64 45N 13 25 E
Tunxi **43** 29 42N 118 25 E
Tuoy-Khaya **31** 62 32N 111 25 E
Tupelo **66** 34 15N 88 42W
Tupik **31** 54 26N 119 57 E
Tupiza **72** 21 30 S 65 40W
Tupper Lake **62** 44 18N 74 30W
Tuque, La **62** 47 30N 72 50W
Túquerres **72** 1 5N 77 37W
Tura **31** 64 20N 100 17 E
Turan **31** 51 55N 95 0 E
Turda **25** 46 34N 23 47 E
Turek **17** 52 3N 18 30 E
Turgutlu **45** 38 30N 27 48 E
Turia → **19** 39 27N 0 19W
Turin = Torino **20** 45 4N 7 40 E
Turkana, L. **51** 3 30N 36 5 E
Turkestan **30** 43 17N 68 16 E
Turkey ■ **45** 39 0N 36 0 E
Turkmen S.S.R. □ **30** 39 0N 59 0 E
Turks Is. **70** 21 20N 71 20W
Turku **27** 60 30N 22 19 E
Turlock **68** 37 30N 120 55W
Turnhout **12** 51 19N 4 57 E
Tŭrnovo **25** 43 5N 25 41 E
Turnu Măgurele **25** 43 46N 24 56 E
Turnu Rosu Pasul **25** 45 33N 24 17 E
Turnu-Severin **25** 44 39N 22 41 E
Turpan **42** 43 58N 89 10 E
Turpan Hami **42** 42 40N 89 25 E
Turriff **6** 57 32N 2 28W
Turukhansk **31** 65 21N 88 5 E
Turun ja Porin lääni □ **27** 60 27N 22 15 E
Tuscaloosa **66** 33 13N 87 31W
Tuscany = Toscana **20** 43 30N 11 5 E
Tuskar Rock **7** 52 12N 6 10W
Tuskegee **66** 32 24N 85 39W
Tutrakan **25** 44 2N 26 40 E
Tuttlingen **13** 47 59N 8 50 E
Tutuila **57** 14 19 S 170 50W
Tuva A.S.S.R. □ **31** 51 30N 95 0 E
Tuvalu ■ **57** 8 0 S 178 0 E
Tuxpan **69** 20 57N 97 24W
Tuxtla Gutiérrez **69** 16 45N 93 7W
Tuy **18** 42 3N 8 39W
Tuy Hoa **41** 13 5N 109 10 E
Tuyen Hoa **41** 17 50N 106 10 E
Tuz Gölü **45** 38 45N 33 30 E
Ţūz Khurmātū **45** 34 56N 44 38 E
Tuzla **24** 44 34N 18 41 E
Tweed → **6** 55 42N 2 10W
Twillingate **63** 49 42N 54 45W
Twin Falls **68** 42 30N 114 30W
Twofold B. **56** 37 8 S 149 59 E
Tyler **67** 32 18N 95 18W
Tynda **31** 55 10N 124 43 E
Tyne → **5** 54 58N 1 28W
Tyne & Wear □ **5** 54 55N 1 35W
Tynemouth **5** 55 1N 1 27W
Tyrifjorden **28** 60 2N 10 8 E
Tyrol = Tirol □ **14** 47 3N 10 43 E
Tyrrhenian Sea **22** 40 0N 12 30 E
Tysfjorden **27** 68 7N 16 25 E
Tyumen **30** 57 11N 65 29 E
Tywi → **5** 51 48N 4 20W
Tywyn **5** 52 36N 4 5W
Tzaneen **53** 23 47 S 30 9 E

U

Uarsciek **47** 2 28N 45 55 E
Uaupés **72** 0 8 S 67 5W
Ubangi = Oubangi → **51** 0 30 S 17 50 E
Ubauro **36** 28 15N 69 45 E
Ubaye → **11** 44 28N 6 18 E
Ube **44** 33 56N 131 15 E
Ubeda **19** 38 3N 3 23W
Uberaba **73** 19 50 S 47 55W
Uberlândia **73** 19 0 S 48 20W
Ubon Ratchathani **41** 15 15N 104 50 E
Ubundu **51** 0 22 S 25 30 E
Ucayali → **72** 4 30 S 73 30W
Uchi Lake **65** 51 5N 92 35W
Uchiura-Wan **44** 42 25N 140 40 E
Uchur → **31** 58 48N 130 35 E
Uda → **31** 54 42N 135 14 E
Udaipur **36** 24 36N 73 44 E
Udaipur Garhi **37** 27 0N 86 35 E
Uddevalla **28** 58 21N 11 55 E
Uddjaur **27** 65 25N 21 15 E
Udgir **38** 18 25N 77 5 E
Udi **49** 6 17N 7 21 E
Údine **21** 46 5N 13 10 E
Udmurt A.S.S.R. □ **30** 57 30N 52 30 E
Udon Thani **41** 17 29N 102 46 E
Udupi **38** 13 25N 74 42 E
Ueda **44** 36 24N 138 16 E
Uedineniya, Os. **3** 78 0N 85 0 E
Uele → **51** 3 45N 24 45 E
Uelen **31** 66 10N 170 0W
Uelzen **13** 53 0N 10 33 E
Ufa **30** 54 45N 55 55 E
Ugab → **52** 20 55 S 13 30 E
Ugalla → **51** 5 8 S 30 42 E
Uganda ■ **51** 2 0N 32 0 E
Ugine **11** 45 45N 6 25 E
Uglegorsk **31** 49 5N 142 2 E
Ugolyak **31** 64 33N 120 30 E
Uíge **51** 7 30 S 14 40 E
Uinta Mts. **68** 40 45N 110 30W
Uitenhage **52** 33 40 S 25 28 E
Uithuizen **12** 53 24N 6 41 E
Ujjain **36** 23 9N 75 43 E
Újpest **15** 47 32N 19 6 E
Ujung Pandang **40** 5 10 S 119 20 E
Uka **31** 57 50N 162 0 E
Ukerewe I. **51** 2 0 S 33 0 E
Ukhta **30** 63 55N 54 0 E
Ukiah **68** 39 10N 123 9W
Ukrainian S.S.R. □ **34** 49 0N 32 0 E
Ulaanbaatar **42** 47 55N 106 53 E
Ulan Bator = Ulaanbaatar **42** 47 55N 106 53 E
Ulan Ude **31** 51 45N 107 40 E
Ulcinj **24** 41 58N 19 10 E
Ulhasnagar **38** 19 15N 73 10 E
Ullapool **6** 57 54N 5 10W
Ullswater **5** 54 35N 2 52W
Ulm **13** 48 23N 10 0 E
Ulonguè **51** 14 37 S 34 19 E
Ulricehamn **28** 57 46N 13 26 E
Ulster □ **7** 54 35N 6 30W
Ulverston **5** 54 13N 3 7W
Ulverstone **56** 41 11 S 146 11 E
Ulya **31** 59 10N 142 0 E
Ulyanovsk **33** 54 20N 48 25 E
Ulyasutay **42** 47 56N 97 28 E
Uman **34** 48 40N 30 12 E
Umba **30** 66 50N 34 20 E
Umboi I. **56** 5 40 S 148 0 E
Umbria □ **21** 42 53N 12 30 E
Ume älv → **27** 63 45N 20 20 E
Umeå **27** 63 45N 20 20 E
Umm al Qaywayn **46** 25 30N 55 35 E
Umm Bel **50** 13 35N 28 0 E
Umm Ruwaba **50** 12 50N 31 20 E
Umniati → **51** 16 49 S 28 45 E
Umpang **41** 16 3N 98 54 E
Umtata **53** 31 36 S 28 49 E
Unac → **21** 44 30N 16 9 E
União da Vitória **74** 26 13 S 51 5W
Union City **67** 36 25N 89 0W
Union of Soviet Socialist Republics ■ **31** 60 0N 100 0 E
Uniontown **66** 39 54N 79 45W
United Arab Emirates ■ **46** 23 50N 54 0 E
United Kingdom ■ **4** 55 0N 3 0W
United States of America ■ **61** 37 0N 96 0W
United States Trust Terr. of the Pacific Is. □ **57** 10 0N 160 0 E
Unity **65** 52 30N 109 5W
Unnao **37** 26 35N 80 30 E
Unst **6** 60 50N 0 55W
Upata **72** 8 1N 62 24W
Upemba, L. **51** 8 30 S 26 20 E
Upernavik **3** 72 49N 56 20W
Upington **52** 28 25 S 21 15 E
Upper L. Erne **7** 54 14N 7 22W
Upper Taimyr → **31** 74 15N 99 48 E
Upper Volta = Burkina Faso ■ **49** 12 0N 1 0W
Uppsala **28** 59 53N 17 38 E
Uppsala län □ **28** 60 0N 17 30 E
Ur **45** 30 55N 46 25 E
Ural → **30** 47 0N 51 48 E
Ural Mts. = Uralskie Gory **30** 60 0N 59 0 E
Uralsk **30** 51 20N 51 20 E
Uralskie Gory **30** 60 0N 59 0 E
Urandangi **56** 21 32 S 138 14 E
Urawa **44** 35 50N 139 40 E
Urbana, Ill., U.S.A. **67** 40 7N 88 12W
Urbana, Ohio, U.S.A. **66** 40 9N 83 44W
Urbana, La **72** 7 8N 66 56W
Urbino **21** 43 43N 12 38 E
Urbión, Picos de **19** 42 1N 2 52W
Urcos **72** 13 40 S 71 38W
Urda **35** 48 52N 47 23 E
Urdos **10** 42 51N 0 35W
Ure → **5** 54 20N 1 25W
Ures **69** 29 26N 110 24W
Urfa **45** 37 12N 38 50 E
Urfahr **14** 48 19N 14 17 E
Urgench **30** 41 40N 60 41 E
Uribia **72** 11 43N 72 16W
Urk **12** 52 39N 5 36 E
Urmia = Orūmīyeh **45** 37 40N 45 0 E
Urmia, L. = Orūmīyeh, Daryācheh-ye **45** 37 50N 45 30 E
Uruapan **69** 19 30N 102 0W
Uruçuí **73** 7 20 S 44 28W
Uruguaiana **74** 29 50 S 57 0W
Uruguay ■ **74** 32 30 S 56 30W
Uruguay → **74** 34 12 S 58 18W
Ürümqi **42** 43 45N 87 45 E
Urup, Os. **31** 46 0N 151 0 E
Uryung-Khaya **31** 72 48N 113 23 E
Usa **30** 2 23 S 36 52 E
Uşak **45** 38 43N 29 28 E
Usakos **52** 21 54 S 15 31 E
Ushakova, O. **3** 82 0N 80 0 E
Ushant = Ouessant, I. d' **8** 48 28N 5 6W
Ushuaia **74** 54 50 S 68 23W
Ushumun **31** 52 47N 126 32 E
Usk → **5** 51 37N 2 56W
Üsküdar **45** 41 0N 29 5 E
Usman **33** 52 5N 39 48 E
Usoke **51** 5 8 S 32 24 E
Usolye Sibirskoye **31** 52 48N 103 40 E
Uspallata, P. de **74** 32 37 S 69 22W
Uspenskiy **30** 48 41N 72 43 E
Ussel **10** 45 32N 2 18 E
Ussuriysk **31** 43 48N 131 59 E
Ust-Bolsheretsk **31** 52 50N 156 15 E
Ust chaun **31** 68 47N 170 30 E
Ust'-Ilga **31** 55 5N 104 55 E
Ust-Ilimsk **31** 58 3N 102 39 E
Ust-Kamchatsk **31** 56 10N 162 28 E
Ust-Kamenogorsk **30** 50 0N 82 36 E
Ust-Karenga **31** 54 25N 116 30 E
Ust Khayryuzova **31** 57 15N 156 45 E
Ust-Kut **31** 56 50N 105 42 E
Ust Kuyga **31** 70 1N 135 43 E
Ust Maya **31** 60 30N 134 28 E
Ust-Mil **31** 59 40N 133 11 E
Ust-Nera **31** 64 35N 143 15 E
Ust-Nyukzha **31** 56 34N 121 37 E
Ust Olenek **31** 73 0N 119 48 E
Ust-Omchug **31** 61 9N 149 38 E
Ust Port **30** 69 40N 84 26 E
Ust Tsilma **30** 65 25N 52 0 E
Ust-Tungir **31** 55 25N 120 36 E
Ust Vorkuta **30** 67 24N 64 0 E
Ustaritz **10** 43 24N 1 27W
Ústí nad Labem **14** 50 41N 14 3 E
Ustica **22** 38 42N 13 10 E
Ustinov **30** 56 51N 53 14 E
Ustye **31** 57 46N 94 37 E
Ustyurt, Plato **30** 44 0N 55 0 E
Usu **42** 44 27N 84 40 E
Usuki **44** 33 8N 131 49 E
Utah □ **68** 39 30N 111 30W
Ütersen **13** 53 40N 9 40 E
Utete **51** 8 0 S 38 45 E
Uthai Thani **41** 15 22N 100 3 E
Utica **66** 43 5N 75 18W
Utrecht **12** 52 5N 5 8 E
Utrecht □ **12** 52 6N 5 7 E
Utrera **18** 37 12N 5 48W
Utsjoki **27** 69 51N 26 59 E
Utsunomiya **44** 36 30N 139 50 E
Uttar Pradesh □ **37** 27 0N 80 0 E
Uttoxeter **5** 52 53N 1 50W
Uusikaarlepyy **27** 63 32N 22 31 E
Uusikaupunki **27** 60 47N 21 25 E
Uvinza **51** 5 5 S 30 24 E
Uvira **51** 3 22 S 29 3 E
Uwajima **44** 33 10N 132 35 E
Uyandi **31** 69 19N 141 0 E
Uzbek S.S.R. □ **30** 41 30N 65 0 E
Uzerche **10** 45 25N 1 34 E
Uzès **11** 44 1N 4 26 E

V

Vaal → **52** 29 4 S 23 38 E
Vaasa **27** 63 6N 21 38 E
Vaasan lääni □ **27** 63 2N 22 50 E
Vabre **10** 43 42N 2 24 E
Vác **15** 47 49N 19 10 E
Vaccarès, Étang de **11** 43 32N 4 34 E
Vach → **30** 60 45N 76 45 E
Vadodara **36** 22 20N 73 10 E
Vadsø **27** 70 3N 29 50 E
Værøy **27** 67 40N 12 40 E
Váh → **15** 47 55N 18 0 E
Vaigach **30** 70 10N 59 0 E
Vaiges **8** 48 2N 0 30W
Vailly-sur-Aisne **9** 49 24N 3 31 E
Vaison-la-Romaine **11** 44 14N 5 4 E
Val-d'Ajol, Le **9** 47 55N 6 30 E
Val-de-Marne □ **9** 48 45N 2 28 E
Val-d'Oise □ **9** 49 5N 2 10 E
Val d'Or **62** 48 7N 77 47W
Valahia **25** 44 35N 25 0 E
Valcheta **74** 40 40 S 66 8W
Valdayskaya Vozvyshennost **32** 57 0N 33 30 E
Valdepeñas **18** 38 43N 3 25W
Valdés, Pen. **74** 42 30 S 63 45W
Valdivia **74** 39 50 S 73 14W
Valdosta **66** 30 50N 83 20W
Valençay **9** 47 9N 1 34 E
Valence, Drôme, France **11** 44 57N 4 54 E
Valence, Tarn-et-Garonne, France **10** 44 6N 0 53 E
Valencia, Spain **19** 39 27N 0 23W
Valencia, Venezuela **72** 10 11N 68 0W
Valencia □ **19** 39 20N 0 40W
Valencia, Albufera de **19** 39 20N 0 27W
Valencia, G. de **19** 39 30N 0 20 E
Valencia de Alcántara **18** 39 25N 7 14W
Valenciennes **9** 50 20N 3 34 E
Valensole **11** 43 50N 5 59 E
Valentia Hr. **7** 51 56N 10 17W
Valentia I. **7** 51 54N 10 22W
Valera **72** 9 19N 70 37W
Valinco, G. de **11** 41 40N 8 52 E
Valjevo **24** 44 18N 19 53 E
Valkenswaard **12** 51 21N 5 29 E
Valladolid, Mexico **69** 20 41N 88 12W
Valladolid, Spain **18** 41 38N 4 43W
Valle d'Aosta □ **20** 45 45N 7 22 E
Valle de la Pascua **72** 9 13N 66 0W
Valle de Santiago **69** 20 23N 101 12W
Vallecas **18** 40 23N 3 41W
Vallejo **68** 38 12N 122 15W
Valleraugue **10** 44 6N 3 39 E
Vallet **8** 47 10N 1 15W
Valley View **64** 40 39N 76 33W
Vallon-Pont-d'Arc **11** 44 24N 4 24 E
Valls **19** 41 18N 1 15 E
Valmont **8** 49 45N 0 30 E
Valmy **9** 49 5N 4 45 E
Valognes **8** 49 30N 1 28W
Valparaíso, Chile **74** 33 2 S 71 40W
Valparaíso, Mexico **69** 22 46N 103 34W
Valréas **11** 44 24N 5 0 E
Vals-les-Bains **11** 44 42N 4 24 E
Valsad **36** 20 40N 72 58 E
Valverde del Camino **18** 37 35N 6 47W
Van **45** 38 30N 43 20 E
Van, L. = Van Gölü **45** 38 30N 43 0 E
Van Buren, Canada **63** 47 10N 67 55W
Van Buren, U.S.A. **67** 35 28N 94 18W
Van Diemen, C. **56** 16 30 S 139 46 E
Van Diemen G. **54** 11 45 S 132 0 E
Van Gölü **45** 38 30N 43 0 E
Van Wert **66** 40 52N 84 31W
Vanavara **31** 60 22N 102 16 E
Vancouver, Canada **64** 49 15N 123 10W
Vancouver, U.S.A. **68** 45 44N 122 41W
Vancouver I. **64** 49 50N 126 0W
Vandalia **67** 38 57N 89 4W
Vanderhoof **64** 54 0N 124 0W
Vanderlin I. **55** 15 44 S 137 2 E
Vänern **28** 58 47N 13 30 E
Vänersborg **28** 58 26N 12 19 E
Vanga **51** 4 35 S 39 12 E
Vangaindrano **53** 23 21 S 47 36 E
Vanier **62** 45 27N 75 40W
Vankarem **31** 67 51N 175 50 E
Vanna **27** 70 6N 19 50 E
Vännäs **27** 63 58N 19 48 E
Vannes **8** 47 40N 2 47W
Vanoise, Massif de la **11** 45 25N 6 40 E
Vanrhynsdorp **52** 31 36 S 18 44 E
Vans, Les **11** 44 25N 4 7 E
Vansbro **28** 60 32N 14 15 E
Vansittart B. **54** 14 3 S 126 17 E
Vanua Levu **57** 16 33 S 179 15 E
Vanuatu ■ **57** 15 0 S 168 0 E
Var □ **11** 43 27N 6 18 E
Var → **11** 43 39N 7 12 E
Varades **8** 47 25N 1 1W
Varanasi **37** 25 22N 83 0 E
Varangerfjorden **27** 70 3N 29 25 E
Varaždin **21** 46 20N 16 20 E
Varberg **28** 57 6N 12 20 E
Vardak □ **46** 34 0N 68 0 E
Vardar → **24** 40 35N 22 50 E
Varennes-sur-Allier **10** 46 19N 3 24 E
Varese **20** 45 49N 8 50 E
Värmlands län □ **28** 60 0N 13 20 E
Varna **25** 43 13N 27 56 E
Värnamo **28** 57 10N 14 3 E
Varzy **9** 47 22N 3 20 E
Vasa **27** 63 6N 21 38 E
Vascongadas □ **19** 42 50N 2 45W
Vaslui **25** 46 38N 27 42 E
Västerås **28** 59 37N 16 38 E
Västerbottens län □ **27** 64 58N 18 0 E
Västernorrlands län □ **27** 63 30N 17 30 E
Västervik **28** 57 43N 16 43 E
Västmanlands län □ **28** 59 45N 16 20 E
Vasto **21** 42 8N 14 40 E
Vatan **9** 47 4N 1 50 E
Vatican City ■ **4** 41 54N 12 27 E
Vatnajökull **27** 64 30N 16 48W
Vatneyri **27** 65 35N 24 0W
Vatomandry **53** 19 20 S 48 59 E
Vatra-Dornei **15** 47 22N 25 22 E
Vättern **28** 58 25N 14 30 E
Vaucluse □ **11** 43 50N 5 20 E
Vaucouleurs **9** 48 37N 5 40 E
Vauvert **11** 43 42N 4 17 E
Växjö **28** 56 52N 14 50 E
Vaygach, Ostrov **30** 70 0N 60 0 E
Vechta **13** 52 47N 8 18 E
Vechte → **12** 52 34N 6 6 E
Vedea → **25** 44 0N 25 20 E
Veendam **12** 53 5N 6 52 E
Veenendaal **12** 52 2N 5 34 E
Vefsna → **27** 65 48N 13 10 E
Vega **27** 65 40N 11 55 E
Vega, La **70** 19 20N 70 30W
Vegafjorden **27** 65 37N 12 0 E
Veghel **12** 51 37N 5 32 E
Vegreville **64** 53 30N 112 5W
Vejer de la Frontera **18** 36 15N 5 59W
Vejle **28** 55 43N 9 30 E
Vela, La **72** 11 27N 69 34W
Velay, Mts. du **10** 45 0N 3 40 E
Velebit Planina **21** 44 50N 15 20 E
Vélez Málaga **18** 36 48N 4 5W
Vélez Rubio **19** 37 41N 2 5W
Velikaya → **32** 57 48N 28 20 E
Velikiye Luki **32** 56 25N 30 32 E
Velikonda Range **38** 14 45N 79 10 E
Velletri **22** 41 43N 12 43 E
Vellore **38** 12 57N 79 10 E
Velsen-Noord **12** 52 27N 4 40 E
Venaco **11** 42 14N 9 11 E
Venado Tuerto **74** 33 50 S 62 0W
Venarey-les-Laumes **9** 47 32N 4 26 E
Vence **11** 43 43N 7 6 E
Vendée □ **8** 46 50N 1 35W
Vendée → **8** 46 20N 1 10W
Vendéen, Bocage **10** 46 40N 1 20W
Vendeuvre-sur-Barse **9** 48 14N 4 28 E
Vendôme **8** 47 47N 1 3 E
Véneto □ **21** 45 40N 12 0 E
Venézia **21** 45 27N 12 20 E
Venézia, G. di **21** 45 20N 13 0 E
Venezuela ■ **72** 8 0N 65 0W
Venezuela, G. de **72** 11 30N 71 0W
Vengurla **38** 15 53N 73 45 E
Venice = Venézia **21** 45 27N 12 20 E
Venkatapuram **38** 18 20N 80 30 E
Venlo **12** 51 22N 6 11 E
Venraij **12** 51 31N 6 0 E
Ventnor **5** 50 35N 1 12W
Ventoux, Mt. **11** 44 10N 5 17 E
Ventspils **32** 57 25N 21 32 E
Ventura **68** 34 16N 119 18W
Vera **19** 37 15N 1 51W
Veracruz **69** 19 10N 96 10W

Veracruz □ 69 19 20N 96 40W
Veraval 36 20 53N 70 27 E
Vercelli 20 45 19N 8 25 E
Verdalsøra 27 63 48N 11 30 E
Verde → 69 15 59N 97 50W
Verden 13 52 58N 9 18 E
Verdon → 11 43 43N 5 46 E
Verdon-sur-Mer, Le 10 45 33N 1 4W
Verdun 9 49 9N 5 24 E
Verdun-sur-le-Doubs 9 46 54N 5 2 E
Vereeniging 53 26 38 S 27 57 E
Verga, C. 49 10 30N 14 10W
Vergt 10 45 2N 0 43 E
Verkhnevilyuysk 31 63 27N 120 18 E
Verkhneye Kalinino 31 59 54N 108 8 E
Verkhniy Baskunchak 35 48 14N 46 44 E
Verkhoyansk 31 67 35N 133 25 E
Verkhoyanskiy Khrebet 31 66 0N 129 0 E
Vermenton 9 47 40N 3 42 E
Vermilion 65 53 20N 110 50W
Vermont □ 66 43 40N 72 50W
Verneuil-sur-Avre 8 48 45N 0 55 E
Vernon, Canada 64 50 20N 119 15W
Vernon, France 8 49 5N 1 30 E
Vernon, U.S.A. 67 34 10N 99 20W
Véroia 26 40 34N 22 12 E
Verona 20 45 27N 11 0 E
Veropol 31 65 15N 168 40 E
Versailles 9 48 48N 2 8 E
Vert, C. 49 14 45N 17 30W
Vertou 8 47 10N 1 28W
Vertus 9 48 54N 4 0 E
Verviers 12 50 37N 5 52 E
Vervins 9 49 50N 3 53 E
Vescavoto 11 42 30N 9 27 E
Veselovskoye Vdkhr. 35 47 0N 41 0 E
Vesle → 9 49 23N 3 28 E
Vesoul 9 47 40N 6 11 E
Vest-Agder fylke □ 27 58 30N 7 15 E
Vesterålen 27 68 45N 15 0 E
Vestfjorden 27 67 55N 14 0 E
Vestmannaeyjar 27 63 27N 20 15W
Vestspitsbergen 3 78 40N 17 0 E
Vestvågøy 27 68 18N 13 50 E
Vesuvio 23 40 50N 14 22 E
Vesuvius, Mt. = Vesuvio 23 40 50N 14 22 E
Veszprém 15 47 8N 17 57 E
Vetlanda 28 57 24N 15 3 E
Vetluga → 30 56 18N 46 24 E
Veurne 12 51 5N 2 40 E
Veynes 11 44 32N 5 49 E
Vézelise 9 48 30N 6 5 E
Vézère → 10 44 53N 0 53 E
Vezhen 25 42 50N 24 20 E
Viacha 72 16 39 S 68 18W
Viana do Castelo 18 41 42N 8 50W
Viaur → 10 44 8N 1 58 E
Viborg 28 56 27N 9 23 E
Vibraye 8 48 3N 0 44 E
Vic-en-Bigorre 10 43 24N 0 3 E
Vic-Fézensac 10 43 47N 0 19 E
Vic-sur-Cère 10 44 59N 2 38 E
Vicenza 21 45 32N 11 31 E
Vich 19 41 58N 2 19 E
Vichy 10 46 9N 3 26 E
Vicksburg 67 32 22N 90 56W
Victor 36 21 0N 71 30 E
Victor Harbor 56 35 30 S 138 37 E
Victoria, Canada 64 48 30N 123 25W
Victoria, Chile 74 38 13 S 72 20W
Victoria, Guinea 49 10 50N 14 32W
Victoria, U.S.A. 67 28 50N 97 0W
Victoria □ 55 37 0 S 144 0 E
Victoria → 54 15 10 S 129 40 E
Victoria, L. 51 1 0 S 33 0 E
Victoria, Mt. 56 8 55 S 147 32 E
Victoria de Durango 69 24 3N 104 39W
Victoria de las Tunas 70 20 58N 76 59W
Victoria Falls 51 17 58 S 25 52 E
Victoria I. 61 71 0N 111 0W
Victoria River Downs 54 16 25 S 131 0 E
Victoria West 52 31 25 S 23 4 E
Victoriaville 63 46 4N 71 56W
Vidalia 67 32 13N 82 25W
Vidauban 11 43 25N 6 27 E
Vidin 24 43 59N 22 50 E
Vidisha 36 23 28N 77 53 E
Viedma 74 40 50 S 63 0W
Vienna = Wien 15 48 12N 16 22 E
Vienne 11 45 31N 4 53 E
Vienne □ 10 46 30N 0 42 E
Vienne → 8 47 13N 0 5 E
Vientiane 41 17 58N 102 36 E
Vientos, Paso de los 70 20 0N 74 0W
Viersen 13 51 15N 6 23 E
Vierzon 9 47 13N 2 5 E
Vietnam ■ 29 19 0N 106 0 E
Vieux-Boucau-les-Bains 10 43 48N 1 23W
Vif 11 45 5N 5 41 E
Vigan, Le 10 43 59N 3 36 E
Vignemale, Pic du 10 42 47N 0 10W
Vigneulles-lès-Hattonchâtel 9 48 59N 5 43 E
Vigo 18 42 12N 8 41W
Vihiers 8 47 10N 0 30W
Vijayawada 38 16 31N 80 39 E
Vikna 27 64 55N 10 58 E
Vila da Maganja 51 17 18 S 37 30 E
Vila de João Belo = Xai-Xai 53 25 6 S 33 31 E
Vila Franca de Xira 18 38 57N 8 59W
Vila Machado 51 19 15 S 34 14 E
Vila Real 18 41 17N 7 48W
Vila Real de Santo António 18 37 10N 7 28W
Vilaine → 8 47 30N 2 27W
Vilanculos 53 22 1 S 35 17 E
Vilhelmina 27 64 35N 16 39 E
Vilhena 72 12 40 S 60 5W
Viliga 31 61 36N 156 56 E
Villa Bella 72 10 25 S 65 22W
Villa Cisneros = Dakhla 49 23 50N 15 53W
Villa Dolores 74 31 58 S 65 15W
Villa María 74 32 20 S 63 10W
Villa Montes 72 21 10 S 63 30W
Villach 14 46 37N 13 51 E
Villagarcía de Arosa 18 42 34N 8 46W
Villaguay 74 32 0 S 59 0W
Villahermosa 69 17 59N 92 55W
Villaines-la-Juhel 8 48 21N 0 20W
Villalba 18 43 26N 7 40W
Villamblard 10 45 2N 0 32 E
Villanueva de la Serena 18 38 59N 5 50W
Villard-Bonnot 11 45 14N 5 53 E
Villard-de-Lans 11 45 3N 5 33 E
Villarreal 19 39 55N 0 3W
Villarrica 74 39 15 S 72 15W
Villarrobledo 19 39 18N 2 36W
Villars-les-Dombes 11 46 0N 5 3 E
Villaviciosa 18 43 32N 5 27W
Villazón 72 22 0 S 65 35W
Ville Platte 67 30 45N 92 17W
Villedieu-les-Poêlles 8 48 50N 1 13W
Villefort 10 44 28N 3 56 E
Villefranche-de-Lauragais 10 43 25N 1 44 E
Villefranche-de-Rouergue 10 44 21N 2 2 E
Villefranche-du-Périgord 10 44 38N 1 5 E
Villefranche-sur-Cher 9 47 18N 1 46 E
Villefranche-sur-Saône 11 45 59N 4 43 E
Villemaur-sur-Vanne 9 48 15N 3 44 E
Villemur-sur-Tarn 10 43 51N 1 31 E
Villena 19 38 39N 0 52W
Villenauxe-la-Grande 9 48 35N 3 33 E
Villenave-d'Ornon 10 44 46N 0 33W
Villeneuve-l'Archevêque 9 48 14N 3 32 E
Villeneuve-lès-Avignon 11 43 58N 4 49 E
Villeneuve-St.-Georges 9 48 44N 2 28 E
Villeneuve-sur-Allier 10 46 40N 3 13 E
Villeneuve-sur-Lot 10 44 24N 0 42 E
Villeréal 10 44 38N 0 45 E
Villers-Bocage 8 49 3N 0 40W
Villers-Bretonneux 9 49 50N 2 30 E
Villers-Cotterêts 9 49 15N 3 4 E
Villers-sur-Mer 8 49 21N 0 2W
Villersexel 9 47 33N 6 26 E
Villerupt 9 49 28N 5 55 E
Villerville 8 49 26N 0 5 E
Villingen 13 48 4N 8 28 E
Villingen-Schwenningen 13 48 3N 8 29 E
Vilnius 32 54 38N 25 19 E
Vilskutskogo, Proliv 31 78 0N 103 0 E
Vilvoorde 12 50 56N 4 26 E
Vilyuy → 31 64 24N 126 26 E
Vilyuysk 31 63 40N 121 35 E
Vimoutiers 8 48 57N 0 10 E
Viña del Mar 74 33 0 S 71 30W
Vinaroz 19 40 30N 0 27 E
Vincennes 66 38 42N 87 29W
Vindel älven → 27 63 55N 19 50 E
Vindeln 27 64 12N 19 43 E
Vindhya Ra. 36 22 50N 77 0 E
Vinh 41 18 45N 105 38 E
Vinita 67 36 40N 95 12W
Vinkovci 24 45 19N 18 48 E
Vinnitsa 34 49 15N 28 30 E
Viramgam 36 23 5N 72 0 E
Virden 65 49 50N 100 56W
Vire 8 48 50N 0 53W
Vire → 8 49 20N 1 7W
Vírgenes, C. 74 52 19 S 68 21W
Virgin → 68 36 50N 114 10W
Virgin Is. 70 18 40N 64 30W
Virginia □ 66 37 45N 78 0W
Virginia Beach 66 36 54N 75 58W
Virieu-le-Grand 11 45 51N 5 39 E
Virton 12 49 35N 5 32 E
Virudunagar 38 9 30N 78 0 E
Vis 21 43 0N 16 10 E
Visalia 68 36 25N 119 18W
Visby 28 57 37N 18 18 E
Viscount Melville Sd. 3 74 10N 108 0W
Visé 12 50 44N 5 41 E
Višegrad 24 43 47N 19 17 E
Viseu 18 40 40N 7 55W
Vishakhapatnam 38 17 45N 83 20 E
Viso, Mte. 20 44 38N 7 5 E
Vistula = Wisła → 17 54 22N 18 55 E
Vitebsk 32 55 10N 30 15 E
Viterbo 21 42 25N 12 8 E
Viti Levu 57 17 30 S 177 30 E
Vitiaz Str. 56 5 40 S 147 10 E
Vitim 31 59 28N 112 35 E
Vitim → 31 59 26N 112 34 E
Vitória, Brazil 73 20 20 S 40 22W
Vitoria, Spain 19 42 50N 2 41W
Vitória da Conquista 73 14 51 S 40 51W
Vitré 8 48 8N 1 12W
Vitry-le-François 9 48 43N 4 33 E
Vitteaux 9 47 24N 4 30 E
Vittel 9 48 12N 5 57 E
Vittória 23 36 58N 14 30 E
Vittório Véneto 21 45 59N 12 18 E
Vitu Is. 56 4 50 S 149 25 E
Vivario 11 42 10N 9 11 E
Vivero 18 43 39N 7 38W
Viviers 11 44 30N 4 40 E
Vivonne 10 46 25N 0 15 E
Vizianagaram 38 18 6N 83 30 E
Vizille 11 45 5N 5 46 E
Vlaardingen 12 51 55N 4 21 E
Vladimir 33 56 15N 40 30 E
Vladivostok 31 43 10N 131 53 E
Vlieland 12 53 16N 4 55 E
Vlissingen 12 51 26N 3 34 E
Vltava → 14 50 21N 14 30 E
Vogelsberg 13 50 37N 9 15 E
Vohibinany 53 18 49 S 49 4 E
Vohimarina 53 13 25 S 50 0 E
Vohimena, Tanjon' i 53 25 36 S 45 8 E
Vohipeno 53 22 22 S 47 51 E
Voi 51 3 25 S 38 32 E
Void 9 48 40N 5 36 E
Voiron 11 45 22N 5 35 E
Vojmsjön 27 64 55N 16 40 E
Volcano Is. 57 25 0N 141 0 E
Volchayevka 31 48 40N 134 30 E
Volda 27 62 9N 6 5 E
Volga → 35 48 30N 46 0 E
Volga Hts. = Privolzhskaya Vozvyshennost 33 51 0N 46 0 E
Volgograd 35 48 40N 44 25 E
Volgogradskoye Vdkhr. 33 50 0N 45 20 E
Volkhov → 32 60 8N 32 20 E
Völklingen 13 49 15N 6 50 E
Vollenhove 12 52 40N 5 58 E
Volochanka 31 71 0N 94 28 E
Vologda 33 59 10N 40 0 E
Vólos 26 39 24N 22 59 E
Volsk 33 52 5N 47 22 E
Volta, L. 49 7 30N 0 15 E
Volta Redonda 73 22 31 S 44 5W
Volterra 20 43 24N 10 50 E
Volturno → 23 41 1N 13 55 E
Volzhskiy 35 48 56N 44 46 E
Voorburg 12 52 5N 4 24 E
Vopnafjörður 27 65 45N 14 40W
Vorarlberg □ 14 47 20N 10 0 E
Voreppe 11 45 18N 5 39 E
Voríai Sporádhes 26 39 15N 23 30 E
Vorkuta 30 67 48N 64 20 E
Voronezh 33 51 40N 39 10 E
Voroshilovgrad 35 48 38N 39 15 E
Vorovskoye 31 54 30N 155 50 E
Vosges 9 48 20N 7 10 E
Vosges □ 9 48 12N 6 20 E
Voss 27 60 38N 6 26 E
Vostochnyy Sayan 31 54 0N 96 0 E
Vostok I. 58 10 5 S 152 23W
Vouga → 18 40 41N 8 40W
Vouillé 8 46 38N 0 10 E
Voulte-sur-Rhône, La 11 44 48N 4 46 E
Vouvray 8 47 25N 0 48 E
Vouziers 9 49 22N 4 40 E
Voves 9 48 15N 1 38 E
Voznesenka 31 56 40N 95 3 E
Voznesensk 34 47 35N 31 21 E
Voznesenye 30 61 0N 35 45 E
Vrangelya, Ostrov 31 71 0N 180 0 E
Vranje 24 42 34N 21 54 E
Vratsa 25 43 13N 23 30 E
Vrbas → 24 45 8N 17 29 E
Vrede 53 27 24 S 29 6 E
Vredenburg 52 32 56 S 18 0 E
Vršac 24 45 8N 21 18 E
Vryburg 52 26 55 S 24 45 E
Vryheid 53 27 45 S 30 47 E
Vught 12 51 38N 5 20 E
Vulcan 64 50 25N 113 15W
Vulcano 23 38 25N 14 58 E
Vyazemskiy 31 47 32N 134 45 E
Vyazma 32 55 10N 34 15 E
Vyborg 30 60 43N 28 47 E
Vychegda → 30 61 18N 46 36 E
Vychodné Beskydy 15 49 30N 22 0 E
Vyrnwy, L. 5 52 48N 3 30W
Vyshniy Volochek 32 57 30N 34 30 E

W

Wa 49 10 7N 2 25W
Waal → 12 51 59N 4 30 E
Wabash 66 40 48N 85 46W
Wabash → 66 37 46N 88 2W
Wąbrzeźno 17 53 16N 18 57 E
Waco 67 31 33N 97 5W
Wad Banda 50 13 10N 27 56 E
Wad Hamid 50 16 30N 32 45 E
Wâd Medani 50 14 28N 33 30 E
Waddeneilanden 12 53 25N 5 10 E
Waddenzee 12 53 6N 5 10 E
Waddington, Mt. 64 51 23N 125 15W
Wadena 65 51 57N 103 47W
Wadi Halfa 50 21 53N 31 19 E
Wageningen 12 51 58N 5 40 E
Wagga Wagga 56 35 7 S 147 24 E
Wagin 54 33 17 S 117 25 E
Waiblingen 13 48 49N 9 20 E
Waigeo 40 0 20 S 130 40 E
Waikato → 59 37 23 S 174 43 E
Wainganga → 36 18 50N 79 55 E
Wainwright 65 52 50N 110 50W
Waitaki → 59 44 56 S 171 7 E
Wajima 44 37 30N 137 0 E
Wajir 51 1 42N 40 5 E
Wakasa-Wan 44 35 40N 135 30 E
Wakayama 44 34 15N 135 15 E
Wakayama-ken □ 44 33 50N 135 30 E
Wake I. 57 19 18N 166 36 E
Wakefield 5 53 41N 1 31W
Wakkanai 44 45 28N 141 35 E
Wałbrzych 17 50 45N 16 18 E
Walbury Hill 5 51 22N 1 28W
Walcheren 12 51 30N 3 35 E
Wales □ 5 52 30N 3 30W
Walgett 55 30 0 S 148 5 E
Walkerton 62 44 10N 81 10W
Walla Walla 68 46 3N 118 25W
Wallaceburg 62 42 34N 82 23W
Wallachia = Valahia 25 44 35N 25 0 E
Wallaroo 56 33 56 S 137 39 E
Wallasey 5 53 26N 3 2W
Wallingford 5 51 40N 1 15W
Wallis & Futuna 57 13 18 S 176 10W
Wallowa, Mts. 68 45 20N 117 30W
Wallsend 5 54 59N 1 30W
Walney, Isle of 5 54 5N 3 15W
Walsall 5 52 36N 1 59W
Walsrode 13 52 51N 9 37 E
Walvisbaai 52 23 0 S 14 28 E
Wamba 51 2 10N 27 57 E
Wana 36 32 20N 69 32 E
Wandoan 56 26 5 S 149 55 E
Wang Saphung 41 17 18N 101 46 E
Wanganui 59 39 56 S 175 3 E
Wangaratta 56 36 21 S 146 19 E
Wanxian 43 30 42N 108 20 E
Warangal 38 17 58N 79 35 E
Warburton → 55 28 4 S 137 28 E
Wardha 36 20 45N 78 39 E
Warialda 56 29 29 S 150 33 E
Warley 5 52 30N 2 0W
Warmbad, Namibia 52 28 25 S 18 42 E
Warmbad, S. Africa 53 24 51 S 28 19 E
Warmeriville 9 49 20N 4 13 E
Warner Mts. 68 41 30N 120 20W
Warrego → 56 30 24 S 145 21 E
Warrego Ra. 56 24 58 S 146 0 E
Warren, Ark., U.S.A. 67 33 35N 92 3W
Warren, Mich., U.S.A. 66 42 31N 83 2W
Warren, Ohio, U.S.A. 66 41 18N 80 52W
Warren, Pa., U.S.A. 66 41 52N 79 10W
Warrenpoint 7 54 7N 6 15W
Warrensburg 67 38 45N 93 45W
Warrenton 52 28 9 S 24 47 E
Warri 49 5 30N 5 41 E
Warrina 54 28 12 S 135 50 E
Warrington, U.K. 5 53 25N 2 38W
Warrington, U.S.A. 66 30 22N 87 16W
Warrnambool 56 38 25 S 142 30 E
Warsaw = Warszawa 17 52 13N 21 0 E
Warszawa 17 52 13N 21 0 E
Warta → 17 52 35N 14 39 E
Warthe = Warta → 17 52 35N 14 39 E
Warwick, Australia 56 28 10 S 152 1 E
Warwick, U.K. 5 52 17N 1 36W
Warwick, U.S.A. 66 41 43N 71 25W
Warwick □ 5 52 20N 1 30W
Wasatch Ra. 68 40 30N 111 15W
Wasco 68 35 37N 119 16W
Wash, The 5 52 58N 0 20 E
Washim 38 20 3N 77 0 E
Washington, D.C., U.S.A. 66 38 52N 77 0W
Washington, Ind., U.S.A. 66 38 40N 87 8W
Washington, Mo., U.S.A. 67 38 35N 91 1W
Washington, Pa., U.S.A. 66 40 10N 80 20W
Washington □ 68 47 45N 120 30W
Wassenaar 12 52 8N 4 24 E
Wassy 9 48 30N 4 58 E
Waterbury 66 41 32N 73 0W
Waterford 7 52 16N 7 8W
Waterford □ 7 52 10N 7 40W
Waterford Harb. 7 52 10N 6 58W
Waterloo, Belgium 12 50 43N 4 25 E
Waterloo, Canada 62 43 30N 80 32W
Waterloo, S. Leone 49 8 26N 13 8W
Waterloo, U.S.A. 67 42 27N 92 20W
Waterton Glacier Int. Peace Park 68 48 35N 113 40W
Watertown, N.Y., U.S.A. 66 43 58N 75 57W
Watertown, Wis., U.S.A. 66 43 15N 88 45W
Waterville 66 44 35N 69 40W
Watford 5 51 38N 0 23W
Watling I. = San Salvador 70 24 0N 74 40W
Watrous 65 51 40N 105 25W
Watsa 51 3 4N 29 30 E
Watson Lake 64 60 6N 128 49W
Watsonville 68 36 55N 121 49W
Watubela, Kepulauan 40 4 28 S 131 35 E
Waukegan 67 42 22N 87 54W
Waukesha 67 43 0N 88 15W
Wausau 67 44 57N 89 40W
Wauwatosa 67 43 6N 87 59W
Wave Hill 54 17 32 S 131 0 E
Waveney → 5 52 24N 1 20 E
Wavre 12 50 43N 4 38 E
Wâw 50 7 45N 28 1 E
Wâw al Kabīr 50 25 20N 16 43 E
Waxahachie 67 32 22N 96 53W
Waycross 66 31 12N 82 25W
Waynesboro, Pa., U.S.A. 66 39 46N 77 32W
Waynesboro, Va., U.S.A. 66 38 4N 78 57W
Waynesville 66 35 31N 83 0W
Wazirabad 36 32 30N 74 8 E
Weald, The 5 51 7N 0 9 E
Wear → 5 54 55N 1 22W
Weddell Sea 60 72 30 S 40 0W
Weert 12 51 15N 5 43 E
Weimar 13 51 0N 11 20 E
Weingarten 13 47 49N 9 39 E
Weinheim 13 49 33N 8 40 E
Weipa 56 12 40 S 141 50 E
Weiser 68 44 10N 117 0W
Weissenburg 13 49 2N 10 58 E
Wejherowo 17 54 35N 18 12 E
Welch 66 37 29N 81 36W
Welkom 52 28 0 S 26 46 E
Welland 62 43 0N 79 15W
Welland → 5 52 43N 0 10W
Wellesley Is. 56 16 42 S 139 30 E
Wellin 12 50 5N 5 6 E
Wellingborough 5 52 18N 0 41W
Wellington, Australia 56 32 35 S 148 59 E
Wellington, N.Z. 59 41 19 S 174 46 E
Wellington, Salop, U.K. 5 52 42N 2 31W
Wellington, Somerset, U.K. 5 50 58N 3 13W
Wellington, I. 74 49 30 S 75 0W
Wells, Norfolk, U.K. 5 52 57N 0 51 E
Wells, Somerset, U.K. 5 51 12N 2 39W
Wells, U.S.A. 68 41 8N 115 0W
Wells L. 54 26 44 S 123 15 E
Wellsville, N.Y., U.S.A. 66 42 9N 77 53W
Wellsville, Ohio, U.S.A. 66 40 36N 80 40W
Wels 14 48 9N 14 1 E
Welshpool 5 52 40N 3 9W
Wem 5 52 52N 2 45W
Wenatchee 68 47 30N 120 17W
Wenchi 49 7 46N 2 8W
Wenlock → 55 12 2 S 141 55 E
Wentworth 56 34 2 S 141 54 E
Wenzhou 43 28 0N 120 38 E
Werda 52 25 24 S 23 15 E
Werder 47 6 58N 45 1 E
Wertach → 13 48 24N 10 53 E
Wertheim 13 49 44N 9 32 E
Weser → 13 53 33N 8 30 E
Wessel Is. 55 11 10 S 136 45 E
West Bengal □ 37 23 0N 88 0 E
West Bromwich 5 52 32N 2 1W
West Falkland 74 51 40 S 60 0W
West Frankfort 67 37 56N 89 0W
West Glamorgan □ 5 51 40N 3 55W
West Memphis 67 35 5N 90 11W
West Midlands □ 5 52 30N 1 55W
West Moors 5 50 49N 1 50W
West Nicholson 51 21 2 S 29 20 E
West Palm Beach 66 26 44N 80 3W
West Sussex □ 5 50 55N 0 30W
West-Terschelling 12 53 22N 5 13 E
West Virginia □ 66 39 0N 81 0W
West-Vlaanderen □ 12 51 0N 3 0 E
West Yorkshire □ 5 53 45N 1 40W
Westerland 13 54 51N 8 20 E
Western Australia □ 54 25 0 S 118 0 E
Western Ghats 38 14 0N 75 0 E
Western Isles □ 6 57 30N 7 10W
Western Sahara ■ 49 25 0N 13 0W
Western Samoa ■ 57 14 0 S 172 0W
Westerschelde → 12 51 25N 3 25 E
Westerstede 13 53 15N 7 55 E
Westerwald 13 50 39N 8 0 E
Westlock 64 54 9N 113 55W
Westmeath □ 7 53 30N 7 30W
Westminster 66 39 34N 77 1W
Weston 66 39 3N 80 29W
Weston-super-Mare 5 51 20N 2 59W
Westport 7 53 44N 9 31W
Westray 6 59 18N 3 0W
Wetar 40 7 30 S 126 30 E
Wetaskiwin 64 52 55N 113 24W
Wetteren 12 51 0N 3 52 E
Wetzlar 13 50 33N 8 30 E
Wewak 56 3 38 S 143 41 E
Wewaka 67 35 10N 96 35W
Wexford 7 52 20N 6 28W
Wexford □ 7 52 20N 6 25W
Wexford Harb. 7 52 20N 6 25W
Weyburn 65 49 40N 103 50W
Weymouth 5 50 36N 2 28W
Weymouth, C. 55 12 37 S 143 27 E
Whale → 63 58 15N 67 40W
Whalsay 6 60 22N 1 0W
Whangarei 59 35 43 S 174 21 E
Wharfe → 5 53 55N 1 30W
Wharfedale 5 54 7N 2 4W
Wheeler Pk. 68 38 57N 114 15W
Wheeling 66 40 2N 80 41W
Whernside 5 54 14N 2 24W
Whidbey Is. 54 34 30 S 135 3 E
Whitby 5 54 29N 0 37W
White →, Ark., U.S.A. 67 33 53N 91 3W
White →, Ind., U.S.A. 66 38 25N 87 45W
White Nile = Nil el Abyad → 50 15 38N 32 31 E
White Russia = Byelorussian S.S.R. □ 32 53 30N 27 0 E
White Sea = Beloye More 30 66 30N 38 0 E
Whitehaven 5 54 33N 3 35W
Whitehorse 64 60 43N 135 3W
Whitehorse, Vale of 5 51 37N 1 30W
Whithorn 6 54 44N 4 25W
Whitney, Mt. 68 36 35N 118 14W
Whitstable 5 51 21N 1 2 E
Whitsunday I. 56 20 15 S 149 4 E
Whyalla 56 33 2 S 137 30 E
Wichita 67 37 40N 97 20W
Wichita Falls 67 33 57N 98 30W
Wick 6 58 26N 3 5W
Wicklow 7 53 0N 6 2W
Wicklow □ 7 52 59N 6 25W
Wicklow Hd. 7 52 59N 6 3W
Wicklow Mts. 7 53 0N 6 30W
Widnes 5 53 22N 2 44W
Wiedenbrück 13 51 52N 8 15 E
Wieliczka 15 50 0N 20 5 E
Wieluń 17 51 15N 18 34 E
Wien 15 48 12N 16 22 E
Wiener Neustadt 15 47 49N 16 16 E
Wierden 12 52 22N 6 35 E
Wiesbaden 13 50 7N 8 17 E
Wigan 5 53 33N 2 38W
Wight, I. of 5 50 40N 1 20W
Wigtown 6 54 52N 4 27W
Wigtown B. 6 54 46N 4 15W
Wilberforce, C. 55 11 54 S 136 35 E
Wilcannia 56 31 30 S 143 26 E
Wildwood 66 38 59N 74 46W
Wilhelm Mt. 56 5 50 S 145 1 E
Wilhelmsburg 13 53 28N 10 1 E
Wilhelmshaven 13 53 30N 8 9 E
Wilkes Barre 66 41 15N 75 52W
Wilkie 65 52 27N 108 42W
Willamina 68 45 9N 123 32W
Willemstad 70 12 5N 69 0W
Williams L. 64 51 48N 90 45W
Williams Lake 64 52 10N 122 10W
Williamsburg 66 37 17N 76 44W
Williamson 66 37 46N 82 17W
Williamsport 66 41 18N 77 1W
Williston 67 48 10N 103 35W
Willits 68 39 28N 123 17W

Willowmore 52 33 15 S 23 30 E
Wilmette 66 42 6N 87 44W
Wilmington, Del., U.S.A. 66 39 45N 75 32W
Wilmington, N.C., U.S.A. 66 34 14N 77 54W
Wilson 66 35 44N 77 54W
Wilsons Promontory 56 38 55 S 146 25 E
Wilton 5 51 5N 1 52W
Wiltshire □ 5 51 20N 2 0W
Wiltz 12 49 57N 5 55 E
Wiluna 54 26 36 S 120 14 E
Wimereux 9 50 45N 1 37 E
Wimmera 55 36 30 S 142 0 E
Winchester, U.K. 5 51 4N 1 19W
Winchester, Ind., U.S.A. 66 40 10N 84 56W
Winchester, Ky., U.S.A. 66 38 0N 84 8W
Winchester, Va., U.S.A. 66 39 14N 78 8W
Wind River Range 68 43 0N 109 30W
Windermere, L. 5 54 20N 2 57W
Windhoek 52 22 35 S 17 4 E
Windorah 56 25 24 S 142 36 E
Windrush → 5 51 48N 1 35W
Windsor, N.S., Canada 63 44 59N 64 5W
Windsor, Nfld., Canada 63 48 57N 55 40W
Windsor, Ont., Canada 62 42 18N 83 0W
Windsor, U.K. 5 51 28N 0 36W
Windward Is., Atl. Oc. 70 13 0N 63 0W
Windward Is., Pac. Oc. 58 18 0 S 149 0W
Windward Passage = Vientos, Paso de los 70 20 0N 74 0W
Winisk → 62 55 17N 85 5W
Winkler 65 49 10N 97 56W
Winneba 49 5 25N 0 36W
Winnemucca 68 41 0N 117 45W
Winnfield 67 31 57N 92 38W
Winnipeg 65 49 54N 97 9W
Winnipeg, L. 65 52 0N 97 0W
Winnipegosis L. 65 52 30N 100 0W
Winona 67 44 2N 91 39W
Winooski 62 44 31N 73 11W
Winschoten 12 53 9N 7 3 E
Winston-Salem 66 36 7N 80 15W
Winter Haven 66 28 0N 81 42W
Winter Park 66 28 34N 81 19W
Winterswijk 12 51 58N 6 43 E
Winterthur 13 47 30N 8 44 E
Winton 56 22 24 S 143 3 E
Wintzenheim 9 48 4N 7 17 E
Wirral 5 53 25N 3 0W
Wisbech 5 52 39N 0 10 E
Wisconsin □ 67 44 30N 90 0W
Wisconsin → 67 43 0N 91 15W
Wisconsin Rapids 67 44 25N 89 50W
Wishaw 6 55 46N 3 55W
Wisła → 17 54 22N 18 55 E
Wissant 9 50 52N 1 40 E
Wissembourg 9 49 2N 7 57 E
Witbank 53 25 51 S 29 14 E
Witham → 5 53 3N 0 8W
Withernsea 5 53 43N 0 2 E
Witney 5 51 47N 1 29W
Witten 13 51 26N 7 19 E
Wittenberge 13 53 0N 11 44 E
Wittenoom 54 22 15 S 118 20 E
Woerth 9 48 57N 7 45 E
Woëvre 9 49 15N 5 45 E
Wokam 40 5 45 S 134 28 E
Wolfenbüttel 13 52 10N 10 33 E
Wolfsburg 13 52 27N 10 49 E
Wolin 17 53 50N 14 37 E
Wollongong 56 34 25 S 150 54 E
Wolstenholme Fjord 3 76 0N 70 0W
Wolvega 12 52 52N 6 0 E
Wolverhampton 5 52 35N 2 6W
Wondai 56 26 20 S 151 49 E
Wŏnsan 43 39 11N 127 27 E
Wonthaggi 56 38 37 S 145 37 E
Woodland 68 38 40N 121 50W
Woodlark I. 56 9 10 S 152 50 E
Woodroffe, Mt. 54 26 20 S 131 45 E
Woods, L. 54 17 50 S 133 30 E
Woods, L. of the 65 49 15N 94 45W
Woodstock, N.B., Canada 63 46 11N 67 37W
Woodstock, Ont., Canada 62 43 10N 80 45W
Woodstock, U.K. 5 51 51N 1 20W
Woomera 55 31 30 S 137 10 E
Woonsocket 66 42 0N 71 30W
Wooramel → 54 25 47 S 114 10 E
Worcester, S. Africa 52 33 39 S 19 27 E
Worcester, U.K. 5 52 12N 2 12W
Worcester, U.S.A. 66 42 14N 71 49W
Workington 5 54 39N 3 34W
Worksop 5 53 19N 1 9W
Workum 12 52 59N 5 26 E
Wormhoudt 9 50 52N 2 28 E
Worms 13 49 37N 8 21 E
Worthing 5 50 49N 0 21W
Worthington 67 43 35N 95 36W
Wour 50 21 14N 16 0 E
Wrath, C. 6 58 38N 5 0W
Wrekin, The 5 52 41N 2 35W
Wrexham 5 53 5N 3 0W
Wrocław 17 51 5N 17 5 E
Września 17 52 21N 17 36 E
Wu Jiang → 43 29 40N 107 20 E
Wuhan 43 30 31N 114 18 E
Wuhu 43 31 22N 118 21 E
Wukari 49 7 51N 9 42 E
Wulumuchi = Ürümqi 42 43 45N 87 45 E
Wum 49 6 24N 10 2 E
Wuppertal 13 51 15N 7 8 E
Würzburg 13 49 46N 9 55 E
Wutach → 13 47 37N 8 15 E
Wutongqiao 42 29 22N 103 50 E
Wuxi 43 31 33N 120 18 E
Wuzhong 42 38 2N 106 12 E
Wuzhou 43 23 30N 111 18 E
Wyandotte 66 42 14N 83 13W
Wyandra 56 27 12 S 145 56 E
Wye → 5 51 36N 2 40W
Wymondham 5 52 45N 0 42W
Wyndham 54 15 33 S 128 3 E
Wynyard 65 51 45N 104 10W
Wyoming □ 68 42 48N 109 0W
Wytheville 66 37 0N 81 3W

X

Xai-Xai 53 25 6 S 33 31 E
Xangongo 52 16 45 S 15 5 E
Xánthi 26 41 10N 24 58 E
Xapuri 72 10 35 S 68 35W
Xenia 66 39 42N 83 57W
Xiaguan 42 25 32N 100 16 E
Xiamen 43 24 25N 118 4 E
Xi'an 43 34 15N 109 0 E
Xiangfan 43 32 2N 112 8 E
Xiangtan 43 27 51N 112 54 E
Xiao Hinggan Ling 42 49 0N 127 0 E
Xigazê 42 29 5N 88 45 E
Xinavane 53 25 2 S 32 47 E
Xingtai 42 37 3N 114 32 E
Xingu → 73 1 30 S 51 53W
Xining 42 36 34N 101 40 E
Xinjiang Uygur Zizhiqu □ 42 42 0N 86 0 E
Xinjin 42 39 25N 121 58 E
Xinxiang 43 35 18N 113 50 E
Xinyang 43 32 6N 114 3 E
Xinzhu 43 24 49N 120 57 E
Xique-Xique 73 10 50 S 42 40W
Xizang □ 42 32 0N 88 0 E
Xuanhua 42 40 40N 115 2 E
Xuchang 43 34 2N 113 48 E
Xuzhou 43 34 18N 117 10 E

Y

Ya'an 42 29 58N 103 5 E
Yabelo 50 4 50N 38 8 E
Yablonovy Khrebet 31 53 0N 114 0 E
Yacuiba 72 22 0 S 63 43W
Yadgir 38 16 45N 77 5 E
Yagodnoye 31 62 33N 149 40 E
Yahuma 51 1 0N 23 10 E
Yakima 68 46 42N 120 30W
Yakut A.S.S.R. □ 31 62 0N 130 0 E
Yakutsk 31 62 5N 129 50 E
Yalgoo 54 28 16 S 116 39 E
Yalinga 50 6 33N 23 10 E
Yalta 34 44 30N 34 10 E
Yamagata 44 38 15N 140 15 E
Yamaguchi 44 34 10N 131 32 E
Yamaguchi □ 44 34 20N 131 40 E
Yamal, Poluostrov 30 71 0N 70 0 E
Yamanashi □ 44 35 40N 138 40 E
Yamantau 30 54 20N 57 40 E
Yâmbiô 50 4 35N 28 16 E
Yambol 25 42 30N 26 36 E
Yamdena 40 7 45 S 131 20 E
Yamma-Yamma, L. 56 26 16 S 141 20 E
Yampi Sd. 54 16 8 S 123 38 E
Yamuna → 37 25 30N 81 53 E
Yamzho Yumco 42 28 48N 90 35 E
Yana → 31 71 30N 136 0 E
Yanai 44 33 58N 132 7 E
Yangambi 51 0 47N 24 20 E
Yangquan 42 37 58N 113 31 E
Yangtze Kiang = Chang Jiang → 43 31 48N 121 10 E
Yanji 42 42 59N 129 30 E
Yantai 42 37 34N 121 22 E
Yao 50 12 56N 17 33 E
Yaoundé 49 3 50N 11 35 E
Yap 57 9 31N 138 6 E
Yaqui → 69 27 37N 110 39W
Yaraka 56 24 53 S 144 3 E
Yaransk 33 57 22N 47 49 E
Yare → 5 52 36N 1 28 E
Yarensk 30 61 10N 49 8 E
Yarmouth 63 43 50N 66 7W
Yaroslavl 33 57 35N 39 55 E
Yartsevo 31 60 20N 90 0 E
Yass 56 34 49 S 148 54 E
Yatsushiro 44 32 30N 130 40 E
Yavari → 72 4 21 S 70 2W
Yavatmal 38 20 20N 78 15 E
Yawatahama 44 33 27N 132 24 E
Yazd 46 31 55N 54 27 E
Yazoo → 67 32 35N 90 50W
Yazoo City 67 32 48N 90 28W
Ye Xian 42 37 8N 119 57 E
Yecla 19 38 35N 1 5W
Yegros 74 26 20 S 56 25W
Yei 50 4 9N 30 40 E
Yelanskoye 31 61 25N 128 0 E
Yelets 33 52 40N 38 30 E
Yell 6 60 35N 1 5W
Yell Sd. 6 60 33N 1 15W
Yellow Sea 43 35 0N 123 0 E
Yellowhead P. 64 52 53N 118 25W
Yellowknife 64 62 27N 114 29W
Yellowknife → 64 62 31N 114 19W
Yellowstone → 67 47 58N 103 59W
Yellowstone National Park 68 44 35N 110 0W
Yemen ■ 47 15 0N 44 0 E
Yenisey → 30 71 50N 82 40 E
Yeniseysk 31 58 27N 92 13 E
Yeniseyskiy Zaliv 30 72 20N 81 0 E
Yenne 11 45 43N 5 44 E
Yenyuka 31 57 57N 121 15 E
Yeo, L. 54 28 0 S 124 30 E
Yeola 38 20 0N 74 30 E
Yeovil 5 50 57N 2 38W
Yeppoon 56 23 5 S 150 47 E
Yerbogachen 31 61 16N 108 0 E
Yerevan 35 40 10N 44 31 E
Yermakovo 31 52 25N 126 20 E
Yerofey Pavlovich 31 54 0N 122 0 E
Yershov 33 51 22N 48 16 E
Yerville 8 49 40N 0 53 E
Yes Tor 5 50 41N 3 59W
Yessey 31 68 29N 102 10 E
Yeu, I. d' 8 46 42N 2 20W
Yevpatoriya 34 45 15N 33 20 E
Yeysk 34 46 40N 38 12 E
Yiannitsa 26 40 46N 22 24 E
Yibin 42 28 45N 104 32 E
Yichang 43 30 40N 111 20 E
Yichun 42 47 44N 128 52 E
Yilan 43 24 51N 121 44 E
Yinchuan 42 38 30N 106 15 E
Yingkou 42 40 37N 122 18 E
Yingtan 42 28 12N 117 0 E
Yining 42 43 58N 81 10 E
Yinnietharra 54 24 39 S 116 12 E
Yíthion 26 36 46N 22 34 E
Ylitornio 27 66 19N 23 39 E
Ylivieska 27 64 4N 24 28 E
Ynykchanskiy 31 60 15N 137 35 E
Yogyakarta 40 7 49 S 110 22 E
Yokadouma 51 3 26N 14 55 E
Yokkaichi 44 35 0N 136 38 E
Yoko 50 5 32N 12 20 E
Yokohama 44 35 27N 139 28 E
Yokosuka 44 35 20N 139 40 E
Yola 50 9 10N 12 29 E
Yonago 44 35 25N 133 19 E
Yongji 43 34 52N 110 28 E
Yonibana 49 8 30N 12 19W
Yonkers 66 40 57N 73 51W
Yonne □ 9 47 50N 3 40 E
Yonne → 9 48 23N 2 58 E
York, Australia 54 31 52 S 116 47 E
York, U.K. 5 53 58N 1 7W
York, U.S.A. 66 39 57N 76 43W
York, C. 56 10 42 S 142 31 E
York, Kap 3 75 55N 66 25W
York Sd. 54 14 50 S 125 5 E
Yorke Pen. 56 34 50 S 137 40 E
Yorkshire Wolds 5 54 0N 0 30W
Yorkton 65 51 11N 102 28W
Yosemite National Park 68 38 0N 119 30W
Yoshkar Ola 33 56 38N 47 55 E
Youghal 7 51 58N 7 51W
Youghal B. 7 51 55N 7 50W
Young 56 34 19 S 148 18 E
Youngstown 66 41 7N 80 41W
Yport 8 49 45N 0 15 E
Ypres = Ieper 12 50 51N 2 53 E
Yssingeaux 11 45 9N 4 8 E
Ystad 28 55 26N 13 50 E
Ythan → 6 57 26N 2 12W
Ytyk-Kel 31 62 30N 133 45 E
Yuba City 68 39 12N 121 37W
Yucatán □ 69 20 50N 89 0W
Yucatán, Canal de 70 22 0N 86 30W
Yuci 42 37 42N 112 46 E
Yugoslavia ■ 24 44 0N 20 0 E
Yukon → 61 65 30N 150 0W
Yukti 31 63 26N 105 42 E
Yule → 54 20 41 S 118 17 E
Yuma 68 32 45N 114 37W
Yur 31 59 52N 137 41 E
Yuribei 30 71 8N 76 58 E
Yurimaguas 72 5 55 S 76 7W
Yushu 42 33 5N 96 55 E
Yuzhno-Sakhalinsk 31 46 58N 142 45 E
Yvelines □ 9 48 40N 1 45 E
Yvetot 8 49 37N 0 44 E

Z

Zaandam 12 52 26N 4 49 E
Zabaykalskiy 31 49 40N 117 25 E
Zabid 47 14 0N 43 10 E
Zābol 46 31 0N 61 32 E
Zābol □ 46 32 0N 67 0 E
Zabrze 17 50 18N 18 50 E
Zacapa 69 14 59N 89 31W
Zacatecas 69 22 47N 102 35W
Zacatecas □ 69 23 0N 103 0W
Zacatecoluca 69 13 29N 88 51W
Zadar 21 44 8N 15 14 E
Zadetkyi Kyun 41 10 0N 98 25 E
Zafra 18 38 26N 6 30W
Żagań 17 51 39N 15 22 E
Zagazig 50 30 40N 31 30 E
Zagreb 21 45 50N 16 0 E
Zāgros, Kuhhā-ye 45 33 45N 47 0 E
Zāhedān 46 29 30N 60 50 E
Zahlah 45 33 52N 35 50 E
Zaïre ■ 51 3 0 S 23 0 E
Zaïre → 51 6 4 S 12 24 E
Zaječar 24 43 53N 22 18 E
Zakamensk 31 50 23N 103 17 E
Zakavkazye 35 42 0N 44 0 E
Zákinthos 26 37 47N 20 57 E
Zalingei 50 12 51N 23 29 E
Zambeze → 51 18 35 S 36 20 E
Zambezi = Zambeze → 51 18 35 S 36 20 E
Zambezi 51 13 30 S 23 15 E
Zambia ■ 51 15 0 S 28 0 E
Zamboanga 40 6 59N 122 3 E
Zamora, Mexico 69 20 0N 102 21W
Zamora, Spain 18 41 30N 5 45W
Zamość 17 50 43N 23 15 E
Zanaga 51 2 48 S 13 48 E
Zandvoort 12 52 22N 4 32 E
Zanesville 66 39 56N 82 2W
Zanjan 45 36 40N 48 35 E
Zanthus 54 31 2 S 123 34 E
Zanzibar 51 6 12 S 39 12 E
Zaouiet Reggane 49 26 32N 0 3 E
Zapadnaya Dvina 30 56 15N 32 3 E
Zapadnaya Dvina → 32 57 4N 24 3 E
Západné Beskydy 15 49 30N 19 0 E
Zapala 74 39 0 S 70 5W
Zapodnyy Sayan 31 52 30N 94 0 E
Zaporozhye 34 47 50N 35 10 E
Zaragoza, Mexico 69 28 29N 100 55W
Zaragoza, Spain 19 41 39N 0 53W
Zaragoza □ 19 41 35N 1 0W
Zaranj 46 30 55N 61 55 E
Zaria 49 11 0N 7 40 E
Zaruma 72 3 40 S 79 38W
Żary 17 51 37N 15 10 E
Zarzis 50 33 31N 11 2 E
Zashiversk 31 67 25N 142 40 E
Zavitinsk 31 50 10N 129 20 E
Zawiercie 17 50 30N 19 24 E
Zāwiyat al Bayḍā 50 32 30N 21 40 E
Zayarsk 31 56 12N 102 55 E
Zaysan, Oz. 30 48 0N 83 0 E
Zduńska Wola 17 51 37N 18 59 E
Zeebrugge 12 51 19N 3 12 E
Zeehan 56 41 52 S 145 25 E
Zeeland □ 12 51 30N 3 50 E
Zeerust 52 25 31 S 26 4 E
Zeila 47 11 21N 43 30 E
Zeist 12 52 5N 5 15 E
Zelzate 12 51 13N 3 47 E
Zémio 51 5 2N 25 5 E
Zemlya Frantsa Iosifa 3 81 0N 55 0 E
Zemun 24 44 51N 20 25 E
Zerbst 13 51 59N 12 8 E
Zeya 31 53 48N 127 14 E
Zeya → 31 53 13N 127 35 E
Zhailma 30 51 37N 61 33 E
Zhanghua 43 24 6N 120 29 E
Zhangjiakou 42 40 48N 114 55 E
Zhangzhou 43 24 30N 117 35 E
Zhanjiang 43 21 15N 110 20 E
Zhdanov 34 47 5N 37 31 E
Zhejiang □ 43 29 0N 120 0 E
Zheleznogorsk-Ilimskiy 31 56 34N 104 8 E
Zhengzhou 43 34 45N 113 34 E
Zhenjiang 43 32 11N 119 26 E
Zhenyuan 43 27 4N 108 21 E
Zhigansk 31 66 48N 123 27 E
Zhijiang 43 27 27N 109 42 E
Zhitomir 32 50 20N 28 40 E
Zhlobin 32 52 55N 30 0 E
Zhokhova, Ostrov 31 76 4N 152 40 E
Zhumadian 43 32 59N 114 2 E
Zhupanovo 31 53 40N 159 52 E
Zhuzhou 43 27 49N 113 12 E
Zibo 42 36 47N 118 3 E
Zielona Góra 17 51 57N 15 31 E
Zierikzee 12 51 40N 3 55 E
Zigey 50 14 43N 15 50 E
Zigong 43 29 15N 104 48 E
Ziguinchor 49 12 35N 16 20W
Zile 45 40 15N 35 52 E
Žilina 15 49 12N 18 42 E
Zillah 50 28 30N 17 33 E
Zima 31 54 0N 102 5 E
Zimbabwe ■ 51 19 0 S 30 0 E
Zinder 49 13 48N 9 0 E
Zion Nat. Park 68 37 25N 112 50W
Zipaquirá 72 5 0N 74 0W
Zitácuaro 69 19 24N 100 22W
Ziway, L. 50 8 0N 38 50 E
Zlatograd 25 41 22N 25 7 E
Zlatoust 30 55 10N 59 40 E
Zlitan 50 32 32N 14 35 E
Znojmo 14 48 50N 16 2 E
Zomba 51 15 22 S 35 19 E
Zongo 51 4 20N 18 35 E
Zonguldak 45 41 28N 31 50 E
Zonza 11 41 45N 9 11 E
Zorritos 72 3 43 S 80 40W
Zouar 50 20 30N 16 32 E
Zouérate 49 22 44N 12 21W
Zoutkamp 12 53 20N 6 18 E
Zrenjanin 24 45 22N 20 23 E
Zuetina 50 30 58N 20 7 E
Zufar 47 17 40N 54 0 E
Zug 13 47 10N 8 31 E
Zuid-Holland □ 12 52 0N 4 35 E
Zuidhorn 12 53 15N 6 23 E
Zula 50 15 17N 39 40 E
Zumbo 51 15 35 S 30 26 E
Zungeru 49 9 48N 6 8 E
Zunyi 43 27 42N 106 53 E
Zürich 13 47 22N 8 32 E
Zutphen 12 52 9N 6 12 E
Zuwārah 50 32 58N 12 1 E
Zverinogolovskoye 30 54 23N 64 40 E
Zvishavane 51 20 17 S 30 2 E
Zvolen 15 48 33N 19 10 E
Zweibrücken 13 49 15N 7 20 E
Zwettl 14 48 35N 15 9 E
Zwickau 13 50 43N 12 30 E
Zwolle 12 52 31N 6 6 E
Żyrardów 17 52 3N 20 28 E
Zyryanka 31 65 45N 150 51 E
Zyryanovsk 30 49 43N 84 20 E

Picture Credits

The publishers wish to thank the following photographers, picture agencies and companies who have supplied photographs for this book. The photographs have been credited by page number, and position on the page where appropriate: B (Bottom), T (Top), L (Left) etc.
Australian Tourist Commission: 2-3, 109, 110 (T), 110 (R), 112.
Austrian National Tourist Office: 37.
Canadian Film Library: 121 (T), 121 (B), 123, 124.
China Tourist Service: 81.
Danish Tourist Board: 62 (T).
Vic Guy: 20 (T)
Neil Holmes: 17.
The Image Bank: 15 (B), 20 (B), 27 (L), 27 (T), 28, 31 (B), 33, 34 (T), 35 (B), 38, 43 (T), 47, 48 (T), 48 (B), 49 (T), 49 (B), 51, 56 (T), 57 (T), 59 (T), 60 (T), 60 (B), 62 (B), 65, 66, 68, 71, 72, 73, 75 (B), 80 (B), 82 (T), 82 (B), 86 (B), 90-91, 91, 93, 107, 114, 117 (L), 119, 129 (T), 129 (B).
Irish Tourist Board: 22 (T), 22 (B), 23.
Japan National Tourist Organization: 86 (T).
Luxembourg National Tourist Office: 30.
Neill Menneer: 4-5, 18 (T), 25, 26, 34 (B), 43 (B), 56 (R), 57 (L), 75 (T), 79 (TL), 79 (TR), 79 (B), 85, 110-111, 117 (R), 118 (T), 118 (B), 130.
Netherlands Board of Tourism: 31 (T).
Scandinavian Airlines System (SAS): 15 (T), 59 (B), 76, 126 (B).
Tim Sharman: 18 (B), 39, 40 (L), 40 (R), 41, 54 (B).
South American Pictures: 6-7, 132 (T), 132 (B), 134 (T), 134 (B), 135, 137 (T), 137 (B), 138, 140 (T), 140 (R), 141 (T), 141 (B), 142 (T), 142 (B), 143.
Spanish National Tourist Office: 45.
Swedish National Tourist Office: 35 (T).
Tropix: 94, 95 (L), 95 (R), 96 (T), 96 (B), 97 (T), 97 (B), 99, 100, 101 (T), 101 (B), 102 (T), 102 (B), 104 (T), 104 (B), 105.
John Woodward: 10-11.
Yugoslav National Tourist Office: 53, 54 (T).